Lecture Notes in Computer Science 4254

Commenced Publication in 1973
Founding and Former Series Editors:
Gerhard Goos, Juris Hartmanis, and Jan van Leeuwen

Torsten Grust Hagen Höpfner
Arantza Illarramendi Stefan Jablonski
Marco Mesiti Sascha Müller
Paula-Lavinia Patranjan Kai-Uwe Sattler
Myra Spiliopoulou Jef Wijsen (Eds.)

Current Trends in Database Technology – EDBT 2006

EDBT 2006 Workshops PhD, DataX, IIDB, IIHA, ICSNW
QLQP, PIM, PaRMA, and Reactivity on the Web
Munich, Germany, March 26-31, 2006
Revised Selected Papers

Springer

Volume Editors

Torsten Grust, Technische Universität München, Germany
E-mail: grust@in.tum.de

Hagen Höpfner, International University in Germany, Germany
E-mail: hoepfner@acm.org

Arantza Illarramendi, The University of the Basque Country, Spain
E-mail: a.illarramendi@ehu.es

Stefan Jablonski, University of Bayreuth, Germany
E-mail: Stefan.Jablonski@uni-bayreuth.de

Marco Mesiti, University of Milan, Italy
E-mail: mesiti@dico.unimi.it

Sascha Müller, University of Erlangen-Nuernberg, Germany
E-mail: sascha.mueller@informatik.uni-erlangen.de

Paula-Lavinia Patranjan, Ludwig-Maximilians University Munich, Germany
E-mail: paula.patranjan@pms.ifi.lmu.de

Kai-Uwe Sattler, Technical University of Ilmenau, Germany
E-mail: kus@tu-ilmenau.de

Myra Spiliopoulou, Otto-von-Guericke-University Magdeburg, Germany
E-mail: myra@iti.cs.uni-magdeburg.de

Jef Wijsen, Université de Mons-Hainaut, Belgium
E-mail: Jef.Wijsen@umh.ac.be

Library of Congress Control Number: 2006934112

CR Subject Classification (1998): H.2, H.3, H.4, C.2.4, K.4.4, J.3
LNCS Sublibrary: SL 3 – Information Systems and Application, incl. Internet/Web and HCI

ISSN 0302-9743
ISBN-10 3-540-46788-2 Springer Berlin Heidelberg New York
ISBN-13 978-3-540-46788-5 Springer Berlin Heidelberg New York

Springer is a part of Springer Science+Business Media

springer.com

Printed in Germany

Typesetting: Camera-ready by author, data conversion by Scientific Publishing Services, Chennai, India
Printed on acid-free paper SPIN: 11896548 06/3142 5 4 3 2 1 0

Preface

You are studying the joint proceedings of the scientific workshops that were held just before and after the 10th *International Conference on Extending Database Technology* (EDBT 2006) in the historic Munich Künstlerhaus, Germany, in late March 2006. The workshops contributing to this volume are:

- **The 4th EDBT Ph.D. Workshop**
- **DataX 2006** (DB Technologies for Handling XML Information on the Web)
- **IIDB** (Inconsistency and Incompleteness in Databases)
- **IIHA** (Information Integration in Healthcare Applications)
- **ICSNW 2006** (Semantics of a Networked World)
- **QLQP 2006** (Query Languages and Query Processing)
- **PIM 2006** (Pervasive Information Management)
- **PaRMa 2006** (Pattern Representation and Management)
- **Reactivity on the Web**

If we let the raw numbers speak, then, compared with EDBT 2004, the number of collocated workshops almost doubled (from five in 2004 to nine in 2006). The nine events attracted circa 170 attendees from all over the globe. Approximately one third of the participants exclusively registered for workshops. These numbers indicate that the satellite workshop idea continues to play a significant role and that the orbited core conference clearly benefits as well. As the EDBT 2006 Workshop Chair, I enjoyed the privilege of being able to sneak into almost all workshops, and throughout I found the direct, to-the-point, and thus effective style of presentation and discourse that you may hope for when "birds of a feather" flock together.

In this post-workshop proceedings volume you will find a selection of 70 contributions, grouped by workshop, whose authors were asked to prepare revised and enhanced versions of their original workshop submissions. The present papers reflect program committee comments as well as feedback collected when the work was presented and discussed in Munich.

I am confident that you will appreciate the diligence with which the authors prepared the papers of this volume. My sincere thanks go to all workshop program committees—more than 150 colleagues in total—and, last but not least, the workshop organizers who stepped up and devoted significant effort and time to shape and run the workshops. You can find their individual forewords on the pages that follow.

August 2006 Torsten Grust

EDBT Ph.D. Workshop

Continuing in its tradition, the Ph.D. Workshop brings together Ph.D. students in the field of database technology outside of the EDBT conference series. It offers Ph.D. students the opportunity to present, discuss, and receive feedback on their research in a constructive and international atmosphere.

The Program Committee, comprised of 30 members from 14 countries, evaluated 70 submissions (received from 20 countries). After a careful review process (each paper was evaluated by three committee members followed by an online discussion), 12 papers were selected for presentation at the workshop. After several intensive and fruitful discussions led by the session chairs, all authors were invited to submit a revised and extended version of their paper for these proceedings.

The EDBT 2006 Ph.D. Workshop was made possible through the cooperation of many different organizations and individuals. In particular, we would like to thank the members of the Program Committee, as well as the Local Organization Committee, for their professional work and time commitment. We are very thankful to the three session chairs at the workshop: Klaus R. Dittrich from the University of Zürich (Switzerland), Klaus Meyer-Wegener from the University of Erlangen-Nuremberg (Germany) and Theo Härder from the Technische Universität Kaiserslautern (Germany).

Special thanks goes to the members of the Database Research Group at the University of Erlangen-Nuremberg (Germany) for providing a submission and review system that worked flawlessly and to Torsten Grust, from the Technische Universität München (Germany), for his outstanding support in the preparation and execution of the workshop.

For their gracious help and kind advice during the workshop preparation, we are particularly indebted to the EDBT 2006 General Chair, Marc H. Scholl, from the University of Konstanz (Germany); the Program Committee Chair, Yannis Ioannidis, from the University of Athens (Greece); and the Executive Chair, Florian Matthes, from the Technische Universität München (Germany).

News and updates can be found at the workshop's website: `http://www6.informatik.uni-erlangen.de/edbt06phd`.

Workshop Chairs

Wolfgang Lindner	Massachusetts Institute of Technology, USA
Sascha Müller	University of Erlangen-Nuremberg, Germany

Program Committee

Walid Aref	Purdue University, USA
Michela Bertolotto	University College Dublin, Ireland
Stefano Ceri	University of Milan, Italy

Stavros Christodoulakis	Technical University of Crete, Greece
Olivier Curé	Université de Marne-la-Vallée, France
Klaus Dittrich	University of Zürich, Switzerland
Georgios Evangelidis	University of Macedonia, Greece
Torsten Grust	Technische Universität München, Germany
Theo Härder	Technische Universität Kaiserslautern, Germany
Leonid Kalinichenko	Russian Academy of Sciences, Russia
Wolfgang Klas	University of Vienna, Austria
George Kollios	Boston University, USA
Alberto Laender	Universidade Federal de Minas Gerais, Brazil
Ulf Leser	Humboldt-Universität zu Berlin, Germany
Wolfgang Lindner	Massachusetts Institute of Technology, USA
Stefan Manegold	CWI, The Netherlands
Ioana Manolescu	INRIA, France
Marco Mesiti	University of Genova, Italy
Klaus Meyer-Wegener	University of Erlangen-Nuremberg, Germany
Mohamed Mokbel	University of Minnesota, USA
Erich Neuhold	University of Vienna, Austria
Beng Chin Ooi	National University of Singapore, Singapore
M. Tamer Özsu	University of Waterloo, Canada
Dimitris Plexousakis	University of Crete, Greece
Jaroslav Pokorny	Charles University, Czech Republic
Andreas Reuter	European Media Laboratory, Germany
Marc H. Scholl	University of Konstanz, Germany
Peter Tabeling	Hasso-Plattner-Institut, Germany
Tan Kian-Lee	National University of Singapore, Singapore
Athena Vakali	Aristotle University of Thessaloniki, Greece

Sponsors

Massachusetts Institute of Technology (MIT), USA
University of Erlangen-Nuremberg (FAU), Germany
10th International Conference on Extending Database Technology (EDBT 2006)

Second International Workshop on Database Technologies for Handling XML Information on the Web (DataX 2006)

The second EDBT 2006 Workshop on *Database Technologies for Handling XML Information on the Web* (*DataX 2006*) was held in Munich, Germany, on Sunday, March 26, 2006, and attracted approximately 30 participants from different countries. The first DataX workshop was held in conjunction with EDBT 2004.

XML seems to be one of the main means towards the next generation of database technology. The workshop goal was to give the participants the opportunity to debate new issues and directions for the XML and database community with specific interest in innovative environments.

In response to the call for papers, 35 high quality submissions were received. Each paper was carefully reviewed by at least three members of the program committee and external reviewers. As result of this process, 10 papers were selected for the workshop, covering a large variety of topics. In addition, H.V. Jagadish accepted our invitation to discuss new and interesting topics in XML and database research.

The workshop opened with a session on *Querying XML Documents*, devoted to efficient query processing and to queries on non-valid documents. A section on *Updating XML Documents* followed, discussing update languages, updates through views, and efficient integrity checking. The following section, *XML Biology*, discussed the use of XML for representing and analyzing molecular interactions. The invited talk, advocating the need for an algebra in practical XML query processing, followed. The workshop was concluded by a section devoted to *XML Security*, referring to both confidentiality of outsourced data and security views, and *XML Schema Mapping* for XML data interchange.

This volume contains improved versions of the workshop papers, revised by authors according to the program committee's and workshop participants' comments.

We would like to thank the invited speaker, the program committee members, and the external reviewers for their efforts in the realization of this workshop and in helping authors to revise their papers. All the workshop participants deserve to be thanked for making the workshop very fruitful. Finally, we wish to express our gratitude to the EDBT Organization and the EDBT Workshop Chair, Torsten Grust, for their support in all the phases of the workshop preparation as well as for the preparation of the post-workshop proceedings.

Workshop Chairs

Barbara Catania	DISI - University of Genova (Italy)
Akmal B. Chaudhri	IBM developerWorks (UK)
Giovanna Guerrini	DISI - University of Genova (Italy)
Marco Mesiti	DICO - University of Milan (Italy)

Program Committee

Sihem Amer-Yahia	Yahoo! Research (USA)
Ricardo Baeza-Yates	University of Chile (Chile)
Zohra Bellahsene	LIRMM (France)
Angela Bonifati	Icar-CNR (Italy)
Stéphane Bressan	NUS (Singapore)
Klaus R. Dittrich	University of Zurich (Switzerland)
Elena Ferrari	University of Insubria (Italy)
Minos Garofalakis	Intel Research, Berkeley (USA)
Sven Helmer	Universität Mannheim (Germany)
Ela Hunt	Glasgow University (UK)
Zoé Lacroix	Arizona State University (USA)
Mounia Lalmas	Queen Mary University of London (UK)
Anna Maddalena	University of Genova (Italy)
Maarten Marx	University of Amsterdam (The Netherlands)
Beng Chin Ooi	NUS (Singapore)
M. Tamer Özsu	University of Waterloo (Canada)
Elisa Quintarelli	Politecnico di Milano (Italy)
Ismael Sanz	Universitat Jaume I (Spain)
Ralf Schenkel	MPI für Informatik, Saarbrücken (Germany)
Michael Schrefl	Johannes Kepler Universität (Austria)
Oded Shmueli	Technion - Israel Institute of Technology (Israel)
Jérôme Siméon	IBM Almaden Research Center (USA)
Divesh Srivastava	AT&T Research (USA)
Athena I. Vakali	Aristotle University of Thessaloniki (Greece)
Vasilis Vassalos	Athens University of Economics and Business (Greece)

External Reviewers

Michelle Cart
Yi Chen
Suo Cong
Anca Dobre
Christian Eichinger
Jean Ferrie
Massimo Franceschet
Irini Fundulaki
Haris Georgiadis
Christian Grün
Jaudoin Hélène
Wouter Kuijper
Stefania Leone
Xu Linhao
Roberto Montagna
Paola Podestà
Paolo Rosso
Mark Roantree
Christoph Sturm
Maria Esther Vidal
Jurate Vysniauskaite
Wenqiang Wang
Rui Yang
Huaxin Zhang
Patrick Ziegler

Inconsistency and Incompleteness in Databases (IIDB)

IIDB 2006, the International Workshop on Inconsistency and Incompleteness in Databases, was held on March 26, 2006, in Munich, Germany, as a collocated event of EDBT 2006, the 10th International Conference on Extending Database Technology. The motivation for this workshop was to bring together database researchers working on inconsistency, incompleteness, and uncertainty to review recent progress and outline future research directions.

In response to the call for papers, ten papers were submitted. Each submission was reviewed by at least three program committee members. Five papers were accepted for regular and three for short, position paper presentation. Additionally, program committee members contributed position papers describing their ongoing research. IIDB 2006 also featured an invited talk by Maurizio Lenzerini on *"Inconsistency Tolerance in P2P Data Integration"* in addition to the technical program.

During the workshop only informal proceedings were distributed. The articles in this volume are revised versions of the five papers accepted for regular presentation at the workshop. The authors were able to make improvements to their papers based on the comments of the reviewers and the discussions during the workshop. The revised articles were subjected to a final check by the program committee.

Workshop Chairs

Jan Chomicki	University at Buffalo, USA
Jef Wijsen	University of Mons-Hainaut, Belgium

Program Committee

Marcelo Arenas	PUC Chile, Chile
Ofer Arieli	Academic College of Tel-Aviv, Israel
Leopoldo Bertossi	Carleton University, Canada
Patrick Bosc	IRISA/ENSSAT, France
Andrea Calì	Free University of Bozen-Bolzano, Italy
Nilesh Dalvi	University of Washington, USA
Thomas Eiter	Vienna University of Technology, Austria
Wenfei Fan	University of Edinburgh, UK & Bell Labs, USA
Enrico Franconi	Free University of Bozen-Bolzano, Italy
Ariel Fuxman	University of Toronto, Canada
Gösta Grahne	Concordia University, Canada
Sergio Greco	University of Calabria, Italy
Maurizio Lenzerini	University of Rome "La Sapienza", Italy
Jerzy Marcinkowski	Wroclaw University, Poland
V.S. Subrahmanian	University of Maryland, USA

External Reviewers

L. Caroprese
V. Kiricenko
A. Lopatenko
O. Pivert
E. Zumpano

Workshop on Information Integration in Healthcare Applications (IIHA)

In the line with the banner theme of the EDBT 2006 conference "From Database Systems to Universal Data Management" this workshop focused on topics concerning information integration in healthcare applications.

Healthcare information systems continuously have to be adapted to meet new requirements, standards, laws, etc. Cost pressure is increasing massively, and at the same time, system complexity is growing. This constantly changing environment is also characterized by highly interdisciplinary processes which depend on the timely provision of patient-related information at the point of care in order to prevent medical errors. In addition, medical knowledge should be provided in a way that enables effective decision support for clinicians. The core challenge is to establish flexible and responsive IT infrastructures that are capable of effectively adapting to changing requirements. Information integration is thus a key factor for healthcare applications, as most medical applications are determined by a huge variety of heterogeneous and independent health care institutions that have to share data. The continuity of medical processes has to be improved, and medical pathways will play an important integrational role within institutions and across institutional borders.

The Program Committee, comprising 10 members from 6 countries, evaluated 18 submissions. After a careful review process (each paper was evaluated by 3 committee members followed by an online discussion), 8 papers were selected for presentation at the workshop, of which one was withdrawn by the authors. After the workshop the authors of 6 papers were finally invited to submit a revised version for these proceedings.

The workshop was a very lively one. There was lot of discussion, and the idea of a continuation workshop arose. One of the highlights of the workshop was Klaus Kuhn's keynote address about the current state of healthcare information systems.

We would like to thank the members of the Program Committee, as well as the local Organization Committee, for their professional work and time commitment. Special thanks goes to the EDBT 2006 workshop chair, Torsten Grust, from the Technische Universität München (Germany) who perfectly supported us during the whole workshop preparation and post processing. Last but not least, we would like to thank Klaus Kuhn from the Technische Universität München (Germany), for giving a superb keynote address at the workshop.

News and updates can be found via the workshop website:
`http://www6.informatik.uni-erlangen.de/edbt06-WSIIHA`.

Workshop Chair

Stefan Jablonski — Chair for Databases and Information Systems, University of Bayreuth, Germany

Program Committee

Wolfgang Deiters	Fraunhofer Institute for Software and Systems Engineering, Dortmund, Germany
Evelyn Hovenga	School of Information Systems, Central Queensland University, Australia
Stan Huff	Intermountain Health Care, Salt Lake City, USA
Stefan Jablonski	Chair for Databases and Information Systems, University of Bayreuth, Germany (Chair)
Klaus Kuhn	Chair for Medical Informatics, Technische Universität München, Germany
Richard Lenz	Institute of Medical Informatics, University of Marburg, Germany
Christian Lovis	Service of Medical Informatics, University Hospitals of Geneva, Switzerland
John Mantas	Health Informatics Lab, University of Athens, Greece
Sascha Müller	Chair for Database Systems, University of Erlangen-Nuremberg, Germany (Organization)
Manfred Reichert	Information Systems Group, University of Twente, The Netherlands

Sponsors

University of Erlangen-Nuremberg
Technische Universität München
10th International Conference on Extending Database Technology (EDBT 2006)

International Conference on Semantics of a Networked World: Semantics of Sequence and Time Dependent Data (ICSNW 2006)

The explosion in information exchange fostered by the success of the Web has led to the identification of semantics as a critical issue in the development of services providing data and information to users and applications worldwide. A newly designated conference series on "Semantics of a Networked World" promoted by the IFIP WG 2.6 intends to continue the exploration of novel emerging trends that raise challenging research issues related to the understanding and management of semantics. Each conference, in addition to soliciting contributions of generic relevance in the semantics domain, plans to focus on a specific theme that conveys exciting promises of innovation.

The theme for ICSNW 2006 was "Semantics of Sequence and Time Dependent Data". Sequence and time dependent data are distinguished by the important role played by order, in modeling and querying the data. For example, monitoring dynamic phenomena produces data that arrive as a stream of temporal observations, whose querying and analysis make essential use of its temporal or sequential nature. Data warehouses give considerable prominence to the temporal dimension for decision support. Applications in the biological and financial domains naturally model their data using sequences, and the mining of such data makes critical use of this property. The purpose of ICSNW 2006, like its predecessors, was to provide an active forum for researchers and practitioners for the presentation and exchange of research results and the discussion of practical issues in the management of data, in particular applied to sequence and time dependent data.

The conference was held on March 30, 2006 in Munich, Germany. The technical program featured two invited keynote talks, one given by Tamer Ozsu (Sliding Window Query Processing over Data Streams), and another one given by John Mylopoulos (Data Semantics Revisited). Eight papers were accepted for the research track, with an acceptance rate of 1 in 3, and were presented in three sessions: Streams, Ontology Applications and Ontology Semantics.

Finally, the conference chairs would like to thank all the people who worked hard to make this conference a success. This includes the members of the steering committee, the members of the program committee, the invited speakers, the authors of the papers presented at the conference and the people who attended the conference.

Conference Chairs

A. Illarramendi (PC Co-chair)	University of the Basque Country, Spain
M.H. Scholl (General Chair)	University of Konstanz, Germany
D. Srivastava (PC Co-chair)	AT&T Labs-Research, USA

Program Committee

K. Aberer	EPFL, Lausanne, Switzerland
A. Borgida	Rutgers University, USA
M. Boehlen	Free University of Bozen-Bolzano, Italy
M. Bouzeghoub	University of Versailles, France
U. Cetintemel	Brown University, USA
G. Cormode	Bell Labs, USA
P. Fankhauser	IPSI Darmstadt, Germany
A. Goni	University of the Basque Country, Spain
S. Hacid	University of Claude Bernard, Lyon 1, France
F. Korn	AT&T Labs-Research, USA
N. Koudas	University of Toronto, Canada
M. Lenzerini	University of "La Sapienza", Rome, Italy
R. Meersman	VU Brussels, Belgium
E. Mena	University of Zaragoza, Spain
G. Moro	University of Bologna, Italy
J. Mylopoulos	University of Toronto, Canada
T. Pedersen	Aalborg University, Denmark
R. Ramakrishnan	University of Wisconsin, Madison, USA
R. Snodgrass	University of Arizona, USA
R. Studer	University of Karlsruhe, Germany
S. Spaccapietra	EPFL, Lausanne, Switzerland
D. Toman	University of Waterloo, Canada
V. Tsotras	University of California, Riverside, USA
J. Wang	New Jersey Institute of Technology, USA
W. Wang	University of North Carolina, USA
C. Zaniolo	University of California, Los Angeles, USA

Query Languages and Query Processing (QLQP 2006)

QLQP 2006 was the 11th workshop in the international workshop series on Foundations of Models and Languages for Data and Objects (FoMLaDO), a series initiated and run by the Working Group on Foundations of Information Systems of the German Computer Society (Gesellschaft für Informatik e.V.). QLQP 2006 addressed topics like

- semantics of query languages,
- query languages for XML, RDF, etc,
- query optimization for semistructured data,
- query languages for sensors and data streams,
- query processing in large scale distributed and autonomous systems,
- processing continuous queries,
- adaptive and robust query processors.

Workshop Chairs

Stefan Conrad	University of Düsseldorf, Germany
Cristian Pérez de Laborda	University of Düsseldorf, Germany
Kai-Uwe Sattler	TU Ilmenau, Germany

Program Committee

Wolf-Tilo Balke	L3S Research Center, University of Hanover
Stefan Conrad	University of Düsseldorf
Jens Dittrich	ETH Zurich
Johann-Christoph Freytag	HU Berlin
Torsten Grust	TU München
Ihab F. Ilyas	University of Waterloo
Wolfgang Lehner	TU Dresden
Stefan Manegold	CWI Amsterdam
Volker Markl	IBM Almaden
Holger Meyer	University of Rostock
Norman Paton	University of Manchester
Torben Bach Pedersen	Aalborg Univ.
Norbert Ritter	University of Hamburg
Kai-Uwe Sattler	TU Ilmenau
Ralf Schenkel	MPI Saarbrücken
Bernhard Seeger	University of Marburg

External Reviewers

Martin Husemann
Iryna Kozlova
Asem Omari
Christopher Popfinger
Jens Teubner

Second International Workshop on Pervasive Information Management (PIM 2006)

The number of mobile devices in use is growing at a tremendous rate. On the one hand, this is true for rather powerful devices like PDAs and smartphones, on the other hand, very lightweight devices like sensors and RFID tags are starting to be deployed in considerable numbers. This development opens the doors for new application areas where information stemming from a multitude of different sources is used to satisfy user demands. However, data management for these applications is a complex task since it has to deal with the mobility of users, devices and data as well as the specifics of wireless connectivity and the resource restrictions many of these devices exhibit. Therefore, new solutions that consider all these dimensions are needed for pervasive data management.

Information is becoming ubiquitous, highly distributed and at the same time accessible from everywhere at any time. However, accessing it takes place in highly dynamic and instable networks often using devices with limited I/O-capabilities and restricted power resources. Information obtained from different sources, among them sensors, needs to be integrated. From the user's point of view, all these difficulties should be invisible. Information access should be as similar to access from the desktop environment as possible.

These post-proceedings contain a selection of the accepted papers of the 2nd International Workshop on Pervasive Information Management, held in conjunction with the 10th International Conference on Extending Database Technology (EDBT 2006) on March 30th, 2006 in Munich, Germany. These papers address a broad range of issues in pervasive information systems. New and existing concepts and techniques are developed in the light of the rapidly increasing mobility of users and the great advances in system infrastructures, mobile devices, and sensor technologies.

Workshop Chairs

Hagen Höpfner	International University in Germany, Bruchsal, Germany
Can Türker	FGCZ Zurich, Switzerland
Birgitta König-Ries	University of Jena, Germany

Program Committee

Michel E. Adiba	Université de Grenoble, France
Susanne Boll	University of Oldenburg, Germany
Thomas Fanghänel	IBM San Jose, USA
Le Gruenwald	University of Oklahoma, USA
Manfred Hauswirth	Ecole Polytechnique Federale de Lausanne, Switzerland

Hagen Höpfner	International University in Germany, Germany, chair
Birgitta König-Ries	University of Jena, Germany, co-chair
Sanjay Kumar Madria	University of Missouri-Rolla, USA
Eduardo Mena	Universidad de Zaragoza, Spain
Boris Novikov	University of St. Petersburg, Russia
Evaggelia Pitoura	University of Ioannina, Greece
Peter Reiher	UCLA, USA
Kai-Uwe Sattler	University of Ilmenau, Germany
Heiko Schuldt	UMIT Innsbruck, Austria
Can Türker	FGCZ Zurich, Switzerland, co-chair
Özgür Ulusoy	Bilkent University, Turkey
Jari Veijalainen	University of Jyväskylä, Finland
Ouri Wolfson	University of Illinois, USA
Arkady Zaslavsky	Monash University, Australia

External Reviewers

Dirk Ahlers	OFFIS, Oldenburg, Germany
Christophe Bobineau	LSR-IMAG, Grenoble, France
Wojciech Galuba	Ecole Polytechnique Federale de Lausanne, Switzerland
Sarunas Girdzijauskas	Ecole Polytechnique Federale de Lausanne, Switzerland
Sergio Ilarri	University of Zaragoza, Spain
Thorsten Möller	University of Basel, Switzerland
Thorsten Steenweg	OFFIS, Oldenburg, Germany

Second International Workshop on Pattern Representation and Management (PaRMa 2006)

PaRMa 2006 was the second international workshop on pattern representation and management, again taking place in conjunction with the International Conference on Extending Database Technology. PaRMa workshops accommodate advances on the management of patterns as database objects with conventional and extended/dedicated database operations.

The vast volumes of data in conventional form, in documents and in multimedia files demand for methods for the discovery of useful patterns from them. Such methods from the domain of knowledge discovery deliver patterns in the form of association rules, classifiers, clusters or time series. Similarly to the need for maintaining, retrieving and updating data, there is the same paramount need to administer patterns: To store them in databases in an efficient way and to provide appropriate query languages for retrieving them; to update them as new data reveal population drifts and to identify such drifts; to design methods for the querying, presentation, evaluation and comparison of patterns.

This year, the PaRMa workshop focussed on systems and query languages. The four papers of the post-workshop proceedings present four systems and underlying conceptual models for pattern management and querying. The system PSYCHO by Catania and Maddalena manages arbitrary types of patterns, working on top of a conventional DBMS architecture. The pattern management model XDM by Meo and Psaila focusses on the integration of data and patterns in an inductive database and builds upon XML as basis for a unifying framework. The system NaviMoz by Christodoulou, Dalamagas and Sellis manages navigation patterns in the Web and shows how portal owners and administrators can gain insights on users' habitual behaviour through pattern querying and inspection. The Précis query framework by Simitsis and Koutrika deals with free-form query answering over databases and delivers query results as multi-relational tables. The PaRMa 2006 workshop also featured an invited talk on PMML by Michael Thess (prudsys). PMML is an obvious candidate for the modeling of data mining patterns, since its emphasis is on pattern specification for exchange among data mining suites. However, PMML evolved independently of database advances. The potential of interplays between database pattern management methods and PMML has been the subject of a vivid panel that followed the invited talk.

The organizers of PaRMa 2006 would like to thank the authors, the reviewers and the invited speaker for their contribution to a successful workshop. Moreover, we would like to express our gratitude to the members of the Organizing Committee of EDBT 2006 for their support.

Workshop Chairs

Myra Spiliopoulou — University of Magdeburg, Germany
Yannis Theodoridis — University of Piraeus, Greece
Panos Vassiliadis — University of Ioannina, Greece

Program Committee

Charu Aggarwal	IBM Research, USA
Jean-Francois Boulicaut	INSA Lyon, France
Barbara Catania	Univ. Genova, Italy
Paolo Ciaccia	Univ. Bologna, Italy
Sašo Džeroski	Josef Stefan Institute, Slovenia
Minos Garofalakis	Intel Research Berkeley, USA
Fabio Grandi	Univ. Bologna, Italy
Daniel A. Keim	Univ. Konstanz, Germany
Rosa Meo	Univ. Torino, Italy
Nikos Pelekis	Univ. Piraeus, Greece
Stefano Rizzi	Univ. Bologna, Italy
Timos Sellis	NTU Athens, Greece
Michalis Vazirgiannis	Athens UEB, Greece

External Reviewers

Jörn Schneidewind	Univ. Konstanz, Germany

Reactivity on the Web

Reactivity on the Web, the ability to detect simple and composite events that occur on the Web and respond to them in a timely manner, has recently emerged as an issue of concern in Web and Semantic Web circles such as the W3C (`http://www.w3.org`) and several international Semantic Web research initiatives such as REWERSE (`http://rewerse.net`). Although a common perception of the Web is that of a distributed information system giving rise to access data in a read only manner, many Web-based systems need to have the capability to update data found at (local or remote) Web resources, to exchange information about events (such as executed updates), and to detect and react not only to simple events but also to complex, real-life situations. The issue of updating data plays an important role, for example, in e-commerce systems receiving and processing buying or reservation orders, and e-learning systems selecting and delivering teaching materials depending on the students' performances on tests. The issues of notifying, detecting, and reacting upon events of interest are now beginning to play an increasingly important role within business strategies on the Web, and event-driven applications are being more widely deployed: Terms such as *zero latency enterprise*, the *real-time enterprise* and *on-demand computing* are being used to describe a vision in which events recognised anywhere within a business, can immediately activate appropriate actions across the entire enterprise and beyond. Businesses that are able to react to events quickly and take appropriate decisions are likely to have a competitive advantage.

The issue of automatic reaction in response to events of interest has its roots in the field of active databases; in particular, the issue of detecting composite events has received considerable attention. However, differences between (generally centralised) active databases and the Web, where a central clock and a central management are missing, give reasons for developing new approaches. Moreover, approaches that cope with existing and upcoming Semantic Web technologies (by gradually evolving together with these technologies) are more likely to leverage the Semantic Web endeavour. Along this line, of crucial importance for the Web and the Semantic Web is the ease of technologies' usage (in particular the languages' usage) that should be approachable also by non-programmers.

The workshop *Reactivity on the Web* was co-located with the 10th International Conference on Extending Database Technology (EDBT 2006) and represents an attempt to establish a more connected research community on Web reactivity. These proceedings contain the research articles accepted for presentation at the workshop. A total of 12 submissions were received and, based on three reviews per paper provided by the Programme Committee members, a 50 percent acceptance rate was decided. For the accepted papers a second round of reviewing was organized so as to provide high-quality workshop post-proceedings. These proceedings contain also two invited articles that were the base of the workshop's invited talks given by François Bry (University of Munich) and Alexandra Poulovassilis (University of London): one article on theses on reactive rules for the Web and one on event-condition-action languages for the Semantic Web.

Workshop Chairs

James Bailey	University of Melbourne, Australia
Sara Comai	Politecnico di Milano, Italy
Wolfgang May	Universität Göttingen, Germany
Paula-Lavinia Pătrânjan	Ludwig-Maximilians-Universität München, Germany

Program Committee

José Júlio Alves Alferes	Universidade Nova de Lisboa, Portugal
Mikael Berndtsson	Högskolan i Skövde, Sweden
Angela Bonifati	Icar-CNR, Italy
Piero Fraternali	Politecnico di Milano, Italy
Bertram Ludäscher	University of California at Davis, USA
Sebastian Schaffert	Salzburg Research, Austria (PC Chair)
Silvie Spreeuwenberg	LibRT, The Netherlands
Laurenţiu Vasiliu	Digital Enterprise Research Institute, Ireland
Marianne Winslett	University of Illinois, USA

External Reviewers

C. Viegas Damásio	R. Hasan	A. Termehchy
T. Groza	A. Lee	C. Zhang

Table of Contents

EDBT Ph.D. Workshop

Second International Workshop on Database Technologies for Handling XML Information on the Web (DataX'06)

Inconsistency and Incompleteness in Databases (IIDB)

Workshop on Information in Health Care (IIHA)

International Conference on Semantics of a Networked World: Semantics of Sequence and Time Dependent Data (ICSNW'06)

Query Languages and Query Processing (QLQP-2006)

Second International Workshop on Pervasive Information Management (PIM 2006)

Second International Workshop on Pattern Representation and Management (PaRMa'06)

Reactivity on the Web

Phenomenon-Aware Sensor Database Systems

M.H. Ali

Department of Computer Science, Purdue University
mhali@cs.purdue.edu

Abstract. Recent advances in large-scale sensor-network technologies enable the deployment of a huge number of sensors in the surrounding environment. Sensors do not live in isolation. Instead, close-by sensors experience similar environmental conditions. Hence, close-by sensors may indulge in a correlated behavior and generate a "phenomenon". A phenomenon is characterized by a group of sensors that show "similar" behavior over a period of time. Examples of detectable phenomena include the propagation over time of a pollution cloud or an oil spill region. In this research, we propose a framework to detect and track various forms of phenomena in a sensor field. This framework empowers sensor database systems with phenomenon-awareness capabilities. Phenomenon-aware sensor database systems use high-level knowledge about phenomena in the sensor field to control the acquisition of sensor data and to optimize subsequent user queries. As a vehicle for our research, we build the *Nile-PDT* system, a framework for Phenomenon Detection and Tracking inside *Nile*, a prototype data stream management system developed at Purdue University.

1 Introduction

A large body of research in the database systems area focuses on handling massive amounts of data that is streamed from sensor networks, e.g., see [7,9,10,12,19,20,29]. The main goal is to provide efficient query processing techniques for sensor data. However, emerging sensor-network applications call for new capabilities that are beyond traditional online query processing techniques. Examples of these applications include surveillance [24], object tracking [12], and environmental monitoring [25]. Mainly, these applications go past simple data retrieval to show their evolving interest in data analysis and field understanding.

In this research, we focus on extending sensor database systems with phenomenon-awareness capabilities as a step towards the understanding of sensor data. A phenomenon appears in a sensor field if a group of sensors show "similar" behavior over a period of time. In particular, phenomenon-aware sensor databases (or PhenomenaBases, for short) have two major tasks: First, it detects and tracks various forms of phenomena in space. Second, it utilizes the knowledge about phenomena in the space to optimize subsequent user queries. Although individual sensor readings can be useful by themselves, *phenomenon*

T. Grust et al. (Eds.): EDBT 2006 Workshops, LNCS 4254, pp. 1–11, 2006.

detection exploits various notions of correlation among sensor data and provides a global view of the underlying environment. Then, *phenomenon tracking* monitors the propagation of detected phenomena to reflect the changes in the surrounding environmental conditions. Given the knowledge about phenomena in the surrounding space, phenomenon-aware optimizers bridge the gap between the low-level sensor readings and the high-level understanding of phenomena to answer user queries efficiently.

1.1 Motivation

In this section, we identify five major points through which sensor-network applications benefit from *Phenomenon Detection and Tracking* (*PDT*, for short) techniques. These points can be summarized as follows:

1. **High-level description of the sensor field.** With the aid of *PDT* techniques, an application may ask for "What is going on in a sensor field?" instead of asking "What are the sensor readings?" *PDT* techniques describe the underlying sensor field using a higher level of knowledge (e.g., report a fire alarm instead of a bunch of high temperature readings).
2. **Phenomenon-guided data acquisition.** Data acquisition can be guided by detected phenomena in the sense that we reduce the sampling rate of *non-interesting* sensors (i.e., sensors that do not contribute to any phenomena). Also, we reduce the sampling rate of sensors that are (and will remain) involved in a phenomenon. Such sensors with persistent phenomena are temporarily turned off with the assumption that their phenomena will not disappear instantaneously. Sensors on the *boundaries* of a phenomenon tend to be more interesting and are likely to change their values quickly. We increase the sampling rate of boundary sensors such that we capture the possible change in their state as quickly as possible. Reducing the sampling rate of a sensor will result in a general reduction in the sensor's energy consumed in sampling, processing, and communication. Also, the processing load over the centralized DSMS (or the sink node of the sensor network) will be reduced.
3. **Data compression.** Voluminous sensor data can be compressed using *PDT* techniques. Instead of maintaining the readings of each individual sensor, we maintain phenomenon pairs (R, B), where R is the region that bounds a phenomenon with behavior B.
4. **Prediction.** Tracking a phenomenon movement and predicting its future trajectory foresees the next state of the sensor field. Based on the boundaries of a phenomenon and their trajectories, we can predict the movement of various phenomena in the space. Prediction of phenomenon-movement enables us to decide which sensors to turn on and off in order to conserve energy without losing useful information.
5. **Phenomenon-guided query processing.** Given a query and given a set of phenomena, query processing can be guided to regions with phenomena that satisfy the query predicates. Hence, the query space is reduced. All phenomena in the space are maintained and their contributing sensors are

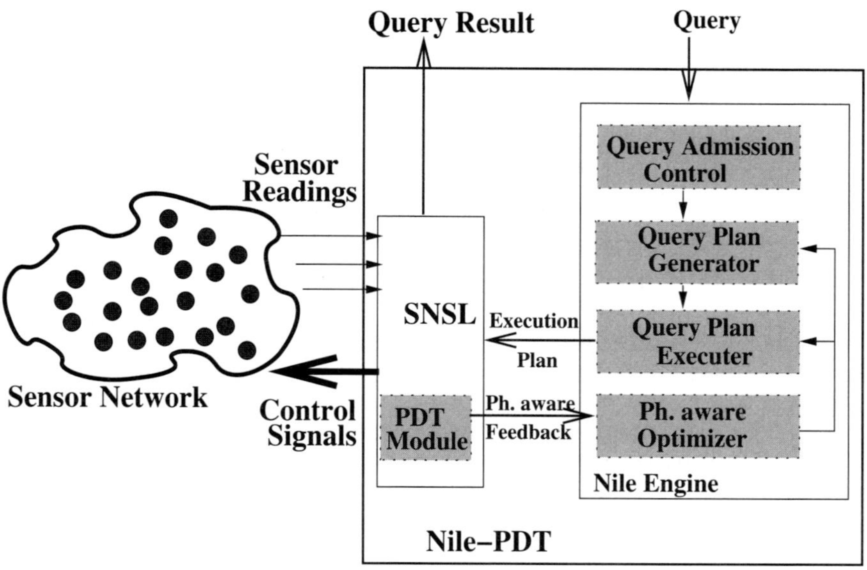

Fig. 1. Nile-PDT architecture

indexed. Then, a user query is mapped to a set of system-detected phenomena. Regions that are covered by this set of phenomena are processed to answer the query.

1.2 Applications

Several applications benefit from the detection and tracking of various phenomena in the sensor field. Examples of these applications include:

1. Tracing pollutants in the environment, e.g., oil spills, or gas leakage.
2. Reporting the excessive purchase of an item at different branches of a retail store.
3. Detecting computer worms that strike various computer sub-networks.

Notice that a phenomenon may or may not have spatial properties. The phenomenon in the first example has spatial properties, where an oil spill is a contiguous portion of the ocean surface. If a phenomenon has spatial properties, it is referred to by the term *cloud*. Retail store applications may not have the notion of spatial attributes, where retail stores can be spread arbitrary over the region. In the third application, the notion of spatial distance is relative to the network connectivity. Also, to generalize the concept of phenomena, a sensor may be a physical device that acquires readings from the environment, (e.g., temperature, light, humidity, or substance identifiers as in the first example) or a virtual sensor like the cashier machine that reads item identifiers as in the second example. A sensor may even be a piece of software that detects computer worms as in the third example.

This Ph.D. research is done in the context of *Nile* [14], a prototype data stream management system developed at Purdue University. We extend *Nile* with a *Sensor Network Support Layer* (*SNSL*) where a Phenomenon Detection and Tracking (*PDT*) module is placed. *PDT* monitors phenomena as they propagate in the sensor field and returns feedback to a phenomenon-aware query optimizer which, in turn, controls the generation and execution of query plans. Figure 1 illustrates the architecture of *Nile-PDT*.

2 Research Plan

In this section, we identify the major challenges in the design and the implementation of phenomenon-aware systems. In particular, we address the following challenges:

1. **The phenomenon-extraction challenge,** where we separate sensors that participate in a phenomenon from sensors that participate in no phenomena.
2. **The sensor-network processing requirements challenge,** where we develop algorithms that comply with the requirements of large-scale dynamically-configured sensor-networks with distributed processing capabilities.
3. **The similarity-notion challenge,** where we define various notions of similarity among sensors' behavior and develop techniques that comply with these notions.
4. **The phenomenon-interpretation challenge,** where we develop a query optimizer that makes use of knowledge about detected phenomena to answer user queries.

In the remainder of this section, we devote a subsection to explore each challenge, emphasize its associated research tasks, and propose preliminary ideas.

2.1 The Phenomenon-Extraction Challenge

As a first step towards phenomenon detection, we propose a concrete definition of a phenomenon. Two parameters control the *phenomenon* definition, the *strength* (α) and the *time span* (w). The *strength* of a phenomenon indicates that a certain phenomenon should occur at least α times to qualify as a phenomenon. (This measure is similar to the notion of support in mining association rules, e.g., see [1].) Reading a value less than α times is considered noise, e.g., impurities that affect the sensor readings. The time span w limits how far a sensor can be lagging in reporting a phenomenon. w can be viewed as a time-tolerant parameter, given the common delays in a sensor network. (This measure is similar to the notion of gaps in mining generalized sequential patterns [23].) In the light of these two parameters, a phenomenon can be defined as follows:

Definition 1. *In a sensor network SN, a phenomenon P takes place only when a set of sensors $S \subset SN$ report similar reading values more than α times within a time window w.*

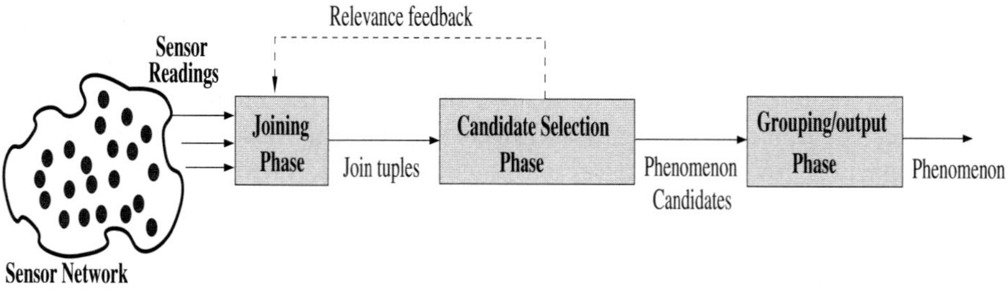

Fig. 2. Phases of the phenomenon detection Process

In [5], we simplify the definition by considering the discrete case of the phenomenon where the notion of similarity reduces to equality. (In Section 2.3, we consider other notions of similarity.) The process of *phenomenon detection* and *tracking* (*PDT*) is divided into three phases (Figure 2):

1. The *joining* that applies an in-memory *multi-way* join over the entire sensor network to detect sensors with the same value within a time frame of length w from each other.
2. The *candidate selection* phase that enforces the (α) and (w) constraints on join pairs to report phenomenon candidate members.
3. The *grouping/output* phase that groups phenomenon candidate members and investigates the application semantics to form and report phenomena to the user.

2.2 The Sensor-Network Processing Requirements Challenge

To implement a phenomenon-aware sensor database system, we need to shift the phenomenon detection phases to the sensor-network level. Distributed algorithms need to replace the centralized ones. We address five major challenges in sensor network processing:

1. **Scalability,** to face the excessive deployment of sensors in the space.
2. **Adaptivity,** to handle the gradual/abrupt appearance/disappearance of phenomena.
3. **Distributed processing,** to relieve the centralized system from possible congestions and to reduce the communication cost by filtering irrelevant data as early as possible.
4. **Dynamic configuration,** where sensors may be added or removed from the network based on the network conditions, the sensor's lifetime, and the availability of additional sensors.
5. **Limited energy,** to reduce the frequency of battery replacement in environments where the existence of a human being is either tough or dangerous, e.g., habitat monitoring [25].

To address the above challenges, we place a new operator (the *SNJoin* operator [3]) at the core of the *PDT* module. *SNJoin* is a distributed multi-way join operator that is specially designed for large-scale dynamically-configured sensor networks. We model the sensor network as an ad-hoc network of sensor nodes that are grouped into clusters based on their energy level and their spatial locations. One node per cluster is dedicated to serve as the cluster head. *SNJoin* decomposes the join operation into multiple smaller join operations that are performed separately over each cluster at the cluster head. Then, each cluster head chooses a cluster-head probing sequence to probe other cluster heads looking for matches. Ideally, the cluster-head probing sequence spans all cluster heads in the network to produce as much output results as possible. However, due to the large size of the network and its associated communication cost, it is practical to probe only clusters where it is more likely to find matches. Notice that only a small number of sensors (compared to the thousands of sensors in the network) join with each other. In *SNJoin*, we introduce the concept of query processing with relevance feedback. As illustrated in Figure 2, a relevance feedback is given from the candidate selection phase to the joining phase. The objective of query processing with relevance feedback is to guide the join operation to process only relevant cluster heads, i.e., clusters that generate the same values. This selective probing reduces both the processing cost and the communication cost at the price of losing some streams that could have participated in the join if they were included in the probing sequence.

2.3 The Similarity-Notion Challenge

In this section, we generalize our work to include continuous phenomena. Continuous phenomena are generated by sensors whose values are drawn from continuous ranges. The major challenge in continuous phenomena comes from the fact that similarity among sensors' behavior does not necessarily mean equality. Instead, various notions of similarity need to be explored. We plan to examine the following notions of similarity:

1. **Similar values,** where similarity is assessed based on a distance function "dist". Two values v_1 and v_2 are considered similar if $dist(v_1, v_2) < D$.
2. **Similar behavior,** where we extract summaries from the sensor data (e.g., histograms, count sketches, or user-defined summaries) that capture the sensors' behavior over a window of time. Similarity is assessed based on the distance between the summaries.
3. **Similar trend,** where the increase/decrease in one sensor readings implies the increase/decrease of another sensor's readings. Generally, the change in the readings of one sensor is related to the change in the other sensor's readings by a function f (i.e., $\triangle v_1 = f(\triangle v_2)$). For example, the increase in the readings of smoke detectors is usually accompanied by an increase in the readings of temperature sensors.

We investigate two approaches to handle continuous phenomena: First, as a preprocessing phase, we group sensor readings into clusters, represent each reading by its cluster identifier, and apply discrete *PDT* techniques over cluster identifiers. Second, we replace the equality join by a similarity join, where the similarity function is a user-defined function that is provided as part of the query syntax. Initial implementation of *PDT* using similarity join is conducted in [2].

2.4 The Phenomenon-Interpretation Challenge

A phenomenon-aware system implies that the phenomenon detection and tracking process is always running in the background to detect new phenomena and to track the propagation of already-detected phenomena. Based on the understanding of surrounding phenomena, phenomenon-aware systems answer user queries. The ultimate goal of our research is to build a sensor database system that optimizes user queries on a *"phenomenon detection guides query processing"* basis. We view phenomenon-aware query optimization as a rich area of research where phenomenon understanding alters the construction/execution of query plans. We explore phenomenon-aware query optimization along two directions:

1. Increasing the sampling rate of sensors that contribute to phenomena associated with active queries.
2. Controlling the join probing sequence such that a reading coming from one sensor probes only sensors where a match is likely to be found. The join probing sequence is tuned to favor the joins that affect the appearance or the disappearance of a phenomenon.

3 Experiments

As a proof of concept, we conduct an experimental study to show the performance gains a phenomenon-aware optimizer may achieve. We generate a set of 2000 sensors using the Nile-PDT simulator [2]. Each sensor generates a stream of readings at a rate of 1 reading per second. We detect and track discrete phenomena as discussed in [5]. Detected phenomena are fed into a naive phenomenon-aware query optimizer. The naive optimizer searches the list of detected phenomena, determines interesting phenomenon regions (i.e., phenomenon regions that satisfy the query predicates), and deploys the query only over regions of its interesting phenomena. We process a set of 100 selection query with predicate selectivities that range from 1% to 20% of the whole space.

Two experiments are conducted. First, we measure the energy saved (in terms of the number of transmitted messages) using a phenomenon-guided data acquisition. Sensors that contribute to phenomena are sampled more frequently than sensors that contribute to no phenomena. The number of transmitted sensor readings is reduced by up to 65%. Second, we measure the accuracy of the query result in terms of the average number of output tuples. Figure 3 illustrates the performance of the query processor in the following cases:

1. **No-PDT,** where no PDT-capabilities are used.
2. **Exact,** where infinite resources are given to calculate the answer.
3. **Naive-PDT,** where a naive PDT phenomenon-aware optimizer is used.
4. **Target-PDT**, which is an imaginary curve that reflects where we expect the performance of a non-naive optimizer will fall.

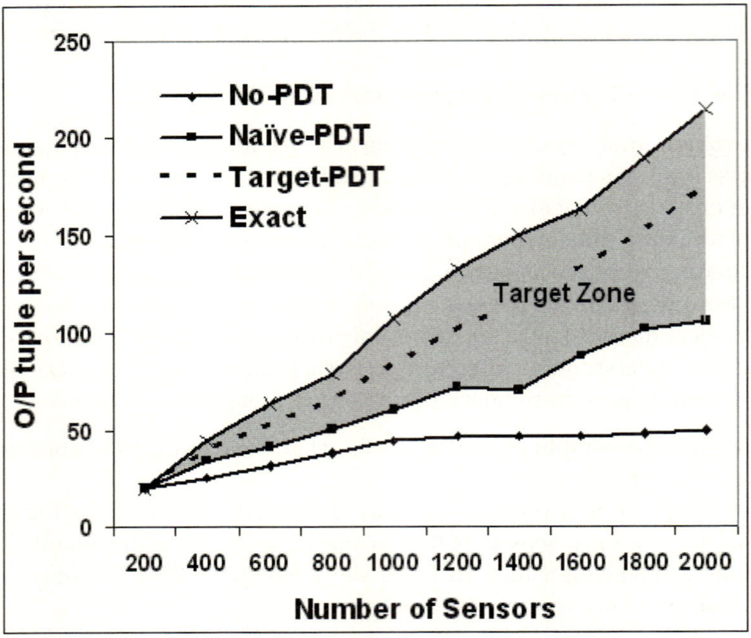

Fig. 3. Performance of Nile-PDT

The Target-PDT curve is somewhere between the *naive-PDT* and the *Exact* curves (i.e., the target zone in the figure).

4 Related Work

Sensors are devices that are capable of sampling, processing, and transmitting readings from the surrounding environment. Various techniques have been proposed to handle the *sampling* [4,6,10,20], *processing* [9,29], and *transmission* [8,16,18] tasks. In this section, we overview other techniques that analyze sensor data to track objects and/or regions as they move in the space. We also highlight the join operation over data streams due to its important role in the process of phenomenon detection and tracking.

To reduce the overall power consumption of the sensor network while object tracking, [28] proposes a prediction-based strategy that focuses on regions where the moving object is likely to appear. In [30], the tree-like communication structure of the sensor network is reconfigured dynamically to reduce the number of hops between a sensor and the sink node as the sensor comes closer to the moving object. Instead of tracking a single object, [2,5] provide a framework to detect and track phenomena in a sensor field once a region of sensors exhibit a common behavior. The work in [22] investigates how to detect boundaries that separate homogeneous regions. In [15], continuous regions with similar values are grouped into homogeneous regions called *isobars*.

The join operation detects similarities in value among sensors along the trajectory of a moving object or among sensors in the same phenomenon region. For example, [12] tracks moving objects in a sensor field through a window join algorithm (*w-join*). The join operation has been studied thoroughly in the literature, e.g., [11,12,13]. Symmetric Hash Join [27] is the first algorithm that takes care of the infiniteness of the data source. XJoin [26] provides disk management to store overflowing tuples on disk for later processing. An asymmetric window join over two data streams with different arrival rates is discussed in [17]. The Hash-Merge Join (*HMJ*) [21] is a recent non-blocking join algorithm that produces early join results. In our work, we propose the *SNJoin* operator [3], a multi-way join operator that is specially designed for large-scale dynamically-configured sensor networks.

5 Conclusions

In this paper, we proposed a framework for phenomenon-aware sensor database systems. We provided a concrete definition for the phenomenon and explored various notions of similarity among sensors' behavior. In a phenomenon-aware sensor database system, the knowledge gained through detected phenomena guides query processing to regions of interest in the sensor field. The proposed research plan has four phases. The first phase is concerned with detecting and tracking discrete phenomena (i.e., the notion of similarity reduces to equality) in a centralized data stream management system. The second phase pushes the detection and tracking of phenomena to the sensor-network level in a distributed-processing fashion. The third phase addresses various notions of similarity among sensors' behavior and generalizes the phenomenon concept to include continuous phenomena. The fourth phase achieves, through a phenomenon-aware optimizer, the ultimate goal of answering user queries efficiently based on the knowledge about phenomena in the space.

References

1. R. Agrawal and R. Srikant. Fast algorithms for mining association rules in large databases. In *Proc. of VLDB*, 1994.
2. M. H. Ali, W. G. Aref, R. Bose, A. K. Elmagarmid, A. Helal, I. Kamel, and M. F. Mokbel. Nile-pdt: A phenomena detection and tracking framework for data stream management systems. In *Proc. of VLDB*, 2005.
3. M. H. Ali, W. G. Aref, and I. Kamel. Multi-way joins for sensor-network databases. Technical Report CSD-05-21, Department of Computer Science, Purdue University, 2005.
4. M. H. Ali, W. G. Aref, and C. Nita-Rotaru. Spass: Scalable and energy-efficient data acquisition in sensor databases. In *Proc. of the International ACM Workshop on Data Engineering for Wireless and Mobile Access (MobiDE)*, 2005.
5. M. H. Ali, M. F. Mokbel, W. G. Aref, and I. Kamel. Detection and tracking of discrete phenomena in sensor-network databases. In *Proc. of SSDBM*, 2005.

6. B. Babcoc, M. Datar, and R. Motwani. Sampling from a moving window over streaming data. In *Proc. of the Annual ACM-SIAM Symp. on Discrete Algorithms*, 2002.
7. P. Bonnet, J. E. Gehrke, and P. Seshadri. Towards sensor database systems. In *Proc. of MDM*, 2001.
8. A. Cerpa and D. Estrin. Ascent: Adaptive self-configuring sensor networks topologies. In *Proc. of INFOCOM*, 2002.
9. J. Considine, F. Li, G. Kollios, and J. W. Byers. Approximate aggregation techniques for sensor databases. In *Proc. of ICDE*, 2004.
10. A. Deshpande, C. Guestrin, S. Madden, J. M. Hellerstein, and W. Hong. Model-driven data acquisition in sensor networks. In *Proc. of VLDB*, 2004.
11. L. Golab and M. T. Ozsu. Processing sliding window multi-joins in continuous queries over data streams. In *Proc. of VLDB*, 2003.
12. M. A. Hammad, W. G. Aref, and A. K. Elmagarmid. Stream window join: Tracking moving objects in sensor-network databases. In *Proc. of SSDBM*, 2003.
13. M. A. Hammad, M. Franklin, W. G. Aref, and A. K. Elmagarmid. Scheduling for shared window joins over data streams. In *Proc. of VLDB*, 2003.
14. M. A. Hammad, M. F. Mokbel, M. H. Ali, W. G. Aref, A. C. Catlin, A. K. Elmagarmid, M. Eltabakh, M. G. Elfeky, T. Ghanem, R. Gwadera, I. F. Ilyas, M. Marzouk, and X. Xiong. Nile: A query processing engine for data streams. In *Proc. of ICDE*, 2004.
15. J. M. Hellerstein, W. Hong, S. Madden, and K. Stanek. Beyond average: Toward sophisticated sensing with queries. In *Proc. of IPSN*, 2003.
16. C. Intanagonwiwat, R. Govindan, and D. Estrin. Directed diffusion: a scalable and robust communication paradigm for sensor networks. In *Proc. of MOBICOM*, 2000.
17. J. Kang, J. F. Naughton, and S. D. Viglas. Evaluating window joins over unbounded streams. In *Proc. of ICDE*, 2003.
18. J. Kulik, W. R. Heinzelman, and H. Balakrishnan. Negotiation-based protocols for disseminating information in wireless sensor networks. *ACM Wireless Networks*, 8(2-3):169–185, 2002.
19. S. Madden and M. Franklin. Fjording the stream: An architecture for queries over streaming sensor data. In *Proc. of ICDE*, 2002.
20. S. Madden, M. Franklin, J. M. Hellerstein, and W. Hong. The design of an acquisitional query processor for sensor networks. In *Proc. of SIGMOD*, 2003.
21. M. Mokbel, M. Lu, and W. Aref. Hash-merge join: A non-blocking join algorithm for producing fast and early join results. In *Proc. of ICDE*, 2004.
22. R. Nowak and U. Mitra. Boundary estimation in sensor networks: Theory and methods. In *Proc. of IPSN*, 2003.
23. R. Srikant and R. Agrawal. Mining sequential patterns: Generalizations and performance improvements. In *Proc. of EDBT*, 1996.
24. S. Srinivasan, H. Latchman, J. Shea, T. Wong, and J. McNair. Airborne traffic surveillance systems: video surveillance of highway traffic. In *the 2nd ACM international workshop on Video surveillance & sensor networks*, 2004.
25. R. Szewczyk, E. Osterweil, J. Polastre, M. Hamilton, A. Mainwaring, and D. Estrin. Habitat monitoring with sensor networks. *Communications of ACM*, 47(6):34–40, 2004.
26. T. Urhan and M. Franklin. Xjoin: A reactively-scheduled pipelined join operator. *IEEE Data Eng. Bull.*, 23(2):27–33, 2000.

27. A. N. Wilschut and E. M. G. Apers. Pipelining in query execution. In *Proc. of the International Conference on Databases, Parallel Architectures and their Applications*, 1991.
28. Y. Xu, J. Winter, and W.-C. Lee. Prediction-based strategies for energy saving in object tracking sensor networks. In *Proc. of MDM*, 2004.
29. Y. Yao and J. Gehrke. Query processing in sensor networks. In *Proc. of CIDR*, 2003.
30. W. Zhang and G. Cao. Optimizing tree reconfiguration for mobile target tracking in sensor networks. In *Proc. of INFOCOM*, 2004.

Scalable Continuous Query Processing and Moving Object Indexing in Spatio-temporal Databases

Xiaopeng Xiong

Department of Computer Science, Purdue University
xxiong@cs.purdue.edu

Abstract. Spatio-temporal database systems aim to answer continuous spatio-temporal queries issued over moving objects. In many scenarios such as in a wide area, the number of outstanding queries and the number of moving objects are so large that a server fails to process queries promptly. In our work, we aim to develop scalable techniques for spatio-temporal database systems. We focus on two aspects of spatio-temporal database systems: 1) the query processing algorithms for a large set of concurrent queries, and 2) the underlying indexing structures for constantly moving objects. For continuous query processing, we explore the techniques of *Incremental Evaluation* and *Shared Execution*, especially to k-nearest-neighbor queries. For moving object indexing, we utilize *Update Memos* to support frequent updates efficiently in spatial indexes such as R-trees. In this paper, we first identify the challenges towards scalable spatio-temporal databases, then review the current contributions we have achieved so far and discuss future research directions.

1 Challenges and Motivations

The integration of position locators and mobile devices enables new pervasive location-aware computing environments [3,32] where all objects of interest can determine their locations. In such environments, moving objects move continuously and send location updates periodically to spatio-temporal databases. Spatio-temporal database servers index the locations of moving objects and process outstanding continuous queries. Characterized by a large number of moving objects and a large number of continuous spatio-temporal queries, spatio-temporal databases are required to exhibit high scalability in terms of the number of moving objects and the number of continuous queries.

To increase the scalability of spatio-temporal databases, there exist two main challenges. The first challenge is to support a large set of continuous queries concurrently. With the ubiquity and pervasiveness of location-aware devices and services, a set of continuous queries execute simultaneously in a spatio-temporal database server. In the case that the number of queries is too large, the performance of the database degrades and queries suffer long response time. Because of the real-timeliness of the location-aware applications, long delay makes the query answers obsolete. Therefore, new query processing algorithms addressing

T. Grust et al. (Eds.): EDBT 2006 Workshops, LNCS 4254, pp. 12–21, 2006.

both efficiency and scalability are required for answering a set of concurrent spatio-temporal queries.

The second challenge for building scalable spatio-temporal databases is to index moving objects efficiently. Building indexes on moving objects can facilitate significantly query processing in spatio-temporal databases. However, due to the dynamic property of moving objects, the underlying indexing structures will receive numerous updates during a short period of time. Given the fact that update processing is costly, traditional spatial indexes may not be applied directly to spatio-temporal databases. This situation calls for new indexing techniques supporting frequent updates.

The above two challenges motivate us to develop scalable techniques for both continuous query processing and moving object indexing in spatio-temporal databases. Specifically, we propose the *SEA-CNN* algorithm for evaluating a large set of continuous k-Nearest-Neighbor queries. While SEA-CNN addresses continuous k-nearest-neighbor queries, it has potential to extend to other types of queries. Meanwhile, we propose the *RUM-tree* for indexing moving objects by enhancing the standard R-trees with *Update Memos*. The update scheme utilized in the RUM-tree can be applied to other indexes to improve their update performance.

In the rest of the paper, we review our research works conducted so far and discuss future Ph.D. research directions.

2 Current PhD Contributions

In this section, we review the contributions we have achieved to build highly scalable spatio-temporal database management systems. The efforts focus on two aspects: (1) Continuous query processing, especially, k-Nearest-Neighbor query processing and (2) Moving object indexing. For each aspect, we first summarize the related works and then generalize our current work. In the following discussion, we assume a two-dimensional environment where objects move continuously and their locations are sampled to the server from time to time. However, the proposed techniques can be applied to higher dimensional environments as well.

2.1 SEA-CNN: Shared Execution Algorithm for Continuous k-Nearest Neighbor Queries

Related Work. The scalability in spatio-temporal queries has been addressed recently in [9,19,23,34,39,54]. The main idea is to provide the ability to evaluate concurrently a set of continuous spatio-temporal queries. Specifically, these algorithms work for stationary range queries [9,39], distributed systems [19], or continuous range queries [34,54]. Utilizing a *shared-execution* paradigm as a means to achieve scalability has been used successfully in many applications, e.g., in NiagaraCQ [14] for web queries, in PSoup [12,13] for streaming queries, and in SINA [34] for continuous spatio-temporal range query. However, to our best knowledge, there has no former work that addresses the scalability issue of k-Nearest-Neighbor queries.

K-nearest-neighbor queries are well-studied in traditional databases (e.g., see [21,26,36,41]). The main idea is to traverse a static R-tree-like structure [20] using *"branch and bound"* algorithms. For spatio-temporal databases, a direct extension of traditional techniques is to use branch and bound techniques for TPR-tree-like structures [7,29]. The TPR-tree family (e.g., [42,43,49]) indexes moving objects given their future trajectory movements. Continuous k-nearest-neighbor queries (CkNN) are first addressed in [44] from the modeling and query language perspectives. Recently, three approaches have been proposed to address CkNN queries [22,46,48]. Mainly, these approaches are based on: (1) Sampling [46]. Snapshot queries are reevaluated with each location change of the moving query. At each evaluation time, the query may get benefit from the previous result of the last evaluation. (2) Trajectory [22,48]. Snapshot queries are evaluated based on the knowledge of the future trajectory. Once the trajectory information is changed, the query needs to be reevaluated. However, the scalability issue of k-Nearest-Neighbor query has not been addressed by the above works yet.

Orthogonal but related to our work, are the recently proposed k-NN join algorithms [8,51]. The k-nearest-neighbor join operation combines each point of one data set with its k-nearest-neighbors in another data set. The main idea is to use either an R-tree [8] or the so-called *G-ordering* [51] for indexing static objects from both data sets. Then, both R-trees or G-ordered sorted data from the two data sets are joined either with an R-tree join or a nested-loops join algorithm, respectively. The CkNN problem is similar in spirit to that of [8,51]. However, we focus on spatio-temporal applications where both objects and queries are highly dynamic and continuously change their locations.

Our Contributions. In [53], we propose, SEA-CNN, a *Shared Execution Algorithm* for evaluating a large set of CkNN queries continuously. SEA-CNN introduces a general framework for processing large numbers of simultaneous CkNN queries. SEA-CNN is applicable to all mutability combinations of objects and queries, namely, SEA-CNN can deal with: (1) Stationary queries issued on moving objects (e.g., "Continuously find the three nearest taxis to my hotel"). (2) Moving queries issued on stationary objects (e.g., "Continuously report the 5 nearest gas stations while I am driving"). (3) Moving queries issued on moving objects (e.g., "Continuously find the nearest tank in the battlefield until I reach my destination"). In contrast to former work, SEA-CNN does not make any assumptions about the movement of objects, e.g., the objects' velocities and shapes of trajectories.

Unlike traditional snapshot queries, the most important issue in processing continuous queries is to maintain the query answer continuously rather than to obtain the initial answer. The cost of evaluating an initial query answer is amortized by the long running time of continuous queries. Thus, our objective in SEA-CNN is not to propose another kNN algorithm. In fact, any existing algorithm for kNN queries can be utilized by SEA-CNN to initialize the answer of a CkNN query. In contrast, SEA-CNN focuses on maintaining the query answer continuously during the motion of objects/queries.

SEA-CNN is designed with two distinguishing features: (1) Incremental evaluation based on former query answers, and (2) Scalability in terms of the number of moving objects and the number of CkNN queries. Incremental evaluation entails that only queries whose answers are affected by the motion of objects or queries are reevaluated. SEA-CNN associates a searching region with each CkNN query. The searching region narrows the scope of a CkNN's reevaluation. The scalability of SEA-CNN is achieved by employing a *shared execution* paradigm on concurrently running queries. Shared execution entails that all the concurrent CkNNs along with their associated searching regions are grouped into a common query table. Thus, the problem of evaluating numerous CkNN queries reduces to performing a spatial join operation between the query table and the set of moving objects (the object table).

During the course of execution, SEA-CNN groups CkNN queries in a query table. Each entry stores the information of the corresponding query along with its searching region. Instead of processing the incoming update information as soon as they arrive, SEA-CNN buffers the updates and periodically flushes them into a disk-based structure. During the flushing of updates, SEA-CNN associates a searching region with each query entry. Then, SEA-CNN performs a spatial join between the moving objects table and the moving queries table.

By combining incremental evaluation and shared execution, SEA-CNN achieves both efficiency and scalability. In [53], we provide theoretical analysis of SEA-CNN in terms of its execution cost and memory requirements, and the effects of other tunable parameters. We also provide a comprehensive set of experiments demonstrating that, in comparison to other R-tree-based CkNN techniques, SEA-CNN is highly scalable and is more efficient in terms of I/O and CPU costs.

2.2 RUM-Tree: R-Trees with Update Memos

Related Work. As one of the dominant choices for indexing spatial objects, the R-tree [20] and the R*-tree [6] exhibit superior search performance in spatial databases. However, R-trees were originally designed for static data where updates rarely happen. The R-tree is not directly applicable to dynamic location-aware environments due to their costly update operation. To facilitate the processing of continuous spatio-temporal queries, for the past decade, many research efforts focus on developing indexes on spatio-temporal objects (e.g., see [33] for a survey). There are two main categories for indexing spatio-temporal objects: (1) trajectory-based, and (2) sampling-based. For the object trajectory based indexing, four approaches have been investigated: (1) Duality transformation (e.g., see [1,16,27,37]), (2) Quad-tree-based methods (e.g., see [50]), (3) R-tree-based index structures (e.g., see [38,39,42,43,49]), and (4) B-tree-based structures [24]. For the sampling-based indexing, the Lazy-update R-tree (LUR-tree) [28] modifies the original R-tree structure to support frequent updates. A hash-based structure is used in [45,47] where the space is partitioned into a set of overlapped zones. SETI [10] is a logical index structure that divides the space into non-overlapped zones. Grid-based structures have been used to maintain only the current locations of moving objects (e.g., see [19,34,53]). One common limitation of the above techniques is that the corresponding old entry has to be removed from the index when an update happens. On the contrary, one unique feature of our work is to allow old entries of an object co-exist with the latest entry.

Our Contributions. In [52], we propose the RUM-tree (stands for R-tree with Update Memo) that aims to minimize the update cost in R-trees. The main idea behind the RUM-tree is as follows. When an update happens, the old entry of the data item is not required to be removed. Instead, the old entry is allowed to co-exist with newer entries before it is removed later. In the RUM-tree, specially designed *Garbage Cleaners* are employed to periodically remove obsolete entries in bulks.

In the RUM-tree, each leaf entry is assigned a *stamp* when the entry is inserted into the tree. The stamp places a temporal relationship among leaf entries, i.e., an entry with a smaller stamp was inserted before an entry with a larger stamp. Accordingly, the leaf entry of the RUM-tree is extended to enclose the identifier of the stored object and the assigned stamp number.

The RUM-tree maintains an auxiliary structure, termed the *Update Memo* (UM, for short). The main purpose of UM is to distinguish the obsolete entries from the latest entries. UM contains entries of the form: $(oid, S_{latest}, N_{old})$, where *oid* is an object identifier, S_{latest} is the *stamp* of the *latest* entry of the object *oid*, and N_{old} is the maximum number of *obsolete* entries for the object *oid* in the RUM-tree. As an example, a UM entry $(O_{99}, 1000, 2)$ entails that in the RUM-tree there exist at most two *obsolete* entries for the object O_{99}, and that the *latest* entry of O_{99} bears the *stamp* of 1000. To accelerate searching, the update memo is hashed on the *oid* attribute.

The RUM-tree employs *Garbage Cleaners* to limit the number of obsolete entries in the tree and to limit the size of UM. The garbage cleaner deletes the obsolete entries *lazily* and in *batches*. Deleting *lazily* means that obsolete entries are not removed immediately; Deleting in *batches* means that multiple obsolete entries in the same leaf node are removed at the same time.

We explore two mechanisms of garbage cleaning in the RUM-tree. The first mechanism of garbage cleaning makes use of the notion of *cleaning tokens*. A *cleaning token* is a logical token that traverses all leaf nodes of the RUM-tree horizontally. The token is passed from one leaf node to the next every time when the RUM-tree receives a certain number of updates. The node holding a cleaning token inspects all entries in the node and cleans its obsolete entries, and then passes the token to the next leaf node after I updates. To locate the next leaf node quickly, the leaf nodes of the RUM-tree are doubly-linked in cycle. To speed up the cleaning process, multiple cleaning tokens may work in parallel in the garbage cleaner. In this case, each token serves a subset of the leaf nodes. Besides the cleaning tokens, another *clean-upon-touch* mechanism of garbage cleaning is performed whenever a leaf node is accessed during an insert/update. As a side effect of insert/update, such clean-upon-touch process does not incur extra disk accesses. When working with the cleaning tokens, the clean-upon-touch reduces the garbage ratio and the size of UM dramatically.

With *garbage cleaners*, the size of UM is kept rather small and can practically fit in main memory of nowadays machines. To check whether an RUM-tree entry is an obsolete entry or not, we just need to compare the stamp number of entry with the S_{latest} of the corresponding UM entry. If the two values are equivalent, the RUM-tree entry is the latest entry for the object. Otherwise, the entry is an obsolete entry.

The Update Memo eliminates the need to delete the old data item from the index during an update. Therefore, the total cost for update processing is reduced dramatically. The RUM-tree has the following distinguishing advantages: (1) The RUM-tree achieves significantly lower update cost than other R-tree variants while offering similar search performance; (2) The update memo is much smaller than the secondary index used in other approaches, e.g., in [28,30]. The *garbage cleaner* guarantees an upper-bound on the size of the Update Memo making it practically suitable for main memory; (3) The update performance of the RUM-tree is stable with respect to the changes between consecutive updates, to the extents of moving objects, and to the number of moving objects.

In [52], we present the RUM-tree along with the associated update, insert, delete and range search algorithms inside the RUM-tree. We design a garbage cleaner based on the concept of cleaning tokens to remove obsolete entries efficiently. Further, we theoretically analyze the update costs for the RUM-tree and for other R-tree variants employing top-down or bottom-up update approaches. We also derive an upper-bound on the size of the Update Memo. Furthermore, we conduct a comprehensive set of experiments. The experimental results indicate that the RUM-tree outperforms other R-tree variants, e.g., R*-tree [6] and FUR-tree [30], by up to a factor of eight in the presence of frequent updates.

3 Future Research Directions

There are still many research issues that can be extended from our current work. The future work can be generalized in the following two aspects.

3.1 Continuous Query Processing

Alternative Underlying Indexing Structure. In our current work, the SEA-CNN framework utilizes a grid-based structure to index the current locations of moving objects. In this case, auxiliary indexing structures are required to index the identifiers of both objects and queries. In this research direction, we aim to utilize a more efficient underlying index structure in the SEA-CNN to further boost the query processing. Specifically, we plan to incorporate the memo-based techniques as employed in the RUM-tree into the grid-based structure to avoid the overhead of auxiliary indexes. In this way, we expect the performance of SEA-CNN can be further improved.

Historical and Predicative Queries. Currently, the *SEA-CNN* framework mainly supports NOW queries, namely, queries only ask for the current status of moving objects. In this research direction, we plan to extend the SEA-CNN framework to support queries that require historical information and future movement predication. To support historical query, SEA-CNN should be coped with efficient indexing structures applicable for historical search. To support future query, SEA-CNN needs to be extended from the sample-based model to the trajectory-based model, thus future movement can be predicted based on the trajectory information.

3.2 Moving Object Indexing

Crash Recovery. In this direction, we address the issue of recovering the RUM-tree in the case of system failure. When the system crashes, the information in the update memo is lost. Therefore, our goal is to rebuild the update memo based on the tree on disk. Since the recovery problem is closely related to the logging problem, we aim to design different recovery algorithms based on various logging policies.

Concurrency Control. Concurrency control in standard R-trees is provided by Dynamic Granular Locking (DGL) [11]. In this direction, we aim to extend the DGL to support concurrency accesses in the RUM-tree. We investigate the throughput of the RUM-tree under concurrency accesses and compare the performance with other R-tree variants.

Bulk Updates. Bulk loading [18,25,31,40] and bulk insertions [2,5,15,17] in R-trees have been explored during the last decade. However, none of the previous works addresses the issue of updating indexed R-tree entries in bulk manners. The main reason is that for a set of updates that will go to the same R-tree node, the corresponding old entries are most likely to reside in different R-tree nodes. Identifying these R-tree nodes containing old entries causes high overhead. On the contrary, reducing an update operation to an insert operation enables the RUM-tree to support bulk updates efficiently. Since there are no deletions of old entries, bulk updates in the RUM-tree can be performed in a way similar to bulk insertions in ordinary R-trees. In this research direction, we aim to propose efficient and scalable bulk update approaches based on the RUM-tree structure.

Extensions to Other Indexing Structures. The proposed update memo inside the RUM-tree is general in the sense that it is not limited to the R-trees, or limited to spatial indexes. The update scheme employed by the RUM-tree can potentially be applied to many other spatial and non-spatial indexes to enhance their update performance. Currently, we are investigating the update performance of the enhanced Grid File [35] by applying an update memo to the original structure. In the near future, we plan to apply our techniques to more index structures, e.g., SP-GiST [4] and B-trees.

Acknowledgements

This work is supported in part by the National Science Foundation under Grants IIS-0093116 and IIS-0209120.

References

1. Pankaj K. Agarwal, Lars Arge, and Jeff Erickson. Indexing Moving Points. In *PODS*, May 2000.
2. Ning An, Kothuri Venkata Ravi Kanth, and Siva Ravada. Improving performance with bulk-inserts in oracle r-trees. In *VLDB*, 2003.
3. Walid G. Aref, Susanne E. Hambrusch, and Sunil Prabhakar. Pervasive Location Aware Computing Environments (PLACE). http://www.cs.purdue.edu/place/.
4. Walid G. Aref and Ihab F. Ilyas. SP-GiST: An Extensible Database Index for Supporting Space Partitioning Trees. *Journal of Intelligent Information Systems , JIIS*, 17(2-3), 2001.
5. Lars Arge, Klaus Hinrichs, Jan Vahrenhold, and Jeffrey Scott Vitter. Efficient bulk operations on dynamic r-trees. *Algorithmica*, 33(1), 2002.
6. Norbert Beckmann, Hans-Peter Kriegel, Ralf Schneider, and Bernhard Seeger. The R*-Tree: An Efficient and Robust Access Method for Points and Rectangles. In *SIGMOD*, 1990.
7. Rimantas Benetis, Christian S. Jensen, Gytis Karciauskas, and Simonas Saltenis. Nearest Neighbor and Reverse Nearest Neighbor Queries for Moving Objects. In *IDEAS*, 2002.
8. Christian Bohm and Florian Krebs. The k-Nearest Neighbor Join: Turbo Charging the KDD Process. In *Knowledge and Information Systems (KAIS), in print*, 2004.
9. Ying Cai, Kien A. Hua, and Guohong Cao. Processing Range-Monitoring Queries on Heterogeneous Mobile Objects. In *Mobile Data Management, MDM*, 2004.
10. V. Prasad Chakka, Adam Everspaugh, and Jignesh M. Patel. Indexing Large Trajectory Data Sets with SETI. In *Proc. of the Conf. on Innovative Data Systems Research, CIDR*, 2003.
11. Kaushik Chakrabarti and Sharad Mehrotra. Dynamic granular locking approach to phantom protection in r-trees. In *ICDE*, 1998.
12. Sirish Chandrasekaran and Michael J. Franklin. Streaming Queries over Streaming Data. In *VLDB*, 2002.
13. Sirish Chandrasekaran and Michael J. Franklin. Psoup: a system for streaming queries over streaming data. *VLDB Journal*, 12(2), 2003.
14. Jianjun Chen, David J. DeWitt, Feng Tian, and Yuan Wang. NiagaraCQ: A Scalable Continuous Query System for Internet Databases. In *SIGMOD*, 2000.
15. Li Chen, Rupesh Choubey, and Elke A. Rundensteiner. Bulk-insertions into r-trees using the small-tree-large-tree approach. In *GIS*, 1998.
16. Hae Don Chon, Divyakant Agrawal, and Amr El Abbadi. Storage and Retrieval of Moving Objects. In *Mobile Data Management*, January 2001.
17. Rupesh Choubey, Li Chen, and Elke A. Rundensteiner. Gbi: A generalized r-tree bulk-insertion strategy. In *SSD*, 1999.
18. Jochen Van den Bercken, Bernhard Seeger, and Peter Widmayer. A generic approach to bulk loading multidimensional index structures. In *VLDB*, 1997.
19. Bugra Gedik and Ling Liu. MobiEyes: Distributed Processing of Continuously Moving Queries on Moving Objects in a Mobile System. In *EDBT*, 2004.
20. Antonin Guttman. R-Trees: A Dynamic Index Structure for Spatial Searching. In *SIGMOD*, 1984.
21. Gsli R. Hjaltason and Hanan Samet. Distance browsing in spatial databases. *TODS*, 24(2), 1999.
22. Glenn S. Iwerks, Hanan Samet, and Ken Smith. Continuous K-Nearest Neighbor Queries for Continuously Moving Points with Updates. In *VLDB*, 2003.

23. Glenn S. Iwerks, Hanan Samet, and Kenneth P. Smith. Maintenance of Spatial Semijoin Queries on Moving Points. In *VLDB*, 2004.
24. Christian S. Jensen, Dan Lin, and Beng Chin Ooi. Query and Update Efficient B+-Tree Based Indexing of Moving Objects. In *VLDB*, 2004.
25. Ibrahim Kamel and Christos Faloutsos. On packing r-trees. In *CIKM*, 1993.
26. Norio Katayama and Shin'ichi Satoh. The SR-tree: An Index Structure for High-Dimensional Nearest Neighbor Queries. In *SIGMOD*, May 1997.
27. George Kollios, Dimitrios Gunopulos, and Vassilis J. Tsotras. On Indexing Mobile Objects. In *PODS*, 1999.
28. Dongseop Kwon, Sangjun Lee, and Sukho Lee. Indexing the Current Positions of Moving Objects Using the Lazy Update R-tree. In *Mobile Data Management, MDM*, 2002.
29. Iosif Lazaridis, Kriengkrai Porkaew, and Sharad Mehrotra. Dynamic Queries over Mobile Objects. In *EDBT*, 2002.
30. Mong-Li Lee, Wynne Hsu, Christian S. Jensen, and Keng Lik Teo. Supporting Frequent Updates in R-Trees: A Bottom-Up Approach. In *VLDB*, 2003.
31. Scott T. Leutenegger, J. M. Edgington, and Mario A. Lopez. Str: A simple and efficient algorithm for r-tree packing. In *ICDE*, 1997.
32. Mohamed F. Mokbel, Walid G. Aref, Susanne E. Hambrusch, and Sunil Prabhakar. Towards Scalable Location-aware Services: Requirements and Research Issues. In *GIS*, 2003.
33. Mohamed F. Mokbel, Thanaa M. Ghanem, and Walid G. Aref. Spatio-temporal Access Methods. *IEEE Data Engineering Bulletin*, 26(2), 2003.
34. Mohamed F. Mokbel, Xiaopeng Xiong, and Walid G. Aref. SINA: Scalable Incremental Processing of Continuous Queries in Spatio-temporal Databases. In *SIGMOD*, 2004.
35. J. Nievergelt, Hans Hinterberger, and Kenneth C. Sevcik. The Grid File: An Adaptable, Symmetric Multikey File Structure. *TODS*, 9(1), 1984.
36. Apostolos Papadopoulos and Yannis Manolopoulos. Performance of Nearest Neighbor Queries in R-Trees. In *ICDT*, 1997.
37. Jignesh M. Patel, Yun Chen, and V. Prasad Chakka. STRIPES: An Efficient Index for Predicted Trajectories. In *SIGMOD*, 2004.
38. Kriengkrai Porkaew, Iosif Lazaridis, and Sharad Mehrotra. Querying Mobile Objects in Spatio-Temporal Databases. In *SSTD*, Redondo Beach, CA, July 2001.
39. Sunil Prabhakar, Yuni Xia, Dmitri V. Kalashnikov, Walid G. Aref, and Susanne E. Hambrusch. Query Indexing and Velocity Constrained Indexing: Scalable Techniques for Continuous Queries on Moving Objects. *IEEE Transactions on Computers*, 51(10), 2002.
40. Yvn J. Garca R, Mario A. Lpez, and Scott T. Leutenegger. A greedy algorithm for bulk loading r-trees. In *GIS*, 1998.
41. Nick Roussopoulos, Stephen Kelley, and Frederic Vincent. Nearest Neighbor Queries. In *SIGMOD*, 1995.
42. Simonas Saltenis and Christian S. Jensen. Indexing of Moving Objects for Location-Based Services. In *ICDE*, 2002.
43. Simonas Saltenis, Christian S. Jensen, Scott T. Leutenegger, and Mario A. Lopez. Indexing the Positions of Continuously Moving Objects. In *SIGMOD*, 2000.
44. A. Prasad Sistla, Ouri Wolfson, Sam Chamberlain, and Son Dao. Modeling and Querying Moving Objects. In *ICDE*, 1997.
45. Zhexuan Song and Nick Roussopoulos. Hashing Moving Objects. In *Mobile Data Management*, 2001.

46. Zhexuan Song and Nick Roussopoulos. K-Nearest Neighbor Search for Moving Query Point. In *SSTD*, 2001.
47. Zhexuan Song and Nick Roussopoulos. SEB-tree: An Approach to Index Continuously Moving Objects. In *Mobile Data Management, MDM*, January 2003.
48. Yufei Tao, Dimitris Papadias, and Qiongmao Shen. Continuous Nearest Neighbor Search. In *VLDB*, 2002.
49. Yufei Tao, Dimitris Papadias, and Jimeng Sun. The TPR*-Tree: An Optimized Spatio-temporal Access Method for Predictive Queries. In *VLDB*, 2003.
50. Jamel Tayeb, Özgür Ulusoy, and Ouri Wolfson. A Quadtree-Based Dynamic Attribute Indexing Method. *The Computer Journal*, 41(3), 1998.
51. Chenyi Xia, Hongjun Lu, Beng Chin Ooi, and Jin Hu. Gorder: An Efficient Method for KNN Join Processing. In *VLDB*, 2004.
52. Xiaopeng Xiong and Walid G. Aref. R-trees with Update Memos. In *ICDE*, 2006.
53. Xiaopeng Xiong, Mohamed F. Mokbel, and Walid G. Aref. SEA-CNN: Scalable Processing of Continuous K-Nearest Neighbor Queries in Spatio-temporal Databases. In *ICDE*, 2005.
54. Xiaopeng Xiong, Mohamed F. Mokbel, Walid G. Aref, Susanne Hambrusch, and Sunil Prabhakar. Scalable Spatio-temporal Continuous Query Processing for Location-aware Services. In *SSDBM*, 2004.

Tolerant Ad Hoc Data Propagation with Error Quantification

Philipp Rösch

Database Technology Group
Technische Universität Dresden, Germany
philipp.roesch@tu-dresden.de

Abstract. Nowadays everybody uses a variety of different systems managing similar information, for example in the home entertainment sector. Unfortunately, these systems are largely heterogeneous, mostly with respect to the data model but at least with respect to the schema, making synchronization and propagation of data a daunting task. Our goal is to cope with this situation in a best-effort manner. To meet this claim, we introduce a symmetric instance-level matching approach that allows to establish mappings without any user interaction, schema information or dictionaries and ontologies. In awareness of dealing with inexact and incomplete mappings, the quality of the propagation has to be quantified. For this purpose, different quality dimensions like accuracy or completeness are introduced. Additionally, visualizing the quality allows users to evaluate the performance of the data propagation process.

1 Introduction

With the flood of gadgets managing personal information, data propagation becomes ever more important. Take the home entertainment sector, for example: a variety of products like MP3 players, hand-helds, mobile phones, car radios, hi-fi systems or PCs store your music files. Since users want to listen to their favorite songs wherever they are, there is a strong need for *ubiquitous access* to personal data, e.g. to favorite playlists. This process should be as simple as possible to allow for the smooth integration of new systems. However, aside from the propagation of data between users' gadgets, where once established mappings could be re-used for every data propagation process, there are also application scenarios where ad hoc data propagation is required. Imagine a rental car comes with a collection of music files. Here, users want to select songs according to their favorite playlists easily and quickly. Consequently, performing this task without the requirement of user interaction or expertise would be a great benefit. This scenario also applies to planes, trains or hotel rooms. Moreover, other types of personal data can be considered, like preferences and highscores of games or settings of programs.

Unfortunately, the huge variety of products and the many different manufacturers complicate this need. Different data models, like hierarchical, relational or flat models, as well as different schemas within the data models create a

T. Grust et al. (Eds.): EDBT 2006 Workshops, LNCS 4254, pp. 22–31, 2006.

large heterogeneity among the data. Together with the inconsistent availability of schema information, a perfect synchronization or propagation of the data will be impossible. Neither will the manufacturers provide mappings from their data models and schemas to all the other models nor does a standard format seem to evolve. Being in this unpromising situation, our goal has to be to propagate the data as efficiently as possible.

All in all, consider the application area: There are small datasets with no schema information available; the propagation of the data may not be perfect; and the user would not or even cannot manually establish these mappings. Therefore, we introduce an instance-level matching approach, where the key is to detect matchings between the current data in the documents. The pleasant consequence is that concentrating on the content allows mapping between documents with *arbitrary namings and structure*. The only prerequisites are 1) an intersection of the content, which is usually given in scenarios concerned with synchronization and data propagation, 2) the absence of complex data types, which is common if there is no schema, and 3) a hierarchical structure of the data.

Subsuming all demands above, we detect a strong need for

- a fully automated matching approach that does not rely on provided schema information, references like dictionaries or thesauri, and user interaction,
- a mapping and propagation technique which considers similarity matches and strongly varying sizes of the documents, and
- the quantification of the error which possibly occurred to give the user feedback on the quality of the results of the data propagation process.

The remainder of the paper is structured as follows: Section 2 gives a brief overview of related work. In Section 3, we introduce the symmetric instance-level matching, which avoids problems of schema matching approaches by efficiently comparing the content of the documents. In Section 4, we present a normalization approach of the matching results and show how to compute the mapping probabilities in order to establish meaningful mappings. The quantification of possible errors of the data propagation process is discussed in Section 5. Finally, a summary and open topics for future work are given in Section 6.

2 Related Work

In the area of data integration, the idea of best-effort data propagation is surprisingly disregarded. Here current solutions like [1,2,3,4] among others consider *schema matching*. These approaches require the existence of schema information as well as similar or semantically meaningful names of elements and attributes. Even if missing schema information may be created from the data, as shown in [5,6], there often are generated schemas with cryptic namings. Additionally, even in the case of semantically meaningful names, application-specific dictionaries and synonym tables must be available. Furthermore, some approaches require user interaction [1,7,8] and can lead to incorrect interpretations of ambiguous names. Moreover, since these solutions claim to deliver perfect results and are intended for large datasets containing hundreds of relations or documents with known schemas, they are oversized and inapplicable in this context.

Dealing with error quantification touches another research topic: *quality*. Unfortunately, there is no common definition in the literature for the ambiguous concept of quality. A variety of publications [9,10,11,12,13,14] show aspects of quality within different application scenarios and define more or less varying quality parameters. An overview can be found in [15,16]. [9,10,17] care about the definition of an *overall measure* for the quality by combining different quality parameters. However, those approaches are mostly subjective and application-dependent. Quality-driven query optimization in integrated environments is given in [18]. Here, queries are optimized with respect to the quality of the result. Ideas from all of these different approaches can be adopted; however, they have to be adapted to create an objective quality measure of the data propagation process.

3 Preprocessing: Symmetric Instance-Level Matching

Visualizing the problem, Fig. 1 shows fragments of a sample source and target document containing information about music albums. Despite being small, even this example already points out problems of schema matching techniques; e.g. consider the element <title> that represents the name of a music album in the first data source, whereas it contains the name of a track in the second data source. Similarly the element <track> would probably be erroneously identified as a match. Besides avoiding invalid mappings due to equal or similar element names, we also have to find valid mappings of elements with different names but equal content, such as information on the release date, the artist, and the position of the track in the current example.

```
<favorites>
  <disc>
    <published>2002</published>
    <title>Hits</title>
    <artist>The Singer</artist>
    <rating>2</rating>
    <song>
      <name>firstTrack</name>
      <track>1</track>
      <duration>2:35</duration>
    </song>
    <song>...</song>
  </disc>
  ...
</favorites>
```

```
<playlist>
  <entry>
    <album>Hits</album>
    <year>2002</year>
    <genre>Pop</genre>
    <tracks>
      <track>
        <singer>The Singer</singer>
        <trackno>1</trackno>
        <title>firstTrack</title>
      </track>
      <track>...</track>
    </tracks>
  </entry>
  ...
</playlist>
```

Fig. 1. XML-fragments of a source and a target document

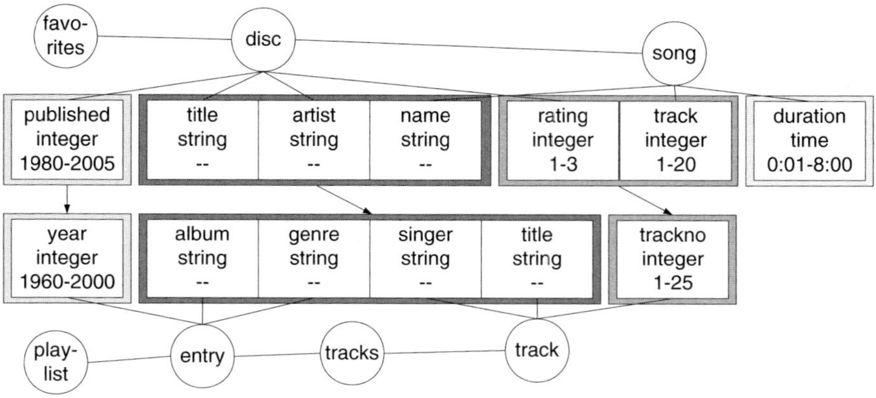

Fig. 2. Clusters (shaded) and cluster groups (linked by arrows)

While this small example identifies problems of finding matches solely with schema information, naive instance-level matching also comes with some challenges we have to face. Although the data sources in the application scenario of this project are moderate in size, it would be very expensive to compare each element of one data source with each element of the other data source. So, to avoid unnecessary comparisons between incompatible types and domains, a *fingerprint* is created on the fly for each element[1] by generating the most specific data type and the domain. Elements with 'compatible' fingerprints, i.e. with the same data types and overlapping domains, are put into a cluster. Figure 2 shows the clusters of the source document (top) and the target document (bottom). The first shaded box of the source document shows the cluster of integers ranging from 1980 to 2005 and the second cluster contains the elements of type string. In the third cluster, elements of type integer ranging from 1 to 20 are collected and the last cluster manages elements with time information.

Now, *cluster groups* can be established by combining each cluster of the source document with all clusters of the target document with compatible fingerprints. Clusters with no compatible target cluster remain unlinked. In Fig. 2, these cluster groups are denoted by arrows between the clusters. In the current simple example, each source cluster is only connected with at most one target cluster, but this is no limitation.

For each cluster group a three-dimensional matrix can be constructed. The three dimensions are 1) the elements of the source document, 2) the elements of the target document, and 3) the direction of comparison. The reason for considering both directions of comparison is given in Sect. 4 while explaining the mapping. Figure 3 shows the matrix for elements of type integer ranging from 1 to 25.

Within the cluster groups, each element of the source document is compared with each element of the target document and vice versa. While integer and

[1] Attributes are treated like elements.

	$d_s \rightarrow d_t / d_t \rightarrow d_s$
d_s.rating (7)	7/15
d_s.track (84)	84/60
	d_t.trackno (60)

Fig. 3. Matrix for elements of type integer and with domain from 1 to 25

floating-point numbers are compared for equality, strings additionally allow similarity matching, like edit distance or soundex. In general, specific comparison operations can be chosen for each data type. The number of matches for each element is annotated in the corresponding matrix. In Fig. 3, for example, the given numbers can be explained with the following sample: The source document d_s contains information about seven albums with a total of 84 tracks, while the target document d_t manages five albums with a total of 60 tracks. The number of occurrences of each element is given in brackets. The rating ranges from 1 to 3, so each of the seven rating entries matches with some track numbers. Moreover, consider that each possible rating occurs. Consequently, each of the first three <trackno>-elements matches with a <rating>-element resulting in a count of 15; that is, 7 of the 7 <rating>-elements of d_s match with some <trackno>-elements of d_t while only 15 of the 60 <trackno>-elements match with some <rating>-elements. For the track numbers, consider a simplified scenario where each album has 12 tracks resulting in 84 and 60 matches respectively.

4 Element Mapping

The generation of a mapping raises another challenge: How can documents of strongly varying sizes or with small intersections be compared? For example, consider the case that both the source and the target document manage 100 albums each and that the intersection consists of just one album. Most of the matches would provide values close to one, making conclusions about the mapping quality difficult. To overcome this problem, we propose a normalization of the matching results. This normalization requires the number of common objects managed in both documents, that is, the intersection size $s_\cap$. Unfortunately, $s_\cap$ is not known in advance; however it can be *estimated.* If there is a pair of elements with unique values[2] having the same number of matches in both directions, this number can be regarded as intersection size. Together with the number of occurrences of these elements, the scaling factors can be calculated. For the source document the scaling factor is given by

$$SF_{d_s} = \frac{occ_x}{s_\cap} \tag{1}$$

with occ_x as the number of occurrences of the source element. The scaling factor for the target document SF_{d_t} can be calculated in the same way.

[2] The uniqueness of an element can be determined from its fingerprint.

For the string-valued elements of the current example we have the unnormalized matching values given in Fig. 4.

	$d_s \to d_t / d_t \to d_s$	$d_s \to d_t / d_t \to d_s$	$d_s \to d_t / d_t \to d_s$	$d_s \to d_t / d_t \to d_s$
d_s.title (7)	4/4	0/0	0/0	2/2
d_s.artist (7)	0/0	0/0	6/60	0/0
d_s.name (84)	2/2	0/0	0/0	48/48
	d_t.album(5)	d_t.genre(5)	d_t.singer(60)	d_t.title(60)

Fig. 4. Matrix for elements of type string

Assuming that album names are unique, the pair (d_s.title, d_t.album) indicates an intersection size of $s_\cap = 4$. Using this intersection size and the number of occurrences of these two elements together with (1), we get the scaling factors of $SF_{d_s} = \frac{7}{4}$ for the source document and $SF_{d_t} = \frac{5}{4}$ for the target document. Once the scaling factors have been determined, they are applied to *all* values in *all* clusters where the normalized number of matches are calculated by

$$\bar{m}_{x,y} = SF_{d_p} * m_{x,y} \tag{2}$$

with $m_{x,y}$ as the number of matches of element x with respect to element y and $p \in s, t$. Obviously, an element cannot have more matches than occurrences, thus (2) has to be extended to

$$\bar{m}_{x,y} = max(SF_{d_p} * m_{x,y}, occ_x) \ . \tag{3}$$

Figure 5 shows the normalized values of the string-typed elements.

	$d_s \to d_t / d_t \to d_s$	$d_s \to d_t / d_t \to d_s$	$d_s \to d_t / d_t \to d_s$	$d_s \to d_t / d_t \to d_s$
d_s.title (7)	7/5	0/0	0/0	3.5/2.5
d_s.artist (7)	0/0	0/0	7/60	0/0
d_s.name (84)	3.5/2.5	0/0	0/0	84/60
	d_t.album(5)	d_t.genre(5)	d_t.singer(60)	d_t.title(60)

Fig. 5. Normalized elements of type string

Now, the mappings from elements of the source document to elements of the target document can be established. Therefore, the ratio of the (normalized) matches and the occurrences of an element are regarded, resulting in a mapping probability of

$$P_{x,y} = \frac{\bar{m}_{x,y}}{occ_x} \ . \tag{4}$$

However, this may lead to bad results. Consider the matching result of d_s.rating and d_t.trackno, which is $\bar{m}_{\text{rating,trackno}} = 7$. This would erroneously generate a perfect mapping $P_{\text{rating,trackno}} = 7/7 = 1$. Otherwise, if the mapping would be the other way around, the considered matching result would be $\bar{m}_{\text{trackno,rating}} = 18.75$, leading to a reasonable result of $P_{\text{trackno,rating}} = 18.75/60 \approx 0.3$. Actually, this is the reason for the *symmetric* instance-level matching. Now, the computation of the mapping probability is extended to

$$P_{x,y} = P_{y,x} = min\left(\frac{\bar{m}_{x,y}}{occ_x}, \frac{\bar{m}_{y,x}}{occ_y}\right) \tag{5}$$

taking both directions of comparison into account.

Figure 6 shows the mapping probabilities of the integer-valued elements with domain 1 to 25 (left) and the string-valued elements (right) of the current example. The possible mappings between elements which are not used for the final mapping generation are illustrated with dashed lines.

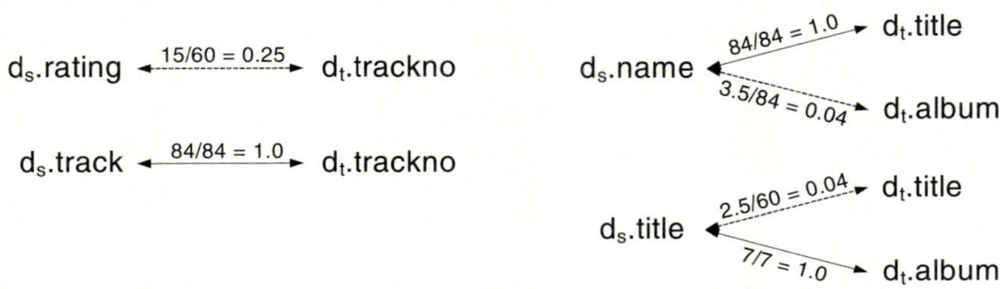

Fig. 6. Mapping probabilities

Now, we have mappings based on the content of the leaves of the hierarchical structure of the documents. However, this hierarchical structure gives further information about semantically meaningful mappings. The relationship between the elements represents *context information*. Consequently, the structure of the content has to be taken into account to further improve the results.

To utilize this additional information, we infer *higher-level mappings*. Beginning at the bottom of the hierarchy, for each node we check if all the mapping partners of its child nodes themselves are children of one common parent node. In this case, the corresponding parents can be seen as mapping candidates. Child nodes without mapping partners are dismissed and considered as not transferable. Now, this information can be used to adapt the mapping probabilities in a way that mappings between child nodes of higher-level mapping candidates are regarded as more likely, since they appear in a similar context, while possible mappings between elements within different contexts are accounted as rather unlikely.

Take the <song>-node of the current example. Without a matching partner, <duration> is dismissed. The other child nodes (<name> and <track>) both have matching partners (<title> and <trackno>), which are child nodes of <track>, thus leading to a higher-level mapping between d_s.song and d_t.track (cf. Fig. 7).

Obviously, a somewhat weaker proceeding is reasonable since the structure of the given documents would rather be equal. Consider the direction from the

```
<song>
  <name>firstTrack</name>
  <track>1</track>
  <duration>2:35</duration>
</song>
```

```
<track>
  <singer>who knows</singer>
  <trackno>1</trackno>
  <title>firstTrack</title>
</track>
```

Fig. 7. Section of the XML-fragments illustrating higher-level mappings

target to the source document. Here, the element <singer> would prevent the meaningful higher-level mapping between d_s.song and d_t.track since the mapping partner <artist> sits on an upper level. Consequently, the results of both directions have to be regarded in this stage as well in order to identify some higher-level mappings. Finally, the partner with the highest mapping probability is chosen for each element to establish the mapping.

5 Error Quantification

Since the data propagation process is fully automated and thus not supervised, some errors may occur. In order to give the user feedback on the quality of the data propagation process, possible errors have to be quantified. One aspect of the result's quality is its *completeness*. This aspect is generally independent of the matching and mapping procedure and is caused by the differences within the schemas of the source and the target document. There are two facets of completeness. On the one hand, we have elements of the source document having no counterpart in the target document and thus cannot be transferred. Those information is *lost*. On the other hand, we have elements of the target document without any counterpart in the source document, which can thus not be filled. The information is *unknown*.

Another aspect of the result's quality depends on the matching procedure. Here, the algorithms for defining similarity of values affect the overall result. If they are too 'tight' some meaningful mappings may be missed; otherwise, if they are too 'lax' some senseless mappings may occur. This aspect is referenced to as *matching accuracy*.

Closely related to the matching accuracy is the *mapping accuracy*. Again, two facets can be considered. The two factors which contribute to the mapping probability and thus to the mapping accuracy are the number of similar or equal values as well as the respective similarity value itself.

Now, to quantify these quality parameters, information of the matching and mapping procedure have to be evaluated. The number of lost and unknown elements can be determined from the clustering process, where unlinked clusters lead to incompleteness. Also the elements which are part of cluster groups but are not part of the final mapping cause incomplete results. Accuracy information can be computed with the number and the similarity of the matchings managed in the matrices of the cluster groups.

6 Conclusion and Future Work

In this paper, we presented an approach for propagating data, like personal information, in a fast and easy way. By concentrating on the content, we avoid—contrary to existing techniques—the requirement of schema information, user interaction and references like dictionaries or thesauri. Furthermore, we presented a mapping technique that copes with strongly varying sizes of documents and defined some quality parameters to give the user feedback on the quality of the results of the data propagation process.

Our prototype TRANSMITTER (ToleRANt ScheMa-Independent daTa propagaTion with ERror quantification), a JAVA implementation of the functionality described above, shows already promising results. Nevertheless, some tasks remain open. To reduce the complexity of the matching, the fingerprints have to be refined. Here, domain information for strings, like patterns of regular expressions, have to be regarded. Also, it has to be examined if histograms can be used in a meaningful way. The resolution of conflicts within the establishment of mappings has to be considered. Moreover, the adaptation of the mapping probabilities based on the higher-level mappings has to be advanced.

In addition, the quality feedback can be extended by taking further quality parameters into account, and even more important, a convenient representation of the current quality for an intuitive interpretation has to be developed.

References

1. Do, H.H., Rahm, E.: COMA - A System for Flexible Combination of Schema Matching Approaches. In: Proceedings of the 28th VLDB Conference, Hong Kong, China. (2002) 610–621
2. Madhavan, J., Bernstein, P.A., Rahm, E.: Generic Schema Matching with Cupid. In: Proceedings of the 27th VLDB Conference, Rome, Italy. (2001) 49–58
3. Milo, T., Zohar, S.: Using Schema Matching to Simplify Heterogeneous Data Translation. In: Proceedings of the 24th VLDB Conference, New York City, USA. (1998) 122–133
4. Melnik, S., Garcia-Molina, H., Rahm, E.: Similarity Flooding: A Versatile Graph Matching Algorithm and its Application to Schema Matching. In: Proceedings of the 18th International Conference on Data Engineering (ICDE'02), San Jose, USA. (2002) 117–128
5. Wang, Q.Y., Yu, J.X., Wong, K.F.: Approximate Graph Schema Extraction for Semi-Structured Data. In: Proceedings of the 7th EDBT Conference, Konstanz, Germany. (2000) 302–316
6. Goldman, R., Widom, J.: DataGuides: Enabling Query Formulation and Optimization in Semistructured Databases. In: Proceedings of the 2rd VLDB Conference, Athens, Greece. (1997) 436–445
7. Mandreoli, F., Martoglia, R., Tiberio, P.: Approximate Query Answering for a Heterogeneous XML Document Base. In: Proceedings of WISE 2004, Brisbane, Australia. (2004) 337–351
8. Rahm, E., Bernstein, P.A.: On Matching Schemas Automatically. Technical Report MSR-TR-2001-17, Microsoft Research, Microsoft Corporation, One Microsoft Way, Redmond, WA 98052-6399 (2001)

9. Bovee, M., Srivastava, R.P., Mak, B.: A Conceptual Framework and Belief-Function Approach to Assessing Overall Information Quality. International Journal of Intelligent Systems **18**(1) (2003) 51–74
10. Lee, Y.W., Strong, D.M., Kahn, B.K., Wang, R.Y.: AIMQ: A Methodology for Information Quality Assessment. Information & Management **40** (2002) 133–146
11. Martinez, A., Hammer, J.: Making Quality Count in Biological Data Sources. In: Proceedings of the IQIS Workshop, Baltimore, USA. (2005) 16–27
12. Motro, A., Rakov, I.: Estimating the Quality of Databases. In: Proceedings of the 3rd FQAS Conference, Roskilde, Denmark. (1998) 298–307
13. Naumann, F., Rolker, C.: Do Metadata Models meet IQ Requirements? In: Proceedings of the 4th IQ Conference, Cambridge, USA. (1999) 99–114
14. Naumann, F., Rolker, C.: Assessment Methods for Information Quality Criteria. In: Proceedings of the 5th IQ Conference, Cambridge, USA. (2000) 148–162
15. Scannapieco, M., Missier, P., Batini, C.: Data Quality at a Glance. Datenbank-Spektrum **14** (2005) 6–14
16. Tayi, G.K., Ballou, D.P.: Examining Data Quality - Introduction. Communications of the ACM **41**(2) (1998) 54–57
17. Pipino, L., Lee, Y.W., Wang, R.Y.: Data Quality Assessment. Communications of the ACM **45**(4) (2002) 211–218
18. Naumann, F.: From Databases to Information Systems - Information Quality Makes the Difference. In: Proceedings of the 6th IQ Conference, Cambridge, USA. (2001) 244–260

Spatio-temporal Aggregates over Streaming Geospatial Image Data

Jie Zhang

Department of Computer Science
University of California, Davis, CA 95616, U.S.A.
zhangji@cs.ucdavis.edu

Abstract. Geospatial image data obtained by satellites and aircraft are increasingly important to a wide range of applications, such as disaster management, climatology, and environmental monitoring. Because of the size of the data and the speed at which it is generated, computing spatio-temporal aggregates over geospatial image data is extremely demanding. Due to the special characteristics of the data, existing spatio-temporal aggregation model and evaluation approaches are not suitable for computing aggregates over such data.

In this paper, we outline the key challenges of computing spatio-temporal aggregates over streaming geospatial image data, and present three goals of our research work. We also discuss several preliminary results and future research directions.

1 Introduction and Motivation

Driven by major advances in remote sensing technology, geospatial image data from satellites and aircraft have become one of the fastest-growing sources of spatio-temporal data sets. The remotely-sensed imagery collected by NASA alone are expected to exceed dozens of terabytes per day within the next few years. Such data have become increasingly important to a wide range of applications, such as disaster management, climatology, and environmental monitoring.

In a typical data processing setting for streaming geospatial image data, the data are transmitted continuously in the form of raster images. Each image can be regarded as a rectangular grid in which each cell (*point*) consists of a point location and point value. Figure 1 gives an example of a sequence of raster images transmitted from the National Oceanic and Atmospheric Administration's (NOAA) Geostationary Environmental Operational Satellite (GOES) West [4] over a period of about one hour. Since GOES West scans different regions of Earth's surface over time, each image in Figure 1 has a different spatial extent.

In general, such image data continuously arrive at a very high rate and volume. For example, GOES West satellite images are transmitted at 2.1Mbits/second – about 22GBytes/day. As a result, it is very important to have operations that summarize the data. One such operation, known as *spatio-temporal aggregation*, summarizes the data in both spatial and time dimension. For example, a typical spatio-temporal aggregate query is: "Calculate the average soil temperature in

T. Grust et al. (Eds.): EDBT 2006 Workshops, LNCS 4254, pp. 32–43, 2006.

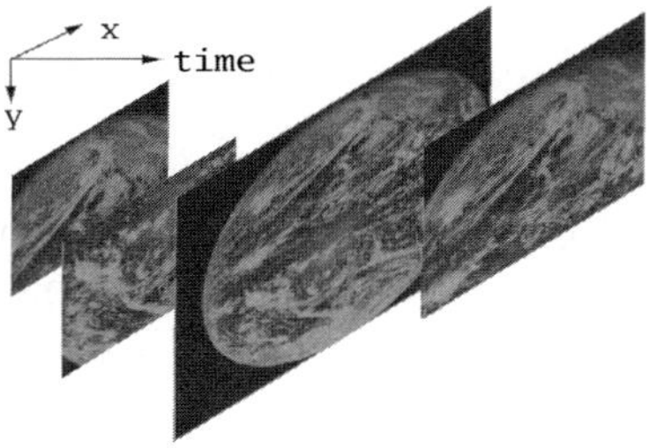

Fig. 1. Sequence of GOES West images. Different regions of Earth's surface are scanned over time, resulting in images with different spatial extents.

Davis, California, from July to September every year for the last ten years." Spatio-temporal aggregates are not only one of the most fundamental operations for various applications, such as detecting changes in the environmental landscape, but also the most demanding in terms of space and time complexity.

The efficient processing of spatio-temporal aggregate queries, which specify a region of interest and some time interval, have been studied in several works [7,10,15,16,17,18,20]. However, there are several limitations in these approaches.

First of all, existing **aggregation models** do not provide a meaningful answer to a query over streaming geospatial image data. All existing approaches use traditional aggregation models, in which data that satisfy the given query region is aggregated, and a *single* aggregate value is returned as the answer. This is not always meaningful in the context of streaming geospatial image data, since they falsely imply that high-quality data is always available for the entire query region.

Secondly, existing **evaluation approaches** are not suitable for streaming geospatial image data. Some of these approaches are optimized for static data in such ways that they are not suitable for streaming data. Some approaches have such high construction or maintenance costs that they can not catch up with the arrival rate of streaming geospatial image data. Moreover, some approaches primarily focus on spatial objects, each of which contains its own spatial component. To apply these approaches to geospatial images, they consider each point in an image as an individual spatial object, and store its spatial component by itself. As a result, these approaches do not take advantages of the gridded point set structure inherent to raster image data. In particular, they do not exploit cases where neighboring points have similar or identical point values – but such cases occur frequently for some regions in raster images. Therefore, these approaches tend to have extremely high storage costs, which in turn lead to poor construction and query performance.

In this PhD research work, we aim to *design effective spatio-temporal aggregate computations for streaming geospatial image data*. Here, "effectiveness" represents both spatio-temporal aggregation models and evaluation approaches. The objectives for this goal include:

1. Develop a new spatio-temporal aggregation model that provides more fine-grained (intuitive) results for the spatio-temporal aggregate computation over streaming geospatial image data.
2. Develop a query processing framework to evaluate spatio-temporal aggregate queries using the new aggregation model.
3. Design efficient supporting index structures to evaluate spatio-temporal aggregate queries over streaming geospatial image data, in terms of construction time, space requirements, and query performance.

2 Related Work

Most of the existing approaches for computing spatial and spatio-temporal aggregates [6,7,9,10,16,18,20] focus on spatial objects and not field-based data, such as gridded point data or raster images. The aR-tree [6,9] is an R-tree in which each MBR (minimum bounding rectangle) of an internal node has a pre-computed aggregate value that summarizes the values for all objects that are contained by the MBR. As a result, the partial aggregate result can be obtained in the intermediate nodes of the tree without accessing all the contained objects.

Papadias et al. [10] presented another structure –the *aRB-tree*– that extends the aR-tree and considers the spatial and temporal information separately. The aRB-tree consists of an R-tree to index the regions of spatial objects, and a B-tree structure associated with each region in the R-tree to store the temporal information. Similar to the aR-tree, partial aggregate results can be obtained from intermediate nodes. The disadvantage of the aR-tree and the aRB-tree is that multiple paths from the root node may be needed to answer an aggregate query. Zhang et al. [21] proposed an indexing scheme –the *BA-tree*– to overcome this limitation. The BA-tree is based on a k-d-B tree. Similar to the aR-tree and aRB-tree, with each region of an internal nodes in a BA-tree a pre-computed aggregate value is associated. In addition to this, the BA-tree maintains some extra data for each region of the internal nodes, which guarantees that only one path is searched during an aggregate computation. Furthermore, based on the BA-tree, Zhang et al. [20] proposed an indexing scheme to maintain aggregate information at multiple temporal granularities for streaming data. Tao et al. [16] pointed out that the aRB-tree has a problem with *distinct counts* and presented an approximate approach to evaluate distinct *count/sum* aggregate queries.

However, none of these approaches is suitable for streaming geospatial image data. The reasons are as follows. First, all the above approaches provide a single value as the final answer to an aggregate query, which is not always meaningful in the context of streaming raster image data, especially when the image data contribute only partially to the query region. Secondly, since these approaches are designed for spatial objects and not for large amounts of points in streaming image data, the location for each point needs to be stored. This results in extremely high space consumption. Finally, the relationship of values among neighboring points is not considered in these approaches, something that one should take advantage of.

3 Preliminary Results

In this section, we describe several preliminary results for this PhD research work. First, we present a new aggregation model – *Segment-based Spatio-temporal Aggregation (SST-Aggregation)* – for answering spatio-temporal aggregate queries over streaming geospatial image data, in particular, raster image data. Secondly, we give a brief description of a query processing architecture for this new model. Thirdly, we present data structures that support such computations. Finally, we present some experimental results.

3.1 Segment-Based Spatio-temporal Aggregation (SST-Aggregation) Model

Consider the scenario in Figure 2, which gives an abstract view of a raster image stream (*RIS*). There are four images $I_1, \cdots, I_4$ with different sizes and spatial locations. A typical spatio-temporal aggregate query is, for example, "Calculate the average soil temperature in a given query region R=[lp, hp] (shown as the bold rectangle box in Figure 2) during the time interval $[t_1, t_2]$." Here, we primarily focus on regions with shapes of a multi-dimensional box.

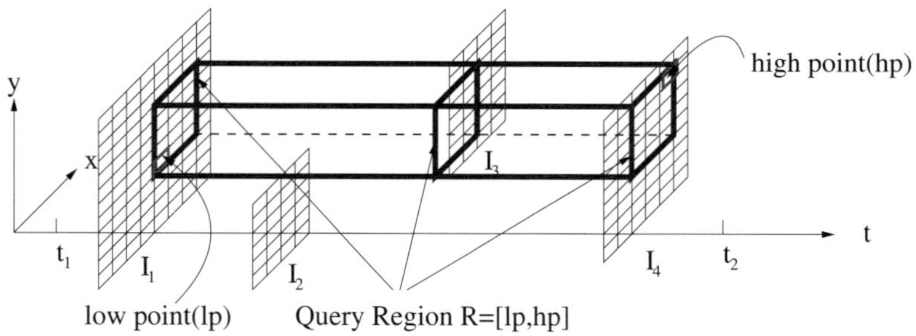

Fig. 2. Example scenario of a spatio-temporal aggregate query over a RIS

Applying existing approaches and index structures to compute spatio-temporal aggregates will provide us with a single value for the query box. An interesting observation for this query is that image I_3 only contributes partially to the query box. That is, at different points in time during $[t_1, t_2]$, not all images contribute all their points (and thus point values) to the query result. Thus, a single aggregate value does not necessarily represent an accurate result since such a result might be skewed, depending on what stream data is available during $[t_1, t_2]$.

Motivated by this observation, we propose a new aggregation model – *Segment-based Spatio-Temporal Aggregation (SST-Aggregation)*. This model overcomes the limitation of the traditional aggregation model in the context of streaming raster image data, and provides more meaningful answers to queries. The definition for SST-Aggregation is given in Definition 2. First, we define a *Segmented Query Region*.

Definition 1. *[**Segmented Query Region**] Given a query region $R = [lp, hp]$, and a RIS $\mathcal{I} = \{I_1, I_2, \cdots, I_n\}$. The **segmented query region** R_{seg} consists of disjoint sub-regions $R_1 = [lp_1, hp_1], R_2 = [lp_2, hp_2], \cdots, R_k = [lp_k, hp_k]$ such that*

1. $R = R_1 \cup R_2 \cup \cdots \cup R_k$;
2. *Each sub-region $R_i = [lp_i, hp_i], i = 1, \cdots, k$, has the same timestamp for the low and high point as R;*
3. *For each image $I_j \in \mathcal{I}(j \in [1, n])$ such that $R \wedge I_j \neq 0$, each sub-region $R_i = [lp_i, hp_i], i = 1, \cdots, k$, satisfies exactly one of the following **segment properties**:*
   - $I_j \geq_S R_i$. *That is, the image I_j fully covers the spatial extent of R_i. The set of all images that cover R_i is denoted $\mathcal{I}_i$, termed the **contribution image set** for R_i.*
   - $I_j \wedge R_i = 0$. *That is, the image I_j does not intersect with R_i.*
4. *Given any two sub-regions R_1 and R_2 whose contribution image sets are $\mathcal{I}_1$ and $\mathcal{I}_2$, respectively. If $R_1 \cup R_2$ is a region, then $\mathcal{I}_1 \neq \mathcal{I}_2$.*

Definition 2. *[**SST-Aggregation**] A **Segment-based Spatio-temporal Aggregation (SST-Aggregation)** over a RIS $\mathcal{I}$ is an aggregate operation that computes summarized information (specified by an aggregate function f) for a query region R. The SST-Aggregation constructs the segmented query region R_{seg} for R, and computes an aggregate value for each sub-region in R_{seg} with the aggregation function f. The SST-Aggregation is defined as follows.*

$$SST\text{-}Aggregation\ (\mathcal{I}, f, R) = \{< r_i, f(\mathcal{I}|_{r_i}) > | r_i \in R_{seg}\ for\ all\ i\}$$

The SST-Aggregation model supports those aggregate functions that are defined in the SQL:2003 standard [8]. This model can be easily extended to support continuous queries, including moving window queries.

3.2 Query Processing Architecture

Based on this new SST-Aggregation model, we propose a two-component query processing architecture to evaluate a spatio-temporal aggregate query, as illustrated in Figure 3. When a query is entered into the stream management systems, it is first passed to the *segmentation component*, which segments the query region into a segmented query region, as defined in Definition 1.

Next, the segmented query regions generated by the segmentation are passed to the aggregate-computation component, which computes and constructs the final result to the query.

Both segmentation and aggregate-computation rely on the images (as spatio-temporal objects) from the stream that have entered the system so far. The aggregate-computation component relies on the image point data, while the segmentation component relies on the image metadata, such as the spatial extent and the timestamp of each image.

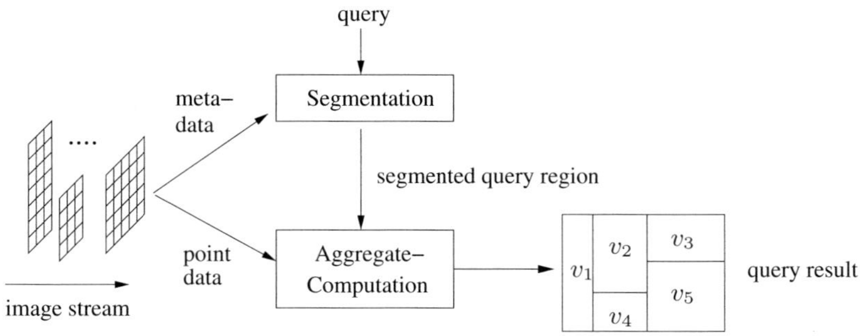

Fig. 3. Conceptual approach for computing SST-Aggregate queries

3.3 Index Structures

To evaluate the effectiveness of our SST-Aggregation model and the proposed query processing architecture, we consider two different index structures for image metadata and point data. Since image metadata is typically much smaller than image point data, we maintain a main-memory data structure –the *Metadata index* – to store the metadata, while disk-based structures are used for image point data.

Metadata Index. The metadata index that we proposed in [22] consists of two Red-Black trees [2], one for each spatial dimension. We call these trees the x-tree and the y-tree. Consider an image I created at time t, which has the spatial region represented by two points (x_{low}, y_{low}) and (x_{high}, y_{high}). The x-tree stores the values of x_{low} and x_{high} along with the timestamp t, where each of x_{low} and x_{high} is a key and t is the value. The y-tree has the same structure as the x-tree except that it stores y values. In both trees, we do not store duplicate key values. To achieve this, we maintain a circular buffer inside each node in the trees. This circular buffer stores the list of timestamp values.

Point Data Index. Our focus has been on summation-related spatio-temporal aggregate queries (*range-sum* queries), such as *Sum*, *Count* and *Avg*, over user-defined query regions. *Dominance-sum (dom-sum)* is a technique to support the efficient computation of box aggregate queries over objects with non-zero extent in some d-dimensional space [21]. It has been widely used for computations on the data cube [3,5] and for spatial and spatio-temporal aggregates in the context of spatial objects [20,21]. In general, for a point set $\mathcal{P}$ in some d-dimensional space, a range-sum query can be computed using the values of 2^d dom-sums. For example, consider the 2-dimensional raster image shown in Figure 4. We want to compute the sum of all values of points located in the region $[(1,1),(2,2)]$. Four dom-sum values are required to compute the sum, as illustrated in Figure 4. It is easy to verify that this value is 8, computed from the dom-sum values of four points shown in bold rectangles, that is, $ds((2,2)) - ds((2,0)) - ds((0,2)) + ds((0,0)) = 8$.

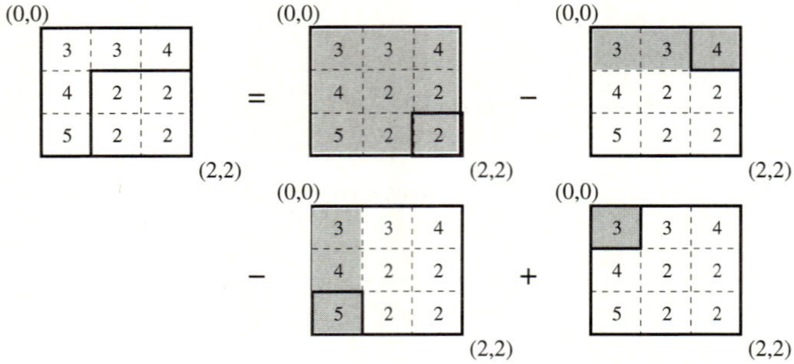

Fig. 4. Computing the range-sum for region $[(1,1),(2,2)]$ by using 4 dom-sum values

Our design and implementation of point data indexes are based on the dominance-sum technique. We first implemented and improved the BA-Tree [21] proposed by Zhang et al., which is a k-d-B tree [11] with some additional aggregate-related information stored at internal nodes. The BA-Tree supports fast dom-sum computations. One improvement we have added to the BA-Tree is as follows. As images stream in, we insert the data for each image spatio-temporal point one by one into the BA-Tree. For a single raster image, all its spatio-temporal points share the same timestamp value. For any two raster images, their spatio-temporal points are likely to share one or both values for the spatial dimensions. In our BA-Tree implementation, we take advantage of this property and introduce an *optimized insert operation* for point data into the BA-Tree. Every time when a point is inserted into the tree, if this point already exists in the tree, we simply add the value of the new point to the value of the existing point. This way, we can significantly reduce the size of the BA-Tree and also improve the performance of querying (refer to [22] for more information).

The major disadvantages of the BA-Tree are that it stores each point in a raster image separately, and does not take advantage of the gridded point set structure inherent to raster images, in particular of the cases where neighboring points have similar or same point values. This causes significantly high storage cost and consequently bad insertion and query performance. To address these shortcomings, we proposed a novel data structure, called the *compressed raster cube (CRC)*. The CRC integrates the *linear region quadtree* [1,12,19] and the dominance-sum computation technique, thus allowing efficient management of streaming image point data in a scalable fashion.

The CRC can be thought of as a cube containing a constantly growing sequence of compressed raster images, each of which is essentially a *linear region quadtree* with some *auxiliary information* with each node, namely dom-sum values for the points contained by the node. These dom-sum values are stored in a novel *dominance-sum compression scheme*, which significantly reduces the number of dom-sum values that need to be stored with nodes in a region quadtree. This compression scheme can be illustrated as follows. In general, given a node k in a quadtree such that k contains $m \times m$ points *that all have the same point value*. Only $2m-1$ dom-sum values need to be stored for k in order to compute the dom-sum value for any point contained by k, as shown in Figure 5. The dom-sum value for any point (x_1, y_1) contained by k can be computed in the following formula:

$$ds((x_1, y_1)) = ds((x_1, y)) + ds((x, y_1)) - ds((x, y)) + (x_1 - x) \times (y_1 - y) \times v$$

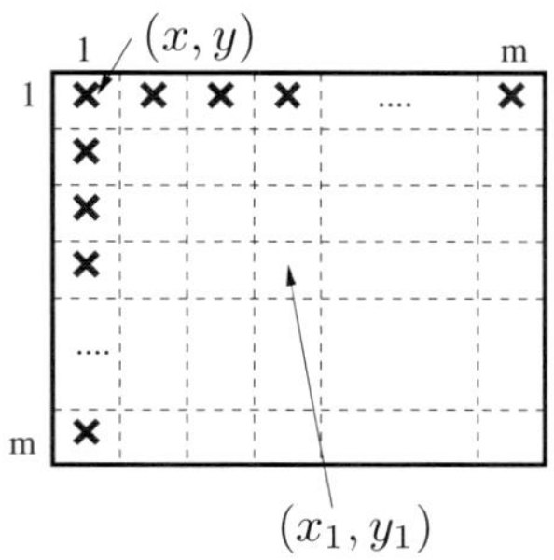

Fig. 5. All required dom-sum values (marked with 'X') for a $m \times m$-size node in which all points have the same point value

To construct such a CRC, we extended the OPTIMAL_BUILD algorithm [12,13,14] to convert a raster image into a quadtree and at the same time employ our dominance-sum compression scheme. Our experiments on NOAA's GOES West Satellite image data show that the CRC can efficiently evaluate both fix-box aggregate queries and moving window queries.

3.4 Experimental Results

Our experimental data is extracted from NOAA's GOES West satellite data. The GOES satellite carries two types of instruments: the Imager and the Sounder. The Imager scans various regions of the Earth's surface, West-to-East and North-to-South. The data are continually transmitted as frames at a rate of 2.1M bits/sec. In our experiments, we are interested in the image data of the visible band from the Imager. We extract this data from GOES data format into a sequence of lines, each of which has the following format:

```
frameId rowId startColId numOfPoints <point-values>
```

The "frameId" is assigned by the satellite to identify a frame. We use it as a logical timestamp in our experiments. "rowId" represents the absolute id of a row in a scan of an image. "startColId" represents the absolute start column id of a scan. "numOfPoints" gives the number of points in this row. Finally, "<point-values>" represents a list of point values where the list has the size of "numOfPoints".

The first objective of our experiments is to determine how query segmentation affects the overall running time for answering SST-Aggregate queries. We implement our metadata index and the BA-Tree in the Java programming language, and run the programs on a Redhat Enterprise machine with a 2GHz CPU and 512M RAM. The size of each node in the BA-Tree is 4096 bytes.

Figure 6 compares the running time of inserting the image metadata into the metadata index with the running time of inserting the image point data into the BA-Tree. Intuitively, since the amount of the image metadata is much smaller than the amount of point data, the time to insert the metadata should be significantly smaller than the time to insert the point data. Figure 6 verifies this intuition. Figure 7 compares the running time of segmenting a query region with the running time of computing aggregate results for that query region. As one expects, the running time of segmentation is significantly smaller than the running time of computing aggregate results.

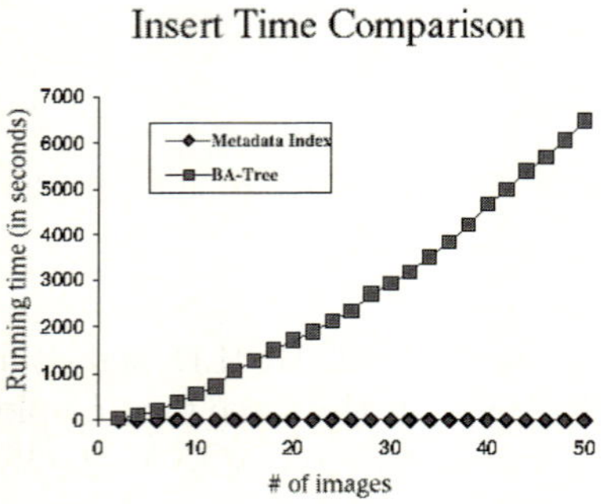

Fig. 6. Time comparison for maintaining two different data structures: Metadata index (bottom line), BA-Tree (upper curve)

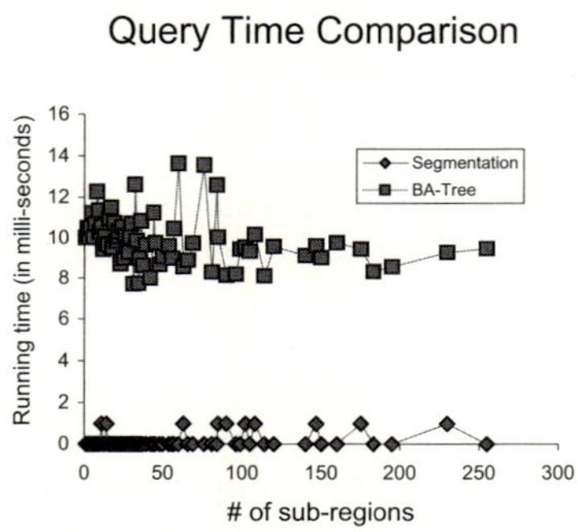

Fig. 7. Time comparison to answer an aggregate query: query segmentation (bottom) and computing aggregate for a single region (top)

The second objective of our experiments is to evaluate the effectiveness of our CRC structure, in terms of space consumption, construction time, and query performance. Our algorithms are implemented using GNU C++. The programs run on a Linux Redhat Enterprise 3 machine with an Intel Pentium 4 $3G$ CPU, $1024K$ cache and $1G$ RAM. For the B^+-tree implementation realizing the linear region quadtree, we choose a node size of 4096 bytes and buffer size of $80M$ bytes.

In this set of experiments, we quantize point values of incoming images by ignoring the $0, 2, 4, 6$ least significant bits, respectively, and collect the results for each of the quantized data. In Figures 8-10, we label these quantized point data sets with CRC-0 ($\triangleq$ original point data), CRC-2, CRC-4, and CRC-6. For the different quantized data, Figure 8 shows the changes in the number of nodes in the B^+-tree for each image as image point data is inserted into the CRC.

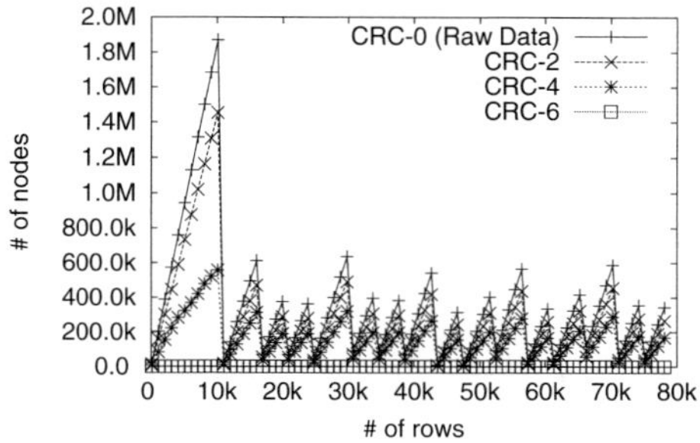

Fig. 8. B^+-tree space consumption for different quantized data

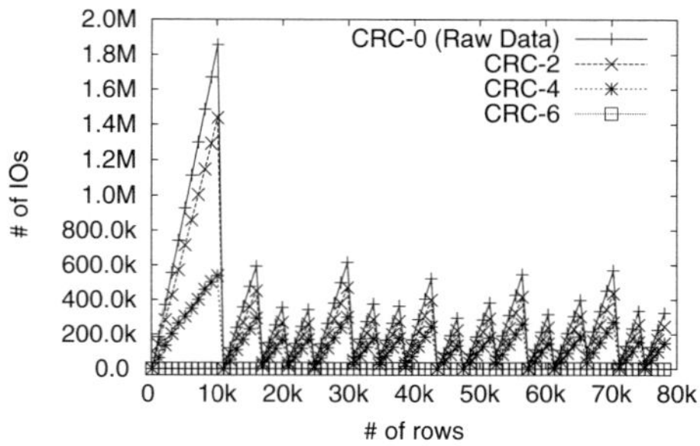

Fig. 9. Number of IOs for different quantized data as points are inserted into the CRC

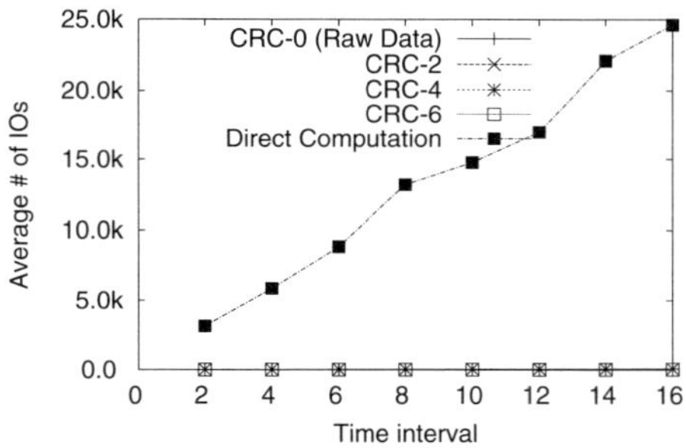

Fig. 10. Comparison of query performance, in IOs, for different quantized data and a direct computation over raw image data. Since the number for a direct computation is much greater than that of any CRCs, all CRCs appear in the same line.

As expected, the more least significant bits are ignored for the point values, the more the size of the CRC decreases. Figure 9 shows the number of IOs to construct the CRC for the different quantized data. Figure 10 shows the query performance of the CRCs and a direct computation from the raw image data. This direct computation is done as follows. The raw image point data are stored point by point in a file. This direct computation extracts the points that satisfy the query and aggregates their values. As one can see, the CRC significantly outperforms this direct computation on the raw data.

4 Conclusions and Future Work

In this paper, we have outlined the key challenges of computing spatio-temporal aggregate queries over streaming geospatial image data. Several preliminary results have been presented. Our focus has been on summation-related aggregations – range-sum aggregations. Range-min/max aggregations are another important fundamental operations that support complex data analysis. We are looking into some evaluation approaches that are able to efficiently support both range-sum and range-min/max aggregate queries.

Since we are dealing with streaming data, the management of large volumes of history data is a very important and challenging task. We are investigating *data vacuuming schemes* to compress or eliminate history data in the stream, and then integrating such schemes into our SST-Aggregation model and query processing framework.

Acknowledgment. This work is supported in part by the NSF under award IIS-0326517.

References

1. D. Abel. A B+-tree structure for large quadtrees. *Computer Vision, Graphics, and Image Processing*, 10(2):167–170, 1984.
2. R. Bayer. Symmetric binary B-trees: Data structure and maintenance algorithms. In *Acta Informatica*, 290–306, 1972.
3. S. Geffner, D. Agrawal, and A. E. Abbadi. The dynamic data cube. In *EDBT'00*, 237–253, 2000.
4. *GOES I-M DataBook*. Space Systems-Loral, 1996.
5. C.-T. Ho, R. Agrawal, N. Megiddo, and R. Srikant. Range queries in OLAP data cubes. *SIGMOD Rec.*, 26(2):73–88, 1997.
6. M. Jurgens and H. Lenz. The RA*-tree: An improved R-tree with materialized data for supporting range queries on OLAP-data. In *DEXA'98*, 1998.
7. I. F. V. Lopez and B. Moon. Spatiotemporal aggregate computation: A survey. *IEEE TKDE*, 17(2):271–286, 2005.
8. J. Melton. SQL:2003. *ISO (International Organization for Standardization) and ANSI (American National Standards Institute)*, 2003.
9. D. Papadias, P. Kalnis, J. Zhang, and Y. Tao. Efficient OLAP operations in spatial data warehouses. In *SSTD'01*, 443–459. Springer-Verlag, 2001.
10. D. Papadias, Y. Tao, P. Kalnis, and J. Zhang. Indexing spatio-temporal data warehouses. In *ICDE'02*, 166. IEEE Computer Society, 2002.
11. J. T. Robinson. The k-d-b tree: A search structure for large multi-dimensional dynamic indexes. In *ACM SIGMOD*, 10–18, 1981.
12. H. Samet. *Applications of Spatial Data Structures: Computer Graphics, Image Processing, and GIS*. Addison-Wesley, 1990.
13. C. A. Shaffer. *Application of alternative quadtree representations (VLSI, data structures)*. PhD thesis, University of Maryland, Computer Science TR-1672, 1986.
14. C. A. Shaffer, H. Samet. Optimal quadtree construction algorithms. *Comput. Vision Graph. Image Process.*, 37(3):402–419, 1987.
15. J. Sun, D. Papadias, Y. Tao, and B. Liu *Querying about the Past, the Present, and the Future in Spatio-Temporal Databases*. In *ICDE'04*, 202. 2004
16. Y. Tao, G. Kollios, J. Considine, F. Li, and D. Papadias. Spatio-temporal aggregation using sketches. In *ICDE'04*, 2004.
17. Y. Tao and D. Papadias. Historical spatio-temporal aggregation. *ACM Trans. Inf. Syst.*, 23(1):61–102, 2005.
18. Y. Tao, D. Papadias, and J. Zhang. Aggregate processing of planar points. In *EDBT'02*, 682–700, 2002.

19. T. Tzouramanis, M. Vassilakopoulos, and Y. Manolopoulos. Overlapping linear quadtrees: a spatio-temporal access method. In *ACM GIS'98*, 1–7, 1998.
20. D. Zhang, D. Gunopulos, V. J. Tsotras, and B. Seeger. Temporal and spatio-temporal aggregations over data streams using multiple time granularities. *Inf. Syst.*, 28(1-2):61–84, 2002.
21. D. Zhang, V. J. Tsotras, and D. Gunopulos. Efficient aggregation over objects with extent. In *PODS'02*, 121–132. ACM Press, 2002.
22. J. Zhang, M. Gertz, and D. Aksoy. Spatio-temporal aggregates over raster image data. In *ACM GIS'04*, 39–46. ACM Press, 2004.

Interoperation Between Information Spaces on the Web

Andreas Harth

Digital Enterprise Research Institute
National University of Ireland, Galway
andreas.harth@deri.org

Abstract. In my thesis I will address the problem of interoperation between information spaces on the web. We explain how this problem is different to traditional database integration scenarios. In particular, we focus on one issue of the information integration problem peculiar to the web environment, namely linking information across sources. We use a graph-based data model and representation format, and define a query and rule language where queries can span multiple sources. We show how such a language can be used to relate information among sources.

1 Introduction

In recent years, there has been a transition from a traditional view in data integration systems with a hierarchical architecture towards a completely distributed model associated with peer-to-peer (p2p) systems [6], [1], [13], [3], [10]. Rather than integrating a set of disparate information sources into a single global schema residing at one server, the p2p view assumes a complex system comprising a large number of autonomous sources that relate information among themselves.

The p2p scenario shares many of the characteristics of the web. Web servers are autonomous sources providing documents that are related to each other using hyperlinks. Similarly, the web is a self-organizing system in a sense that its global structure emerges from and evolves by collective creation and linkage of HTML pages, without the need for a central server or coordination authority.[1] In addition, the web community has recently developed a number of languages that aim at representing semistructured data or ontologies and thus facilitate the exchange of information.

Although there are many similarities, the web environment differs from the typical p2p data integration scenario in the following ways:

- the network structure on the web is relatively stable; servers are up most of the time, in contrast to peers joining and leaving frequently
- relating information on the web is done manually; the network structure is not emerging randomly as assumed by the p2p model, but *users* put in hyperlinks to connect related pages

[1] Except maybe W3C which standardizes languages, formats and protocols to provide interoperability.

T. Grust et al. (Eds.): EDBT 2006 Workshops, LNCS 4254, pp. 44–53, 2006.

- on the web, identifiers and their meaning may be shared across sources; databases identifiers are local and may mean different things in different databases

We assume it is neither desirable nor possible to completely mechanize all integration activities for data on the web. In fact, the manually created hyperlink structure of the HTML web provides a rich source of information which is useful e.g., for ranking purposes.

We believe that a typical system for information integration and sharing on the web can comprise at least the following components:

1. **Query and reasoning.** Infrastructure that allows to execute queries which take into account the link structure between sources; in particular recursive query processing facilities are needed because the network structure can contain cycles.
2. **Link creation and exchange.** Agents (users or software) may create associations between data in the form of coordination rules, and store, publish, and exchange these coordination rules with other agents.
3. **Information browsing.** User interfaces are needed to browse and explore the integrated information set.
4. **Caching and replication.** Caching and replication mechanisms are required at some stage to make the system fast, scalable, and reliable.

In the thesis, we focus on the problem discussed in point 1, since we believe that problem has to be solved before the other components become useful or are required. We assume that all data is available in RDF (Resource Description Framework); data in other formats can be aligned using wrappers.

Example. *To motivate the problem, consider three autonomous data sources with connections and dependencies among them as illustrated in Figure 1: one data source contains information about people expressed in FOAF*[2] *vocabulary collected from the web, another data source holds publication metadata from DBLP*[3]*, and the third data source contains Citeseer*[4] *publication data. Since the data sources contain overlapping or complementary information, we can use the following links to relate data in one source to data in another source:*

- *information about people from FOAF files should be also made available in the DBLP data source, e.g., the DBLP admin wants to show a picture of the authors of a publication*
- *publications in the DBLP source should also include abstracts which are available in the Citeseer data set*
- *the administrator of the FOAF source wants to show information about the publications of a person*

---

[2] `http://www.foaf-project.org/`

[3] `http://www.informatik.uni-trier.de/~ley/db/`

[4] `http://citeseer.ist.psu.edu/`

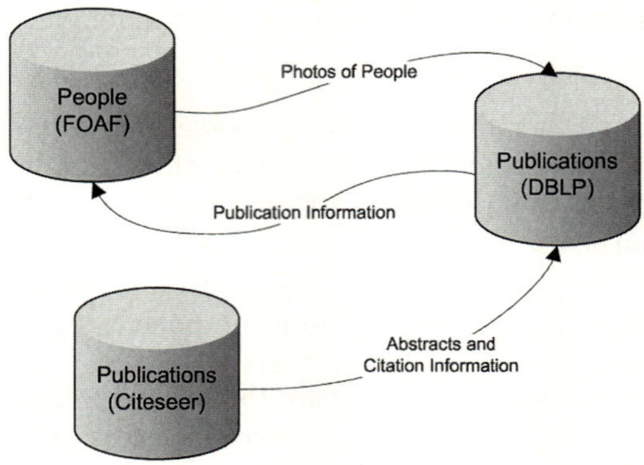

Fig. 1. Three data sources connected via coordination links

The research question this thesis aims to answer is two-fold:

- How to link RDF data sources on the web to arrive at a distributed, self-organized system comprising a large number of autonomous interoperable information sources?
- How to utilize these links to interoperate (share, exchange, and integrate information) among the connected sources?

The remainder of the paper is organized as follows. In Section 2 we introduce the data model for our framework. Section 3 introduces syntax and semantics of the query and rule language. In Section 4 we describe how to encode and integrate the formal semantics of vocabulary descriptions into the framework. Section 5 discusses the current state of the system and presents some ideas for future work, and Section 6 concludes.

2 Data Model

In this section we first review traditional data models, then describe RDF, the data model we use, and finally introduce our notion of context, which is mandatory in a distributed environment.

2.1 Related Approaches

The relational data model is by far the most popular, but has some drawbacks when it comes to data exchange and integration. In particular, data cannot be exchanged before an agreement is reached on how different relational schemas relate to each other.

Semistructured data formats such as OEM [19] or XML try to alleviate some of the problems because data in these formats can be merged without the need for integrating the schema first. However, one drawback of XML is the lack of the notion of objects and object identity.

We employ the notion of context which we believe is mandatory in the distributed web environment. Context frameworks such as [9], [12], [23] track the processing steps performed (e.g. data exchange, joining information from multiple sources) to derive the associated piece of information. TRIPLE [21] has the notion of parameterized contexts, where parameters can be passed to a set of facts and rules. Our notion of context is relatively basic in a sense that we just capture the physical location of a given piece of information.

2.2 RDF Data Model

Before we describe our notion of context, we define the standard RDF data model. RDF is a schema-less, self-describing graph-based data model, which facilitates merging information from different sources without performing schema integration at the merging stage. The data model consists of RDF triples.

Definition 1 (RDF Triple). *Given a set of URI references $\mathcal{U}$, a set of blank nodes $\mathcal{B}$, and a set of literals $\mathcal{L}$, a triple (s, p, o) $\in (\mathcal{U} \cup \mathcal{B}) \times \mathcal{U} \times (\mathcal{U} \cup \mathcal{B} \cup \mathcal{L})$ is called an RDF triple.*

In such a triple, s is called the subject, p the predicate, and o the object. We refer the interested reader to [17] which describes the RDF model in more detail, including blank nodes, containers, and reification.

We use N3 (Notation3) as a syntax for RDF. To make this paper self-contained, we introduce the basic syntactic N3 primitives. Brackets (<>) denote URIs, quotes ("") denote RDF literals, and blank node identifiers start with "_ :". There exists a number of syntactic shortcuts, for example ";" to introduce another predicate and object for the same subject. Namespaces are introduced with the @prefix keyword. For a full description see [5]. Figure 2 shows a small example in N3 syntax describing a paper and a person.

In RDF, the concept of URI acts as a global identifier for entities, which represents a form of agreement among multiple sources about how to name things. RDF has a notion of object identity via URIs and object nesting via predicates which refer to other URIs. More advanced object-oriented features such as classes and inheritance can be layered on top of the simple graph-based data model of RDF, which is discussed in Section 4.

2.3 Context

Although the RDF specification itself does not define the notion of context, usually applications require context to store various kinds of metadata for a given set of RDF triples. In typical integration scenarios where data is gathered from a large number of sources, it is mandatory to track the provenance of information, that is, the physical location of the RDF file addressable via a URI. Capturing provenance is one of the fundamental necessities in open distributed environments like the web, where the quality of data has to be judged by its origin.

```
@prefix foaf: <http://xmlns.com/foaf/0.1/> .
@prefix dc: <http://purl.org/dc/elements/1.1/> .
@prefix rdf: <http://www.w3.org/1999/02/22-rdf-syntax-ns#> .
@prefix ley: <http://www.informatik.uni-trier.de/~ley/> .

ley:db/journals/computer/computer25.html#Wiederhold92
  dc:title "Mediators in the Architecture of Future Information Systems.";
  dc:creator <http://www.example.org/dblp/GioWiederhold> ;
  rdf:type foaf:Document .

<http://www.example.org/dblp/GioWiederhold> foaf:name "Gio Wiederhold" ;
  foaf:homepage <http://www-db.stanford.edu/people/gio.html> ;
  rdf:type foaf:Person .
```

Fig. 2. Small N3 example describing a document and a person

In the following we define our basic notion of context.

Definition 2 (Triple in Context). *A pair (t, c) with t be a triple and* $c \in (\mathcal{U} \cup \mathcal{B})$ *is called a triple in context c.*

Please note that a pair ((s, p, o), c) is equivalent to a quadruple (s, p, o, c). In our model, we assume a finite set of spaces which are accessible via HTTP. Each information space can host multiple contexts. A context c can be a relative URI or an absolute URI. A relative URI denotes a context relative to the current context, which allows to move the location of entire data sets while keeping the internal link structure intact.

Example. *For our running example, the context for information from DBLP is* `http://example.org/dblp`*, for FOAF* `http://example.com/foaf`*, and for Citeseer* `http://example.org/citeseer`*. For brevity we will use* `exo:dblp`*,* `exc:foaf`*, and* `exo:citeseer` *to denote the data sources in the rest of the paper.*

N3 extends the RDF data model with means to quote graphs. Within N3, RDF subgraphs can become the subject or object of a statement, using "{}". To be able to express our notion of context within the RDF data model we introduce the namespace `yars`[5]. The `yars:context` predicate denotes that the subgraph grouped in the subject occurs in the context provided as the object.

3 Query and Rule Language

Rules are used to pose queries, or to specify how pieces of information, possibly in different contexts, are related to each other. We first review some related approaches, and then define syntax and semantics of our rule language.

[5] `http://sw.deri.org/2004/06/yars#`

3.1 Related Approaches

Unlike traditional data integration approaches, we can postpone the schema integration to a later stage, since RDF is semistructured and schema-less. We only need to relate identifiers to each other, similar to what is done in [16]. We believe that rule unfolding is a sufficient evaluation method that is somewhat between full schema mapping and merely relating identifiers to each other.

Many query and rule languages for RDF have been proposed [4]. We discuss here only SPARQL[6] due to space limitations. SPARQL is a query language for RDF that shares many of the features of our framework. The most notable distinctions between our approach based on N3 and SPARQL are that we use N3 syntax to encode both facts and rules, which can be used to write rules that return other rules, and we allow recursion in our language.

3.2 Notation3 Rule Syntax

To be able to express rules, N3 extends the RDF data model with variables. Variables in N3 are prefixed with a question mark ("?"). With variables, we can define the notion of quad patterns, which allow us to specify patterns where constants may be replaced by variables.

Definition 3 (Quad Pattern). *Given a set of variables $\mathcal{V}$, a quad (s, p, o, c) $\in (\mathcal{U} \cup \mathcal{B} \cup \mathcal{V}) \times (\mathcal{U} \cup \mathcal{V}) \times (\mathcal{U} \cup \mathcal{B} \cup \mathcal{L} \cup \mathcal{V}) \times (\mathcal{U} \cup \mathcal{B})$ is called an RDF quad pattern.*

To be able to formulate rules within the RDF data model we use the graph quoting feature of N3 and introduce the `log:implies` predicate in namespace `log`[7].

Definition 4 (Rule). *A rule is in the form $\{b_1 \ldots b_n\}$ `log:implies` $\{h\}$. where $b_1 \ldots b_n$ and h are quad patterns.*

The quad patterns $b_1 \ldots b_n$ are called the body, and h the head of a rule. A rule is safe if all variables occurring in the head also occur in the body.

Definition 5 (Program). *A program P at context C_P is a finite set of facts and rules accessible on the web by dereferencing C_P.*

If the context C_P is a query-able endpoint it is possible to push selections during query processing and retrieve only the necessary information to answer a query, thus reducing the amount of data transferred.

Example. *Recall the running example given in the introduction. We are now able to give an example of a rule that expresses a link between repositories. Figure 3 shows a rule which is stored at* `exo:dblp` *and relates photos in* `exc:foaf` *to people in* `exo:dblp`*, given identical homepage URIs.*

---

[6] Currently a W3C Working Draft.

[7] `http://www.w3.org/2000/10/swap/log#`

```
@prefix foaf: <http://xmlns.com/foaf/0.1/> .
@prefix yars: <http://sw.deri.org/2004/06/yars#> .
@prefix log: <http://www.w3.org/2000/10/swap/log#> .

{{ ?x foaf:homepage ?hp .
   ?x foaf:depiction ?img . } yars:context exc:foaf .
   ?y foaf:homepage ?hp .
} log:implies {
   ?y foaf:depiction ?img .
} .
```

Fig. 3. Rule to relate photos in the FOAF data source to people in DBLP

3.3 Operational Semantics

We have defined the syntax of rules, but not yet their meaning. In the following, we define an operator that can be used to calculate a fixpoint taking into account recursive rules.

Definition 6 (Immediate Consequence). *Let P be a program at context C_P. A fact h is an immediate consequence of P if (i) $h \in C_P$ or (ii) $\{b_1 \ldots b_n\}$ `log:implies` $\{h\}$. is an instantiation of a rule in P and each $b_i \in C_i$. T_P denotes all facts that are immediate consequences of P.*

In our framework we anticipate a large number of rules, possibly recursively referencing each other. There is no way to escape the need for recursion, since there is no central control over the network, and each actor can put in rules without coordinating with others, which makes it possible (and very likely) that one actor references triples inferred by a rule of another actor. In addition, we need recursion to be able to define the semantics of transitivity.

Given that our rules language has no function symbols that can be used to generate new symbols, the set of rules are guaranteed to reach the fixpoint (i.e. no new facts are generated by the T_P operator) after a finite number of steps [2]. The expressivity of our language is equivalent to (recursive) datalog under the least-model semantics.

We employ the open world assumption; results to queries are not guaranteed to be complete, since complete knowledge of a huge distributed system such as the web is somewhat illusory. Thus, our framework returns sound answers but is an incomplete procedure (i.e. all answers returned are sound but we might miss some answers due to the distributed nature of the web).

4 Vocabulary Descriptions and Ontologies

So far we have operated on a sub-schema level without taking into account formal descriptions about the data. Object-oriented features such as classes, instances, properties, and inheritance can be layered on top of RDF. Vocabulary descriptions, such as RDF Schema (RDFS) [8], or ontologies, such as OWL, the Web Ontology Language [18], are commonly used to formally describe information on the web.

4.1 Related Approaches

[11] discusses the intersection of logic programming rules and OWL called description logic programs (DLP) which is the fragment common to both paradigms. The paper also argues that language layering is a desirable feature from an architectural viewpoint.

TRIPLE's notion of parameterized context in combination with a set of rules that (partially) axiomatize the semantics of RDFS can be used to derive additional information from an RDFS specification [21].

C-OWL [7] is a proposed extension to OWL with the notion of context and bridge rules. An interesting feature of this language is that its semantics makes use of the so-called local model semantics where for each context there exists a local model and a local domain of interpretation.

4.2 Axiomatic Semantics

To be able to interpret a set of triples under the semantics of e.g. RDFS or OWL DLP we need a formalization of that semantics. For RDFS, we use a set of rules that axiomatize the RDFS semantics. The main feature of RDFS is the transitivity of `rdfs:subClassOf` and `rdfs:subPropertyOf` properties, which can be encoded using our rule language. We also use rules to encode the semantics of `rdfs:domain` and `rdfs:range` for properties.

The OWL variant that is expressible in our rule language is OWL DLP. We plan to axiomatize the OWL DLP subset using N3 rules, similar to what has been done in [15]. Once the RDFS or OWL DLP rules are added to a context, queries against the RDF graph there take into account the semantics of the respective vocabulary description or ontology.

5 Discussion and Ongoing Work

We have implemented a prototype that allows to answer conjunctive queries that span multiple contexts. We are experimenting with an RDF version of DBLP (around 1.5 GB in size) and a web crawl of RDF data (around 1 GB in size). [14] has more information on the index organization and query processing techniques used in our prototype. One immediate next step is to implement the operational semantics described in Section 3.3. We plan to investigate the use of (hybrid) top-down methods such as QRGT [22] or QSQ [2].

Ongoing work includes extending the rule language with scoped negation [20]. The idea here is that we close off the world for data sources that contain complete information about a subject; then we are able to employ a form of default negation.

An interesting theoretical question which requires some more in-depth investigation is what extensions (possibly within second-order logic) are needed to be able to query rule bases.

6 Conclusion

The aim of the thesis is to investigate methods for interoperation among autonomous RDF information spaces on the web. Our framework allows to operate with only local information, that is, creating links between sources or evaluating queries can be done without any global knowledge about the network.

We have shown how to use coordination links expressed in the query and rule language N3 with context to interlink data sources. We have defined both syntax and operational fixpoint semantics of the query and rule language, and have sketched a number of questions we intend to tackle as part of the Ph.D. thesis.

Acknowledgements

I gratefully acknowledge the support of my thesis advisor Stefan Decker. This work has been partially supported by the EU IST program under the DIP project (FP6-507483) and by Science Foundation Ireland (SFI/02/CE1/I131).

References

1. K. Aberer, M. Punceva, M. Hauswirth, and R. Schmidt. Improving data access in p2p systems. *IEEE Internet Computing*, January/February 2002.
2. S. Abiteboul, R. Hull, and V. Vianu. *Foundations of Databases.* Addison-Wesley Publishing Co., 1995.
3. M. Arenas, V. Kantere, A. Kementsietsidis, I. Kiringa, R. J. Miller, and J. Mylopoulos. The hyperion project: From data integration to data coordination. *SIGMOD Record*, 32, 2003.
4. J. Bailey, F. Bry, T. Furche, and S. Schaffert. Web and semantic web query languages: A survey. In *Reasoning Web, First International Summer School*, 2005.
5. T. Berners-Lee. Notation 3 – ideas about web architecture. http://www.w3.org/DesignIssues/Notation3.html.
6. P. A. Bernstein, F. Giunchiglia, A. Kementsietsidis, J. Mylopoulos, L. Serafini, and I. Zaihrayeu. Data management for peer-to-peer computing: A vision. In *Workshop on the Web and Databases, WebDB 2002*, 2002.
7. P. Bouquet, F. Giunchiglia, F. van Harmelen, L. Serafini, and H. Stuckenschmidt. C-OWL: Contextualizing ontologies. In *Proceedings of the 2nd International Semantic Web Conference.* Springer, 2003.
8. D. Brickley and R. V. Guha. Rdf vocabulary description language 1.0: Rdf schema. W3C Recommendation, Feb. 2004. http://www.w3.org/TR/rdf-schema/.
9. P. P. de Siliva and D. McGuiness. Knowledge provenance infrastructure. *IEEE Data Engineering Bulletin*, 26(4):26–32, 2003.
10. E. Franconi, G. Kuper, A. Lopatenko, and I. Zaihrayeu. The codb robust peer-to-peer database system. In *Proc. of the 2nd Workshop on Semantics in Peer-to-Peer and Grid Computing (SemPGrid'04)*, 2004.

11. B. N. Grosof, I. Horrocks, R. Volz, and S. Decker. Description logic programs: Combining logic programs with description logic. In *Proceedings of the 12th International WWW Conference.* ACM Press, 2003.
12. R. V. Guha, R. McCool, and R. Fikes. Contexts for the semantic web. In *Proceedings of the 3rd International Semantic Web Conference.* Springer, Nov 2004.
13. A. Y. Halevy, Z. G. Ives, P. Mork, and I. Tatarinov. Piazza: Data management infrastructure for semantic web applications. In *Proceedings of the 12th International WWW Conference.* ACM Press, 2003.
14. A. Harth and S. Decker. Optimized index structures for querying rdf from the web. In *Proceedings of the 3rd Latin American Web Congress.* IEEE Press, 2005.
15. A. Harth and S. Decker. Owl lite- reasoning with rules, 2005. WSML Working Draft.
16. A. Kementsietsidis, M. Arenas, and R. J. Miller. Managing data mappings in the hyperion project. In *Proceedings of the 19th International Conference on Data Engineering (ICDE)*, 2003.
17. F. Manola and E. Miller. Rdf primer. W3C Recommendation, Feb. 2004. http://www.w3.org/TR/rdf-primer/.
18. D. L. McGuinness and F. van Harmelen. Owl web ontology language overview. W3C Recommendation, Feb. 2004. http://www.w3.org/TR/owl-features/.
19. Y. Papakonstantinou, H. Garcia-Molina, and J. Widom. Object exchange across heterogeneous information sources. In *Proceedings of the 11th International Conference on Data Engineering (ICDE)*, pages 251–260, 1995.
20. A. Polleres. Logic programs with contextually scoped negation. In *20th Workshop on Logic Programming (WLP 2006)*, February 2006.
21. M. Sintek and S. Decker. Triple - an rdf query, inference, and transformation language. In *Proceedings of the 1st International Semantic Web Conference.* Springer, 2002.
22. J. D. Ullman. *Principles of Database and Knowledge-Base Systems*, volume 2: The New Technologies. Computer Science Press, 1989.
23. Y. Velegrakis, R. J. Miller, and J. Mylopoulos. Representing and querying data transformations. In *Proceedings of the 21st International Conference on Data Engineering (ICDE)*, 2005.

Enhancing User Interaction and Efficiency with Structural Summaries for Fast and Intuitive Access to XML Databases

Felix Weigel

Centre for Information and Language Processing (CIS)
University of Munich (LMU), Germany
weigel@informatik.uni-muenchen.de

Abstract. This paper describes an ongoing Ph. D. project whose goal is to improve both the user interaction and the efficiency of XML databases. Based on *structural summaries* for indexing and visualizing the structure of XML data, we describe a highly interactive, intuitive GUI targeted at non-experts, and present sophisticated algorithms and data structures for efficient query evaluation which enable a smooth user interaction. Preliminary results illustrate how XML exploration, indexing, querying, caching, ranking and user feedback in XML databases can benefit significantly from the structural summaries.

1 Introduction

XML has by now become a de-facto standard for modelling, querying, exchanging and storing a broad range of data with different characteristics. At the one end of the spectrum, there are text-centric documents with little structure to be queried, e.g., web pages, Wikis, Blogs, news feeds, e-mail and FAQ archives. At the other end, there is XML content with a much more rigid and meaningful structure and little text, e.g., product catalogues, tax payer's data submitted via electronic forms and bibliography servers. While traditional Information Retrieval (IR) techniques have been established for the former class of data, XPath and XQuery [1] are the languages of choice for the latter.

However, XML is most commonly used for a wide variety of truly semistructured data in between those two extremes, with complex and irregular structure adding significant information to the rich textual content. Examples are documents in digital libraries or publishing houses, electronic encyclopedias, on-line manuals, linguistic databases and scientific taxonomies. For querying such data neither database nor IR-style methods are well suited. On the one hand, we cannot expect unskilled users of these applications to express their information need in XPath or XQuery, languages which are also inapt for ranked retrieval in XML data with an irregular or (partly) unknown schema. On the other hand, flat-text IR disregards valuable structural hints which can help not only to formulate more precise queries, but also to rank and present query results in a meaningful form. Although there is much recent work on ranking structured documents, the user interaction in such systems mostly follows the database paradigm[1].

[1] See, e.g., the IR extensions to XPath (in the *INEX* benchmark [2]) or XQuery [3].

T. Grust et al. (Eds.): EDBT 2006 Workshops, LNCS 4254, pp. 54–65, 2006.

We argue that to make the full spectrum of XML applications accessible to non-experts, a new way of user interaction with XML databases is needed which helps them understand and use the schema of the data in an intuitive way. It is known from earlier experience with relational databases (RDBSs) and IR engines that sophisticated query languages alone are not enough for serving the information needs of unexperienced users. Making users *benefit* from the XML structure poses *challenges* to both the user interface and the query kernel:

Schema exploration. Exploiting the inherent document structure allows for more precise and useful queries and answers. However, sometimes users find the markup just meaningless, either because they ignore the underlying schema or because they are faced with instructions for layout, document processing, namespaces, etc.[2] Rather than to present the structure of the data one-to-one, interfaces to XML databases should therefore allow users to explore the schema and selected sample data, as well as to create views customized to their information need and degree of expertise.

Structured query results. When presenting query results to users, the XML structure relates distinct parts of the result and defines boundaries for highlighting matches in a meaningful context. Yet users also need to recognize how results relate to the query and schema. When exploring results, users often wish to change part of the query and reevaluate it. Ideally this could be done in a seamless iterative feedback without leaving the result view.

Efficient query evaluation. Encouraging vivid user interaction via integrated schema exploration, querying and result browsing makes sense only with a fast query kernel ensuring prompt system reaction. A major challenge is the incremental query evaluation based on previously retrieved results in an XML query cache, which is needed for smooth user interaction and feedback.

Structured ranking. Structural query hints can be used to present retrieved elements in order of relevance. However, computing relevance scores for structured documents is non-trivial. Open problems are, e.g., how to find elements which cover exactly a relevant portion of text, how to handle structural near-misses and how to avoid overlapping elements in the query result efficiently.

We believe that the key to easy, intuitive user interaction with XML databases is the tight integration of graphical views on the document schema, sample data, user queries and retrieval results on top of an efficient and scalable query kernel. The goal of the Ph. D. project is to address the above challenges with (1) a novel graphical user interface (GUI) providing integrated schema, query and result views, (2) index structures and algorithms for efficient, scalable and incremental query evaluation, (3) efficient and effective techniques for XML ranking. In a first phase, we have investigated how *structural summaries* visualizing the document schema also improve the efficiency of the query kernel. Most of this work, though targeting enhanced user interaction, applies to XML databases in general. Hence

[2] For instance, with its 30,000 distinct label paths, the schema of the INEX collection of scientific articles [2] is much more complex than the actual logical structure of the documents, and therefore hard to understand for non-expert users.

we present our contributions in the context of more recent approaches which have appeared since the beginning of the project in late 2003. To the best of our knowledge our approach to intuitive and efficient user interaction is unique in that we employ the same structural summary for (a) exploring the schema and samples of the data, (b) formulating, planning, evaluating and caching queries, (c) ranking query results and (d) enabling iterative user feedback.

The next section sketches the state of the art in XML retrieval, highlighting techniques we build upon. Section 3 explains in detail our solutions to the aforementioned challenges, presenting the main contributions of the project. These are summarized and briefly contrasted with existing approaches in Section 4, which also gives a snapshot of the accomplished work and remaining issues.

2 XML Retrieval: State of the Art and Open Problems

User interaction with XML databases. As mentioned in the introduction, XML retrieval is typically addressed either from an IR or a database viewpoint, which is also reflected in the main features of the systems. While the focus of XML databases is efficient XQuery processing, IR engines optimize ranking effectiveness (precision/recall). By contrast, user interaction has been somewhat neglected so far[3]. Most systems from both camps offer only a text interface to queries and results, rendering query results as XML fragments [4]. More sophisticated GUIs focus on visual query creation [5,6,7,8,9,10] while disregarding the exploration of query results. In particular, it is hard to figure out how results relate to the query and schema. [11] introduces a compact result view which reflects the query structure, but is not linked to the query view. All these tools assume prior knowledge of the document schema for creating meaningful queries. [8,10] support DTD-driven query assistance and restructuring, but lack schema and result browsing. In [6,12] structural summaries are used to visualize the document schema, provide sample content and facilitate manual query formulation to some extent. However, there is little work on adapting IR-style relevance feedback for smooth iterative XML retrieval. In particular, we are not aware of any solution to efficient incremental query evaluation based on user feedback.

Index and Storage Structures. As more and more multi-gigabyte data sets need to be stored and queried, efficiency and scalability of XML databases have received much attention. IR systems often use inverted lists built over tag names or keywords as index structures. This hinders scalability, joins of large node lists being expensive. Many database approaches are based on the *DataGuide* [6], a compact representation of the document structure where each distinct label path appears exactly once. Query paths are matched on this *structural summary* in main memory rather than the entire data set on disk, which avoids some joins and disk I/O. The DataGuide has been combined with different IR techniques for text matching, such as signature files, tries and inverted lists.

[3] No new approaches to user interaction were presented at the *Interactive* and *Relevance Feedback* tracks of INEX 2004 [2].

A complementary indexing technique are *labelling schemes*, which assign elements specific IDs from which part of the document structure is inferred without accessing the entire data set. Recently many new schemes addressing different query problems on XML trees have been proposed. For instance, *interval schemes* [13] encode the descendant axis by representing an element v as a numeric interval I_v such that v is a descendant of v' iff $I_v \subset I_{v'}$. They are space-efficient but sensitive to node insertions and join-intensive. *Prefix schemes* [14] represent an element as the sequence of sibling positions on its root path, similar to the section numbers in this paper. Simple label manipulations allow to infer ancestors and siblings. Binary encodings have been applied to reduce the space overhead of prefix schemes. Node insertions can be handled gracefully [15], whereas the problem of labelling graph-shaped XML remains open.

While earlier semistructured [16] and most IR engines are native systems, recent approaches treat XML retrieval as an application for RDBSs. Different methods of storing and querying XML in tables have been proposed [17,15,13]. Supporters of the native approach [18,4,19] argue that the best performance is achieved by tailoring the system to the XML data model. However, the question whether native or relational systems are more efficient, which largely affects indexing, joining as well as query planning and optimization, is still unresolved.

Caching of XML Query Results. Reusing cached query results is an instance of the more general problem of query processing in the presence of *views* on the database, which has been studied extensively for RDBSs. Major problems are *query containment/overlap* (compare the definitions of queries/views to decide whether their extension overlap or contain one another) and *query answering* (based on the view definitions and extensions, decide whether a given piece of data is part of the result of a specific query). Many papers have studied the theoretical complexity of these problems with different query languages for semistructured data. For instance, [20] shows that both are PSPACE-complete for tree-shaped and EXPSPACE-complete for arbitrary conjunctive queries of regular path expressions. Despite the high theoretical complexity, a number of different approaches strive to push the practical efficiency to its limits, building on native XQuery engines [21,22], two-way finite state automata [20], tree automata [23], incomplete trees [24,25], or LDAP servers [26].

Ranked XML Retrieval. Unlike flat-text IR, XML ranking must cope with (1) relaxing query structure in order to capture near misses, (2) balancing structural and textual query conditions when computing relevance scores, (3) defining an inverted element frequency, (4) choosing suitable elements to return (rather than entire documents), and (5) avoiding result overlap. Since the first INEX benchmark [2] in 2002, many performance metrics and new ranking models have been proposed, most of which adopt flat-text methods such as *tf·idf* [27,28,29]. A web-inspired technique is to exploit the link structure in document collections [30,31]. Recently the use of ontologies for query expansion has been studied more thoroughly [32,31]. However, little work is concerned with the efficient implementation of XML ranking techniques.

3 Contributions of the Project

3.1 Indexing and Exploring XML Data with the CADG Index

At the core of our efficiency enhancements is the *Content-Aware DataGuide (CADG)*, a path summary inspired by the DataGuide [6] which tightly integrates IR techniques for efficient keyword search. Those parts of the schema which do not lead to occurrences of query terms are pruned early during path matching. Experiments show that this considerably reduces disk I/O, improving the performance of the original DataGuide by up to a factor 200 [33]. As a first step toward enhanced user interaction (Sect. 3.6), we created a graphical CADG [34] which extends the DataGuide visualization in [6] (Fig. 1). The schema is rendered as a tree with highlightable nodes. The user can view sample keywords occurring under specific label paths and statistical information about their distribution in the data. For complex schemata (e.g., INEX benchmark), the user may simplify the CADG by hiding subtrees based on tag names or textual content. Unlike [6], we also use the CADG for creating complex tree queries in a semiautomated manner.

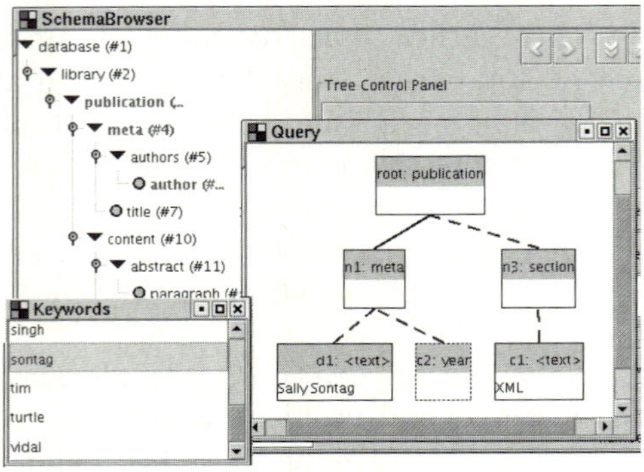

Fig. 1. CADG visualization

3.2 Ranked XML Retrieval with the CADG Index

As mentioned above, the question how to rank structured documents both efficiently and effectively is still open. Rather than to commit ourselves to a particular model, we therefore classified existing approaches w.r.t. the path and term frequencies they use for computing relevance scores. In [35] we show how to adapt the CADG to indexing precomputed frequencies for different classes of ranking model, which speeds up the retrieval process. To evaluate our approach experimentally, we implemented the *S-Term* ranking model [36] and tested it with the INEX 2004 benchmark [2]. The system scaled up well to over 500 MB in terms of retrieval speed, but we discovered that even with precomputed frequencies the scoring of certain queries takes quite long [37]. Clearly this is due to deficiencies inherent to the S-Term model. Although not central to the Ph. D. project, we might therefore develop a simplified model which avoids too complex scoring and at the same time addresses some of the challenges mentioned in Sect. 2.

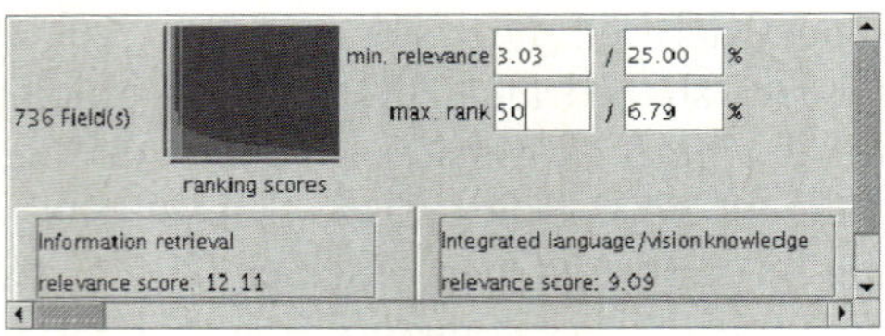

Fig. 2. Ranking visualization

We also use ranking in our preliminary GUI for rendering result lists, which may become large for unselective queries. With a new *threshold histogram* (Fig. 2) the user specifies a minimum relevance score (or alternatively, a maximum rank) for items to be displayed, dynamically adapting the number of items in the result list below the widget.

3.3 The BIRD Labelling Scheme

In a third step we developed the *BIRD* labelling scheme [38] for avoiding joins of large node sets, a common bottleneck in XML query evaluation. Although the CADG matches leaves of query paths without such joins, BIRD achieves huge benefits when retrieving nodes higher on the path, or common ancestors in tree queries. The key to reducing the join effort is that BIRD not only *decides* all XPath axes for two given elements, but also infers ancestors, siblings and children of a single element from its label alone, for which we coined the term *reconstruction.* Combined with the CADG, reconstruction avoids additional disk I/O for looking up matches to the branching nodes of a tree query. As shown in Fig. 3, BIRD labels (small numbers) are multiples of integer *weights* (large numbers), which are stored in the CADG. For instance, to reconstruct the parent of element 43, we look up the parent weight (5) in the CADG and simply compute the parent label as $43 - (43 \bmod 5) = 40$, and likewise for other ancestors.

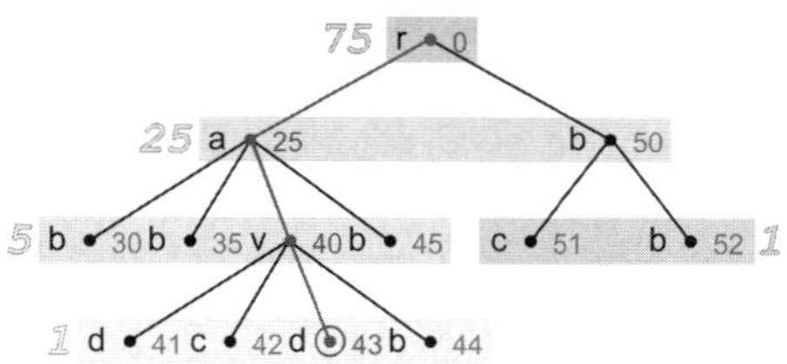

Fig. 3. BIRD ancestor reconstruction. Small numbers denote BIRD node labels, whereas large numbers indicate BIRD weights. Here all children of the same node have the same weight regardless of their label paths.

In [38] we study (1) the benefit of reconstruction over decision and (2) how BIRD compares to other labelling schemes in terms of expressivity (reconstruction/decision of different axes), processing time, space consumption and robustness against updates. In our experiments with five labelling schemes BIRD outperforms all competitors with equal expressivity in terms of space and time. The only comparable approach, μPID [39], generates smaller labels but is less expressive than BIRD. Although BIRD is not as robust against updates as other schemes such as ORDPATH [15], further experiments illustrate that a simple strategy minimizes the impact of node insertions at least for a certain class of data set. Still we would like to investigate advanced updating techniques for BIRD sketched in [38]. Finally, a comparison of different query algorithms in the paper confirms that (1) reconstruction is indeed most effective for speeding up query evaluation, (2) schemes with excessive label size may incur a performance overhead due to inefficient node comparison, and (3) labelling schemes respecting document order (such as BIRD, e.g.) benefit from extra optimization techniques. These encouraging results motivated the combination of BIRD and the CADG in a relational setting (see the next section).

Currently we are surveying a multitude of new approaches with distinct features which have appeared meanwhile, including an extensive comparative analysis and evaluation of more than twenty labelling schemes in terms of time and space efficiency, robustness against node insertions and expressivity. While a previous survey [40] classifies a small number of approaches into *bit-vector*, *interval* and *prefix* schemes, we subsume BIRD and a few other encodings under a fourth class, *multiplicative schemes.*

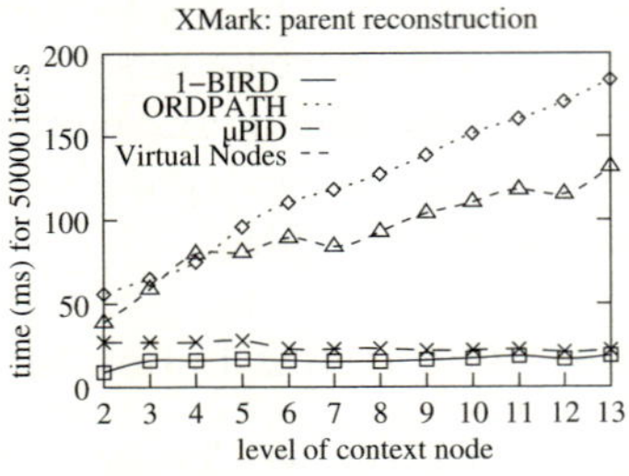

Fig. 4. Reconstruction speed of BIRD and other approaches

3.4 Relational XML Retrieval with the RCADG Index

The following work contributes to the discussion of native vs. relational XML retrieval systems (see Section 1). Given that both approaches have been established and pursued without much cross-fertilization taking place so far, we examined how our native XML indexing techniques can boost the retrieval of XML stored in an RDBS. The goals in the context of the Ph. D. project were (1) to improve the scalability of our native prototype system whose performance degraded for unselective queries, (2) to benefit from RDBS features such as concurrency or recovery and (3) to store intermediate results temporarily during query evaluation, in anticipation of a future incremental query kernel (see the next section). In [41] we show how to migrate the CADG and BIRD to the relational data model, applying interval labelling [42] to CADG nodes and BIRD labelling to document nodes. The resulting *Relational CADG (RCADG)* replaces the structural summary in main memory with a single table containing one row for each CADG node (see Figure 5), including its interval-scheme labels (columns *pid*, *max*), BIRD weight (*weight*), CADG-specific keyword signatures (*csig*, *gsig*) and statistical path information for query planning and ranking (*keys*, *elts*).

pid	*par*	*max*	*lab*	*type*	*lev*	*weight*	*csig*	*gsig*	*keys*	*elts*
#0		#5	people	elt	0	27	000000	111111	0	1
#1	#0	#5	person	elt	1	9	000000	111111	0	1
#2	#1	#2	name	elt	2	3	010010	010010	2	2
#3	#1	#5	profile	elt	2	3	000000	101111	0	2
#4	#3	#4	edu	elt	3	1	101100	101100	2	2
#5	#3	#5	gender	elt	3	1	001011	001011	2	2

Fig. 5. Relational CADG (RCADG)

XML queries against the RCADG are evaluated entirely within an RDBS as a sequence of SQL statements. The translation algorithm makes heavy use of BIRD's reconstruction capabilities to minimize the number and the size of intermediate result node sets to be joined. For instance, to evaluate the query in Figure 6 only q_3 and q_5 are matched by joining the RCADG table with the element table, whereas matches to q_1, q_4 and q_6 are obtained via reconstruction. Thus the number of joins is reduced by 50% compared to other relational approaches. Subsequent evaluation steps each produce a more complete intermediate result table from prior results, which also enables relational index support for elements reconstructed on the fly. This technique is rewarded in the

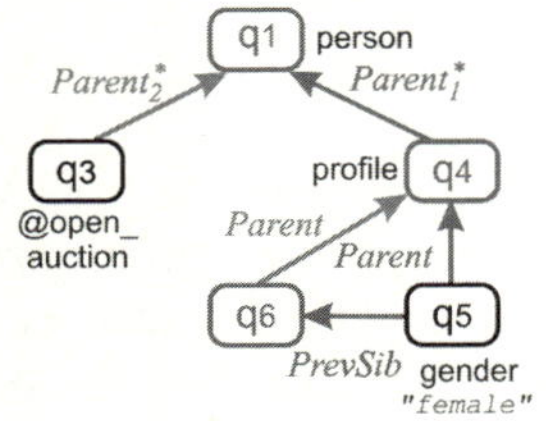

Fig. 6. RCADG query

experiments where we compare the RCADG to the native CADG/BIRD system, a relational version of the interval scheme and another relational DataGuide variant that uses string matching on paths [17]. Unlike the two relational competitors, the RCADG fully preserves the underlying document schema in the RDBS. This avoids false hits for certain queries on recursive data sets (which we observed for the string-matching approach) and also enables query optimization techniques that take into account XML path statistics ignored by the relational optimizer.

From the study on relational XML retrieval with the RCADG, we learned that (1) exploiting native indexing techniques such as BIRD and the CADG in an RDBS boosts the query performance by up to three orders of magnitude compared to both native and relational approaches, (2) the proposed techniques significantly improve the scalability both in terms of the query complexity and selectivity, (3) these benefits are achieved with only a negligible space overhead, but (4) the performance gains may be deteriorated by inappropriate query planning and rewriting. Our preliminary planning algorithm needs to be refined to cope with more involved cases where the selectivity of a particular query node on the one hand and the analysis of applicable reconstruction steps on the other hand favour conflicting query plans.

3.5 Incremental Query Evaluation with an XML Query Cache

The user interaction described below encourages the continuous modification of prior queries in an iterative relevance feedback process. To this end, queries need to be evaluated *incrementally*, i.e., common subsets of results to different queries should not be retrieved repeatedly from scratch but reused with the least possible computational effort. This means that (1) final or intermediate results to previous queries must be materialized at least temporarily and (2) subsequent queries must be analyzed to find out which parts of the results they share with previous ones. The first requirement is satisfied in a natural way by the RCADG (see above). To meet the second requirement, we have developed a novel XML query cache [43] from which reusable result subsets can be retrieved efficiently with the help of schema information. A new query is first matched on the schema level (which can be done very fast in the RCADG's path table). The resulting *schema hits* are decomposed into pairs of label paths which are then looked up in the query cache to find prior queries with overlapping schema hits. The results of these queries are available in their RCADG result tables for further processing.

This approach has three benefits, which distinguish it from the earlier work we know of. First, comparing query *extensions* (i.e., results) rather than *intensions* (i.e., tree patterns or XQuery expressions) works around the high complexity of query containment (Sect. 2). Second, comparing schema hits before accessing the full query results helps to discard useless cached queries efficiently. Third, by caching intermediate and final matches to all parts of a query we can reuse partial query results and create new query plans to compute the complete result incrementally. Note also that only schema hits are kept in the main-memory part of the cache, whereas the full query extensions reside in the RDBS backend.

3.6 Integrated Schema Exploration, Querying and Result Browsing

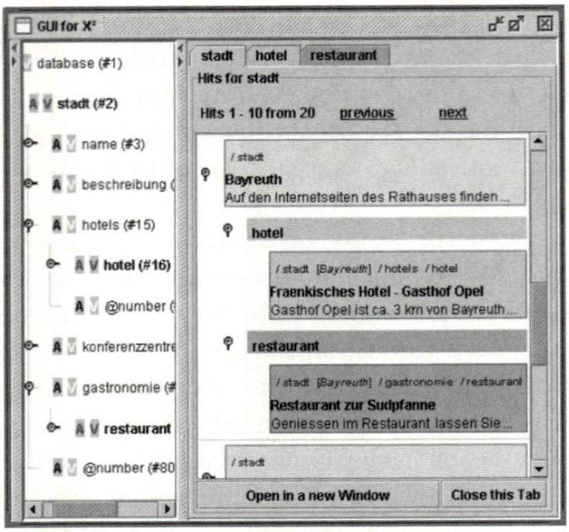

Fig. 7. Preliminary GUI

The current GUI described in [34] provides separate views on the schema, queries and results. Once a query has been formulated and evaluated, the retrieved hits are explored in a graphical representation reflecting the query structure. While browsing the result view, users often wish to modify the query, realizing mismatches with their information need. Currently this requires re-editing and re-running the query outside the result view (perhaps after consulting the schema again). This not only causes needless computations to find data that is already known, but also makes it hard for the user to keep track of updates to the query result.

The most salient feature of the new GUI to be developed is the tight integration of the schema, query and result views. Ideally the user would silently issue new queries or modify previous ones while browsing the document schema or query result, as follows. First the user activates interesting label paths, possibly with keyword constraints as before. The occurrences of these label paths span a substructure in the documents which in turn induces a partial schema specific to the current activation. In the schema view, the CADG is immediately updated, e.g., by hiding paths outside the reduced schema. Note that finding the current substructure requires efficient tree matching in the documents, just like for processing explicit user queries.

At any point in time the user can either narrow down or expand the CADG by changing the path activation. Moreover, distinct paths can be *merged*, i.e., treated as equivalent both in query evaluation and in the GUI. Conversely, occurrences of the same label path can be distinguished, based on their textual content or statistics such as subtree size, by *splitting* the corresponding node in the schema view. To some extent this blurs the distinction between the schema and the actual data. However, query results for user-specified parts of the schema

a. Tree view.

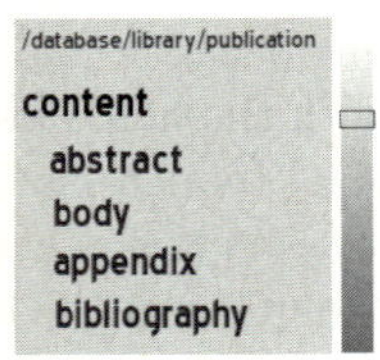

b. Hotspot view.

c. Bird's eye overview.

Fig. 8. Alternative schema views

are still displayed in a dedicated view (see Figure 7, right-hand side), using different profiles determining the desired level of detailedness as well as backlinks into the schema view for locating the corresponding label paths.

Inspired by the capabilities of common file system browsers, we intend to provide alternative views on the schema. Fig. 8 sketches two possible schema presentations, the *tree view* (*a.*) introduced before and the *hotspot view* (*b.*) which displays the root path and children of a single schema node. The *level widget* to the right in Fig. 8 *b.* indicates how deep the node is buried in the document hierarchy. Multiple hotspot views may be opened in separate frames or integrated with the tree view. A *bird's eye overview* locates the hotspots in the document hierarchy (Fig. 8 *c.*). Individual schema nodes may be rendered at distinct levels of detailedness. Two alternatives to the simplistic rendering in Fig. 8 *a.* are illustrated in Fig. 9. In a concise read-only profile (Fig. 9 *a.*), sample keywords and user-specified query keywords are shown. By contrast, the full profile (Fig. 9 *b.*) provides widgets to edit these properties and also displays some path statistics.

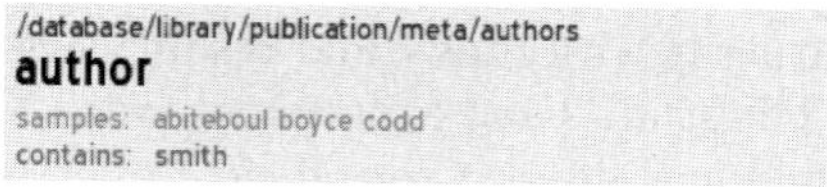

a. Concise schema node profile.

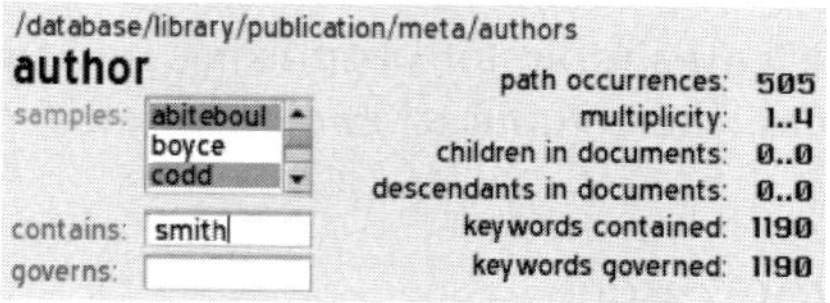

b. Full schema node profile.

Fig. 9. Alternative schema node profiles

Meanwhile we have specified the intended user interaction with the new GUI in terms of a clean formal algebra. More specifically, we compiled a set of *A-operations* for activating label paths in the schema view, and *E-operations* for exploring the query results. A preliminary implementation covers some A- and E-operations in the GUI, but does not yet trigger the appropriate evaluation steps. Further remaining tasks include the merging and splitting of label paths and an analysis of the expressiveness of the interaction algebra.

4 Summary and Discussion

The Ph. D. project presented here aims to improve both the user interaction and the efficiency of XML databases. Major contributions are (1) a highly interactive, intuitive *GUI for non-expert users*, (2) *index and storage structures* for efficient exact or ranked XML retrieval and (3) algorithms for the *incremental evaluation of XML queries*. The work on index and storage structures is finished. We have thoroughly analyzed our techniques in comparison with existing methods and demonstrated their practical use in extensive experiments, including scalability tests for various data sets up to 9 GB in size. The use of structural summaries such as the CADG has been shown to be particularly apt for the envisaged user interaction, because it provides an intuitive graphical access to the document schema and at the same time accelerates query evaluation. This twofold benefit was already discussed in the context of the *Lore* system [6]. We significantly extend that work by (1) combining the DataGuide with IR techniques for keyword search and ranking (*CADG*), (2) boosting its performance by means of a novel labelling scheme (*BIRD*), (3) migrating the resulting index to an RDBS (*RCADG*), (4) using it for similarity search in an XML query cache, (5) integrating it with query and result views for iterative feedback-driven search.

The studies and experiments with XML ranking have shown that our indexing techniques support the efficient query evaluation with different models, and have given us a clear picture of what needs to be improved. As far as the quality of the S-Term ranking is concerned, the performance at INEX 2004 is encouraging but leaves room for optimizing the specificity of the results. For better response times, the computation of relevance scores needs to be simplified.

References

1. Boag, S., Chamberlin, D., et al.: XQuery 1.0. W3C Cand. Rec. (2005)
2. INEX: (Initiative for the Evaluation of XML Retrieval)
3. Amer-Yahia, S., et al.: XQuery 1.0 and XPath 2.0 Full-Text. W3C W. Dr. (2005)
4. Paparizos, S., Al-Khalifa, S., Chapman, A., Jagadish, H., et al.: TIMBER: A Native System for Quering XML. In: Proc. SIGMOD Conf. (2003)
5. Gemis, M., Paredaens, J., Thyssens, I.: A Visual Database Management Interface based on GOOD. In: Proc. Int. Worksh. on Interfaces to Database Systems. (1993)
6. Goldman, R., Widom, J.: DataGuides: Enabling Query Formulation and Optimization in Semistructured Databases. In: Proc. VLDB Conf. (1997) 436–445
7. Munroe, K.D., Papakonstantinou, Y.: BBQ: A Visual Interface for Browsing and Querying of XML. In: Proc. Conf. on Visual Database Systems. (2000) 277–296
8. Comai, S., Damiani, E., Fraternali, P.: Computing Graphical Queries over XML Data. Trans. Inf. Syst. **19** (2001) 371–430
9. Berger, S., et al.: Xcerpt and visXcerpt: From Pattern-Based to Visual Querying of XML and Semistructured Data. In: Proc. VLDB Conf. (2003) 1053–1056 (Demo).
10. Braga, D., Campi, A., Ceri, S.: XQBE (XQuery By Example): A Visual Interface to the Standard XML Query Language. Trans. Database Syst. **30** (2005) 398–443
11. Meuss, H., Schulz, K.U.: Complete Answer Aggregates for Tree-like DBs: A Novel Approach to Combine Querying and Navig. Trans. Inf. Syst. **19** (2001) 161–215
12. Chawathe, S.S., Baby, T., Yeo, J.: VQBD: Exploring Semistructured Data. In: Proc. SIGMOD Conf. (2001) 603 (Demo).
13. Boncz, P., Grust, T., van Keulen, M., Manegold, S., et al.: Pathfinder: XQuery—The Relational Way. In: Proc. VLDB Conf. (2005) 1322–1325
14. Tatarinov, I., Viglas, S., Beyer, K.S., et al.: Storing and Querying Ordered XML Using a Relational Database System. In: Proc. SIGMOD Conf. (2002) 204–215
15. O'Neil, P., O'Neil, E., Pal, S., Cseri, I., et al.: ORDPATHs: Insert-Friendly XML Node Labels. In: Proc. SIGMOD Conf. (2004) 903–908
16. McHugh, J., Abiteboul, S., Goldman, R., Quass, D., Widom, J.: Lore: A Database Management System for Semistructured Data. SIGMOD Record **26** (1997) 54–66
17. Yoshikawa, M., et al.: XRel: A Path-Based Approach to Storage and Retrieval of XML Documents Using Relational Databases. Trans. Int. Tech. **1** (2001) 110–141
18. Fiebig, T., Helmer, S., Kanne, C.C., Moerkotte, G., Neumann, J., et al.: Anatomy of a Native XML Database Management System. VLDB Journal **11** (2002) 292–314
19. Galax: Open-source XQuery reference implementation. (`www.galaxquery.org`)

20. Calvanese, D., et al.: View-based Query Answering and Query Containment over Semistructured Data. In: Proc. Int. Worksh. Database Prog. Lang. (2002) 40–61
21. Chen, L., Rundensteiner, E.A.: XQuery Containment in Presence of Variable Binding Dependencies. In: Proc. Int. Conf. World Wide Web. (2005) 288–297
22. Shah, A., et al.: Improving Query Perf. using Materialized XML Views: A Learning-based Approach. In: Proc. Int. Worksh. XML Schema Data Mgt. (2003) 297–310
23. Chen, L., Rundensteiner, E.A., Wang, S.: XCache: a Semantic Caching System for XML Queries. In: Proc. SIGMOD Conf. (2002) 618–618 (Demo).
24. Hristidis, V., Petropoulos, M.: Semantic Caching of XML Databases. In: Proc. Int. Worksh. Web and Databases. (2002) 25–30
25. Abiteboul, S., Segoufin, L., Vianu, V.: Representing and Querying XML with Incomplete Information. In: Proc. Symp. Principles of Database Systems. (2001)
26. Marrón, P.J., Lausen, G.: Efficient Cache Answerability for XPath Queries. In: Proc. Int. Worksh. Data Integration over the Web. (2002)
27. Wolff, J.E., Flörke, H., Cremers, A.B.: XPRES: A Ranking Approach to Retrieval on Structured Documents. Technical Report IAI-TR-99-12, Univ. Bonn (1999)
28. Fuhr, N., Großjohann, K.: XIRQL: A Query Language for Information Retrieval in XML Documents. In: Proc. Int. Conf. Research Developm. IR. (2001) 172–180
29. Theobald, M., Schenkel, R., Weikum, G.: An Efficient and Versatile Query Engine for TopX Search. In: Proc. VLDB Conf. (2005) 625–636
30. Guo, L., Shao, F., Botev, C., et al.: XRANK: Ranked Keyword Search over XML Documents. In: Proc. SIGMOD Conf. (2003) 16–27
31. Graupmann, J., et al.: The SphereSearch Engine for Unified Ranked Retrieval of Heterogeneous XML and Web Documents. In: Proc. VLDB Conf. (2005) 529–540
32. Theobald, A., Weikum, G.: The Index-Based XXL Search Engine for Querying XML Data with Relevance Ranking. In: Proc. EDBT Conf. (2002) 477–495
33. Weigel, F., Meuss, H., Bry, F., Schulz, K.U.: Content-Aware DataGuides: Interleaving IR and DB Indexing Techniques for Efficient Retrieval of Textual XML Data. In: Proc. Europ. Conf. Information Retrieval. (2004) 378–393
34. Meuss, H., Schulz, K.U., Weigel, F., et al.: Visual Exploration and Retrieval of XML Document Collections with the Generic System X^2. Dig. Lib. **5** (2005) 3–17
35. Weigel, F., Meuss, H., Schulz, K.U., Bry, F.: Content and Structure in Indexing and Ranking XML. In: Proc. Int. Worksh. Web and Databases. (2004)
36. Schlieder, T., Meuss, H.: Querying and Ranking XML Documents. Journ. American Society for Information Science and Technology **53** (2002) 489–503
37. Weigel, F., Meuss, H., Schulz, K.U., Bry, F.: Ranked Retrieval of Structured Documents with the S-Term Vector Space Model. In: Proc. INEX Worksh. (2004)
38. Weigel, F., Schulz, K.U., Meuss, H.: The BIRD Numbering Scheme for XML and Tree Databases – Deciding and Reconstructing Tree Relations using Efficient Arithmetic Operations. In: Proc. Int. XML Database Symposium. (2005) 49–67
39. Bremer, J.M., Gertz, M.: Integrating XML Document and Data Retrieval Based on XML. VLDB Journal (2005) Online First.
40. Christophides, V., Scholl, M., Tourtounis, S.: On Labeling Schemes for the Semantic Web. In: Proc. Int. Conf. World Wide Web. (2003)
41. Weigel, F., Schulz, K.U., Meuss, H.: Exploiting Native XML Indexing Techniques for XML Retrieval in Relational Database Systems. In: Proc. Int. Worksh. Web Information and Data Management. (2005)
42. Li, Q., Moon, B.: Indexing and Querying XML Data for Regular Path Expressions. In: Proc. 27th VLDB Conf. (2001) 361–370
43. Weigel, F., Schulz, K.U.: Caching Schema Information and Intermediate Results for Fast Incremental XML Query Processing in RDBSs. Submitted for publ. (2006)

Orchestrating Access Control in Peer Data Management Systems

Christoph Sturm

Department of Informatics
University of Zurich
sturm@ifi.unizh.ch

Abstract. This paper describes an approach to establish access control mechanisms in a peer data management system (PDMS). Based on the research on security in Peer-to-Peer networks, we develop a decentralized access control component for PDMS. For this purpose, information resident in local access control components in the peers is used, and mappings between the peer access control policies are established. A client side access control mechanism enforces access rights in the whole PDMS.

1 Introduction

The use of Peer-to-Peer (P2P) networks introduced new challenges for database management systems. These new databases, called Peer Data Management Systems (PDMS), are defined as follows: A PDMS is a Peer-to-Peer network where every peer has its own database management system and intends to share parts of its database with other peers. To share data, the peers need to establish data mappings between their schemas [10,13,9,16]. Query processing is done by traversing these mappings, rewriting the queries, executing them on the peers and gathering the results at the peer that requested data. Because every peer can leave and join the network at its will, there is no permanent global schema. In fact, a kind of global schema is only established during query execution. Many security problems arise in such an environment, and, therefore, many projects deal with security in P2P networks (a good overview is given in [18]). But to our knowledge there is no approach which considers the creation of an access control mechanism in the special case of PDMS.

To illustrate the need for such an access control component, let us consider the following scenario. Several databases store health information about a person A. Database db_x holds data on the doctor, database db_y has details of health insurance, and database db_z is at a hospital which provided medical treatment for A. In an emergency, this information should be combined to give A the best possible medical care. A PDMS might provide such a service, because the mappings between those databases can be established fast and remain flexible. Let us assume that we have established all mappings between relevant data sources. Without access control in the newly established PDMS, every user can see all data. This is definitely not appropriate. We need a fine grained PDMS access control, similar to what is common in relational databases.

T. Grust et al. (Eds.): EDBT 2006 Workshops, LNCS 4254, pp. 66–74, 2006.

2 The Research Question

The following questions are being addressed in my research:

- How can a fine grained access control for PDMSs be established?
- How can the PDMS access control component be distributed in the network?
- How can the information inside local access control components be used for the PDMS?
- What is the relationship between local and global access control rules?
- How can one prevent PDMS access control bypassing?

The intention is to build on existing research work in P2P security mechanisms. With these mechanisms we can guarantee a secure authentication and communication inside PDMSs.

The next step is to establish the PDMS access control component. Here, the solution can be based on the security mechanisms of loosely coupled federated databases. But the mechanism proposed by Heimbigner and McLeod [11] seems to be insufficient for a PDMS. It is only based on peers and not on users, and it depends on access lists. Each database item which needs to be protected has its own access list where all authorized peers are recorded. This approach will also work in a PDMS; however, it is very costly and scales poorly. Therefore, we need a new approach that matches the requirements of a PDMS.

3 Significant Issues in the Field of Research

The basic problem in the research field is the missing central authority. Access control in data integration systems is a well studied research topic, see for example [2,20]. But up till now, every control mechanism relies on such a central authority. Furthermore, the high dynamics of PDMSs is a major problem. Peers leave and join the system at arbitrary times. Moreover, peers normally belong to different organizations and establish cooperations for a short period of time. Therefore, trust between peers is very important. Finally, if obstacles to join the PDMS are too high, the flexibility that P2P systems are famous for is going to disappear.

4 State of the Art

Before we can think of access control in PDMSs, some basic requirements need to be fulfilled. These are secure authentication and communication, and client based access control. A lot of research has been done to enable these services in a PDMS, as detailed below.

4.1 Secure Authentication and Communication

The basis of every security consideration is secure authentication of users and peers. Every user must own a single, specific and distinct ID. But without a central authority there is no instance that gives the guarantee that a newly generated ID is distinct. As shown by Berket et al. [3], this problem can be solved via a public key infrastructure (PKI) and certificates. A central certification authority guarantees distinct user IDs. Nevertheless, one problem remains. Normally, every peer should be able to have only one identity. Otherwise, the P2P network is vulnerable to "Sybil" attacks [8]. This can be prevented through the assignment of peer certificates from a certification authority, guaranteeing PDMS-wide distinct peer IDs. Peer hardware information, for example the MAC address of the network card in a certificate, can preclude multiple peer identities. Such a solution gives us the possibility, besides secure authentication, to establish secure communication between the peers and between users.

4.2 Trust Management

There are several proposals for trust management systems in P2P networks, e.g. [1] and [19]. Without trust between the participants, there will be no collaboration, and, without this, no working network. Besides, trust management systems that are based on peer reputation are able to detect malicious peers and exclude them from the network, if the authentication problem described in Sect. 4.1 is solved. Trust information can further be used to optimize the selection of peers and therefore network performance. These trust management systems must be immune to attacks of malicious peers.

4.3 Client Based Access Control

In a P2P network, one needs a new access control approach. As stated by Miklau and Suciu [14], trust domains in PDMSs differ from domains in traditional client server databases. The data owner trusts and controls only the data, whereas the execution of the query, and the query itself, may be beyond the control of the data provider. Hence, a PDMS peer is forced to give away its raw data to enable other peers to execute their queries and establish their mappings. When a peer gives away its data it also gives away the control over this data. It cannot restrict access to the data given away or protect it from changes. Even worse, one cannot prove where the data originates from.

One solution to solve this problem is to perform access control on the client and not on the data provider side. This can be done via trusted software on the client. The software enforces access and distribution restrictions of the data provider, and the client can only operate on the data through this trusted software. The data provider therefore encrypts the content and gives the encrypted data, together with the information needed to decrypt the data, to the data requester. Only the trustful software from the requestor is able to decrypt and display the data.

Another approach to enforce client based access control can be a solution based on the encryption and distribution of keys [14,4,5]. In the current solution, we opt for the trusted software approach, because we need this technology to enable the distribution of access control anyway (see Sect. 5.2). Besides, trusted software can make it much harder for a malicious peer to gain raw unencrypted data from the system.

4.4 Access Control in Peer-to-Peer Networks

Recent papers consider access control in P2P networks. Sandhu and Zhang [17] present a general framework for the use of trusted computing technology for access control in P2P networks. The work of Berket et al. [3] presents an access control mechanism for a P2P network. Secure communication and authentication of peers is provided via PKI. In addition, every peer establishes its own rights management policy for its own data and enforces this policy through a special authorization manager. A related approach from Crispo and others [6] uses more flexible policies. These two approaches do not address the problem of client based access control that causes problems as stated before (see Sect. 4.3). None of these approaches considers existing access control components and information residing on the peers, which is essential for a PDMS.

5 Problem Solution

As a basis, every peer and every PDMS user requires a certificate from a central certification authority. This enables secure authentication and communication between peers and PDMS users. Furthermore, we postulate that every peer has a fully fledged DBMS with an access control component that offers fine grained access control including roles, users, access rights and grant rights. Access control information contained in these components can be considered as a kind of meta data that can be connected through mappings to other peers. Of course, access control data is special and so are the mappings. What we need is a general data exchange format for access control information. Afterwards, we need to design a mapping language and appropriate transformation rules that can map/transform this information between different peers. This situation is illustrated in Fig. 1.

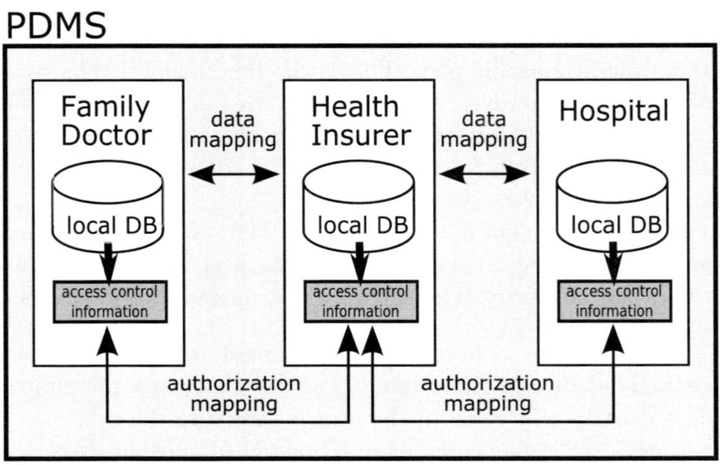

Fig. 1. PDMS with authorization mappings

The creation of authorization mappings is a collaborative task, because two peers, between whom an access control mapping should be established, need to coordinate their access control mechanisms. That might cause changes to the local access control rules of both peers.

To make a valid and secure authorization mapping (AM) contract, the mapping should be encrypted and signed by both peers. The encryption ensures that only the two contractual partners can see the mapping rules and the signatures guarantee that changes to the mappings are done collaboratively. It is clear that the AMs and the certificates increase the effort to join a PDMS, but we believe it is worth doing, due to the additional security control achieved in this way.

5.1 Two Level Access Control

A basic principle of our approach is that there are two levels of access control inside a PDMS. On the one hand, we have access control inside the individual peer. On the other hand, we have authorization mappings between single peers. These mappings are established in such a way that users have appropriate rights on the relevant databases. To make things easier, especially to avoid the need to map each individual user, it may be useful to map roles or groups of users. It is important to note that the individual peer has full control over its local user management component. So it can always change local access rights, which ensures peer autonomy. In contrast, mappings between the peers can only be composed or changed in cooperation. An exception is the dissolution of an AM contract, which can be done without the other partner.

5.2 Indirect Mappings

This problem results from the underlying assumption of data distribution and data processing in a PDMS. When we look at mappings from the point of view of authorization, we deserve an "indirect mapping" problem, shown in Fig. 2. A peer which has access to data can grant this access privilege to other peers without asking the originating peer. This is the fundamental "share your data" principle of a PDMS. However, we think that this is not a good solution for access rights. There might be situations where the sharing of access rights is exactly what we want. But for the majority of cases, we need a mechanism which restricts these indirect mappings.

A solution to this problem is the trusted PDMS software mentioned in Sect. 4.3. This must be installed on every contributing peer and is distributed by the central certification authority. The software guarantees several things:

- The data provided by a particular peer cannot be rewrapped as someone else's data. That means, the origin of the data is clearly announced.
- Only data exactly addressed to the user is shown to the user.
- Data addressed to a user cannot be redirected to another user.
- In case of indirect AMs, the peer and user ID has to be added to the request to show the authorization path.

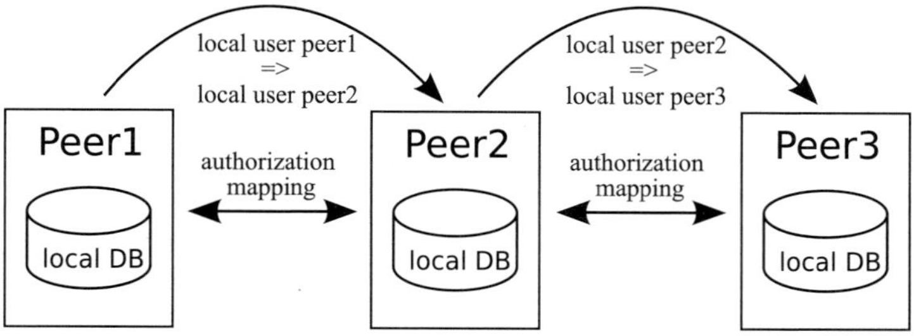

Fig. 2. The indirect mapping problem

That means that the middle peer, *Peer2* from Fig. 2, is not able to redirect queries from *Peer1* with other user rights than the user rights of the originating requestor. *Peer2* can execute queries over data provided by *Peer3* but it is not able to republish the data as its own. This is the default mode for AMs between peers. However, a peer can explicitly assign so called "indirect authorization mapping rights" to another peer. If *Peer3* has granted such a right to *Peer2*, *Peer2* is allowed to give *Peer1* access to data of *Peer3*.

In addition, the trusted PDMS connection software guarantees that the data owner has always full control over his data.

5.3 Diversity of Access Control Methods

Another problem to be considered is the high diversity of access control methods (positive or negative access rights, open or closed world assumption, etc.) residing on different peers. This is a well known problem in federated databases [12,7]. To solve these inequalities, one can think about conversion peers that convert one access control method into another. This is only possible if indirect AMs are allowed. Without indirect mappings, the conversion between the different methods must be done inside/through the mapping. This approach is more flexible but requires a more powerful mapping language.

5.4 Authorization Mapping Content

The AM consists of both peer IDs and a mapping of the users and roles (in our scenario from the introduction: $user\,f$ of $databasedb_x \Leftrightarrow user\ g$ of $databasedb_y$, or $role\ w$ of $database\,db_x \Leftrightarrow role\ v$ of $database\,db_y$). In addition, it needs to be specified whether indirect mappings to a particular user or role are allowed. Note that only mappings between local users or roles of the partners are allowed. Therefore, an indirect (inherited) AM always needs to be resolved through the granting middle peers. Only a direct AM, which can be derived semi-automatically from the indirect ones, can shorten the detour. To make the mapping secure, the signature of the two peers has to be added. The content of the mappings should be minimal to reduce the complexity and performance impact of access control.

5.5 Decentralized User Management Component

Up till now we only have a mechanism to connect local access control components of peer databases. The missing link is an authority that manages these connections for a number of peers. Here the idea of islands of trust comes into play. Due to the high trust barrier in a PDMS, the best starting point is to establish a small group of peers that highly trust each other. Such a group is called an island of trust. Referring to our scenario, a health insurance company can establish a trust island for hospitals. In the next step, this island can be connected to the other islands established by other health insurers, etc. If every participant in an island trusts the others, they might grant each other further rights, especially indirect AMs.

Highly reliable and trustful peers (e.g., the health insurance company) in the island of trust will hold many indirect AM rights. This makes them responsible for connecting access rights of the island of trust to the rest of the PDMS. In fact, every peer with the right to grant access to data of other peers (indirect AM right) is a kind of substitute for all peers connected through indirect mappings. The most reliable and trustful peers establish therefore something like a decentralized user management component. The more trust there is inside the PDMS, the more centralized access control will be. The drawback is that as access control becomes more and more centralized, it will become increasingly vulnerable to attacks. Therefore, it is a good idea for each peer to grant more than one peer indirect AM rights. Because we treat access rights as data and establish mappings between them, we can use similar methods as we use for data mappings to make them more reliable or scalable.

With our approach we dynamically connect already available access control components to establish a PDMS wide access control system. Due to these mappings, that are as flexible as the data mappings, we are now able to support a range of solutions, from centralized to completely decentralized PDMS access control, exactly arranged to the requirements of each individual peer.

5.6 Correlation Between Data and Rights Mappings

There is a strong correlation between data and authorization mappings. Data mappings are established at peer level. That is, mappings are shared by all users on a peer. Of course, it makes sense to hide the mappings from the user who has no access; nevertheless, every peer user can see all mappings in principle. It is clear that such data mappings should coincide with the corresponding rights to access the mapped data. Therefore, an AM always accompanies a data mapping. As a result, the authorization path can easily be found.

6 How PDMS Access Control Works

When an access request from a connected peer arrives, several things need to be checked. First of all, the sender of the request has to be proven through PKI decryption. Additional IP address and challenge response tests can increase security. Then the rights mappings have to be considered. If there is a direct rights mapping between the two peers, the user sending the request has to be tested via challenge response. Otherwise, we need to check all peers and users of the current authorization path. If everything is all right so far, we can start with real access control. First, the corresponding local user rights are derived from AMs. Afterwards, the request has to be executed using the permissions of the according local user. During the execution, the rights of the local user have to be considered as usual. Afterwards, the result is encrypted with the public key of the requestor and sent to the requestor. If the peer is not the endpoint of the request, we rewrite the query using the data mapping, add the local user/role the rights mapping corresponds to and forward it to connected peers.

7 Future Work

First, we are going to specify the export schema of the access control information. The international standard XACML [15] can be such an export schema. In that case mappings will be established between XACML documents. Next, the design of the mapping and transformation language of the AMs will be developed. Here we may benefit from former research in federated databases [12]. In addition, tools to assist the creation of AMs are essential.

As a proof of concept, we are going to implement our security framework on top of a P2P enhanced version of SIRUP [21]. The implementation will focus on performance and scalability of access control mechanisms, because these are central issues in a PDMS.

References

1. Karl Aberer and Zoran Despotovic. Managing Trust in a Peer-2-Peer Information System. In *Proceedings of the Tenth International Conference on Information and Knowledge Management (CIKM '01)*, pages 310–317, 2001.
2. Christian Altenschmidt, Joachim Biskup, Ulrich Flegel, and Yücel Karabulut. Secure Mediation: Requirements, Design, and Architecture. *Journal of Computer Security*, 11(3):365–398, 2003.
3. Karlo Berket, Abdelilah Essiari, and Artur Muratas. PKI-Based Security for Peer-to-Peer Information Sharing. In *Proceesings of the Fourth International Conference on Peer-to-Peer Computing (P2P 2004)*, pages 45–52, 2004.
4. Elisa Bertino, Barbara Carminati, Elena Ferrari, Bhavani Thuraisingham, and Amar Gupta. Selective and Authentic Third-Party Distribution of XML Documents. *IEEE Transactions on Knowledge and Data Engineering*, 16(10):1263–1278, 2004.
5. Luc Bouganim, François Dang Ngoc, and Philippe Pucheral. Client-Based Access Control Management for XML documents. In *Proceedings of the 30th International Conference on Very Large Data Bases (VLDB 2004)*, pages 84–95, 2004.
6. Bruno Crispo, Swaminathan Sivasubramanian, Pietro Mazzoleni, and Elisa Bertino. P-Hera: Scalable Fine-grained Access Control for P2P Infrastructures. In *Proceedings of the 11th International Conference on Parallel and Distributed Systems (ICPADS'05)*, pages 585–591, 2005.

7. Sabrina De Capitani di Vimercati and Pierangela Samarati. Authorization specification and enforcement in federated database systems. *Journal of Computer Security*, 5(2):155–188, 1997.
8. John R. Douceur. The Sybil Attack. In *Revised Papers from the First International Workshop on Peer-to-Peer Systems (IPTPS '01)*, pages 251–260, 2001.
9. Enrico Franconi, Gabriel M. Kuper, Andrei Lopatenko, and Ilya Zaihrayeu. The coDB Robust Peer-to-Peer Database System. In *Proceedings of the Twelfth Italian Symposium on Advanced Database Systems (SEBD 2004)*, pages 382–393, 2004.
10. Alon Y. Halevy, Zachary G. Ives, Dan Suciu, and Igor Tatarinov. Schema Mediation in Peer Data Management Systems. In *Proceedings of the 19th International Conference on Data Engineering (ICDE 2003)*, pages 505–516, 2003.
11. Dennis Heimbigner and Dennis McLeod. A Federated Architecture for Information Management. *ACM Transactions on Information Systems (TOIS)*, 3(3):253–278, 1985.
12. Dirk Jonscher and Klaus R. Dittrich. An Approach for Building Secure Database Federations. In *Proceedings of 20th International Conference on Very Large Databases (VLDB 94)*, pages 24–35, 1994.
13. Anastasios Kementsietsidis, Marcelo Arenas, and Renée J. Miller. Mapping Data in Peer-to-Peer Systems: Semantics and Algorithmic Issues. In *Proceedings of the 2003 ACM SIGMOD International Conference on Management of Data*, pages 325–336, 2003.
14. Gerome Miklau and Dan Suciu. Controlling Access to Published Data Using Cryptography. In *Proceedings of 29th International Conference on Very Large Databases (VLDB 2003)*, pages 898–909, 2003.
15. Tim Moses. eXtensible Access Control Markup Language (XACML) Version 2.0. OASIS Standard, February 2005.
16. Wee Siong Ng, Beng Chin Ooi, Kian-Lee Tan, and Aoying Zhou. PeerDB: A P2P-based System for Distributed Data Sharing. In *Proceedings of the 19th International Conference on Data Engineering (ICDE 2003)*, pages 633–644, 2003.
17. Ravi Sandhu and Xinwen Zhang. Peer-to-Peer Access Control Architecture Using Trusted Computing Technology. In *Proceedings of the Tenth ACM Symposium on Access Control Models and Technologies (SACMAT '05)*, pages 147–158, 2005.
18. Dan S. Wallach. A Survey of Peer-to-Peer Security Issues. In *Software Security – Theories and Systems, Mext-NSF-JSPS International Symposium (ISSS 2002)*, pages 42–57, 2002.
19. Li Xiong and Ling Liu. PeerTrust: Supporting Reputation-Based Trust for Peer-to-Peer Electronic Communities. *IEEE Transactions on Knowledge and Data Engineering*, 16(7):843–857, 2004.
20. Jacqueline Yang, Duminda Wijesekera, and Sushil Jajodia. Subject Switching Algorithms for Access Control in Federated Databases. In *Proceedings of the 15th Annual Working Conference on Database and Application Security (DBSec '01)*, pages 61–74, 2002.
21. Patrick Ziegler and Klaus R. Dittrich. User-Specific Semantic Integration of Heterogeneous Data: The SIRUP Approach. In *First International IFIP Conference on Semantics of a Networked World (ICSNW 2004)*, pages 44–64, 2004.

Moving Objects in Networks Databases*

Victor Teixeira de Almeida

LG Datenbanksysteme für neue Anwendungen
Fachbereich Informatik, Fernuniversität Hagen
D-58084 Hagen, Germany
victor.almeida@fernuni-hagen.de

Abstract. Moving objects databases have become an intensive field of research in recent years with many applications such as location-based services, traffic monitoring, fleet management, etc. Most of the works in the literature assume free movement in the 2-dimensional space, although in some cases, the objects move within spatially embedded networks, e.g. vehicles in highways and trains in railways. Moreover, these works are focused on isolated aspects such as efficient query processing with specialized index structures. The aim of this PhD. project is to present a prototype of a complete database management system for efficiently storing and querying moving objects in networks, providing a comprehensive data model supporting the description of complete histories of movement, index structures for efficient query processing, an extended model handling uncertainty, and a complete integrated implementation as an algebra inside the SECONDO extensible database system.

1 Introduction

With the development of wireless network communications (e.g. the IEEE 802.11 protocol) and positioning technologies such as the Global Positioning System (GPS) and the European Satellite Navigation System (GALILEO), devices equipped with such technologies like handheld devices, on-board units in vehicles, or even mobile phones have become relatively cheap and are predicted to be in widespread use in the near future. This trend will lead to many new kinds of applications, e.g. location-based services and spatio-temporal data mining. The challenge to the database community is how to handle such complex spatio-temporal data in database management systems assuming the presence of huge amounts of historical data.

There are two main approaches in the literature that try to model this problem. These can be characterized as the *location management* and the *spatio-temporal database* perspectives. First, Wolfson et al. in [25,28] developed a model called Moving Object Spatio-Temporal (MOST) and the Future Temporal Logic

* This work was partially supported by grants Gu 293/8-1 and Gu 293/8-2 from the Deutsche Forschungsgemeinschaft (DFG), project "Datenbanken für bewegte Objekte" (Databases for Moving Objects).

T. Grust et al. (Eds.): EDBT 2006 Workshops, LNCS 4254, pp. 75–85, 2006.

(FTL) language for querying current and anticipated future locations of moving objects. Motion vectors are stored into dynamic attributes for the moving objects. Only moving point objects are considered.

Second, the spatio-temporal database perspective was explored, which means that the complete trajectories of the moving objects are stored such that querying past states is possible. Güting et al. in [9, 6] provide a complete framework for the representation and querying of spatio-temporal data, namely *moving point* and *moving region*. Such data types can be embedded as attribute types into extensible database management systems. Our work follows this approach and therefore throughout this paper when we mention moving objects we are interested in the spatio-temporal database perspective.

Since then, the field has flourished and a lot of work has been done especially on efficient query processing providing index structures mainly focused on the range and nearest neighbor queries, e.g. [21,18,8,13] just to mention some of the most recent ones.

An important observation that has not been addressed in the research mentioned above is that in many cases objects do not move freely in the 2-dimensional space but rather within spatially embedded networks, e.g. roads or highways. One could then describe movement relative to the network rather than 2-dimensional space which would enable easier formulation of queries and, even more important, more efficient representations and indexing of moving objects.

There exist some works in the literature focusing on modeling issues for moving objects in networks and some presenting specialized index structures and query processing algorithms for the range query, which are discussed on Section 2. However, there is a big gap between data modeling and query processing. A comprehensive data model and query language for objects moving in networks does not yet exist. As long as this is so, it is not clear how the proposals for efficient indexing and query processing can be integrated and used in a database system.

The purpose of this PhD. project is then to build a complete prototype of a vertical database system for moving objects in networks, i.e. to provide a model containing data types for the network as well as for static and moving objects together with a comprehensive set of operations among them, efficient algorithms for the operations, index structures to improve query processing, optimization rules that enable the usage of such indexes, and a complete integrated implementation inside the SECONDO extensible database system [12, 10, 5].

This paper is organized as follows: Section 2 presents the most closely related work. Section 3 details the PhD. project proposal, the results achieved so far, and the future work that needs to be done. Finally, Section 4 concludes the paper.

2 Related Work

Network query processing, in particular shortest path computation, has been considered by Shekhar et al. in [23, 24] and Rundensteiner et al. in [15, 16].

In [24] an adjacency list data structure clustered into pages is based on the z-order of node positions. A similar one using the Hilbert ordering is presented in [19]. These works are considered inside the internal structures of our proposed network representation.

Considering models, Vazirgiannis and Wolfson in [27] present a first model for querying moving objects in road networks. The network model basically corresponds to an undirected graph, where nodes are street crossings and edges are city road blocks. Moving objects are described by geometric polylines, as in the earlier work for unconstrained movement mentioned in Section 1. Besides, the network model and the query language are limited compared to our proposal.

Two papers by Jensen et al. [17, 14] have also looked at data modeling issues for spatial networks with respect to possible uses for location-based services. They describe as a case study the data model used by the Danish road directory and a Danish company. The emphasis is to explain that real road networks are quite complex, and that just simple directed graph models are not sufficient. The case study suggests a model that uses several interrelated representations which are expressed in terms of relational tables. This is an interesting application study, and we have drawn some of our motivation to use a route-oriented model from the first of these papers. However, moving objects are not considered.

The same group has described a more formalized model incorporating some of these ideas into [26]. They propose to use two complementary models of a network together, namely the 2-dimensional representation and the graph representation. The first is geared to describing a network at very high detail, while the second should support efficient computations. Data and query points are available in both models to represent static objects (e.g. facilities) and moving query objects (e.g. vehicles). The paper further describes how the graph representation can be derived from the 2-dimensional representation.

This model is the closest to our network model, but both representations are graph-oriented, i.e. they do not offer a route-oriented model as we do (see Section 3.2, and they do not offer a model for moving objects in networks, in the sense that trajectories of moving points relative to the network are not available. Furthermore, only point objects are considered.

The route-oriented model is closely related to the kilometer-post representation in [17] and to the concept of *linear referencing* widely used in the GIS-T (Geographic Information Systems in Transportation) literature, e.g. the work from Scarponcini in [22], where positions are described relative to the length of a road. Linear referencing is also already available in commercial database products such as Oracle Spatial.

Finally, index structures for the trajectories of moving objects in networks are presented by Frentzos in [7] and by Pfoser and Jensen in [20]. Both use the same idea of converting a 3-dimensional problem into two sub-problems with lower dimensions, where the first one is to index the network data and the second is to index the moving objects. It is shown that the problem then becomes simpler using this approach and their index structures outperform 3-dimensional structures.

3 The PhD. Project

3.1 The Proposal

The PhD. work started in September 2002 as part of a Deutsche Forschungsgemeinschaft (DFG) project named "Datenbanken für bewegte Objekte" (Databases for Moving Objects) under supervision of Prof. Dr. Güting. The project is divided into two parts having two years duration each. The main goals of the first part, related to the PhD. work presented in this paper, were to build the main model for moving objects in networks, and extensions to this model supporting dynamic networks and to cope with uncertainty, all integrated; to define an implementation strategy; and to start building a prototype given the implementation strategy.

The second part of the project is still in progress and is more focused on implementing a prototype running inside SECONDO, on proposing efficient algorithms for the operations, on studying efficient execution of query processing using indexes, and finally on extending the optimizer to cope with complex objects such as moving objects (constrained to networks or not).

Inserted into this project, the main goal of this PhD. work is to build a complete database system for moving objects in networks providing a vertical solution from a model with data types and operations, efficient algorithms for the operations, indexing structures for efficient query processing, and optimization rules enabling the usage of such indexes.

3.2 Results Achieved so Far

A model for moving objects in networks is presented in [11]. The core of this model are the data types *network*[1], *gpoint*, and *gline* to represent the underlying network (highway network), network positions (motels or gas stations), and network regions (speed limit or construction areas), respectively. Obviously, the corresponding moving data types for network positions (vehicles or trains) and regions (traffic jam area or part of the network affected by a snow storm) are defined, namely *moving*(*gpoint*) and *moving*(*gline*).

One should note that the model is consistent with (and can be seen as an extension of) the one in [9] allowing us to re-use many concepts and facilities provided there and to completely integrate them in order to be able to handle interactions between both network constrained and unconstrained spatial and spatio-temporal data. An example is the second **inside** operation in the list of operations below which uses a 2-dimensional region (*region* data type defined in [9]) as argument.

The main novelty on the network data type is that it is modeled in terms of *routes* and *junctions* and not in terms of nodes and edges of a graph, and we name it the *route-oriented model.* A route corresponds to a path over a graph possibly containing several edges, and junctions store intersections between pairs of routes. This representation has several advantages, which are detailed in [11],

[1] We write data types in italics underlined, and operations in bold face.

but the perhaps most practical one is that the representation of a moving object becomes much more compact in this way. If positions are given relative to edges, then for example a vehicle going along a highway at constant speed needs a change of description at every node (exit/junction) because the edge identifier changes. If positions are given relative to routes, then the description needs to change only when the vehicle leaves the highway.

Another important point is that the description of the network is not too simplistic. Routes can be bi-directional, i.e., admit movement in two directions, and positions on the two sides of a route, e.g. on a highway, can be distinguished, so that the distance between positions on each side of a route can be quite big in some cases. On the other hand, there are also cases where one does not want to distinguish between positions on two sides of a road, e.g. people moving around in a pedestrian zone. Therefore, two kinds of routes called *simple* and *dual routes* are provided. Furthermore, we do not assume that all transitions are possible in a junction, which is not realistic. The possible transitions between routes at junctions are stored into 4x4 matrices encoded into integer numbers, namely the *connectivity code.*

Object data types are then described relative to the network rather than the embedding 2-dimensional space, leading to a more compact representation of moving objects, since no geometric information needs to be stored. Geometry is stored once and for all with the network. Besides, discovering relationships between objects and parts of the network becomes much simpler and more efficient in this way.

The point data type ($\underline{gpoint}$) is represented by a route location containing a route id, a relative position on that route, and its side, for dual routes. The network region data type ($\underline{gline}$) is represented by a set of intervals of route locations. To the best of our knowledge, this is the first work that handles network regions. For the moving counterparts of these data types, we provide linear functions for the time-dependent location ($\underline{moving}(\underline{gpoint})$) and for the route interval boundaries ($\underline{moving}(\underline{gline})$).

Operations are then provided for these data types. Some examples are

$$\begin{array}{lll}
\underline{mgpoint} \times \underline{gline} & \rightarrow \underline{mbool} & \textbf{inside} \\
\underline{mgpoint} \times \underline{region} & \rightarrow \underline{mbool} & \textbf{inside} \\
\underline{mgline} & \rightarrow \underline{mreal} & \textbf{length} \\
\underline{mgpoint} \times \underline{gpoint} & \rightarrow \underline{mreal} & \textbf{distance}
\end{array}$$

Their semantics are straightforward and can be found in [11] together with the complete set of operations. Three applications containing some sample queries are presented in [11] as well as some implementation issues.

An index structure to store the trajectories of moving objects supporting the route-oriented model is presented in [2, 3], namely the MON-Tree. It supports the range query employing a similar approach of dividing the problem into two sub-problems presented in [7, 20], where a top R-Tree indexes the routes in the network and bottom R-Trees index objects' movements inside each route (Figure 1. Given the advantages of using the route-oriented model, the MON-Tree outperforms the competing index structures.

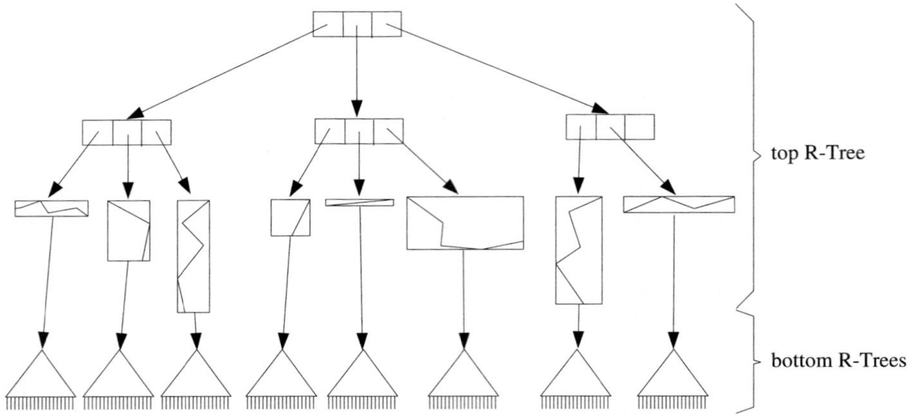

Fig. 1. The index structure of the MON-Tree

An extension to the model in [11] to cope with uncertainty is presented in [4]. Most of the data types were extended to their uncertain counterparts, e.g. the 2-dimensional point is now expressed as a region with uniform distribution function and the boolean data type has a new *maybe* value. The geometry of the uncertain trajectories of point objects with movement constrained to networks is presented (Figure 2), as well as the data type representation and the operations from [9,11] are extended. Finally, it is explained how we could modify the MON-Tree to index the trajectories of such moving objects with uncertainty.

Before starting the implementation of moving objects in networks, several implementation tasks have been done in the SECONDO system. A persistent version of the *Relational Algebra* containing almost all operations such as selection, projection, sorting, hash join, sort-merge join, loop join, etc. supporting large objects in tuples was implemented, which was demonstrated at ICDE'05 ([10]). The data types and the most important operations from the model in [9] were also implemented as an algebra in SECONDO, namely the *Spatial Algebra*. A demonstration of all these features together is accepted to the demo session at MDM'06 ([5]). Finally, several other improvements in the SECONDO system have been done during this PhD. project, which are not here discussed given space limitations.

3.3 Further Work

The SECONDO extensible database system is composed by three major components written in different languages:

– the kernel, written in C++, implements specific data models, is extensible by algebra modules, and provides query processing at executable level over the implemented algebras;

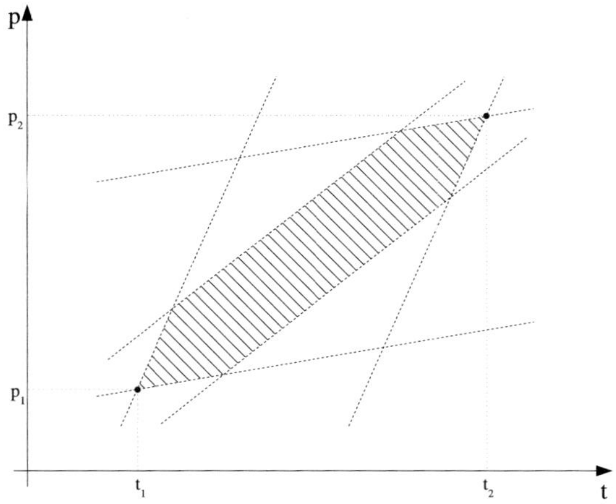

Fig. 2. The uncertain geometry of a moving object between two measurement points p_1 and p_2

– the optimizer, written in Prolog, provides as its core capability conjunctive query optimization, currently for a relational environment and also implements the essential part of SQL-like queries;
– and the graphical user interface (GUI), written in Java, which is an extensible interface for such an extensible system like SECONDO, where new data types or models can provide their own way to be displayed.

The implementation of the data types and operations presented in the models in [11,4] as an algebra in the SECONDO kernel is still in progress and we plan to finish it in the near future.

In the optimizer, we are currently investigating how to convert from SQL queries to the best executable plan, or at least to an efficient one, in the presence of such complex data types. In this case, it is important to note that the choice of SECONDO as a database system was a good one, because we do not need to provide complex selectivity estimation functions. SECONDO uses the sampling approach to estimate selectivities.

For cost estimation, since we use abstract data types, and in this case instances of these data types can be very big, the execution time of some operations in one object (inside a tuple) is not negligible in the query processing time and must be taken into account by the optimizer. We plan to estimate the time for complex operations also using the sampling approach.

In order to provide efficient query processing, we need to identify the operations where an index can be helpful, provide such an index (if needed), and provide some optimization rules in order to use such indexes. In some cases, we discovered that we can re-write the query adding some predicates in the *where* clause to enforce the usage of such indexes.

As an example, let us take the parcel delivery application presented in [11]. The application models a company offering express delivery of packages in the city network of Hagen, Germany. We assume that we have the road network of the city of Hagen as a data object, a relation *road* mapping road names to route identifiers in the network, and a relation called *postman* describing post workers' trips.

```
road( name: string, route: int )
postman( name: string, trip: mgpoint )
```

We focus our discussion on query **P4**, which returns all post workers who stayed in the street "Hagener Strasse" for more than one hour yesterday. This query should be written as

```
SELECT p.name
FROM   postman AS p, road AS r
WHERE  r.name = 'Hagener Strasse' AND
       duration(deftime(at(atperiods(trip, yesterday), route)))
         < one_hour
```

assuming that *yesterday* and *one_hour* are pre-defined objects storing the period of yesterday and the duration of one hour, respectively. This query first reduces the trips to the period of yesterday (**atperiods**) then to the times where they were at the route named "Hagener Strasse" (**at**), computes their temporal dimension (**deftime**) and compares their duration (**duration**) to the *one_hour* duration. The most expensive part of this query is

```
at(atperiods(trip, yesterday), route)
```

which is a selection in time and integer spaces. A temporal index could be available in the system with entries in the format ⟨*time_interval*, *route_id*⟩. An example of such an index is [1]. Moreover, the query optimizer should be smart enough to recognize this pattern and to add further conditions to the query so that this index is used. The query that would be then evaluated is

```
SELECT p.name
FROM   postman AS p, road AS r
WHERE  r.name = 'Hagener Strasse' AND
       duration(deftime(at(atperiods(trip, yesterday), route)))
         < one_hour
       present(trip, yesterday)
       passes(trip, route)
```

where **present** and **passes** are the counterpart predicates for **atperiods** and **at**, respectively.

Finally, we will also provide specific methods for displaying the data types in the SECONDO GUI. We think that a visualization tool is very helpful for doing research in moving object databases. An example of the GUI with spatio-temporal data of some trains of the city of Berlin is shown in Figure 3.

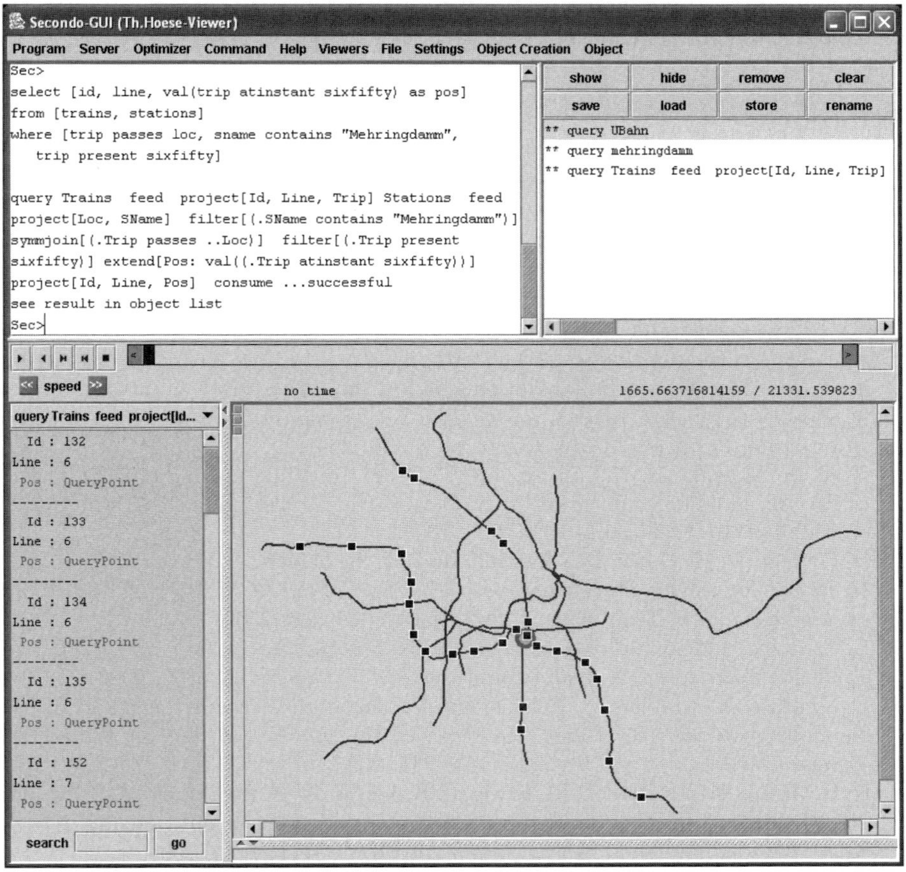

Fig. 3. The SECONDO graphical user interface

4 Conclusions

The proposed PhD. work investigates the problem of building a prototype of a complete database system for moving objects in networks. We showed the importance of this field of research and the lack of such solution in the literature. We believe that this is the first attempt to build such a prototype of a complete database system for both unconstrained and network constrained moving objects.

Acknowledgments

I would like to thank Prof. Dr. Ralf Güting for giving me the opportunity to come to Germany and to work with his group, Dr. Zhiming Ding who contributed a lot with the project, to all my colleagues in the FernUniversität in Hagen that helped me during my PhD. work, and to all students that contributed to the SECONDO extensible database system.

References

1. B. Becker, S. Gschwind, T. Ohler, B. Seeger, and P. Widmayer. An asymptotically optimal multiversion B-tree. *VLDB Journal*, 5(4):264–275, 1996.
2. V. T. de Almeida and R. H. Güting. Indexing the trajectories of moving objects in networks (Extended Abstract). In *Proc. of the 16th Intl. Conf. on Scientific and Statistical Database Management (SSDBM)*, pages 115–118, 2004.
3. V. T. de Almeida and R. H. Güting. Indexing the trajectories of moving objects in networks. *GeoInformatica*, 9(1):33–60, 2005.
4. V. T. de Almeida and R. H. Güting. Supporting uncertainty in moving objects in network databases. In *Proc. of the 13th Intl. Symp. on Advances in Geographic Information Systems (ACM-GIS)*, pages 31–40, 2005.
5. V. T. de Almeida, R. H. Güting, and T. Behr. Querying moving objects in SECONDO. Accepted for publication at the Demonstration Session in the 7th Intl. Conf. on Mobile Data Management (MDM), 2006.
6. L. Forlizzi, R. H. Güting, E. Nardelli, and M. Schneider. A data model and data structures for moving objects databases. In *Proc. of the ACM SIGMOD Intl. Conf. on Management of Data*, volume 29(2), pages 319–330, 2000.
7. E. Frentzos. Indexing objects moving on fixed networks. In *Proc. of the 8th Intl. Symp. on Spatial and Temporal Databases (SSTD)*, pages 289–305, 2003.
8. E. Frentzos, K. Gratsias, N. Pelekis, and Y. Theodoridis. Nearest neighbor search on moving object trajectories. In *Proc. of the 9th Intl. Symp. on Spatial and Temporal Databases (SSTD)*, pages 328–345, 2005.
9. R. H. Güting, M. H. Böhlen, M. Erwig, C. S. Jensen, N. A. Lorentzos, M. Schneider, and M. Vazirgiannis. A foundation for representing and querying moving objects. *ACM Transactions on Database Systems (TODS)*, 25(1):1–42, 2000.
10. R. H. Güting, V. T. de Almeida, D. Ansorge, T. Behr, Z. Ding, T. Höse, F. Hoffmann, M. Spiekermann, and U. Telle. SECONDO: An extensible dbms platform for research prototyping and teaching. In *Proc. of the 21st Intl. Conf. on Data Engineering (ICDE)*, pages 1115–1116, 2005.
11. R. H. Güting, V. T. de Almeida, and Z. Ding. Modeling and querying moving objects in networks. Technical Report 308, Fernuniversität Hagen, Fachbereich Informatik, 2004. *Accepted for publication in the VLDB Journal.*
12. R.H. Güting, T. Behr, V. T. de Almeida, Z. Ding, F. Hoffmann, and M. Spiekermann. SECONDO: An extensible DBMS architecture and prototype. Technical Report 313, Fernuniversität Hagen, Fachbereich Informatik, 2004.
13. M. Hadjieleftheriou, G. Kollios, P. Bakalov, and V. J. Tsotras. Complex spatio-temporal pattern queries. In *Proc. of the 31st Very Large Data Bases Conference (VLDB)*, pages 877–888, 2005.
14. C. Hage, C. S. Jensen, T. B. Pedersen, L. Speicys, and I. Timko. Integrated data management for mobile services in the real world. In *Proc. of the 29th Intl. Conf. on Very Large Data Bases (VLDB)*, pages 1019–1030, 2003.
15. Y. Huang, N. Jing, and E. A. Rundensteiner. Path queries for transportation networks: Dynamic reordering and sliding window paging techniques. In *Proc. of the 4th Intl. Symp. on Advances in Geographic Information Systems (ACM-GIS)*, pages 9–16, 1996.

16. Y. Huang, N. Jing, and E. A. Rundensteiner. Integrated query processing strategies for spatial path queries. In *Proc. of the 13th Intl. Conf. on Data Engineering (ICDE)*, pages 477–486, 1997.
17. C. S. Jensen, T. B. Pedersen, L. Speicys, and I. Timko. Data modeling for mobile services in the real world. In *Proc. of the 8th Intl. Symp. on Spatial and Temporal Databases (SSTD)*, pages 1–9, 2003.
18. J. Ni and C. V. Ravishankar. PA-Tree: A parametric indexing scheme for spatio-temporal trajectories. In *Proc. of the 9th Intl. Symp. on Spatial and Temporal Databases (SSTD)*, pages 254–272, 2005.
19. D. Papadias, J. Zhang, Nikos Mamoulis, and Yufei Tao. Query processing in spatial network databases. In *Proc. of 29th Intl. Conf. on Very Large Data Bases (VLDB)*, pages 802–813, 2003.
20. D. Pfoser and C. S. Jensen. Trajectory indexing using movement constraints. *GeoInformatica*, 9(2):93–115, 2005.
21. S. Rasetic, J. Sander, J. Elding, and M. A. Nascimento. A trajectory splitting model for efficient spatio-temporal indexing. In *Proc. of the 31st Very Large Data Bases Conference (VLDB)*, pages 934–945, 2005.
22. P. Scarponcini. Generalized model for linear referencing in transportation. *GeoInformatica*, 6(1):35–55, 2002.
23. S. Shekhar, A. Kohli, and M. Coyle. Path computation algorithms for advanced traveller information system (atis). In *Proc. of the 9th Intl. Conf. on Data Engineering (ICDE)*, pages 31–39, 1993.
24. S. Shekhar and D. Liu. CCAM: A connectivity-clustered access method for networks and network computations. *IEEE Trans. Knowl. Data Eng.*, 9(1):102–119, 1997.
25. A. P. Sistla, O. Wolfson, S. Chamberlain, and S. Dao. Modeling and querying moving objects. In *Proceedings of the 13th Intl. Conf. on Data Engineering (ICDE)*, pages 422–432, 1997.
26. L. Speicys, C. S. Jensen, and A. Kligys. Computational data modeling for network-constrained moving objects. In *Proc. of the 11th Intl. Symp. on Advances in Geographic Information Systems (ACM-GIS)*, pages 118–125, 2003.
27. M. Vazirgiannis and O. Wolfson. A spatiotemporal model and language for moving objects on road networks. In *Proc. of the 7th Intl. Symp. on Spatial and Temporal Databases (SSTD)*, pages 20–35, 2001.
28. O. Wolfson, S. Chamberlain, S. Dao, L. Jiang, and G. Mendez. Cost and imprecision in modeling the position of moving objects. In *Proceedings of the 14th Intl. Conf. on Data Engineering (ICDE)*, pages 588–596, 1998.

Change Management in Large-Scale Enterprise Information Systems

Boris Stumm

University of Kaiserslautern
stumm@informatik.uni-kl.de

Abstract. The information infrastructure in today's businesses consists of many interoperating autonomous systems. Changes to a single system can therefore have an unexpected impact on other, dependent systems. In our Caro approach we try to cope with this problem by observing each system participating in the infrastructure and analyzing the impact of any change that occurs. The analysis process is driven by declaratively defined rules and works with a generic and extensible graph model to represent the relevant metadata that is subject to changes. This makes Caro applicable to heterogeneous scenarios and customizable to special needs.

1 Introduction

In today's businesses, information infrastructures are getting more and more complex. There are many heterogeneous systems with a manifold of mutual dependencies leading to unmanageability of the overall infrastructure. New dependencies between existing systems evolve and new systems are added. Generally, there is no central management of all systems.

Small, local changes can have a major impact at company-wide scale due to the dependencies between systems. To keep everything running, it is therefore necessary to *preventively* analyze the impact of a change, to be able to make adjustments in case of conflicts without compromising the infrastructure. While the heterogeneity of systems and the problem of incomplete metadata make change impact analysis already a hard task, the situation becomes even more difficult as changes are not always planned globally and in advance. Thus, unexpected problems may occur after a change is carried out, making a *reactive* change impact analysis necessary. We present Caro, an approach for change impact analysis (CIA) that is able to operate even under these adverse conditions.

When speaking of changes, we refer to metadata changes. In our context, metadata includes not only data schemas, but also APIs, configuration files, assertions about data quality and performance, etc., in short, everything that other systems could rely on.

Problem Statement. The problems that we face in change management and which we address with our approach can be divided into three categories:

- Heterogeneity. The connected systems often have different data models (e.g. XML or SQL), different interfaces (e.g. query or function calls), etc.

T. Grust et al. (Eds.): EDBT 2006 Workshops, LNCS 4254, pp. 86–96, 2006.

- Incomplete metadata. In general, it is not possible or feasible to get all metadata for an exact CIA. There may be no easy way to query the metadata of a system, documentation is often outdated or non-existent, and dependencies between systems can be hidden in procedural code, which in the worst case would have to be decompiled to get the required information. While it is theoretically possible to get exact metadata, in practice, the costs may be too high.
- System autonomy and missing global management. In practice, many systems are black boxes that cannot be controlled from outside. This especially holds true if an integration environment spans over several departments or even several companies, and complicates access to such systems. Changes are applied without global analysis, and without notification to the affected systems. Thus, problems emerge unexpectedly, and it is hard to find the cause.

Contribution. Caro is a concept which includes three main components responsible for addressing the discussed problems:

- We propose an *architecture* which allows a central or distributed approach to change impact analysis. We have software components called *metadata agents*, which, amongst other things, monitor the systems participating in the integration infrastructure for changes. The *change manager* allows for preventive CIA as well as reactive CIA.
- We present a *metamodel* which allows us to handle and homogenize the heterogeneous metadata encountered. It is designed to be extensible to describe arbitrary metadata at arbitrary granularities.
- We use a robust and generic *analysis algorithm* which can handle incomplete metadata. It works on a best-effort basis based on the input metadata, and the quality of the analysis results will gracefully degradate as input metadata gets less complete or more coarse-grained.

With these concepts, Caro is applicable to a wide range of different systems, and thus a wide range of different changes can be detected and analyzed.

Related Work. In the context of information integration, much research has been done. Some approaches are complementary to ours, and others are similar to Caro in some aspects. The most important distinguishing facts of Caro are its genericity, robustness and scope. It makes no assumptions about the environment it operates in, and can be used for any scenario where change impact analysis is necessary.

Dorda et al. [8] present an approach which is quite similar to Caro with respect to the problems addressed. However, the solution they propose is different in two fundamental points: They require a central documentation (or metadata) repository and a strict process policy. This constrains their approach to scenarios where it is feasible to have a central repository and to enforce adherence to defined processes. While they want to avoid integration clusters[1], we think that such a clustering (and thus decentralization) in large EIS cannot be avoided.

[1] Integration clusters are called "integration islands" in [8].

Deruelle et al. [7] present another approach to change impact analysis. They use a multigraph and change propagation rules for analysis, which is very similar to Caro. Their approach has several limitations. The focus lies on preventive change impact analysis, thus they lack a framework to support reactive CIA. Apparently, they do not consider the problem of incomplete metadata. Also, their meta-model and rules are rather specialized, which makes the extension to support other data models and change types more difficult than with Caro.

Various other approaches to CIA in information systems exist that are limited with respect to the supported data models [10] or scope and support of exact analysis [12]. The concepts of change impact analysis in software systems [6,3,16] are similar to the ones we use. However, the models and analysis procedures focus on the elements that are found in software: methods, signatures, classes, attributes and so on. In addition, CIA for software systems is usually done preventively. Aspects of heterogeneity, metadata incompleteness and distribution are not that relevant as they are in information systems.

Research done in the field of schema evolution [15,4,17], schema matching [14,13,11] or model management [5] are complementary to our approach. Especially the latter approaches are used to plan and realize integration, generally between only two or a small group of systems, as well as adapt systems to changing requirements. Caro is not designed for use in the initial stages of an integration project. It will take the results of such a project, namely the dependencies between the systems that were created based on schema matches or mapping definitions, and monitor them for changes. When a change occurs, Caro will analyze the impact of it and notify the responsible person. If problems are encountered, the output of Caro can be the input for the information integration tools that are used to repair the impacted systems. Caro focuses on the monitoring of systems participating in the overall information infrastructure and the detection of the global impact of changes. As such, it "fills the gap" to an overall management of a heterogeneous integrated environment.

Structure of the Paper. In the following sections, we will first give an overview over the architecture of our CIA approach (Sect. 2). We discuss the conceptual meta-model on which our approach is based on in Sect. 3. In Sect. 4 our approach to conduct the analysis is presented. In Sect. 5 we will discuss some of the issues that arise during the preceeding sections. Finally we finish with conlusions and outlook in Sect. 6.

2 Overview

Central architectural components of Caro are the metadata repository (MDR) and the change manager (CM) (see Fig. 1). The MDR is a passive component that holds the metadata of the different information systems in a common representation. It provides an interface to query and update the stored metadata. All metadata is versioned, to be able to keep track of any changes that happened in the past. The CM is a reactive component responsible for the analysis of changes. It can analyze change proposals issued via the user interface, or react to changes that have happened in an observed system. The third component in our architecture is constituted by metadata agents (MDA). Every system participating in CIA is monitored by an MDA responsible for mediating

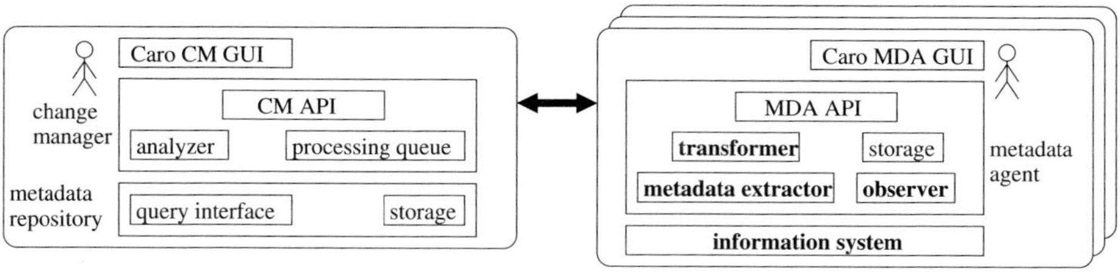

Fig. 1. Caro architecture

between the CM, the observed information system and the human responsible for it. An MDA consists of various subcomponents. The metadata extractor is needed to initially extract all metadata from the underlying system and to later pick up changes. A transformer component maps the extracted metadata to the Caro format. The observer component serves as a guard and watches for changes in the information system. For caching purposes there is a storage component. The MDA communicates with the CM via asynchronously to not block either component. The MDA parts written in bold face are those that need to be customized for each information system. Caro provides generic functionality, and specific functionality can be added via a plugin mechanism. To configure the components, GUIs for the CM and the MDAs will be provided. Furthermore, the GUIs give a global (CM GUI) or local (MDA GUI) view of metadata and dependencies and are used as interface for preventive CIA. The MDA GUI is constrained to a local analysis, which is also useful (e.g., to analyze how views are affected if a base table changes). In the following sections, the main focus lies on the metadata model and the analysis approach. The issues that arise in the functionality of the MDAs, such as detecting changes in system metadata, conversion from a source's native metadata representation or modeling dependencies, are discussed in Sect. 5.

Caro can also be used in a distributed way. Several change managers, each responsible for a part of the overall system, can communicate with each other and pass on their analysis results. This enables the use of Caro in cases where a centralized solution is not feasible. An example scenario for this is shown in Fig. 2. This way it is possible to restrict the data passed on to the other servers, which can be important for security reasons.

Our base assumption is that every single system in an integrated information infrastructure provides various kinds of services to other systems. We refer to this set of services as the system's *provision*. For each accessing client system, there may exist a different provision set, depending on the authorizations of it. Complementary to this, the part of the provision that is used by the client system is called *usage*. A client system as a usage for each system it depends on. Note that the usage of the client needs not to be identical to the provision of the server system. In general, the usage will be a subset of the provision, or may even contain elements not present in the provision. If that happens, there exists a problem which will be recognized by our approach.

We do not use the more common terms import or export schema, since provisions and usages can contain more than only schema data, and may, for example, include configuration data, technical metadata, quality assertions ("The data provided is less than

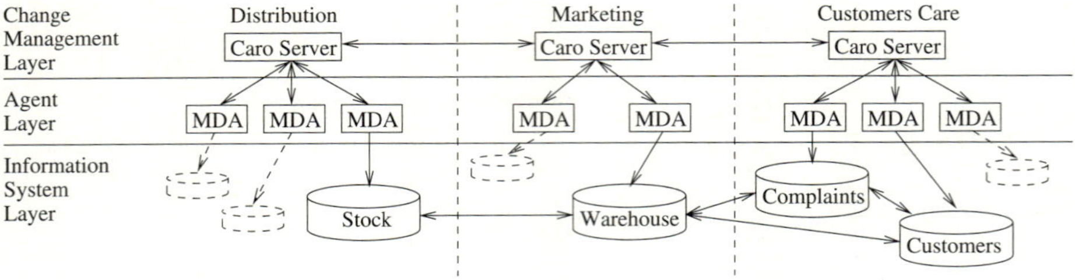

Fig. 2. Distributed Caro architecture

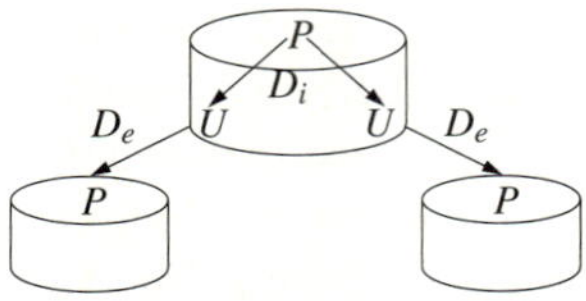

Fig. 3. Provision and usage specifications, internal and external dependencies

a day old.") or activity information ("The ETL process runs every Saturday at 0:00."). Figure 3 illustrates provisions P, usages U and the dependencies D between them. *External dependencies* (D_e) exist between a provision and a usage of different systems. The usage depends on the corresponding provision to be made. *Internal dependencies* (D_i) exist between the provision and usages *within* a system. Services provided (in the provision) may be dependent on the use (in the usage) of other system's services. A simple example is a federated DBMS, whose provision is basically a view on the provisions of the base systems. In this case, the internal dependencies are represented by the view definitions in the federated DBMS.

Change impact analysis is an integral part of a larger *system evolution process*, which is happening in every information infrastructure. System evolution includes all changes that occur to systems that are part of the infrastructure. In ideal scenarios, before any change is applied, its impact will be analyzed. We call this *preventive CIA*. Depending on the analysis result, some adjustments may be made to minimize the impact or to adapt the impacted systems. Caro supports this process by providing tools and interfaces to do preventive CIA before changes are made. In practice, such ideal scenarios do not exist, mostly due to the autonomy of systems involved. The larger the number of integrated systems, the more probable it is that changes are made without prior analysis or coordination. Caro monitors every system and detects changes shortly after they occur. *Reactive CIA* is then initiated automatically, and administrators of impacted systems are notified. The analysis process itself is identical for both cases. The difference lies only in the type of input data (proposed changes vs. already applied changes) and in the actions taken after analysis. With preventive CIA, results will have no effect on running systems, whereas with reactive CIA, affected systems may be disabled, or other measures may be taken, to prevent data corruption or incorrect query results.

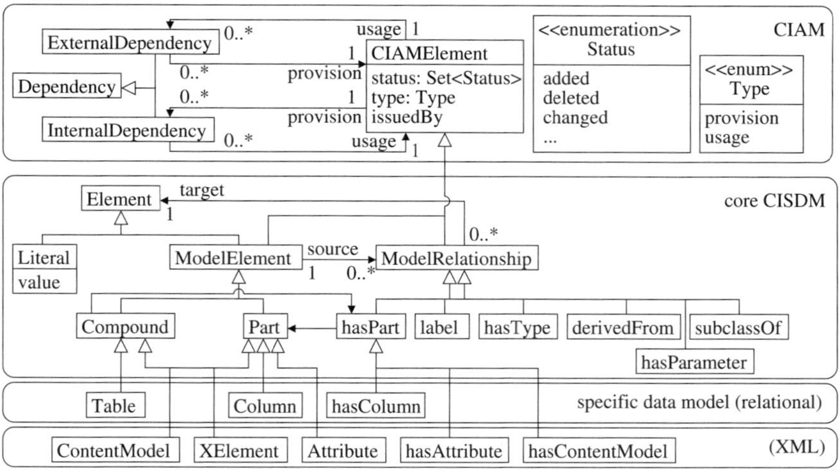

Fig. 4. Caro meta-models

3 Conceptual Model

An important consideration was the choice of the meta-model to use in our approach. It must be possible to represent arbitrary metadata and dependencies, without assuming any data model (like SQL or XML) or types of dependencies. There has to be support for a declarative specification of change impact, and the possibility to describe metadata at different granularities. These requirements are met by our conceptual model.

The base assumption we build our model on is the following: A metadata description consists of *elements* and the *relationships* between them. Elements are *atomic information units*. In the relational world, a table definition consists of many elements, namely the element representing the table itself, the name of the table, elements for every column, column name and column type, and so on. A metadata description can then be expressed as a bipartite digraph with node types E and R representing elements and relationships, similar to the ER-model. Relationship nodes represent a binary relation between element nodes and thus always have one incoming and one outgoing edge. Expressing relationships as nodes and not as edges has its reason in that there can be dependencies between relationships.

The elements in the metadata graph are instances of elements defined in the Caro meta-model. This meta-model has two parts, the *change-impact system description model* (CISDM) and the *change-impact analysis meta-model* (CIAM). Both of them are depicted in Fig. 4. We aim to provide more complex class-building constructs, like it is possible in OWL [1], but for readability we used an UML-like syntax in the figure.

The CISDM defines classes that capture the semantics that are relevant to CIA. The figure shows a selection of these. The top level classes are Element, which all element nodes are instances of, and ModelRelationship for the relationship nodes. ModelRelationships connect two Elements, as we have stated before. Literals have no outgoing edges, since they only function as containers for values of other Nodes. For each CIA-relevant "role" that a node may have, the top level classes are subclassed. In the figure, two roles for element nodes (Compound and Part), and several roles for relationship nodes are shown. The CISDM itself is not intended to model metadata graphs directly. It is an abstract meta-model from which concrete meta-models can inherit, assigning CIA semantics to their elements. In the lower part of the figure, this is shown for some elements of the relational and XML data model. The change impact analysis is done only with the information that the generic part of the CISDM provides, whereas the metadata is described in terms of the corresponding data model. Change impact properties are assigned to meta-model elements by inheritance, which makes it easy to adapt existing meta-models for use in Caro by simply adding the CISDM classes as superclasses to the model.

While the CISDM is used to model the change impact properties of metadata descriptions, the CIAM provides means to connect different graphs via dependencies and enables setting the status of nodes (e.g., to added or deleted). The upper part of Fig. 4 shows the CIAM. Main classes are Dependency and CIAMElement. Each dependency connects two CIAMElements, which are either ModelElements or ModelRelationships. The connected elements have one of two roles: provision or usage. CIAMElement has two other properties. The status property holds the current analysis result for this element. For simplicity, only the three status values added, deleted and changed are shown in the figure. The issuedBy property denotes the observed system which the graph belongs to. With this model, not only dependencies between elements, but also between relationships can be expressed.

There is no requirement for metadata graphs to be complete, or every dependency to be modeled. If there is a dependency between a table in a source system and a federated DBMS, the individual column elements need not be connected via dependencies. The most coarse-grained metadata graph would consist only in one element node per system, and dependency nodes showing how systems are related to each other. This does not allow a very precise analysis, but in this way no system will be "forgotten" if a change occurs somewhere. Since fine-grained metadata can be very expensive to get, it can be decided on a case-by-case basis if an exact analysis is required or if more false alarms are acceptable. There are no constraints on the types of metadata changes that can be captured. If the corresponding elements and their dependencies are modeled, changes will be detected. Although in our prototype we focus on schema changes, Caro is not limited to that. Some examples that come to mind are function signatures, classes, methods, directory layouts, application configuration files, installed software. Even more dynamic metadata such as network capacity, free disk space, or CPU performance can be modeled and analyzed. Of course, the CISDM will probably have to be extended, and some more analysis rules may be required. We will discuss this in Sect. 5.

4 Analysis

The analysis of a change is done by applying impact rules to the metadata graph until no more rules can fire. Conceptually the rules and the graphs they operate on have the following characteristics:

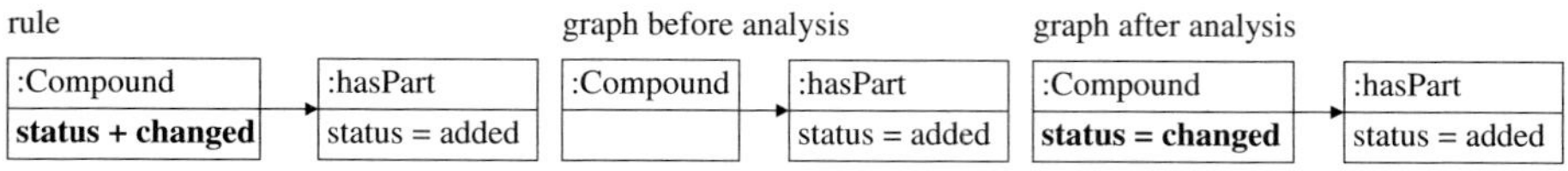

Fig. 5. Example rule

- Each rule has a *premise*, which is a graph pattern specifying nodes and their properties. If the premise matches a subgraph, the *conclusion* of the rule is applied. The conclusion is always a list of property values that will be added to a specific node.
- Each node has a finite set of properties that are identified by property names.
- If a part of a conclusion already exists in the graph, only the missing part is added.

These characteristics make the appliance of rules monotonic. Besides that, order of rule appliance does not matter. This ensures that analysis will always produce the same output if given the same input and that the calculation will always terminate.

Figure 5 shows a simple rule in a graphical notation on the left. Text written in normal font constitutes the premise. The conclusion is written in boldface. The analysis rule shown in the figure adds the changed-status to a compound if a part was added. Although the rule is quite simple, we argue that in the majority of cases, such simple rules suffice, making the analysis procedure similar transitive closure algorithm. In some cases, more complex rules which contain more nodes and edges may be needed, therefore the reasoner used must not rely on having only simple rules. Our current implementation uses RDF [2] and the Jena framework [9] with its generic rule reasoner for analysis. We mapped our conceptual model to RDF triples. The implementation details cannot be discussed here due to space restrictions. Rules always specify the most general class to which they apply, but also match subclasses. For the example analysis rule this means that a hasColumn relationship, which is a specialization of hasPart, between a table and its columns will also be matched. If a meta-model needs to be analyzed in a way not covered by the standard ruleset, special rules can easily be added by using the corresponding subclasses in the rule definitions.

5 Deploying Caro

In the previous two sections we introduced the conceptual meta-model and the analysis rules that work on it. We showed that we can handle arbitrary metadata models, and even cope with incomplete data. For this to work, we make several basic assumptions: for all metadata there is a specific meta-model extending the CISDM, and all metadata to analyze will be transformed automatically into our common format. Further, the metadata agents detect all changes and notify the change manager component. In this section we will discuss the manual effort that is needed to fulfill these assumptions.

Extending the CISDM. All metadata needs to be described by a meta-model which is an extension of the CISDM. Although we aim to provide meta-models for SQL and XML directly, there will in general be the need to define custom meta-models. We believe that for most cases the effort will be rather small, and depending on the resources available, one can decide to have a not-so-detailed model at the cost of a more coarse-grained analysis. Tightly coupled with the extension of the CISDM is the addition of new analysis rules. As we mentioned, rules will generally have a very simple structure, so this is also an unproblematic task.

Transforming the Metadata. Since Caro needs all metadata in form of a graph, the system metadata will need to be transformed to the graph format. This basically amounts to writing custom transformer components for the corresponding MDA. This is not a scientific effort, only a technical one, since there is already a meta-model for the system. While this is a manual task, it can be accomplished in a straightforward way.

Monitoring and Extracting the Metadata. Perhaps the biggest problems that Caro and all similar approaches are facing is how to monitor systems for changes, and how to extract the metadata in an automated way. All relational DBMS have an information schema[2], which makes it very easy create a custom MDA-component to extract the schema and other metadata. Listening for changes gets more difficult, since triggers on system tables are usually not allowed. A solution here can be a periodic poll and use of a "diff" tool to find out what changed, or inspecting logfiles. In this and similar cases, monitoring and metadata extraction poses no problems. But there are other scenarios, e.g., systems only allowing function calls with no simple query mechanism to inspect metadata, or where access rights prevent the MDA from inspection. There is no general solution for these scenarios. An implementation of a custom MDA-component might, e.g., analyze the source code, do probing or check the timestamps of files. Even if the information that is gathered this way is incomplete, Caro is still able to do analysis on a more coarse-grained level.

While the manual effort to make the assumptions work may seem high, it is far less than the manual effort needed when integrating information systems. In information integration, specific data schemas (models) have to be integrated, matched and mapped to each other. In Caro, we work with meta-models. Most of the work has to be done only once for all instances of a proprietary system type, or could be provided by third parties.

6 Conclusions and Outlook

We presented a generic approach to change impact analysis which uses inference rules for processing. The approach can be applied to a wide range of scenarios. There are no constraints on which systems can be monitored and analyzed for changes. If a system with a proprietary metadata format is to be analyzed, only some custom MDA-components need to be developed. Since Caro can also function with incomplete and coarse-grained metadata, the initial development time and cost of these components can be kept low, at the cost of a less precise analysis leading to more false alarms.

An important question that arises is how Caro handles metadata other than SQL and XML schemas. It is neither possible nor desirable to include elements for all possible

[2] Not all DBMS may have a information schema conforming to the newer SQL standards, but all have a proprietary variant of it.

metadata descriptions in the CISDM or CIAM. Instead, these meta-models themselves can be extended by adding more possible values to the status property or subclassing ModelRelationship and ModelElement. In addition to the model extensions, new analysis rules need to be defined, too. This imposes no problem, since the rules are generally very simple. The main goal of our work is to analyze the impact of changes in an integrated environment of heterogeneous information systems. It would be interesting to know to which extent our approach could be used in other areas where the analysis of change impact is important, like CIA in software development.

One of the next steps is to extend Caro to not only be able to automatically analyze changes but also to handle problems that are detected, and help the developers by correlating the "old" and the "new" elements (i.e., to better recognize renaming or moving of elements). Furthermore, it is necessary to provide possibilities to give behavioral advice to systems affected by a change, to enable automatic reaction to problems. By using additional properties for element and relationship nodes, this can happen without interference with the current system. While the existing system was developed with this in mind, the details are subject to future work.

References

1. OWL Web Ontology Language Guide, 2004. http://www.w3.org/TR/2004/REC-owl-guide-20040210/.
2. RDF/XML Syntax Specification (Revised), 2004. http://www.w3.org/TR/2004/REC-rdf-syntax-grammar-20040210/.
3. S. Ajila. Software Maintenance: An Approach to Impact Analysis of Objects Change. *Software – Practice and Experience*, 25(10):1155–1181, October 1995.
4. P. Andritsos, A. Fuxman, A. Kementsietsidis, R. J. Miller, and Y. Velegrakis. Kanata: Adaptation and Evolution in Data Sharing Systems. *SIGMOD Record*, 33(4):32–37, December 2004.
5. P. A. Bernstein. Applying Model Management to Classical Meta Data Problems. In *Proc. of the 1st Conference on Innovative Data Systems Research (CIDR)*, 2003.
6. S. A. Bohner and R. S. Arnold, editors. *Software Change Impact Analysis*. IEEE Computer Society Press, Los Alamitos, CA, USA, 1996.
7. L. Deruelle, M. Bouneffa, G. Goncalves, and J.-C. Nicolas. Local and Federated Database Schemas Evolution: An Impact Propagation Model. In *Proc. of the 10th International Conference on Database and Expert Systems Applications (DEXA)*, pages 902–911, 1999.
8. C. Dorda, H.-P. Steiert, and J. Sellentin. Modellbasierter Ansatz zur Anwendungsintegration. *it – Information Technology*, 46(4):200–210, 2004.
9. Hewlett-Packard. Jena – A Semantic Web Framework for Java, 2005. http://jena.sourceforge.net/.
10. A. Keller and C. Ensel. An Approach for Managing Service Dependencies with XML and the Resource Description Framework. Technical report, IBM, 2002.
11. P. McBrien and A. Poulovassilis. Automatic migration and wrapping of database applications – a schema transformation approach. In *Int. Conf. on Conceptual Modeling/the Entity Relationship Approach*, 1999.
12. R. McCann, B. AlShebli, Q. Le, H. Nguyen, L. Vu, and A. Doan. Mapping Maintenance for Data Integration Systems. In *Proceedings of the 31st VLDB Conference*, 2005.
13. S. Melnik, E. Rahm, and P. A. Bernstein. Developing Metadata-Intensive Applications with Rondo. *Journal of Web Semantics*, 1(1), 2004.

14. E. Rahm and P. A. Bernstein. A survey of approaches to automatic schema matching. *VLDB Journal*, 10:334–350, 2001.
15. J. F. Roddick. Schema Evolution in Database Systems – An Annotated Bibliography. *SIGMOD Record*, 21(4):35–40, 1992.
16. B. G. Ryder and F. Tip. Change Impact Analysis for Object-Oriented Programs. In *Proceedings of PASTE*, 2001.
17. X. Zhang and E. A. Rundensteiner. Data Warehouse Maintenance Under Concurrent Schema and Data Updates. Technical report, Worcester Polytechnic Institute, 1998.

Constructing Optimal Wavelet Synopses

Dimitris Sacharidis

Knowledge and Database Systems Lab
School of Electrical and Computer Engineering
National Technical University of Athens
Zographou 157 73, Athens, Greece
dsachar@dblab.ntua.gr

Abstract. The wavelet decomposition is a proven tool for constructing concise synopses of massive data sets and rapid changing data streams, which can be used to obtain fast approximate, with accuracy guarantees, answers. In this work we present a generic formulation for the problem of constructing optimal wavelet synopses under space constraints for various error metrics, both for static and streaming data sets. We explicitly associate existing work and categorize it according to the previous problem formulation and, further, we present our current work and identify its contributions in this context. Various interesting open problems are described and our future work directions are clearly stated.

1 Introduction

Approximate query processing over compact precomputed data synopses has attracted a lot of attention recently as an effective approach for dealing with massive data sets in interactive decision support and data exploration environments. In such settings, users typically pose complex queries, which require considerable amounts of time to produce exact answers, over large parts of the stored data. However, due to exploratory behavior, users can often tolerate small imprecisions in query results, as long as these results are quickly generated and accompanied with accuracy guarantees.

Several studies have demonstrated the applicability of wavelets as a data reduction tool for a variety of database problems. Briefly, the key idea is to first apply the decomposition process over an input data set, thus producing a set of wavelet coefficients. One, then, retains only a subset, composing the *wavelet synopsis*, of the coefficients by performing a thresholding procedure. Clearly, such a lossy compression procedure introduces some error when reconstructing the original data. The bulk of recent work focuses on defining useful metrics that capture this reconstruction error and, further, provide algorithms for constructing optimal synopses given a space constraint.

In a data streaming setting, usually one needs to resort to approximation in order to deal with the high volume and rate of incoming data. Wavelet synopses seem to be an effective summarization technique that can be applied in such a setting as well. Unfortunately, algorithms for constructing wavelet synopses designed to operate on static disk-resident data cannot be easily extended to

T. Grust et al. (Eds.): EDBT 2006 Workshops, LNCS 4254, pp. 97–104, 2006.

process data streams. For example, most of the static algorithms require many passes over the data, whereas, in a streaming context only one-pass algorithms can be applied. In other words, once a data stream item has been processed it cannot be examined again in the future, unless explicitly stored; of course, explicitly storing the entire data stream is not an option.

In this work, we briefly introduce the wavelet decomposition in Section 2. We present our problem formulation for constructing wavelet synopses, discuss the challenges that arise within a data streaming environment and describe our contributions in Section 3. Finally, we conclude our discussion and propose future research directions in Section 4.

2 Background on Wavelet Decomposition

The wavelet decomposition is a mathematical tool for the hierarchical decomposition of functions with a long history of successful applications in signal and image processing [15]. Let us briefly introduce the wavelet decomposition process through a simple example. Consider the *data vector* $a = [2, 2, 0, 2, 3, 5, 4, 4]$, of domain size $N = 8$. The Haar wavelet decomposition, the simplest of all wavelet decompositions, of a is computed as follows. We first average the values together pairwise to get a new "lower-resolution" representation of the data with the pairwise averages $[\frac{2+2}{2}, \frac{0+2}{2}, \frac{3+5}{2}, \frac{4+4}{2}] = [2, 1, 4, 4]$. This averaging loses some of the information in a. To restore the original a values, we need *detail coefficients*, that capture the missing information. In the Haar decomposition, these detail coefficients are the differences of the (second of the) averaged values from the computed pairwise average. Thus, in our simple example, for the first pair of averaged values, the detail coefficient is 0 since $2 - 2 = 0$, for the second it is -1 since $1 - 2 = -1$. No information is lost in this process – one can reconstruct the eight values of the original data array from the lower-resolution array containing the four averages and the four detail coefficients. We recursively apply this pairwise averaging and differencing process on the lower-resolution array of averages until we reach the overall average, to get the full Haar decomposition, depicted in Figure 1(a). The transform of a is given by $w_a = [11/4,\ -5/4,\ 1/2,\ 0,\ 0,\ -1,\ -1,\ 0]$, that is, the overall average followed by the detail coefficients in order of increasing resolution. Each entry in w_a, be it a detail or average, is called a *wavelet coefficient*.

A B-term *wavelet synopsis* is simply defined as any subset $\Lambda \subset w_a$ of wavelet coefficients, where usually $B = |\Lambda| \ll N$. Implicitly, all non-stored coefficients are set to 0. Thus, a wavelet synopsis is typically stored by B $\langle$coeff-index, coeff-value$\rangle$ pairs.

A useful conceptual tool for visualizing and understanding the hierarchical nature of the Haar decomposition process is the *error tree* structure [12] (shown in Fig. 1(b) for the example array a). Each internal tree node c_i corresponds to a wavelet coefficient (with the root node c_0 being the overall average), and leaf nodes $a[i]$ correspond to the original data-array entries. This view allows us to see that the reconstruction of any $a[i]$ depends only on the $\log N + 1$ coefficients

Resolution	Averages	Detail Coefficients
3	[2, 2, 0, 2, 3, 5, 4, 4]	-----
2	[2, 1, 4, 4]	[0, −1, −1, 0]
1	[3/2, 4]	[1/2, 0]
0	[11/4]	[−5/4]

(a)

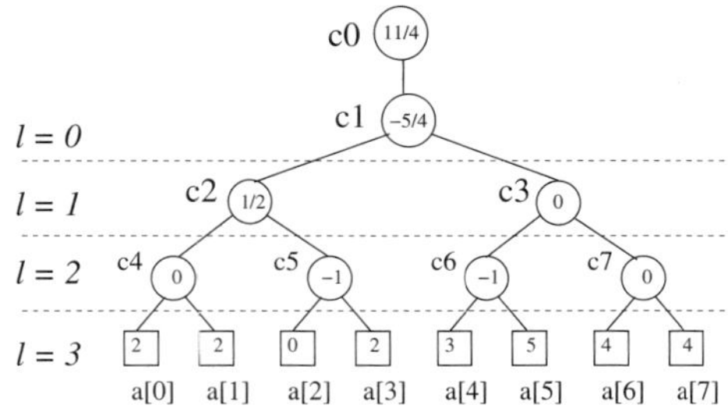

(b)

Fig. 1. Example error-tree structure for the example array a

in the path between the root and $a[i]$. Without going into detail, observe that $a[5]$ can be reconstructed by adding or subtracting coefficients in the path from the root down to $a[5]$, depending on whether we descend to a left or right child respectively; i.e., $a[5] = c_0 - c_1 + c_3 - c_6 \Leftrightarrow 5 = \frac{11}{4} - (-\frac{5}{4}) + 0 - (-1)$. Similarly, notice that the value of a wavelet coefficient only depends on a subset of the original values, depending on the height of the tree they belong to; e.g., the value of coefficient c_5 depends only on the values $a[2]$ and $a[3]$.

Intuitively, wavelet coefficients towards the root of the error tree carry a higher weight in the reconstruction of the original data values. To equalize the importance of all coefficients, a common normalization scheme is to scale the coefficient values at level l by a factor of $\sqrt{N/2^l}$. Letting c_i^* denote the normalized coefficient values, this fact has two important consequences: (1) The *energy* (a.k.a., the L_2 norm) of the a vector is preserved in the wavelet domain, that is, $||a||_2^2 = \sum_i a[i]^2 = \sum_i (c_i^*)^2$ (by Parseval's theorem); and, (2) Retaining the B largest coefficients in terms of *absolute normalized value* gives the (provably) optimal B-term wavelet synopsis in terms of Sum-Squared-Error (SSE) in the data reconstruction (for a given budget of coefficients B) [15]. More formally, assuming a synopsis Λ and denoting by $\widetilde{a}$ the vector of reconstructed data values, the SSE is defined as $\sum_i (a[i] - \widetilde{a}[i])^2 = \sum_{\forall c_j \notin \Lambda} (c_j^*)^2$, where the latter equation is due to Parseval's theorem. In other words, SSE is equal to the sum of squared normalized values of the non-stored coefficients, hence the previous observation.

3 Constructing Optimal Wavelet Synopses

In this section we present a generic problem formulation for constructing optimal wavelet synopses. To this end we distinguish among various error metrics and also differentiate on static (disk-resident) and streaming data. Further, we explicitly relate the contributions of our current work with respect to the aforementioned problem formulation.

A *B-term optimal wavelet synopsis* is a wavelet synopsis that minimizes some aggregate reconstruction error metric under a space constraint of B coefficients — therefore, its construction depends on the definition of such an error metric.

Minimizing Weighted L_p Norm of Point Errors. Given a wavelet synopsis Λ of some data vector a, let $\mathrm{err}(i)$ denote the *point error*, that is, the reconstruction error for the i-th data value $a[i]$. In Section 2 we considered the point to be the absolute error $\mathrm{err}_{abs}(i) = |a[i] - \widetilde{a}[i]|$ and further applied the L_2 norm to aggregate across all data values, leading to the SSE error metric. Finding the optimal wavelet synopsis for SSE is quite trivial, as discussed. However, the extension to other point errors, such as, for example, the relative error (with sanity bound s) $\mathrm{err}_{rel}(i) = \frac{|a[i]-\widetilde{a}[i]|}{\max\{s,a[i]\}}$ and using other norms, such as the maximum L_∞ norm, to aggregate individual data reconstruction errors, is not as straightforward.

Let $\mathrm{err}(i)$ denote the i-th point error and w_i denote a weight (or, importance) assigned to this error. Using a weighted L_p norm for aggregation we obtain the following generic error metric: $\sum_i w_i \cdot (\mathrm{err}(i))^p$. Unfortunately, since Parseval's theorem can only be applied in the unweighted L_2 norm of absolute errors, no easy to process rewriting of arbitrary aggregate error metrics exists.

There are two approaches to constructing an optimal wavelet synopsis for general weighted aggregated point errors. The first approach, used in [16] for the weighted L_2 error, tries to incorporate the error metric in the decomposition process. The decomposition step for obtaining the average coefficient changes to a weighted average, that is, for two values a, b we obtain $\frac{w_a a + w_b b}{2}$, where weights w_a, w_b can be constructed from the given reconstruction error weights. This approach leads to a different, Haar-like, decomposition in which the SSE metric is exactly the weighted L_2 error metric measured in the conventional Haar decomposition. Therefore, the construction of the optimal, under weighted L_2 norm, synopsis problem translates to the conventional SSE minimization problem.

The second approach, such as the one taken in [3,4,14,6], is the design of algorithms that incorporate the error metric in their operation by exploiting the error tree structure. In short, due to the distributive nature of error metrics, the algorithms solve a dynamic programming recurrence, where the optimal error incurred at a node i in the error tree (for a specified space budget and for a specified set of ancestor nodes retained in the synopsis) depends on the optimal errors incurred at the two children nodes $2i, 2i+1$. The choice to be made involves distributing available space to children nodes and deciding whether to include node i in the set of retained nodes, or not.

Recently [7], it has been observed that restricting the retained synopsis values to the actual decomposition values is suboptimal for other than SSE error metrics. Indeed, consider the case where just one coefficient, the average, is to be maintained in the synopsis. In the case of an SSE-optimal synopsis the optimal value would be the value in the original decomposition, that is, the average. However, in the case of the maximum absolute error metric the optimal value would rather be $(\min + \max)/2$, where min and max are the minimum and maximum values, respectively, in the original data. In light of this observation, one has to construct a synopsis by searching not only for the best coefficients to choose, but also for their optimal values. The term used for this more generic and computationally harder optimization problem is the construction of optimal *unrestricted wavelet synopses.*

Extending results to multi-dimensional data sets is not straightforward, as it usually requires the design of external memory algorithms. Our work in [9] presents I/O efficient algorithms for constructing SSE optimal wavelet synopses for massive multi-dimensional data sets. In brief, the main idea is to put into memory a part of the data set such that when the wavelet decomposition is performed on this data, we obtain an as large as possible set of finalized coefficient values. The wavelet decomposition of the in-memory data values is performed efficiently by the SHIFT and SPLIT operations, that intuitively: (i) shift the indices of the detail coefficients to their corresponding indices in the final decomposed data set; and (ii) split the energy of the average coefficients to properly update some already calculated coefficients.

Minimizing Weighted L_p Norm of Range-Sum Errors. For this case we define the *range-sum error*, denoted by $\text{err}(i:j)$, as the summation of reconstruction errors for data values $a[i]$ through $a[j]$: $\text{err}(i:j) = \sum_{k=i}^{j} \text{err}(k)$. Similar to the case of point errors, one can use weighted L_p norms to aggregate across all $N(N+1)/2$ range-sum errors. Further, the first approach for finding a point error optimal synopsis, described previously, apply to the case of range-sum error optimal synopses as well. The work in [11] operates on the prefix-sum array of a and show that one has to follow a similar to the SSE-optimal synopses thresholding procedure for the case of unweighted L_2 aggregation of range-sum absolute errors. Unfortunately, the second approach of incorporating the error metric in the synopsis construction algorithm cannot be directly applied, since no nice distributive property for aggregating range-sum errors can be exploited.

3.1 Streaming Wavelet Synopses

A data streaming environment introduces resource restrictions to conventional static data processing algorithms, due to the high volumes and rates associated with incoming data. Namely: (i) there is not enough space to store the entire stream, as it can be of potentially unbounded size, and thus, data stream items can only be seen once; (ii) data stream items must be processed quickly in real time; and (iii) queries over data streams are of persistent nature and must be continuously and, most importantly, quickly evaluated. Under these restrictions, data stream processing algorithms must have small space requirements and exhibit fast per-item processing and querying time — here, small and quickly should be read as poly-logarithmic to data stream size.

In our context, we are to construct and maintain the optimal wavelet synopsis of a data vector a whose values are continuously updated by the data stream. There are two conceptually different ways to model [5,13] how the data stream updates the values of a: (i) the *time series model*, where data stream items are appended to the data vector a, that is, the i-th data stream item is the value $a[i]$; and (ii) the *turnstile model*, where data stream items update the data vector

a, that is, each data stream item (i, u) is an update for one of the data values, implying that $a^{new}[i] \leftarrow a^{old}[i] + u$.

Time Series Model. In this data stream model, since the data stream items are appended at the end of the data vector a, only those coefficients, termed the wavelet *fringe*, in the path from the root down to the most recently appended data value change. This means that the bulk of wavelet coefficients (except for the logarithmically small subset that lies in the fringe) have a data value that it is not going to be affected by subsequent data stream items. For a B-term SSE optimal synopsis, this observation leads to a very simple algorithm [5]: maintain the B highest in absolute normalized value coefficients among those whose value is finalized and additionally keep all the coefficients in the fringe. Once a fringe coefficient is finalized the algorithm simply needs to compare its value with the B stored values and construct the new set of stored values by either dropping the coefficient at hand or the smallest one in the stored set. However, in the case of arbitrary error metrics no algorithm that produces an optimal synopsis exists, to the best of our knowledge. The work in [10] provides with a heuristic as to which coefficients to maintain for a maximum (relative or absolute) error optimal synopsis in the time series model: each time a coefficient needs to be dropped, the one which leads to the smallest increase in error is greedily picked.

For the problem of maintaining SSE optimal wavelet synopses, our work in [9] introduces some interesting results. In data streaming applications, as also argued in [2], it is often more appropriate to keep update times small to accommodate for multiple bursty streams, rather that try to save on memory footprint. To this end, the SHIFT/SPLIT operations defined in [9] allow for a trade-off between per-item processing time and available space for maintaining streaming wavelet synopses. Further, in [9] we present the first time and space requirements results for maintaining wavelet synopses over a multi-dimensional time series data stream. All results are provided for both forms of multi-dimensional wavelet decomposition, standard and non-standard [15].

Turnstile Model. The turnstile model is more general in that it allows arbitrary updates to the data vector, and thus, potentially any wavelet coefficient can be affected by a data stream item. This makes keeping track of wavelet coefficients a very hard task, let alone constructing an optimal synopsis. The work in [5] uses a sketch [1] as a means of (probabilistically) maintaining the energy/magnitude of the data vector a. Then, one can estimate any wavelet coefficient by multiplying the energy of the data vector with that of the corresponding wavelet basis vector, as long as the angle among the two vectors is sufficiently large. Constructing an optimal in terms of SSE synopsis, however, requires super-linear in N time. To make matters worse, no results exist for other error metrics.

Our work in [2] deals with maintaining SSE optimal synopses under this more general model (where sketching techniques are the only option) and offers significant time improvements over previous approaches. The crux of our work lies in two novel technical ideas. First, our algorithms work entirely in the wavelet domain: instead of maintaining a sketch over a data vector we choose to sketch its wavelet decomposition. This is possible as a single data stream update item can be translated to only poly-logarithmically more update items in the wavelet domain. Second and most importantly, our algorithms employ a novel hierarchical group organization of wavelet coefficients to accommodate for efficient binary-search-like identification of high in absolute normalized value coefficients. In addition, a trade-off between query time and update time is established, by varying the hierarchical structure of groups, allowing the right balance to be found for specific data stream scenarios. The algorithms presented in [2] can easily scale to large domain sizes and, further, can be applied to multi-dimensional data streams for both decomposition forms.

4 Conclusions and Future Work Directions

In this work we have presented a problem formulation for constructing wavelet synopses, general enough to embody the majority of existing work in this area. Further, we have explicitly illustrated the contributions of our current work and described, in context, how it relates to the general formulation. From our discussion one can easily deduce that many interesting and challenging issues remain open for constructing optimal wavelet synopses, especially in a data streaming environment. Our future work will try to address some of these.

In particular, when aggregating point errors, the approach of incorporating the desired minimization metric into the wavelet decomposition seems to be the most promising one, as choosing the coefficients can be done in a similar to the SSE minimization process. Further, such an approach can then be easily adapted to operate over data streams for both models. However, similar results for other L_p norms, including minimizing for the maximum error (L_∞), do not exist. It would be interesting to see whether modified Haar wavelet bases, or even other wavelet bases, are suitable for this task.

Optimizing for arbitrary workloads, such as those that include range-sum queries, seem more useful than simply optimizing for point query workloads. However, as also discussed in [11], optimizing for arbitrary workloads seems to be a difficult task. Perhaps, optimizing for a simpler case, such as that of a workload containing just dyadic range-sum queries, can provide some nice heuristics for arbitrary workloads.

Finally, another interesting issue to consider would be devising techniques for space-efficient compression of wavelet synopses. As recently suggested in [8], adaptive quantization can be applied to the coefficient values, and even some clever indexing can be employed to reduce the overhead of identifying retained wavelet coefficients.

References

1. N. Alon, Y. Matias, and M. Szegedy. The space complexity of approximating the frequency moments. In *Proceedings ACM symposium on Theory of computing (STOC)*, 1996.

2. G. Cormode, M. Garofalakis, and D. Sacharidis. Fast approximate wavelet tracking on streams. To appear in *International Conference on Extending Database Technology (EDBT)*, 2006.
3. M. Garofalakis and P. B. Gibbons. Wavelet synopses with error guarantees. In *Proceedings ACM International Conference on Management of Data (SIGMOD)*, 2002.
4. M. Garofalakis and A. Kumar. Deterministic wavelet thresholding for maximum-error metrics. In *Proceedings ACM Principles of Database Systems (PODS)*, 2004.
5. A. C. Gilbert, Y. Kotidis, S. Muthukrishnan, and M. J. Strauss. Surfing wavelets on streams: One-pass summaries for approximate aggregate queries. In *Proceedings International Conference on Very Large Data Bases (VLDB)*, 2001.
6. S. Guha. Space efficiency in synopsis construction algorithms. In *Proceedings International Conference on Very Large Data Bases (VLDB)*, 2005.
7. S. Guha and B. Harb. Wavelet synopsis for data streams: minimizing non-euclidean error. In *Proceedings ACM International Conference on Knowledge Discovery in Data Mining (SIGKDD)*, 2005.
8. S. Guha and B. Harb. Approximation Algorithms for Wavelet Transform Coding of Data Streams. In *Proceedings ACM-SIAM Symposium on Discrete Algorithms (SODA)*, 2006.
9. M. Jahangiri, D. Sacharidis, and C. Shahabi. Shift-Split: I/O efficient maintenance of wavelet-transformed multidimensional data. In *Proceedings ACM International Conference on Management of Data (SIGMOD)*, 2005.
10. P. Karras and N. Mamoulis. One-pass wavelet synopses for maximum-error metrics. In *Proceedings International Conference on Very Large Data Bases (VLDB)*, 2005.
11. Y. Matias and D. Urieli. On the optimality of the greedy heuristic in wavelet synopses for range queries. Technical Report TR-TAU, 2005.
12. Y. Matias, J. S. Vitter, and M. Wang. Wavelet-based histograms for selectivity estimation. In *Proceedings ACM International Conference on Management of Data (SIGMOD)*, 1998.
13. S. Muthukrishnan. Data streams: algorithms and applications. In *Proceedings ACM Symposium of Discrete Algorithms (SODA)*, 2003.
14. S. Muthukrishnan. Subquadratic algorithms for workload-aware haar wavelet synopses. In *Proceedings Conference on Foundations of Software Technology and Theoretical Computer Science (FSTTCS)*, 2005.
15. E. J. Stollnitz, T. D. Derose, and D. H. Salesin. *Wavelets for computer graphics: theory and applications.* Morgan Kaufmann Publishers Inc., 1996.
16. D. Urieli and Y. Matias. Optimal workload-based weighted wavelet synopses. In *Proceedings International Conference on Database Theory (ICDT)*, 2005.

Towards a Secure Service Coordination

Thi-Huong-Giang Vu

LSR-IMAG Laboratory, BP 72, 38402 Saint Martin d'Hères, France
Thi-Huong-Giang.Vu@imag.fr
http://www-lsr.imag.fr/Les.Personnes/Thi-Huong-Giang.Vu/

Abstract. This paper presents an approach for building secure service-based coordinated systems. Secure coordination is considered at two levels: abstraction (i.e., specification) and execution (i.e., run level). At the abstraction level, we define a general model enabling to specify coordination and its related non functional properties (such as security). The idea is to use constraints for expressing the application logic of a coordinated system and its required security strategies. Coordination activities are the key concepts used for controlling the execution of participating services. Constraints are specified as pre and post conditions of these coordination activities. At the execution level, we propose an architecture which implements strategies to verify constraints and manage the secure execution of coordination. We propose also an instantiating vade-mecum to configure execution level components according to a specific set of constraints.

1 Context and Motivations

The democratization of Internet along with recent advances in information technologies has made the global networked marketplace vision a reality. In such an environment, companies form alliances for building information systems that aggregate their respective services, and thereby enabling them to stay competitive. Effective service sharing and integration is a critical step towards developing next generation of information systems for supporting the new online economy. Given the time-to-market, rapid development and deployment requirements, information systems are made up of the services of different service providers, accessible through networks, e.g., Internet. Such information systems are called *coordinated systems*. A service performs functionalities associated with a goal desired by its provider. Services are heterogeneous, and use different data formats and transport protocols. A service provider is an autonomous organism that keeps control on the service execution with respect to some non-functional aspects such as security. A service can evolve independently of its users (applications) by both aggregating new functionalities or, conversely, removing existing ones. A service provider predefines also instructions and descriptions for using its services (e.g., where and when functionalities of these services can be accessed). Using a service implies invoking a provided method and (possibly) waiting for execution results.

Numerous systems, models and languages have been proposed for supporting service coordination, i.e., the way services invocations are orchestrated according

T. Grust et al. (Eds.): EDBT 2006 Workshops, LNCS 4254, pp. 105–114, 2006.

to the application logic of a given coordinated system. Existing solutions such as workflow models [16,7] or Petri nets [13] tackle the specification and enactment of service coordination. Using a workflow model, the execution of a coordinated system is controlled by a data flow and a control flow. The data flow specifies data exchange among participating services. The control flow describes their dependencies and it is expressed by ordering operators such as sequence, selection (OR-split, OR-joint) and synchronization (AND-split, AND-joint). Using a Petri net, the execution of a coordinated system is expressed in form of rules applied on data delivered to or consumed by participating services (i.e., places). It implies (i) rules for abstracting the structure of exchanged data (i.e., tokens) between services and (ii) rules for scheduling and firing input and output data of service execution (i.e., transitions). The execution of interaction among services has been facilitated by current technologies, such as technologies driven by the interoperation approach [5,15] and the intercommunication approach [4].

While particular attention has been devoted to service coordination, non-functional aspects such as security have been poorly addressed by existing coordination models, languages and execution engines. It is hard to accurately specify what a coordinated system has to do under specific security requirements such as authentication, reliability, non repudiation and messages integrity. It is also often difficult to consider in advance the coordination of participating services under a large set of interactions and interdependencies among them. A loose specification of application logic can lead to a wrong order of interactions among services. We can also mistreat real situations during the coordination execution, e.g., invoked service is undesirably replaced by another. Furthermore, at execution time managing secure coordination implies:

- Authentication of the services that participate in a coordination process (i.e., identify the invoked service and the service that provides results after an invocation).
- Verifying messages integrity (i.e., those exchanged among services) in order to avoid their unauthorised alteration.
- Ensuring non repudiation of coordination: post-check the validity of coordinated system execution and prevent a participating service from denying previous actions.

The challenges are to avoid security vulnerabilities that can reach the service coordination and to provide strategies and measures for ensuring security at run-time. Moreover, the proposed strategies and measures should not contradict the facility of the coordinated system construction and the flexibility of services. It should be possible to adapt coordination and security aspects of coordinated systems on different topologies, usage scenarios, delegation requirements and security configurations. It should imply also the way to customize security levels for different types of participating services when they take part in different coordinated systems. Therefore, we aim at adding security properties service coordination.

Our approach enables secure service coordination by combining security properties of services. It also defines the general architecture of components for managing secure coordination at run-time. We assume that services and network security is ensured by the communication and the execution environments. Particularly, we suppose that there is no backdoor for accessing public instructions and descriptions exported by services; and that exchanged information confidentiality is ensured by underlying network services (e.g., by cipher mechanisms). We also assume that security properties are exported by services and that they are implemented by heterogeneous tools (e.g., different encryption algorithms).

The remainder of this paper is organized as follows. Section 2 introduces the model for secure service coordination. Section 3 presents the run-time architecture for verifying constraints and managing the secure execution of coordination. Section 4 describes the instantiating vade-mecum for programming security tools supported by the execution and communication environments. Section 5 compares our work with existing ones. Finally, section 6 concludes the paper and discusses further research directions.

2 Model for Secure Service Coordination

We propose a model (see Fig. 1) that offers concepts to describe service coordination as coordination activities and their associated constraints.

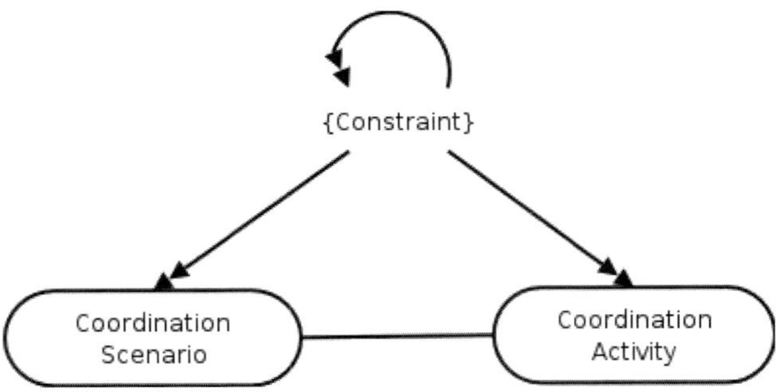

Fig. 1. Secure service coordination model

A *coordination activity* specifies an interaction between two services, where one invokes a function provided by the other and (possibly) waits for execution results.

A *coordination scenario* is the history containing information about the execution of a coordinated system. It is built by tracing the execution of coordination activities.

A *constraint* specifies the behaviour, the data, the characteristic or the interface associated to a coordination activity or to a coordination scenario. A constraint can be enabled, enforced, observed and verified.

In our model, the application logic of a service-based coordinated system is specified as a set of constraints. These constraints are added to coordination activities (in form of their preconditions, post-conditions and invariants) and refer to a given coordination scenario. In this way, an application logic can address different types of requirements imposed to the execution of coordination activities: ordering (e.g., their temporal relationships), firing (e.g., the moment in which a participating service must be invoked) and data interdependencies (e.g., input/output data relationships).

Security strategies required by a coordinated system are specified in a similar way. Constraints expressed on security properties provided by services are coupled with constraints used to control the execution of coordination activities. These constraints are also added to coordination activities and refer to a given coordination scenario. A security strategy addresses integrity, authentication, authorisation and non repudiation for coordination. The coordination can be then controlled and managed to be performed with respect to specific functional safety requirements such as in the correct time, in the correct communication cross-links, by the correct actors, etc.

Let us consider a flight booking application built out of three existing services:

- Adventurer service manages clients that are interested in booking flights.
- Payment service executes online payment transactions on given client accounts.
- Seeking service looks for available seats and performs flight pre-booking operations on a flight database.

The application logic of such a coordinated system is explained as follows. The flight booking application first interacts with Adventurer service to get information about client and her/his needs by invoking the method get_Requirements. This information is used by the method seek_Flights of the Seeking service for looking for available flights. This service returns a list of possible flights that are displayed by the method display_Results of the Adventurer service.

Constraints (ordering, firing and data interdependencies) express this application logic as pre and post conditions associated to the three following coordination activities:

- A_1: getFlightInformation(AdventurerService) where reservation requirements are retrieved.
- A_2: seekFlights(SeekingService) for looking for available flights according to the information received as input (from A_1).
- A_3: showResults(AdventurerService) for displaying the booking result.

Required security properties such as authentication and authorisation are also expressed in form of pre and post conditions of these coordination activities. Corresponding security strategies specify that these identified coordination activities are permitted for invoking their relating methods and that received results really stem from the invoked services.

For example, examine the coordination activity A_2 and its related coordination activities A_1 and A_3. The following constraints specify coordination and security aspects associated to A_2:

- Obligate(S_1 = COMMIT): once the execution status of A_1 (i.e., S_1) is succesful, the method seekFlights of the Seeking service can be invoked.
- Match(O_1): information about customer's needs (i.e., O_1) produced by the method getFlightInformation of the Adventurer service is used as input data of the method seekFlights provided by the Seeking service.
- After(getFlightInformation): the end of the execution of the method getFlightInformation must precede the beginning of the execution of the method seekFlights.
- Approved(seekFlights): the identity of the service providing the invoked method seekFlights must belong to the approved list of the coordinated system.

Similarly, the following post conditions of A_2 must hold:

- Permit(S_3 = READY): A_3 can fire the invocation to a method of the Adventurer service. This constraint plays also the role of an authorisation constraint for A_3.
- Invariant(O_2): the flight search result cannot be altered until it is redelivered to the Adventurer service.
- Received(seekFlights, invocation) $\wedge$ Sent(seekFlights, result): it ensures that the invocation and the transmission of results are done within the same execution scope. In the example, the invocation of the method seekFlights is received and its results are sent within the scope of the coordination activity A_2. This constraint is used for avoiding non-repudiation.

3 Execution Manager General Architecture

We propose an architecture for realising strategies to execute secure service coordination. This execution architecture provides components that can be adapted to manage security strategies to specific application requirements. It provides components for managing functional aspects and non functional aspects, in particular security. For example, at the participating services side, functional aspects are the methods they provide. In our example a security aspect of the Adventurer service is client authentication. The functional aspect of a coordinated system is its application logic and its non-functional aspects concern functional safety.

We define execution managers, which consist of control components that are associated to services and coordination activities. It is extended with other trusted third-party components. For a given coordination activity, each participating service is associated to a connector and a partner controller. A coordination activity is executed by a builder and it has an associated security controller that supervises its execution and the execution of the related participating services. There are three types of security controllers: constraint builders, strategy controllers and aspect controllers. Security properties of services are homogenised by wrappers which are also responsible of managing secure interaction between services.

3.1 Coordination Activity Builder

Fig. 2 shows the components that execute coordination activities.

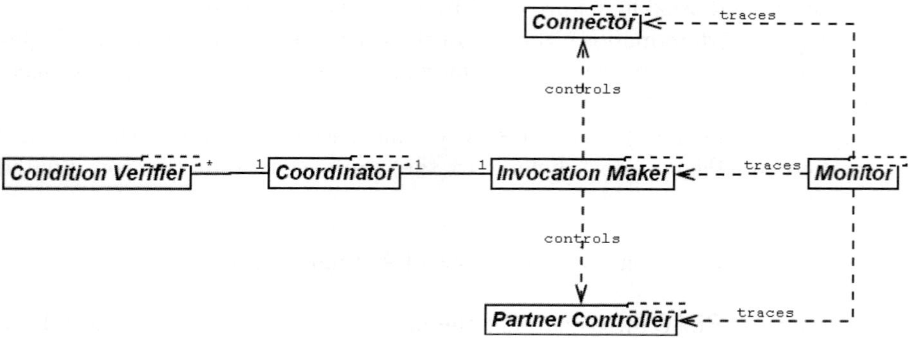

Fig. 2. Components for implementing coordination activities

A *coordinator* controls the execution of a coordination activity with the support of an *invocation maker* and *condition verifier*s. It builds a schedule that specifies the moment in which one or several constraints must be verified with respect to the invocation of a method.

An *invocation maker* performs the invocation of a method specified within a coordination activity.

A *partner controller* manages the interaction with the service related to a specific invocation.

A *connector* is used as a specific communication channel for the interaction between the partners of an invocation.

A *monitor* traces the execution of these components and notifies the execution status to build the coordination scenario.

3.2 Constraint Builder

Fig. 3 shows the components used for managing constraints: *constraint solver*s, *exception handler*s and *condition verifier*s.

A *constraint solver* verifies a set of constraints. It returns a Boolean result. The *false* value is considered as an exception and it is managed by another component.

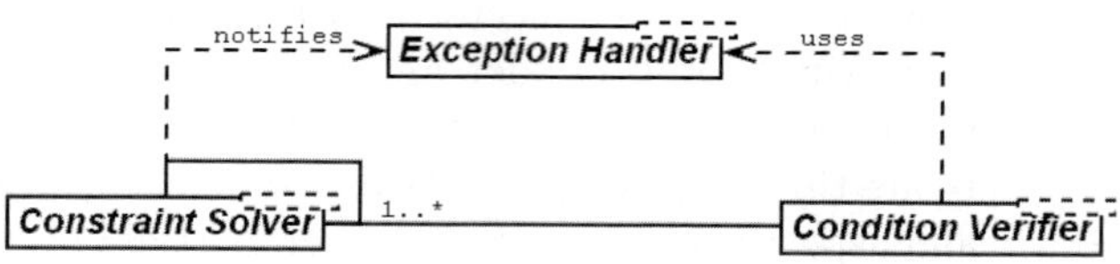

Fig. 3. Constraint builder components

An *exception handler* manages exceptions raised within the execution of a coordinated application. It collects the execution results of other components an generates information associated to the coordination scenario.

A *condition verifier* combines the results of constraint solvers to evaluate pre and post conditions of a specific coordination activity. It translates invariants to equivalent pre and post conditions. All preconditions are checked before launching an invocation. All post conditions are checked after receiving the result from the corresponding invocation.

3.3 Strategy Controller

Fig. 4 shows the components that implement strategies associated to a coordination.

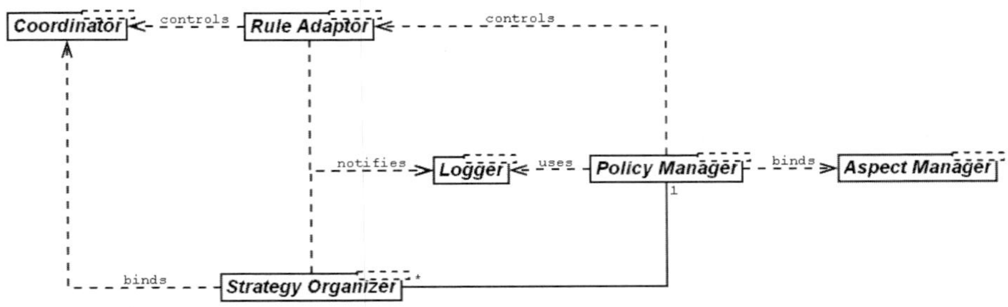

Fig. 4. Strategy controller components

A *rule adaptor* schedules coordination activities according to pre-defined strategies. It controls the execution of a set of coordination activities.

A *strategy organizer* implements a strategy specified by constraints using properties of the participating services.

A *policy controller* controls and manages the execution of the strategies for a given coordinated application.

A *logger* collects information about the execution state of strategies and the notifications from monitors, exception handlers and stores them in a log.

3.4 Aspect Controller

Fig. 5 shows the components for managing security policies of participating services.

Aspect form generator describes security properties of a participating service and exports it.

Aspect manager manages security properties of a service.

Monitor traces modifications on security properties and matches properties with application requirements.

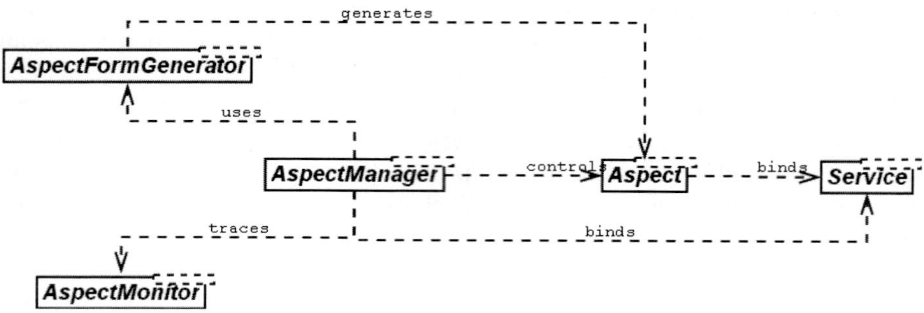

Fig. 5. Aspect controllers - wrappers for participating services

4 Instantiating Vade-Mecum

We describe an instantiating vade-mecum for programming security tools supported by the execution and communication environments (e.g., secure data exchange among services). Our instantiating vade-mecum assists programmers to configure the components of a service-based coordinated system according to a specific set of constraints. The vade-mecum helps to avoid conflicts and redundancy of coordination and security strategies supported by the components of the proposed architecture and those supported by real environment. The vade-mecum provides a technical catalogue of security strategies that can be associated to given coordination contexts, and a guide for combining security strategies with given coordination constructors.

Reinforce Coordination Rule. Security constraints associated to a coordination activity are explicitly specified in our model. Those associated to participating services are implicit to the description of such services. For giving supplementary effects of protection at run-time (e.g., for supervising exchanged information and for notifying the potentially dangerous scripts), security strategies which are not (or implicitly) specified by constraints can be implemented and instantiated as an instance of a *Strategy Organizer*.

Establish Privileges for Actors Related to a Coordination Activity. Authorisation constraints associated to a coordination activity specify in which conditions such an activity can be executed. The role of an actor plays and his/her associated privileges are important elements for verifying constraints. We describe how to grant and manage invoking privileges, and how to associate them to the corresponding connectors.

Supervise Coordination Activity Orchestration. We describe how to construct an activity state-transition automaton for pre-checking the causality of coordination activities for a given set of participating services.

5 Related Works

Existing works can be classified into two categories according to their service interaction mechanisms. In the first category, services interact through a shared space [6,8,1]. Security policies are associated to the shared space: access control (authorisation, control privilege, etc.) and services authentication. Target coordinated system configuration is specified by suitable coordination languages, e.g., the Linda family [11,12,14].

In the second category, coordination is based on data exchange among participating services. Services are considered black box processes that produce and consume data via well defined interfaces. Services communicate directly for establishing connections, exchanging data, diffusing control events among processes [10,8,2].

In [1] security strategies are applied to tools and the environments that support interconnection and communication among participating services (i.e., only at coordination execution level). WS-Policy and WS-Secure-Conversation combined with WS-Security and WS-Trust are going in this direction. [6] presents an approach for building a secure mobile agent environment. [3] specifies secure exchanged messages among Web services based on SOAP protocols. [9] proposes a formal security model to identify and quantify security properties of component functionalities to protect user data by evaluating and certifying the components and their composition.

6 Conclusion and Future Work

This paper presented our approach towards secure service coordination. We described our coordination model and an associated architecture for addressing services authentication.

In conclusion, the main contribution of our work is to provide secure service coordination by specifying security strategies and an associated architecture for executing them. Security properties provided by services are homogenized under a pivot view that can be used for specifying well suited security strategies according to specific requirements.

We are currently specifying and implementing a secure coordination framework called MEOBI. Future work includes evaluating MEOBI for component-based and Web services based systems. Further research focuses on the extension of secure coordination strategies by including performance requirements.

Acknowledgment

This research is supported by the French National Research Council (CNRS). I would like to thank Prof. Christine Collet and Dr. Genoveva Vargas-Solar for their support, guidance and attentive comments, Dr. Christophe Bobineau for his constructive discussions during the preparation of this paper. I would like to extend my appreciation to the reviewers for their feedbacks on the previous draft of this paper.

References

1. Alvarez, P., Banares, J.A., Muro-Medrano, P.R.,Nogueras, J.,Zarazaga, F.J.: A Java Coordination Tool for Web-service Architectures: The Location-Based Service Context. In *FIDJI'01: Revised Papers from the International Workshop on Scientific Engineering for Distributed Java Applications*, Springer-Verlag (2003) 1–14
2. BEA Systems, IBM Corporation, Microsoft Corporation: Web Services Coordination (2003)
3. Belhajjame, K., Vargas-Solar, G., Collet, C.: Defining and coordinating open-services using Workflow. In: *Proceedings of the Eleventh International Conference on Cooperative Information Systems, Lecture Notes in Computer Science* (2003)
4. IBM Corporation: http://www-306.ibm.com/software/htp/cics/ (1999)
5. Object Management Group: http://www.corba.org/ (2002)
6. Cremonini, M., Omicini, A.,Zambonelli, F.: Coordination in Context: Authentication, Authorisation and Topology in Mobile Agent Applications. In: *3rd International Conference on Coordination Languages and Models*, Springer-Verlag (1999)
7. Georgakopoulos, D., Hornick, M.F., Sheth, A.P.: An Overview of Workflow Management: From Process Modeling to Workflow Automation Infrastructure. *Distributed and Parallel Databases* (1995) 119-153
8. Issarny, V., Bidan, C., Saridakis, T.: Characterizing Coordination Architectures According to Their Non-Functional Execution Properties. In: *31st IEEE International Conference on System Science* (1998)
9. Khan, K.M., Han, J.: A Security Characterisation Framework for Trustworthy Component Based Software Systems. In: *IEEE International Computer Software and Applications Conference* (2003)
10. Klint, P., Olivier, P.: The TOOLBUS Coordination Architecture: A Demonstration. In: *5th International Conference on Algebraic Methodology and Software Technology*, Springer Verlag (1996) 575–578
11. Malone, T.W.: What is Coordination Theory and How Can it Help Design Cooperative Work Systems?. In *CSCW '90: Proceedings of the 1990 ACM conference on Computer-supported cooperative work* (1990) 357–370
12. Papadopoulos, G.A., Arbab, F.: Coordination models and languages. *Advances in Computers* (1998)
13. Peterson, J.L.: Petri Net Theory and the Modeling of Systems. Prentice Hall PTR (1981)
14. Tolksdorf, R.: Coordination Technology for Workflows on the Web: Workspaces. In *COORDINATION '00: Proceedings of the 4th International Conference on Coordination Languages and Models*, Springer-Verlag (2000) 36–50
15. Microsoft Corporation: http://msdn.microsoft.com/webservices/building/interop/ (2003)
16. Workflow Management Coalition: Terminology and Glossary (1996)

Document Interrogation: Architecture, Information Extraction and Approximate Answers

Soraya Abad-Mota[1,2]

[1] University of New Mexico
soraya@cs.unm.edu
[2] Universidad Simón Bolívar
abadmota@usb.ve

Abstract. We present an architecture for structuring and querying the contents of a set of documents which belong to an organization. The structure is a database which is semi-automatically populated using information extraction techniques. We provide an ontology-based language to interrogate the contents of the documents. The processing of queries in this language can give approximate answers and triggers a mechanism for improving the answers by doing additional information extraction of the textual sources. Individual database items have associated quality metadata which can be used when evaluating the quality of answers. The interaction between information extraction and query processing is a pivotal aspect of this research.

1 Introduction

Many organizations produce large amounts of documents and their contents never reach the operational databases or the data warehouses of the organization. With the world-wide accessibility to the web these documents are made available to a wide audience, but browsing through them manually is cumbersome, at best. The definition of the *semantic web* [1], has led to fascinating possibilities of research in making explicit the semantics of terabytes of unstructured data available today. Our research seeks to improve the use of these unstructured sources, in particular, textual sources.

Florescu et al. in [2] have clearly defined three tasks in databases related to information management on the www. One of these tasks is *information extraction and data integration*. The data integration task deals with processing queries that require access to heterogeneous data. The queries are posed against data sources after information extraction has taken place. The extraction task is performed by a set of *wrapper programs* and the integration is addressed by *mediator systems* (see [3]).

In this research, each document is a data source from which data are extracted. Each document type has a schema of its contents and all document type schemas that belong to the same organization are integrated into a global schema. The

T. Grust et al. (Eds.): EDBT 2006 Workshops, LNCS 4254, pp. 115–125, 2006.

individual document schemas are used in the task of information extraction from the documents to populate a single relational database.

As a motivating example let us think of a university where each year there is a period when faculty apply for a sabbatical leave for the following academic year. Each sabbatical application is a document which includes the dates, a plan and the institution where this plan will be carried out. The sabbatical application is a type of document which has an associated conceptual schema; each particular application instantiates this schema.

There is not a schema for each instance of a document, but for each type of document. The document type and global schemas are expressed in an extension of the ER model as defined in [4].

The *broad information extraction* phase of the architecture proposed in this work (see figure 1) uses some annotated documents of a particular type to generate extraction rules. The rules are used to extract data slots from the documents. The data extracted can then be used to populate the portion of the integrated database schema which corresponds to the document type schema. When another type of document is processed, new extraction rules are generated; all the documents of this new type are subject to the information extraction process and another portion of the global schema in the relational database is populated with extracted data.

The main idea in this ongoing work is to develop a mechanism that takes advantage of the contents of the documents of an organization. The approach proposed is to structure these contents in a database that is semi-automatically populated using information extraction techniques. The global and individual schemas of documents are produced manually. The *broad information extraction* phase allows a massive population of the database. Later, with the user queries and the answers provided to these queries, more information might be extracted from the documents in an attempt to improve previous answers. It is therefore the interaction between information extraction and query processing a crucial aspect of this research.

In the next section the architecture for document interrogation is briefly described with an emphasis on its ontology. Section 3 contains a description of the information extraction results of this work. In section 4 we introduce the need for a mechanism to provide approximate answers and present a discussion about data quality in this architecture. In section 5 we present a case study which illustrates the components of the arquitecture and their use. Finally, section 6 contains the conclusions and a plan for future work.

2 The Architecture

The Document Interrogation Architecture (*DIA*) presented in [4] and shown in figure 1, addresses the problem of providing mechanisms for structuring the data contained in textual documents and providing an ontology-based language to interrogate the documents through the database built with extracted data.

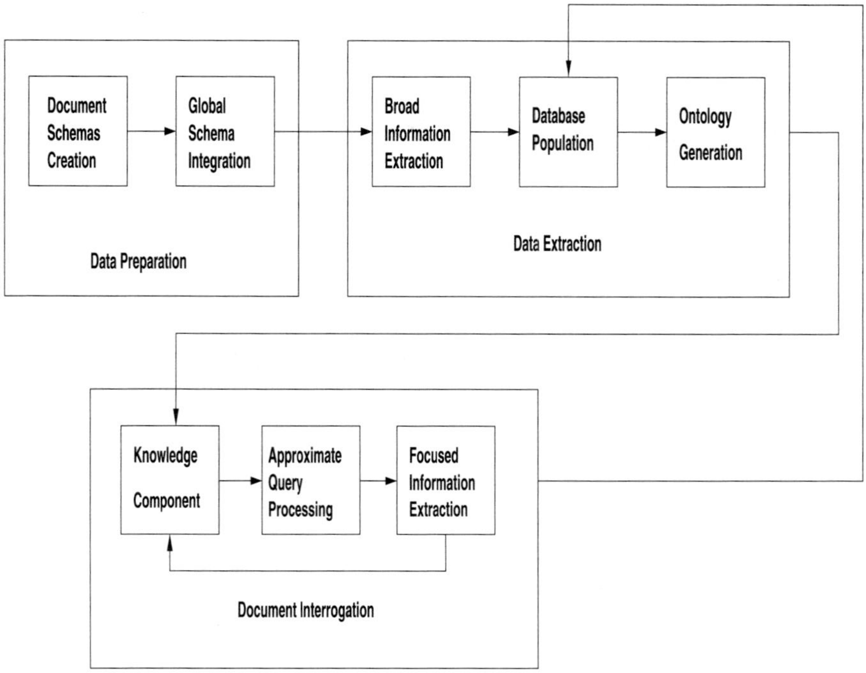

Fig. 1. Document Interrogation Architecture

Our proposed architecture deals with data integration from different data sources but within an organization.

The architecture has three phases. The preparation phase is where training and test documents are annotated and the information extractor is built, by generating extraction rules which are learned from the training examples. The second phase extracts data items from the documents and populates a relational database. Once the database is populated with data, the user may ask questions; the answers are provided by the third phase, the document interrogation phase of the architecture. When computing an answer, the available data is analyzed in order to determine missing data or differences in their quality with respect to the query being posed.

The database of *DIA* is represented at three levels of abstraction: the relational representation, the ER representation in which the schema integration is done, and a higher level, ontology-based representation (see [5]). This latter representation is the basis for the interrogation language. The concepts in the ontology are extended with concepts defined by the user and all these concepts are mapped to the global ER schema of documents and then to the relational database in order to answer queries.

The ontology of *DIA* is initially built with all the concepts contained in the global ER schema of the documents and their relationships. Mostly concepts and not instances are included in the ontology; the relational database contains all the instances. Suppose for example, that we have in the ER schema an entity COUNTRY with instances stored in the relational database. The initial ontology contains the concept COUNTRY, defined as an aggregation of the attributes of the entity, but without instances.

The ontology-based document interrogation language, ODIL, is defined to interrogate and extend the concepts contained in the database. We presented the specification of the language and the mappings between the three models of the database in [6].

Following the example above, the user may extend the ontology by defining a new concept, REGION, as an aggregation of countries; this definition will be stored in the ontology with the mappings between the new concept and the corresponding concepts in the ER schema. If the user defines a particular region, for example, the "Andean Region", with the five countries that comprise it, that instance is stored in the ontology as an instance of REGION, with references to the five instances of COUNTRY that are contained in it. The user may now ask queries about REGION and the mappings between this new concept and the ER schema will let the system compose an answer using the data for the countries that compose a region. This is why we say that the ontology grows with the user queries.

3 Information Extraction in DIA

Information Extraction is a fairly recent research field which has received the attention of researchers from different areas such as: Natural Language Processing (NLP), (see [7] for empirical methods in NLP and [8] for a summary of specific information extraction methods), Machine Learning (ML) (see [9] and [10] for a description of some techniques) and Databases (DB) ([2], [11] and [12]).

Information Extraction is the process by which several pieces of relevant data are extracted from natural language documents. This process includes: locating the relevant data, extracting the phrases which contain the data, separating the facts contained in these phrases and structuring the data in a database for future use.

The approaches to IE taken by the researchers in the areas mentioned above are varied. The natural language processing and machine learning approaches to IE expect mainly natural language text as input and apply empirical methods to it. The research in IE from the database perspective has concentrated on extracting data from web sources of semi-structured data; these include two main approaches, conceptual model-based extraction as developed in the Data Extraction Group of BYU ([11]) and the "Wrapper-Mediator" Approach ([2]). The field of IE has experienced great acceleration recently in response to the increasing amount of textual documents available on the web.

The architecture proposed in [8] defines a generic architecture for an Information Extraction System, which has five phases: tokenization and tagging, sentence analysis, extraction, merging, and template generation. A very effective mechanism for implementing the extraction phase is the definition of extraction rules using patterns. The different alternatives for generating these rules are commonly called *corpus-based methods for learning IE patterns.* The methods to produce the extraction patterns do it in three steps, sentence analysis and preprocessing, training/test case generation, and learning algorithm. Several successful tools have used this technique (see [9]), some representative examples of which are: RAPIER ([13]), WHISK ([14]), and $(LP)^2$ ([15]).

Both "wrappers" and the *corpus-based methods for learning IE patterns* work very well on structured text, a precision near 100% is not unusual. But the former assume a strict regularity in the format of the document; therefore if the format changes, the "wrapper" needs to be modified.

The database approach to IE exploits the problem domain knowledge in contrast with most of the ML approaches to IE, which focus on the natural language semantics of text. In particular, the work of Embley et al. in [11], even though motivated by web page exploration, is an attempt to build an IE system which strongly relies on a conceptual data model of the domain of the source documents. The challenge of this approach is how to represent the domain knowledge in a compact and simple form and how to find ways of acquiring such knowledge automatically.

We have developed an extractor for *DIA* as a combination of the preprocessing activities of the NLP extractors (as classified in [16]), a variation of the learning algorithm of$(LP)^2$ ([15]), and the use of the document schema to build the database tuples. The method for generating extraction rules is fully implemented. Our learning algorithm was tested in several well-known corpora and we obtained similar results to the best reported algorithms (see results of the Pascal Challenge in [17] and our results in [18]).

4 Data Quality and Approximate Answers

The canonical approach for using a database to provide answers to queries is to assume that the database has *the whole truth and nothing but the truth* ([19]). The data which populates the database of DIA is obtained through information extraction procedures from a set of documents. The extracted data might not be complete due to possible mistakes in the extraction process (mostly omissions) and due to the data items in the documents having varying degrees of accuracy or recency (see [20] for a good summary of data quality definitions).

Most of the approaches to data quality within the data integration literature consider the overall quality of a data source. We are interested in a lower granularity measure of quality. Each data item must have a description which includes: the source of the item, the date, the units if it is a measure, the object being described by it, among other metadata. The work of Rakov in [21] considers the quality of database components rather than the whole database. This is a useful measure, but we also want to produce qualitative measures that we can express in text, so that we can go back to the documents to extract more data, based on the text that describes which data are missing.

The problem is that we want to give an answer to a query but in order to build the answer we might use several data items which have different quality metadata associated with them. For example, if we want to answer what the total population of the Andean Region is, we need the current population of the five countries which constitute this region, Bolivia, Colombia, Ecuador, Peru and Venezuela. But we might not have data for the population of Bolivia, we might have census data for Venezuela from 2000 and data for the three other countries from 2004. If we consider these differences a canonical approach would give no answer. If we add up all the population values that we have, Bolivia is not represented in that sum and the other values do not correspond to the same year. Our system should provide the sum of these values as an answer, with a measure of the quality of the answer. Additionally, it will provide a textual phrase that describes the missing data, which triggers further information extraction from the documents.

Approximate query processing in *DIA* distinguishes two cases. The first case occurs when some of the components of the answer are missing. The other case is when there is data for all the components, but their individual quality measures differ greatly from each other. We discuss the first case in the following paragraphs.

When data are missing we have two options, one is to compute an answer without the missing components, but present it as a bound for the real answer. In the case of the total population of the Andean Region, if we add up the existing data for four countries, that sum would be a lower bound for the total population, because the population of Bolivia is greater than zero.

Another option is to try to estimate the missing components. In the statistical literature there are several ways of estimating missing data; for an application of one of these methods to query processing in statistical databases see [22]. Some of the ways of computing missing data consider total uncertainty, but if there is additional information which can be used, the query processor could compute an informed guess. In particular, in the context of an answer which needs several components, it is very relevant to know the relative order of the components and the percentage of the total which can be attributed to the missing components.

The web is a good source of general facts and we can use it to bootstrap our estimating method. On a quick look at the web, we did a search of Bolivia and the other four andean countries. Since the query requires the population of the five countries and we only have these data for four countries, we searched all five countries and got the number of pages about those countries. Then we added one word to the name of each country and performed more searches.

We tried 5 searches with only the name of the country and 95 searches of one word together with the names of the countries. With the results of these trials we computed the global ranking of the countries in terms of the number of pages found by the search engine for each country. The computed order of the five countries was: Colombia, Venezuela, Peru, Ecuador and Bolivia, almost the real order of population size which is: Colombia, Peru, Venezuela, Ecuador and Bolivia.

The computed value of the population of Bolivia, used in the calculation of the total population of the region is an estimate and we include it as such in the database; it is a statistical measure of the missing value. Together with the estimated value we store metadata which describe how it was computed.

These first experiments were performed using words selected manually, but we can use words from the ontology which are close to the concept of the "population of Bolivia" and their synonyms. Additionally, we can also select words from the conceptual schemas or we can generate words by other means.

In this case we used the web as a source of additional information, in general we can use other sources of information that are available.

Regarding the quality of the answer, at first we can say that one out of five components of the answer to the query about the population of the Andean Region is missing, that is, 20 % is missing, or equivalently, four out of five components are correct. This relation could be taken as a measurement of quality, which we could call the *uniform metric*, analogous to the *freshness-rate metric* used for data freshness in [23]. However the 20 % figure is improved to 16.12 % when we perform the procedure of searching words on the web and compute the average proportion of the number of pages about Bolivia with respect to the number of pages for the whole Andean Region. We call this estimate the *bootstrap metric*. The real data reveals that the Bolivian population is 7.43 % of the total of the region. Therefore the distance between the *bootstrap metric* and the real proportion is smaller than that between the real proportion and the *uniform metric*.

There is a qualitative difference between these two metrics. Whereas the *uniform metric* provides no information with regard to the ranking of the missing components, the computations involved when calculating the *bootstrap metric* provide additional information on the ranking of the missing components. For instance, in the case under consideration, Bolivia ranked fourth in nine out of 20 words and ranked fifth in eleven out of those 20 words. We think that this ranking observation deserves further research.

5 A Case Study: CENDA

CENDA is the Center for Document Archives of Universidad Simón Bolívar (USB). This office receives boxes of paper documents from all the organizational units of the university. The documents contained in these boxes are official and are archived for preservation and query answering purposes.

The personnel of CENDA have to manually inspect the boxes, classify the documents contained in them, verify for document duplicity and place each document physically on a drawer or a shelf. A big effort to digitize the documents is underway, but the documents are saved in an image format, which is not the best way to exploit the contents of them or to find answers to queries, because it still needs a great deal of human intervention. A typical query takes 3 days in average to be attended, if the documents needed are already in place.

The *DIA* architecture provides a solution for CENDA's needs. Instead of working with an image of the document, each document is scanned and converted into text with an OCR software. The most requested documents processed by

CENDA can be categorized into 17 major classes. Examples of these document classes are: resolutions of the councils of the university, appointments, admissions, student records, among others. In order to use *DIA* in this problem, each document class needs a document schema. All the document schemas are then integrated into the global schema for the database to be used as the primary means of query answering.

The initial ontology for CENDA is defined using the results of the database construction. The *ODIL* language is then used to pose queries and to extend the ontology.

When a user comes to CENDA with a query, the database of *DIA* is the first resource to be accessed, and the answer could be facts contained in the database or a reference to a document. In many cases, the user needs a copy of the document which contains the answer. The documents would still be classified and stored, but the answers can be processed in the database and the document could be directly accessed and retrieved using the reference to it that resides in the database. This way a huge amount of manual work can be saved for validation of the data stored which was automatically processed.

The answer to a user query in CENDA can often be found in several documents. This is due to the nature of these official documents where several instances have to approve the same fact. For example, an application for sabbatical leave is presented in several documents, one from the faculty member, one from her department and yet another one being the official communication which informs the faculty of the decision regarding the approval or the rejection of the sabbatical. For efficiency reasons and since these documents are somewhat redundant, only one of them is scanned and "loaded" into the database.

The ability of *DIA* to reason about the quality of its answers is particularly useful in the CENDA environment. When an approximate answer is produced it could be due to a missing component. In order to overcome the absence of this missing component in cases like the one just described, where several documents contain redundant information, the documents which were not scanned can be processed to try to extract additional information which might provide a more accurate answer.

Currently there is a teamwork that will select a few classes of documents to be scanned and an integrated schema is being designed to perform a test of the use of the *DIA* architecture in CENDA.

6 Conclusions and Future Work

The *DIA* architecture was defined to take advantage of the contents of textual documents, restricting human intervention to a minimum to make it feasible. One of the aspects in which we try to reduce interaction with a user is in the use of information extraction methods, which learn from a set of annotated examples. We have designed a broad information extractor for DIA, the generation of extraction rules has been implemented and tested and it provides good results; we are working on reducing the number of training examples. The implementation of the module of the extractor that inserts the tuples in the database, using the document schemas, is under construction.

The motivating goal of this research is to provide a tool for humans to query the contents of a set of related documents, without having to manually inspect all the documents. The definition of a high-level language, based on the main concepts abstracted from the documents is a response to this goal. The language has an SQL-like syntax and its main value is in the way it is processed, with the ability to provide approximate answers, to evaluate the quality of the data used in providing an answer and with a mechanism for searching for more data in the documents, if the answer is not good enough.

We have a prototype implementation of the query processor of ODIL. The prototype includes the primitives for defining new concepts and their mapping to the ER schema. It also includes some of the procedures to compute answers. Our immediate plan is to complete the prototype with the generation of approximate answers and also with the evaluation of the metrics described. For the answers which had a missing component, a phrase describing the missing data should be produced, so that a procedure could extract more data from the documents. After concluding the implementation we will run tests to evaluate the improvement in the answers and the ability of the system to extract more data guided by the descriptive phrase.

DIA provides data integration when determining the combination of data required to provide an answer to a document query. Query processing is done over a database of facts obtained from the documents, but since the facts that populate the database do not have a homogeneous quality, a metric for the quality of the combined answer must be searched. In particular, there might be differing qualities of the stored data which are used in the computation of an answer. These qualities are relative to the query being processed. We need to find a metric that will take into account the metadata associated with each component of the answer and that will give a quality value to it. In this aspect the work of Motro et al. in [24] is relevant.

Our system also provides a description of the incomplete or inaccurate data, to perform further extraction from the documents guided by the description of the missing data. This is what we call *focused information extraction* and to the best of our knowledge this is a novel approach which has not been explored.

References

1. James Hendler Tim Berners-Lee and Ora Lassila, "The semantic web," *Scientific American*, may 2001.
2. Daniela Florescu, Alon Levy, and Alberto Mendelzon, "Database techniques for the world-wide-web: A survey," *SIGMOD Record*, vol. 27, no. 3, pp. 59–74, September 1998.
3. G. Wiederhold, "Mediators in the architecture of future information systems," *IEEE Computer*, vol. 25, no. 3, pp. 38–49, 1992.

4. Soraya Abad-Mota and Paul A. Helman, "Dia: A document interrogation architecture," in *Proceedings of the Text Mining Workshop in conjunction with the Sixth Pacific-Asia Conference on Knowledge Discovery and Data Mining (PAKDD-02)*, 2002, pp. 35–45.
5. N. Guarino, Ed., *Formal Ontology and Information Systems*, IOS Press, 1998.
6. Soraya Abad-Mota and Paul A. Helman, "Odil: Ontology-based document interrogation language," in *Proceedings of the 2004 Information Resources Management Association International Conference*, Mehdi Khosrow-Pour, Ed. IRMA, 2004, pp. 517–520, Idea Group Publishing.
7. Eric Brill and Raymond J. Mooney, "An overview of empirical natural language processing," *AI Magazine*, , no. Winter, pp. 13–24, 1997.
8. Claire Cardie, "Empirical methods in information extraction," *AI Magazine*, vol. 18, no. 4, pp. 65–80, 1997.
9. Ion Muslea, "Extraction patterns for information extraction tasks: A survey," in *AAAI-99 Workshop on Machine Learning for Information Extraction*, July 19 1999, Orlando, Florida.
10. Un Yong Nahm and Raymond J. Mooney, "A mutually beneficial integration of data mining and information extraction," in *Proceedings of the Seventeenth National Conference on Artificial Intelligence (AAAI-00)*, July 2000.
11. David W. Embley, Douglas M. Campbell, Y. S. Jiang, Stephen W. Liddle, Yiu-Kai Ng, Dallan Quass, and Randy D. Smith, "Conceptual-model-based data extraction from multiple-record web pages," *Data Knowledge Engineering*, vol. 31, no. 3, pp. 227–251, 1999.
12. David W. Embley, "Toward semantic understanding: an approach based on information extraction ontologies," in *CRPIT '04: Proceedings of the fifteenth conference on Australasian database*, Darlinghurst, Australia, Australia, 2004, pp. 3–12, Australian Computer Society, Inc.
13. Mary Elaine Califf, "Relational learning techniques for natural language extraction," Tech. Rep. AI98-276, University of Texas, 1 1998.
14. Stephen Soderland, "Learning information extraction rules for semi-structured and free text," *Machine Learning*, vol. 34, no. 1-3, pp. 233–272, 1999.
15. Fabio Ciarvegna, "(lp)2, an adaptative algorithm from information extraction from web-related texts," in *Proceedings of the IJCAI-2001 Workshop on Adaptative Text Extraction and Mining*. IJCAI-2001, August 2001.
16. A. Laender B., Ribeiro-Neto, A. da Silva, and J. Teixeira, "A brief survey of web data extraction tools," *SIGMOD Record*, vol. 31, no. (2), pp. 84–93, 2002.
17. Neil Ireson, Fabio Ciarvegna, Marie Elaine Califf, Dayne Freitag, Nicholas Kushmerick, and Alberto Lavelli, "Evaluating machine learning for information extraction," in *Proceedings of the 22nd International Conference on Machine Learning (ICML 2005)*. IJCAI-2001, August 2005.
18. Soraya Abad-Mota and Eduardo Ruiz, "Experiments in information extraction," in *To appear in the Proceedings of the 2006 Information Resources Management Association International Conference*, Mehdi Khosrow-Pour, Ed. IRMA, 2006, Idea Group Publishing.
19. Amihai Motro, "Integrity = validity + completeness," *ACM Transactions on Database Systems*, vol. 14, no. 4, pp. 481–502, december 1989.
20. George Andrei Mihaila, *Publishing, Locating, and Querying Networked Information Sources*, Ph.D. thesis, University of Toronto, 2000.
21. Igor Rakov, "Quality of information in relational databases and its use for reconciling inconsistent answers in multidatabases. electronic document, citeseer.ist.psu.edu/133297.html," .

22. Soraya Abad-Mota, "Approximate query processing with summary tables in statistical databases," in *Proceedings of the 3rd International Conference on Extending Database Technology, Advances in Database Technology - EDBT '92. Vienna, Austria.* March 1992, number 580 in Lecture Notes in Computer Science, pp. 499–515, Springer-Verlag.
23. Mokrane Bouzeghoub and Verónika Peralta, "A framework for analysis of data freshness," in *IQIS '04: Proceedings of the 2004 international workshop on Information quality in information systems*, New York, NY, USA, 2004, pp. 59–67, ACM Press.
24. Amihai Motro and Igor Rakov, *Flexible query answering systems*, chapter Not all answers are equally good: estimating the quality of database answers, pp. 1–21, Kluwer Academic Publishers, Norwell, MA, USA, 1997.

The Importance of Algebra for XML Query Processing

Stelios Paparizos* and H.V. Jagadish*

University of Michigan, Ann Arbor, MI, USA
{spapariz, jag}@umich.edu

Abstract. Relational algebra has been a crucial foundation for relational database systems, and has played a large role in enabling their success. A corresponding XML algebra for XML query processing has been more elusive, due to the comparative complexity of XML, and its history. We argue that having a sound algebraic basis remains important nonetheless. In this paper, we show how the complexity of XML can be modeled effectively in a simple algebra, and how the conceptual clarity attained thereby can lead to significant benefits.

1 Introduction

XML is in wide use today, in large part on account of its flexibility in allowing repeated and missing sub-elements. However, this flexibility makes it challenging to develop an XML data management system.

The first XML enabled systems used a native navigational model to query documents. They showed a lot of promise and the interest shifted into them. In such model, an XML document is first loaded into memory as one big tree and then path expressions are matched via traversals in this tree. Examples of systems using this model include [2,7,15]. A big limitation of such systems is that the biggest XML document they can process is limited by the amount of physical memory in the system. Since they are essentially instance-at-a-time systems, they have little room for optimization and indices. In general they are known to provide full support of XQuery but poor performance – a traversal for a descendant node can force a search of the entire database.

Another popular approach (perhaps, due to existing system support) was to use relational databases and map XML documents into relations. Such solutions were presented in [1,3,14,16,18]. But these mappings may come at the expense of efficiency and performance since relational databases were not designed for XML data. The data transformation process and the query time can be lengthy. Many expensive operations (e.g. joins) needed to determine structural relationships between elements. Due to the variations possible in parallel elements within XML, and the possibility of repeated and missing sub-elements, the mapping becomes non-trivial, and frequently requires liberal use of null values or of un-normalized relations. Overall, with relational support for XML expressiveness is not the issue - with sufficient effort, many mappings are possible. The issue is how natural the mapping is, how well it preserves the original structure and how expensive the resulting relational expressions can be to evaluate.

The solution to this problem would be to use a native XML system while taking advantage of the knowledge of many years of research in the relational world. For example, one of the lessons we learned is that for efficiency purposes, it is essential to use

* Supported in part by NSF, under grant IIS-0208852.

T. Grust et al. (Eds.): EDBT 2006 Workshops, LNCS 4254, pp. 126–135, 2006.

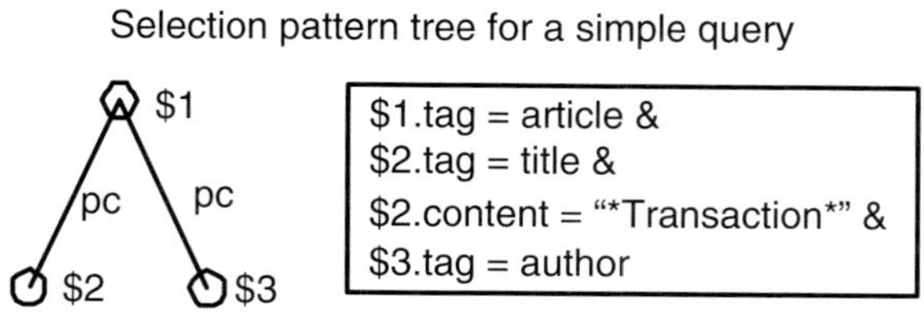

Fig. 1. A pattern tree corresponding to the query 'Select articles with some author and with title that contains Transaction'

'set-at-a-time' processing instead of 'instance-at-a-time'. We also know that the careful choice of evaluation plan can make orders of magnitude difference in query cost. And finally, the relational algebra is long recognized as a useful intermediate form in query processing. From all of the above we conclude that a set-oriented bulk algebra is essential in XML query processing.

Yet, although native algebraic solutions appear to be the better system approach (with significant existing efforts like those in [6,17]), there is no universally accepted XML algebra. In this paper we present our algebraic XML solution and demonstrate its strengths. We start by introducing our basis, the pattern trees and show a Tree Algebra for XML in Section 2. We continue with a discussion in XML and XQuery order related issues in Section 3. Then we show some practical advances in XML algebras in Section 4 and some optimization opportunities that arise in Section 5. We conclude the paper with a few final words in Section 6.

2 Ideal Algebra - Tree Algebra for XML

In the relational model, a tuple is the basic unit of operation and a relation is a set of tuples. In XML, a database is often described as a forest of rooted node-labeled trees. Hence, for the basic unit and central construct of our algebra, we choose an *XML query pattern* (or *twig*), which is represented as a rooted node-labeled tree. An example of such tree, we call it *pattern tree*, is shown in Figure 1. An edge in such tree represents a structural inclusion relationship, between the elements represented by the respective pattern tree nodes. The inclusion relationship can be specified to be either immediate (parent-child relationship) or of arbitrary depth (ancestor-descendant relationship). Nodes in the pattern tree usually have associated conditions on tag names or content values.

Given an XML database and a query pattern, the *witness trees* (pattern tree matchings) of the query pattern against the database are a forest such that each witness tree consists of a vector of data nodes from the database, each matches to one pattern tree node in the query pattern, and the relationships between the nodes in the database satisfy the desired structural relationship specified by the edges in the query pattern. The set of witness trees obtained from a pattern tree match are all structurally identical. Thus, a pattern tree match against a variegated input can be used to generate a structurally homogeneous input to an algebraic operator. Sample of witness trees can be found in Figure 2.

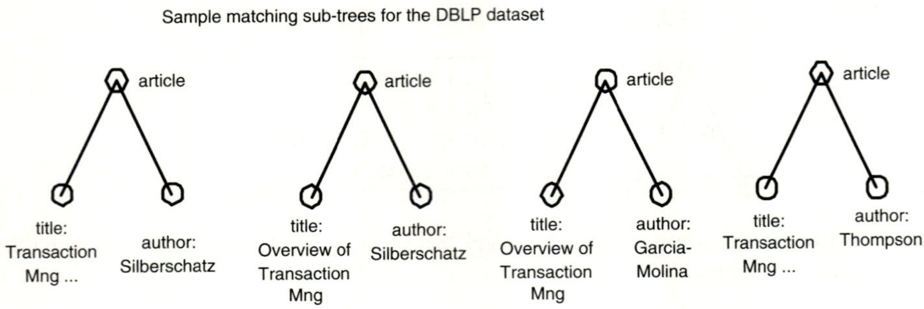

Fig. 2. A sample of the resulting witness trees produced from the matching of the tree in Figure 1 to the DBLP dataset

1. ORDER BY clause,
   explicit, depends on value.
2. Re-establish original document order,
   implicit, required by XML .
3. Binding order of variables,
   implicit, depends on variable binding predicates.

Fig. 3. Ordering Requirements for XML and XQuery

Using this basic primitives, we developed an algebra, called *Tree Algebra for XML* (TAX), for manipulating XML data modeled as forests of labeled ordered trees. Motivated both by aesthetic considerations of intuitiveness, and by efficient computability and amenability to optimization, we developed TAX as a natural extension of relational algebra, with a small set of operators. TAX is complete for relational algebra extended with aggregation, and can express most queries expressible in popular XML query languages. Details about the algebra, with illustrative examples can be found in [5].

3 Ordering and Duplicates

XML itself incorporates semantics in the order data is specified. XML queries have to respect that and produce results based on the order of the original document. XQuery takes this concept even further and adds an extra implicit ordering requirement. The order of the generated output is sensitive to the order the variable binding occurred in the query, we call this notion *'binding order'*. Additionally, a FLWOR statement in XQuery may include an explicit *ORDERBY* clause, specifying the ordering of the output based on the value of some expression – this is similar in concept with ordering in the relational world and SQL. To facilitate our discussion we summarize the XML and XQuery order properties in Figure 3.

Although XML and XQuery require ordering, many "database-style" applications could not care less about order. This leaves the query processing engine designer in a quandary: should order be maintained, as required by the semantics, irrespective of

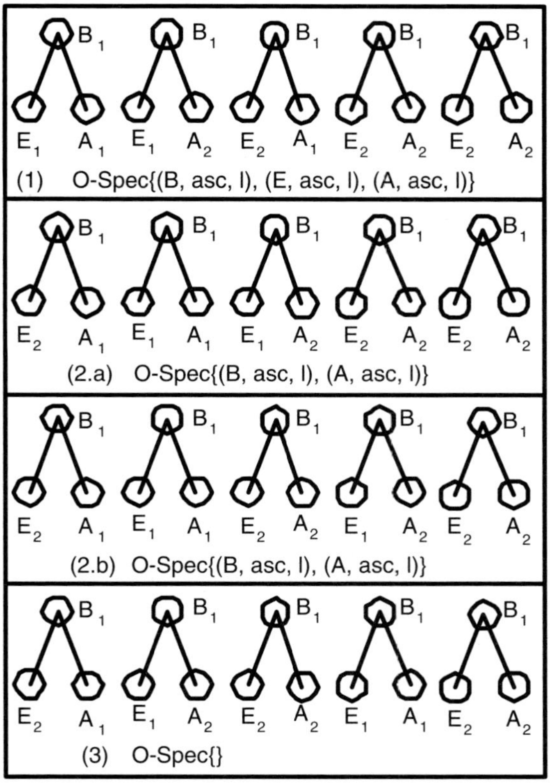

Fig. 4. Collections with Ordering Specification O-Spec. A "fully-ordered" collection in (1), two variations of a "partially-ordered" collection in (2.a) and (2.b) and an unordered collection in (3). Duplicates are allowed in these examples, so (3) is not a set.

the additional cost; or can order be ignored for performance reasons. What we would like is an engine where we pay the cost to maintain order when we need it, and do not incur this overhead when it is not necessary. In algebraic terms, the question we ask is whether we are manipulating sets, which do not establish order among their elements, or manipulating sequences, which do.

The solution we propose is to define a new generic *Hybrid Collection* type, which could be a set or a sequence or even something else. We associate with each collection an *Ordering Specification O-Spec* that indicates precisely what type of order, if any, is to be maintained in this collection.

As an example, in Figure 4, we can see a few ordered collections using the *Ordering Specification*. A simple sorting procedure using all `B` nodes (identifiers), sorting them in ascending order and placing all empty entries in the beginning is described by (B, asc, l). In part (1) of the Figure we see a "fully-ordered" collection; all the nodes in every tree were used to perform the sort. A "fully-ordered" collection has one and only one way that the trees can be ordered (absolute order). In parts (2.a) and (2.b) we see

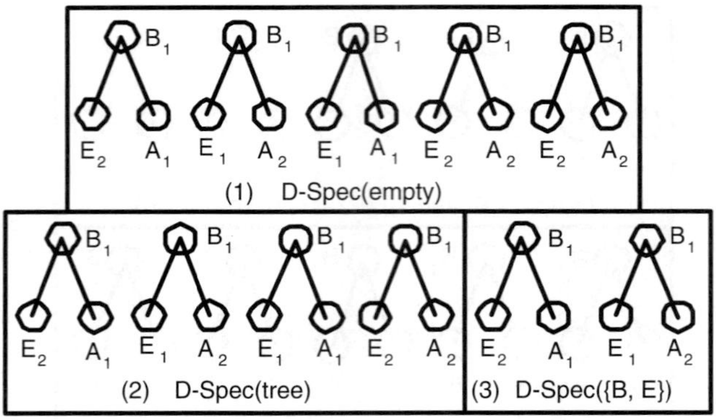

Fig. 5. Collections of trees coupled with their Duplicate Specification D-Spec. All types of duplicates are allowed in (1), deep-tree comparison is used to eliminate duplicates in (2) and duplicates are eliminated in (3) using a partial comparison on B and E nodes. Both (2) and (3) can be thought as sets since no duplicates exist.

the same "partially-ordered" collection; only nodes in parts of every tree were used to perform the sort. A "partially-ordered" collection can potentially have multiple ways it can be ordered. Parts (2.a) and (2.b) show the same collection ordered by the same key with clearly more than one representations of the absolute tree order. In part (3) we see a collection with unspecified order (any order).

Duplicates in collections are also a topic of interest, not just for XML, but for relational data as well. In relational query processing, duplicate removal is generally considered expensive, and avoided where possible even though relational algebra formally manipulates sets that do not admit duplicates.The more complex structure of XML data raises more questions of what is equality and what is a duplicate. Therefore there is room for more options than just sets and multi-sets. Our solution is to extend the *Hybrid Collection* type with an explicit *Duplicate Specification D-Spec* as well.

An example of collections with *D-Spec* describing how duplicates were previously removed from them can be found in Figure 5. Notice the duplicates that exist in part (1), how the last tree from (1) is removed in part (2) and how multiple trees are removed in part (3).

Using our Hybrid Collections we extended our algebra. Thus, we were able to develop query plans that maintain as little order as possible during query execution, while producing the correct query results and managing to optimize duplicate elimination steps. Formal definitions of our collections, extensions to algebraic operations along with the algorithm for correct order can be found in [12]. We believe our approach can be adopted in any XML algebra, providing correctness and flexibility.

4 Tree Logical Classes (TLC) for XML

XQuery semantics frequently requires that nodes be clustered based on the presence of specified structural relationships. For example the RETURN clause requires the

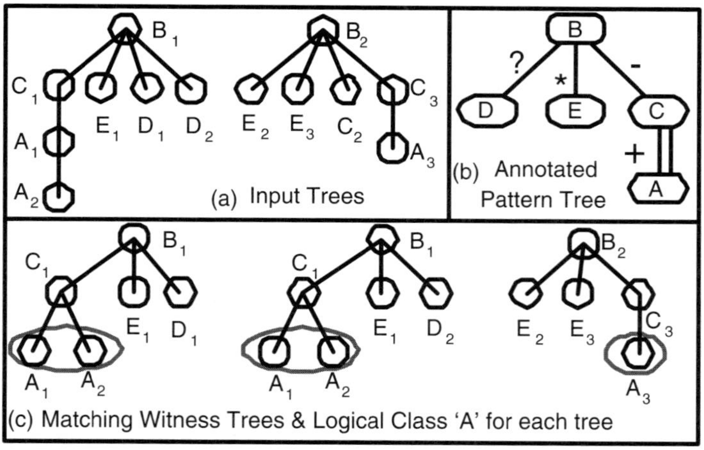

Fig. 6. A sample match for an Annotated Pattern Tree

complete subtree rooted at each qualifying node. A traditional pattern tree match returns a set of 'flat' witness trees satisfying the pattern, thus requiring a succeeding grouping step on the parent (or root) node. Additionally, in tree algebras, each algebraic operator typically performs its own pattern tree match, redoing the same selection time and time again. Intermediate results may lose track of previous pattern matching information and can no longer identify data nodes that match to a specific pattern tree node in an earlier operator. This redundant work is unavoidable for operators that require a homogeneous set as their input without the means for that procedure to persist.

The loss of *Structural Clustering*, the *Redundant Accesses* and the *Redundant Tree Matching* procedures are problems caused due to the witness trees having to be similar to the input pattern tree, i.e. have the same size and structure. This requirement resulted in homogeneous witness trees in an inherently heterogeneous XML world with missing and repeated sub-elements, thus requiring extra work to reconstruct the appropriate structure when needed in a query plan. Our solution uses *Annotated Pattern Trees (APTs)* and *Logical Classes (LCs)* to overcome that limitation.

Annotated Pattern Trees accept edge matching specifications that can lift the restriction of the traditional one-to-one relationship between pattern tree node and witness tree node. These specifications can be "-" (exactly one), "?" (zero or one),"+" (one or more) and "*" (zero or more). Figure 6 shows the example match for an annotated pattern tree. The figure illustrates how annotated pattern trees address heterogeneity on both dimensions (height and width) using variations of annotated edges. So A_1, A_2 and E_2, E_3 are matched into clustered siblings due to the "+" and "*" edges in the APT. On the flip side D_1, D_2 matchings will produce two witness trees for the first input tree (the second tree is let through, although there is no D matching) due to the "?" edge in the APT.

Once the pattern tree match has occurred we must have a logical method to access the matched nodes without having to reapply a pattern tree matching or navigate to them. For example, if we would like to evaluate a predicate on (some attribute of) the

```
FOR $a IN distinct-values(document("bib.xml")//author)
RETURN
   <authorpubs>
      { $a }
      {FOR $b IN document("bib.xml")//article
         WHERE $a = $b/author
         RETURN $b/title}
   </authorpubs>
```

Fig. 7. Query 1: Group by *author* query (After XQuery use case 1.1.9.4 Q4)

"A" node in Figure 6, how can we say precisely which node we mean? The solution to his problem is provided by our Logical Classes. Basically, each node in an annotated pattern tree is mapped to a set of matching nodes in *each* resulting witness tree – such set of nodes is called a *Logical Class*. For example in Figure 6, the red(gray) circle indicates how the A nodes form a logical class for each witness tree. Every node in every tree in any intermediate result is marked as member of at least one logical class[1]. We also permit predicates on logical class membership as part of an annotated pattern tree specification, thus allowing operators late in the plan to reuse pattern tree matches computed earlier.

Using this techniques we extended TAX into our *Tree Logical Class* (TLC) algebra. We discuss our operators and our translation algorithm for XQuery to TLC along with other details in [13]. We base our discussion on our physical algebra seen in [11].

5 Algebraic Optimizations

In this section we demonstrate some of the advantages we get by using algebraic primitives to produce more efficient solutions. We discuss how we address grouping in XQuery and also show some algebraic rewrites that focus on smart placement of ordering and duplicate operations.

Grouping: While SQL allows for grouping operations to be specified explicitly, XQuery provides only implicit methods to write such queries. For example consider a query that seeks to output, for each `author`, `titles` of `articles` he or she is an `author` of (in a bibliography database). A possible XQuery statement for this query is shown in Figure 7. A direct implementation of this query as written would involve two distinct retrievals from the bibliography database, one for `authors` and one for `articles`, followed by a join. Yet, one of our basic primitives of our algebra is a GROUPBY operator, thus enabling us to produce a 'smarter' plan than the one dictated by XQuery.

The procedure uses a rewrite that operates in the following way. In the beginning, the parser will 'naïvely' try to interpret the query from Figure 7 as a join following the logic specified in XQuery. Then a rewrite will transform the plan into a more efficient

[1] Base data, read directly from the database, has no such association.

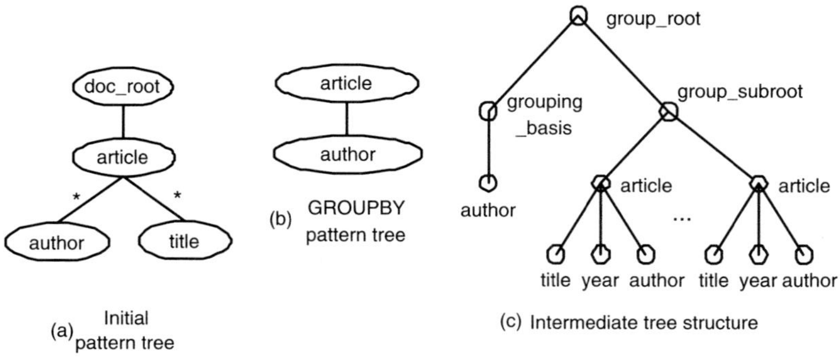

Fig. 8. GROUPBY rewrite for Query 1

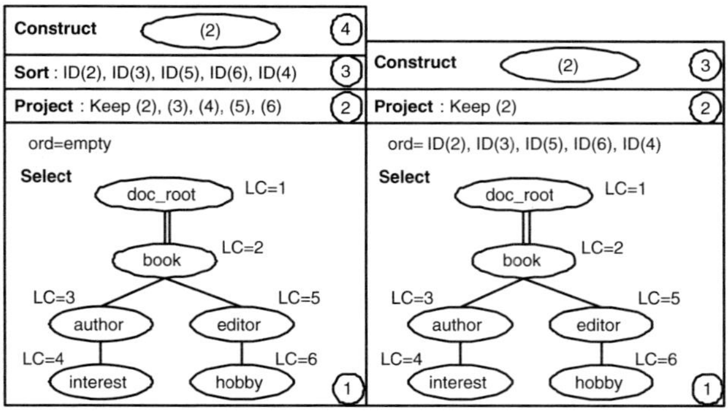

Fig. 9. On the right the rewritten plan having pushed the *Sort* into the *Select*

one using the GROUPBY operator. First, a selection will be applied on the database using the pattern tree of Figure 8.a followed by a projection. This will produce a collection of trees containing all `article` elements and their `author` and `title` children. Next the input pattern tree to be used by the GROUPBY operator will be generated. For Query 1 this is shown at Figure 8.b. The GROUPBY operator (grouping basis : *author*) will be applied on the generated collection of trees and the intermediate tree structures in Figure 8.c are produced. Finally a projection is done keeping only the necessary nodes.

The power of the algebra allows for the transformation of the 'naïve' join plan into a more efficient query plan using grouping – overcoming the XQuery nuances and making it similar to a relational query asking for the same information. Details of the rewrite algorithm along with more complex scenarios can be found in [10].

Duplicates and Ordering: As we discussed in Section 3, smart operation placement of ordering and duplicate elimination procedures can cause orders of magnitude difference in evaluation performance. We show two examples of such rewrites. Details for both techniques along with other examples are found in [12].

We start by showing an example on how we optimize ordering in Figure 9. The rewrite takes advantage of our extended operations that use *Ordering Specification*

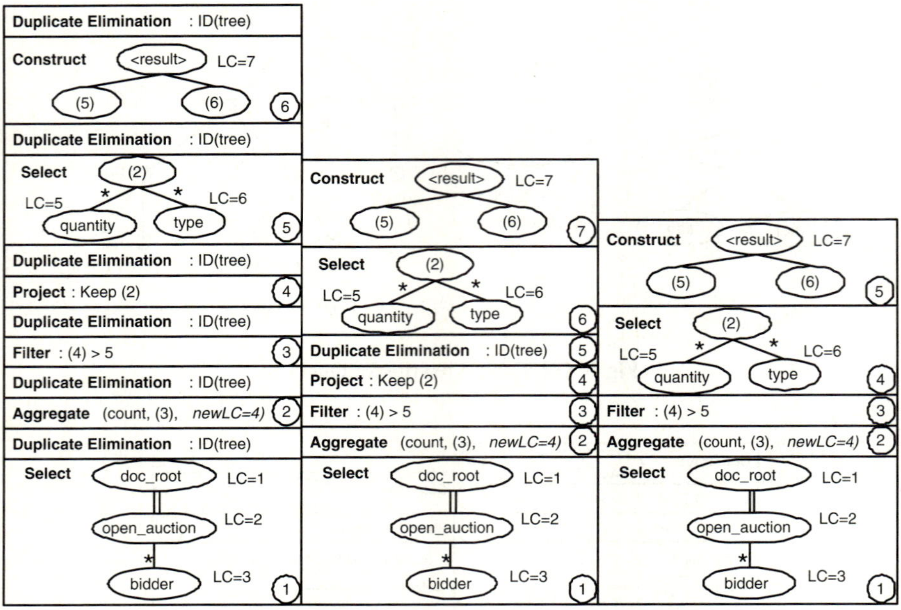

Fig. 10. Minimizing Duplicate Elimination procedures

annotations to push the `Sort` procedure into the original `Select`. Thus, the rewrite provides the cost based optimizer with the means to efficiently plan the pattern tree match using the appropriate physical access methods, without having to satisfy a blocking `Sort` operation at the final step of the query plan.

Additionally, we show an example on how duplicate elimination procedures can be minimized in Figure 10. First, we 'naïvely' force a duplicate elimination after every operation to produce the correct behavior. Then our technique detects and removes all redundant procedures by checking which operations will potentially produce duplicates. With the last step, we take advantage of our 'partial' duplicate collections and manage to remove the duplicate elimination procedure completely.

6 Final Words

The flexibility of XML poses a significant challenge to query processing: it is hard to perform set-oriented bulk operations on heterogeneous sets. In this paper, we proposed our algebraic framework as an effective means to address this problem. We introduced the *Pattern Tree* as the basic unit of operations and developed an algebra that consumes and produces collections of trees in TAX. We discussed how we address efficiently the very complex ordering requirements of XML and XQuery using our *Hybrid Collections*. We showed some practical extensions to tree algebras with the *Annotated Pattern Trees* and *Logical Classes* of TLC. Finally, we hinted on some optimization opportunities that arise with the use of algebra.

It is our belief that a good algebra is central to a good database system, whether relational or XML. The algebraic infrastructure we described in this paper is the basis for the TIMBER [4,8,9] native XML database system developed at the University of Michigan. The experience we gained from implementing our system strengthens our belief in an algebraic approach. We hope in the near future the XML community can converge on an algebra that combines the best characteristics of the various proposed solutions and provides an alternative formal representation of XQuery.

References

1. D. DeHaan, D. Toman, M. P. Consens, and M. T. Ozsu. A comprehensive XQuery to SQL translation using dynamic interval encoding. In *Proc. SIGMOD Conf.*, Jun. 2003.
2. T. Fiebig, S. Helmer, C.-C. Kanne, G. Moerkotte, J. Neumann, R. Schiele, and T. Westmann. Anatomy of a native XML base management system. *VLDB Journal*, 11(4), 2002.
3. D. Florescu and D. Kossman. Storing and querying XML data using an RDMBS. *IEEE Data Eng. Bull.*, 22(3), 1999.
4. H. V. Jagadish, S. Al-Khalifa, A. Chapman, L. V. S. Lakshmanan, A. Nierman, S. Paparizos, J. M. Patel, D. Srivastava, N. Wiwatwattana, Y. Wu, and C.Yu. TIMBER: A native XML database. *VLDB Journal*, 11(4), 2002.
5. H. V. Jagadish, L. V. S. Lakshmanan, D. Srivastava, and K. Thompson. TAX: A tree algebra for XML. In *Proc. DBPL Conf.*, Sep. 2001.
6. B. Ludascher, Y. Papakonstantinou, and P. Velikhov. Navigation-driven evaluation of virtual mediated views. In *Proc. EDBT Conf.*, Mar. 2000.
7. J. McHugh, S. Abiteboul, R. Goldman, D. Quass, and J. Widom. Lore: A database management system for semistructured data. *SIGMOD Record*, 26(3), 1997.
8. U. of Michigan. The TIMBER project. `http://www.eecs.umich.edu/db/timber`.
9. S. Paparizos, S. Al-Khalifa, A. Chapman, H. V. Jagadish, L. V. S. Lakshmanan, A. Nierman, J. M. Patel, D. Srivastava, N. Wiwatwattana, Y. Wu, and C. Yu. TIMBER: A native system for quering XML. In *Proc. SIGMOD Conf.*, Jun. 2003.
10. S. Paparizos, S. Al-Khalifa, H. V. Jagadish, L. V. S. Lakshmanan, A. Nierman, D. Srivastava, and Y. Wu. Grouping in XML. *Lecture Notes in Computer Science*, 2490:128–147, 2002. Presented at EBDT'02 workshop on XML data management.
11. S. Paparizos, S. Al-Khalifa, H. V. Jagadish, A. Nierman, and Y. Wu. A physical algebra for XML. `http://www.eecs.umich.edu/db/timber/`, Technical Report, 2002.
12. S. Paparizos and H. V. Jagadish. Pattern tree algebras: sets or sequences? In *Proc. VLDB Conf.*, 2005.
13. S. Paparizos, Y. Wu, L. V. S. Lakshmanan, and H. V. Jagadish. Tree logical classes for efficient evaluation of XQuery. In *Proc. SIGMOD Conf.*, Jun. 2004.
14. J. Shanmugasundaram, K. Tufte, C. Zhang, G. He, D. J. DeWitt, and J. F. Naughton. Relational databases for querying XML documents: Limitations and opportunities. In *Proc. VLDB Conf.*, 1999.
15. J. Simeon and M. F. Fernandez. Galax, an open implementation of XQuery. `http://db.bell-labs.com/galax/`.
16. I. Tatarinov, S. Viglas, K. Beyer, J. Shanmugasundaram, E. Shekita, and C. Zhang. Storing and querying ordered XML using a relational database system. In *Proc. SIGMOD Conf.*, 2002.
17. S. D. Viglas, L. Galanis, D. J. DeWitt, D. Maier, and J. F. Naughtonn. Putting XML query algebras into context. `http://www.cs.wisc.edu/niagara/`.
18. X. Zhang, B. Pielech, and E. A. Rundensteier. Honey, i shrunk the XQuery! — an XML algebra optimization approach. In *Workshop on Web Information and Data Management*, 2002.

Hash-Based Structural Join Algorithms

Christian Mathis and Theo Härder

University of Kaiserslautern
Database and Information Systems, D-67653 Kaiserslautern, Germany
{mathis, haerder}@informatik.uni-kl.de

Abstract. Algorithms for processing Structural Joins embody essential building blocks for XML query evaluation. Their design is a difficult task, because they have to satisfy many requirements, e. g., guarantee linear worst-case runtime; generate sorted, duplicate-free output; adapt to fiercely varying input sizes and element distributions; enable pipelining; and (probably) more. Therefore, it is not possible to design *the* structural join algorithm. Rather, the provision of different specialized operators, from which the query optimizer can choose, is beneficial for query efficiency. We propose new hash-based structural joins that can process unordered input sequences possibly containing duplicates. We also show that these algorithms can substantially reduce the number of sort operations on intermediate results for (complex) tree structured queries (twigs).

1 Introduction

Because XML data is based on a tree-structured data model, it is natural to use path and tree patterns for the search of structurally related XML elements. Therefore, expressions specifying those patterns are a common and frequently used idiom in many XML query languages and their effective evaluation is of utmost importance for every XML query processor. A particular path pattern—the *twig*—has gained much attention in recent publications, because it represents a small but frequently used class of queries, for which effective evaluation algorithms have been found [1,3,7,11,14,16].

Basically, a twig, as depicted in Fig. 1, is a small tree, whose nodes n represent simple predicates p_n on the content (text) or the structure (elements) of an XML document, whereas its edges define the relationship between the items to match. In the graphical notation, we use the double line for the descendant and the single line for the child relationship. For twig query matching, the query processor has to find all possible embeddings of the given twig in the queried document, such that each node corresponds to an XML item and the defined relationship among the matched items is fulfilled. The result of a twig is represented as an ordered[1] sequence of tuples, where the fields of each tuple

a) **Queries**
Q1) //book[title="XML"]//author[.//city="Rome"]/name
Q2) **for** $b **in** //book, $a **in** $b//author
where $b//title="XML" **and** $a//city="Rome"
return ($a, $a/name)

b) **Twig for Q1 and Q2**

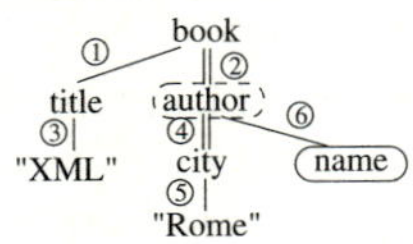

Fig. 1. Sample Query and Twig

[1] Here, "ordered" means: sorted in document order from the root to the leaf items.

T. Grust et al. (Eds.): EDBT 2006 Workshops, LNCS 4254, pp. 136–149, 2006.

correspond to matched items. Usually, not all nodes of a twig generate output, but are mere (path) predicates. Therefore, we use the term *extraction point* [7] to denote twig nodes that do generate output (the boxed nodes in Fig. 1).

1.1 Related Work

For twig query matching, a large class of effective methods builds on two basic ideas: the *structural join* [1] and the *holistic twig join* [3]. The first approach decomposes the twig into a set of binary join operations, each applied to neighbor nodes of the twig (for an example, see Fig. 2). The result of a single join operation is a sequence of tuples S_{out} whose degree (number of fields) is equal to the sum of the degrees of its input tuples from sequences S_{inA} and S_{inB}. S_{out} may serve as an input sequence for further join operations. In the following, we denote the tuple fields that correspond to the twig nodes to join as the *join fields*. The underlying structural join algorithms are interchangeable and subject to current research (see the discussion below).

In [3], the authors argue that, intrinsic for the structural join approach, intermediate result sizes may get very large, even if the final result is small, because the intermediate result has to be unnested. In the worst case, the size of an intermediate result sequence is in the order of the product of the sizes of the input sequences. To remedy this drawback, twig join algorithms [3,7] evaluate the twig as a whole, avoiding intermediate result unnesting by encoding the qualifying elements on a set of stacks.

Of course, holistic twig join algorithms are good candidates for physical operators supporting query evaluation in XDBMSs. However, they only provide for a small fraction of the functionality required by complete XPath and XQuery processors (e. g., no processing of axes other than *child* and *descendant*; no processing of order-based queries). Therefore, the development of new structural join algorithms is still valuable, because they can act as complemental operators in case the restricted functionality of twig joins is too small, or as alternatives if they promise faster query evaluation.

Existing structural join approaches can roughly be divided into four classes by the requirements they pose on their input sequences: A) *no requirements* [8,11,14]; B) *indexed input* [16], C) *sorted input* [1,10,16]; D) *indexed and sorted input* [4]. Especially for classes C and D, efficient algorithms have been found that generate results in linear time depending on the size of their input lists. In contrast, for class A, there is—to the best of our knowledge—no such algorithm. All proposed approaches either sort at least one input sequence [11], or create an in-memory data structure (a heap) requiring $O(nlog_2n)$ processing steps [14]. By utilizing hash tables that can be built and probed in (nearly) linear time, the algorithms we introduce in this paper can remedy this problem. Note, the strategies in [11,14] elaborate on partition-based processing schemes, i. e., they assume a small amount of main memory and large input sequences, requiring their partition-wise processing. Their core join algorithm, however, is main-memory–based, as ours is. Therefore, our new join operators can be—at least theoretically[2]—combined with the partitioning schemes proposed in these earlier works.

[2] [14] uses a perfect binary tree (PBiTree) to generate XML identifiers. In real-world scenarios, we assume document modifications that can hardly be handled with PBiTrees. Therefore, we used SPLIDs (Sect. 2.1) instead. As a consequence, this "gap" had to be bridged to support the proposed partition schemes with our ideas.

Answering twig (and more complex queries) using binary structural join algorithms imposes three non-trivial problems: selecting the best (cheapest) join order (*P1*) to produce a sorted (*P2*) and duplicate-free (*P3*) output. P1 is tackled in [15], where a dynamic programming framework is presented that produces query executions plans (QEPs) based on cost estimations. The authors assume class C (and D) algorithms, which means that even intermediate results are required to be in document order on the two join fields. As a consequence, sort operators have to be embedded into a plan to fulfill this requirement. Consider for example the twig in Fig. 1. Let the circled numbers denote the join order selected by an algorithm from [15]. Then, three sort operators have to be embedded into the QEP (see[3] Fig. 2). Sort operators are expensive and should be avoided whenever possible. With structural join algorithms not relying on a special input order—like those presented in this paper—we can simply omit the sort operators in this plan. However, a final sort may still be necessary in some cases.

Problem P3 was studied in [8]. The authors show that duplicate removal is also important for intermediate results, because otherwise, the complexity of query evaluation depending on the number of joins for a query Q can lead to an exponential worst-case runtime behavior. Therefore, for query evaluation using binary structural joins, tuplewise duplicate-free intermediate result sequences have to be assured after each join execution. Note, due to result unnesting, even a (single) field in the tuple may contain duplicates. This circumstance is unavoidable and, thus, we have to cope with it. Because duplicate removal—like the sort operator—is an expensive operation, it should be minimized. For example in [6], the authors present an automaton that rewrites a QEP for Q, thereby removing unnecessary sort and duplicate removal operations. Their strategy is based on plans generated by normalization of XPath expressions, resulting in the XPath core language expressions. However, this approach does not take join reordering into account, as we do. Our solution to P3 is a class of algorithms that do not produce any duplicates if their input is duplicate free.

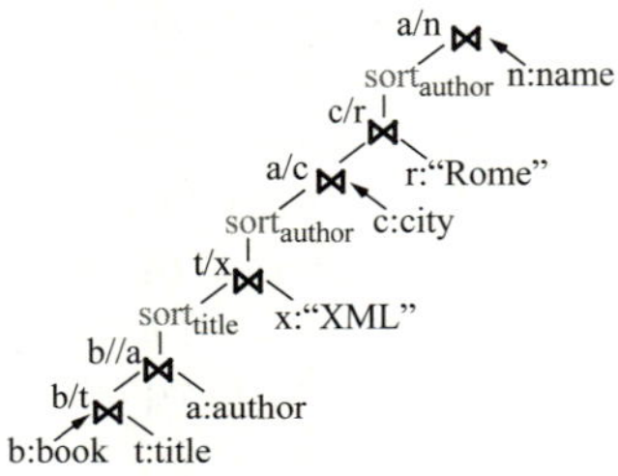

Fig. 2. Sample Plan

1.2 Contribution

We explore the use of hash-based joins for path processing steps of XML queries and identify the selectivity ranges when they are beneficial. In particular, we propose a class of hash-based binary structural join operators for the axes *parent*, *child*, *ancestor*, *descendant*, *preceding-sibling*, and *following-sibling* that process unordered input sequences and produce (unordered) duplicate-free output sequences. Furthermore, we show by extensive tests using the XTC (XML Transaction Coordinator)—our prototype of a native XDBMS—that our approach leads to a better runtime performance than sort-based schemes.

The remainder of this paper is organized as follows: Sect. 2 briefly describes some important internals of XTC, namely our node labeling scheme and an access method for

[3] An arrow declares the input node of a join by which the output is ordered, where important. Possible are *root to leaf*, e. g., between "book" and "title", and *leaf to root*, e. g., the final join.

element sequences. Sect. 3 introduces new hash-based algorithms. In Sect. 4 we present our quantitative results before we conclude in Sect. 5.

2 System Testbed

XTC adheres to the well-known layered hierarchical architecture: The concepts of the storage system and buffer management could be adopted from existing relational DBMSs. The access system, however, required new concepts for document storage, indexing, and modification including locking. The data system available only in a slim version is of minor importance for our considerations.

2.1 Path Labels

Our comparison and evaluation of node labeling schemes in [9] recommends node labeling schemes which are based on the Dewey Decimal Classification [5]. The abstract properties of Dewey order encoding—each label represents the path from the documents root to the node and the local order w. r. t. the parent node; in addition, sparse numbering facilitates node insertions and deletions—are described in [13]. Refining this idea, similar labeling schemes were proposed which differ in some aspects such as overflow technique for dynamically inserted nodes, attribute node labeling, or encoding mechanism. Examples of these schemes are ORDPATH [12], DeweyID [9], or DLN [2]. Because all of them are adequate and equivalent for our processing tasks, we prefer to use the substitutional name *stable path labeling identifiers* (SPLIDs) for them.

Here we only summarize the benefits of the SPLID concept which provides holistic system support. Existing SPLIDs are immutable, that is, they allow the assignment of new IDs without the need to reorganize the IDs of nodes present. Comparison of two SPLIDs allows ordering of the respective nodes in document order, as well as the decision of all XPath axis relations. As opposed to competing schemes, SPLIDs easily provide the IDs of all ancestors to enable direct parent/ancestor identification or access. This property is very helpful for navigation and for fine-grained lock management in the XML documents. Finally, the representation of SPLIDs, e. g., label 1.3.7 for a node at level 3 and also used as an index reference to this node, facilitates the application of hashing in our join algorithms.

2.2 Accessing Ordered Element Sequences

A B*-tree is used as a document store where the SPLIDs in inner B*-tree nodes serve as fingerposts to the leaf pages. The set of doubly chained leaf pages forms the so-called document container where the XML tree nodes are stored using the format (SPLID, data) in document order. Important for our discussion, the XDBMS creates an *element index* for each XML document. This index consists of a *name directory* with (potentially) all element names occurring in the XML document

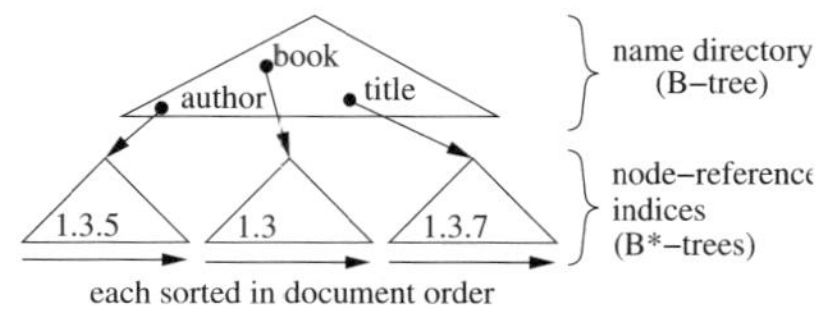

Fig. 3. Element Index

(Fig. 3). For each specific element name, in turn, a *node-reference index* is maintained which addresses the corresponding elements using their SPLIDs. Note, for the document store and the element index, prefix compression of SPLID keys is very effective because both are organized in document order directly reflected by the SPLIDs [9].

The leaf nodes in our QEPs are either element names or values. By accessing the corresponding node reference indexes, we obtain for them ordered lists of SPLIDs and, if required lists of nodes in document order by accessing the document store.

3 Hash-Based Structural Join Algorithms

To be able to compete with existing structural join algorithms, we had to design our new algorithms with special care. In particular, the use of semi-joins has several important benefits. The processing algorithms become simpler and the intermediate result size is reduced (because the absolute byte size is smaller and we avoid unnesting). Several important design objectives can be pointed out:

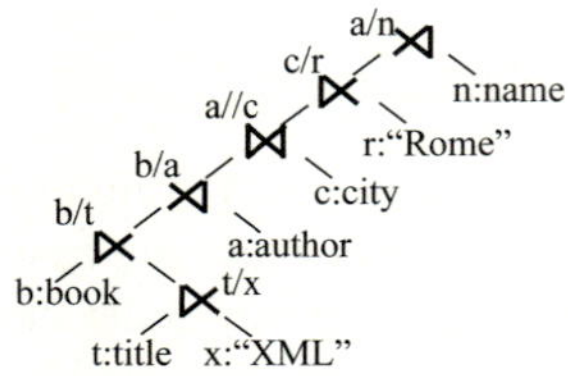

Fig. 4. Plan for Query 1

- *Design single-pass algorithms.* As in almost all other structural join proposals, we have to avoid multiple scans over input sequences.
- *Exploit extraction points.* With knowledge about extraction points, the query optimizer can pick semi-join algorithms instead of full joins for the generation of a QEP. For example, consider the plan in Fig. 4 which embodies one way to evaluate the twig for the XPath expression in Fig. 1. After having joined the *title* elements with the content elements "XML", the latter ones are not needed anymore for the evaluation of the rest of the query; a semi-join suffices.
- *Enable join reordering.* Join reordering is crucial for the query optimizer which should be able to plan the query evaluation with any join order to exploit given data distributions. As a consequence, we need operators for the reverse axes *ancestor* and *parent*, too (e. g., the semi-join operator between *title* and "XML" in Fig. 4 actually calculates the parent axis).
- *Avoid duplicate removal and sort operations whenever possible.* By using only algorithms that do not generate duplicates and operate on unordered input sequences, the query optimizer can ignore these problems. However, the optimizer has to ensure the correct output order, requiring a final sort operator. In some cases, this operator can be skipped: If we assume that the element scans at the leaf nodes of the operator tree in Fig. 4 return the queried element sequences in document order (as, for example, our element index assures), then, because the last semi-join operator is simply a filter for name elements (see Sect. 3.1), the correct output order is automatically established.
- *Design dual algorithms that can hash the smaller input sequence.* The construction of an in-memory hash table is still an expensive operation. Therefore, our set of algorithms should enable the query optimizer to pick an operator that hashes the smaller of both input sequences and probes the other one, yielding the same result.

Table 1. Classification of Hash-Join Operators

Hashed	Output: *ancestor/parent*	*descendant/child*	*full join*
	Class 1: UpStep	Class 2: TopFilter	Class 3: FullTopJoin
parent	//**a**[b]	//**a**/b	//**a**/b, //**a**[b]
	ParHashA	ChildHashA	ChildFullHashA
ancestor	//**a**[.//b]	//**a**//b	//**a**//b, //**a**[.//b]
	AncHashA	DescHashA	DescFullHashA
	Class 4: BottomFilter	Class 5: DownStep	Class 6: FullBottomJoin
child	//a[**b**]	//a/**b**	//a/**b**, //a[**b**]
	ParHashB	ChildHashB	ChildFullHashB
descendant	//a[.//**b**]	//a//**b**	//a//**b**, //a[.//**b**]
	AncHashB	DescHashB	DescFullHashB

3.1 Classification of Algorithms

We can infer three orthogonal degrees of freedom for structural hash-join algorithms: the *axis* that has to be evaluated (*parent/child/ancestor/descendant*); the *mode* of the join (*semi/full*); and the choice of which input sequence to *hash* (*A* or *B*)[4]. The following naming scheme is used for our operators: `<axis> + <mode> + <hash>`: `{Par|Child|Anc|Desc} {Semi|Full} Hash{A|B}` ("Semi" is omitted for brevity). For example, the join operator between *title* and "XML" in Fig. 4 is a `ParHashB` operator, because it calculates the parent axis, is a semi-join operator, and hashes the sequence of possible children.

For an overview of all possible operators refer to Table 1: The column header defines the input to be hashed, whereas the row header defines the output. For clarification of the semantics, each operator is additionally described by an XPath expression where the input sequence to hash is marked in bold face. The names of the operator classes describe the evaluation strategy of the join. They will be discussed in the following. Note, class 1–3 algorithms are dual to class 4–6 algorithms, i. e., they calculate the same result as their corresponding algorithms, but hash a different input sequence.

3.2 Implementation

To abstract from operator scheduling and dataflow control, we let all operators act in the same operating system thread and use the well-known iterator-based *open-next-close* protocol as a basis for the evaluation. Each algorithm receives two input sequences of tuples, where, due to intermediate result unnesting, duplicates on the join fields have to be expected.

All proposed algorithms in this paper consist of two phases. In phase one, a hash table `ht` is constructed using the join field of the tuples of one input sequence (either sequence A or B). In phase 2, the join field of the other input sequence is probed against `ht`. Depending on how a result tuple is constructed, the operators can be assigned to one of the six classes: *Full*Join* operators return a sequence of joined result tuples just as earlier proposals for structural join algorithms (e. g., [1]). Note, the qualifiers "Top" and "Bottom" denote which input sequence is hashed. The remaining classes contain

[4] Note, in the following, *A* denotes the sequence of possible ancestors or parents (depending on the context), whereas *B* denotes descendants or children.

```
Input: TupSeq A,B, Axis aixs, bool hashA
Output: TupSeq results,Local:HashTable ht

1  // phase 1: build hash table
2  if (hashA)
3    foreach (Tuple a in A)
4      hash a.jField() in ht;
5  else if (axis is 'Par' or 'Child')
6    foreach (Tuple b in B)
7      hash b.jField().parent() in ht;
8  else if (axis is 'Anc')
9    List levelOcc = getLevels(A);
10   foreach (Tuple b in B)
11     foreach (level in levelOcc)
12      hash b.jField().anc(level) in ht;
13
14 // phase 2: probe
15 foreach (Tuple t in ((hashA) ? B : A)
16   if (! hashA and
17      t.jField() in ht) results.add(t);
18   else if (axis == 'Child' or 'Par')
19      if (t.jField().parent() in ht)
20       results.add(t);
21
22   else if (axis == 'Desc' or 'Anc')
23     List levelOcc = getLevelsByProb(A);
24     foreach (level in levelOcc)
25       if (t.jField().anc(level) in ht)
26         results.add(t);
27         break inner loop;
28
29 function hashEnqueue
30       (SPLID s, Tuple t, HT ht)
31   Queue q = ht.get(s);
32   q.enqueue(t);
33   hash (s, q) in ht;
34
35 function hashDelete (SPLID s, HT ht)
36   Queue q = ht.get(s);
37   foreach (Tuple t in q)
38     results.add(t);
39   ht.delete(s);
40
41 function hashFull
42       (SPLID s, Tuple current, HT ht)
43   Queue q = ht.get(s);
44   foreach (Tuple t in q)
45     results.add(new Tuple(t, current));
```

Fig. 5. *Filter Operator and Auxiliary Functions for *Step and Full*Join

semi-join algorithms. **Filter* operators use the hash table, constructed for one input sequence to filter the other one, i. e., tuples are only returned from the probed sequence. **Step* operators work the other way around, i. e., they construct the result tuples from the hashed input sequence.

**Filter Operators* (see Fig. 5): In phase one, for `ChildHashA` and `DescHashA`, the algorithm simply hashes the SPLID of the elements of the join fields (accessed via method `jField()`) into `ht` (line 4). Then, in phase two, the algorithm checks for each tuple *t* in B, whether the parent SPLID (line 19 for `ChildHashA`) or any ancestor SPLID (line 25 for `DescHashA`) of the join field is contained in `ht`. If so, *t* is a match and is appended to the result. Actually, for the descendant operator, we had to check all possible ancestor SPLIDs which could be very costly. To narrow down the search, we use the meta-information, at which levels and by which probability an element of the join field of A occurs (line 23). This information can be derived dynamically, e. g., when the corresponding elements are accessed via an element index scan, or kept statically in the document catalog.

The strategy for `ParHashB` and `AncHashB` is similar, with the difference, that in the hash phase the algorithm uses the join fields of input B to precalculate SPLIDs that might occur in A (lines 7 and 12). Again for the descendant operator, we use the level information (line 9), but this time the probability distribution does not matter. In the probing phase it only has to be checked, whether the current join field value is in `ht`.

Obviously, the output order of the result tuples is equal to the order of the probed input sequence. Furthermore, if the probed input sequence is tuplewise duplicate free, the algorithm does not produce any duplicates. The *hashed* input sequence may contain duplicates. However, these are automatically skipped, whereas collisions are internally resolved by the hash table implementation.

**Step Operators* conceptually work in the same way as their corresponding **Filter* operators. However, they do not return tuples from the probed, but from the hashed input sequence. Accordingly, tuples that have duplicates on the *key* they use for hashing (e. g., TupSeq A of Fig. 7a) may not be skipped (as above) but have to be memorized for later output. The new algorithms work as follows: In the hash phase, the function `hashEnqueue()` (Fig. 5 line 29) is called instead of the simple hash statements in lines 4, 7, and 12). The first argument is the SPLID *s* of the join field (or its *parent/ancestor* SPLID). Function hashEnqueue() checks for *s* whether or not an entry is found in hash table `ht` (line 31). If so, the corresponding value, a queue *q*, is returned to which the current tuple is appended (line 32). Finally, *q* is written back into the hash table (line 33).

In the probing phase, we substitute the hash table lookup and result generation (lines 17, 19–20, 25–26) with the `hashDelete()` method (Fig. 5 line 35). For the given SPLID s to probe, this method looks up the corresponding tuple queue in the hash table and adds each contained tuple *t* to the result. Finally, the entry for *s* and its queue are removed from the hash table, because the result tuples have to be returned exactly once to avoid duplicates. The sort order of these algorithms is dictated by the sort order of the input sequence used for probing. If the hashed input sequence did not contain any duplicates, the result is also duplicate free.

The technique to memorize tuples with the same hash key works fine for the step operators `ParHashA`, `ParHashB`, and `AncHashA`. For `DescHashB`, however, the following problem occurs: In phase 1, the algorithm has to anticipate for each node *b* in tuple sequence B, on which level the ancestor nodes in the tuple sequence A can possibly reside. Then—following the technique above—it had to insert *b* into all queues of possible ancestors. As an example, consider the document shown in Fig. 6a and the element with the SPLID 1.3.3.5. In phase 1, the algorithm inserts 1.3.3.5 in the queue for the possible ancestor elements 1.3.3 and 1 (1.3 does not belong to any input). This is not only unfavorable because of the redundant storage of element 1.3.3.5 and the implied higher memory consumption, but it may also lead to duplicates in the final result: in the probing phase, the algorithm 1) *checks* for each *a* in input sequence A, if there is a corresponding tuple queue in the hash table, 2) *appends* all elements in the queue to the result sequence, and 3) *removes* the matched entry from the hash table. In the example, if the algorithm processes the possible ancestor 1.3.3, it would return the result tuple containing 1.3.3.5 and remove this entry for 1.3.3 from the hash table. If later on, possible ancestor 1 is probed, 1.3.3.5 is again returned. Thus, a duplicate would be generated.

To remedy these problems, a distinguished algorithm for the `DescHashB` operator is designed (see Fig. 6c). In the first phase, the operator builds two hash tables, named `htB` and `htA`, instead of only one. Hash table `htB` has the same function as in the other step operators: it keeps track of mappings from possible ancestor elements to queues of possible descendants. To avoid redundant storage, the possible descendant element *b* is only stored in the queue for the anticipated *lowest ancestor element* (line 4 to 6), which corresponds to the SPLID with the highest level that can still be an ancestor of *b*. For example, the tuple corresponding to 1.3.3.5 is only stored in the queue for

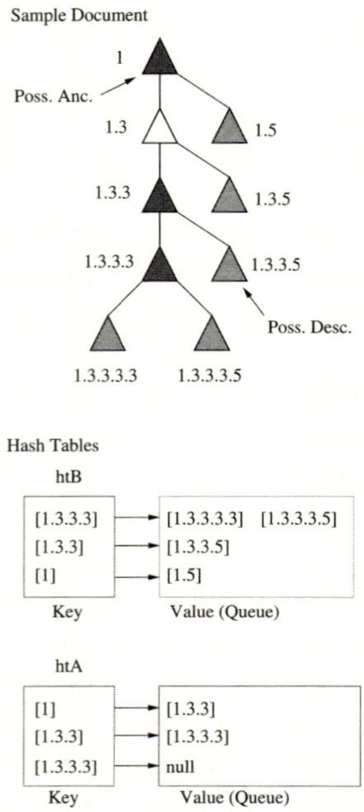


```
Input: TupSeq A,B
Output: TupSeq results
Local: HashTable htB,htA

1  // phase 1: build hash table
2  List levelOcc = getLevels(A);
3  foreach (Tuple b in B)
4    SPLID lowestAnc =
5      b.jField().lowestAnc(levelOcc);
6    hashEnqueue(lowestAnc, b, htB);
7    SPLID highestAnc =
8      b.jField().highestAnc
9                          (levelOcc,htA);
10
11   foreach (level in levelOcc between
12       highestAnc.level() and
13       lowestAnc.level() descending)
14     SPLID ancAnc =
15           b.jField().anc(level);
16     SPLID anc =
17           b.jField().anc(level+1);
18     Queue ancQ = htA.get(ancAnc);
19     ancQ.enqueue(anc);
20     ancQ = htA.get(anc);
21     ancQ.enqueue(null);
22
23 // phase 2: probe
24 foreach (Tuple a in A)
25   hashDelete(a, htB);
26   Queue q = new Queue();
27   q.addAll(htA.get(a.jField());
28   htA.remove(a.jField());
29   while (!q.isEmpty())
30     SPLID id = q.removeFirst();
31     hashDelete(id, htB);
32     q.addAll(htA.get(id));
33     htB.remove(id);
```

Fig. 6. a) Sample Document, b) Hash Tables, c) DescHashB Operator

1.3.3, because 1.3.3 is the anticipated lowest ancestor (the storage of 1.3.3.5 in the queue of element 1 is thus omitted). Then, another hash table (htA) is built which keeps track of ancestor/descendant relationships among the possible ancestor elements. In essence, htA stores a forest of trees. In the example, when element *b*=1.3.3.5 is processed, the key-value pairs (1, 1.3.3) and (1.3.3, null) are inserted into htA. Later on, when for example *b*=1.3.3.3.3 is processed, only the pair (1.3.3, 1.3.3.3) has to be inserted into htA, because the relationship of their ancestors is already contained in htA. This functionality is implemented in lines 7 to 21. First the highest possible ancestor SPLID, whose relationship is not yet contained in htA is computed. This can easily be done by comparing the keys already contained in htA. In the above example, when (1, 1.3.3) and (1.3.3, null) are present in htA, the highest possible ancestor for *b*=1.3.3.3.3 is 1.3.3. Afterwards the structural relationships down to the lowest possible ancestor are inserted into htA (lines 11 to 21).

In the probing phase, the algorithm calls hashDelete() (line 25). I. e., it probes each element a of the ancestor sequence A against htB. If there is a queue for the key a, the found tuples are written to the result and the matched key-value pair is removed from `htB`. For example, the lookup of a=1.3.3 immediately returns the tuple corresponding to 1.3.3.5 and the pair (1.3.3, 1.3.3.5) is removed from `htB`. Because the algorithm has to return *all* descendants, it follows the tree stored in `htA` rooted at a and calls `hashDelete()` for all possible ancestors found (lines 26 to 33). In the example, the algorithm looks up a=1.3.3 in `htA`, finds x=1.3.3.3, and calls hashDelete for x, which returns the descendants 1.3.3.3.3 and 1.3.3.3.5. All touched entries are removed from `htA`. Note, the operator fulfills our requirements: it does not produce any duplicates and can operate on unsorted input sequences.

*Full*Join Operators* resemble the **Step* operators. The only difference is the result generation. While **Step* algorithms are semi-join operators that do not produce a joined result tuple, *Full*Join* operators append the current result tuple with all tuples matched (as depicted in method `hashFull()`, Fig. 5 line 41). Note, opposed to `hashDelete()`, in `hashFull()` no matched entries from `ht`/`htA`/`htB` are deleted. For a brief *full join* example see Fig.7a: input sequence A for the `ChildFullHashA` operator is hashed on join field 1, thereby memorizing tuples with duplicates in the related queues. Then, the tuples from sequence B are probed against the hash table. For each match, each tuple in the queue is joined with the current tuple from B and appended to the result.

Space and Time Complexity. The space complexity (number of tuples stored) and time complexity (number of hashes computed) of the operators depend on the axis to be evaluated. Let $n = |A|$ and $m = |B|$ be the sizes of the input sequences. For the *parent/child* axis, the space and time complexity is $O(n+m)$. For the *ancestor/descendant* axis, the height h of the document also plays a role. Here the space complexity for classes 1–3 is also $O(n + m)$, whereas the time complexity is $O(n + h * m)$ (for each tuple in sequence B up to h hashes have to be computed). For classes 4–6, both space and time complexity are $O(n+h*m)$, except for the `DescHashB` operator, where the time complexity is $O(h * (n + m))$.

Beyond Twig Functionality: Calculation of Sibling Axes. With hash-based schemes and a labeling mechanism enabling the parent identification, the *preceding-sibling* and the *following-sibling* axes are—in contrast to holistic twig join algorithms—computable, too. Due to space restrictions, we can only show filtering algorithms, corresponding to the **Filter* classes above: In phase 1 operators `PreSiblHashA` and `FollSiblHashA` (see Fig. 7b) create a hash table `ht` to store key-value pairs of *parent/child* SPLIDs. For each element in A, parent *p* is calculated. Then the following-sibling (preceding-sibling) axis is evaluated as follows: For each parent SPLID *p*, the smallest (largest) child SPLID *c* in A is stored in `ht`. This hash table instance is calculated by successive calls to the `checkAndHash()` method (lines 14 to 21). While probing a tuple *b* of input B, the algorithm checks whether the SPLID on the join field of *b* is a following-sibling (preceding-sibling) of *c*, that has the same parent (lines 6 to 12). If so, the current *b* tuple is added to the result. Clearly, these algorithms reveal the same characteristics as their corresponding **Filter* algorithms: They do not produce any tuplewise duplicates and preserve the order of input sequence B.

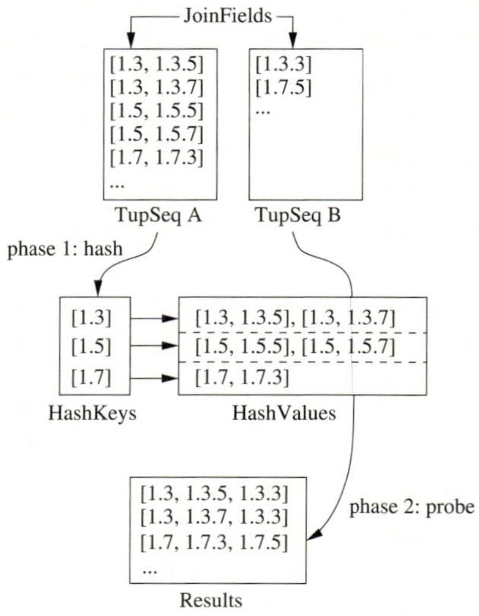


```
Input: TupSeq A, B, Axis aixs
Output: TupSeq results, Local:HashTable ht

// phase 1: build hash table
foreach (Tuple a in A)
  checkAndHash(a.jField(), axis)

// phase 2: probe
foreach (Tuple b in B)
  SPLID s = ht.get(b.parent());
  if( (axis == 'PreSibl' and
       b.jField().isPreSibl(s)) or
      (axis == 'FollSibl' and
       b.jField().isFollSibl(s)) )
    results.add(b);

function checkAndHash(SPLID a, Axis axis)
  SPLID s = ht.get(a.parent());
  if( (s is NULL) or
      (axis == 'PreSibl' and
       not s.isPreSibl(a)) or
      (axis == 'FollSibl' and
       not s.isFollSibl(a)) )
    ht.put(a.parent(), a);
```

Fig. 7. a) Full*Join Example and b) Sibling Operator

4 Quantitative Results

To substantiate our findings, we compared the different algorithms by one-to-one operator comparison on a single-user system. All tests were run on an Intel XEON computer (four 1.5 GHz CPUs, 2 GB main memory, 300 GB external memory, Java Sun JDK 1.5.0) as the XDBMS server machine and a PC (1.4 GHz Pentium IV CPU, 512 MB main memory, JDK 1.5.0) as the client, connected via 100 MBit ethernet to the server.

To test the dependency between runtime performance and query selectivity, we generated a collection of synthetic XML documents, whose structure is sketched in Fig. 8. Each document has a size of 200 MB and contains bibliographic information. Because we were mainly interested in structural join operators for element sequences, the generated documents do not contain much text content. The schema graph is a directed acyclic graph (and not a tree), because an author element may be the child of either a book or an article element. We generated the documents in such a way, that we obtained the following selectivity values for the execution of structural joins between input nodes: 1%, 5%, 10%, 50%, and 100%. For example, for the query `//book[title]`, selectivity 1% means that 1% of all *title* elements have a *book* element as their parent (all others have the *article* element as parent). Additionally, we created 10% noise on each input node, e. g., 10% of all *book* elements have the child *booktitle* instead of *title*.

4.1 Join Selectivity Dependency of Hash-Based Operators

In a first experiment, we want to explore the influence of the join selectivities of the input sequences and, in case of varying input sequence sizes, their sensitivity on the hash operator performance. All operators presented in Table 1 revealed the same performance characteristics as a function of the join selectivity. Hence, it is sufficient to

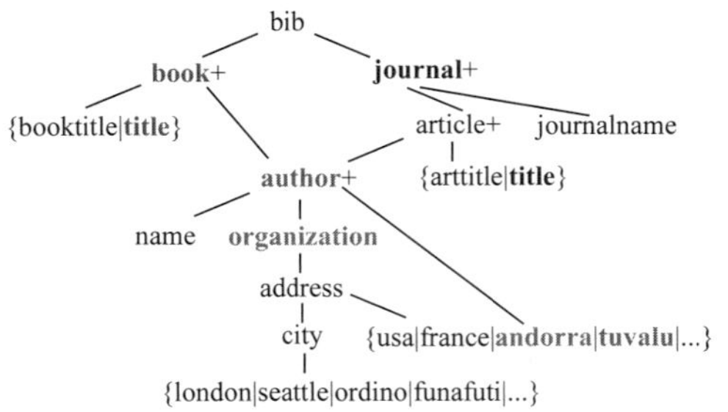

*Filter Queries:
a) `//book[title]` **or** `//book/title`
b) `//journal[.//title]` **or** `//journal//title`

*Step and Full*Join Queries:
a) `//author[tuvalu]` **or** `//author/tuvalu`
b) `//organization[.//andorra]` **or** `//organization//andorra`

Fig. 8. Document Schema and Sample Queries

present an indicative example for which we have chosen the `DescFullHash*` operators. For the query `//journal//title`, the size of the input sequence containing *journal* elements varies from around 2,000 to 200,000 elements, whereas the size of the *title* sequence remains stable (roughly 200,000 elements). Fig. 9a illustrates the runtime performance of the *DescFullHashA* operator and the *DescFullHashB* operator for the same query. For selectivities smaller than 10%, the runtime of each operator remains quite the same, because in these cases external memory access costs for the node reference indexes (column sockets) dominate the execution time, whereas the time for the hash table creation and probing remains roughly the same. However for selectivities > 10%, the runtime increases due to higher CPU costs for hashing and probing of larger input sequences. The gap between the `DescFullHashA` and the `DescFullHashB` operator results from hashing the wrong—i. e., the larger—input sequence (*title*) instead of the smaller one (in operator `DescFullHashB`). Therefore, it is important that the query optimizer chooses the right operator for an anticipated data distribution.

4.2 Hash-Based vs. Sort-Based Schemes

In the next test, we want to identify the performance differences of our hash-based schemes as compared to sort-based schemes. For this purpose, we implemented the

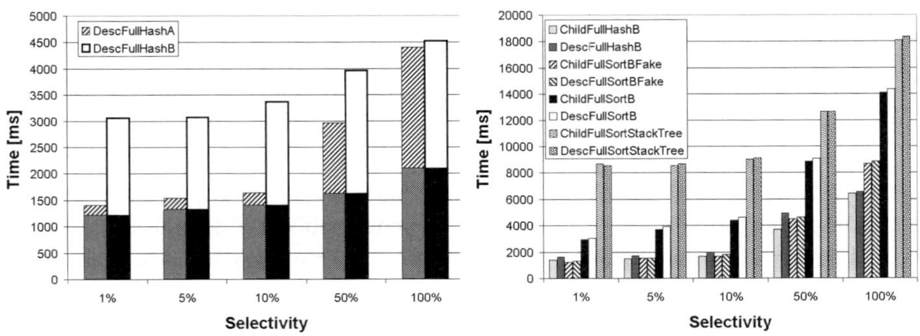

Fig. 9. a) DescFullHash* Characteristics, b) Operator Comparison

StackTree algorithm [1] and the structural join strategy from [14] called *AxisSort** in the following. Both operators work in two phases: In phase 1, input sequences are sorted using the *QuickSort* algorithm. While *StackTree* needs to sort both input sequences, *AxisSort** only needs to sort the smaller one. In phase 2, *StackTree* accomplishes its ordinary join strategy, while *AxisSort** performs a binary search on the sorted input for each element of the other input sequence. To compare our operators with minimal-cost sort-based schemes, we introduce hypothetical operators which also sort the smaller input sequence, but omit the probing phase. Thus, so-called **Fake* operators do not produce any output tuples. The result comparison is presented in Fig. 9b. Having the same join selectivity dependency, our hash-based operators are approximately twice as fast as the sort-based operators (with result construction). The figures for the *StackTree* algorithm impressively demonstrate that sort operations on intermediate results in query plans should really be avoided if possible. Finally, the hash-based operators—with their "handicap" to produce a result—match the sort-based fake operators.

4.3 Memory Consumption

Finally, we measured the memory consumption of hash-based and sort-based operators. On the generated document collection, we issued the query `//organization[.//andorra]`, where the number of andorra elements varied from 2000 to 200.000, whereas organization elements remained stable (at roughly 200.000). For comparison, we used the `DescFullHashB`[5] and the `DescFullSortB` operator. In all selectivity ranges, the internal hash table of the hash-based operator consumed three to four times more memory than the plain array of the sort-based one. To reduce this gap, a space optimization for hash-based operators is possible: Each key contained in the hash-table (as depicted in Fig. 7a) is repeated (as a prefix) in the join field value of the tuples contained in the key's queue. This redundant information can safely be disposed for a more compact hash table.

In a last experiment, we compare `DescFullHashB` with `AncHashB`. Here, the semi-join alternative required around three times fewer memory than the full join variant on all selectivities. This circumstance is also a strong argument for our proposal, that the query optimizer should pick semi-join operators whenever possible.

5 Conclusions

In this paper, we have considered the improvement of twig pattern queries—a key requirement for XML query evaluation. For this purpose, we have substantially extended the work on structural join algorithms thereby focussing on hashing support. While processing twig patterns, our algorithms, supported by appropriate document store and index structures, primarily rely on SPLIDs which flexibly enable and improve path processing steps by introducing several new degrees of freedom when designing physical operators for path processing steps.

Performance measurements approved our expectations about hash-based operators. They are, in the selectivity range 1%–100%, twice as fast as sort-based schemes and

[5] Note, regarding the space complexity, `DescFullHashB` is one of the more expensive representative among the hash-based operators (see 3.2).

not slower than the **Fake* operators. As another beneficial aspect, intermediate sorts in QEPs can be drastically reduced. Such hash-based operators should be provided—possibly with other kinds of index-based join operators—in a tool box for the cost-based query optimizer to provide for the best QEP generation in all situations.

References

1. S. Al-Khalifa et al.: Structural Joins: A Primitive for Efficient XML Query Pattern Matching. Proc. ICDE: 141-152 (2002)
2. T. Böhme, E. Rahm: Supporting Efficient Streaming and Insertion of XML Data in RDBMS. Proc. 3rd DIWeb Workshop: 70-81 (2004)
3. N. Bruno, N. Koudas, D. Srivastava: Holistic twig joins: optimal XML pattern matching. Proc. SIGMOD: 310-321 (2002)
4. S.-Y. Chien, Z. Vagena, D. Zhang, V. J. Tsotras, C. Zaniolo: Efficient Structural Joins on Indexed XML Documents. Proc. VLDB: 263-274 (2002)
5. M. Dewey: Dewey Decimal Classification System. http://www.mtsu.edu/ vvesper/dewey.html
6. M. Fernandez, J. Hidders, P. Michiels, J. Simeon, R. Vercammen: Optimizing Sorting and Duplicate Elimination. Proc DEXA: 554-563 (2005).
7. M. Fontoura, V. Josifovski, E. Shekita, B. Yang: Optimizing Cursor Movement in Holistic Twig Joins, Proc. 14th CIKM: 784-791 (2005)
8. G. Gottlob, C. Koch, R. Pichler: Efficient algorithms for processing XPath queries. ACM Trans. Database Syst. 30(2): 444-491 (2005)
9. T. Härder, M. Haustein, C. Mathis, M. Wagner: Node Labeling Schemes for Dynamic XML Documents Reconsidered, accepted for Data & Knowledge Engineering (2006)
10. Q. Li, B. Moon: Indexing and Querying XML Data for Regular Path Expressions. Proc. VLDB: 361-370 (2001)
11. Q. Li, B. Moon: Partition Based Path Join Algorithms for XML Data. Proc. DEXA: 160-170 (2003)
12. P. E. O'Neil, E. J. O'Neil, S. Pal, I. Cseri, G. Schaller, N. Westbury: ORDPATHs: Insert-Friendly XML Node Labels. Proc. SIGMOD: 903-908 (2004)
13. I. Tatarinov et al.: Storing and Querying Ordered XML Using a Relational Database System. Proc. SIGMOD: 204-215 (2002)
14. Z. Vagena, M. M. Moro, V. J. Tsotras: Efficient Processing of XML Containment Queries using Partition-Based Schemes. Proc. IDEAS: 161-170 (2004)
15. Y. Wu, J. M. Patel, H. V. Jagadish: Structural Join Order Selection for XML Query Optimization. Proc. ICDE: 443-454 (2003).
16. C. Zhang, J. Naughton, D. DeWitt, Q. Luo, G. Lohmann, On Supporting Containment Queries in Relational Database Management Systems. Proc. SIGMOD: 425-436 (2001)

Efficiently Processing XML Queries over Fragmented Repositories with PartiX

Alexandre Andrade[1], Gabriela Ruberg[1], Fernanda Baião[2], Vanessa P. Braganholo[1], and Marta Mattoso[1]

[1] Computer Science Department, COPPE/Federal Univ. of Rio de Janeiro, Brazil
[2] Applied Informatics Department, University of Rio de Janeiro, Brazil
{alexsilv, gruberg, vanessa, marta}@cos.ufrj.br,
fernanda.baiao@uniriotec.br

Abstract. The data volume of XML repositories and the response time of query processing have become critical issues for many applications, especially for those in the Web. An interesting alternative to improve query processing performance consists in reducing the size of XML databases through fragmentation techniques. However, traditional fragmentation definitions do not directly apply to collections of XML documents. This work formalizes the fragmentation definition for collections of XML documents, and shows the performance of query processing over fragmented XML data. Our prototype, PartiX, exploits intra-query parallelism on top of XQuery-enabled sequential DBMS modules. We have analyzed several experimental settings, and our results showed a performance improvement of up to a 72 scale up factor against centralized databases.

1 Introduction

In the relational [15] and object-oriented data models [4], data fragmentation has been used successfully to efficiently process queries. One of the key factors to this success is the formal definition of fragments and their correctness rules for transparent query decomposition. Recently, several fragmentation techniques for XML data have been proposed in literature [1,2,6,7,8,12]. Each of these techniques aims at a specific scenario: data streams [7], peer-to-peer [1,6], Web-Service based systems [2], etc.

In our work, we focus on high performance of XML data servers. In this scenario, we may have a single large document (SD), or large collections of documents (MD) over which XML queries are posed. For this scenario, however, existent fragmentation techniques [1,2,6,7,8,12] do not apply. This is due to several reasons. First of all, they do not clearly distinguish between horizontal, vertical and hybrid fragmentation, which makes it difficult to automatically decompose queries to run over the fragments. Second, none of them present the fragmentation correctness rules, which are essential for the XML data server to verify the correctness of the XML fragments and then apply the reconstruction rule to properly decompose queries. Also, for large XML repositories, it is important to have a fragmentation model close to the traditional fragmentation techniques, so it can profit as much as possible from well-known results. Third, the query processing techniques are specific for the scenarios where they were proposed, and thus do not apply to our scenario. For instance, the model proposed in [7] for stream data

T. Grust et al. (Eds.): EDBT 2006 Workshops, LNCS 4254, pp. 150–163, 2006.

does not support horizontal fragmentation. The same happens in [2], where fragmentation is used for efficient XML data exchange through Web services. Finally, the lack of distinction between SD and MD prevents the distributed query processing of the MD collection [6,12].

Thus, to efficiently answer queries over large XML repositories using an XML data server, we need a precise definition of XML fragmentation and a high performance environment, such as a cluster of PCs. This way, queries can be decomposed in subqueries which may run in parallel at each cluster node, depending on how the database is fragmented. In this paper, we are interested in the empirical assessment of data fragmentation techniques for XML repositories. We formalize the main fragmentation alternatives for collections of XML documents. We also contribute by defining the rules that verify the correctness of a fragment definition. Our fragmentation model is formal and yet simple when compared to related work. We consider both SD and MD repositories. To address the lack of information on the potential gains that can be achieved with partitioned XML repositories, we present experimental results for horizontal, vertical and hybrid fragmentation of collections of XML documents. The experiments were run with our prototype named PartiX. Sketches of algorithms for query decomposition and result composition are available at [3]. Our results show substantial performance improvements, of up to a 72 scale up factor compared to the centralized setting, in some relevant scenarios.

This paper is organized as follows. In Section 2, we discuss related work. Section 3 presents some basic concepts on XML data model and query language, and formalizes our fragmentation model. Section 4 shows the architecture of PartiX. Our experimental results and corresponding analysis are presented in Section 5. Section 6 closes this work with some final remarks and research perspectives.

2 Related Work

In this section, we briefly present related work. A more detailed discussion can be found in [3]. Foundations of distributed database design for XML were first addressed in [8] and [12]. Ma and Schewe [12] propose three types of XML fragmentation: *horizontal*, which groups elements of a single XML document according to some selection criteria; *vertical*, to restructure a document by unnesting some elements; and a special type named *split*, to break an XML document into a set of new documents. However, these fragmentation types are not clearly distinguished. For example, horizontal fragmentation involves data restructuring and elements projection, thus yielding fragments with different schema definitions.

Our definition of vertical XML fragmentation is inspired in the work of Bremer and Gertz [8]. They propose an approach for distributed XML design, covering both data fragmentation and allocation. Nevertheless, their approach only addresses SD repositories. Moreover, their formalism does not distinguish between horizontal and vertical fragmentation, which are combined in a hybrid type of fragment definition. They maximize local query evaluation by replicating global information, and distributing some indexes. They present performance improvements, but their evaluation focuses on the benefits of such indexes.

Different definitions of XML fragments have been used in query processing over streamed data [7], peer-to-peer environments [1,6], and Web-Service based scenarios [2]. However, they either do not present fragmentation alternatives to SD and MD [6], or do not distinguish between the different fragmentation types [1,2,6,7]. In PartiX, we support horizontal, vertical and hybrid fragmentation of XML data for SD and MD repositories. Furthermore, we have implemented a PartiX prototype, and performed several tests to evaluate the performance of these fragmentation alternatives. No work in the literature presents experimental analysis of the query processing response time on fragmented XML repositories.

3 XML Data Fragmentation

3.1 Basic Concepts

XML documents consist of trees with nodes labeled by element names, attribute names or constant values. Let $\mathcal{L}$ be the set of distinct element names, $\mathcal{A}$ the set of distinct attribute names, and $\mathcal{D}$ the set of distinct data values. An *XML data tree* is denoted by the expression $\Delta := \langle t, \ell, \Psi \rangle$, where: t is a finite ordered tree, ℓ is a function that labels nodes in t with symbols in $\mathcal{L} \cup \mathcal{A}$; and Ψ maps leaf nodes in t to values in $\mathcal{D}$. The root node of Δ is denoted by $root_\Delta$. We assume nodes in Δ do not have mixed content; if a given node v is mapped into $\mathcal{D}$, then v does not have siblings in Δ. Notice, however, that this is not a limitation, but rather a presentation simplification. Furthermore, nodes with labels in $\mathcal{A}$ have a single child whose label must be in $\mathcal{D}$. An XML document is a data tree.

Basically, names of XML elements correspond to names of data types, described in a DTD or XML Schema. Let S be a schema. We say that document $\Delta := \langle t, \ell, \Psi \rangle$ *satisfies* a type τ, where $\tau \in S$, iff $\langle t, \ell \rangle$ is a tree derived from the grammar defined by S such that $\ell(root_\Delta) \rightarrow \tau$. A *collection* C of XML documents is a set of data trees. We say it is *homogeneous* if all the documents in C satisfy the same XML type. If not, we say the collection is *heterogeneous*. Given a schema S, a homogeneous collection C is denoted by the expression $C := \langle S, \tau_{root} \rangle$, where τ_{root} is a type in S and all instances Δ of C satisfy τ_{root}.

Figure 1(a) shows the $S_{virtual\_store}$ schema tree, which we use in the examples throughout the paper. In this Figure, we indicate the minimum and maximum cardinalities (assuming cardinality 1..1 when omitted). The main types in $S_{virtual\_store}$ are `Store` and `Item`, which describe a virtual store and the items it sells. Items are associated with sections and may have descriptive characteristics. Items may also have a list of pictures to be used in the virtual store, and a history of prices. Figure 1(b) shows the definition of the homogeneous collections C_{store} and C_{items}, based on $S_{virtual\_store}$.

We consider two types of XML repositories, as mentioned in [17]. An XML repository may be composed of several documents (*Multiple Documents*, MD) or by a single large document which contains all the information needed (*Single Document*, SD). The collection C_{items} of Figure 1(b) corresponds to an MD repository, whereas the collection C_{store} is an SD repository.

A *path expression* P is a sequence $/\mathsf{e}_1/\ldots/\{\mathsf{e}_k \mid @\mathsf{a}_k\}$, where $\mathsf{e}_x \in \mathcal{L}$, $1 \leq x \leq k$, and $\mathsf{a}_k \in \mathcal{A}$. P may optionally contain the symbols "$*$" to indicate any element, and "//"

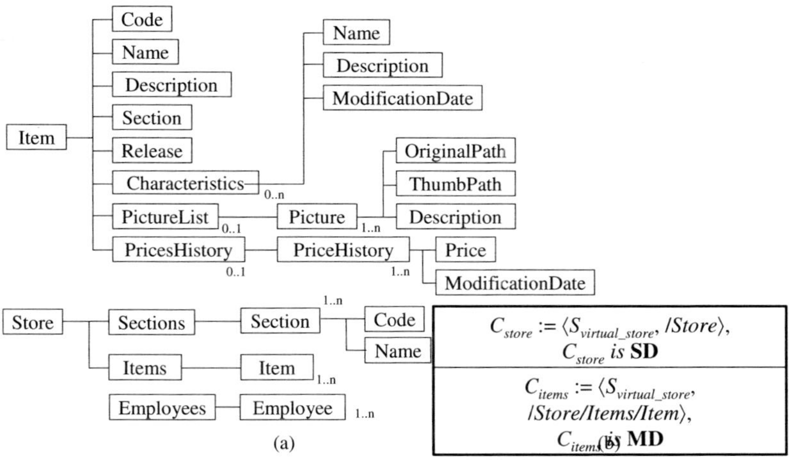

Fig. 1. (a) $S_{virtual\_store}$ schema (b) Specification of collections C_{Store} and C_{Items}

to indicate any sequence of descendant elements. Besides, the term e$[i]$ may be used to denote the i-th occurrence of element e. The evaluation of a path expression P in a document Δ represents the selection of all nodes with label e_k (or a_k) whose steps from $root_\Delta$ satisfy P. P is said to be *terminal* if the content of the selected nodes is simple (that is, if they have domain in $\mathcal{D}$). On the other hand, a *simple predicate* p is a logical expression: $p := \;\; P \; \theta \; value \;\mid\; \phi_v(P) \; \theta \; value \;\mid\; \phi_b(P) \;\mid\; Q$, where P is a terminal path expression, $\theta \in \{=, <, >, \neq, \leq, \geq\}$, $value \in \mathcal{D}$, ϕ_v is a function that returns values in $\mathcal{D}$, ϕ_b is a boolean function and Q denotes an arbitrary path expression. In the latter case, p is true if there are nodes selected by Q (existential test).

3.2 XML Fragmentation Techniques

The subject of data fragmentation is well known in relational [15] and object databases [4]. Traditionally, we can have three types of fragments: *horizontal*, where instances are grouped by selection predicates; *vertical*, which "cuts" the data structure through projections; and/or *hybrid*, which combines selection and projection operations in its definition. Our XML fragmentation definition follows the semantics of the operators from the TLC algebra [16], since it is one of the few XML algebras [9,10,18] that uses collections of documents, and thus is adequate to the XML data model defined in Section 3.1. In [3], we show how fragment definitions in PartiX can be expressed with TLC operators. In XML repositories, we consider that the fragmentation is defined over the schema of an XML collection. In the case of an MD XML database, we assume that the fragmentation can only be applied to homogeneous collections.

Definition 1. *A fragment F of a homogeneous collection C is a collection represented by $F := \langle C, \gamma \rangle$, where γ denotes an operation defined over C. F is horizontal if γ denotes a selection; vertical, if operator γ is a projection; or hybrid, when there is a composition of select and project operators.*

(a)	$F1_{CD} := \langle C_{items}, \sigma_{\text{/Item/Section="CD"}} \rangle$ $F2_{CD} := \langle C_{items}, \sigma_{\text{/Item/Section}\neq\text{"CD"}} \rangle$	(b)	$F1_{good} := \langle C_{items}, \sigma_{\text{contains(//Desciption, "good")}} \rangle$ $F2_{good} := \langle C_{items}, \sigma_{\text{not(contains(//Desciption, "good"))}} \rangle$
		(c)	$F1_{with\_pictures} := \langle C_{items}, \sigma_{\text{/Item/PictureList}} \rangle$ $F2_{with\_pictures} := \langle C_{items}, \sigma_{\text{empty(/Item/PictureList)}} \rangle$

Fig. 2. Examples of three alternative fragments definitions over the collection C_{items}

Instances of a fragment F are obtained by applying γ to each document in C. The set of the resulting documents form the fragment F, which is valid if all documents generated by γ are well-formed (i.e., they must have a single root).

We now detail and analyze the main types of fragmentation in XML. However, we first want to make clear our goal in this paper. Our goal is to show the advantages of fragmenting XML repositories in query processing. Therefore, we formally define the three typical types of XML fragmentation, present correctness criteria for each of them, and compare the performance of queries stated over fragmented databases with queries over centralized databases.

Horizontal Fragmentation. This technique aims to group data that is frequently accessed in isolation by queries with a given selection predicate. A horizontal fragment F of a collection C is defined by the selection operator (σ) [10] applied over documents in C, where the predicate of σ is a boolean expression with one or more simple predicates. Thus, F has the same schema of C.

Definition 2. *Let μ be a conjunction of simple predicates over a collection C. The horizontal fragment of C defined by μ is given by the expression $F := \langle C, \sigma_\mu \rangle$, where σ_μ denotes the selection of documents in C that satisfy μ, that is, F contains documents of C for which σ_μ is true.*

Figure 2 shows the specification of some alternative horizontal fragments for the collection C_{items} of Figure 1(b). For instance, fragment $F1_{good}$ (Figure 2(b)) groups documents from C_{items} which have `Description` nodes that satisfy the path expression `//Description` (that is, `Description` may be at any level in C_{items}) and that contain the word "good". Alternatively, one can be interested in separating, in different fragments, documents that have/have not a given structure. This can be done by using an existential test, and it is shown in Figure 2(c). Although $F1_{with\_pictures}$ and C_{items} have the same schema, in practice they can have different structures, since the element used in the existential test is mandatory in $F1_{with\_pictures}$. Observe that $F1_{with\_pictures}$ cannot be classified as a vertical nor hybrid fragment.

Notice that, by definition, SD repositories may not be horizontally fragmented, since horizontal fragmentation is defined over documents (instead of nodes). However, the elements in an SD repository may be distributed over fragments using a hybrid fragmentation, as described later in this paper.

Vertical Fragmentation. It is obtained by applying the projection operator (π) [16] to "split" a data structure into smaller parts that are frequently accessed in queries. Observe that, in XML repositories, the projection operator has a quite sophisticated semantics: it is possible to specify projections that exclude subtrees whose root is located in any level of an XML tree. A projection over a collection C retrieves, in each document of

(a)	$F1_{items} := \langle C_{items}, \pi_{/Item, \{/Item/PictureList\}} \rangle$ $F2_{items} := \langle C_{items}, \pi_{/Item/PictureList, \{\}} \rangle$	(b)	$F1_{sections} := \langle C_{store}, \pi_{/Store/Sections, \{\}} \rangle$ $F2_{section} := \langle C_{store}, \pi_{/Store, \{/Store/Sections\}} \rangle$

Fig. 3. Examples of vertical fragments definitions over collections C_{items} and C_{store}

$F1_{items} := \langle C_{store}, \pi_{/Store/Items, \{\}} \bullet \sigma_{/Item/Section="CD"} \rangle$
$F2_{items} := \langle C_{store}, \pi_{/Store/Items, \{\}} \bullet \sigma_{/Item/Section="DVD"} \rangle$
$F3_{items} := \langle C_{store}, \pi_{/Store/Items, \{\}} \bullet \sigma_{/Item/Section \neq "CD" \wedge /Item/Section \neq "DVD"} \rangle$
$F4_{items} := \langle C_{store}, \pi_{/Store, \{/Store/Items\}} \rangle$

Fig. 4. Examples of hybrid fragments over collection C_{store}

C (notice that C may have a single document, in case it is of type SD), a set of subtrees represented by a path expression, which are possibly pruned in some descendant nodes.

Definition 3. *Let P be a path expression over collection C. Let $\Gamma := \{E_1, \ldots, E_x\}$ be a (possibly empty) set of path expressions contained in P (that is, path expressions in which P is a prefix). A vertical fragment of C defined by P is denoted $F := \langle C, \pi_{P,\Gamma} \rangle$, where $\pi_{P,\Gamma}$ denotes the projection of the subtrees rooted by nodes selected by P, excluding from the result the nodes selected by the expressions in Γ. The set Γ is called the prune criterion of F.*

It is worth mentioning that the path expression P cannot retrieve nodes that may have cardinality greater than one (as it is the case of `/Item/PictureList/Picture`, in Figure 1(a)), except when the element order is indicated (e.g. `/Item/PictureList/Picture[1]`). This restriction assures that the fragmentation results in well-formed documents, without the need of generating artificial elements to reorganize the subtrees projected in a fragment.

Figure 3 shows examples of vertical fragments of the collections C_{items} and C_{store}, defined on Figure 1(b). Fragment $F2_{items}$ represents the documents that contain all `PictureList` nodes that satisfy the path `/Item/PictureList` in the collection C_{items} (no prune criterion is used). On the other hand, nodes that satisfy `/Item/PictureList` are exactly the ones pruned out the subtrees rooted in `/Item` in the fragment $F1_{items}$, thus preserving disjointness with respect to $F2_{items}$.

Hybrid Fragmentation. The idea here is to apply a vertical fragmentation followed by a horizontal fragmentation, or vice-versa. An interesting use of this technique is to normalize the schema of XML collections in SD repositories, thereby allowing horizontal fragmentation.

Definition 4. *Let σ_μ and $\pi_{P,\Gamma}$ be selection and projection operators, respectively, defined over a collection C. A hybrid fragment of C is represented by $F := \langle C, \pi_{P,\Gamma} \bullet \sigma_\mu \rangle$, where $\pi_{P,\Gamma} \bullet \sigma_\mu$ denotes the selection of the subtrees projected by $\pi_{P,\Gamma}$ that satisfy σ_μ.*

The order of the application of the operations in $\pi_{P,\Gamma} \bullet \sigma_\mu$ depends on the fragmentation design. Examples of hybrid fragmentation are shown in Figure 4.

3.3 Correctness Rules of the Fragmentation

An XML distribution design consists of fragmenting collections of documents (SD or MD) and allocating the resulting fragments in sites of a distributed system, where each collection is associated to a set of fragments. Consider that a collection C is decomposed into a set of fragments $\Phi := \{F_1, ..., F_n\}$. The following rules must be verified to guarantee the fragmentation of C is correct:

- *Completeness*: each data item in C must appear in at least one fragment $F_i \in \Phi$. In the horizontal fragmentation, the data item consists of an XML document, while in the vertical fragmentation, it is a node.
- *Disjointness*: for each data item d in C, if $d \in F_i$, $F_i \in \Phi$, then d cannot be in any other fragment $F_j \in \Phi$, $j \neq i$.
- *Reconstruction*: it must be possible to define an operator ∇ such that $C := \nabla F_i$, $\forall F_i \in \Phi$, where ∇ depends on the type of fragmentation. For horizontal fragmentation, the union ($\cup$) operator [10] is used (TLC is an extension of TAX [10]), and for vertical fragmentation, the join ($\bowtie$) operator [16] is used. We keep an ID in each vertical fragment for reconstruction purposes.

These rules are important to guarantee that queries are correctly translated from the centralized environment to the fragmented one, and that results are correctly reconstructed. Procedures to verify correctness depend on the algorithms adopted in the fragmentation design. As an example, some fragmentation algorithms for relations guarantee the correctness of the resulting fragmentation design [15]. Still others [14] require use of additional techniques to check for correctness. Such automatic verification is out of the scope of this paper.

Query Processing. By using our fragmentation definition, we can adopt a query processing methodology similar to the relational model [15]. The query expressed on the global XML documents can be mapped to its corresponding fragmented XML documents by using the fragmentation schema definition and reconstruction program. Then an analysis on query specification versus schema definition can proceed with data localization. Finally global query optimization techniques can be adopted [10,16].

Figure 5 sketches the query processing in PartiX. The overall idea is that PartiX works as a middleware between the user application and a set of DBMS servers, which actually store the distributed XML data. Information on data distribution is kept by PartiX: when a query arrives, PartiX analyzes the fragmentation schema to properly split it

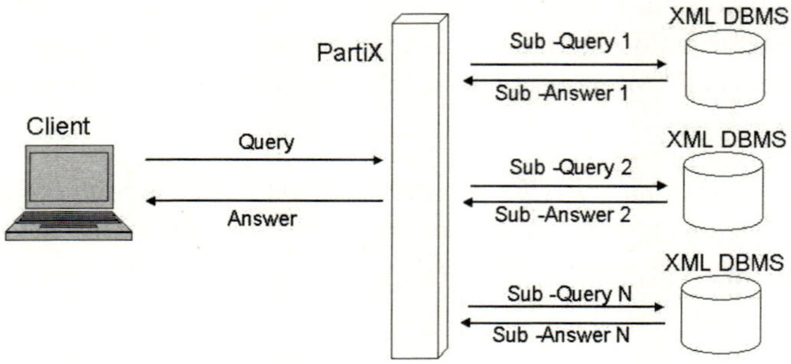

Fig. 5. Query Processing in PartiX

into sub-queries, and then sends each sub-query to its respective fragment. Also, PartiX gathers the results of the sub-queries and reconstructs the query answer. Notice some queries may involve a single fragment, and that in this case, no result reconstruction is needed. In general, defining query rewriting and data localization is a complex research issue, which can benefit from our formal fragmentation model. Yet, we leave such a definition as future work. In the next section, we detail the PartiX architecture.

4 The PartiX Architecture

We propose an architecture to process XQuery queries in distributed XML data sets. Our architecture uses DBMS with no distribution support, and applies our XML fragmentation model, shown in Section 3. The goal of this architecture, named PartiX, is to offer a system which coordinates the distributed processing of XQuery queries. In our distributed environment, a sequencial XML-enabled DBMS is installed at all nodes, which are coordinated by PartiX. In this way, there is no need of buying a specific distributed DBMS.

Generally speaking, PartiX intercepts an XQuery query before it reaches the XML DBMS. PartiX analyzes the definition of the fragments and rewrites the query as sub-queries accordingly (see details for horizontal fragmentation in [3]). Then, it sends these sub-queries to the PartiX components installed in the corresponding DBMS nodes, and collects the partial results. Our architecture is illustrated in the PartiX system, shown in Figure 6. It is composed of three main parts: (i) *catalog services*, which are used to publish schema and distribution metadata; (ii) *publishing service* for distributed XML data; and (iii) distributed *query service*.

The *XML Schema Catalog Service* registers the data types used by the distributed collections, while the *XML Distribution Catalog Service* stores the fragment definitions. The *Distributed XML Data Publisher* receives XML documents from users, applies the fragmentation that was previously defined to the collections, and sends the resulting fragments to be stored in the remote DBMS nodes. XQuery queries are submitted to the *Distributed XML Query Service*, which analyzes their path expressions and identifies the fragments referenced in each query. It writes the sub-queries that are sent to the corresponding DBMS nodes, constructs the result, and sends it to the user.

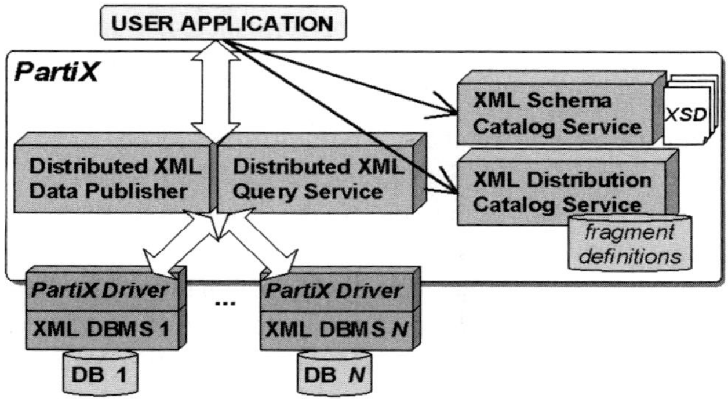

Fig. 6. PartiX Architecture

Our architecture considers that there is a *PartiX Driver*, which allows accessing remote DBMSs to store and retrieve XML documents. This driver provides a uniform communication interface between the PartiX modules and the XML DBMS nodes that host the distributed collections. The *PartiX driver* allows different XML DBMSs to participate in the system. The only requirement is that they are able to process XQuery.

The proposed architecture is implemented in a prototype of the PartiX system. We have developed a PartiX *driver* to the eXist DBMS [13]. The *Data Publisher* interprets loading scripts and stores the documents of a collection in the XML DBMSs. In the PartiX prototype, we did not implement automatic query decomposition, and we consider that data location is provided along with sub-queries. However, given a decomposed query, the *query service* is capable of coordinating the distributed execution of the sub-queries annotated with the location of the required data fragments.

In the next section we show a performance evaluation of queries over fragmented repositories using PartiX.

5 Experimental Evaluation

This section presents experimental results obtained with the PartiX implementation for horizontal, vertical and hybrid fragmentation. We evaluate the benefits of data fragmentation for the performance of query processing in XML databases. We used a 2.4Ghz Athlon XP with 512Mb RAM memory in our tests. We describe the experimental scenario we have used for each of the fragmentation types: horizontal, vertical and hybrid, and show that applying them in XML data collections have reduced the query processing times.

We applied the ToXgene [5] XML database generator to create the C_{store} and C_{items} collections, as defined in Figures 1(a) and (b), and also a collection for the schema defined in the XBench benchmark [17]. All of them were stored in the eXist DBMS [13]. Four databases were generated for the tests: *database ItemsSHor*, with document sizes of 2K in average, and elements `PriceHistory` and `ImagesList` with zero occurrences (Figure 1(a)); *database ItemsLHor*, with document sizes of 80Kb in average (Figure 1(a)); *database XBenchVer*, with the XBench collections, with document sizes varying from 5Mb to 15Mb each; and database StoreHyb (Figure 1(a)), with document sizes from 5Mb to 500Mb. Experiments were conducted varying the number of documents in each database to evaluate the performance of fragmentation for different database sizes (5Mb, 20Mb, 100Mb and 250Mb for all databases, and 500Mb for databases ItemsLHor and StoreHyb). (Due to space restrictions, in this paper we show only the results for the 250Mb database. The remaining results are available at [3].) Some indexes were automatically created by the eXist DBMS to speed up text search operations and path expressions evaluation. No other indexes were created.

Each query was decomposed in sub-queries (according to [3]) to be processed with specific data fragments. When the query predicates match the fragmentation predicates, the sub-queries are issued only to the corresponding fragments. After each sub-query is executed, we compose the result to compute the final query answer [3]. The parallel execution of a query was simulated assuming that all fragments are placed at different sites and that the sub-queries are executed in parallel in each site. For instance, in Figure

7(a) with 8 fragments, we can have at most 8 sub-queries running in parallel. We have used the time spent by the slowest site to produce the result. We measured the communication time for sending the sub-queries to the sites and for transmitting their partial results, since there is no inter-node communication. This was done by calculating the average size of the result and dividing it by the Gigabit Ethernet transmission speed. For all queries we have measured the time between the moment PartiX receives the query until final result composition.

In our experiments, each query was submitted 10 times, and the execution time was calculated by discarding the first execution time and calculating the average of the remaining results. We have measured the execution times of each sub-query. More details on our experiments are available in [3].

Horizontal Fragmentation. For horizontal fragmentation, the tests were run using a set of 8 queries [3], which illustrates diverse access patterns to XML collections, including the usage of predicates, text searches and aggregation operations. The XML database was fragmented as follows. The C_{Items} collection was horizontally fragmented by the "Section" element, following the correctness rules of Section 3.3. We varied the number of fragments (2, 4 and 8) with a non-uniform document distribution. The fragments definitions are shown in [3].

Figure 7(a) contains the performance results of the PartiX execution on top of database ItemsSHor, and Figure 7(b) on database ItemsLHor, in the scenarios previously described. The results show that the fragmentation reduces the response time for most of the queries. When comparing the results of databases ItemsSHor and ItemsLHor with a large number of documents, we observe that the eXist DBMS presents better results when dealing with large documents. This is due to some pre-processing operations (e.g., parsing) that are carried out for each XML tree. For example, when using a 250Mb database size and centralized databases, query Q8 is executed in 1200s in ItemsSHor, and in 31s in ItemsLHor. When using 2 fragments, these times are reduced to 300s and 14s, respectively. Notice this is a superlinear speedup. This is very common also in relational databases, and is due to reduction of I/O operations and better use of machine resources such as cache and memory, since a smaller portion of data is being processed at each site.

An important conclusion obtained from the experiments relates to the benefit of horizontal fragmentation. The execution time of queries with text searches and aggregation operations (Q5, Q6, Q7 and Q8) is significantly reduced when the database is horizontally fragmented. It is worth mentioning that text searches are very common in XML applications, and typically present poor performance in centralized environments, sometimes prohibiting their execution. This problem also occurs with aggregation operations. It is important to notice that our tests included an aggregation function (count) that may be entirely evaluated in parallel, not requiring additional time for reconstructing the global result.

Another interesting result can be seen in the execution of Q6. As the number of fragments increases, the execution time of Q6 increases in some cases. This happens because eXist generates different execution plans for each sub-query, thus favoring the query performance in case of few fragments. Yet, all the distributed configurations performed better than the centralized database.

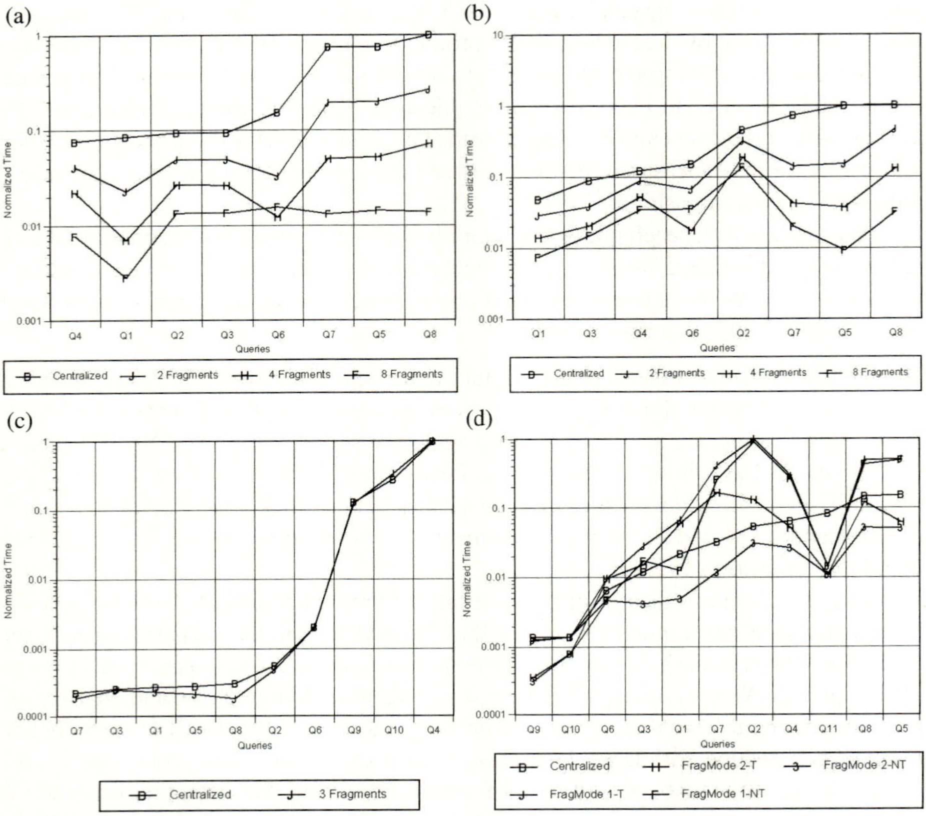

Fig. 7. Experimental results for databases (a) ItemsSHor and (b) ItemsLHor - horizontal fragmentation; (c) XBenchVer - vertical fragmentation; (d) StoreHyb with and without transmission times - hybrid fragmentation

As expected, in small databases (i.e., 5Mb) the performance gain obtained is not enough to justify the use of fragmentation [3]. Moreover, we concluded that the document size is very important for defining the fragmentation schema. Database ItemsLHor (Figure 7(b)) presents better results with few fragments, while database ItemsSHor presents better results with many fragments.

Vertical Fragmentation. For the experiments with vertical fragmentation, we have used the XBenchVer database and some of the queries specified in XBench [17], which are shown in [3]. We have named them Q1 to Q10, although these names do not correspond to the names used in the XBench document.

Database *XBenchVer* was vertically fragmented in three fragments:

- $F1_{papers} := \left\langle C_{papers}, \pi_{/article/prolog} \right\rangle$,
- $F2_{papers} := \left\langle C_{atigos}, \pi_{/article/body} \right\rangle$, and
- $F3_{papers} := \left\langle C_{artigos}, \pi_{/article/epilog} \right\rangle$.

Figure 7(c) shows the performance results of PartiX in this scenario. In the 5Mb database, we had gains in all queries, except for Q4 and Q10 [3]. With vertical fragmentation, the main benefits occur for queries that use a single fragment. Since queries Q4, Q7, Q8 and Q9 need more than one fragment, they can be slowed down by fragmentation. Query Q4 does not present performance gains in any case, except for a minor improvement in the 100Mb database [3]. We believe once more that some statistics or query execution plan has favored the execution of Q4 in this database. In the 20Mb database, all queries presented performance gains (except for Q4), including Q10, which had presented poor performance in the 5Mb database.

As the database size grows, the performance gains decreases. In the 250Mb database, queries Q6, Q9 and Q3 perform equivalently to the centralized approach. With these results, we can see that vertical fragmentation is useful when the queries use few fragments. The queries with bad performance were those involving text search, since in general, they must be applied to all fragments. In such case, the performance is worse than for horizontal fragmentation, since the result reconstruction requires a join (much more expensive than a union).

Hybrid Fragmentation. In the experiments with hybrid fragmentation, we have used the C_{Store} collection fragmented into 5 different fragments. Fragment F_1 prunes */Store/Items*, while the remaining 4 fragments are all about Items, each of them horizontally fragmented over */Store/Items/Item/Section*. We call this database *StoreHyb*, and the set of queries defined over it is shown in [3].

As we will see later on, the experimental results with hybrid fragmentation were heavily influenced by the size of the returning documents. Because of this, we show the performance results with and without the transmission times.

We consider the same queries and selection criteria adopted for databases ItemsSHor e ItemsLHor, with some modifications. With this, most of the queries returned all the content of the "Item" element. This was the main performance problem we have encountered, and it affected all queries. This serves to demonstrate that, besides a good fragmentation design, queries must be carefully specified, so that they do not return unnecessary data. Because XML is a verbose format, an unnecessary element may carry a subtree of significant size, and this will certainly impact in the query execution time.

Another general feature we have noticed while making our tests was that the implementation of the horizontal fragment affects the performance results of the hybrid fragmentation. To us, it was natural to take the single document representing the collection, use the prune operation, and, for each "Item" node selected, to generate an independent document and store it. This approach, which we call *FragMode1*, has proved to be very inefficient. The main reason for this is that, in these cases, the query processor has to parse hundreds of small documents (the ones corresponding to the "Item" fragments), which is slower than parsing a huge document a single time. To solve this problem, we have implemented the horizontal fragmentation with a single document (SD), exactly like the original document, but with only the item elements obtained by the selection operator. We have called this approach *FragMode2*. As we will see, this fragmentation mode beats the centralized approach in most of the cases.

When we consider the transmission times (*FragModeX-T* in Figure 7(e)), FragMode1 performs worse for all database sizes, for all queries, except for queries Q9, Q10 and Q11. Queries Q9 and Q10 are those that prune the "Items" element, which makes the parsing of the document more efficient. Query Q11 uses an aggregation function that presented a good performance in the 100Mb database and in larger ones. In the remaining databases, it presented poor performance (5Mb database) or an anomalous behavior (20Mb database) [3].

Notice the FragMode2 performs better, although it does not beat the centralized approach in all cases. In the 5Mb database, it wins in queries Q3, Q4, Q5 and Q6, which benefit from the parallelism of the fragments and from the use of a specific fragment. As in the FragMode1, queries Q9 and Q10 always performs better than the centralized case; query Q11 only looses in the 5Mb database.

As the database size grows, the query results also increase, thus increasing the total query processing time. In the 20Mb database, query Q6 performs equivalently to the centralized approach. In the 100Mb database, this also happens to Q3 and Q6. In the 250Mb database, these two queries perform worse than in the centralized approach. Finally, in the 500Mb database, query Q4 also performs equivalently to the centralized case, and the remaining ones loose.

As we could see, the transmission times were decisive in the obtained results. Without considering this time, FragMode2 wins in all databases, in all queries, except for query Q11 in the 5Mb database. However, FragMode1 has shown to be effective in some cases. Figure 7(e) shows the experimental results without the transmission times (*FragModeX-NT*). It shows that hybrid fragmentation reduces the query processing times significantly.

6 Conclusions

This work presents a solution to improve the performance in the execution of XQuery queries over XML repositories. This is achieved through the fragmentation of XML databases. We present a formal definition for the different types of XML fragments, and define correctness criteria for the proposed fragmentation model. By specifying the concept of collections of XML documents, we create an abstraction where fragment definitions apply to both single and multiple document repositories (SD and MD). These concepts are not found in related work, and they are fundamental to perform query decomposition and result composition.

Our experiments highlight the potential for significant gains of performance through XML fragmentation. The reduction in the time of query execution is obtained by intra-query parallelism, and also by the local execution, avoiding scanning unnecessary fragments. The queries executed by PartiX with the eXist DBMS present an estimated execution time up to 72 times smaller (for horizontal fragmentation) when compared to centralized executions. The PartiX architecture [3] is generic, and can be plugged to any XML DBMS that process XQuery queries. This architecture follows the approach of *database clusters* that have been presenting excellent performance results over relational DBMSs [11].

As future work, we intend to use the proposed fragmentation model to define a methodology for fragmenting XML databases. This methodology could be used define algorithms for the fragmentation design [18], and to implement tools to automate this fragmentation process. We are also working on detailing algorithms to automatically rewrite queries to run over the fragmented database.

Acknowledgements. The authors thank CNPq for partially funding this work. V. Braganholo thanks FAPERJ and G. Ruberg thanks the Central Bank of Brazil for their support. The contents of this paper express the viewpoint of the authors only.

References

1. S. Abiteboul, A. Bonifati, G. Cobena, I. Manolescu, and T. Milo. Dynamic XML documents with distribution and replication. In *SIGMOD*, pages 527–538, 2003.
2. S. Amer-Yahia and Y. Kotidis. A web-services architecture for efficient XML data exchange. In *ICDE*, pages 523–534, 2004.
3. A. Andrade, G. Ruberg, F. Baião, V. Braganholo, and M. Mattoso. Partix: Processing XQueries over fragmented XML repositories. Technical Report ES-691, COPPE/UFRJ, 2005. `http://www.cos.ufrj.br/~vanessa`.
4. F. Baião, M. Mattoso, and G. Zaverucha. A distribution design methodology for object DBMS. *Distributed and Parallel Databases*, 16(1):45–90, 2004.
5. D. Barbosa, A. Mendelzon, J. Keenleyside, and K. Lyons. ToXgene: a template-based data generator for XML. In *WebDB*, pages 621–632, 2002.
6. A. Bonifati, U. Matrangolo, A. Cuzzocrea, and M. Jain. XPath lookup queries in P2P networks. In *WIDM*, pages 48–55, 2004.
7. S. Bose, L. Fegaras, D. Levine, and V. Chaluvadi. XPath lookup queries in p2p networks. In *WIDM*, pages 48–55, 2004.
8. J.-M. Bremer and M. Gertz. On distributing XML repositories. In *WebDB*, 2003.
9. M. Fernández, J. Siméon, and P. Wadler. An algebra for XML query. In *FSTTCS*, pages 11–45, 2000.
10. H. Jagadish, L. Lakshmanan, D. Srivastava, and K. Thompson. TAX: A tree algebra for XML. In *DBPL*, pages 149–164, 2001.
11. A. Lima, M. Mattoso, and P. Valduriez. Adaptive virtual partitioning for olap query processing in a database cluster. In *SBBD*, pages 92–105, 2004.
12. H. Ma and K.-D. Schewe. Fragmentation of XML documents. In *SBBD*, 2003.
13. W. Meier. eXist: Open source native XML database, 2000. Available at: `http://exist.sourceforge.net`.
14. S. Navathe, K. Karlapalem, and M. Ra. A mixed fragmentation methodology for initial distributed database design. *Journal of Computer and Software Engineering*, 3(4), 1995.
15. T. Ozsu and P. Valduriez. *Principles of Distributed Database Systems*. Prentice Hall, 1999.
16. S. Paparizos, Y. Wu, L. Lakshmanan, and H. Jagadish. Tree logical classes for efficient evaluation of XQuery. In *SIGMOD*, pages 71–82, 2004.
17. B. Yao, M. Ozsu, and N. Khandelwal. Xbench benchmark and performance testing of XML DBMSs. In *ICDE*, pages 621–632, 2004.
18. X. Zhang, B. Pielech, and E. Rundesnteiner. Honey, I shrunk the XQuery!: an XML algebra optimization approach. In *WIDM*, pages 15–22, 2002.

Validity-Sensitive Querying of XML Databases*

Slawomir Staworko and Jan Chomicki

University at Buffalo
{staworko, chomicki}@cse.buffalo.edu

Abstract. We consider the problem of querying XML documents which are not valid with respect to given DTDs. We propose a framework for measuring the invalidity of XML documents and compactly representing minimal repairing scenarios. Furthermore, we present a validity-sensitive method of querying XML documents, which extracts more information from invalid XML documents than does the standard query evaluation. Finally, we provide experimental results which validate our approach.

1 Introduction

XML is rapidly becoming the standard format for the representation and exchange of semi-structured data (documents) over the Internet. In most contexts, documents are processed in the presence of a schema, typically a Document Type Definition (DTD) or an XML Schema. Although currently there exist various methods for maintaining the validity of semi-structured databases, many XML-based applications operate on data which is invalid with respect to a given schema. A document may be the result of integrating several documents of which some are not valid. Parts of an XML document could be imported from a document that is valid with respect to a schema slightly different than the given one. For example, the schemas may differ with respect to the constraints on the cardinalities of elements. The presence of legacy data sources may even result in situations where schema constraints cannot be enforced at all. Also, temporary violations of the schema may arise during the updating of an XML database in an incremental fashion or during data entry.

At the same time, DTDs and XML Schemas capture important information about the expected structure of an XML document. The way a user formulates queries in an XML query language is directly influenced by her knowledge of the schema. However, if the document is not valid, then the result of query evaluation may be insufficiently informative or may fail to conform to the expectations of the user.

Example 1. Consider the DTD D_0 in Figure 1 specifying a collection of project descriptions: Each project description consists of a name, a manager, a collection of subprojects, and a collection of employees involved in the project. The following query Q_0 computes the salaries of all employees that are not managers:

$$/projs//proj/name/emp/following\_sibling::emp/salary$$

* Research supported by NSF Grants IIS-0119186 and IIS-0307434.

T. Grust et al. (Eds.): EDBT 2006 Workshops, LNCS 4254, pp. 164–177, 2006.

```
<!ELEMENT projs  (proj*)>
<!ELEMENT proj   (name,emp,proj*,emp*)>
<!ELEMENT emp    (name,salary)>
<!ELEMENT name   (#PCDATA)>
<!ELEMENT salary (#PCDATA)>
```

Fig. 1. DTD D_0

```
<projs><proj>
  <name> Cooking Pierogies </name>
  <proj>
    <name> Preparing Stuffing </name>
    <emp><name> John </name>
         <salary> 80K </salary></emp>
    <emp><name> Mary </name>
         <salary> 40K </salary></emp>
  </proj>
  <emp><name> Peter </name>
       <salary> 30K </salary></emp>
  <emp><name> Steve </name>
       <salary> 50K </salary></emp>
</proj></projs>
```

Fig. 2. An invalid document T_0

Now consider the document T_0 in Figure 2 which lacks the information about the manager of the main project. Such a document can be the result of the main project not having the manager assigned yet or the manager being changed.

The standard evaluation of the query Q_0 will yield the salaries of *Mary* and *Steve*. However, knowing the DTD D_0, we can determine that an `emp` element following the `name` element ``Cooking Pierogies'' is likely to be missing, and conclude that the salary of *Peter* should also be returned.

Our research addresses the impact of invalidity of XML documents on the result of query evaluation. The problem of querying invalid XML documents has been addressed in the literature in two different ways: through *query modification* or through *document repair*. Query modification involves various techniques of distorting, relaxing, or approximating queries [14,21,3]. Document repair involves techniques of cleaning and correcting databases [9,17]. Our approach follows the second direction, document repair, by adapting the framework of *repairs* and *consistent query answers* developed in the context of inconsistent relational databases [4]. A *repair* is a consistent database instance which is *minimally* different from the original database. Various different notions of minimality have been studied, e.g., set- or cardinality-based minimality. A *consistent query answer* is an answer obtained in *every* repair. The framework of [4] is used as a foundation for most of the work in the area of querying inconsistent databases (for recent developments see [8,12]).

In our approach, differences between XML documents are captured using sequences of atomic operations on documents: inserting/deleting a leaf. Such operations are used in the context of incremental integrity maintenance of XML documents [1,5,6] (modification of a node's label is also handled but we omit it because of space limitations). We define *repairs* to be valid documents obtained from a given invalid document using sequences of atomic operations of *minimum cost*, where the cost is measured simply as the number of operations. Valid answers are defined analogously to consistent answers. We consider schemas of XML documents defined using DTDs.

Example 2. The validity of the document T_1 from Example 1 can be restored in two alternative ways:

1. by inserting in the main project a missing `emp` element (together with its subelements `name` and `salary`, and two text elements). The cost is 5.
2. by deleting the main project node and all its subelements. The cost is 19.

Because of the minimum-cost requirement, only the first way leads to a repair. Therefore, the valid answers to Q_0 consist of the salaries of *Mary*, *Steve*, and *Peter*.

In our opinion, the set of atomic document operations proposed here is sufficient for the correction of *local* violations of validity created by missing or superfluous nodes. The notion of valid query answer provides a way to query possibly invalid XML documents in a *validity-sensitive* way. It is an open question if other sets of operations can be used to effectively query XML documents in a similar fashion.

The contributions of this paper include:

- A framework for validity-sensitive querying of such documents based on measuring the invalidity of XML documents;
- The notion of a *trace graph* which is a compact representation of all repairs of a possibly invalid XML document;
- Efficient algorithms, based on the trace graph, for the computation of valid query answers to a broad class of queries;
- Experimental evaluation of the proposed algorithms.

Because of space limitations we omitted the proofs of most of the theorems. These will be included in a forthcoming technical report.

2 Basic Definitions

In our paper we use a model of XML documents and DTDs similar to those commonly used in the literature [5,6,16,19].

Ordered Labeled Trees. We view XML documents as labeled ordered trees with text values. For simplicity we ignore attributes: they can be easily simulated using text values. By Σ we denote a fixed (and finite) set of tree node labels and we distinguish a label $\mathtt{PCDATA} \in \Sigma$ to identify *text nodes*. A text node has no children and is additionally labeled with an element from an infinite domain Γ of text constants. For clarity of presentation, we use capital letters $\mathtt{A},\mathtt{B},\mathtt{C},\mathtt{D},\mathtt{E},\ldots$ for elements from Σ and capital letters $X,Y,Z\ldots$ for variables ranging over Σ.

We assume that the data structure used to store a document allows for any given node to get its label, its parent, its first child, and its following sibling in time $O(1)$. For the purpose of presentation, we represent trees as terms over the signature $\Sigma \setminus \{\mathtt{PCDATA}\}$ with constants from Γ.

Example 3. The tree T_1 from Figure 3 can be represented with the term $\mathtt{C}(\mathtt{A}(\mathtt{a}), B(\mathtt{b}),\mathtt{B}())$.

DTDs. For simplicity our view of DTDs omits the specification of the root label. A *DTD* is a function D that maps labels from $\Sigma \setminus \{PCDATA\}$ to regular expressions

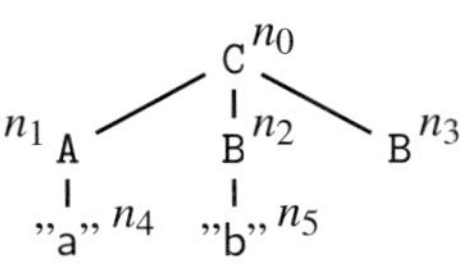

Fig. 3. A running example

over Σ. The size of D, denoted $|D|$, is the sum of the lengths of the regular expressions occurring in D.

A tree $T = X(T_1, \ldots, T_n)$ is *valid* w.r.t. a DTD D if: (1) T_i is valid w.r.t. D for every i and, (2) if $X_1, \ldots, X_n$ are labels of root nodes of $T_1, \ldots, T_n$ respectively and $E = D(X)$, then $X_1 \cdots X_n \in L(E)$.

Example 4. Consider the DTD $D_1(\texttt{A}) = \texttt{PCDATA} + \varepsilon$, $D_1(\texttt{B}) = \varepsilon$, $D_1(\texttt{C}) = (\texttt{A} \cdot \texttt{B})^*$. The tree $\texttt{C}(\texttt{A}(\texttt{a}), \texttt{B}(\texttt{b}), \texttt{B}())$ is not valid w.r.t. D_1 but the tree $\texttt{C}(\texttt{A}(\texttt{a}), \texttt{B}())$ is.

To recognize strings satisfying regular expressions we use the standard notion of *non-deterministic finite automaton* (NDFA) [15] $M = \langle \Sigma, S, q_0, \Delta, F \rangle$, where S is a finite set of *states*, $q_0 \in S$ is a distinguished *starting state*, $F \subseteq S$ is the set of *final states*, and $\Delta \subseteq S \times \Sigma \times S$ is the *transition relation*.

2.1 Tree Edit Distance and Repairs

Tree Operations. A *location* is a sequence of natural numbers defined as follows: ε is the location of the root node, and $v \cdot i$ is the location of i-th child of the node at location v. This notion allows us to identify nodes without fixing a tree.

We consider two *atomic tree operations* (or *operations* for short) commonly used in the context of managing XML document integrity [1,5,6]:

1. *Deleting* a leaf at a specified location.
2. *Inserting* a leaf at a specified location. If the tree has already a node at this location, we shift the existing node to the right together with any following siblings.

We note that our approach can be easily extended to handle the operation of *Modifying* the label of a node (omitted here because of space limitations). We use sequences of editing operations to transform the documents. The *cost* of a sequence of operations is defined to be its length, i.e., the number of operations performed when applying the sequence. Two sequences of operations are *equivalent* on a tree T if their application to T yields the same tree. We observe that some sequences may perform redundant operations, for instance inserting a leaf and then removing it. Because we focus on finding cheapest sequences of operations, we restrict our considerations to redundancy-free sequences (those for which there is no equivalent but cheaper sequence).

Note that a deletion (an insertion) of a whole subtree can be performed with a sequence of deletions (resp. insertions) of length equal to the size of the tree.

Definition 1 (Edit distance). *Given two trees T and S, the* edit distance *$dist(T,S)$ between T and S is the minimum cost of transforming T into S.*

Note that the distance between two documents is a metric, i.e. it is positively defined, symmetric, and satisfies the triangle inequality.

For a DTD D and a (possibly invalid) tree T, a sequence of operations is a sequence *repairing* T w.r.t. D if the document resulting from applying the sequence to T is valid w.r.t. D. We are interested in the cheapest repairing sequences of T.

Definition 2 (Distance to a DTD). *Given a document T and a DTD D, the* distance *$dist(T,D)$ of T to D is the minimum cost of repairing T, i.e.*

$$dist(T,D) = \min\{dist(T,S) | S \text{ is valid w.r.t } D\}.$$

Repairs. The notions of distance introduced above allow us to capture the minimality of change required to repair a document.

Definition 3 (Repair). *Given a document T and a DTD D, a document T' is a* repair *of T w.r.t. D if T' is valid w.r.t. D and $dist(T,T') = dist(T,D)$.*

Note that, if repairing a document involves inserting a text node, the corresponding text label can have infinitely many values, and thus in general there can be infinitely many repairs. However, as shown in the following example, even if the operations are restricted to deletions there can be an exponential number of non-isomorphic repairs of a given document.

Example 5. Suppose we work with documents labeled only with $\Sigma = \{\mathtt{A},\mathtt{B},\mathtt{T},\mathtt{F}\}$ and consider the following DTD: $D(\mathtt{A}) = \mathtt{T}\cdot\mathtt{A}+\mathtt{A}\cdot\mathtt{F}+\mathtt{B}\cdot\mathtt{B}$, $(\mathtt{B}) = \varepsilon$, $D(\mathtt{T}) = \varepsilon$, $D(\mathtt{F}) = \varepsilon$. The tree $\mathtt{A}(\mathtt{T}(),\mathtt{A}(\ldots\mathtt{A}(\mathtt{T}(),\mathtt{A}(\mathtt{B}(),\mathtt{B}()),\mathtt{F}())\ldots),\mathtt{F}())$ consisting of $3n+2$ elements has 2^{n-1} repairs w.r.t. D.

3 Computing the Edit Distance

In this section we present an efficient algorithm for computing the distance $dist(T,D)$ between a document T and a DTD D. The algorithm works in a bottom-up fashion: we compute the distance between a node and the DTD after finding the distance between the DTD and every child of the node.

3.1 Macro Operations

Now, we fix a DTD D and a tree $T = X(T_1,\ldots,T_n)$. The base case, when T is a leaf, is handled by taking $n = 0$. We assume that the values $dist(T_i,D)$ have been computed earlier. We recall that the value $dist(T_i,D)$ is the minimum cost of a sequence of atomic tree operations that transforms T_i into a valid tree. Similarly, the value $dist(T,D)$ corresponds to the cheapest sequence *repairing* T. We model the process of repairing T with 3 *macro operations* applied to the root of T:

1. *Deleting* a subtree rooted at a child.
2. *Repairing* recursively the subtree rooted at a child.
3. *Inserting* as a child a minimum-size valid tree whose root's label is Y for some $Y \in \Sigma$.

Each of these macro operations can be translated to a sequence of atomic tree operations. In the case of a repairing operation there can be an exponential number of possible translations (see Example 5), however, for the purpose of computing $dist(T,D)$ we only need to know their cost. Obviously, the cost of deleting T_i is equal to $|T_i|$ and the cost of repairing T_i is equal to $dist(T_i,D)$ (computed earlier). The cost of inserting a minimal subtree can be found using a simple algorithm (omitted here). A sequence of macro operations is a sequence repairing T if the resulting document is valid. The cost of a sequence of macro operations is the sum of the costs of its elements. A sequence of macro operations is equivalent on T to a sequence of atomic operations if their applications to T yield the same tree. Using the macro operations to repair trees is equivalent to atomic operations.

3.2 Restoration Graph

Now, let $X_1,\ldots,X_n$ be the sequence of the labels of roots of $T_1,\ldots,T_n$ respectively. Suppose $E = D(X)$ defines the labels of children of the root and let $M_E = \langle \Sigma, S, q_0, \Delta, F\rangle$ be the NDFA recognizing $L(E)$ such that $|S| = O(|E|)$ [15].

To find an optimal sequence of macro operations repairing T, we construct a directed *restoration graph* U_T. The vertices of U_T are of the form q^i for $q \in S$ and $i \in \{0,\ldots,n\}$. The vertex q^i is referred as the *state* q *in the i-th column* of U_T and corresponds to the state q being reached by M_E after reading $X_1,\ldots,X_i$ processed earlier with some macro operations. The edges of the restoration graph correspond to the macro operations applied to the children of T:

- $q^{i-1} \xrightarrow{Del} q^i$ corresponds to deleting T_i and such an edge exists for any state $q \in S$ and any $i \in \{1,\ldots,n\}$,
- $q^{i-1} \xrightarrow{Rep} p^i$ corresponds to repairing T_i recursively and such an edge exists only if $\Delta(q,X_i,p)$,
- $q^i \xrightarrow{Ins_Y} p^i$ corresponds to inserting before T_i a minimal subtree labeled with Y and such an edge exists only if $\Delta(q,Y,p)$.

A *repairing path* in U_T is a path from q_0^0 to any accepting state in the last column of U_T.

Lemma 1. *For any sequence of macro operations v, v is a sequence repairing T w.r.t. D iff there exists a repairing path (possibly cyclic) in U_T labeled with the consecutive elements of v.*

If we assign to each edge the cost of the corresponding macro operation, the problem of finding a cheapest repairing sequence of macro operations is reduced to the problem finding a shortest path in U_T.

Theorem 1. *$dist(T,D)$ is equal to the minimum cost of a repairing path in U_T.*

Example 6. Figure 4 illustrates the construction of the restoration graph for the document `C(A(a),B(b),B())` and the DTD from Example 4. The automaton $M_{(\mathtt{A}\cdot\mathtt{B})^*}$ consists of two states q_0 and q_1; q_0 is both the starting and the only accepting state; $\Delta = \{(q_0,\mathtt{A},q_1),(q_1,\mathtt{B},q_0)\}$. The cheapest repairing paths are indicated with bold lines.

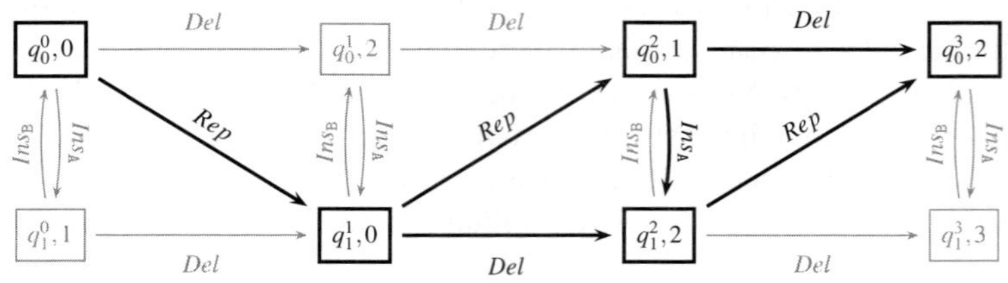

Fig. 4. Construction of the restoration graph

In each vertex we additionally put the minimum cost of reaching that vertex from q_0^0. Note that the restoration graph represents 3 different repairs: (1) $\texttt{C}(\texttt{A}(\texttt{a}),\texttt{B}(),\texttt{A}(),\texttt{B}())$, obtained by inserting $\texttt{A}()$; (2) $\texttt{C}(\texttt{A}(\texttt{a}),\texttt{B}())$ obtained by deleting the second child; (3) $\texttt{C}(\texttt{A}(\texttt{a}),\texttt{B}())$ obtained by repairing the second child (removing the text node b) and removing the third child. We note that although isomorphic, the repairs (2) and (3) are not the same because the nodes labeled with B are obtained from different nodes in the original tree.

3.3 Trace Graph

The *trace graph* U_T^* is the subgraph of U_T consisting of only the cheapest repairing paths. Note that if U_T has cycles, only arcs labeled with inserting macro operations can be involved in them. Since the costs of inserting operations are positive, U_T^* is a directed acyclic graph.

Repairs and Paths in the Trace Graph. Suppose now that we have constructed a trace graph in every node of T. Every repair can be characterized by selecting a path on each of the trace graphs. Similarly a choice of paths in each of the trace graphs yields a repair. We note that a choice of a path on the top-level trace graph of T may correspond to more than one repair (this happens when some subtree has more than one repair).

Complexity Analysis. First, note that for any vertex from the restoration graph U_T the incoming edges come from the same or the preceding column. Therefore, when computing the minimum cost of a path to a given vertex we need to consider at most $(|\Sigma|+1)\times|S|+1$ values.

Moreover, we don't need to store the whole restoration graph in memory, but only its two consecutive columns. Also, note that we need the values $dist(T_i,D)$ and $|T_i|$ only when we compute the minimum cost for the i-th column of U_T, so there is no need for extra space to store these values. We assume that Σ is fixed and $|S|$ is bounded by $|D|$.

Theorem 2. *The distance between a document T and a DTD D can be computed in $O(|D|^2\times|T|)$ time using $O(|D|^2\times height(T))$ space.*

4 Valid Query Answers

In our paper we use the negation-free fragment of XPath 1.0 [26] restricted to its logical *core* (only element and text nodes, and only functions selecting the string value of nodes). Our approach, however, is applicable to a wider class of negation-free Regular XPath Queries [18]. We assume the standard semantics of XPath queries and by $QA^Q(T)$ we denote the answers to the query Q in the tree T.

We use an evaluation method that is geared towards the computation of valid answers. The basic notion is this of a *tree fact* (n, p, x) which states that an *object* x (a node, a label, or a string constant) is reachable from the node n with an XPath expression p.

We distinguish *basic* tree facts which use only $parent::*$, $following\text{-}sibling::*$, $name(.)$, and $text(.)$ path expressions. We note that basic tree facts capture all structural and textual information contained in XML documents. For the tree T_1=$\mathtt{C}(\mathtt{A}(\mathtt{a}),\mathtt{B}(\mathtt{b}),\mathtt{B}())$ from Figure 3 examples of basic facts are: $(n_0, parent::*, n_3)$, $(n_3, parent::*, n_4)$, and $(n_4, text(), \mathtt{a})$. Other tree facts can be derived from the basic facts using simple Horn rules that follow the standard semantics of XPath. For example:

$$(x, descendant::*, y) \leftarrow (x, parent::*, y)$$
$$(x, descendant::*, y) \leftarrow (x, descendant::*, z) \wedge (z, parent::*, y)$$
$$(x, p_1/p_2, y) \leftarrow (x, p_1, z) \wedge (z, p_2, y)$$

For instance, for the document T_1 we can derive $(n_0, descendant::*/text(.), \mathtt{a})$. Since we consider only positive queries, the used rules don't contain negation. Therefore, the derivation process, similarly to negation-free Datalog programs, is monotonic i.e., adding new (basic) facts does not invalidate facts derived previously.

Given a document T and a query Q we construct the set of all relevant tree facts B by adding to B all the basic facts of T. If adding a fact allows to derive new facts involving subexpressions of Q, these facts are also added to B. To find the answers to Q we simply select the facts that originate in the root of T and involve Q.

4.1 Validity-Sensitive Query Evaluation

Definition 4 (Valid query answers). *Given a tree T, a query Q, and a DTD D, an object x is a* valid answer *to Q in T w.r.t D if x is an answer to Q in every repair of T w.r.t. D.*

Computing Valid Query Answers. We construct a bottom-up algorithm that for every node constructs the set of *certain* tree facts that hold in every repair of the subtree rooted in this node. The set of certain tree facts computed for the root node is used to obtain the valid answers to the query (similarly to standard answers).

We now fix the tree T, the DTD D, and the query Q, and assume that we have constructed the trace graph U_T^* for T as described in Section 3. We also assume that the sets of certain tree facts for the children of the root of T have been computed earlier.

Recall that the macro operation Ins_Y corresponds to inserting a minimum-size tree valid w.r.t. the DTD, whose root label is Y. Thus for every label Y our algorithm needs the set C_Y of (certain) tree facts present in every minimal valid tree with the root's label Y. This set can be constructed with a simple algorithm (omitted here).

4.2 Naive Computation of Valid Answers

We start with a naive solution, which may need an exponential time for computation. Later on we present a modification which guarantees a polynomial execution time.

For each repairing path in U_T^* the algorithm constructs the set of certain tree facts present in every repair corresponding to this path. Assume now that $T = X(T_1,\dots,T_n)$, and the root nodes of $T, T_1, \dots, T_n$ are respectively $r, r_1, \dots, r_n$.

For a path $q_0^0 = v_0, v_1, \dots, v_m$ in U_T^* we compute the corresponding set C of certain facts in an incremental fashion (in every step we keep adding any facts that can be derived for subexpressions of the query Q):

1. for q_0^0 the set of certain facts consists of all the basic fact for the root node;
2. if C is the set corresponding to $v_0,\dots,v_{k-1}$, then the set C' corresponding to $v_0,\dots,v_k$ is obtained by one of the 3 following cases depending on the type of edge from v_{k-1} to v_k:
   - for $q^{i-1} \xrightarrow{Del} q^i$ no additional facts are added, i.e., $C' = C$;
   - for $q^{i-1} \xrightarrow{Rep} p^i$ we *append* the tree facts of T_i to C, i.e., we add to C certain facts of the tree T_i with the basic fact $(r, /*, r_i)$; if on the path $v_0,\dots,v_{k-1}$ other trees have been appended (with either *Rep* or Ins_Y instruction), then we also add the fact $(r', \mathit{following\text{-}sibling} :: *, r_i)$ where r' is the root node of the last appended tree;
   - $q^i \xrightarrow{Ins_Y} p^i$ is treated similarly to the previous case, but we append (a copy of) C_Y.

Naturally, the set of certain facts for T is the intersection of all sets corresponding to repairing paths in U_T^*. We implement this algorithm by computing for every v the collection $\mathbb{C}(v)$ of sets of tree facts corresponding to every path from q_0^0 to v.

Example 7. Recall the document $T_1 = \mathtt{C(A(a),B(b),B())}$ and the trace graph from Figure 4 constructed for T_1 and DTD D_1 (Example 6). We consider the query $Q_1 = \mathit{descendant}::*/\mathit{text}(.)$ and we denote the operation of deriving tree facts involving subqueries of Q_1 with the superscript $(\cdot)^{Q_1}$. The collections for the trace graph U_T^* are constructed as follows:

$\mathbb{C}(q_0^0) = \{B_0\}$, where

$$B_0 = (\{(n_0, \mathit{name}(.), \mathtt{C}, n_0)\})^{Q_1}.$$

$\mathbb{C}(q_1^1) = \{B_1\}$, where

$$B_1 = (B_0 \cup C_1 \cup \{(n_0, \mathit{parent}::*, n_1)\})^{Q_1},$$

and C_1 is the set of certain facts for $\mathtt{A(d)}$

$$C_1 = (\{(n_1, \mathit{name}(.), \mathtt{A}), (n_1, \mathit{parent}::*, n_2), (n_2, \mathit{name}(.), \mathtt{PCDATA}), (n_2, \mathit{text}(.), \mathtt{d})\})^{Q_1}.$$

$\mathbb{C}(q_2^0) = \{B_2\}$, where

$$B_2 = (B_1 \cup C_2 \cup \{(n_0, \mathit{parent}::*, n_3), (n_1, \mathit{following\text{-}sibling}::*, n_3)\})^{Q_1},$$

and C_2 is the set of certain facts for the second child

$$C_2 = (\{, (n_3, \mathit{name}(.), \mathtt{B})\})^{Q_1}.$$

$\mathbb{C}(q_1^2) = \{B_1, B_3\}$, where

$$B_3 = (B_1 \cup C_{\mathtt{A}} \cup \{(n_0, \mathit{parent}::*, i_1), (n_3, \mathit{following\text{-}sibling}::*, i_1)\})^{Q_1},$$

where $C_{\mathtt{A}}$ is the set of certain facts for every valid tree with the root label A (i_1 is a new node)

$$C_{\mathtt{A}} = (\{(i_1, name(.), \mathtt{A})\})^{Q_1}.$$

$\mathbb{C}(q_0^3) = \{B_2, B_4, B_5\}$, where

$$B_4 = (B_3 \cup C_3 \cup \{(n_0, parent::*, n_5), (i_1, following\text{-}sibling::*, n_5)\})^{Q_1},$$

$$B_5 = (B_1 \cup C_3 \cup \{(n_0, parent::*, n_5), (n_1, following\text{-}sibling::*, n_5)\})^{Q_1},$$

where C_3 is the set of certain facts for the third child

$$C_3 = (\{(n_5, name(.), \mathtt{B})\})^{Q_1}.$$

In order to prevent an exponential explosion of the sizes of the consecutive collections, we use the following optimization of *eager intersection*:

> Let B_1 and B_2 be two sets from $\mathbb{C}(v)$ for some vertex v. Suppose that $v \longrightarrow v'$ and the edge is labeled with an operation that appends a tree (either *Rep* or *Ins*). Let B_1' and B_2' be the sets for v' obtained from B_1 and B_2 respectively. Instead of storing in $\mathbb{C}(v')$ both sets B_1' and B_2' we only store their intersection $B_1' \cap B_2'$.

In Example 7 this optimization give us: $\mathbb{C}(q_0^3) = \{B_2, B_{4,5}'\}$, where $B_{4,5}' = B_4 \cap B_5$.

With a simple induction over the column number we show that the number of sets of tree facts stored in a vertex in the i-th column is $O(i \times |S| \times |\Sigma|)$. We use the notion of *data complexity* [24] which allows to express the complexity of the algorithm in terms of the size of the document only (by assuming other input components to be fixed).

Theorem 3. *The data-complexity of computation of valid answers to negation-free core XPath queries is PTIME.*

We note that if we include the query into the input, the problem becomes co-NP-complete (we omit the proof). This shows that computing valid query answers is considerably more complex than computation of standard answers (whose combined complexity is known to be in PTIME [13]).

5 Experimental Evaluation

In our experiments, we tested 2 algorithms: DIST computing $dist(D,T)$ and VQA computing valid answers. We compared these algorithms with an algorithm VALIDATE for validation of a document and an algorithm QA computing standard answers. All compared algorithms have been implemented using a common set of programming tools including: the parser, the representation of regular expressions and corresponding NDFA's, the representation for tree facts, and algorithms maintaining closure of the set of tree facts. For ease of implementation, we considered only a restricted class of *non-ascending path queries* which use only simple filter conditions (testing tag and text elements), do not use union, and involve only *child*, *descendant*, and *following-sibling* axises. We note that those queries are most commonly used in practice and the restrictions allow to construct algorithms that compute standard answers to such queries in time linear in the size of the document. This is also the complexity of the QA algorithm.

Data Generation. To observe the impact of the document size on the performance of algorithms, we randomly generated a valid document and we introduced the violations of validity to a document by randomly removing and inserting nodes. To measure the invalidity of a document T we use the *invalidity ratio* $dist(T,D)/|T|$. All the documents used for tests had a small height, 8-10.

For most of the experiments we used the DTD D_0 and the query Q_0 from Example 1. To measure the impact of the DTD size on the performance, we generated a family of DTDs D_n, $n \geq 0$: $D_n(\mathtt{A}) = (\ldots((\mathtt{PCDATA}+\mathtt{A}_1)\cdot\mathtt{A}_2+\mathtt{A}_3)\cdot\mathtt{A}_4+\ldots\mathtt{A}_n)^*$,$D_n(\mathtt{A}_i) = \mathtt{A}^*$. For those documents we used a simple query $//*/text(.)$.

Environment. The system was implemented in Java 5.0 and tested on an Intel Pentium M 1000MHz machine running Windows XP with 512 MB RAM and 40 GB hard drive.

5.1 Experimental Results

Results in Figure 5(a) and in Figure 5(b) confirm our analysis: edit distance between a document and a DTD can be computed in time linear in the document size and quadratic in the size of the DTD. If we take as the base line the time needed to parse the whole file (PARSE), then we observe that the overhead needed to perform computations is small. Because our approach to computing edit distance doesn't assume any particular

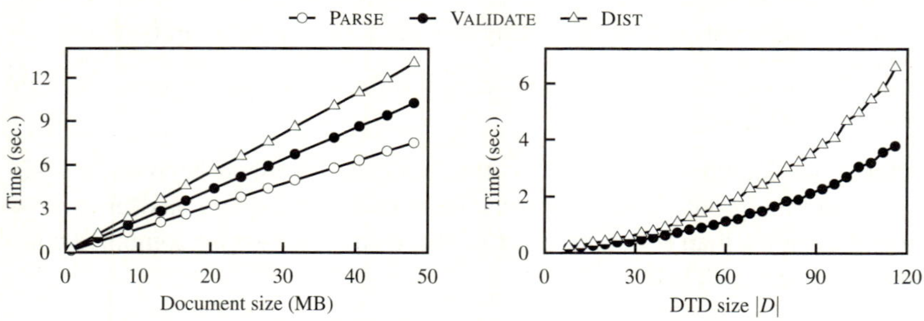

(a) for variable document size (b) for variable DTD size

Fig. 5. Edit distance computation time (0.1% invalidity ratio)

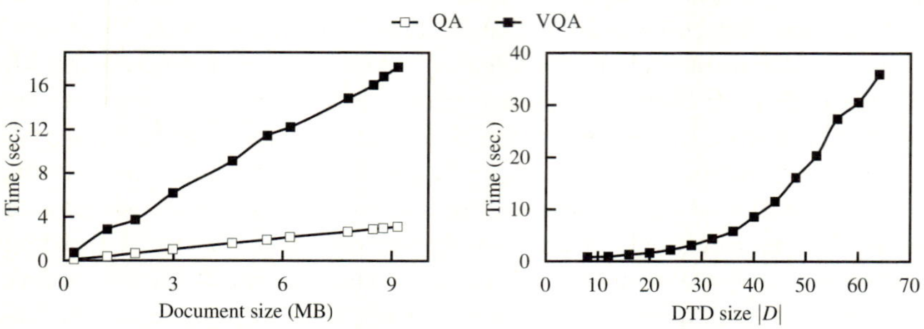

(a) for variable document size (b) for variable DTD size

Fig. 6. Valid answers computation time (0.1% invalidity ratio) properties of the automata used to construct the trace graph, Figure 5(b) allows us to make the following conjecture: Any techniques that optimize the automata to efficiently validate XML documents should also be applicable to the algorithm for computing the distance of XML documents to DTDs.

Figure 6(a) shows that for the DTD D_0 computing valid query answers is about 6 times longer than computing query answers with QA. Similarly to computing edit distance, computing valid answers involves constructing the restoration graph. This explains the quadratic dependency between the performance time and the size of DTD observed for VQA in Figure 6(b).

6 Related Work

Tree Edit Distance. Tree edit distance is a generalization of the classical string edit distance. There are several different versions of the former notion varying with the semantics of tree operations [7]. In the most studied approach [23], the deleting operation also can be performed on a internal node, in which case the children are *promoted up*. Conversely, the inserting operation can *push down* a contiguous sequence of nodes. The implied notion of edit distance is not equivalent to ours (our notion is sometimes called *1-degree edit distance* [22]). In the area of data integration, insertions and deletions of internal document nodes could be used for the resolution of major structural discrepancies between documents. However, such operations require shifting nodes between levels and thus it is not clear if our approach can be adapted to that context. The notion of edit distance identical to ours has been used in papers dealing with the maintenance of XML integrity [1,5,6] and to measure structural similarity between XML documents [20]. [9] studies an extension of the basic tree edit framework with *moves*: a subtree can be shifted to a new location. In the context of validity-sensitive querying, extending our approach with move operations would allow to properly handle situations where invalidity of the document is caused by transposition of elements.

Almost every formulation of edit distance, including ours, allows to assign a non-unit cost to each operation.

Structural Restoration. A problem of correcting a *slightly invalid* document is considered in [9]. Under certain conditions, the proposed algorithm returns a valid document whose distance from the original one is guaranteed to be within a multiplicative constant of the minimum distance. The setting is different from ours: XML documents are encoded as binary trees, so performing editing operations on a encoded XML document may shift nodes between levels in terms of the original tree.

A notion equivalent to the distance of a document to a DTD (Definition 2) was used to construct error-correcting parsers for context-free languages [2].

Consistent Query Answers for XML. [10] investigates querying XML documents that are valid but violate functional dependencies. Two repairing actions are considered: updating element values with a *null* value and marking nodes as unreliable. This choice of actions prevents from introducing invalidity in the document upon repairing it. Nodes with null values or marked as unreliable do not cause violations of functional dependencies but also are not returned in the answers to queries. Repairs are consistent instances with a minimal set of nodes affected by the repairing actions.

A set of operations similar to ours is considered for consistent querying of XML documents that violate functional dependencies in [11]. Depending on the operations used different notions of repairs are considered: *cleaning* repairs obtained only by deleting elements, *completing* repairs obtained by inserting nodes, and *general* repairs obtained by both operations.

[25] is another adaptation of consistent query answers to XML databases closely based on the framework of [4].

7 Conclusions and Future Work

In this paper we investigated the problem of querying XML documents containing violations of validity of a local nature caused by missing or superfluous nodes. We proposed a framework which considers possible repairs of a given document obtained by applying a minimum number of operations that insert or delete nodes. We demonstrated algorithms for (a) measuring invalidity in terms of document-to-DTD distance, and (b) validity-sensitive querying based on the notion of valid query answer.

We envision several possible directions for future work. First, one can investigate if valid answers can be obtained using query rewriting [14]. Second, it is an open question if negation could be introduced into our framework. Third, it would be of significant interest to establish a complete picture of how the complexity of the computational problems considered in this paper (computing document-to-DTD distance, computing valid query answers) depends on the query language and the repertoire of the available tree operations (other operations include subtree swap, restricted subtree move). Finally, it would be interesting to find out to what extent our framework can be adapted to handle semantic inconsistencies in XML documents, for example violations of key dependencies.

References

1. S. Abiteboul, J. McHugh, M. Rys, V. Vassalos, and J. L. Wiener. Incremental Maintenance for Materialized Views over Semistructured Data. In *International Conference on Very Large Data Bases (VLDB)*, pages 38–49, 1998.
2. A. V. Aho and T. G. Peterson. A Minimum Distance Error-Correcting Parser for Context-Free Languages. *SIAM Journal on Computing*, 1(4):305–312, 1972.
3. S. Amer-Yahia, S. Cho, and D. Srivastava. Tree Pattern Relaxation. In *International Conference on Extending Database Technology (EDBT)*, pages 496–513, 2002.
4. M. Arenas, L. Bertossi, and J. Chomicki. Consistent Query Answers in Inconsistent Databases. In *ACM Symposium on Principles of Database Systems (PODS)*, 1999.
5. A. Balmin, Y. Papakonstantinou, and V. Vianu. Incremental Validation of XML Documents. *ACM Transactions on Database Systems (TODS)*, 29(4):710–751, December 2004.
6. M. Benedikt, W. Fan, and F. Geerts. XPath Satisfiability in the Presence of DTDs. In *ACM Symposium on Principles of Database Systems (PODS)*, 2005.
7. P. Bille. Tree Edit Distance, Aligment and Inclusion. Technical Report TR-2003-23, The IT University of Copenhagen, 2003.
8. P. Bohannon, M. Flaster, W. Fan, and R. Rastogi. A Cost-Based Model and Effective Heuristic for Repairing Constraints by Value Modification. In *ACM SIGMOD International Conference on Management of Data*, 2005.

9. U. Boobna and M. de Rougemont. Correctors for XML Data. In *International XML Database Symposium*, pages 97–111, 2004.
10. S. Flesca, F. Furfaro, S. Greco, and E. Zumpano. Repairs and Consistent Answers for XML Data with Functional Dependencies. In *International XML Database Symposium*, 2003.
11. S. Flesca, F. Furfaro, S. Greco, and E. Zumpano. Querying and Repairing Inconsistent XML Data. In *Web Information Systems Engineering (WISE)*, pages 175–188, 2005.
12. A. Fuxman, E. Fazli, and R. J. Miller. ConQuer: Efficient Management of Inconsistent Databases. In *ACM SIGMOD International Conference on Management of Data*, 2005.
13. G. Gottlob, C. Koch, and R. Pichler. XPath Processing in a Nutshell. *SIGMOD Record*, 32(2):21–27, 2003.
14. G. Grahne and A. Thomo. Query Answering and Containment for Regular Path Queries under Distortions. In *Foundations of Information and Knowledge Systems (FOIKS)*, 2004.
15. J. E. Hopcroft, R. Motwani, and J. D. Ullman. *Introduction to Automata Theory, Languages, and Computation*. Addison Wesley, 2nd edition, 2001.
16. A. Klarlund, T. Schwentick, and D. Suciu. XML: Model, Schemas, Types, Logics and Queries. In J. Chomicki, R. van der Meyden, and G. Saake, editors, *Logics for Emerging Applications of Databases*. Springer-Verlag, 2003.
17. W. L. Low, W. H. Tok, M. Lee, and T. W. Ling. Data Cleaning and XML: The DBLP Experience. In *International Conference on Data Engineering (ICDE)*, page 269, 2002.
18. M. Marx. Conditional XPath, the First Order Complete XPath Dialect. In *ACM Symposium on Principles of Database Systems (PODS)*, pages 13–22, 2004.
19. F. Neven. Automata, Logic, and XML. In *Workshop on Computer Science Logic (CSL)*, volume 2471 of *Lecture Notes in Computer Science*, pages 2–26. Springer, 2002.
20. A. Nierman and H. V. Jagadish. Evaluating Structural Similarity in XML Documents. In *Workshop on the Web and Databases (WebDB)*, pages 61–66, 2002.
21. P. Polyzotis, M. N. Garofalakis, and Y. E. Ioannidis. Approximate XML Query Answers. In *ACM SIGMOD International Conference on Management of Data*, pages 263–274, 2004.
22. S. M. Selkow. The Tree-to-Tree Editing Problem. *Information Processing Letters*, 1977.
23. D. Shasha and K. Zhang. Approximate Tree Pattern Matching. In A. Apostolico and Z. Galil, editors, *Pattern Matching in Strings, Trees, and Arrays*, pages 341–371. Oxford University Press, 1997.
24. M. Y. Vardi. The Complexity of Relational Query Languages. In *ACM Symposium on Theory of Computing (STOC)*, pages 137–146, 1982.
25. S. Vllalobos. Consistent Answers to Queries Posed to Inconsistent XML Databases. Master's thesis, Catholic University of Chile (PUC), 2003. In Spanish.
26. W3C. XML path language (XPath 1.0), 1999.

XQuery!: An XML Query Language with Side Effects

Giorgio Ghelli[1], Christopher Ré[2], and Jérôme Siméon[3]

[1] Università di Pisa
[2] University of Washington
[3] IBM T.J. Watson Research Center

Abstract. As XML applications become more complex, there is a growing interest in extending XQuery with side-effect operations, notably XML updates. However, the presence of side-effects is at odds with XQuery's declarative semantics in which evaluation order is unspecified. In this paper, we define "XQuery!", an extension of XQuery 1.0 that supports first-class XML updates and user-level control over update application, preserving the benefits of XQuery's declarative semantics when possible. Our extensions can be easily implemented within an existing XQuery processor and we show how to recover basic database optimizations for such a language.

1 Introduction

As XML applications grow in complexity, developers are calling for advanced features in XML query languages. Many of the most requested extensions, such as XML updates, support for references, and variable assignment, involve side-effects. So far, proposed update extensions for XQuery [16,21,23,1,4] have been based on restricted compositionality and a "snapshot semantics", where updates are only applied at the end of query execution. This approach preserves as much of XQuery's declarative semantics as possible, but the query cannot use the result of an update for further processing, limiting expressiveness in a way which is not always acceptable for applications.

In this paper, we develop the semantic foundations for extending XQuery 1.0 with side-effect operations in a fully compositional way. We use that framework to define XQuery! (read: "XQuery Bang"), an extension of XQuery 1.0 [2] that supports compositional XML updates and user-level control over update application. We show such a language can be obtained with limited impact on XQuery's declarative semantics and classical optimization techniques. To the best of our knowledge, this is the first complete treatment and implementation of a compositional side-effect extension of XQuery. The semantic framework is characterized by the presence of an operator (`snap`) that allows users to identify declarative fragments within their side-effecting programs, and which enables the recovery of traditional database optimizations.

XQuery! supports the same basic update operations as previous proposals [16,21,23,4]. However, the ability to use updates in any context (e.g., in function calls) and to control update application makes it more expressive than previous proposals. For instance, it allows to write programs which both return a value and have a side effect, or it allows part of the query to exploit the result of an update. Compositionality is one of the main design principles in XQuery 1.0, resulting in a language simpler to explain

T. Grust et al. (Eds.): EDBT 2006 Workshops, LNCS 4254, pp. 178–191, 2006.

to users and specify. Our experience with a more restricted update language [23] shows that applications often require the additional expressiveness. We illustrate how compositionality between queries and updates in XQuery! can be used to develop a simple Web service that includes logging of service calls.

The contributions of this paper are:

- A formal description of a semantic framework for extending XML query languages with side-effect operations which can appear anywhere in the query.
- The description of a new construct (`snap`) that can be used to control update application. The semantics of `snap` enables unlimited nesting and allows the optimizer to recover standard database optimizations, even in the presence of side-effects.
- The definition of XQuery!, an extension to XQuery 1.0 with first-class updates, and an example of its use in a Web service usecase.
- The description of a complete implementation of XQuery!. We show that such an implementation can easily be obtained from an existing XQuery engine.

The main novelty in our framework lies in the ability to control update application through the `snap` construct. The notion of delaying update application to the end of query evaluation (so called *snapshot* semantics) was first proposed in [21,16], and has been studied further in [9,8,1]. Previous proposals apply that approach to the whole query, while XQuery! provides programmer control of the snapshot scope through the `snap` operator. Languages with explicit control of the snapshot semantics are mentioned explicitly in the XQuery update requirements document [5], and have been explored by the W3C XML update task force [11,3]. Work on the XL programming language [12] indicates support for fully compositional updates, but not for control of update application. To the best of our knowledge, our work is the first to propose a complete treatment of such an operator, and to explicit its relationship with optimization properties of the language.

Due to space limitations, we restrict the presentation to the main aspects of the language and its semantics. We first introduce XQuery! through a Web service usecase, before giving a formal definition of the language semantics. We then give an overview of our implementation, and discuss optimization issues. More details of the language, its complete formal semantics and more details about the implementation can be found in the complete paper [13].

2 XQuery! Use Case: Adding Logging to an XQuery Web Service

2.1 Snapshot Semantics

Before we illustrate the use of XQuery!, we introduce the notion of snapshot semantics. All the update extensions to XQuery we are aware of [21,16,9,8,1] delay update applications up to the end of query execution, in order to retain the declarative semantics of XQuery. For instance, consider the following query which inserts a new `buyer` element for each person who buys an item.

```
for $p in $auction//person
for $t in $auction//closed_auction
```

```
where $t/buyer/@person = $p/@id
return insert { <buyer name="{$p/name}"
                        itemid="{$t/itemref/@item}" /> }
       into { $purchasers }
```

This is a typical join query, and the snapshot semantics ensures that traditional optimization techniques, such as algebraic rewritings and lazy evaluation, can be applied. In XQuery!, where the snapshot semantics is controlled explicitly, the absence of any internal `snap` allows similar optimizations. We come back to this point in more details in Section 4.

In addition, in order to facilitate rewritings, previous proposals limit the use of updates to specific sub-expressions, typically in the return clause of a FLWOR, as in the above example. In the rest of this section, we give a more advanced Web service use-case which requires complex composition of side-effects and queries, and control over update application.

2.2 The Web Service Scenario: Updates Inside Functions

We assume a simple Web service application in which service calls are implemented as XQuery functions organized in a module. Because of space limitations, we focus on the single function `get_item`, which, given an itemid and the userid of the requester, returns the item with the given itemid; the userid is ignored for now. The server stores the auction document from XMark [22] in a variable `$auction`. The following is a possible implementation for that function using standard XQuery.

```
declare function get_item($itemid,$userid) {
  let $item := $auction//item[@id = $itemid]
  return $item
};
```

Now, let's assume that the Web service wants to log each item access. This can be easily done in XQuery! by adding an insert operation in the body of the function.

```
declare function get_item($itemid,$userid) {
  let $item := $auction//item[@id = $itemid]
  return (
    ( let $name := $auction//person[@id = $userid]/name return
      insert { <logentry user="{$name}" itemid="{$itemid}"/> }
      into { $log }),
    $item
  )
};
```

This simple example illustrates the need for expressions that have a side-effect (the log entry insertion) and also return a value (the item itself).

Note that in the above example we use XQuery's sequence construction (`,`) to compose the conditional insert operation with the result `$item`. This is a convenience made possible by the fact that the value returned by atomic update operations is always the empty sequence.

2.3 Controlling Update Application

The other central feature of our approach is the ability to control the "snapshot scope". A single global scope is often too restrictive, since many applications, at some stage of their computation, need to see the result of previous side-effects. For this reason, XQuery! supports a `snap { Expr }` operator which evaluates *Expr*, collects its update requests, and makes the effects of these updates visible to the rest of the query. A `snap` is always implicitly present around the top-level query in the main XQuery! module, so that the usual "delay until the end" semantics is obtained by default. However, when needed, the code can decide to see its own effects. For example, consider the following simple variant for the logging code, where the log is summarized into an archive once every *$maxlog* insertions. (`snap insert{} into{}` abbreviates `snap {insert{} into{}}`, and similarly for the other update primitives).

```
( let $name := $auction//person[@id = $userid]/name
  return
   (snap insert { <logentry user="{$name}"
                             itemid="{$item/@id}"/> }
         into { $log },
    if (count($log/logentry) >= $maxlog)
    then (archivelog($log,$archive),
          snap delete $log/logentry )
    else ())),
```

Here, the `snap` around `insert` makes the insertion happen. The insertion is visible to the code inside the subsequent if-then-else because XQuery! semantics imposes that in the sequence constructor `(e1,e2)`, `e1` be evaluated before `e2`. Hence, XQuery!'s ability to support the above example relies on the combination of the `snap` operator and of an explicit evaluation order. This is an important departure from XQuery 1.0 semantics, and is discussed in the next subsection.

In many situations, different scopes for the `snap` would lead to the same result. In such cases, the programmer can adopt a simple criterion: make `snap` scope as broad as possible, since a broader `snap` favors optimization. A `snap` should only be closed when the rest of the program relies on the effect of the updates.

2.4 Sequence Order, Evaluation Order, and Update Order

In XQuery 1.0, queries return sequences of items. Although sequences of items are ordered, the evaluation order for most operators is left to the implementation. For instance, in the expression (e_1, e_2), if e_1 and e_2 evaluate respectively to v_1 and v_2, then the value of e_1, e_2 must be v_1, v_2, in this order. However, the engine can evaluate e_2 before e_1, provided the result is presented in the correct sequence order. This freedom is visible for instance, if both expressions e_1 and e_2 were to raise an error, as which of those errors is reported may vary from implementation to implementation.

Although that approach is reasonable in an almost-purely functional language as XQuery 1.0, it is widely believed that programs with side-effects are impossible to reason about unless the evaluation order is easy to grasp.[1] For this reason, in XQuery!

[1] Simon Peyton-Jones: "lazy evaluation and side effects are, from a practical point of view, incompatible" [15].

we adopt the standard semantics used in popular functional languages with side-effects [18,17], based on the definition of a precise evaluation order. This semantics is easy to understand for a programmer and easy to formalize using the XQuery 1.0 formal semantic style, but is quite constraining for the compiler. However, as we discuss in Section 3, inside an innermost snap no side-effect takes place, hence we recover XQuery 1.0 freedom of evaluation order in those cases. In other words, inside an innermost snap, both the pure subexpressions and the update operations can be evaluated in any order, provided that, at the end of the snap scope, both the item sequence and the list of update requests are presented in the correct order.

The order of update requests is a bit harder to maintain than sequence order, since a FLWOR expression may generate updates in the *for*, *where*, and *return* clause, while result items are only generated in the *return* clause. For this reason, XQuery! supports alternative semantics for update application, discussed in Section 3.2, which do not depend on order.

2.5 Nested Snap

Support for nested snap is central to our proposal, and is essential for compositionality. Assume, for example, that a counter is implemented using the following function.

```
declare variable $d := element counter { 0 };
declare function nextid() as xs:integer {
  snap { replace { $d/text() } with { $d + 1 },
         $d }
};
```

The snap around the function body ensures that the counter function performs as expected, returning an increasing value after each call. Obviously, the nextid() function may be used in the scope of another snap. For instance, the following variant of the logging code computes a new id for every log entry.

```
(::: Logging code :::)
( let $name := $auction//person[@id = $userid]/name
  return
   (snap insert { <logentry id="{nextid()}"
                            user="{$name}"
                            itemid="{$item/@id}"/> }
         into { $log },
     if (count($log/logentry) >= $maxlog) ...
(::: End logging code :::)
```

The example shows that the snap operator must not freeze the state when its scope is opened, but just delay the updates that are in its immediate scope until it is closed. Any nested snap opens a nested scope, and makes its updates visible as soon as it is closed. The details of this semantics are explained in Section 3.

3 XQuery! Semantics

The original semantics of XQuery is defined in [7] as follows. First, each expression is normalized to a *core* expression. Then, the meaning of core expressions is defined by a semantic judgment *dynEnv* $\vdash$ *Expr* $\Rightarrow$ *value*. This judgment states that, in the dynamic context *dynEnv*, the expression *Expr* yields the value *value*, where *value* is an instance of the XQuery data model [6] (XDM).

To support side-effect operations, we extend the data model with a notion of store that maintains the state of the instances that are being processed. It should be clear from the discussion in Section 2 that only snap expressions actually modify the store. We extend the semantic judgment so that expressions may modify the store, and produce both a value and a list of pending updates. In the rest of this section, we introduce the update primitives supported by the XQuery! language, followed by the data model extensions. We then shortly describe normalization, and finally define the new semantic judgment.

3.1 Update Primitives

At the language level, XQuery! supports a set of standard updates primitives: insertion, deletion, replacement, and renaming of XML nodes [16,21,23,1,9,8]. The language also includes an explicit deep-copy operator, written `copy { ... }`. The full grammar for the XQuery! extension to XQuery 1.0 is given in [13].

The detailed semantics of these primitives is also standard: insertion allows a sequence of nodes to be inserted below a parent at a specified position. Replacement allows a node to be replaced by another, and renaming allows the node name to be updated. Finally, to better deal with aliasing issues in the context of a compositional language, the semantics of the delete operation does not actually delete nodes, but merely *detaches* nodes from their parents. If a "deleted" (actually, detached) node is still accessible from a variable, it can still be queried, or inserted somewhere.

3.2 XDM Stores and Update Requests

Store. To represent the state of XQuery! computation, we need a notion of *store*, which specifies the valid node ids and, for each node id, its kind (element, attribute, text...), parent, name, and content. A formal definition can be found in [13,14,10]. On this store, we define accessors and constructors corresponding to those of the XDM. Note that this presentation focuses on well-formed documents, and does not consider the impact of types on the data model representation and language semantics.

Update Requests. We then define, for each XQuery! update primitive, the corresponding *update request*, which is a tuple that contains the operation name and its parameters, written as "opname(par_1,...,par_n)". For each update request, its *application* is a partial function from stores to stores. The application of "insert (*nodeseq*,*nodepar*,*nodepos*)" inserts all nodes of *nodeseq* as children of *nodepar*, after *nodepos*. For each update request we also define some preconditions for its parameters. In the insert case, they include the fact that nodes in *nodeseq* must have no parent, and that *nodepos* must be a child of *nodepar*. When the preconditions are not met, the update application is undefined.

Update Lists. An update list, denoted Δ, is a list of update requests. Update lists are collected during the execution of the code inside a `snap`, and are applied when the `snap` scope is closed. An update list is an *ordered* list, whose order is fully specified by the language semantics.

Applying an Update List to the Store. For optimization reasons, XQuery! supports three semantics for update list application: *ordered*, *non-deterministic*, and *conflict-detection*. The programmer chooses the semantics through an optional keyword after each `snap`.

In the *ordered* semantics, the update requests are applied in the order specified by Δ. In the *non-deterministic* semantics, the update requests are applied in an arbitrary order. In the *conflict-detection* semantics, update application is divided into conflict verification followed by store modification. The first phase tries to prove, by some simple rules, that the update sequence is actually conflict-free, meaning that the ordered application of every permutation of Δ would produce the same result. If verification fails, update application fails. If verification succeeds, the store is modified, and the order of application is immaterial.

The *ordered* approach is simple and deterministic, but imposes more restrictions on the optimizer. The *non-deterministic* approach is simpler to implement and optimize, but makes code development harder, especially in the testing phase. Finally, the *conflict-detection* approach gives the optimizer the same re-ordering freedom as the non-deterministic approach while avoiding non-determinism. However, it rules out many reasonable pieces of code, as exemplified in the full paper. Moreover, it can raise run-time failures which may be difficult to understand and to prevent.

3.3 Normalization

Normalization simplifies the semantics specification by first transforming each XQuery! expression into a *core* expression, so that the semantics only needs to be defined on the core language. The syntax of XQuery! core for update operations is almost identical to that of the surface language. The only non-trivial normalization effect is the insertion of a deep copy operator around the first argument of `insert`, as specified by the following normalization rule; the same happens to the second argument of `replace`. As with element construction in XQuery 1.0, this copy prevents the inserted tree from having two parents.

$$\frac{[\![\texttt{insert }\{\mathit{Expr}_1\}\texttt{ into }\{\mathit{Expr}_2\}]\!]}{\texttt{insert }\{\texttt{copy }\{[\![\mathit{Expr}_1]\!]\}\}\texttt{ as last into }\{[\![\mathit{Expr}_2]\!]\}}$$

3.4 Formal Semantics

Dynamic Evaluation Judgment. We extend the semantic judgment "$\mathit{dynEnv} \vdash \mathit{Expr} \Rightarrow \mathit{value}$", in order to deal with delayed updates and side-effects, as follows:

$$\mathit{store}_0;\ \mathit{dynEnv} \vdash \mathit{Expr} \Rightarrow \mathit{value};\ \Delta;\ \mathit{store}_1$$

Here, store_0 is the initial store, *dynEnv* is the dynamic context, *Expr* is the expression being evaluated, *value* and Δ are the value and the list of update requests returned by the expression, and store_1 is the new store after the expression has been evaluated. The updates in Δ have not been applied to $store_1$ yet, but *Expr* may have modified $store_1$ thanks to a nested `snap`, or by allocating new elements.

Observe that, while the store is modified, the update list Δ is just returned by the expression, exactly as the *value*. This property hints at the fact that an expression which just produces update requests, without applying them, is actually side-effects free, hence can be evaluated with the same approaches used to evaluate pure functional expressions. This is the main reason to use a snapshot semantics: inside the innermost `snap`, where updates are collected but not applied, lazy evaluation techniques can be applied.

Dynamic Semantics of XQuery Expressions. The presence of stores and Δ means that every judgment in XQuery 1.0 must be extended in order to properly deal with them. Specifically, every semantic judgment which contains at least two subexpressions has to be extended in order to specify which subexpression has to be evaluated first. Consider for example the XQuery! rule for the sequence constructor.

$$\frac{\begin{array}{c} store_0;\ dynEnv \vdash Expr_1 \ \Rightarrow\ value_1;\ \Delta_1;\ store_1 \\ store_1;\ dynEnv \vdash Expr_2 \ \Rightarrow\ value_2;\ \Delta_2;\ store_2 \end{array}}{store_0;\ dynEnv \vdash Expr_1, Expr_2 \ \Rightarrow\ value_1, value_2;\ (\Delta_1, \Delta_2);\ store_2}$$

As written, $Expr_1$ must be evaluated first in order for $store_1$ to be computed and passed for the evaluation of $Expr_2$.

If a sub-expression is guaranteed not to invoke a `snap`, the compiler can again choose evaluation order as in the original XQuery 1.0 semantics for that sub-expression. Of course, Δ_1 must precede Δ_2 in the result, when the *ordered* approach is followed, but this is not harder than preserving the order of ($value_1$, $value_2$); preserving update order is more complex in the case of FLWOR expressions and function calls (see [13]).

Dynamic Semantics of XQuery! Operations. We have to define the semantics of `copy`, of the update operators, and of `snap`. `copy` just invokes the corresponding operation at the data model level, adding the corresponding nodes to the store. The evaluation of an update operation produces an update request, which is added to the list of the pending update requests produced by the subexpressions, while `replace` produces *two* update requests, insertion and deletion. Here is the semantics of `replace`. The metavariables express constraints on rule applicability: *node* and *nodepar* can only be matched to node ids, and *nodeseq* only to a sequence of node ids.

$$\frac{\begin{array}{c} store_0;\ dynEnv \vdash Expr_1 \ \Rightarrow\ node;\ \Delta_1;\ store_1 \\ store_1;\ dynEnv \vdash Expr_2 \ \Rightarrow\ nodeseq;\ \Delta_2;\ store_2 \\ store_2;\ dynEnv \vdash \mathrm{parent}(node) \ \Rightarrow\ nodepar;\ ();\ store_2 \\ \Delta_3 = (\Delta_1, \Delta_2, \mathrm{insert}(nodeseq, nodepar, node), \mathrm{delete}(node)) \end{array}}{store_0;\ dynEnv \vdash \texttt{replace}\ \{Expr_1\}\ \texttt{with}\ \{Expr_2\} \ \Rightarrow\ ();\ \Delta_3;\ store_2}$$

The evaluation produces an empty sequence and an update list Δ_3. It may also modify the store, but only if either $Expr_1$ or $Expr_2$ modify it. If they only perform allocations or copies, their evaluation can still be commuted or interleaved. If either executes a `snap`, the processor must follow the order specified by the rule, since, for example, $Expr_2$ may depend on the part of the store which has been modified by a `snap` in $Expr_1$.

The two update requests produced by the operation are just inserted into the pending update list Δ_3 after every update requested by the two subexpressions. The actual order is only relevant if the *ordered* semantics has been requested for the smallest enclosing snap.

The rule for snap $\{Expr\}$ looks very simple: *Expr* is evaluated, it produces its own update list Δ, Δ is applied to the store, and the value of *Expr* is returned.

$$\frac{store_0;\ dynEnv \vdash Expr \Rightarrow value;\ \Delta;\ store_1 \qquad store_2 = \text{apply } \Delta \text{ to } store_1}{store_0;\ dynEnv \vdash \texttt{snap}\ \{Expr\} \Rightarrow value;\ ();\ store_2}$$

The evaluation of *Expr* may itself modify the store, and snap updates this modified store. For example, the following piece of code inserts <b/><a/><c/> into $x, in this order, since the internal snap is closed first, and it only applies the updates in its own scope.

```
snap ordered { insert {<a/>} into $x,
               snap   { insert {<b/>} into $x },
               insert {<c/>} into $x }
```

Hence, the formal semantics implicitly specifies a stack-like behavior, reflected by the actual stack-based implementation that we adopted (see [13]).

In the appendix we list the semantic rules for the other update operations, and for the most important core XQuery 1.0 expressions.

4 Implementation and Optimization

XQuery! has been implemented as an extension to the Galax XQuery engine [20,19], and a preliminary version is available for download[2]. In this section, we review the modifications that were required to the original Galax compiler to support side-effects, notably changes to the optimizer.

4.1 Data Model and Run-Time

Changes to the data model implementation to support atomic updates were not terribly invasive. The only two significant challenges relate to dealing with document order maintenance, and garbage collection of persistent but unreachable nodes, which is made necessary by the use of the detach semantics for the delete expression (See Section 3.1). Both of these aspects are beyond the scope of this paper.

The run-time must be modified to support update lists, which are computed in addition to the value for each expression. The way the update lists are represented internally depends on whether the snap operator uses the ordered semantics or not (See Section 3.2). Because the nondeterministic and conflict-detection semantics are both independent of the actual order of the atomic updates collected in a snap scope, they

[2] http://xquerybang.cs.washington.edu/

can be easily implemented using a stack of update lists, where each update list on the stack corresponds to a given `snap` scope, and where the order inside a list is irrelevant. The invocation of an update operation adds an update to the update list on the top of the stack. When exiting a `snap`, the top-most update list is popped from the stack and applied. In the case of conflict-detection semantics, it is also checked for conflicts, in linear time, using a pair of hash-tables over node ids.

This implementation strategy has the virtue that it does not require substantial modifications to an existing compiler. The implementation of the ordered semantics is more involved, as we must rely on a specialized tree structure to represent the update lists in a way that allows the compiler to lazily evaluate FLWOR expressions and still retain the order in which each update must be applied. We refer to the full paper [13] for more details.

4.2 Compilation Architecture

Implementing XQuery! does not require modifications to the XQuery processing model. The XQuery! compiler in Galax proceeds by first *parsing* the query into an AST and *normalization*, followed by a phase of syntactic *rewriting*, *compilation* into the XML algebra of [20] with some simple update extensions, *optimization* and finally *evaluation*.

Changes to parsing and normalization are trivial (See Section 3). To preserve the XQuery! semantics, some of the syntactic rewritings must be guarded by a judgment checking whether side effects may occur in a given sub-expression. Of course, this is not necessary when the query is guarded by an innermost `snap`, i.e., a `snap` whose scope contains no other `snap`, nor any call to any function which may cause a `snap` to be evaluated. Inside such innermost `snap`, all the rewritings immediately apply.

4.3 XQuery! Optimizer

Galax uses a rule-based approach in several phases of the logical optimization. Most rewrite rules require some modifications. To illustrate the way the optimizer works, let us consider the following variant of XMark query 8 which, for each person, stores information about the purchased items.

```
for $p in $auction//person
let $a :=
  for $t in $auction//closed_auction
  where $t/buyer/@person = $p/@id
  return (insert { <buyer person="{$t/buyer/@person}"
                          itemid="{$t/itemref/@item}" /> }
          into { $purchasers }, $t)
return <item person="{ $p/name }">{ count($a) }</item>
```

Ignoring the insert operation for a moment, the query is essentially the same as XMark 8, and can be evaluated efficiently with an outer join followed by a group by. Such a query plan can be produced using query unnesting techniques such as those proposed in e.g., [20]. A naive nested-loop evaluation has complexity O($|person| * |closed\_auction|$). Using an outer join/group by with a typed hash join, we can recover the join complexity of $O(|person| + |closed\_auction| + |matches|)$, resulting in a substantial improvement.

In XQuery!, recall that the query is always wrapped into a top-level snap. Because that top-level snap does not contain any nested snap, the state of the database will not change during the evaluation of the query, and a outer-join/group-by plan can be used. The optimized plan generated by our XQuery! compiler is shown below. The syntax used for that query plan is that of [20], where algebraic operators are written as follows:

$$\mathsf{Op}[\mathsf{p}_1,\ldots,\mathsf{p}_i]\{\mathsf{DOp}_1,\ldots,\mathsf{DOp}_h\}(\mathsf{Op}_1,\ldots,\mathsf{Op}_k)$$

with Op being the operator name; p_i's being the static parameters of the operator; DOp_i's being dependent sub-operators; and Op_i's are input (or independent) operators. [...] stands for tuple construction, # for tuple field access, and IN is the input of dependent sub-operators (as passed by the operator from the result of its independents sub-operators). Path expressions, constructors, and update operators are written in XQuery! syntax for conciseness.

```
Snap (
  MapFromItem{
    <person name="{ IN#p/name }">{ count(IN#a) }</person>
   }
   (GroupBy [a,index,null]
        { IN }
        { (insert { <buyer person="{IN#t/buyer/@person}"
                             itemid="{IN#t/itemref/@item}" /> }
           as last into { $purchasers }, IN#t) }
    (LOuterJoin[null]{ IN#t/buyer/@person = IN#p/@id }
         (MapIndexStep[index]
            (MapFromItem{[p:IN]}($auction//person)),
          MapFromItem{[t:IN]}($auction//closed_auction)))))
```

In general, the optimization rules must be guarded by appropriate preconditions to ensure that not only the resulting value is correct, but also that the order (when applicable) and the values of side-effects are preserved. Those preconditions check for properties related to cardinality and a notion of independence between expressions. The former ensures that expressions are evaluated with the correct cardinality, as changing the number of invocation may change the number of effects applied to the store. The latter is used to check that a part of the query cannot observe the effects resulting from another part of the query, hence allowing certain rewritings to occur.

More specifically, consider the compilation of a join from nested for loops (maps): we must check that the inner branch of a join does not have updates. If the inner branch of the join does have update operations, they would be applied once for each element of the outer loop. Merge join and hash joins are efficient because they only evaluate their inputs once, however doing so may change the cardinality for the side-effect portion of the query. Additionally, we must ensure that applying these new updates does not change the values returned in the outer branch, thus changing the value returned by the join. The first problem requires some analysis of the query plan, while the latter is difficult to ensure without the use of snap. In our example, if we had used a `snap insert` at line 5 of the source code, the group-by optimization would be more difficult to detect as one would have to know that the effect of the inserts are not observed in the rest of the query. This property has some similarity with the notion binding independance proposed in [1], although it needs to be applied here on a much more expressive language.

5 Related Work

Nested Transactions. The `snap` operator groups update requests to apply them all at once, which is reminiscent of transactions. However, their purpose and semantics are essentially orthogonal. Flat transactions are meant to protect a piece of code from concurrently running transactions, while nested transactions allow the programmer to isolate different concurrent threads within its own code.

On the other side, without concurrency and failures, transactions have no effect. In particular, within a given transaction, access to a variable x that has been modified will return the new value for that variable. On the contrary, an update to x requested inside a `snap` scope will not affect the result of queries to x inside the same scope. In a nutshell, transactions isolate against external actions, while `snap` delays internal actions.

Monads in Pure Functional Languages. Our approach allows the programmer to write essentially imperative code containing code fragments which are purely functional, and hence can be optimized more easily. The motivation is similar to that of monadic approaches in languages such as Haskell [15]. In those approaches, the type system distinguishes between purely functional code, which can be lazily evaluated, from impure "monadic" code, for which evaluation order is constrained. The type system will not allow pure code to call monadic code, while monadic code may invoke pure code at will.

An XQuery! processor must also distinguish the case where the query has some pending updates but no effect, going beyond the pure-impure distinction. Those pieces of code in XQuery! do not block every optimizations, provided that some "independence" constraints are verified. It seems that these constraints are too complex to be represented through types. Hence, we let the optimizer collect the relevant information, and in particular flag the scope of each innermost `snap` as *pure*. To be fair, we believe that a bit of typing would be useful: the signature of functions coming from other modules should contain an *updating* flag, with the "monadic" rule that a function that calls an updating function is *updating* as well. We are currently investigating the systematic translation of XQuery! to a core monadic language, which should give us a more complete understanding of the relationship between the two approaches.

Snapshot Semantics and Optimization. The optimization opportunities enabled by the snapshot semantics are explored in [1]. An important difference is that we consider similar optimization in the context of a fully compositional language.

6 Conclusion

We presented a semantic framework, and an extension of XQuery 1.0 that supports fully compositional updates. The main contribution of our work is the definition of a `snap` operator which enables control over update application and supports arbitrary nesting. We described a prototype implementation which is available for download. Many important issues are still open for research, such as static typing, optimization, and transactional mechanisms. We are currently working on those issues.

Acknowledgments. We want to thank the members of the W3C XML Query working group update task for numerous discussions on updates. Thanks to Daniela Florescu, Don Chamberlin, Ioana Manolescu, Andrew Eisenberg, Kristoffer Rose, Mukund Raghavachari, Rajesh Bordawekar, and Michael Benedikt for their feedback on earlier versions of this draft. Special thanks go to Dan Suciu for proposing `snap` as the keyword used in XQuery!.

References

1. Michael Benedikt, Angela Bonifati, Sergio Flesca, and Avinash Vyas. Adding updates to XQuery: Semantics, optimization, and static analysis. In *XIME-P'05*, 2005.
2. Scott Boag, Don Chamberlin, Mary F. Fernandez, Daniela Florescu, Jonathan Robie, and Jérôme Simeon. XQuery 1.0: An XML query language. W3C Candidate Recommendation, November 2005.
3. Don Chamberlin. Communication regarding an update proposal. W3C XML Query Update Task Force, May 2005.
4. Don Chamberlin, Daniela Florescu, and Jonathan Robie. XQuery update facility. W3C Working Draft, January 2006.
5. Don Chamberlin and Jonathan Robie. XQuery update facility requirements. W3C Working Draft, June 2005.
6. XQuery 1.0 and XPath 2.0 data model (XDM). W3C Candidate Recommendation, November 2005.
7. Denise Draper, Peter Fankhauser, Mary Fernández, Ashok Malhotra, Kristoffer Rose, Michael Rys, Jerôme Siméon, and Philip Wadler. XQuery 1.0 and XPath 2.0 formal semantics. W3C Candidate Recommendation, November 2005.
8. Daniela Florescu et al. Communication regarding an XQuery update facility. W3C XML Query Working Group, July 2005.
9. Don Chamberlin et al. Communication regarding updates for XQuery. W3C XML Query Working Group, October 2002.
10. Mary Fernández, Jerôme Siméon, and Philip Wadler. *XQuery from the experts*, chapter Introduction to the Formal Semantics. Addison Wesley, 2004.
11. Daniela Florescu. Communication regarding update grammar. W3C XML Query Update Task Force, April 2005.
12. Daniela Florescu, Andreas Grünhagen, and Donald Kossmann. XL: An XML programming language for Web service specification and composition. In *Proceedings of International World Wide Web Conference*, pages 65–76, May 2002.
13. Giorgio Ghelli, Christopher Ré, and Jérôme Siméon. XQuery!: An XML query language with side effects, full paper, 2005. `http://xquerybang.cs.washington.edu/papers/XQueryBangTR.pdf`.
14. Jan Hidders, Jan Paredaens, Roel Vercammen, and Serge Demeyer. A light but formal introduction to XQuery. In *Database and XML Technologies (XSym)*, pages 5–20, May 2004.
15. Simon Peyton Jones. Tackling the awkward squad: monadic input/output, concurrency, exceptions, and foreign-language calls in Haskell. In "Engineering theories of software construction", ed Tony Hoare, Manfred Broy, Ralf Steinbruggen, IOS Press, 2001.

16. Patrick Lehti. Design and implementation of a data manipulation processor for an XML query processor, Technical University of Darmstadt, Germany, Diplomarbeit, 2001.
17. Xavier Leroy. *The Objective Caml system, release 3.08, Documentation and user's manual.* Institut National de Recherche en Informatique et en Automatique, july 2004.
18. Robin Milner, Mads Tofte, Robert Harper, and David MacQueen. *The definition of Standard ML (revised).* MIT Press, 1997.
19. Christopher Ré, Jerome Simeon, and Mary Fernandez. A complete and efficient algebraic compiler for XQuery. Technical report, AT&T Labs Research, 2005.
20. Christopher Ré, Jerome Simeon, and Mary Fernandez. A complete and efficient algebraic compiler for XQuery. In *ICDE*, Atlanta,GA, April 2006.
21. Michael Rys. Proposal for an XML data modification language, version 3, May 2002. Microsoft Corp., Redmond, WA.
22. A. Schmidt, F. Waas, M. Kersten, M. Carey, Ioana Manolescu, and Ralph Busse. XMark: A benchmark for XML data management. In *VLDB*, pages 974–985, August 2002.
23. Gargi M. Sur, Joachim Hammer, and Jérôme Siméon. An XQuery-based language for processing updates in XML. In *PLAN-X*, 2004.

Conflict Resolution in Updates Through XML Views

André Prisco Vargas[1], Vanessa P. Braganholo[2], and Carlos A. Heuser[1]

[1] Instituto de Informática - Federal University of Rio Grande do Sul - Brazil
[2] COPPE - Federal University of Rio de Janeiro - Brazil
{apvargas, heuser}@inf.ufrgs.br, vanessa@cos.ufrj.br

Abstract. In this paper, we focus on B2B scenarios where XML views are extracted from relational databases and sent over the Web to another application that edits them and sends them back after a certain (usually long) period of time. In such transactions, it is unrealistic to lock the base tuples that are in the view to achieve concurrency control. Thus, there are some issues that need to be solved: first, to identify what changes were made in the view and second, to identify and solve conflicts that may arise due to changes in the database state during the transaction. We address both of these issues in this paper by proposing an approach that uses our XML view update system PATAXÓ.

1 Introduction

XML is increasingly being used as an exchange format between business to business (B2B) applications. In this context, a very common scenario is one in which data is stored in relational databases (mainly due to the maturity of the technology) and exported in XML format [14,9] before being sent over the Web. The proposes in [14,9], however, address only part of the problem, that is, they know how to generate and query XML views over relational databases, but they do not know how to update those views. In B2B environments, enterprises need not only to obtain XML views, but also to update them. An example is a company B (buyer) that buys products from another company S (supplier). One could think on B asking S for an *order form*. B would them receive this form (an empty XML view) in a PDA of one of its employees who would fill it in and send it back to S. S would them have to process it and place the new order in its relational database. This scenario is not so complicated, since the initial XML view was empty. There are, however, more complicated cases. Consider the case where B changes its mind and asks S its order back, because it wants to change the quantities of some of the products it had ordered before. In this case, the initial XML view is not empty, and S needs to know what changes B made to it, so it can reflect the changes back to the database.

In previous work [2], we have proposed PATAXÓ, an approach to update relational databases through XML views. In this approach, XML views are constructed using UXQuery [3], an extension of XQuery, and updates are issued through a very simple update language. The scenario we address in this paper is different in the following senses: (i) In PATAXÓ [2], updates are issued through an update language that allows insertions, deletions and modifications. In this paper, we deal with updates done directly over the XML view, that is, users directly *edit* the XML view. Thus, we need to know

T. Grust et al. (Eds.): EDBT 2006 Workshops, LNCS 4254, pp. 192–205, 2006.

exactly what changes were made to the view. We address this by calculating the *delta* between the original and the updated view. Algorithms in literature [6,4,17,7] may be used in this case, but need to be adapted for the special features of the updatable XML views produced by PATAXÓ; (ii) In PATAXÓ [2], we rely on the transaction manager of the underlying DBMS. As most DBMS apply the ACID transaction model, this means that we simple lock the database tuples involved in a view until all the updates have been translated to the database. In B2B environments, this is impractical because the transactions may take a long time to complete [5]. Returning to our example, company B could take days to submit the changes to its order back to S. The problem in this case is what to do when the database state changes during the transaction (because of external updates). In such cases, the original XML view may not be valid anymore, and conflicts may occur.

In this paper, we propose an approach to solve the open problems listed above. We use PATAXÓ [2] to both generate the XML view and to translate the updates over the XML view back to the underlying relational database. For this to be possible, the update operations that were executed over the XML view need to be detected and specified using the PATAXÓ update language. It is important to notice that not all update operations are valid in this context. For example, PATAXÓ does not allow changing the tags of the XML elements, since this modifies the view schema – this kind of modification can not be mapped back to the underlying relational database.

We assume the XML view is updatable. This means that all updates applied to it can be successfully mapped to the underlying relational database. In [2], we present a set of rules the view definition query must obey in order for the resulting XML view to be updatable. Basically, this means that primary keys are preserved in the view, joins are made by key-foreign keys, and nesting is done from the owner relation to the owned relation. An example of non-updatable view would be a view that repeats the customer name for each item of a given order. This redundancy causes problems in updates, thus the view is not updatable.

Application Scenario. Consider companies B and S, introduced above. Company S has a relational DB that stores orders, products and customers. The DB schema is shown in Figure 1(a). Now, let's exemplify the scenario previously described. Company B requests its order to company S so it can alter it. The result of this request is the XML view shown in Figure 2 (the numbers near the nodes, shown in red in the Figure, are used so we can refer to a specific node in our examples). While company B is analyzing the view and deciding what changes it will make over it, the relational database of company S is updated as shown in Figure 1(b). These updates may have been made directly over the database, or through some other XML view. The main point is that the update over *LineOrder* affects the XML view that is being analyzed by company B. Specifically, it changes the price of one of the products that B has ordered (blue pen).

Meanwhile, B is still analyzing its order (XML view) and deciding what to change. It does not have any idea that product "BLUEPEN" had its price doubled. After 5 hours, it decides to make the changes shown in Figure 3 (the changes are shown in boldface in the figure). The changes are: increase the quantity of blue pens to 200, increase the quantity of red pens to 300, and order a new item (100 notebooks (NTBK)). Notice

(a)
```
Customer (custId, name, address),
   primary key (custId)
Product (prodId, description, curPrice),
   primary key (prodId)
Order (numOrder, date, custId, status),
   primary key (numOrder),
   foreign key (custId) references Customer
LineOrder (numOrder, prodId, quantity, price),
   primary key (numOrder, prodId),
   foreign key (prodId) references Product,
   foreign key (numOrder) references Order
```

(b)
```
//increases price of "blue pen"
UPDATE Product
SET curPrice = 0.10
WHERE prodId = "BLUEPEN";

UPDATE LineOrder
SET price = 0.10
WHERE prodId = "BLUEPEN" AND
numOrder IN (SELECT numOrder
  FROM Order WHERE status="open");
```

Fig. 1. (a) Sample database of company S (b) Updates made over the database

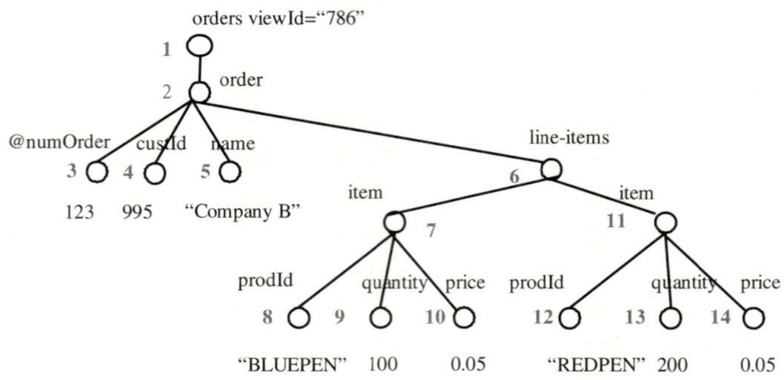

Fig. 2. Original XML view

there that, in order to add a new product in its order, B has to query S for a catalog of products. We assume this has already been done.

When S receives the updated view, it will have to: (i) Detect what were the changes made by B in the XML view; (ii) Detect that the updates shown in Figure 1(b) affect the view returned by B, and detect exactly what are the conflicts; (iii) Decide how to solve the conflicts, and update the database using PATAXÓ.

Contributions and Organization of the Text. The main contributions of this paper are: (i) A delta detection technique tailored to the PATAXÓ XML views; (ii) An approach to verify the status of the database during the transaction. This is done by comparing the status of the database in the beginning of the transaction with the status of the database in the time the updated view is returned to the system; (iii) A conflict resolution technique, based on the structure of the XML view; (iv) A merge algorithm to XML views that emphasizes the conflicts caused by changes in the database state during the transaction.

The remaining of this paper is organized as follows. Section 2 discusses related work. Section 3 presents an overview of the PATAXÓ approach. Section 4.1 presents our technique to detect deltas in XML views, and Section 4.2 presents a solution to the problems caused by conflicts. Finally, we conclude in Section 5.

2 Related Work

Extended Transactions. As we mentioned in the introduction, in this paper we do not rely only on the ACID transaction model implemented by most of the DBMS. Instead,

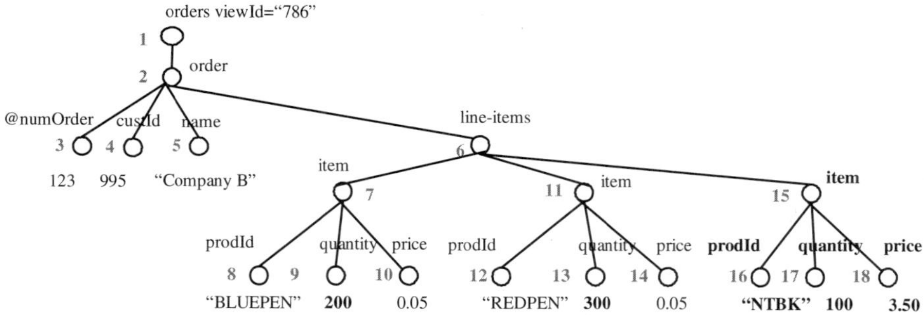

Fig. 3. XML view updated by company B and returned to company S

we propose a mechanism to detect changes that were done offline. This mechanism is responsible for detecting the cases where the offline changes done through the view may conflict to changes done directly through the database. [5] discusses the effects of transaction on objects and the interactions between transactions on several extended transaction models. In our paper, we use the terminology presented in [5], but do not use any of the extended transaction models proposed there. We discuss the reason for that below.

In our paper, although we externally detect conflicts between update operations, we still depend on the ACID transaction model, since the updates are actually executed by the underlying DBMS (we do not want to change the DBMS in anyway). Because of this, even if we have several views being updated at the same time, it is enough to detect conflicts between the database and the view that has just been returned to the system. To exemplify, assume we have a database D and a set of views $V_1, ..., V_n$ specified over D using the exact same view definition query (i.e., the views are identical). Assume also that all of these views are being updated offline. When the updated views are returned to PATAXÓ, we have an order in which they will be analyzed. Assume this order is $V_1, ..., V_n$ (the order in which the views were returned to the system). We then compare V_1 with the current state of D to detect conflicts, and translate non conflicting updates to D. Then, we proceed with the next view in the queue. Notice that the updates done through V_1 are already reflected in D, so we do not need to compare V_1 with V_2 to detect conflicts. Thus, we have isolated transactions.

On a similar line of thought, [1] criticizes the ANSI SQL-92 *Isolation Levels*, and discusses the problems that may occur when several transactions interact over the same data. Since we are not proposing a new transaction manager in our approach, we claim we do not need to worry about such things in our approach.

Harmony. Work related to our approach is the Harmony Project [13], in which the authors propose the use of *lenses* to synchronize data in different formats. In [10], the authors propose to use the semantic foundation of *lenses* to support updates through views. Their formal framework treats the database as a concrete format, and views over the database as an abstract format. Then, lenses are used to map concrete data to abstract views (*get component*), and the inverse mapping (the one required to update the database - *putback component*) derives automatically from the get component. After defined, two abstract views v_1 and v_2 can be synchronized. Comparing to our scenario, we may assume v_1 is the original view and v_2 is the updated view. The concrete format of v_1 is the database D, while the concrete format of v_2 is v_2 itself (in this case we use the identity lens to perform the mapping from v_2 to v_2). When the database is updated, v_1 reflects the changes. The problem here is that when we synchronize v_1 and v_2, we may erroneously reinsert old things in the database. As an example, suppose we have tuples t_1 and t_2 in D. Suppose also that t_1 and t_2 are both in v_1. View v_2, at the beginning, is equal to v_1, so it also has t_1 and t_2. Suppose that, while v_2 is being updated, D is updated to delete t_2. Thus, v_1 will reflect this change, and now it has only t_1. Meanwhile, v_2 is updated to insert t_3, and so it now has t_1, t_2 and t_3. When v_1 is synchronized with v_2, the system finds out that t_2 and t_3 needs to be inserted into v_1 (and consequently into D). It is thus erroneously reinserting t_2. Our approach, in this case, would insert only t_3.

Consistency control of disconnected replicas. A problem closely related to our work is the problem of consistency control of disconnected database replicas [11,15,12]. To solve such problem, Phatak and Badrinath [12] propose a reconciliation phase that synchronizes operations. [11] uses conflict detection and dependencies between operations. However, these approaches do not deal with the XML views problem or require the semantics of the data to be known. In our paper, we use some of the ideas of [11] in the XML context.

3 The PATAXÓ Approach

As mentioned before, PATAXÓ [2] is a system that is capable of constructing XML views over relational databases and mapping updates specified over this view back into the underlying relational database. To do so, it uses an existing approach on updates through relational views [8]. Basically, a view query definition expressed in UXQuery [3] is internally mapped to a query tree [2]. Query trees are a formalism that captures the structure and the source of each XML element/attribute of the XML view, together with the restrictions applied to build the view. As an example, the query tree that corresponds to the view query that generates the XML view of Figure 2 is shown if Figure 4. The interested reader can refer to [2] for a full specification of query trees.

In this paper, it will be important to recognize certain types of nodes in the query tree and in the corresponding view instance. In the query tree of Figure 4, node *order* is a *starred-node* (*-node) [1]. Each starred node generates a collection of (possibly complex) elements. Each such element carries data from a database tuple, or from a join between two or more tuples (tables Customer and Order, in the example). We call each element of this collection a *starred subtree*. The element itself (the root of the subtree), is called

[1] Notice that, despite the fact that the condition *numOrder=123* restricts this view to a single order, node *order* is defined as a starred node. This is because the formal definition of query trees requires that nodes with *source annotations* be starred [2]. In [2], this decision was made to simplify the mapping to relational views – this way, the algorithm does not need to check the *where* annotations to find out whether a given node will have single or multiple instances. More details about the formal definition of query trees can be found in [2]. Notice further that this view would not be *updatable* if it had multiple orders, since the *name* of the customer could be redundant. To solve this problem, orders would have to be nested within customer.

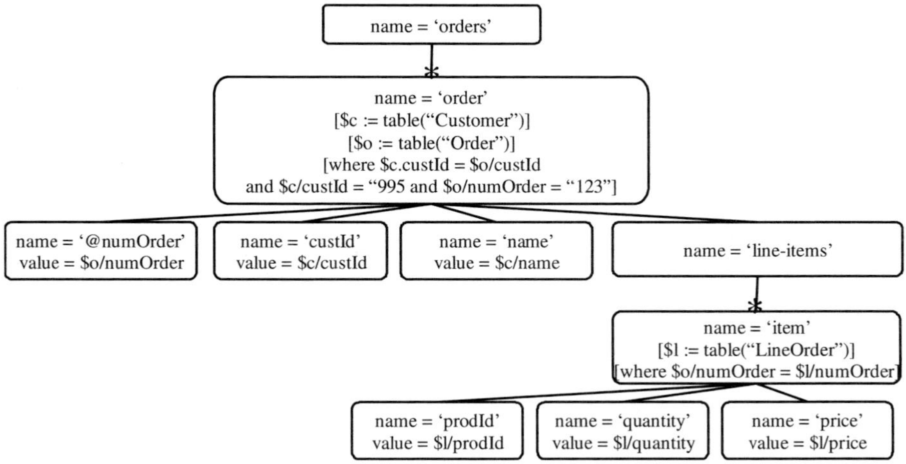

Fig. 4. Query tree that generated the XML view of Figure 2

starred element. In the example of Figure 2 (which is generated from the query tree of Figure 4), nodes 2, 7 and 11 are *starred elements* (since they are produced by starred nodes of the corresponding query tree).

Updates in PATAXÓ. As mentioned before, PATAXÓ uses a very simple update language. Basically, it is expressed by a triple $\langle t, \Delta, \mathit{ref}\rangle$, where t is the type of the operation (*insert*, *delete* or *update*), Δ is the subtree to be inserted or an atomic value to be modified, and *ref* is a path expression that points to the update point in the XML view. The update point *ref* is expressed by a simple XPath expression that only contains child access (/) and conjunctive filters.

Not all update specifications are valid, since they need to be mapped back to the underlying relational database. Mainly, the updates applied to the view need to follow the view DTD. PATAXÓ generates the view together with its DTD, and both the view and the DTD are sent to the client application. The DTD of the XML view of Figure 2 is available in [16]. The remaining restrictions regarding updates are as follows: (i) subtrees inserted must represent a (possibly complex/nested) database tuple. This restriction corresponds to adding only subtrees rooted at starred nodes in the query trees of [2]. Such elements correspond to elements with cardinality "*" in the DTD. Thus, in this paper, it is enough to know that only subtrees rooted at elements with cardinality "*" in the DTD can be inserted. In Figure 3 the inserted subtree `item` (node 15) satisfies this condition. (ii) The above restriction is the same for deletions. Subtrees deleted must be rooted at a starred node in the query tree. This means that in the example view, we could delete `order` and `item` subtrees.

All of these restrictions can be verified by checking the updated XML view against the DTD of the original view. As an example, it would not be possible to delete node `name` (which is not a starred element, and so contradicts rule (ii) above), since this is a required element in the DTD. Also, it is necessary to check that updates, insertions and deletions satisfy the view definition query. As an example, it would not be possible to insert another `order` element in the view, since the view definition requires that this view has only an order with `numOrder` equals "123" (see the restrictions on node *order* of Figure 4).

Notice that we do not support "?" cardinality in our model. This is because we map updates over the view to updates of the same type in the relational database (insertions map to insertions, deletions map to deletions, and so on). Supporting optional elements would make us to break this rule. Inserting an optional leaf element would map to modifying a database tuple. In the same way, deleting an optional element would map to modifying the corresponding tuple to NULL. We discuss this in more details in [3].

4 Supporting Disconnected Transactions

In this section, we describe our approach and illustrate it using the order example of Section 1. Our architecture [16] has three main modules: the *Transaction Manager*, *Diff Finder* and *Update Manager*. The *Transaction Manager* is responsible for controlling the currently opened transactions of the system. It receives a view definition query, passes it to PATAXÓ, receives PATAXÓ's answer (the resulting XML view and its DTD), and before sending it to the client, it: (i) adds an `viewId` to the root of the XML view (this attribute is set to 786 in the example view of Figure 2; the value that will be assigned to attribute `viewId` is controlled by a sequential counter in the Transaction Manager); (ii) adds this same attribute, with the same value, to the root of the view definition query; (iii) adds an attribute declaration in the view DTD for the `viewId`; (iv) stores the XML view, the view definition query and the view DTD in a *Temporary Storage* facility, since they will have to be used later when the updated view is returned to the system.

When the updated view is returned by the user to the system, the Transaction Manager checks its `viewId` (it is a requirement of our approach that the `viewID` is not modified during the transaction) and uses it to find the view DTD and the definition query, which are stored in the Temporary Storage facility. Then it uses the DTD to validate the updated view. If the view is not valid, then the transaction is aborted and the user is notified. In the case it is valid, then the Transaction Manager sends the view definition query to PATAXÓ, and receives a new XML view reflecting the database state at this moment as a response (we will call it *view'*). This new XML view will be used to check the database state. If it is exactly the same as the original XML view (which is also stored in the temporary storage facility), then the updates made to the database during this transaction do not affect the XML view. In this case all view updates made in the updated XML view may be translated back to the database. Notice that, at this stage, we have three copies of the XML view in the system:

- The *original* XML view (O): the view that was sent to the client at the first place. In our example, the original view is shown in Figure 2.
- The *updated* XML view (U): the view that was updated by the client and returned to the system. The updated XML view is shown in Figure 3.
- The *view'*: a new XML view which is the result of running the view definition query again, right after the updated view arrives in the system. *View'* is used to

(a)

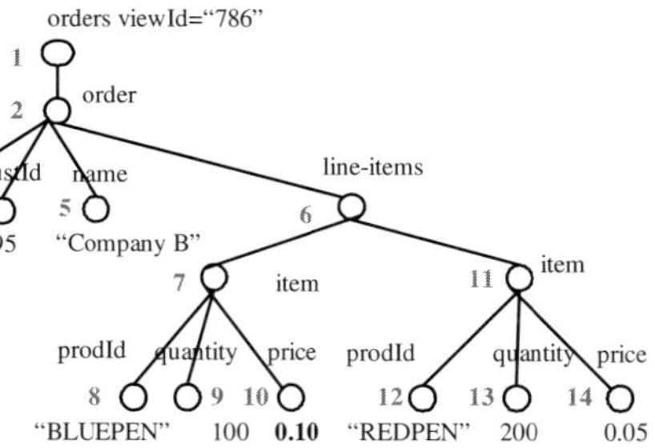

(b)

$E_1(O \rightarrow U)$ = *Update(9, 200), Update(13, 300), Insert(t_1, 6))*

```
t1 = <item>
       <prodId>NTBK</prodId>
       <quantity>100</quatity>
       <price>3.50</price>
     </item>
```

$E_2(O \rightarrow$ *view'*) = *Update(10, 0.10)*

Fig. 5. (a) View' (b) Edit scripts for our example

capture possible conflicts caused by external updates in the base tuples that are in the original view. As an example, view' is shown in Figure 5(a). Notice that it reflects the base updates shown in Figure 1(b).

These views are sent to the *Diff Finder* module. In this module, two comparisons take place. First, the *original* view is compared to the *updated* view, to find what were the updates made over the view. Next, the *original* view is compared to *view'* to find out if the database state has changed during the transaction (Section 4.1). The deltas found by *Diff Finder* are sent to the *Update Manager*, which analyzes them and detects conflicts. In case there are no conflicts, the Update Manager transforms the updates into updates using the PATAXÓ update language and sends them to PATAXÓ. PATAXÓ then translates them to the relational database. If there are conflicts we try to solve them (Section 4.2), and then notify the user of the result of the updates (Section 4.3).

4.1 Detecting Deltas in XML Views

As mentioned before, the *Diff Finder* is responsible for detecting the changes made in the XML view, and also in the database (through the comparison of *view'* with the original view). To accomplish this, it makes use of an existing diff algorithm that finds *deltas* between two XML views. A *delta* is a set of operations that denotes the difference between two data structures D_1 and D_2 in a way that if we apply *delta* to D_1, we obtain D_2. Using the notation of [17], this delta can be expressed by $E(D_1 \rightarrow D_2)$.

We adopt X-Diff [17] as our diff algorithm, mainly because it is capable of detecting the operations supported by PATAXÓ (insertion of subtrees, deletion of subtrees and modification of text values), and considers an unordered model. MH-DIFF [4] does not support insertion and deletion of subtrees, (it supports only insertion and deletion of single nodes), thus it is not appropriate in our context. Xy-Diff [6] and XMLTreeDiff [7] consider ordered models, which does not match the unordered model of our source data (relations).

X-DIFF. According to [17], the operations detected by X-Diff are as follows:

Insertion of leaf node. The operation *Insert(x(name, value), y)* inserts a leaf node x with name *name* and value *value*. Node x is inserted as a child of y.

Deletion of leaf node. Operation *Delete(x)* deletes a leaf node x.

Modification of leaf value. A modification of a leaf value is expressed as *Update(*x*, new-value)*, and it changes the value of node x to *new-value*.

Insertion of subtree. Operation *Insert(*T_x*,* y*)* inserts a subtree T_x (rooted at node x) as a child of node y.

Deletion of subtree. The operation *Delete(*T_x*)* deletes a subtree T_x (rooted at node x). When there is no doubts about which is x, this operation can be expressed as *Delete(*x*)*.

An important characteristic of X-Diff is that it uses parent-child relationships to calculate the minimum-cost matching between two trees T_1 and T_2. This parent-child relationship is captured by the use of a node *signature* and also by a hash function. The hash function applied to node y considers its entire subtree. Thus, two equal subtrees in T_1 and T_2 have the same hash value. The node signature of a node x is expressed by *Name(*x_1*)/.../Name(*x_n*)/Name(*x*)/Type(*x*)*, where (x_1/.../x_n/x) is the path from the root to x, and *Type(*x*)* is the type of node x. In case x is not an atomic element, its signature does not include *Type(*x*)* [17]. Matches are made in a way that only nodes with the same signature are matched. Also, nodes with the same hash value are identical subtrees, and thus they are matched by X-Diff.

To exemplify, Figure 5(b) shows the edit script generated by X-Diff for the original (O) and updated (U) views. This Figure also shows the edit script for the original (O) view and view', which is also calculated by *Diff Finder*.

Update Manager. The Update Manager takes the edit script generated by X-Diff and produces a set of update operations in the PATAXÓ update language. Here, there are some issues that need to be taken care of. The main one regards the *update path expressions* (they are referred to as *ref* in the update specification). In PATAXÓ, update operations need to specify an update path, and those are not provided by the edit script generated by X-Diff.

To generate the update path *ref*, we use the DB primary keys as filters in the path expression. Notice that keys must be kept in the view for it to be updatable [2]. Specifically, for an operation on node x, we take the path p from x to the view root, and find all the keys that are descendants of nodes in p.

In our example, the keys are *custId, numOrder* and *prodId*. The rules for translating an X-Diff operation into a PATAXÓ operation are as follows. The function *generateRef* uses the primary keys to construct filters, as mentioned above. The general form of a PATAXÓ update operation is $\langle t, \Delta, ref\rangle$.

- *Insert (*x *(name, value),* y*)* is mapped to $\langle insert, x, generateRef(y)\rangle$.
- *Delete (*x*)* is mapped to $\langle delete, \{\}, generateRef(x)\rangle$.
- *Update (*x*, new-value)* is mapped to $\langle modify, \{new\text{-}value\}, generateRef(x)\rangle$.
- *Insert (*T_x*,* y*)* is mapped to $\langle insert, T_x, generateRef(y)\rangle$.
- *Delete (*T_x*)* is mapped to $\langle delete, \{\}, generateRef(x)\rangle$.

Function *generateRef*(x) works as follows. First, it gets the parent x_n of x, then the parent x_{n-1} of x_n, and continues to get their parents until the root is reached. The obtained elements form a path $p = x_1/.../x_{n-1}/x_n/x$. Then, for each node y in p, it searches for leaf children that are primary keys in the relational database. Use this set of nodes to specify a conjunctive filter that uses the node name and its value in the view. As an example, we show the translation of an operation of E_1 (Figure 5(b)):

– *Update(9, 200)* ≡ *<modify*, {200}, *orders/order[@numOrder="123" and custId="995"]/line-item/item[prodId="BLUEPEN"]/quantity>*

PATAXÓ uses the values in the filters in the translation of modifications and deletions, and the values of leaf nodes in the path from the update point to the root in the translation of insertions. This approach, however, causes a problem when some of these values were modified by the user in the view. To solve this, we need to establish an order for the updates. This order must make sure that if an update operation u references a node value x that was modified in the view, then the update operation that modifies x must be issued *before* u. Given this scenario, we establish the following order for the updates: (1) Modifications; (2) Insertions; (3) Deletions.

There is no possibility of deleting a subtree that was previously inserted, since this kind of operation would not be generated by X-Diff. When there is more than one update in each category, then the updates that have the shortest update path (*ref*) are issued first. To illustrate, consider a case where the numOrder is changed (u_1), and the quantity of an item is changed by u_2. Since the numOrder is referenced in the filter of the update path of u_2, then u_1 has to be issued first, so that when u_2 is executed, the database already has the correct value of the numOrder. Notice that this example is not very common in practice, since normally primary key values are not changed.

4.2 Guaranteeing Database Consistency

The detection of conflicts is difficult, because a conflict can have different impacts depending on the application. To illustrate, in our example of orders, the removal of a product from the database means that the customer can not order it anymore. As a counter example, if a user increases the quantity of an item in its order, she may not want to proceed with this increase when she knows that the price of the item has increased.

The issues above are semantic issues. Unfortunately, a generic system does not know about these issues, and so we take the following approach: The *Diff Finder* uses X-Diff to calculate the edit script for the original XML view O and the view that has the current database state (*view'*). If the edit script is empty the updates over the updated view can be translated to the database with no conflict. In this case, the Update Manager translates the updates to updates in the PATAXÓ update language (Section 4.1) and sends them to PATAXÓ so it can map them to the underlying relational database.

However, most of the times the views (O and view') will not be equal, which implies in conflicts. A conflict is any update operation that has been issued in the database during the transaction lifetime, and that affects the updates made by the user through the view. We will provide more details on this later on.

In our approach, there are three *operational modes* to deal with conflicts: *restrictive, relaxed* and *super-relaxed* modes. The first one, the *restrictive mode*, no updates are translated when there are differences between the views original and view'. This is a very restrictive approach, where all modifications made over the view are treated as a single atomic transaction.

The second, *relaxed mode*, is a bit less restrictive. In this mode, updates that do not cause conflicts are translated to the underlying database. The remaining ones are aborted. To keep database consistency, we assume that some updates may coexist with others done externally, without causing inconsistencies in the database. To recognize such cases, we define a set of rules that are based on the view structure only. Notice that we do not know the semantics of the data in the view nor in the database. Thus, sometimes we may detect an operation to cause conflict even tough semantically it does not cause conflicts. This is the price we pay for not requiring the user to inform the semantics of the data in the view.

Conflict Detection Rules for Relaxed Mode. We now present rules for the resolution of conflicts in modifications for the relaxed mode. We leave insertions and deletions for future work.

RULE 1 (*Leaf node within the same starred-element). Let* $L = \{l_1, ..., l_n\}$ $(n \geq 1))$ *be the set of leaf nodes descending from a starred node* s *in a given XML view* v. *Additionally, ensure that* s *is the first starred ancestor of the nodes in L. If any* $l_i \in L$ *is modified in the updated view, and some* l_j *is modified in view' (*$i = j$ *or* $i \neq j$*), then the updates in nodes of L are rejected.*

An example of such case can be seen in the modification of node 9 (quantity of blue pens) in Figure 3 from 100 to 200. This operation can not proceed because it conflicts with the update of node 10 (price of blue pens) in view'.

RULE 2 (*Dependant starred-subtrees). Let* s_1 *and* s_2 *be two starred subtrees in a given XML view* v*. Let* $L_1 = \{l_{1_1}, ..., l_{1_n}\}$ $(n \geq 1))$ *be the set of leaf nodes descending from* s_1*, but not from its starred subtrees, and* $L_2 = \{l_{2_1}, ..., l_{2_k}\}$ $(k \geq 1))$ *be the set of leaf nodes descending from* s_2*, but not from its starred subtrees. Further, let* s_1 *be an ancestor of* s_2*. If any* $l_{2_i} \in L_2$ *is modified in the updated view, and some* $l_{1_j} \in L_1$ *is modified in view', then the updates conflict, and the modification of* l_{2_i} *is aborted.*

This rule captures the dependency between starred subtrees. In the XML view of Figure 3, it is easy to see that each *item* subtree is semantically connected to its parent *order* tree. Thus, rule 2 defines that modifications done in the database that affect the *order* subtree conflicts with modifications to the *item* subtree done through the view.

Notice that in all the above rules, we need to know the correspondence of nodes in views U and *view'*. For example, we need to know that node 12 in the updated view (Figure 3) correspond to node 12 in *view'* (Figure 5(a)). This can be easily done by using a variation of our *merge* algorithm presented later on.

To check for conflicts, each modify operation detected in $E_1(O \rightarrow U)$ is checked against each modify operation in $E_2(O \rightarrow \textit{view'})$ using the rules above. In [16], we present the algorithm. The checking is very simple, and once we detect a conflict due to one rule, we do not need to check the other one.

Conflict Detection Rules for Super-Relaxed Mode. Finally, the third, less restrictive operational mode is the *super-relaxed* mode. In this mode, we consider a conflict happens only when the update occurs over the same leaf node, or the tuple key has been changed in the database. Formally, we have:

RULE 3 (*Same leaf node). Let* l *be a leaf node in a given XML view* v*. If* l *is modified in the updated view to a value* v_1*, and* l *is modified in view' to a value* v_2*,* $v_1 \neq v_2$*, then the update on node* l *is rejected.*

RULE 4 (*Key node*). *Let l and k be two leaf nodes in a given XML view v. Let k represent the primary key of the tuple from which l was extracted in the database. If l is modified in the updated view, and k is modified in view', then the update on node l is rejected.*

We consider this a conflict because we use the key value to translate the update. If the key has changed, we can not reach the tuple to update it anymore.

4.3 Notifying the User

In all operational modes of our system, we need to inform the user of which update operations were actually translated to the base tables, and which were aborted. To do so, the system generates a *merge* of the updated data and the current database state. The algorithm starts with the original XML view. Consider $E1 = E(O \rightarrow U)$ and $E2 = E(O \rightarrow \textit{view'})$.

1. Take each delete operation u=Delete(x) in $E2$ and mark x in the original XML view. The markup is made by adding a new parent *pataxo:DB-DELETE* to x, where *pataxo* is a namespace prefix (we omit it in the remaining definitions). This new element is connected to the parent of x.
2. Take each insert operation u=Insert(T_x, y) in $E2$, insert T_x under y and add a new parent *DB-INSERT* to T_x. Connect the new element as a child of y.
3. Take each modify operation u=Update(x, new-value) in $E2$, add a *DB-MODIFY* element with value *new-value*. Connect it as a child of x.

After this, it is necessary to apply the update operations that are in the updated view to the original view, and mark them too. In this step, the markup elements receive a STATUS attribute to describe if the update operation was accepted or aborted. Since we are currently detecting conflicts only between modify operations, we are assuming the remaining ones are always accepted.

1. Take each delete operation u=Delete(x) in $E1$, add a new parent *CLIENT-DELETE STATUS="ACCEPT"* to x and connect it to the parent of x.
2. Take each insert operation u=Insert(T_x, y) in $E1$, insert T_x under y and add a new parent *CLIENT-INSERT STATUS="ACCEPT"* to T_x. Connect the new created element as a child of y.
3. Take each modify operation u=Update(x, new-value) in $E1$, add a new element *CLIENT-MODIFY* with value *new-value*. Connect the *CLIENT-MODIFY* element as a child of x. If u is marked in $E1$, then add a *STATUS* attribute to the *CLIENT-MODIFY* with value *ABORT*. If not, then add the *STATUS* attribute with value *ACCEPT*.

The result of this merge in our example is shown in Figure 6. There may be elements with more than one conflict markup. For example, suppose the client had altered the price of blue pens to 0.02 (the issue of whether this is allowed by the application or not, is out of the scope of this paper). In this case, the element price would have two markups.

After the execution of the merge algorithm, the Transaction Manager receives the new *merged* view (notice that the merged view is an XML document not valid according

```
<orders viewId="786">
   <order numOrder="123">
      <custId>995</custId>
      <name>Company B</name>
      <line-items>
         <item>
            <prodId>BLUEPEN</prodId>
            <quantity>100
                <pataxo:CLIENT-MODIFY STATUS="ABORT">200</pataxo:CLIENT-MODIFY>
            </quantity>
            <price>0.05
                <pataxo:DB-MODIFY>0.10</pataxo:DB-MODIFY>
            </price>
         </item>
         <item>
            <prodId>REDPEN</prodId>
            <quantity>200
                <pataxo:CLIENT-MODIFY STATUS="ACCEPT">300<pataxo:CLIENT-MODIFY>
            </quatity>
            <price>0.05</price>
         </item>
         <pataxo:CLIENT-INSERT STATUS="ACCEPT">
            <item>
              <prodId>NTBK</prodId>
              <quantity>100</quantity>
              <price>3.50</price>
            </item>
         </pataxo:CLIENT-INSERT>
      </line-items>
   </order>
</orders>
```

Fig. 6. Result of the *merge* algorithm

to the view DTD, since new markup elements were added). It re-generates the view (which is now the original view O), and stores it in the temporary storage facility, since now this is the new *original view*. Then, it sends the *merged* view and view O back to the client application. The client may want to analyze the merged view and to resubmit updates through view O. This second "round" will follow the same execution flow as before. The system will proceed as if it was the first time that updated view arrives in the system.

5 Discussion and Future Work

We have presented an approach to support disconnected transactions in updates over relational databases through XML views. Our approach uses PATAXÓ [2] to both generate the views and to translate the updates to the underlying relational database. In this paper, we allow views to be edited, and we automatically detect the changes using X-Diff [17]. We present an algorithm to transform the changes detected by X-Diff into the update language accepted by PATAXÓ. Also, we present a technique to detect conflicts that may be caused by updates over the base relations during the transaction execution. Currently, we only detect conflicts for modifications.

One of the benefits of our approach is that it does not require that updates are done online. In our previous approach [2], the client application must be connected to PATAXÓ in order to issue updates. In this paper, however, we support offline update operations that can be done in offline devices, like PDAs.

This scenario is very common in practice, and we believe that industry will greatly benefit from our work. In the future, we plan to evaluate our approach in real enterprises. Also, we are working on rules to detect conflicts on insertions and deletions. We plan to work on algorithms to solve such conflicts.

References

1. H. Berenson, P. Bernstein, J. Gray, J. Melton, E. O'Neil and P. O'Neil. A critique of ANSI SQL isolation levels. In *SIGMOD*, pages 1–10, San Jose, California, May 1995.
2. V. Braganholo, S. B. Davidson, and C. A. Heuser. From XML view updates to relational view updates: old solutions to a new problem. In *VLDB*, pages 276–287, Toronto, Canada, Sept. 2004.
3. V. Braganholo, S. B. Davidson, and C. A. Heuser. PATAXÓ: A framework to allow updates through XML views. *ACM Transactions on Database Systems, TODS*, to appear, 2006.
4. S. S. Chawathe and H. Garcia-Molina. Meaningful change detection in structured data. In *SIGMOD*, pages 26–37, Tucson, Arizona, May 1997.
5. P. Chrysanthis and K. Ramamritham. Synthesis of extended transaction models using acta. *ACM Transactions on Database Systems, TODS*, 19(3):450–491, 1994.
6. G. Cobena, S. Abiteboul, and A. Marian. Detecting changes in XML documents. In *ICDE*, pages 41–52, San Jose, California, Feb. 2002.
7. F. Curbera and D. Epstein. Fast difference and update of XML documents. In *XTech*, San Jose, California, Mar. 1999.
8. U. Dayal and P. A. Bernstein. On the correct translation of update operations on relational views. *ACM TODS*, 8(2):381–416, Sept. 1982.
9. M. Fernández, Y. Kadiyska, D. Suciu, A. Morishima, and W.-C. Tan. Silkroute: A framework for publishing relational data in XML. *ACM TODS*, 27(4):438–493, Dec. 2002.
10. J. Foster, M. Greenwald, J. Moore, B. Pierce and A. Schmitt. Combinators for bi-directional tree transformations: a linguistic approach to the view update problem. In *Symposium on Principles of Programming Languages (POPL)*, pages 233–246, Long Beach, CA, USA, 2005. ACM Press.
11. L. Klieb. Distributed disconnected databases. In *Symposium on Applied Computing (SAC)*, pages 322–326, New York, NY, USA, 1996. ACM Press.
12. S. H. Phatak and B. R. Badrinath. Conflict resolution and reconciliation in disconnected databases. In *DEXA*, 1999.
13. B. Pierce, A. Schmitt and M. Greenwald. Bringing Harmony to optimism: A synchronization framework for heterogeneous tree-structured data. Technical Report MS-CIS-03-42, University of Pennsylvania, USA, 2003. Superceded by MS-CIS-05-02.
14. J. Shanmugasundaram, J. Kiernan, E. Shekita, C. Fan, and J. Funderburk. Querying XML views of relational data. In *VLDB*, Rome, Sept. 2001.
15. D. Terry, M. Theimer, K. Petersen, A. Demers, M. Spreitzer, and C. Hauser. Managing update conflicts in bayou, a weakly connected replicated storage system. In *SOSP*, pages 172–183, 1995.
16. A. Vargas, V. Braganholo, and C. Heuser. Conflict resolution and difference detection in updates through XML views. Technical Report RP-352, UFRGS, Brazil, Dec. 2005. Available at `www.cos.ufrj.br/~vanessa`.
17. Y. Wang, D. J. DeWitt, and J.-Y. Cai. X-diff: An effective change detection algorithm for XML documents. In *ICDE*, pages 519–530, India, March 2003.

Efficient Integrity Checking over XML Documents

Daniele Braga[1], Alessandro Campi[1], and Davide Martinenghi[2]

[1] Politecnico di Milano – Dip. di Elettronica e Informazione
p.zza L. da Vinci 32, 20133 Milano, Italy
{braga, campi}@elet.polimi.it
[2] Free University of Bozen/Bolzano – Faculty of Computer Science
p.zza Domenicani, 3, 39100 Bolzano, Italy
martinenghi@inf.unibz.it

Abstract. The need for incremental constraint maintenance within collections of semi-structured documents has been ever increasing in the last years due to the widespread diffusion of XML. This problem is addressed here by adapting to the XML data model some constraint verification techniques known in the context of deductive databases. Our approach allows the declarative specification of constraints as well as their optimization w.r.t. given update patterns. Such optimized constraints are automatically translated into equivalent XQuery expressions in order to avoid illegal updates. This automatic process guarantees an efficient integrity checking that combines the advantages of declarativity with incrementality and early detection of inconsistencies.

1 Introduction

It is well-known that expressing, verifying and automatically enforcing data correctness is a difficult task as well as a pressing need in any data management context. In this respect, XML is no exception; moreover, there is no standard means of specifying generic constraints over large XML document collections. XML Schema offers a rich set of predefined constraints, such as structural, domain and cardinality constraints. However, it lacks full extensibility, as it is not possible to express general integrity requirements in the same way as SQL assertions, typically used to specify business rules at the application level in a declarative way. A large body of research, starting from [21], gave rise to a number of methods for incremental integrity checking within the framework of deductive databases and w.r.t. the relational data model. Indeed, a brute force approach to integrity checking, i.e., verifying the whole database each time data are updated, is unfeasible. This paper addresses this problem in the context of semi-structured data, and namely XML, in order to tackle the difficulties inherent in its hierarchical data model. A suitable formalism for the declarative specification of integrity constraints over XML data is therefore required in order to apply optimization techniques similar to those developed for the relational world. More specifically, we adopt for this purpose a formalism called XPathLog, a logical language inspired by Datalog and defined in [18]. In our approach, the tree structure of XPathLog constraints is mapped to a relational representation (in Datalog) which lends itself well to the above mentioned optimization techniques. The optimization only needs to take place once, at schema design time: it takes as input a set of constraints and an update pattern and, using the hypothesis that

T. Grust et al. (Eds.): EDBT 2006 Workshops, LNCS 4254, pp. 206–219, 2006.

the database is always consistent prior to the update, it produces as output a set of optimized constraints, which are as instantiated as possible. These optimized constraints are finally translated into XQuery expressions that can be matched against the XML document so as to check that the update does not introduce any violation of the constraints. At runtime, the optimized checks are performed instead of the full ones, whenever the updates are recognized as matching the patterns used in the simplification.

In particular, the constraint simplification method we adopt generates optimized constraints that can be tested *before* the execution of an update (and without simulating the updated state), so that inconsistent database states are completely avoided.

2 Constraint Verification

Semantic information in databases is typically represented in the form of integrity constraints, which are properties that must always be satisfied for the data to be considered *consistent*. In this respect, database management systems should provide means to automatically verify, in an efficient way, that database updates do not introduce any violation of integrity. A complete check of generic constraints is too costly in any nontrivial case; in view of this, verification of integrity constraints can be rendered more efficient by deriving specialized checks that are easier to execute at each update. Even better performance is achieved if these checks can be tested before illegal updates. Nevertheless, the common practice is still based on *ad hoc* techniques: domain experts hand-code tests in the application program producing the update requests or design triggers within the database management system that respond to certain update actions. However, both methods are prone to errors and little flexibility w.r.t. changes in the schema or design of the database, which motivates the need for automated integrity verification methods.

In order to formalize the notion of consistency, and thus the constraint verification problem, we refer to deductive databases, in which a *database state* is the set of database facts and rules (tuples and views). As semantics of a database state D we take its *standard model*: the truth value of a closed formula F, relative to D, is defined as its valuation in the standard model and denoted $D(F)$.

Definition 1 (Consistency). *A database state D is* consistent *with a set of integrity constraints Γ iff $D(\Gamma) = true$.*

An *update* U is a mapping $U : \mathscr{D} \mapsto \mathscr{D}$, where $\mathscr{D}$ is the space of database states. For convenience, for any database state D, we indicate the state arising after update U as D^U. The constraint verification problem may be formulated as follows. Given a database state D, a set of integrity constraints Γ, such that $D(\Gamma) = true$, and an update U, does $D^U(\Gamma) = true$ hold too? As mentioned, evaluating $D^U(\Gamma)$ may be too expensive, so a suitable reformulation of the problem can be given in the following terms: is there a set of integrity constraints Γ^U such that $D^U(\Gamma) = D(\Gamma^U)$ and Γ^U is easier to evaluate than Γ? In other words, the looked for condition Γ^U should specialize the original Γ, as specific information coming from U is available, and avoid redundant checks by exploiting the fact that $D(\Gamma) = true$. We observe that reasoning about the future database state D^U with a condition (Γ^U) that is tested in the present state D, complies with the semantics of *deferred* integrity checking (i.e., integrity constraints do *not* have to hold in intermediate transaction states).

3 General Constraints over Semi-structured Data

Consistency requirements for XML data are not different from those holding for relational data, and constraint definition and enforcement are expected to become fundamental aspects of XML data management. In current XML specifications, fixed-format structural integrity constraints can already be defined by using XML Schema definitions; they are concerned with type definitions, occurrence cardinalities, unique constraints, and referential integrity. However, a generic constraint definition language for XML, with expressive power comparable to assertions and checks of SQL, is still not present in the XML Schema specification. We deem this a crucial issue, as this lack of expressiveness does not allow one to specify business rules to be directly included in the schema. Moreover, generic mechanisms for constraint enforcement are also lacking. In this paper we cover both aspects.

Our approach moves from a recently proposed adaptation of the framework of deductive databases to the world of semi-structured data. More precisely, we refer to XPathLog [18] as the language for specifying generic XML constraints, which are expressed in terms of queries that must have an empty result.

Even though, in principle, we could write denials in XQuery, a declarative, first-order logic language is closer to what is usually done for relational data [14]; a logical approach leads to cleaner constraint definitions, and the direct mapping from XPathLog to Datalog helps the optimization process.

3.1 XPathLog

XPathLog [18] is an extension of XPath modeled on Datalog. In particular, the XPath language is extended with variable bindings and is embedded into first-order logic to form XPath-Logic; XPathLog is then the Horn fragment of XPath-Logic. Thanks to its logic-based nature, XPathLog is well-suited to querying XML data and providing declarative specifications of integrity constraints.

It uses an *edge-labeled graph* model in which subelements are ordered and attributes are unordered. Path expressions have the form root/axisStep/.../axisStep where root specifies the starting point of the expressions (such as the root of a document or a variable bound to a node) and every axisStep has the form axis::nodetest[qualifier]*. An axis defines a navigation direction in the XML tree: child, attribute, parent, ancestor, descendant, preceding-sibling and following-sibling. All elements satisfying along the chosen axis nodetest are selected, then the qualifier(s) are applied to the selection to further filter it. Axes are abbreviated as usual, e.g. path/nodetest stands for path/child::nodetest and path/@nodetest for path/attribute::nodetest.

XPath-Logic formulas are built as follows. An infinite set of variables is assumed along with a signature of element names, attribute names, function names, constant symbols and predicate names. A *reference expression* is a path expression that may be extended to bind selected nodes to variables with the construct "→ *Var*". Reference expressions have the form root/refAxisStep/.../refAxisStep, where the syntax of refAxisStep is as follows:

$$\text{axis::(nodetest}|Var)\text{[qualifier]}^*[\rightarrow Var]\text{[qualifier]}^*.$$

XPath-Logic predicates are predicates over reference expressions and atoms and literals are defined as usual. Formulas are thus obtained by combining atoms with connectives ($\wedge$, $\vee$, $\neg$) and with quantified ($\exists$, $\forall$) variables. Clauses are written in the form *Head*$\leftarrow$*Body* where the head, if present, is an atom and the body a conjunction of literals. In particular, a *denial* is a headless clause; integrity constraints will be written as denials, which indicates that there must be no variable binding satisfying the condition in the denial body for the data to be consistent. Unless otherwise indicated, clause variables (written with capital letters) are implicitly universally quantified.

Aggregates are written with the syntax $\text{agg}(V[G_1,\ldots,G_n];\text{reference-expression})$, where agg is an aggregate (such as Sum, Cnt, etc.), V, if present, is the variable on which the aggregate operation is performed and $G_1,\ldots,G_n$ are the group-by variables. A D subscript (e.g., Cnt_D) indicates that only *distinct* values are considered. Note that V is absent for Cnt and Cnt_D.

3.2 Examples

Consider two documents: `pub.xml` containing a collection of published articles and `rev.xml` containing information on reviewer/paper assignment for all tracks of a given conference. The DTDs are as follows.

```
<!-- pub.xml -->
<!ELEMENT dblp (pub)*>
<!ELEMENT pub (title,aut+)>
<!ELEMENT title (#PCDATA)>
<!ELEMENT aut (name)>
<!ELEMENT name (#PCDATA)>
```

```
<!-- rev.xml -->
<!ELEMENT review (track)+>
<!ELEMENT track (name,rev+)>
<!ELEMENT name (#PCDATA)>
<!ELEMENT rev (name,sub+)>
<!ELEMENT sub(title,auts+)>
<!ELEMENT title (#PCDATA)>
<!ELEMENT auts (name)>
```

Example 1. Consider the following integrity constraint, which imposes the absence of *conflict of interests* in the submission review process (i.e., no one can review papers written by a coauthor or by him/herself):

$$\begin{aligned}\leftarrow\ & //rev[name/text() \rightarrow R]/sub/auts/name/text() \rightarrow A \\ & \wedge(A = R \vee //pub[aut/name/text() \rightarrow A \wedge aut/name/text() \rightarrow R])\end{aligned}$$

The text() function refers to the text content of the enclosing element. The condition in the body of this constraint indicates that there is a reviewer named R who is assigned a submission whose author has name A and, in turn, either A and R are the same or two authors of a same publication have names A and R, respectively.

Example 2. Consider a conference policy imposing that a reviewer involved in three or more tracks cannot review more than 10 papers. This is expressed as follows:

$$\begin{aligned}\leftarrow\ & \text{Cnt}_\text{D}\{[R];//track[/rev/name/\text{text}() \rightarrow R]\} \geq 3\wedge \\ & \text{Cnt}_\text{D}\{[R];//rev[/name/\text{text}() \rightarrow R]/sub\} \geq 10\end{aligned}$$

4 Mapping XML Constraints to the Relational Data Model

In order to apply our simplification framework to XML constraints, as will be described in Section 5, schemata, update patterns, and constraints need to be mapped from the XML domain to the relational model. Note that these mappings take place statically and thus do not affect runtime performance.

4.1 Mapping of the Schema and of Update Statements

The problem of representing XML data in relations was considered, e.g., in [25]. Our approach is targeted to deductive databases: each node type is mapped to a corresponding predicate. The first three attributes of all predicates respectively represent, for each XML item: its (unique) node identifier, its position and the node identifier of its parent node. It is worth noting that the second attribute is crucial, as the XML data model is ordered. Whenever a parent-child relationship within a DTD is a one-to-one correspondence (or an optional inclusion), a more compact form is possible, because a new predicate for the child node is not necessary: the attributes of the child may be equivalently represented within the predicate that corresponds to the parent (allowing null values in case of optional child nodes). The documents of the previous section map to the relational schema

```
pub(Id,Pos,IdParent_{dblp},Title)          aut(Id,Pos,IdParent_{pub},Name)
track(Id,Pos,IdParent_{review},Name)       rev(Id,Pos,IdParent_{track},Name)
sub(Id,Pos,IdParent_{rev},Title)           auts(Id,Pos,IdParent_{sub},Name)
```

where Id, Pos and $IdParent_{tagname}$ preserve the hierarchy of the documents and where the PCDATA content of the `name` and `title` node types is systematically embedded into the container nodes, so as to reduce the number of predicates.

As already mentioned, mapping a hierarchical ordered structure to a flat unordered data model forces the exposition of information that is typically hidden within XML repositories, such as the order of the sub-nodes of a given node and unique node identifiers. The root nodes of the documents (`dblp` and `review`) are not represented as predicates, as they have no local attributes but only subelements; however, such nodes are referenced in the database as values for the IdParent_{dblp} and IdParent_{review} attributes respectively, within the representation of their child nodes. Publications map to the *pub* predicate, authors in `pub.xml` map to *aut*, while authors in `rev.xml` map to *auts*, and so on, with predicates corresponding to tagnames. Last, `names` and `titles` map to attributes within the predicates corresponding to their containers.

Data mapping criteria influence update mapping. We express updates with the XUpdate language [13], but other formalisms that allows the specification of insertions of data fragments would also apply. Consider the following statement:

```
<xupdate:modifications version="1.0" xmlns:xupdate="http://www.xmldb.org/xupdate">
  <xupdate:insert-after select="/review/track[2]/rev[5]/sub[6]" >
    <xupdate:element name="sub">
      <title> Taming Web Services </title> <auts> <name> Jack </name> </auts>
    </xupdate:element> </xupdate:insert-after> </xupdate:modifications>
```

In the corresponding relational model, this update statement corresponds to adding $\{$ $sub(id_s, 7, id_r,$ "Taming Web Services"$)$, $auts(id_a, 2, id_s,$ "Jack"$)$ $\}$ where id_a and id_s

represent the identifiers that are to be associated to the new nodes and id_r is the identifier associated to the target `rev` element. Their value is immaterial to the semantics of the update, provided that a mechanism to impose their uniqueness is available. On the other hand, the actual value of id_r depends on the dataset and needs to be retrieved by interpreting the `select` clause of the XUpdate statement. Namely, id_r is the identifier for the fifth (`reviewer`) child of the second (`track`) node, in turn contained into the root (`review`) node of the document `rev.xml`. Positions (7 and 2 in the second argument of both predicates) are also derived by parsing the update statement: 7 is determined as the successor of 6, according to the `insert-after` semantics of the update; 2 is due to the ordering, since the `auts` comes after the `title` element. Finally, note that the *same* value id_s occurs both as the first argument of $sub()$ and the third argument of $auts()$, since the latter represents a subelement of the former.

4.2 Mapping of Integrity Constraints

The last step in the mapping from XML to the framework of deductive databases is to compile denials into Datalog. We express constraints as Datalog denials: clauses with an empty head (understood as *false*), whose body indicates not holding conditions. Input to this phase are the schemata (XML and relational) and an XPathLog denial in a normal form without disjunctions [1]. All p.e. in XPathLog generate chains of conditions over the predicates corresponding to the node types traversed by the path expression. to the traversed node types. Containment in terms of parent-child relationship translates to correspondences between variables in the first position of the container and in the third position of the contained item.

Quite straightforwardly, XPathLog denial expressing that the author of the "Duckburg tales" cannot be Goofy and its mapping (anonymous variables are indicated with an underscore):

$$\leftrightsquigarrow //pub[title = \text{“}Duckburg\ tales''\text{”}]/aut/name \rightarrow N \wedge N = \text{“}Goofy''$$

$$\leftarrow pub(I_p, \_, \_, \text{“}Duckburg\ tales''\text{”}) \wedge aut(\_, \_, I_p, N) \wedge N = \text{“}Goofy''.$$

The fact that the XML data model is ordered impacts the translation. Either the `position()` function is used in the original denial or a filter is used that contains an expression returning an integer. In both cases, the second argument in the relational predicate is associated to a variable that is matched against a suitable comparison expression (containing the variable associated to the `position()` function or directly to the expression that returns the value).

Example 3. The XPathLog constraint of example 1, is translated into the following couple of Datalog denials (due to the presence of a disjunction).

$$\begin{aligned}\Gamma = \{ &\leftarrow rev(I_r, \_, \_, R) \wedge sub(I_s, \_, I_r, \_) \wedge auts(\_, \_, I_s, R),\\ &\leftarrow rev(I_r, \_, \_, R) \wedge sub(I_s, \_, I_r, \_) \wedge auts(\_, \_, I_s, A)\\ &\quad \wedge aut(\_, \_, I_p, R) \wedge aut(\_, \_, I_p, A)\}\end{aligned}$$

[1] A default rewriting allows one to reduce to such normal form any denial expressed with disjunctions, so that we can restrict to this case without loss of generality.

5 Simplification of Integrity Constraints

Several methods for optimized and incremental constraint checking in deductive databases, known as *simplification* methods, were produced since the landmark contribution by Nicolas [21]. Simplification in this context means to derive specialized versions of the integrity constraints w.r.t. given update patterns, employing the hypothesis that the database is initially consistent. In the following, we briefly describe the approach of [16]. To illustrate the framework, we limit our attention to tuple insertions, consistently with the fact that XML documents typically grow. An update transaction is expressed as a set of ground atoms representing the tuples that will be added to the database. Placeholders for constants, called *parameters* (written in boldface: **a**, **b**, ...), allow one to indicate update *patterns*. For example, the notation $\{p(\mathbf{a}), q(\mathbf{a})\}$, where **a** is a parameter, refers to the class of update transactions that add the same tuple to both unary relation p and unary relation q. The first step in the simplification process is to introduce a syntactic transformation After that translates a set of denials Γ referring to the updated database state into another set Σ that holds in the present state if and only if Γ holds after the update.

Definition 2. *Let Γ be a set of denials and U an update. The notation* $\mathsf{After}^U(\Gamma)$ *refers to a copy of Γ in which all atoms of the form $p(\vec{t})$ have been simultaneously replaced by $(p(\vec{t}) \vee \vec{t} = \vec{a}_1 \vee \cdots \vee \vec{t} = \vec{a}_n)$, where $p(\vec{a}_1), \ldots, p(\vec{a}_n)$ are all additions on p in U, $\vec{t}$ is a sequence of terms and $\vec{a}_1, \ldots, \vec{a}_n$ are sequences of constants or parameters (we assume that the result of this transformation is always given as a set of denials which can be produced by using, e.g., De Morgan's laws).*

Example 4. Consider a relation $p(ISSN, TITLE)$ and let $U = \{p(\mathbf{i}, \mathbf{t})\}$ be the addition of a publication with title **t** and ISSN number **i** and $\phi = \leftarrow p(X,Y) \wedge p(X,Z) \wedge Y \neq Z$ the denial imposing uniqueness of ISSN. $\mathsf{After}^U(\{\phi\})$ is as follows:

$$\begin{aligned}
&\{ \leftarrow [p(X,Y) \vee (X = \mathbf{i} \wedge Y = \mathbf{t})] \wedge [p(X,Z) \vee (X = \mathbf{i} \wedge Z = \mathbf{t})] \wedge Y \neq Z\} \\
\equiv &\{ \leftarrow p(X,Y) \wedge p(X,Z) \wedge Y \neq Z, \\
&\leftarrow p(X,Y) \wedge X = \mathbf{i} \wedge Z = \mathbf{t} \wedge Y \neq Z, \\
&\leftarrow X = \mathbf{i} \wedge Y = \mathbf{t} \wedge p(X,Z) \wedge Y \neq Z, \\
&\leftarrow X = \mathbf{i} \wedge Y = \mathbf{t} \wedge X = \mathbf{i} \wedge Z = \mathbf{t} \wedge Y \neq Z\}.
\end{aligned}$$

Clearly, After's output is not in any "normalized" form, as it may contain redundant denials and sub-formulas (such as, e.g., $a = a$). Moreover, assuming that the original denials hold in the current database state can be used to achieve further simplification. For this purpose, a transformation $\mathsf{Optimize}_\Delta(\Gamma)$ is defined that exploits a given set of denials Δ consisting of trusted hypotheses to simplify the input set Γ. The proposed implementation [17] is described in [16] in terms of sound rewrite rules, whose application reduces denials in size and number and instantiates them as much as possible. For reasons of space, we refrain from giving a complete list of the rewrite rules in the Optimize operator and we describe its behavior as follows.

Given a set of denials Γ, a denial $\phi \in \Gamma$ is removed if it can be proved redundant from $\Gamma \setminus \{\phi\}$; ϕ is replaced by a denial ψ that can be proved from Γ if ψ subsumes ϕ; equalities involving variables are eliminated as needed. The resulting procedure is terminating, as it is based on resolution proofs restricted in size. The operators After and Optimize can be assembled to define a procedure for simplification of integrity constraints.

Definition 3. *For an update U and two sets of denials Γ and Δ, we define* $\mathsf{Simp}^U_\Delta(\Gamma) = \mathsf{Optimize}_{\Gamma\cup\Delta}(\mathsf{After}^U(\Gamma))$.

Theorem 1 ([16]). Simp *terminates on any input and, for any two set of denials Γ,Δ and update U,* $\mathsf{Simp}^U_\Delta(\Gamma)$ *holds in a database state D consistent with Δ iff Γ holds in D^U.*

We use $\mathsf{Simp}^U(\Gamma)$ as a shorthand for $\mathsf{Simp}^U_\Gamma(\Gamma)$.

Example 5. [4 cont.] The first denial in $\mathsf{After}^U(\{\phi\})$ is the same as ϕ and is thus redundant; the last one is a tautology; both the second and third reduce to the same denial; therefore the resulting simplification is $\mathsf{Simp}^U(\{\phi\}) = \{\leftarrow p(\mathbf{i},Y)\wedge Y \neq \mathbf{t}\}$, which indicates that, upon insertion of a new publication, there must not already exist another publication with the same ISSN and a different title.

5.1 Examples

We now consider some examples based on the relational schema of documents `pub.xml` and `rev.xml` given in section 4.

Example 6. [1 continued] Let us consider constraint Γ from example 3 imposing the absence of conflict of interests in the submission review process. An update of interest is, e.g., the insertion of a new submission to the attention of a reviewer.

For instance, a submission with a single author complies with the pattern
$U = \{sub(\mathbf{i}_s,\mathbf{p}_s,\mathbf{i}_r,\mathbf{t}), auts(\mathbf{i}_a,\mathbf{p}_a,\mathbf{i}_s,\mathbf{n})\}$,
where the parameter ($\mathbf{i}_s$) is the same in both added tuples. The fact that $\mathbf{i}_s$ and $\mathbf{i}_a$ are new node identifiers can be expressed as a set of extra hypotheses to be exploited in the constraint simplification process:
$\Delta = \{\leftarrow sub(\mathbf{i}_s,\_,\_,\_), \leftarrow auts(\_,\_,\mathbf{i}_s,\_), \leftarrow auts(\mathbf{i}_a,\_,\_,\_)\}$.
The simplified integrity check w.r.t. update U and constraint Γ is given by
$\mathsf{Simp}^U_\Delta(\Gamma)$: $\{\leftarrow rev(\mathbf{i}_r,\_,\_,\mathbf{n}), \leftarrow rev(\mathbf{i}_r,\_,\_,R)\wedge aut(\_,\_,I_p,\mathbf{n})\wedge aut(\_,\_,I_p,R)\}$.

The first denial requires that the added author of the submission ($\mathbf{n}$) is not the same person as the assigned reviewer ($\mathbf{i}_r$). The second denial imposes that the assigned reviewer is not a coauthor of the added author $\mathbf{n}$. These conditions are clearly much cheaper to evaluate than the original constraints Γ, as they are instantiated to specific values and involve fewer relations.

Example 7. Consider the denial $\phi = \leftarrow rev(I_r,\_,\_,\_)\wedge \mathsf{Cnt_D}(sub(\_,\_,\underline{I_r},\_)) > 4$ imposing a maximum of 4 reviews per reviewer per track. The simplified integrity check of ϕ w.r.t. update U from example 6 is $\mathsf{Simp}^U_\Delta(\{\phi\}) = \{\leftarrow rev(\mathbf{i}_r,\_,\_,\_)\wedge \mathsf{Cnt_D}(sub(\_,\_,\mathbf{i}_r,\_)) > 3\}$, which checks that the specific reviewer $\mathbf{i}_r$ is not already assigned 3 different reviews in that track.

6 Translation into XQuery

The simplified constraints obtained with the technique described in the previous section are useful only if they can be checked before the corresponding update, so as to prevent the execution of statements that would violate integrity. Under the hypothesis that the dataset is stored into an XML repository capable of executing XQuery statements, the simplified constraints need to be translated into suitable equivalent XQuery expressions in order to be checked. This section discusses the translation of Datalog denials into XQuery. We exemplify the translation process using the (non-simplified) set of constraints Γ defined in example 3. For brevity, we only show the translation of the second denial.

The first step is the expansion of the Datalog denial. It consists in replacing every constant in a database predicate (or variable already appearing elsewhere in database predicates) by a new variable and adding the equality between the new variable and the replaced item. This process is applied to all positions, but the first and the third one, which refer to element and parent identifiers and thus keeps information on the parent-child relationship of the XML nodes. In our case, the expansion is:

$$\leftarrow rev(I_r,B,C,R) \wedge sub(I_s,D,I_r,E) \wedge auts(F,G,I_s,A)$$
$$\wedge aut(H,I,I_p,J) \wedge aut(K,L,I_p,M) \wedge J = R \wedge M = A$$

The atoms in the denial must be sorted so that, if a variable referring to the parent of a node also occurs as the id of another node, then the occurrence as an id comes first. Here, no such rearrangement is needed. Then, for each atom $p(Id, Pos, Par, D_1, \ldots, D_n)$ where $D_1, \ldots, D_n$ are the values of tags d1, ..., dn, resp., we do as follows. If the definition of `$Par` has not yet been created, then we generate `$Id in //p` and `$Par in $Id/..`; otherwise we just generate `$Id in $Par/p`. This is followed by `$Pos in $Id/position()`, `$D1 in $Id/d1/text(), ..., $Dn in $Id/dn/text()`.

Then we build an XQuery boolean expression (returning `true` in case of violation) by prefixing the definitions with the `some` keyword and by suffixing them with the `satisfies` keyword followed by all the remaining conditions in the denial separated by `and`. This is a well-formed XQuery expression. Here we have:

```
some $Ir in //rev, $C in $Ir/.., $B in $Ir/position(),     $R in $Ir/name/text(),
     $Is in $Ir/sub,              $D in $Is/position(),     $E in $Is/title/text(),
     $F in $Is/auts,              $G in $F/position(),      $A in $F/name/text(),
     $H in //aut,                 $Ip in $H/..,             $I in $H/position(),
     $J in $H/name/text(),        $K in $Ip/aut,            $L in $K/position(),
     $M in $K/name/text()
satisfies $J = $R and $M = $A
```

Such expression can be optimized by eliminating definitions of variables which are never used, unless they refer to node identifiers. Such variables are to be retained because they express an existential condition on the element they are bound to. Variables referring to the position of an element are to be retained only if used in other parts of the denial. In the example, we can therefore eliminate the definitions of variables `$B`, `$C`, `$D`, `$E`, `$G`, `$I`, `$L`. If a variable is used only once outside its definition, its occurrence is replaced with its definition. Here, e.g., the definition of `$Is` is removed and `$Is` is replaced by `$Ir/sub` in the definition of `$F`, obtaining `$F in $Ir/sub/auts`.

Variables occurring in the `satisfies` part are replaced by their definition. Here we obtain the following query.

```
some      $Ir in //rev, $H in //aut
satisfies $H/name/text()=$Ir/name/text()
      and $H/../aut/name/text()=$Ir/sub/auts/name/text()
```

The translation of the simplified version $\mathsf{Simp}^U_\Delta(\Gamma)$ is made along the same lines. Again, we only consider the simplified version of the second constraint (the denial $\leftarrow rev(\mathbf{i}_r,\_,\_,R) \wedge aut(\_,\_,I_p,\mathbf{n}) \wedge aut(\_,\_,I_p,R)$). Now, a parameter can occur in the first or third position of an atom. In such case, the parameter must be replaced by a suitable representation of the element it refers to. Here we obtain:

```
some      $D in //aut
satisfies $D/name/text()=%n
      and $D/../aut/name/text()= /review/track[%i]/rev[%j]/name/text()
```

where `/review/track[%i]/rev[%j]` conveniently represents $\mathbf{i}_r$. Similarly, `\%n` corresponds to $\mathbf{n}$. The placeholders `%i`, `%j` and `%n` will be known at update time and replaced in the query.

The general strategy described above needs to be modified in the presence of aggregates. Aggregates apply to sequences of nodes; therefore, the most suitable constructs to define such sequences are `let` clauses. In particular, there is a `let` clause for each aggregate. This does not affect generality, as variables bound in the `let` clauses correspond to the aggregate's target path expression possibly defined starting from variables already bound in the `for` clauses above. The expression is wrapped inside an `exists(...)` construct in order to obtain a boolean result; for this purpose, an empty `<idle/>` tag is returned if the condition is verified. Again, integrity is violated if the query returns `true`. Constraint $\leftarrow rev(I_r,\_,\_,\_) \wedge \mathsf{Cnt}_{\mathsf{D}}(sub(\_,\_,\underline{I_r},\_)) > 4$, shown in example 7, is mapped to XQuery as shown below.

```
exists( for $Ir in //rev  let $D := $R/sub  where count($D) > 4  return <idle/> )
```

The other constraints in the examples can be translated according to the same strategy.

7 Evaluation

We now present some experiments conducted on a series of XML datasets matching the DTD presented in section 2, varying in size from 32 to 256 MB, on the examples described in order to evaluate the performance of our approach. Figures 1(a), 1(b) refer to the integrity constraints of examples 1, 2, respectively. The data were generated remapping data from the DBLP repository [15] into the schema of our running examples. Our tests were run on a machine with a 3.4 GHz processor, 1 GB of RAM and 140 GB of hard disk, using eXist [8] as XQuery engine. Execution times are indicated in milliseconds and represent the average of the measured times of 200 attempts for each experiment (plus 50 additional operations that were used as a "warm-up" procedure and thus not measured). The size of the documents is indicated in MB on the x-axis. Each figure corresponds to one of the running examples and reports three curves representing respectively the time needed (i) to verify the original constraint (diamonds), (ii) to verify the optimized constraint (squares), and (iii) to execute an update, verify the original constraint, and undo the update (triangles). We observe that we do not have to take into account the time spent to produce the optimized constraints, nor the cost of mapping schemata and constraints to the relational model, as in our framework these are generated at schema design time and thus do not interfere with run time performance[2]. The curves with diamonds and squares are used to compare integrity checking in the non-simplified and, resp., simplified case, when the update is legal. The execution time needed to perform the update is not included, as this is identical (and unavoidable) in both the optimized and un-optimized case. The curve with triangles includes both the update execution time and the time needed to rollback the update, which is necessary when the update is illegal; when the update is illegal, we then compare the curve with triangles to the curve with squares. Rollbacks, needed since constraints are checked after an update, were simulated by performing a compensating action to re-construct the state prior to the update. The interpretation of these results is twofold, as we must consider two possible scenarios.

The update is legal: in the un-optimized framework the update is executed first and the full constraint is then checked against the updated database (showing that the update is legal); on the other hand, with the optimized strategy of our approach, the simplified constraint is checked first and the update is performed afterwards, as it is possible to check properties of the future database state in the present state (see Section 5).

The update is illegal: in the un-optimized framework execution is as in the previous case, but this time the check shows that there is some inconsistency and, finally, a compensative action is performed. On the contrary, with our optimized strategy, the simplified constraint is checked first, which reports an integrity violation w.r.t. the proposed update; therefore the update statement is *not* executed.

From the experimental results shown in figures 1(a) and 1(b) we observe two features. The comparison between the performance of the optimized and un-optimized checks shows that the optimized version is always more efficient than the original one. In some cases, as shown in figure 1(a), the difference is remarkable, since the simplified version contains specific values coming from the concrete update statement which allow one to filter the values on which complex computations are applied. Further improvement is due to the elimination of a join condition in the optimized query. In other cases the improvement is not as evident because introduction of filters does not completely eliminate the complexity of evaluation of subsequent steps, such as the calculation of aggregate operations (figure 1(b)). The gain of early detection of inconsistency, which

[2] The only activity to be performed at runtime is the matching of the actual update with a suitable known pattern, so as to apply the right optimized constraint. In our framework, we consider the case in which such recognition is trivially achieved and its cost is negligible, either because the patterns are very simple or because the user declares which pattern is in use while performing the update itself, choosing among a set of patterns published at schema design time. Otherwise, efficient representations of patterns and ad-hoc matching techniques should be investigated, so as to minimize this cost, which should of course be considered in the runtime evaluation. Unrecognized updates can either be processed w.r.t. the full integrity check or undergo a runtime simplification, but this case was not considered in our experiments. Nevertheless, we point out that the cost of the simplification itself is not dramatic: for instance, the simplified constraints of examples 1 and 6 were generated in less than 50 ms. Further details on the complexity analysis and the evaluation of the simplification procedure are in [5].

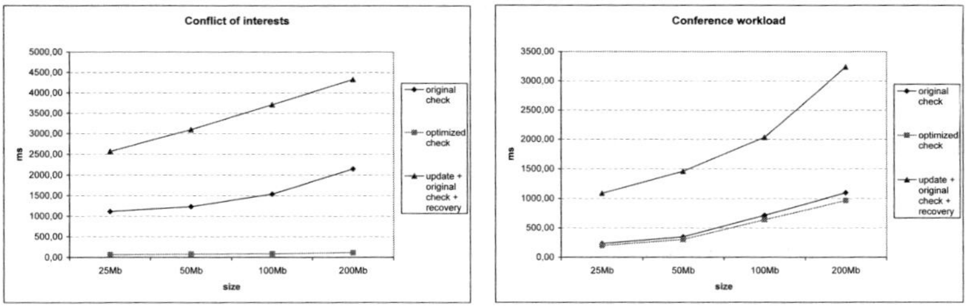

(a) (b)

Fig. 1. Conflict of interests (a) and Conference workload (b)

is a distinctive feature of our approach, is unquestionable in the case of illegal updates. This is prominently apparent in the cases considered in figures 1(a) and 1(b), since, as is well-known, the modification of XML documents is an expensive task.

8 Related Work

Integrity checking is often regarded as an instance of materialized view maintenance: integrity constraints are defined as views that must always remain empty for the database to be consistent. The database literature is rich in methods that deal with relational view/integrity maintenance; insightful discussions are in [11] and [7].

A large body of research in the field has also been produced by the logic programming and artificial intelligence communities, starting from [21]. Logic-based methods that produce *simplified* integrity tests can be classified according to different criteria, e.g., whether these tests can be checked before or only after the update, whether updates can be compound or only singleton, whether the tests are necessary and sufficient or only sufficient conditions for consistency, whether the language includes aggregates. Some of these methods are surveyed in [19]. In this respect, the choice of the simplification method of [16] seems ideal, as it matches all the above criteria, and is further motivated by the availability of an implementation.

An attempt to adapt view maintenance techniques to the semi-structured data model has been made in [26] and in [22]. Incremental approaches have been proposed with respect to validation of structural constraints in [1], as well as to key and foreign key constraints in [4], where the validating algorithm parses the document with SAX and constructs an index of standard XML keys in one pass, with the help of suitable automata which recognize the context, the target, and the paths of such keys. Later, [24] addressed incremental validation in the context of streaming data under memory limitation. DTDs are considered as grammars and condition are provided on such grammars for the recognition of their languages to be performed by finite state automata instead of pushdown automata. Here the focus is again on validation w.r.t. DTD-like structural constraints only, and constraints upon values or involving aggregates are not addressed.

An attempt to simplification of general integrity constraints for XML has been made in [2], where, however, constraints are specified in a procedural fashion with an extension of XML Schema that includes loops with embedded assertions.

We are not aware of other works addressing validation w.r.t. general constraints for XML. However, integrity constraint simplification can be reduced to query containment if the constraints can be viewed as queries. Relevant works to this end are [23,20].

There are several proposals and studies of constraint specification languages for XML by now. In [9] a unified constraint model (UCM) is proposed, which captures in a single framework the main features of o-o schemata and XML DTDs. UCM builds on the W3C XML query algebra and focuses on trading expressivity of the constraint language with simplicity of reasoning about the properties of the constraints. UCM leverages key/foreign key constraints and the XML type system, for expressing a restricted class of constraints whose consistency is proved decidable. This work addresses core algorithms for enforcing a particular class of constraints within a query engine, while our work relies on the availability of a query engine and addresses the simplification of constraints of arbitrary complexity (as long as they are expressible in XPathLog).

The XUpdate language, which was used for the experimental evaluation, is described in [13]. A discussion on update languages for XML is in [27].

As for XML-relational mappings, there exist several approaches to the problem of representing semi-structured data in relations [25,3,6,10]. For a survey, see [12].

9 Conclusion and Future Work

In this paper we presented a technique enabling efficient constraint maintenance for XML datasets. We described the scenario in which integrity constraints are declaratively expressed in XPathLog, an intuitive logical language. These constraints are translated into Datalog denials that apply to an equivalent relational representation of the same data. Such denials are then simplified w.r.t. given update patterns so as to produce optimized consistency checks that are finally mapped into XQuery expressions that can be evaluated against the original XML document.

Besides the possibility to declaratively specify constraints, the main benefits of our approach are as follows. Firstly, the ability to produce optimized constraints typically allows a much faster integrity checking. Secondly, performance is further improved by completely avoiding the execution of illegal updates: the optimized check is executed first and the update is performed only if it does not violate integrity.

In this paper we focused on updates whose contents are specified extensionally, as in the XUpdate language. More complex updates may be specified with a rule-based language such as XPathLog, i.e., intensionally in terms of other queries. Yet, introducing such updates would not increase complexity, as these are already dealt with by the relational simplification framework of section 5 and can be translated from XPathLog to Datalog as indicated in section 4.

Several future directions are possible to improve the proposed method. We are studying the feasibility of a trigger-based view/integrity maintenance approach for XML that would combine active behavior with constraint simplification. Further lines of investigation include integrating visual query specification to allow the intuitive specification of constraints: domain experts lacking specific competencies in logic would be provided with the ability to design constraints to be further processed with our approach.

Acknowledgements. D. Martinenghi is supported by EU's IST project FP6-7603 ("TONES").

References

1. A. Balmin, Y. Papakonstantinou, and V. Vianu. Incremental validation of XML documents. *ACM Trans. Database Syst.*, 29(4):710–751, 2004.
2. M. Benedikt, G. Bruns, J. Gibson, R. Kuss, and A. Ng. Automated Update Management for XML Integrity Constraints. In *Inf. Proc. of PLAN-X Workshop*, 2002.
3. P. Bohannon, J. Freire, P. Roy, and J. Siméon. From XML schema to relations: A cost-based approach to XML storage. *ICDE*, 64–75, 2002.
4. Y. Chen, S. B. Davidson, and Y. Zheng. Xkvalidator: a constraint validator for XML. In *CIKM*, 446–452, New York, NY, USA, 2002. ACM Press.
5. H. Christiansen and D. Martinenghi. On simplification of database integrity constraints. *Fundamenta Informaticae*, 71(4):371–417, 2006.
6. A. Deutsch, M. Fernandez, and D. Suciu. Storing semi-struct-ured data with STORED. *SIGMOD*, 431–442, 1999.
7. G. Dong and J. Su. Incremental Maintenance of Recursive Views Using Relational Calculus/SQL. *SIGMOD Record*, 29(1):44–51, 2000.
8. eXist. Open source native xml database. `http://exist.sourceforge.net`.
9. W. Fan, G. M. Kuper, and J. Siméon. A unified constraint model for XML. *Computer Networks*, 39(5):489–505, 2002.
10. D. Florescu and D. Kossman. Storing and Querying XML Data using an RDMBS. *IEEE Data Eng. Bull.*, 22(3):27–34, 1999.
11. A. Gupta and I. S. Mumick (eds.). *Materialized views: techniques, implementations, and applications*. MIT Press, 1999.
12. R. Krishnamurthy, R. Kaushik, and J. Naughton. XML-SQL query translation literature: The state of the art and open problems. *XSym*, 1–18, 2003.
13. A. Laux and L. Matin. XUpdate working draft. Technical report, `http://www.xmldb.org/xupdate`, 2000.
14. A. Levy and Y. Sagiv. Constraints and redundancy in datalog. In *PODS*, 67–80, New York, NY, USA, 1992.
15. M. Ley. Digital Bibliography & Library Project. `http://dblp.uni-trier.de/`.
16. D. Martinenghi. Simplification of integrity constraints with aggregates and arithmetic built-ins. In *Flexible Query-Answering Systems*, 348–361, 2004.
17. D. Martinenghi. A simplification procedure for integrity constraints. `http://www.ruc.dk/~dm/spic`, 2004.
18. W. May. XPath-Logic and XPathLog: a logic-programming-style XML data manipulation language. *TPLP*, 4(3):239–287, 2004.
19. E. Mayol and E. Teniente. A Survey of Current Methods for Integrity Constraint Maintenance and View Updating. In *ER Workshops*, 62–73, 1999.
20. F. Neven and T. Schwentick. XPath Containment in the Presence of Disjunction, DTDs, and Variables. In *ICDT*, 315–329, 2003.
21. J.-M. Nicolas. Logic for improving integrity checking in relational data bases. *Acta Informatica*, 18:227–253, 1982.
22. A. Sawires, J. Tatemura, O. Po, D. Agrawal, and K. S. Candan. Incremental maintenance of path expression views. In *SIGMOD*, 2005.
23. T. Schwentick. XPath query containment. *SIGMOD Record*, 33(1):101–109, 2004.
24. L. Segoufin and V. Vianu. Validating Streaming XML Documents. In *PODS*, 53–64, 2002.
25. J. Shanmugasundaram, K. Tufte, C. Zhang, G. He, D. DeWitt, J. Naughton. Relational Databases for Querying XML Documents: Limitations and Opportunities. In *VLDB*, 302–314, 1999.
26. D. Suciu. Query Decomposition and View Maintenance for Query Languages for Unstructured Data. In *VLDB*, 227–238, 1996.
27. I. Tatarinov, Z. G. Ives, A. Y. Halevy, and D. S. Weld. Updating XML. In *SIGMOD*, 2001.

An Evaluation of the Use of XML for Representation, Querying, and Analysis of Molecular Interactions

Lena Strömbäck and David Hall

Department of Computer and Information Science,
Linköping University, Sweden
lestr@ida.liu.se

Abstract. Currently, biology researchers rapidly generate new information on how genes, proteins and other molecules interact in living organisms. To completely understand the machinery underlying life it is necessary to integrate and analyze these large quantities of data. As one step in this direction, new standards for describing molecular interactions have been defined based on XML. This work evaluates the usage of the XML Query language XQuery for molecular interactions, as it would be of great benefit to the user to work directly on data represented in the new standards. We use and compare a set of available XQuery implementations, eXist, X-Hive, Sedna and QizX/open for querying and analysis on data exported from available databases. Our conclusion is that XQuery can easily be used for the most common queries in this domain but is not feasible for more complex analyses. In particular, for queries containing path analysis the available XQuery implementations have poor performance and an extension of the GTL package clearly outperforms XQuery. The paper ends with a discussion regarding the usability of XQuery in this domain. In particular we point out the need for more efficient graph handling and that XQuery also requires the user to understand the exact XML format of each dataset.

1 Introduction

During the past few years XML has become one of the most used formats for representation of information in a wide variety of domains and applications. In this paper we will discuss the current use of XML for molecular interactions, which is one important sub-area of bioinformatics. In this area the goal is to understand how proteins, genes, and other substances interact with each other within living cells. Proteins are the fundamental building blocks of life, and today biology researchers are gaining small pieces of information on each protein and how it interacts with other proteins and substances in the cell. To understand how the proteins and genes work together is the key to understanding the secret of life, and as such this has been set as a major goal for bioinformatics research by the Human Proteome Organization [8] and the US National Human Genome

T. Grust et al. (Eds.): EDBT 2006 Workshops, LNCS 4254, pp. 220–233, 2006.

Research Institute [5], since this would be the key to new medical treatments for many diseases.

Within the area of molecular interactions the tradition has been to publish results from experiments on the web, making it possible for researchers to compare and reuse results from other research groups. This has resulted in a situation with a large number of available databases on Internet [2,9,12,13,14,15,20,26] with information about experimental results. However, the information content, data model and functionality is different between the different databases, which makes it hard for a researcher to track the specific information he needs.

There is, however, ongoing development within the field with the goal of making the datasets from each of the databases available for downloading and further analysis. Evaluations [1,16] have shown that XML is beneficial for information representation within bioinformatics. Most of the existing molecular interaction databases allow export of data in XML. Recently, there have also been proposals for XML-based exchange formats for protein interactions, e.g. SBML [10], PSI MI [8], and BioPAX [3]. However, to allow for easy analysis and understanding of these datasets there is still a need for software for integration, querying and analysis based on XML.

The aim of this paper is to evaluate the use of available XML tools for direct usage of molecular interaction data available in XML. The paper starts with a brief introduction to the chosen data formats. After that we report on two experiments on analysis of data with XQuery. Finally we conclude the paper with a discussion on future needs for XML tools for this application.

2 XML Standards for Molecular Interactions

There are currently a number of different XML formats for molecular interaction data available from different databases. In this work we will focus on the two formats SBML [10] and PSI MI [8]. We've chosen these formats because they have been proposed as future standards and there are currently large datasets of data available in these formats. Here, we give a short introduction to these standards; for a more extensive description and comparison with other formats see [23,24].

Systems Biology Markup Language (SBML) [10] was created by the Systems Biology Workbench Development group in cooperation with representatives from many system and tool developers within the bioinformatics field. A brief example of an SBML model is given in Figure 1. As we can see, an SBML model contains a number of compartments, each of which is a description of the container or environment in which the reaction takes place. The substances or entities that take part in the reactions are represented as species. The interactions between molecules are represented as reactions, defined as processes that change one or more of the species. Reactants, products and modifiers for reactions are specified by references to the relevant species.

The Proteomics Standards Initiative Molecular Interaction XML format (PSI MI) [8] was developed by the Proteomics Standards Initiative, one initiative of

SBML

```
<model name="Example">
 <listOfCompartments>
  <compartment name="Mithocondrial Matrix"
            id="MM">
 </listOfCompartments>
 <listOfSpecies>
  <species name="Succinate"
      compartment="MM" id="Succinate">
  <species name="Fumarate"
      compartment="MM" id="Fumarate">
  <species name="Succinate dehydrogenase"
      compartment="MM" id="Succdeh">
 </listOfSpecies>
 <listOfReactions>
  <reaction name="Succinate dehydrogenas
       catalysis" id="R1">
   <listOfReactants>
    <speciesReference species="Succinate">
   </listOfReactants>
   <listOfProducts>
    <speciesReference species="Fumarate">
   </listOfProducts>
   <listOfModifiers>
     <modifierSpeciesReference
                 species="Succdeh">
   </listOfModifiers>
  </reaction>
 </listOfReactions>
</model>
```

PSI MI

```
<entry>
 <interactorList>
  <proteinInteractor id="Succinate>
   <names>
    <shortLabel>Succinate</shortLabel>
    <fullName>Succinate</fullName>
   </names>
  </proteinInteractor> ...
 </interactorList>
 <interactionList>
  <interaction>
   <names>
    <shortLabel> Succinate dehydrogenas
         catalysis </shortLabel>
     <fullName>Interaction between ....
     </fullName>
    </names>
   <participantList>
    <proteinParticipant>
     <proteinInteractorRef ref="Succinate">
     <role>neutral</role>
    </proteinParticipant>
    <proteinParticipant>
     <proteinInteractorRef ref="Fumarate">
     <role>neutral</role>
    </proteinParticipant>
    <proteinParticipant>
     <proteinInteractorRef ref="Succdeh">
     <role>neutral</role>
    </proteinParticipant>
   </participantList>
  </interaction>
 </interactionList>
</entry>
```

Fig. 1. Examples of data in SBML and PSI MI

the Human Proteome Organization (HUPO). An abbreviated example pathway represented in PSI MI is shown in Figure 1. In PSI MI the *experimentList* describes experiments and links to publications where the interactions are verified. The pathway itself is described via the *interactorList*, which is a list of proteins participating in the interaction, and the *interactionList*, a list of the actual interactions. For each *interaction* it is possible to set one or more names. The participating proteins are described by their names or by references to the *interactorList*. Note that, where the intention of SBML is to describe an actual interaction, i.e. that interacting substances produce some product, the purpose of PSI MI is to describe the result of an experiment, i.e. that there is some chemical interaction between the substances but roles of the substances in the interaction are not always known.

As we can see, the two formats are similar. Even so, there are several important differences between them. As previously discussed PSI MI contains more detailed information and there are differences in how participants in an interaction are represented. In addition to this there is also an important

1.1 *Find all information on a given compartment. Compartment id is given.*
1.2 *Find all information on a given species. Species id is given.*
1.3 *Find all information on a given reaction. Reaction id is given.*
2.1 *Find all reactions which a given modifier participates in. The species of the modifier is given.*
3.1 *Find all the reactions whose reactants are the products of some reactions which a given modifier participates in. The species of the modifier is given.*
3.2 *Find all the reactions whose reactants and products are the same but modifiers are different.*
4.1 *Count the number of species in the database.*
4.2 *Count the number of reactions in the database.*

Fig. 2. Queries for the SBML dataset

difference in the fact that SBML makes more use of XML attributes while PSI MI prefers to represent information as extra children in the tree structure. In the remainder of this paper we will look at possibilities for the researcher to work directly on the dataset, i.e. to analyze it by querying directly against the XML document.

3 Experiment 1: XQuery Querying

For our first experiment we want to test some common queries within the molecular interaction domain. For the experiments we use XQuery [32], the proposed standard query language for XML. The experiment consists of three parts: first the selection of queries and datasets for the test, next the formulation of the XQuery queries, and finally execution on XQuery implementations.

3.1 Definition of Queries and Datasets

Since the two standards SBML and PSI MI contain partly different information we define one set of interesting queries for each of the standards. The selected queries are based on an investigation of the query possibilities within available databases or investigating what are interesting questions from a biological point of view. The queries are divided into four different groups:

1. Simple selection of one data item.
2. Combination of information on two kinds of data types.
3. Complex queries, combination of several items.
4. Counting information in the datasets.

The selected queries for SBML are presented in Figure 2, the first number of each query shows which of the query groups it belongs to. Since the PSI MI data model is richer than the one for SBML we could use more queries compared to the SBML dataset. Here we also wanted to test some combined queries, i.e.

1.1 *Find information on a given protein. Protein id is given.*
1.2 *Find information on a given experiment description. Experiment description id is given.*
1.3 *Find information on a given interaction. Interaction id is given.*
2.1 *Find the protein information for the proteins that participate in a given interaction. Interaction id is given.*
2.2 *Find the experiment description information for an experiment description that is part of an interaction. Interaction id is given.*
2.3 *Find all interactions that a given protein participates in. Protein id is given.*
2.4 *Find all interactions that a given experiment description is part of. Experiment description id is given.*
2.5 *Find any interactions that two given proteins are a part of. Protein ids for the two proteins are given.*
3.1 *Find information on the proteins that could interact with a given protein. Protein id is given.*
3.2 *Find the description of the experiments which involve some interactions which a given protein participate in. Protein id is given.*
3.3 *Find the interactions which some given proteins participate in. The proteins secondary attribute is given.*
4.1 *Count the number of proteins in the database.*
4.2 *Count the number of interactions in the database.*

Fig. 3. Queries for the PSI MI dataset

forcing XQuery to join information from different parts of the data file. The selected queries for the PSI MI dataset are presented in Figure 3.

The database currently providing the largest subsets of SBML data is Reactome [12]. It is a database on biological pathways, mainly human but there are pathways from other species as well. We selected two datasets from Reactome of sizes 3 and 6 MB. They are available in SBML level 2, version 1. PSI MI is the most supported format for protein interaction databases. It is available as an alternative download format in a number of databases, for instance DIP [20], MINT [26], and IntAct [9]. Here, the IntAct database is the one currently providing the largest portions of PSI MI data. It is an open source database and toolkit for protein interactions. It currently contains nearly 40,000 interactions. We selected three datafiles from IntAct of sizes 9.5, 29.3 and 37.3 MB.

3.2 Expressing Queries in XQuery

In this section we discuss some issues in formulating queries for the first experiment. An extensive description of the queries is given in [7]. Many of the queries are written as simple path expressions with arbitrary depth (nesting) using // and some conditional. This is used in, for instance, the first three queries for both test cases which are very basic queries consisting of paths. Here we exemplify this with query 2.1 for PSI MI:

```
document("rat_small.xml")//proteinInteractor[@id="EBI-77471"]
```

For the more complicated queries, join over path expressions or in some cases the XQuery FLWOR expressions are used, since these make the queries more readable and easier to express. As an example of this we present query 2.1 for PSI MI which uses a FLWOR expression. Here we find the interaction with the appropriate ID and iterate over the proteins participating in this interaction. For each of these proteins we find the desired information in the list of protein-interactors.

```
for $ref in document("rat_small.xml")//interaction
  [names/shortLabel="interaction1"]
  /participantList/proteinParticipant/proteinInteractorRef/@ref
return document("rat_small.xml")//proteinInteractor[@id=$ref]
```

The last two queries for each standard use the count aggregate function to give a measure of the size of the datasets. Here we exemplify this with query 4.1 for PSI MI counting the number of proteins in the database.

```
count(document("rat_small.xml")//proteinInteractor)
```

From this discussion we can conclude that for a user that is accustomed to the concepts and constructions in the molecular interaction standards, and who has a reasonable knowledge of XQuery, these queries can easily be expressed.

3.3 Efficiency

Having formulated the queries, we were interested in the performance of the different XML database systems. There are a large number of implementations of XQuery, ranging from implementations for direct querying on XML files to systems aiming at more efficient storage and treatment of larger XML files, so-called native XML databases. We selected three native XML database implementations: eXist [27], Sedna [30] and X-Hive [31] and the XQuery API QizX/open [29] which does not support indexing and thus is expected to yield lower performance than the other systems.

Since the exact times can depend on external factors such as other processes running on the system the computer results would differ from time to time for the same queries. To decrease the influence of sudden spikes in measured time all queries were run several times and we base our values on the mean times. We have run several sets of tests on our selected datasets on two different computers. Here we will present a selection of results that represents our general findings. Figure 4 shows a general comparison of the systems for queries on the IntAct 29.3 MB dataset run on a IBM X40, Intel Pentium 1200 MHz processor with 512 MB RAM. All the Native database systems have similar and good performance, where X-Hive has slightly higher response time than the other systems. QizX/open performs worse than the other systems for all queries, as expected

We also wanted to compare how the response time varied if we varied data size. Figure 5 show a comparison of response times on eXist and Sedna on the

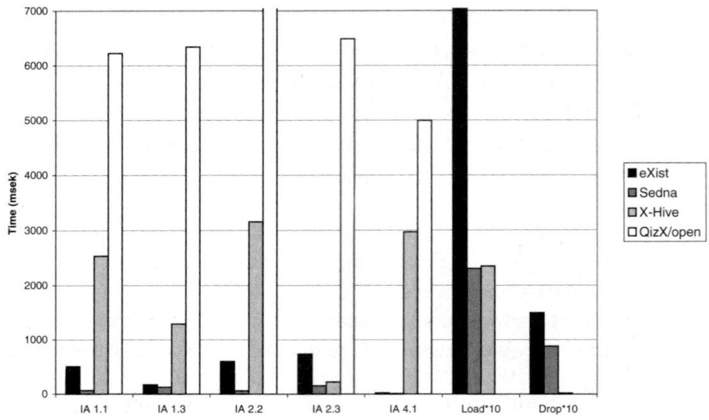

Fig. 4. Query times for different systems

9.5 and 37.3 IntAct datasets. This queries were run on an AMD Athlon 1000 MHz computer with 512 MB RAM. From the figure we can conclude that Sedna is the better performing system, with some exceptions where we have a very high response time for Sedna. For both systems we can also see an increase in response time when complexity of queries increase. Here performance of the systems is highly dependent on the number of intermediate results generated by a query, and thus by evaluation order on parts of the query. In general, the response time increases when the data size increases. There are however some exceptions to this. These exceptions can be explained with the different composition of datasets. For a particular query the data size for an intermediate step can be higher even if the total data size is smaller.

Finally we wanted to compare the performance between SBML and PSI MI. For this we used the Reactome 6MB and IntAct 9.15 MB datasets, which are reasonably comparable in number of items stored. A comparison on corresponding queries are given in Figure 6, this time run on the AMD computer. The figure shows that there is no larger difference between the datasets in terms of performance.

To conclude this section we can see that all the queries run with a reasonable response time on the selected datasets. Comparing the systems we can see that all the native databases provide similar performance with Sedna being the fastest and X-Hive being the most stable implementation.

4 Experiment 2: Pathway Analyses

In addition to queries similar to those currently available through conventional systems, we also wanted to test advanced analysis on the datasets. In this case, we want to search for interaction chains between given proteins. As explained, it

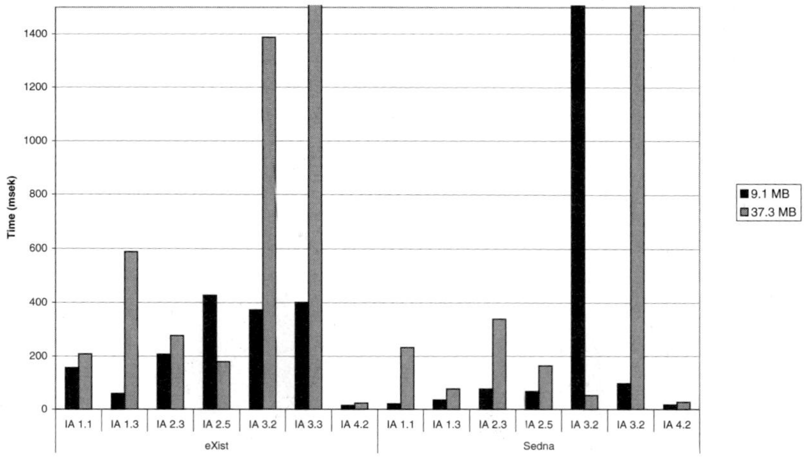

Fig. 5. Query times for different data sizes

is not possible to make out reactant and products in PSI MI interactions since there is no order of the reactions defined in this format. Therefore we decided to concentrate the pathway searching efforts to the SBML dataset and used the following query: textit

> Given two proteins find out if there is a given pathway between them in maximum n steps. Protein ids are given for the two proteins.

This analysis is very important, since it is often important to identify connections between interacting proteins in a given dataset. To express this in XQuery, recursion is required. The query is shown in Figure 7. As we wanted to be able to test the query for various lengths of the pathways the query contains a recursive function *findMolecule* that returns elements for found connected proteins within a specified maximum length of the path. The function takes the start and goal reactants together with the cut-off depth as parameters.

The response times for this query run on the IBM 1200 GHz computer on the 3MB Reactome file are presented in Table 1. eXist, Sedna and QizX/open ran out of memory at 4 steps. Sedna query times increase more slowly than for X-Hive, but X-Hive is the only XML tool reaching 4 steps.

These results are disappointing, both in the sense that formulating recursive XQuery queries gets rather complicated and that the response times are too high, especially taking into account that a real application would often need to do queries on larger datasets and longer paths than the ones we used.

For the molecular interaction applications there is a need for more efficient handling of these kinds of queries. One possibility would be to include an existing graph package into the XQuery language. For this reason we made an experiment with the graph package GTL (Graph Template Library) [28]. GTL is an extension of the Standard Template Library for graphs and graph algorithms in C++. The function we wanted to test, finding all paths between two proteins,

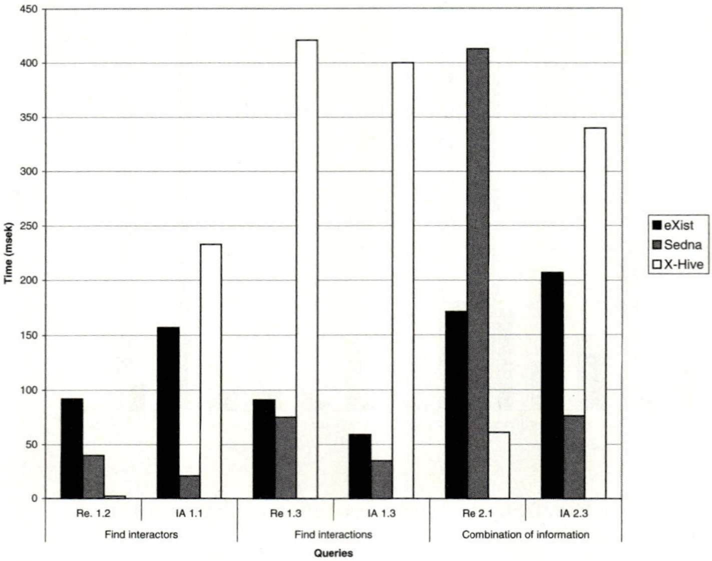

Fig. 6. Comparison between SBML and PSI MI

was not implemented in GTL and we had to extend the package [7]. Before GTL can be used the protein interaction, data in SBML format is transformed to GML, a non-XML-based graph representation format provided by GTL. In our translation nodes are substances and edges are reactions. The transformation is done using the MSXSL command line transformation utility from Microsoft and it takes about 2 seconds to transform the 3 MB Reactome file.

The first step of our algorithm would be a search using GTL's built-in breadth-first search algorithm to verify that the end node really can be reached from the start node. The search between the start and end node is done by a recursive function, which works outwards from the start node and follows outgoing edges. In addition to this we use a cut-off depth at which to stop searching, as with the corresponding XQuery. The graph sent as an argument has already-visited nodes marked as hidden to avoid loops. Table 2 shows the performance of the pathway searches using our extension of GTL. The numbers given in the relevant

Table 1. Test case 3: Pathway searches with XQuery

Steps	eXist Mean time	X-Hive Mean time	Sedna Mean time	QizX/open Mean time
1	422 ms	334 ms	121 ms	906 ms
2	951 ms	646 ms	245 ms	1125 ms
3	33323 ms	9053 ms	3493 ms	7172 ms
4	-	700443 ms	-	-

```
declare function local:findMolecule($molecule as xs:string,
            $goalMol as xs:string, $n as xs:integer) {
  for $i in document("sbml.xml")//reaction
        [listOfReactants/speciesReference/@species=$molecule]
        /listOfProducts/speciesReference/@species
  return <item>{$i} {
    if($i = $goalMol) then <found/> else
      if($i = $molecule) then <loop /> else
        if ($n = 1) then <max/> else
          local:findMolecule($i, $goalMol, $n - 1)}
    </item>};
<path>{local:findMolecule("H2O", "sodium ion",2)}</path>
```

Fig. 7. Query for path searches

Table 2. Test case 3: Pathway searches using the extended GTL package

Steps	1	2	3	4	5	6	7	8
Time	0.3 ms	3 ms	15 ms	101 ms	823 ms	5,55 s	35,8 s	215 s

table are based on a mean value of ten iterations. Figure 8 shows a comparison between the GTL implementation and the tested databases.

As shown by this table the C++ program developed for graph searches is magnitudes faster than using the XQuery searches. This depends on a number of things with the most important probably being that the C++ program has graph and loop detection and that the representation is optimal for graph searches.

5 Discussion and Implications for the Future

The development of web databases and new standards within the area of molecular interaction indicates that XML representations will be of high importance for the area in the future. This means that there will also be a high degree of interest in existing XML technology as well as a need for development of new technology for the specific needs of the application. In this section we will put our results into context by providing a discussion on the generality of the results and requirements for the molecular interaction application.

For our experiments the most central criteria has been to test whether XQuery is useful for finding relevant information from a molecular interaction dataset with reasonable simple query formulations and a reasonable level of efficiency. To determine this we have based our queries on an investigation of available queries on existing databases for molecular interactions and cellular pathways available over the Internet [2,9,12,13,14,15,20,26]. This ensures that our selected queries capture the most important features of the application.

Another measure of generality is to compare our queries to available test benches for XML [4,17,21,25]. These test benches define either particular

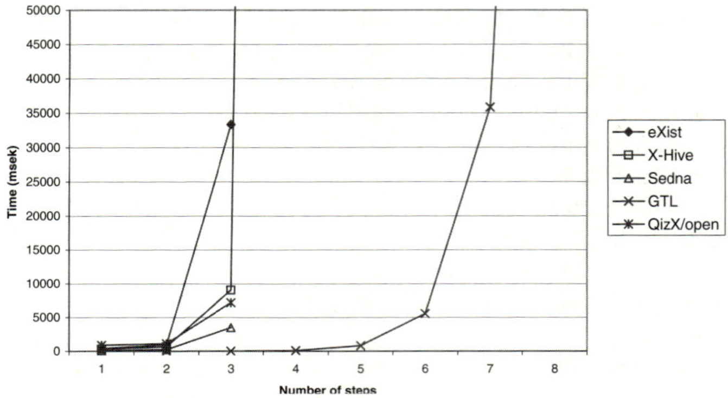

Fig. 8. Comparison of query times for pathway searches

XQuery queries or sets of XQuery queries, where the idea is to cover as many features of XQuery as possible. Such a comparison shows that our selected test queries cover the query groups relevant to this domain. Certain kinds of queries that were not relevant to this application or these datasets were naturally excluded from our tests, for example queries based on order.

For the queries in experiment 1, it was feasible to write queries on the protein-interaction data using the XQuery language. For a small dataset all three tested NXD's gave response times acceptable for interactive use with the exception for pathway queries. Our previous comparison with relational databases [22] also shows that these results are comparable with what can be achieved using a relational approach.

However, an interesting question is whether XQuery is a suitable query language for the domain. Even though it is possible to express queries, querying with XQuery requires a solid knowledge of the specific XML format of a dataset, which requires the user to have a high degree of knowledge about the specific XML formats. Since it is very likely that a typical user would need to handle several of these formats, there is a need for developing higher-level query languages for the domain.

In the case of more complex analyses, e.g. pathway analysis, the search times become large after just a few steps and the tested XQuery implementations do not cope with pathway queries longer than three steps. A C++ program for performing this query was developed using a graph package and resulted in searches that were orders of magnitude faster than for the XML databases, making it possible to search even larger graphs.

XQuery does not provide any special support for graph processing, while queries of this kind are doubtless very interesting in many applications. XGMML (Extensible Graph Markup and Modeling Language) [18] is a general format for describing graphs using XML based on GML, used in these tests. Other more specialized formats, such as the already-existing PSI MI and SBML formats for biological data, may emerge in a number of different subject areas.

This means there is a need for graph-capable XML in combination with XQuery. To be able to perform larger graph searches there must be special support for this. One possibility would be to extend XQuery with a number of internal functions for path searches and graph analyses. This is possible by using, for example, a Java binding such as those offered by eXist and QizX/open, which makes it possible to call functions in Java in the same way as XQuery's internal functions.

A final issue is the situation where the user needs to query over several datasets and integrate the resulting information into one query. Here we see several solutions. One is to provide a higher level query language capable of translating the query into several specific query languages. This is similar to what has been proposed for general databases within bioinformatics [11]. Another option would be to provide tools for fast data integration between the different XML formats in the line of the work within schema matching [6,19].

6 Summary

XML is more and more commonly used within the area of molecular interactions and new XML standards are arising within the area. Because of this it would be very appealing if existing XML technology could be used for querying and analyses on this data. This work evaluates the use of XQuery and Native XML databases on datasets in two of the available standards, SBML and PSI MI.

Our experiments show that XQuery is a suitable language for most of the queries expected for the domain. We also saw a reasonable level of efficiency in the tested native XML implementations. There are, however, several obvious points for future research. One is the need for extended query languages and methods for graph analyses. A second issue is methods for the user to query over several different standard formats without having an exact knowledge of the specific XML format for each of the datasets.

Acknowledgements. Thanks to Patrick Lambrix for valuable comments on this work. We are also grateful to Liu Ke for performing some of the tests.

References

1. Achard F, Vaysseix G, and Barillot E: XML, bioinformatics and data integration. *Bioinformatics* **17**(2):115-125, 2001.
2. Bader GD, Donaldson I, Wolting C, Oulette BF, Tony BF, Pawson TBF, and Hogue CWV: BIND - The Biomolecular Network Database. *Nucleic Acids Research* **29**(1):242-245, 2001.
3. BioPAX working Group: BioPAX – Biological Pathways Exchange Language. Level 1, Version 1.0 Documentation. Available at http://www.biopax.org, 2004.
4. Bressan S, Lee M-L, Li YG, Lacroix Z, Nambiar U: The XOO7 Benchmark. EEXTT 2002: 146-147, 2002.
5. Collins FS, Green ED, Guttmacher AE, and Guyer MS: A vision for the future of genomics research: A blueprint for the genomic era. *Nature* **422**: 835-847, 2003.

6. Doan, A, Halevy AY: Semantic Integration Research in the Database Community: A brief Survey. *AI Magazine, Special Issue on Semantic Integration, Spring 2005*, 2004.
7. Hall D. *An XML-based Database of Molecular Pathways.* Master Thesis, Department of Computer and Information Science, Linköpings universitet, LITH-IDA-EX–05/049–SE, 2005.
8. Hermjakob H, Montecchi-Palazzi L, Bader G, Wojcik J, Salwinski L, Ceol A, Moore S, Orchard S, Sarkans U, von Mering C, Roechert B, Poux S, Jung E, Mersch H, Kersey P, Lappe M, Li Y, Zeng R, Rana D, Nikolski M, Husi H, Brun C, Shanker K, Grant SGN, Sander C, Boork P, Zhu W, Akhilesh P, Brazma A, Jacq B, Vidal M, Sherman D, Legrain P, Cesareni G, Xenarios I, Eisenberg D, Steipe B, Hogue C, and Apweiler R: The HUPO PSI's Molecular Interaction format - a community standard for the representation of protein interaction data. *Nature Biotechnology* **22**(2):177-183, 2004.
9. Hermjakob H, Montecchi-Palazzi L, Lewington C, Mudali S, Kerrien S, Orchard S, Vingron M, Roechert B, Roepstorff P, Valencia A, Margalit H, Armstrong J, Bairoch A, Cesareni G, Sherman D, Apweiler R: IntAct - an open source molecular interaction database. *Nucl. Acids. Res.* 32: D452-D455, 2004.
10. Hucka M, Finney A, Sauro HM, Bolouri H, Doyle JC, Kitano H, Arkin AP, Bornstein BJ, Bray D, Cornish-Bowden A, Cuellar AA, Dronov S,. Gilles ED, Ginkel M, Gor V, Goryanin II, Hedley W-J, Hodgman TC, Hofmeyr J-H, Hunter PJ, Juty NS, Kasberger JL, Kremling A, Kummer U, Le Novere N, Loew LM, Lucio D, Mendes P, Minch E, Mjolsness ED, Nakayama Y, Nelson MR, Nielsen PF, Sakurada T, Schaff JC, Shapiro BE, Shimizu TS, Spence HD, Stelling J, Takahashi K, Tomita M, Wagner J, and Wang J: The systems biology markup language (SBML): a medium for representation and exchange of biochemical network models. *Bioinformatics* **19**(4):524-531, 2003.
11. Jakoniene V, Lambrix P: Ontology-based Integration for Bioinformatics. Proceedings of the VLDB Workshop on Ontologies-based techniques for DataBases and Information Systems - ODBIS 2005, pp 55-58, Trondheim, Norway.
12. Joshi-Tope G, Gillespie M, Vastrik I, D'Eustachio P, Schmidt E, de Bono B, Jassal B, Gopinath GR, Wu GR, Matthews L, Lewis S, Birney E, Stein L: Reactome: a knowledgebase of biological pathways. *Nucleic Acids Res.* 1;33 Database Issue:D428-32. PMID: 15608231, 2005.
13. Kanehisa, M and Goto, S: KEGG: Kyoto Encyclopedia of Genes and Genomes. *Nucleic Acids Res.* **28**, 27-30, 2000.
14. Kanehisa M, Goto S, Kawashima S, Okuno Y, and Hattori M: The KEGG resources for deciphering the genome. *Nucleic Acids Res.* **32**, D277-D280, 2004.
15. Karp P.D, Arnaud M, Collado-Vides J, Ingraham J, Paulsen IT, and Saier MH Jr: The E. coli EcoCyc Database: No Longer Just a Metabolic Pathway Database. *ASM News* **70**(1): 25-30, 2004.
16. McEntire R, Karp P, Abrenethy N, Benton D, Helt G, DeJongh M, Kent R, Kosky A, Lewis S, Hodnett D, Neumann E, Olken F, Pathak D, Tarzy-Hornoch P, Tolda L, and Topaloglou T: An evaluation of Ontology Exchange Languages for Bioinformatics. *Proceedings International Conference on Intelligent Systems for Molecular Biology* **8**:239-250, 2000.
17. Nambiar U, Lacroix Z, Bressan S, Lee M-L, Li YG: Current Approaches to XML Management. IEEE Internet Computing 6(4): 43-51, 2002.
18. Punin J, Krishnamoorthy M: XGMML (eXtensible Graph Markup and Modeling Language) http://www.cs.rpi.edu/~puninj/XGMML/, 2001 (Accessed April 2005).

19. Rahm, E and PA Bernstein: A survey of approaches to semantic schema matching. *The VLDB Journal 10:334-350.* DOI 10-1007/s007780100057, 2001.
20. Salvinski L, Miller CS, Smith AJ, Bowie JU, and Eisenberg D: The Database of Interacting Proteins: 2004 Update. *Nucleic Acids Research* **32** Database Issue D449-451, 2004.
21. Schmidt AR, Waas F, Kersten ML, Florescu D, Carey MJ, Manolescu I, and Busse R: Why and How to Benchmark XML Databases. ACM SIGMOD Record, 3(30):27-32, 2001.
22. Strömbäck, L: Storage and Integration of Molecular Interactions: Evaluating the Use of XML Technology. *Proc of the 3rd International Workshop on Biological Data Management (BIDM'05).* Copenhagen, Denmark, 2005.
23. Strömbäck, L: XML representations of pathway data: a comparison. *Proc. of the ACM SIGIR'04 Workshop on Search and Discovery within Bioinformatics.* Sheffield UK, 2004.
24. Strömbäck, L and Lambrix P: Representations of molecular pathways: An evaluation of SBML, PSI MI and BioPAX. Accepted for publication in *Bioinformatics* **21**(24):4401-4407, 2005.
25. Yao BB, Özsu MT, and Khandelwal N: XBench Benchmark and Performance Testing of XML DBMSs. In *Proceedings of 20th International Conference on Data Engineering*, Boston, MA, pp 621-632, March 2004.
26. Zanzoni A, Montecchi-Palazzi L, Quondam M, Ausiello G, Helmer-Citterich M, and Cesareni G: MINT: a Molecular INTeraction database. *FEBS Letters* **513**(1):135-140, 2002.
27. eXist http://exist.sourceforge.net (Accessed May 2005)
28. GTL The Graph Template Library http://infosun.fmi.uni-passau.de/GTL/index.html (Accessed May 2005)
29. QizX/open http://www.xfra.net/qizxopen/ (Accessed May 2005)
30. Sedna http://www.modis.ispras.ru/Development/sedna.htm (Accessed May 2005)
31. X-Hivehttp://www.x-hive.com (Accessed May 2005)
32. XQuery http://www.w3c.org (Accessed May 2005)

Confidentiality Enforcement for XML Outsourced Data*

Barbara Carminati and Elena Ferrari

University of Insubria at Como, Via Carloni, 78 - 22100 Como, Italy
barbara.carminati, elena.ferrari@uninsubria.it

Abstract. Data outsourcing is today receiving growing attention due to its benefits in terms of cost reduction and better services. According to such paradigm, the data owner is no more responsible for data management, rather it outsources its data to one or more service providers (referred to as publishers) that provide management services and query processing functionalities. Clearly, data outsourcing leads to challenging security issues in that, by outsourcing its data, the data owner may potentially loose control over them. Therefore, a lot of research is currently carrying on to ensure secure management of data even in the presence of an untrusted publisher. One of the key issues is confidentiality enforcement, that is, how to ensure that data are not read by unauthorized users. In this paper, we propose a solution for XML data, which exploits cryptographic techniques and it is robust to the most common and relevant security threats. In the paper, we present the encryption methods and query processing strategies.

1 Introduction

Data outsourcing is today emerging as one of the most important trend in the area of data management. According to such paradigm, the data owner is no more totally responsible for data management. Rather it outsources its data (or portions of them) to one or more publishers that provide data management services and query processing functionalities. Main benefit of data outsourcing is cost reduction for the owner, in that it pays only for the services it uses and not for the deployment, installation, maintenance, and upgrades of DBMSs. By contrast, when data are outsourced such costs are amortized across several users. Another important benefit is scalability in that data owners could not become bottlenecks for the system, rather they can outsource their data to as many publishers as they needs according to the amount of data and the number of managed users. Clearly, data outsourcing leads to many research challenges. One of the most significant is related to security. The key problem is that, since the owner does not anymore manage its data, it may potentially loose control

* The work reported in this paper has been partially supported by the Italian MIUR under the project 'Web-based management and representation of spatial and geographical data'.

T. Grust et al. (Eds.): EDBT 2006 Workshops, LNCS 4254, pp. 234–249, 2006.

over them. The challenge is therefore how to ensure the most important security properties (e.g., confidentiality, integrity, authenticity) even if data are managed by a third party. A naive solution is to assume the publisher to be *trusted*, that is, to assume it always operates according to the owner's security policies. However, making this assumption is not realistic, especially for web-based systems that can be easily attacked and penetrated. Additionally, verifying that a publisher is trusted is a very costly operation. Therefore, the research is now focusing on techniques to satisfy main security properties even in the presence of an untrusted publisher that can not always follow owner's security policies (for instance it can maliciously modify/delete the data it manages or it can send data to non authorized users). In this paper, we make a contribution to this research by focusing on confidentiality, that is, protection against non authorized reading operations, since it represents one of the most relevant security properties. Moreover, we cast our techniques in the framework of XML [11], since it is today the de-facto standard for data modeling and exchange over the web.

When data are outsourced confidentiality has two main aspects. The first, which we call *confidentiality wrt users*, refers to protect data against unauthorized read operations by users. The second, which we call *confidentiality wrt publishers*, deals with protecting owner's data from read operations by publishers. Our solution enforces confidentiality by using cryptographic techniques: publishers manage ciphered data instead of clear-text ones. In that way confidentiality wrt publishers is always ensured. Data encryption is generated by the owner and it is driven by the specified access control policies: all data portions to which the same policies apply are encrypted with the same key. Then, each user receives only the keys corresponding to the policies he/she satisfies. This ensures confidentiality wrt users. Enforcing confidentiality through the use of encryption requires dealing with several issues. The first is encryption generation in that there is the need to devise an encryption scheme which is robust to the most relevant security attacks. For instance, if you consider keyword-based searches on textual data, if the same keyword is always encrypted with the same key, both publishers and users can infer information by analyzing the document encryption. The same problem arises at the schema level, that is, with encrypted tags or attributes names. In this work we propose an encryption scheme that avoids information leakage due to data dictionary attacks. The second main issue is how publishers can query encrypted data. In the literature, several methods exist to this purpose.[1] Some of them have been designed for relational databases [6,7], others have been designed to query textual data [10]. Our work is inspired by both of them, since an XML document contains both text and attributes with standard domains. In the paper, we present our strategy to query XML encrypted data and we describe both publisher side and user side query processing. The work described in this paper is part of a wider project whose goal is to ensure the most relevant security properties (i.e., authenticity/integrity and completeness in addition to confidentiality) when data are managed by a third party. Therefore, before going into the details of confidentiality protection we

[1] Some of them are surveyed in Section 2.

describe the overall architecture of the system we propose. Details on techniques for authenticity/integrity and completeness verification can be found in [1]. The remainder of this paper is organized as follows. Next section surveys related work that are the basis of our proposal. Section 3 deals with confidentiality enforcement. Section 4 illustrates client-side query processing. Finally, Section 5 concludes the paper.

2 Related Work

In recent years the problem of inquiring encrypted data managed by a third party has been deeply investigated by several researchers, that proposed different solutions [6,7,10] for different data models and domains. In general, the most appropriate solution to query encrypted data mainly depends on the nature of the data being queried, that is, the data domain and the underlying data model. Thus, in order to select the most appropriate technique to inquire XML encrypted data, we need to take into account the characteristics of XML data. XML documents often contain data with heterogeneous domains (e.g, textual data, date, integer). For this reason, we believe that in the scenario considered in this paper, it is not enough to use a single technique to inquiry encrypted XML data. Rather, different techniques should be combined into a unified framework to manage data with different domains. For instance, the work by Hacigumus et al. [6,7] develops a method to query encrypted data stored in relational databases. From such work we borrow the method to query non textual data. By contrast [10] deals with keyword-based searches on textual data. We use some of the methods proposed in [10] to solve a twofold issue, that is, querying textual data and avoiding information leakage due to data dictionary attacks at the schema level. However, with difference to our proposal, such approaches only consider confidentiality wrt publishers, whereas they do not consider confidentiality wrt users. In what follows, we briefly introduce the techniques proposed in [6,7] and [10], whereas details on how these two techniques are used in our framework are presented in Section 3. Confidentiality enforcement through the use of encryption techniques has also been investigated by us in [4]. The current work extends our previous work along several relevant directions. The first is that in this paper we provide a comprehensive method to query encrypted XML documents, which exploits a variety of strategies to query XML documents with heterogeneous content. In [4] we adapt the strategy proposed in [6,7] to query both textual and non textual attributes as well as data with textual domain. The technique proposed in [6,7] has a major shortcoming, i.e., to be prone to data dictionary attacks by both publishers and users. This kind of attack can be for instance perpetrated when the same data portion (e.g., attribute value, tag name) repeatedly appears in an XML document ciphered with the same key. In this paper, we solve this problem by applying a combination of strategies to treat XML data, able to trade-off between query expressivity and robustness to security threats. Another weak point of the solution proposed in [4] is information leakage due to inferences at the schema level in that tags/attributes with the same names and covered by the same access control policies are encrypted with the same key. Therefore, by analyzing document encryptions both publishers and users can infer information on the schema of some document portions, even if they are not allowed to access such portions. This is a relevant security threat since tags and attributes names can convey semantic relevant information (for instance, by exploiting such kind of attack a user can infer the existence of an element named `salary` even if he/she is not allowed to access it according to owner's security policies).

2.1 Hacigums et al.

The approach proposed by Hacigumus et. al [6,7] exploits binning techniques and privacy homomorphisms to inquiry encrypted relational data. Binning techniques are used to perform selection queries on encrypted relation data, whereas privacy homomorphisms are used to make a third party able to perform aggregate queries over encrypted tuples. In our framework, we assume that users submit queries through XPath [11], with the obvious intention to extend the approach to support XQuery [11]. Thus, since XPath expressions do not contain aggregate functions, in what follows we review only the approach for selection queries.

The underlying idea of the approach is the following: given a relation R, the owner divides the domain of each attribute in R into distinguished partitions, to which it assigns a different id. Then, the owner sends the publisher the encrypted tuples, together with the ids of the partitions corresponding to each attribute value in R. The publisher is able to perform queries directly on the encrypted tuples, by exploiting the received partition ids. The idea is that a user, before submitting a query to a publisher, rewrites it in terms of partition ids. As an example, consider the relation $Employee(eid, ename, salary)$, and, for simplicity, consider only the *salary* attribute. Suppose that the domain of *salary* is in the interval [500k, 5000k], and that an equi-partition with 100k as range is applied on that domain. Suppose that a user wants to perform the following query: "SELECT * FROM Employee WHERE salary =1000k". It translates it into the query: "SELECT * FROM Employee WHERE salary=id_{1000k}", where id_{1000k} is the id of the partition containing the value 1000k. Clearly, users should receive by the owner information on the techniques used to partition data and generate ids. The publisher is then able to answer such query by exploiting only the received ids. The publisher returns an approximate result wrt the original query. For instance, with reference to the above example, it returns all the tuples of the *Employee* relation whose *salary* attribute belongs to the range [1000K, 1099K). A further query processing has thus to be performed by the user to refine the received answer.

2.2 Song et al.

Another approach that has greatly inspired the present work is the one proposed by Song et al. [10] for keyword searching on encrypted textual data. Given a text consisting of a sequence of words: $W_1, W_2, \dots W_n$, the basic scheme proposed in

[10] first encrypts each word using a symmetric encryption algorithm $E_k()$, with a single secret key k. Then the scheme generates the XOR of each encrypted word with a pseudorandom number. The resulting ciphered words are then outsourced to the third party. According to this scheme, when a user needs to search for a keyword W, it generates the encrypted word $E_k(W)$ and computes $E_k(W) \oplus S$, where S is the corresponding pseudorandom number. This simple scheme allows the third party to search for keyword W in the encrypted data, by simply looking for $E(W) \oplus S$, thus without gaining any information on the clear text. Since occurrences of the same word are xored with different pseudorandom numbers, by analyzing the distribution of the encrypted words, no information could be inferred regarding the clear text. In particular, in [10] the authors propose a generation process for pseudorandom numbers, that makes users able to locally compute pseudorandom numbers, without any interaction with the data owner. The scheme exploits a symmetric encryption function $E()$, and two pseudorandom numbers generator functions, namely F and f. In the following, with the notation $E_k(x)$ ($F_k(x)$, $f_k(x)$, respectively), we denote the result of applying E (F, f, respectively) to input x with key k. The scheme considers as input a set of clear-text words, $W_1, W_2, \ldots, W_l$, with the same length n.[2] Given these set of words, the steps needed to generate the corresponding ciphered words are the following:

- data owner generates a sequence of pseudorandom values: $S_1 \ldots S_l$, of length $n - m$;[3]
- for each word W_j, the outsourced ciphered word C_j is generated according to the following formula: $C_j = E_k(W_j) \oplus < S_j, F_{K_j}(S_j) >$, where $K_j = f_k(FB_j)$, and FB_j denotes the first $n - m$ bits of $E_k(W_j)$.

Let us see now how query evaluation and decryption take place. When a user needs to search for a keyword W_i, he/she sends the third party $E_k(W_i)$ and key K_i, which can be locally computed by the user. Then, for each outsourced ciphered word C_i, the third party: *1)* calculates $C_i \oplus E_k(W_i)$; *2)* takes the first $n-m$ bits bts of the resulting value, and computes $F_{K_i}(bts)$, where K_i is the key received by the requiring user; *3)* if the result of $F_{K_i}(bts)$ is equal to the $n-m+1$ remaining bits, then the ciphered word C_i is returned. Indeed, if C_i contains the searched encrypted word, then $E_k(W_i) \oplus < S_i, F_{K_i}(S_i) > \oplus E_k(W_i) =< S_i, F_{K_i}(S_i) >$, for the properties of the XOR operator. When a user receives C_i as answer of a query, he/she is not able to extract the value $E_k(W_i)$ from C_i and thus to decrypt it, by simply using the decryption key k. Therefore, the scheme proposed in [10] assumes that users know S_i.[4] In such a way, user is able to

[2] This set of words can be obtained by partitioning the input clear-text into atomic quantities (on the basis of the application domain), and by padding and splitting the shortest and longest words.

[3] Parameter m can be properly adjusted to minimize the number of erroneous answers due to collision of pseudorandom numbers generator $F()$ and $f()$.

[4] Users are able to generate it using the pseudorandom number generator and knowing the seed.

recover FB_i, by xoring S_i with the first $n - m$ bits of C_i. Having FB_i, the user can generate K_i (i.e., $K_i = f_k(FB_i)$)), which can be used to compute $F_{K_i}(S_i)$. Finally, having $< S_i, F_{K_i}(S_i) >$ the user is able to extract from C_i the encrypted word $E_k(W_i)$, and to decrypt it.

3 Confidentiality Enforcement

Enforcing confidentiality in an outsourced-based architecture requires to address confidentiality wrt both publishers and users. Since publishers could be untrusted, it is necessary to devise some mechanisms to avoid their malicious usage of owner's data. On the other hand, users are usually entitled to access only selected portions of owner's data based on their characteristics and profiles.

Confidentiality requirements wrt users are usually modelled through a set of access control policies stating who can access what portions of the owner's data. In traditional client-server architectures confidentiality wrt users is usually enforced by means of access control mechanisms (i.e., reference monitors), which mediate each user access request by authorizing only those in accordance with the owner's access control policies. A fundamental requirement is therefore the presence of a trusted environment hosting the reference monitor. In traditional scenarios, this environment is provided by the entity managing the data, i.e., the owner's DBMS server. Enforcing access control in a third party scenario would imply the delegation of the reference monitor tasks to publishers. However, since we are considering a scenario where assumptions on publisher trustworthiness cannot be done, such solution is no longer applicable.

To enforce confidentiality wrt both users and publishers we therefore propose an alternative solution based on cryptographic techniques. The underlying idea is that data owners outsource to publishers an encrypted version of the data they are entitled to manage, without providing them the corresponding decryption keys. Such encryption is generated in such a way to minimize the risks of data dictionary attacks. Therefore, the publisher is not able to access and, as a consequence, to misuse the outsourced data, since they are ciphered. To enforce confidentiality wrt users we propose a particular document encryption, hereafter called *well-formed encryption*, where different portions of the same document are encrypted with different keys, on the basis of the access control policies specified by the owner. In order to correctly enforce access control, it is therefore necessary to selectively distribute secret keys to users. According to the proposed architecture (see [4]), the appropriate keys are distributed by owner in such a way that each user obtains all and only the keys corresponding to the policies he/she satisfies. Policies are specified according to a credential-based access control model for XML data proposed by us in [2]. Appropriate keys for each user are therefore determined by evaluating user credentials against the specified policies. The well-formed encryption and the selective distribution of secret keys ensure confidentiality wrt users. Indeed, each node of the resulting encrypted document is accessible only to authorized users, that is, those users who have received the appropriate keys directly by owners. Even in the case that an untrusted publisher returns unauthorized nodes to a user, he/she is not able to access it, since he/she has not been provided with the corresponding keys.

Applying a cryptographic-based solution in a third party scenario implies to address two main issues. The first is related to the fact that publishers operate on ciphered data. Therefore, we need some mechanisms to make them able to perform queries over them. In Section 3.1, we show how Hacigumus et al. and Song et al. approach can be adopted in the context of XML. The second issue is the definition of encryption strategies able to reduce as much as possible security threats that can be perpetrated against the system. In particular, we have addressed information inference threat that a publisher (user) can perpetrate by analyzing the distribution of encrypted nodes. To overcome this drawback, in Section 3.2, we show how Song et al. scheme can be adopted to encrypt tagnames and attribute names and values, thus to avoid inference.

3.1 Inquiring Encrypted XML Data

As introduced in Section 2, selecting the most appropriate solution to query encrypted data mainly depends on the nature of the data, that is, the data domain and the underlying data model. Usually, an XML document contains data to be modeled into elements, which in turn could contain other elements in accordance to the structure of the modelled data. Whereas attributes are usually exploited to better describe data contained into the corresponding elements. Let us consider, for instance, an XML document modelling a book. It is reasonable to suppose that in such an XML document, `Chapter` elements contain book's chapters, whereas their attributes `Title` and `Number` store additional information about book's chapters. Therefore, in devising methods to query XML encrypted data, we need to consider that elements could be searched based on their attributes values and/or their contents. Thus, we need a method that makes the publisher able to perform logical comparisons on encrypted attribute values, as well as keyword-based searches on encrypted element contents and textual attributes.

To cope with this requirement, we have adopted two different strategies to query XML encrypted data. In particular, we use an approach similar to the one proposed by Song et al.'s [10] to query elements and attributes with textual domain. By contrast, for non textual elements and attributes, we exploit the method proposed by Hacigumus et al. [6]. Thus, we assume that before encrypting a node n, the encryption process determines n's data domain. This task can be performed by means of information contained in the XMLSchema. Let us see in more details which are the query strategies for textual and non-textual encrypted data.

Textual data. Song et al.'s approach [10]. In particular makes a publisher able to search for a specific keyword on encrypted textual data without loss of data confidentiality. Applying such an approach to our scenario requires two adjustments wrt the original formulation. The first is because the scheme proposed in [10] works for words of the same length, whereas we need to consider words of variable length. Therefore, we adapt the scheme proposed in [10] to the management of variable length words, as follows. Let $\mathbf{W}$ be the longest word in the owner's dictionary, and let $L_{\mathbf{W}}$ be the length of $\mathbf{W}$. Thus, for each sequence of clear-text words: $W_1, W_2, \ldots, W_l$, with length $L_j \leq L_{\mathbf{W}}$, the steps for ciphered words generation are the following:

- for each word W_j, data owner pads it with a sequence *pdbts* of $L_{\mathbf{W}} - L_j$ bits;
- data owner generates a sequence of pseudorandom values $S_1 \ldots S_l$, of length $L_{\mathbf{W}} - m$;
- for each keyword W_j the outsourced ciphered word C_j is generated by the following formula: $C_j = E_k(W_j||pdbts) \oplus < S_j, F_{K_j}(S_j) >$, where $K_j = f_k(FB_j))$, and FB_j denotes the first $n - m$ bits of $E_k(W_j||pdbts)$.

According to this scheme, users have to know $L_{\mathbf{W}}$, that is, the length of the longest word managed by the data owner, to be able to pad the searched keyword W_i, before submitting the query.

Finally, we need to define a method for keywords selection. In particular, given a node n, we need to state how to select keywords from n's content. A naive solution is to split the content into separate $L_{\mathbf{W}}$ blocks, and to treat them as distinguished keywords. This solution however is useless if we consider that the resulting ciphered words should be exploited for the search. Thus, it is obvious that some content analysis should be performed over the node's content before keywords selection. In particular, the solution we propose requires a first phase during which the owner preprocesses the textual data contained into an XML node and extracts a set of keywords.[5] Then, each keyword is ciphered according to the scheme introduced above.

Non-textual data. To make publishers able to evaluate queries on encrypted non-textual data, we adapt Hacigums et al.'s approach [6]. First, we have to deal with partition generation. In general, the choice of the most appropriate partitioning technique mainly depends on the node domain. For instance, for numeric data (such as integer, real, etc.), a strategy based on an equi-partitioning of the domain could be appropriate. By contrast, for temporal data a partitioning based on time intervals could be more appropriate. Therefore, in our system we associate a different partitioning function with each possible data domain, with the exception of textual domain. Thus, given a node n of a document d, by analyzing the XML schema defining d it is possible to select the appropriate partitioning function. The partitioning function takes as input the node value and returns the id of the partition to which the node belong to, generated according to the data domain.

3.2 Document Encryption

Document encryption requires a first phase during which each node of the input document is associated with the proper secret key. Therefore, each node of the input document is first marked with the set of access control policies applied

[5] Several techniques developed in the Information Retrieval field can be used to this purpose [9].

```
<Sec-Info>
  <Node-Info   Name='C_{K_1}(CD)'>
    < Query-Info> ...</Query-Info>
  </ Node-Info>
  <Attributes>
    <Node-Info   Name='C_{K_2}(Price)'   Value='C_{K_2}(30)'>
      <Query-Info> ... </Query-Info>
    </ Node-Info>
  </Attributes>
</Sec-Info>
```

Fig. 1. An example of `Sec-Info` element

to it, and then a different secret key is generated for each different configuration of policies that applies to a document portion. Then, all the nodes are encrypted with the corresponding secret keys. In particular, we use an encryption strategy that preserves as much as possible the original structure of the XML document. In the well-formed encryption, the encryption of an XML element e is an XML element $\overline{e}$ having as tagname the encryption of *e.tagname*[6] and as element content the encryption of *e.content*. The well-formed encryption is therefore an XML document that preserves the elements relationships of the original document. We have decided to preserve as much as possible the structure of the original document in the well-formed encryption since this simplifies query formulation. Indeed, users formulate queries through XPath expressions that exploit the structure of the XML document.

However, preserving the original document structure implies some security threats. An untrusted publisher (or user) could infer information by analyzing the distribution of encrypted nodes. This threat could be easily perpetrated against tagnames, attribute names and values, since an XML document may often contain repeated elements and several attributes with the same names (or values). To overcome this drawback, rather than symmetric encryption we apply the scheme proposed by Song et al. (see Section 2.2) to encrypt tagnames and attribute names and values. By contrast, for element contents we have decided to adopt traditional symmetric encryption (e.g., TDES, AES), that requires less computational resources. This choice is motivated by the fact that probability of having a number of occurrences of the same encrypted element content sufficient for data dictionary attacks is small. This probability is further reduced in our context, where elements with the same content are encrypted with different keys, if they are protected by different access control policies.

To make publishers able to evaluate queries on encrypted XML documents, the resulting document encryption is complemented with additional information, called *query processing information*. This information consists of partition's ids or ciphered keywords associated with attribute values or element contents. Query processing information are encoded by an XML element, called `Sec-Info`, which is inserted into each element of the well-formed encryption (see Figure 1) and encodes query processing information of both the element itself and all its at-

[6] In the paper, given an element e (i.e., an attribute a) we use the dot notation to identify its tagname (name) *e.tagname* (i.e., *a.name*) and content (value) *e.content* (i.e., *a.value*).

tributes. The `Sec-Info` element associated with an element e contains a mandatory subelement, named `Node-Info`, whose `Query-Info` subelement stores the query processing information corresponding to e. The `Query-Info` subelement contains the ciphered words extracted from $e.content$ or the id of the partition to which e belongs to, if element e has non-textual domain. By contrast, to model query processing information corresponding to each attribute of element e, the `Sec-Info` contains an `Attributes` subelement, which in turn contains a different `Node-Info` subelement for each attribute of e. The `Node-Info` subelement corresponding to attribute a of element e contains a `Query-Info` subelement storing the id of the partition to which the value of a belongs to or the ciphered keywords extracted from it, if attribute a has textual domain.

Algorithm 1. *The element encryption algorithm*

INPUT:
  1. An XML element e
  2. The encryption key K corresponding to the policy configuration applied to e

OUTPUT:
  An XML element, $\overline{e}$, containing the encryption of e and its query processing information

1. Let $\overline{e}$ be an empty XML node;
2. Set $\overline{e}.tagname$ equal to $C_K(e.tagname)$;
3. Set $\overline{e}.content$ equal to $E_K(e.content)$;
4. Let se be an empty `Sec-Info` element;
5. Let ni be an empty `Node-Info` element subelement of se;
6. Set the `Name` attribute of ni equal to $C_K(e.tagname)$;
7. **If** the domain of e is textual:
   Let WS be the set of keywords extracted from $e.content$;
   For each $w \in WS$: Insert $C_K(w)$ into the `Query-Info` subelement of ni;
   Else
   Let $PF()$ be the partitioning function associated with e's domain;
   Insert $PF(e.content)$ into the `Query-Info` subelement of ni;
8. Return $\overline{e}$;

Let us now see in more details how given a document d, the generation of $\overline{d}$, that is, the document to be outsourced, is carried on. This process is realized by means of two different phases. During the first phase, each element e of d is encrypted, according to the strategy previously explained, and inserted into $\overline{d}$. Additionally, the `Sec-Info` element associated with e is generated. Then, attribute encryption is performed and the `Sec-Info` element is updated accordingly. Algorithm 1 deals with element encryption. The algorithm takes as input an element e and the encryption key corresponding to the policy configuration applied to e. First, it generates the encryption of the tagname and element content (steps 2 and 3). This is done by means of $C_K()$ function implementing the Song et al.'s scheme, and $E_K()$ function that performs symmetric encryption. Then, Algorithm 1 generates the query processing information associated with the input element. In particular, in case of textual domain, the system extracts the set of meaningful keywords from *e.content* and generates the corresponding ciphered keywords, which are then inserted into the `Query-Info` element. By contrast, for element with non-textual domain, the query processing information consists of the id of the partition to which e belongs to.[7] In order to complete the well-formed encryption we need to consider all attributes of e. This is done during a second phase, implemented by Algorithm 2. This phase considers each attribute a and generates the encryption of its name and value, according to Song et al.'s scheme. Moreover, it generates the query processing information related to a, in the same way as Algorithm 1. The resulting information is then inserted into the `Sec-Info` element associated with the element to which a belongs to. This information is stored as a new `Node-Info` element inside the `Attributes` subelement of `Sec-Info`.

Algorithm 2. *The attribute encryption algorithm*

INPUT:
1. An XML attribute a
2. The encryption key K corresponding to the policy configuration applied to a

OUTPUT:
The updated `Sec-Info` containing the encryption of a and its query processing information

1. Let f be the element containing a;
2. Let se be the `Sec-Info` element in f;
3. Let ni be an empty `Node-Info` element;
4. Set the `Name` attribute of ni equal to $C_K(a.name)$;
5. Set the `Value` attribute of ni equal to $C_K(a.value)$;
6. **If** a has a textual domain:
   Let WS be the set of keywords extracted from $a.value$;
   For each $w \in WS$: Insert $C_K(w)$ into the `Query-Info` subelement of ni;
   Else
   Let $PF()$ be the partitioning function associated with a's domain;
   Insert $PF(a.value)$ into the `Query-Info` subelement of ni;
7. Insert ni in the `Attributes` subelement of se;
8. Return se;

---

4 Client Side Query Processing

In the proposed system, users submit queries through a *client*, i.e., a program that users download from the owner site, and which makes them able to submit encrypted queries to publishers, and verify security properties on the received answers. In this section we show how the client is able to submit queries to publisher and decrypt the resulting nodes. Before going into the details we introduce the *query template*.

[7] We assume that our system manages a library of partitioning functions, which associates with each different data domain a unique partitioning function.

4.1 Query Template

The query template has a twofold goal. The first is to make a user able to verify the completeness of a query result,[8] the second is to make a user able to formulate queries and to decrypt the received results. We do not go into the details of completeness verification, since it is outside the scope of this paper (interested readers could refer to [4]). Rather, we focus on the information the query template contains for query processing.

Query templates are generated by the owner for each outsourced document and make available to all users for downloading. Query template contains the encrypted structure of the corresponding XML document and it is generated by using the same encryption strategy employed for XML documents. Moreover, the query template contains the encrypted pseudorandom numbers associated with each node, and needed by clients for document decryption. More precisely, all additional information associated with an element e needed for both query processing and completeness verification are encoded by an XML element, which is inserted as direct child of e into the query template. The element is defined according the syntax of the `Sec-Info` element (cfr. Section 3.2). All information is therefore stored into the `Node-Info` element. Each `Node-Info` element contains an additional attribute called `N` storing the encrypted pseudorandom number associated with the element tagname or attribute name to which the `Node-Info` element refers to.[9] Pseudorandom number is encrypted with the encryption key associated with the element/attribute to which it refers to. By contrast, attribute values can be often split into several words, where each of them is associated with a different pseudorandom number. Therefore, the encryption of these numbers are placed as content of an additional subelement, called `Numbers`, inside the `Node-Info` element.

By having the query template users are able to generate the authorized view of the structure of the document to be inquired, which can be exploited to formulate queries.

4.2 Query Generation

In proposed framework, we assume that users submit queries through XPath expressions. XPath allows one to traverse the graph structure of an XML document and to select specific portions on the document according to some properties, such as the type of the elements, or specified content-based conditions. In general, an XPath expression consists of a *location path*, that allows one to select a set of nodes from target documents, which in turn consists of one or more *location steps*, separated among each other by a slash. A location step contains: an *axis*, specifying the tree relationships between the nodes selected by the location step and the current node (e.g., ancestor, ancestor-or-self, attribute, child,

---

[8] By completeness we mean that a user receives all document portions he/she is authorized to see according to the owner's access control policies.

[9] We assume that tagnames and attribute names are shorten than $L_{\mathbf{W}}$, i.e., the max length, and thus are treated as a unique word. Therefore, they are associated with a unique pseudorandom number.

descendant, descendant-or-self); a *node test*, used to identify a node within an axis, by specifying a node type or the node name (e.g., text(), node()); and zero or more *predicates*, placed inside square brackets, used to further refine the set of nodes selected by the location step (e.g., [@Price='30']). By means of predicates an XPath expression can specify conditions on attributes through comparison operators (e.g., <,>,=), as well as conditions on textual data, in that it is possible to retrieve XML nodes containing a specified keyword (supported by the *contains()* function).

In order to submit a query to a publisher, the first step that a user has to perform is to download the query template of the requested document from the owner site. By decrypting the query template, the client can locally generate the structure of the authorized view, which can be displayed to the user in order to formulate XPath queries on it. Such queries should then be translated by the client into one or more XPath expressions that could be evaluated by publishers on the encrypted XML documents. In order to do that there are two main transformations to which each location step of a user XPath expression must undergo before being submitted to a publisher. The first implies to cipher the tagnames specified in the node test of the location steps with the proper keys. Note that according to the well-formed encryption, nodes with the same name could be ciphered with different keys, based on the access control policies applied to them. Thus, the ciphering of a location step does not always return a unique value, which implies that for each user's query the client could generate more ciphered queries. The second transformation implies the translation of the query conditions in terms of partition ids and/or encrypted keywords. This is applied to each predicate composing the input XPath expression. If the predicate contains comparison operators (e.g., <,>,=), the client substitutes the values appearing in the predicate with the id of the partition to which it belongs to. This is done by using the information about the partitioning functions obtained during the subscription phase. By contrast, if the predicate exploits the contains() function, the client translates the condition by replacing the searched keyword W_j, with the corresponding encrypted word. We recall that according to the adopted scheme, for searching a keyword W_j publishers must be provided with its encryption and with key K_j, which must be sent by the client to publishers together with the submitted query.

To better understand query processing, let us consider an example. In particular, consider an XML document modelling a CD catalog, where a different `CD` element is inserted for each different CD in the catalog. The `CD` element contains an attribute, i.e., `Price`, storing the CD's price and two subelements, i.e., `Title` and `Author`, containing the CD's title and author, respectively. Let us suppose moreover that on this document two different access control policies apply, namely P_1 and P_2. The first authorizes all users to access all the nodes except for `Price` attributes. By contrast, P_2 grants store-staff users the access to the whole document. The outsourced document is thus encrypted with two different encryption keys, namely K_1 and K_2. K_1 is associated with policy configuration consisting of both P_1 and P_2 and encrypts all the nodes except for `Price` attributes. K_2

corresponds to policy P_2 and encrypts only the `Price` attributes. A store-staff member u receives by the owner both K_1 and K_2. Suppose now that u wants to submit the following query: `/CD`[@`Price`=30K]/`Title`[contains(.,'Overture')], which returns all the CDs having price equal to 30K and the keyword *Overture* in the title. Before submitting this query the client transforms it, by, at first, ciphering the tagname in each location step obtaining thus the following expression: $/C_{K_1}$(`CD`) [@C_{K_2}(`Price`)='30K']/C_{K_1}(`Title`)[contains(.,'Overture')]. Note that clients can easily cipher a tagname by simply extracting from the query template the corresponding pseudorandom number. Then, each condition specified in the predicates is translated. This is done by considering the query processing information of the node on which the predicate is specified. Let us for instance consider the predicate "contains(.,'Overture')" on element `Title`. According to the proposed strategy this can be evaluated by searching a ciphered word among those contained in the query processing information of the `Title` element that matches E_{K_1}('Overture'). Thus, the predicate that should be evaluated by the publisher is:

$/C_{K_1}$(`CD`)/C_{K_1}(`Title`)/`Sec-Info` /`Node-Info`/`Query-Info` [contains(.,'$E_{K_1}(Overture)$')].[10]

Furthermore, we have to note that in the proposed encoding the ciphered name of an attribute a is stored into the `Name` attribute of a `Node-Info` subelement of `Attributes`, which is contained into the `Sec-Info` element associated with the element e to which a belongs to. This implies that in our example conditions on price should be verified against the query processing information contained into the `Node-Info` element, whose `Name` attribute is equal to C_{K_2}(`Price`). Thus, predicates on the price attributes should be evaluated by the publisher as:

$/C_{K_1}$(`CD`)//`Attributes`/ `Node-Info`[@`Name`=C_{K_2}(`Price`)/`Query-Info` [contains(.,'PF(30')],

where PF(30) returns the id of the partition to which the value 30 belongs to. The resulting XPath expression generated by the client is thus:

"$/C_{K_1}$(`CD`)/ C_{K_1}(`Title`)/`Sec-Info`/`Node-Info`/`Query-Info`[contains(.,'$E_{K_1}(Overture)$')]
AND
$/C_{K_1}$(`CD`)//`Attributes`/`Node-Info`[@`Name`=C_{K_2}(`Price`)/`Query-Info`[contains(.,'PF(30')]".

4.3 Decryption of Query Answers

Once the query has been evaluated, the publisher returns to client the encrypted nodes identified by the submitted XPath expressions. According to the adopted document encryption strategy, the client needs to perform two different decryption processes in order to decrypt the obtained nodes: one for tagnames, attribute names and values, and the other for decrypting element contents.

Decryption of tagnames, attribute names and values. Tagnames, attribute names and values are ciphered according to Song et al.'s scheme (cfr.

[10] Note that publishers implement a different contains() function wrt Xpath parsers, by, however, preserving the semantics.

Section 2.2). Given a ciphered word C_j, in order to extract from it the encrypted word $E_K(W_j)$, and thus to decrypt it, the client must be provided with the corresponding pseudorandom numbers. Such numbers are retrieved by the client from the query template (cfr. Section 4.1). By decrypting the pseudorandom numbers, the client is thus able to decrypt the ciphered tagnames, attribute names, and attribute values.

Decryption of element contents. Element contents are encrypted by means of a symmetric encryption algorithm. Therefore, the decryption of element content is simply performed by first retrieving the encryption key associated with the element, and then by executing the proper symmetric decryption algorithm.

5 Conclusions

In this paper, we have proposed a method based on cryptographic techniques for confidentiality enforcement on outsourced XML data. Main benefits of the proposed solution are that it does not make any assumption on the trustworthiness of publishers and it is robust to data dictionary attacks both at the schema and document content level. In the paper, besides illustrating the cryptographic schemes, we show by an example how client-side query processing takes place. Due to space limitations, we have not considered other important issues related to key management, for instance those related to the number of keys that need to be managed. To limit the number of keys we use a hierarchical key management scheme similar to the one proposed by us for temporal access control policies [3], which requires to permanently store a number of keys linear in the number of access control policies.

We are currently implementing the proposed strategies to test the performance of the system in different environments. Moreover, we are currently investigating techniques to efficiently manage updates to policies and documents, that would require a partial re-encryption of documents as well as an update of the related security information. In particular, in order to efficiently manage update operations, we plan to adopt a strategy similar to the one in [5] that incrementally maintains document encryptions, by changing all and only those portions which are really affected by the administrative operation, without the need of re-encrypting the document from scratch.

References

1. E.Bertino, B.Carminati, E.Ferrari, B. Thuraisingham, A. Gupta. Selective and Authentic Third-Party Distribution of XML Documents. *IEEE Transactions on Knowledge and Data Engineering (TKDE)*, 16(10):1263–1278, 2004.
2. E. Bertino and E. Ferrari. Secure and Selective Dissemination of XML Documents. *ACM Transactions on Information and System Security (TISSEC)*, 5(3):290–331, 2002.
3. E. Bertino, B. Carminati, and E. Ferrari. A Temporal Key Management Scheme for Broadcasting XML Documents, In Proc. of the *9th ACM Conference on Computer and Communications Security (CCS'02)*, Washington, November, 2002.

4. B. Carminati, E. Ferrari, and E. Bertino. Securing XML Data in Third-Party Distribution Systems. In Proc. of the *ACM Fourteenth Conference on Information and Knowledge Management (CIKM'05)*, Bremen, Germany, November, 2005.
5. B. Carminati, E.Ferrari. Management of Access Control Policies for XML Document Sources. *International Journal of Information Security*, 1(4):236–260, 2003, Springer.
6. H. Hacigumus, B. Iyer, C. Li, and S. Mehrotra. Executing SQL over Encrypted Data in the Database Service Provider Model. In Proc. of the *ACM SIGMOD 2002*, Madison, WI, USA, June 2002.
7. H. Hacigumus, B. R. Iyer, and S. Mehrotra. Efficient execution of aggregation queries over encrypted relational databases. In Proc. of the *9th International Conference on Database Systems for Advanced Applications*, Jeju Island, Korea, March 2004.
8. R.C. Merkle. A Certified Digital Signature. In *Advances in Cryptology-Crypto '89*, 1989.
9. G. Salton and M. McGill. *Introduction to Modern Information Retrival.* McGraw-Hill, 1983.
10. D. X. Song, D. Wagner and A. Perrig. Practical Techniques for Searches on Encrypted Data, In Proc. of the *IEEE Symposium on Security and Privacy*, Oakland, California, 2000.
11. World Wide Web Consortium. `http://www.w3.org`.

Query Translation for XPath-Based Security Views

Roel Vercammen*, Jan Hidders, and Jan Paredaens

University of Antwerp, Belgium

Abstract. Since XML is used as a storage format in an increasing number of applications, security has become an important issue in XML databases. One aspect of security is restricting access to data by certain users. This can, for example, be achieved by means of access rules or XML security views, which define projections over XML documents. The usage of security views avoids information leakage that may occur when we use certain access rules. XML views can be implemented by materialized views, but materialization and maintenance of views may cause considerable overhead. Therefore, we study translations from queries on views to equivalent queries on the original XML documents, assuming both the security views and the queries are specified by XPath expressions. Especially, we investigate which XPath fragments are closed under the composition of a view and a query.

1 Introduction

Access control mechanisms are essential for database systems used to store and share sensitive information. XML is used in an increasing number of applications, including those handling confidential information. As a consequence, some standards for XML access control have already emerged, such as XACL [11] and XACML [9]. Furthermore, several approaches for XML access control mechanisms have been proposed in the literature [6,13,4]. In most of these approaches, the policies are specified at the DTD level. Fundulaki and Marx developed a framework to compare XML access control mechanisms in terms of XPath [8]. Query answering that incorporates these access control policies can, for example, be performed by computing some (materialized) security view [14,12] and then evaluating the query against this security view. This ensures that no information is exposed that is not supposed to be seen by the user, since the query is evaluated against an XML tree that contains exactly the information the user is allowed to see. However, the materialization of views causes an overhead that might be avoided if we can translate queries on the view to equivalent queries on the original data, without leaking information on "hidden" nodes [6,2].

In this paper, we will not introduce a new XML access control mechanism, but instead we assume that security views are defined by path expressions p such

* Roel Vercammen is supported by IWT – Institute for the Encouragement of Innovation by Science and Technology Flanders, grant number 33581.

T. Grust et al. (Eds.): EDBT 2006 Workshops, LNCS 4254, pp. 250–263, 2006.

that access to a node is never granted, except when it is the root node or in the result of p. The obtained XML security views are similar to those of [6] and [12], but we specify them by means of path expressions instead of annotated DTDs. We investigate how to translate queriesst on views to equivalent queries on the original data. Since it is known that some XPath fragments can be evaluated very efficiently [10], we look at a number of XPath fragments to see which of these fragments are closed under the composition of a view and a query.

The rest of the paper is structured as follows. In Section 2 we introduce our XPath-based security views and some preliminary notions. In Section 3 we study the problem of translating queries on XML views to queries on the original (XML) data. We then use these results in Section 4 to examine which XPath fragments are closed under the composition of a view and a query. Finally, we compare our approach to existing query translation mechanisms for queries on XML views in Section 5 and conclude the paper in Section 6.

2 Preliminaries

In this section we introduce some preliminary notions that are used in the rest of our paper. First, we define the data model and the query language that we use in the theoretical exploration of this paper. Next, we introduce our XPath-based security views. Finally, we define the fragments that we investigate.

2.1 Data Model

Our data model is a simplification and abstraction of the full XML data model [7] and restricts itself to the element nodes. First of all, we postulate an infinite set of tag names Σ and an infinite set of nodes $\mathcal{N}$.

Definition 1 (XML Tree). *An* XML tree *is a tuple* $T = (N, \lhd, r, \lambda, \prec)$ *such that* $(N, \lhd, r)$ *is a rooted tree where* $N \subset \mathcal{N}$ *is a finite set of* nodes, $\lhd$ *is the* parent-child relationship, r *is the root,* $\lambda : N \to \Sigma$ *labels nodes with their tag name and* $\prec$ *is a strict total order*[1] *over* N *that represents the* document order *and defines a pre-order tree-walk, i.e., (1) every child is smaller than its parent, and (2) if two nodes are siblings then all descendants of the smaller sibling are smaller than the larger sibling*

In the following we let $\rhd$ denote the inverse relation of $\lhd$, $\lhd^+$ and $\rhd^+$ the transitive closure of resp. $\lhd$ and $\rhd$, and $\lhd^*$ and $\rhd^*$ the transitive and reflexive closure of resp. $\lhd$ and $\rhd$. The set of all XML trees is denoted by $\mathcal{T}$.

2.2 XPath Queries

We now define the set of XPath expressions we consider. We use a syntax in the style of [1] that abstracts from the official syntax [3] and is more suitable

[1] A strict total order is a binary relation that is irreflexive, transitive and total.

for formal presentations. The largest fragment of XPath that we study in this paper, called $\mathcal{P}$, is defined by the following abstract grammar:

$$p ::= \epsilon \mid \Uparrow \mid l \mid \downarrow \mid \uparrow \mid \downarrow^* \mid \downarrow^+ \mid \uparrow^* \mid \uparrow^+ \mid \leftarrow^+ \mid \rightarrow^+ \mid \twoheadleftarrow \mid \twoheadrightarrow \mid \\ p/p \mid p[p] \mid p \cap p \mid p \cup p \mid p - p$$

where ϵ represents the empty path expression or *self* axis, $l \in \Sigma$ denotes a label test, $\uparrow$ and $\downarrow$ represent the *parent* and *child* axis, $\uparrow^*$, $\uparrow^+$, $\downarrow^*$ and $\downarrow^+$ represent the *ancestor-or-self*, *ancestor*, *descendant-or-self* and *descendant* axis, $\leftarrow^+$ and $\rightarrow^+$ represent the *preceding-sibling* and *following-sibling* axis, $\twoheadrightarrow$ and $\twoheadleftarrow$ represent the *following* and *preceding* axis, $\Uparrow$ represents the document root, p_1/p_2 represents the concatenation of p_1 and p_2, $p_1[p_2]$ represents a path p_1 with a *predicate* p_2 and finally $\cap$, $\cup$ and $-$ represent the set intersection, set union and set difference. For disambiguation, parentheses are added and the concatenation is assumed to have the highest precedence. The label tests of the form $l \in \Sigma$ behave as if they follow the *self* axis. This means that `a/b` corresponds to the conventional XPath expression `self::a/self::b` and *not* to the expression `child::a/child::b` as is the case for the so-called abbreviated XPath syntax. Based on [5] and similar to [1] we define the semantics as follows:

Definition 2 (XPath Semantics). *Given an XML tree* $T = (N, \lhd, r, \lambda, \prec)$ *we define the* semantics of a path expression p, $[\![p]\!]_T \subseteq N \times N$ *as follows:*

$$\begin{array}{llll}
[\![\Uparrow]\!]_T & = \{(n,n')|n' = r\} & & \\
[\![\uparrow]\!]_T & = \rhd & [\![\downarrow]\!]_T & = \lhd \\
[\![\uparrow^*]\!]_T & = \rhd^* & [\![\downarrow^*]\!]_T & = \lhd^* \\
[\![\uparrow^+]\!]_T & = \rhd^+ & [\![\downarrow^+]\!]_T & = \lhd^+ \\
[\![\twoheadleftarrow]\!]_T & = \succ - \rhd^+ & [\![\twoheadrightarrow]\!]_T & = \prec - \lhd^+ \\
[\![\leftarrow^+]\!]_T & = \succ \cap (\rhd \circ \lhd) & [\![\rightarrow^+]\!]_T & = \prec \cap (\rhd \circ \lhd) \\
[\![\epsilon]\!]_T & = \{(n,n')|n = n'\} & [\![l]\!]_T & = \{(n,n')|n = n' \wedge \lambda(n) = l\} \\
[\![p_1/p_2]\!]_T & = [\![p_1]\!]_T \circ [\![p_2]\!]_T & [\![p_1 \cap p_2]\!]_T & = [\![p_1]\!]_T \cap [\![p_2]\!]_T \\
[\![p_1 \cup p_2]\!]_T & = [\![p_1]\!]_T \cup [\![p_2]\!]_T & [\![p_1 - p_2]\!]_T & = [\![p_1]\!]_T - [\![p_2]\!]_T \\
[\![p_1[p_2]]\!]_T & = \{(n,n')|(n,n') \in [\![p_1]\!]_T \wedge \exists n'' : (n',n'') \in [\![p_2]\!]_T\} & &
\end{array}$$

Note that "$\circ$" denotes the concatenation of binary relations (and therefore also functions), i.e., $(x, y) \in (f \circ g) \Leftrightarrow \exists z : (x, z) \in f \wedge (z, y) \in g$. This is the reverse of the usual semantics. The length of a path expression p is denoted by $|p|$ and equals the size of the abstract syntax tree of p. Let p be a path expression. We define p^k as the concatenation of k times p, i.e., $p^0 = \epsilon$ and $p^{n+1} = p^n/p$.

Definition 3 (Query). *Let p be a path expression. The query $\mathcal{Q}[p]$ is a function $\mathcal{T} \to 2^{\mathcal{N}}$, defined as follows: $\forall T = (N, \lhd, r, \lambda, \prec) : (n \in \mathcal{Q}[p](T) \Leftrightarrow (r, n) \in [\![p]\!]_T)$*

Note that $\forall T \in \mathcal{T} : [\![p_1]\!]_T = [\![p_2]\!]_T$ implies $\mathcal{Q}[p_1] = \mathcal{Q}[p_2]$, but the reverse does not necessarily hold. For example, we know that $\mathcal{Q}[\downarrow/\uparrow^+] = \mathcal{Q}[\epsilon[\downarrow]]$, but for many XML trees T, $[\![\downarrow/\uparrow^+]\!]_T \neq [\![\epsilon[\downarrow]]\!]_T$.

2.3 XPath-Based Security Views

The XPath-based security views that we consider are similar to the XML security views of [6,12]. However, we define security views by means of path expressions instead of annotating the DTD. Informally, a view defined by a path expression p maps an XML tree, called *input tree*, to an XML tree, called *view tree*, such that the view tree is the projection of the input tree on the nodes selected by p and the root of the input tree. We always include the root of the input tree in order to ensure that the projection yields a valid XML tree instead of a forest.

Definition 4 (View). *Let p be a path expression. The view $\mathcal{V}[p]$ is a function $\mathcal{T} \to \mathcal{T}$, defined as follows: $\forall T_1 = (N_1, \lhd_1, r_1, \lambda_1, \prec_1), T_2 = (N_2, \lhd_2, r_2, \lambda_2, \prec_2)$: $\mathcal{V}[p](T_1) = T_2 \Leftrightarrow$*

- $N_2 = \{n | (n = r_1) \vee ((r_1, n) \in [\![p]\!]_{T_1})\}$
- $\lhd_2 = \{(m, n) | (m, n \in N_2) \wedge (m \lhd_1^+ n) \wedge (\not\exists n' \in N_2 : (m \lhd_1^+ n') \wedge (n' \lhd_1^+ n))\}$
- $r_2 = r_1$
- $\lambda_2 = \{(n, s) | (n \in N_2) \wedge (\lambda_1(n) = s)\}$
- $\prec_2 = \{(m, n) | (m, n \in N_2) \wedge (m \prec_1 n)\}$[2]

Example 1. A governmental organization has to check hospitals and the treatments that are performed by their doctors. For privacy reasons, hospitals are not allowed to transfer *any* information on their patients to this institute. The doctors of this hospital, however, have internally organized the information on treatments by collecting them per patient. Suppose the hospital database is the left tree in Fig. 1 and the government wants the data in the form of the right tree in this figure. We can obtain the right tree using an XPath-based security view, more precisely the view $\mathcal{V}[\downarrow/\texttt{Doctor}/(\epsilon \cup \downarrow^+/\texttt{Treatment}/\downarrow^*)]$ transforms input trees of the left form to view trees of the right form.

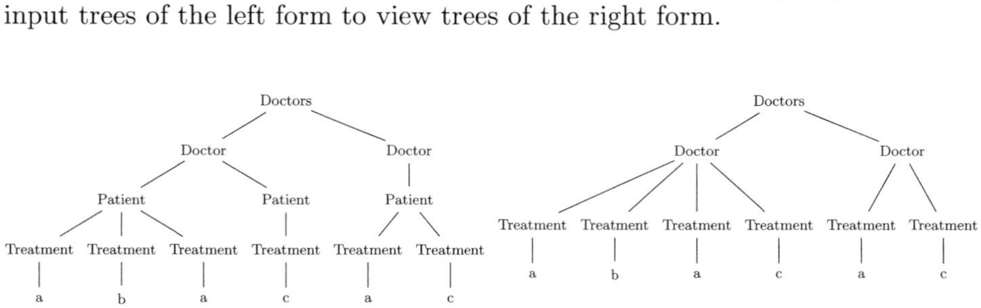

Fig. 1. Input and View Tree of Example 1

Note that the semantics of path expressions on the view tree in terms of the input tree differs from the semantics of the same path expression on the input tree. For example, in Fig. 1 a 'Treatment' node is a child of a 'Doctor' node in the view, while this is not true in the input tree. However, for some axes a it holds that they are "robust under view definition", i.e., $[\![a]\!]_{\mathcal{V}[p](T)} \subseteq [\![a]\!]_T$. The robust axes are $\epsilon, \uparrow^*, \uparrow^+, \downarrow^*, \downarrow^+, \twoheadleftarrow$, and $\twoheadrightarrow$. As we show in Section 3, these axes can easily be translated. Moreover, we can express all other axes in terms of these axes as follows: $[\![\downarrow]\!]_T = [\![\downarrow^+ - \downarrow^+/\downarrow^+]\!]_T$, $[\![\uparrow]\!]_T = [\![\uparrow^+ - \uparrow^+/\uparrow^+]\!]_T$, $[\![\rightarrow^+]\!]_T = [\![(\uparrow^+ - \uparrow^+/\uparrow^+)/(\downarrow^+ - \downarrow^+/\downarrow^+) \cap \twoheadrightarrow]\!]_T$, and $[\![\leftarrow^+]\!]_T = [\![(\uparrow^+ - \uparrow^+/\uparrow^+)/(\downarrow^+ - \downarrow^+/\downarrow^+) \cap \twoheadleftarrow]\!]_T$.

[2] This defines a pre-order tree-walk, since $\prec_1$ is a strict total order and $\lhd_2^+ \subseteq \lhd_1^+$.

In some query translations, we first transform path expressions to equivalent expressions only containing robust axes. Since none of our fragments contain the following and preceding axes, we afterwards remove them using following equalities: $\llbracket \twoheadrightarrow \rrbracket_T = \llbracket \uparrow^* / \rightarrow^+ / \downarrow^* \rrbracket_T$ and $\llbracket \twoheadleftarrow \rrbracket_T = \llbracket \uparrow^* / \leftarrow^+ / \downarrow^* \rrbracket_T$.

2.4 XPath Fragments

We now define the XPath fragments that we study in this paper and discuss some of their properties. These fragments are inspired by the fragments introduced in [1], but we have added sibling axes, intersection, union and set difference. Furthermore, their label tests l correspond to $\downarrow/l$ in our XPath model. Our fragments are defined by the axes that can occur in path expressions and the different operations we can use to combine two path expressions to a new path expression. We consider two groups of fragments. One is defined by a base fragment $\mathcal{X}$ and loosely corresponds to the fragments introduced in [1]; the other is defined by a base fragment $\mathcal{A}$ which is based on the abbreviated syntax [3].
The fragment $\mathcal{X}$ is defined as

$$p ::= \epsilon \mid \Uparrow \mid l \mid \downarrow \mid p/p.$$

We can extend this fragment by adding the parent axis ($\uparrow$), adding the sibling axes ($\leftarrow^+$ and $\rightarrow^+$), and adding the transitive and reflexive closure of axes (i.e., adding $\downarrow^*$ and if $\uparrow$ is in the fragment then also $\uparrow^*$). The three possible extensions can be combined arbitrarily and are respectively denoted by superscripts $\uparrow$, $\leftrightarrow$, and r.

The fragment $\mathcal{A}$ is defined as

$$p ::= \epsilon \mid \Uparrow \mid \downarrow \mid \downarrow/l \mid \downarrow^* \mid \uparrow \mid p/p.$$

All previous fragments can be extended with predicates ([ ]), set intersection ($\cap$), set union ($\cup$), and set difference ($-$). The addition of these extensions is denoted by subscripts.

Some fragments F contain path expressions that are equivalent to path expressions that are not in F. If the addition of a certain operation o to a fragment F does not increase the expressive power of path expressions defined in F then we say that o can be expressed in F. Furthermore, for some fragments F it holds that we cannot in general express an operation o in F, but we can express o if we assume that all path expressions are evaluated against the root. We then say that o can be expressed in queries of F. We now give some expressibility results for the XPath fragments that we have just defined.

Lemma 1. *The following expressibility properties hold for queries, i.e., path expressions evaluated against the root of a tree:*

1. *The union of two path expressions can be expressed in all fragments that can express the set difference and the descendant-or-self axis.*
2. *The intersection of two path expressions can be expressed in all fragments that can express the set difference.*

3. *Predicates can be expressed in all fragments that can express intersection.*
4. *Parent, ancestor and ancestor-or-self axes can be expressed in all fragments that can express intersection and descendant-or-self axes.*

The first two properties also hold for path expressions in general.

Proof. (Sketch)

1. This follows from $[\![p_1 \cup p_2]\!]_T = [\![(\Uparrow/\downarrow^*) - ((\Uparrow/\downarrow^*) - p_1 - p_2)]\!]_T$.
2. This follows from $[\![p_1 \cap p_2]\!]_T = [\![p_1 - (p_1 - p_2)]\!]_T$.
3. We can define a function $e : \mathcal{P} \times \mathcal{P} \to \mathcal{P}$ such that $\mathcal{Q}[p_c/p] = \mathcal{Q}[p_c/e(p, p_c)]$ and its result does not contain predicates if the second argument does not contain predicates. For predicate operations the mapping is defined by $e(p_1[p_2], p_c) = e(p_1, p_c)/(\epsilon \cap e(p_2, p_c/e(p_1, p_c))/\Uparrow/p_c/e(p_1, p_c))$. For all other operations the definition is straightforward, e.g., $e(p_1 \cup p_2, p_c) = e(p_1, p_c) \cup e(p_2, p_c)$, and $e(p_1/p_2, p_c) = e(p_1, p_c)/e(p_2, p_c/e(p_1, p_c))$.
4. Similar to the previous part of this proof, we can define a function $e : \mathcal{P} \times \mathcal{P} \to \mathcal{P}$ such that $\mathcal{Q}[p_c/p] = \mathcal{Q}[p_c/e(p, p_c)]$ and $e(p, p_c)$ does not contain $\uparrow$, $\uparrow^+$ or $\uparrow^*$ if the second argument does not contain these axes. The mapping for $\uparrow^*$ is defined by $e(\uparrow^*, p_c) = \Uparrow/\downarrow^*[\downarrow^* \cap \Uparrow/p_c]$ and similar mappings can be defined for $\uparrow$ and $\uparrow^+$. The mapping of predicate operations differs from part 3: $e(p_1[p_2], p_c) = e(p_1, p_c)[e(p_2, p_c/e(p_1, p_c))]$. Since predicates can be expressed using intersection, we only need $\cap$ and $\downarrow^*$ axes to express $\uparrow$, $\uparrow^+$, and $\uparrow^*$. □

From the previous lemma follows that $\mathcal{P}$ has the same expressive power as $\mathcal{X}^{r,\leftrightarrow}_{-}$. We conclude this section by showing that for some queries $\mathcal{Q}[p]$ we know that all nodes in $\mathcal{Q}[p](T)$ are on the same depth in T.

Lemma 2. *For all path expressions $p \in \mathcal{X}^{\uparrow,\leftrightarrow}_{[\,],\cap,-}$ it holds that for all XML trees T all nodes in the result of $\mathcal{Q}[p](T)$ are on the same level $d(p, 0)$, inductively defined as follows:*

$d(\Uparrow, n)$	$= 0$	$d(\epsilon, n)$	$= n$	$d(l, n)$	$= n$
$d(\downarrow, n)$	$= n + 1$	$d(\uparrow, n)$	$= n - 1$	$d(p_1/p_2, n)$	$= d(p_2, d(p_1, n))$
$d(\leftarrow^+, n)$	$= n$	$d(\rightarrow^+, n)$	$= n$	$d(p_1[p_2], n)$	$= d(p_1, n)$
$d(p_1 \cap p_2, n)$	$= d(p_1, n)$	$d(p_1 - p_2, n)$	$= d(p_1, n)$		

Proof. (Sketch) For all $p \in \mathcal{X}^{\uparrow,\leftrightarrow}_{[\,],\cap,-}$ it can be shown by induction on the length of p that if n_1 is a node in T at depth n and $(n_1, n_2) \in [\![p]\!]_T$ then n_2 is a node at depth $d(p, n)$ in T. □

3 Composing Views and Queries

In this section we study the problem of composing a view and a query to a new query on the input tree that is equivalent to the query on the view tree. We propose two translations, one that can be used to translate path expressions on view trees to path expressions on input trees and one that can only be used to translate queries on view trees to queries on input trees.

The first translaction assumes that all axes in path expressions are robust, such that after each step we can restrict the result of the axis step to the nodes that are in the view tree.

Definition 5. *Let p be a path expression. The function $\tau_p : \mathcal{P} \to \mathcal{P}$ is defined as follows:*

$$
\begin{array}{llll}
\tau_p(\Uparrow) & = \Uparrow & \tau_p(\epsilon) & = \epsilon \\
\tau_p(l) & = l & \tau_p(q_1/q_2) & = \tau_p(q_1)/\tau_p(q_2) \\
\tau_p(q_1[q_2]) & = \tau_p(q_1)[\tau_p(q_2)] & \tau_p(q_1 \cap q_2) & = \tau_p(q_1) \cap \tau_p(q_2) \\
\tau_p(q_1 \cup q_2) & = \tau_p(q_1) \cup \tau_p(q_2) & \tau_p(q_1 - q_2) & = \tau_p(q_1) - \tau_p(q_2) \\
\tau_p(\downarrow^*) & = \downarrow^* \cap \Uparrow/(p \cup \epsilon) & \tau_p(\uparrow^*) & = \uparrow^* \cap \Uparrow/(p \cup \epsilon) \\
\tau_p(\twoheadrightarrow) & = \twoheadrightarrow \cap \Uparrow/(p \cup \epsilon) & \tau_p(\twoheadleftarrow) & = \twoheadleftarrow \cap \Uparrow/(p \cup \epsilon)
\end{array}
$$

We now show that this definition can be used to translate path expressions on view trees to path expressions on input trees.

Lemma 3. *Let p, q be path expressions. For all XML trees $T = (N, \lhd, r, \lambda, \prec)$ and $T' = (N', \lhd', r, \lambda', \prec')$ it holds that if $\mathcal{V}[\![p]\!](T) = T'$ then $[\![\tau_p(q)]\!]_T \cap (N' \times N) = [\![q]\!]_{T'}$ and therefore $\mathcal{V}[\![p]\!] \circ \mathcal{Q}[\![q]\!] = \mathcal{Q}[\![\tau_p(q)]\!]$. Furthermore, $|\tau_p(q)| = O(|p| \times |q|)$*

Proof. (Sketch) This lemma can be shown by induction on $|q|$. Note that since $\uparrow^*, \downarrow^*, \twoheadleftarrow$ and $\twoheadrightarrow$ are robust axes, they can be translated by following the same axis and restricting the result nodes to nodes in T', which are the result nodes of $\Uparrow/(p \cup \epsilon)$. Finally, $|\tau_p(q)| = O(|p| \times |q|)$, since each of the $|q|$ steps is translated into a path expression of size $O(|p|)$. □

The following example illustrates this translation.

Example 2. Consider the view defined in Example 1. Suppose the government wants to have a list of doctors who have performed "operation b". The query on the view can then be written as $\mathcal{Q}[\![\downarrow/\texttt{Doctor}[\downarrow/\texttt{Treatment}/\downarrow/b]]\!]$. Intuitively, this expression can be translated to $\mathcal{Q}[\![\downarrow/\texttt{Doctor}[\downarrow^+/\texttt{Treatment}/\downarrow/b]]\!]$, but according to the translation of Definition 5, we obtain the following query[3]:

$$
\begin{array}{l}
\mathcal{Q}[\![(((\downarrow^* \cap \Uparrow/((\downarrow/\texttt{Doctor}/(\epsilon \ \cup \ \downarrow^+/\texttt{Treatment}/\downarrow^*)) \cup \epsilon)) - \epsilon) - \\
\quad (((\downarrow^* \cap \Uparrow/(((\downarrow^+ - (\downarrow^+/\downarrow^+))/\texttt{Doctor}/(\epsilon \ \cup \ \downarrow^+/\texttt{Treatment}/\downarrow^*)) \cup \epsilon)) - \epsilon)/ \\
\qquad ((\downarrow^* \cap \Uparrow/((\downarrow/\texttt{Doctor}/(\epsilon \ \cup \ \downarrow^+/\texttt{Treatment}/\downarrow^*)) \cup \epsilon)) - \epsilon) \\
\quad))/ \\
\ \ \texttt{Doctor}[(((\downarrow^* \cap \Uparrow/((\downarrow/\texttt{Doctor}/(\epsilon \ \cup \ \downarrow^+/\texttt{Treatment}/\downarrow^*)) \cup \epsilon)) - \epsilon) - \\
\quad (((\downarrow^* \cap \Uparrow/((\downarrow/\texttt{Doctor}/(\epsilon \ \cup \ \downarrow^+/\texttt{Treatment}/\downarrow^*)) \cup \epsilon)) - \epsilon)/ \\
\qquad ((\downarrow^* \cap \Uparrow/((\downarrow/\texttt{Doctor}/(\epsilon \ \cup \ \downarrow^+/\texttt{Treatment}/\downarrow^*)) \cup \epsilon)) - \epsilon) \\
\quad))/\texttt{Treatment}/ \\
\quad (((\downarrow^* \cap \Uparrow/((\downarrow/\texttt{Doctor}/(\epsilon \ \cup \ \downarrow^+/\texttt{Treatment}/\downarrow^*)) \cup \epsilon)) - \epsilon) - \\
\qquad (((\downarrow^* \cap \Uparrow/((\downarrow/\texttt{Doctor}/(\epsilon \ \cup \ \downarrow^+/\texttt{Treatment}/\downarrow^*)) \cup \epsilon)) - \epsilon)/ \\
\qquad\quad ((\downarrow^* \cap \Uparrow/((\downarrow/\texttt{Doctor}/(\epsilon \ \cup \ \downarrow^+/\texttt{Treatment}/\downarrow^*)) \cup \epsilon)) - \epsilon) \\
\qquad))/\texttt{b}] \\
]\!]
\end{array}
$$

[3] Note that in order to use τ_p, we have to rewrite the path expression in the query such that it only contains robust axes.

Using the previous result, we can translate q to $\tau_p(q)$ such that q evaluated against a node n in the view tree and $\tau_p(q)$ evaluated against a node n' in the input tree always return the same result when $n' = n$. This property might be too strong, since for some fragments it can be impossible to find such a translation, but we can find a translation for path expressions evaluated against the root. Therefore, we introduce a second translation, which can only be used if we know that all nodes are on the same level.

Definition 6. *Let p, q be path expressions in $\mathcal{X}^{\uparrow,\leftrightarrow}_{[\,],\cap,-}$. The function $\rho_p : \mathcal{P}\times\mathbb{N} \rightarrow \mathcal{P}$ is defined as follows:*

$$\begin{array}{llll}
\rho_p(q,n) & = q & (\textit{if } n \in \{0,1\} \textit{ and } q \in \{\Uparrow, \epsilon\} \cup \Sigma) & \\
\rho_p(\downarrow,0) & = p & (\textit{if } d(p,0) > 0) & \\
\rho_p(\uparrow,1) & = \Uparrow & (\textit{if } d(p,0) > 0) & \\
\rho_p(\leftarrow^+,n) & = \Uparrow/p \cap (\bigcup_{l=0}^{d(p,0)} \uparrow^l/\leftarrow^+/\downarrow^l) & \rho_p(\rightarrow^+,n) & = \Uparrow/p \cap (\bigcup_{l=0}^{d(p,0)} \uparrow^l/\rightarrow^+/\downarrow^l) \\
\rho_p(q_1/q_2,n) & = \rho_p(q_1,n)/\rho_p(q_2,d(q_1,n)) & \rho_p(q_1[q_2],n) & = \rho_p(q_1,n)[\rho_p(q_2,d(q_1,n))] \\
\rho_p(q_1 \cap q_2,n) & = \rho_p(q_1,n) \cap \rho_p(q_2,n) & \rho_p(q_1 - q_2,n) & = \rho_p(q_1,n) - \rho_p(q_2,n)
\end{array}$$

In the cases not covered by the above equations, $\rho_p(q,n) = p_\emptyset$, where $p_\emptyset$ is a shorthand for a path expression that is not satisfiable, e.g., a/b with $a,b \in \Sigma$ and $a \neq b$.

Lemma 4. *If $p, q \in \mathcal{X}^{\uparrow,\leftrightarrow}_{[\,],\cap,-}$ then $\mathcal{Q}[\rho_p(q,0)] = \mathcal{V}[p] \circ \mathcal{Q}[q]$. Furthermore, $|\rho_p(q,0)| = O(|p|^2 \times |q|)$.*

Proof. (Sketch) We show by induction on $|q|$ that for all $p, q \in \mathcal{X}^{\uparrow,\leftrightarrow}_{[\,],\cap,-}$ it holds that if n_1 is a node at depth n in $\mathcal{V}[p](T)$ then $(n_1,n_2) \in [\![q]\!]_{\mathcal{V}[p](T)}$ iff $(n_1,n_2) \in [\![\rho_p(q,n)]\!]_T$. Afterwards, it clearly holds that $\mathcal{Q}[\rho_p(q,0)] = \mathcal{V}[p] \circ \mathcal{Q}[q]$, since a query is always evaluated from the root node. From Lemma 2 we know that all nodes selected by p are on the same level and hence the view tree does not contain nodes at depth 2 or more. Consequently, we can sometimes determine statically whether a certain operation jumps out of the view tree, yielding an empty result set. If $d(p,0) > 0$ then the set of nodes on level 1 in the view tree is $\mathcal{Q}[p](T)$. Hence following $\downarrow$ from level 0 in the view tree corresponds to evaluating p against the root in the input tree and following $\uparrow$ from level 1 corresponds to $\Uparrow$. The evaluation of $\rightarrow^+$ in the view tree corresponds to getting all following nodes on level $d(p,0)$ in the input tree and checking whether they are in $\mathcal{Q}[p](T)$. The translation of $\leftarrow^+$ is similar and the translation for the other operations is straightforward and similar to τ_p.

Finally, $|\rho_p(q,0)| = O(|p|^2 \times |q|)$, since each of the $|q|$ steps is translated into a path expression of size $O(|p|^2)$ (and $O(|p|)$ if q does not contain sibling axes). □

4 Closure of XPath Fragments Under View Composition

In the previous section, we defined two translations, τ_p and ρ_p, but as was shown in Example 2, the resulting path expressions can be large[4]. Moreover,

[4] The size of the translated path expression is in this case still linear to the product of the sizes of the path expressions of the view and the query.

the translation introduced set difference, which makes query answering more complex. Therefore, we will investigate in this section for each XPath fragment F, defined in Subsection 2.4, whether it is closed under view composition, i.e., $\forall p_1, p_2 \in F : \exists p_3 \in F : \mathcal{V}[p_1] \circ \mathcal{Q}[p_2] = \mathcal{Q}[p_3]$. Note that the purpose of this paper is to establish whether it is feasible to find translations within the same fragment. Whether an efficient translation exists, is left for further research.

4.1 View Composition for Positive XPath Fragments

The following table summarizes which positive fragments are closed under view composition. Each cell in this table denotes one fragment, i.e., the fragment that can be obtained by adding the operations in the column head to the fragment that is in the row head. If a "∘" is in a certain cell then this fragment is not closed under view composition, otherwise there is a "•" to denote that the fragment is closed under view composition. Next to each "•" and "∘" symbol there is a number that refers to the theorem that shows the result for this fragment.

		[ ]	∩	∪	[ ],∩	[ ],∪	∩,∪	[ ],∩,∪
$\mathcal{X}$	•1	•1	•1	∘2	•1	∘2	∘2	∘2
$\mathcal{X}^{\uparrow}$	•1	•1	•1	∘2	•1	∘2	∘2	∘2
$\mathcal{X}^{\leftrightarrow}$	∘4	∘4	∘4	∘2	∘4	∘2	∘2	∘2
$\mathcal{X}^{r}$	∘3	∘3	∘3	∘2	∘3	∘2	∘2	∘2
$\mathcal{X}^{\uparrow,\leftrightarrow}$	∘4	∘4	∘4	∘2	∘4	∘2	∘2	∘2
$\mathcal{X}^{\leftrightarrow,r}$	∘3	∘3	∘3	∘2	∘3	∘2	∘2	∘2
$\mathcal{X}^{\uparrow,r}$	∘3	∘3	∘3	∘2	∘3	∘2	∘2	∘2
$\mathcal{X}^{\uparrow,\leftrightarrow,r}$	∘3	∘3	∘3	∘2	∘3	∘2	∘2	∘2
$\mathcal{A}$	∘3	∘3	∘3	∘3	∘3	∘3	∘3	∘3

Theorem 1. *All fragments from $\mathcal{X}$ to $\mathcal{X}^{\uparrow}_{[\,],\cap}$ are closed under view composition.*

Proof. (Sketch) From Lemma 4 we know that if p, q in $\mathcal{X}^{\uparrow}_{[\,],\cap}$ then $\mathcal{Q}[\rho_p(q, 0)] = \mathcal{V}[p] \circ \mathcal{Q}[q]$. Note that in ρ_p parent axes, predicates and intersection only occur in the resulting path expression iff they occur in q or p. □

The following lemma introduces a monotonicity property of path expressions that do not contain set difference. As we will see in the two following theorems, many composed queries do not have this property and hence they cannot be expressed by a query defined by a positive XPath expression, i.e., a path expression without set difference.

Lemma 5. *Let $p \in \mathcal{X}^{\uparrow,\leftrightarrow,r}_{[\,],\cap,\cup}$ and T an XML tree. If T' is T where some nodes are renamed to a new node name that does not occur in p, then $[\![p]\!]_{T'} \subseteq [\![p]\!]_T$.*

Proof. (Sketch) We prove this lemma by induction on $|p|$. The semantics of axes in T and T' are the same. The semantics of label tests changes, but for all label tests l that occur in p it holds that $[\![l]\!]_{T'} \subseteq [\![l]\!]_T$. Finally, if $[\![p_1]\!]_{T'} \subseteq [\![p_1]\!]_T$ and $[\![p_2]\!]_{T'} \subseteq [\![p_2]\!]_T$, then for path expressions p of the form $p_1[p_2]$, $p_1 \cap p_2$ or $p_1 \cup p_2$ it clearly holds that $[\![p]\!]_{T'} \subseteq [\![p]\!]_T$. □

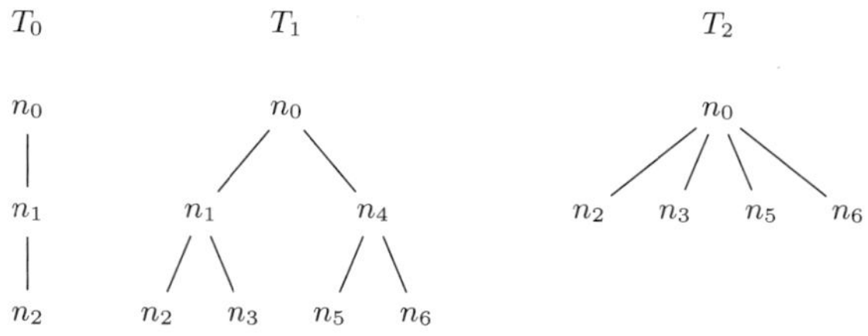

Fig. 2. Counter examples for proofs of Theorems 2, 3, and 4

Theorem 2. *All fragments from $\mathcal{X}_{\cup}$ to $\mathcal{X}_{[\,],\cap,\cup}^{\uparrow,\leftrightarrow,r}$ are not closed under view composition.*

Proof. (Sketch) Suppose $p \in \mathcal{X}_{[\,],\cap,\cup}^{\uparrow,\leftrightarrow,r}$ and $\mathcal{Q}[p] = \mathcal{V}[(\downarrow/a) \cup (\downarrow/\downarrow)] \circ \mathcal{Q}[\downarrow]$. Let T be the tree T_0 shown in Fig. 2 with $\lambda(n_1) =$ "a" and T' be the same XML tree as T except that n_1 has a label which is different from "a" and all labels for which a test occurs in p. From Lemma 5 it follows that $[\![p]\!]_{T'} \subseteq [\![p]\!]_{T}$. However, $\mathcal{Q}[p](T) = \{n_1\}$ and $\mathcal{Q}[p](T') = \{n_2\}$. □

Theorem 3. *All fragments from $\mathcal{X}^{r}$ to $\mathcal{X}_{[\,],\cap,\cup}^{\uparrow,\leftrightarrow,r}$ and from $\mathcal{A}$ to $\mathcal{A}_{[\,],\cap,\cup}$ are not closed under view composition.*

Proof. (Sketch) Suppose $p \in \mathcal{X}_{[\,],\cap,\cup}^{\uparrow,\leftrightarrow,r}$ and $\mathcal{Q}[p] = \mathcal{V}[\downarrow^{*}/\downarrow/a] \circ \mathcal{Q}[\downarrow]$. Let T be the tree T_0 shown in Fig. 2 with $\lambda(n_1) = \lambda(n_2) =$ "a" and T' be the same XML tree as T except that n_1 has a label which is different from "a" and all labels for which a test occurs in p. From Lemma 5 it follows that $[\![p]\!]_{T'} \subseteq [\![p]\!]_{T}$. However, $\mathcal{Q}[p](T) = \{n_1\}$ and $\mathcal{Q}[p](T') = \{n_2\}$. □

Finally, we show that positive XPath fragments with sibling axes and without set union or recursive axes are also not closed under view composition.

Theorem 4. *All fragments from $\mathcal{X}^{\leftrightarrow}$ to $\mathcal{X}_{[\,],\cap}^{\uparrow,\leftrightarrow}$ are not closed under view composition.*

Proof. (Sketch) Suppose $p \in \mathcal{X}_{\cap}^{\uparrow,\leftrightarrow}$ and $\mathcal{Q}[p] = \mathcal{V}[\downarrow/\downarrow] \circ \mathcal{Q}[\downarrow/\rightarrow^{+}]$. Since both the view and the query do not contain label tests, we may assume that p does not contain label tests. Let T_1 be a tree of the form shown in Fig. 2. The tree T_2 in this figure is obviously $\mathcal{V}[\downarrow/\downarrow](T_1)$ and hence $\mathcal{Q}[p](T_1) = \mathcal{Q}[\downarrow/\rightarrow^{+}](T_2) = \{n_3, n_5, n_6\}$. From Lemma 2 we know $\mathcal{Q}[p](T_1)$ only contains nodes at depth $d(p,0)$ in T_1. We can encode $\mathcal{Q}[p](T_1)$ as a string of $0's$ and $1's$, where a 0 at position i denotes the absence of, and a 1 the presence of the ith node at level $d(p,0)$ in $\mathcal{Q}[p](T)$. For example, $\mathcal{Q}[p](T_1)$, which is $\{n_3, n_5, n_6\}$, is encoded by 0111.

We show by induction on $|p|$ that $\mathcal{Q}[p](T_1)$ cannot be encoded by 0111. Since queries start from the root, the result of ϵ is encoded by 1. The following diagram shows all possible "state transitions" of $\uparrow, \downarrow, \leftarrow^{+}$, and $\rightarrow^{+}$. Note that we omit transitions to empty results, since these states are sink states.

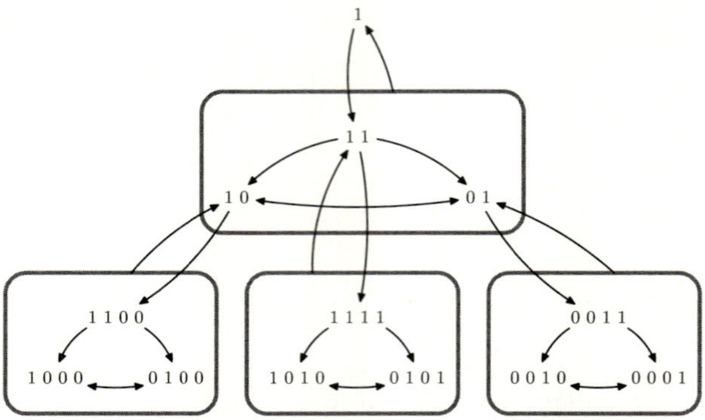

Finally, the intersection combines two of the states in the previous diagram and, as can easily be verified, goes again to one of the states in this diagram. Hence, the encodings for all possible results of path expressions on T_1 in $\mathcal{X}_{\cap}^{\uparrow,\leftrightarrow}$ (without node tests) are listed in this diagram, which does not contain 0111, so p cannot be expressed in $\mathcal{X}_{\cap}^{\uparrow,\leftrightarrow}$ and by Lemma 1 also not in $\mathcal{X}_{[\,],\cap}^{\uparrow,\leftrightarrow}$. □

4.2 View Composition for Fragments with Set Difference

The following table summarizes shows that all fragments with set difference are closed (•) under view composition and next to each "•" symbol there is a number that refers to the theorem that shows the result for this fragment.

	-	$[\,],-$	$\cap,-$	$\cup,-$	$[\,],\cap,-$	$[\,],\cup,-$	$\cap,\cup,-$	$[\,],\cap,\cup,-$
$\mathcal{X}$	•5	•5	•5	•7	•5	•7	•7	•7
$\mathcal{X}^{\uparrow}$	•5	•5	•5	•7	•5	•7	•7	•7
$\mathcal{X}^{\leftrightarrow}$	•5	•5	•5	•7	•5	•7	•7	•7
$\mathcal{X}^{r}$	•6	•6	•6	•6	•6	•6	•6	•6
$\mathcal{X}^{\uparrow,\leftrightarrow}$	•5	•5	•5	•7	•5	•7	•7	•7
$\mathcal{X}^{\uparrow,r}$	•6	•6	•6	•6	•6	•6	•6	•6
$\mathcal{X}^{\leftrightarrow,r}$	•6	•6	•6	•6	•6	•6	•6	•6
$\mathcal{X}^{\uparrow,\leftrightarrow,r}$	•6	•6	•6	•6	•6	•6	•6	•6
$\mathcal{A}$	•6	•6	•6	•6	•6	•6	•6	•6

Theorem 5. *All fragments from $\mathcal{X}_{-}$ to $\mathcal{X}_{[\,],\cap,-}^{\uparrow,\leftrightarrow}$ are closed under view composition.*

Proof. (Sketch) Let $p, q \in \mathcal{X}_{[\,],\cap}^{\uparrow,\leftrightarrow}$. Using ρ_p we can create a query $\mathcal{Q}[\rho_p(q,0)] = \mathcal{V}[p] \circ \mathcal{Q}[q]$. Note that predicates only occur in $\rho_p(q,0)$ iff they occur in q or p. Since we have set difference, by Lemma 1 we can express intersection and hence predicates. We also can express a parent axis in $\mathcal{X}_{-}$, which can be shown by changing $e(\uparrow, p_c)$ of part 4 of the proof of Lemma 1 to $\Uparrow/(\downarrow)^{d(p_c,0)-1}[\downarrow \cap \Uparrow/p_c]$, because all "candidate parents" are at depth $d(p_c,0)-1$. Finally, the translation of the sibling axes can be expressed in $\mathcal{X}_{-}$. For example, $[\![\rho_p(\leftarrow^+, n)]\!]_T = [\![\Uparrow/p - (\Uparrow/p - \leftarrow^+ - \uparrow/\leftarrow^+/\downarrow - \ldots - (\uparrow)^{d(p,0)}/\leftarrow^+/(\downarrow)^{d(p,0)})]\!]_T$ as can be verified. □

Theorem 6. *All fragments from* $\mathcal{X}^r_{-}$ *to* $\mathcal{X}^{\uparrow,\leftrightarrow,r}_{[\,],\cap,\cup,-}$, *and from* $\mathcal{A}_{-}$ *to* $\mathcal{A}_{[\,],\cap,\cup,-}$ *are closed under view composition.*

Proof. (Sketch) We use τ_p, for which we know that $\tau_p(q)$ does not contain sibling axes if they do not occur in p and q. Moreover, from Lemma 1 we know that $\uparrow^*$, $\cup$, $\cap$ and predicates can be expressed using set difference and $\downarrow^*$. □

Theorem 7. *All fragments from* $\mathcal{X}_{\cup,-}$ *to* $\mathcal{X}^{\uparrow,\leftrightarrow}_{[\,],\cap,\cup,-}$ *are closed under view composition.*

Proof. (Sketch) We use τ_p to prove this theorem. Since we can express intersection and predicates using set difference, we can eliminate these operations in $\tau_p(q)$. No recursive axes ($\downarrow^*, \uparrow^*$) are allowed in p and hence there is a depth k such that all nodes deeper than k cannot influence the result of q, since they can simply never be in the view. Hence, we can simulate the $\downarrow^*$ axes in $\tau_p(q)$ by $\bigcup_{i=0}^{k} \downarrow^i$ for some k of which the value depends on p. From part 4 of Lemma 1 then follows that we also can simulate the $\uparrow^*$ axes. Finally, $\tau_p(q)$ does not contain sibling axes if they do not occur in p and q. □

4.3 Summary of Results

All fragments with recursive axes, sibling axes, or set union and without set difference are not closed under view composition, while all other fragments are closed. It can easily be verified that for all fragments that are closed under view composition the size of translated queries for $\mathcal{V}[p] \circ \mathcal{Q}[q]$ is $O(|p| \times |q|)$, except for (1) fragments containing sibling axes and no recursive axes, where the size of the translated query is $O(|p|^2 \times |q|)$, due to the translation of sibling axes in ρ_p, and (2) fragments containing set union and set difference, and no recursive axis steps, where the size of the translated query is also $O(|p|^2 \times |q|)$ (see proof of Theorem 7).

5 Related Work

We briefly discuss two existing approaches for translating queries on XML views to queries on the original (XML) data and compare them to our approach.

Fan, Chan, and Garofalakis introduce the notion of XML security views in [6], where they specify views in terms of normalized DTDs. They present a query translation mechanism for their XPath fragment, which more or less corresponds to our fragment $\mathcal{X}^r_{[\,],\cup}$, augmented with predicates containing boolean operators ($\wedge, \vee, \neg$) and comparisons of the contents of a node with constant values. They also look at the optimization of the obtained path expressions and their work is mainly geared towards finding efficient translations for path expressions in general, i.e., the translation can use all XPath features, whereas our work mainly focuses on the closure properties of XPath fragments under view composition, to see whether the composed query still has the same characteristics of the view and query.

Benedikt and Fundulaki investigate the specification and composition of XML subtree queries [2]. A subtree query is specified by a path expression and is, just like our XPath-based security views, a projection of nodes from an input tree. While in our views intermediate nodes can be hidden, subtree queries show also all descendants and ancestors. It is for example true that if one node in a view is a child of another node in the same view then the former is also a child of the latter in the input tree, which is not necessarily true in our notion of views. More fragments are closed under the composition of subtree queries than under the composition of our XPath-based views and queries. Note that our notion of views can also be used to express subtree queries: if p is a path expression that specifies a subtree query then this subtree query is equivalent to the view specified by $p/\downarrow^*/\uparrow^*$.

6 Conclusion and Future Work

In this paper we introduce XPath-based security views that define a projection of a tree that only contains the root and the nodes that are selected by an XPath expression. We investigate how to translate XPath queries on such views to XPath queries on the original trees. More specifically, we show which fragments are closed under such a composition of a view and a query. In future work we plan to investigate the translation of path expressions that start from arbitrary nodes in the view. We also plan to include extra knowledge that we can obtain from DTDs. Moreover, we want to see whether a DTD for the view tree can automatically be derived from the DTD of the input tree and the view definition.

References

1. M. Benedikt, W. Fan, and G. M. Kuper. Structural properties of XPath fragments. In *ICDT 2003*, pages 79–95, 2003.
2. M. Benedikt and I. Fundulaki. XML subtree queries: Specification and composition. In *DBPL 2005*, pages 138–153, 2005.
3. A. Berglund, S. Boag, D. Chamberlin, M. Fernández, M. Kay, J. Robie, and J. Siméon. XML path language (XPath) 2.0, W3C working draft, 2005. `http://www.w3.org/TR/xpath20`.
4. E. Bertino and E. Ferrari. Secure and selective dissemination of XML documents. *ACM Trans. Inf. Syst. Secur.*, 5(3):290–331, 2002.
5. D. Draper, P. Frankhauser, M. Fernández, A. Malhotra, K. Rose, M. Rys, J. Siméon, and P. Wadler. XQuery 1.0 and XPath 2.0 formal semantics. W3C Working Draft, 2005.
6. W. Fan, C. Y. Chan, and M. N. Garofalakis. Secure XML querying with security views. In *SIGMOD Conference*, pages 587–598, 2004.
7. M. Fernández, A. Malhotra, J. Marsh, M. Nagy, and N. Walsh. XQuery 1.0 and XPath 2.0 data model (XDM), 2005. `http://www.w3.org/TR/xpath-datamodel/`.
8. I. Fundulaki and M. Marx. Specifying access control policies for XML documents with XPath. In *SACMAT 2004*, pages 61–69, 2004.
9. S. Godik and T. Moses, editors. *eXtensible Access Control Markup Language (XACML) Version 1.0.* February 2003.

10. G. Gottlob, C. Koch, and R. Pichler. The complexity of XPath query evaluation. In *PODS 2003*, pages 179–190, San Diego, California, 2003.
11. M. Kudo and S. Hada. XML access control. `http://www.trl.ibm.com/projects/xml/xacl/`.
12. G. Kuper, M. Fabio, and R. Nataliya. Generalized XML security views. In *SACMAT 2005*, pages 77–84, 2005.
13. M. Murata, A. Tozawa, M. Kudo, and S. Hada. XML access control using static analysis. In *CCS*, pages 73–84, 2003.
14. A. Stoica and C. Farkas. Secure XML views. In E. Gudes and S. Shenoi, editors, *DBSec*, volume 256 of *IFIP Conference Proceedings*, pages 133–146. Kluwer, 2002.

Management of Executable Schema Mappings for XML Data Exchange

Tadeusz Pankowski[1,2]

[1] Institute of Control and Information Engineering,
Poznań University of Technology, Poland
[2] Faculty of Mathematics and Computer Science,
Adam Mickiewicz University, Poznań, Poland
tadeusz.pankowski@put.poznan.pl

Abstract. Executable schema mappings between XML schemas are essential to support numerous data management tasks such as data exchange, data integration and schema evolution. The novelty of this paper consists in a method for automatic generation of automappings (automorphisms) from key constraints and value dependencies over XML schemas, and designing algebraic operations on mappings and schemas represented by automappings. During execution of mappings some missing or incomplete data may be inferred. A well-defined executable semantics for mappings and operations on mappings are proposed. A mapping language XDMap to specify XML schema mappings is discussed. The language allows to specify executable mappings that can be used to compute target instances from source instances preserving key constraints and value dependencies. The significance of mappings and operators over mappings is discussed on a scenario of data exchange in a P2P setting.

1 Introduction

Schema mapping is a basic problem for many applications such as data exchange, data integration, P2P databases or e-commerce, where data may be available at many different peers in many different schemas [3,6,10,11,17,20]. A schema mapping specifies a constraint that holds between schemas and can be thought of as a relation on instances. Executable mappings are mappings that are able to compute target instances from source instances preserving a set of given constraints [11]. The main contributions of this work are as follows:

1. We propose a method for generating *automappings* over schemas from key and value dependency constraints defined in schemas. Automappings are then used to create mappings between schemas (*Match* operator). Mappings can be combined (using *Compose* and *Merge* operators) to give new mappings. We propose a mapping language, called XDMap, to specify mappings.
2. In the process of data transformation some missing or incomplete data, which are not given explicitly in sources, can be deduced based on value dependency constraints enforced by the target schema. This is achieved by representing missing data by terms defining the constraints. In some cases such terms may be resolved and replaced by the actual data.

T. Grust et al. (Eds.): EDBT 2006 Workshops, LNCS 4254, pp. 264–277, 2006.

The following section discuss the contribution of the paper against related work. The next section shows a scenario of data exchange. Section 4 illustrates the problem of using constraints to mapping specifications and to inferring some missing data. Section 5 describes basic ideas of our approach and proposes syntax and semantics for the mapping language XDMap. Operations on mappings are discussed in Section 6. Section 7 concludes the paper.

2 Related Work

We discuss our contribution from the following three points of view.

1. A language for mapping specification. It is commonly accepted that the basic relationships between a source and a target relational schemas can be expressed as a source-to-target dependencies (STD) [2,6,11,13]. In [3] $STDs$ are adopted to XML data in such a way that if a certain pattern occurs in the source, another pattern has to occur in the target. In our approach, the main idea of using $STDs$ consists in specifying how nodes in a target instance depend on key paths, how these key paths correspond to paths in sources, and how target values depend on other values. So, our approach is more operational and uses DOM interpretation of XML documents. To generate the instance of a target schema from instances of source schemas, we use the idea of *chasing* [2,19]. In our mapping language XDMap we use Skolem functions with text-valued arguments from a source instance to create nodes (node identifiers) in a target instance. A concept of using Skolem functions for creation and manipulation object identifiers has been previously proposed in ILOG [8] and in [1,7]. Recently, Skolem functions are also used in some approaches to schema mappings, in Clio [16] are used for generating missing target values if the target element cannot be null (e.g. components of keys), in [19] are used in a query rewriting based on data mapping. Our mapping language can be compared with the mapping language proposed in [19]. However, XDMap is more powerful because we can use arbitrary Skolem functions for intermediate (non leaf-level) nodes, while in [19] these Skolem functions are system generated in a controlled way. Consequently, in our mappings, node generation is controlled by the mapping itself.

2. Generating mappings from key constraints. To define mappings we assume that key and some value constraints are specified within schema (using XML Schema [18] notation). We show how an automapping (a mapping from a schema onto itself) may be automatically generated from these constraints. It is significant in our approach that the constraints are specified outside the mapping by means of constraint-oriented notation. The generated automapping preserves these constraints. In contrast, in other mapping languages (e.g. in [19]) constraints must be explicitly encoded in the mapping language. This can make difficulties for future management when schemas evolve. To define correspondences between schema elements we use the method proposed in [9,16] where a correspondence is defined between single elements from a source and a target schema. Establishing of a correspondence may be supported by automated techniques [17].

3. Algebra of mappings. Since a schema is represented by its automapping, we can operate over schemas and mappings in a uniform way. We discuss three operators over mappings (schemas): *Match* – creates a mapping between two schemas (it is a special case of composition), *Compose* – combines two successive mappings, and *Merge* – produces a mapping that merges two source schemas. Operations on mappings, mainly composition, was recently studied in [6,10,11,12,13].

3 A Scenario of Data Exchange

We illustrate XML data exchange on a scenario of a P2P data exchanging system. Suppose there are three peers with schemas $\mathbf{S}_1$, $\mathbf{S}_2$, and $\mathbf{S}_3$, respectively (Fig. 1). Only $\mathbf{S}_2$ and $\mathbf{S}_3$ are associated with data, while $\mathbf{S}_1$ is a mediated (or target) schema that does not store any data. The meaning of labels are: author (A), name (N) and university (U) of the author; paper (P) title (T), year (Y) of publication and the conference (C) where the paper has been presented. Elements labeled with R and K are used to join authors with their papers. I_2 and I_3 are instances of $\mathbf{S}_2$ and $\mathbf{S}_3$, respectively. In such scenario we meet the problem of data exchange, i.e. computing target instances from source instances [3,5,11,16,19]. Mappings are needed to perform these functions effectively.

An instance of $\mathbf{S}_1$ can be obtained in different ways (Fig. 2): (1) and (2) by simple transformation of instance I_2 or I_3 by means of mappings $\mathcal{M}_{21}$ or $\mathcal{M}_{31}$; (3) as a merge $\mathcal{M}_{21} \cup \mathcal{M}_{31}$ over instances; (4) by means of composition $(\mathcal{M}_{32} \circ \mathcal{M}_{21})(\mathrm{I}_3)$ (when the $\mathbf{S}_2$'s peer is unavailable); (5) using combination of merge and composition, $((\mathcal{M}_{22} \cup \mathcal{M}_{32}) \circ \mathcal{M}_{21})(\mathrm{I}_2, \mathrm{I}_3)$. This shows that we often need to create new mappings from existing ones [6,10,11].

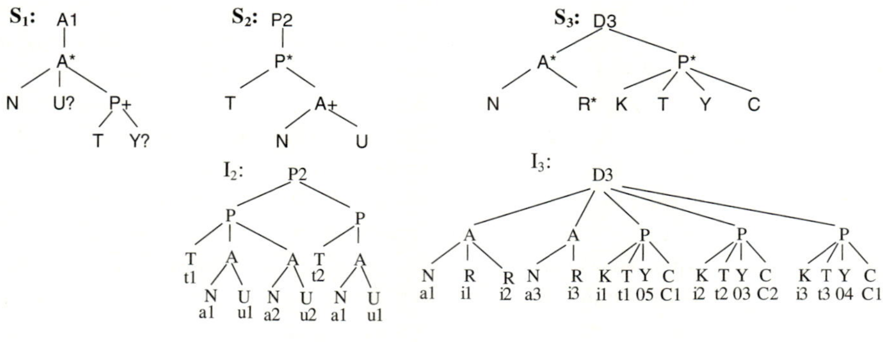

Fig. 1. Schemas: $\mathbf{S}_1, \mathbf{S}_2, \mathbf{S}_3$, and schema instances I_2 and I_3

4 Using Constraints for Mapping Specification

In our approach, we use two kinds of constraints to define mappings, namely:

1. *Value dependency constraints* (on the target) imposing that a value of a path depends on a tuple of values of other paths. We will declare them in

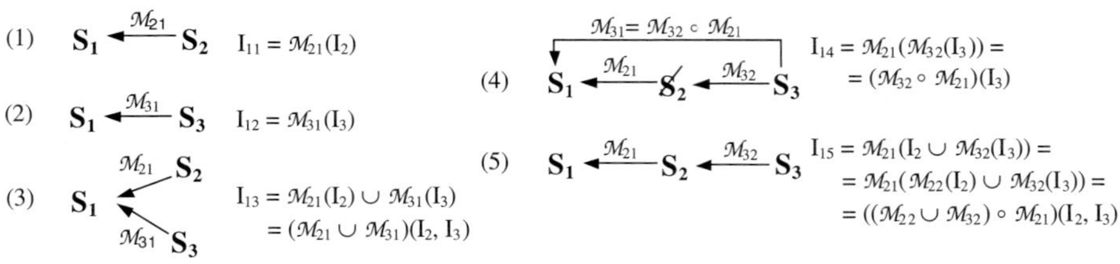

Fig. 2. Scenarios of data exchange – an instance of $\mathbf{S}_1$ may be computed in many ways

the `<xs:valdep>` section of XML Schema (Fig. 4) that is a non-standard element within XML Schema.

2. *Key constraints* (on a source) stating that a subtree is uniquely identified by a tuple of values of key paths [4,18]. They are specified within `<xs:key>` and `<xs:keyref>` sections of XML Schema (Fig. 4).

Value dependencies can be used to infer missing data. Suppose we want to transform the instance I_2 under the target schema $\mathbf{S}_1$, i.e. an instance $\mathrm{I}_{11} = \mathcal{M}_{21}(\mathrm{I}_2)$ must be produced (Fig. 3(a)). The original instance provides no data about publication year. However, we know that the publication year (Y) uniquely depends on the title (T) of the paper that is denoted by the constraint $Y = y(T)$, where y is the name of a function mapping titles into publication years. So the term $y(t)$, where t is the title, is assigned to Y as its text value. This forces some elements of type Y to have the same values (Fig. 3(a)). Such constraints are defined within the `<xs:valdep>` section in XML Schema (Fig. 4). Next, a term like $y(t)$ may be resolved using other mappings.

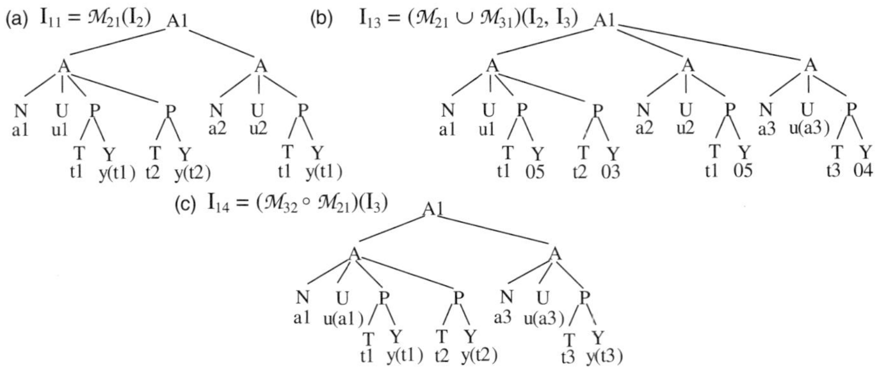

Fig. 3. Instances of schema $\mathbf{S}_1$ produced by mappings using constraints

Suppose that under $\mathbf{S}_1$ we want to merge the instances I_{11} (Fig. 3(a)) and I_3 (Fig. 1). In this process terms denoting years will be replaced with actual values (Fig. 3(b)). In this way we are able to infer the publication year of the paper written by $a2$. This information is not given explicitly neither in I_2 nor in I_3. The

```
<xs:schema xmlns:xs="http://www.w3.org/2001/XMLSchema">
  <xs:element name="A1">
    <xs:complexType>
      <xs:sequence>
        <xs:element ref="A"/>
      </xs:sequence>
    </xs:complexType>
  </xs:element>
  <xs:element name="A">
    <xs:complexType>
      <xs:sequence>
        <xs:element name="N" type="xs:string"/>
        <xs:element name="U" type="xs:string" minOccurs="0"/>
        <xs:element ref="P" minOccurs="1" maxOccurs="unbounded"/>
      </xs:sequence>
    </xs:complexType>
    <xs:key name="AKey">
      <xs:selector xpath="."/>
      <xs:field xpath="N"/>
    </xs:key>
    <xs:valdep>
      <xs:dependent xpath="N"/>
      <xs:function name="u"/>
      <xs:argument xpath="N"/>
    </xs:valdep>
  </xs:element>
  <xs:element name="P">
    <xs:complexType>
      <xs:sequence>
        <xs:element name="T" type="xs:string"/>
        <xs:element name="Y" type="xs:string" minOccurs="0"/>
      </xs:sequence>
    </xs:complexType>
    <xs:key name="PKey">
      <xs:selector xpath="."/>
      <xs:field xpath="T"/>
    </xs:key>
    <xs:valdep>
      <xs:dependent xpath="Y"/>
      <xs:function name="y"/>
      <xs:argument xpath="T"/>
    </xs:valdep>
  </xs:element>
</xs:schema>
```

Fig. 4. XML Schema of $\mathbf{S}_1$, extended with <xs:valdep> declaration instances in Fig. 3(a)-(c) illustrate execution of composed mappings. In detail, we will address this issue in Section 6.

Information provided by key constraints will be used to specify how many instances (nodes) of an element type must be in the computed target instance. For example, the element of type $/A1/A$ in $\mathbf{S}_1$ is uniquely identified by the key path N. So, there are as many nodes of type $/A1/A$ as there are different values of $/A1/A/N$. In $\mathbf{S}_2$, however, elements of type $/P2/P/A$ are identified by N but only in a context determined by the element type $/P2/P$ that is identified by T. Thus, to identify $/P2/P/A$ we need a pair of values determined by paths $/P2/P/T$ and $/P2/P/A/N$. In XML Schema such keys are defined using `<xs:key>`, and a declaration within a subelement denotes that the key identification is satisfied only in the context of superelement. In Fig. 4 there is a definition of the schema $\mathbf{S}_1$ written in an extended variant of XML Schema.

5 Executable XML Schema Mappings

5.1 Basic Ideas of Mappings

From the definition in Fig. 4 we can generate the automapping $\mathcal{M}_{11}$ over $\mathbf{S}_1$ (Fig. 5), i.e. a mapping from $\mathbf{S}_1$ onto itself (numbers of lines provided here are for explanation only). It is formalized in Definition 2.

$\mathcal{M}_{11}$ = **foreach** G_{11} **where** Φ_{11} **when** C_{11} **exists** Δ_{11} =

(1) **foreach** $\$y_{A1}$ $\underline{\text{in}}$ $/A1$, $\$y_A$ $\underline{\text{in}}$ $\$y_{A1}/A$, $\$y_N$ $\underline{\text{in}}$ $\$y_A/N$,
$\$y_U$ $\underline{\text{in}}$ $\$y_A/U$, $\$y_P$ $\underline{\text{in}}$ $\$y_A/P$, $\$y_T$ $\underline{\text{in}}$ $\$y_P/T$, $\$y_Y$ $\underline{\text{in}}$ $\$y_P/Y$
(2) **where true**
(3) **when** $\$y_U = u(\$y_N), \$y_Y = y(\$y_T)$
exists
(4) $F_{/A1}()$ **in** $F_{()}()/A1$
(5) $F_{/A1/A}(\$y_N)$ **in** $F_{/A1}()/A$
(6) $F_{/A1/A/N}(\$y_N)$ **in** $F_{/A1/A}(\$y_N)/N$ **with** $\$y_N$
(7) $F_{/A1/A/U}(\$y_N, \$y_U)$ **in** $F_{/A1/A}(\$y_N)/U$ **with** $\$y_U$
(8) $F_{/A1/A/P}(\$y_N, \$y_T)$ **in** $F_{/A1/A}(\$y_N)/P$
(9) $F_{/A1/A/P/T}(\$y_N, \$y_T)$ **in** $F_{/A1/A/P}(\$y_N, \$y_T)/T$ **with** $\$y_T$
(10) $F_{/A1/A/P/Y}(\$y_N, \$y_T, \$y_Y)$ **in** $F_{/A1/A/P}(\$y_N, \$y_T)/Y$ **with** $\$y_Y$

Fig. 5. Automapping $\mathcal{M}_{11}$ over $\mathbf{S}_1$

(1) The clause **foreach** defines *source variables*. Every source variable ranges over a set of nodes. Variables ranging over non-leaf nodes are *auxiliary variables* whereas variables ranging over leaves are *text variables*. Note that auxiliary variables appear only in the **foreach** clause. We assume that any text variable is partially bound to text values of leaves over which it ranges. By Ω we will denote a set of all (partial) bindings for source text variables.
(2) The **where** clause restricts values of variables. The restrictions can be consequences of key references defined in the schema (see $\mathcal{M}_{33}$ in Fig. 6).

(3) Equalities in (3) reflect value dependency constraints specified in the schema. They are interpreted as follows. Let $y = f(\overline{\$x})$ be a value dependency, where $\overline{\$x}$ is a vector of (totally bound) source variables, f is the name of a text valued Skolem function, and $\$y$ is a *dependent variable* that denotes a text value in the target (e.g. $\$y_U$ and $\$y_Y$). The value of $f(\overline{\$x})$ is determined by a binding $\omega \in \Omega$ and is equivalent to the term "$f(\omega(\overline{\$x}))$" being the result of the concatenation of the name "f" and the text value $\omega(\overline{\$x})$ created from the current values of variables. We assume that we have a set Ω'_Ω of *dependent bindings* such that for any value dependency $\$y = f(\overline{\$x})$ and for any $\omega \in \Omega$ there exists $\omega'_\omega \in \Omega'_\Omega$ such that $\omega'_\omega(\$y) :=$ "$f(\omega(\overline{\$x}))$". If $\omega(\$y)$ is defined, then there are two bindings for $\$y$: $\omega(\$y)$ and $\omega'_\omega(\$y)$, otherwise the only binding for $\$y$ is $\omega'_\omega(\$y)$. In some cases, dependent bindings can be used to infer missing bindings (i.e. values of variables) by applying the following inference rule:

$$\omega'_{\omega_1}(\$y_1) = \omega'_{\omega_2}(\$y_2) \Rightarrow \omega_1(\$y_1) = \omega_2(\$y_2) \tag{1}$$

In this way we can obtain the value of $\omega_1(\$y_1)$(see Example 4).
(4) Two new nodes are created, the root r and the node n of the outermost element of type $/A1$, as results of Skolem functions $F_{()}()$ and $F_{/A1}()$, respectively. The node n is a child of type $A1$ of r.
(5) A new node n' for any distinct value of $\$y_N$ is created. Each such node has the type $/A1/A$ and is a child of type A of the node n created by $F_{/A1}()$ in (4).
(6) For any distinct value of $\$y_N$ a new node n'' of type $/A1/A/N$ is created. Each such node is a child of type N of the node created by invocation of $F_{/A1/A}(\$y_N)$ in (5) for the same value of $\$y_N$. Because n'' is a leaf, it obtains the text value equal to the current value of $\$y_N$.
(7) Analogously for the rest of the specification (7-10).

5.2 Capturing Key Constraints by Automappings

In a specification of automapping, Skolem functions and their arguments play a crucial role. We assume that:

- for any (rooted) path P in the schema there is exactly one Skolem function, $F_P(...)$, where F_P is the name of the Skolem function,
- arguments of a Skolem function $F_P(...)$ are determined by key paths defined for the element of type P in the schema.

In $\mathbf{S}_1$ there is exactly one root and one outermost element, so the corresponding Skolem functions have empty lists of arguments. Element of type $/A1/A$ has a key path N. Each its subelement inherits this key path and additionally has its local (relative) key paths. The local key paths for non-leaf elements are defined in the schema. The local key path for a leaf element is, by default, this leaf element itself. Thus, for $\mathbf{S}_1$ we have the following key paths: N for $/A1/A$ and $/A1/A/N$; (N,T) for $/A1/A/P$ and $/A1/A/P/T$; and (N,T,Y) for $/A1/A/P/Y$.

Text values of these key paths are bound to variables and are used as arguments of Skolem functions.

In definition of $\mathbf{S}_3$ (Fig. 6), the schema specifies the *key* and *keyref* relationships between the K child element of the P element (the *referenced key*) and the R child element of the A element (the *foreign key*).

In the automapping specification over $\mathbf{S}_3$, key references are captured by the equality $\$z_R = \$z_K$ in the **where** clause (Fig. 6).

```
...
<xs:element name="A">
  <xs:complexType>
  ...
  </xs:complexType>...
  <xs:keyref name="AKeyref"
             refer="PKey">
    <xs:selector xpath="."/>
    <xs:field xpath="R"/>
  </xs:keyref>
</xs:element>
```

```
<xs:element name="P">
  <xs:complexType>
  ...
  </xs:complexType>
  <xs:key name="PKey">
    <xs:selector xpath="."/>
    <xs:field xpath="K"/>
  </xs:key>
  <xs:valdep>
    <xs:dependent name="Y"/>
    <xs:function name="y"/>
    <xs:argument xpath="T"/>
  </xs:valdep>   ...
</xs:element>
...
```

$$
\begin{array}{l}
\mathcal{M}_{33} = \textbf{foreach } \$z_{D3} \ \underline{\text{in}}\ /D3,\ \$z_A \ \underline{\text{in}}\ \$z_{D3}/A,\ \$z_N \ \underline{\text{in}}\ \$z_A/N, \$z_R \ \underline{\text{in}}\ \$z_A/R, \\
\qquad\qquad\qquad \$z_P \ \underline{\text{in}}\ \$z_{D3}/P,\ \$z_K \ \underline{\text{in}}\ \$z_P/K,\ \$z_T \ \underline{\text{in}}\ \$z_P/T, \\
\qquad\qquad\qquad \$z_Y \ \underline{\text{in}}\ \$z_P/Y,\ \$z_C \ \underline{\text{in}}\ \$z_P/C \\
\qquad \textbf{where } \$z_R = \$z_K \\
\qquad \textbf{when } \$z_K = k(\$z_N, \$z_T), \$z_Y = y(\$z_T), \$z_C = c(\$z_T) \\
\qquad \textbf{exists} \\
\qquad\quad F_{/D3}() \textbf{ in } F_{()}()/D3 \\
\qquad\quad F_{/D3/A}(\$z_N) \textbf{ in } F_{/D3}()/A \\
\qquad\quad F_{/D3/A/N}(\$z_N) \textbf{ in } F_{/D3/A}(\$z_N)/N \textbf{ with } \$z_N \\
\qquad\quad F_{/D3/A/R}(\$z_N, \$z_R) \textbf{ in } F_{/D3/A}(\$z_N)/R \textbf{ with } \$z_R \\
\qquad\quad F_{/D3/P}(\$z_K) \textbf{ in } F_{/D3}()/P \\
\qquad\quad F_{/D3/P/K}(\$z_K) \textbf{ in } F_{/D3/P}(\$z_K)/K \textbf{ with } \$z_K \\
\qquad\quad F_{/D3/P/T}(\$z_K, \$z_T) \textbf{ in } F_{/D3/P}(\$z_K)/T \textbf{ with } \$z_T \\
\qquad\quad F_{/D3/P/Y}(\$z_K, \$z_Y) \textbf{ in } F_{/D3/P}(\$z_K)/Y \textbf{ with } \$z_Y \\
\qquad\quad F_{/D3/P/C}(\$z_K, \$z_C) \textbf{ in } F_{/D3/P}(\$z_K)/C \textbf{ with } \$z_C
\end{array}
$$

Fig. 6. Fragment of XML Schema defining $\mathbf{S}_3$ and the automapping $\mathcal{M}_{33}$ over $\mathbf{S}_3$

5.3 Syntax and Semantics for Mappings

In general, there are two vectors of variables $\overline{\$x}$ and $\overline{\$y}$ in a mapping $\mathcal{M}$. Variables from $\overline{\$x}$ are bound in a source by means of the **foreach** clause, and variables from $\overline{\$y}$ are bound to terms in the **when** clause as a consequence of value dependency constraints. The part **foreach/where/when** of a mapping $\mathcal{M}(\overline{\$x}; \overline{\$y})$ determines a partially ordered set $(\Omega, \leq)$ of bindings of $\mathcal{M}$'s variables. For example, in the mapping $\mathcal{M}_{21}$ (Fig. 7) for two bindings $\omega_1, \omega_2 \in \Omega$ over I_2, where $\omega_1 = (\$x_T \rightarrow t_1, \$x_N \rightarrow a_1, \$x_U \rightarrow u_1, \$y_Y \rightarrow y(t_1))$ and $\omega_2 = (\$x_T \rightarrow t_1, \$x_N \rightarrow a_2, \$x_U \rightarrow u_2, \$y_Y \rightarrow y(t_2))$, we have $\omega_1 < \omega_2$, because the tuple of leaf nodes providing values for ω_1 precedes the tuple of leaf nodes providing values for ω_2. Bindings from Ω are used in the **exists** part to produce the result target instance. The ordering imposed in Ω by a source instance should be preserved in the target instance.

If the **foreach/where** clause is defined over $\mathbf{S}_2$, while the **when/exists** concerns $\mathbf{S}_1$, then we deal with a mapping $\mathcal{M}_{21}$ from $\mathbf{S}_2$ into $\mathbf{S}_1$. Then, after the given replacement of variables (the result of the replacement $\phi[\$y \rightarrow \$x]$ is the expression created from ϕ by replacing all occurrences of $\$y$ with $\$x$), we obtain:

$$
\begin{aligned}
\mathcal{M}_{21} = \ & \textbf{foreach } \$x_{P2} \ \underline{\text{in}} \ /P2,\ \$x_P \ \underline{\text{in}} \ \$x_{P2}/P,\ \$x_T \ \underline{\text{in}} \ \$x_P/T, \\
& \qquad\qquad \$x_A \ \underline{\text{in}} \ \$x_P/A,\ \$x_N \ \underline{\text{in}} \ \$x_A/N,\ \$x_U \ \underline{\text{in}} \ \$x_A/U \\
& \textbf{where true} \\
& \textbf{when } C_{11}(\$y_N, \$y_U, \$y_T, \$y_Y)[\$y_N \rightarrow \$x_N, \$y_U \rightarrow \$x_U, \$y_T \rightarrow \$x_T] \\
& \textbf{exists } \Delta_{11}(\$y_N, \$y_U, \$y_T, \$y_Y)[\$y_N \rightarrow \$x_N, \$y_U \rightarrow \$x_U, \$y_T \rightarrow \$x_T]
\end{aligned}
$$

Fig. 7. Mapping $\mathcal{M}_{21}$ from $\mathbf{S}_2$ into $\mathbf{S}_1$

Thus, the **when** clause of $\mathcal{M}_{21}$ is equal to $\$x_U = u(\$x_N), \$y_Y = y(\$x_T)$. There is no replacement for $\$y_Y$, so its value must be set as the current value of the term $y(\$x_T)$, according to the inference rule (1) proposed in 5.1. We set it as the term $y(t)$, where t is the current value of $\$x_T$ (see Fig. 3(a)). It is a form of *Skolemization*.

Observe that a mapping specification in XDMap conforms to the general form of *source-to-target generating dependencies* [2,6,13]:

$$\forall \overline{\$x}(G(\overline{\$x}) \wedge \Phi(\overline{\$x}) \Rightarrow \exists \overline{\$y} C(\overline{\$x}; \overline{\$y}) \wedge \Delta(\overline{\$x}; \overline{\$y})),$$

where $G(\overline{\$x})$ and $\Phi(\overline{\$x})$ are conjunctions of atomic formulas over a source, and $C(\overline{\$x}; \overline{\$y})$ and $\Delta(\overline{\$x}; \overline{\$y})$ are conjunctions of atomic formulas over a target.

Definition 1. *An executable schema mapping in XDMap (or mapping for short) between a source schema* $\mathbf{S}$ *and a target schema* $\mathbf{T}$ *is a sequence* $\mathcal{M} ::= (M, ..., M)$ *of mapping rules between* $\mathbf{S}$ *and* $\mathbf{T}$*, where:*

$$
\begin{aligned}
M = (G, \Phi, C, \Delta)(\overline{\$x}; \overline{\$y}) := \ & \textbf{foreach } G(\overline{\$x}) \\
& \textbf{where } \Phi(\overline{\$x}) \\
& \textbf{when } C(\overline{\$x}; \overline{\$y}) \\
& \textbf{exists } F_{P/l}(\overline{\$x'}; \overline{\$y'}) \textbf{ in } F_P(\overline{\$x''}; \overline{\$y''})/l[\textbf{ with } \$z\ ]
\end{aligned}
$$

- *G is a list of variable definitions over a source schema;*
- *Φ is a conjunction of atomic conditions: $\$x = \$x'$;*

- *C is a list of target value dependency constraints:* $\$x = f(\overline{\$x})$ *or* $\$y = f(\overline{\$x})$, $\$x \in \overline{\$x}$, $\$y \in \overline{\$y}$;
- $F_P(\overline{\$x}; \overline{\$y})$ *is a Skolem term, where P is a rooted path in a target schema;*
- $(\overline{\$x'}; \overline{\$y'}) \subseteq (\overline{\$x}; \overline{\$y})$, $(\overline{\$x''}; \overline{\$y''}) \subseteq (\overline{\$x'}; \overline{\$y'})$, $\$z \in (\overline{\$x'}; \overline{\$y'})$. □

Semantics for XDMap is defined as follows:

Definition 2. *Let* $\mathcal{M} = (G, \Phi, C, \Delta)(\overline{\$x}; \overline{\$y})$ *be a mapping, and* $(\Omega, \leq)$ *be a partially ordered set of bindings of variables* $(\overline{\$x}; \overline{\$y})$ *determined by* (G, Φ, C). *A target instance J of a target schema* $\mathbf{T}$ *is then obtained as follows:*

1. $F_{()}()$ *– the root of J.*
2. $F_P(\overline{\$x'}; \overline{\$y'})(\omega) = n$ *– a node of type P.*
3. *If* $F_{P/l}(\overline{\$x'}; \overline{\$y'})(\omega) = n$, $F_P(\overline{\$x''}; \overline{\$y''})(\omega) = n'$, *then n is a child of type l of n'.*
4. *Let* $F_{P/l}(\overline{\$x'}; \overline{\$y'})(\omega_1) = n_1$, $F_{P/l}(\overline{\$x'}; \overline{\$y'})(\omega_2) = n_2$, *and* $\omega_1 \leq \omega_2$. *Then* $n_1 \leq n_2$ *in the document order.*
5. *If* $F_{P/l}(\overline{\$x'}; \overline{\$y'})(\omega) = n$ *is a leaf, then the text value of n is* $\omega(\$z)$.

6 Operations on Mappings

Mappings can be combined by means of some operators giving a result that in turn is a mapping. We define the following operations: *Match*, *Compose*, and *Merge*. First, we have to define a *correspondence* between paths of different schemas. Establishing the correspondence is a crucial task in definition of data mappings [17].

Definition 3. *Let $\mathcal{P}$ and $\mathcal{P}'$ be sets of paths from schemas* $\mathbf{S}$ *and* $\mathbf{S}'$, *respectively. A correspondence from* $\mathbf{S}$ *into* $\mathbf{S}'$ *is a partial function* $\sigma : \mathcal{P} \to \mathcal{P}'$ *which maps a path* $P \in \mathcal{P}$ *on a path* $P' = \sigma(P) \in \mathcal{P}'$. □

Example 1. Correspondence σ_{12} from $\mathbf{S}_1$ to $\mathbf{S}_2$, and σ_{23} from $\mathbf{S}_2$ to $\mathbf{S}_3$ (Fig. 1) are:

$\sigma_{12}(/A1/A/N) = /P2/P/A/N$ $\quad$ $\sigma_{23}(/P2/P/T) = /D3/P/T$
$\sigma_{12}(/A1/A/U) = /P2/P/A/U$ $\quad$ $\sigma_{23}(/P2/P/A/N) = /D3/A/A$
$\sigma_{12}(/A1/A/P/T) = /P2/P/T$

6.1 *Match* Operator

The *Match* operator was proposed in [11] as an operator to create a mapping between two schemas (modes). In our approach each schema is represented by automappings, thus *Match* is defined on two automappings and returns a mapping between schemas over which these automappings are defined. Because *Match* is in fact a special kind of composition, we will denote it, like the *Compose* operator (see p. 6.2), by $\circ$, i.e. $Match(\mathcal{M}_s, \mathcal{M}_t)$ will be abbreviated by $\mathcal{M}_s \circ \mathcal{M}_t$, where $\mathcal{M}_s$ and $\mathcal{M}_t$ are automappings over source and target schemas, respectively. Then $\mathcal{M}_{st} = \mathcal{M}_s \circ \mathcal{M}_t$ is a mapping from the source schema into the target schema.

Definition 4. *Let* $\mathcal{M}_s = (G_s, \Phi_s, C_s, \Delta_s)(\overline{\$x_s}; \overline{\$y_s})$ *be an automapping over* **S**, $\mathcal{M}_t = (G_t, \Phi_t, C_t, \Delta_t)(\overline{\$x_t}; \overline{\$y_t})$ *be an automapping over* $\mathbf{T}_t$, *and* σ *be a correspondence between* **T** *and* **S**. *Then the* $Match_\sigma(\mathcal{M}_s, \mathcal{M}_t)$ *is the mapping*

$$\mathcal{M}_s \circ_\sigma \mathcal{M}_t = (G_s, \Phi_s, C_t, \Delta_t)[\overline{\$x_t} \rightarrow \sigma(\overline{\$x_t})](\overline{\$x}; \overline{\$y}), \tag{2}$$

where the result of the replacement $[\overline{\$x_t} \rightarrow \sigma(\overline{\$x_t})]$ *is defined as follows:*

- *any occurrence of a variable* $\$x_t \in \overline{\$x_t}$ *of type* P *in* $(G_s, \Phi_s, C_t, \Delta_t)$ *is replaced by a variable* $\$x_s \in \overline{\$x_s}$ *of type* $\sigma(P)$, $\$x_s$ *is the replacing variable; and* $\overline{\$x}$ *is a tuple of all replacing variables and all variables occurring in* Φ_s;
- $\overline{\$y} \subseteq (\overline{\$x_t}; \overline{\$y_t})$ *and consists of all variables which have not been replaced; and all unnecessary variable definitions are removed from* G_s. □

Example 2. The mapping $\mathcal{M}_{21}$ (Fig. 7) is the result of matching from $\mathcal{M}_{22}$ to $\mathcal{M}_{11}$ using the correspondence σ_{12} from $\mathbf{S}_1$ to $\mathbf{S}_2$ (see Example 1), i.e.
$\mathcal{M}_{21}(\$x_N, \$x_U, \$x_T; \$y_Y) = \mathcal{M}_{22}(\$x_T, \$x_N, \$x_U) \circ_{\sigma_{12}} \mathcal{M}_{11}(\$y_N, \$y_U, \$y_T, \$y_Y)$.
Similarly,
$\mathcal{M}_{32}(\$z_T, \$z_N, \$z_R, \$z_K; \$v_U) =$
$= \mathcal{M}_{33}(\$z_N, \$z_R, \$z_K, \$z_T, \$z_Y, \$z_C) \circ_{\sigma_{23}} \mathcal{M}_{22}(\$v_T, \$v_N, \$v_U)$. □

6.2 *Compose* Operator

The *Compose* operator combines two successive mappings into one.

Definition 5. *Let* $\mathcal{M}_{12}$ *and* $\mathcal{M}_{23}$ *be mappings from* $\mathbf{S}_1$ *into* $\mathbf{S}_2$ *and from* $\mathbf{S}_2$ *into* $\mathbf{S}_3$, *respectively. Let* σ_{21} *and* σ_{32} *be correspondences from* $\mathbf{S}_2$ *into* $\mathbf{S}_1$ *and from* $\mathbf{S}_3$ *into* $\mathbf{S}_2$. *Let* $\mathcal{M}_{11}$ *and* $\mathcal{M}_{33}$ *be automappings over* $\mathbf{S}_1$ *and* $\mathbf{S}_3$, *respectively, and* $\sigma = \sigma_{32} \circ \sigma_{21}$ *be the correspondence from* $\mathbf{S}_3$ *into* $\mathbf{S}_2$ *obtained as the result of composition of correspondences* σ_{32} *and* σ_{21}. *Then*

$$Compose_\sigma(\mathcal{M}_{12}, \mathcal{M}_{23}) = \mathcal{M}_{11} \circ_\sigma \mathcal{M}_{33} \tag{3}$$

is a mapping from $\mathbf{S}_1$ *to* $\mathbf{S}_3$, *and* $\mathcal{M}_{11} \circ_\sigma \mathcal{M}_{33}$ *is defined by (2).*

Example 3. It is easily to show that:
$\mathcal{M}_{321}(\$z_T, \$z_N, \$z_R, \$z_K; \$y_U, \$y_Y) = Compose_{(\sigma_{12} \circ \sigma_{23})}(\mathcal{M}_{32}, \mathcal{M}_{21}) =$
$\mathcal{M}_{33}(\$z_N, \$z_R, \$z_K, \$z_T, \$z_Y, \$z_C) \circ_{(\sigma_{12} \circ \sigma_{23})} \mathcal{M}_{11}(\$y_N, \$y_U, \$y_T, \$y_Y) =$
= **foreach** $G_{33}(\$z_N, \$z_R, \$z_K, \$z_T)$
where $\$z_R = \$z_K$
when $\$y_U = u(\$z_N), \$y_Y = y(\$z_T)$
exists
$F_{/A1}()$ **in** $F_{()}()/A1$
$F_{/A1/A}(\$z_N)$ **in** $F_{/A1}()/A$
$F_{/A1/A/N}(\$z_N)$ **in** $F_{/A1/A}(\$z_N)/N$ **with** $\$z_N$
$F_{/A1/A/U}(\$z_N, \$y_U)$ **in** $F_{/A1/A}(\$z_N)/U$ **with** $\$y_U$
$F_{/A1/A/P}(\$z_N, \$z_T)$ **in** $F_{/A1/A}(\$z_N)/P$
$F_{/A1/A/P/T}(\$z_N, \$z_T)$ **in** $F_{/A1/A/P}(\$z_N, \$z_T)/T$ **with** $\$z_T$
$F_{/A1/A/P/Y}(\$z_N, \$z_T, \$y_Y)$ **in** $F_{/A1/A/P}(\$z_N, \$z_T)/Y$ **with** $\$y_Y$

$\mathcal{M}_{321}$ has two variables, $\$y_U$ and $\$y_Y$, which are not bound in the source. Instead, they are bound in the **when** clause to target terms $u(\$z_N)$ and $y(\$z_T)$, respectively. An instance of the mapping is given in Fig. 3(c). In the final result all term-valued leaves may be either removed, replaced with nulls, or left as they are (they may be resolved and replaced with actual values in next mappings (e.g. by *Merge*) as in Fig. 3(a)-(b)).

6.3 *Merge* Operator

Definition 6. *Let* $\mathcal{M}_1 = (G_1, \Phi_1, C_1, \Delta_1)(\overline{\$x_1}; \overline{\$y_1})$ *and* $\mathcal{M}_2 = (G_2, \Phi_2, C_2, \Delta_2)(\overline{\$x_2}; \overline{\$y_2})$, *where* $(\overline{\$x_1}; \overline{\$y_1})$ *and* $(\overline{\$x_2}; \overline{\$y_2})$ *are disjoint, be mappings from* $\mathbf{S}_1$ *and* $\mathbf{S}_2$*, respectively, into* $\mathbf{S}_3$*. Then merging of* $\mathcal{M}_1$ *and* $\mathcal{M}_2$ *is the mapping defined as follows:*

$$\mathcal{M}_1 \cup \mathcal{M}_2 = (G_1 \cup G_2, \Phi_1 \cup \Phi_2, C_1 \cup C_2, \Delta_1 \cup \Delta_2)(\overline{\$x_1} \cup \overline{\$x_2}; \overline{\$y_1} \cup \overline{\$y_2}).$$

If mappings $\mathcal{M}_1$ and $\mathcal{M}_2$ are mappings from $\mathbf{S}_1$ and $\mathbf{S}_2$, respectively, into $\mathbf{S}_3$ then $\mathcal{M}_1 \cup \mathcal{M}_2$ is a mapping that *merges* $\mathbf{S}_1$ and $\mathbf{S}_2$ under $\mathbf{S}_3$.

Example 4. Let

$$\mathcal{M}_{21} = (G_{21}(\$x_T, \$x_N, \$x_U), \{\mathbf{true}\}, \{x_U = u(\$x_N), \$y_Y = y(\$x_T)\}, \Delta_{21}(\$x_T, \$x_N, \$x_U; \$y_Y))$$

be a mapping from $\mathbf{S}_2$ into $\mathbf{S}_1$ (Example 2), and

$$\mathcal{M}_{31} = (G_{31}(\$z_N, \$z_R, \$z_K, \$z_T, \$z_Y), \{\$z_R = \$z_K\}, \{\$v_U = u(\$z_N), \$z_Y = y(\$z_T)\}, \Delta_{31}(\$z_N, \$z_T, \$z_Y; \$v_U))$$

be a mapping from $\mathbf{S}_3$ into $\mathbf{S}_1$.

The merge $\mathcal{M}_{21} \cup \mathcal{M}_{31}$ is a mapping consisting of all mapping rules from $\mathcal{M}_{21}$ and all mapping rules from $\mathcal{M}_{31}$. Below, we show only these rules that involve variables from constraints in the **when** clause.

$\mathcal{M}_{21} \cup \mathcal{M}_{31} =$

foreach $G_{21}(\$x_T, \$x_N, \$x_U), G_{31}(\$z_N, \$z_R, \$z_K, \$z_T, \$z_Y)$
where $\$z_R = \$z_K$
when $x_U = u(\$x_N), \$y_Y = y(\$x_T), \$v_U = u(\$z_N), \$z_Y = y(\$z_T)$
exists ...
$F_{/A1/A/U}(\$x_N, \$x_U)$ **in** $F_{/A1/A}(\$x_N)/U$ **with** $\$x_U$
$F_{/A1/A/P/Y}(\$x_N, \$x_T, \$y_Y)$ **in** $F_{/A1/A/P}(\$x_N, \$x_T)/Y$ **with** $\$y_Y$
$F_{/A1/A/U}(\$z_N, \$v_U)$ **in** $F_{/A1/A}(\$z_N)/U$ **with** $\$v_U$
$F_{/A1/A/P/Y}(\$z_N, \$z_T, \$z_Y)$ **in** $F_{/A1/A/P}(\$z_N, \$z_T)/Y$ **with** $\$z_Y$
...

For variables occurring in G_{21} and in G_{31}, the **foreach** clause defines a set Ω of bindings. Term values of dependent variables, i.e. of $\$x_U$, $\$y_Y$, $\$z_Y$, and $\$v_U$, are defined in the **when** clause and are represented by Ω'. Missing values in Ω (e.g. for variables $\$y_Y$ and $\$v_U$) are replaced by appropriate term values from Ω', i.e. $\omega(\$y) := \omega'_{\omega}(\$y)$.

Before resolving: $\Omega := \Omega_{21} \cup \Omega_{31}$

Ω	$\$x_T$	$\$x_N$	$\$x_U$	$\$y_Y$	$\$z_N$	$\$z_K$	$\$z_T$	$\$z_Y$	$\$v_U$
ω_1	$t1$	$a1$	$u1$	$y(t1)$					
ω_2	$t1$	$a2$	$u2$	$y(t1)$					
ω_3	$t2$	$a1$	$u1$	$y(t2)$					
ω_4					$a1$	$i1$	$t1$	05	$u(a1)$
ω_5					$a1$	$i2$	$t2$	03	$u(a1)$
ω_6					$a3$	$i3$	$t3$	04	$u(a3)$

Ω'_Ω	$\$x_U$	$\$y_Y$	$\$z_Y$	$\$v_U$
ω'_{ω_1}	$u(a1)$	$y(t1)$		
ω'_{ω_2}	$u(a2)$	$y(t1)$		
ω'_{ω_3}	$u(a1)$	$y(t2)$		
ω'_{ω_4}			$y(t1)$	$u(a1)$
ω'_{ω_5}			$y(t2)$	$u(a1)$
ω'_{ω_6}			$y(t3)$	$u(a3)$

Next, in the *resolving process* we try to resolve term values in Ω. The resolving process is based on the rule (1) discussed in Subsection 5.1.

After resolving: $\Omega := Resolve(\Omega_{21} \cup \Omega_{31})$

Ω	$\$x_T$	$\$x_N$	$\$x_U$	$\$y_Y$	$\$z_N$	$\$z_K$	$\$z_T$	$\$z_Y$	$\$v_U$
ω_1	$t1$	$a1$	$u1$	05					
ω_2	$t1$	$a2$	$u2$	05					
ω_3	$t2$	$a1$	$u1$	03					
ω_4					$a1$	$i1$	$t1$	05	$u1$
ω_5					$a1$	$i2$	$t2$	03	$u1$
ω_6					$a3$	$i3$	$t3$	04	$u(a3)$

Execution of the mapping $\mathcal{M}_{21} \cup \mathcal{M}_{31}$ is illustrated in Fig. 3. Fig. 3(a) shows the result produced by the part corresponding to $\mathcal{M}_{21}$, and Fig. 3(b) is the final result. Note, that the term $u(a_3)$ cannot be resolved. □

7 Conclusion

We have described a novel approach to XML schema mapping specification and operations over schema mappings. We discussed how automappings may be generated using key constraints [4,18], keyref constraints [18], and some value dependency constraints defined in XML Schema. Constraints on values can be used to infer some missing data. Mappings between two schemas can be generated automatically from their automappings and correspondences between paths of these two schemas. Automappings represent schemas, so operations over schemas and mappings can be defined and performed in a uniform way. We propose some algebraic operations over mappings. The syntax and semantics for the mapping language XDMap are defined and discussed. Our techniques can be applied in various XML data exchange scenarios, and are especially useful when the set of data sources change dynamically (e.g. in P2P environment) [14,15].

References

1. Abiteboul, S., Buneman, P., Suciu, D.: *Data on the Web. From Relational to Semistructured Data and XML*, Morgan Kaufmann, San Francisco, 2000.
2. Abiteboul, S., Hull, R., Vianu, V.: *Foundations of Databases*, Addison-Wesley, Reading, Massachusetts, 1995.

3. Arenas, M., Libkin, L.: XML Data Exchange: Consistency and Query Answering, *PODS Conference*, 2005, 13–24.
4. Buneman, P., Davidson, S. B., Fan, W., Hara, C. S., Tan, W. C.: Reasoning about keys for XML, *Information Systems*, **28**(8), 2003, 1037–1063.
5. Fagin, R., Kolaitis, P. G., Popa, L.: Data exchange: getting to the core., *ACM Trans. Database Syst.*, **30**(1), 2005, 174–210.
6. Fagin, R., Kolaitis, P. G., Popa, L., Tan, W. C.: Composing Schema Mappings: Second-Order Dependencies to the Rescue., *PODS*, 2004, 83–94.
7. Fernandez, M. F., Florescu, D., Kang, J., Levy, A. Y., Suciu, D.: Catching the Boat with Strudel: Experiences with a Web-Site Management System., *SIGMOD Conference*, 1998, 414–425.
8. Hull, R., Yoshikawa, M.: ILOG: Declarative Creation and Manipulation of Object Identifiers., *VLDB*, 1990, 455–468.
9. Kuikka, E., Leinonen, P., Penttonen, M.: Towards automating of document structure transformations., *ACM Symposium on Document Engineering*, 2002, 103–110.
10. Madhavan, J., Halevy, A. Y.: Composing Mappings Among Data Sources., *VLDB*, 2003, 572–583.
11. Melnik, S., Bernstein, P. A., Halevy, A. Y., Rahm, E.: Supporting Executable Mappings in Model Management., *SIGMOD Conference*, 2005, 167–178.
12. Melnik, S., Rahm, E., Bernstein, P. A.: Rondo: A Programming Platform for Generic Model Management., *SIGMOD Conference*, 2003, 193–204.
13. Nash, A., Bernstein, P. A., Melnik, S.: Composition of Mappings Given by Embedded Dependencies., *PODS*, 2005.
14. Pankowski, T.: Specifying Schema Mappings for Query Reformulation in Data Integration Systems, 3rd *Atlantic Web Intelligence Conference - AWIC'2005,* Lecture Notes in Computer Science 3528, Springer-Verlag, 2005, 361–365.
15. Pankowski, T.: Integration of XML Data in Peer-To-Peer E-commerce Applications, 5th *IFIP Conference I3E'2005*, Springer, New York, 2005, 481–496.
16. Popa, L., Velegrakis, Y., Miller, R. J., Hernández, M. A., Fagin, R.: Translating Web Data., *VLDB*, 2002, 598–609.
17. Rahm, E., Bernstein, P. A.: A survey of approaches to automatic schema matching, *The VLDB Journal*, **10**(4), 2001, 334–350.
18. XML Schema Part 1: Structures 2d Edition: 2004. www.w3.org/TR/xmlschema-1
19. Yu, C., Popa, L.: Constraint-Based XML Query Rewriting For Data Integration., *SIGMOD Conference*, 2004, 371–382.
20. Yu, C., Popa, L.: Semantic Adaptation of Schema Mappings when Schemas Evolve., *VLDB*, 2005, 1006–1017.

Models for Incomplete and Probabilistic Information

Todd J. Green* and Val Tannen**

University of Pennsylvania
{tjgreen, val}@cis.upenn.edu

Abstract. We discuss, compare and relate some old and some new models for incomplete and probabilistic databases. We characterize the expressive power of *c*-tables over infinite domains and we introduce a new kind of result, algebraic completion, for studying less expressive models. By viewing probabilistic models as incompleteness models with additional probability information, we define completeness and closure under query languages of general probabilistic database models and we introduce a new such model, probabilistic *c*-tables, that is shown to be complete and closed under the relational algebra.

1 Introduction

The representation of incomplete information in databases has been an important research topic for a long time, see the references in [18], in Ch.19 of [2], in [31], in [35,25], as well as the recent [33,30,29]. Moreover, this work is closely related to recently active research topics such as inconsistent databases and repairs [4], answering queries using views [1], and data exchange [13]. The classic reference on incomplete databases remains [20] with the fundamental concept of *c*-table and its restrictions to simpler tables with variables. The most important result of [20] is the query answering algorithm that defines an algebra on *c*-tables that corresponds exactly to the usual relational algebra ($\mathcal{RA}$). A recent paper [29] has defined a hierarchy of incomplete database models based on finite sets of choices and optional inclusion. One of our contributions consists of **comparisons** between the models [29] and the tables with variables from [20].

Two criteria have been provided for comparisons among all these models: [20, 29] discuss *closure* under relational algebra operations, while [29] also emphasizes *completeness*, specifically the ability to represent all finite incomplete databases. We point out that the latter is not appropriate for tables with variables over an infinite domain, and we contribute another criterion, $\mathcal{RA}$**-completeness**, that fully characterizes the expressive power of *c*-tables.

We also introduce a new idea for the study of models that are not complete. Namely, we consider combining existing models with queries in various fragments of relational algebra. We then ask how big these fragments need to be to

* Partially supported by NSF IIS-0477972 and NSF SEIII IIS-0513778.
** Partially supported by NSF SEIII IIS-0513778.

T. Grust et al. (Eds.): EDBT 2006 Workshops, LNCS 4254, pp. 278–296, 2006.

obtain a combined model that is complete. We give a number of such **algebraic completion** results.

Early on, probabilistic models of databases were studied less intensively than incompleteness models, with some notable exceptions [7, 5, 28, 23, 10]. Essential progress was made independently in three papers [15,22,34] that were published at about the same time. [15, 34] assume a model in which tuples are taken independently in a relation with given probabilities. [22] assumes a model with a separate distribution for each attribute in each tuple. All three papers attacked the problem of calculating the probability of tuples occurring in query answers. They solved the problem by developing more general models in which rows contain additional information ("event expressions","paths","traces"), and they noted the similarity with the conditions in c-tables.

We go beyond the problem of individual tuples in query answers by defining **closure** under a query language for probabilistic models. Then we develop a new model, **probabilistic c-tables** that adds *to the c-tables themselves* probability distributions for the values taken by their variables. Here is an example of such a representation that captures the set of instances in which Alice is taking a course that is Math with probability 0.3; Physics (0.3); or Chemistry (0.4), while Bob takes the same course as Alice, provided that course is Physics or Chemistry and Theo takes Math with probability 0.85:

Student	*Course*	*Condition*
Alice	x	
Bob	x	$x = \text{phys} \lor x = \text{chem}$
Theo	math	$t = 1$

$$x = \begin{cases} \text{math} : 0.3 \\ \text{phys} : 0.3 \\ \text{chem} : 0.4 \end{cases} \qquad t = \begin{cases} 0 : 0.15 \\ 1 : 0.85 \end{cases}$$

The concept of probabilistic c-table allows us to solve the closure problem by using the same algebra on c-tables defined in [20].

We also give a **completeness** result by showing that probabilistic boolean c-tables (all variables are two-valued and can appear only in the conditions, not in the tuples) can represent *any* probabilistic database.

An important conceptual contribution is that we show that, at least for the models we consider, the probabilistic database models can be seen, as **probabilistic counterparts** of incomplete database models. In an incompleteness model a tuple or an attribute value in a tuple may or may not be in the database. In its probabilistic counterpart, these are seen as elementary events with an assigned probability. For example, the models used in [15, 22, 34] are probabilistic counterparts of the two simplest incompleteness models discussed in [29]. As another example, the model used in [10] can be seen as the probabilistic counterpart of an incompleteness model one in which tuples sharing the same key have an exclusive-or relationship.

A consequence of this observation is that, in particular, query answering for probabilistic c-tables will allow us to solve the problem of calculating probabilities about query answers for any model that can be defined as a probabilistic counterpart of the incompleteness models considered in [20, 29].

This paper is purely theoretical. Nonetheless, it was motivated by the work the authors are doing with others on the Orchestra[1] and SHARQ[2] projects. These projects are concerned with certain aspects of collaborative information sharing. Incompleteness arises in Orchestra (a peer-to-peer data exchange system) in the process of update propagation between sites. Incompleteness is also exploited in query answering algorithms. Probabilistic models are used in SHARQ (a bio-informatics data sharing system) to model approximate mappings between schemas used by groups of researchers. The sources of uncertainty here include data from error-prone experiments and accepted scientific hypotheses that allow for the limited mismatch. We expect that the results of this paper will help us in choosing appropriate representation systems that will be used internally in the Orchestra and SHARQ systems.

2 Incomplete Information and Representation Systems

Our starting point is suggested by the work surveyed in [18], in Ch. 19 of [2], and in [31]. A database that provides incomplete information consists of a *set of possible instances.* At one end of this spectrum we have the conventional single instances, which provide "complete information." At the other end we have the set of *all* allowable instances which provides "no information" at all, or "zero information."

We adopt the formalism of relational databases over a fixed countably infinite domain $\mathbb{D}$. We use the unnamed form of the relational algebra. To simplify the notation we will work with relational schemas that consist of a single relation name of arity n. Everything we say can be easily reformulated for arbitrary relational schemas. We shall need a notation for the set of *all* (conventional) instances of this schema, i.e., all the finite n-ary relations over $\mathbb{D}$:

$$\mathcal{N} := \{I \mid I \subseteq \mathbb{D}^n,\ I \text{ finite}\}$$

Definition 1. *An* **incomplete(-information) database** *(***i-database** *for short), $\mathcal{I}$, is a set of conventional instances, i.e., a subset $\mathcal{I} \subseteq \mathcal{N}$.*

The usual relational databases correspond to the cases when $\mathcal{I} = \{I\}$. The **no-information** or **zero-information database** consists of *all* the relations: $\mathcal{N}$.

Conventional relational instances are finite. However, because $\mathbb{D}$ is infinite incomplete databases are in general infinite. Hence the interest in finite, syntactical, representations for incomplete information.

Definition 2. *A* **representation system** *consists of a set (usually a syntactically defined "language") whose elements we call tables, and a function Mod that associates to each table T an incomplete database $Mod(T)$.*

The notation corresponds to the fact that T can be seen as a logical assertion such that the conventional instances in $Mod(T)$ are in fact the *models* of T (see also [27,32]).

[1] `http://www.cis.upenn.edu/~zives/orchestra`
[2] `http://db.cis.upenn.edu/projects/SHARQ`

The classical reference [20] considers three representation systems: **Codd tables**, **v-tables**, and **c-tables**. v-tables are conventional instances in which variables can appear in addition to constants from $\mathbb{D}$. If T is a v-table then[3]

$$Mod(T) := \{\nu(T) \mid \nu : Var(T) \to \mathbb{D} \ \text{ is a valuation for the variables of } T\}$$

Codd tables are v-tables in which all the variables are distinct. They correspond roughly to the current use of nulls in SQL, while v-tables model "labeled" or "marked" nulls. c-tables are v-tables in which each tuple is associated with a condition — a boolean combination of equalities involving variables and constants. We typically use the letter φ for conditions. The tuple condition is tested for each valuation ν and the tuple is discarded from $\nu(T)$ if the condition is not satisfied.

Example 1. Here is an example of a v-table.

$$R := \begin{array}{|c|}\hline 1\ 2\ x \\ 3\ x\ y \\ z\ 4\ 5 \\ \hline\end{array} \qquad Mod(R) = \left\{ \begin{array}{|c|}\hline 1\ 2\ 1 \\ 3\ 1\ 1 \\ 1\ 4\ 5 \\ \hline\end{array}, \begin{array}{|c|}\hline 1\ 2\ 2 \\ 3\ 2\ 1 \\ 1\ 4\ 5 \\ \hline\end{array}, \begin{array}{|c|}\hline 1\ 2\ 1 \\ 3\ 1\ 2 \\ 1\ 4\ 5 \\ \hline\end{array}, \ldots, \begin{array}{|ccc|}\hline 1 & 2 & 77 \\ 3 & 77 & 89 \\ 97 & 4 & 5 \\ \hline\end{array}, \ldots \right\}$$

Example 2. Here is an example of a c-table.

$$S := \begin{array}{|c|c|}\hline 1\ 2\ x & \\ 3\ x\ y & x = y \wedge z \neq 2 \\ z\ 4\ 5 & x \neq 1 \vee x \neq y \\ \hline\end{array} \quad Mod(S) = \left\{ \begin{array}{|c|}\hline 1\ 2\ 1 \\ 3\ 1\ 1 \\ \hline\end{array}, \begin{array}{|c|}\hline 1\ 2\ 2 \\ 1\ 4\ 5 \\ \hline\end{array}, \ldots, \begin{array}{|ccc|}\hline 1 & 2 & 77 \\ 97 & 4 & 5 \\ \hline\end{array}, \ldots \right\}$$

Several other representation systems have been proposed in a recent paper [29]. We illustrate here three of them and we discuss several others later. A **?-table** is a conventional instance in which tuples are optionally labeled with "?," meaning that the tuple may be missing. An **or-set-table** looks like a conventional instance but or-set values [21, 26] are allowed. An or-set value $\langle 1, 2, 3\rangle$ signifies that exactly one of 1, 2, or 3 is the "actual" (but unknown) value. Clearly, the two ideas can be combined yielding another representation systems that we might (awkwardly) call **or-set-?-tables**.[4]

Example 3. Here is an example of an or-set-?-table.

$$T := \begin{array}{|ccc|c|}\hline 1 & 2 & \langle 1,2\rangle & \\ 3 & \langle 1,2\rangle & \langle 3,4\rangle & \\ \langle 4,5\rangle & 4 & 5 & ? \\ \hline\end{array} \quad Mod(T) = \left\{ \begin{array}{|c|}\hline 1\ 2\ 1 \\ 3\ 1\ 3 \\ 4\ 4\ 5 \\ \hline\end{array}, \begin{array}{|c|}\hline 1\ 2\ 1 \\ 3\ 1\ 3 \\ \hline\end{array}, \begin{array}{|c|}\hline 1\ 2\ 2 \\ 3\ 1\ 3 \\ 4\ 4\ 5 \\ \hline\end{array}, \ldots, \begin{array}{|c|}\hline 1\ 2\ 2 \\ 3\ 2\ 4 \\ \hline\end{array} \right\}$$

3 $\mathcal{RA}$-Completeness and Finite Completeness

"Completeness" of expressive power is the first obvious question to ask about representation systems. This brings up a fundamental difference between the

[3] We follow [2, 29] and use the *closed-world assumption (CWA)*. [20] uses the *open-world assumption (OWA)*, but their results hold for CWA as well.

[4] In [29] these three systems are denoted by $\mathcal{R}_?$, $\mathcal{R}^A$ and $\mathcal{R}^A_?$.

representation systems of [20] and those of [29]. The presence of variables in a table T and the fact that $\mathbb{D}$ is infinite means that *Mod*(T) may be infinite. For the tables considered in [29], *Mod*(T) is always finite.

[29] defines completeness as the ability of a representation system to represent "all" possible incomplete databases. For the kind of tables considered in [29] the question makes sense. But in the case of the tables with variables in [20] this is hopeless for trivial reasons. Indeed, in such systems there are only countably many tables while there are uncountably many incomplete databases (the subsets of $\mathcal{N}$, which is infinite). We will discuss separately below *finite completeness* for systems that only represent finite database. Meanwhile, we will develop a different yardstick for the expressive power of tables with variables that range over an infinite domain.

c-tables and their restrictions (v-tables and Codd tables) have an inherent limitation: the cardinality of the instances in *Mod*(T) is at most the cardinality of T. For example, the zero-information database $\mathcal{N}$ *cannot* be represented with c-tables. It also follows that among the incomplete databases that are representable by c-tables the "minimal"-information ones are those consisting for some m of all instances of cardinality up to m (which are in fact representable by Codd tables with m rows). Among these, we make special use of the ones of cardinality 1:

$$\mathcal{Z}_k := \{\{t\} \mid t \in \mathbb{D}^k\}.$$

Hence, $\mathcal{Z}_k$ consists of *all* the one-tuple relations of arity k. Note that $\mathcal{Z}_k = \mathit{Mod}(Z_k)$ where Z_k is the Codd table consisting of a single row of k distinct variables.

Definition 3. *An incomplete database $\mathcal{I}$ is* $\mathcal{RA}$**-definable** *if there exists a relational algebra query q such that $\mathcal{I} = q(\mathcal{Z}_k)$, where k is the arity of the input relation name in q.*

Theorem 1. *If $\mathcal{I}$ is an incomplete database representable by a c-table T, i.e., $\mathcal{I} = \mathit{Mod}(T)$, then $\mathcal{I}$ is $\mathcal{RA}$-definable.*

Proof. Let T be a c-table, and let $\{x_1, \ldots, x_k\}$ denote the variables in T. We want to show that there exists a query q in $\mathcal{RA}$ such that $q(\mathit{Mod}(Z_k)) = \mathit{Mod}(T)$. Let n be the arity of T. For every tuple $t = (a_1, \ldots, a_n)$ in T with condition φ_t, let $\{x_{i_1}, \ldots, x_{i_j}\}$ be the variables in φ_t which do not appear in t. For $1 \leq i \leq n$, define C_i to be the singleton $\{c\}$, if $a_i = c$ for some constant c, or $\pi_j(Z_k)$, if $a_i = x_j$ for some variable x_j. For $1 \leq j \leq k$, define C_{n+j} to be the expression $\pi_{i_j}(Z_k)$, where x_j is the jth variable in φ_t which does not appear in t. Define q to be the query

$$q := \bigcup_{t \in T} \pi_{1,\ldots,n}(\sigma_{\psi_t}(C_1 \times \cdots \times C_{n+k})),$$

where ψ_t is obtained from φ_t by replacing each occurrence of a variable x_i with the index j of the term C_j in which x_i appears. To see that $q(\mathit{Mod}(Z_k)) = \mathit{Mod}(T)$, since Z_k is a c-table, we can use Theorem 4 and check that, in fact, $\bar{q}(Z_k) = T$ where $\bar{q}$ is the translation of q into the c-tables algebra (see the proof of Theorem 4). Note that we only need the *SPJU* fragment of $\mathcal{RA}$. □

Example 4. The c-table from Example 2 is definable as $Mod(S) = q(\mathcal{Z}_3)$ where q is the following query with input relation name V of arity 3: $q(V) := \pi_{123}(\{1\} \times \{2\} \times V) \cup \pi_{123}(\sigma_{2=3,4\neq`2'}(\{3\} \times V)) \cup \pi_{512}(\sigma_{3\neq`1',3\neq 4}(\{4\} \times \{5\} \times V))$.

Remark 1. It turns out that the i-databases representable by c-tables are also definable via $\mathcal{RA}$ starting from the absolute zero-information instance, $\mathcal{N}$. Indeed, it can be shown (Proposition 4) that for each k there exists an $\mathcal{RA}$ query q such that $\mathcal{Z}_k = q(\mathcal{N})$. From there we can apply Theorem 1. The class of incomplete databases $\{\mathcal{I} \mid \exists q \in \mathcal{RA} \text{ s.t. } \mathcal{I} = q(\mathcal{N})\}$ is strictly larger than that representable by c-tables, but it is still countable hence strictly smaller than that of all incomplete databases. Its connections with FO-definability in finite model theory might be interesting to investigate.

Hence, c-tables are in some sense "no more powerful" than the relational algebra. But are they "as powerful"? This justifies the following:

Definition 4. *A representation system is* **$\mathcal{RA}$-complete** *if it can represent any $\mathcal{RA}$-definable i-database.*

Since Z_k is itself a c-table the following is an immediate corollary of the fundamental result of [20] (see Theorem 4 below). It also states that the converse of Theorem 1 holds.

Theorem 2. *c-tables are $\mathcal{RA}$-complete.*

This result is similar in nature to Corollary 3.1 in [18]. However, the exact technical connection, if any, is unclear, since Corollary 3.1 in [18] relies on the certain answers semantics for queries.

We now turn to the kind of completeness considered in [29].

Definition 5. *A representation system is* **finitely complete** *if it can represent any finite i-database.*

The finite incompleteness of ?-tables, or-set-tables, or-set-?-tables and other systems is discussed in [29] where a finitely complete representation system $\mathcal{R}^A_{\text{prop}}$ is also given (we repeat the definition in the Appendix). Is finite completeness a reasonable question for c-tables, v-tables, and Codd tables? In general, for such tables $Mod(T)$ is infinite (all that is needed is a tuple with at least one variable and with an infinitely satisfiable condition). To facilitate comparison with the systems in [29] we define *finite-domain* versions of tables with variables.

Definition 6. *A* **finite-domain** *c-table (v-table, Codd table) consists of a c-table (v-table, Codd table) T together with a* finite *$dom(x) \subset \mathbb{D}$ for each variable x that occurs in T.*

Note that finite-domain Codd tables are equivalent to or-set tables. Indeed, to obtain an or-set table from a Codd table, one can see $\text{dom}(x)$ as an or-set and substitute it for x in the table. Conversely, to obtain a Codd table from an or-set table, one can substitute a fresh variable x for each or-set and define $\mathrm{dom}(x)$ as the contents of the or-set.

In light of this connection, finite-domain v-tables can be thought of as a kind of "correlated" or-set tables. Finite-domain v-tables are strictly more expressive than finite Codd tables. Indeed, every finite Codd table is also a finite v-table. But, the set of instances represented by e.g. the finite v-table $\{(1,x),(x,1)\}$ where $\mathrm{dom}(x) = \{1,2\}$ cannot be represented by any finite Codd table. Finite-domain v-tables are themselves finitely incomplete. For example, the i-database $\{\{(1,2)\},\{(2,1)\}\}$ cannot be represented by any finite v-table.

It is easy to see that finite-domain c-tables are finitely complete and hence equivalent to [29]'s $\mathcal{R}^A_{\mathrm{prop}}$ in terms of expressive power. In fact, this is true even for the fragment of finite-domain c-tables which we will call *boolean c-tables*, where the variables take only boolean values and are only allowed to appear in conditions (never as attribute values).

Theorem 3. *Boolean c-tables are finitely complete (hence finite-domain c-tables are also finitely complete).*

Proof. Let $\mathcal{I} = \{I_1, I_2, \ldots, I_m\}$ be a finite i-database. Construct a boolean c-table T such that $Mod(T) = \mathcal{I}$ as follows. Let $\ell := \lceil \lg m \rceil$. For $1 \le i < m$, put all the tuples from I_i into T with condition φ_i, defined

$$\varphi_i := \bigwedge_j \neg x_j \wedge \bigwedge_k x_k,$$

where the first conjunction is over all $1 \le j \le \ell$ such that jth digit in the ℓ-digit binary representation of $i-1$ is 0, and the second conjunction is over all $1 \le k \le \ell$ such that the kth digit in the ℓ-digit binary representation of $i-1$ is 1. Finally, put all the tuples from I_m into T with condition $\varphi_m \vee \cdots \vee \varphi_{2^\ell}$. □

Although boolean c-tables are complete there are clear advantages to using variables in tuples also, chief among them being *compactness* of representations

Example 5. Consider the finite c-table $\{(x_1, x_2, \ldots, x_m : \mathit{true})\}$ where $\mathrm{dom}(x_1) = \mathrm{dom}(x_2) = \cdots = \mathrm{dom}(x_m) = \{1, 2, \ldots, n\}$. The equivalent boolean c-table has n^m tuples.

If we additionally restrict boolean c-tables to allow conditions to contain only true or a single variable which appears in no other condition, then we obtain a representation system which is equivalent to ?-tables.

Since finite c-tables and $\mathcal{R}^A_{\mathrm{prop}}$ are each finitely complete there is an obvious naïve algorithm to translate back and forth between them: list all the instances the one represents, then use the construction from the proof of finite completeness for the other. Finding a more practical "syntactic" algorithm is an interesting open question.

4 Closure Under Relational Operations

Definition 7. *A representation system is* **closed** *under a query language if for any query q and any table T there is a table T' that represents $q(Mod(T))$.*

(For notational simplicity we consider only queries with one input relation name, but everything generalizes smoothly to multiple relation names.)

This definition is from [29]. In [2], a *strong* representation system is defined in the same way, with the significant addition that T' should be *computable* from T and q. It is not hard to show, using general recursion-theoretic principles, that there exist representation systems (even ones that only represent finite i-databases) which are closed as above but not strong in the sense of [2]. However, the concrete systems studied so far are either not closed or if they are closed then the proof provides also the algorithm required by the definition of strong systems. Hence, we see no need to insist upon the distinction.

Theorem 4 ([20]). *c-tables, finite-domain c-tables, and boolean c-tables are closed under the relational algebra.*

Proof. (Sketch.) We repeat here the essentials of the proof, including most of the definition of the c-table algebra. For each operation u of the relational algebra [20] defines an operation $\bar{u}$ on c-tables as follows. For projection, we have

$$\bar{\pi}_\ell(T) := \{(t' : \varphi_{t'}) \mid t \in T \text{ s.t. } \pi_\ell(t) = t', \varphi_{t'} = \bigvee \varphi_t\}$$

where ℓ is a list of indexes and the disjunction is over all t in T such that $\pi_\ell(t) = t'$. For selection, we have

$$\bar{\sigma}_c(T) := \{(t : \varphi_t \wedge c(t)) \mid (t, \varphi_t) \in T\}$$

where $c(t)$ denotes the result of evaluating the selection predicate c on the values in t (for a boolean c-table, this will always be true or false, while for c-tables and finite-domain c-tables, this will be in general a boolean formula on constants and variables). For cross product and union, we have

$$T_1 \mathbin{\bar{\times}} T_2 := \{(t_1 \times t_2 : \varphi_{t_1} \wedge \varphi_{t_2}) \mid t_1 \in T_1, t_2 \in T_2\}$$
$$T_1 \mathbin{\bar{\cup}} T_2 := T_1 \cup T_2$$

Difference and intersection are handled similarly. By replacing u's by $\bar{u}$ we translate any relational algebra expression q into a c-table algebra expression $\bar{q}$ and it can be shown that

Lemma 1. *For all valuations* ν, $\nu(\bar{q}(T)) = q(\nu(T))$.

From this, $Mod(\bar{q}(T)) = q(Mod(T))$ follows immediately. □

5 Algebraic Completion

None of the incomplete representation systems we have seen so far is closed under the full relational algebra. Nor are two more representation systems considered in [29], $\mathcal{R}_{\text{sets}}$and $\mathcal{R}_{\oplus\equiv}$ (we repeat their definitions in the Appendix).

Proposition 1 ([20, 29]). *Codd tables and v-tables are not closed under e.g. selection. Or-set tables and finite v-tables are also not closed under e.g. selection. ?-tables, $\mathcal{R}_{sets}$, and $\mathcal{R}_{\oplus\equiv}$ are not closed under e.g. join.*

We have seen that "closing" minimal-information one-row Codd tables (see before Definition 4) $\{Z_1, Z_2, \ldots\}$, by relational algebra queries yields equivalence with the c-tables. In this spirit, we will investigate "how much" of the relational algebra would be needed to complete the other representation systems considered. We call this kind of result *algebraic completion.*

Definition 8. *If $(\mathcal{T}, Mod)$ is a representation system and $\mathcal{L}$ is a query language, then the representation system* obtained by closing $\mathcal{T}$ under $\mathcal{L}$ *is the set of tables $\{(T, q) \mid T \in \mathcal{T}, q \in \mathcal{L}\}$ with the function $Mod : \mathcal{T} \times \mathcal{L} \to \mathcal{N}$ defined by $Mod(T, q) := q(Mod(T))$.*

We are now ready to state our results regarding algebraic completion.

Theorem 5 ($\mathcal{RA}$-Completion).

1. *The representation system obtained by closing Codd tables under SPJU queries is $\mathcal{RA}$-complete.*
2. *The representation system obtained by closing v-tables under SP queries is $\mathcal{RA}$-complete.*

Proof. (Sketch.) For each case we show that given a arbitrary c-table T one can construct a table S and a query q of the required type such that $\bar{q}(S) = T$. Case 1 is a trivial corollary of Theorem 1. The details for Case 2 are in the Appendix. □

Note that in general there may be a "gap" between the language for which closure fails for a representation system and the language required for completion. For example, Codd tables are not closed under selection, but at the same time closing Codd tables under selection does not yield an $\mathcal{RA}$-complete representation system. (To see this, consider the incomplete database represented by the v-table $\{(x, 1), (x, 2)\}$. Intuitively, selection alone is not powerful enough to yield this incomplete database from a Codd table, as, selection operates on one tuple at a time and cannot correlate two un-correlated tuples.) On the other hand, it is possible that some of the results we present here may be able to be "tightened" to hold for smaller query languages, or else proved to be "tight" already. This is an issue we hope to address in future work.

We give now a set of analogous completion results for the finite case.

Theorem 6 (Finite-Completion).

1. *The representation system obtained by closing or-set-tables under PJ queries is finitely complete.*
2. *The representation system obtained by closing finite v-tables under PJ or S^+P queries is finitely complete.*
3. *The representation system obtained by closing $\mathcal{R}_{sets}$ under PJ or PU queries is finitely complete.*

4. The representation system obtained by closing $\mathcal{R}_{\oplus\equiv}$ under S^+PJ queries is finitely complete.

Proof. (Sketch.) In each case, given an arbitrary finite incomplete database, we construct a table and query of the required type which yields the incomplete database. The details are in the Appendix. □

Note that there is a gap between the $\mathcal{RA}$-completion result for Codd tables, which requires $SPJU$ queries, and the finite-completion result for finite Codd tables, which requires only PJ queries. A partial explanation is that proof of the latter result relies essentially on the finiteness of the i-database.

More generally, if a representation system can represent arbitrarily-large i-databases, then closing it under $\mathcal{RA}$ yields a finitely complete representation system, as the following theorem makes precise (see Appendix for proof).

Theorem 7 (General Finite-Completion). *Let $\mathcal{T}$ be a representation system such that for all $n \geq 1$ there exists a table T in $\mathcal{T}$ such that $|Mod(T)| \geq n$. Then the representation system obtained by closing $\mathcal{T}$ under $\mathcal{RA}$ is finitely-complete.*

Corollary 1. *The representation system obtained by closing ?-tables under $\mathcal{RA}$ queries is finitely complete.*

6 Probabilistic Databases and Representation Systems

Finiteness assumption. For the entire discussion of probabilistic database models we will assume that *the domain of values $\mathbb{D}$ is finite.* Infinite domains of values are certainly interesting in practice; for some examples see [22, 33, 29]. Moreover, in the case of incomplete databases we have seen that they allow for interesting distinctions.[5] However, finite probability spaces are much simpler than infinite ones and we will take advantage of this simplicity. We leave for future investigations the issues related to probabilistic databases over infinite domains.

We wish to model probabilistic information using a probability space whose possible outcomes are all the conventional instances. Recall that for simplicity we assume a schema consisting of just one relation of arity n. The finiteness of $\mathbb{D}$ implies that there are only finitely many instances, $I \subseteq \mathbb{D}^n$.

By **finite probability space** we mean a probability space (see e.g. [11]) $(\Omega, \mathcal{F}, \mathbb{P}[\ ])$ in which the set of outcomes Ω is *finite* and the σ-field of events $\mathcal{F}$ consists of *all* subsets of Ω. We shall use the equivalent formulation of pairs (Ω, p) where Ω is the finite set of outcomes and where the *outcome probability assignment* $p : \Omega \to [0, 1]$ satisfies $\sum_{\omega \in \Omega} p(\omega) = 1$. Indeed, we take $\mathbb{P}[A] = \sum_{\omega \in A} p(\omega)$.

[5] Note however that the results remain true if $\mathbb{D}$ is finite; we just require an infinite supply of *variables*.

Definition 9. *A* **probabilistic(-information) database** *(sometimes called in this paper a p-***database***) is a finite probability space whose outcomes are all the conventional instances, i.e., a pair* $(\mathcal{N}, p)$ *where* $\sum_{I \in \mathcal{N}} p(I) = 1$.

Demanding the direct specification of such probabilistic databases is unrealistic because there are 2^N possible instances, where $N := |\mathbb{D}|^n$, and we would need that many (minus one) probability values. Thus, as in the case of incomplete databases we define **probabilistic representation systems** consisting of "probabilistic tables" (prob. tables for short) and a function *Mod* that associates to each prob. table T a probabilistic database $Mod(T)$. Similarly, we define **completeness** (finite completeness is the only kind we have in our setting).

To define closure under a query language we face the following problem. Given a probabilistic database $(\mathcal{N}, p)$ and a query q (with just one input relation name), how do we define the probability assignment for the instances in $q(\mathcal{N})$? It turns out that this is a common construction in probability theory: image spaces.

Definition 10. *Let* (Ω, p) *be a finite probability space and let* $f : \Omega \to \Omega'$ *where* Ω' *is some finite set. The* **image** *of* (Ω, p) *under* f *is the finite probability space* (Ω', p') *where* [6] $p'(\omega') := \sum_{f(\omega)=\omega'} p(\omega)$.

Again we consider as query languages the relational algebra and its sublanguages defined by subsets of operations.

Definition 11. *A probabilistic representation system is* **closed** *under a query language if for any query* q *and any prob. table* T *there exists a prob. table* T' *that represents* $q(Mod(T))$*, the image space of* $Mod(T)$ *under* q.

7 Probabilistic ?-Tables and Probabilistic Or-Set Tables

Probabilistic ?-tables (p-?-tables for short) are commonly used for probabilistic models of databases [34, 15, 16, 9] (they are called "independent tuple representation in [30]). Such tables are the probabilistic counterpart of ?-tables where each "?" is replaced by a probability value. Example 6 below shows such a table. The tuples not explicitly shown are assumed tagged with probability 0. Therefore, we define a p-?-table as a mapping that associates to each $t \in \mathbb{D}^n$ a probability value p_t. In order to represent a probabilistic database, papers using this model typically include a statement like "every tuple t is in the outcome instance with probability p_t, independently from the other tuples" and then a statement like

$$\mathbb{P}[I] = \Big(\prod_{t \in I} p_t\Big)\Big(\prod_{t \notin I} (1 - p_t)\Big).$$

In fact, to give a rigorous semantics, one needs to define the events $E_t \subseteq \mathcal{N}$, $E_t := \{I \mid t \in I\}$ and then to prove the following.

Proposition 2. *There exists a unique probabilistic database such that the events* E_t *are jointly independent and* $\mathbb{P}[E_t] = p_t$.

[6] It is easy to check that the $p'(\omega')$'s do actually add up to 1.

This defines p-?-tables as a probabilistic representation system. We shall however provide an equivalent but more perspicuous definition. We shall need here another common construction from probability theory: product spaces.

Definition 12. *Let* $(\Omega_1, p_1), \ldots, (\Omega_n, p_n)$ *be finite probability spaces. Their* **product** *is the space* $(\Omega_1 \times \cdots \times \Omega_n, p)$ *where*[7] $p(\omega_1, \ldots, \omega_n) := p_1(\omega_1) \cdots p_n(\omega_n)$.

This definition corresponds to the intuition that the n systems or phenomena that are modeled by the spaces $(\Omega_1, p_1), \ldots, (\Omega_n, p_n)$ behave without "interfering" with each other. The following formal statements summarize this intuition.

Proposition 3. *Consider the product of the spaces* $(\Omega_1, p_1), \ldots, (\Omega_n, p_n)$. *Let* $A_1 \subseteq \Omega_1, \ldots, A_n \subseteq \Omega_n$.

1. *We have* $\mathbb{P}[A_1 \times \cdots \times A_n] = \mathbb{P}[A_1] \cdots \mathbb{P}[A_n]$.
2. *The events* $A_1 \times \Omega_2 \times \cdots \times \Omega_n$, $\Omega_1 \times A_2 \times \cdots \times \Omega_n$, $\ldots$, $\Omega_1 \times \Omega_2 \times \cdots \times A_n$ *are jointly independent in the product space.*

Turning back to p-?-tables, for each tuple $t \in \mathbb{D}^n$ consider the finite probability space $B_t := (\{\mathsf{true}, \mathsf{false}\}, p)$ where $p(\mathsf{true}) := p_t$ and $p(\mathsf{false}) = 1 - p_t$. Now consider the product space

$$P := \prod_{t \in \mathbb{D}^n} B_t$$

We can think of its set of outcomes (abusing notation, we will call this set P also) as the set of functions from $\mathbb{D}^n$ to $\{\mathsf{true}, \mathsf{false}\}$, in other words, predicates on $\mathbb{D}^n$. There is an obvious function $f : P \to \mathcal{N}$ that associates to each predicate the set of tuples it maps to true.

All this gives us a p-database, namely the image of P under f. It remains to show that it satisfies the properties in Proposition 2. Indeed, since f is a bijection, this probabilistic database is in fact *isomorphic* to P. In P the events that are in bijection with the E_t's are the Cartesian product in which there is exactly one component $\{\mathsf{true}\}$ and the rest are $\{\mathsf{true}, \mathsf{false}\}$. The desired properties then follow from Proposition 3.

We define now another simple probabilistic representation system called **probabilistic or-set-tables** (p-or-set-tables for short). These are the probabilistic counterpart of or-set-tables where the attribute values are, instead of or-sets, finite probability spaces whose outcomes are the values in the or-set. p-or-set-tables correspond to a simplified version of the ProbView model presented in [22], in which plain probability values are used instead of confidence intervals.

Example 6. A p-or-set-table S, and a p-?-table T.

$S :=$

1	$\langle 2 : 0.3, 3 : 0.7 \rangle$
4	5
$\langle 6 : 0.5, 7 : 0.5 \rangle$	$\langle 8 : 0.1, 9 : 0.9 \rangle$

$T :=$

1	2	0.4
3	4	0.3
5	6	1.0

[7] Again, it is easy to check that the outcome probability assignments add up to 1.

A p-or-set-table determines an instance by choosing an outcome in each of the spaces that appear as attribute values, *independently*. Recall that or-set tables are equivalent to finite-domain Codd tables. Similarly, a p-or-set-table corresponds to a Codd table T plus for each variable x in T a finite probability space $\text{dom}(x)$ whose outcomes are in $\mathbb{D}$. This yields a p-database, again by image space construction, as shown more generally for c-tables next in section 8.

Query answering. The papers [15,34,22] have considered, independently, the problem of calculating the probability of tuples appearing in query answers. This does *not* mean that in general $q(Mod(T))$ can be represented by another tuple table when T is some p-?-table and $q \in \mathcal{RA}$ (neither does this hold for p-or-set-tables). This follows from Proposition 1. Indeed, if the probabilistic counterpart of an incompleteness representation system $\mathcal{T}$ is closed, then so is $\mathcal{T}$. Hence the lifting of the results in Proposition 1 and other similar results.

Each of the papers [15, 34, 22] recognizes the problem of query answering and solves it by developing a more general model in which rows contain additional information *similar in spirit* to the conditions that appear in c-tables (in fact [15]'s model is essentially what we call probabilistic boolean c-tables, see next section). We will show that we can actually use a probabilistic counterpart to c-tables themselves together with the algebra on c-tables given in [20] to achieve the same effect.

8 Probabilistic c-Tables

Definition 13. *A* **probabilistic** c**-table** *(pc-***tables** *for short) consists of a c-table T together with a* finite probability space *$dom(x)$ (whose outcomes are values in $\mathbb{D}$) for each variable x that occurs in T.*

To get a probabilistic representation system consider the product space

$$V := \prod_{x \in Var(T)} \text{dom}(x)$$

The outcomes of this space are in fact the *valuations* for the c-table T! Hence we can define the function $g : V \to \mathcal{N}, g(\nu) := \nu(T)$ and then define $Mod(T)$ as the image of V under g.

Similarly, we can talk about boolean pc-tables, pv-tables and probabilistic Codd tables (the latter related to [22], see previous section). Moreover, the p-?-tables correspond to restricted boolean pc-tables, just like ?-tables.

Theorem 8. *Boolean pc-tables are complete (hence pc-tables are also complete).*

Proof. Let $I_1, \ldots, I_k$ denote the instances with non-zero probability in an arbitrary probabilistic database, and let $p_1, \ldots, p_k$ denote their probabilities. Construct a probabilistic boolean c-table T as follows. For $1 \leq i \leq k-1$, put the tuples from I_i in T with condition $\neg x_1 \wedge \cdots \wedge \neg x_{i-1} \wedge x_i$. Put the tuples from I_k in T with condition $\neg x_1 \wedge \cdots \wedge \neg x_{k-1}$. For $1 \leq i \leq k-1$, set $\mathbb{P}[x_i = \text{true}] := p_i/(1 - \sum_{j=1}^{i-1} p_j)$. It is straightforward to check that this yields a table such that $\mathbb{P}[I_i] = p_i$. □

The previous theorem was independently observed in [30].

Theorem 9. *pc-tables (and boolean pc-tables) are closed under the relational algebra.*

Proof. (Sketch.) For any *pc*-table T and any $\mathcal{RA}$ query q we show that the probability space $q(Mod(T))$ (the image of $Mod(T)$ under q) is in fact the same as the space $Mod(\bar{q}(T))$. The proof of Theorem 4 already shows that the outcomes of the two spaces are the same. The fact that the probabilities assigned to each outcome are the same follows from Lemma 1. □

The proof of this theorem gives in fact an algorithm for constructing the answer as a *p*-database itself, represented by a *pc*-table. In particular this will work for the models of [15, 22, 34] or for models we might invent by adding probabilistic information to *v*-tables or to the representation systems considered in [29]. The interesting result of [9] about the applicability of an "extensional" algorithm to calculating answer tuple probabilities can be seen also as characterizing the conjunctive queries q which for any *p*-?-table T are such that the *c*-table $\bar{q}(T)$ is in fact equivalent to some *p*-?-table.

9 Some Ideas for Further Work

The new results on algebraic completion may not be as tight as they can be. Ideally, we would like to be able show that for each representation system we consider, the fragment of $\mathcal{RA}$ we use is minimal in the sense that closing the representation system under a more restricted fragment does not obtain a complete representation system.

We did not consider *c*-tables with global conditions [17] nor did we describe the exact connection to logical databases [27, 32]. Even more importantly, we did not consider complexity issues as in [3]. All of the above are important topics for further work, especially the complexity issues and the related issues of *succinctness/compactness* of the table representations.

As we see, in *pc*-tables the probability distribution is on the values taken by the variables that occur in the table. The variables are assumed independent here. This is a lot more flexible (as the example shows) than independent tuples, but still debatable. Consequently, as part of the proposed work, trying to make *pc*-tables even more flexible, we plan to investigate models in which the assumption that the variables take values independently is relaxed by using conditional probability distributions [14].

Space limitations prevent us from giving details, but there is a good reason why the *c*-table algebra was in essence rediscovered in [15, 22, 34] and to some extent in [28]. The condition that decorates a tuple t in $\bar{q}(T)$ can be seen as the *lineage* [8], a.k.a. the *why-provenance* [6], of the tuple t. We plan to discuss elsewhere the connection between algorithms for computing why-provenance and the *c*-table algebra.

It would be interesting to connect this work to the extensive literature on *disjunctive databases*, see e.g., [24], and to the work on probabilistic object-oriented databases [12].

Probabilistic modeling is by no means the only way to model uncertainty in information systems. In particular it would be interesting to investigate *possibilistic* models [19] for databases, perhaps following again, as we did here, the parallel with incompleteness.

References

1. S. Abiteboul and O. M. Duschka. Complexity of Answering Queries Using Materialized Views. In *PODS*, pages 254–263, 1998.
2. S. Abiteboul, R. Hull, and V. Vianu. *Foundations of Databases.* Addison–Wesley, Reading, MA, 1995.
3. S. Abiteboul, P. Kanellakis, and G. Grahne. On the representation and querying of sets of possible worlds. *Theor. Comput. Sci.*, 78(1):159–187, 1991.
4. M. Arenas, L. E. Bertossi, and J. Chomicki. Answer sets for consistent query answering in inconsistent databases. *TPLP*, 3(4-5):393–424, 2003.
5. D. Barbara, H. Garcia-Molina, and D. Porter. A probabilistic relational data model. In *EDBT*, pages 60–74, New York, NY, USA, 1990.
6. P. Buneman, S. Khanna, and W. C. Tan. Why and Where: A Characterization of Data Provenance. In *ICDT*, pages 316–330, 2001.
7. R. Cavallo and M. Pittarelli. The Theory of Probabilistic Databases. In *VLDB*, pages 71–81, 1987.
8. Y. Cui, J. Widom, and J. L. Wiener. Tracing the lineage of view data in a warehousing environment. *ACM Trans. Database Syst.*, 25(2):179–227, 2000.
9. N. Dalvi and D. Suciu. Efficient Query Evaluation on Probabilistic Databases. In *VLDB*, pages 864–875, 2004.
10. D. Dey and S. Sarkar. A Probabilistic Relational Model and Algebra. *ACM TODS*, 21(3):339–369, 1996.
11. R. Durrett. *Probability: Theory and Examples.* Duxbury Press, 3rd edition, 2004.
12. T. Eiter, J. J. Lu, T. Lukasiewicz, and V. S. Subrahmanian. Probabilistic object bases. *ACM Trans. Database Syst.*, 26(3):264–312, 2001.
13. R. Fagin, P. G. Kolaitis, R. J. Miller, and L. Popa. Data exchange: Semantics and query answering. In *ICDT*, pages 207–224, London, UK, 2003. Springer-Verlag.
14. N. Friedman, L. Getoor, D. Koller, and A. Pfeffer. Learning probabilistic relational models with structural uncertainty. In *Proc. ICML*, 2001.
15. N. Fuhr and T. Rölleke. A Probabilistic Relational Algebra for the Integration of Information Retrieval and Database Systems. *ACM TODS*, 14(1):32–66, 1997.
16. E. Grädel, Y. Gurevich, and C. Hirch. The Complexity of Query Reliability. In *PODS*, pages 227–234, 1998.
17. G. Grahne. Horn Tables - An Efficient Tool for Handling Incomplete Information in Databases. In *PODS*, pages 75–82. ACM Press, 1989.
18. G. Grahne. *The Problem of Incomplete Information in Relational Databases*, volume 554 of *Lecture Notes in Computer Science.* Springer-Verlag, Berlin, 1991.
19. J. Y. Halpern. *Reasoning About Uncertainty.* MIT Press, Cambridge, MA, 2003.
20. T. Imieliński and W. Lipski, Jr. Incomplete Information in Relational Databases. *J. ACM*, 31(4):761–791, 1984.

21. T. Imieliński, S. A. Naqvi, and K. V. Vadaparty. Incomplete objects — a data model for design and planning applications. In *SIGMOD*, pages 288–297, 1991.
22. L. V. S. Lakshmanan, N. Leone, R. Ross, and V. S. Subrahmanian. ProbView: a Flexible Probabilistic Database System. *ACM TODS*, 22(3):419–469, 1997.
23. L. V. S. Lakshmanan and F. Sadri. Probabilistic deductive databases. In *ILPS*, pages 254–268, Cambridge, MA, USA, 1994. MIT Press.
24. N. Leone, F. Scarcello, and V. S. Subrahmanian. Optimal Models of Disjunctive Logic Programs: Semantics, Complexity, and Computation. *IEEE Trans. Knowl. Data Eng.*, 16(4):487–503, 2004.
25. L. Libkin. *Aspects of Partial Information in Databases.* PhD thesis, University of Pennsylvania, 1994.
26. L. Libkin and L. Wong. Semantic representations and query languages for or-sets. *J. Computer and System Sci.*, 52(1):125–142, 1996.
27. R. Reiter. A sound and sometimes complete query evaluation algorithm for relational databases with null values. *J. ACM*, 33(2):349–370, 1986.
28. F. Sadri. Modeling Uncertainty in Databases. In *ICDE*, pages 122–131. IEEE Computer Society, 1991.
29. A. D. Sarma, O. Benjelloun, A. Halevy, and J. Widom. Working Models for Uncertain Data. In *To appear in ICDE*, April 2006.
30. D. Suciu and N. Dalvi. Foundations of probabilistic answers to queries (tutorial). In *SIGMOD*, pages 963–963, New York, NY, USA, 2005. ACM Press.
31. R. van der Meyden. Logical Approaches to Incomplete Information: A Survey. In J. Chomicki and G. Saake, editors, *Logics for Databases and Information Systems.* Kluwer Academic Publishers, Boston, 1998.
32. M. Y. Vardi. Querying Logical Databases. *JCSS*, 33(2):142–160, 1986.
33. J. Widom. Trio: A System for Integrated Management of Data, Accuracy, and Lineage. In *CIDR*, Jan. 2005.
34. E. Zimányi. Query evaluation in probabilistic databases. *Theoretical Computer Science*, 171(1–2):179–219, 1997.
35. E. Zimányi and A. Pirotte. Imperfect information in relational databases. In *Uncertainty Management in Information Systems*, pages 35–88. Kluwer, 1996.

Appendix

Proposition 4. *There exists a relational query q such that $q(\mathcal{N}) = \mathcal{Z}_n$.*

Proof. Define sub-query q' to be the relational query

$$q'(V) := V - \pi_\ell(\sigma_{\ell \neq r}(V \times V)),$$

where ℓ is short for $1, \ldots, n$ and $\ell \neq r$ is short for $1 \neq n+1 \vee \cdots \vee n \neq 2n$. Note that q' yields V if V consists of a single tuple and $\emptyset$ otherwise. Now define q to be the relational query

$$q(V) := q'(V) \cup (\{t\} - \pi_\ell(\{t\} \times q'(V))),$$

where t is a tuple chosen arbitrarily from $\mathbb{D}^n$. It is clear that $q(\mathcal{N}) = \mathcal{Z}_n$. $\square$

Definition 14. *A table in the representation system $\mathcal{R}_{sets}$ is a multiset of sets of tuples, or* blocks, *each such block optionally labeled with a '?'. If T is an $\mathcal{R}_{sets}$ table, then Mod(T) is the set of instances obtained by choosing one tuple from each block not labeled with a '?', and at most one tuple from each block labeled with a '?'.*

Definition 15. *A table in the representation system $\mathcal{R}_{\oplus\equiv}$ is a multiset of tuples $\{t_1, \ldots, t_m\}$ and a conjunction of logical assertions of the form $i \oplus j$ (meaning t_i or t_j must be present in an instance, but not both) or $i \equiv j$ (meaning t_i is present in an instance iff t_j is present in the instance). If T is an $\mathcal{R}_{\oplus\equiv}$ table then Mod(T) consists of all subsets of the tuples satisfying the conjunction of assertions.*

Definition 16. *A table in the representation system $\mathcal{R}^A_{prop}$ is a multiset of or-set tuples $\{t_1, \ldots, t_m\}$ and a boolean formula on the variables $\{t_1, \ldots, t_m\}$. If T is an $\mathcal{R}^A_{prop}$ table then Mod(T) consists of all subsets of the tuples satisfying the boolean assertion, where the variable t_i has value* true *iff the tuple t_i is present in the subset.*

Theorem 5 ($\mathcal{RA}$-Completion).

1. *The representation system obtained by closing Codd tables under SPJU queries is $\mathcal{RA}$-complete.*
2. *The representation system obtained by closing v-tables under SP queries is $\mathcal{RA}$-complete.*

Proof. In each case we show that given an arbitrary c-table T, one can construct a table S and a query q such that $\bar{q}(S) = T$.

1. Trivial corollary of Theorem 1.
2. Let k be the arity of T. Let $\{t_1, \ldots, t_m\}$ be an enumeration of the tuples of T, and let $\{x_1, \ldots, x_n\}$ be an enumeration of the variables which appear in T. Construct a v-table S with arity $k + n + 1$ as follows. For every tuple t_i in T, put exactly one tuple t'_i in S, where t'_i agrees with t_i on the first k columns, the $k+1$st column contains the constant i, and the last m columns contain the variables $x_1, \ldots, x_m$. Now let q be the SP query defined

$$q := \pi_{1,\ldots,k}(\sigma_{\bigvee_{i=1}^{m} k+1=`i' \wedge \psi_i}(S))$$

where ψ_i is obtained from the condition φ_{t_i} of tuple t_i by replacing variable names with their corresponding indexes in S. □

Theorem 6 (Finite Completion).

1. *The representation system obtained by closing or-set-tables under PJ queries is finitely complete.*
2. *The representation system obtained by closing finite v-tables under PJ or S^+P queries is finitely complete.*

3. *The representation system obtained by closing $\mathcal{R}_{sets}$ under PJ or PU queries is finitely complete.*
4. *The representation system obtained by closing $\mathcal{R}_{\oplus\equiv}$ under S^+PJ queries is finitely complete.*

Proof. Fix an arbitrary finite incomplete database $\mathcal{I} = \{I_1, \ldots, I_n\}$ of arity k. It suffices to show in each case that one can construct a table T in the given representation system and a query q in the given language such that $q(Mod(T)) = \mathcal{I}$.

1. We construct a pair of or-set-tables S and T as follows. (They can be combined together into a single table, but we keep them separate to simplify the presentation.) For each instance I_i in $\mathcal{I}$, we put all the tuples of I_i in S, appending an extra column containing value i. Let T be the or-set-table of arity 1 containing a single tuple whose single value is the or-set $\langle 1, 2, \ldots, n\rangle$. Now let q be the S^+PJ query defined:
$$q := \pi_{1,\ldots,k}\sigma_{k+1=k+2}(S \times T).$$
2. Completion for PJ follows from Case 1 and the fact that finite v-tables are strictly more expressive than or-set tables. For S^+P, take the finite v-table representing the cross product of S and T in the construction from Case 1, and let q be the obvious S^+P query.
3. Completion for PJ follows from Case 1 and the fact (shown in [29]) that or-set-tables are strictly less expressive than $\mathcal{R}_{\text{sets}}$. Thus we just need show the construction for PU. We construct an $\mathcal{R}_{\text{sets}}$ table T as follows. Let m be the cardinality of the largest instance in $\mathcal{I}$. Then T will have arity km and will consist of a single block of tuples. For every instance I_i in $\mathcal{I}$, we put one tuple in T which has every tuple from I_i arranged in a row. (If the cardinality of I_i is less than m, we pad the remainder with arbitrary tuples from I_i.) Now let q be the PU query defined as follows:
$$q := \bigcup_{i=0}^{m-1} \pi_{ki,\ldots,ki+k-1}(T)$$
4. We construct a pair of $\mathcal{R}_{\oplus\equiv}$-tables S and T as follows. (S can be encoded as a special tuple in T, but we keep it separate to simplify the presentation.) Let $m = \lceil \lg n \rceil$. T is constructed as in Case 2. S is a binary table containing, for each i, $1 \le i \le m$, a pair of tuples $(0, i)$ and $(1, i)$ with an exclusive-or constraint between them. Let sub-query q' be defined
$$q' := \prod_{i=1}^{m} \pi_1(\sigma_{2=`i'}(S))$$
The S^+PJ query q is defined as in Case 2, but using this definition of q'. □

Theorem 7 (General Finite Completion). *Let $\mathcal{T}$ be a representation system such that for all $n \geq 1$ there exists a table T in $\mathcal{T}$ such that $|Mod(T)| \geq n$. Then the representation system obtained by closing $\mathcal{T}$ under $\mathcal{RA}$ is finitely-complete.*

Proof. Let $\mathcal{T}$ be a representation system such that for all $n \geq 1$ there is a table T in $\mathcal{T}$ such that $|Mod(T)| \geq n$. Let $\mathcal{I} = \{I_1, ..., I_k\}$ be an arbitrary non-empty finite set of instances of arity m. Let T be a table in $\mathcal{T}$ such that $Mod(T) = \{J_1, \ldots, J_\ell\}$, with $\ell \geq k$. Define $\mathcal{RA}$ query q to be

$$q(V) := \bigcup_{1 \leq i \leq k-1} I_i \times q_i(V) \cup \bigcup_{k \leq i \leq \ell} I_k \times q_i(V),$$

where I_i is the query which constructs instance I_i and $q_i(V)$ is the boolean query which returns true iff V is identical to I_i (which can be done in $\mathcal{RA}$). Then $q(Mod(T)) = \mathcal{I}$. □

DART: A Data Acquisition and Repairing Tool

Bettina Fazzinga, Sergio Flesca, Filippo Furfaro, and Francesco Parisi

DEIS - Università della Calabria
Via Bucci - 87036 Rende (CS) Italy
{bfazzinga, flesca, furfaro, fparisi}@deis.unical.it

Abstract. An architecture is proposed providing robust data acquisition facilities from input documents containing tabular data. This architecture is based on a data-repairing framework exploiting integrity constraints defined on the input data to support the detection and the repair of inconsistencies in the data arising from errors occurring in the acquisition phase. In particular, a specific but expressive form of integrity constraints (*steady aggregate constraints*) is defined which enables the computation of a repair to be expressed as a mixed integer linear programming problem.

1 Introduction

The need to acquire data from different sources of information often arises in many application scenarios, such as e-procurement, competitor analysis, business intelligence. In several cases these sources are heterogenous documents, possibly represented according to different formats, ranging from paper documents to electronic ones (PDF, MSWord, HTML files). In order to be exploited to provide valuable knowledge, information must be extracted from the original documents and re-organized into a machine-readable format. The problem of defining efficient and effective approaches accomplishing this task is a challenging issue in the context of Information Extraction (IE). Most of traditional IE techniques focus on efficiency, providing unsupervised extraction algorithms which automatically extract records from documents. However, it frequently happens that some of the extracted records are not correctly recognized, i.e. the value of one (or more) field has been misspelled. In several contexts (such as balance analysis) extracted information must be 100% error free in order to be profitably exploited, thus unsupervised approaches are not well-suited. In these cases, data transcription from input documents into a machine-readable format requires massive human intervention, thus compromising efficiency and making valuable resources be wasted. Human intervention is mainly devoted to verifying the correctness of acquired data by comparing them with the content of source documents.

Indeed, if integrity constraints are defined on the input data, this kind of human intervention can be reduced by automatically verifying whether acquired data satisfy these constraints, thus limiting manual corrections to those pieces of acquired data which do not satisfy them. In fact current approaches exploiting integrity constraints on source documents require inconsistent acquired data to be manually edited by a human operator. This editing task is likely to be onerous, since a large amount of data in the input documents need to be accessed and compared with the acquired ones.

T. Grust et al. (Eds.): EDBT 2006 Workshops, LNCS 4254, pp. 297–317, 2006.

The idea underlying this paper is that human intervention can be reduced by exploiting some repairing technique to suggest the "most likely" way of fixing inconsistent data. We introduce the architecture of a system (namely, *DART* - Data Acquisition and Repairing Tool) based on this idea. The motivation of this work and the contribution provided by this system can be better understood after reading the following example, describing a specific application scenario (that is, data acquisition from balance sheets).

Example 1. The balance sheet is a financial statement of a company providing information on what the company owns (its assets), what it owes (its liabilities), and the value of the business to its stockholders. A thorough analysis of a company balance sheet is extremely important for both stock and bond investors, since it allows potential liquidity problems to be detected, thus determining the company financial reliability as well as its ability to satisfy financial obligations.

Figure 1 is a portion of a document containing two *cash budgets* for a firm, each of them related to a year. Each cash budget is a summary of cash flows (receipts, disbursements, and cash balances) over the specified periods.

2003	Receipts	beginning cash	20
		cash sales	100
		receivables	120
		total cash receipts	220
	Disbursements	payment of accounts	120
		capital expenditure	0
		long-term financing	40
		total disbursements	160
	Balance	net cash inflow	60
		ending cash balance	80

2004	Receipts	beginning cash	80
		cash sales	100
		receivables	100
		total cash receipts	200
	Disbursements	payment of accounts	130
		capital expenditure	40
		long-term financing	20
		total disbursements	190
	Balance	net cash inflow	10
		ending cash balance	90

Fig. 1. An input document

This cash budget satisfies the following integrity constraints:

a) for each year, the sum of *cash sales* and *receivables* in section *Receipts* must be equal to *total cash receipts*;
b) for each year, the sum of *payment of accounts*, *capital expenditure* and *long-term financing* must be equal to *total disbursements* (in section *Disbursements*);
c) for each year, the *net cash inflow* must be equal to the difference between *total cash receipts* and *total disbursements*;
d) for each year, the *ending cash balance* must be equal to the sum of the *beginning cash* and the *net cash inflow*;

Generally balance sheets like the ones depicted in Figure 1 are available as paper documents, thus they cannot be automatically processed by balance analysis tools, since these work only on electronic data. In fact, some companies do business acquiring electronic balance data and reselling them in a format suitable for being processed by commercial analysis tools. Currently electronic versions are obtained by means of either human transcriptions or OCR acquisition tools. Both these approaches are likely to result in erroneous acquisition, thus compromising the reliability of the analysis task.

An example of numerical value recognition error occurring during the acquisition phase is the recognition of the value 250 instead of 220 for "total cash receipts" in the year 2003. Consequently, some constraints are not satisfied on the acquired data for year 2003:

i) in section *Receipts*, the value of *total cash receipts* is not equal to the sum of values of *cash sales* and *receivables*;

ii) the value of *net cash inflow* is not to equal the difference between *total cash receipts* and *total disbursements*.

Furthermore, some symbol recognition errors in non-numerical strings may occur in the acquisition phase. For instance, the item "bgnning cesh" could be recognized instead of "beginning cash". □

DART is a system supporting the acquisition of heterogeneous documents and the supervised repairing of the acquired data. With respect to Example 1, DART will suggest to change the "total cash receipts" value for year 2003 from 250 (i.e. the acquired value) to 220, thus reducing the human intervention, as the human operator is no longer required to access the whole input document to fix acquisition errors making integrity constraints violated. In particular, DART is based on the notion of *card*-minimal repair introduced in [16], where the problem of repairing numerical data which are inconsistent w.r.t. aggregate constraints is addressed. Aggregate constraints defined in [16] can express constraints like those defined in the context of balance-sheet data. The notion of *card*-minimal repair is well-suited for our context, where data inconsistency is due to bad symbol recognition during the acquisition phase. Indeed, applying the *card*-minimal semantics means searching for repairs changing the minimum number of acquired values, which corresponds to the assumption that the minimum number of errors occurred in the acquisition phase.

This work stems from a specific application context, where data to be acquired are balance sheets. In this scenario, the relevant information is formatted according to a tabular layout. Therefore, our acquisition approach is targeted to tabular data. However, observe that this feature does not limit DART to the acquisition of balance sheets, as tabular data often occur in many different application contexts, such as web sites publishing product catalogs.

Related Work

The most widely used notion of repair and consistent query answer on inconsistent data is that of [2]: a repair of an inconsistent database D is a database D' satisfying the given integrity constraints and which is minimally different from D. The consistent answer of a query q posed on D is the answer which is in every result of q on each repair D'. Different approaches to the problem of extracting reliable information from inconsistent data had been introduced in [1,8].

Based on the notions of repair and consistent query answer introduced in [2], several works investigated more expressive classes of queries and constraints. In [3] extended disjunctive logic programs with exceptions were used for the computation of repairs, and in [4] the evaluation of aggregate queries on inconsistent data was investigated. A further generalization was proposed in [19], where the authors defined a sound and complete technique (in presence of universally quantified constraints) based on the rewriting of constraints into extended disjunctive rules with two different forms of negation (negation as failure and classical negation). In [9,10] a practical framework for computing consistent query answer for large relational database has been presented, and the system *Hippo* supporting projection-free relational algebra queries and denial integrity constraints was presented.

All the above-cited approaches assume that tuple insertions and deletions are the basic primitives for repairing inconsistent data. More recently, in [11] a repairing strategy using only tuple deletions was proposed, and in [7,24,25] repairs consisting of also value-update operations were considered. The latter are the first approaches performing repairs at the attribute-value level.

In [6] the problem of repairing databases by fixing numerical data at attribute level was investigated in presence of both denial constraints (where built-in comparison predicates are allowed) and a non-linear form of multi-attribute aggregate constraints (when constraints of this form are defined, the repair existence problem was shown to be undecidable). In [16] the problem of repairing and extracting reliable information from data violating a given set of aggregate constraints was investigated. These constraints consist of linear inequalities on aggregate-sum queries issued on measure values stored in the database. This syntactic form enables meaningful constraints to be expressed, such as those of Example 1 as well as other forms which often occur in practice.

In this work we define a restricted class of aggregate constraints and provide a method to compute a *card*-minimal repair defined in [16] (according to the *card*-minimal semantics, a repaired database D' minimally differs from the original database D iff the number of value updates yielding D' is minimum w.r.t. all other possible repairs). We exploit this computation method in the DART system where data are acquired by means of acquisition tool and information is extracted and transformed by a wrapping system.

There has been a lot of research work related to web information extraction. Specialized information extraction procedures, called *wrappers*, represent an effective solution to capture text contents of interest from a source-native format and encode such contents into a structured format suitable for further application-oriented processing. Web wrappers typically exploit markup-tag and lexical token information to infer the template structuring the contents in a web page.

Traditional issues concerning wrapper systems are the development of powerful languages for expressing extraction patterns and the ability of generating these patterns with the lowest human effort [5,13]. Several systems for generating web wrappers have been recently proposed. We mention here DEByE [20], XWRAP [21], Lixto [5], SCRAP [15,17], RoadRunner [13]. All these systems do not provide any facility for effectively handling tabular data. Indeed, there are no systems that address data extraction from HTML tables in a satisfactory way. In [14] data extraction from HTML tables with unknown structure is addressed. This system fails when dealing with small tables and in finding mappings related to numeric attributes. A wrapper-learning system called WL2 is presented in [12]. It uses very specific extraction rules which can be applied only to documents which are structurally similar to the documents in the training example.

Main contributions

In this work we introduce a system architecture aiming at supervised acquiring of information encoded into tabular data inside documents with possibly heterogeneous formats. Main novelties of our proposal are the following:

1. Our system embeds a wrapping module for extracting information from tabular data. This module can manage tables having "variable" structures, i.e. tables whose cells can span multiple rows and columns, according to no pre-determined scheme. This is a valuable feature, as all existing wrapping techniques do not work at all or are far from being satisfactory on tabular data without a "rigid" structure.
2. A framework for computing *card*-minimal repairs on wrongly acquired data is introduced to drive the data validation process. This framework exploits a specific form of aggregate constraints (namely, *steady aggregate constraints*) defined on the source documents to check the consistency of the acquired data and computing a repair.

Describing our wrapping technique in detail is out of the scope of this paper. Here we will focus on presenting the architecture of our system and the technique adopted for computing repairs.

2 DART in a Nutshell

DART (*Data Acquisition and Repairing Tool*) is a system providing robust data acquisition facilities. It takes as input documents containing tabular data, and it exploits integrity constraints defined on the input data to support the detecting and the repairing of inconsistencies due to errors occurring in the acquisition phase. If acquisition errors are detected, the system proposes a way to correct these errors. Proposed corrections are validated by means of human intervention. In order to detect and repair inconsistencies, integrity constraints are considered expressing algebraic relations among the numerical data reported in the cells of the input tables. These constraints are exploited only to fix the acquired numerical values. Moreover, a dictionary of the terms used in the specific scenario which the input documents refer to is exploited to provide spelling error corrections on non-numerical strings.

Two kinds of user interact with DART, namely the *acquisition designer* and the *operator*. The former is an expert on the application context and specifies the metadata which are used to support both the extraction of tabular data and the repairing process. The latter interacts with the system during the acquisition of each document: if the acquired data need to be corrected, he is prompted to validate proposed corrections.

As shown in Figure 2, DART consists of two macro-modules. The first module takes as input documents containing tabular data and returns a relational database where the extracted tabular data are stored. It performs three steps: it loads the input document and convert it in HTML format, it extracts the tabular data from the HTML document and it transforms them into a database instance. This module exploits metadata specified by the acquisition designer, which describe the structure and the semantics of the input documents[1]. The second module takes as input the database instance D generated by the *acquisition and extraction module*. It locates possible inconsistencies in D and returns a repair for D. Both the inconsistency detection and the repair computation are

[1] As it will be clear in the following, designing an extraction module taking as input HTML documents will make it possible to exploit its features also in Web applications, where the problem of automatically extracting information from HTML pages often arises in many scenarios.

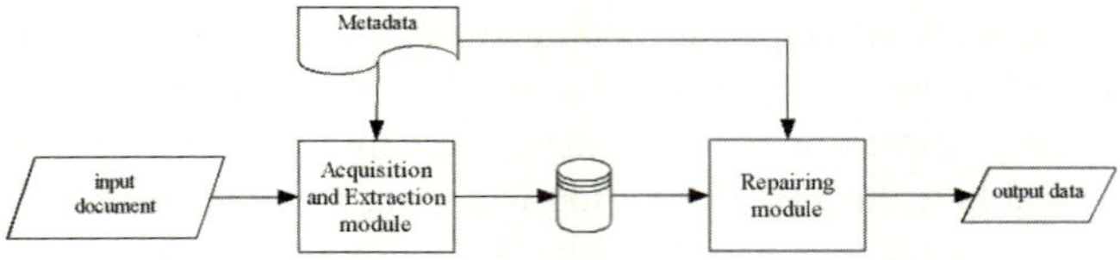

Fig. 2. Data flow in DART

accomplished according to a set of aggregate constraints $\mathcal{AC}$ defined by acquisition designer and represented in the metadata. In more detail, the *repairing module* transforms the problem of finding a *card*-minimal repair[2] for D w.r.t. $\mathcal{AC}$ into an MILP instance (Mixed-Integer Linear Programming problem) and solves it providing a repair for D. The proposed repair is then validated by the operator, who either accepts it or requires to compute a different repair. In fact, it can be the case that the proposed repair is unsatisfactory since the operator realizes that it consists of value updates which do not correspond to the actual content of the source document. In this case the operator inserts further constraints on the acquired data. Basically, he drives the repairing process by specifying the exact values that some pieces of the repaired data must take.

3 Preliminaries

We assume classical notions of database scheme, relational scheme, and relations. In the following we will also use a logical formalism to represent relational databases, and relational schemes will be represented by means of sorted predicates of the form $R(A_1 : \Delta_1, \ldots, A_n : \Delta_n)$, where $A_1, \ldots, A_n$ are attribute names and $\Delta_1, \ldots, \Delta_n$ are the corresponding domains. Each Δ_i can be either $\mathbb{Z}$ (infinite domain of integers), $\mathbb{R}$ (reals), or $\mathbb{S}$ (strings). Domains $\mathbb{R}$ and $\mathbb{Z}$ will be said to be *numerical domains*, and attributes defined over $\mathbb{R}$ or $\mathbb{Z}$ will be said to be *numerical attributes*. Given a ground atom t denoting a tuple, the value of attribute A of t will be denoted as $t[A]$.

Given a database scheme $\mathcal{D}$, we will denote as $\mathcal{M}_\mathcal{D}$ (namely, *Measure attributes*) the set of numerical attributes representing measure data. That is, $\mathcal{M}_\mathcal{D}$ specifies the set of attributes representing measure values, such as weights, lengths, prices, etc. For instance, in Figure 3, $\mathcal{M}_\mathcal{D}$ consists of the only attribute *Value*.

3.1 Aggregate Constraints

Given a relational scheme $R(A_1 : \Delta_1, \ldots, A_n : \Delta_n)$, an *attribute expression* on R is defined recursively as follows:

- a numerical constant is an attribute expression;
  each A_i (with $i \in [1..n]$) is an attribute expression;
- $e_1 \psi e_2$ is an attribute expression on R, if e_1, e_2 are attribute expressions on R and ψ is an arithmetic operator in $\{+, -\}$;
- $c \times (e)$ is an attribute expressions on R, if e is an attribute expression on R and c a numerical constant.

[2] As it will be shown in Section 3.2, a *card*-minimal repair for a database is a repair changing the minimum number of values w.r.t. all possible repairs.

Let R be a relational scheme and e an attribute expression on R. An *aggregation function* on R is a function $\chi : (\Lambda_1 \times \cdots \times \Lambda_k) \to \mathbb{R}$, where each Λ_i is either $\mathbb{Z}$, or $\mathbb{R}$, or $\mathbb{S}$, and it is defined as follows:

$$\chi(x_1, \ldots, x_k) = \texttt{SELECT sum(e)} \quad \texttt{FROM R} \quad \texttt{WHERE } \alpha(x_1, \ldots, x_k)$$

where $\alpha(x_1, \ldots, x_k)$ is a boolean formula on $x_1, \ldots, x_k$, constants and attributes of R.

Example 2. Consider the database scheme $\mathcal{D}$ consisting of the single relation scheme *CashBudget(Year, Section, Subsection, Type, Value)*, and its instance reported in Figure 3. This instance represents a possible output of the *acquisition and extraction module* when DART takes as input the document in Figure 1 (it results from the case that a symbol recognition error occurred in the acquisition phase, so that the acquired value of *total cash receipts* is 250 instead of 220). Values '*det*', '*aggr*' and '*drv*' in column *Type* stand for *detail*, *aggregate* and *derived*, respectively. In particular, an item of the table is *aggregate* if it is obtained by aggregating items of type *detail* of the same section, whereas a *derived* item is an item whose value can be computed using the values of other items of any type and belonging to any section.

Year	*Section*	*Subsection*	*Type*	*Value*
2003	Receipts	beginning cash	drv	20
2003	Receipts	cash sales	det	100
2003	Receipts	receivables	det	120
2003	Receipts	total cash receipts	aggr	250
2003	Disbursements	payment of accounts	det	120
2003	Disbursements	capital expenditure	det	0
2003	Disbursements	long-term financing	det	40
2003	Disbursements	total disbursements	aggr	160
2003	Balance	net cash inflow	drv	60
2003	Balance	ending cash balance	drv	80
...	...	...	...	...
...	...	...	...	...
2004	Receipts	beginning cash	drv	80
2004	Receipts	cash sales	det	100
2004	Receipts	receivables	det	100
2004	Receipts	total cash receipts	aggr	200
2004	Disbursements	payment of accounts	det	130
2004	Disbursements	capital expenditure	det	40
2004	Disbursements	long-term financing	det	20
2004	Disbursements	total disbursements	aggr	190
2004	Balance	net cash inflow	drv	10
2004	Balance	ending cash balance	drv	90

Fig. 3. A cash budget

The following aggregation functions are defined on the relational scheme *CashBudget*:

$$\chi_1(x, y, z) = \texttt{SELECT sum(Value)} \quad \texttt{FROM CashBudget} \quad \texttt{WHERE Section=x AND Year=y AND Type=z}$$

$$\chi_2(x, y) = \texttt{SELECT sum(Value)} \quad \texttt{FROM CashBudget} \quad \texttt{WHERE Year = x AND Subsection=y}$$

Function χ_1 returns the sum of *Value* of all the tuples having *Section* x, *Year* y and *Type* z. For instance, χ_1('Receipts', '2003', 'det') returns $100 + 120 = 220$, whereas χ_1('Disbursements', '2003', 'aggr') returns 160. Function χ_2 returns the sum of *Value* of all the tuples where *Year=x* and *Subsection=y*. In our running example, as the pair *Year*, *Subsection* is a key for the tuples of *CashBudget*, the sum returned by χ_2 is an attribute value of a single tuple. For instance, χ_2('2003', 'cash sales') returns 100, whereas χ_2('2004', 'net cash inflow') returns 10. □

Definition 1 (Aggregate constraint). *Given a database scheme $\mathcal{D}$, an aggregate constraint on $\mathcal{D}$ is an expression of the form:*

$$\forall x_1,\ldots,x_k \left(\phi(x_1,\ldots,x_k) \Longrightarrow \sum_{i=1}^{n} c_i \cdot \chi_i(X_i) \le K \right) \quad (1)$$

where:

1. $c_1,\ldots,c_n,K$ *are constants;*

2. $\phi(x_1,\ldots,x_k)$ *is a conjunction of atoms containing the variables* $x_1,\ldots,x_k$*;*

3. each $\chi_i(X_i)$ *is an aggregation function, where* X_i *is a list of variables and constants, and variables appearing in* X_i *are a subset of* $\{x_1,\ldots,x_k\}$.

Given a database D and a set of aggregate constraints $\mathcal{AC}$, we will use the notation $D \models \mathcal{AC}$ [resp. $D \not\models \mathcal{AC}$] to say that D is consistent [resp. inconsistent] w.r.t. $\mathcal{AC}$. Observe that aggregate constraints enable equalities to be expressed as well, since an equality can be viewed as a pair of inequalities. For the sake of brevity, in the following equalities will be written explicitly.

Example 3. Constraints a) and b) defined in Example 1 can be expressed as: for each section and year, the sum of the values of all *detail* items must be equal to the value of the *aggregate* item of the same section and year, that is:

Constraint 1:

$\forall\, x,y,s,t,v \quad CashBudget(y,x,s,t,v) \Longrightarrow \chi_1(x,y,\text{'det'}) - \chi_1(x,y,\text{'aggr'}) = 0$

□

For the sake of simplicity, in the following we will use a shorter notation for denoting aggregate constraints, where universal quantification is implied and variables in ϕ which do not occur in any aggregation function are replaced with the symbol '_'. For instance, Constraint 1 of Example 3 can be written as:

$CashBudget(y,x,\_,\_,\_) \Longrightarrow \chi_1(x,y,\text{'}det\text{'}) - \chi_1(x,y,\text{'}aggr\text{'}) = 0$

Example 4. Constraints c) and d) of Example 1 can be expressed as follows:

Constraint 2: $CashBudget(x,\_,\_,\_,\_) \Longrightarrow$
$\chi_2(x,\text{'net cash inflow'}) - (\chi_2(x,\text{'total cash receipts'}) - \chi_2(x,\text{'total disbursements'})) = 0$

Constraint 3: $CashBudget(x,\_,\_,\_,\_) \Longrightarrow$
$\chi_2(x,\text{'ending cash balance'}) - (\chi_2(x,\text{'beginning cash'}) + \chi_2(x,\text{'net cash balance'})) = 0$

3.2 Repairing Inconsistent Databases

Updates at attribute-level will be used in the following as the basic primitives for repairing data violating aggregate constraints. Given a relational scheme R in the database scheme $\mathcal{D}$, let $\mathcal{M}_R = \{A_1,\ldots,A_k\}$ be the subset of $\mathcal{M}_\mathcal{D}$ containing all the attributes in R belonging to $\mathcal{M}_\mathcal{D}$.

Definition 2 (Atomic update). *Let* $t = R(v_1,\ldots,v_n)$ *be a tuple on the relational scheme* $R(A_1:\Delta_1,\ldots,A_n:\Delta_n)$*. An* atomic update *on* t *is a triplet* $< t, A_i, v'_i >$*, where* $A_i \in \mathcal{M}_R$ *and* v'_i *is a value in* Δ_i *and* $v'_i \neq v_i$.

Update $u =< t, A_i, v'_i >$ replaces $t[A_i]$ with v'_i, thus yielding the tuple $u(t) = R(v_1,\ldots,v_{i-1},v'_i,v_{i+1},\ldots,v_n)$.

Observe that atomic updates work on the set $\mathcal{M}_R$ of measure attributes, as our framework is based on the assumption that data inconsistency is due to errors in the acquisition phase. Therefore we only consider repairs aiming at re-constructing the correct measure data.

Example 5. Update $u =< t, \mathit{Value}, 130 >$ issued on the following tuple:
$t = \mathit{CashBudget}$(2003, 'Receipts', 'cash sales', 'det', 100)
returns the tuple: $u(t) = \mathit{CashBudget}$(2003, 'Receipts', 'cash sales', 'det', 130). □

Given an update u, we denote the pair $< \mathit{tuple}, \mathit{attribute} >$ updated by u as $\lambda(u)$. That is, if $u = < t, A_i, v >$ then $\lambda(u) =< t, A_i >$.

Definition 3 (Consistent database update). *Let D be a database and $U = \{u_1, \ldots, u_n\}$ be a set of atomic updates on tuples of D. The set U is said to be a* consistent database update *iff $\forall\, j, k \in [1..n]$ if $j \neq k$ then $\lambda(u_j) \neq \lambda(u_k)$.*

Informally, a set of atomic updates U is a consistent database update iff for each pair of updates $u_1, u_2 \in U$, u_1 and u_2 do not work on the same tuples, or they change different attributes of the same tuple.

The set of pairs $< \mathit{tuple}, \mathit{attribute} >$ updated by a consistent database update U will be denoted as $\lambda(U) = \cup_{u_i \in U}\{\lambda(u_i)\}$.

Given a database D and a consistent database update U, performing U on D results in the database $U(D)$ obtained by applying all atomic updates in U.

Definition 4 (Repair). *Let $\mathcal{D}$ be a database scheme, $\mathcal{AC}$ a set of aggregate constraints on $\mathcal{D}$, and D an instance of $\mathcal{D}$ such that $D \not\models \mathcal{AC}$. A* repair *$\rho$ for D is a consistent database update such that $\rho(D) \models \mathcal{AC}$.*

Example 6. A repair ρ for *CashBudget* w.r.t. constraints 1), 2) and 3) consists in decreasing attribute *Value* in the tuple: $t = \mathit{CashBudget}$(2003, 'Receipts', 'total cash receipts', 'aggr', 250) down to 220; that is, $\rho = \{ < t, \mathit{Value}, 220 > \}$. □

If a repair exists, different repairs can be performed on D yielding a new database consistent w.r.t. $\mathcal{AC}$, although not all of them can be considered "reasonable". For instance, if a repair exists for D changing only one value in one tuple of D, any repair updating all values in all tuples of D can be reasonably disregarded. To evaluate whether a repair should be considered "relevant" or not, we use an ordering criteria stating that a repair ρ_1 is preferred w.r.t. a repair ρ_2 if the number of changes issued by ρ_1 is less than ρ_2.

Example 7. Another repair for *CashBudget* is: $\rho' = \{\langle t_1, \mathit{Value}, 130\rangle, \langle t_2, \mathit{Value}, 70\rangle, \langle t_3, \mathit{Value}, 190\rangle\}$, where:

$t_1 = \mathit{CashBudget}$(2003, 'Receipts', cash sales', 'det', 100),
$t_2 = \mathit{CashBudget}$(2003, 'Disbursements', 'long-term financing', 'det', 40),
$t_3 = \mathit{CashBudget}$ (2003, 'Disbursements', 'total disbursements', 'aggr', 160).

Observe that $\rho < \rho'$, where ρ is the repair defined in Example 6. □

Definition 5 (*Card*-minimal repair). *Let $\mathcal{D}$ be a database scheme, $\mathcal{AC}$ a set of aggregate constraints on $\mathcal{D}$, and D an instance of $\mathcal{D}$. A repair ρ for D w.r.t. $\mathcal{AC}$ is* card-minimal repair *iff there is no repair ρ' for D w.r.t. $\mathcal{AC}$ such that $|\lambda(\rho')| < |\lambda(\rho)|$.*

Example 8. Repair ρ of Example 6 is a *card*-minimal repair. □

Given a database D which is not consistent w.r.t. a set of aggregate constraints $\mathcal{AC}$, different *card*-minimal repairs can exist on D. In our running example, repair ρ of Example 6 is the unique *card*-minimal repair.

In [16] the problem of repairing and extracting reliable information from data violating a given set of aggregate constraints has been investigated. It has been shown that 1) given a database D violating a set of aggregate constraints, deciding whether a repair for D exists is NP-complete, and 2) given a database D violating a set of aggregate constraints and a repair ρ for D, deciding whether ρ is a *card*-minimal repair is coNP-complete. Furthermore, the consistent query answer under both the set-minimal and the *card*-minimal semantics has been studied.

Observe that, as the repair-existence problem is NP-complete, there is no ε-approximation algorithm $\mathcal{A}$ [23] for the computation of a *card*-minimal repair for D, unless $P = NP$. Otherwise, running $\mathcal{A}$ would result in obtaining a possible repair for D (not necessarily a *card*-minimal one) in polynomial time.

4 Steady Aggregate Constraints

In this section we introduce a restricted form of aggregate constraints, namely *steady aggregate constraints*. On the one hand, steady aggregate constraints are less expressive than (general) aggregate constraints, but, on the other hand, computing a *card*-minimal repair w.r.t. a set of steady aggregate constraints can be accomplished by solving an instance of an MILP (Mixed Integer Linear Programming) problem. This allows us to adopt standard techniques addressing MILP problems to accomplish the computation of a *card*-minimal repair (as it will be clear in the following, this would not be possible for general aggregate constraints). However, observe that the loss in expressiveness is not dramatic, as steady aggregate constraints suffice to express relevant integrity constraints in many real-life scenarios. For instance, all the aggregate constraints introduced in our running example can be expressed by means of steady aggregate constraints.

Before providing the formal definition of steady aggregate constraint, we introduce some preliminary notations.

Given a relational scheme $R(A_1, \ldots, A_n)$ and a conjunction of atoms ϕ containing the atom $R(x_1, \ldots, x_n)$, we say that the attribute A_j corresponds to the variable x_j, for each $j \in [1..n]$. Given an aggregation function χ_i, we will denote as $\mathcal{W}(\chi_i)$ the union of the set of the attributes appearing in the WHERE clause of χ_i and the set of attributes corresponding to variables appearing in the WHERE clause of χ_i. Given an aggregate constraint κ where the aggregation functions $\chi_1, \ldots, \chi_n$ occur, we will denote as $\mathcal{A}(\kappa)$ the set of attributes $\bigcup_{i=1}^{n} \mathcal{W}(\chi_i)$. Given an aggregate constraint κ, we will denote as $\mathcal{J}(\kappa)$ the set of attributes such that for each $A \in \mathcal{J}(\kappa)$ there are two atoms $R_i(x_{i_1}, \ldots, x_{i_n})$ and $R_j(x_{j_1}, \ldots, x_{j_m})$ in $\phi(x_1, \ldots, x_k)$ satisfying both the following conditions:

1. there are $i_l \in [i_1..i_n]$ and $j_h \in [j_1..j_m]$ such that $x_{i_l} = x_{j_h}$;
2. A corresponds to either x_{i_l} or x_{j_h}.

Basically, $\mathcal{J}(\kappa)$ contains attributes A corresponding to variables shared by two atoms in ϕ.

The reason why sets $\mathcal{A}(\kappa)$ and $\mathcal{J}(\kappa)$ have been introduced is that they allow us to detect a useful property. In fact, in the case that $\mathcal{A}(\kappa) \cup \mathcal{J}(\kappa)$ does not contain any measure attribute, the tuples in the database instance D which are "involved" in κ (i.e. the tuples where ϕ and the WHERE clauses of the aggregation functions in κ evaluate to true) can be detected without looking at the values of their measure attributes. As it will be clear in the following, if this syntactic property holds we can translate κ into a set of linear inequalities and then express the computation of a *card*-minimal repair w.r.t. κ as an instance of MILP.

Definition 6 (Steady aggregate constraint). *Let $\mathcal{D}$ be a database scheme, $\mathcal{M}_{\mathcal{D}}$ the set of measure attributes of $\mathcal{D}$ and κ an aggregate constraint on $\mathcal{D}$. An aggregate constraint κ is said to be a* steady aggregate constraint *if:*

$$(\mathcal{A}(\kappa) \cup \mathcal{J}(\kappa)) \cap \mathcal{M}_{\mathcal{D}} = \emptyset \tag{2}$$

Example 9. Consider a database scheme $\mathcal{D}$ containing the relational schemes $R_1(A_1, A_2, A_3)$ and $R_2(A_4, A_5, A_6)$, where $\mathcal{M}_{\mathcal{D}} = \{A_2, A_4\}$. Let κ be the following aggregate constraint on $\mathcal{D}$:

$$\forall\, x_1, x_2, x_3, x_4, x_5\ (R_1(x_1, x_2, x_3), R_2(x_3, x_4, x_5) \implies \chi(x_2) \leq K) \tag{3}$$

where:

$$\begin{aligned}\chi(x) = &\ \texttt{SELECT sum}(\texttt{A}_6)\\ &\ \texttt{FROM}\quad \texttt{R}_2\\ &\ \texttt{WHERE}\ \ A_5 = x\end{aligned}$$

We have that $\mathcal{A}(\kappa) = \{A_5, A_2\}$ and $\mathcal{J}(\kappa) = \{A_3, A_4\}$, therefore κ is not a steady aggregate constraint.

Consider *Constraint 1* of our running example. We have that $\mathcal{A}(\textit{Constraint 1}) = \{Year, Section, Type\}$ and $\mathcal{J}(\textit{Constraint 1}) = \emptyset$. Since $\mathcal{M}_{\mathcal{D}} = \{Value\}$, Constraint 1 is a steady aggregate constraint. Similarly, it is straightforward to show that also constraints 2) and 3) are steady aggregate constraints. □

5 Computing a *Card*-Minimal Repair

Several theoretical issues regarding the consistent query answer (CQA) problem have been widely investigated for different classes of constraints, and some techniques for evaluating the CQA have been proposed too (see Related Work section). It can be shown that all complexity results (characterizing either the repair existence problem and the consistent query answer problem) given in [16] (where general aggregate constraints were considered) are still valid for our restricted class of aggregate constraints.

Indeed, in our specific application scenario, we are more interested in computing a repair (fixing all the acquired values) than evaluating whether a single acquired value is "reliable". The main contribution of this section is the definition of a technique for computing a *card*-minimal repair for a database w.r.t a set of steady aggregate constraints, which is based on the translation of the repair-evaluation problem into an instance of a mixed-integer linear programming (MILP) problem [18]. Our technique exploits the restrictions imposed on steady aggregate constraints w.r.t. general aggregate constraints to accomplish the computation of a repair. As it will be clear later, this approach does not work for (general) aggregate constraints.

Consider a database scheme $\mathcal{D}$ and a set of steady aggregate constraints $\mathcal{AC}$ on $\mathcal{D}$. In this case, we can model the problem of finding a *card*-minimal repair as MILP problem (if the domain of numerical attributes is restricted to $\mathbb{Z}$ then it can be formulated as an ILP problem).

We first show how a steady aggregate constraint can be expressed by a set of linear inequalities.

Consider the steady aggregate constraint κ:

$$\forall x_1, \ldots, x_k \left(\phi(x_1, \ldots, x_k) \implies \sum_{i=1}^{n} c_i \cdot \chi_i(y_{i_1}, \ldots, y_{i_{m_i}}) \leq K \right) \tag{4}$$

where $\cup_{i=1}^{n}\{y_{i_1}, \ldots y_{i_{m_i}}\}$ is a subset of $\{x_1, \ldots, x_k\}$ and for each $i \in [1..n]$:

$$\begin{aligned} \chi_i(y_{i_1}, \ldots y_{i_{m_i}}) = \ & \texttt{SELECT sum}(\texttt{e}_\texttt{i}) \\ & \texttt{FROM} \quad \texttt{R}_{\chi_\texttt{i}} \\ & \texttt{WHERE} \quad \alpha_i(y_{i_1}, \ldots, y_{i_{m_i}}) \end{aligned}$$

Without loss of generality, we assume that each attribute expression e_i occurring in the aggregation function χ_i is either an attribute or a constant.

We associate a variable z_{t,A_j} to each database value $t[A_j]$, where t is a tuple in the database instance D and A_j is an attribute in $\mathcal{M}_{\mathcal{D}}$. z_{t,A_j} is defined on the same domain as A_j. For every ground substitution θ of $x_1, \ldots, x_k$ such that $\phi(\theta x_1, \ldots, \theta x_k)$ is true, we will denote as T_{χ_i} the set of the tuples involved in the aggregation function χ_i, that is $T_{\chi_i} = \{t : t \models \alpha_i(\theta y_{i_1}, \ldots, \theta y_{i_{m_i}})\}$.
The translation of χ_i, denoted as $\mathcal{P}(\chi_i)$, is defined as follows:

$$\mathcal{P}(\chi_i) = \begin{cases} \sum_{t \in T_{\chi_i}} z_{t,A_j} & \text{if } e_i = A_j; \\ e_i \cdot |T_{\chi_i}| & \text{if } e_i \text{ is a constant.} \end{cases}$$

Starting from $\mathcal{P}(\chi_i)$, the whole constraint κ can be expressed as a set $\mathcal{S}$ of linear inequalities as follows. For every ground substitution θ of $x_1, \ldots, x_k$ such that $\phi(\theta x_1, \ldots, \theta x_k)$ is true, $\mathcal{S}$ contains the following inequality:

$$\sum_{i=1}^{n} c_i \cdot \mathcal{P}(\chi_i) \leq K \tag{5}$$

Observe that this construction is not possible for a non-steady aggregate constraint since, given a database instance D and an aggregation function χ_i in the constraint, we cannot determine T_{χ_i}: changing a measure value might result in changing the set of the tuples involved the aggregation function.

For the sake of simplicity, in the following we associate to each pair $\langle t, A_j \rangle$ an integer index i, therefore we write z_i instead of z_{t,A_j}. If we assume that the number of values involved in constraints in $\mathcal{AC}$ concerning the given database instance D is N then the index i will take values in $[1..N]$.

As shown above, we can translate each steady aggregate constraint into a system linear inequalities. The translation of all aggregate constraints in $\mathcal{AC}$ produces the system of linear inequalities $A \cdot Z \leq B$, where $Z = [z_1, z_2, \ldots, z_N]^T$. This system will be denoted as $\mathcal{S}(\mathcal{AC})$.

Example 10. Consider the database scheme $\mathcal{D}$ of our running example, the database instance in Figure 3 and the set of aggregate constraints $\mathcal{AC}$ consisting of constraints 1), 2) and 3). The values involved in constraints in $\mathcal{AC}$ w.r.t. the given database instance in Figure 3 are as many as the number of tuples, that is $N = 20$. Therefore, z_i, with $i \in [1..20]$ is the variable associated to the database value $t[Value]$, where t is the i-th tuple in Figure 3. For instance, z_2 is the variable associated with the value of attribute *Value* in the tuple $t =$ *CashBudget*(2003, 'Receipts', 'cash sales', 'det', 100).

The translation of constraints 1), 2) and 3) is the following, where we explicitly write equalities instead of inequalities:

$$1) \begin{cases} z_2 + z_3 = z_4 \\ z_5 + z_6 + z_7 = z_8 \\ z_{12} + z_{13} = z_{14} \\ z_{15} + z_{16} + z_{17} = z_{18} \end{cases} \quad 2) \begin{cases} z_4 - z_8 = z_9 \\ z_{14} - z_{18} = z_{19} \end{cases} \quad 3) \begin{cases} z_1 - z_9 = z_{10} \\ z_{11} - z_{19} = z_{20} \end{cases}$$

$\mathcal{S}(\mathcal{AC})$ consists of the system obtained by assembling all the equalities reported above (basically, it is the intersection of systems 1,2,3). □

In the following we will denote the current database value corresponding to the variable z_i as v_i. That is, if z_i is associated with $t[A_j]$, then $v_i = t[A_j]$. Every solution s of $\mathcal{S}(\mathcal{AC})$ corresponds to a (possibly non-minimal) repair $\rho(s)$ of D w.r.t. $\mathcal{AC}$. In particular, for each variable z_i which is assigned a value different from v_i, repair $\rho(s)$ contains an atomic update assigning the value z_i to the database item corresponding to z_i.

In order to decide whether a solution s of $\mathcal{S}(\mathcal{AC})$ corresponds to a *card*-minimal repair, we must count the number of variables of s which are assigned a value different from the corresponding source value in D. This is accomplished as follows. For each $i \in [1..N]$, we define a variable $y_i = z_i - v_i$ on the same domain as z_i. Consider the following system of linear inequalities, which will be denoted as $\mathcal{S}'(\mathcal{AC})$:

$$\begin{cases} AZ \leq B \\ y_i = z_i - v_i \quad \forall i \in [1..N] \end{cases} \tag{6}$$

As shown in [22], if a system of equalities has a solution, it has also a solution where each variable takes a value in $[-M, M]$, where M is a constant equal to $n \cdot (ma)^{2m+1}$, where m is the number of equalities, n is the number of variables and a is the maximum value among the modules of the system coefficients. It is straightforward to see that $\mathcal{S}'(\mathcal{AC})$ can be translated into a system of linear equalities in augmented form with $m = N + r$ and $n = 2 \cdot N + r$, where r is the number of rows of A[3].

In order to detect if a variable z_i is assigned (for each solution of $\mathcal{S}'(\mathcal{AC})$ bounded by M) a value different from the original value v_i (that is, if $|y_i| > 0$), a new binary variable δ_i will be defined. δ_i will have value 1 if the value of z_i differs from v_i, 0 otherwise. To express this condition, we add the following constraints to $\mathcal{S}'(\mathcal{AC})$:

$$\begin{cases} y_i \leq M\delta_i \quad \forall i \in [1..N] \\ -M\delta_i \leq y_i \quad \forall i \in [1..N] \\ \delta_i \in \{0,1\} \quad \forall i \in [1..N] \end{cases} \tag{7}$$

[3] Observe that the size of M is polynomial in the size of the database, as it is bounded by $\log n + (2 \cdot m + 1) \cdot \log(ma)$.

The system obtained by assembling $\mathcal{S}'(\mathcal{AC})$ with inequalities (7) will be denoted as $\mathcal{S}''(\mathcal{AC})$. For each solution s'' of $\mathcal{S}''(\mathcal{AC})$, the following hold: 1) for each z_i which is assigned in s'' a value greater than v_i, the variable δ_i is assigned 1 (this is entailed by constraint $y_i \leq M\delta_i$); 2) for each z_i which is assigned in s'' a value less than v_i, the variable δ_i is assigned 1 (this is entailed by constraint $-M\delta_i \leq y_i$). Moreover, for each z_i which is assigned in s'' the same value as v_i (that is, $y_i = 0$), variable δ_i is assigned either 0 or 1.

Obviously each solution of $\mathcal{S}''(\mathcal{AC})$ corresponds to exactly one solution for $\mathcal{S}(\mathcal{AC})$ (or, analogously, for $\mathcal{S}'(\mathcal{AC})$) with the same values for variables z_i, and, vice versa, for each solution of $\mathcal{S}(\mathcal{AC})$ whose variables are bounded by M there is at least one solution of $\mathcal{S}''(\mathcal{AC})$ with the same values for variables z_i. As solutions of $\mathcal{S}(\mathcal{AC})$ correspond to repairs for D, each solution of $\mathcal{S}''(\mathcal{AC})$ corresponds to a repair ρ for D w.r.t. $\mathcal{AC}$ such that, for each update $u = \langle t, A, v\rangle$ in ρ it holds that $|v| \leq M$. Repairs satisfying this property will be said to be *M-bounded repairs*.

In order to consider only the solutions of $\mathcal{S}''(\mathcal{AC})$ where each δ_i is 0 if $y_i = 0$, we consider the following optimization problem $\mathcal{S}^*(\mathcal{AC})$, whose goal is minimizing the sum of the values assigned to the variables $\delta_1, \ldots, \delta_N$:

$$\min \sum_{i=1}^{N} \delta_i \\ \begin{cases} AZ \leq B \\ y_i = z_i - v_i \quad \forall i \in [1..N] \\ y_i - M\delta_i \leq 0 \quad \forall i \in [1..N] \\ -y_i - M\delta_i \leq 0 \quad \forall i \in [1..N] \\ z_i, y_i \in \mathbb{R} \quad \forall i \in I_{\mathbb{R}} \\ z_i, y_i \in \mathbb{Z} \quad \forall i \in I_{\mathbb{Z}} \\ \delta_i \in \{0,1\} \quad \forall i \in [1..N] \end{cases} \tag{8}$$

where $I_{\mathbb{R}} \subseteq \{1, \ldots, N\}$ and $I_{\mathbb{Z}} \subseteq \{1, \ldots, N\}$ are the sets of the indexes of the variables $z_1, \ldots, z_N$ (and, equivalently, $y_1, \ldots, y_N$) defined on the domains $\mathbb{R}$ and $\mathbb{Z}$, respectively.

It is straightforward to see that any solution of $\mathcal{S}^*(\mathcal{AC})$ corresponds to an M-bounded repair ρ for D w.r.t. $\mathcal{AC}$ having minimum cardinality w.r.t. all M-bounded repairs for D w.r.t. $\mathcal{AC}$. It can be shown that if there is a repair for D w.r.t. $\mathcal{AC}$, then there is an M-bounded *card*-minimal repair ρ^* for D (this follows from Lemma 1 in [16]). This implies that any solution of $\mathcal{S}^*(\mathcal{AC})$ corresponds to a *card*-minimal repair for D w.r.t. $\mathcal{AC}$.

Basically, the minimum value of the objective function of $\mathcal{S}^*(\mathcal{AC})$ represents the number of atomic updates performed by any *card*-minimal repair, whereas the values of variables $z_1, \ldots, z_N, y_1, \ldots, y_N, \delta_1, \ldots, \delta_N$ corresponding to an optimum solution s^* of $\mathcal{S}^*(\mathcal{AC})$ define the atomic updates performed by the *card*-minimal repair $\rho(s^*)$.

Example 11. The optimization problem obtained starting from the database in the Figure 3 of our running example and from the set of steady aggregate constraints consisting of 1), 2) and 3) is shown in Figure 4. Specifically, since it is assumed that the domain of attribute $Value$ of relation $CashBudget$ is $\mathbb{Z}$, then $I_{\mathbb{Z}} = \{1, \ldots, 20\}$ and $I_{\mathbb{R}} = \emptyset$. The value of the constant M is $20 \cdot (28 \cdot 250)^{2 \cdot 28+1}$.

The minimum value of the objective function of this optimization problem is 1 (only $\delta_4 = 1$). This problem admits only one optimum solution where the value of each variable $y_1, \ldots, y_{20}$ is 0 except for y_4 that takes value -30. The *card*-minimal repair corresponding to this solution is that of Example 6. □

$$\min \sum_{i=1}^{20} \delta_i$$
$$\begin{cases}
z_2 + z_3 = z_4 & y_4 = z_4 - 250 & y_{15} = z_{15} - 130 \\
z_5 + z_6 + z_7 = z_8 & y_5 = z_5 - 120 & y_{16} = z_{16} - 40 \\
z_{12} + z_{13} = z_{14} & y_6 = z_6 - 0 & y_{17} = z_{17} - 20 \\
z_{15} + z_{16} + z_{17} = z_{18} & y_7 = z_7 - 40 & y_{18} = z_{18} - 190 \\
z_4 - z_8 = z_9 & y_8 = z_8 - 160 & y_{19} = z_{19} - 10 \\
z_{14} - z_{18} = z_{19} & y_9 = z_9 - 60 & y_{20} = z_{20} - 90 \\
z_1 - z_9 = z_{10} & y_{10} = z_{10} - 80 & y_i - M\delta_i \leq 0 \quad \forall i \in [1..20] \\
z_{11} - z_{19} = z_{20} & y_{11} = z_{11} - 80 & -y_i - M\delta_i \leq 0 \quad \forall i \in [1..20] \\
y_1 = z_1 - 20 & y_{12} = z_{12} - 100 & z_i, y_i \in \mathbb{Z} \quad \forall i \in [1..20] \\
y_2 = z_2 - 100 & y_{13} = z_{13} - 100 & \delta_i \in \{0, 1\} \quad \forall i \in [1..20] \\
y_3 = z_3 - 120 & y_{14} = z_{14} - 200 &
\end{cases}$$

Fig. 4. MILP-problem instance for the running example

6 DART Architecture

The DART architecture is shown in Figure 5, where the organization of both the *Acquisition and extraction module* and the *Repairing module* of Figure 2 are described in more detail. In the following we discuss the tasks accomplished by these modules.

6.1 Acquisition Module

This module performs the task of acquiring the information contained in the (either electronic or paper) input documents, and represents it into an electronic document whose format is suitable for the extraction phase accomplished by the *Data Extraction Module*. As the current implementation of DART embeds a wrapper working on HTML documents, input documents which are not already in this format are converted into an HTML document by means of a format-conversion tool (in the current implementation this tool supports the conversion of PDF, MSWord, RTF documents). In particular, paper documents are first digitized and processed by means of an OCR tool (yielding PDF documents) whose output is then processed by the converter.

6.2 Data Extraction Module

The *Data extraction module* carries out both the information extraction and the database generation tasks. The former task is accomplished by a wrapping sub-module which takes as input the HTML document generated by the *Acquisition module* as well as a set of extraction metadata providing information on the semantics and the structure of data contained into the input document.

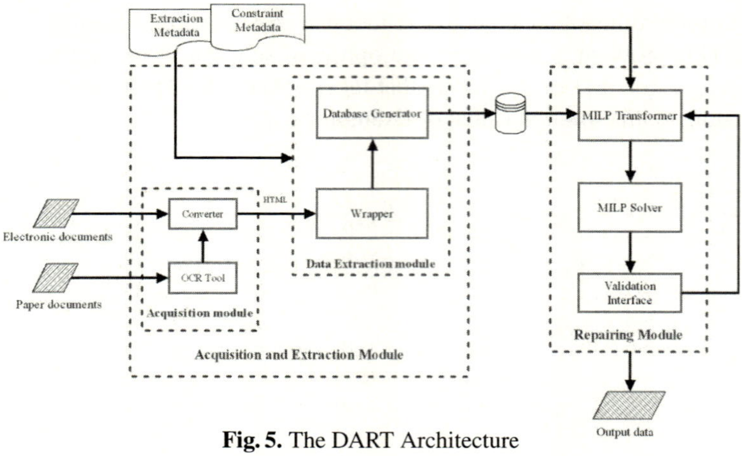

Fig. 5. The DART Architecture

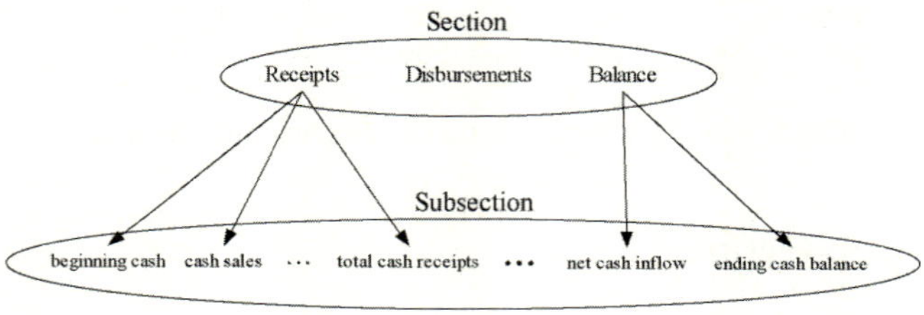

Fig. 6. Domains and hierarchical relationships

Wrapper

Data to be extracted from the input HTML document are contained into tables whose position inside the document is specified inside the extraction metadata. The information encoded into each table is extracted by evaluating whether its rows match some patterns (namely *row patterns*) defining structure and content of the data to be extracted.

Before explaining how the wrapping sub-module works, we give some details about the set of extraction metadata.

This set contains *domain descriptions*, *row patterns* and *hierarchical relationships*. *Domain descriptions* specify a set of domains and the sets of lexical items that belongs to each domain. For instance, considering the balance sheet analysis context, *Section* and *Subsection* are domains. Some lexical items belonging to the former are "Receipts", "Disbursements", "Balance", whereas some lexical items belonging to the latter are "beginning cash", "receivables", "payment of accounts" and "capital expenditure". In the following we will denote the set of these domains as Dom. *Hierarchical relationships* are relations among lexical items belonging to different domains. For instance, the items "beginning cash", "cash sales", "receivables" and "total cash receipts" are specializations of "Receipts". Figure 6 depicts some domains, some lexical items belonging to them and some hierarchical relationships represented by means of arrows. A *row pattern* specifies the structure and the content of a table row. The structure is given specifying an ordered set of cells. The content of a cell is either a domain belonging to Dom or a *standard domain* such as *Integer*, *String*, etc. A row pattern r matches a row r_t of a table in an input document if r and r_t have the same number of cells and if the content of the i-th cell of r_t matches the domain specified into the i-th cell of r. A row pattern contains an headline indicating the semantics of the domains specified in the cells. The headline will be exploited in the database generation task to construct a relation scheme. In a row pattern, hierarchical relationships can be specified among lexical items expected in some cells. For instance, it is possible to require that a lexical item expected in a cell must be a generalization of another lexical item required in another cell.

Example 12. Consider the row pattern shown in Figure 7(a). The headline consists of the cells with the dashed border. The row pattern indicates that the rows which must be extracted from the input table consist of 4 cells. In particular, both the first and the last cells specify that a value of type *Integer* is required, and the headline specifies that the first value is interpreted as *Year* and the last as *Value*. The second cell indicates that a lexical item s_1 belonging to the *Section* domain is expected. The third cell imposes a hierarchical relationship, indicated by an arrow. It specifies that a lexical item s_2 belonging to the *Subsection* domain is required, and that s_2 must be specialization of s_1. □

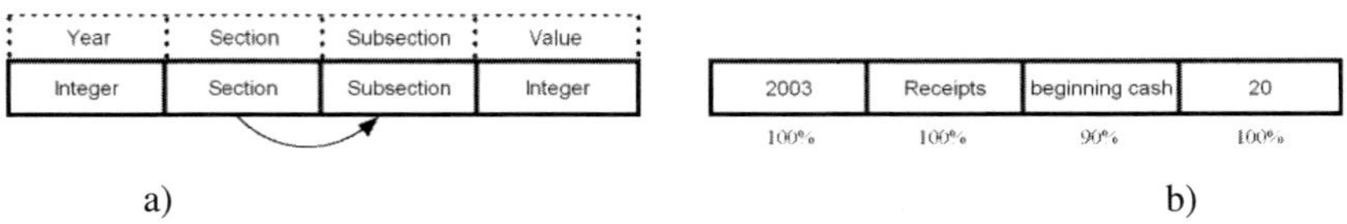

Fig. 7. a)A row pattern b)A row pattern instance

The wrapper takes as input a set of row patterns and the HTML document returned by the acquisition module, and returns a set of *row pattern instances*. A row pattern instance is the result of the matching between a table row and the set of row patterns. First, for each row r_t of the input table, the wrapper identifies the row pattern r that matches r_t at best, i.e. it chooses the row pattern having the most similar structure and the most compatible content w.r.t. r_t. After this choice the wrapper constructs the row pattern instance p relative to r.

In more detail, the evaluation of the matching between a table row and a row pattern yields a score representing the matching degree. The matching is performed comparing the table cells and the corresponding row pattern cells. The comparison between a row pattern cell and an input table cell yields a cell matching score. The whole row pattern instance is associated with a score obtained by applying a suitable t-norm to all the matching scores of its cells.

Each cell matching score results from "validating" the string s in the table cell w.r.t the domain d specified in the cell of the row pattern. The validation of s w.r.t. d is accomplished by identifying the item s' in d which is the most similar [4] to s, and returning the similarity degree between s' and s. Given a string s and a domain d we denote the item in d which is the most similar to s as $msi(d, s)$. The string [resp. the domain] contained in the i-th cell of a document row r_t [resp. row pattern r] will be denoted as $r_t(i)$ [resp. $r(i)$].

[4] s' must also satisfy the hierarchical relationships specified in the row pattern.

For each document row r_t, the row pattern r for which the matching degree is maximum is chosen. Then a row pattern instance p is constructed, where the i-th cell of p contains the item $msi(r(i), r_t(i))$.

Observe that the construction of the row pattern instance is a form of repair on the input data. Indeed, incorrect items in the input tables (i.e. items which do not belong to the corresponding domain in the specified row pattern) are transformed into the most similar valid lexical items.

Finally, we obtain a set of row pattern instances such that each document row is mapped on a row pattern instance.

Example 13. Consider the document in Figure 1 and the row pattern in Figure 7(a). Assume that a symbol recognition error in non-numerical string occurs, like the recognizing of the item "bgnning cesh" instead of "beginning cash". The matching between the first document row and this row pattern returns the row pattern instance in Figure 7(b), where *Integer* in the first cell is bound to "2003", *Section* to "Receipts", *Subsection* to "beginning cash" and *Integer* in the last cell is bound to "20". In Figure 7(b) the matching scores for the cells are also depicted. The third cell score (90%) is lower than the others (100%), since it comes from a non-exact match.

Note that the value "2003" is coded into a multi-row cell of the input table, and it is bound in this row pattern instance since the wrapper considers this value associated to all the document rows which are adjacent to the multi-row cell. □

Database Generator

The *Database generator* sub-module takes as input the set of row pattern instances returned by the wrapper module and returns a database instance D conforming to the database scheme defined in the extraction metadata.

Extraction metadata specify also *classification information* providing classification of lexical items depending on the role they play in aggregation constraints. For instance, in Example 1 lexical items in the domain *Subsection* are classified as *detail*, *aggregate* and *derived* items (the meaning of these classes has been defined in Example 2).

The definition of the database scheme contained in the extraction metadata contains both the definition of the relational scheme (that is, the name of the relations and, for each relation, the names of its attributes) and the correspondence between each relation scheme and the row pattern instances taken as input. For instance in our running example the relational scheme specified in the extraction metadata consists of *CashBudget(Year, Section, Subsection, Type, Value)*. Moreover, the extraction metadata contain the specification that attributes *Year, Section, Subsection, Value* correspond to the cells of the row pattern instances described by the same names in the headline, whereas the attribute *Type* is determined by classification information.

Each row pattern instance taken as input is exploited to insert a new tuple in the corresponding relation. For instance, each tuple t in Figure 3 is obtained from a row pattern instance r returned by the wrapper. In particular, the values of the attributes *Year, Section, Subsection, Value* in t are taken from the corresponding cells of the row pattern instance r. Moreover the value of the attribute *Type* is implied by the value of the attribute *Subsection* according to classification information.

6.3 Repairing Module

The input of the repairing module is the database D obtained by the data extraction module and a set $\mathcal{AC}$ of steady aggregate constraints implied by the constraint metadata. The repairing module returns a *card*-minimal repair for D w.r.t. $\mathcal{AC}$. This is accomplished by means two phases: first, the problem of finding a *card*-minimal repair for D w.r.t. $\mathcal{AC}$ is translated into an instance of an MILP problem (as we have shown in Section 5), and then such an obtained MILP instance is solved by means of an MILP solver, which is implemented using LINDO API 4.0 (available at `www.lindo.com`).

Validation Interface
The *Validation Interface* is the component allowing the *operator* to interact with DART. When a document is processed, the *Validation Interface* displays the repair computed by the *Repairing module* by showing the suggested set of value updates. Then, the operator examines the proposed repair by comparing every updated value with the corresponding source value in the input document. If the operator verifies that the suggested updated values are equal to the corresponding source values, then the repair is accepted and the repaired data is considered as consistent. Otherwise, a new repair is computed by the *Repairing module* according to operator "instructions". That is, for each suggested update u which has not been accepted by the operator, the operator can specify the actual source value v corresponding to the database item d changed by u. Then an aggregate constraint is added to the set of constraints inputted into the MILP transformer, forcing the value of d to be equal to v. Similarly, accepting an update u on the database item d is translated into an aggregate constraint forcing the value of d to be equal to the value suggested by the repair. After this, a new repair is computed, corresponding to the solution of the new MILP instance obtained by assembling the aggregate constraints resulting from *Constraint Metadata* with those resulting from operator validation. This process goes on until the generated repair is accepted by the operator.

At each iteration, the operator is not requested to validate values which had been already validated in a previous iteration. Moreover, the computation of a repair can be re-started after validating only some of the suggested updates. Every repair is proposed to the operator by displaying its updates in a specific order. That is, an update u_2 is displayed before another update u_2 if the database item d_1 changed by u_1 is involved in a larger number of ground aggregate constraints than the database item d_2 changed by u_2 (i.e. if the variable corresponding to d_1 occurs in the MILP instance in a larger number of inequalities than the variable corresponding to d_2). This ordered displaying is an heuristics which is useful in the case that the operator chooses to re-start the repair computation after a small number of validations, and it aims at finding an acceptable repair in a small number of iterations.

7 Conclusions and Future Works

DART is currently being developed. Both the *Acquisition and extraction* module and the *Repairing* module have been implemented, but no user-friendly interface is currently available. Preliminary tests show that DART effectively supports the acquisition of balance data, providing the correct repair of wrongly acquired data in a few iterations in most cases. A more extensive experimental evaluation of system effectiveness will be accomplished on larger data sets when a user-friendly visual interface will be available.

References

1. Agarwal, S., Keller, A. M., Wiederhold, G., Saraswat, K., Flexible Relation: An Approach for Integrating Data from Multiple, Possibly Inconsistent Databases, *Proc. International Conference on Data Engineering (ICDE)*, 495–504, 1995.
2. Arenas, M., Bertossi, L. E., Chomicki, J., Consistent Query Answers in Inconsistent Databases, *Proc. Symposium on Principles of Database Systems (PODS)*, 68–79, 1999.
3. Arenas, M., Bertossi, L. E., Chomicki, J., Specifying and Querying Database Repairs using Logic Programs with Exceptions, *Proc. International Conference on Flexible Query Answering Systems (FQAS)*, 27–41, 2000.
4. Arenas, M., Bertossi, L. E., Chomicki, J., He, X., Raghavan, V., Spinrad, J., Scalar aggregation in inconsistent databases, *Theoretical Computer Science*, Vol. 3(296), 405–434, 2003.
5. Baumgartner, R., Flesca, S., Gottlob, G., Visual Web Information Extraction with Lixto, *Proc. International Conference on Very Large Data Bases (VLDB)*, 119–128, 2001.
6. Bertossi, L., Bravo, L., Franconi, E., Lopatenko, A., Complexity and Approximation of Fixing Numerical Attributes in Databases Under Integrity Constraints, *Proc. International Symposium on Database Programming Languages (DBPL)*, 262–278, 2005.
7. Bohannon, P., Flaster, M., Fan, W., Rastogi, R., A Cost-Based Model and Effective Heuristic for Repairing Constraints by Value Modification, *Proc. ACM SIGMOD International Conference on Management of Data (SIGMOD)*, 143–154, 2005.
8. Bry, F., Query Answering in Information Systems with Integrity Constraints, *IFIP WG 11.5 Working Conference on Integrity and Control in Information Systems*, 113–130, 1997.
9. Chomicki, J., Marcinkowski, J., Staworko, S., Computing consistent query answers using conflict hypergraphs, *Proc. International Conference on Information and Knowledge Management (CIKM)*, 417–426, 2004.
10. Chomicki, J., Marcinkowski, J., Staworko, S., Hippo: A System for Computing Consistent Answers to a Class of SQL Queries, *Proc. International Conference on Extending Database Technology (EDBT)*, 841–844, 2004.
11. Chomicki, J., Marcinkowski, J., Minimal-Change Integrity Maintenance Using Tuple Deletions, *Information and Computation (IC)*, Vol. 197(1-2), 90–121, 2005.
12. Cohen, W. W., Hurst, M., Jensen, L. S., A flexible learning system for wrapping tables and lists in HTML documents, *Proc. International World Wide Web Conference (WWW)*, 232–241, 2002.
13. Crescenzi, V., Mecca, G., Merialdo, P., RoadRunner: Towards Automatic Data Extraction from Large Web Sites, *Proc. International Conference on Very Large Data Bases (VLDB)*, 109–118, 2001.
14. Embley, D. W., Tao, C., Liddle, S. W., Automating the extraction of data from HTML tables with unknown structure, *Data & Knowledge Engineering*, Vol. 54(1) 3–28, 2005.
15. Fazzinga, B., Flesca, S., Tagarelli, A., Learning Robust Web Wrappers, *Proc. International Conference on Database and Expert Systems Applications (DEXA)*, 736–745, 2005.
16. Flesca, S., Furfaro, F., Parisi, F., Consistent Query Answer on Numerical Databases under Aggregate Constraint, *Proc. International Symposium on Database Programming Languages (DBPL)*, 279–294 2005.
17. Flesca, S., Tagarelli, A., Schema-Based Web Wrapping, *Proc. International Conference on Conceptual Modeling (ER)*, 286–299, 2004.

18. Gass, S.I., Linear Programming Methods and Applications, *McGrawHill*, 1985.
19. Greco, G., Greco, S., Zumpano, E., A Logical Framework for Querying and Repairing Inconsistent Databases, *IEEE Transactions on Knowledge and Data Engineering (TKDE)*, Vol. 15(6), 1389–1408, 2003.
20. Laender, A. H. F., Ribeiro-Neto, B. A., da Silva, A. S., DEByE - Data Extraction By Example, *Data & Knowledge Engineering*, Vol. 40(2), 121–154, 2002.
21. Liu, L., Pu, C., Han, W., XWRAP: An XML-Enabled Wrapper Construction System for Web Information Sources, *Proc. International Conference on Data Engineering (ICDE)*, 611–621, 2000.
22. Papadimitriou, C. H., On the complexity of integer programming, *Journal of the Association for Computing Machinery (JACM)*, Vol. 28(4), 765–768, 1981.
23. Papadimitriou, C. H., Computational Complexity, *Addison-Wesley*, 1994.
24. Wijsen, J., Condensed Representation of Database Repairs for Consistent Query Answering, *Proc. International Conference on Database Theory (ICDT)*, 378–393, 2003.
25. Wijsen, J., Making More Out of an Inconsistent Database, *Proc. International Conference on Advances in Databases and Information Systems (ADBIS)*, 291–305, 2004.

Preference-Driven Querying of Inconsistent Relational Databases*

Slawomir Staworko[1], Jan Chomicki[1], and Jerzy Marcinkowski[2]

[1] University at Buffalo
{staworko, chomicki}@cse.buffalo.edu
[2] Wroclaw University
Jerzy.Marcinkowski@ii.uni.wroc.pl

Abstract. One of the goals of cleaning an inconsistent database is to remove conflicts between tuples. Typically, the user specifies how the conflicts should be resolved. Sometimes this specification is incomplete, and the cleaned database may still be inconsistent. At the same time, data cleaning is a rather drastic approach to conflict resolution: It removes tuples from the database, which may lead to information loss and inaccurate query answers.

We investigate an approach which constitutes an alternative to data cleaning. The approach incorporates preference-driven conflict resolution into query answering. The database is not changed. These goals are achieved by augmenting the framework of consistent query answers through various notions of preferred repair. We axiomatize desirable properties of preferred repair families and propose different notions of repair optimality. Finally, we investigate the computational complexity implications of introducing preferences into the computation of consistent query answers.

1 Introduction

In many novel database applications, violations of integrity constraints cannot be avoided. A typical example is integration of two consistent data sources that contribute conflicting information. At the same time the sources are autonomous and cannot be changed. Inconsistencies also occur in the context of long running operations. Finally, integrity enforcement may be neglected because of efficiency considerations.

Integrity constraints, however, often capture important semantic properties of the stored data. These properties directly influence the way a user formulates a query. Evaluation of the query over an inconsistent database may negatively affect the meaning of the answers.

Example 1. Consider the schema

$$Mgr(Name, Dept, Salary, Reports)$$

* Research supported by NSF Grants IIS-0119186 and IIS-0307434.

T. Grust et al. (Eds.): EDBT 2006 Workshops, LNCS 4254, pp. 318–335, 2006.

together with with two key dependencies:

$$Dept \rightarrow Name\,Salary\,Reports, \qquad (fd_1)$$
$$Name \rightarrow Dept\,Salary\,Reports, \qquad (fd_2)$$

In an instance of this schema a tuple (x, y, z, v) denotes the fact that x manages the department y, receives a salary z, and is required to write v reports annually.

Now suppose we integrate the following (consistent) sources:

$$s_1 = \{(Mary, R\&D, 40k, 3)\}, \quad s_2 = \{(John, R\&D, 10k, 2)\},$$
$$s_3 = \{(Mary, IT, 20k, 1), (John, PR, 30k, 4)\}.$$

The integrated instance $r = s_1 \cup s_2 \cup s_3$ contains 3 conflicts:

1. $(Mary, R\&D, 40k, 3)$ and $(John, R\&D, 10k, 2)$ w.r.t. fd_1,
2. $(Mary, R\&D, 40k, 3)$ and $(Mary, IT, 20k, 1)$ w.r.t. fd_2,
3. $(John, R\&D, 10k, 2)$ and $(John, PR, 30k, 4)$ w.r.t. fd_2.

These inconsistencies may result from changes that are not yet fully propagated. For example, $Mary$ may have been promoted to manage $R\&D$ whose previous manager $John$ was moved to manage PR, or conversely, $John$ may have been moved to manage $R\&D$, while $Mary$ was moved from $R\&D$ to manage IT.

Consider the query Q_1 asking if $John$ earns more than $Mary$:

$$\exists x_1, y_1, z_1, x_2, y_2, z_2. Mgr(Mary, x_1, y_1, z_1) \wedge Mgr(John, x_2, y_2, z_2) \wedge y_1 < y_2.$$

The answer to Q_1 in r is true but this is misleading because r may not correspond to any actual state of the world.

One way to deal with the impact of inconsistencies in the results of the query evaluation is *data cleaning* [18]. Although there exist a wide variety of tools for automatic elimination of duplicates, extraction and standardization of information, there are practically no tools that automatically resolve integrity constraint violations [20]. Usually, the user is responsible for providing a procedure that decides how the conflicts should be resolved. The standard repertoire of actions that can be performed on a conflicting tuple is [24]: removing the tuple, leaving the tuple, or reporting the tuple to an auxiliary (*contingency*) table. Typically, the data cleaning system provides useful information which may include:

– the timestamp of creation/last modification of the tuple (the conflicts can be resolved by removing from consideration old, outdated tuples),
– the source of the information of the tuple (a user can consider the data from one source more reliable than the data from the other).

Applying of data cleaning has several shortcomings:

– If the user provides insufficient information to resolve all the conflicts then data cleaning results in an inconsistent database; this again may lead to misleading answers.

- Physically removing the tuples from the database may lead to information loss.
- Data cleaning does not allow to utilize the incomplete information often present in inconsistencies.

The framework of *repairs* and *consistent query answers* [1] incorporates an alternative approach to deal with inconsistent databases, geared toward utilizing incomplete information. A *repair* is a consistent database minimally different from the given one, and a *consistent answer* to a query is the answer present in *every* repair. This approach does not remove physically any tuples from the database. The framework of [1] has served as a foundation for most of the subsequent work in the area of querying inconsistent databases (for recent developments see [5,13], for the surveys of the area see [4,3,8]).

Example 2. The instance r of Example 1 has 3 repairs:

$$\begin{aligned} r_1 &= \{(Mary, R\&D, 40k, 3), (John, PR, 30k, 4)\}, \\ r_2 &= \{(John, R\&D, 10k, 2), (Mary, IT, 20k, 1)\}, \\ r_3 &= \{(Mary, IT, 20k, 1), (John, PR, 30k, 4)\}. \end{aligned}$$

Because Q_1 is false in r_1 and r_2, true is not a consistent answer to Q_1.

The standard framework of consistent query answers does not contain any way to incorporate additional user input about how to resolve some conflicts. One can attempt to first clean the database and then use the consistent query answers approach. However, this is a radical approach: removing tuples may lead to information loss. Instead, we propose to use additional user input in the form of preferences to select only the *preferred* repairs. Query answers present in every preferred repair are called *preferred consistent query answers.*

Example 3. Suppose the user finds the source s_3 to be less reliable than s_1 and less reliable than s_2. The user does not know, however, the relative reliability of the sources s_1 and s_2. The cleaning of r with this information yields an inconsistent database:

$$r' = \{(Mary, R\&D, 40k, 3), (John, R\&D, 10k, 2)\}.$$

Consider the query Q_2 asking if $Mary$ earns more and has fewer reports to write than $John$:

$$\exists x_1, y_1, z_1, x_2, y_2, z_2. Mgr(Mary, x_1, y_1, z_1) \wedge Mgr(John, x_2, y_2, z_2) \wedge y_1 > y_2 \wedge z_1 < z_2.$$

The answer to this query in the "cleaned" database r' is false. False is also the consistent answer to Q_2 in r'. Note, however, that, neither false nor true is a consistent answer to Q_2 in r.

Intuitively, however, the repairs r_1 and r_2 incorporate more of reliable information than the repair r_3 (all tuples of r_3 come from a less reliable source s_3). If we consider r_1 and r_2 as the only preferred repairs, then true is the preferred consistent answer to Q_2.

In this paper we extend the framework of consistent query answers with additional input consisting of preference information Φ. We use Φ to define the set of preferred repairs Rep^{Φ}. When we compute preferred consistent answers, instead of considering the set of all repairs Rep, we use the set of preferred repairs. We assume that there exists a (possibly partial) operation of extending Φ with some additional preference information and we write $\Phi \subseteq \Psi$ when Ψ is an *extension* of Φ. Φ is *total* if it cannot be extended further. We identify the following desirable properties of families of preferred repairs:

$\mathcal{P}1$ **Non-emptiness**

$$Rep^{\Phi} \neq \varnothing.$$

$\mathcal{P}2$ **Monotonicity**: extending preferences can only narrow the set of preferred repairs

$$\Phi \subseteq \Psi \Rightarrow Rep^{\Psi} \subseteq Rep^{\Phi}.$$

$\mathcal{P}3$ **Non-discrimination**: if no preference information is given, then no repair is removed from consideration

$$Rep^{\varnothing} = Rep.$$

$\mathcal{P}4$ **Categoricity**: given maximal preference information we obtain exactly one repair

$$\Phi \text{ is total} \Rightarrow |Rep^{\Phi}| = 1.$$

We also note that properties $\mathcal{P}2$ and $\mathcal{P}3$ imply an important property

$\mathcal{P}5$ **Conservativeness**: preferred repairs are a subset of all repairs

$$Rep^{\Phi} \subseteq Rep.$$

In Section 3 we also study various notions of repair *optimality* which ensure a proper use of preference information to select preferred repairs.

2 Preliminaries

In this paper, we work with databases over a schema consisting of only one relation R with attributes from U. We use $A, B, \ldots$ to denote elements of U and $X, Y, \ldots$ to denote subsets of U. We consider two disjoint domains: uninterpreted names D and natural numbers N. Every attribute in U is typed. We assume that constants with different names are different and that symbols $=, \neq, <, >$ have the natural interpretation over N.

The instances of R, denoted by $r, r', \ldots$, can be seen as finite, first-order structures, that share the domains D and N. For any tuple t from r by $t.A$ we denote the value associated with the attribute A. In this paper we consider first-order queries over the alphabet consisting of R and binary relation symbols $=, \neq, <$, and $>$.

The limitation to only one relation is made only for the sake of clarity and along the lines of [9] the framework can be easily extended to handle databases with multiple relations.

2.1 Inconsistency and Repairs

The class of integrity constraints we study consists of functional dependencies (FD). We use $X \to Y$ to denote the following constraint:

$$\forall t_1, t_2 \in R. \bigwedge_{A \in X} t_1.A = t_2.A \Rightarrow \bigwedge_{B \in Y} t_1.B = t_2.B \tag{1}$$

We identify conflicts as follows: tuples t_1 and t_2 are *mutually conflicting* in the database r w.r.t. the set of functional dependencies F if t_1 and t_2 belong to r and there exists a functional dependency of the form (1) in F such that $t_1.A = t_2.A$ for all $A \in X$ and $t_1.B \neq t_2.B$ for some $B \in Y$. A database r is *inconsistent* with a set of constraints F if and only if r contains some conflicting tuples w.r.t. F. Otherwise, the database is *consistent.*

In the framework of [1] when repairing a database two operations are considered: adding or removing a tuple. In the presence of functional dependencies adding new tuples cannot remove conflicts and hence only repairs obtained by deleting tuples have to be considered.

Definition 1 (Repair). *Given a database r and a set of integrity constraints F, a database r' is a* repair *of r w.r.t. F if r' is a maximal subset of r consistent with F. By $Rep(r, F)$ we denote the set of all repairs of r w.r.t F.*

A repair can be viewed as the result of a process of cleaning the input relation. Note that since every conflict can be resolved in two different ways and conflict are often independent, there may be an exponential number of repairs.

Example 4. For any natural number n consider an instance

$$r_n = \{(0,0), (0,1), \ldots, (n-1,0), (n-1,1)\}$$

of the schema $R(A, B)$. Note that the set of all repairs of r_n w.r.t. the functional dependency $A \to B$ is equal to the set of all functions from $\{0, \ldots, n-1\}$ to $\{0, 1\}$.

Also note that the set of repairs of a consistent relation r contains only r.

Given a relation instance r and a set of functional dependencies F, a *conflict graph* $G(r, E)$ is a graph whose vertices are the tuples of r and two tuples are adjacent if only if they are mutually conflicting w.r.t. F. Conflict graphs are *compact representations of repairs* because the set of all repairs is equal to the set of all maximal independent sets of the corresponding conflict graph.

Example 5. The conflict graph for the instance r_n for $n = 4$ and the functional dependency $A \to B$ from Example 4 is presented in Figure 1.

For a given tuple t, by $n(t)$ we denote its *neighborhood* in the conflict graph, i.e. all tuples conflicting with t; and the *vicinity* of t is $v(t) = \{t\} \cup n(t)$.

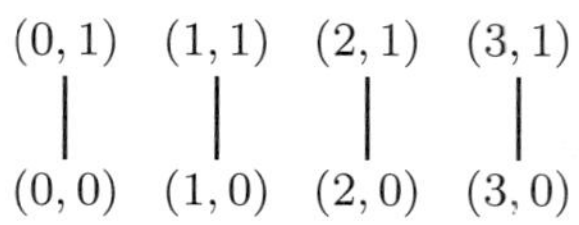

Fig. 1. A conflict graph

2.2 Priorities and Preferred Repairs

For the clarity of presentation we assume a fixed database instance r with a fixed set of functional dependencies F.

To represent the preference information, we use acyclic orientations of some (not necessarily all) edges of the conflict graph. Orientations allow us to express the preferences at the level of single conflicts and acyclicity ensures unambiguity of the preference.

Definition 2 (Priority). *A* priority *(in r w.r.t. F) is a binary relation $\succ \subseteq r \times r$ such that $\succ$ is acyclic and $x \succ y$ implies that x and y are mutually conflicting (in r w.r.t. F). If $x \succ y$ we say that that x* dominates *y. A priority $\succ$ is* total *if for every pair x, y of mutually conflicting tuples (in r w.r.t. F) either $x \succ y$ or $y \succ x$.*

From the point of the user interface it is often more natural to define the priority as some acyclic binary relation on r and then consider the priority relation only on conflicting tuples. Naturally, those approaches are equivalent.

Extending an orientation consists of orienting some conflicting edges that were not oriented before; formally, a priority $\succ'$ is an *extension* of $\succ$ if $\succ' \supseteq \succ$. Note that an extension $\succ'$ is also a priority and therefore $\succ'$ is acyclic and defined only on mutually conflicting tuples. Also observe that a priority cannot be extended further if and only if it is total.

Conflict resolution. A total priority provides an unambiguous information on how each conflict should be resolved. The Algorithm $\mathcal{CR}$ uses a total priority to construct a consistent database by iteratively selecting tuples that are not dominated by any other tuples, i.e. tuples selected by the *winnow operator* [7]:

$$\omega_{\succ}(r) = \{t \in r | \neg \exists t' \in r. t' \succ t\}.$$

After selecting a tuple t, t is removed together with its neighbors from further consideration.

Proposition 1. *Given a total priority $\succ$, the Algorithm $\mathcal{CR}$ computes a unique repair for any sequence of choices in Step 3.*

Preferred repairs. In our work we investigate families of preferred repairs. Formally, a *family of preferred repairs* is a function $\mathcal{X}$-*Rep* defined on triplets $(r, F, \succ)$, where $\succ$ is a priority in r w.r.t. a set of FDs F, such that $\mathcal{X}$-*Rep*$(r, F, \succ)$ is a set of repairs. We say that a family $\mathcal{X}_1$-*Rep subsumes* a family $\mathcal{X}_2$-*Rep*, denoted $\mathcal{X}_1$-*Rep* $\sqsubseteq$ $\mathcal{X}_2$-*Rep*, if for every $(r, F, \succ)$ we have that $\mathcal{X}_1$-*Rep*$(r, F, \succ) \subseteq$ $\mathcal{X}_2$-*Rep*$(r, F, \succ)$.

Algorithm $\mathcal{CR}$: Conflict Resolution

$r' \leftarrow \varnothing$
while $\omega_{\succ}(r) \neq \varnothing$ **do**
    choose any $x \in \omega_{\succ}(r)$
    $r' \leftarrow r' \cup \{x\}$
    $r \leftarrow r \setminus (\{x\} \cup n(x))$ ▷ where $n(x)$ – the neighborhood of x.
return r'

2.3 Preferred Consistent Query Answers

We generalize the notion of consistent query answer [1] by considering only preferred repairs when evaluating a query (instead of all repairs). We only study closed first-order logic queries. We can easily generalize our approach to open queries along the lines of [1,9]. For a given query Q we say that *true* is an answer to Q in r, if $r \models Q$ in the standard model-theoretic sense.

Definition 3 ($\mathcal{X}$-Consistent query answer). *Given a database r, a set of FDs F, a closed query Q, a priority $\succ$, and a family of repairs $\mathcal{X}$-Rep,* true *(*false*) is the $\mathcal{X}$-*consistent query answer *to a query Q in r w.r.t. F and $\succ$ if for every repair $r' \in \mathcal{X}\text{-}Rep(r, F, \succ)$ we have $r' \models Q$ (resp. $r' \not\models Q$).*

Note that we obtain the original notion of consistent query answer [1] if we consider the whole set of repairs $Rep(r, F)$.

3 Priority-Based Repairing

The main purpose of introducing $\mathcal{P}1$–$\mathcal{P}4$ is the identification of the desired properties of families of preferred repairs. We note that all properties except for $\mathcal{P}4$ do not require any use of the priority itself to eliminate repairs. This makes it possible to construct a family of preferred repairs which satisfies $\mathcal{P}1$–$\mathcal{P}4$ but which practically makes no use of the given priority.

Example 6. Consider a family of repairs, which for a total priority consists of the clean database obtained with Algorithm $\mathcal{CR}$ and for non-total priorities it consists of all repairs. This family of repairs fulfills properties $\mathcal{P}1$–$\mathcal{P}4$.

Thus we investigate a number of increasingly complex notions of repair optimality that ensure an effective use of the preference information:

1. r' is a *locally optimal* repair, if no tuple x from r' can be replaced with a tuple y such that $y \succ x$ and the resulting set of tuples is consistent;
2. r' is a *Pareto optimal* if no nonempty subset X of tuples from r' can be replaced with a tuple y such that $\forall x \in X. y \succ x$ and the resulting set of tuples is consistent;
3. r' is a *globally optimal* if no nonempty subset X of tuples from r can be replaced with a set of tuples Y such that $\forall x \in X. \exists y \in Y. y \succ x$ and the resulting set of tuples is consistent.

We note that global optimality implies Pareto optimality which in turn implies local optimality. Intuitively, global optimality makes an aggressive use of priorities to select repairs, while local optimality does so in a less aggressive manner.

3.1 Locally Optimal Repairs

By $\mathcal{L}$-*Rep* we denote the family selecting all locally optimal repairs. The following example illustrates that the notion of local optimality allows to effectively use priorities to handle relations with one key dependency.

Example 7. Consider the relational schema $R(A, B)$ with a key dependency $F = \{A \to B\}$ and take an instance $r = \{t_a = (1,1), t_b = (1,2), t_c = (1,3)\}$ with the priority $\succ = \{(t_a, t_c), (t_a, t_b)\}$. Figure 2 contains the corresponding conflict graph and its orientation. The repairs are $Rep(r, F) = \{r_1 = \{t_a\}, r_2 = \{t_b\}, r_3 = \{t_c\}\}$. Only r_1 is locally preferred.

Proposition 2. *$\mathcal{L}$-Rep satisfies properties $\mathcal{P}1$–$\mathcal{P}3$.*

As it's shown on the following example, locally optimal repairs do not satisfy $\mathcal{P}4$.

Example 8. Consider the relational schema $R(A, B, C)$ with a functional dependency $A \to B$ and take an instance $r = \{t_a = (1,1,1), t_b = (1,1,2), t_c = (1,2,3)\}$ with the total priority $\succ = \{(t_c, t_a), (t_c, t_b)\}$. The corresponding conflict graph can be found in Figure 3. The set of repairs consists of two repairs $Rep(r, F) = \{r_1 = \{t_a, t_b\}, r_2 = \{t_c\}\}$. All repairs are locally optimal.

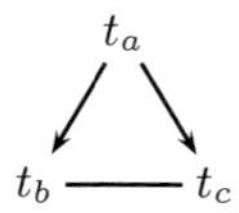

Fig. 2. Use of $\mathcal{L}$-*Rep*

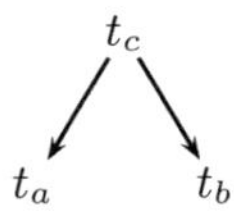

Fig. 3. Non-categoricity of $\mathcal{L}$-*Rep*

3.2 Pareto Optimal Repairs

In Example 8, we note that even though the priority suggests rejecting r_1 from consideration, the notion of local optimality is too weak to do so. The main reason is the existence of violations of functional dependency with duplicates (t_a and t_b which are not conflicting, but both of them conflict with t_c). The notion of Pareto optimality, on the other hand, effectively applies the priority in the situations of violations of one non-key functional dependency: the repair r_1 is not Pareto optimal and r_2 is. By $\mathcal{P}$-*Rep* we denote the family selecting all Pareto optimal repairs. We note that $\mathcal{P}$-*Rep* is as effective in enforcing priorities as $\mathcal{L}$-*Rep*.

Proposition 3. *$\mathcal{P}$-Rep satisfies properties $\mathcal{P}1$–$\mathcal{P}4$. Moreover $\mathcal{P}$-Rep $\sqsubseteq$ $\mathcal{L}$-Rep and for one key dependency $\mathcal{L}$-Rep coincides with $\mathcal{P}$-Rep.*

3.3 Globally Optimal Repairs

Pareto optimality selects repairs whose compliance with the priority cannot be improved by exchanging a set of tuples with a dominating tuple. The following example presents a situation where one may decide to use global optimality to provide a finer selection of repairs.

Example 9. Consider the schema $R(A, B, C, D)$ with two functional dependencies $F = \{A \to B, C \to D\}$ and suppose we have a database: $r = \{t_a = (1,1,0,0), t_b = (1,2,0,0), t_c = (1,1,1,1), t_d = (1,2,2,1), t_e = (0,0,2,2)\}$ with a priority $\succ = \{(t_a, t_b), (t_b, t_c), (t_c, t_d), (t_d, t_e)\}$. The conflict graph is presented on Figure 4. The set of repairs is $Rep(r, F) = \{r_1 = \{t_b, t_e\}, r_2 = \{t_b, t_d\}, r_3 = \{t_a, t_c, t_e\}\}$. Repairs r_2 and r_3 are Pareto optimal. However, only the repair r_3 is globally optimal.

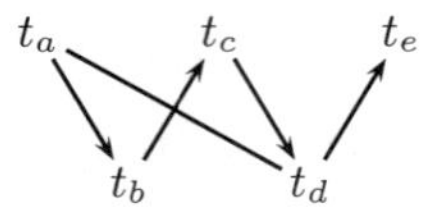

Fig. 4. Pareto vs. global optimality

Let $\mathcal{G}$-*Rep* be the family selecting all globally optimal repairs.

Proposition 4. *$\mathcal{G}$-Rep satisfies properties $\mathcal{P}1$–$\mathcal{P}4$. Moreover $\mathcal{G}$-Rep $\sqsubseteq$ $\mathcal{P}$-Rep and for one functional dependency $\mathcal{G}$-Rep coincides with $\mathcal{P}$-Rep.*

Globally optimal repairs can be characterized in an alternative way.

Proposition 5. *For a given priority $\succ$ and two repairs, we say that r_2 is* preferred *over r_1, denoted $r_1 \ll r_2$, if*

$$\forall x \in r_1 \setminus r_2.\ \exists y \in r_2 \setminus r_1.\ y \succ x.$$

A repair r' is globally optimal if and only if it is $\ll$-maximal (there is no repair r'' such that $r' \ll r''$).

This particular "lifting" of a preference on objects to a preference on sets of objects can be found in other contexts. For example, a similar definition is used for a preference among different models of a logic program [22], or for a preference among different worlds [17].

3.4 Common Optimal Repairs

Now, we investigate the question whether there are repairs common for any family of optimal repairs that satisfies the properties $\mathcal{P}1$ and $\mathcal{P}2$, i.e. given any $(r, F, \succ)$ is there a repair r' which is in $\mathcal{X}$-*Rep*$(r, F, \succ)$ for any family $\mathcal{X}$-*Rep* of optimal repairs satisfying $\mathcal{P}1$ and $\mathcal{P}2$? The answer is negative for families of locally optimal repairs. For instance we can construct two families of locally optimal repairs that define the same set of preferred repairs as $\mathcal{L}$-*Rep* except that for the setting in Example 8 one returns only r_1 while the other only r_2. Surprisingly, the situation is different for families of Pareto (and thus also globally) optimal repairs.

Theorem 1. *For every instance r, every set of functional dependencies F, and every priority $\succ$ in r w.r.t. F, there exists a repair r' such that $r' \in \mathcal{X}$-Rep$(r, F, \succ)$ for any family $\mathcal{X}$-Rep of Pareto optimal repairs that satisfies $\mathcal{P}1$ and $\mathcal{P}2$.*

We define a new family of $\mathcal{C}$-*Rep* which selects only *common* repairs of all families of Pareto optimal repairs satisfying the properties $\mathcal{P}1$ and $\mathcal{P}2$. $\mathcal{C}$-*Rep* is another family of preferred repairs that satisfies all properties.

Proposition 6. *$\mathcal{C}$-Rep is a family of globally optimal repairs, i.e. $\mathcal{C}$-Rep $\sqsubseteq$ $\mathcal{G}$-Rep, and $\mathcal{C}$-Rep satisfies properties $\mathcal{P}1$-$\mathcal{P}4$.*

Interestingly the family of common repairs has an alternative *procedural* characterization.

Proposition 7. *For a given instance r, a given set of functional dependencies F, and a given priority $\succ$, the set $\mathcal{C}$-Rep$(r, F, \succ)$ consists of all results of Algorithm $\mathcal{CR}$ for any sequence of choices in Step 3.*

We also note that under some conditions, the properties $\mathcal{P}1$ and $\mathcal{P}2$ specify exactly one family of globally optimal repairs.

Theorem 2. *$\mathcal{C}$-Rep and $\mathcal{G}$-Rep coincide for priorities that cannot be extended to a cyclic orientation of the conflict graph.*

4 Computational Properties

In this section we study the computational implications of using priorities to handle inconsistent databases. Because of space restriction we skip the proofs (they can be found in [10] or derived using the techniques presented there).

4.1 Data Complexity

In our paper we use the notion of *data complexity* [23] which captures the complexity of a problem as a function of the number of tuples in the database. The input consists of the relation instance and the priority relation, while the database schema, the integrity constraints, and the query are assumed to be fixed. For a family $\mathcal{X}$-*Rep* of preferred repairs we study two fundamental computational problems:

(*i*) $\mathcal{X}$-*repair checking* – determining if a database is a preferred repair of a given database i.e., the complexity of the following set

$$\mathcal{B}_F^{\mathcal{X}} = \{(r, \succ, r') : r' \in \mathcal{X}\text{-}Rep(r, F, \succ)\}.$$

(*ii*) $\mathcal{X}$-*consistent query answers* – checking if *true* is an answer to a given query in every preferred repair i.e., the complexity of the following set

$$\mathcal{D}_{F,Q}^{\mathcal{X}} = \{(r, \succ) : \forall r' \in \mathcal{X}\text{-}Rep(r, F, \succ). r' \models Q\}.$$

4.2 Negative Results

First we state that computing preferred consistent query answers with any family of Pareto (and thus also globally) optimal repairs that satisfies $\mathcal{P}1$ and $\mathcal{P}2$ leads to intractability.

Theorem 3. *For any family $\mathcal{X}$-Rep of Pareto optimal repairs that satisfies $\mathcal{P}1$ and $\mathcal{P}2$, there exists a set of two functional dependencies F and a quantifier-free ground query Q (consisting of one atom) to which computing the $\mathcal{X}$-consistent answer is co-NP-hard.*

Proof. We reduce computing $\mathcal{X}$-consistent query answers to the complement of SAT. Take then any CNF formula $\varphi = c_1 \wedge \ldots \wedge c_k$ over variables $x_1, \ldots, x_n$ and let $c_j = l_{j,1} \vee \ldots \vee l_{j,m_j}$. We assume that there are no repetitions of literals in a clause (i.e., $l_{j,k_1} \neq l_{j,k_2}$). We construct a relation instance r_φ over the schema $R(A_1, B_1, A_2, B_2)$ in the presence of two functional dependencies $F = \{A_1 \to B_1, A_2 \to B_2\}$. The instance r_φ consists of the following tuples:

- $w_i = (i, 1, i, 1)$ corresponds to the positive valuation of the variable x_i (for every $i = 1, \ldots, n$),
- $\bar{w}_i = (i, -1, -i, 1)$ corresponds to the negative valuation of the variable x_i (for every $i = 1, \ldots, n$),
- $v_i^j = (n + j, 1, -i, 0)$ corresponds to the use of the literal x_i in the clause c_j,
- $v_i^j = (n + j, 1, i, 0)$ corresponds to the use of the literal $\neg x_i$ in the clause c_j,
- $d_j = (n + j, 1, 0, 1)$ corresponds to the clause c_j,
- $b = (0, 0, 0, 0)$ corresponds to the formula φ.

The constructed priority $\succ_\varphi$ is the minimal priority on r_φ (w.r.t. F) such that:

$$\begin{aligned} &\bar{w}_i \succ_\varphi v_i^j, && v_i^j \succ_\varphi d_j, && d_j \succ_\varphi b, \\ &w_i \succ_\varphi \bar{v}_i^j, && \bar{v}_i^j \succ_\varphi d_j. && \end{aligned}$$

The query we consider is $Q = \neg R(b)$. On Figure 5 we can find a conflict graph of an instance received from reduction of a formula $\varphi = (\neg x_1 \vee x_2 \vee x_3) \wedge (x_3 \vee \neg x_4 \vee x_5 \vee \neg x_6)$.

Now we show that

$$(r_\varphi, \succ_\varphi) \in \mathcal{D}_{F,Q} \iff \forall r' \in \mathcal{X}\text{-}Rep(r_\varphi, F, \succ_\varphi). b \notin r' \iff \varphi \notin SAT.$$

$\Rightarrow$ Suppose there exists a valuation V such that $V \models \varphi$. Consider then the following instance

$$\begin{aligned} r' = &\{w_i | V(x_i) = true\} \cup \{\bar{w}_i | V(x_i) = false\} \cup \\ &\{v_i^j | V(x_i) = true\} \cup \{\bar{v}_i^j | V(x_i) = false\} \cup \{b\}. \end{aligned}$$

We claim that $r \in \mathcal{X}\text{-}Rep(r_\varphi, F, \succ_\varphi)$. To prove this consider the following priority $\succ' = \succ_\varphi \cup \{(v_i, \bar{v}_i) | V(x_i) = true\} \cup \{(\bar{v}_i, v_i) | V(x_i) = false\}$. By $\mathcal{P}1$ we have that $\mathcal{X}\text{-}Rep(r_\varphi, F, \succ')$ is non-empty. We can prove that

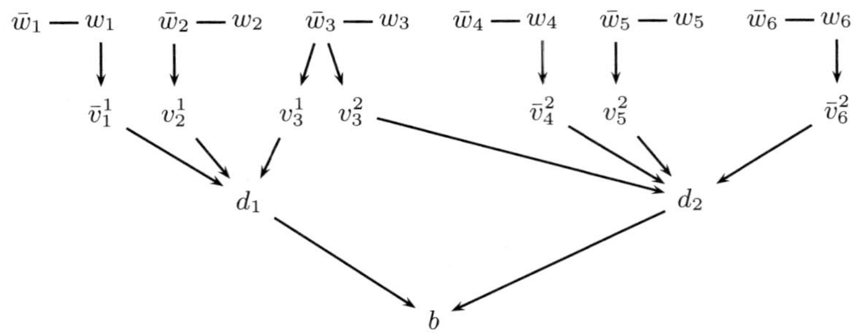

Fig. 5. Conflict graph for $\varphi = (\neg x_1 \vee x_2 \vee x_3) \wedge (x_3 \vee \neg x_4 \vee x_5 \vee \neg x_6)$ with $\succ_\varphi$

r' belongs to $\mathcal{X}$-*Rep*$(r_\varphi, F, \succ')$ using the fact that $\mathcal{X}$-*Rep* is a family of Pareto optimal repairs (for brevity we skip this step). And from $\mathcal{P}2$ we get that $\mathcal{X}$-*Rep*$(r_\varphi, F, \succ')\subseteq \mathcal{X}$-*Rep*$(r_\varphi, F, \succ_\varphi)$ and hence r' belongs to $\mathcal{X}$-*Rep*$(r_\varphi, F, \succ')$. Since $b \in r$ this contradicts $(r_\varphi, \succ_\varphi) \in \mathcal{D}_{F,Q}$.

$\Leftarrow$ For brevity we just sketch this part of the proof. Suppose there exists a repair $r' \in \mathcal{X}$-*Rep*$(r_\varphi, F, \succ_\varphi)$ such that $b \in r'$. We can prove that the following valuation

$$V(x_i) = \begin{cases} true & \text{if } v_i \in r', \\ false & \text{if } \bar{v}_i \in r', \\ true & \text{otherwise} \end{cases}$$

satisfies φ which is a contradiction.

It's an open question whether a similar statement holds for families of locally optimal repairs. We note that computing preferred consistent query answers is co-NP-hard if we consider slightly restricted locally optimal repairs: locally optimal repairs for which there doesn't exists a pair of tuples x_1, x_2 which can be replaced with a tuple y such that $y \succ x_1$ and $y \succ x_2$ and the resulting set of tuples is consistent. Therefore we state the following conjecture.

Conjecture 1. For any family $\mathcal{X}$-*Rep* of preferred repairs satisfying $\mathcal{P}1$, $\mathcal{P}2$, and global local optimality computing $\mathcal{X}$-consistent answers is co-NP-hard.

Another argument for this conjecture is the intractability of computing $\mathcal{L}$-consistent query answers (the proof of co-NP-hardness is omitted here, however, it uses the reduction from the proof of Theorem 3.)

Theorem 4. *$\mathcal{L}$-repair checking is in PTIME and $\mathcal{L}$-consistent query answers are co-NP-complete.*

To find if a repair r' is Pareto optimal we seek a tuple $y \in r \setminus r'$ whose all neighbors in r' are dominated by y. Such a tuple exists if and only if r' is not Pareto optimal. The tractability of $\mathcal{P}$-checking implies that computing $\mathcal{P}$-consistent answers is in co-NP: the nondeterministic machine uses a polynomial (in the size of r) number of nondeterministic steps to construct a repair r', checks if r' is Pareto optimal; the machine finds the answer to the query in r' (if r' is not Pareto then the machine halts with the answer 'yes'). With Theorem 3 we obtain:

Corollary 1. *$\mathcal{P}$-repair checking is in PTIME and $\mathcal{P}$-consistent query answers are co-NP-complete.*

Checking if a repair is globally optimal requires, however, an essential use of non-determinism. This also promotes computing preferred consistent query answers to a higher level of the polynomial hierarchy (proofs of the following claims can be found in [10].)

Theorem 5. *$\mathcal{G}$-repair checking is co-NP-complete and $\mathcal{G}$-consistent query answers are Π_2^p-complete.*

The procedural nature of common repairs makes it possible to check if a repair r' belongs to $\mathcal{C}$-$Rep(r, F, \succ)$ with a simulation of Algorithm $\mathcal{CR}$ with the choices in Step 3 restricted to $\omega_\succ(r) \cap r'$. Naturally this process can be performed in polynomial time. Again using Theorem 3 we get:

Corollary 2. *$\mathcal{C}$-repair checking is in PTIME and $\mathcal{C}$-consistent query answers is co-NP-complete.*

4.3 Positive Results

We show how to compute consistent query answers if only one key dependency is present. Note that under one key dependency all previously introduced families of repairs coincide and hence we simply talk about preferred repairs. We note that under one key dependency the corresponding conflict graph consists of disjoint cliques. A repair is obtained by choosing one tuple from each clique. If a priority is given then a preferred repair is obtained by choosing a non-dominated tuple from each clique, i.e. a tuple selected with the winnow operator.

Now, we show how to adopt the algorithm from [8] to find if true is the preferred consistent answer to a query Φ in r for a given priority $\succ$ w.r.t. one key dependency. We assume that the query is in CNF: $\Phi = \Phi_1 \wedge \ldots \Phi_n$. We note that true is not a preferred consistent query answer if and only if there exists a preferred repair r' such that $r' \not\models \Phi_i$ for some i. The algorithm attempts to find if such a repair exists for every i. If the algorithm is successful for some i then the answer is false; otherwise the answer is true. Let's fix i and consider $\neg\Phi_i$

$$\neg\Phi_i = R(t_1) \wedge \ldots \wedge R(t_k) \wedge \neg R(t_{k+1}) \wedge \ldots \wedge \neg R(t_m).$$

We use the following test:

Claim. For every $j \in \{1, \ldots, m\}$ if $t_j \in r$ we identify the clique C_j the tuple t_j belongs to. A preferred repair r' such that $r' \models \neg\Phi_i$ exists if and only if:

1. $\{t_1, \ldots, t_k\} \subseteq r$,
2. $\{t_1, \ldots, t_k\}$ is independent,

3. $\{t_1, \ldots, t_k\} \cap \{t_{k+1}, \ldots, t_n\} = \varnothing$,
4. $t_j \in \omega_{\succ}(C_j)$ for every $j \in \{1, \ldots, k\}$,
5. $\omega_{\succ}(C_j) \setminus \{t_{k+1}, \ldots, t_m\} \neq \varnothing$ for every $j \in \{k+1, \ldots, n\}$ such that $t_j \in r$.

Proof. $\Rightarrow$ The conditions 1, 2, and 3 are trivially implied. We observe that every tuple in r' is selected among non-dominated tuples from the clique it belongs to (with $\{t_1, \ldots, t_k\} \subseteq r'$ this proves 4) and r' is maximal, i.e. r' contains a tuple selected from every clique (with $\{t_{k+1}, \ldots, t_m\} \cap r' = \varnothing$ this proves 5).

$\Leftarrow$ We construct the repair r' as follows. First, for every $j \in \{1, \ldots, k\}$ we select the tuple t_j from C_j (feasible by 1, 2, and 3). The condition 4 guarantees that none of the tuples $t_{k+1}, \ldots, t_m$ is selected in this step. Next, for every $j \in \{k+1, \ldots, m\}$, such that $t_j \in r$, from the clique C_j we select a tuple different from $t_{k+1}, \ldots, t_m$ (feasible by 5). Finally, we select an arbitrary non-dominated tuple from every remaining clique. Obviously, $r' \models \neg\Phi_i$.

We also observe that the described test can be performed in time polynomial in the size of the database.

Along the lines of [2,8] this algorithm can be further extended to handle one functional dependency. Because for one FD the family of locally optimal repairs does not coincide with other families of preferred repairs, we can extend this algorithm is two different directions: computing the preferred consistent query answers w.r.t. locally optimal repairs and w.r.t. Pareto optimal repairs.

Theorem 6. *For one functional dependency computing preferred consistent query answers is in PTIME for $\mathcal{L}$-Rep, $\mathcal{P}$-Rep, $\mathcal{G}$-Rep, and $\mathcal{C}$-Rep.*

5 Related Work

We limit our discussion to the work on using priorities to maintain consistency and facilitate resolution of conflicts.

The first article to notice the importance of priorities in information systems is [11]. The authors study there the problem of updates of databases containing propositional sentences. The priority is expressed by storing a natural number with each clause. If during an update (inserting or deleting a sentence) the inconsistency arises, then the priorities are used in a fashion similar to $\mathcal{G}$-repairs to select minimally different repairs. We note, however, that the chosen representation of priorities imposes a significant restriction on the class of considered priorities. In particular it assumes transitivity of the priority on conflicting facts i.e. if facts a, b, and c are pair-wise conflicting and a has a higher priority than b and b has a higher priority than c, then the priority of a is higher than c. This assumption cannot be always fulfilled in the context of inconsistent databases. For example the conflicts between a and b, and between b and c may be caused by violation of one integrity constraint while the conflict between a and c is introduced by a different constraint. While the user may supply us with a rule assigning priorities to conflicts created by the first integrity constraint, the user may not wish to put any priorities on any conflicts created by the other constraint.

A similar representation of priorities used to resolve inconsistency in first-order theories is studied in [6], where the inconsistent set of clauses is stratified (again the lowest strata has the highest priority). Then preferred maximal consistent subtheories are constructed in a manner analogous to $\mathcal{C}$-repairs. Furthermore, this approach is generalized to priorities being a partial order, by considering all extensions to weak orders. Again, however, this approach assumes the transitivity of priority on conflicts, which as we explained previously may be considered a significant restriction.

In the context of logic programs, priorities among rules can be used to handle inconsistent logic programs (where rules imply contradictory facts). More preferred rules are satisfied, possibly at the cost of violating less important ones. In a manner analogous to Proposition 5, [22] lifts a total order on rules to a preference on (extended) answers sets. When computing answers only maximally preferred answers sets are considered.

[21] investigate disjunctive logic programs with priorities on facts. A transitive and reflexive closure of user supplied priorities on facts is used to define a relation of preference on models of the program. The definition of preference on models of the disjunctive program is essentially different from the characterization of globally optimal repairs in Proposition 5. The answer to a program in the extended framework consists of all maximally preferred answer sets. The main shortcoming of using this framework is it computational infeasibility (which is specific to decision problems involving general disjunctive programs): computing answers to ground queries to disjunctive prioritized logic programs under cautious (brave) semantics is Π_3^p-complete (resp. Σ_3^p-complete). We note that a family of preferred repairs defined in analogous manner does not satisfy $\mathcal{P}2$ and $\mathcal{P}4$ but satisfies $\mathcal{P}1$, $\mathcal{P}3$, and $\mathcal{P}5$.

A simpler approach to the problem of inconsistent logic programs is presented in [16]. There, conflicting facts are removed from the model unless the priority specifies how to resolve the conflict. Because only programs without disjunction are considered, this approach always returns exactly one model of the input program. Constructing preferred repairs in a corresponding fashion (by removing all conflicts unless the priority indicates a resolution) would similarly return exactly one database instance (fulfillment of $\mathcal{P}1$ and $\mathcal{P}4$). However, if the priority is not total, the returned instance is not a repair and therefore the $\mathcal{P}5$ is not satisfied. Such an approach leads to a loss of (disjunctive) information and does not satisfy $\mathcal{P}2$ and $\mathcal{P}3$.

[12] proposes a framework of *conditioned active integrity constraints*, which allows the user to specify the way some of the conflicts created with the constraint can be resolved. This framework satisfies properties $\mathcal{P}1$ and $\mathcal{P}3$ and doesn't satisfy $\mathcal{P}2$ and $\mathcal{P}4$. [12] also describes how to translate conditioned active integrity constraints into a prioritized logic program [21], whose preferred models correspond to maximally preferred repairs. We note that the framework of prioritized logic programming is computationally more powerful (computing answers under the brave semantics is Σ_3^p-complete) than required by the problem of finding if an atom is present in any repair (Σ_2^p-complete). It is yet to be seen if less power-

ful programming environments (like general disjunctive logic programs) can be used to compute preferred answers.

[19] uses ranking functions on tuples to resolve conflicts by taking only the tuple with highest rank and removing others. This approach constructs a unique repair under the assumption that no two different tuples are of equal rank (satisfaction of $\mathcal{P}4$). If this assumption is not satisfied and the tuples contain numeric values, a new value, called the fusion, can be calculated from the conflicting tuples (then, however, the constructed instance is not a repair in the sense of Definition 1 which means a possible loss of information).

A different approach based on ranking is studied in [15]. The authors consider polynomial functions that are used to rank repairs. When computing preferred consistent query answers, only repairs with the highest rank are considered. The properties $\mathcal{P}3$ and $\mathcal{P}5$ are trivially satisfied, but because this form of preference information does not have natural notions of extensions and maximality, it is hard to discuss postulates $\mathcal{P}2$ and $\mathcal{P}4$. Also, the preference among repairs in this method is not based on the way in which the conflicts are resolved.

An approach where the user has a certain degree of control over the way the conflicts are resolved is presented in [14]. Using repair constraints the user can restrict considered repairs to those where tuples from one relation have been removed only if similar tuples have been removed from some other relation. This approach satisfies $\mathcal{P}2$ but not $\mathcal{P}1$. A method of weakening the repair constraints is propose to get $\mathcal{P}1$, however this comes at the price of losing $\mathcal{P}2$.

6 Conclusions and Future Work

In this paper we proposed a general framework of preferred repairs and preferred consistent query answer. We also proposed a set of desired properties a family of preferred repairs should satisfy. We presented 4 families of preferred repairs: $\mathcal{L}$-*Rep*, $\mathcal{P}$-*Rep*, $\mathcal{G}$-*Rep*, and $\mathcal{C}$-*Rep*. Figure 6 summarizes the computational complexity results; its first row is taken from [8].

	Repair Check	Consistent Answers to		Possible Applications
		$\{\forall,\exists\}$-free queries	conjunctive queries	
Rep	PTIME	PTIME	co-NP-complete	no priorities given
$\mathcal{L}$-*Rep*	PTIME	co-NP-complete		key
$\mathcal{P}$-*Rep*	PTIME	co-NP-complete		one FD
$\mathcal{G}$-*Rep*	co-NP-complete	Π_p^2-complete		many FDs with mutual conflicts
$\mathcal{C}$-*Rep*	PTIME	co-NP-complete		

Fig. 6. Summary of complexity results

We envision several directions for further work. Along the lines of [2], the computational complexity results could be further studied, by assuming the conformance of functional dependencies with BCNF.

Extending our approach to cyclic priorities is an interesting and challenging issue. Including priorities in similar frameworks of preferences [14] leads to losing the monotonicity. A modified, conditional, version of monotonicity may be necessary to capture non-trivial families of repairs.

Finally, one can extend our framework to handle a broader class of constraints. Conflict graphs can be generalized to hypergraphs [8], necessary to deal with denial constraints. Then, more than two tuples can be involved in a single conflict and the current notion of priority does not have a clear meaning.

References

1. M. Arenas, L. Bertossi, and J. Chomicki. Consistent Query Answers in Inconsistent Databases. In *ACM Symposium on Principles of Database Systems (PODS)*, pages 68–79, 1999.
2. M. Arenas, L. Bertossi, J. Chomicki, X. He, V. Raghavan, and J. Spinrad. Scalar Aggregation in Inconsistent Databases. *Theoretical Computer Science (TCS)*, 296(3):405–434, 2003.
3. L. Bertossi. Consistent Query Answering in Databases. *SIGMOD Record*, 2006. *To appear.*
4. L. Bertossi and J. Chomicki. Query Answering in Inconsistent Databases. In J. Chomicki, R. van der Meyden, and G. Saake, editors, *Logics for Emerging Applications of Databases*, pages 43–83. Springer-Verlag, 2003.
5. P. Bohannon, M. Flaster, W. Fan, and R. Rastogi. A Cost-Based Model and Effective Heuristic for Repairing Constraints by Value Modification. In *ACM SIGMOD International Conference on Management of Data*, 2005.
6. G. Brewka. Preferred Subtheories: An Extended Logical Framework for Default Reasoning. In *International Joint Conference on Artificial Intelligence (IJCAI)*, pages 1043 – 1048, 1989.
7. J. Chomicki. Preference Formulas in Relational Queries. *ACM Transactions on Database Systems (TODS)*, 28(4):427–466, December 2003.
8. J. Chomicki and J. Marcinkowski. Minimal-Change Integrity Maintenance Using Tuple Deletions. *Information and Computation*, pages 90–121, 2005.
9. J. Chomicki, J. Marcinkowski, and S. Staworko. Computing Consistent Query Answers Using Conflict Hypergraphs. In *International Conference on Information and Knowledge Management (CIKM)*, pages 417–426. ACM Press, November 2004.
10. J. Chomicki, J. Marcinkowski, and S. Staworko. Priority-Based Conflict Resolution in Inconsistent Relational Databases. Technical Report cs.DB/0506063, arXiv.org e-Print archive, June 2004.
11. R. Fagin, J. D. Ullman, and M. Y. Vardi. On the Semantics of Updates in Databases. In *ACM Symposium on Principles of Database Systems (PODS)*, pages 352–356, 1983.
12. S. Flesca, S. Greco, and E. Zumpano. Active Integrity Constraints. In *ACM SIGPLAN International Conference on Principles and Practice of Declarative Programming (PPDP)*, pages 98–107, 2004.
13. A. Fuxman, E. Fazli, and R. J. Miller. ConQuer: Efficient Management of Inconsistent Databases. In *ACM SIGMOD International Conference on Management of Data*, 2005.

14. G. Greco and D. Lembo. Data Integration with Preferences Among Sources. In *International Conference on Conceptual Modeling (ER)*, pages 231–244. Springer, November 2004.
15. S. Greco, C. Sirangelo, I. Trubitsyna, and E. Zumpano. Feasibility Conditions and Preference Criteria in Quering and Repairing Inconsistent Databases. In *International Conference on Database and Expert Systems Applications (DEXA)*, pages 44–55, 2004.
16. B. N. Grosof. Prioritized Conflict Handling for Logic Programs. In *International Logic Programming Symposium*, pages 197–211, 1997.
17. J. Y. Halpern. Defining Relative Likehood in Partially-Ordered Preferential Structures. *Journal of Artificial Intelligence Research*, 1997.
18. D. B. Lomet. Letter from the Editor-in-Chief. *IEEE Data Eng. Bull.*, 23(4), 2000.
19. A. Motro, P. Anokhin, and A. C. Acar. Utility-based Resolution of Data Inconsistencies. In *International Workshop on Information Quality in Information Systems (IQIS)*, pages 35–43. ACM, 2004.
20. E. Rahm and H. H. Do. Data Cleaning: Problems and Current Approaches. *IEEE Data Eng. Bull.*, 23(4):3–13, 2000.
21. C. Sakama and K. Inoue. Prioritized logic programming and its application to commonsense reasoning. *Artificial Intelligence*, 123:185–222, 2000.
22. D. Van Nieuwenborgh and D. Vermeir. Preferred Answer Sets for Ordered Logic Programs. In *European Conference on Logics for Artificial Intelligence (JELIA)*, pages 432–443. Springer-Verlag, LNCS 2424, 2002.
23. M. Y. Vardi. The Complexity of Relational Query Languages. In *ACM Symposium on Theory of Computing (STOC)*, pages 137–146, 1982.
24. P. Vassiliadis, Z. Vagena, S. Skiadopoulos, and N. Karayannidis. ARKTOS: A Tool For Data Cleaning and Transformation in Data Warehouse Environments. *IEEE Data Eng. Bull.*, 23(4):42–47, 2000.

Semantically Correct Query Answers in the Presence of Null Values

Loreto Bravo and Leopoldo Bertossi

Carleton University, School of Computer Science
Ottawa, Canada
{lbravo, bertossi}@scs.carleton.ca

Abstract. For several reasons a database may not satisfy a given set of integrity constraints (ICs), but most likely most of the information in it is still consistent with those ICs; and could be retrieved when queries are answered. Consistent answers to queries wrt a set of ICs have been characterized as answers that can be obtained from every possible minimally repaired consistent version of the original database. In this paper we consider databases that contain null values and are also repaired, if necessary, using null values. For this purpose, we propose first a precise semantics for IC satisfaction in a database with null values that is compatible with the way null values are treated in commercial database management systems. Next, a precise notion of repair is introduced that privileges the introduction of null values when repairing foreign key constraints, in such a way that these new values do not create an infinite cycle of new inconsistencies. Finally, we analyze how to specify this kind of repairs of a database that contains null values using disjunctive logic programs with stable model semantics.

1 Introduction

In databases, integrity constraints (ICs) capture the semantics of the application domain, and help maintain the correspondence between this domain and the database when updates are performed. However, there are several reasons for a database to be or become inconsistent wrt a given set of ICs [6]; and sometimes it could be difficult, impossible or undesirable to repair the database in order to restore consistency [6]. This process might be too expensive; useful data might be lost; it may not be clear how to restore the consistency, and sometimes even impossible, e.g. in virtual data integration, where the access to the autonomous data sources may be restricted [9].

In those situations, possibly most of the data is still consistent and can be retrieved when queries are posed to the database. In [2], consistent data is characterized as the data that is invariant under certain minimal forms of restoration of consistency, i.e. as the data that is present in all minimally repaired and consistent versions of the original instance, the so-called *repairs*. In particular, an answer to a query is defined as consistent when it can be obtained as a standard answer to the query from *every possible* repair.

T. Grust et al. (Eds.): EDBT 2006 Workshops, LNCS 4254, pp. 336–357, 2006.

More precisely, a repair of a database instance D, as introduced in [2], is a new instance of the same schema as D that satisfies the given ICs, and makes minimal under set inclusion the symmetric set difference with the original instance, taken both instances as sets of ground database atoms.

In [2, 13, 14, 17] algorithms and implementations for consistent query answering (CQA) have been presented, i.e. for retrieving consistent answers from inconsistent databases. All of them work only with the original, inconsistent database, without restoring its consistency. That is, inconsistencies are solved at query time. This is in correspondence with the idea that the above mentioned repairs provide an auxiliary concept for defining the right semantics for consistent query answers. However, those algorithms apply to restricted classes of queries and constraints, basically those for which the intrinsic complexity of CQA is still manageable [15].

In [3, 20, 5, 6] a different approach is taken: database repairs are specified as the stable models of disjunctive logic programs, and in consequence consistent query answering amounts to doing *cautious* or *certain* reasoning from logic programs under the stable model semantics. In this way, it is possible to handle any set of universal ICs and any first-order query, and even beyond that, e.g. queries expressed in extensions of Datalog. It is important to realize that the data complexity of query evaluation in disjunctive logic programs with stable model semantics [16] matches the intrinsic data complexity of CQA [15], namely both of them are Π^P_2-complete.

All the previous work cited before did not consider the possible presence of null values in the database, and even less their peculiar semantics. Using null values to repair ICs was only slightly considered in [3, 5, 6]. This strategy to deal with referential ICs seemed to be the right way to proceed given the results presented in [11] that show that repairing cyclic sets of referential ICs by introducing arbitrary values from the underlying database domain leads to the undecidability of CQA.

In [10] the methodology presented in [5, 6], based on specifying repairs using logic programs withe extra annotation constants, was systematically extended in order to handle both; (a) databases containing null values, and (b) referential integrity constraints (RICs) whose satisfaction is restored via introduction of null values. According to the notion of IC satisfaction implicit in [10], those introduced null values do not generate any new inconsistencies.

Here, we extend the approach and results in [10] in several ways. First, we give a precise semantics for integrity constraint satisfaction in the presence of null values that is both sensitive to *the relevance of the occurrence of a null value* in a relation, and also compatible with the way null values are usually treated in commercial database management systems (the one given in [10] was much more restrictive). The introduced null values do not generate infinite repair cycles through the same or other ICs, which requires a semantics for integrity constraint satisfaction under null values that sanctions that tuples with null values in attributes relevant for checking the IC do not generate any new inconsistencies. A new notion of repair is given accordingly. With the new repair semantics CQA becomes decidable for a quite general class of ICs that includes universal constraints, referential ICs, *NOT NULL*-constraints, and foreign key constraints, even the cyclic cases.

The logic programs that specify the repairs are modified wrt those given in [10], in such a way that the expected one-to-one correspondence between the stable models and repairs is recovered for *acyclic* sets of RICs. Finally, we study classes of ICs for which the specification can be optimized and a lower complexity for CQA can be obtained.

2 Preliminaries

We concentrate on relational databases, and we assume we have a fixed relational schema $\Sigma = (\mathcal{U}, \mathcal{R}, \mathcal{B})$, where $\mathcal{U}$ is the possibly infinite database domain such that $null \in \mathcal{U}$, $\mathcal{R}$ is a fixed set of database predicates, each of them with a finite, ordered set of attributes, and $\mathcal{B}$ is a fixed set of built-in predicates, like comparison predicates. $R[i]$ denotes the attribute in position i of predicate $R \in \mathcal{R}$. The schema determines a language $\mathcal{L}(\Sigma)$ of first-order predicate logic. A database instance D compatible with Σ can be seen as a finite collection of ground atoms of the form $R(c_1, ..., c_n)$,[1] where R is a predicate in $\mathcal{R}$ and $c_1, ..., c_n$ are constants in $\mathcal{U}$. Built-in predicates have a fixed extension in every database instance, not subject to changes. We need to define ICs because their syntax is fundamental for what follows.

An *integrity constraint* is a sentence $\psi \in \mathcal{L}(\Sigma)$ of the form:

$$\forall \bar{x}(\bigwedge_{i=1}^{m} P_i(\bar{x}_i) \longrightarrow \exists \bar{z}(\bigvee_{j=1}^{n} Q_j(\bar{y}_j, \bar{z}_j) \vee \varphi)), \tag{1}$$

where $P_i, Q_j \in \mathcal{R}$, $\bar{x} = \bigcup_{i=1}^{m} \bar{x}_i$, $\bar{z} = \bigcup_{j=1}^{n} \bar{z}_j$, $\bar{y}_j \subseteq \bar{x}$, $\bar{x} \cap \bar{z} = \emptyset$, $\bar{z}_i \cap \bar{z}_j = \emptyset$ for $i \neq j$, and $m \geq 1$. Formula φ is a disjunction of built-in atoms from $\mathcal{B}$, whose variables appear in the antecedent of the implication. We will assume that there is a propositional atom **false** $\in \mathcal{B}$ that is always false in a database. Domain constants other than *null* may appear instead of some of the variables in a constraint of the form (1). When writing ICs, we will usually leave the prefix of universal quantifiers implicit. A wide class of ICs can be accommodated in this general syntactic class by appropriate renaming of variables if necessary.

A *universal integrity constraint* (UIC) has the form (1), but with $\bar{z} = \emptyset$, i.e. without existentially quantified variables:

$$\bar{\forall} \bar{x}(\bigwedge_{i=1}^{m} P_i(\bar{x}_i) \longrightarrow \bigvee_{j=1}^{n} Q_j(\bar{y}_j) \vee \varphi). \tag{2}$$

A *referential integrity constraint* (RIC) is of the form (1), but with $m = n = 1$ and $\varphi = \emptyset$, i.e. of the form[2]: (here $\bar{x}' \subseteq \bar{x}$ and $P, Q \in \mathcal{R}$)

$$\forall \bar{x}\ (P(\bar{x}) \longrightarrow \exists \bar{y}\ Q(\bar{x}', \bar{y})). \tag{3}$$

[1] Also called *database tuples.* Finite sequences of constants in $\mathcal{U}$ are simply called *tuples.*

[2] To simplify the presentation, we are assuming the existential variables appear in the last attributes of Q, but they may appear anywhere else in Q.

Class (1) includes most ICs commonly found in database practice, e.g. a *denial constraint* can be expressed as $\forall\bar{x}(\bigwedge_{i=1}^{m} P_i(\bar{x}_i) \longrightarrow \textbf{false})$. Functional dependencies can be expressed by several implications of the form (1), each of them with a single equality in the consequent. Partial inclusion dependencies are RICs, and full inclusion dependencies are universal constraints. We can also specify (single row) *check constraints* that allow to express conditions on each row in a table, so they can be formulated with one predicate in the antecedent of (1) and only a formula φ in the consequent. For example, $\forall xy(P(x,y) \rightarrow y > 0)$ is a check constraint.

In the following we will assume that we have a fixed finite set IC of ICs of the form (1). Notice that sets of constraints of this form are always consistent in the classical sense, because empty database always satisfy them.

Example 1. For $\mathcal{R} = \{P, R, S\}$ and $\mathcal{B} = \{>, =, \textbf{false}\}$, the following are ICs: (a) $\forall xyzw\,(P(x,y) \wedge R(y,z,w) \rightarrow S(x) \vee (z \neq 2 \vee w \leq y))$ (universal). (b)$\forall xy(P(x, y) \rightarrow \exists z\, R(x,y,z))$ (referential). (c)$\forall x(S(x) \rightarrow \exists yz(R(x,y) \vee R(x,y,z)))$. □

Notice that defining φ in (1) as a disjunction of built-in atoms is not an important restriction, because an IC that has φ as a more complex formula can be transformed into a set of constraints of the form (1). For example, the formula $\forall xy\,(P(x,y) \rightarrow (x > y \vee (x = 3 \wedge y = 8)))$ can be transformed into: $\forall xy\,(P(x,y) \rightarrow (x > y \vee x = 3))$ and $\forall xy\,(P(x,y) \rightarrow (x > y \vee y = 8))$.

The *dependency graph* $\mathcal{G}(IC)$ [12] for a set of ICs IC of the form (1) is defined as follows: Each database predicate P in $\mathcal{R}$ appearing in IC is a vertex, and there is a directed edge (P_i, P_j) from P_i to P_j iff there exists a constraint $ic \in IC$ such that P_i appears in the antecedent of ic and P_j appears in the consequent of ic.

Example 2. For the set IC containing the UICs $ic_1 : S(x) \rightarrow Q(x)$ and $ic_2 : Q(x) \rightarrow R(x)$, and the RIC $ic_3 : Q(x) \rightarrow \exists y T(x,y)$, the following is the dependency graph $\mathcal{G}(IC)$:

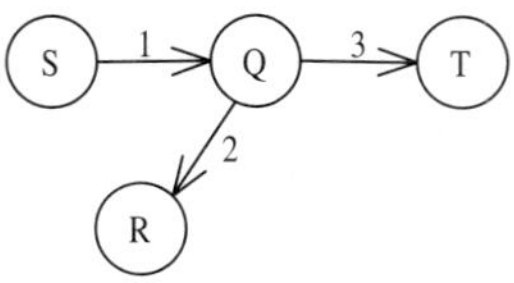

the edges are labelled just for reference. Edges 1 and 2 correspond to the constraints ic_1 and ic_2, resp., and edge 3 to ic_3. □

A *connected component* in a graph is a maximal subgraph such that for every pair $(A,\ B)$ of its vertices, there is a path from A to B or from B to A. For a graph $\mathcal{G}$, $\mathcal{C}(\mathcal{G}) := \{c \mid c$ is a connected component in $\mathcal{G}\}$; and $\mathcal{V}(\mathcal{G})$ is the set of vertices of $\mathcal{G}$.

Definition 1. Given a set IC of UICs and RICs, IC_U denotes the set of UICs in IC. The *contracted dependency graph*, $\mathcal{G}^C(IC)$, of IC is obtained from $\mathcal{G}(IC)$ by replacing, for every $c \in \mathcal{C}(\mathcal{G}(IC_U))$,[3] the vertices in $\mathcal{V}(c)$ by a single vertex and deleting all the edges associated to the elements of IC_U. Finally, IC is said to be *RIC-acyclic* if $\mathcal{G}^C(IC)$ has no cycles. □

[3] Notice that for every $c \in \mathcal{C}(\mathcal{G}(IC_U))$, it holds $c \in \mathcal{C}(\mathcal{G}(IC))$.

Example 3. (example 2 cont.) The contracted dependency graph $\mathcal{G}^C(IC)$ is obtained by replacing in $\mathcal{G}(IC)$ the edges 1 and 2 and their end vertices by a vertex labelled with $\{Q, R, S\}$.

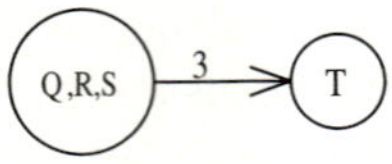

Since there are no loops in $\mathcal{G}^C(IC)$, IC is RIC-acylic. If we add a new UIC: $T(x, y) \rightarrow R(y)$ to IC, all the vertices belong to the same connected component. $\mathcal{G}(IC)$ and $\mathcal{G}^C(IC)$ are, respectively:

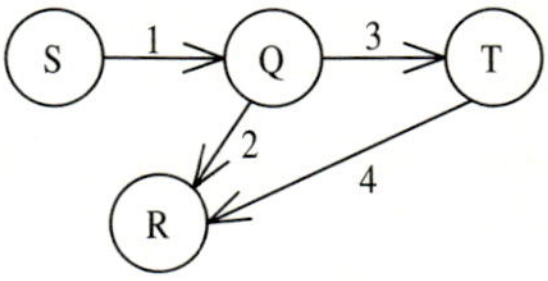

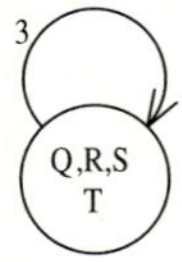

Since there is a self-loop in $\mathcal{G}^C(IC)$, the new IC is *not* RIC-acylic. □

As expected, a set of UICs is always RIC-acyclic.

3 IC Satisfaction in Databases with Null Values

We deal with incomplete databases in the classic sense that some information is represented using null values [21] (cf. also [19]). More recently, the notion of incomplete database has been used in the context of virtual data integration [23, 9], referring to data sources that contain a subset of the data of its kind in the global system; and in inconsistent databases [11, 15], referring to the fact that inconsistencies may have occurred due to missing information and then, repairs are obtained through insertion of new tuples.

There is no agreement in the literature on the semantics of null values in relational databases. There are several different proposals in the research literature [29, 4, 25, 28], in the SQL standard [31, 22], but also implicit semantics in the different ways null values are handled in commercial database management systems (DBMSs).

Not even within the SQL standard there is a homogenous and global semantics of integrity constraint satisfaction in databases with null values; rather, different definitions of satisfaction are given for each type of constraint. Actually, in the case of foreign key constraints, three different semantics are suggested (*simple-*, *partial-* and *full-match*). Commercial DBMSs implement only the simple-match semantics for foreign key constraints. Some criticisms to the treatment of nulls in the SQL standard have been expressed by the database community, c.f. [32].

One of the reasons why it is difficult to agree on a semantics is that a null value can be interpreted as an unknown, inapplicable or even withheld value. Different null constants can be used for each of these different interpretations [27]. Also the use of more than one null value (of the same kind), i.e. labelled nulls, has been suggested [30], but in this case every new null value uses a new fresh constant; for which the *unique names assumption* does not apply. The latter alternative allows to keep a relationship between null values in different attributes or relations. However commercial DBMSs consider only one null value, represented by a single constant, that can be given any of the interpretations mentioned above.

In [10] a semantics for null values was adopted, according to which a tuple with a null value in any of its attributes would not be the cause for any inconsistencies. In other words, it would not be necessary to check tuples with null values wrt possible violations of ICs (except for *NOT NULL*- constraints, of course). This assumption is consistent in some cases with the practice of DBMSs, e.g. in IBM DB2 UDB. Here we will propose a semantics that is less liberal in relation to the participation of null values in inconsistencies; a sort of compromise solution considering the different alternatives available.

Example 4. For *IC* containing only $\psi_1\colon P(x,y,z) \rightarrow R(y,z)$, the database $D = \{P(a,b,null)\}$ would be: (a) Consistent wrt the semantics in [10] because there is a null value in the tuple (b) Consistent wrt the simple-match semantics of SQL:2003 [22], because there is a null value in one of the attributes in the set $\{P[2], P[3], R[1], R[2]\}$ of attributes that are relevant to check the constraint. (c) Inconsistent wrt the partial-match semantics in SQL:2003, because there is no tuple in R with a value b in its first attribute. (d) Inconsistent wrt the full-match semantics in SQL:2003, because there cannot be a *null* in an attribute that is referencing a different table.

If we consider, instead of ψ_1, the constraint $\psi_2 : P(x,y,z) \rightarrow R(x,y)$, the same database would be consistent only for the semantics in [10], because the other semantics consider only the null value in the attributes that are relevant to check the constraint, and in this case there is no null value there. □

Even though there are different possible semantics, we would like to define and concentrate in a null-value semantics that would allow us to integrate our results with commercial databases. This is why we would like to generalize in a declarative and homogenous way the semantics defined in SQL:2003 [22] that is implemented in commercial DBMSs like IBM DB2 UDB. For this reason we consider only one kind of null value. We also want our null-value semantics to be uniform for a wide class of ICs that goes beyond the type of constraints supported by commercial DBMS.

Example 5. Consider a database with a table that stores courses with the professor that taught it and the term, and a table that stores the experience of each professor in each course with the number of times (s)he has taught the course. We have a foreign key constraint based on the RIC $\forall xyz(Course(x,y,z) \rightarrow \exists w\ Exp(y,\ x,\ w))$ together with the constraint expressing that table *Exp* has $\{ID, Code\}$ as a key. We can be sure there are no null values in those two attributes. Now consider the instance D:

Course	Code	ID	Term
	CS27	*21*	W04
	CS18	*34*	*null*
	CS50	*null*	W05

Exp	ID	Code	Times
	21	*CS27*	3
	34	*CS18*	*null*
	45	*CS32*	*2*

In IBM DB2, this database is accepted as consistent. The null values in columns *Term* and *Times* are not relevant to check the satisfaction of the constraints. In order to check the constraint the only attributes that we need to pay attention to are *ID* and *Code*. If *null* is in the one of these attributes in table *Course*, the tuple is considered to be consistent, without checking table *Exp*. For example *Course(CS50,null, W05)* has a null value in *ID*, therefore DB2 does not check if there is a tuple in *Exp* that satisfies the constraint. It does not even check that there exists a tuple in *Exp* with attribute *Code=CS50*.

This behavior for foreign key constraints is called simple-match in the SQL standard, and is the one implemented in all commercial DBMS. The partial- and full-match would not accept the database as consistent, because partial-match would require *Exp* to have a tuple (any non-null value, *CS50*, any value); and full-match would not allow a tuple with *null* in attributes *ID* or *Code* in table *Course*.

If we try to insert tuple *(CS41,18, null)* into table *Course*, it would be rejected by DB2. This is because the attributes *ID* and *Code* are relevant to check the constraint and are different from *null*, but there is no tuple in *Exp* with *ID=18* and *Code=CS41*. □

Example 6. Consider the single-row check constraint $\forall ID\, \forall Name\, \forall Salary\, (Emp\, (ID, Name, Salary) \rightarrow Salary > 100)$ and the database D below. DB2 accepts this database instance as consistent. Here, in order to check the satisfaction of the constraint, we only need to verify that the attribute *Salary* is bigger than 100; therefore the only attribute that is relevant to check the constraint is *Salary*. DBMSs will accept as consistent any state where the condition (the consequent) evaluates to *true* or *unknown*. The latter is the case here. Tuple (32, *null*, 50) could not be inserted because $Salary > 100$ evaluates to *false*. Notice that the null values in attributes other that *Salary* are not even considered in the verification of the satisfaction. □

Emp	ID	Name	Salary
	32	*null*	*1000*
	41	*Paul*	*null*

When dealing with primary keys, DBMSs use a bag semantics instead of the set semantics, that is, a table can have two copies of the same tuple. The following example illustrates the issue.

Example 7. Since the SQL standard allows duplicate rows, i.e. uses the bag semantics, it is possible to have the database D below. If this database had $P[1]$ as the primary key, then D would not have been accepted as a consistent state, i.e. the insertion of the second tuple $P(a, b)$ would have been rejected.

P	A	B
	a	b
	a	b

This is one of the cases in which the SQL standard deviates from the relational model, where duplicates of a row are not considered. In a commercial DBMS a primary key is checked by adding an index to the primary key and then ensuring that there are no duplicates. Therefore if we try to check the primary key by using the associated functional dependency $P(x, y), P(x, z) \rightarrow y = z$ we would not have the same semantics since D satisfies the functional dependency in this classical, first-order representation. □

With the type of first-order constraints that we are considering, we cannot enforce a bag semantics, therefore we will assume that D is consistent.

In order to develop a null-value semantics that goes beyond the ICs supported by DBMSs, we analyze other examples.

Example 8. Consider the UIC $\forall xyzstuw(Person(x,y,z,w) \wedge Person(z,s,t,u) \rightarrow u > w+15)$, and the database D below. This constraint can be considered as a multi-row check constraint. If we want to naturally extend the semantics for single-row check constraints, D would be consistent iff the condition evaluates to *true* or *unknown*. In this case, D would be consistent because the condition evaluates to *unknown* for $u = null$ and $w = 27$. Here the relevant attributes to check the IC are *Name, Mom, Age*. □

Person	Name	Dad	Mom	Age
	Lee	*Rod*	*Mary*	*27*
	Rod	*Joe*	*Tess*	*55*
	Mary	*Adam*	*Ann*	*null*

Example 9. Consider the UIC $\forall xyz(Course(x,y,z) \rightarrow Employee(y,z))$ and the database D:

Course	Code	Term	ID
	CS18	*W04*	*34*

Employee	Term	ID
	W04	*null*

Since *Term, ID* is not a primary key of *Employee*, the constraint is not a foreign key constraint, and therefore it is not supported by commercial DBMS. In contrast to foreign key constraints, now we can have a null value in the referenced attributes. In order to extend the semantics used in commercial DBMS. to this case, we refer to the literature. For example, in [25] the satisfaction of this type of constraints is defined as follows: An IC $\forall \bar{x}\bar{y}P(\bar{x}) \rightarrow \exists \bar{z}Q(\bar{y},\bar{z})$ is satisfied if, for every tuple $t_1 \in P$, there exists a tuple $t_2 \in Q$, such that t_1 provides *less or equal information* than t_2, i.e. for every attribute, the value in t_1 is the same as in t_2 or the value in t_1 is *null*. In this example we have the opposite situation: (*W04,34*) does *not* provide less or equal information than (*W04,null*). Therefore, we consider the database to be inconsistent wrt the constraint. Note that the only attributes that are relevant to check the constraint are *Term* and *ID*. □

Examples 6, 5, 8 and 9 show that there are some attributes that are "relevant" when the satisfaction of a constraint is checked against a database.

Definition 2. For t a term, i.e. a variable or a domain constant, let $pos^R(\psi,t)$ be the set of positions in predicate $R \in \mathcal{R}$ where t appears in ψ. The set $\mathcal{A}$ of *relevant attributes* for an IC ψ of the form (1) is
$\mathcal{A}(\psi) = \{R[i] \mid x \text{ is variable present at least twice in } \psi, \text{ and } i \in pos^R(\psi,x)\} \cup$
$\{R[i] \mid c \text{ is a constant in } \psi \text{ and } i \in pos^R(\psi,c)\}$. □

Remember that $R[i]$ denotes a position (or the correspondent attribute) in relation R. In short, the relevant attributes for a constraint are those involved in joins, those appearing both in the antecedent and consequent of (1), and those in φ.

Definition 3. For a set of attributes $\mathcal{A}$ and a predicate $P \in \mathcal{R}$, we denote by $P^{\mathcal{A}}$ the predicate P restricted to the attributes in $\mathcal{A}$. $D^{\mathcal{A}}$ denotes the database D with all its database atoms projected onto the attributes in $\mathcal{A}$, i.e. $D^{\mathcal{A}} = \{P^{\mathcal{A}}(\Pi_{\mathcal{A}}(\bar{t})) \mid P(\bar{t}) \in D\}$, where $\Pi_{\mathcal{A}}(\bar{t})$ is the projection on $\mathcal{A}$ of tuple $\bar{t}$. $D^{\mathcal{A}}$ has the same underlying domain $\mathcal{U}$ as D. □

Example 10. Consider a UIC $\psi: \forall xyz(P(x,y,z) \rightarrow R(x,y))$ and D below.

P	A	B	C
	a	b	a
	b	c	a

R	A	B
	a	5
	a	2

Since x and y appear twice in ψ, $\mathcal{A}(\psi) = \{P[1], R[1], P[2], R[2]\}$. The value in z should not be relevant to check the satisfaction of the constraint, because we only want to make sure that the values in the first two attributes in P also appear in R. Then, checking this is equivalent to checking if $\forall xy(P^{\mathcal{A}(\psi)}(x,y) \rightarrow R^{\mathcal{A}(\psi)}(x,y))$ is satisfied by $D^{\mathcal{A}(\psi)}$. For a more complex constraint, such as γ: $\forall xyzw(P(x,y,z) \wedge R(z,w) \rightarrow \exists v R(x,v) \vee w > 3)$, variable x is relevant to check the implication, z is needed to do the join, and w is needed to check the comparison, therefore $\mathcal{A}(\gamma) = \{P[1], R[1], P[3], R[2]\}$.

$D^{\mathcal{A}(\psi)}$:

$P^{\mathcal{A}(\psi)}$	A	B
	a	b
	b	c

$R^{\mathcal{A}(\psi)}$	A	B
	a	5
	a	2

$D^{\mathcal{A}(\gamma)}$:

$P^{\mathcal{A}(\gamma)}$	A	C
	a	a
	b	a

$R^{\mathcal{A}(\gamma)}$	A	B
	a	5
	a	2

□

An important observation we can make from Examples 6, 5, 8 and 9 is that, roughly speaking, a constraint is satisfied if any of the relevant attributes has a *null* or the constraint is satisfied in the traditional way (i.e. first-order satisfaction and null values treated as any other constant). We introduce a special predicate *IsNull*$(\cdot)$, with *IsNull*(c) true iff c is *null*, instead of using the built-in comparison atom $c = null$, because in traditional DBMS this equality would be always evaluated as *unknown* (as observed in [29], the *unique names assumption* does not apply to null values).

Definition 4. A constraint ψ as in (1) is satisfied in the database instance D, denoted $D \models_N \psi$ iff $D^{\mathcal{A}(\psi)} \models \psi^N$, where ψ^N is

$$\forall \bar{x}(\bigwedge_{i=1}^{m} P_i^{\mathcal{A}(\psi)}(\bar{x}_i) \rightarrow (\bigvee_{v_j \in \mathcal{A}(\psi) \cap \bar{x}} IsNull(v_j) \vee \exists \bar{z}(\bigvee_{j=1}^{n} Q_j^{\mathcal{A}(\psi)}(\bar{y}_j, \bar{z}_j) \vee \varphi))), \quad (4)$$

where $\bar{x} = \cup_{i=1}^{m} \bar{x}_i$ and $\bar{z} = \cup_{j=1}^{n} \bar{z}_j$. $D^{\mathcal{A}(\psi)} \models \psi^N$ refers to classical first-order satisfaction where *null* is treated as any other constant in $\mathcal{U}$. □

We can see from Definition 4 that there are basically two cases for constraint satisfaction: (a) If there is a *null* in any of the relevant attributes in the antecedent, then the constraint is satisfied. (b) If no null values appear in them, then the second disjunct in the consequent of formula (4) has to be checked, i.e, the consequent of the original IC restricted to the relevant attributes. This can be done as usual, treating nulls as any other constant.

Formula (4) is a direct translation of formula (1) that keeps the relevant attributes. In particular, if the original constraint is universal, so is the transformed version. Notice that the transformed constraint is domain independent, and then its satisfaction can be checked by restriction to the active domain.

As mentioned before, the semantics for IC satisfaction introduced in [10] considered that tuples with *null* never generated any inconsistencies, even when the null value was not in a relevant attribute. For example, under the semantics in [10], the instance $\{P(b, null)\}$ would be consistent wrt the IC $\forall xy(P(x,y) \rightarrow R(x))$, but it is intuitively clear that there should be a tuple $R(b)$. The new semantics corrects this, and adjusts to the semantics implemented in commercial DBMS.

Notice that in a database without null values, Definition 4 (so as the definition in [10]) coincides with the traditional, first-order definition of IC satisfaction.

Example 11. Given the ICs: (a) $\forall xyz(P(x,y,z) \rightarrow R(x,y))$, (b) $\forall x(T(x) \rightarrow \exists yz P(x, y, z))$, the database instance D below is consistent.

P	A	B	C
	a	d	e
	b	*null*	g

R	D	E
	a	d

T	F
	b

For (a), the variables x and y are relevant to check the constraint, therefore $\mathcal{A}_1 = \{P[1], R[1], P[2], R[2]\}$; and for (b), the variable x is relevant to check the constraint; therefore $\mathcal{A}_2 = \{P[1], T[1]\}$.

$D^{\mathcal{A}_1}$:

$P^{\mathcal{A}_1}$	A	B
	a	d
	b	*null*

$R^{\mathcal{A}_1}$	D	E
	a	d

$D^{\mathcal{A}_2}$:

$P^{\mathcal{A}_2}$	A
	a
	b

$T^{\mathcal{A}_2}$	F
	b

To check if $D \models_N \forall xyz(P(x,y,z) \rightarrow R(x,y))$, we need to check if $D^{\mathcal{A}_1} \models \forall xy(P^{\mathcal{A}_1}(x,y) \rightarrow (IsNull(x) \vee IsNull(y) \vee R^{\mathcal{A}_1}(x,y)))$ For $x = a$ and $y = d$, $D^{\mathcal{A}_1} \models P^{\mathcal{A}_1}(a,d)$, but none of them is a null value, i.e. $IsNull(a)$ and $IsNull(d)$ are both false, therefore we need to check if $D^{\mathcal{A}_1} \models R^{\mathcal{A}_1}(a,d)$. For $x = b$ and $y = null$, $D^{\mathcal{A}_1} \models P^{\mathcal{A}_1}(b, null)$, and since $D^{\mathcal{A}_1} \models IsNull(null)$, the constraint is satisfied. The same analysis can be done to prove that D satisfies constraint (b), this is by checking $D^{\mathcal{A}_2} \models \forall x(T^{\mathcal{A}_2}(x) \rightarrow (IsNull(x) \vee P^{\mathcal{A}_2}(x)))$

If we add tuple $P(f, d, null)$ to D, it would become inconsistent wrt constraint (a), because $D^{\mathcal{A}_1} \not\models (P^{\mathcal{A}_1}(f,d) \rightarrow (IsNull(f) \vee IsNull(d) \vee R^{\mathcal{A}_1}(f,d)))$. □

Example 12. Consider the IC ψ: $\forall xywz\ ((P_1(x,y,w) \wedge P_2(y,z)) \rightarrow \exists u\ Q(x,z,u))$ and the database D:

P_1	A	B	C
	a	*b*	*c*
	d	*null*	*c*
	b	*e*	*null*
	null	*b*	*b*

P_2	D	E
	b	*a*
	e	*c*
	d	*null*
	null	*b*

Q	F	G	H
	a	*a*	*c*
	b	*null*	*c*
	b	*c*	*d*
	null	*c*	*a*

Variables x, y and z are relevant to check the constraint, therefore the set of relevant attributes is $\mathcal{A}(\psi) = \{P_1[1], P_1[2], P_2[1], P_2[2], Q[1], Q[2]\}$. Then we need to check if $D^{\mathcal{A}(\psi)} \models \forall xyz\ ((P_1^{\mathcal{A}(\psi)}(x,y) \wedge P_2^{\mathcal{A}(\psi)}(y,z)) \rightarrow (IsNull(x) \vee IsNull(y) \vee IsNull(z) \vee Q^{\mathcal{A}(\psi)}(x,z))$, where $D^{\mathcal{A}(\psi)}$ is

$P_1^{\mathcal{A}(\psi)}$	A	B
	a	b
	d	$null$
	b	e
	$null$	b

$P_2^{\mathcal{A}(\psi)}$	D	E
	b	a
	e	c
	d	$null$
	$null$	b

$Q^{\mathcal{A}(\psi)}$	F	G
	a	a
	b	$null$
	b	c
	$null$	c

When checking the satisfaction of $D^{\mathcal{A}(\psi)} \models \psi^N$, *null* is treated as any other constant. For example for $x = d$, $y = null$ and $z = b$, the antecedent of the rule is satisfied since $P_1^{\mathcal{A}(\psi)}(d, null) \in D^{\mathcal{A}}$ and $P_2^{\mathcal{A}(\psi)}(null, b) \in D^{\mathcal{A}}$. If *null* had been treated as a special constant, with no unique names assumption applied to it, the antecedent would have been false. For these values the consequence is also satisfied, because *IsNull*(*null*) is true. In this example, $D^{\mathcal{A}(\psi)} \models \psi^N$, and the database satisfies the constraint. □

Notice that in order for formula (4) to have $\bar{z} \neq \emptyset$, i.e. existential quantifiers, there must exist an atom $Q_j(\bar{y}_j, \bar{z}_j)$ in the corresponding IC of the form (1), such that $\bar{z}_j$ has a repeated variable. This is because that is the only case in which a constraint can have $(\mathcal{A}(\psi) \smallsetminus \bar{x}) \neq \emptyset$.

Example 13. Given $\psi\colon \forall x(P(x, y) \rightarrow \exists z Q(x, z, z))$ and $D = \{P(a, b), P(null, c), Q(a, null, null)\}$, $\mathcal{A}(\psi) = \{P[1], Q[1], Q[2], Q[3]\}$. D satisfies ψ iff $D^{\mathcal{A}} \models \psi^N$, with $D^{\mathcal{A}(\psi)} = \{P^{\mathcal{A}}(a), P^{\mathcal{A}}(null), Q^{\mathcal{A}}(a, null, null)\}$ and $\psi^N : \forall x(P^{\mathcal{A}(\psi)}(x) \rightarrow (IsNull(x) \vee \exists z Q^{\mathcal{A}(\psi)}(x, z, z)))$. The constraint is satisfied, because for $x = a$ it is satisfied given that there exists the satisfying value *null* for z; and for $x = null$ the constraint is satisfied given that *IsNull*(*null*) is true. □

The predicate *IsNull* also allows us to specify *NOT NULL*-constraints, which are common in commercial DBMS, and prevent certain attributes from taking a null value. As discussed before, this constraint is different from having $x \neq null$.

Definition 5. A *NOT NULL*-constraint (NNC) is a denial constraint of the form

$$\bar{\forall} \bar{x}(P(\bar{x}) \wedge IsNull(x_i) \rightarrow \textbf{false}), \tag{5}$$

where $x_i \in \bar{x}$ is in the position of the attribute that cannot take null values. For a NNC ψ, we define $D \models_N \psi$ iff $D \models \psi$ in the classical sense, treating *null* as any other constant. □

Notice that a NNC is not of the form (1), because it contains the constant *null*. This is why we give a separate definitions for them. By adding NNCs we are able to represent all the constraints of commercial DBMS, i.e. primary keys, foreign key constraints, check constraints and *NOT NULL*-constraints.

Our semantics is a natural extension of the semantics used in commercial DBMSs. Note that: (a) In a DBMS there will never be a join between a null and another value (null or not). (b) Any check constraint with comparison, e.g $<, >, =$, will never create an inconsistency when comparing a null value with any other value. These two features justify our decision in Definition 4 to include the attributes in the joins and the elements in φ among the attributes that are checked to be null with *IsNull*, because if there is a null in them an inconsistency will never arise.

Our semantics of IC satisfaction with null values allows us to integrate our results in a compatible way with current commercial implementations; in the sense that the database repairs we will introduce later on would be accepted as consistent by current commercial implementations (for the classes of constraints that can be defined and maintained by them).

4 Repairs of Incomplete Databases

Given a database instance D, possibly with null values, that is inconsistent, i.e. D does not satisfy a given set IC of ICs of the kind defined in Section 3 or NNCs. A *repair* of D will be a new instance with the same schema as D that satisfies IC and minimally differs from D.

More formally, for database instances D, D' over the same schema, the *distance* between them was defined in [2] by means of the symmetric difference $\Delta(D, D') = (D \smallsetminus D') \cup (D' \smallsetminus D)$. Correspondingly, a repair of D wrt IC was defined as an instance D' that satisfies IC and minimizes $\Delta(D, D')$ under set inclusion. Finally, a tuple $\bar{t}$ was defined as a consistent answer to a query $Q(\bar{x})$ in D wrt IC if $\bar{t}$ is an answer to $Q(\bar{x})$ from every repair of D wrt IC. The definition of repair given in [2] implicitly ignored the possible presence of null values. Similarly, in [3, 5, 11], that followed the repair semantics in [2], no null values were used in repairs.

Example 14. Consider the database D below and the RIC: $Course(ID, Code) \rightarrow \exists Name\ Student(ID, Name)$. D is inconsistent, because there is no tuple in *Student* for tuple *Course(34,C18)* in *Course*. The database can be minimally repaired by deleting the inconsistent tuple or by inserting a new tuple into table *Student*. In the latter case, since the value for attribute *Name* is unknown, we should consider repairs with all the possible values in the domain. Therefore, for the repair semantics introduced in [2], the repairs are of the two following forms

Course	ID	Code
	21	*C15*
	34	*C18*

Student	ID	Name
	21	*Ann*
	45	*Paul*

Course	ID	Code
	21	*C15*

Student	ID	Name
	21	*Ann*
	45	*Paul*

Course	ID	Code
	21	*C15*
	34	*C18*

Student	ID	Name
	21	*Ann*
	45	*Paul*
	34	μ

for all the possible values of μ in the domain, obtaining a possibly infinite number of repairs. □

The problem of deciding if a tuple is a consistent answer to a query wrt to a set of universal and referential ICs is undecidable for this repair semantics [11].

An alternative approach is to consider that, in a way, the value μ in Example 14 is an unknown value, and therefore, instead of making it take all the values in the domain, we could use it as a null value. We will pursue this idea, which requires to modify the notion of repair accordingly. It will turn out that consistent query answering will become decidable for universal and referential constraints.

Example 15. (example 14 cont.) By using null values, there will be two repairs:

Repair 1:

Course	ID	Code
	21	*C15*

Student	ID	Name
	21	*Ann*
	45	*Paul*

Repair 2:

Course	ID	Code
	21	*C15*
	34	*C18*

Student	ID	Name
	21	*Ann*
	45	*Paul*
	34	*null*

Here *null* tells us that there is a tuple with 34 in the first attribute, but unknown value in the second. □

Now we define in precise terms the notion of repair of a database with null values.

Definition 6. [6] Let D, D', D'' be database instances over the same schema and domain $\mathcal{U}$. It holds $D' \leq_D D''$ iff: (a) For every database atom $P(\bar{a}) \in \Delta(D, D')$, with $\bar{a} \in (\mathcal{U} \smallsetminus \{null\})$,[4] it holds $P(\bar{a}) \in \Delta(D, D'')$; and (b) For every atom $Q(\bar{a}, \overline{null})$[5] $\in \Delta(D, D')$, with $\bar{a} \in (\mathcal{U} \smallsetminus \{null\})$, there exists a $\bar{b} \in \mathcal{U}$ such that $Q(\bar{a}, \bar{b}) \in \Delta(D, D'')$ and $Q(\bar{a}, \bar{b}) \notin \Delta(D, D')$. □

Definition 7. Given a database instance D and a set IC of ICs of the form (1) and NNCs, a repair of D wrt IC is a database instance D' over the same schema, such that $D' \models_N IC$ and D' is $\leq_D$-*minimal* in the class of database instances that satisfy IC wrt $\models_N$, and share the schema with D, i.e. there is no database D'' in this class with $D'' <_D D'$, where $D'' <_D D'$ means $D'' \leq_D D'$ but not $D' \leq_D D''$. The set of repairs of D wrt IC is denoted with $Rep(D, IC)$. □

In the absence of *null*, this definition of repair coincides with the one in [2].

Example 16. The database instance $D = \{Q(a,b), P(a,c)\}$ is inconsistent wrt the ICs $\psi_1 : (P(x,y) \rightarrow \exists z Q(x,z))$ and $\psi_2 : (Q(x,y) \rightarrow y \neq b)$.[6] because $D \not\models_N \psi_2$. The database has two repairs wrt $\{\psi_1, \psi_2\}$, namely $D_1 = \{\}$, with $\Delta(D, D_1) = \{Q(a,b), P(a,c)\}$, and $D_2 = \{P(a,b), Q(a, null))\}$, with $\Delta(D, D_2) = \{Q(a,b), Q(a, null)\}$. Notice that $D_2 \not\leq_D D_1$ because $Q(a, null) \in \Delta(D, D_2)$ and there is no constant $d \in \mathcal{U}$ such that $Q(a,d) \in \Delta(D, D_1)$ and $Q(a,d) \notin \Delta(D, D_2)$. Similarly, $D_1 \not\leq_D D_2$, because $P(a,c) \in \Delta(D, D_1)$ and $P(a,c) \notin \Delta(D, D_1)$. □

Example 17. If the database instance is $\{P(a, null), P(b,c), R(a,b)\}$ and IC consists only of $(P(x,y) \rightarrow \exists z\, R(x,z))$, then there are two repairs: $D_1 = \{P(a, null)$, $P(b,c)$, $R(a,b)$, $R(b, null)\}$, with $\Delta(D, D_1) = \{R(b, null)\}$, and $D_2 = \{P(a, null)$, $R(a,b)\}$, with $\Delta(D, D_2) = \{P(b,c)\}$. Notice, for example, that $D_3 = \{P(a, null)$, $P(b,c)$, $R(a,b)$, $R(b,d)\}$, for any $d \in \mathcal{U}$ different from *null*, is not a repair: Since $\Delta(D, D_3) = \{R(b,d)\}$, we have $D_2 <_D D_3$ and, therefore D_3 is not $\leq_D$-minimal. □

---

4 That $\bar{a} \in (\mathcal{U} \smallsetminus \{null\})$ means that each of the elements in tuple $\bar{a}$ belongs to $(\mathcal{U} \smallsetminus \{null\})$.

5 $\overline{null}$ is a tuple of null values, that, to simplify the presentation, are placed in the last attributes of Q, but could be anywhere else in Q.

6 The second IC is *non-generic* [7] in the sense that it implies some ground database literals. Non generic ICs have in general been left aside in the literature on CQA.

Example 18. Consider the UIC $\forall xy(P(x,y) \rightarrow T(x))$ and the RIC $\forall x(T(x) \rightarrow \exists y P(y,x))$, and the inconsistent database $D = \{P(a,b), P(null,a), T(c)\}$. In this case, we have a RIC-cyclic set of ICs. The four repairs are

i	D_i	$\Delta(D, D_i)$
1	$\{P(a,b), P(null,a), T(c), P(null,c), T(a)\}$	$\{T(a), P(null,c)\}$
2	$\{P(a,b), P(null,a), T(a)\}$	$\{T(a), T(c)\}$
3	$\{P(null,a), T(c), P(null,c)\}$	$\{P(a,b), P(null,c)\}$
4	$\{P(null,a)\}$	$\{P(a,b), T(c)\}$

Notice that, for example, the additional instance $D_5 = \{P(a,b), P(null,a), T(c), P(c,a), T(c)\}$, with $\Delta(D, D_5) = \{T(a), P(c,a)\}$, satisfies IC, but is not a repair because $D_1 <_D D_5$. □

The previous example shows that we obtain a finite number of repairs (with finite extension). If we repaired the database by using the non-null constants in the infinite domain with the repair semantics of [2], we would obtain an infinite number of repairs and infinitely many of them with infinite extension, as considered in [11].

Example 19. Consider a schema with relations $R(X,Y)$, with primary key $R[1]$, and a table $S(U,V)$, with $S[2]$ a foreign key to table R. The ICs are $\forall xyz\ (R(x,y) \wedge R(x,z) \rightarrow y = z)$ and $\forall uv\ (S(u,v) \rightarrow \exists y\ R(v,y))$, plus the NNC $\forall xy(R(x,y) \wedge \mathit{IsNull}(x) \rightarrow \mathbf{false})$. Since the original database satisfies the NNC and there is no constraint with an existential quantifier over $R[1]$, the NNC will not be violated while trying to solve other inconsistencies. We would have a *non-conflicting interaction* of RICs and NNCs. Here $D = \{R(a,b), R(a,c), S(e,f), S(null,a)\}$ is inconsistent and its repairs are $D_1 = \{R(a,b), S(e,f), S(null,a), R(f,null)\}$, $D_2 = \{R(a,c), S(e,f), S(null,a), R(f,null)\}$, $D_3 = \{R(a,b), S(null,a)\}$ and $D_4 = \{R(a,c), S(null,a)\}$. □

If a given database D is consistent wrt a set of ICs, then there is only one repair, that coincides with D. The following example shows what can happen if we have a *conflicting interaction* of a RIC containing an existential quantifier over a variable with an additional NNC that prevents that variable from taking null values.

Example 20. Consider the database $D = \{P(a), P(b), Q(b,c)\}$, the RIC $\forall x\ (P(x) \rightarrow \exists y\ Q(x,y))$, and the NNC $\forall xy(Q(x,y) \wedge \mathit{IsNull}(y) \rightarrow \mathbf{false})$ over an existentially quantified attribute in the RIC. We cannot repair as expected using null values. Actually, the repairs are $\{P(b), Q(b,c)\}$, corresponding to a tuple deletion, but also those of the form $\{P(a), P(b), Q(b,c), Q(a,\ \mu)\}$, for every $\mu \in (\mathcal{U} \smallsetminus \{null\})$, that are obtained by tuple insertions. We thus recover the repair semantics of [2]. □

With an appropriate conflicting interaction of RICs and NNCs we could recover in our setting the situation where infinitely many repairs and infinitely many with finite extension appear (c.f. remark after Example 18). Our repair semantics above could be modified in order to repair only through tuple deletions in this case, when null values cannot be used due to the presence of conflicting NNCs. This could be done as follows: If $Rep(D, IC)$ is the class of repairs according to Definitions 6 and 7, the alternative class of repairs, $Rep_d(D, IC)$, that prefers tuple deletions over insertions with arbitrary non-null elements of the domain due to the presence of conflicting NNCs, can be defined by $Rep_d(D, IC) := \{D' \mid D' \in Rep(D, IC)$ and there is no $D'' \in Rep(D, IC')$ with $D'' <_D D'\}$, where IC' is IC without the (conflicting) NNCs.

Since the semantics introduced Definitions 6 and 7 is easier to deal with, and in order to avoid repairs like those in Example 20, we will make the following

Assumption: Our sets IC, consisting of ICs of the form (1) and NNCs, are *non-conflicting*, in the sense that there is no NNC on an attribute that is existentially quantified in an IC of the form (1).

In this way, we will always be able to repair RICs by tuple deletions or tuple insertions with null values. Notice that every set of ICs consisting of primary key constraints (with the keys set to be non-null), foreign key constraints, and check constraints satisfies this condition. Also note that if there are non conflicting NNCs, the original semantics and the one based on Rep_d-repairs coincide. The repair programs introduced in Section 5 compute specify the Rep_d-repairs, so our assumption is also relevant from the computational point of view.

It is possible to prove that under our repair semantics there will always exists a repair for a database D wrt a set of non-conflicting ICs. This follows from the fact that a database instance with no tuples always satisfies the ICs. Furthermore, the set of repairs is finite and each of them is finite in extension (i.e. each database relation is finite). This can be proved establishing first by contradiction that the repairs are restricted to have constants in $adom(D) \cup const(IC) \cup \{null\}$, where $adom(D)$ is the active domain of the original instance D and $const(IC)$ is the set of constants that appear in the ICs. Since the constants that can appear in the repairs are finite there is a finite set of candidates to repairs, and each of them is finite.

Proposition 1. Given a database D and a set IC of non-conflicting ICs: (a) For every repair $D' \in Rep(D, IC)$, $adom(D') \subseteq adom(D) \cup const(IC) \cup \{null\}$. (b) The set $Rep(D, IC)$ of repairs is non-empty and finite; and every $D' \in Rep(D, IC)$ is finite.[7] □

Theorem 1. The problem of determining if a database D' is a repair of D wrt a set IC consisting of ICs of the form (1) and NNCs[8] is *coNP*-complete. □

Definition 8. [2] Given a database D, a set of ICs IC, and a query $Q(\bar{x})$, a ground tuple $\bar{t}$ is a *consistent answer* to Q wrt IC in D iff for every $D' \in Rep(D, IC)$, $D' \models Q[\bar{t}]$. If Q is a sentence (boolean query), then *yes* is a consistent answer iff $D' \models Q$ for every $D' \in Rep(D, IC)$. Otherwise, the consistent answer is *no*. □

[7] For proofs of all results go to `www.scs.carleton.ca/~lbravo/IIDBdemos.pdf`

[8] In this case we do not need the assumption of non-conflicting ICs.

In this formulation of CQA we are using a notion $D' \models Q[\bar{t}]$ of satisfaction of queries in a database with null values. At this stage, we are not committing to any particular semantics for query answering in this kind of databases. In the rest of the paper, we will assume that we have such a notion, say $\models_N^q$, that can be applied to queries in databases with null values. Some proposals can be found in the literature [22, 26, 34]. In principle, $\models_N^q$ may be orthogonal to the notion $\models_N$ for satisfaction of ICs. However, in the extended version of this paper we will present a semantics for query answering that is compatible with the one for IC satisfaction. For the moment we are going to assume that $\models_N^q$ can be computed in polynomial time in data for safe first-order queries, and that it coincides with the classical first-order semantics for queries and databases without null values. We will also assume in the following that queries are safe [33], a sufficient syntactic condition for domain independence.

The decision problem of consistent query answering is

$$CQA(Q, IC) = \{(D, \bar{t}) \mid \bar{t} \text{ is a consistent answer to } Q(\bar{x}) \text{ wrt } IC \text{ in } D\}.$$

Since we have Q and IC as parameters of the problem, we are interested in the data complexity of this problem, i.e. in terms of the size of the database [1]. It turns out that CQA for FOL queries is decidable, in contrast to what happens with the classic repair semantics [2], as established in [11].

Theorem 2. Consistent query answering for first-order queries wrt to non-conflicting sets of ICs of the form (1) and NNCs is decidable. □

The ideas behind the proof are as follows: (a) There is a finite number of database instances that are candidates to be repair given that the use only the active domain of the original instance, *null* and the constants in the ICs. (b) The satisfaction of ICs in the candidates can de decided by restriction to the active domain given that the ICs are domain independent. (c) Checking if $D_1 \leq_D D_2$ can be effectively decided. (d) The answers to safe first-order queries can be effectively computed.

The following proposition can be obtained by using a similar result [15] and the fact that our tuple deletion based repairs are exactly those considered in [15], and every repair in our sense that is not one of those contains at least one tuple insertion.

Theorem 3. Consistent query answering for first-order queries and non-conflicting sets of ICs of the form (1) or NNCs is Π_2^p-complete. □

In the proof of this theorem NNCs are not needed for hardness. Actually, hardness can be obtained with boolean queries.

5 Repair Logic Programs

The stable models semantics was introduced in [18] to give a semantics to disjunctive logic programs that are non-stratified, i.e. that contain recursive definitions that contain weak negation. By now it is the standard semantics for such programs. Under this semantics, a program may have several stable models; and what is true of the program is what is true in all its stable models (a cautious semantics).

Repairs of relational databases can be specified as stable models of disjunctive logic programs. In [6, 10, 12] such programs were presented, but they were based on classic IC satisfaction, that differs from the one introduced in Section 3.

The repair programs we will present now implement the repair semantics introduced in Section 3 for a set of RIC-acyclic constraints. The repair programs use annotation constants with the intended, informal semantics shown in the table below. The annotations are used in an extra attribute introduced in each database predicate; so for a predicate $P \in \mathcal{R}$, the new version of it, $P\_$, contains an extra attribute.

Annotation	Atom	The tuple $P(\bar{a})$ is...
$\mathbf{t_a}$	$P\_(\bar{a}, \mathbf{t_a})$	advised to be made true
$\mathbf{f_a}$	$P\_(\bar{a}, \mathbf{f_a})$	advised to be made false
$\mathbf{t^\star}$	$P\_(\bar{a}, \mathbf{t^\star})$	true or becomes true
$\mathbf{t^{\star\star}}$	$P\_(\bar{a}, \mathbf{t^{\star\star}})$	it is true in the repair

In the repair program, *null* is treated as any other constant in $\mathcal{U}$, and therefore the $IsNull(x)$ atom can be replaced by $x = null$.

Definition 9. Given a database instance D, a set IC of UICs, RICs and NNCs, the repair program $\Pi(D, IC)$ contains the following rules:

1. Facts: $P(\bar{a})$ for each atom $P(\bar{a}) \in D$.
2. For every UIC ψ of form (2), the rules:
   $\bigvee_{i=1}^{n} P_i\_(\bar{x}_i, \mathbf{f_a}) \vee \bigvee_{j=1}^{m} Q_j\_(\bar{y}_j, \mathbf{t_a}) \leftarrow \bigwedge_{i=1}^{n} P_i\_(\bar{x}_i, \mathbf{t^\star}), \bigwedge_{Q_j\_\in Q'} Q_j\_(\bar{y}_j, \mathbf{f_a}),$
   $\bigwedge_{Q_k \in Q''} \; not \; Q_k(\bar{y}_k), \bigwedge_{x_l \in \mathcal{A}(\psi) \cap \bar{x}} x_l \neq null, \bar{\varphi}.$
   for every set Q' and Q'' of atoms appearing in formula (2) such that $Q' \cup Q'' = \bigcup_{j=1}^{m} Q_j(\bar{y}_j)$ and $Q' \cap Q'' = \emptyset$.[9] Here $\mathcal{A}(\psi)$ is the set of relevant attributes for ψ, $\bar{x} = \bigcup_{i=1}^{n} x_i$ and $\bar{\varphi}$ is a conjunction of built-ins that is equivalent to the negation of φ.
3. For every RIC of form (3), the rules:
   $P\_(\bar{x}, \mathbf{f_a}) \vee Q\_(\bar{x}', \overline{null}, \mathbf{t_a}) \leftarrow P\_(\bar{x}, \mathbf{t^\star}), \; not \;\; aux(\bar{x}'), \bar{x}' \neq null.$
   And for every $y_i \in \bar{y}$:
   $aux(\bar{x}') \leftarrow Q\_(\bar{x}', \bar{y}, \mathbf{t^\star}), \; not \; Q\_(\bar{x}', \bar{y}, \mathbf{f_a}), \bar{x}' \neq null, \; y_i \neq null.$
4. For every NNC of the form (5), the rule:
   $P\_(\bar{x}, \mathbf{f_a}) \leftarrow P\_(\bar{x}, \mathbf{t^\star}), x_i = null.$
5. For each predicate $P \in R$, the annotation rules:
   $P\_(\bar{x}, \mathbf{t^\star}) \leftarrow P(\bar{x}).$ $\qquad$ $P\_(\bar{x}, \mathbf{t^\star}) \leftarrow P\_(\bar{x}, \mathbf{t_a}).$
6. For every predicate $P \in \mathcal{R}$, the interpretation rule:
   $P\_(\bar{x}, \mathbf{t^{\star\star}}) \leftarrow P\_(\bar{x}, \mathbf{t^\star}), \; not \; P\_(\bar{x}, \mathbf{f_a}).$
7. For every predicate $P \in \mathcal{R}$, the program denial constraint:
   $\leftarrow \; P\_(\bar{x}, \mathbf{t_a}), P\_(\bar{x}, \mathbf{f_a}).$ □

[9] We are assuming in this definition that the rules are a direct translation of the original ICs introduced in Section 2; in particular, the same variables are used and the standardization conditions about their occurrences are respected in the program.

Facts in 1. are the elements of the database. Rules 2., 3. and 4. capture, in the right-hand side, the violation of ICs of the forms (2), (3), and (5), resp., and, with the left-hand side, the intended way of restoring consistency. The set of predicates Q' and Q'' are used to check that in all the possible combinations, the consequent of a UIC is not being satisfied. Since the satisfaction of UICs and RICs needs to be checked only if none of the relevant attributes of the antecedent are *null*, we use $x \neq null$ in rule 2. and in the first two rules in 3. (as usual, $\bar{x}' \neq null$ means the conjunction of the atoms $x_j \neq null$ for $x_j \in \bar{x}'$). Notice that rules 3. are implicitly based on the fact that the relevant attributes for a RIC of the form (3) are $\mathcal{A} = \{x \mid x \in \bar{x}'\}$. Rules 5. capture the atoms that are part of the inconsistent database or that become true in the repair process; and rules 6. those that become true in the repairs. Rule 7. enforces, by discarding models, that no atom can be made both true and false in a repair.

Example 21. (example 19 cont.) The repair program $\Pi(D, IC)$ is the following:
1. $R(a,b).\quad R(a,c).\quad S(e,f).\quad S(null,a).$
2. $R\_(x,y,\mathbf{f_a}) \vee R\_(x,z,\mathbf{f_a}) \leftarrow R\_(x,y,\mathbf{t^\star}), R\_(x,z,\mathbf{t^\star}),\ y \neq z,\ x \neq null.$
3. $S\_(u,x,\mathbf{f_a}) \vee R\_(x,null,\mathbf{t_a}) \leftarrow S\_(u,x,\mathbf{t^\star}), not\ aux(x),\ x \neq null.$
   $aux(x) \leftarrow R\_(x,y,\mathbf{t^\star}),\ not\ R\_(x,y,\mathbf{f_a}),\ x \neq null,\ y \neq null.$
5. $R\_(x,y,\mathbf{t^\star}) \leftarrow R\_(x,y,\mathbf{t_a}).\quad R\_(x,y,\mathbf{t^\star}) \leftarrow R(x,y).$ (similarly for S)
6. $R\_(x,y,\mathbf{t^{\star\star}}) \leftarrow R\_(x,y,\mathbf{t_a}).$
   $R\_(x,y,\mathbf{t^{\star\star}}) \leftarrow R(x,y),\ not\ R\_(x,y,\mathbf{f_a}).$ (similarly for S)
7. $\leftarrow R\_(x,y,\mathbf{t_a}), R\_(x,y,\mathbf{f_a}).\quad \leftarrow S\_(\bar{x},\mathbf{t_a}), S\_(\bar{x},\mathbf{f_a}).$

Only rules 2. and 3. depend on the ICs: rules 2. for the UIC, and 3. for the RIC. They say how to repair the inconsistencies. In rule 2., $Q' = Q'' = \emptyset$, because there is no database predicate in the consequent of the UIC. There is no rule 4., because there is no NNC. □

Example 22. Consider $D = \{P(a,b), P(c,null)\}$ and the non-conflicting set of ICs: $\{\forall P(x,y) \rightarrow R(x) \vee S(y), P(x,y) \wedge IsNull(y) \rightarrow \mathbf{false}\}$. Then $\Pi(D, IC)$:
1. $P(a,b).\quad P(c,null).$
2. $P\_(x,y,\mathbf{f_a}) \vee R\_(x,\mathbf{t_a}) \vee S\_(y,\mathbf{t_a}) \leftarrow P\_(x,y,\mathbf{t^\star}), R\_(x,\mathbf{f_a}), S\_(y,\mathbf{f_a}), x \neq null, y \neq null.$
   $P\_(x,y,\mathbf{f_a}) \vee R\_(x,\mathbf{t_a}) \vee S\_(y,\mathbf{t_a}) \leftarrow P\_(x,y,\mathbf{t^\star}), R\_(x,\mathbf{f_a}),\ not\ S(y), x \neq null, y \neq null.$
   $P\_(x,y,\mathbf{f_a}) \vee R\_(x,\mathbf{t_a}) \vee S\_(y,\mathbf{t_a}) \leftarrow P\_(x,y,\mathbf{t^\star}),\ not\ R(y), S\_(x,\mathbf{f_a}), x \neq null, y \neq null.$
   $P\_(x,y,\mathbf{f_a}) \vee R\_(x,\mathbf{t_a}) \vee S\_(y,\mathbf{t_a}) \leftarrow P\_(x,y,\mathbf{t^\star}),\ not\ R(y),\ not\ S(y), x \neq null, y \neq null.$
4. $P\_(x,y,\mathbf{f_a}) \leftarrow P\_(x,y,\mathbf{t^\star}), y = null.$
5. $P\_(x,y,\mathbf{t^\star}) \leftarrow P\_(x,y,\mathbf{t_a}).\quad P\_(x,y,\mathbf{t^\star}) \leftarrow P(x,y).$ (similarly for R and S)
6. $P\_(x,y,\mathbf{t^{\star\star}}) \leftarrow P\_(x,y,\mathbf{t_a}).$
   $P\_(x,y,\mathbf{t^{\star\star}}) \leftarrow P(x,y),\ not\ P\_(x,y,\mathbf{f_a}).$ (similarly for R and S)
7. $\leftarrow P\_(x,y,\mathbf{t_a}), P\_(x,y,\mathbf{f_a}).$ (similarly for R and S)

The rules in 2. are constructed by choosing all the possible sets Q' and Q'' such that $Q' \cup Q'' = \{R(x), S(y)\}$ and $Q' \cap Q'' = \emptyset$. The first rule in 2. corresponds to $Q' = \{R(x), S(y)\}$ and $Q'' = \emptyset$, the second for $Q' = \{R(x)\}$ and $Q'' = \{S(y)\}$, the third for $Q' = \{S(y)\}$ and $Q'' = \{R(x)\}$, and the fourth for $Q' = \emptyset$ and $Q'' = \{R(x), S(y)\}$ □

The repair program can be run by a logic programming system that computes the stable models semantics, e.g. DLV system [24]. The repairs can be obtained by collecting the atoms annotated with $\mathbf{t}^{\star\star}$ in the stable models of the program.

Definition 10. Let $\mathcal{M}$ be a stable model of program $\Pi(D, IC)$. The database instance associated with $\mathcal{M}$ is $D_{\mathcal{M}} = \{P(\bar{a}) \mid P \in \mathcal{R} \text{ and } P\_(\bar{a}, \mathbf{t}^{\star\star}) \in \mathcal{M}\}$. □

Example 23. (example 21 continued) The program has four stable models (the facts of the program are omitted for simplicity):

$\mathcal{M}_1 = \{R\_(a,b,\mathbf{t}^\star),\ R\_(a,c,\mathbf{t}^\star),\ S\_(e,f,\mathbf{t}^\star),\ S\_(null,a,\mathbf{t}^\star),\ aux(a),\ \underline{S\_(e,f,\mathbf{t}^{\star\star})},\ \underline{S\_(null,a,\mathbf{t}^{\star\star})},\ R\_(f,null,\mathbf{t_a}),\ \underline{R\_(a,b,\mathbf{t}^{\star\star})},\ R\_(a,c,\mathbf{f_a}),\ R\_(f,null,\mathbf{t}^\star),\ \underline{R\_(f,null,\mathbf{t}^{\star\star})}\ \}$,

$\mathcal{M}_2 = \{R\_(a,b,\mathbf{t}^\star),\ R\_(a,c,\mathbf{t}^\star),\ S\_(e,f,\mathbf{t}^\star),\ S\_(null,a,\mathbf{t}^\star),\ aux(a),\ \underline{S\_(e,f,\mathbf{t}^{\star\star})},\ \underline{S\_(null,a,\mathbf{t}^{\star\star})},\ R\_(f,null,\mathbf{t_a}),\ R\_(a,b,\mathbf{f_a}),\ \underline{R\_(a,c,\mathbf{t}^{\star\star})},\ R\_(f,null,\mathbf{t}^\star),\ \underline{R\_(f,null,\mathbf{t}^{\star\star})}\ \}$,

$\mathcal{M}_3 = \{R\_(a,b,\mathbf{t}^\star),\ R\_(a,c,\mathbf{t}^\star),\ S\_(e,f,\mathbf{t}^\star),\ S\_(null,a,\mathbf{t}^\star),\ aux(a),\ S\_(e,f,\mathbf{f_a}),\ \underline{S\_(null,a,\mathbf{t}^{\star\star})},\ \underline{R\_(a,b,\mathbf{t}^{\star\star})},\ R\_(a,c,\mathbf{f_a})\}$,

$\mathcal{M}_4 = \{R\_(a,b,\mathbf{t}^\star),\ R\_(a,c,\mathbf{t}^\star),\ S\_(e,f,\mathbf{t}^\star),\ S\_(null,a,\mathbf{t}^\star),\ aux(a),\ S\_(e,f,\mathbf{f_a}),\ \underline{S\_(null,a,\mathbf{t}^{\star\star})},\ R\_(a,b,\mathbf{f_a}),\ \underline{R\_(a,c,\mathbf{t}^{\star\star})}\}$.

The databases associated to the models select the underlined atoms: $D_1 = \{S(e,f),\ S(null,a),\ R(a,b),\ R(f,null)\}$, $D_2 = \{S(e,f),\ S(null,a),\ R(a,c),\ R(f,null)\}$ $D_3 = \{S(null,a), R(a,b)\}$ and $D_4 = \{S(null,a), R(a,c)\}$. As expected these are the repairs obtained in Example 19. □

Theorem 4. Let IC be a RIC-acylic set of UICs, RICs and NNCs. If $\mathcal{M}$ is a stable model of $\Pi(D, IC)$, then $D_{\mathcal{M}}$ is a repair of D with respect to IC. Furthermore, the repairs obtained in this way are all the repairs of D. □

6 Head-Cycle-Free Programs

In some cases, the repair programs introduced in Section 5 can be transformed into equivalent non-disjunctive programs. This is the case when they become *head-cycle-free* [8]. Query evaluation from such programs has lower computational complexity than general disjunctive programs, actually the data complexity is reduced from Π_2^P-complete to *coNP*-complete [8, 16]. We briefly recall their definition.

The *dependency graph* of a ground disjunctive program Π is the directed graph that has ground atoms as vertices, and an edge from atom A to atom B iff there is a rule with A (positive) in the body and B (positive) in the head. Π is *head-cycle free* (HCF) iff its dependency graph does not contain any directed cycles passing through two atoms in the head of the same rule. A disjunctive program Π is HCF if its ground version is HCF.

A HCF program Π can be transformed into a non-disjunctive normal program $sh(\Pi)$ that has the same stable models. It is obtained by replacing every disjunctive rule of the form $\bigvee_{i=1}^n P_i(\bar{x}_i) \leftarrow \bigwedge_{j=1}^m Q_j(\bar{y}_j),\ \varphi.$ by the n rules $P_i(\bar{x}_i) \leftarrow \bigwedge_{j=1}^m Q_j(\bar{y}_j),\ \varphi,\ \bigwedge_{k \neq i}\ not\ P_k(\bar{x}_k).$, for $i = 1, ..., n$.

For certain classes of queries and ICs, consistent query answering has a data complexity lower than Π_2^P, a sharp lower bound as seen in Theorem 3 (c.f. also [15]). In those cases, it is natural to consider this kind of transformations of the disjunctive repair program. In the rest of this section we will consider sets IC of integrity constraints formed by UICs, RICs and NNCs.

Definition 11. A predicate P is *bilateral* with respect to IC if it belongs to the antecedent of a constraint $ic_1 \in IC$ and to the consequent of a constraint $ic_2 \in IC$, where ic_1 and ic_2 are not necessarily different. □

Example 24. If $IC = \{\forall x\ (T(x) \rightarrow \exists y\ R(x,y), \forall xy\ (S(x,y) \rightarrow T(x))\}$, the only bilateral predicate is T. □

Theorem 5. For a set IC of UICs, RICs and NNCs, if for every $ic \in IC$, it holds that (a) ic has no bilateral predicates; or (b) ic has exactly one occurrence of a bilateral predicate (without repetitions), then the program $\Pi(D, IC)$ is HCF. □

For example, if in IC we have the constraint $P(x,y) \rightarrow P(y,x)$, then P is a bilateral predicate, and the condition in the theorem is not satisfied. Actually, the program $\Pi(D, IC)$ is not HCF. If we have instead $P(x,a) \rightarrow P(x,b)$, even though the condition is not satisfied, the program is HCF. Therefore, the condition is sufficient, but not necessary for the program to be HCF.

This theorem can be immediately applied to useful classes of ICs, like denial constraints, because they do not have any bilateral literals, and in consequence, the repair program is HCF.

Corollary 1. If IC contains only constraints of the form $\bar{\forall}(\bigwedge_{i=1}^{n} P_i(\bar{t}_i) \rightarrow \varphi)$, where $P_i(\bar{t}_i)$ is a database atom and φ is a formula containing built-in predicates only, then $\Pi(D, IC)$ is HCF. □

As a consequence of this corollary we obtain, for first-order queries and this class of ICs, that CQA belongs to *coNP*, because a query program (that is non-disjunctive) together with the repair program is still HCF. For this class of constraints, with the classical tuple-deletion based semantics, this problem becomes *coNP*-complete [15]. Actually, CQA for this class with our tuple-deletion/null-value based semantics is still *coNP*-complete, because the same reduction found in [15] can be used in our case.

7 Conclusions

We have introduced a new repair semantics that considers, systematically and for the first time, the possible occurrence of null values in a database in the form we find them present and treated in current commercial implementations. Null values of the same kind are also used to restore the consistency of the database. The new semantics applies to a wide class of ICs, including cyclic sets of referential ICs.

We established the decidability of CQA under this semantics, and a tight lower and upper bound was presented. The repairs under this semantics can be specified as stable models of a disjunctive logic program with a stable model semantics for acyclic foreign key constraints, universal ICs and *NOT NULL*-constraints, covering all the usual ICs found in database practice.

In an extended version of this paper we will provide: (a) An extension of our semantics of IC satisfaction in databases with null values that can also be applied to query answering in the same kind of databases. (b) A more detailed analysis of the way null-values are propagated in a controlled manner, in such a way that no infinite loops are created. (c) Construction of repairs based on a sequence of "local" repairs for the individual ICs.

Acknowledgments. Research supported by NSERC, CITO/IBM-CAS Student Internship Program. L. Bertossi is Faculty Fellow of IBM Center for Advanced Studies (Toronto Lab.).

References

[1] Abiteboul, S., Hull, R., and Vianu, V. *Foundations of Databases.* Addison-Wesley, 1995.

[2] Arenas, M., Bertossi, L. and Chomicki, J. Consistent Query Answers in Inconsistent Databases. In *Proc. ACM Symposium on Principles of Database Systems (PODS 99)*, ACM Press, 1999, pp. 68-79.

[3] Arenas, M., Bertossi, L. and Chomicki, J. Answer Sets for Consistent Query Answers. *Theory and Practice of Logic Programming*, 2003, 3(4-5):393-424.

[4] Atzeni, P. and Morfuni, N. Functional Dependencies and Constraints on Null Values in Database Relations. *Information and Control*, 1986, 70(1):1-31.

[5] Barcelo, P. and Bertossi, L. Logic Programs for Querying Inconsistent Databases. In *Proc. Fifth International Symposium on Practical Aspects of Declarative Languages (PADL 03)*, Springer LNCS 2562, 2003, pp. 208-222.

[6] Barcelo, P., Bertossi, L. and Bravo, L. Characterizing and Computing Semantically Correct Answers from Databases with Annotated Logic and Answer Sets. In *Semantics of Databases*, Springer LNCS 2582, 2003, pp. 1-27.

[7] Bertossi, L. and Chomicki, J. Query Answering in Inconsistent Databases. In *Logics for Emerging Applications of Databases.* Springer, 2003, pp. 43-83.

[8] Ben-Eliyahu, R. and Dechter, R. Propositional Semantics for Disjunctive Logic Programs. *Annals of Mathematics in Artificial Intelligence*, 1994, 12:53-87.

[9] Bertossi, L. and Bravo, L. Consistent Query Answers in Virtual Data Integration Systems. In *Inconsistency Tolerance*, Springer LNCS 3300, State of the Art Survey Series, 2004, pp. 42-83.

[10] Bravo, L. and Bertossi, L. Consistent Query Answering under Inclusion Dependencies. In *Proc. Annual IBM Centers for Advanced Studies Conference (CASCON 04)*, 2004, pp. 202-216.

[11] Cali, A., Lembo, D. and Rosati, R. On the Decidability and Complexity of Query Answering over Inconsistent and Incomplete Databases. In *Proc. ACM Symposium on Principles of Database Systems (PODS 03)*, ACM Press, 2003, pp. 260-271.

[12] Caniupan, M. and Bertossi, L. Optimizing Repair Programs for Consistent Query Answering. In *Proc. International Conference of the Chilean Computer Science Society (SCCC 05)*, IEEE Computer Society Press, 2005, pp. 3-12.

[13] Celle, A. and Bertossi, L. Querying Inconsistent Databases: Algorithms and Implementation. In *Computational Logic* , Springer LNCS 1861, 2000, pp. 942-956.

[14] Chomicki, J., Marcinkowski, J. and Staworko, S. Computing Consistent Query Answers Using Conflict Hypergraphs. In *Proc. ACM International Conference on Information and Knowledge Management*, ACM Press, 2004, pp. 417-426.
[15] Chomicki, J. and Marcinkowski, J. Minimal-Change Integrity Maintenance using Tuple Deletions. *Information and Computation*, 2005, 197(1-2):90-121.
[16] Dantsin, E., Eiter, T., Gottlob, G. and Voronkov, A. Complexity and Expressive Power of Logic Programming. *ACM Computing Surveys*, 2001, 33(3): 374-425.
[17] Fuxman, A., Fazli, E. and Miller, R.J. ConQuer: Efficient Management of Inconsistent Databases. In *Proc. ACM International Conference on Management of Data (SIGMOD 05)*, ACM Press, 2005, pp. 155-166.
[18] Gelfond, M. and Lifschitz, V. Classical Negation in Logic Programs and Disjunctive Databases. *New Generation Computing*, 1991, 9:365–385.
[19] Grahne, G. *The Problem of Incomplete Information in Relational Databases.* Springer LNCS 554, 1991.
[20] Greco, G., Greco, S. and Zumpano, E. A Logical Framework for Querying and Repairing Inconsistent Databases. *IEEE Transactions in Knowledge and Data Engineering*, 2003, 15(6):1389-1408.
[21] Imielinski, T. and Lipski, W. Incomplete Information in Relational Databases. *Journal of the ACM*, 1984, 31(4):761-791.
[22] International Organization for Standardization (ISO). *ISO International Standard: Database Language SQL - Part 2: SQL/Foundation*, Melton, J. (ed), ISO/IEC 9075-2:2003, 2003.
[23] Lenzerini, M. Data Integration: A Theoretical Perspective. In *Proc. ACM Symposium on Principles of Database Systems (PODS 02)*, ACM Press, 2002, pp. 233-246.
[24] Leone, N., Pfeifer, G., Faber, W., Eiter, T., Gottlob, G., Perri, S. and Scarcello, F. The DLV System for Knowledge Representation and Reasoning. To appear in *ACM Transactions on Computational Logic.*
[25] Levene, M. and Loizou, G. Null Inclusion Dependencies in Relational Databases. *Information and Computation*, 1997, 136(2):67–108.
[26] Levene, M. and Loizou, G. *A Guided Tour of Relational Databases and Beyond*, Springer-Verlag, 1999.
[27] Libkin, L. A Semantics-based Approach to Design of Query Languages for Partial Information. In *Semantics in Databases*, Springer LNCS 1358, 1998, pp. 170-208.
[28] Lien, E. On the Equivalence of Database Models. *Journal of the ACM*, 1982, 29(2):333–362.
[29] Reiter, R. Towards a Logical Reconstruction of Relational Database Theory. In *On Conceptual Modelling*, M.L. Brodie, J. Mylopoulos, J.W. Schmidt (eds.), Springer, 1984, pp. 191-233.
[30] Reiter, R. A Sound and Sometimes Complete Query Evaluation Algorithm for Relational Databases with Null Values. *Journal of the ACM*, 1986, 33(2):349-370.
[31] Türker, C. and Gertz, M. Semantic Integrity Support in SQL:1999 and Commercial (Object–) Relational Database Management Systems. *The VLDB Journal*, 2001, 10(4):241-269.
[32] Van der Meyden, R. Logical Approaches to Incomplete Information: A Survey. In *Logics for Databases and Information Systems*, Kluwer, 1998, pp. 307-356.
[33] Van Gelder, A. and Topor, R. Safety and Correct Translation of Relational Calculus Formulas. In *Proc. ACM Symposium on Principles of Database Systems (PODS 87)*, ACM Press, 1987, pp. 313–327.
[34] Zaniolo, C. Database Relation with Null Values. In *Journal of Computer and System Sciences*, 1984, 28(1):142-166.

On the First-Order Reducibility of Unions of Conjunctive Queries over Inconsistent Databases

Domenico Lembo, Riccardo Rosati, and Marco Ruzzi

Dipartimento di Informatica e Sistemistica
Università di Roma "La Sapienza"
Via Salaria 113, I-00198 Roma, Italy
{lembo, rosati, ruzzi}@dis.uniroma1.it

Abstract. Recent approaches in the research on inconsistent databases have started analyzing the *first-order reducibility* of consistent query answering, i.e., the possibility of identifying classes of queries whose consistent answers can be obtained by a first-order (FOL) rewriting of the query, which in turn can be easily formulated in SQL and directly evaluated through any relational DBMS. So far, the investigations in this direction have only concerned subsets of conjunctive queries over databases with key dependencies. In this paper we extend the study of first-order reducibility of consistent query answering under key dependencies to more expressive queries, in particular to unions of conjunctive queries. More specifically: (i) we analyze the applicability of known FOL-rewriting techniques for conjunctive queries in the case of unions of conjunctive queries. It turns out that such techniques are applicable only to a very restricted class of unions of conjunctive queries; (ii) to overcome the above limitations, we define a new rewriting method which is specifically tailored for unions of conjunctive queries. The method can be applied only to unions of conjunctive queries that satisfy an acyclicity condition on unions of conjunctive queries.

1 Introduction

Consistent query answering. Research in *consistent query answering* (CQA) studies the definition (and computation) of "meaningful" answers to queries posed to databases whose data do not satisfy the integrity constraints (ICs) declared on the database schema [2,11,4].

Recent studies in this area have established declarative semantic characterizations of consistent query answering over relational databases, decidability and complexity results for consistent query answering, as well as techniques for query processing [2,6,11,4,3,5]. In particular, it has been shown that computing consistent answers of conjunctive queries (CQs) is coNP-hard in data complexity, i.e., in the size of the database instance, even in the presence of very restricted forms of ICs (single, unary keys).

From the algorithmic viewpoint, the approach mainly followed is query answering via query rewriting: (i) First, the query that must be processed (usually a conjunctive query) is reformulated in terms of another, more complex query.

T. Grust et al. (Eds.): EDBT 2006 Workshops, LNCS 4254, pp. 358–374, 2006.

Such a reformulation is purely intensional, i.e., the rewritten query is independent of the database instance; (ii) Then, the reformulated query is evaluated over the database instance. Due to the semantic nature and the inherent complexity of consistent query answering, Answer Set Programming (ASP) is usually adopted in the above reformulation step [11,3,5], and stable model engines like DLV [13] can be used for query processing.

First-order reducibility of Consistent Query Answering. An orthogonal approach to consistent query answering is the one followed by recent theoretical works [2,6,10,12], whose aim is to identify classes of *first-order reducible* queries, i.e., queries whose consistent answers can be obtained by rewriting the query in terms of a first-order (FOL) query.

The advantage of such an approach is twofold: first, this technique allows for computing consistent answers efficiently in data complexity. More specifically, in this case, the data complexity of consistent query answering is the one of standard evaluation of FOL queries over databases, i.e., LogSpace. Second, consistent query answering in these cases can be performed through standard database technology, since the FOL query synthesized can be easily translated into SQL and then evaluated by any relational database management system. On the other hand, this approach is only limited to particular subclasses of the problem. In particular, Fuxman and Miller in [10] have studied databases with key dependencies, and have identified a broad subclass of CQs that can be treated according to the above strategy.

Our contribution. In this paper we study first-order reducibility of consistent query answering for unions of conjunctive queries in the presence of key dependencies. More specifically, our contribution can be summarized as follows:

1. first, we analyze the direct applicability of the rewriting technique of [10] to unions of conjunctive queries. In particular, we characterize the subclass of unions of conjunctive queries for which a first-order rewriting can be computed in a modular way, such that the FOL rewriting of a union of conjunctive queries corresponds to the union of the FOL rewritings of each single conjunctive query. Each query belonging to such a subclass is a union of conjunctive queries in which (i) every disjunct can be rewritten exploiting the rewriting technique presented in [10], and (ii) repetition of atom symbols in different disjuncts is limited according to a suitable condition (see Section 3). It turns out that this way of FOL-reducing unions of conjunctive queries is possible only for a very restricted class of unions of conjunctive queries;
2. to overcome the limitations of the previous approach, we define a new rewriting method which is specifically tailored for unions of conjunctive queries. The method can be applied only to a subclass of unions of conjunctive queries, in particular the queries that satisfy an *acyclicity* condition on unions of conjunctive queries: for each such query q, the method produces a FOL-rewriting of the query whose evalutation produces the consistent answers to q. Note that this new defined subclass, properly contains the one described in the previous item.

Relevance of our results. We believe that the relevance of our study is twofold:

1. Extending the study of first-order reducibility of consistent query answering from conjunctive (i.e., select-project-join) queries to more expressive queries is certainly interesting: in this respect, the extension to unions of conjunctive queries is particularly important, since the possibility of expressing unions is probably the most important expressive feature which is missed by the language of conjunctive queries.
2. As explained in Section 5, we argue that the ability of handling unions of conjunctive queries is necessary in order to extend the first-order reduction techniques of consistent query answering to other forms of integrity constraints, specifically to *inclusion dependencies.* Besides key dependencies, inclusion dependencies, and in particular *foreign keys*, are certainly the most important form of integrity constraints in relational schemas. At the best of our knowledge this problem has not been studied yet. Notably, the analysis of first-order reduction of consistent query answering of unions of conjunctive queries constitutes a necessary first step in order to arrive at the definition of analogous methods for (unions of) conjunctive queries under key and foreign key dependencies.

Structure of the paper. In the next section, we present some preliminary definitions. In Section 3 we recall the method for first-order reducibility of conjunctive queries under key dependencies and study under which conditions this technique can be directly applied to unions of conjunctive queries. Then, in Section 4 we define a new query rewriting algorithm specifically designed for unions of conjunctive queries, and discuss formal properties of the method. Finally, we conclude in Section 5.

2 Inconsistent Databases and Consistent Answers

Syntax. We consider to have an infinite, fixed alphabet Γ of constants representing real world objects, and we take into account only database instances having Γ as domain. Moreover, we assume that different constants in Γ denote different objects, i.e., we adopt the so-called *unique name assumption.*

A *database schema* $\mathcal{S}$ is constituted by a *relational signature* $\mathcal{A}$, i.e., a set of relation symbols in which each relation is associated with an arity (positive integer) indicating the number of its attributes, and a set of integrity constraints specified over $\mathcal{A}$. An *attribute* of a relation symbol r is an integer b such that $1 \leq b \leq n$, where n is the arity of r. We consider schemas which contain only *key dependencies* specified over $\mathcal{A}$. A key dependency (KD) over $\mathcal{A}$ is an expression of the form $key(r) = \{i_1, \ldots, i_k\}$, where r is a relation symbol of $\mathcal{A}$, and, if n is the arity of r, $1 \leq i_j \leq n$ for each j such that $1 \leq j \leq k$. We assume that at most one KD is specified over a relation r and we say that an attribute of r is a *key attribute* if it belongs to the set $key(r)$ (otherwise we say that it is a *non-key attribute*). We denote with the pair $\langle \mathcal{A}, \mathcal{K} \rangle$, a database schema $\mathcal{S}$ with signature $\mathcal{A}$ and set of key dependencies $\mathcal{K}$ over $\mathcal{A}$.

A *term* is either a variable or a constant of Γ. An *atom* is an expression of the form $p(t_1, \ldots, t_n)$ where p is a relation symbol of arity n and $t_1, \ldots, t_n$ is a sequence of n terms. An atom is called *fact* if all the terms occurring in it are constants. A *database instance* $\mathcal{D}$ for $\mathcal{S}$ is a set of facts over $\mathcal{A}$. We denote as $r^{\mathcal{D}}$ the set $\{\boldsymbol{t} \mid r(\boldsymbol{t}) \in \mathcal{D}\}$.

A *union of conjunctive queries* (UCQ) q of arity n over a (database schema with) signature $\mathcal{A}$ is an expression of the form

$$h(x_1, \ldots, x_n) :- d_1 \vee \ldots \vee d_m$$

where the atom $h(x_1, \ldots, x_n)$ is called the *head* of the query (denoted by *head*(q)), $d_1 \vee \ldots \vee d_m$ is called the *body* of the query (denoted by *body*(q)), and for each $i \in \{1 \ldots m\}$, d_i, called the *i-th disjunct* of q, is a conjunction of atoms $a_{i,1} \wedge \ldots \wedge a_{i,k}$, whose predicate symbols are in $\mathcal{A}$, such that all the variables occurring in the query head also occur in d_i. If $m = 1$, q is simply called *conjunctive query* (CQ). In a UCQ q, we say that a variable is a *head variable* if it occurs in the query head, while we say that a variable is *existential* if it only occurs in the query body. Moreover, we call an existential variable *shared in a disjunct d of q* if it occurs at least twice in d (otherwise we say that it is *non-shared in d*). Obviously, if q is a CQ, an existential variable shared (resp. non-shared) in the unique disjunct of q will be simply called shared (resp. non-shared) in q.

A *FOL query* of arity n is an expression of the form

$$\{x_1, \ldots, x_n \mid \Phi(x_1, \ldots, x_n)\}$$

where $x_1, \ldots, x_n$ are variable symbols and Φ is a first-order formula with free variables $x_1, \ldots, x_n$.

Semantics. First, we briefly recall the standard evaluation of queries over a database instance. Let q be the UCQ $h(x_1, \ldots, x_n) :- d_1 \ldots\ldots\ldots d_m$ and let $\boldsymbol{t} = \langle c_1, \ldots, c_n \rangle$ be a tuple of constants of Γ. A set of facts I is an *image of $\boldsymbol{t}$ w.r.t. q* if there exists a substitution σ of the variables occurring in a disjunct d_i of q such that $\sigma(head(q)) = h(\boldsymbol{t})$ and $\sigma(d_i) = I$. Given a database instance $\mathcal{D}$, we denote by $q^{\mathcal{D}}$ the evaluation of q over $\mathcal{D}$, i.e., $q^{\mathcal{D}}$ is the set of tuples $\boldsymbol{t}$ such that there exists an image I of $\boldsymbol{t}$ w.r.t. q such that $I \subseteq \mathcal{D}$.

Given a FOL query q and a database instance $\mathcal{D}$, we denote by $q^{\mathcal{D}}$ the evaluation of q over $\mathcal{D}$, i.e., $q^{\mathcal{D}} = \{\langle c_1, \ldots, c_n \rangle \mid \mathcal{D} \models \Phi(c_1, \ldots, c_n)\}$, where each t_i is a constant symbol and $\Phi(c_1, \ldots, c_n)$ is the first-order sentence obtained from Φ by replacing each free variable x_i with the constant c_i.

Then, we define the semantics of queries over inconsistent databases. A database instance $\mathcal{D}$ *violates* the KD $key(r) = \{i_1, \ldots, i_k\}$ iff there exist two *distinct* facts $r(c_1, \ldots, c_n)$, $r(d_1, \ldots, d_n)$ in $\mathcal{D}$ such that $c_{i_j} = d_{i_j}$ for each j such that $1 \leq j \leq k$.

Let $\mathcal{S} = \langle \mathcal{A}, \mathcal{K} \rangle$ be a database schema. A database instance $\mathcal{D}$ is *legal for $\mathcal{S}$* if $\mathcal{D}$ does not violate any KD in $\mathcal{K}$.

A set of ground atoms $\mathcal{D}'$ is a *repair of $\mathcal{D}$ under $\mathcal{S}$* iff: (i) $\mathcal{D}' \subseteq \mathcal{D}$; (ii) $\mathcal{D}'$ is legal for $\mathcal{S}$; (iii) for each $\mathcal{D}''$ such that $\mathcal{D}' \subset \mathcal{D}'' \subseteq \mathcal{D}$, $\mathcal{D}''$ is not legal for $\mathcal{S}$. In words, a repair for $\mathcal{D}$ under $\mathcal{S}$ is a maximal subset of $\mathcal{D}$ that is legal for $\mathcal{S}$.

The problem in which we are interested is *consistent query answering* [2,6]: given a database schema $\mathcal{S}$, a database instance $\mathcal{D}$, and a UCQ q, return all tuples $\boldsymbol{t}$ of constants of Γ such that, for each repair $\mathcal{D}'$ of $\mathcal{D}$ under $\mathcal{S}$, $\boldsymbol{t} \in q^{\mathcal{D}'}$. Each such tuple is called consistent answer to q in $\mathcal{D}$ under $\mathcal{S}$.

Furthermore, analogously to [10], we say that consistent query answering for a class $\mathcal{C}$ of UCQs is *FOL-reducible* (or simply that the class $\mathcal{C}$ is FOL-reducible), if for every database schema $\mathcal{S} = \langle \mathcal{A}, \mathcal{K} \rangle$ and every query $q \in \mathcal{C}$ over $\mathcal{A}$, there exists a FOL query q_f over $\mathcal{A}$ such that for every database instance $\mathcal{D}$, $\boldsymbol{t}$ is a consistent answer to q in $\mathcal{D}$ under $\mathcal{S}$ iff $\boldsymbol{t} \in q_f^{\mathcal{D}}$. We call such a q_f a *FOL-rewriting* of q under $\mathcal{S}$. Notice that FOL-reducibility is a very interesting property from a practical point of view, since FOL queries correspond to queries expressed in relational algebra (i.e., in SQL). Observe also that every FOL query can be evaluated in LogSpace wrt data complexity, i.e., computational complexity w.r.t. the size of the database instance (see e.g., [1]). It follows that if a class $\mathcal{C}$ is FOL-reducible, then consistent query answering for $\mathcal{C}$ is in LogSpace wrt data complexity.

3 FOL-Rewriting of UCQs Via FOL-Rewriting of CQs

It is well known that the consistent query answering problem studied in this paper is coNP-hard in data complexity for generic conjunctive queries (and thus for generic unions of conjunctive queries) [4,6]. As a consequence, the issue of scalability of query answering with respect to (large) database instances turns out to be crucial [3,8]. In this respect, an interesting approach is the one that aims at identifying *subclasses* of queries for which the problem is tractable [7,6], or FOL-reducible [2,10,9]. In particular, in [10] the authors study the problem for the class of conjunctive queries, and define a subclass of CQs, called $\mathcal{C}_{tree}$, for which they provide an algorithm for FOL-rewriting under schemas which contain only KDs. The class $\mathcal{C}_{tree}$ is based on the notion of join graph: a *join graph of a conjunctive query* q is the graph that contains (i) a node N_i for every atom in the query body, (ii) an arc from N_i to N_j if an existential shared variable occurs in a non-key position in N_i and occurs also in N_j, (iii) an arc from N_i to N_i if an existential shared variable occurs at least twice in N_i, and at least one occurrence is in a non-key position. According to [10], $\mathcal{C}_{tree}$ is the class of conjunctive queries (a) without repeated relation symbols, (b) in which every join from non-key to key attributes involves the entire key of at least one relation and (c) whose join graph is acyclic. As pointed out in [10], this class of queries is very common, since cycles are rarely present in queries used in practice.

A class of CQs slightly more general than $\mathcal{C}_{tree}$, called $\mathcal{C}^{+}_{tree}$, has been considered in [12], and a new algorithm, called CQ-FolRewrite, for FOL-rewriting of such CQs has been proposed. Conjunctive queries belonging to such a class respect condition (a) and (c) above, but admit also joins from non-key attributes that not necessarily involve the entire key of a relation (i.e., condition (b) above has been removed)[1].

In what follows we consider the algorithm CQ-FolRewrite and study a possible extension of it in order to deal with queries specified in the more expressive language of unions of conjunctive queries. In particular, we consider UCQs where each disjunct is of class $\mathcal{C}^{+}_{tree}$. Notice that, even if CQA of CQs in the class $\mathcal{C}^{+}_{tree}$ is FOL-reducible, CQA for queries that are unions of $\mathcal{C}^{+}_{tree}$ queries is not in general FOL-reducible as shown by the following theorem.

Theorem 1. *Let $\mathcal{S} = \langle \mathcal{A}, \mathcal{K} \rangle$ be a database schema, $\mathcal{D}$ a database instance for $\mathcal{S}$, q a UCQ of arity n over $\mathcal{S}$, and t an n-tuple of constants in Γ. The problem of establishing whether t is a consistent answer to q in $\mathcal{D}$ under $\mathcal{S}$ is coNP-hard with respect to data complexity.*

Proof. (Sketch) The proof is by reduction of the three-colorability problem to the complement of our problem. □

For the sake of completeness, we show the algorithm CQ-FolRewrite and its subroutine NodeRewrite in Figure 1 and Figure 2, respectively.

Algorithm CQ-FolRewrite($q, \mathcal{S}$)
Input: CQ $q \in \mathcal{C}^{+}_{tree}$ with $q = h(x_1, \ldots, x_n) \text{ :- } d$
  schema $\mathcal{S} = \langle \mathcal{A}, \mathcal{K} \rangle$
Output: FOL query
begin
  compute $JG(q)$;
  return $\{x_1, \ldots, x_n \mid \bigwedge_{N \in roots(JG(q))} \text{NodeRewrite}(JG(q), N, \mathcal{S})\}$
end

Fig. 1. The algorithm CQ-FolRewrite

In the algorithm, we exploit a refined notion of join graph, in which we associate to each node an adornment which specifies the different nature of terms in the atoms, as formally specified below.

Definition 1. *Let $\mathcal{S} = \langle \mathcal{A}, \mathcal{K} \rangle$ be a database schema, q be a CQ over $\mathcal{A}$, and $a = r(x_1, \ldots, x_n)$ be an atom (of arity n) occurring in the body of q. Then, let $key(r) = \{i_1, \ldots, i_k\}$ belong to $\mathcal{K}$, and let $1 \leq i \leq n$. The* type *of the* i-th *argument of* a *in* q, *denoted by* $type(a, i, q)$ *is defined as follows:*

[1] The algorithm CQ-FolRewrite takes into account also other forms of integrity constraints specified on the database schema (a.k.a. exclusion dependencies), which are not considered in the present paper.

Algorithm NodeRewrite($JG(q), N, \mathcal{S}$)
Input: Join Graph $JG(q)$;
node N of $JG(q)$
schema $\mathcal{S} = \langle \mathcal{A}, \mathcal{K} \rangle$
Output: FOL formula
begin
let $a = r(x_1/t_1, \ldots, x_n/t_n)$ be the label of N;
for $i := 1$ **to** n **do**
if $t_i \in \{KB, B\}$ **then** $v_i := x_i$
else $v_i := y_i$, where y_i is a new variable
if each argument of a is of type B or KB **then** $f_1 := r(x_1, \ldots, x_n)$
else begin
let $i_1, \ldots, i_m$ be the positions of the arguments of a of type S, U, KU;
$f_1 := \exists y_{i_1}, \ldots, y_{i_m}. r(v_1, \ldots, v_n)$
end;
if there exists no argument in a of type B or S **then return** f_1
else begin
let $p_1, \ldots, p_c$ be the positions of the arguments of a of type U, S or B;
let $\ell_1, \ldots, \ell_h$ be the positions of the arguments of a of type B;
for $i := 1$ **to** c **do**
if $t_{p_i} = S$ **then** $z_{p_i} := x_{p_i}$ **else** $z_{p_i} := y'_i$, where y'_i is a new variable
for $i := 1$ **to** n **do**
if $t_i \in \{KB, KU\}$ **then** $w_i := v_i$ **else** $w_i := z_i$;

$$f_2 := \forall z_{p_1}, \ldots, z_{p_c}. r(w_1, \ldots, w_n) \rightarrow \left(\bigwedge_{N' \in jgsucc(N)} \mathsf{NodeRewrite}(JG(q), N', \mathcal{S}) \right) \wedge \bigwedge_{i \in \{\ell_1, \ldots, \ell_h\}} w_i = x_i$$

return $f_1 \wedge f_2$
end
end

Fig. 2. The algorithm NodeRewrite

1. *If $i_1 \leq i \leq i_k$, then:*
   - *if x_i is a head variable of q, a constant, or an existential shared variable, then type$(a, i, q) = KB$;*
   - *if x_i is an existential non-shared variable of q, then type$(a, i, q) = KU$.*
2. *Otherwise ($i \notin \{i_1, \ldots, i_k\}$):*
   - *if x_i is a head variable of q or a constant, then type$(a, i, q) = B$;*
   - *if x_i is an existential shared variable of q, then type$(a, i, q) = S$;*
   - *if x_i is an existential non-shared variable of q, then type$(a, i, q) = U$.*

Terms typed by KB or B are called *bound terms*, otherwise they are called *unbound.* We call the *typing of a in q* the expression of the form $r(x_1/t_1, \ldots, x_n/t_n)$, where each t_i is the type of the argument x_i in q.

In the algorithm, $JG(q)$ denotes the join graph of q, in which each node N_i is labelled with the typing of the corresponding atom a_i in q, and $jgsucc(N)$

denotes the set of node which are successors on N in the join graph. Furthermore, $roots(JG(q))$ denotes the set of nodes that are roots in $JG(q)$ (notice that each join graph for a query of class $\mathcal{C}^+_{tree}$ is actually a set of trees, i.e. a forest). For a detailed description of the algorithm we refer the reader to [12], where also soundness and completeness of CQ-FolRewrite with respect to the problem of consistent query answering for CQs belonging to the $\mathcal{C}^+_{tree}$ class are established.

We are now ready to attack the study of consistent query answering for UCQs specified over database schemas with key dependencies. We start by analyzing the possibility of solving the problem for a UCQ q by simply applying the algorithm CQ-FolRewrite to each disjunct d_i of q, and taking as result the query q_f obtained by the union of the FOL queries produced by each such execution of CQ-FolRewrite. In order to do that, in the following we obviously consider UCQs whose disjuncts are of class $\mathcal{C}^+_{tree}$. Formally, we provide the algorithm UCQ-FolRewrite shown in Figure 3.

Algorithm UCQ-FolRewrite($q, \mathcal{S}$)
Input: UCQ $q = h(x_1, \ldots, x_n) \coloneq d_1 \vee \ldots \vee d_m$ such that $d_i \in \mathcal{C}^+_{tree}$ for $i \in \{1, \ldots, m\}$;
schema $\mathcal{S} = \langle \mathcal{A}, \mathcal{K} \rangle$
Output: FOL query
begin
for $i := 1$ **to** m **do**
begin
$q_i = h(x_1, \ldots, x_n) \coloneq d_i$;
compute $JG(q_i)$;
end
return $\{x_1, \ldots, x_n \mid \bigvee_{i=1}^{m} \bigwedge_{N \in roots(JG(q_i))} \mathsf{NodeRewrite}(JG(q_i), N, \mathcal{S})\}$;
end

Fig. 3. The algorithm UCQ-FolRewrite

Example 1. Consider a database schema $\mathcal{S} = \langle \mathcal{A}, \mathcal{K} \rangle$, such that $\mathcal{A}$ contains the binary relation symbols r_1, r_2 and r_3, and $\mathcal{K}$ contains the dependencies $key(r_1) = \{1\}$, $key(r_2) = \{1\}$, $key(r_3) = \{1\}$. Consider the UCQ

$$q \coloneq (r_1(x, y) \wedge r_2(y, z)) \vee (r_3(x, y) \wedge r_2(y, z))$$

over $\mathcal{A}$. The join graphs of each disjunct are as follows:

$$\begin{array}{lcl} r_1(x/KU, y/S)\,(N1) & \longrightarrow & (N2)\, r_2(y/KB, z/U) \\ r_3(x/KU, y/S)\,(N1) & \longrightarrow & (N2)\, r_2(y/KB, z/U) \end{array}$$

Now it is easy to see that any disjunct in the query is in class $\mathcal{C}^+_{tree}$. Then, the first-order query returned by the execution of UCQ-FolRewrite($q, \mathcal{S}$) is

$$\begin{array}{rl} q_f = \{ \mid & (\exists x, y.r_1(x, y) \wedge \forall y'.r_1(x, y') \rightarrow \exists z.r_2(y', z)) \vee \\ & (\exists x, y.r_3(x, y) \wedge \forall y'.r_3(x, y') \rightarrow \exists z.r_2(y', z))\} \end{array}$$

For such an example it is possible to verify that the query above is actually the FOL-rewriting of the input query q, i.e., for every database instance $\mathcal{D}$, $\boldsymbol{t}$ is a consistent answer to q in $\mathcal{D}$ under $\mathcal{S}$ iff $\boldsymbol{t} \in q_f^{\mathcal{D}}$. □

Now, the question arises whether the condition that any disjunct in the input query q is in class C^+_{tree} is sufficient in order to guarantee soundness and, in particular, completeness of the algorithm. The following example shows that actually this is not the case.

Example 2. Assume to have a database schema $\mathcal{S} = \langle \mathcal{A}, \mathcal{K} \rangle$, such that $\mathcal{A}$ contains the relation symbol r of arity 2, and $\mathcal{K}$ contains the dependency $key(r) = \{1\}$. Consider the UCQ q :- $r(x, c_1) \vee r(x', c_2)$ over $\mathcal{A}$, in which c_1 and c_2 are different constant symbols. It is immediate to verify that any disjunct in the query is in class C^+_{tree}. Then, the first-order query returned by the execution of UCQ-FolRewrite$(q, \mathcal{S})$ is

$$q_f = \{ \mid (\exists x, y.r(x, y) \wedge \forall y'.r(x, y') \rightarrow y' = c_1) \vee \\ (\exists x, y.r(x, y) \wedge (\forall y'.r(x, y') \rightarrow y' = c_2) \}.$$

Now, assume to have the database instance $\mathcal{D} = \{r(a, c_1), r(a, c_2)\}$, which is not legal for $\mathcal{S}$. It is easy to see that $\mathcal{D} \not\models \Phi$, where Φ is the sentence corresponding to the body of q_f, i.e., according to a notation commonly adopted in the database theory for boolean queries, $\langle\rangle \notin \mathcal{D}$, where $\langle\rangle$ indicates the empty tuple. On the other hand, the repairs of $\mathcal{D}$ under $\mathcal{S}$ are $\mathcal{R}_1 = \{r(a, c_1)\}$ and $\mathcal{R}_2 = \{r(a, c_2)\}$, and the body of the query q evaluates to true in both $\mathcal{R}_1$ and $\mathcal{R}_2$, i.e. $\langle\rangle$ is a consistent answer to q in $\mathcal{D}$ under $\mathcal{S}$. □

The example above shows that the algorithm UCQ-FolRewrite is in general incomplete (even if it is easy to see that it is always sound). This is mainly due to the fact that separately rewriting single disjuncts does not take into account the interaction that may exist between them. Indeed, the body of the FOL-rewriting that the algorithm constructs for each single disjunct d_i (i.e., $\bigwedge_{N \in roots(JG(q_i))}$ NodeRewrite$(JG(q_i), N)$) is a FOL formula, which we denote with ϕ, such that, given an assignment of the free variables of ϕ (i.e., a tuple of constants $\boldsymbol{t}$), the sentence $\phi(\boldsymbol{t})$ is satisfied only by those database instances $\mathcal{D}$ such that in any repair of $\mathcal{D}$ there is an image of $\boldsymbol{t}$ w.r.t the disjunct d_i. On the other hand, for a union of conjunctive queries q, for a tuple $\boldsymbol{t}$ to be a consistent answer to q it is sufficient that in any repair of $\mathcal{D}$ there exists an image of the tuple w.r.t. q, i.e. with respect to *any* disjunct d_j of q (in other words, the disjunct which provides the image has not to be the same in any repair). This is actually the case we have in Example 2.

Despite the above limitations of the algorithm, we are able to identify a subclass of conjunctive queries for which the algorithm UCQ-FolRewrite is sound and complete. To this aim, we provide the following definition.

Definition 2. *Let $\mathcal{S} = \langle \mathcal{A}, \mathcal{K} \rangle$ be a database schema, let r be a relation symbol of $\mathcal{A}$ such that $key(r) = \{1, \ldots, n\} \in \mathcal{K}$. Let q be a UCQ over $\mathcal{A}$ and let $a_1 = r(\boldsymbol{x}, \boldsymbol{y})$ and $a_2 = r(\boldsymbol{z}, \boldsymbol{w})$ be two different atoms occurring respectively in two different disjuncts d_1 and d_2 of q, such that $\boldsymbol{x} = x_1, \ldots, x_n$, $\boldsymbol{y} = y_1, \ldots, y_m$, $\boldsymbol{z} = z_1, \ldots, z_n$, $\boldsymbol{w} = w_1, \ldots, w_m$ are sequences of terms. Then, we say that a_1 and a_2 are* interacting *in q if*

1. *the sequences of terms in key position in a_1 and a_2 unify, i.e., there exists a unifier between $\boldsymbol{x}$ and $\boldsymbol{z}$;*
2. *there exists $j \in \{1, \ldots, m\}$ such that y_j and w_j are not identical constants;*
3. *a_1 (resp. a_2) is such that either a_1 is not a leaf in the join graph of d_1 (resp. d_2) or there exists a non-key argument of a_1 (resp. a_2) which is bound.*

Notice that the atoms $r(a, c_1)$ and $r(a, c_2)$ in the example above are interacting atoms in the query q. Now we are able to define the class we were looking for.

Definition 3. *A UCQ q belongs to the class UCQ_{NI} of* non-interacting *UCQs if:*

- *each disjunct d_i of q is in $\mathcal{C}^+_{tree}$;*
- *there do not exist two interacting atoms a_1 and a_2 in q.*

It is easy to see that the query in Example 1 belongs to the class UCQ_{NI}, whereas the query in in Example 2 does not.

Theorem 2. *Let $\mathcal{S} = \langle \mathcal{A}, \mathcal{K} \rangle$ be a database schema, $q \in UCQ_{NI}$ be a query over $\mathcal{S}$. Then, the FOL query q_f returned by the algorithm* UCQ-FolRewrite$(q, \mathcal{S})$ *is a FOL-rewriting of q under $\mathcal{S}$.*

In other words, the above theorem states that the problem of consistent query answering under key dependencies is FOL-reducible for the class UCQ_{NI}.

4 Algorithm

In this section we try to overcome the limitations of the rewriting technique presented in the previous section, by defining a new FOL-rewriting algorithm for UCQs. Based on such an algorithm, we are able to identify the class of acyclically interacting queries, a class of UCQs which extends the class UCQ_{NI} defined in Section 3, and to prove that acyclically interacting queries constitute a class of FOL-reducible queries under key dependencies.

4.1 The Algorithm UCQ-FolRewriteNew

We are now ready to define the algorithm UCQ-FolRewriteNew, a FOL rewriting algorithm for UCQs that, differently from the previous algorithm UCQ-FolRewrite, takes into account the semantic interactions between the query disjuncts.

In the algorithm UCQ-FolRewriteNew(and in the other algorithms iteratively invoked by UCQ-FolRewriteNew and presented in this section), with a little abuse of terminology we call *typed query associated to a query* q the query q^t obtained from q by replacing each atom with its typing. Analogously, the *typed disjunct associated to a disjunct* d is the disjunct d^t obtained from d by replacing each atom with its typing. Coherently to the above definitions, when the operator JG, used for constructing the join graph of a query, is applied to a typed query q^t, the nodes of $JG(q^t)$ respect the typing specified by q^t, i.e., each node of the graph is labeled with the corresponding typing indicated in q^t. We also point out that in the query Q in input to UCQ-FolRewriteNew, each variable symbol only occurs in a single disjunct of Q, and the new variables introduced by the algorithm NodeRewriteNew(see below) are always fresh symbols with respect to all the executions of the algorithm.

The algorithm UCQ-FolRewriteNew is presented in Figure 4.

Algorithm UCQ-FolRewriteNew(Q,$\mathcal{S}$)
Input: a first-order reducible UCQ $Q = h(x_1, \ldots, x_n) :- d_1 \vee \ldots \vee d_m$;
 schema $\mathcal{S} = \langle \mathcal{A}, \mathcal{K} \rangle$
Output: FOL query (representing the rewriting of Q)
begin
 let Q^t be the typed query associated to Q;
 for $i := 1$ **to** m **do**
  let d_i^t be the typed disjunct associated to d_i;
 return $\{x_1, \ldots, x_n \mid \bigvee_{i=1,\ldots,m}$ DisjunctRewrite$(d_i^t, Q^t, \mathcal{S}, (\emptyset, \emptyset))$ $\}$
end

Fig. 4. The algorithm UCQ-FolRewriteNew

Algorithm DisjunctRewrite($d, Q, \mathcal{S}, \mathcal{P}$)
Input:
 a typed union of conjunctive queries $Q = h(x_1, \ldots, x_n) :- d_1 \vee \ldots \vee d_m$;
 a typed disjunct d that appears in Q;
 schema $\mathcal{S} = \langle \mathcal{A}, \mathcal{K} \rangle$;
 $\mathcal{P} = (M, E)$ where M is a list of atoms and E is a set of equalities;
Output: FOL query (representing the rewriting of the disjunct d)
begin
 $q = h(x_1, \ldots, x_n) :- d$;
 compute $JG(q)$;
 return $\{ \bigwedge_{N \in roots(JG(q))}$ NodeRewriteNew$(JG(q), N, Q, \mathcal{S}, \mathcal{P})\}$
end

Fig. 5. The algorithm DisjunctRewrite

Such algorithm calls the algorithm DisjunctRewrite, described in Figure 5, which computes the rewriting of a single disjunct d_i of the UCQ, by recursively calling the subroutine NodeRewriteNew, presented in Figure 6.

The algorithm NodeRewriteNew is actually a new version of the algorithm NodeRewrite presented in Section 3. Notably, NodeRewriteNew (executed on a

Algorithm NodeRewriteNew$(JG(q), N, Q, \mathcal{S}, \mathcal{P})$
Input: join graph $JG(q)$;
node N of $JG(q)$;
a typed query $Q = h(x_1, \ldots, x_n) :- d_1 \vee \ldots \vee d_m$;
schema $\mathcal{S} = \langle \mathcal{A}, \mathcal{K} \rangle$;
$\mathcal{P} = (M, E)$ where M is a list of atoms and E is a set of equalities;
Output: FOL formula
begin
let $a = r(x_1/t_1, \ldots, x_n/t_n)$ be the label of N;
for $i := 1$ **to** n **do**
if $t_i \in \{KB, B\}$ **then** $v_i := x_i$
else $v_i := y_i$, where y_i is a new variable;
if each argument of a is of type B or KB **then** $f_1 := r(x_1, \ldots, x_n)$
else begin
let $i_1, \ldots, i_m$ be the positions of the arguments of a of type S, U, KU;
$f_1 := \exists y_{i_1}, \ldots, y_{i_m}. r(v_1, \ldots, v_n)$
end;
if there exists no argument in a of type B or S
then return f_1
else begin
let $p_1, \ldots, p_c$ be the positions of the arguments of a of type U, S or B;
let $\ell_1, \ldots, \ell_h$ be the positions of the arguments of a of type B;
for $i := 1$ **to** c **do**
if $t_{p_i} = S$ **then** $z_{p_i} := x_{p_i}$ **else** $z_{p_i} := y'_i$, where y'_i is a new variable
for $i := 1$ **to** n **do**
if $t_i \in \{KB, KU\}$ **then** $w_i := v_i$ **else** $w_i := z_i$;
if $occurs(\Pi_{kd}(a), \mathcal{P})$
then $f_2 = \left(\bigwedge_{N' \in jgsucc(N)} \text{NodeRewriteNew}(JG(q), N', Q, \mathcal{S}, \mathcal{P}) \wedge \bigwedge_{i \in \{\ell_1, \ldots, \ell_h\}} w_i = x_i \right)$
else begin
$M = M \cup \{\Pi_{kd}(a)\}$;
$E = E \cup \{w_1 = u_1, \ldots, w_n = u_n\}$;
$f_2 := \forall z_{p_1}, \ldots, z_{p_c}. r(w_1, \ldots, w_n) \rightarrow$
$\left(\bigwedge_{N' \in jgsucc(N)} \text{NodeRewriteNew}(JG(q), N', Q, \mathcal{S}, \mathcal{P}) \wedge \bigwedge_{i \in \{\ell_1, \ldots, \ell_h\}} w_i = x_i \right) \vee$
$\bigvee_{d_j \in Int(N)} \exists u_{j_1}, \ldots, u_{j_s}. w_1 = u_1 \wedge \ldots \wedge w_n = u_n \wedge$
$\wedge$ DisjunctRewrite$(\tau(d_j), \tau(Q), \mathcal{S}, \mathcal{P})$;
return $f_1 \wedge f_2$
end
end
end

Fig. 6. The subroutine NodeRewriteNew

disjunct d) recursively calls DisjunctRewrite to properly take into account the role of other disjuncts which have relation symbols in common with d. More precisely, the rewriting produced by the algorithm NodeRewriteNew suitably encodes the possibility that, given an assignment of the head variables of the UCQ Q (i.e., a tuple of constants $\boldsymbol{t}$), an "opponent fact" $r(\boldsymbol{c}')$ to a fact $r(\boldsymbol{c})$ (i.e., such that $r(\boldsymbol{c})$ and $r(\boldsymbol{c}')$ have the same key) that belongs to an image of $\boldsymbol{t}$ w.r.t. a disjunct d_i of Q, might not be part of any image of the same disjunct d_i but may be part of an image of $\boldsymbol{t}$ w.r.t. *another* disjunct d_j of the query. Thus, the formula in the FOL-rewriting must look for the existence of such an image of d_j. It can be shown that this *non-local* check must be performed only in the presence of interacting atoms in Q. More precisely, when NodeRewriteNew is computing the rewriting of a node corresponding to an atom a, it must recursively invoke DisjunctRewrite only for each disjunct d_j such that there is an atom b in d_j that is interacting with a in Q.

In the algorithms DisjunctRewrite and NodeRewriteNew, $\mathcal{P}$ is the pair (M, E) in which M is a list of atoms and E is a set of equalities of terms. Each atom in the list M is obtained by means of the operator Π_{kd} applied to a typing $a = r(x_1/t_1, \ldots, x_n/t_n)$ (i.e., a label of a node of a join graph). $\Pi_{kd}(a)$ returns the atom $r(x_{i_1}, \ldots, x_{i_a})$, where $i_1, \ldots, i_a$ are positions of the arguments of a of type KU or KB, i.e., $x_{i_1}, \ldots, x_{i_a}$ are the key-arguments of the atom $r(x_1, \ldots, x_n)$. The function call $occurs(\Pi_{kd}(a), \mathcal{P})$ returns true if the atom $\Pi_{kd}(a)$ is in the list M or it can be constructed from an atom of M according to the equalities of terms contained in E. Otherwise $occurs(\Pi_{kd}(a), \mathcal{P})$ returns false. This check avoids useless calls of the algorithm DisjunctRewrite and guarantees termination of the procedure. Furthermore, $Int(N)$ denotes the set of disjuncts of Q that contain atoms interacting with the atom corresponding to the node N (and different from the disjunct which N belongs to); $u_1, \ldots, u_n$ denote the terms occurring the interacting atom in the disjunct d_j, and $u_{j_1}, \ldots, u_{j_s}$ are the variables occurring in such atom; τ is an operator which modifies the typing of each atom (in the disjunct d_j and in the query Q in the two invocations $\tau(d_j)$ and $\tau(Q)$, respectively) by assigning KB to the key arguments of the interacting atom, and B to the other (non-key) arguments.

Example 3. Consider again the query q of Example 2, and execute the algorithm UCQ-FolRewriteNew$(q, \mathcal{S})$. Then the FOL-rewriting produced by the algorithm is as follows

$$\{ \mid (\exists y_1.r(y_1, c_1) \wedge \forall y_2.r(y_1, y_2) \rightarrow y_2 = c_1 \vee (\exists y_3.y_1 = y_3 \wedge y_2 = c_2 \wedge r(y_3, c_2))) \vee$$
$$(\exists y_1.r(y_1, c_2) \wedge \forall y_2.r(y_1, y_2) \rightarrow y_2 = c_2 \vee (\exists y_3.y_1 = y_3 \wedge y_2 = c_1 \wedge r(y_3, c_1)))\}.$$

Notice that in such a case the check on the execution of DisjunctRewrite, which we have talked about above, avoids the execution of identical calls of such a procedure. □

We finally point out that the rewriting produced by the algorithm can be refined in order to get a simplified version of it (which could be evaluated in a more efficient way). However, this is outside the scope of the present paper.

4.2 Termination and Correctness

The algorithm UCQ-FolRewriteNew in general does not terminate. In order to charaterize the class of queries for which the algorithm terminates, we give the following definitions.

Definition 4. *Given two atoms $a = r(x_1, \ldots, x_n, w_1, \ldots, w_m)$, $b = r(y_1, \ldots, y_n, z_1, \ldots, z_m)$, where $key(r) = \{1, \ldots, n\}$, we say that a and b are* key-unifiable *if, for each i s.t. $1 \leq i \leq n$: (i) x_i is a variable; or (ii) y_i is a variable; or (iii) $x_i = y_i$. If a and b are key-unifiable, we denote by $\sigma_{a \to b}$ the substitution $\{y_i \leftarrow x_i \mid 1 \leq i \leq n$ and y_i is a variable$\}$.*[2]

Definition 5. *A UCQ $Q = \{x_1, \ldots, x_m \mid d_1 \vee \ldots \vee d_n\}$ has a $\vee$-cycle if there exists a sequence $d^1_{i_1}, \ldots, d^k_{i_k}$ (with $k > 1$) and a sequence of relation symbols $r_{j_1}, \ldots, r_{j_{k-1}}$ such that:*

- *$d^1_{i_1} = d_{i_1}$;*
- *$i_k = i_1$;*
- *for each h s.t. $1 \leq h \leq k-1$, r_{j_h} occurs both in $d^h_{i_h}$ and in $d^{h+1}_{i_{h+1}}$;*
- *let a be the atom with relation r_{j_h} in $d^h_{i_h}$ and let b be the atom with relation r_{j_h} in $d_{i_{h+1}}$. Then, a and b are key-unifiable. Moreover, for each h s.t. $1 \leq h \leq k-1$, $d^{h+1}_{i_{h+1}} = \sigma_{a \to b}(d_{i_{h+1}})$;*
- *the key arguments of $r_{j_1}(d^k_{i_k})$ contain at least one existential variable not occurring in the key arguments of $r_{j_1}(d^1_{i_1})$.*

In a $\vee$-cycle, the disjuncts $d^j_{i_j}$ and $d^{j+1}_{i_{j+1}}$ are connected through two atoms a (occurring in d_{i_j}) and b (occurring in $d_{i_{j+1}}$) such that a and b are on the same relation symbol r. The key arguments of a are "passed" to b, thus $d_{i_{j+1}}$ is transformed according to such a substitution.

Example 4. Let us consider the UCQ

$$q :- (r_1(x, y) \wedge r_2(y, z)) \vee (r_2(x, y) \wedge r_1(y, z))$$

We now show that there is an $\vee$-cycle in q which starts from the atom $r_1(x, y)$ of the first disjunct. Indeed, the $\vee$-cycle is due to: (i) the presence of the atom $r_1(x, y)$ in the first disjunct and the atom $r_1(y, z)$ in the second disjunct, which constitutes the first part of the cycle; (ii) the presence of the atom $r_2(x, y)$ in the second disjunct and the atom $r_2(y, z)$ in the first disjunct, which constitutes the second part of the cycle; (iii) the fact that, after this cycle, the key argument of the atom $r_1(x, y)$ in the first disjunct is unbound. □

It is easy to verify that a a necessary condition for a UCQ Q to have a $\vee$-cycle is the presence of interacting atoms in Q.

Definition 6. *A UCQ $Q = \{x_1, \ldots, x_m \mid d_1 \vee \ldots \vee d_n\}$ belongs to the class UCQ_{AI} of* acyclically interacting *UCQs if:*

[2] In the definition of key-unifiable atoms, head variables are considered as constants.

1. *each conjunction d_i is such that the CQ $\{x_1, \ldots, x_m \mid d_i\}$ belongs to $\mathcal{C}^+_{tree}$;*
2. *there are no $\vee$-cycles in Q.*

Informally, according to the above definition, a UCQ Q is acyclically interacting if the interacting atoms in the query disjuncts are such that they do not constitute a $\vee$-cycle in Q, i.e., a cycle of interactions that, starting from an atom $r(\boldsymbol{x})$, cycles back to the same atom introducing at least one existential variable in the key arguments of the atom.

From the semantic viewpoint, the presence of an $\vee$-cycle implies that, when checking for the opponents of an image $r(\boldsymbol{t})$ of a query atom a, we need to check for the opponents of another image $r(\boldsymbol{t}')$ of a, where $\boldsymbol{t}'$ has in its key arguments a new value that does not occur neither in $\boldsymbol{t}$ nor in the query Q. This immediately implies non-termination of the algorithm UCQ-FolRewriteNew, since at every such iteration there are new key arguments in the call to NodeRewriteNew for the atom a. Vice versa, the absence of such a cycle implies termination of the algorithm, since no new term (with respect to the terms occurring in the query Q) is introduced in the calls to NodeRewriteNew, hence the number of possible instantiations of the calls to NodeRewriteNew is finite.

The following property formalizes the fact that the class of acyclically interacting queries is precisely the class of UCQs for which the algorithm UCQ-FolRewriteNew terminates.

Theorem 3. *Let Q be a UCQ, and let $\mathcal{S}$ be a schema. The execution of the algorithm UCQ-FolRewriteNew with input Q terminates if and only if Q is acyclically interacting.*

Moreover, the following theorem establishes soundness and completeness of the algorithm UCQ-FolRewriteNew for the class of acyclically interacting UCQs.

Theorem 4. *If Q is acyclically interacting, then for every database instance $\mathcal{D}$ for $\mathcal{S}$, a tuple t is a consistent answer to Q in $\mathcal{D}$ under $\mathcal{S}$ iff $t \in Q_r^{\mathcal{D}}$, where Q_r is the FOL query returned by UCQ-FolRewriteNew(Q) (i.e., the FOL query returned by the algorithm UCQ-FolRewrite(Q) is a FOL-rewriting of q under $\mathcal{S}$).*

As a corollary of the above theorem, we obtain that the class UCQ_{AI} is FOL-reducible.

Finally, we point out that:

- the class of UCQ_{AI} is a proper superset of the class of UCQs UCQ_{NI} analyzed in Section 3 and for which the algorithm UCQ-FolRewrite is complete;
- if Q is a query in the class UCQ_{NI}, the algorithms UCQ-FolRewrite(Q) and UCQ-FolRewriteNew(Q) return exactly the same FOL query.

5 Discussion and Conclusions

We believe that the study of first-order reducibility of consistent query answering for unions of conjunctive queries is relevant per se, since the possibility of expressing unions in queries is an important feature which has practical relevance. However, we argue that the ability of handling unions of conjunctive queries is necessary in order to solve via FOL-rewriting techniques the problem of consistent query answering for (unions of) conjunctive queries issued over database schemas which contain keys and foreign keys under the *loosely-sound* semantics, a repair semantics which allows for properly dealing with both incomplete and inconsistent databases[3] [4,5].

Formally, given a database schema $\mathcal{S}$ which contains keys and foreign keys, a *loosely-sound repair* of a database $\mathcal{D}$ is any database legal for $\mathcal{S}$ that contains a repair (as so far intended in the present paper and formally specified in Section 2) of $\mathcal{D}$ under $\mathcal{S}'$, where $\mathcal{S}'$ is obtained from $\mathcal{S}$ disregarding foreign key dependencies. Roughly speaking, such semantics adds the ability to deal with inconsistent databases to the first-order semantics commonly adopted for dealing with incomplete databases. Indeed, in intuitive terms, it maintains the ability of the first-order semantics to deliberately add facts to a database instance (property that can be exploited to satisfy those dependencies that can be satisfied by adding facts, as foreign keys), but it also allows for a (minimal) deletion of facts, thus enabling the repairing of database instances with respect to those dependencies, as key dependencies, that may generate inconsistency according to the first-order semantics.

Notably, as showed in [5], in order to solve consistent query answering for (unions of) conjunctive queries under the loosely-sound semantics, it is possible to separately dealing with keys and foreign keys. According to the procedure provided in [5], a query q is first processed only according to the foreign keys issued over the database schema. Such a pre-processing produces a union of conjunctive queries Q. Then, it is sufficient to solve consistent query answering for the UCQ Q over the same database schema in which foreign keys have been dropped. It is immediate to see, that if the query Q obtained is of class UCQ_{AI}, then to solve the second problem we can apply the algorithm UCQ-FolRewrite presented in this paper.

Consequently, even if still preliminary, the analysis of first-order reduction of unions of conjunctive queries we have presented turns out to be a necessary first step in order to arrive to the definition of analogous methods for (unions of) conjunctive queries under key and foreign key dependencies.

Acknowledgments

This research has been partially supported by the FET project INFOMIX: Boosting Information Integration, funded by EU under contract number IST-2001-33570, the FET project TONES: Thinking ONtologiES, funded by the EU under contract number FP6-7603, and by MIUR FIRB 2005 project "Tecnologie Orientate alla Conoscenza per Aggregazioni di Imprese in Internet" (TOCAI.IT).

[3] Notice that also inclusion dependencies of a particular form which guarantees decidability of the consistent query answering problem might be considered [4].

References

1. Serge Abiteboul, Richard Hull, and Victor Vianu. *Foundations of Databases.* Addison Wesley Publ. Co., 1995.
2. Marcelo Arenas, Leopoldo E. Bertossi, and Jan Chomicki. Consistent query answers in inconsistent databases. In *Proceedings of the Eighteenth ACM SIGACT SIGMOD SIGART Symposium on Principles of Database Systems (PODS'99)*, pages 68–79, 1999.
3. Loreto Bravo and Leopoldo Bertossi. Logic programming for consistently querying data integration systems. In *Proceedings of the Eighteenth International Joint Conference on Artificial Intelligence (IJCAI 2003)*, pages 10–15, 2003.
4. Andrea Calì, Domenico Lembo, and Riccardo Rosati. On the decidability and complexity of query answering over inconsistent and incomplete databases. In *Proceedings of the Twentysecond ACM SIGACT SIGMOD SIGART Symposium on Principles of Database Systems (PODS 2003)*, pages 260–271, 2003.
5. Andrea Calì, Domenico Lembo, and Riccardo Rosati. Query rewriting and answering under constraints in data integration systems. In *Proceedings of the Eighteenth International Joint Conference on Artificial Intelligence (IJCAI 2003)*, pages 16–21, 2003.
6. Jan Chomicki and Jerzy Marcinkowski. On the computational complexity of minimal-change integrity maintenance in relational databases. In Leopoldo Bertossi, Anthony Hunter, and Torsten Schaub, editors, *Inconsistency Tolerance*, volume 3300 of *Lecture Notes in Computer Science*, pages 119–150. Springer, 2005.
7. Jan Chomicki, Jerzy Marcinkowski, and Slawomir Staworko. Computing consistent query answers using conflict hypergraphs. In *Proceedings of the Thirteenth International Conference on Information and Knowledge Management (CIKM 2004)*, pages 417–426, 2004.
8. Thomas Eiter, Michael Fink, Gianluigi Greco, and Domenico Lembo. Efficient evaluation of logic programs for querying data integration systems. In *Proceedings of the Nineteenth International Conference on Logic Programming (ICLP'03)*, pages 163–177, 2003.
9. Ariel Fuxman, Elham Fazli, and Renée J. Miller. ConQuer: Efficient management of inconsistent databases. In *Proceedings of the ACM SIGMOD International Conference on Management of Data*, pages 155–166, 2005.
10. Ariel Fuxman and Renée J. Miller. First-order query rewriting for inconsistent databases. In *Proceedings of the Tenth International Conference on Database Theory (ICDT 2005)*, volume 3363 of *LNCS*, pages 337–351. Springer, 2005.
11. Gianluigi Greco, Sergio Greco, and Ester Zumpano. A logical framework for querying and repairing inconsistent databases. *IEEE Transactions on Knowledge and Data Engineering*, 15(6):1389–1408, 2003.
12. Luca Grieco, Domenico Lembo, Marco Ruzzi, and Riccardo Rosati. Consistent query answering under key and exclusion dependencies: Algorithms and experiments. In *Proceedings of the Fourteenth International Conference on Information and Knowledge Management (CIKM 2005)*, pages 792–799, 2005.
13. Nicola Leone, Gerald Pfeifer, Wolfgang Faber, Thomas Eiter, Georg Gottlob, Simona Perri, and Francesco Scarcello. The DLV system for knowledge representation and reasoning. *ACM Transactions on Computational Logic*, 2006. To appear.

Managing Valid Time Semantics for Semistructured Multimedia Clinical Data

Carlo Combi and Barbara Oliboni

Department of Computer Science — University of Verona
Ca' Vignal 2 — Strada le Grazie 15 — 37134 Verona, Italy
{carlo.combi, barbara.oliboni}@univr.it

Abstract. In this paper we propose an approach to manage in a correct way valid time semantics for semistructured temporal clinical information. In particular, we use a graph-based data model to represent radiological clinical data, focusing on the patient model of the well known DICOM standard, and define the set of (graphical) constraints needed to guarantee that the history of the given application domain is consistent.

1 Introduction

In the clinical context the amount of multimedia temporal data is growing up. Recently, there has been an increasing attention on semistructured multimedia clinical data motivated also by the growing usage of XML (eXtensible Markup Language) [14] for exchanging medical data and knowledge [6,12]. Semistructured data have some structure, that may be irregular or incomplete and does not necessarily conform to a schema fixed in advance [1]. In the semistructured data context, the same information can be structured in different ways within the same document, and documents about the same topics can be structured in different ways, thus an important issue is related to the integration of semistructured (XML) data. At this aim, in this paper we use a graphical data model to represent in a simple and intuitive way semistructured documents coming from different sources and (possibly) structured in different ways.

A further aspect which has gained increasing attention also for clinical data is the management of the temporal dimension of information [6]. The time dimension usually considered for clinical data is *valid time* (VT), which is user-provided, and represents the time when a fact is true in the considered domain [7]. Both for conceptual models and for the relational model, several proposals deal with the issue of formalizing and managing valid time semantics of related data [9]: for example, we could require that the database system must be able to constrain the valid time of a visit, i.e. the time during which the visit happened, to be *during* the valid time of the patient, i.e. the time during which a person was hospitalized; on the other hand, we could require that the valid time of the diagnosis starts after the beginning of the symptoms, the diagnosis is based on.

The main issue we consider in this paper is related to the management of valid time semantics for temporal semistructured multimedia clinical data. To

T. Grust et al. (Eds.): EDBT 2006 Workshops, LNCS 4254, pp. 375–386, 2006.

represent semistructured multimedia temporal information we use the Multimedia Temporal Graphical Model (MTGM) [6], which is a general data model for representing semistructured data, having multimedia and temporal features.

We propose a simple approach to manage valid time semantics in the semistructured data context allowing the definition of the set of constraints needed to manage in a correct way the valid time dimension of information represented by means of MTGM. Being MTGM a graph-based data model, we use a graphical approach also to represent the constraints. A constraint will be composed by a *graph*, used to identify the portions of the semistructured data where the constraint has to be applied, and a set of *formulae*, representing restrictions to impose on those information.

In particular, we apply our approach to clinical data, considering DICOM [2] data. DICOM (Digital Imaging and Communications in Medicine) is a standard method to encode and transfer images and related information between heterogeneous sources. DICOM is considered one of the most important standards in radiology, and allows the physicians to store documents containing a diagnostic report related to radiology images. Each report contains the interpretation and the impressions of the radiologist. This kind of document is a typical example of a semistructured document. It has a structure (defined by the DICOM standard) that could be irregular or incomplete: for example the interpretation of the radiologist could be missing in a particular report.

The structure of the paper is as follows: in Section 2 we briefly describe some research directions on multimedia temporal data and then introduce MTGM through general clinical examples. Then, in Section 3, we describe how MTGM allows us to model DICOM data, and in Section 4 we define the constraints needed to manage in a correct way the valid time dimension. In Section 5 we describe a prototype, developed by using the Java technology, managing multimedia temporal clinical data, together with the defined constraints related to the valid time semantics. Finally, in Section 6 we sketch some conclusions.

2 Managing Multimedia Temporal Data

In the context of multimedia database systems, it is possible to distinguish two main research directions: the first one focuses on data modeling and querying issues [4,5], while the second one is addressed to model multimedia presentations [3,11]. As examples of the first research direction, in [4] the authors present a unified data model for multimedia types, such as images, sounds, videos and long text data, while in [5] the author faces the problem of modeling temporal aspects (at different granularities and with indeterminacy) of visual and related textual entities in multimedia databases. As for the second research direction, in [3] the authors deal with the mechanisms for the specification of synchronization constraints between different media objects, while in [11] the authors present a methodological approach for checking the temporal integrity of interactive multimedia documents.

To this regard, MTGM deals with both the above research issues, in the management of clinical data [6]. MTGM can be considered as a logical model for semistructured and multimedia data: the main advantages of this model are related to (i) the chance of representing in a flexible and common way information having different structures, and (ii) the possibility of representing, in a seamless way, both temporal aspects of multimedia data and their temporal presentation requirements. In this paper, we do not focus on the graphical description of multimedia presentations, composed by semistructured and multimedia information represented by means of MTGM, even though in the clinical context, the possibility of composing presentations starting from the stored information is an important feature. Details on multimedia presentations with MTGM can be found in [6]. As for data modeling, multimedia temporal data are represented through graphs: an MTGM graph is a directed, labeled graph, with a single root. Figure 1 shows a portion of an MTGM graph representing information about a pregnant patient and her ultrasound exam.

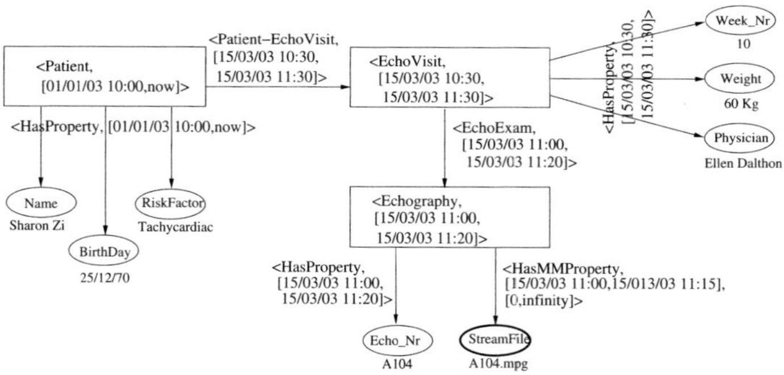

Fig. 1. A portion of an MTGM graph

MTGM has *complex*, *atomic* and *stream* nodes: complex nodes represent abstract entities and are depicted as rectangles, atomic nodes represent primitive values and are depicted as ovals, and stream nodes (which are a particular kind of atomic node) contain multimedia information and are depicted as thick ovals. In the example of Figure 1, there are three complex nodes, *Patient*, *EchoVisit* and *Echography*, and seven atomic nodes as, for example, *Name*, *Birthday* and *RiskFactor*. The atomic node *StreamFile* (child of *Echography*) is a stream node and contains the string "A104.mpg", which refers to the file that encodes the movie of the echography.

Nodes are connected through direct labeled edges (*relational edges*). Relational edges between complex nodes and their atomic nodes have labels with name "*HasProperty*", while relational edges between complex nodes and their stream nodes have labels with name "*HasMMProperty*".

Valid time is explicitly managed by MTGM both for nodes and edges. The valid time[1] of a complex node is represented in its label. The valid time of an

[1] In this work dates are represented in the format DD/MM/YY. Format and granularity of timestamps can be chosen with respect to the considered domain.

atomic (stream) node is represented in the label of the edge between the atomic node and its parent. For example, in Figure 1, the valid time of the node *Patient* is [01/01/03 10:00, *now*] where "*now*" indicates that the represented fact is currently true (i.e., Sharon Zi is still a patient), while the valid time of the simple node *Physician* related to the complex node *Echo_visit* is [15/03/03 10:30, 15/03/03 11:30] (i.e., the visit has been executed by Ellen Dalthon during the specified interval). The label of a relational edge is composed by the name of the relationship and its valid time. The label of the edge relating a complex node to a stream node contains also the specific subpart of the stream object the complex node is related to. As shown in Figure 1, the label of the edge between *Echography* and *StreamNode* is ⟨*HasMMProperty*, [15/03/03 11:10, 15/03/03 11:15], [0, *infinity*]⟩ and represents the time during which the movie of the echography has been recorded. In particular, the interval [0, *infinity*] describes the fact that all the frames of the movie are related to the echography.

3 Modeling DICOM Data by the Multimedia Temporal Graphical Model

DICOM is a standard method to represent images and related information, and in particular it is considered as a standard in radiology. DICOM allows one to store diagnostic reports containing radiology images and the interpretation and the impressions of the radiologist [2].

The DICOM standard aims at allowing interoperability of medical image equipment and considers several aspects: from network communication, to syntax and semantics of exchanged information, to media storage services and file format, to requirements for verifying standard conformance. In particular, in this work, we consider the *DICOM information model* [2], which is an ER-based schema of the domain considered by DICOM. Let us now focus on the representation of (part of) the DICOM model through MTGM [6].

In Figure 2 we show an example of an MTGM graph representing information about a patient and her radiological data, according to the DICOM information model. In Figure 2 *Patient* and *Study* are complex nodes, while nodes *Name* of *Patient* and *Physician's_Name* of *Study* are simple nodes. The node *Raw_Data* of *Image* is a stream node. As for the temporal dimension, the valid time of the *Patient* is [10/01/05, *now*] where "*now*" indicates that the considered fact is currently true. The valid time of an atomic (stream) node is represented in the label of the edge connecting the atomic node and its parent. The label of a relational edge is composed by the already mentioned name of the relationship and by its valid time: for example, the label of the edge between *Patient* and *Study* in Figure 2 is ⟨*References*, $[10/01/05, now]$⟩. The label of the edge relating a complex node to a stream node contains also the specific subpart of the stream object the complex node is related to. In case of images the subpart is specified by $[x, y, width, height]$ that represents the portion of the image with origin in *(x,y)* and dimensions *width* and *height*: as an example in Figure 2, the label of the edge between the *Image* (with *Number* equal to 60) and *Raw Data*

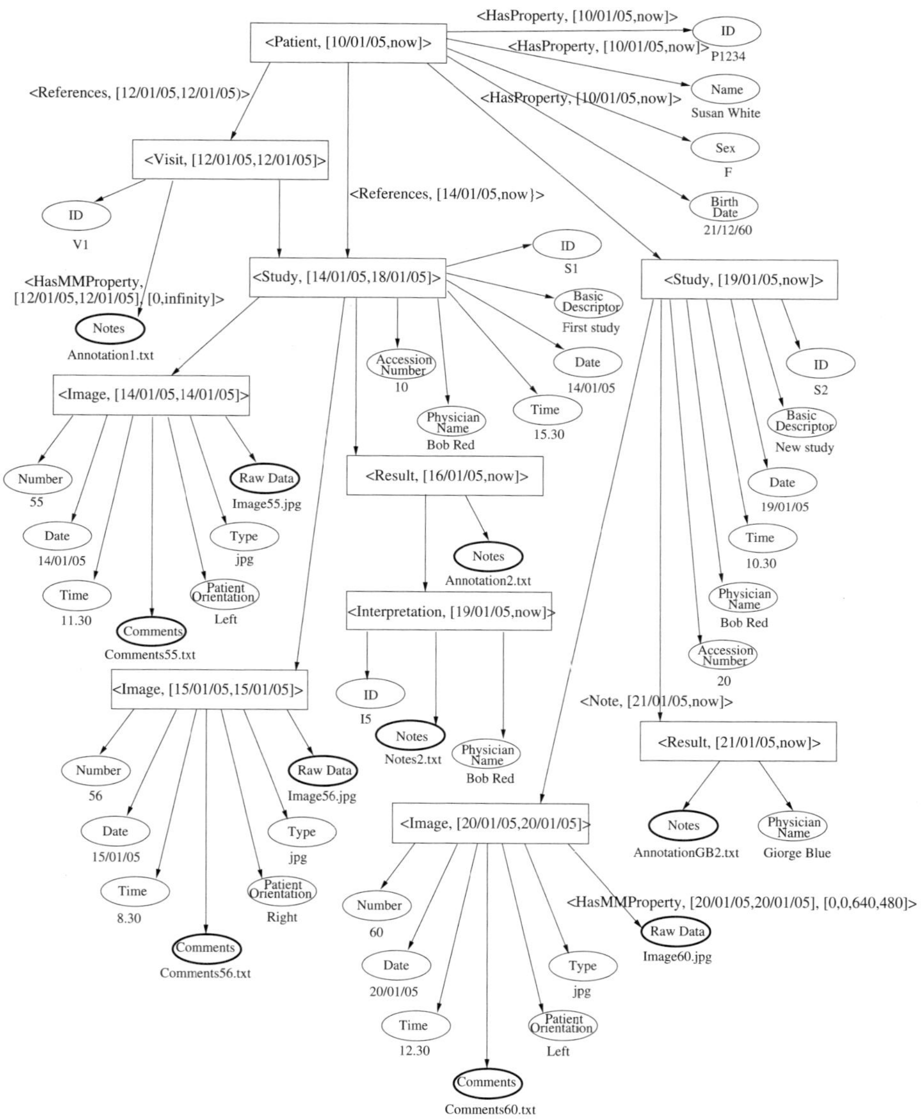

Fig. 2. An example of an MTGM graph

is $\langle HasMMProperty, [20/01/05, now], [0, 0, 640, 480]\rangle$. For readability reasons, in Figure 2 we do not report all the edge labels.

4 Expressing Valid Time Semantics

Constraints on valid times must be able to guarantee that the history of the given application domain is consistent. As an example, at a specific time instant, between two nodes it cannot exist more than one edge representing the same relation.

The graphical formalism we use in the following constraints has been described in [8,13]: a constraint is composed by a *graph*, which is used to identify the subgraphs (i.e., the portions of a semistructured database) where the constraint has to be applied, and a set of *formulae*, which represent restrictions imposed on those subgraphs.

We distinguish two different categories of constraints for valid time values of nodes and edges: *basic constraints* must be satisfied by every MTGM graph; *domain-dependent constraints* are further constraints, which can be defined either for some specific nodes and edges or for the whole graph for a specific clinical domain. In the following, part a) of Figures from 3 to 9 identifies the subgraphs where the constraint has to be applied, and part b) the set of *formulae* representing restrictions imposed on those subgraphs. Part c) shows an example of intervals satisfying the related constraint.

4.1 Basic Constraints

In an MTGM graph, we identified the following basic constraints:

1. The time interval of an edge between a complex node and a simple node must be related to the time interval of the complex node (Figure 3). Intuitively, the relation between a complex node and a simple node cannot survive the complex node; thus, the time interval of the edge cannot start before and cannot end after the valid time of the complex node. This is due to the fact that we suppose that a complex node is related to its properties (simple nodes) while it is valid.

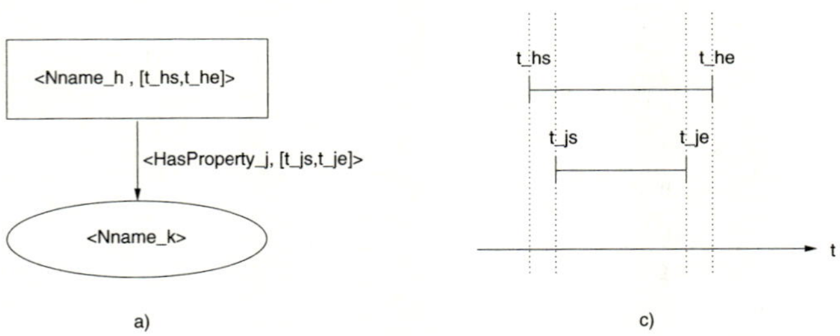

b) $t_{js} \geq t_{hs} \wedge t_{je} \leq t_{he}$

Fig. 3. The VT constraint on the time interval of edges pointing a simple node

2. A complex node cannot have, at a given time, different values for the same property, and thus at a specific time instant, a complex node can be related to at most one simple node with a particular name.
3. At a specific time instant, between two complex nodes it cannot exist more than one edge with the same name. Intuitively, an edge represents a relationship between two complex nodes, thus it makes no sense representing with two edges the same relationship.

4.2 Domain Dependent Constraints

Other possible optional constraints that can be considered are the ones for imposing restrictions on the time interval of an edge connecting two complex nodes. These constraints are strictly related to the semantics of the represented objects and relationships. In this work, we consider radiological clinical data represented by means of DICOM, and thus we define the set of constraints needed to manage this kind of information in a consistent way. In Figure 2 we represented information about the DICOM patient information model, related to radiology images, by means of MTGM, and now we define the related set of domain dependent constraints.

1. A patient can be examined only in the period of time in which she is valid (i.e., she is alive), thus the valid time of the visit must be contained in the valid time of the patient. Moreover the valid time of the edge must start at the same time of the visit (Figure 4).

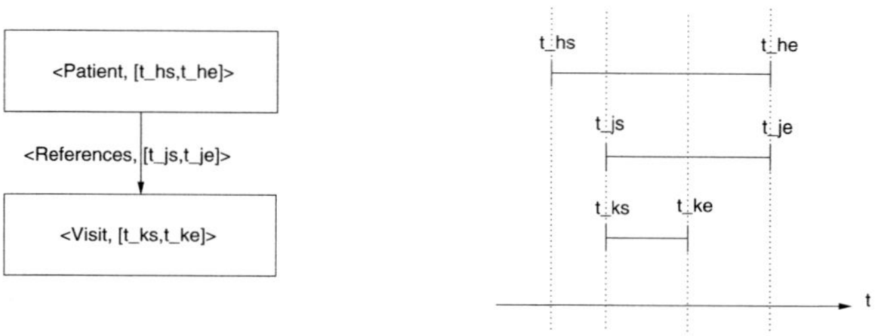

a) c)

b) $t_{ks} \geq t_{hs} \wedge t_{ke} \leq t_{he} \wedge t_{js} = t_{ks}$

Fig. 4. The VT constraint on the relation between a patient and a visit

In this constraint we do not consider the end time of the edge, because we do not fix a rigid relation between its value and the valid times of the patient and the visit. Modifying the constraint, it is possible to require that the start time of the edge is related to the start time of the visit, and that the end time of the edge is related to the end time of the patient. In this case, for each subgraph satisfying the structure shown in part a) of Figure 4 we require that $t_{ks} \geq t_{hs} \wedge t_{ke} \leq t_{he} \wedge t_{js} = t_{ks} \wedge t_{je} = t_{he}$. Intervals reported in part c) of Figure 4 satisfy also this version of the constraint.
2. The situation of the patient with respect to the visit can be studied during the visit or after the visit; thus the start time of the study must start at the same time or after the valid time of the visit (Figure 5).
3. The result of the study can be defined during or after the study, thus the valid time of the result must start after the start of the valid time of the study (Figure 6).
4. The result can be interpreted after the creation of the result itself, thus the valid time of the interpretation must start after the valid time of the result (Figure 7).

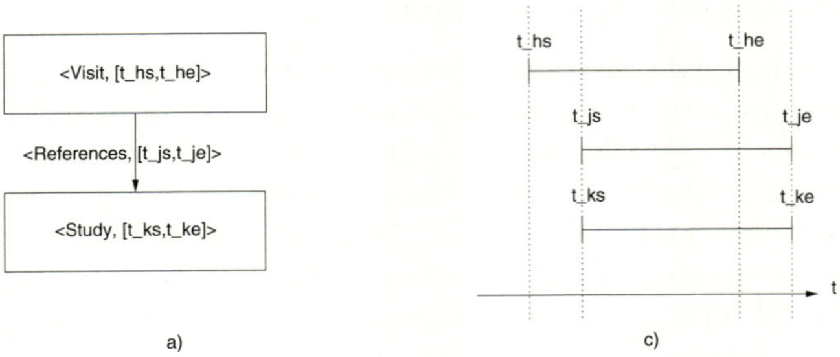

b) $t_{ks} \geq t_{hs}$

Fig. 5. The VT constraint on the relation between a visit and a study

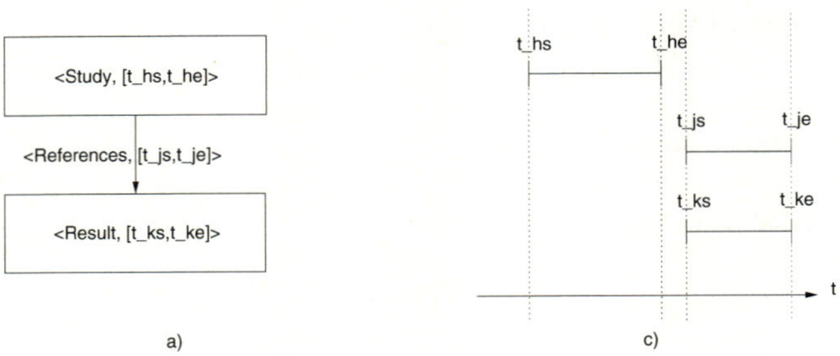

b) $t_{ks} > t_{hs}$

Fig. 6. The VT constraint on the relation between a study and a result

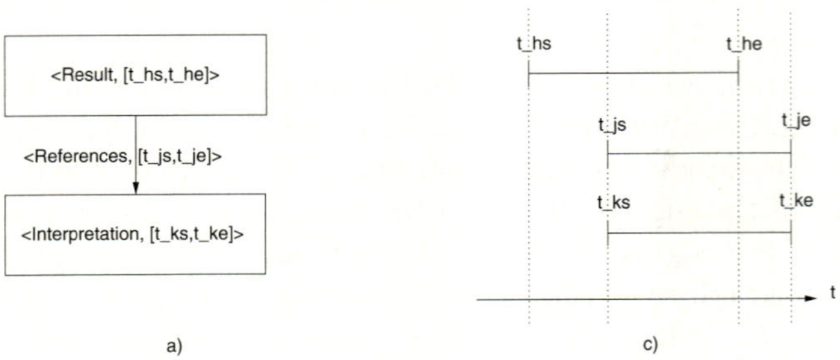

b) $t_{ks} > t_{hs} \wedge t_{ke} \geq t_{he}$

Fig. 7. The VT constraint on the relation between a result and an interpretation

5. A patient can be considered for a study after the moment in which she becomes a patient, thus the valid time of the study must start after the start of the valid time of the patient (Figure 8).
6. An image must be related to a study, thus the valid time of the image must be contained in the valid time of the study (Figure 9).

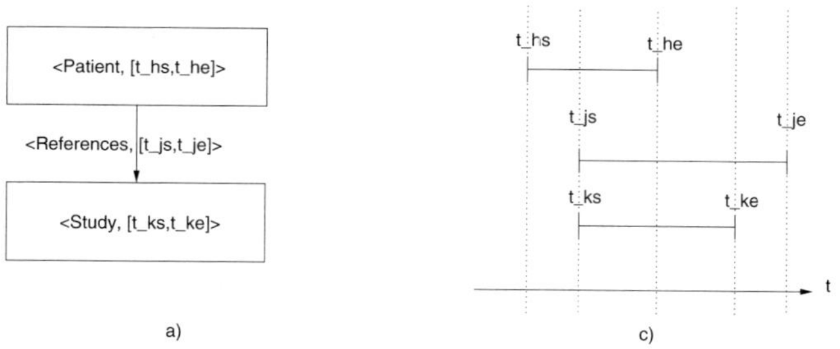

b) $t_{ks} > t_{hs}$

Fig. 8. The VT constraint on the relation between a patient and a study

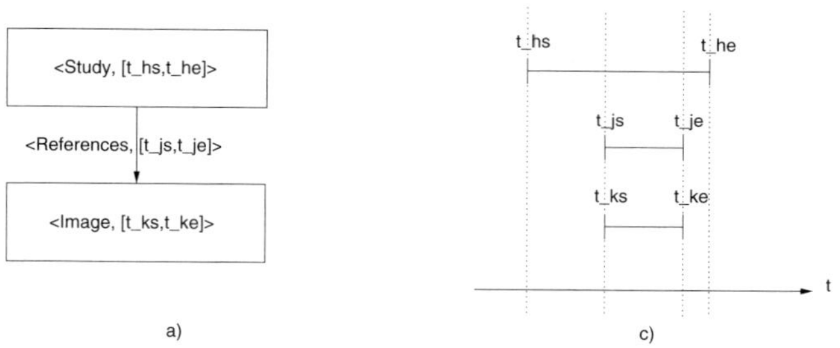

b) $t_{ks} \geq t_{hs} \wedge t_{ke} \leq t_{he}$

Fig. 9. The VT constraint on the relation between a study and an image

Further, and more complex constraints could be defined: for example we could require that the valid times of two studies related to the same patient do not overlap.

4.3 Translating MTGM Graphs into XML Documents

MTGM can be seen as a logical model for semistructured data; an MTGM graph can be physically realized through the emerging XML technology. Among the main differences between MTGM and the data model underlying XML, we have to consider (i) the fact that MTGM considers labeled graphs, while XML mainly deals with trees, and (ii) that, while in MTGM both nodes and edges are labeled, in XML only labeled nodes are allowed. Another important difference is that XML node labels are in some way atomic, while in MTGM we deal with compound labels.

The overall, main ideas underlying the designed translation technique can be summarized as follows:

1. Complex nodes are translated into complex elements (i.e., elements which contain other elements); in particular, they have a (nested) element for the corresponding valid time and an element for each outgoing edge.

2. Atomic (stream) nodes are translated into mixed elements (i.e., elements containing both string values and other elements); in particular, they contain the string representing their values and an element for their valid times (which are contained, in the related MTGM graph, in the label of the ingoing relational edge).
3. Edges between complex nodes are represented through complex elements nested into the element corresponding to the complex node, which the edge originates from. The element corresponding to the node the edge points to, is referred through a suitable attribute in the element representing the edge.
4. Edges between a complex node and an atomic (stream) one are not translated (see point 2.).
5. Compound labels are managed by introducing suitable sub-elements (i.e., nested elements), as for representing valid times of nodes and edges.
6. Elements corresponding to MTGM nodes have an attribute (of type ID), which allows one to refer to them in an unambiguous way.

5 Managing Temporal Clinical Data by XML Native Database Systems

Semistructured temporal DICOM data are managed by means of a system prototype developed by the Java technology, and based on the native XML database

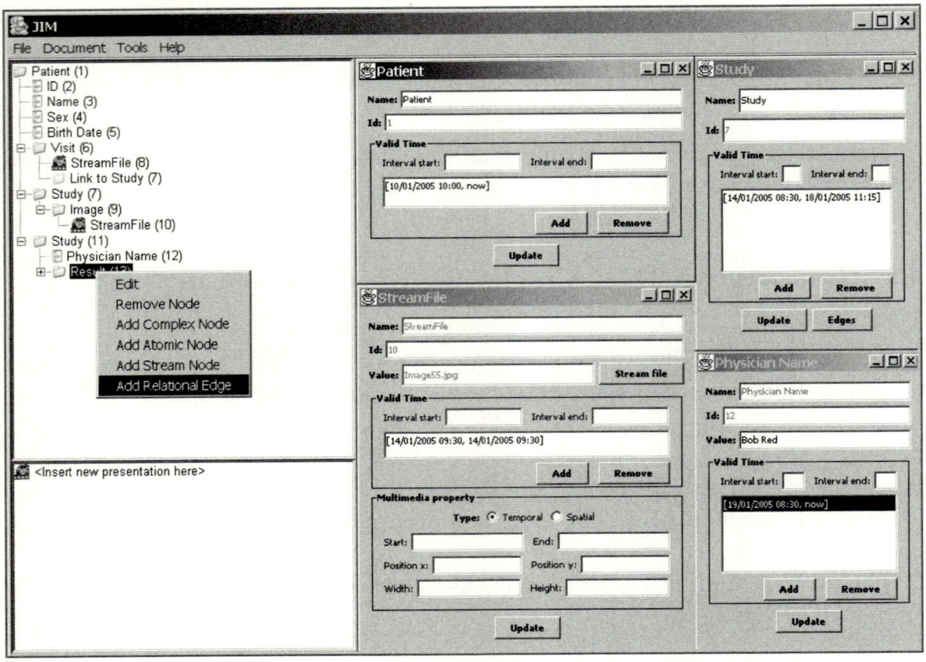

Fig. 10. A screen shot of the described prototype

system eXist [10]. The system prototype has been designed according to the architecture described in [6] and allows us to store clinical radiological data (represented by means of MTGM as shown in Figure 2) in an XML database, as reported in Figure 10.

In the left part of Figure 10 it is possible to see the description of a portion of the MTGM graph reported in Figure 2. The prototype allows us to create and modify an MTGM graph by adding nodes and edges. The description of them can be inserted by means of suitable windows (see the right part of Figure 10). At the end of these operations, the MTGM graph is represented through an XML document and stored in the eXist database.

The constraints described in Section 4 can be managed by the prototype, which allows us to define a set of constraints on a graph-based representation of information. The defined constraints are verified at each operation on the graph: the graph can be modified only if the constraints are verified.

6 Conclusions

In this work we introduced a graph-based approach to manage in a correct way valid time semantics for semistructured clinical information. In particular we considered the patient data model proposed by the DICOM standard and showed how to represent it by the semistructured temporal data model MTGM; moreover we modeled valid time semantics of DICOM data through graphical constraints. Finally, we showed how to use our system prototype to manage radiological data. We plan to study and define more complex constraints related for example to nodes connected by complex paths involving several edges, and to further extend the implemented system to manage them.

References

1. S. Abiteboul. Querying Semi-Structured Data. In *Proceedings of the International Conference on Database Theory*, volume 1186 of *Lecture Notes in Computer Science*, pages 262–275, 1997.
2. National Electrical Manufactures Association. Digital Imaging and Communications in Medicine (DICOM). 2003. `http://medical.nema.org/dicom/2004.html`.
3. E. Bertino and E. Ferrari. Temporal synchronization models for multimedia data. *IEEE TKDE*, 10(2):612–631, 1998.
4. A. F. Cárdenas and J. D. N. Dionisio. A Unified Data Model for Representing Multimedia, Timeline and Simulation Data. *IEEE TKDE*, 10(5):746–767, 1998.
5. C. Combi. Modeling Temporal Aspects of Visual and Textual Objects in Multimedia Databases. In *TIME 2000*, pages 59–68. IEEE Computer Society Press, 2000.
6. C. Combi, B. Oliboni, and R. Rossato. Merging multimedia presentations and semistructured temporal data: a graph-based model and its application to clinical information. *International Journal Artificial Intelligence in Medicine*, 34(2):89–112, 2005.
7. Carlo Combi and Angelo Montanari. Data models with multiple temporal dimensions: Completing the picture. In *CAiSE*, pages 187–202, 2001.

8. E. Damiani, B. Oliboni, E. Quintarelli, and L. Tanca. Modeling semistructured data by using graph-based constraints. In *OTM Workshops Proceedings*, Lecture Notes in Computer Science, pages 20–21. Springer-Verlag, Berlin, 2003.
9. C. S. Jensen and R. Snodgrass. Temporal data management. *IEEE Transactions on Knowledge and Data Engineering*, 11(1):36–44, 1999.
10. W. Meier. An Open Source Native XML Database. In *Web, Web-Services, and Database Systems*, volume 2593 of *Lecture Notes in Computer Science*, pages 169–183. Springer, 2003.
11. I. Mirbel, B. Pernici, T.K. Sellis, S. Tserkezoglou, and M. Vazirgiannis. Checking the Temporal Integrity of Interactive Multimedia Documents. *VLDB Journal*, 9(2):111–130, 2000.
12. R. Noumeir. Dicom structured report document type definition. *IEEE Transactions on Information Technology in Biomedicine*, 7(4):318–328, 2003.
13. B. Oliboni. *Blind queries and constraints: representing flexibility and time in semistructured data.* PhD thesis, Politecnico di Milano, 2003.
14. World Wide Web Consortium. Extensible Markup Language (XML) 1.0, 1998. `http://www.w3C.org/TR/REC-xml/`.

Context-Sensitive Clinical Data Integration

James F. Terwilliger[1], Lois M.L. Delcambre[1], and Judith Logan[2]

[1] Department of Computer Science
Portland State University, Portland OR 97207, USA
{jterwill, lmd}@cs.pdx.edu,
[2] Department of Medical Informatics and Clinical Epidemiology
School of Medicine, Oregon Health and Science University, Portland OR 97239, USA
loganju@ohsu.edu

Abstract. Current methods for data integration are as difficult to use as they are powerful. Motivated by our work with clinical data and the people who analyze it, we present two components that allow non-technical users that are domain experts to create and reuse complex data integration processes. The GUAVA (GUI As View Apparatus) component enables data analysts to make informed data integration decisions based on detailed accounts of the user interface that was used to generate the data. The MultiClass component allows analysts to revisit decisions made for prior studies and reuse them or not each time the data is used. We describe these two components with examples where a warehouse of clinical data is used to support research studies. We describe the state of our implementation and why we believe the two components can be automatically translated into ETL workflows.

1 Introduction

In a traditional data warehouse, database specialists construct an ETL (Extract-Transform-Load) workflow to combine, and transform data from heterogeneous data sources and accumulate it in a central place. Because ETL can include programming code of any complexity, if a warehouse-building process can be done, it can be done using ETL. However, an ETL workflow, once defined, encapsulates only one set of decisions about how to integrate various source databases, and is almost entirely inaccessible to those who are not database experts or programmers. If health-related databases are to be used in research, data must be extracted from data sources and transformed differently for different studies, at multiple points in time, using methods to be specified by clinical experts rather than database experts.

In a clinical setting, there are additional weaknesses to the classical approach of full data integration. First, it may be necessary to lose information. A data source A with two categories, smokers or non-smokers, cannot be fully integrated with a data source B with three related categories, non-smokers, cigar smokers, or cigarette smokers without making a classification decision or declaring the integration impossible. Many integration techniques [1,9,15] identify similarities

T. Grust et al. (Eds.): EDBT 2006 Workshops, LNCS 4254, pp. 387–398, 2006.

between data sources, without offering any guidance on how to answer the classification decision appropriately.

Second, integration techniques that do address the classification decision [6,7] assume that there will be a single, integrated data source. We are interested in supporting an environment where data is used in different studies and may require different classifiers.

Because data integration solutions often require a person to read and understand a database, it is often left to technical experts to decide how to integrate data, even if they do not fully understand the data they are integrating. But, the data in the database is not sufficient for most clinical inquiries. The user interface of a software tool used to capture data defines the precise meaning of data. A "1" in the field "smoker" might mean that the patient is a current smoker, or instead could mean that they quit smoking one year ago.

We present two complementary components that allow domain experts to make their own integration and classification decisions, as needed, for each study. The first, GUI As View Apparatus (GUAVA), provides the user with a rich query interface that is derived from the same GUI that clinical providers used to assemble and view the data originally. Users can thus view data in its original context rather than the potentially obscure environment of a database. The second component, MultiClass, allows domain experts to integrate and classify data again and again, as needed. MultiClass captures these decisions and uses them to generate ordinary ETL workflows. Analysts are also able to use MultiClass to document, inspect, reuse, and modify integration decisions from prior studies.

Section 2 motivates this work by describing patient data used in clinical outcomes research. We describe the GUAVA and MultiClass components in Section 3. Section 4 looks at current results. Section 5 briefly presents related research. Section 6 describes our plans for future work and offers some conclusions.

2 The Status Quo

The primary actor in our scenario is the data analyst, a person trained in statistical methodology with good domain knowledge. For clinical studies, this means the analyst understands medical terminology and data. The data analysts that we are observing work for the *C*linical *O*utcomes *R*esearch *I*nitiative[1] (CORI), an organization that studies clinical data to improve the practice of clinical endoscopy. To encourage clinics to submit data, CORI developed a software reporting tool that clinics can use to document endoscopic procedures. Data from the CORI software tool is periodically sent for inclusion in the CORI warehouse. An ETL workflow performs schema transformation and data cleaning while moving the data into the warehouse. Analysts then identify and extract relevant reports for import into a statistical package for each study. Here are two studies that the analysts may run:

[1] More information about CORI can be found at http://www.cori.org.

Study 1: *We would like to find out, of all patients undergoing upper GI endoscopy, how many (what proportion) had the indication of "Asthma-specific ENT/Pulmonary Reflux symptoms"? Of these, include only those with no history of renal failure and with cardiopulmonary and abdominal examinations within normal limits. How many of these suffered the complication of transient hypoxia? Of these, how many required each of the following interventions: surgery, IV fluids, or oxygen administration?*

Study 2: *Of all procedures on ex-smokers, how many had a complication of hypoxia?*

These research studies as performed by an analyst are more than just queries. A study comprises all of the decisions that a data analyst makes from the time a request arrives to when final statistical analyses are run, and those decisions can change over time. Those decisions are also based on the precise semantics of both the study and the data; if a study defines an ex-smoker to be someone who has quit in the last year, but the user interface indicates that an ex-smoker is anyone who has ever smoked, the data may not be appropriate to use in that study.

The technical demands of writing an ETL workflow are beyond the capabilities of the CORI analysts. It is left to the development team to write the ETL workflow, and as a consequence, the analysts do not completely understand the process by which data arrives in the warehouse. Thus, they also cannot modify that process as new research questions arise. To complicate matters, several commercial reporting tool vendors have expressed an interest in contributing data to CORI's clinical data warehouse. Each new vendor necessitates a new ETL workflow, potentially for each study.

3 Architectural Overview

The GUAVA and MultiClass components of our architecture enable data analysts to express their own data extraction, integration, and cleaning for each study. We introduce three artifacts (Figure 1):

- *GUAVA trees (g-trees)* that allow an analyst to explore the user interface of a data capture tool to select the data of interest
- *Study schemas* that document the data that analysts want in studies
- *Classifiers* that relate elements of g-trees with the study schema

Anyone using the system can annotate and timestamp each of these artifacts, as well as the studies themselves, so that it is clear who generated them, when, and why.

To perform a study, the data analyst chooses data elements from (or adds data elements to) a study schema, writes conditions similar to a WHERE clause in SQL to filter out unwanted data, and then selects or defines new classifiers. The analyst may choose to look at other studies that use the same study schema to make informed decisions as to which classifiers to use.

MultiClass uses the specifications set out by the analyst to create an ETL workflow that is tailored to a specific study. Thus, we can leverage existing ETL

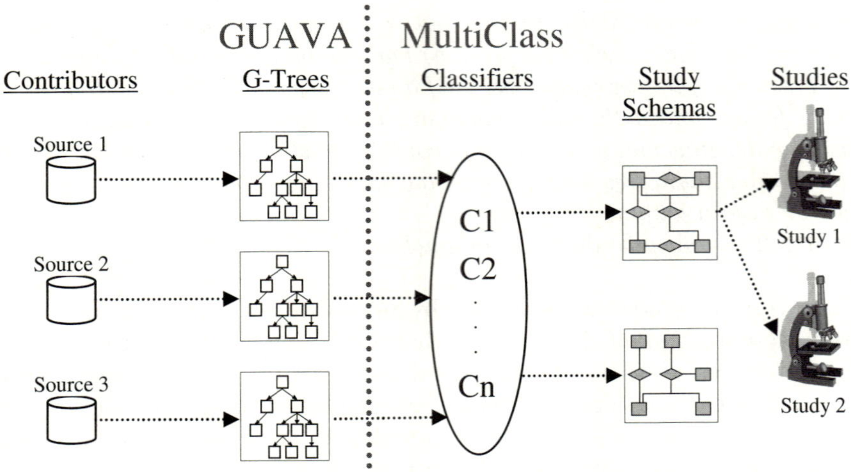

Fig. 1. GUAVA and MultiClass components and how they interface

and still offer the flexibility that analysts require when running studies over semantically-rich data.

3.1 Scope

We do not expect our architecture to be a universal data integration solution. GUAVA expects that a GUI accompanies each data source. The user interfaces that interest us are *reporting tools*, where the primary purpose of the interface is to facilitate data entry.

We are not working on resolving naming conflicts or automated schema matching [1,10]. We assume that, because data analysts are domain experts, they are capable of making judgments about domain-specific vocabulary, such as the fact that "interventions" in one source refers to the same data as "complications" in another source. Note that controlled vocabularies [4] or ontology, or other automated schema matching tools [10] may be useful in conjunction with GUAVA to assist the user.

Also, we are not addressing instance identification problem [15]. Since an endoscopy report is likely not created twice, MultiClass simply unions together the results of ETL workflows from different contributors.

3.2 GUAVA: GUI as View Apparatus

Each contributor schema in Figure 1 is associated with a GUAVA tree (or g-tree) that captures the structure and content of the user interface (Figure 2). The g-tree demonstrates relationships that may not be present in the database alone, such as a question that becomes enabled only if one answered a previous question in a specific way. Each node in a g-tree (Figure 3) captures context

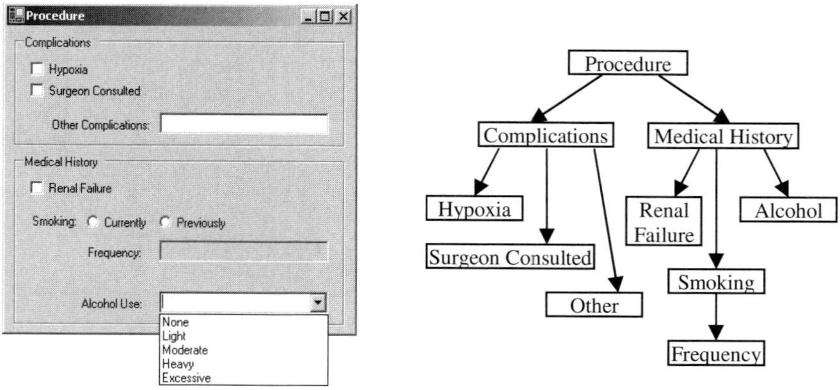

(a) (b)

Fig. 2. An example dialog from a clinical tool and its corresponding g-tree. There is a node in the g-tree for every control on the screen, even those that do not normally store data, such as group boxes. Because the "frequency" textbox does not become enabled until someone answers the "smoking" question, the "frequency" node appears as a child of the "smoking" node.

information about a control on the interface, including the exact wording of a control's question and answer options, whether there is a default value, and whether the control is required to be filled in.

The g-tree behaves like a view; when analysts write classifiers, they express queries against the g-trees. Thus, each node in the g-tree must refer back to the contributor's database to get data. As a normal part of using the reporting tool, when the user enters data into a field, the reporting tool places that data into the database. In GUAVA, we exploit that connection between UI elements and the database to generate mappings between the UI and the database automatically.

One benefit of our approach comes from how we deal with schematic heterogeneity, when information of interest appears as schema (such as table or column names) in one data source and as data (a field in a table extent) in another data source. The most frequent type of schematic heterogeneity arises because contributors often use a generic database layout, where each row in the database looks like "Entity, Attribute, Value". The user interface, however, is not generic and does not have a generic layout; if one considers a single screen in the interface as a row in the database, then each control represents a column.

Informally, we have noticed that reporting tools maintain an in-memory structure with a simple design: each screen of the tool corresponds to a table, and each control corresponds to a column. We call this design the *naïve schema* for a tool. The physical database design is far different, typically with a generic layout. We believe that the differences between the naïve schema and the real database can be encapsulated by specific design patterns (Table 1). Each pattern

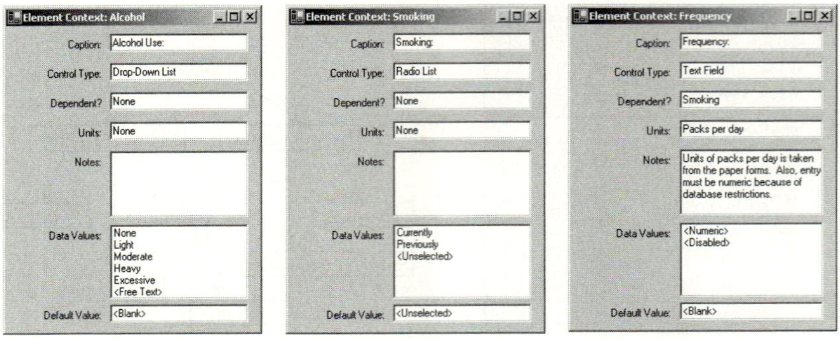

(a) (b) (c)

Fig. 3. Details for three nodes from the g-tree in Figure 2. The alcohol node (a) has one data value each for the selections in the drop-down list, and an option for free text. The smoking node (b) has an option for "unselected" because the radio list starts out with no option selected. The frequency node (c) records that the control does not become enabled unless the smoking control has an answer.

describes a data transformation; several put together describe how to translate a query against the g-tree into one against the database.

Since the code for a user interface can be arbitrarily complex, there may be an arbitrarily complex relationship between the UI and the underlying data source. By exploring the utility of database patterns, we hope to show that most such complex relationships can be expressed using a small number of design patterns.

3.3 MultiClass: Study Schema

A study schema collects all of the things that analysts want to study — like a patient's gender or smoking habits — and organizes them at a conceptual level. The study schema may be incomplete compared to a global schema. Data elements not needed in any study are simply omitted. Analysts can expand the study schema as needed for new studies. For the data analysts at CORI, the primary entity of interest is always the procedure; we expect that CORI would only need to have one study schema. We allow multiple study schemas, e.g., with patient or medications as the primary entity of interest.

A study schema simplifies the traditional ER model in that the only relationship type is "has-a" with a single entity of primary interest sitting atop a tree, much like a "part-of" hierarchy in a CAD database [13]. Using such a hierarchical model (Figure 4) meets the needs of clinical studies where the primary entity of interest is the procedure. The biggest difference between a study schema and an ER diagram is the addition of multiple *domains* for an attribute. Depending on the study, analysts may want to represent an attribute like smoking habits in different ways (Table 2).

Table 1. Example database design patterns. Each design pattern represents a transformation that one must perform when reading data into memory.

Pattern	Description	Data Transformation
Naïve	No transformations are applied to the data.	None — this is just the in-memory database
Merge	Data from several forms are drawn from the same table.	Pull only data where C = form name (C is a column that holds forms)
Split	Attributes from a single form are distributed over several tables	Join
Generic	Each row in a table represents an attribute, rather than each column.	Execute an un-pivot operation, either in code or SQL if the operator exists in the DBMS
Audit	No rows are ever deleted or updated. Rows can be deprecated by setting the value in a column. The reporting tool only displays current data.	Pull only data where C = 0 (0 is a sentinel to indicate that the row has not been deleted)

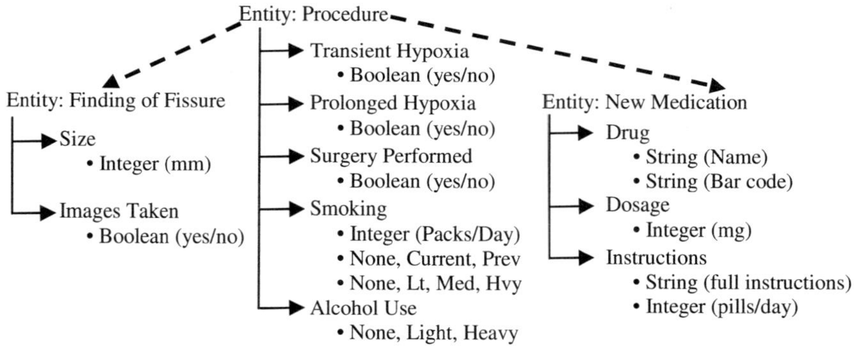

Fig. 4. A study schema. Entities have attributes, which in turn have domain(s) that correspond to different ways to represent them. The dashed lines indicate "has-a" relationships between entities, with the primary entity "Procedure" at the top of the tree.

Table 2. Three different domains for the "smoking" attribute. There is no way to translate any one representation into another without losing information.

Domain	Elements	Description
1	Positive Integers	Number of packs smoked per day
2	None, Current, Previous	No smoking, current smoker, or has smoked in the past
3	None, Light, Moderate, Heavy	General classification of smoking habits

3.4 MultiClass: Classifiers

An analyst creates a classifier to relate nodes in a g-tree with domain entries in a study schema. Each classifier is a list of declarative statements of the form $A \leftarrow B$, where A is an arithmetic calculation and B is a Boolean condition. Both clauses use nodes in a g-tree as arguments (see Figure 5 for examples). Thus, the input to a classifier is contributor data, but as displayed as it appears in a user interface rather than as stored in a database.

MultiClass allows more than one classifier to map data from the same contributor to the same domain. Different studies may interpret domain values differently; a "previous" smoker may mean someone who has quit in the last year, or in the last ten years, or at any time at all. MultiClass needs *entity classifiers* to identify unique objects in a g-tree and bring them forward into a study schema. An analyst creates an entity classifier just like any other classifier, except the target object of the classifier is an entity rather than a domain. Also, the classifier must refer to at least one node in the g-tree that represents a form rather than an attribute.

Classifier Habits (Cancer)
Classifies packs per day according to conversations with cancer study on 5/3/02

None	←	PacksPerDay = 0
Light	←	0 < PacksPerDay < 2
Moderate	←	2 ≤ PacksPerDay < 5
Heavy	←	PacksPerDay ≥ 5

Classifier Habits (Chemistry)
Classifies packs per day according to flier from chemical studies

None	←	PacksPerDay = 0
Light	←	0 < PacksPerDay < 1
Moderate	←	1 ≤ PacksPerDay < 2
Heavy	←	PacksPerDay ≥ 2

(a)

Classifier Tumor Size
Estimates tumor volume based on dimensions in 3-space. Assumes 52% occupancy from sphere-to-cube ratio.

TumorX * TumorY * TumorZ * 0.52 ← TumorX > 0 AND TumorY > 0 AND TumorZ > 0

(b)

Entity Classifier Relevant Procedures
Only consider procedures where surgery was performed

Procedure ← Procedure AND SurgeryPerformed = TRUE

(c)

Fig. 5. Example classifiers. Two classifiers (a) can relate data from a contributor to the same domain for different studies. Another classifier (b) shows how to write classifiers that refer to more than one g-tree node. An entity classifier (c) tells MultiClass how to relate forms in the application with entities in the study schema, where "Procedure" is a node in the g-tree that represents the form in Figure 2.

4 Analysis

We have shown a number of analysts our architecture with examples of g-trees, classifiers, and study schemas and compared them with the statistical software tools that they currently use. They confirm that g-trees are easy to read and that classifiers are simple to write and organize.

4.1 Research Directions

In the process of our research, we will investigate the validity of three hypotheses.

Hypothesis #1: It is possible to automatically generate a g-tree and database mappings using an Integrated Development Environment (IDE). The prototype of GUAVA that we are developing extends Visual Studio .Net to generate a g-tree from the code that makes up the GUI of a reporting tool. The prototype allows the developer to specify database design patterns that relate the g-tree to the database.

Hypothesis #2: The artifacts of GUAVA and MultiClass are simple enough that data analysts can use them without technical assistance. We assert that g-trees are significantly simpler to read than database schemas, that classifiers are easy to specify, and that domains are simple to understand because they are a concept from statistics. Usability testing will include measuring precision and recall; analysts should be able to extract only and all relevant data from contributors without technical help.

Hypothesis #3: It is possible to compile studies into ETL workflows. A study in MultiClass consists of classifiers that draw from databases using GUAVA. At this early stage, we can show how to translate these objects into an ETL workflow in specific cases. We aim to show that we can generate ETL workflows by comparing the expressive power of our classifier language against a set of common ETL components.

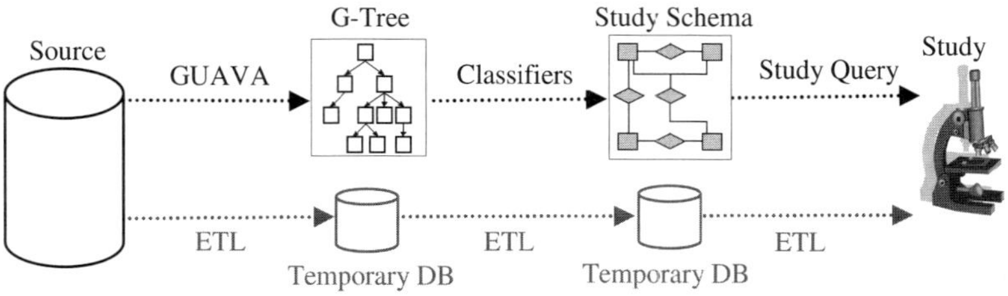

Fig. 6. Translating GUAVA and MultiClass artifacts into ETL

We believe that the classifier language as specified here is equivalent in expressive power to conjunctive queries with union. We can translate queries specified against the g-tree into predefined SQL queries and ETL components that depend on the database patterns used. At present, a study created over GUAVA and MultiClass has a logical translation to a sequence of three ETL components, each executing a query over the previous one's results (Figure 6).

4.2 Implementation Status and Options

A prototype implementation of GUAVA is underway. Though we have identified 11 distinct database patterns so far, our initial prototype only considers the patterns listed in Table 1. The prototype takes the standard .Net form components and extends them with methods that allow the IDE to generate a g-tree. The g-tree is stored as an XML Schema, which mimics the hierarchical nature of the form interface and allows queries to return XML documents in a standard format. Currently, we are working on developing the mechanism to translate queries against the tree.

We are still in the early stages of development for MultiClass. We have developed the algorithms for translating the classifier language into XQuery. Our approach is to identify all of the nodes in a g-tree that are referenced by the set of classifiers. Then, treat each entity classifier as a "for-each" to iterate through objects, each domain classifier as a variable assignment, and each rule in a classifier as a conditional statement. To date, we have successfully hand-translated several collections of classifiers into both XQuery and Datalog.

We are still considering our options for implementing a study schema. The naïve approach is to materialize the output of individual classifiers into relational tables or XML documents. In the relational model, the result is a collection of tables, one table per entity classifier per entity, with columns representing classifier output (Figure 7). This option allows for simple data retrieval because getting data from the study schema reduces to select-project-join queries. If the classifiers/domains ratio is high, then a comprehensive materialized study schema may be too large to manage. Alternatives include materializing only often-used classifiers or determining relationships between classifiers. The latter implies that if classifier A and classifier B share a simple algebraic relationship, then we can materialize A's output and compute B as needed.

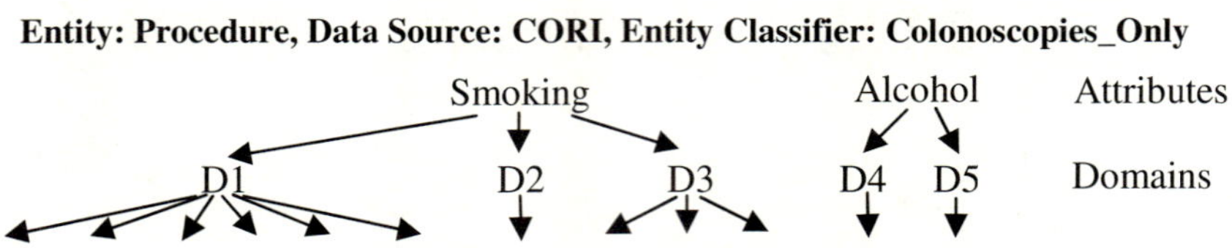

Classifiers

C1	C2	C3	C4	C5	C6	C7	C8	C9	CA	CB	CC
T	T	T	T	T	F	0	A	A	A	T	H
T	T	T	T	F	F	1	B	B	B	T	M
T	F	F	F	T	F	2	A	A	B	T	L
F	F	F	F	F	F	0	C	B	C	F	N

Fig. 7. A fully-materialized study schema must also materialize every classifier, where each classifier serves as a column in the table

5 Related Work

SEMEX. The SEMantic EXplorer project [2] also supports on-demand data integration by non-technical users. SEMEX uses outside sources such as search engines to suggest matches, but does not consult any user interface that may have generated data. Also, SEMEX does not provide any way to classify values.

Schematic Heterogeneity. SchemaSQL [8] and nD-SQL [5] demonstrate how to extend SQL to accommodate schematic heterogeneity; however, few of these features are available in commercial databases. They are also very difficult to learn, even for expert SQL users, so even if we decide to use these languages in our implementation, we will not require data analysts to learn them.
Mediated Schemas. A mediated schema serves a similar function as a study schema: presenting a unified view of heterogeneous data sources to the end user — in our case, a data analyst. A mediated schema uses Inter-schema Correspondence Assertions (ICAs) to establish relationships between databases. Database patterns and classifiers both act as ICAs, if one were to consider g-trees to be schemas. There exist both a simple notation [12] and more complex notations such as GLAV [7] for representing ICAs. These notations only express relationships between sets of objects, such as equality or containment. They do not express any transformation of data elements as is required for classifiers.
Context. The COIN project [11] stores context alongside data in the form of metadata, and also automatically transforms data based on that context. Because a g-tree resides outside of the underlying database, GUAVA can attach context information over an existing database regardless of implementation. MultiClass allows for multiple classifiers to transform data from the same context to the same domain in different ways according to need.

6 Future Work and Conclusion

We want to extend the classifier language to allow data cleaning, since analysts may also choose to discard data based on the needs of the particular study they wish to run. We are also interested in handling new versions of a reporting tool by propagating classifiers to the next version if their input nodes did not change, and suggest new classifiers if there is a change. Finally, we are interested in exploring whether GUAVA or MultiClass is able to provide benefits in other domains, such as traffic data and financial applications.

Acknowledgements

This work is supported in part by Collins Medical Trust, and by DHHS NIH National Institute of Diabetes Digestive and Kidney Diseases No. 5-R33-DK061778-03 awarded to Oregon Health & Science University (OHSU).

References

1. R. Dhamankar, Y. Lee, A. Doan, A. Halevy, P. Domingos. iMAP: discovering complex semantic matches between database schemas. In *Proceedings of the 2004 ACM SIGMOD International Conference on Management of Data*, Paris, France, 2004, 383–394.

2. X. Dong, A. Y. Halevy. A Platform for Personal Information Management and Integration. In *Proceedings of the Second Biennial Conference on Innovative Data Systems Research (CIDR)*, Asilomar, CA, USA, January 4-7, 2005, 119–130.
3. F. Du, S. Amir-Yahia, J. Freire. A comprehensive solution to the XML-to-relational mapping problem. In *Proceedings of the 6th Annual ACM International Workshop on Web Information and Data Management*, Washington DC, November 12-13, 2004, 31–38.
4. M. Evens. Thesaural Relations in Information Retrieval. In R. Green, C. A. Bean, and S. H. Myaeng (eds.), *The Semantics of Relationships: An Interdisciplinary Perspective*, Kluwer Academic Publishers, Dordrecht, Netherlands, ©2002, 143–160.
5. F. Gingras and L. V. S. Lakshmanan. nD-SQL: A multi-dimensional language for interoperability and OLAP. In *Proceedings of the 24th International Conference on Very Large Data Bases (VLDB)*, New York City, USA, 1998, 134–145.
6. J. A. Larson, S. B. Navathe, and R. Elmasri. A Theory of Attribute Equivalence in Databases with Application to Schema Integration. *IEEE Transactions on Software Engineering*, April 1989, 15(4):449–463.
7. J. Madhavan and A. Y. Halevy. Composing Mappings Among Data Sources. In *Proceedings of the 29th International Conference on Very Large Data Bases (VLDB)*, Berlin, Germany, September 2003, 572–583.
8. R. J. Miller. Using Schematically Heterogeneous Structures. In *Proceedings of ACM SIGMOD*, Seattle, WA, June 1998, 27(2):189–200.
9. R. J. Miller, M. A. Hernandez, L. M. Haas, L.-L. Yan, C. T. H. Ho, R. Fagin, and L. Popa. The Clio Project: Managing Heterogeneity. *SIGMOD Record*, 2001, 30(1):78–83.
10. E. Rahm and P.A. Bernstein. A survey of approaches to automatic schema matching. In *Proceedings of the 27th International Conferences on Very Large Databases*, 2001, 10(4):334–350.
11. E. Sciore, M. Siegel, and A. Rosenthal. Using semantic values to facilitate interoperability among heterogeneous information systems. *ACM Transactions on Database Systems*, June 1994, 19(2):254–290.
12. S. Spaccapietra, C. Parent, and Y. Dupont. Model independent assertions for integration of heterogeneous schemas. *VLDB Journal*, 1992, 1:81–126.
13. D. L. Spooner. Towards an Object-Oriented Data Model for a Mechanical CAD Database System. In K. R. Dittrich, U. Dayal, and A. P. Buchmann (eds.), *On Object-Oriented Database Systems*, Springer-Verlag, Berlin, Germany, 1991, 189–205.
14. P. Vassiliadis, A. Simitsis, P. Georgantas, M. Terrovitis, and S. Skiadopoulos. A generic and customizable framework for the design of ETL scenarios. *Information Systems*, November 2005, 30(7):492–525.
15. Y. R. Wang and S. E. Madnick. The inter-database instance identification problem in integrating autonomous systems. In *Proceedings of the Fifth International Conference on Data Engineering (ICDE)*, Los Angeles, CA, February 6-10, 1989, IEEE Computer Society Press, Washington, DC, pages 46–55.

An Integrated Platform for Analyzing Molecular-Biological Data Within Clinical Studies

Toralf Kirsten[1], Jörg Lange[1], and Erhard Rahm[1,2]

[1] Interdisciplinary Center for Bioinformatics Leipzig, University of Leipzig
[2] Dept. of Computer Science, University of Leipzig
{tkirsten, lange}@izbi.uni-leipzig.de,
rahm@informatik.uni-leipzig.de

Abstract. To investigate molecular-biological causes and effects of diseases and their therapies it becomes increasingly important to combine data from clinical trials with high volumes of experimental genetic data and annotations. We present our approach to integrate such data for two large collaborative cancer research studies in Germany. Our platform interconnects a commercial study management system (eRN) with a data warehouse-based gene expression analysis system (GeWare). We utilize a generic approach to import different anonymized pathological and patient-related annotations into the warehouse. The platform also integrates different forms of experimental data and public molecular-biological annotation data and thus supports a wide range of genetic analyses for both clinical and non-clinical parameters.

1 Introduction

Clinical trials help to study the cure process and survival rate of patients for new or modified therapies and drugs, e.g. to deal with specific types of cancer. For this purpose, many patient and treatment parameters are observed and analyzed. In addition to analyzing the success of entire therapies, one can also find parameters acting as classifiers, for which participating patients show a different therapy course and success. On the other hand, diseases and therapy processes are deeply affected by molecular-biological conditions for genes, proteins and their complex inter- and intra-cellular interactions. For instance, cancer cells underlie genomic mutations and thus have a modified gene expression that is often increased in higher states of the disease. To better understand the genotype-phenotype interrelationships for diseases and their therapies it becomes increasingly important to combine clinical and molecular-biological data, e.g. to investigate the relationship between pathological classifications and genomic disparities [Co03]. These studies utilize new experimental high throughput techniques for patients like microarray-based gene expression analysis [Ka05]. An ultimate goal is to support personalized therapies with respect to individual genetic patient conditions.

The need to combine clinical and molecular-biological data poses specific data integration requirements. So far these different types of data are not only maintained in a variety of different data sources but are also managed by different complex data

T. Grust et al. (Eds.): EDBT 2006 Workshops, LNCS 4254, pp. 399 – 410, 2006.

management and analysis systems. Clinical trials typically involve many institutions and complex workflows. They are usually managed by commercial study management software, such as eResearch Network[1] (eRN), Oracle Clinical[2], and MACRO[3]. Most of these systems are certified by public authorities, such as *Federal Drug Administration* (FDA) in the USA and *European Medicines Agency* (EMEA) in Europe [Ku03]. On the other hand, molecular-biological experimental data is typically maintained in specific genomic databases, such as ArrayExpress [Bra03], Stanford Microarray Database (SMD) [She01], and Gene Expression Omnibus (GEO) [Ba05]. They support the analysis of huge amounts of gene expression data but without considering clinical parameters. In addition, there are numerous publicly available data sources providing annotations for molecular-biological analysis, e.g. Entrez [Ma05], SwissProt [Ba04], GeneOntology [GOC04], and OMIM [OMIM00].

Overviews of currently available approaches and tools for data integration in bioinformatics are given in [St03, LC03]. Most of the approaches focus on the integration of publicly available annotation data. [Na04] proposes a data warehouse platform to integrate patient-related data with data from different types of molecular-biological experiments and annotations. However, the platform is limited in the number of annotation sources and does not support clinical trials across different institutions. NCICB (National Cancer Institute Center for Bioinformatics) has started a large biomedical data integration effort within the caBIG initiative (cancer Biomedical Informatics Grid) [Bu05,Co03].

In this paper, we present our analysis platform integrating clinical and molecular-biological data for two large collaborative cancer research studies in Germany. One study aims at investigating molecular mechanisms of malignant lymphoma[4], the other focuses on glioma[5]. First results [Hu06] are recently published. Our platform interconnects the commercial study management system eRN with a data warehouse-based gene expression analysis platform (GeWare). We utilize a generic approach to import different pathological and anonymized patient-related annotations into the warehouse where it is used for improved data analysis. The platform also supports integration of different forms of experimental data and public molecular-biological annotation data. We believe our approach is quite general and applicable in similar research studies on analyzing molecular mechanisms for different types of diseases and therapies.

In the next section we introduce the project environment and resulting requirements. Section 3 presents the overall architecture of our integration approach and platform. In section 4 we present our generic approach to import and maintain annotations. Section 5 explains the multidimensional data warehouse model and different analysis capabilities before we conclude.

2 Project Requirements

Clinical trials typically involve complex workflows across different organizations. Fig. 1 visualizes some process portion of a clinical trial focusing on major data acquisition

[1] http://www.ert.com
[2] http://www.oracle.com/industries/life_sciences/clinical.html
[3] http://www.infermed.com/macro/
[4] http://www.lymphome.de/en/Projects/MMML/index.jsp
[5] http://www.gliomnetzwerk.de/

steps. It starts with the identification of relevant patients to participate in the clinical trial based on defined inclusion criteria. These criteria have to be carefully specified to select patients relevant for the respective research question while preserving enough patients to support statistically valid analysis. For selected patients *personal data* is captured, such as age, sex, material status or non-/smoker distinction. Some properties reflect habits and peculiarities of patients that can have a great impact in the later analysis, e.g. when the data is partitioned in non-/smoker portions.

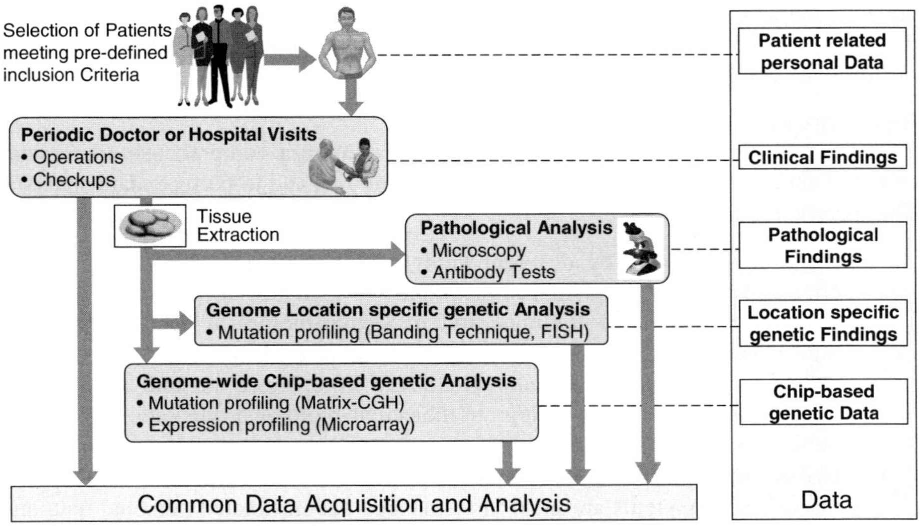

Fig. 1. Project environment and resulting data

A *clinical finding* is produced whenever a patient visits a doctor or the hospital. That can happen regularly, e.g. for quarterly checkups, or when an adverse event happens. In both cases, the clinical finding describes the current clinical state of the patient and makes it possible to track the therapy status by utilizing precisely defined parameters. Typically, such clinical findings are stored in a study management system. In addition, it could be necessary to extract diseased tissue material for a patient within an operation, e.g. cancer nodes. This material is then analyzed by pathologists, e.g. using light microscopy or antibody tests. The pathologists describe the properties of the extracted tissue material and hence create a *pathological finding* that can influence the decisions of doctors in the therapy process.

Moreover, parts of the extracted tissue material can be utilized to experimentally measure properties at the genetic level, particularly using expression profiling and mutation profiling. *Expression profiling* studies the so-called expression behavior (activity) of interesting genes w.r.t. different conditions, e.g. healthy vs. diseased tissues or for different points in time. Microarrays [She95, Lo96] are the currently prevalent tools measuring the expression of thousands of genes at the same time.

The second experimental approach, mutation profiling, focuses on the genetic diversity of patients. Normally, genes are located at fixed positions on a chromosome. However, individual mutations (insertions, deletions, moves) of sequences can have a significant impact on the development and therapy of diseases. This holds particularly for large block-wise mutations, such as copies and movements across different chromosomes. Current techniques to measure such genetic imbalances include the banding analysis [Ca70], the Fluorescent in situ-Hybridization (FISH) [Me95], and Matrix-based comparative genomic hybridization (Matrix-CGH) [Ka92]. The first two techniques focus on a specific genome location and bring out a relative small number of data or just a description. By contrast, the Microarray-based gene expression and the Matrix-CGH mutation profiling operate genome-wide and, hence, generate huge amounts of data. Typically, the banding and FISH analyses are performed in different hospitals, while the Microarray-based expression and Matrix-CGH mutation profiling are centrally conducted by specialized labs.

Requirements

The sketched project environment and workflow require a comprehensive and standardized approach to integrate the different types of data and to perform data analysis. The specific requirements are:

- **Data integration:** The different kinds of data obtained from the described clinical workflow need to be integrated for analysis, in particular personal data, several types of findings, and molecular-biological data produced by high-throughput techniques. The high volume of experimental data asks for a central management of the integrated data. To enhance the analysis capabilities it is also desirable to integrate molecular-biological annotation data from publicly available sources.
- **Utilization of existing information systems:** Typically, commercial study management systems are utilized to manage patient-related personal data and her corresponding finding data, whereas different genomic databases manage expression and mutation profiling data. In order to save time and cost such already existing systems should be used and connected instead of designing a new comprehensive system from scratch.
- **Uniform data specification:** Data of different steps such as clinical and pathological findings are generated in different hospitals and organizations. To keep the data comparable it is imperative to enforce uniform data acquisition procedures and standardized data formats. This concerns not only the metadata such as the sets of parameters to be provided but also the permissible data (instance) values and their meaning. The latter may be enforced by conformed vocabularies.
- **Autonomous data input:** Manual data input into paper forms should largely be avoided and replaced by direct data entry into the study management system. The data entry should be autonomously take place where the data is generated by using pre-defined web templates. The study management can centrally store the data and should perform extensive validity tests to ensure high data quality.
- **Central molecular-biological experiments:** Molecular biological experiments should be performed in a central laboratory for each type of experimental data. This ensures uniform laboratory conditions and device properties as needed for a comparative analysis of experimental data.

- **Privacy aspects:** Legal requirements demand the protection of the patients' privacy. In particular, identifying data such as id card number, social insurance number or the person's name must not be stored together with other data, e.g. clinical and pathological findings.
- **Advanced data analysis:** Comprehensive molecular-biological data analysis should be supported for different theoretical and biological researchers to fully leverage the collected and integrated set of data.

3 Platform Architecture

To meet these requirements for two large collaborative cancer research studies we have developed a comprehensive data integration and analysis platform at the University of Leipzig. Fig. 2 shows the overall architecture of this platform. It interconnects two existing data management systems, the study management system eRN and the gene expression warehouse GeWare [KHR04]. Both systems themselves integrate data from several sources, permit interactive user input and support analysis of their data.

The study management system eRN allows users at participating institutions to autonomously specify patient-related personal, clinical, and pathological data using predefined web forms. To enforce the anonymity of patient-related data, a *technical patient identifier* is generated whenever a new patient enters the clinical study. All personal identifications such as patient names or social security number are excluded and only anonymous patient data tagged with the technical patient identifier is entered in the study management system. To support high data quality the system implements different rule-based input and consistency checks (e.g. minimum and maximum values) as well as cross validations. Specific data validation reports indicate input imbalances or missing data to be corrected by users before the data is accepted and made available for analysis. All analysis routines on study management data can be performed via web interfaces but are typically restricted to basic statistical reports (e.g., number of examined patients at various stages of the therapy).

While the eRN system manages patient-related data, the GeWare system deals with chip-based expression and mutation data. Currently, this data is generated at central labs by Microarray-based and Matrix-CGH chip experiments. This data is much more voluminous than the patient-related data and cannot be stored within eRN. GeWare provides web interfaces to upload new experimental data and to specify their technical annotations on laboratory conditions, such as hybridization temperature.

To combine patient-related data with chip-based data for combined analysis, GeWare also imports a subset of patient-related data from eRN. The selection depends on the research project and currently subsumes about 100 to 130 parameter values per patient. While the patient-related data is identified by the patient identifier, the chip-based data utilizes a chip identifier from which the patient identifier can not be derived. We thus provide a *mapping table* associating each chip identifier with the corresponding patient identifier to correctly combine clinical, pathological and experimental data and to permit an over-spanning data analysis. In addition, GeWare integrates publicly available gene/clone annotation data for extended analysis possibilities. This data integration is performed by a query mediator approach and outlined in [Ki05].

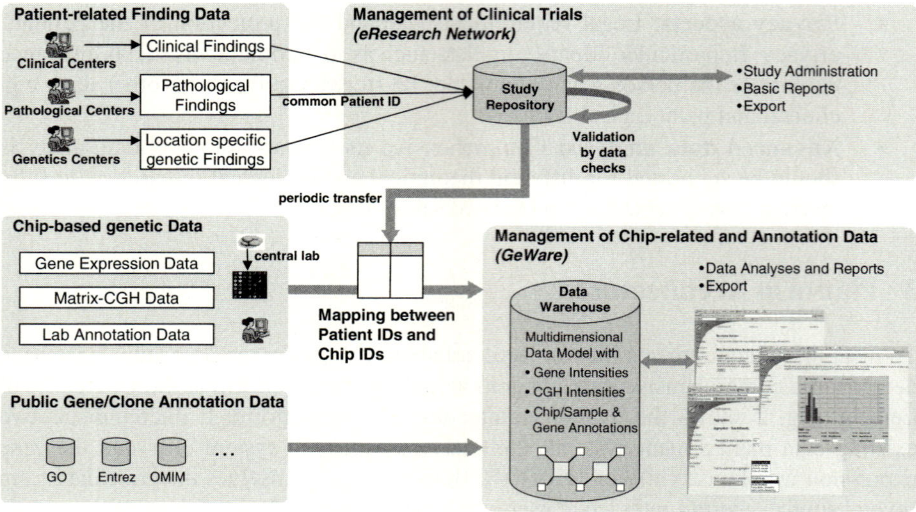

Fig. 2. Overall Architecture of the Platform

GeWare comprises different reports and analysis methods. For instance, it is possible to find lists of differentially expressed genes according to different clinical circumstances by analyzing experimentally generated data together with biological and selected patient-related annotations. Furthermore, data can be exported for external analysis by specialized statistical or data mining software.

The platform not only preserves the anonymity of personal data but also utilizes a sophisticated authentication and authorization concept for different user groups. In particular, access rights can be granted/revoked not only for the access to both systems and its data (patient-related annotations and experimental data), but also for the functions on the data, such as import, export, query etc. According to the user profile, e.g. doctors in a hospital, pathologists and biostatisticians, the web user interface is automatically generated to only cover the allowed functions of both systems.

4 Annotation Integration

Depending on the clinical focus, the trials can be conducted and documented in different ways. For instance, clinical lymphoma studies usually describe diseased cancer nodes using parameters such as node size and node type, but also the state of thyroids due to its important role in the metabolism. On the other hand, in glioma studies the specific brain region is important to annotate. Hence, the captured parameters typically differ between studies. Similarly, annotations of experimental conditions for microarray data and Matrix-CGH arrays may differ substantially. While standards like MIAME[6]/ MIAME-CGH [Bra01] give a recommendation about the minimal information to be captured, they do not specify what values should be used for each parameter. Hence, additional standardizations are needed to avoid non-comparable or conflicting data.

[6] MIAME stands for Minimal Information about a Microarray Experiment.

Addressing these problems thus requires support for different sets of annotations for different studies and consistent data values. For this purpose, our platform provides a *generic* approach to specify and maintain annotations so that adding or changing annotation specifications are easily possible. For these specifications we provide so-called *annotation templates* to prescribe the parameters to be annotated and controlled vocabularies to constrain permissible parameter values. A template consists of pages that group together related parameters, e.g. for personal data, pathological findings or experimental parameters. Each page can be hierarchically organized. Annotation parameters and their corresponding values (metadata and data) are stored generically using the so-called Generic Annotation Model (GAM) introduced in [DR04]. These approaches for specifying and storing annotations avoid changing the database schema for new or changed annotations. This makes it easy to support additional clinical studies or additional types of annotations in our platform.

Fig. 3 illustrates the process to specify annotations for a clinical study, to map annotation data from the study management system eRN to GeWare, and to use (query) annotations in GeWare. Initially, the annotation parameters for which values have to be captured in a new clinical trial are specified (Step 1). Furthermore, the

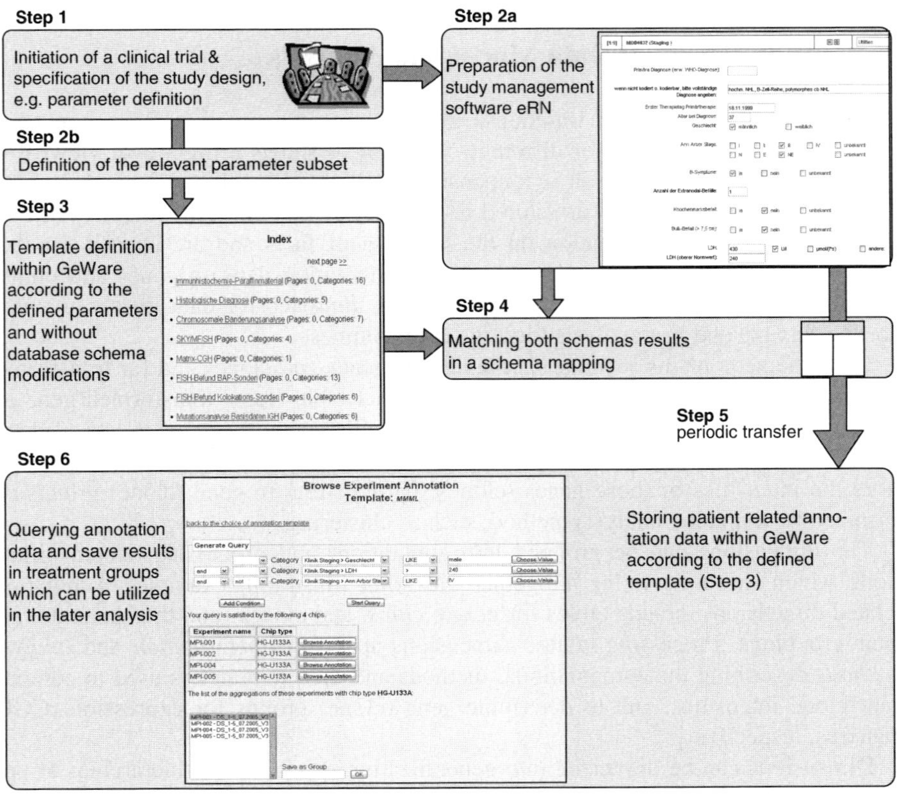

Fig. 3. Defining, transferring, and querying patient-related annotations

study management system eRN is configured to manage data for the clinical trial (Step 2a). In addition, the subset of parameters to be transferred from eRN to GeWare for analysis purposes are specified (Step 2b). Based on these parameters a new template can then be created in GeWare (Step 3) consisting of hierarchically arranged pages. Based on the database schema of eRN and the tree-based annotation schema of the template, a schema mapping (Step 4) is created for the relevant subset of parameters. The result of this schema mapping associates each source element, i.e. the parameter specific attribute and table of the relational database schema of eRN, with the corresponding target element, i.e. the parameter-specific path in the annotation schema. While this schema mapping is currently performed manually, it could also be done semi-automatically by utilizing schema matching algorithms [RB01]. The resulting schema mapping is regularly used to transfer new patient-related annotation values from eRN to GeWare (Step 5).

GeWare allows browsing through the annotations, querying them and applying them to extract and analyze experimental data (Step 6). For querying, the user can define multiple conditions that are combined with the logical operators AND, OR, and NOT. The query result identifies lists of chips, patients or genes that can be used to specify experimental data portions for further analysis.

5 Multidimensional Data Model and Analysis

GeWare is a relational data warehouse integrating and maintaining both annotation data and experimental data of different types. Fig. 4 shows a high-level view of its multidimensional schema built of dimension and fact tables. Experimental data like numerical expression values are stored in fact tables containing the majority of data. Dimensions provide information on the meaning of facts and are needed for their analysis. In particular they maintain selected annotation data on genes and chips / patients. Multidimensional modeling is a proven approach for data warehouses supporting flexible and fast analysis for large data volumes.

Our schema contains separate fact tables for genes and clones and for transformed and analyzed data values. The *Gene Intensity* fact table stores transformed gene expression data, whereas the *Clone Intensity* fact table contains intensity data of determined clones. Additional fact tables are kept for *Expression* and *CGH Matrices*, to store the intensities of those genes (clones) participating in gene (clone) groups determined by a specific analysis method, such as clustering.

The dimensions can be grouped into annotation- and processing-related dimensions, which are shown in Fig. 4 together with some illustrating examples. Annotation-related dimensions include tables for *genes*, *chips,* and *clones* (and thus patients) and their groupings. Processing-related dimensions specify *transformation* and *analysis methods* describing the computational methods and their parameters used to compute gene/clone intensities, and to determine gene (clone) groups for expression (CGH) matrices, respectively.

Dimensions can be organized into generalization/specialization hierarchies to provide different levels of abstraction for analysis. For example, the chip dimension is organized into three levels, experiment, treatment group and chip. Experiment is the most abstract level describing a clinical trial encompassing many chips which can be

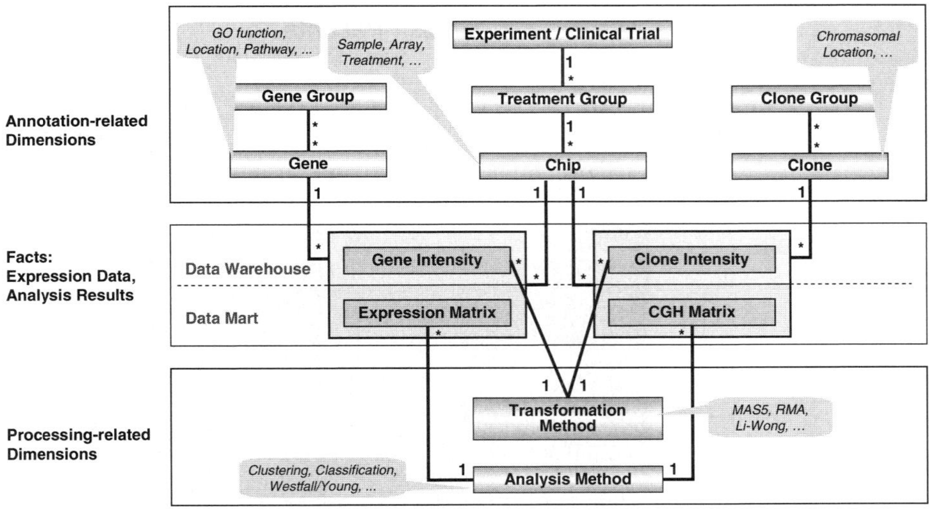

Fig. 4. Multidimensional data warehouse model

grouped into so-called treatment groups. Each of these treatment groups may include chips for a specific experimental condition, e.g. for tissue probes from the same patient at a specific time point in the clinical trial.

The sketched multidimensional data model supports high analysis flexibility. While current approaches typically evaluate a complete data matrix, i.e. gene expression and CGH matrix, containing the intensity values for all measured genes/clones and several/all chips, we now can focus on individual or comparative analysis to an arbitrary subset of intensity values determined by specific annotation values of interest. The selection may be based on a value at a specific level of a single dimension or any combination for several dimensions, e.g. to consider both gene and clinical parameters. A variety of analysis methods can be applied to the selected data set, e.g. queries to determine differentially expressed genes or clustering to find co-expressed genes. Such result groups can in turn be saved for further queries and analysis. The platform also supports the export of the pre-computed analysis results, e.g. gene/clone groups and expression/CGH matrices, to perform analysis in external tools.

As an example for a combined analysis of experimental and annotation data, Fig. 5 shows a gene expression heatmap for a selected group of 25 genes (rows) and a treatment group of 25 chips/patients (columns). Furthermore, the expression data is analyzed by hierarchical clustering for both, chips and genes. The dendrogram on the top represents the chip hierarchy while the one on the left hand side shows the gene hierarchy. In addition, a classification of the chip data by pre-defined classifiers, in this case the cancer stage which was acquired by the clinical diagnoses, using available patient-related annotation data is visualized by a colored band (different colors represent different values) above the heatmap. Thus the user can determine if there is a correlation between the hierarchical order resulting from the clustering and the fragmentation stemming from the classification.

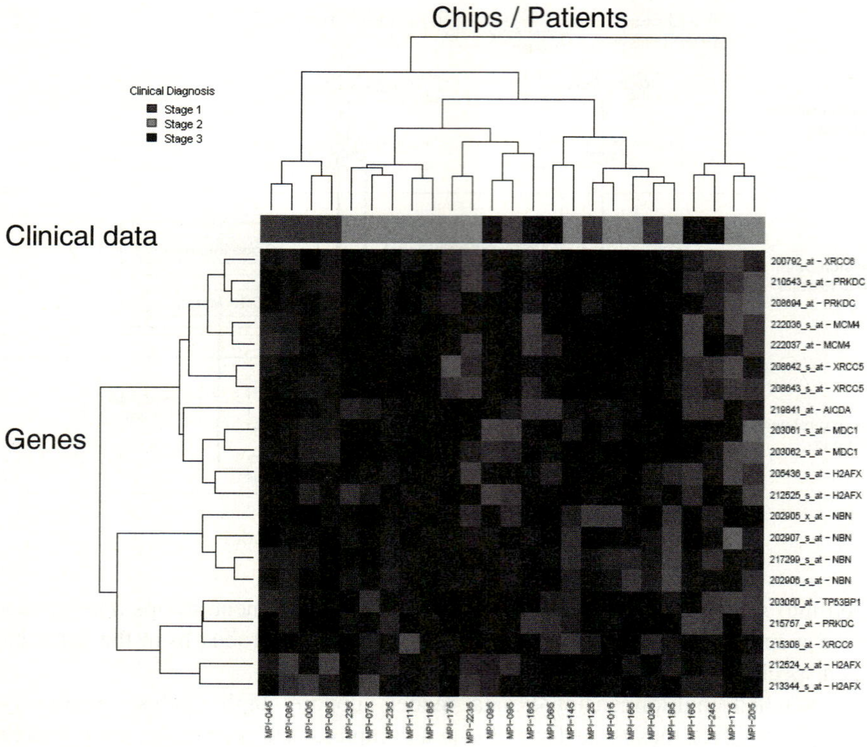

Fig. 5. Heatmap utilizing patient-related annotations

6 Conclusions

We presented a platform combining clinical and molecular-biological data for large-scale collaborative clinical research studies. The approach combines two proven subsystems for managing clinical trials and gene expression analysis. The clinical study system uniformly captures patient-related data from several participating hospitals. All patient-related data is kept in anonymous form and is interrelated with other data by a technical patient id only. The warehouse-based platform imports selected clinical annotations from the study system and combines them with data of centrally performed molecular-biological high-throughput experiments. Annotations are managed generically to easily support different studies and changing analysis needs. Currently, the platform is fully operational and is in use in two large clinical collaborative research projects in Germany.

Acknowledgements

The authors are thankful for useful hints and discussions with Markus Löffler and Hilmar Berger who are involved in the clinical studies and made this work possible.

We would also like to thank Hans Binder for fruitful discussions. The work is supported by the German Research Foundation (Deutsche Forschungsgemeinschaft) grant BIZ 1/3-1 and the German Cancer Aid (Deutsche Krebshilfe) grant 70-3173-Tr3.

References

[Ba04] Bairoch, A. et al.: Swiss-Prot: Juggling between evolution and stability. Briefings in Bioinformatics. 5:39-55, 2004

[Ba05] Barrett, Tanya et al.: NCBI GEO: mining millions of expression profiles - database and tools. Nucleic Acids Research, 33: D562-D566 (Database issue), 2005

[Bra01] Brazma, Alvis et al.: Minimum Information about a Microarray Experiment (MIAME) – Towards Standards for Microarray Data. Nature Genetics, 19, 2001

[Bra03] Brazma, Alvis et al.: ArrayExpress: A public database of gene expression data at EBI. C. R. Biologies, 326(10-11), 1075-8

[Bu05] Buetov, Kenneth H.: Cyberinfrastructure: Empowering a Third Way in Biomedical Research. Science, 308: 821-24, 2005

[Ca70] Caspersson et al., Identification of human chromosomes by DNA-binding fluorescent agents, Chromosoma 30: 215 - 227, 1970

[Co03] Covitz, P.A.: Class struggle: Expression profiling and categorizing cancer. The Pharmacogenomcs Journal, 3:257-60, 2003

[DR04] Do, Hong-Hai; Rahm, Erhard: Flexible Integration of Molecular-biological Annotation Data: The GenMapper Approach. Proc. EDBT, Heraklion, Greece, Springer LNCS, March 2004.

[GOC04] The Gene Ontology Consortium: The Gene Ontology (GO) database and informatics resource. Nucleic Acids Research, 32: D258-D261, 2004

[Hu06] Hummel, M. et al.: Transcriptional and genomic profiling provides a biological definition of Burkitt lymphoma and identifies novel prognostic groups within mature aggressive B-cell lymphoma. (submitted)

[Ka92] Kallioniemi, A. et al.: Comparative genomic hybridization for molecular cytogenetic analysis of solid tumors. Science, 258(5083): 818-21, 1992

[Ka05] Kallioniemi, O: Dissection of molecular pathways of cancer by high-throughput biochip technologies and RNA interference. Breast Cancer Research, 7:43, 2005

[KHR04] Kirsten, T., Do, H.-H.; Rahm, E.: A Data Warehouse for Gene Expression Analysis. Technical Report. Univ. of Leipzig, 2004

[Ki05] Kirsten, T.; Do, H.-H.; Rahm, E.; Körner, C.: Hybrid Integration of molecular biological Annotation Data. Proc. 2nd Int. Workshop on Data Integration in the Life Sciences, San Diego, 2005

[Ku03] Kuchinke, W.; Ohmann C., „eTrials“ werden zur Routine, Deutsches Ärzteblatt 2003; 100:A 3081-3084, 2003

[LC03] Lacroix, Zoe; Critchlow, Terence: Bioinformatics: Managing Scientific Data. Morgan Kaufmann, 2003

[Lo96] Lockhart, D.J. et al: Expression Monitoring by Hybridization to High-density Oligonucleotide Arrays. Nature Biotechnology 14, 1996

[Ma05] Maglott, Donna et al.: Entrez Gene: gene-centered information at NCBI. Nucleic Acids Research, 33: D54-D58, (Database issue), 2005

[Me95] Mecucci, C.: FISH (fluorescent in situ hybridization): the second youth of cytogenetics. Haematologica, 80(2):95-7, 1995

[Na04] Nagarajan, R; Ahmed, Mushtaq; Phatak, Aditya: Database Challenges in the Integration of Biomedical Data Sets. Proc. of the 30th VLDB Conf., Toronto, Canada, 2004

[OMIM00] Online Mendelian Inheritance in Man, OMIM. McKusick-Nathans Institute for Genetic Medicine, Johns Hopkins University (Baltimore, MD) and National Center for Biotechnology Information, National Library of Medicine (Bethesda, MD), 2000

[RB01] Rahm, Erhard; Bernstein, Philip A.: A survey of approaches to automatic schema matching. VLDB Journal, 10(4):334-50, 2001

[She95] Shena, M. et al: Quantitative Monitoring of Gene Expression Patterns with a complementary DNA Microarray. Science 270, 1995

[She01] Sherlock, Gavin et al.: The Stanford Microarray Database. Nucleic Acid Research, 29(1), 2001

[St03] Stein, L.: Integrating Biological Databases. Nature Review Genetics, 4(5): 337-45, 2003

Data Integration Targeting a Drug Related Knowledge Base

Olivier Curé and Raphaël Squelbut

Université de Marne-la-Vallée, Laboratoire ISIS
5, boulevard Descartes
Marne-la-Vallée 77454 France
{ocure, rsquelbu}@univ-mlv.fr
77454 Champs-sur-Marne, France

Abstract. We present a patient-oriented computer-based medical system which proposes advices on mild clinical signs treatment and medication. Therefore, this system can be considered a self-medication assistant tool. In a nutshell, this web application validates drug consumptions of a given patient, based on patient information stored in an electronic health care record, with a drug and symptom knowledge base. The efficiency and accuracy of the knowledge base inferences depend on the quality, quantity and recency of the drug instances. A practical source for these information are databases. Thus we developed a data integration solution which enables the mapping of relational databases to a Description Logics knowledge base.

1 Introduction

Nowadays, it becomes obvious that the french public health system has to evolve in order to survive. Among possible evolutions, the act to provide assistance and reliable services to the general public is promising. This approach may result in giving more responsabilities to the patient and hence reducing the costs of care for the health system. This issue is of central importance in countries where drug over-consumption is a general practice. In France, this situation is partly due to a high rate of drug reimbursements by the social security system. Consequently, the adoption by the general public of such services may reduce costs for both the patient and the public health system, prevent medical errors due to drug interactions, and improve efficiency and quality of patient treatment. We believe that these facts can be generalized to most industrial countries and hence will soon cover a central aspect of computer-based medical systems.

We have developed, with the clinical pharmacology department at the Cochin hospital in Paris (France), a system named IMSA (Interactive Multimedia System for Auto-medication) [3] and its extension XIMSA (eXtended IMSA) [4] enabled with Semantic Web technologies. Both of these systems belong to this category of medical information systems. The latest version of this system embeds a drug consumption checking service. The purpose of this module is to check, according to data stored for a given patient, the adequacy, in terms of

T. Grust et al. (Eds.): EDBT 2006 Workshops, LNCS 4254, pp. 411–422, 2006.

drug characteristics, of a medication (self) prescription. This service requires inferences on updated and accurate drug knowledge to detect clinical and drug contraindications, side effects, etc..

We have decided to store these data in a knowledge-based system to enable reasoning from explicit as well as implicit data. As databases become widely used, there is a need to translate data to the knowledge base and therefore to embed a data integration solution in the framework. This solution ensures that the right information is available at the right time from the right source of information. Consequently an ontology has to be designed from the data sources via a mapping solution, permitting tuples from these sources to populate the knowledge base.

The representation of this ontology is based on Description Logics (DL) [1], a fragment of first order logic, which are advocated as the key technology for realizing the Semantic Web. Standardization efforts within the World Wide Web Consortium (W3C) have resulted in the Web Ontology Language (OWL). Numerous tools, such as editors and reasoners, are already available for this language and thus Semantic Web applications can realistically be implemented with recognized standards.

This paper is organized as follows. In section 2, we present and justify the drug consumption checker tool within the context of the XIMSA system. In section 3, we present our data integration system which ensures that data contained in relational databases are integrated in XIMSA's ontology. In section 4, we present some general integration issues related to our information migration solution. Finally, we conclude this paper with some perspective on future works.

2 Drug Consumption Checker Application

The Drug Consumption Checker Application, henceforth DCCA, is a service proposed within XIMSA, and is aimed at the general public. This system assists but is not limited to a popular activity in most industrial countries : self-medication. In this paper, we consider self-medication as the health activities to treat oneself with or without drugs. Within this system, the goal of the DCCA module is to provide patients with a tool that controls the adequacy of a drug (self) prescription. The architecture of the DCCA service is supported by a drug ontology and a Simplified Electronic Health Record (SEHR), especially designed for the XIMSA system.

The goal of the SEHR is to store health related information concerning a particular patient. The formalism adopted for the SEHR is the semi-structured XML language. An instance of such a document stores three different categories of patient information :

- general information concerning the owner of this document : social security number, first and last name, gender, date of birth, etc..
- medical information concerning known diseases, allergies, current states (pregnancy, breast feeding, etc.).

– drug consumption information which distinguishes discrete and continuous (life long treatments) consumptions. Both consumptions require the start date and dosage of the treatment. For a discrete consumption, additional fields concerning the treatment duration and prescription source (either the patient or a health care professional) are required. We consider that non-discrete treatments are the responsability of health care professionals.

Example 1 proposes an XML extract from a SEHR which highlights the consumption of the *Marsilid*© drug between november 1st and november 10th, thus it is a discrete prescription, with a dosage of one pill per day. This drug is identified by the french identifier for drug products (cip code) 3442856 and has been prescribed by a general practitioner.

Example 1. SEHR discrete consumption example

<discretePrescription >
<prescription >
<idnum >3442856 </idnum >
<nomMed >Marsilid </nomMed >
<posologie >1 comprime par jour </posologie >
<prescriptionSource >Dr XXX </prescriptionSource >
<datedebut >1/11/2005 </datedebut >
<datefin >10/11/2005 </datefin >
</prescription >
...
</discretePrescription >

The drug and symptom knowledge base is central to the architecture of XIMSA as it is being used to make inferences in various services. In this paper, we concentrate solely on the DCCA service and on the drug knowledge base. For the following scenario, we consider that our knowledge base contains the Summary of Product Characteristics (SPC) of all french drugs :

Example 2. On november 7th, 2005, a patient connected to the DCCA service wants to self-prescribe the *Pulmodexane*© drug. He selects this drug from the system's graphical user interface, accepts the default dosage and validates his choice. The system then checks the patient's SEHR. We consider that this document contains no continuous prescription and that the only discrete prescription entry corresponds to the one in example 1. The inference engine advises not to use this drug at the moment because a contraindicated drug is currently being medicated. The result of this inference is based on the analysis of the characteristics of the Recommended International Non-proprietary Names (RINN) of *Pulmodexane*, i.e. *dextromethrophan* and the *Marsilid*, i.e. *iproniazide*. Navigating the knowledge base, the system is able to find that these two chemical substances are contraindicated one another. Additionally, the system proposes some drugs belonging to the *Pulmodexane*'s therapeutic class, i.e. anti-coughing, which are coherent with a current *marsilid* treatment.

The quality of the DCCA inferences results from the sufficiency, recency and accuracy of the data contained in the knowledge base. To ensure these quality requirements, it is necessary to consider the knowledge base's domain : pharmacology and its market. In France, the drug market is rapidly evolving due to frequent addition, modification and deletion of drugs, drug switches, reimbursement rate changes, emergence of the generics market, etc.. Given these characteristics, the most reliable source of information for the population of this knowledge base are drug related databases. In the context of XIMSA, we already maintain a drug database, named *self*, which stores all the information contained in the SPCs (posology, composition, contraindication, side effects, therapeutic class, price, social security system reimbursement rate, pharmaceutical laboratory, etc.) plus some extra information provided by collaborating health care professionals, i.e. comments on drugs as well as drug rating. Although databases are widely used in the drug industry, there does not exist an exhaustive and up-to-date french drug database, even from french administrations. Hence, in order to fulfill DCCA's recency and exhaustivity requirements, it is pertinent to translate and integrate data contained in multiple drug databases in XIMSA's knowledge base.

3 Data Integration

The development of the XIMSA application motivated the development of the DBOM (DataBase Ontology Mapping) system. DBOM is a fully-implemented and domain-independent application which enables the creation, population and maintenance of a DL-based ontology from database sources. This solution is based on a declarative mapping document. In order to present our data integration solution, it is necessary to provide some formal and general aspects about the components involved in the mapping.

3.1 Preliminaries

The prototype we have developed adopts a database reverse engineering approach which enables to design an ontology from a set of Entity-Relationship diagrams. This design is materialized through a mapping file whose purpose is to build a DL ontology schema and populate it from tuples of source databases.

We now characterize the system underlying the DBOM system and its cornerstone : the mapping language.

Definition 1. *The DBOM system is supported by a migration system $\mathcal{MI}$ which is a triple $(\mathcal{S}, \mathcal{O}, \mathcal{M})$, where :*

- *$\mathcal{S}$ is a set of source schemas of relational databases.*
- *$\mathcal{O}$ is the (target) ontology schema formalized in OWL DL.*
- *$\mathcal{M}$ is a set of formulas of a language $\mathcal{L}_{\mathcal{M}}$ over $\mathcal{S}$ and $\mathcal{O}$.*

The definition of $\mathcal{MI}$ emphasizes relations with data exchange [12] and data integration [13] systems. We now contrast the DBOM approach with the comparison of data exchange and integration provided in [8] :

- as in both data exchange and integration, the source schemas are given and the mapping is a set of formulas constructed by a human expert.
- as in data integration, the ontology (target) schema is a reconciliation of the sources and is constructed from the processing of the source schemas given a mapping.
- as in data exchange, the target instances are materialized, while they are virtualized in the case of data integration.

The target schema is an ontology designed in a DL. This family of knowledge representation formalisms allow the represention and reasoning over domain knowledge in a formally and well-understood way. In the DBOM approach, a DL ABox (assertional box or extension of the knowledge base) is considered as a view of the relational database. Our contribution to this issue lies in the possibility to richly axiomatized the terminology; thus permitting the creation of expressive ontologies, corresponding to the $\mathcal{SHOIN}$(D) DL, equivalent to the OWL DL language. Another interesting feature is the solution proposed to maintain the synchronization between the database tuples and the ABox of the knowledge base [5]. We assume readers are familiar with the semantics of DL, though we recall that the syntax for concepts in $\mathcal{SHOIN}$(D) [11] are defined as follows, where C_i is a concept, A is an atomic concept, R_i is an object role, S is a simple object role, T is a datatype role, D is a datatype, o_i is an individual and n is a non-negative integer :

$$C \rightarrow \mathrm{A} \mid \neg\, C_1 \mid C_1 \sqcap C_2 \mid C_1 \sqcup C_2 \mid \exists\, R_1.\mathrm{C} \mid \forall\, R_1.\mathrm{C} \mid \geq \mathrm{n\ S} \mid \leq \mathrm{n\ S} \mid \{o_1, .., o_m\} \mid \geq \mathrm{n\ T} \mid \leq \mathrm{n\ T} \mid \exists\, \mathrm{T.D} \mid \forall\, \mathrm{T.D}$$

The reason of our interest in the $\mathcal{SHOIN}$(D) DL is its syntactical equivalence with the OWL DL language [6], an expressive ontology language developed by the W3C and which is already supported by numerous tools (editors, reasoners, etc.). The choice of this formalism is motivated by our need to reason over web compliant data represented in an expressive, formal and decidable knowledge representation language. It is important to emphasize that semantic integration plays a key role in the growth of the Semantic Web and thus motivates many researches in this field, [5] proposes a study of relevant projects in this field.

Finally, regarding the source schema, we assume we have a fixed database schema P=$\{P_1, .., P_n\}$ where P_i, with $1 \leq i \leq n$, are predicates corresponding to the database relations. We also have a fixed, possibly infinite database domain D and a fixed set of built-in predicates B $(=, \neq, <, >, \leq, \geq)$. We define the first-order language $\mathcal{L}$ as $P \cup D \cup B$. Each predicate of $\mathcal{L}$ has an arity, i.e., the number of arguments taken.

3.2 Integration of the *Self* Database

The idea of the DBOM solution is to integrate data contained in relational databases in an ontology as expressive as the $\mathcal{SHOIN}(D)$ DL.

Concretly, data contained in tuples of P, a database instance, are mapped to concepts C_i and roles R_i of the ontology ([1] chap.16). The population of the ABox is performed via the execution of queries contained in the definition of concrete concepts and (binary) roles. The extract of the *self* database, presented in example 3, focuses on drugs and their chemical substances. Primary keys of relations are underlined and they correspond to a french drug identifier code (cip) and an international code for the identification of chemical substances (atcCode). The Anatomical Therapeutic Chemical (ATC) system [14] proposes an international classification of drugs and is part of WHO's initiatives to achieve universal access to needed drugs and rational use of drugs. In this classification, drugs are classified in groups at five different levels. The subset P' of the relational schema P of the *self* database proposes the last level which corresponds to chemical substances. Finally, the *drugRate* attribute contains a drug grade based on a tolerance/efficiency ratio and is designed by health care professionals of our research group.

Example 3. Schema extract of the *self* database
drug (cip, drugName, drugPrice, drugRate)
rinn (atcCode, substanceName)
rinnToDrug (cip, atcCode)

Given the relational schema of example 3, we propose a possible mapping in example 4. This mapping is presented in the form of conjunctive queries as they are more readable and concise than the XML serialization. The mapping provides a complete freedom to the ontology designer and offers the ability to integrate some or all P_i' of P'. It is also possible to define concepts and properties that are not mapped to any P_i' of P', meaning that these members must be abstract because no instantiations will be possible, as there are no queries attached. The abstract (and concrete) members feature have the same meaning than in object-oriented programming, thus abstract member can not be instantiated while concrete ones can. These definitions enable to design rich generalization/specialization relations between members. Example 4 only proposes concrete members as we primarilly focus in this paper on data integration and not on knowledge base inferences. For readability reasons, concepts start with an uppercase letter and properties are lowercased.

Example 4. A valid DBOM mapping file for example 3's relational schema
Drug $\leadsto$ { (W,X,Y,Z) | drug(W,X,Y,Z)}
Rinn $\leadsto$ { (X,Y) | rinn(X,Y)}
rinnToDrug $\leadsto$ { (X,Y) | rinnToDrug(X,Y)}

This example emphasizes that the integration solution adopts a Global-As-View (GAV) approach. The GAV solution means that each assertion in $\mathcal{M}$ relates an element of the target schema $\mathcal{O}$ to a query over a source schema $\mathcal{S}$. The counterpart of GAV is the Local-As-View approach (LAV) where the mapping specifies the content of the source in terms of the global schema. A comparison of the two approaches, and possible translations from one to the other, is available in [2].

The XML serialization of example 4's *Drug* concept is presented in example 5. In this example, we consider that the prolog of the mapping has defined the following elements :

- the *hasName*, *hasPrice*, *hasGrade* datatype properties, binary properties where the domain is an ontology concept instance and the range is an XML schema data type corresponding to the domain D of the P_i mapped attribute.
- the information (database driver, hostname, login, password) necessary for a connection to the *self* database. An alias, named *selfDB*, is declared for this connection.

Example 5. XML serialization of the *Drug* concept

```
<class namespace="drug" className="Drug" >
<instance dbSrc="selfDB" query="SELECT * FROM drug;" >
<id >
<field value="1"/ >
</id >
<data >
<field value="2" datatypeProperty="hasName"/ >
<field value="3" datatypeProperty="hasPrice"/ >
<field value="4" datatypeProperty="hasGrade"/ >
</data >
</instance >
</class >
```

DBOM processes such an XML mapping in the following manner :

- given the attributes of the *instance* element (second line), a SQL query is performed for an identified database connection.
- the tuples resulting from this query processing are mapped to data type properties. A special data type property serves as a primary key, to relate unambiguously database tuples and knowledge base instances, an operation required by the maintenance solution. Agregated primary keys can be defined in DBOM mapping files.

The identification of the database connection for each SQL view definition enables to integrate several databases in a single mapping instance. This can be done by declaring several database connection aliases in the prolog.

3.3 Integrating Several Databases with DBOM

We now consider practical and concrete integrations in DCCA with the *self* database. This database does not contain all drugs available on the french market and may also need to integrate emerging standards. So it may be necessary to integrate data from additional databases. We can distinguish two integration situations :

- "instance integration" where the new source populates a given target schema with instances that are not yet available in the knowledge base.

- "schema integration" where the new source requires modifications of the target schema by adding concepts and properties. These newly created concepts and properties are then populated from this source.

An example of "instance integration" is proposed in the following scenario : a database containing some drugs, and their chemical substances, missing from the *self* database, has been found and is thus integrated. The schema of the database (*db1*) is proposed in example 6 :

Example 6. Schema of the *db1* database
drug (cip, drugName, drugPrice)
molecule (atcCode, moleculeName)
moleculeToDrug (atcCode, cip)

We emphasize that the schema of *db1* does not contain a drug grade column as it is a specificity of the *self* database. Given this relational schema, a possible mapping instance can integrate anti-coughing drugs containing the *dextromethorphan* chemical substance which can be unambiguously identified with the R05DA09 ATC code. This code extract uses a special representation of conjunctive queries where database names are prefixing attribute names.

Example 7. A valid DBOM mapping integrating the *self* and *db1* databases
Drug $\rightsquigarrow$ { (W,X,Y,Z) | SELF.drug(W,X,Y,Z)}
Drug $\rightsquigarrow$ { (X,Y,Z) | DB1.drug(X,Y,Z) $\wedge$ DB1.moleculeToDrug(W,X)
$\wedge$ W='R05AD09'}
RINN $\rightsquigarrow$ { (X,Y) | SELF.rinn(X,Y)}
RINN $\rightsquigarrow$ { (X,Y) | DB1.molecule(X,Y) $\wedge$ X='R05AD09'}
drugToRinn $\rightsquigarrow$ { (X,Y) | SELF.rinnToDrug(X,Y)}
drugToRinn $\rightsquigarrow$ { (X,Y) | DB1.moleculeToDrug(X,Y) $\wedge$ X='R05AD09' }

This mapping highlights several aspects of the integration with DBOM :

- the use of queries for the population of the knowledge base enables the design of 'filters', e.g. we only select drugs with the *dextromethorphan* chemical substance from *db1*.
- the use of set operations on the results of queries. The semantics of this mapping emphasizes the use of the union set operations which allows to combine the results of the several views for the same member, e.g. two definitions for the *Drug* concept.
- the drugs populated from the *db1* database do not contain grade values. In such a situation, the DBOM's processing does not assign any value to this drug, thus such a drug does not have a *hasGrade* data property. This is due to the fact that the first *Drug* definition has four attributes in its view while the second one only has three attributes.

A situation of "schema integration" corresponds to the need to integrate valuable data from health care institutions. We take as an example the integration of a DDD database. The Defined Daily Dose "is the assumed average maintenance dose per day for a drug used for its main indication in adults" [14]. The integration of this classification may serve to propose posology in the absence of such data for a particular drug. Although, the DDD has some drawbacks in the context of compound drugs (with several RINNs), it still is an interesting candidate for integration. The relational schema of example 8 highlights the relation between the ATC/DDD system where each molecule is identified by an ATC code and characterized by the defined daily dose, unit of dosage and notes. Anotehr relation contains all the administration routes avalailable, e.g. oral.

Example 8. Schema of the *ddd* database
ddd (<u>atcCode</u>, ddd, unit, adminId, notes)
administrationRoute(<u>adminId</u>, adminRouteName)

We can propose a mapping instance for the *self* and *ddd* databases which assumes that :

- DDD information (dosage, unit, administration route and notes) are stored in a *Ddd* concept.
- the *adminRouteName* for an *adminId* is stored directly, in the form of a property, in the *Ddd* concept.
- we consider that all RINN that match a DDD are in the *self* database; otherwise the *ddd* database can easily be filtered before the mapping processing to match all the ATC code of the *self* database.
- a *rinnToDrug* property relates an *Rinn* instance to a *Ddd* instance.

Example 9. A valid DBOM mapping file for the *self* and *ddd* schemas
Drug $\rightsquigarrow$ { (W,X,Y,Z) | SELF.drug(W,X,Y,Z)}
Rinn $\rightsquigarrow$ { (X,Y) | SELF.rinn(X,Y)}
Ddd $\rightsquigarrow$ { (T,U,V,Z,X) | DDD.ddd(T,U,V,Y,X) $\wedge$ DDD.administrationRoute (Y,Z)}
drugToRinn $\rightsquigarrow$ { (X,Y) | SELF.rinnToDrug(X,Y)}
rinnToDDD $\rightsquigarrow$ { (X,X) | DDD.ddd(X,Y)}

A more efficient mapping proposition would merge all the information contained in *Ddd* instances in the corresponding *Rinn* instances. But this operation requires to write views in the GAV mapping joining relations from both databases. Such an operation is not yet implemented in the DBOM framework but is on our future works list.

Figure 1 proposes a graph extract of the knowledge base resulting from the processing of example 9's mapping. In the context of DCCA, graph navigation enables to make inferences using explicit as well as implicit knowledge. Enriching Figure 1's graph with a *contraindicatedWith* symmetric property between RINNs R05DA09 and N05AF06, we would be able to detect that any drug containing the *dextromethorphan* chemical substance is contraindicated with a drug containing the *iproniazide* substance.

4 Data Integration Issues in DBOM

DBOM faces all the commonly encountered problems of data integration which are based on heterogeneity, redundancy and inconsistency :

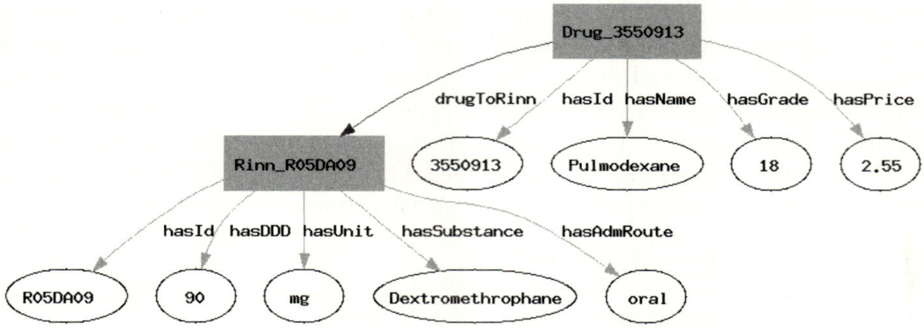

Fig. 1. Ontologie graph resulting from example 9's mapping

- structural heterogeneity is due to structure differences between sources, e.g. naming conflicts, data type conflicts, integrity conflicts, etc..
- semantic heterogeneity is due to different interpretations of the data and domain of sources, e.g. representation conflicts, subsumption conflicts, etc..
- redundancy is due the absence of common key identifier between sources for equivalent relations.
- inconsistency is due to the presence of different values for equivalent data in different source, incomplete information, etc..

Solving these heterogeneity problems is a complex and time-consuming task that is usually left to the user. In the XIMSA system, a particular attention is given to the selection of source candidates. They are generally proposed by health care professionals and validated by the user responsible for the mapping. Several operations, such as data cleaning [9] may be required to process the mapping. Whether these problems are solved manually or in a (semi-)automatic way, semantic is the key issue. This is a challenging problem because there are few reliable and non-subjective information sources for semantic :

- the creator of the database who are generally not accessible or have forgotten about the data.
- documentations are generally missing or tend to be outdated, sketchy and incorrect.

Many solutions are designed to solve these problems in a semi-automatic way, meaning that the user is involved in the processing of the system [7] in terms of validation of the results, providing some clues to solve problems, etc..

An interesting service proposed within DBOM is the maintenance of both the database sources and the knowledge base. This maintenance solution is described in [5] for a single database source. The idea of this maintenance is two fold :

- to automatically maintain the synchronization between the knowledge base instances and the database tuples. This means that whenever a tuple is updated (insertion, deletion and modification) in a source, the corresponding

knowledge base instance has to be modified. [5] emphasizes that the synchronization can be delayed because of integrity constraints expressed on sources relational schema.
- to semi-automatically maintain the database tuples from detection of inconsistencies on the knowledge base's side. The semi-automatic aspect of this maintenance means that the intervention of a user is required to solve the inconsistency.

A practical scenario for the second form of maintenance is now proposed : "A health care professional collaborating to XIMSA inserts a new drug in the *self* database. This drug belongs to the 'anti-coughing' therapeutic class and contains the *iproniazide* chemical substance. This tuple is automatically translated in the form of a concept instance, and its properties, in the knowledge base. XIMSA's inference engine then tries to detect possible inconsistencies in the knowledge base and finds that the relation between the therapeutic class and the RINN was not unknown.". The treament of such inconsistencies is not automatized and XIMSA awaits from the user to correct or validate this new entry.

In a data integration context, the maintenance solution needs to efficiently identify the source of a knowledge base instance. This identification serves to correct the data at the source level, for example the modification of a newly inserted drug in the *self* database. The purpose of these updates is to maintain the *self* database consistent because it is exploited in several other situations : additional services in XIMSA, support of dynamic web sites, a book [10], etc.. These interventions can be processed only on updatable sources, as we are not granted to modify all integrated sources, e.g. a *ddd* database.

5 Conclusion

This paper present an extension to the DBOM system, formerly a migration tool from a unique database to a Semantic Web compliant (OWL DL) knowledge base. This extension now proposes to integrate several sources in an ontology and processes its instantiation from tuples of the sources. This approach considers the DL Abox as a relational view over the relational databases.

We have presented conceptual and functional aspects of this system via practical examples in the context of a drug prescription checking tool. Through data integration, the DCCA is ensured to access an up-to-date drug market knowledge base and hence supports efficient and high-quality patient reasoning procedures. This approach turned out to be very efficient in the context of XIMSA. As a self-medication tool, XIMSA aims to be used by the general public. Hence the content of the drug characteristics (SPCs) have been transformed and translated to be more easily understood by patients.

We are now thinking about developing a XIMSA version tailored to health care professionals. This tool would assist general practitioners to prescribe drugs to their patients in a more secure and cost-effective way. Some tests conducted with medicine students have shown that such a tool may be interesting to this community. We believe that DBOM's functionalities may help to integrate new drug concepts and standards from the pharmaceutical industry , e.g. the french drug efficiency rating (SMR) and amelioration (AMSR).

The DBOM system is also evolving on several aspects and we are currently :

- developing a Protégé plug-in to enable the design of mapping files with a graphical user interface. This plug-in would benefit from a collaboration with other OWL components (class, property tabs, visualization and rule solutions, etc.).
- studying the maintenance of the knowledge given some particular source schema modifications. This is a novel approach as at the moment our maintenance solution only tackles instance modifications.

References

1. Baader, F., Calvanese, D., McGuinness, D., Nardi, D., Patel-Schneider, P. : *The Description Logic Handbook: Theory, Implementation and Applications* Cambridge University Press (2003).
2. Cali, A., Calvanese, D., De Giacomo, G.,Lenzerini, M. : *On the expressive power of data integration* Proceedings of ER 2002. pp 338-350.
3. Curé, O. : *Overview of the IMSA project, a patient-oriented information system* Data Science Journal 1(2): pp 66-75 (2002)
4. Curé, O. : *XIMSA : eXtended Interactive Multimedia System for Auto-medication* IEEE Computer-Based Medical System Symposium (CBMS) 2004. pp 570-575.
5. Curé, O., Squelbut, R. : *A database trigger strategy to maintain knowledge bases developed via dat a migration* EPIA 2005. LNAI 3808 pp 206-217.
6. Dean, M., Schreiber, G. : *OWL Web Ontology Language Reference.* 2004. W3C Recommendation 10 February 2004
7. Doan, A., Halevy, A. : *Semantic integration Research in the database community : a brief survey* AI Magazine, Special Issue on Semantic Integration, Spring 2005. pp 83-94.
8. Fagin, R., Kolaitis, P., Miller, R., Popa, L. : *Data exchange : semantics and query answering* Proceedings of ICDT 2003. LNCS 2572. pp 207-224.
9. Galhardas, H. Florescu, D., Shasha, D., Simon, E., Saita, C-A : *Declarative Data Cleaning: Language, Models, and Algorithms.* In Very Large Data Bases 2001. pp 371-380.
10. Giroud, J.P., Hagege, C. : *Le guide Giroud-Hagege de tous les médicaments* Editions du Rocher, Paris, France. 2001.
11. Horrocks, I., Sattler, U. : *A Tableaux Decision Procedure for SHOIQ.* Proceedings of IJCAI 2005. pp 448-453.
12. Kolaitis, P. : *Schema mappings, data exchange, and metadata management* In ACM Symposium on Principles of Database Systems (PODS) 2005. pp 61-75.
13. Lenzerini, M. : *Data integration : a theoretical perspective.* In ACM Symposium on Principles of Database Systems (PODS) 2002. pp 233-246.
14. WHO Collaborating Centre for Drug Statistics Methodology URL of Web site : http://www.whocc.no/atcddd/

Data Management in Medicine: The EPIweb Information System, a Case Study and Some Open Issues

Pierpaolo Vittorini and Ferdinando di Orio

University of L'Aquila
Department of Internal Medicine and Public Health
67100 L'Aquila (AQ) - Via S. Sisto
Italy
pierpaolo.vittorini@cc.univaq.it

Abstract. Data management in medicine usually takes place through the usage of heterogeneous and legacy systems. So far, these information systems were rarely reusable into other investigations and, expecially in multicenter studies, their development absorbed part of the given funding. To overcome these limitation, we developed the EPIweb system, i.e. a totally configurable web-based information system which helps the epidemiologists/public health practitioners to conduct their (distributed) researches by following a workflow made up of the selection of the remote centers, the creation of the questionnaires, the data entry, the statistical processing of the data, and the generation of the technical reports. The most important EPIweb features are shown in the paper by means of a recent investigation conducted with the system. Finally, we discuss some open issues regarding the improvement of the EPIweb system in the direction of scientific workflow management.

1 Introduction

To support their decisions, clinicians and public health practitioners use both information technology, statistical and operational research methods [1,2,3], usually applied to massive amount of data stored on databases (e.g., [4]).

Recently, the need for "[...] collecting and analyzing morbidity, mortality, and other relevant data and facilitate the timely dissemination of results to appropriate decision makers [...]" [5] has lead to the development of several Internet-based information systems, among the many we mention PHIN [6] which proposes an automated exchange of data between public health partners through ebXML compliant web services [7], ESSENCE system [8] which uses a secure file transfer protocol to send the data over the Internet, RSVP [9] which uses a combination of web and Java technologies to collect the data, and a long list of information systems developed to support their related multicenter studies (e.g., [10,11]).

So far, these sophisticated information systems were rarely reusable and, expecially in multicenter studies, their development absorbed part of the given funding. Furthermore, some of these systems focused only on the data collection activity, and the tasks

T. Grust et al. (Eds.): EDBT 2006 Workshops, LNCS 4254, pp. 423–432, 2006.

of analyse, display, report and map the collected data were demanded to specialized software. To overcome these limitations, we present the EPIweb system [12], i.e. a web-based information system [13] which helps the epidemiologists to conduct their studies by adopting a clear and guided workflow made up of the following phases: the selection of the remote centers (also through randomization), the creation of the questionnaires, the data entry, the statistical processing of the data, and the generation of the technical reports. All these phases are configurable, therefore the system is both flexible and responsive to changing requirements, and also reusable and "tailorable" to different investigations. Furthermore, the underlying database supports information integration since data coming from different sources can be integrated in the form of answers given to different questionnaires.

To show these features, an investigation entirely performed through the EPIweb system regarding the middle school students' nutritional habits in the Municipality of L'Aquila is discussed. The "lesson learned" from this study suggests several implementation improvements and particularly in the direction of scientific workflow management.

2 EPIweb Features and Architecture

EPIweb implements the workflow highlighted in figure 1: an epidemiological study starts with the selection of the remote centers, continues with the questionnaires development, the data entry, the data analysis, the report generation, and ends with a discussion of the achieved results. The following three typologies of users "interact" with the workflow: the epidemiologists (hereafter called study administrators) which organize and manage their studies, the remote centers which participate in the data entry, and the users which read the reports and discuss the published results.

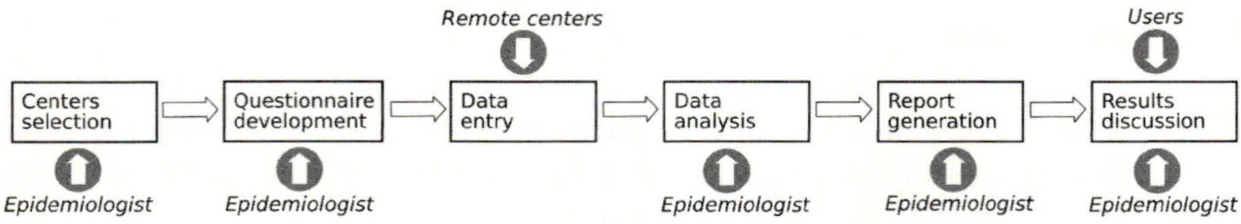

Fig. 1. The EPIweb workflow of an epidemiological study

The EPIweb system is a web-based application following the architecture depicted in figure 2. At the highest level of abstraction, the apache web server [14] takes care of both the communication with the clients – when necessary through a secure connection – and the execution of the PHP scripts [15]. The scripts implement all the EPIweb features, by relying on the MySQL database [16] to store the data, on STATA™ [17] to execute the statistical analyses, and on the LaTeX typesetting system [18] to produce the technical reports. Since the proposed architecture incorporates LaTeX and STATA™ like two software components reused in a wider project, a reduction of the overall development efforts was achieved [19]. This architecture also reduces the deployment efforts,

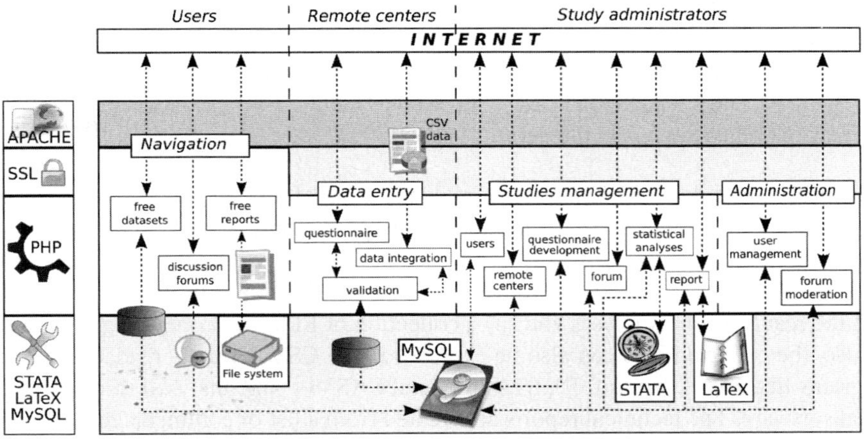

Fig. 2. The EPIweb architecture

i.e. the costs connected with the set of activities which follow the initial release, since the software updates or bug fixes are applied only in the EPIweb system.

In detail, the architecture is divided into four sections, namely: the navigation, the data entry, the studies management and the administration sections.

The navigation section is opened to the users, and offers the possibility to download free datasets and reports, and to debate the results of the available investigations through a discussion forum. The free datasets are generated on-the-fly by a PHP script which extracts from the underlying database the proper tuples. The free reports are available as PDF files stored in the file system.

In the data entry section, the remote centers can fill in the questionnaire and/or integrate into the underlying database any old dataset if available as CSV data. We remark that the entered data is validated towards several constraints defined by the epidemiologist. The constraints may regard:

- that a question must be considered as a primary key;
- an allowed range for a numeric answer;
- when a missing value can be accepted;
- the definition of relationships between questions, i.e. a question can be placed if a certain statement is true. The interface of the EPIweb system currently allows the development of statements in which a question is placed only in connection with the value of a previous answer.

The studies management section allows an epidemiologist to organize its study in terms of the following areas: (i) users, (ii) centers, (iii) questionnaires, (iv) statistical analyses, (v) reports, and (vi) forums. The users area offers the possibility to involve other users in the investigation. In the centers area, remote centers can be included/excluded from the data entry. The questionnaires are organized as a list of questions created through a visual interface, and can be developed to honor the above mentioned constraints. The following kind of data types can be used:

- Free text (limited to 80 characters);
- Integer values (the range is -2147483648 to 2147483647);
- Floating values (the allowable values are $-3.402823466 \cdot 10^{+38}$ to $-1.175494351 \cdot 10^{-38}$, 0, and $1.175494351 \cdot 10^{-38}$ to $3.402823466 \cdot 10^{+38}$);
- Sets of values (stored as integers).

To process the data, the administrators define a list of analyses by selecting the desired one among a set of predefined statistical analyses and graphs, or by creating new variables. Then, STATA™ is invoked in background by providing it with a dataset and a do-file containing the needed commands. As output, STATA™ produces (i) a log file with the results of the analyses and (ii) a collection of EPS files containing the graphs. In case, the collected data can also be exported in the CSV format – readable by most programs like Excel, Epi Info™, STATA™ and SAS™ – and analysed through an external software. The technical reports are created from a list of comments regarding the results of the most significant statistical analyses: the EPIweb system automatically "assembles" all the given comments/results,automatically creates a `tex` file, then invokes LaTeX to produce the PDF file, and finally displays such a file as the resulting technical report. The report contains: (i) a title page, (ii) a page with a note and the list of the participants of the study, (iii) the table of contents, (iv) a chapter with a description of the epidemiological study and a note which foregoes the results, (v) a central chapter with all comments/results regarding the analysis, (vi) the description of the questionnaire and of the dataset, (vii) the list of tables, and (viii) the list of figures.

Finally, in the administration section, a discussion forum regarding the results of a study can be opened and moderated. Furthermore, a user management facility is also provided.

The database was conceptually modelled (see E/R diagram depicted in figure 3) to allow the storage (i) of the epidemiological data organized in terms of answers given to questionnaires, (ii) of the statistical analysis as a collection of processings taken from certain statistical models, and (iii) of the reports from comments given to selected processings. In detail, a dataset comes from a *questionnaire*, whose `name` is stored in the database. A questionnaire is made up of a list of *question*s. The questions are organized as a double-linked list, where the `next`/`prev` attributes point to the next/previous questions, respectively. The `type` attribute indicates the datatype of the expected answer and the `opt` attribute stores its possible options. The `null` attribute indicates whether a missings value might be accepted, and the `text` attribute contains the text of the question. The `ic` attribute is used to store an eventual internal consistency check. Actually, it is under consideration the possibility to model constrainst using the results coming from business rules [20]. To a certain question, an *answer* is given, whose value is stored in the proper attribute (either `int`, `float` or `str80`). The flag `missing` is obviously used to represent a missing value. Furthermore, the time in which the answer was entered is stored in the `time_stamp` attribute. A statistical *processing* is the actual application of a certain *model* in a given analysis. Therefore, a *model* has a `name`, a `type` which specifies whether it is a statistical analysis or a graph, and a `stata_cmds` attribute which contains its abstract STATA implementation. A *model* becomes "tangible" by means of the proper `varlist`, `by` prefix, `if` qualifier and `opt` options, stored in the *processing* entity. Hence, the *model*s represent all the available statistical

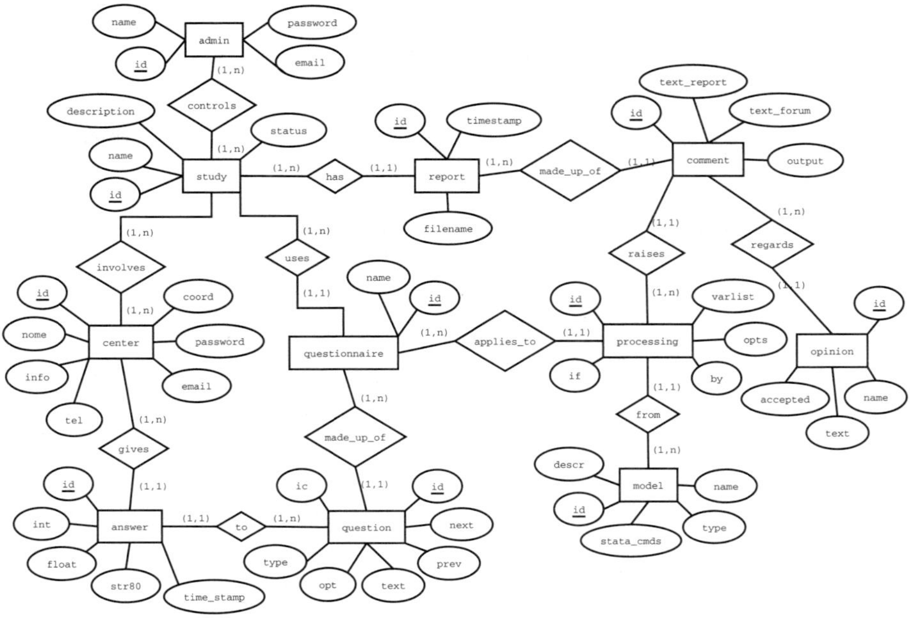

Fig. 3. The E/R diagram of the underlying database

analyses/graphs, while the *processings* are the actual analyses executed by an epidemiologist in his/her investigation.

This conceptual model supports information integration since data coming from different sources can be stored in the database as answers given to ad-hoc developed questionnaires. In other terms, each different data source is represented by a questionnaire, whose questions must reflect the metadata structure of the original data source.

3 The Case Study

Hereafter, a sample system run which shows how EPIweb supported an investigation regarding the middle school students's nutritional habits in the Municipality of L'Aquila (Italy) [21] is reported.

The epidemiologist connects to the server, logs in as an EPIweb administrator, and creates a new study by giving it a name (i.e. "Middle school students' nutritional habits in the Municipality of L'Aquila") and a short description. Hence, the epidemiologist decides to select the remote centers through simple randomization. By clicking on the proper link, a pop-up window is opened, and the epidemiologist (i) adds all the possible remote centers, (ii) randomly selects a subset of a chosen size, and (iii) stores the resulting centers into the database. Then, the epidemiologist develops the questionnaire by sequentially adding the needed questions. In this phase, the epidemiologist has to take attention in specifying e.g. when a missing value might be accepted, the list of the allowed answers (by using the associative sets), the range of acceptance, when a question should be asked, etc.

Figure 4 shows the question regarding if the student has breakfast. The expected answer belongs to a set of choices: 0=Always, 1=Sometimes, and 2=Never. Therefore, the epidemiologist creates the "Do you have breakfast?" question as a "Set of values" with a related associative set specified with the string `0 "Always" 1 "Sometimes" 2 "Never"` (see figure).

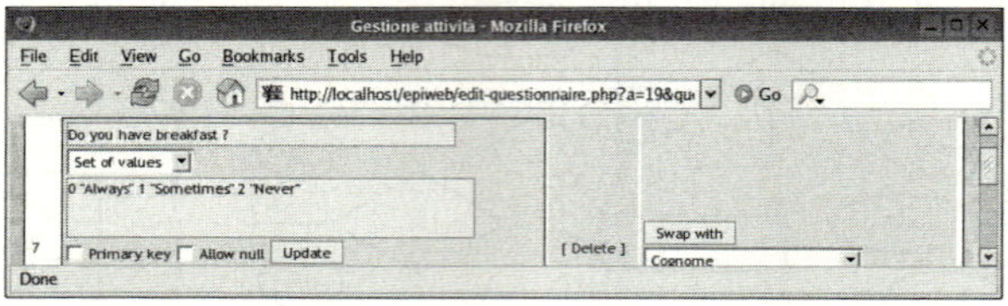

Fig. 4. The questionnaire creation area (first question)

Figure 5 shows the subsequent question, which regards the reason because the student does not have breakfast. Since this question must be asked only to the students who answered "Never" to the previous one, an internal consistency check must be applied: the question is asked only if the answer given to the "Do you have breakfast?" question is equal to 2 (i.e. "Never").

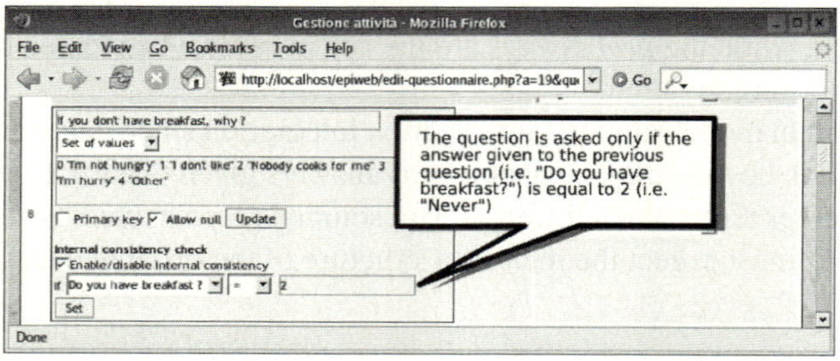

Fig. 5. The questionnaire creation area (subsequent, constrained question)

When the questionnaire is ready, the epidemiologist enables the data entry. The remote centers log in the EPIweb system and fill in their questionnaires question by question. Depending on the constraints given by the epidemiologist, the system either accepts or rejects the questionnaire.

When the data entry is over, the epidemiologist begins the statistical processing of the data. Initially, he decides to investigate the age of the students. To this aim, he creates a table and a pie chart regarding the question "How old are you?". Figure 6 shows the interface used to create the statistical analysis, and the corresponding result. With similar operations, the epidemiologists continues the analysis and adds all the needed statistics, tests and graphs.

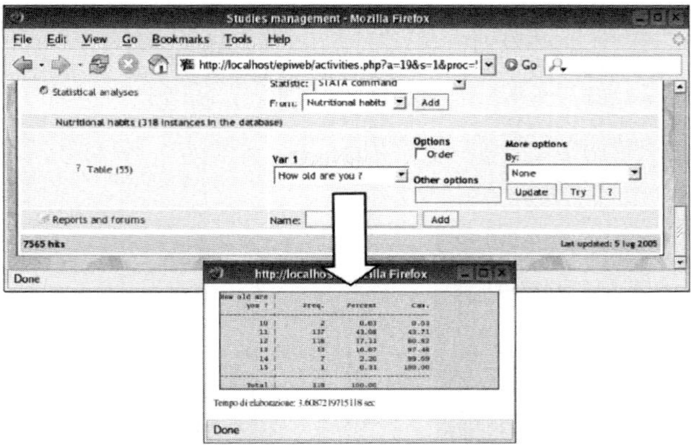

Fig. 6. The age distribution

Finally, he starts the development of the technical report. We recall that the report is created by the EPIweb system by "assembling" the comments given to the analyses/graphs that the epidemiologist considers relevant. Figure 7 finally depicts the produced report.

We remark that a study can be also repeated periodically, since the timestamp of each answer is stored in the dataset. Also the center which entered the answer is stored in the dataset, therefore, comparisons regarding e.g. centers, repeated studies can be performed.

4 Discussion

The paper discussed the need for an integrated and flexible approach to effectively collect, validate, analyse, display and report epidemiological data. We have briefly shown in the sample system run that the EPIweb system can be easily "tailored" to the specificities of an epidemiological study, and that it can handle a large variety of investigations by properly changing the questionnaire and the statistical analyses. It is worth remarking that the EPIweb system implements a centralized flow of information, which makes available both the statistical investigations and/or the technical reports regarding the most important research findings timely.

The study regarding the nutritional habits was also used to assess the advantages of the EPIweb system, throughout its comparison with similar investigations conducted with traditional methods. The physician who supervised the data entry, who also weighed and measured the students, reported that the data collection activity was greatly improved by the adoption of the EPIweb system: the data was collected timely and directly in a digital format, and the entering of typos was prevented. Nevertheless, the epidemiologist who managed this study, even if satisfied of the processing capabilities, asked for improving the report generation interface which allows only a stereotyped organization.

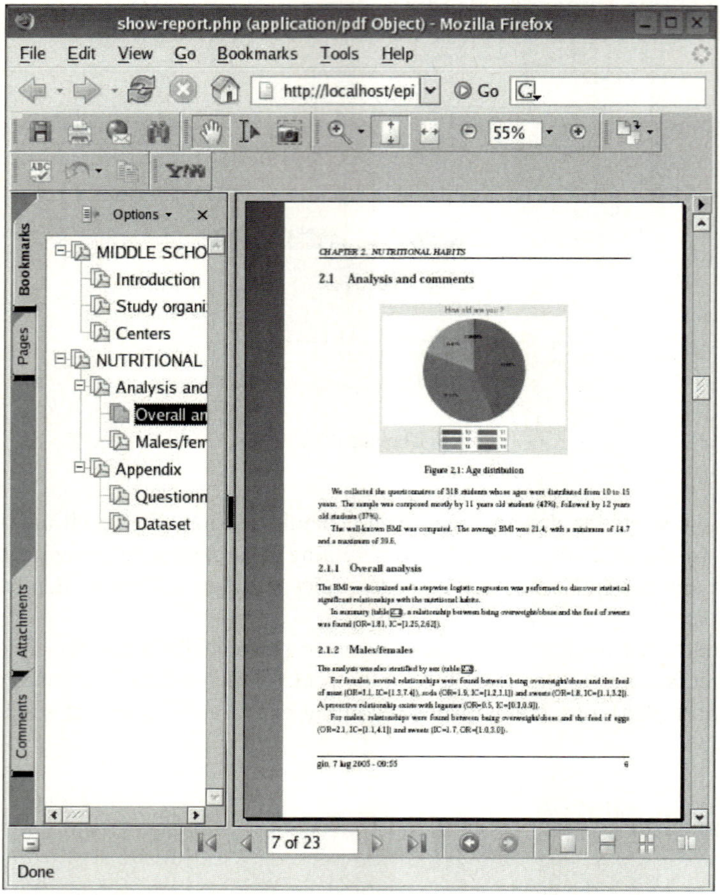

Fig. 7. The technical report

Further open issues arised during the investigation. The workflow embedded in the EPIweb system which "drives" an epidemiological study was not clearly perceived by the epidemiologist, which asked for a more clear and intuitive interface. Furthermore, we state that a fundamental support could be given in the selection of the best statistical analysis useful to reach a certain research objective. We point out that this aim can be achieved by implementing in the next release of the EPIweb system a scientific workflow management based on a hierarchical statistical analyses organization like that highlighted in figure 8, which extends the flowcharts for relating reseach questions to statistical methods available in [22]. In the figure, the research objective is the main question, then further "refinements" are required (e.g., the variable type, if a graph or a measure is needed), until the proper statistics is selected. For instance, to measure the dispersion of a numerical variable (i.e., not expressed in terms of ranks, neither frequencies), the system could propose to evaluate either its variance or standard deviation.

- Which is the central tendency?
  - Variable: numerical
    - * Measure
      - · Mean
    - * Graph
      - · Histogram
      - · Steam-leaf plot
      - · Box graph
      - · Frequency polygon
  - Variable: ranks
    - * Measure
      - · Median
      - · Mode
    - * Graph
      - · Bar graph
      - · Box graph
  - ...
- Which is the dispersion?
  - Variable: numerical
    - * Variance
    - * Standard deviation
  - Variable: ranks
    - * Max-min
    - * IRQ
  - ...
- Do you want to investigate into the normality deviation?
  - Variable: numerical
    - * Skewness
    - * Kurtosis
- Is there a difference? [22]
- Is there an association? [22]
- Are there two or more independent variables? [22]

Fig. 8. A possible hierarchical organization of (a portion of) the statistical analyses useful for medical research

References

1. Raghupathi, W., Tan, J.: Strategic IT applications in health care. Communications of the ACM **45** (2002) 56–61
2. Hauck, K., Smith, P.C., Goddard, M.: The Economics of Priority Setting for Health Care – A Literature Review. The World Bank (2003)
3. Eubank, S., Guclu, H., Kumar, A., Marathe, M., Srinivasan, A., Toroczkal, Z., Wang, N.: Modelling disease outbreaks in realistic urban social networks. Science **429** (2004) 180–4
4. Capocaccia, R., Gatta, G., Roazzi, P., Carrani, E., Santaquilani, M., De Angelis, R., Tavilla, A., the EUROCARE Working Group: The EUROCARE-3 database: methodology of data collection, standardisation, quality control and statistical analysis. Annals of Oncology **14** (2003) 14–27
5. Sosin, D.M.: Draft framework for evaluating syndromic surveillance systems. Journal of Urban Health **2 Suppl 1** (2003) 8–13
6. Loonsk, J.: PHIN overview. In: 1st Annual PHIN Conference. (2003)
7. OASIS: ebXML. Available on-line (2005) http://www.ebxml.org/.
8. Lombardo, J.S., Burkom, H., Pavlin, J.: ESSENCE II and the framework for evaluating syndromic surveillance systems. Morbidity and Mortality Weekly Report **53** (2004) 159–165

9. Zelicoff, A., Brillman, J., Forslund, D.W., George, J.E., Zink, S., Koening, S.: The rapid syndrome validation project (RSVP). Sandia National Laboratories (2001)
10. Sanson, R.L., Morris, R.S., Stern, M.W.: EpiMAN-FMD: a decision support system for managing epidemics of vesicular disease. Revue scientifique et technique (International Office of Epizootics) **18** (1999) 593–605
11. Silva, S., Gouveia-Oliveira, R., Maretzek, A., Carriço, J., Gudnason, T., Kristinsson, K.G., Ekdahl, K., Brito-Avô, A., Tomasz, A., Sanches, I.S., de Lencastre, H., Almeida, J.: EURISWEB – web-based epidemiological surveillance of antibiotic-resistant pneumococci in day care centers. BMC Medical Informatics and Decision Making **3** (2003)
12. Vittorini, P., Necozione, S., di Orio, F.: The information technology for the management of health care data: the EPIweb project. Epidemiologia e Prevenzione (2005) . In press.
13. Deshpande, Y., Hansen, S.: Web engineering: creating a discipline among disciplines. IEEE Multimedia **8** (2001) 82–87
14. Laurie, B., Laurie, P.: Apache: The Definitive Guide (3rd Edition). O'Reilly (2002)
15. Sklar, D.: Learning PHP 5. O'Reilly (2004)
16. DuBois, P.: MySQL, Second Edition. Sams (2003)
17. Stata Corporation: Stata Base Reference Manual (4 volumes). Stata Press (2003)
18. Lamport, L.: LaTeX: A Document Preparation System. Addison Wesley (1994)
19. Mili, H., Mili, A., Yacoub, S., Addy, E.: Reuse Based Software Engineering: Techniques, Organizations, and Measurement. Wiley (2002)
20. Hay, D.C.: Modeling business rules: the business constraint metamodel. The Data Administration Newsletter (TDAN.com) (2004)
21. Cesare, B., Vittorini, P., Sallusti, E., Bontempo, V., Graziani, M., Necozione, S., di Orio, F.: Le abitudini alimentari dei ragazzi di scuola media nel Comune di L'Aquila: risultati di uno studio descrittivo. In: IX Conferenza Nazionale di Sanità Pubblica. (2005) in Italian.
22. Dawson-Saunders, B., Trapp, R.G.: Appendix C: Flowcharts for relating reseach questions to statistical methods. In: Basic & Clinical Biostatistics. Appleton & Lange (1994)

A Tag-Based Data Model for Privacy-Preserving Medical Applications

Surya Nepal, John Zic, Frederic Jaccard, and Gregoire Kraehenbuehl

CSIRO ICT Centre PO Box 76, Epping NSW 1710 Australia[1]
{Surya.Nepal,John.Zic, Frederic.Jaccard, Gregoire.Kraehenbuehl}@csiro.au

Abstract. In autonomous distributed healthcare environments, patients' electronic medical records are controlled and managed by each healthcare facility. It is important to ensure that when records are accessed and transferred that it is done securely, while still respecting patients' rights on privacy and confidentiality of their personal health information. We propose a new tag-based data model for representing patients' electronic medical records as well as access and transfer policy statements. This model helps to categorize the patient information, as well as expressing patients' consent for a variety of domains (individual, health care provider and facility). Unlike most existing data models used in healthcare information systems, our model supports patients' consent expression in terms of healthcare facilities, healthcare providers, their roles, and categories of medical records or any combination of them within a single framework. Our model has been demonstrated by developing a prototype system using some trusted computing components.

1 Introduction

The coordination of individual's health care relies on the sharing of personal health information among healthcare providers such as local clinics, test laboratories and hospitals. It is well known that there are potential benefits and risks associated with sharing patients' electronic medical records [3]. One of the risks is patient's loss of privacy and confidentiality, where patients may not want to share or transfer their personal health information without their knowledge, and retain the rights to both access and transfer of this information.

The effective usage of personal health information systems is hard to achieve without addressing the patients' privacy and confidentiality concerns [2]. Different models have been proposed and demonstrated to address their concerns. An eConsent model has been developed and demonstrated in [1]. The model proposed a novel, privacy-preserving anonymous transfer protocols based on the concept of 'placeholders'. However, the model was based on a number of assumptions that represent a subset of real world application such as medical records are organized in nested structure to resolve the conflicts in policies [1].

[1] This work is completed as part of CeNTIE project that is supported by the Australian Government through the Advanced Networks Program of the Department of Communications, Information Technology and the Arts.

T. Grust et al. (Eds.): EDBT 2006 Workshops, LNCS 4254, pp. 433 – 444, 2006.

This paper offers an alternate way to organize medical records and express access and transfer policies. Our approach, which we call tag-based model, extends the eConsent model so as to address the weaknesses in the current eConsent model.

In our model, an electronic medical record has a number of policy tags associated with them, which we call *eTags*. Each of these tags has two fields: *category* and *policy*. The category field categorizes records into different groups such as heart, head and AIDS. The policy field, which we call *eCo* (electronic consent), consists of rights expressions. Unlike RBAC [6] and the eConsent model [1], our approach allows definition of permission for both transfer and access in terms of (a) roles, (b) healthcare Facilities, (c) healthcare providers, and (d) categories of information.

The following summarizes the key characteristics of our tag-based model.

- **Default policy expression:** each healthcare facility, patient and their families may have different policies for different categories of medical records. Our model supports default policies for patients, their families and healthcare facilities. For example, a patient can define a default policy for his AIDS related record so that all of his AIDS related records are subjected to this default policy. A facility can define its own default policy for AIDS related records, where AIDS related records of all patients in the facility are subjected to this policy. Similarly, a patient's family can define default policies for all the members of their family.
- **Access and transfer policy:** the policy expression mechanism allows the specification of both inter- and intra-facility access and transfer rights expressions. This enables, for example, a patient to deny specific healthcare facilities for receiving their personal health information.
- **Uniform model:** our model used eTags for both categorization and policy expressions, and allows us to define a set of policies for different categories of information.
- **Flat model:** there is no nested and hierarchical structure in information representation, and provides flexible way of representing information and defining policies.
- **Categorization into multiple groups:** in our model, electronic medical records are categorized according to a common, well-defined medical ontology. For example, a prescription related to "headache" that has side effect on heart can be categorized into three different groups – heart, head and prescription- by attaching their respective eTags.
- **Prioritized conflict resolution:** the model has an underlying priority-based conflict resolution mechanism for resolving policy conflicts between varies eCos..
- **General policy expression:** the model extends the usual role-based policy expression to allow policy expressions in terms of healthcare facilities, healthcare providers and categories of information. For example, a policy expression such as "grant access to *AIDS related records* to *Dr. Smith* while working as a *heart specialist* in *North Ryde Medical Center*" is possible in our model.

The rest of the paper is organized as follows. In Section 2, we describe a motivating example and identify some of the privacy and confidentialty problems that need to be solved. The flat data model is described in Section 3. Section 4 briefly describes a prototype implemented in a trusted environment. Section 5 presents the related work and the last section presents the concluding remarks and the future work.

2 A Motivating Scenario

We consider an example distributed healthcare environment that includes two healthcare facilities: Western Sydney Hospital and North Shore Hospital. Each hospital is autonomous and has its own medical information systems. However, as is often required, these hospitals share patients' personal health information in order to provide effective services. For example, Western Sydney Hospital may move a patient to North Shore Hospital and transfer all their medical records with them.

Each hospital has its own set of privacy and confidentiality policies for patient records held within their medical information systems. For example, a doctor working in the emergency department is permitted to have access to all medical records of a patient admitted to an emergency ward. Though the basic policies are setup by government rules and legislation, each hospital may implement these policies differently. That is, each hospital may have different set of policies for different categories of information. For example, Western Sydney Hospital may have different set of policies for AIDS related records to that of North Shore hospital. Any data model must support a variety of *default access policies for hospitals* so that all medical records in the hospital are subjected to these policies.

It is a fundamental assumption that a patient owns their personal health information. A patient may have policies that differ from those of a particular hospital. For example, a patient can define a policy that all AIDS related records are accessible to their doctor, and no other doctor in the hospital can access it except in case of emergency. Similarly, a patient's family may define their own policies for family members. For example, only family doctors may be allowed to access immunization records of the family members. Any data model developed and used must support the definition of *default family and patient policies.*

The discussion so far has been on specific policies of hospitals, patients' families and patients. As we mentioned earlier, a patient is an ultimate owner of his/her health information and thus must be able to define *policies for individual electronic medical records* independently. For example, a patient's AIDS related records policy may grant access to only family doctors. Of course, the patient may require that a particular blood test to be examined by AIDS specialist. Furthermore, the patient may not want to disclose the AIDS related records to the family doctor even though the family has defined a policy that all records of family members are accessible to the family doctor.

The hospitals may share health information with each other to provide better services. Similar to access policies, *transfer policies* are also defined at hospital, family, patient and record levels. The hospital may define its own transfer policy to another facility, but any information sharing is only possible if the patient allows it in their transfer policy

Transfer and access policies may be defined at on entities such as hospitals, patients, families and medical records. However, some policies may also need to be defined on for a group of medical records such as AIDS related records. This means medical records need to be categorized so that it is possible to define policies *for a set of records in a category*.

Hospital default policies are normally expressed on *Roles* within the facility. For example, Western Sydney Hospital may have policy that a *doctor* or *nurse* in an *emergency doctor* role can access all information. However, patient policies are less likely to depend on roles, and rather express *policies in terms of individual doctors*, such as "grant access to AIDS related records to Dr. Smith".

In order to model the above scenario, the data model must be able to express and support (a) agreed upon information categorization such as AIDS and Heart, (b) access and transfer policy rights expression, (c) default policy expressions for hospitals, patients and family, (d) default policy expression for different categories of information, and (e) policy expressions for both indentified individuals and roles.

2.1 Security Features

The discussion so far has presented some of been the characteristics of the data model. This section briefly identifies the security requirements that are necessary to meet the patient's privacy and confidentiality requirements on the access and transfer of their personal health information. They include:

- no loss of privacy and confidentiality for the patient;
- medical records should be accessible to only those providers who need to know;
- access should be limited to those portions of medical records that pertain to the provider's role;
- a log or audit trail must be maintained about all access to any part of the medical records;
- anonymity must be maintained if the medical record is published into the public domain for research purpose;
- the release/transfer of data needs patients' authorization;
- any confidential data must carry the confidentiality information;
- the medical records transfer to other side must be protected;
- a secure transfer mechanism must be established;

These requirements and their impact on the required protocols to implement these requirements are further discussed in a forthcoming paper.

3 The Tag-Based Data Model

This section presents our tag-based data model and how it provides the health information requirements discussed in Section 2.

An electronic record (*eRec*) is our fundamental unit of information. An eRec could be a diagnostic report, X-ray image, or prescription as shown in Fig 1. Each eRec may have an arbitrary number of electronic tags (*eTags*) attached to it.

Each eTag has two fields: *category* and *policy expression* (as shown in Fig. 1) that we refer to as an *eCo* (electronic consent). The *category* field is a tuple, consisting of *type of category* and its associated *value*. The *type* determines whether the category is related to patient, family or facility. The *value* provides the categorization information within the category type. The *eCo* field consists of a set of *access and transfer rights policies* for the category.

Finally, each policy has a timestamp representing the time of creation of the policy. This is used for conflict resolution (as shown later) as well as for audit purposes.

<Category Type, Value>	<eCo>

Fig. 1. eTag Structure

Each eTag can be placed into one of three broad classes: (a) a special NULL category with a non-empty set of policies, used to express *record-specific policies*. (b) An eTag with a NULL policy but with category information, used for *categorization* purposes only. (c) An eTag with both category information and a set of policies that groups the set of records and specifies group-related policies.

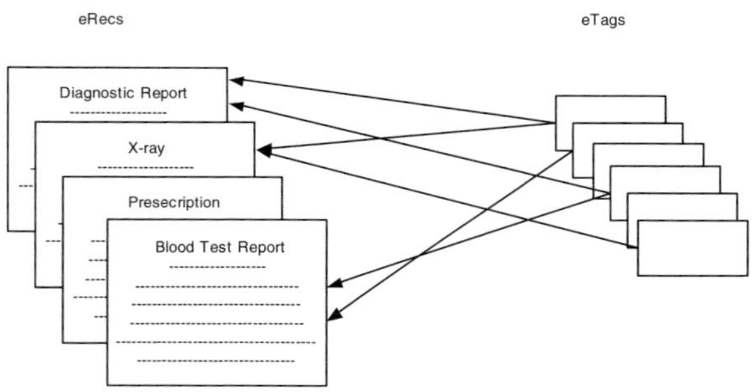

Fig. 2. eRecs and eTags in the data model

Our model allows eTags and eRecs to be related via a many-to-many relation as shown in Fig. 2. This allows an eRec to be categorized into multiple groups by attaching multiple eTags onto the eRec. Further, access and transfer rights are defined by each eTag, allowing complex access and transfer relationships to be defined and enforced.

The information held in the eTag catagory is also sensitive, in that poorly designed systems may result in accidental violation of privacy and confidentiality requirements. Our eTags have an eCo that applies to both an eRec and to category information. This means a medical practitioner will not have access to the eTags if the eCo defined in the eTag denies access to the practitioner.

Our eCo expresses both the transfer and access rights of a particular eRec. One could define an eCo access rights using standard policy languages such as XACML [12] , or EPAL [13]. However, most of the current policy expression languages are primarily used for expressing access policies. Languages that may by used to express *transfer* policies are a recent development, such as those that came out of the Family

Domain effort within Motorola [14] and are now in OMA 2.0 [15]. These languages are very rich and allow generalised application to any DRM application. However, we did not require their full capabilities for this application, and so we defined our own, application-specific rights policy expression language, described in the following section.

Note that we have omitted any formal description of the model due to the limited space available in this paper.

3.1 Policy Expression Language

Fig. 3 shows our rights policy expression language in BNF style.

```
policy :=
  policy_TRANSFER | policy_ACCESS
policy_TRANSFER :=
  ('grant' | 'deny') 'transfer to' (FACILITY)
policy_ACCESS:=
  policy_ACCESS_GRANT | policy_ACCESS_DENY
policy_ACCESS_GRANT:=
  'grant' 'access to'
  (((PRINCIPAL | ROLE)['with append right']) | FACILITY)
policy_ACCESS_DENY :=
  'deny' 'access to' (PRINCIPAL | ROLE | FACILITY)
```

Fig. 3. Policy Expression Language

The transfer policy grants or denies transfer to a certain facility (or hospital). The access policy grants or denies access to health practitioners (or principal), their roles or facilities. The access permission can be granted with append rights for healthcare practitioners or their roles defined in the facility. A doctor can access an electronic record, if and only if the access policies: (a) allow access to the subject or to the Role and (b) allow access to the Facility. That is, both the facility and practitioners need to have access permission in order to access the medical records. Similarly, a doctor can transfer an electronic record if and only if (a) the access policies allow access to the subject and his facility and (b) transfer policies grant transfer permission to the destination facility.

3.2 Policy Enforcement and Conflict Resolution Mechanism

In order to determine whether a principal can access an eRec or not, all the policies listed in the eCo of all eTags attached to the eRec must be evaluated. However, the policies defined in different eTags may conflict each other. To address this, we first define a policy priority, based on the following eTag type partial order:

$$\text{Facility} \subseteq \text{Family} \subseteq \text{Patient} \subseteq \text{NULL} \tag{1}$$

We then use this order to define a *prioritized multi-step conflict resolution mechanism*, as follows.

1. **Higher priority wins:** A simple check is first performed according the order presented in Equation (1), above. Unfortunately, this first step cannot resolve all conflicts, since a single eCo may contain multiple policies. Similarly, an eRec can have multiple eTags from the same level of priority.
2. **More specific wins:** If eTags have identical priorities, we resolve the conflict using a principal of "more specific wins". For example, a policy concerning a doctor wins over a policy concerning a role because a doctor is more specific than the role. If this rule fails to resolve the conflict, we move onto the following step.
3. **Most recent wins:** At this point, we resolve identical priorities and specifities by use of the timestamp and a rule where "most recent wins".
4. **"Deny" wins over "grant":** Should all the rules fail up to this point, the policy with "deny" wins over the policy with "grant".

4 Prototype Implementation

We implemented a demonstration system running on four PCs. Fig. 4 depicts the overall architecture of our "MedicClient/Server" system. The system has six major components:

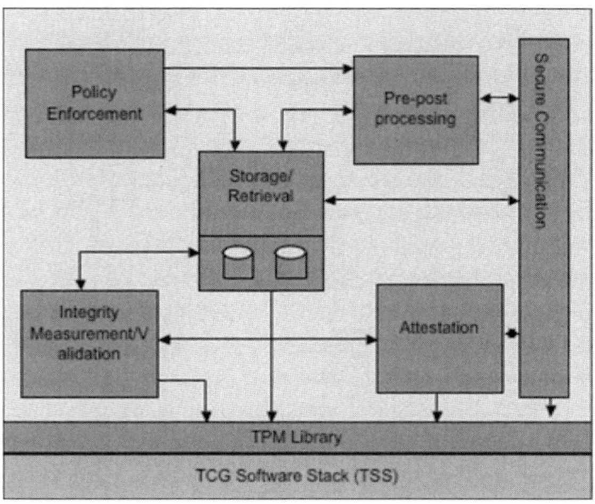

Fig. 4. MedicClient/Server Architecture

1. **Policy enforcement:** responsible for enforcing policies and resolving conflicts while accessing and transferring medical records. It is also responsible for generating and maintaining of audit logs.
2. **Integrity measurement/validation:** is used to measure the current environment of the computer where MedicServer is running and verifies that the measurements sent by other facility are as expected and so can be trusted.

3. **Secure communication:** encrypts the outgoing information and decrypts the incoming information.
4. **Attestation:** is used to determine the identity of the remote facility
5. **Pre/post processing:** processes the eTag for transfer.
6. **Storage and Retrieval:** is responsible for storing and retrieving an eRec from the SQL databases.

We consider only two components: storage and retrieval, and policy enforcement and monitoring since the scope of this paper is the data model. We present the trusted computing components (integrity measurement and validation, attestation and secure protocols) in a forthcoming paper.

Storage and retrieval: Electronic medical records and all other data needed for the functioning of components are stored in a persistent, securely encrypted store implemented using SQL server and ADO.NET classes to connect data sources and to retrieve and update stored data.

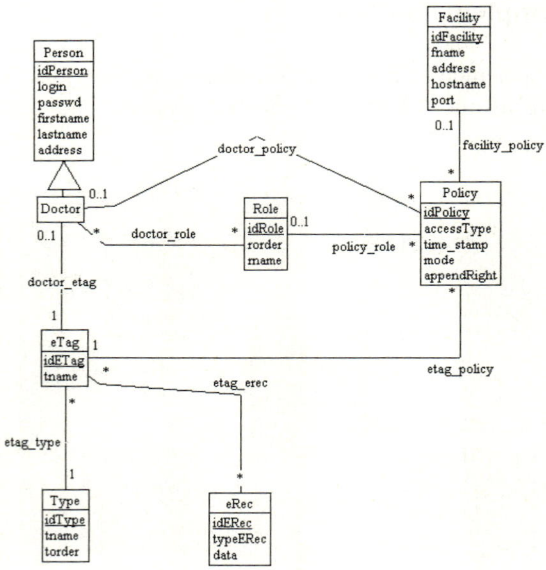

Fig. 5. E-R diagram for the tag-based model

Fig. 5 shows the relationships between the various entities in our tag-based model. It can be seen from the figure that a policy is defined on the roles and facilities as well as individual doctors. It is worthwhile noting that the doctor eTag is a NULL policy, as it does not have any relationship with the policy entities. The entities and their relationships were used to create the SQL tables held on the server, and used trusted computing technology to ensure the privacy and security of the SQL data.

Guided by the requirement that the patient's medical record privacy must be protected, we decided to encrypt the information in an eRec table entry. This is because each table entry contains a patient's medical record. This decision then allowed a simple database implementation, as only the eRec table entry data needs to be secured. Decryption of the information in an eRec could be done without using another access to the database.

The eRec data is encrypted using Triple DES, and requires the use of a symmetric key created at the time of installation of our system. An asymmetric key is created and registered at the same time and is used for the purposes of *sealing* the symmetric key so as to prevent unauthorized access to the symmetric key. *Sealing* can be simply described as an encryption function that allows only the hardware device and its specific software environment that created the object to decrypt it. The implemented mechanisms rely on the support of the Trusted Platform Modules (TPM) and Trusted Software Stack (TSS) library, and are not discussed any further in this paper. These will be presented in a subsequent paper.

Policy enforcement and monitoring: Again, due to space constrains, we only briefly describe only one of the many implemented functions of this component, namely the access policy enforcement. The access policy enforcement mechanism consists of two steps. The first checks whether the doctor is allowed to access the information or not. The second step checks whether the facility where the doctor is trying to access the information is allowed to access it or not. For both steps, all related policies for an eRec are collected from eTags in a list and checked against the conflict resolution mechanism described in Section 3.2 to see whether the winner mode is "grant" or "deny". If both facility and doctor lists come out with the winner mode as "grant", then the access is granted to the doctor in the facility for the eRec. In all other cases, access is denied.

5 Related Work

Heath services can be improved significantly by sharing patient information, but this needs to be balanced with patient's privacy and confidentiality requirements. The electronic medical record systems enable the easy sharing and distribution of patient information. However, the disclosure of a patient's medical records without his/her permission is prohibited. In this section, we first discuss the related work in health informatics in general and then discuss the work closely related to our proposed model.

Huston [8] discusses the general security concerns on implementing e-medical records and technological and administrative tools available for safeguarding the e-medical records. Stein [7] discusses the different scenarios of electronic medical records and highlights the threats and promises. Reliability, Accountability and Privacy are considered as threats, whereas consistency, flexibility, availability, and quality are considered as promises.

One of the major privacy concerns is secure transfer of electronic medical records from one service provider to other. Task force on medical informatics [3] discusses some issues related to transfer of medical records. Chadwick and Mundy [2] look at the security requirements for electronic transfer of prescriptions from the perspectives of confidentiality, integrity and availability. It analyzed the four different transfer models published in UK: Transcript Consortium Model, Pharmacy 2U Consortium Model, SchlumbergerSema Consortium Model, and University of Salford Model.

Evered and Bogeholz [5] present a case study of the access control requirements for a health information system in a small aged care facility. The study was focused on the use of static per-method access control list. The case study found that the method is inadequate as the policy constrains become complex even for a small system taken in the case study.

Reid et al. [6] examined the RBAC as a candidate access control mechanism for health care information and found that the range of access policy expressions supported by RBAC is not adequate. The paper proposed a model where the access control is given through a consumer centric role called care team role. The advantage of this model is that a subgroup of entities within a role can be explicitly granted or denied access to health information. Motta and Furuie [10] extend the RBAC reference model by introducing contextual authorisation. The authorization module not only uses the positive and negative authorization, but also user affiliation, time and location of access, user and patient relationship, patient status, etc.

Khayat and Abdallah [4] present a formal model for flat role-based access control, which we see closer to our model. This model overcomes the some of the problems as it uses the flat model. However, this model does not consider the problem-oriented approach where the patient's medical condition is divided into a list of discrete problems such as diabetes, coronary artery disease and lower back pain as in [7]. The reason behind it is that the model considers only roles. Our approach has overcome this problem by flattening not only roles, but also problems (or categorization of medical records) as well as medical information as done in our model.

Choudhri et al. [9] presents a healthcare systems based on mobile technology. The system delivers different versions of the documents based upon their roles using dynamic trust model. The model is based on transitive trust, that is, a doctor can delegate his role to other doctors. During the delegation process, the doctor may give his full rights or limited rights. This means a doctor who was not denied by patients could have access to the patient information through delegation. We have not dealt with transitive trust in our model.

6 Conclusions and Future Work

Previous eConsent data models were developed on a set of restricted assumptions. By widening the assumptions and examining the realistic use of eConsent within the health care system, we noted that these eConsent data models needed to be changed. As a consequence, we developed a flexible data model for electronic medical records, called tag-based data model. The data model allows representing patients' medical records along their consents. The model also allows us to categorize medical records into different group and define default policies for such categories. Unlike existing role-based access model, our data model supports both access and transfer policies on roles, and on categories of information, facilities and healthcare practitioners.

Our experience has been that the data model allows a great deal of flexibility and autonomy to the end users, and imposes a minimal set of semantic requirements on its use in specifying policies and catagories. Because eTags and eRecs are securely encrypted, indexing and searching requires the extension of the current data model to include metadata information.

Finally, we demonstrated the feasibility of the use of this data model by developing a prototype system based on .NET and trusted computing technologies. The prototype system gave us an insight of difficulties in implemented secure medical applications. One of the issues was the need for a good user interface to allow the complex relationships of the model to be accurately captured as well as easily understood. Other issues such as secure transport protocol, and the establishment of mutual trust will be presented in subsequent papers.

Acknowledgements

Discussion with Paul Greenfield of the prior e-consent model greatly assisted us in developing the tag-based data model. We would also like to thank Michael Cox from NTRU who helped on using some functionalities of NTRU TSS driver. Special thanks go to Alan Fekete from Sydney University and Andre Schiper from EPFL for encouraging Greg and Fred to take this project at CSIRO.

References

1. O'Keefe, C.M., Greenfield, P., and Goodchild, A. (2005): A Decentralised Approach to Electronic Consent and Health Information Access Control. Journal of Research and Practice in Information Technology, Vol. 37(2):161-178, May 2005.
2. Chadwick,D,, and Mundy, D (2004). The secure electronic transfer of prescriptions. Healthcare Computing, 2004.
3. Task Force on Medical Informatics (1996): Safeguard Needed in Transfer of Patient Data. PEDIATRICS Vol. 98 No. 5, pp. 984-986, Nov 1996.
4. Khayat, E.J., and Abdallah, A.E. (2003); A formal model for flat role-based access control. IEEE International Conference on Computer Systems and Applications, Tunisia, July 2003.
5. Evered, M. and Bogeholz, S. (2004); A case study in access control requirements for a health information system. Australasian Information Security Workshop 2004.
6. Reid, J., Cheong, I., Henricksen, M., and Smith, J. (2003) A Novel Use of RBAC to Protect Privacy in Distributed Health Care Information Systems. In Safavi-Naini, Rei and Seberry, Jennifer, Eds. Proceedings 8th Australasian Conference on Information Security and Privacy (ACISP 2003) 2727, pages 403-415, Wollongong
7. Stein, L.D. (1997). The Electronic Medical Record: Promises and Threats. Web Journal, 2(3), 1997.
8. Huston, T. (2001): Security Issues for Implementation of E-medical Records. Communication of the ACM, 44(9) pp. 89-94, September 2001.
9. Choudhri, A., Kagal, L., Joshi, A., Finin, T. and Yesha, Y. (2003). PatientService: Electronic Patient Record Redaction and Delivery in Pervasive Environment. Fifth International Workshop on Enterprise Networking and Computing in Healthcare Industry (Healthcom 2003).
10. Motta, G.H.M.B and Furuie, S.S. (2003). A Contextual Role-Based Access Control Authorization Model for Electronic Patient Record. IEEE Transactions on Information Technology in Biomedicine 7(3):202-207, Sept. 2003.
11. Crook, R., Ince, D. and Nuseibeh, B. (2003). Modelling access policies using roles in requirements engineering. Information and Software Technology, 45:979-991.

12. OASIS (2005). eXtensible Access Control Markup Language (XACML) Version 2.0 3, http://docs.oasis-open.org/xacml/2.0/access_control-xacml-2.0-core-spec-os.pdf, 2005.
13. Paul Ashley, Satoshi Hada, Günter Karjoth, Calvin Powers, and Matthias Schunter (2003), Enterprise Privacy Authorization Language (EPAL 1.1), IBM Technical Report, 2003.
14. Messerges, T. S. and Dabbish, E. A. 2003. Digital rights management in a 3G mobile phone and beyond. In Proceedings of the 2003 ACM Workshop on Digital Rights Management (Washington, DC, USA, October 27 - 27, 2003). DRM '03. ACM Press, New York, NY, 27-38. DOI= http://doi.acm.org/10.1145/947380.947385
15. Open Mobile Alliance, DRM Architecture, version 2.0.6, 2004 (OMA-DRM-ARCH-V2_0_6-20040820-C.zip at http://www.openmobilealliance.org

Window Specification over Data Streams

Kostas Patroumpas and Timos Sellis

School of Electrical and Computer Engineering
National Technical University of Athens, Hellas
{kpatro, timos}@dbnet.ece.ntua.gr

Abstract. Several query languages have been proposed for managing data streams in modern monitoring applications. Continuous queries expressed in these languages usually employ windowing constructs in order to extract finite portions of the potentially unbounded stream. Explicitly or not, window specifications rely on ordering. Usually, timestamps are attached to all tuples flowing into the system as a means to provide ordered access to data items. Several window types have been implemented in stream prototype systems, but a precise definition of their semantics is still lacking. In this paper, we describe a formal framework for expressing windows in continuous queries over data streams. After classifying windows according to their basic characteristics, we give algebraic expressions for the most significant window types commonly appearing in applications. As an essential step towards a stream algebra, we then propose formal definitions for the windowed analogs of typical relational operators, such as join, union or aggregation, and we identify several properties useful to query optimization.

1 Introduction

Data streams have emerged as a modern paradigm for managing time-varying, volatile, unpredicted and possibly unbounded information in various monitoring applications. Typical examples include data generated from telecom calls, financial tickers, sensor readings over large areas or traffic measurements. Such information must be handled online as data items flow rapidly into the system from multiple sources. Over this dynamic data, the system must provide timely and incremental responses to multiple *continuous queries*, ideally keeping in pace with the data arrival rate.

Compared to one-time queries in conventional DBMS's, continuous queries differ substantially in their semantics. Since the size of the stream is potentially unbounded, the state of the data is not known in advance, so responses clearly depend on the set of stream tuples available during query evaluation. Several operations, such as aggregation or join between streams, may need special treatment, e.g., previously arrived tuples must be maintained, at the expense of a significant overhead. Obviously, since streaming data is usually retained in memory and not physically stored on disk, it is not practically feasible to "remember" the entire history of rapidly accumulating stream elements due to resource limitations. Besides, it is probably not worth maintaining stale tuples for long, as the significance of each isolated item is time-decaying for most realistic applications.

T. Grust et al. (Eds.): EDBT 2006 Workshops, LNCS 4254, pp. 445–464, 2006.

To overcome such difficulties, *windows* have been introduced in query formulation. Such constructs generally emphasize on the latest data by taking advantage of an ordering among tuples, usually established through timestamp values attached to every item. Intuitively, at any time instant, a window operator specifies a finite set of recent tuples from the unbounded stream; this finite portion of the stream will be subsequently used to evaluate the query and produce results corresponding to that time instant. As time advances, fresh items get included in the window at the expense of older tuples that stop taking part in computations (and perhaps may get discarded altogether). In general, windows evolve in a prescribed mode keeping up with the continuous arrival of data items. Certain variants have been suggested for effective stream processing, like *sliding*, *landmark* or *tuple-based* windows, whereas several types have been successfully implemented in prototype systems [1,6,8,13]. However, most of these constructs are described in an abstract manner or by giving motivating examples, without paying particular attention to their subtle semantics.

The structure of a window clearly determines the snapshot of the dataset over which the query will be evaluated each time. But how can the extent of that window be defined in order to obtain a particular portion of the stream? Should this extent be allowed to change over time and in which specific pattern? Should window's contents be overlapping between any two successive snapshots? Finally, is it possible for windowing constructs to be intertwined with relational operators and under what semantic interpretation for their results?

In this paper, we provide a foundation for window specification over data streams with precise semantics. First, we sketch out a simple, yet quite robust model for querying data streams that is capable enough to capture their volatile nature. This model adheres to well-founded relational concepts and extends recent approaches in data stream management. Our contributions are as follows:

- We identify certain generic properties of windows that offer a sound basis for their taxonomy in several categories. Through these properties we can then create a mechanism for expressing typical window variants over streams.
- We introduce a parameterized *scope function* as a building block that enables effective specification of both the window's extent and its progression across time. Composite window types may then be defined by simply arranging their basic features according to the semantics of the query at hand.
- We provide formal definitions of well-known relational operators combined with windowing specifications that can be used to express queries on streams. We further investigate characteristic properties that may prove useful to query formulation and transformation.

The remainder of this paper is organized as follows: Section 2 presents a framework for data stream modeling and explains the semantics of continuous queries. In Section 3 a basic algebraic representation is introduced for windows according to their taxonomy into distinct types. Section 4 proposes a combination of windowing constructs with certain relational operators outlining several useful properties. Related work is briefly reviewed in Section 5. Finally, Section 6 offers conclusions and hints to future research directions.

2 A Framework for Querying Data Streams

2.1 Basic Notions on Data Streams

Items of a data stream are commonly represented as relational tuples [3], not excluding a semistructured form [16]. Henceforth we opt for a specification of stream items as relational tuples:

Definition 1 (Schema of tuples). *The tuple schema E of streaming items is represented as a set of elements $\langle e_1, e_2, \ldots, e_N \rangle$ of finite* arity N. *Each element e_i is termed* attribute *with name A_i and its values are drawn from a possibly infinite atomic* data type domain D_i. *Every tuple is an instance of the schema and it is described by its values at the respective attributes.*

A timestamp value is attached to every streaming tuple as a means of providing order among the data items that interminably flow into the system. It is often convenient to represent time as an ordered sequence of distinct moments (like clock ticks). Alternatively, simple sequence numbers may also serve as a means for ordering tuples, i.e., a unique serial number is attached to each tuple upon admission to the system. The following definition covers both interpretations:

Definition 2. Time Domain $\mathbb{T}$ *is regarded as an ordered, infinite set of discrete time instants $\tau \in \mathbb{T}$. A time* interval $[\tau_1, \tau_2] \in \mathbb{T}$ *consists of all distinct time instants $\tau \in \mathbb{T}$ for which $\tau_1 \leq \tau \leq \tau_2$.*

From the definition above, it follows that $\mathbb{T}$ may be considered similar to the domain of natural numbers $\mathbb{N}$. The extent of each interval is also a natural number, as it is simply the count of all distinct time instants occurring between its bounds. At each timestamp $\tau \in \mathbb{T}$, a possibly large, but always finite number of data elements of the stream arrive for processing [3]. Thus, multiset (bag) semantics apply and duplicates are allowed, signifying that zero, one or multiple identical tuples may arrive at any single instant:

Definition 3 (Data Stream). *A Data Stream S is a mapping $S : \mathbb{T} \rightarrow 2^R$ that at each instant $\tau \in \mathbb{T}$ returns a finite subset from the set R of tuples with common schema E. A supplementary attribute A_τ (not included in E) is designated as the* timestamp *of tuples and takes its ever-increasing values from $\mathbb{T}$.*

Note that other temporal indications (e.g., attached at data sources) are still allowed in the schema, although not explicitly considered as timestamps. In contrast, timestamp is a distinctive attribute attached to every stream element.

From a historical perspective, a data stream may be regarded as an ordered sequence of elements evolving in time, so its *current contents* are all tuples accumulated so far. On the other hand, an *instance* of the stream at any distinct time instant is a finite multiset of tuples with that specific timestamp value.

Definition 4. Current Stream Contents *$S(\tau_i)$ of a Data Stream S at time instant $\tau_i \in \mathbb{T}$ is the set $S(\tau_i) = \{s \in S : \ s.A_\tau \leq \tau_i\}$.*

Definition 5. Current Stream Instance *$S_I(\tau_i)$ of a Data Stream S at time instant $\tau_i \in \mathbb{T}$ is the set $S_I(\tau_i) = \{s \in S : \ s.A_\tau = \tau_i\}$.*

Timestamps serve as a unique time indication for the entire tuple and also as a common time reference for all incoming tuples. Each tuple maps to exactly one timestamp, but multiple tuples can have identical timestamp values. Timestamps cannot be assigned a NULL value. Hence, a total order of stream items may be defined by taking advantage of properties inherent in Time Domain:

Definition 6. Temporal Ordering *is defined as a many-to-one mapping* $f_O : D_S \to \mathbb{T}$ *from data type domain* D_S *of the tuples belonging to a data stream* S *to Time Domain* $\mathbb{T}$*, with the following timestamp properties:*
i) Existence: $\forall\ s \in S,\ \exists\ \tau \in \mathbb{T}$, *such that* $f_O(s) = \tau$.
ii) Monotonicity: $\forall\ s_1, s_2 \in S$, *if* $s_1.A_\tau \leq s_2.A_\tau$, *then* $f_O(s_1) \leq f_O(s_2)$.

Temporal ordering is crucial in stream processing because data items must be given for processing in accordance to their timestamps. As a general rule when evaluating a continuous query at time τ, all stream tuples with timestamps upto that particular τ must be available. Hence, no item should propagate for further execution if its timestamp value is less than the latest tuple produced by the system. Handling out-of-order tuples is beyond the scope of this paper.

2.2 Semantics of Continuous Queries

Intuitively, the results of a continuous query on a data stream may be considered as a union of the sets of tuples returned from successive query evaluations over the current stream contents at every distinct time instant. Similarly to [7,19], we may formally define:

Definition 7 (Continuous Query over Stream). *Let* Q *a continuous query submitted at time instant* $\tau_0 \in \mathbb{T}$ *on data stream* S*. The results* Q^c *that would be obtained at* $\tau_i \in \mathbb{T}$ *are the union of the subsets* $Q(S(\tau))$ *of qualifying tuples produced from a series of one-time queries* Q *on successive stream contents* $S(\tau)$*:*

$$\forall\ \tau_i \in \mathbb{T},\ \tau_i \geq \tau_0,\ Q^c(S(\tau_i)) = \bigcup_{\tau_0 \leq \tau \leq \tau_i} Q(S(\tau))$$

The problem with this evaluation method is that it may not be practically feasible each time to compute query results by taking into account all stream contents due to the overwhelming bulk of data that keep accumulating continuously. Periodic evaluation is no better: if only intermediate stream contents are considered in each evaluation, it may happen that newer results may cancel tuples included in formerly given answers.

A conservative approach is to accept queries with *append-only results*, thus not allowing any deletions or modifications at answers already produced. This class of continuous queries is called *monotonic* [7]:

Definition 8 (Monotonic Continuous Query over Stream). *A continuous query* Q *applied over data stream* S *is characterized* monotonic *when*

$$\forall\ \tau_1, \tau_2 \in \mathbb{T},\ \tau_1 \leq \tau_2,\ if\ S(\tau_1) \subseteq S(\tau_2),\ then\ Q(S(\tau_1)) \subseteq Q(S(\tau_2)),$$

where $Q(S(\tau_i))$ *denotes results for query* Q *that have been produced from qualifying tuples of stream contents* $S(\tau_i)$ *at time instant* τ_i.

Obviously, the above definitions can be generalized for multiple input streams. It is important to note that monotonicity refers to query results and not to incoming stream items. As long as tuples may only be added to, but never discarded from results, incremental evaluation of queries involving projections or selections may be carried out as simple filters without particular complications. However, joins or set-theoretic operations may involve stream items that have arrived at previous time instants, so a state must be continuously maintained for them [20]. *Blocking operators*, like aggregation or sorting, cannot produce even a single tuple of their result before reading the entire input. *Stateful operators*, like join or intersection, are equally problematic: in order to execute a join, all tuples from both streams must be maintained, just in case a newly arriving data item matches an older tuple from the other stream.

In order to bound the increasing memory requirements of query operators, sliding windows are usually applied over the infinite streams and always return a finite portion of the most recent data items. However, continuous queries specifying sliding windows over streams are *non-monotonic*, since new results are produced but some older ones get expired due to window movement [10]. Regarding evaluation of sliding window queries, the interesting idea of *negative tuples* [11] has been suggested as a way to cancel previously returned, but no longer valid results. Certainly, this approach entails revision of typical query operators to make them capable to handle positive and negative tuples alike.

The exact role of relational tables in continuous queries is another concern. Whereas in Gigascope [13] there is no support for relations, other approaches allow static tables (e.g., AURORA [1]) or even arbitrary updates in time-varying relations (as in STREAM [3]). In the latter case, insertion and deletion tuples are used to represent the changing state of such a relation. In [10] it is suggested the notion of *non-retroactive relations*, whose updates affect only upcoming results but do not alter any previously given query answers. In this work, our focus is strictly on streams, setting aside for future research their interaction with relations.

We think that our proposition for window semantics presented in the next sections is flexible enough to be used under any of the aforementioned interpretations of continuous queries. Our main focus is on precise specification of windows, i.e., stream portions that may be regarded as temporary relations where typical operators may be applied under well-known relational semantics.

3 An Algebraic Representation for Windows

3.1 Window Semantics and Properties

In all data stream prototype systems, submission of continuous queries is always accompanied by –mostly sliding– window specifications on any stream involved in the query. A *window* is generally considered as a mechanism for adjusting flexible bounds on the unbounded stream in order to fetch a finite, yet ever-changing set of tuples, which may be regarded as a temporary relation.

Definition 9 (Window over Data Stream). *Let W_E a window with conjunctive condition E applied at time instant $\tau_0 \in \mathbb{T}$ over the items of a data stream S, i.e., over its current contents $S(\tau_0)$. Then:*

$$\forall\ \tau_i \in \mathbb{T},\ \tau_i \geq \tau_0,\ W_E(S(\tau_i)) = \{s \in S(\tau_i) :\ E(s, \tau_i)\ holds\}$$

provided that $\mid W_E(S(\tau_i)) \mid \leq n$, for any large, but always finite $n \in \mathbb{N}$.

Therefore, each window is applied over the items of a single data stream S and at every τ_i returns a concrete finite set of tuples $W_E(S(\tau_i)) \subset S(\tau_i)$ which is called the *window state* at this time instant. When a continuous query involves multiple streams (e.g., joins), a separate window must be specified for each one, even if identical semantics are applied to all of them (i.e., similar expressions E).

Window specification is achieved by means of a *windowing attribute* [16] that helps in establishing order among stream items. We adhere to timestamps for ordering stream elements, so in the discussion below we designate timestamp attribute as the one used for obtaining tuples qualifying for condition E. Conjunctive condition E clearly depends on the windowing attribute and in our framework it takes the form of a *scope function.* This condition determines the exact structure of the window through its distinctive properties:

- *upper bound:* the timestamp of the most recent data item of the window, i.e., the greatest time indication or sequence number. Note that this is not necessarily the current timestamp, as the window may be delayed by an offset with regard to the most recent stream tuple.
- *lower bound:* the timestamp of the oldest data item within the window.
- *extent:* the "size" of the window, that may be expressed either as the number of tuples included in it or as the temporal interval spanning its contents.
- *mode of adjustment:* as time advances. This crucial property determines whether and in what way a window changes state over time.

These properties are useful for classifying windows into distinct types according to the following criteria that prescribe their evolution with time:

Measurement Unit. Provided that one of its bounds is specified (e.g., the current time instant) a window can be described through its size, such that its contents may be obtained indirectly through their relative position to the known bound. Therefore, the *scope* of the window can be measured in:

- *logical units*, usually in timestamp values. Hence, a *time-based* window is derived from the time interval spanning its contents.
- *physical units*, implying the number of tuples falling within window's bounds. Typical variants include *count-based* (Fig. 1a) and *partitioned* windows.

Most often, the upper bound is known, as it can be derived easily either from the current timestamp value (under the logical interpretation) or the most recent tuple of the stream (physical interpretation) [6].

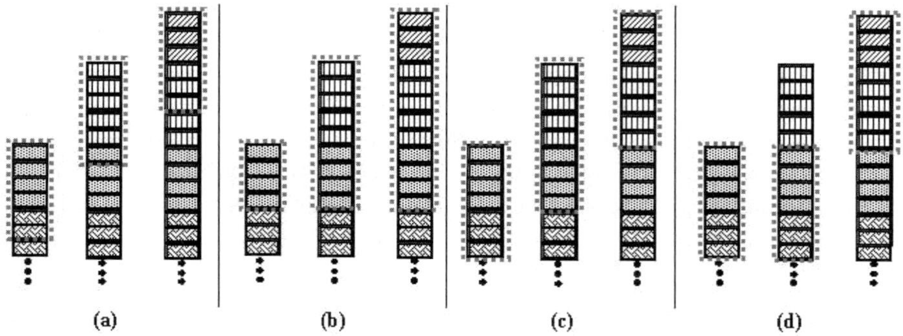

Fig. 1. Typical window variants illustrated for three consecutive states at time instants $\tau_k, \tau_k + 1, \tau_k + 2$. New data items are piling up on top of previously arrived ones. Boxes depicted with the same fill style represent tuples with identical timestamps. (a) *Count-based sliding* window of size $N = 6$. (b) *Landmark* window with lower bound fixed at τ_k. (c) *Sliding time-based* window of temporal extent $\omega = 2$ and progression step $\beta = 1$. (d) *Tumbling* window of temporal extent $\omega = 2$ and progression step $\beta = 2$.

Edge Shift. Alternatively, a window can be explicitly defined by its two bounds (or *edges*), which are commonly expressed as specific timestamp values for each state. Depending on whether edges can change over time, we distinguish between:

- *fixed-bound windows*, where at least one of the bounds remains anchored at a specific time instant. The other edge of the window is allowed to move freely. It is the upper bound that is usually shifted forward in pace with time progression, as occurs in *landmark windows* [8] (Fig. 1b).
- *variable-bound windows*, where both bounds change over time. For instance, in *sliding windows* both edges proceed in tandem at the same pace such that the window size (expressed either in time units or in tuple count) stays fixed.

Progression Step. Except for the case its bounds remain fixed, a window changes progressively its contents either due to the arrival of new streaming tuples or because of the advancement of time[1]. Therefore, transition between any two successive states of a window may be carried out at:

- *Unit step.* In that case, window's bounds advance smoothly one tuple-at-a-time or at every discrete time instant (assuming that a global clock exists). Overlaps should be expected between successive states of a window: when progression step is expressed in time units (*time-based sliding windows*), tuples with the oldest timestamp are discarded and those with the most recent timestamp get inserted; in general, the number of expired tuples is not necessarily equal to those appended (Fig. 1c). As for *count-based sliding windows*,

[1] In general, windows may be allowed to move not only forward in time, but also backwards. However, this approach is of little practical importance for applications that need to process data streams online. In this paper, we assume that windows move along the direction of increase in timestamp values.

each incoming tuple throws away the oldest one. In both cases, window's contents get modified only across its bounds, retaining all tuples in between.
- *Hops* that span multiple time instants or a specific number of tuples. Depending on whether this hop size is smaller or larger than the window size, overlapping or non-overlapping window extents may be created, respectively. For example, non-overlapping *tumbling windows* [1,13] are used to get different portions of the stream, so that no data item takes part in calculations twice (Fig. 1d).

Many window variants can be specified on the basis of the aforementioned classification criteria, depending on the semantics of the respective continuous queries. For instance, a sliding time-based window (Fig. 1c) may be needed so that the time interval covered by its contents remains fixed, although the number of tuples within the window might be varying over time. Besides, conjunctive condition E that identifies qualifying tuples may be extended with additional filtering predicates on other attributes apart from the windowing one, in a way that *value-based windows* may be expressed [6]. However, the main motivation behind windowing constructs is their combination with typical relational operators (join, aggregation, etc.), so that their windowed analogs can be specified in continuous queries over data streams.

In the next subsections, we attempt a rigorous algebraic description of the principal window types that have been proposed in the context of data streams, assuming that timestamps are used as windowing attributes. We adopt from [6] the basic discrimination in *physical* and *logical windows*, according to the unit in which window contents are determined.

3.2 Physical Window Types

Since these windowing constructs are determined by a predefined number of tuples, they are sliding by default, so naturally, their extent spans the most recent stream elements ("backward"). We are not aware of any practical application that might ask for the N data items that will be arriving after the k-th element ("forward"), because it cannot be known in advance whether or even when this specific tuple will be observed in the flow of the unbounded stream. In the following, window states are determined only at single-tuple units, as it seems unlikely to specify a slide parameter of multiple tuples in most cases.

Count-Based Windows. At every time instant $\tau \in \mathbb{T}$ a typical count-based window covers the most recent N tuples of stream S:

$$W_n(S,\tau,N) = \{s \in S(\tau) : \exists\, \tau_1 \in \mathbb{T}\ (\tau_1 \leq \tau \wedge \mid \{s \in S(\tau) :\ \tau_1 \leq s.A_\tau \leq \tau\} \mid \leq N) \\ \wedge \forall\, \tau_2 \in \mathbb{T}\ (\tau_2 < \tau_1 \wedge \mid \{s \in S(\tau) :\ \tau_2 \leq s.A_\tau \leq \tau\} \mid > N)\}$$

The above formula implies the method utilized to identify qualifying tuples: intuitively, starting from the current time instant τ and going steadily backwards in time, tuples are being obtained until their total count exceeds threshold N (cf.

Fig. 1a for a graphical representation of such a window with size $N = 6$ tuples). Nevertheless, subtle issues may arise with this policy. When the contents of count-based windows are derived through their sequence numbers [3], it must be clear how many times possible duplicates are counted and how ties are broken for the N-th element. A similar case, but concerning timestamped tuples, arises in our definition above: ties may still occur when only k elements need be chosen out of a batch of $m > k$ tuples corresponding to the lower bound of the window, in order to reach the predefined total count N. As a convenient workaround to resolve both subtleties, tuples may be selected in a non-deterministic fashion, as suggested for `ROW`-based windows in CQL [3].

Partitioned Windows. The semantics of this window type are applied to the streaming tuples by first partitioning them according to a subset $L = \{A_1, A_2, \ldots, A_k\}$ of *grouping attributes*, as in extended relational algebra. Therefore, several *substreams* are derived, each one corresponding to an existing combination of values $\langle a_1, a_2, \ldots, a_k \rangle$ on the grouping attributes. From each resulting partition the most recent N elements are taken and the union of these subsets provides the final set of window tuples. Note that the windowing attribute (timestamp) is not allowed to participate in the list of grouping attributes. Formally, this operation may be defined as follows:

$$\begin{aligned} W_p(S, \tau, L, N) = \{ & s \in S(\tau) : \forall A_k \in L,\ s.A_k = a_k \ \wedge \ \ a_k \in D_k \ \wedge \\ & \wedge \ \exists\ \tau_1 \in \mathbb{T}\ (\tau_1 \leq \tau \ \wedge \ |\ \{s \in S(\tau) :\ \ s.A_k = a_k \ \wedge \ \tau_1 \leq s.A_\tau \leq \tau\}\ |\leq N) \ \wedge \\ & \wedge \ \forall\ \tau_2 \in \mathbb{T}\ (\tau_2 < \tau_1 \ \wedge \ |\ \{s \in S(\tau) :\ \ s.A_k = a_k \ \wedge \ \tau_2 \leq s.A_\tau \leq \tau\}\ |> N)\} \end{aligned}$$

In contrast to usual relational semantics, aggregate functions (like `SUM`, `AVG`, etc.) are not applied to the partitions formed after grouping stream elements. Instead, a subset of N tuples is obtained from each partition and not just a single value expressing their total count. Observe that *count-based windows* may be regarded as a special case of partitioned windows where all tuples of the stream get assigned to a single partition with no grouping attributes specified.

3.3 Logical Window Types

In logical windows, the timestamp values of streaming tuples are checked for inclusion within a prespecified temporal interval. We conveniently express this requirement by means of a *scope function* that may be defined for each window type as a mapping from Time Domain $\mathbb{T}$ to the domain of possible time intervals:

$$scope : \ \mathbb{T} \rightarrow \{[\tau_1, \tau_2] : \tau_1, \tau_2 \in \mathbb{T},\ \ \tau_1 \leq \tau_2\}$$

Essentially, at every time instant the scope function returns the window bounds (and *not* its actual contents), taking as parameters the properties of the respective window type (extent, progression step, etc.).

Due to lack of space, in the following we present the most representative variants of logical windows that have been implemented for several stream prototypes, although the expressiveness of this approach has a broader applicability.

Landmark Windows maintain one of their bounds fixed at a specific time instant, letting the other follow the evolution of time. We distinguish two cases:

Lower-bounded landmark window. The lower bound (i.e., the starting time τ_l) of the window is permanent, whereas the upper bound proceeds with time. If this construct is applied at time τ_0, then at any subsequent time $\tau \geq \tau_0 \in \mathbb{T}$ the scope function takes the form:

$$scope_l(\tau) = \begin{cases} \emptyset & \text{if } \tau_0 \leq \tau < \tau_l \\ [\tau_l,\ \tau] & \text{if } \tau_0 \leq \tau_l \leq \tau \end{cases}$$

Therefore, streaming tuples of S with timestamps that qualify for the scope of this landmark window are returned as its state at every time instant:

$$W_l(S, \tau, \tau_0, \tau_l) = \{s \in S(\tau) :\ s.A_\tau \in scope_l(\tau)\}$$

Note that this window type will keep appending new tuples indefinitely, unless either the query is explicitly revoked (and hence the window is cancelled) or the stream is exhausted and no tuples enter into the system anymore.

Upper-bounded landmark window. Here it is the upper edge that has been fixed to a future time instant, which might not yet have occurred, but it will eventually occur due to time monotonicity. Assuming that such a window is applied at time τ_0, the scope function is as follows:

$$scope_u(\tau) = \begin{cases} [\tau_0,\ \tau] & \text{if } \tau_0 \leq \tau < \tau_u \\ [\tau_0,\ \tau_u] & \text{if } \tau_0 \leq \tau_u \leq \tau \end{cases}$$

and the upper-bounded landmark window is defined accordingly:

$$W_u(S, \tau, \tau_0, \tau_u) = \{s \in S(\tau) :\ s.A_\tau \in scope_u(\tau)\}$$

Of course, there is no point in specifying upper bounds in the past ($\tau_u < \tau_0$). Intuitively, as long as the upper bound has not been reached yet, the scope of window keeps expanding. After time instant $\tau = \tau_u$, the scope will no longer change, so the window will "close" and its bounds will be fixed. For append-only streams, this means that the contents of the upper-bounded window will thereafter be "frozen", like a materialized snapshot of a particular stream portion.

Fixed-Band Windows. Combining the aforementioned landmark window variants, a *band window* function with fixed upper and lower bounds is constructed:

$$scope_b(\tau) = \begin{cases} \emptyset & \text{if } \tau < \tau_l \\ [\tau_l,\ \tau] & \text{if } \tau_l \leq \tau \leq \tau_u \\ [\tau_l,\ \tau_u] & \text{if } \tau_u < \tau \end{cases}$$

and $$W_b(S, \tau, \tau_l, \tau_u) = \{s \in S(\tau) :\ \tau_l \leq \tau_u\ \wedge\ s.A_\tau \in scope_b(\tau)\}$$

Note that the state is not related to the moment τ_0 this window is initially applied, hence even arbitrary time intervals ("bands") in the past may be expressed. From a semantics point of view, as soon as the current stream timestamp τ exceeds the upper bound (third branch), window's contents will remain unchanged, assuming that they can be maintained in memory indefinitely.

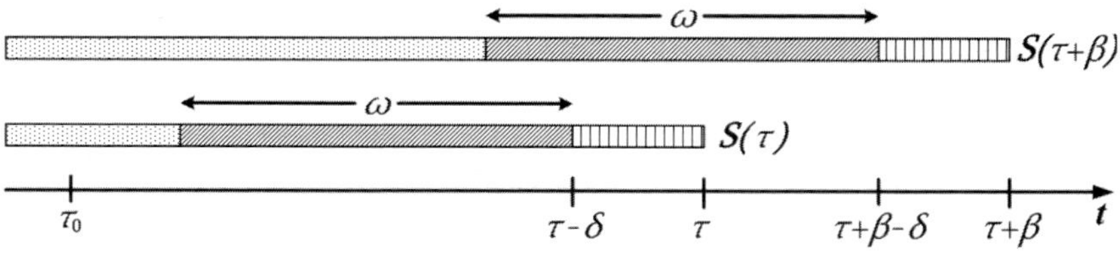

Fig. 2. Two successive states of a *sliding window* at time instants τ and $\tau + \beta$. This window obtains tuples delayed by δ time units with regard to current time (i.e., lagged elements). Since $\beta < \omega$, window states (ω) may have overlapping tuples. In case $\beta \geq \omega$, there is no longer smooth state transition, thus a *tumbling window* is actually applied.

Time-Based Sliding Windows. This is probably the most common class of windows over data streams, defined by means of time units (recall that physical windows also slide as new tuples arrive). Let $\tau_0 \in \mathbb{T}$ be the time instant that a continuous query is initially submitted specifying a sliding window W_s. Let ω denote the invariable temporal extent of this window, β its progression step and suppose that the upper bound of the window has a delay (or *lag*) δ with regard to the current time instant τ. Then the scope of this sliding window may be defined as a function of time:

$$scope_s(\tau) = \begin{cases} \emptyset & \text{if } \tau_0 \leq \tau < \tau_0 + \delta \\ [\tau_0,\ \tau - \delta] & \text{if } \tau_0 \leq \tau - \delta < \tau_0 + \omega \ \wedge\ \texttt{mod}((\tau - \tau_0), \beta) = 0 \\ [\tau - \delta - \omega + 1,\ \tau - \delta] & \text{if } \tau \geq \tau_0 + \delta + \omega \ \wedge\ \texttt{mod}((\tau - \tau_0), \beta) = 0 \\ scope_s(\tau - 1) & \text{if } \texttt{mod}((\tau - \tau_0), \beta) \neq 0 \end{cases}$$

In the most common case, the upper bound of the sliding window coincides with the current timestamp of the stream (i.e., $\delta = 0$), so the previous scope function may be simplified as follows:

$$scope_s(\tau) = \begin{cases} [\tau_0,\ \tau] & \text{if } \tau_0 \leq \tau < \tau_0 + \omega \ \wedge\ \texttt{mod}((\tau - \tau_0), \beta) = 0 \\ [\tau - \omega + 1,\ \tau] & \text{if } \tau \geq \tau_0 + \omega \ \wedge\ \texttt{mod}((\tau - \tau_0), \beta) = 0 \\ scope_s(\tau - 1) & \text{if } \texttt{mod}((\tau - \tau_0), \beta) \neq 0 \end{cases}$$

Note that $\tau_0, \tau \in \mathbb{T}$ are expressed in timestamp values, whereas parameters ω, δ, β are actually sizes of time intervals (hence $\omega, \delta, \beta > 0$). For the sake of clarity, all parameters may be considered as natural numbers according to the definition of the Time Domain $\mathbb{T}$, so the scope function is evaluated at discrete time instants of $\mathbb{T}$. For every time instant $\tau \in \mathbb{T}$, the qualifying tuples are included in the window state:

$$W_s(S, \tau, \tau_0, \omega, \beta, \delta) = \{s \in S(\tau) :\ s.A_\tau \in scope_s(\tau)\}$$

In the most general case where $\beta < \omega$, overlaps are observed between the extents of any two successive states of a sliding window, thus a subset of their contents remains intact across states (common tuples in both ω in Fig. 2). In the meantime of any two successive evaluations that are β units apart, no change occurs to the qualifying tuples. That is exactly the meaning of the recursive expression at the last branch of the function, which provides a warranty that window's bounds change discontinuously at time instants that depend strictly on the pattern stipulated by the progression step β. The definition allows for the existence of "half-filled" windows with extent less than ω at early evaluation stages, so the window may be considered as being gradually filled with tuples. As soon as the extent reaches its capacity, the window starts exchanging some older tuples with newly arriving ones. Since time evolution implies an analogous change of time intervals derived from scope, this function is by definition *monotonic*. Function scope holds even for time instants in the future, thus covering all forthcoming stream elements, no matter when they will actually arrive for processing.

Progression step β is usually set equal to the granularity of time (e.g., seconds), so that the window slides smoothly in pace with the advancement of time. In that case, the recursive branch in the above definition for the scope function is redundant, as window's contents are modified at every time instant.

Finally, by setting $\tau = \texttt{NOW}$, $\omega = 1$, $\delta = 0$ and $\beta = 1$ in the definition of the scope function, it is very easy to express an important class of sliding windows that obtain the current instance $S_I(\tau)$ of the stream, i.e., all its tuples with the current timestamp value (in [3] the shortcut $S\,[\texttt{NOW}]$ is used for this purpose).

Time-Based Tumbling Windows. The scope function defined for sliding windows is generic enough to express windows with arbitrary progression step (even $\beta \geq \omega$). Intuitively, *tumbling windows* accept streaming tuples in "batches" that span a fixed time interval. This is particularly useful when aggregates must be computed over successive, yet non-overlapping portions of the stream, in a way that no tuple takes part in computations more than once [13]. Usually, a new window state is created as soon as the previous one has ceased to exist: the lower bound of the current state and the upper bound of its preceding one are consecutive time instants. This variant can be derived by simply setting $\beta = \omega$ at the scope function $scope_s$ of a sliding window, assuming a standard extent ω is used. At each evaluation, disjoint stream portions of equal extent are returned and thus window contents are obtained in a discontinuous fashion:

$$W_t(S, \tau, \tau_0, \omega, \omega, \delta) = \{s \in S(\tau) : \; s.A_\tau \in scope_s(\tau)\}$$

Alternatively, for several applications (e.g., traffic monitoring), different window sizes might be needed (e.g., for peak or night hours, weekends etc.). In that case, function $scope_s$ is still valid by replacing fixed extent ω with a time-varying $\omega(\tau)$. In [1] tumbling windows may be accompanied with user-defined predicates so as to determine the end of temporary states, but this approach is mainly geared towards implementation efficiency rather than query semantics.

3.4 Monotonicity of Window Types

From the discussion above, it is apparent that monotonicity varies according to the characteristics of window types, since edge shift and progression step clearly determine containment and expiration of timestamped tuples with regard to the window specified. In [10] a characterization on monotonicity has been introduced for query operators with respect to sliding windows. More specifically, sliding windows are described as *weakest non-monotonic*: although new tuples are appended to a window state pushing older ones out of it, order is always preserved, since tuples are included into and excluded from a sliding window (either time- or count-based) in a FIFO fashion.

Here, we will briefly comment upon monotonicity of the remaining window variants. In particular, partitioned windows are *weak non-monotonic*. Although the contents of each of its constituent substreams change in FIFO order, some partitions may be modified more often than others. In fact, depending on the pattern of incoming tuples, some combinations of values on the grouping attributes may be observed more frequently. As a result, the expiration order of tuples does not generally coincide to their insertion order into the window.

However, lower- and upper-bounded landmark windows are *monotonic*. In either case, no tuple is ever removed from window state. Therefore, at any time instant the window state subsumes all previous ones. Accordingly, fixed-band windows are also monotonic, as their bounds remain intact over time.

The case appears more intricate for tumbling windows. At a first glance, each window state has no overlapping tuples with its predecessor, so this type is clearly non-monotonic. However, every state ceases to exist in its entirety as soon as the new one is initiated, so it may be assumed that each participating tuple is removed from that window at the same order it was inserted, emulating some kind of deferred elimination. Therefore, tumbling windows may be considered as *weakest non-monotonic*, exactly like their sliding counterparts.

4 Windowed Queries over Data Streams

As already pointed out, the main motivation behind the introduction of windows is the necessity to unblock query operators in stream processing. In fact, the combination of windows with relational operators creates their windowed analogs that accept streams of timestamped tuples as input and generate temporary relations as answers. If resulting tuples must be reassembled as a stream for further processing, a converse *Streamline* operator (like `ISTREAM`, `DSTREAM`, `RSTREAM` proposed in [3]) is needed to progressively make up the derived stream. However, this transformation does not affect window semantics and it will not be further examined here. Derived items are always given suitable time indications, whose value is operation dependent. Next, we describe these windowed operators and briefly present some of their properties, but a meticulous investigation regarding the minimal set of operators for a stream algebra is left for future work.

4.1 Windowed Operators

Since projection and selection are neither blocking nor stateful operators, application of windows is not strictly necessary, because both operators act like filters over each streaming tuple. However, in many circumstances query semantics either include window specification (e.g., maintain all sensor readings over the past hour) or even impose a suitable one to facilitate query execution [3].

Windowed Projection. We define *windowed projection* π_L^W as an operator that applies a window[2] W over the contents of a stream S and returns all qualifying tuples retaining a restricted set of chosen attributes $L = \{A_1, A_2, \ldots, A_k\}$:

$$\pi_L^W(S(\tau)) = \pi_L\ (W(S(\tau))) = \{\langle s.A_1, s.A_2, \ldots, s.A_k, s.A_\tau \rangle : s \in W(S(\tau))\}$$

This "vertical" operator treats the contents of each window state as a typical relation and it simply projects out any unnecessary attributes. Note that the timestamp values from attribute A_τ of input tuples are attached to the resulting ones as well.

This operation can be further extended to *generalized projection*, in which expressions involving attributes, constants or arithmetic operators may be computed by considering each tuple of S in turn. Occasionally, a *renaming* operator may be utilized to control the names of composite expressions that appear as attributes in derived streams, in the same sense as in relational algebra [2].

Windowed Selection. Assuming that a condition F will be applied to each state of a window W over stream S, the selection operator can be defined as

$$\sigma_F^W(S(\tau)) = \sigma_F\ (W(S(\tau))) = \{s \in W(S(\tau)) : F(s)\ holds\}$$

Condition F may be an *atomic* one, that is, either $s.A_i = a_i$ or $s.A_i = s.A_j$. In the former case, the value of an attribute A_i is checked for equality to an atomic value $a_i \in D_i$ from its data type domain. In the latter case, A_i, A_j can be any two distinct attributes (apart from the timestamp) in the schema of stream tuples. Further, a *generalized* condition F may be defined with comparison operators $\theta \in \{=, \neq, <, \leq, >, \geq\}$ or as a conjunction of atomic selections, exactly as in relational algebra [2], since each predicate is applied over the temporary relation derived from its respective window state. Note that the schema of each tuple is left intact by this "horizontal" operator, hence the original timestamp value is retained in attribute $s.A_\tau$ for each item s at the output.

Windowed Duplicate Elimination. This operator applies a window W over the contents of a stream S and returns the most recent appearance of each tuple, eliminating any other identical tuple within the current extent of W:

$$\begin{aligned}\delta^W(S(\tau)) &= \delta\ (W(S(\tau))) = \\ &\{s \in W(S(\tau)) : \nexists\ s' \in W(S(\tau)), \forall\ A_i \in E, s'.A_i = s.A_i \wedge s'.A_\tau \geq s.A_\tau\}\end{aligned}$$

Note that a more conservative strategy can be adopted, which maintains each distinct tuple as long as its timestamp falls within window's extent. Only when this tuple expires, is it replaced by a more recent identical tuple [10].

---

[2] For clarity, we henceforth eliminate conjunctive condition E in window notation.

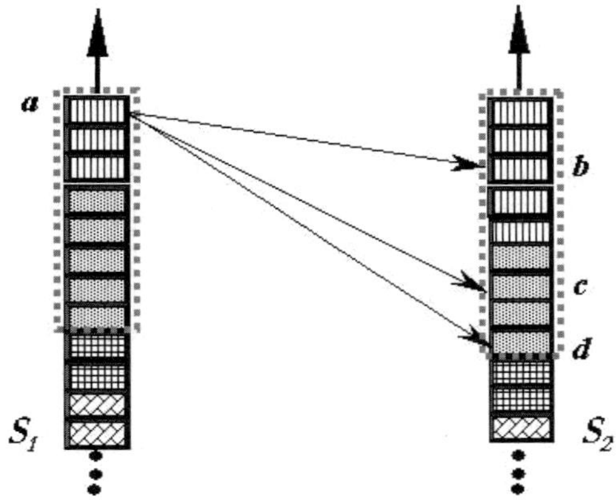

Fig. 3. Join operation between two streams S_1 and S_2 with different windows specified over each one. Each incoming tuple from either stream is tested for possible match with every tuple in the window applied to the other stream such that potential matches (pointed to with arrows) are returned.

Windowed Join. This symmetric binary operator may be applied between two streams (and easily generalized for multi-way joins), but there is no restriction that windows of the same type or the same scope must be specified over each stream[3]. At each time instant $\tau \in \mathbb{T}$, the *windowed join* between two streams returns the concatenation of pairs of matching tuples taken from either window state. In particular:

$$\begin{aligned} S_1(\tau) \underset{W}{\bowtie} S_2(\tau) &= W_1(S_1(\tau)) \bowtie W_2(S_2(\tau)) = \{\langle s_1, s_2, \tau_m \rangle : \\ & s_1 \in W_1(S_1(\tau)),\ s_2 \in W_2(S_2(\tau)) \ \wedge\ J(s_1, s_2) \ \wedge\ \tau_m = \mathtt{min}(s_1.A_\tau, s_2.A_\tau)\} \end{aligned}$$

As illustrated in Fig. 3, each newly arriving tuple within window W_1 of stream S_1 is checked for possible matches against the current state of window W_2 of stream S_2, and vice versa. Matching is performed according to the join condition J involving attributes from both streams (e.g., $S_1.A_i = S_2.A_j$). If matching tuples are found, the resulting joined element must be assigned a new timestamp value. Several policies have been suggested: in [10] the minimum of the two original timestamp values is given to the new tuple, with the natural interpretation that the concatenated tuple should expire from window as soon as one of the original tuples expire. Although this rule is acceptable from a semantics point of view (hence we adopt it in the definition above), it can lead to disorder among the joined tuples and to complications on further processing. Alternatively [4], the most recent from the pair of timestamp values attached to its constituent tuples can be chosen, as a means to preserve ordering in the derived stream. It has also been suggested that each resulting tuple may be assigned to the time instant it was produced from the join operator [6], but this approach might be

[3] In this paper we do not examine interaction of streams with static relational tables (e.g., in joins), as we consider that windows are applied solely over streams.

troublesome for successive joins in complex execution plans. In all cases, the chosen timestamp value substitutes existing ones at the concatenated tuple, so that only one timestamp attribute is retained.

Windowed Aggregation. Similarly to the respective operator in extended relational algebra, at first a grouping of window's tuples takes place according to their values for those attributes specified in grouping list $L = \{A_i, A_j, \ldots, A_n\}$. Next, for each combination of values $\langle a_i, a_j, \ldots, a_n \rangle$, an aggregation function f (like `COUNT`, `SUM`, `MIN`, `MAX` or `AVG`) is applied. If no attributes are specified, then all tuples in the window are regarded as belonging to a single group. Formally:

$$\gamma_L^{f^W}(S,\tau) = \gamma_L^f(W(S(\tau))) = \{ \langle a_i, a_j, \ldots, a_n, f(a_i, a_j, \ldots, a_n), \tau_m \rangle : \tau_m = \tau \wedge \forall A_k \in L, a_k \in D_k, s \in W(S(\tau)) \wedge a_k = s.A_k \}$$

Note that the current time instant (assuming a global system clock exists) is attached to the resulting tuple as its timestamp. Alternatively, the most recent timestamp among all window state elements may be used, so that ordering can be achieved for the operator's output. More adequately, the $\texttt{min}(s.A_\tau)$ among all current tuples $s \in W(S(\tau))$ participating in a group may be assigned as the timestamp τ_m for this group, but that may cause disorder to the derived stream.

Windowed Set-Theoretic Operations. As it will become obvious from the following algebraic expressions, set-theoretic operations on data streams adhere to bag semantics as in relational algebra [9]. Therefore, we extent tuple schema with a positive integer value k that counts the number of duplicate stream elements within each window state. In the following, we denote as $\langle s, k \rangle$ a bag (multiset) where tuple s appears k times. Operations like *Windowed Union*, *Windowed Intersection*, and *Windowed Difference* are applied at each instant $\tau \in \mathbb{T}$ over the respective window states (even of diverse specifications), provided that both streams involved in these operations must have identical schemata:

$$S_1(\tau) \underset{W}{\cup} S_2(\tau) = W_1(S_1(\tau)) \bigcup W_2(S_2(\tau)) = \{\langle s, \tau, k \rangle : \exists\, k_1, k_2 \in \mathbb{N}, (\ \langle s, k_1 \rangle \in W_1(S_1(\tau)) \vee \langle s, k_2 \rangle \in W_2(S_2(\tau))\ ) \wedge k = k_1 + k_2 \wedge k \neq 0\}$$

$$S_1(\tau) \underset{W}{\cap} S_2(\tau) = W_1(S_1(\tau)) \bigcap W_2(S_2(\tau)) = \{\langle s, \tau, k \rangle : \exists\, k_1, k_2 \in \mathbb{N}, \langle s, k_1 \rangle \in W_1(S_1(\tau)) \wedge \langle s, k_2 \rangle \in W_2(S_2(\tau)) \wedge k = \mathsf{min}(k_1, k_2) \wedge k \neq 0\}$$

$$S_1(\tau) \overset{W}{-} S_2(\tau) = W_1(S_1(\tau)) - W_2(S_2(\tau)) = \{\langle s, \tau, k \rangle : \exists\, k_1, k_2 \in \mathbb{N}, \langle s, k_1 \rangle \in W_1(S_1(\tau)) \wedge \langle s, k_2 \rangle \in W_2(S_2(\tau)) \wedge k = \mathsf{max}(0, k_1 - k_2) \wedge k \neq 0\}$$

Observe that these operators essentially treat all copies of a tuple as being distinct to each other, so they simply manipulate their number of occurrences. Also note that the timestamp attached to resulting tuples is the time instant of their evaluation, as existing timestamps are not taken into account when checking for duplicates. This might be reasonable since window contents are treated as transitory multisets. Alternatively, the k most recent (or the k older) tuples of each multiset may be returned each time, with the drawback of unsynchronized results produced from successive window states. Generalization of windowed union and intersection for more than two stream inputs is trivial.

4.2 Properties of Windowed Operators

Due to lack of space, we present just some indicative properties of the windowed operators defined previously, so as to emphasize their usefulness in query rewriting. First, it is obvious that *projection* is commutative with both logical and physical windows, that is, $\pi_L\ (W_E(S(\tau))) = W_E(\pi_L(S(\tau)))$.

Selection commutes with logical time-based windows only, i.e., $\sigma_F\ (W_E(S(\tau))) = W_E(\sigma_F(S(\tau)))$, but not physical ones [3]. Evidently, the state of a count-based window may contain different items if selection has formerly been applied to the stream. Similarly, *duplicate elimination* also commutes solely with logical windows, i.e., $\delta\ (W_E(S(\tau))) = W_E(\delta(S(\tau)))$.

On the other hand, *stateful operators* like joins, intersections or aggregates, generally do not commute with any type of windows. Still, windowed analogs of binary operators have some interesting properties:

Rewriting Rules for Windowed Joins.

i) *Commutative:* $S_1(\tau) \underset{W}{\bowtie} S_2(\tau) = S_2(\tau) \underset{W}{\bowtie} S_1(\tau)$

ii) *Associative:* $(S_1(\tau) \underset{W}{\bowtie} S_2(\tau)) \underset{W}{\bowtie} S_3(\tau) = S_1(\tau) \underset{W}{\bowtie} (S_2(\tau) \underset{W}{\bowtie} S_3(\tau))$

iii) *Distributive over selection:* $\sigma_F(S_1(\tau) \underset{W}{\bowtie} S_2(\tau)) = \sigma_F(S_1(\tau)) \underset{W}{\bowtie} \sigma_F(S_2(\tau))$
Similarly to selections, this property holds for logical windows only.

iv) *Distributive over projection:* $\pi_L(S_1(\tau) \underset{W}{\bowtie} S_2(\tau)) = \pi_L(\pi_{L_1}(S_1(\tau)) \underset{W}{\bowtie} \pi_{L_2}(S_2(\tau)))$
Attribute lists L_1 and L_2 used for the separate projections over each stream must include attributes in list L and attributes involved in join conditions.

As for *Windowed Union* and *Windowed Intersection*, commutativity and associativity hold, but not distribution over selection. Note that union is not a blocking operator for streams, since its result may be produced in an incremental fashion by simply merging the current instances $S_I(\tau)$ of incoming streams.

5 Related Work

Stream processing has become a very fertile topic for database researchers over the past few years, but here we review issues mostly relative to continuous queries and window semantics. The first notion of continuous queries over append-only databases appeared in Tapestry [19] as a means to provide timely responses by utilizing periodic query execution and identifying several rewriting rules for incremental evaluation. In [7], this approach was extended such that continuous semantics could deal with more involved cases, i.e., when deletions or modifications are allowed in the database, and not just insertions. Previous work in sequence databases [18] has provided useful semantics and a declarative language for managing ordered relations, but it is not too expressive for continuous queries over infinite streams. Besides, issues such as temporal modeling, ordering and indexing have been extensively studied in the context of temporal databases [12]. In [14] a temporal foundation for a stream algebra is attempted, which makes a distinction between logical and physical operator levels. Transformation rules are provided between a logical level that refers to query specification and a physical level that covers implementation issues. In terms of windows, only sliding and fixed variants are supported.

There have been several proposals for a query language over data streams. The declarative Continuous Query Language (CQL), which is being developed for the STREAM prototype [3], supports management of both dynamic streams and updatable relations and introduced mappings between them. CQL adopts semantics for queries and windows that are closest in spirit to ours. A more detailed approach on stream and query semantics is provided in [5], but windowing issues are covered briefly for tuple-based and time-based sliding windows only. StreaQuel is a SQL-like query language that is being developed for the TelegraphCQ project [8], although a subset of its functionality has been implemented so far. At present, continuous queries in TelegraphCQ may only be specified through time-based sliding windows, but there are plans to support more window variants (landmark, fixed, band). Several window types have also been implemented in Aurora [1], a prototype system that assumes a work-flow paradigm for data streams, instead of a relational one. Apart from windowed versions of join and sort operations, the main focus is on computing aggregates through sliding and tumbling windows. Gigascope [13] is a system for managing network flow in large data communication networks, where all stream tuples include an ordering attribute, exactly as in sequence databases. No windows are explicitly defined in its stream-only language GSQL, but their semantics can be indirectly expressed into constraints by analyzing the timestamps of input streams and query properties.

Most recently, window semantics are briefly touched in [16] in a more general setting for data stream representation, whereas a more detailed examination of window aggregates is proposed by the same authors in [15]. In brief, they attach explicit identifiers to all window states created during processing and they maintain the window states where each tuple actually participates in. This is performed by means of a special function that is the inverse of the one returning the extent. In essence, an additional attribute is attached to the grouping list used for aggregation; hence, windowed aggregation reduces to a simple relational one. One of their goals is to deal with disorder in incoming stream elements, hence they accept as windowing attribute any one with a totally ordered domain, i.e., not only timestamps or sequence numbers. Further, their view focuses mostly on aggregates, and it covers only sliding, landmark and partitioned windows. The authors in [10] distinguish time-evolving streams from relational tables in order to derive update patterns for continuous queries. These patterns are classified according to monotonicity, in order to develop suitable physical query plans for processing and data structures for state maintenance. However, that insightful framework is limited to time-based sliding windows only, with no formal foundations. Although we set out with a similar overall approach on window semantics, we differ substantially in the development of window formalization. We avoid to assign identifiers to transient window states, since we think that it relates mostly to optimization issues rather than query semantics. We do not focus strictly on window interaction with aggregates, but we tackle all main relational operations. Further, we provide a detailed description of windows' properties and rich semantics for the most typical variants.

6 Conclusions and Future Work

In this paper we developed a foundation with clear semantics for specifying windows over data streams. To the best of our knowledge, our approach is the first to determine several common properties for windows, presenting a sound taxonomy of the most significant variants proposed in the literature. In order to overcome subtle intricacies, we introduced a generic scope function as a building block for effective specification of both the window's extent and its progression across time. More composite window types can then be defined by simply arranging their basic characteristics in consistency with query semantics. Further, our algebraic formulation for the windowed analogs of principal relational operators is of particular importance as a mechanism for expressing queries on streams and checking for syntactic equivalences. Overall, we believe that this approach is an essential step towards creating an algebra and a query language for managing data streams. Of course, several demanding topics remain open for future research, such as inclusion of relations or completeness of stream operators.

We are currently implementing (in C++) several operators to verify feasibility of our semantic foundations. We have begun developing a simplified stream processing engine for submitting continuous queries, which, of course, is far from a full-fledged DSMS. As of the time of writing this paper, all window variants have been successfully constructed, as well as windowed implementations for selection, projection and join in order to support typical SPJ continuous queries. Encouraged by these positive indications, we are in the process of gradually incorporating more operations, particularly aggregation and duplicate elimination.

We also believe that this framework is a promising area for research concerning *multidimensional streams*. In connection to our preliminary work [17], we further plan to investigate modeling of moving objects, introducing algebraic constructs for space-based windows and developing operators for typical spatiotemporal queries, such as range or nearest-neighbor search. Finally, shared execution of various spatiotemporal predicates and window subsumption in multiple dimensions are considered most challenging issues in such a dynamic setting.

References

1. D.J. Abadi, D. Carney, U. Çetintemel, M. Cherniack, C. Convey, S. Lee, M. Stonebraker, N. Tatbul, and S. Zdonik. Aurora: a New Model and Architecture for Data Stream Management. *VLDB Journal*, 12(2):120-139, August 2003.
2. S. Abiteboul, R. Hull, and V. Vianu. *Foundations of Databases*. Addison-Wesley, 1995.
3. A. Arasu, S. Babu, and J. Widom. The CQL Continuous Query Language: Semantic Foundations and Query Execution. *VLDB Journal*, 2006 (to appear).
4. A. Ayad and J. Naughton. Static Optimization of Conjunctive Queries with Sliding Windows over Data Streams. In *ACM SIGMOD*, pp. 419-430, June 2004.
5. A. Arasu and J. Widom. A Denotational Semantics for Continuous Queries over Streams and Relations. *ACM SIGMOD Record*, 33(3):6-12, September 2004.
6. B. Babcock, S. Babu, M. Datar, R. Motwani, and J. Widom. Models and Issues in Data Stream Systems. In *ACM PODS*, pp. 1-16, May 2002.
7. D. Barbarà. The Characterization of Continuous Queries. *International Journal of Cooperative Information Systems*, 8(4): 295-323, December 1999.
8. S. Chandrasekaran, O. Cooper, A. Deshpande, M.J. Franklin, J.M. Hellerstein, W. Hong, S. Krishnamurthy, S.R. Madden, V. Raman, F. Reiss, and M.A. Shah. TelegraphCQ: Continuous Dataflow Processing for an Uncertain World. In *CIDR*, Asilomar, California, January 2003.
9. U. Dayal, N. Goodman, and R.H. Katz. An Extended Relational Algebra with Control over Duplicate Elimination. In *ACM PODS*, pp.117-123, March 1982.
10. L. Golab and M. Tamer Özsu. Update-Pattern-Aware Modeling and Processing of Continuous Queries. In *ACM SIGMOD*, pp. 658-669, June 2005.
11. M. Hammad, W. Aref, M. Franklin, M. Mokbel, and A. Elmagarmid. Efficient Execution of Sliding Window Queries over Data Streams. *Technical Report* CSD-TR-03-035, Purdue University, 2003.
12. C.S. Jensen and R.T. Snodgrass. Temporal Data Management. *IEEE Transactions on Knowledge and Data Engineering*, 11(1): 36-44, January 1999.
13. T. Johnson, S. Muthukrishnan, V. Shkapenyuk, and O. Spatscheck. A Heartbeat Mechanism and its Application in Gigascope. In *VLDB*, pp. 1079-1088, September 2005.
14. J. Krämer and B. Seeger. A Temporal Foundation for Continuous Queries over Data Streams. In *COMAD*, pp. 70-82, January 2005.
15. J. Li, D. Maier, K. Tufte, V. Papadimos and P.A. Tucker. Semantics and Evaluation Techniques for Window Aggregates in Data Streams. In *ACM SIGMOD*, pp. 311-322, June 2005.
16. D. Maier, J. Li, P. Tucker, K. Tufte, and V. Papadimos. Semantics of Data Streams and Operators. In *ICDT*, pp. 37-52, January 2005.
17. K. Patroumpas and T. Sellis. Managing Trajectories of Moving Objects as Data Streams. In *STDBM*, pp. 41-48, August 2004.
18. P. Seshadri, M. Livny, and R. Ramakrishnan. SEQ: A Model for Sequence Databases. In *ICDE*, pp. 232-239, March 1995.
19. D. B. Terry, D. Goldberg, D. Nichols, and B. M. Oki. Continuous Queries over Append-only Databases. In *ACM SIGMOD*, pp. 321-330, June 1992.
20. P. Tucker, D. Maier, T. Sheard, and L. Fegaras. Exploiting Punctuation Semantics in Continuous Data Streams. *IEEE Transactions on Knowledge and Data Engineering*, 15(3): 555-568, May 2003.

Using Temporal Semantics for Live Media Stream Queries

Bin Liu[1], Amarnath Gupta[2], and Ramesh Jain[3]

[1] School of Electrical and Computer Engineering, Georgia Institute of Technology, Atlanta GA 30332, USA
[2] San Diego Supercomputer Center, University of California San Diego, La Jolla, CA 92093, USA
[3] Department of Computer Science, University of California Irvine, Irvine, CA 92697, USA

Abstract. Querying live media streams is a challenging problem that becomes an essential requirement in a growing number of applications. We address the problem of evaluating continuous queries on media streams produced by media sources such as webcams and microphones. The temporal attributes and the order of stream tuples play essential roles in live stream generation and query execution. Furthermore, the temporal constraints and query semantics of related streams provide additional query optimization opportunities. We investigate the modeling issues and introduce the query processing techniques of a live media stream management system (MedSMan), including media capturing, automatic feature generating, declaration and query languages, temporal stream operators and querying algorithms. A prototype is implemented and we present experimental results to show the performance of our prototype using various real-time media experiments.

1 Introduction

In recent times, processing continuous queries over live and unbounded streams has become a major research area in data management. A number of research groups are developing data stream processing systems for a wide variety of problem domains including network data management, traffic monitoring, business data analysis, environmental sensor networks and immersive environments. At the same time, the proliferation of various sensor devices (e.g., webcam, microphone, RFid, etc) has fuelled many applications utilizing massive media streams in a unifying way. We consider the problem of continuous querying on multiple live media streams, by taking advantages of automatic and real-time multimedia information processing techniques. The basic premise behind delivering multimedia information is that while each individual media channel contains some information, it is the synchronous combination of the channels that captures the intended semantics of the content. We use the term *live multimedia* to refer to the scenario where the multimedia information is not "produced" though manual editing, but is captured in a real-life setting by different sensors and streamed to

T. Grust et al. (Eds.): EDBT 2006 Workshops, LNCS 4254, pp. 465–482, 2006.

a central processor. This makes live multimedia stream query systems distinct. First, their primary problem is to effectively combine multiple media streams as well as auxiliary non-media information to answer standing queries about the situations observed by the media sensors. For example, consider a professional conference room equipped with multiple cameras and microphones capturing the activities of both the speaker and audience. A remote user wants to connect to the speaker's video only when he or she talks about "multimedia database". This is different from research issues in the standard image, video and audio database systems which centers around similarity queries and problems like scene detection and shot segmentation using different features. Second, unlike alphanumeric symbolic streams, media streams often cannot be directly queried. Instead, queries on them are evaluated by computing feature streams from them. The data model for media streams need to capture this media-feature dependency. Third, real-life applications often specify their queries in terms of events occurring over intervals of time (i.e., an interval event with a start and a end time). The events need to be expressed in terms of the underlying media streams as well as the derived feature streams.

1.1 Prior Work

There has been considerable prior work on data stream management systems (DSMSs), such as OpenCQ [1], NiagaraCQ [2], Aurora [3], Telegraph [4], COUGAR [5], and STREAM system [6]. A number of research issues of DSMSs have been received significant attentions, including data models, continuous query semantics, query languages, blocking operators, memory requirements, cost metrics and statistics, approximations, adaptivity and query optimizations, and scalability issues. Much of this earlier work has focused on alphanumeric symbolic streams, while live media streams have received less attention - due to the heterogeneity of multimedia and tremendous on-line processing costs (in terms of time, memory and CPU). However, advances in multimedia information systems and digital signal processing techniques are decreasing the media processing costs and making the queries of live media streams viable. As a result, there is a need for a unifying data stream management system effectively combining extensible digital processing techniques and the general DSMS research.

A *media stream* is usually the output of a sensor device such as a video, audio or motion sensor that produces a continuous or discrete signal, but typically cannot be directly used by a data stream processor. To evaluate queries on media streams, one needs to continuously extract content-based descriptors, that we call *features*, from them and identify the qualifying media portions by evaluating queries on the generated *feature streams*, which are post-processed by one or more transformers and correlated to the media streams temporally and in terms of content. We previously studied the media stream generation, as well as feature function implementations (especially for feature streams derived from single media or feature stream) in [7]. Considering the *interval* nature of media tuples, we do not use window based approaches [8], but a per-tuple triggering approach. Temporal sequence research has developed sequence models [9] and access modes (e.g., stream-probe) [10] for accessing sequences. But our problem is different since for any tuple in one stream, there are no fixed corresponding tuple(s) in another stream. Therefore, we treat all joining streams equally in accessing and triggering operations. We cannot directly use many efficient algorithms developed for temporal join, such as RI-tree-based [11], partition-based [12,13], and index-based [14,15] algorithms, because media streams have very high arrival rates compared to typical relation updates. The construction overhead of these algorithms triggered by each tuple arrival may not be offset by the benefit of using them. Further, we studied event modelling and the related environment modelling issues in [16]. In this paper, we focus on stream processing techniques by utilizing temporal constraints and query semantics between related media and feature streams, particularly for the purpose of query optimizations.

1.2 Example

We use a typical live media query example for illustration throughout this paper. Consider a surveillance application in which both live video and audio are used to automatically detect potential intrusions. A video stream ($video1$) is captured by a camera and an audio stream ($audio2$) is produced by a microphone. If abnormal movements occur in $video1$ and abnormal sounds occur in $audio2$ at the same time, a possible intrusion is identified and the corresponding video frames should be displayed.

1.3 Outline

The rest of the paper is organized as follows. Section 2 discusses the modelling issues of media and feature streams. Section 3 presents the query techniques of our system, including query languages, stream operators, query execution, cost metrics and optimizations. A brief introduction of system implementation is introduced in Section 4. We run a number of real-time media stream queries and analyze the results in Section 5. Finally, we conclude our work and future research in Section 6.

2 Media and Feature Stream Model

2.1 Formal Definitions

Because of their continuous nature and the stream dependency, both media and feature elements require explicit and exact timestamps. The time attributes provide valuable information for the stream generating and query processing. In our framework, the element of a media or feature stream is defined as a *tuple*, which consists of a logical sequence number (sqno) indicating its position in a stream, a temporal extent defined by a pair of *start* and *end* timestamps (t_s, t_e] (for a time-point attribute $t_s = t_e$, a single time point is represented as t_d), and any other media or feature attribute. We give a series of conventions and definitions that make more precise the notions of media and feature streams.

Convention 1. *A sequence T, is said to be* ***continuously well-ordered*** *iff (1) T is well-ordered, and (2) for each time-unit $(t_{si}, t_{ei}]$, there must be one and only one directly following time-unit $(t_{si+1}, t_{ei+1}]$ in T, where $t_{ei} = t_{si+1}$. We refer to a continuously well-ordered set of time-units as a* ***continuous time set****. A corresponding tuple value holds in each time-unit.*

Convention 2. *A sequence T is said to be* ***discretely well-ordered*** *if and only if T is well-ordered, i.e., the continuity clause does not apply to two consecutive units. We refer to a discretely well-ordered set of time-points as a* ***discrete time set****. At each time-point t_d, a corresponding tuple value holds.*

Definition 1. *A* ***continuous media stream*** *is a sequence of tuples, each consists of a sequence number (m_{sqno}) uniquely identifying its position in stream, a pair of start and end timestamps $(t_s, t_e]$ whose domain is a continuous time set, and a media valued attribute v_m valid only during $(t_s, t_e]$.*

Definition 2. *A* ***discrete stream*** *is a sequence of tuples, each consists of a sequence number (m_{sqno}) uniquely identifying its position in stream, a media or non-media valued attribute v_m, and a time-point t_d, defined on a discrete time set domain, indicating when v_m arrives intermittently.*

Definition 3. *A* ***feature stream*** *is defined as a sequence of tuples, each consists of a sequence number (f_{sqno}) uniquely identifying its position in stream, a feature value attribute v_f, a time-point attribute t_f indicating when v_f is computed, and a set $\bar{m}_{sqno}$ identifying the media tuples or a set $\bar{f}_{sqno}$ identifying other feature tuples, from which a feature tuple is derived.*

For example, a pixel movement detection is derived from two consecutive video frames. Table 1 shows a feature tuple is derived from two media tuples of same media stream.

Table 1. A feature can be derived from two media tuples

$f_{sqno}(k)$	$v_f(k)$	$t_f(k)$	$m_{sqno}(i)$	$v_m(i)$	t_{bi}	t_{ei}
			$m_{sqno}(j)$	$v_m(j)$	t_{bj}	t_{ej}

Note the start and end time of a tuple are the *valid* time defined in temporal database. In particular, a feature tuple is an entity dependent on its deriving media tuple(s), and its value is *atomic* in that its semantics represents one aspect of all media tuples from which it is derived. Therefore, a feature tuple has a *representing interval* equal to the time-unit or set of time-units of its deriving media tuples. In the above example, the representing interval of $f_{sqno}(k)$ derived from $m_{sqno}(i)$ and $m_{sqno}(j)$ is $(t_{bi}, t_{ej}]$.

2.2 Special Querying Issues

A number of unique issues should be considered in designing a general data model for time-based media and feature streams.

Time Attributes and Order. Our definitions in previous section require explicit time attributes in both media and feature streams. Stream tuples are generated and queried not in isolation but in synchronization. Further, we assume all tuples in a stream are either continually well-ordered by intervals or discretely well-ordered by time-points. Note tuples from different streams may not be totally ordered, but partially ordered. For the presence of explicit time attributes, tuples in a relation produced from a stream by sliding window operators are also ordered in time, rather than a bag of unordered tuples. As we will present in later sections, the order of tuples is necessary to guarantee tuple continuity for queries over intervals.

Stream Uncertainties. Uncertainties exist in media stream capturing, feature stream generating and stream querying. Figure 1 shows a timing diagram of synchronization among related media and feature streams. The notations in the figure are defined as follows:

$t^R_{s(k)}$: The start timestamp of the k-th tuple in stream R.
$t^R_{e(k)}$: The end timestamp of the k-th tuple in stream R.
$T^R_{(k)}$: The interval of the k-th tuple in stream R.
$v^R_{(k)}$: The timestamp indicating when the k-th tuple in stream R is generated.
$D^{R,S}_{(k)}$: The generation delay of the k-th tuple in stream R which is derived from stream S.

In this paper, we assume a feature stream is derived from a single media stream and a tuple in a derived stream has the same sqno as its source tuple in a deriving stream, thus setting up the mapping between two streams. One the one hand, the intervals ($T^R_{(k)}$) of the deriving streams (e.g., media streams M and N) are variable. On the other hand, the generation delays ($D^{R,S}_{(k)}$) of tuples in the derived streams (e.g., feature streams X and Y) are not constant, which depend on the transmission delays and computation delays. In the extreme case, if a deriving tuple takes too long to generate its derived tuple, it might affect the following tuple(s). For example, the $(i+1)$-th tuple in stream N has to be skipped since it arrives before its previous tuple finishes the i-th feature tuple generation for stream Y. As a result, the derived tuples in feature stream Y are not continual. This non-determinism nature of media and feature streams must be addressed by query synchronization.

Query Synchronization. In most multimedia applications, especially for audio-visual applications, the synchronization between different media streams needs to be precise to satisfy perceptual continuity, when viewed by the human user. Synchronization is required not only in media composition but also in many other phases throughout the entire media stream query processing.

Live media query processing contains multiple sub-processings (threads), such as media capturing, feature generating and stream querying, thus forming a "producer - consumer" relation. Each consumer thread depends on the results of its producer thread(s). Because of the uncertainties of streams, specific operations performed on some tuples in a thread may cost longer than the expected times

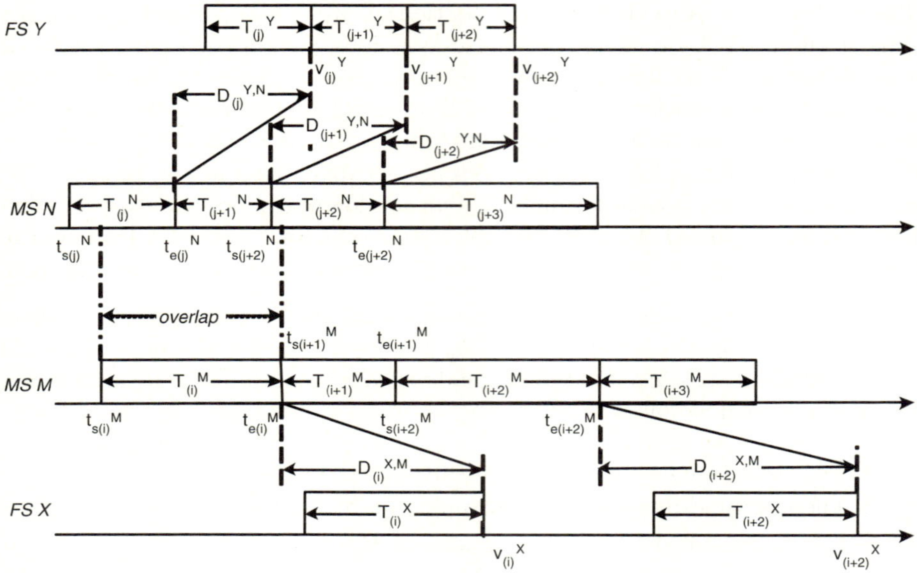

Fig. 1. A timing diagram of synchronization among media and feature streams

of both its producer and consumer threads. In order to preserve the continuity in stream tuple order, we can implement these threads through a *blocking approach*, i.e., a producer thread does not send new input to its consumer until the consumer finishes processing the previous input. By this way, we may slow down the data rate of the producer. An alternative is a *non-blocking approach*, i.e., to skip some inputs that cannot be processed by its consumer (e.g., the $(i+1)$-th tuple in stream N is skipped in Figure 1).

Due to the unbounded nature of streams, continuous queries over streams are often defined in terms of sliding windows, either tuple-based or time-based [8]. Nevertheless, such windows do not take the tuple intervals into account. In those applications, a tuple (e.g., temperature reading) is instant-based, rather than interval-based. This is not true for typical media stream tuples, and may have problems (e.g., false join) in joining tuples with non-overlapping intervals. A loose window including multiple non-overlapping tuples cannot satisfy the strict temporal join constraint for media or feature tuples from different streams. Instead, we require a more precise and strict metric to join them. We apply an overlap join (O_Join) TSJ_1 defined in [17]: *All participating tuples that satisfy the join condition share a common time point.* Tuples whose temporal attributes overlap in time have the *highest temporal relevance*, thus can be joined. Those non-temporal attributes of tuples can only be joined after satisfying the premise that the corresponding temporal attributes are overlapping in time. As shown in Figure 1, the i-th tuple in stream M can be overlap joined with three tuples in stream N, i.e., the j-th, $(j+1)$-th and $(j+2)$-th.

In a query plan involving more than one unsynchronized input streams, it is essential to decide which one(s) act as the trigger stream to execute the query plan. In general, we can make every input stream as the trigger such that each of their arrival tuple will trigger the query execution. By this way, the query delay may be reduced. However, as we show in later section, this is not absolutely true in all cases, due to the complex constraints and synchronization among related streams and threads. Instead, there are scenarios where a "master-slave" approach is preferred to reduce the overall query cost (including query delay, CPU, memory, etc), i.e., to select one input stream as the master stream triggering the query execution and treat all the other input streams as salve streams tuning to the master stream. In particular, this approach allows to reduce unnecessary high-cost feature tuple generations and the overall performance improvement is significant.

Stream Operator Complexities. The stream based operators are quite different from the traditional record based operators. In many cases, it is the responsibility of a stream operator to determine tuple(s) from deriving stream(s) as its input to generate the corresponding output tuple(s) at a specific time. In addition, the uncertainties of tuple arrival and tuple generation cost bring even more complexities to stream operators.

A feature stream is produced by one or more stream operators (called *transformers*) operating on one or multiple related media or other feature streams. Feature streams are complex in terms of tuple values, deriving media or feature streams, feature tuple interval semantics, and generation costs. Moreover, fragments from multiple media streams can be composed to form a media stream of a new format. In general, a stream operator should take N ($N \geq 1$) input (media or feature) stream(s) and generate a new stream of a format defined by users. Our definition of stream operator also applies to the standard query operators, such as selection, projection, join, etc.

The stream operator design and implementation depend on users' specific requirement. Due to the heterogeneity of media streams and different application needs, it is desirable for a querying system to be extendable to user-defined operators, i.e., the system allows users to design and implement their own transformers and plug codes into the querying system [18].

3 Query Processing

3.1 Media and Feature Stream Description Languages

We have designed a Media Stream Description Language (MSDL) and a a Feature Stream Description Language (FSDL) for media stream capturing and feature stream generating [7]. In our example, there are two media streams. First, *video*1 is captured from a webcam connected to a local port (vfw://0) with a data rate of 10 frames per second (FPS):

```
create type frame { integer frame_num primary key,
            time frame_st, time frame_et, image content };
create media stream video1 of frame from
            sensortype cam sensorsource vfw://0 datarate 10.0;
```

Second, *audio*2 is captured from a local port (dsound://) with audio clip buffer size of 40ms:

```
create type audioclip { integer clip_num primary key,
            time clip_st, time clip_et, audiobuffer clip };
create media stream audio2 of audioclip from
            sensortype mic sensorsource dsound:// capturebuffersize 40;
```

Different media streams may have different sensor-dependent initialization parameters. For example, *video*1 is defined with a data rate, while *audio*2 is defined with a clip buffer size.

Further, we can generate one movement detection feature stream from *video*1 and a sound detection feature stream from *audio*2:

```
create type mvFeature { integer mv_sn primary key,
            time mv_bt, time mv_et, integer mv_pixel };
create feature stream mvFStream1 of mvFeature on video1
with   mv_sn:=getFrameNum(frame_num)
       mv_bt:=getFrameTime(frame_bt)
       mv_et:=getFrameTime(frame_et)
       mv_pixel:=getMovementNum(content);

create type sdFeature { integer sd_sn primary key,
            time sd_bt, time sd_et, double sd_energy };
create feature stream sdFStream3 of sdFeature on audio2
with   sd_sn:=getFrameNum(clip_num)
       sd_bt:=getFrameTime(clip_bt)
       sd_et:=getFrameTime(clip_et)
       sd_energy:=getSoundEnergy(clip);
```

Note any feature tuple in both feature streams is derived from a single media tuple of the deriving media stream.

3.2 Query Expression

We also designed a query language, MF-CQL [16], extended from CQL [19]. Our query example can be issued as:

Query 1. Select content From video1, mvFStream1, audio2, sdFStream3 Where mv_pixel > 5000 And sd_energy > 32.0;

The logical query plan is shown in Figure 2, where:

mv: Movement feature transformer for video;
sd: Sound feature transformer for audio;
FSel: Selection operator for feature stream;
Proj$_X$: Projection operator filtering out attribute(s) X;
MFetch: Map operator fetching media tuples via corresponding feature tuples;
Fbi-Join: Binary overlap join operator for two feature streams.

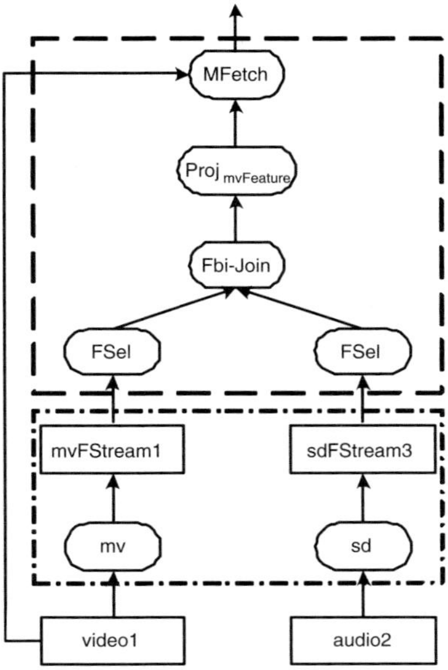

Fig. 2. Query plan example

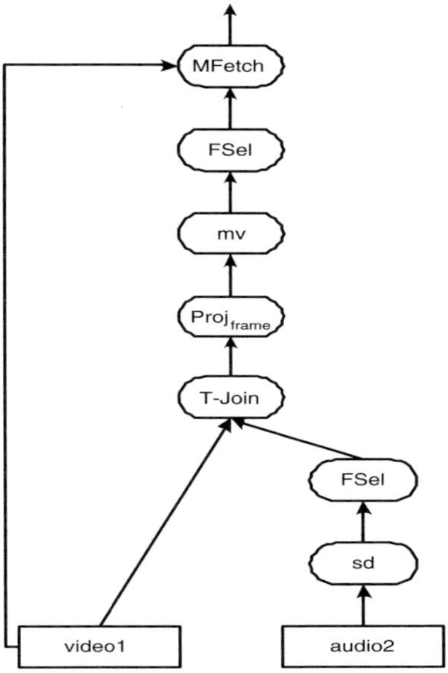

Fig. 3. Optimized query plan

3.3 Cost Model for Operators

Queue length for MFetch. A MFetch operator is used to inactively pull the buffered tuple(s) in its queue at a time, triggered by the corresponding feature tuple(s). The queue length for a stream R at time t is:

$$L_Q(t) = \int_{t-D(t)}^{t} \lambda_R(\tau)\, d\tau, \tag{1}$$

where t is the time when a target tuple is retrieved, and $D(t)$ denotes the delay from the arrival time of the target tuple to t. Note our implementation maintains a common media/feature tuple queue for each media/feature stream, and sets a queue length to maximum satisfying all MFetch operators associated with a given media stream.

O_Join Cost. A traditional, cardinality-based cost model is incapable of producing cost estimates of join over unbounded streams, and a unit-time basis cost model as a new metric should be proposed [20].

Table 2. Notation for cost

Notation	Description
N_{comp}	Comparing number for pairing two tuples
C_{comp}	Unit cost of one comparison
$\lambda_X(t)$	Arrival rate of stream X at time t
$N_{X,Y}(t)$	Number of tuples in stream Y to be paired by a tuple in X at time t

The selection of temporal attributes used in O_Join (including T-Join) depends on the types of joining streams in a join query:

Case(1): If the O_Join operates on two feature streams derived from a same media stream, the comparing attribute is *sqno*, thus $N_{comp} = 1$;
Case(2): Otherwise, the comparing attributes are both the *start* and *end* timestamps of interval, thus $N_{comp} = 2$.

A unit-time based cost formula of O_join between streams R and S during period $[t_1, t_2]$ is:

$$C_{R\bowtie S}(t1, t2) = \frac{C_{comp} \times N_{comp}}{t2 - t1} \times \int_{t1}^{t2} [\lambda_R(t) N_{R,S}(t) + \lambda_S(t) N_{S,R}(t)]\, dt, (t2 > t1). \quad (2)$$

The cost of O_m*_Join* operator joining m $(m > 2)$ streams is:

$$C_{\bowtie m}(t1, t2) = \frac{2C_{comp}}{t2 - t1} \times \int_{t1}^{t2} \sum_{i=1}^{m} \sum_{\substack{j=1 \\ j \neq i}}^{m} \lambda_{S_i}(t) N_{S_i,S_j}(t)\, dt. \quad (3)$$

Query Delay. For one qualified tuple in a media stream, its query delay is defined as the time difference between it enters the system and it leaves the topmost operator. Query delay is both media stream dependent and individual tuple dependent, because (1) different media tuples have different tuple extents and *feature computation delays* (FCDs); (2) a particular media tuple may be joined with multiple tuples from other streams; thus (3) different tuples in one stream joined with a common tuple in another stream may have different delays.

3.4 Query Optimization

By utilizing the temporal constraints and query semantics among media and the derived stream streams, we can apply a number of optimizations.

Reverse Order in O_Join. According to equations (2) and (3), we should minimize the number (NX,Y(t)) of tuples to be paired to reduce the join cost. The ordering nature of sqno and interval timestamps provides optimizations for join operator. The O_Join is a merge scan join by using the ordered sqnos and interval timestamps. This is similar to Temporal Equijoin (TEJ-1) algorithm [21]. Rather than using ascending order in TEJ-1, our implementation takes the descending order, because each new arrival tuple (i.e., trigger tuple) has the latest sqno and timestamp. We pair it with every tuple in the other stream queue from rear to front, i.e., in a reverse order, and terminate pairing at the first tuple that can not be overlap joined in time; thus we minimize the comparison number.

Push Down T-Join. The query plan shown in Figure 2 has two sub-processes – the feature generating and the stream querying. One problem of this approach is that the feature generating thread always runs and is independent of the following querying thread, i.e., whether a feature tuple is really used or not in the querying subprocess, it is always computed. According to our experiments, the feature computation cost (in terms of delay, CPU and memory) is the most significant factor in overall query cost. Nevertheless, the temporal constraints between related streams, together with application semantics, provide optimization opportunities in many scenarios. In our example, The sound feature generation costs much lower than the movement feature generation. The movement feature is only necessary when the predicate of sound feature is qualified (normally only in a small portion of time the abnormal sound is detected). Upon these observations, we develop a optimization rule by using T-Join (a special form of O_Join only joining on time attributes) as follows:

Rule 1. *Push down temporal join* (T-Join)*:*
Proj_f (Sel(FeatTran(R)) Fbi-Join S) =Sel(FeatTran(Proj_m(R T-Join S))), *where* FeatTran *is the feature transformer from media stream R of type m to feature type f, and S is another join (media or feature) stream.*

The rule implies that other operators are processed after applying temporal join operator T-Join first to reduce the number of unnecessary operations, especially the high-cost feature generations. This rule is especially useful in the cases where one feature transformer is expensive while another one is much cheaper. We apply this rule to our example and have an optimized logical query plan shown as Figure 3.

3.5 Query Execution

Figure 3 shows there is no explicit feature stream generating thread. Insteand, the feature generation operators are integrated into the stream query processing thread. This integration not only simplifies issuing queries (i.e., reducing the declaration of feature stream generation), more important, it allows performing optimizations covering every phase of media stream querying in a unifying way.

Note the node of *video*1 can be split into two node instances (i.e., creating two pointers to same memory address); thus we get a tree structured query plan, called *transformation tree* (TT). By taking a post-order serialization, we can get a *serialized transformation tree* (STT) consisting of tree types of nodes:

Data node: It is an input stream and a leaf node of TT. It has a queue buffering tuples at this node at a time.

Transformer node: It is one of the various operators inside TT. It takes one or multiple data nodes as input and produces a new data node of any format.

Number node: It is the number N ($N \geq 1$) of data nodes that a transformer node takes as input.

For example, the STT of Figure 3 is serialized as:

Ex1:

@video1, @video1, @audio2, \$sd, #1, \$$\mathsf{Sel}_{sd}$, #1, \$T-Join, #2, \$$\mathsf{Proj}_{mv}$, #1, \$mv, #1, \$$\mathsf{Sel}_{mv}$, #1, \$MFetch, #2;

where @, $ and # are the token symbols used in our query parser indicating the data node, transformer node and number node, respectively.

The algorithm to execute the STT is:

```
List SST = makeCopy(SST0);  // make a new instance for each run
while (SST is not empty)
    Node node = STT.getFirstNode(); //will remove node from SST
    if (node is a DataNode)
        DataNode dataNode = (DataNode) node
        stack.push(dataNode);
     else  //must be a Transformer Node
        TranNode tranNode = (TranNode) node;
        Node node1 = STT.getFirstNode(); //must be a Number Node
        int num = ((NumNode) node1).intValue();
        DataNode dataNode_im = new DataNode(); //intermediate result
        for (int = 1 to num)   // get num Data Nodes
            Node node2 = stack.pop();
            inputDataList.add((DataNode)node2);
        dataNode_im = TranExec(tranNode, inputDataList); //transform
        stack.push(dataNode_im);
DataNode result = (DataNode) stack.pop();
```

By default, every new arriving tuple in *video*1 or *audio*2 can trigger the query plan. We notice *video*1 is a direct child of T-Join. A fact is that if there is no tuple available in the queue of *audio*2 at a time, it is unnecessary for a new arriving *video*1 tuple to trigger the query plan, since the T-Join will not produce any output at this time. Therefore, a "master-slave" approach is preferred to reduce the number of triggering streams. Only *audio*2's new arriving tuples need to trigger the query plan, and *video*1's tuples just wait in queue for being processed by T-Join when triggered by *audio*2.

4 Implementation

The prototype of MedSMan is implemented using Java (JDK 1.5.0). We use APIs provided by Java Media Framework (JMF2.1.1) and OpenCV (integrated with the Java based query engine via Java Native Interface (JNI)) for real-time audio/video capturing and feature generating. The stream description and query languages are implemented using Java Compiler Compiler (JavaCC).

Our implementation consists of two major components, including media/feature stream generation [7] and stream querying execution. The former permits a designer to directly capture various live data streams from different sensor devices, and form media streams consisting of logical media tuples. Then, more meaningful feature streams can be automatically derived from media streams for the query purpose. Stream queries are parsed and generate physical query plans. MedSMan runs physical plans using an individual tuple triggering approach for media and feature stream query execution, thus reduces query delays. The query execution of the two sub-processes approach (see Figure 2) is presented in [16].

We implement the SST algorithm and provide an open system which enables users to design, implement and upload special operator codes fulfilling their application requirements. These codes are dynamically loaded at run-time [18]. This goal is achieved by using Java's dynamic class loader capabilities. In addition, we also support a language structure allowing users to specify the master stream in the join query for query optimizations. More important, by integrating a set of related individual operators and using our SST algorithm, users can design "super" operators that can take multiple media streams of any formats as input and perform the special transformation or query functionalities.

5 Experiments and Analysis

We run a number of query examples on multiple live media and feature streams, and evaluate performances for two different implementing approaches. We investigate FCDs, query delays, tuple queue and optimization effects. Our experiments run on a XP machine with dual $2.4GHz$ CPUs and $2GB$ RAM.

5.1 Blocking Approach

We begin with the blocking approach which creates a strict "producer-consumer" relationship among media capturing thread, feature generating thread and stream querying thread. We examine the FCDs and their impacts on the deriving media streams. With the media and feature stream defined in Section 3.1, we issue two examples performing single feature queries as follows:

Query 2. Select content From video1, mvFStream1 Where mv_pixel > 5000;

Query 3. Select clip From audio2, sdFStream3 Where sd_energy > 32;

The average frame interval, FCD(mv) and query delay for Query 2 are 204.2 ms, 199.7 ms and 463.3 ms, respectively. Figure 4 (a) shows they vary with the video frame number. The average interval is much greater than the expected value, i.e., 100 ms, since we use the blocking approach and the average FCD(mv) is greater than the expected data rate of *video*1. The video thread only produce a new frame after the previous one is computed by the mv transformer. As a result, the total query delay is accumulated and significant. In Query 3, the average clip interval, FCD(sd) and query delay are 39.99 ms, 5.89 ms and 9.11 ms, respectively. These metrics are much better than those of Query 2, because the average FCD(sd) is quite small compared to its audio clip interval (i.e., 40 ms), although there are a few big jitters as shown in Figure 4 (b).

Then, we perform Query 1 which joins two feature streams derived from two different media streams. Figure 5 (a) shows the query delays for each video frame and each audio clip. Note one video frame overlaps with multiple sequential audio clips (similarly, one audio clip may overlaps with one or two video frames).

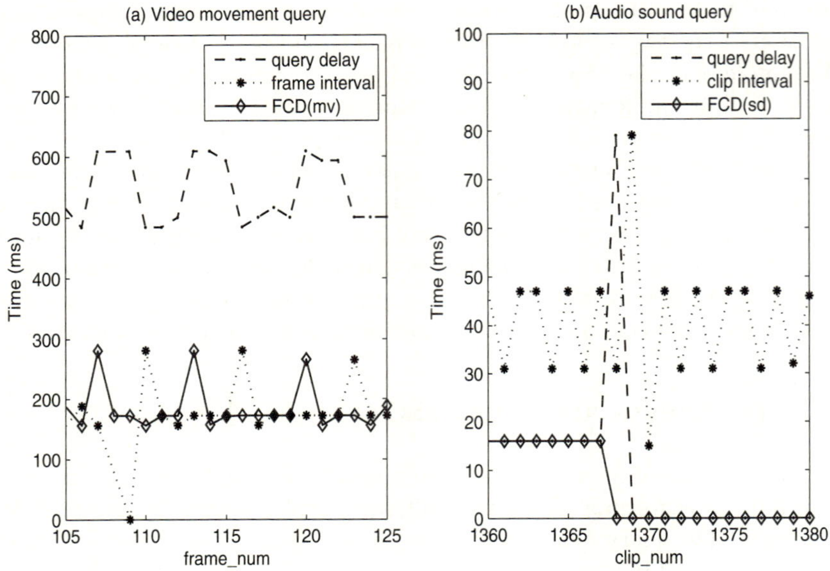

Fig. 4. Performances of single media single feature queries

The average delay of the video frames is 393.1 *ms*, and the average *max* delay of the audio clips is 622.5 *ms* for the oldest one waiting in queue, since an optimization is implemented by making a slower feature (i.e., mvFestream1) tuple trigger the faster feature (i.e., sdFStream3) tuples waiting in queue, in order to remove an unnecessary trigger stream. Figure 5 (b) shows the varying length of sdFStream3's queue with an average of 13.9, which indicates the necessary size of buffering memory of *audio*2 for this query.

The above experiments and results show FCDs play a significant role in determining dynamic tuple intervals and total query delays. However, we can utilize the temporal constraints and query semantics between streams to reduce the number of unnecessary feature generations, thus improve the overall performance.

5.2 Non-blocking Approach

We perform Query 1 by executing the serialized tree expressed in Ex1 through the non-blocking approach. In addition, we indicate *audio*2 as the master stream for the purpose of optimization. We are interested in the performance of T-Join operator which plays a key role in the query execution and optimization. In order to avoid the outside performance affects from other operators, we assume the selectivities of both Sel_{mv} and Sel_{sd} are 1. An important metric discussed here is the *selectivity*(*video*1), i.e., M/N, where M and N are the number of frames entering and leaving the query plan tree, respectively. T-Join determines this metric value when assuming the selectivities of related selection operators as 1.

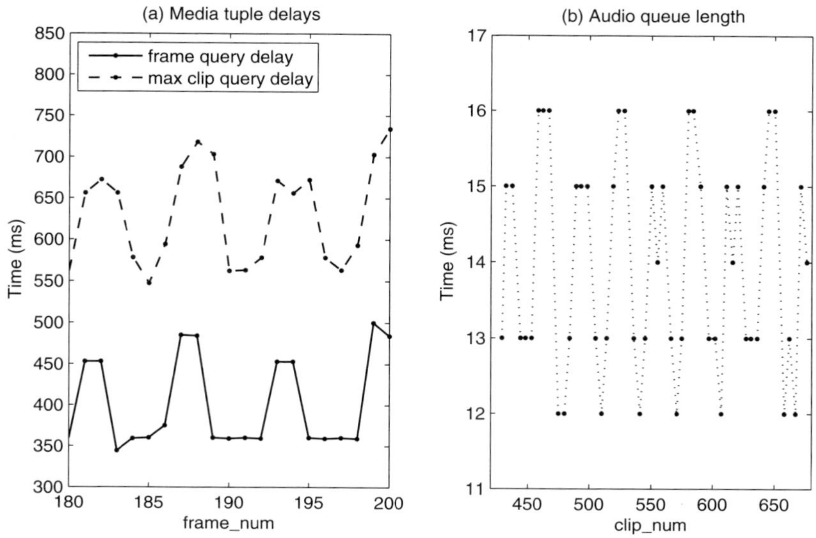

Fig. 5. Performances of video and audio join query

Besides, we define an output window W_{T-Join}, which is the maximum number of tuples that T-Join can output at a time. This metric implies that if the T-Join produces more than W_{T-Join} tuples, only the latest W_{T-Join} tuples are output and the other earlier tuples are skipped. The necessity of W_{T-Join} is explained as follows.

From Figure 3, the qualified M ($M \geq 1$) tuples out of T-Join are projected and then sent to feature transformer mv, which performs the feature generation for every tuple. If FCD(mv) is greater than the expected frame interval or M is large, mv will be a blocking operator which blocks the entire query plan execution for a period of $SUM_{FCD} = \sum_{i=1}^{M} FCD_i$. During a blocking period, *video*1's new arriving tuples are buffered in queue but not processed. However, if SUM_{FCD} is too large, the new tuples will replace the old ones in *video*1's queue, since the size of the queue is limited. As a result, the following M_Fetch operator cannot retrieve the deriving media tuple which is required by a qualified but seriously delayed feature tuple.

As shown in Figure 6 (a), SUM_{FCD} increases linearly as W_{T-Join} increases, so does the query delay. Figure 6 (b) shows the frame interval and FCD(mv) do not change much with W_{T-Join}. The selectivity of *video*1 reaches the climax about 0.38 with $W_{T-Join} = 13$ as shown in (c). After that, it drops dramatically and jumps to 0 after W_{T-Join} is greater 17, because we set the size of *video*1's queue as 50 and the average frame interval is about 97 ms. This implies that a query delay greater than 4850 ms will make the qualified feature tuple fail to fetch its deriving media tuple, which has been dequeued. Note all the metrics in Figure 6 are average values.

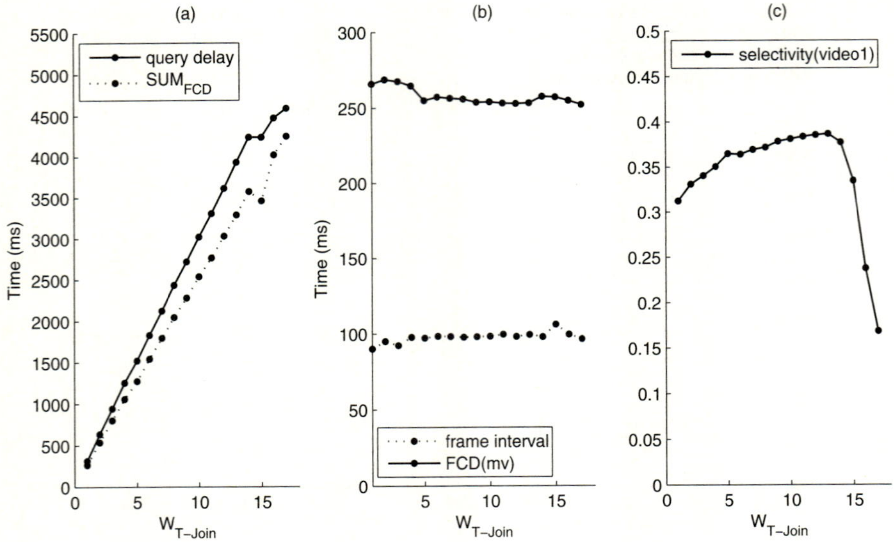

Fig. 6. Performance affects of W_{T-Join}

Figure 7 shows which portions of the original video frames sequences are queried out by choosing different W_{T-Join}. Obviously, in case of $W_{T-Join} = 1$, the output frames are the most evenly distributed and the query delay is minimal (314.8 ms). As W_{T-Join} increases, the selectivity may not reduce and may even increase a little (before reaching the climax), but the output tuples are not evenly distributed, which is not preferred in an application where allocating system resource to monitor evenly across time is important. Moreover, the query delays also increase linearly.

The average number of media tuples getting queried in a unit period by using non-blocking approach may not be greater than that of using the blocking approach (e.g., the ratio of the former to the latter is 70% when W_{T-Join}=1). However, this only holds when assuming the selectivities of related selection as 1, which is not true in typical queries and forces the mv transformer to work in the worst blocking status. In actual cases, SUM_{FCD} is much less; thus the non-blocking approach works more efficiently. Further, the non-blocking approach does not delay the media stream capturing thread. This implies the media signal sampling resolution is not degraded; thus more media tuples have chances to be captured and then queried. This approach also makes the capturing thread independent of querying thread. This is essential when multiple queries share a common media stream. In addition, the average query delay is smaller when setting W_{T-Join} as 1. The optimal value of W_{T-Join} depends on the actual selectivities of related selection operators, the tuple intervals of joining media streams, and the FCDs of feature streams.

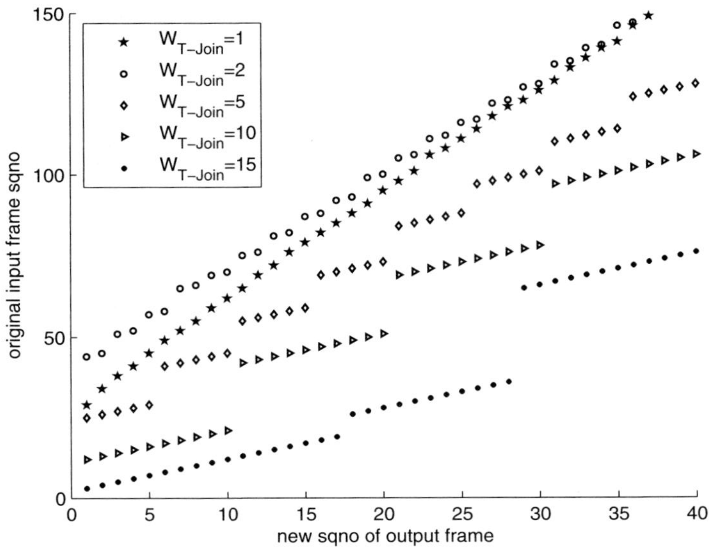

Fig. 7. Temporal distributions of output tuples

6 Conclusion and Future Work

This paper presents our approach to dealing with continuous querying over live heterogeneous media streams by effectively combining extendible digital processing techniques with a general media stream management system. A number of distinct issues in modelling media stream are investigated. By utilizing the coherent temporal constraints, as well as query semantics, of media streams and the derived feature streams, we can design efficient stream operators and query execution algorithm for live media and feature stream querying. We analyze the cost metrics of media stream querying and introduce several optimizations. One additional advantage of our system implementation is its openness for users to design, implement and plug their own operators into our system. A number of experiments are run over live media stream queries by using both blocking and unblocking implementations. We also discuss the metrics and performances of our system.

In the near future, we will investigate scalability issues, sharing of multiple queries, and more complex features derived from multiple media or existing feature streams out of a large number of distributed sensors. We also plan to investigate other factors, such as media transmission delays and compression/decompression, that may affect system performance.

References

1. Liu, L., Pu, C., Tang, W.: Continual queries for internet scale event-driven information delivery. IEEE Transactions on Knowledge and Data Engineering **11**(4) (1999) 610–628

2. Chen, J., DeWitt, D.J., Tian, F., Wang, Y.: Niagaracq: a scalable continuous query system for internet databases. In: International Conference on Management of Data, Dallas, Texas (2000) 379 – 390
3. Abadi, D., Carney, D., Cetintemel, U., et al.: Aurora: A new model and architecture for data stream management. VLDB Journal **12**(2) (2003) 120–139
4. Madden, S., Shah, M., Hellerstein, J.M., Raman, V.: Continously adaptive continous queries over streams. In: ACM SIGMOD International Conference on Management of Data, Madison,Wisconsin (2002)
5. Bonnet, P., Gehrke, J., Seshadri, P.: Towards sensor database systems. In: Proc. 2nd Int. Conf. on Mobile Data Management. (2001) 3–14
6. Babcock, B., Babu, S., Datar, M., Motwani, R., Widom, J.: Models and issues in data stream systems. In: Symposium on Principles of Database Systems, Madison,Wisconsin (2002) 1–16
7. Liu, B., Gupta, A., Jain, R.: A live multimedia stream querying system. In: Proceedings of the 2nd international workshop on Computer Vision Meets Databases. (2005) 35–42
8. Golab, L., Ozsu, M.T.: Issues in data stream management. ACM SIGMOD Record **32**(2) (2003) 5–14
9. Seshadri, P., Livny, M., Ramakrishnan, R.: Seq: A model for sequence databases. ICDE (1995) 232–239
10. Seshadri, P., Livny, M., Ramakrishnan, R.: Sequence query processing. ACM SIGMOD (1994) 430–441
11. Enderle, J., Hampel, M., Seidl, T.: Joining interval data in relational databases. In: Proc. ACM SIGMOD. (2004)
12. Soo, M.D., Snodgrass, R.T., Jensen, C.S.: Efficient evaluation of the valid-time natural join. ICDE (1994) 282–292
13. Lu, H., Ooi, B.C., Tan, K.L.: On spatially partitioned temporal join. VLDB (1994) 546–557
14. Beckmann, N., Kriegel, H.P., Schneider, R., Seeger, B.: The R*-Tree: An efficient and robust access method for points and rectangles. In: SIGMOD Conference. (1990) 322–331
15. Elmasri, R., Wuu, G.T.J., Kim, Y.J.: The time index: An access structure for temporal data. VLDB (1990) 1–12
16. Liu, B., Gupta, A., Jain, R.: Medsman: a streaming data management system over live multimedia. In: Proceedings of the 13th annual ACM international conference on Multimedia. (2005) 171–180
17. Tansel, A.U., Clifford, J., Gadia, S.K., Segev, A., Snodgrass, R.T.: Temporal Databases: Theory, Design, and Implementation. Benjamin/Cummings (1993)
18. Ramachandran, U., Lillethun, D., Liu, B., Nakazawa, J., Hilley, D., Horrigan, S., Cooper, B.: Mediabroker++: A platform for applications in a dynamic pervasive environment. Submitted to International Conference on Distributed Computing Systems (2005)
19. Arasu, A., Babu, S., Widom, J.: The cql continuous query language: Semantic foundations and query execution. Technical report, Stanford University (2003)
20. Kang, J., Naughton, J.F., Viglas, S.D.: Evaluating window joins over unbounded streams. Proc. of the 2003 Intl. Conf. on Data Engineering (2003)
21. Gunadhi, H., Segev, A.: Query processing algorithms for temporal intersection joins. ICDE (1991) 336–344

Summa Contra Ontologiam

Simone Santini

Escuela Politécnica Superior
Universidad Autónoma de Madrid, Madrid, Spain
and University of California, San Diego, USA

Abstract. This paper is a critical analysis of the concept of ontology thus as it is used in contemporary computing science. It identifies three main problems with such a concept, two of which are intrinsic to it and one of which is extrinsic, so to speak, being related to the use that of ontology is made in applications.

The first problem with ontology is that the only accepted definition of its main artifact is teleological rather than structural as it would be proper in computing science. The second problem is that claiming that ontology is in any way a semantic discipline requires such a limited and outdated notion of semantic to be to all practical purposes useless. The third and final problem is that the limitations and misconceptions of ontology might make it a limiting factor, rather than a help, for many of the applications for which it is sought.

The article concludes that a profound reconsideration of the relation between computers and semantics might be overdue.

1 Introduction

The purpose of this paper (the lifting-cum-paraphrase of whose title I hope St. Thomas Aquinas will forgive) is to analyze the foundations and the value (in a rather broad sense) of what today is commonly known, among researchers and practicioners of information systems, as *ontology*. I will make three arguments: the first two will be endemic to computing science, while the third will be of a broader nature, touching upon the relation between the ontological offering of computing science and the disciplines to which the offer is made. Of the two endemic arguments, the first will be of a formal nature, viz. the investigation of an acceptable definition of ontology, while the second is of a more theoretical nature, so to speak, in that it deals with the common assumption that ontology can be used to formally specify the *semantics* of a certain domain of discourse. This division can be seen, *mutatis mutandi*, as a mirror of the linguistic division into which ontology would locate itself: the first section (the one on the definition of ontology) deals with its *syntax*; the second section deals with the *semantics* of ontology, and the third with the way ontology is applied in disciplines outside of computing science, that is, it deals with the *pragmatics* of ontology. The parallel with the three traditional levels of linguistics should not be taken too seriously, of course, but it should be located somewhere between the general guideline and the pure *divertissement*.

Before taking on these subjects, however, I should like to take a little space to settle, once and for all, a terminological matter. The word ontology originates in metaphysics where it is, according to the *Britannica*,

T. Grust et al. (Eds.): EDBT 2006 Workshops, LNCS 4254, pp. 483–496, 2006.

the study of being as such, i.e. of the basic characteristics of all reality.

Ontology, as defined in metaphysics, is the study of *being*, not of *beings*: it is not a taxonomy of existing things and consequently, for instance, Linneus never claimed to be doing ontology (and quite correctly so). It is true that John Scot's *De divisionis Naturae* is generally regarded as an ontological work, but this is due to its Platonic assumption of the universals as the only reality, and not to the taxonomical structure of the work per se. The word ends with the suffix *-logy* and, due to the programmatic rather than methodological connotation of the suffix in this case, it has no plural: there are no different studies of being as such, but any way of studying it is part of the same discipline of ontology. The Oxford English Dictionary, quite correctly, doesn't report any plural for the word ontology.

In computing, the word ontology is used with two different connotations: as a discipline and as the artifacts that the discipline produces. While the term ontology is usable (by an admittedly rather daring metaphorical extension) in the first case, as a name for the artifact it is clearly improper: a better name in this case would be *ontonomy* (plural *ontonomies*)[1]. In this paper, I will keep the distinction and refer to the discipline as ontology and to the artifact as ontonomy.

Some readers might see into all this the expression of too fine a pont, an empty pseudo-intellectualistic annoyance, but I disagree quite emphatically with any such assessment: computing is a mathematical discipline, and precision in the terms that one uses is of the greatest importance for it, the unwanted connotations of a term often leading to confusion. Since confusion is precisely what I ascribe the existence of computational ontology to, it is important to try to avoid falling into easy connotational pitfalls, the risk of pedantry being in any case preferrable to that of imprecision.

2 Syntactic Definition of Ontology

Given the importance that these days is ascribed to ontology in many areas of information management, it is surprisingly hard to come across a mathematically acceptable definition of the discipline or of its artifacts. The most common definition or, at least, the one that I hear around the most, is along the following lines:

an ontology is a formalization of a conceptualization.

The most quoted source of this definition appears to be [7], but the definition is widely accepted (see [12,2], for example). The problems of this definition are of several orders, and I will consider some of them in a short while but, for the moment, I would like to concentrate on the *functional* nature of it: this definition doesn't tell us what an

[1] Quite surprisingly (to me, at least), this is not a neologism. The term was used in 1803 by J. Stewart in his *Opus Maximum* as more or less as synonym of ontology. Given its derivation from $o\nu\tau o\varsigma$, (present participle of *to be*) and $\nu o\mu\iota\alpha$, (*distribution, arrangement*), I think that my connotation is better than Stewart's. A more appropriate name, with less metaphysical baggage, would be (from $o\iota\kappa o\varsigma$, *household*) the word *economy* but, as the readers undoubtedly know, the term is already used for an altogether different discipline.

ontology *is* but, rather, what it is (generally) used for. This kind of definition is of course unacceptable in computing science.

Consider, as a parallel, the definition of formal grammar: if researchers in programming languages had used the same criteria of rigor (or lack thereof) as researchers in ontology, the definition would sound something such as:

> a formal grammar is the specification of a programming language.

But this is unacceptable: for one thing, while computing scientists do use formal grammars in order to formalize programming languges, there is no reason why this should be their only use. Linguists (at least those adhering to the Chomskyan current of the Anglo-American philosophy of language) use it to describe parts of natural language, and there is no reason why other uses should not be found. Finding new uses will not change the nature of the artifact, but will invalidate functional definitions such as the one given above. A functional definition describes the use of an artifact, but it doesn't specify its nature and structure, how we can identify it: given an arbitrary string of symbols, a definition should allow one to determine whether the string is a formal grammar or not. To this end, a *structural* definition is necessary. In the case of formal grammar, the definition is the well known one: a formal grammar is a 4-tuple (N, T, S, P), where N is a finite set (called the set of non-terminals), T is a finite set, disjoint from N (called the set of terminals), etc.

With this definition, one can proceed to define the language recognized by the grammar, and its properties. In the case of ontology, with very few exceptions, a structural definition is not provided: researchers are building a huge edifice on a formal structure without knowing what that structure is. Artificial intelligence does indeed have a definition of ontonomies but, in that case, an ontonomy is defined as the collection of all symbols used in a logic system, with the indication of which names are functions, which are predicates, and which are constants [10]. There is nothing wrong with this definition, but it certainly bears little resemblance to what the information system ontologists are doing. In particular, this definition doesn't include any relation between the terms and doesn't lay any semantic claim.

* * *

Many researchers in information systems are blissfully unaware of the fact that they are building such an enormous edifice on such weak foundations, but not all. One interesting attempt at a formal foundation of ontology has been made by Guarino [8]. Guarino's starting point is the notion of *intensional relation*. Consider a relation such as $[\text{above}](x, y)$ (which contains all pairs x, y such that x is above y). One can consider a set of objects, say a, b, c, and d, and create a relation, say

$$[\text{above}] = \{(a, b), (a, d), (b, d)\}, \tag{1}$$

which states that a is above b and d, and b is above d. This definition makes the concept "above" dependent on the specific configuration of a, b, c, and d: if b were above a, instead of a being above b, the relation would change. This extensional notion of "aboveness" is in this sense unsatisfactory: the *concept* of one thing being above another should be independent of the particular world configuration that we are analyzing. Guarino solves this insufficiency by introducing the notion of *intensional relation*.

Let D be a set of elements. An n-ary relation on D is a subset of D^n and therefore 2^{D^n} is the set of all n-ary relations on D. Let W be a set of worlds, that is, *grosso modo*, a set of legal configurations of the elements of D. An intensional relation r is an assignment, to each possible world in W, of a relation (n-ary, in this example) on D, that is, an intensional relation is a function

$$r : W \rightarrow 2^{D^n} . \tag{2}$$

So, given a world w in which a is above b and nothing else is above anything, we would have

$$[\text{above}](w) = \{(a, b)\} . \tag{3}$$

Given a logical language $L(V)$ built on a vocabulary V, an extensional model for $L(V)$ is a pair (D, R)—where D is a set, and R a set of relations on D—such that V can be mapped to D and predicates of L to elements of R. Similarly to this standard definition, Guarino defines an intensional model for a language by replacing R with a set of intensional relations. An intensional model for $L(V)$ can be seen then as a function that maps any possible world w to an extensional model relative to that world.

This intensional interpretation of a language is also called an *ontological commitment*. An ontonomy (my term, of course, not Guarino's) is then defined as follows:

> Given a language L, with ontological commitment K, an [ontonomy] for L is a set of axioms designed in a way such that the set of its models approximates as best as possible the set of intended models of L according to K ([8])

There are three ways in which this definition is unsatisfactory, at least as a computing science theory (some points of the definition have a certain philosophical interest, but this is besides the point in a computing milieu).

Firstly, the notion of intensional relation is in some way related to the Kripkean notion of possible worlds, but with some important distinguo. In Kripke, possible worlds are formal models indexed by a variable that corresponds to a degree of modality. A predicate is true (false) in a world depending on what it predicates about the extensional relation existing in the model corresponding to the degree of modality of that world. Extensional relations are what determine the essence of the world and, therefore, what determines the structure of a model.

In the case of ontology, however, we have to resort to the notion of possible worlds in order to define extensional relations, which implies that extensional relations can't be expressed in the world (if they were, the extensional relations would be logically prior to the intensional, and the latter could not be used to define the former). But, if this is the case, no possible world can have any structure, and not only can't they be used as a model in the Kripkean sense, but they can't even induce an extensional relation.

To put it in a different way: given a formal world of blocks, in order to instantiate the extensional relation [above], one needs to know whether block a is above block b; but the only way in which this can be known is to check whether $(a, b) \in$ [above]: the worlds, that one needs in order to define the intensional relation, can only have structure by virtue of the extensional relations that the intensional ones are supposed to define. We are stuck in the middle of a circular argument. All this does not imply that intensional relations do not exist, but it does imply that, whetever they are, they are not a function from worlds to extensional relations, as the model requires.

Secondly, an ontology is defined as a system of axioms that defines (approximately, but this will be my third point) the set of models of a language L. On one hand, this definition leaves one with the complete freedom to choose the logic system in which these axioms are drawn while, on the other hand, it makes an ontonomy dependent on the choice of the language L. Given this latitude, it is not clear whether this definition defines anything worth defining. In order to dispense with the dependency on the language L (which runs quite against the common notion of ontonomy), one could say that an ontonomy is a system of axioms for which there is a language L such the axioms define the same set of models as the ontological commitment of L. But, presumably, for all non-contradictory set of axioms it is possible to define such a language so the definition would reduce simply to the statement that an ontonomy is any set of statement in any formal language. Such a definition is formally correct, but it is also so generic as to be of no use.

Thirdly, we have the presence of the word "approximates." With this addendum, any system of statements that admits at least one model that is also a model for a language L is an ontonomy for L. If we abstract from the language, then any set of statements that admits at least a model is an ontonomy. In particular, any set of tautologies is an ontology. Allowing for approximation, in other words, worsens the problem considered in the previous point: the definition is formally consistent, but too broad to be of any use: many things, from a C program to a very well structured grocery list, to a tax return form would qualify.

To this, one should add that Guarino's definition is not innocent of functionalism: given a set of statements in a certain logic system the only thing that makes them into an ontonomy is their intended use: if the statements are used to provide models consistent with an ontological commitment, then they form an ontonomy, otherwise they don't. This is not a *structural* definition of the type that computing science seeks. To come back to my previous example, given the definition of a grammar, and an arbitrary string, then one can decide whether the string is a grammar based on structural considerations only, even if one doesn't know that grammars are used to specify languages. The definition is structural and, in a sense, *closed:* it can be checked by making reference to the definition alone, without any teleological consideration. With Guarino's definition of ontonomy such a possibility does not exist.

* * *

A formally correct, structural definition of ontonomy that has been proposed in the literature is based on the algebraic theory of abstract data type, in particular on the notion of sub-typing. The theory has been proposed, e.g. by Bench-Capon and Malcom in [1], and its theoretical presupposition are in Goguen and Meseguer's *order-sorted algebras* [6]. An order-sorted algebra is a multi-sorted algebra $(\Omega, (A_\alpha | \alpha \in S))$ where the set of sorts S is endowed with a partial order relation called the *sub-sort* relation. Given a partially ordered set of sort names $\mathbb{S} = (S, \leq)$, a collection Σ of types equation symbols, and a set E of equations on the symbols of Σ, one obtains a *order-sorted equational theory* $T = (\mathbb{S}, \Sigma, E)$. If D is a model of T, then call (T, D) a *data domain*.

If we have a set of classes with attributes, Bench-Capon and Malcom use the sorts of the order-sorted equational theory to model the attributes, a data domain to model the attribute values, and a separate order model to model the classes:

Definition 1. *An* ontology signature *is a triple* $(\mathcal{D}, \mathcal{C}, A)$*, where* $\mathcal{D} = (T, D)$ *is a data domain,* $\mathcal{C} = (C, \leq)$ *is a partial order, called a* class hierarchy*, and* A *is a family of sets* $A_{c,e}$ *of* attribute symbols *for* $c \in C$ *and* $e \in C + S$*, where* S *is the set of sorts in* T*. The family is such that* $A_{c',e} \subseteq A_{c,e'}$ *whenever* $c \leq c'$ *and* $e \leq e'$[2].

An ontonomy is then simply a pair (Σ, A), where Σ is an ontology signature and A a set of axioms. A model of such an ontonomy is a model of Σ that satisfies the axioms of A.

While this is a rigorous structural definition, it has the problem of reducing ontology to the specification of a type system whose components are structures[3]. The basic relation between types here is the sub-typing relation (the partial order $\leq$ among classes), while all other relations have to be introduced as attributes. In other words, this model is strongly oriented towards monocriterial taxonomies, although it is more general than a simple taxonomy in that it allows the classification structure to be a partial order (viz. a directed acyclic graph) rather than a tree. It is, in other words, too limited a definition to cover the uses that are being done of the idea of ontology: while the theory can serve as the foundation of *a* discipline of ontology, it is too weak to provide a sound basis to the current uses of the notion.

Even with all these defects, the model of Bench-Capon and Malcom has the clear advantage of providing the type of definition necessary for computing science, without resorting to unacceptable teleological notions. To the best of my knowledge this is, to this date, the most promising attempt at a definition of an ontonomy, and the one most likely to be eventually extended to an acceptable definition.

3 Ontology and Semantics

While a correct structural definition is still very elusive (and while most practicioners seem blissfully unaware of—or unconcerned by—the problem), there is a general consensus that ontology is somehow involved with the *semantics* of an information system, that ontonomies, whatever their structural definition will turn out to be, contain *concepts* and relations between them. The idea is not immediately obvious: ontonomies contain symbols, not unlike any formal system (or not unlike any data base, for that matter), and one should wonder what makes the symbols contained in an ontonomy be concepts. This question constitutes the semantic problem of ontology, which I propose to discuss in this section.

It is worth reminding that, when we are talking about semantics in the context of ontology, we are talking about something very different than, say, the semantics of a programming language. In programming languages, semantics is simply a function from states to states of a certain abstract machine. In ontology, the semantic that is modeled is supposed to be the semantics of the group in which the system is inserted, that is, the relation between the data in an information system and the symbols of an ontology is supposed to be isomorphic to the signification relation between *signifier* and *signified* in human culture. So, while the development of a theory of programming language

[2] [1].

[3] Bench-Capon and Malcom call these elements "classes," but they should not be confused with the classes used in object oriented models: the classes of this model are not abstract, since their attributes are explicitly declared.

semantics doesn't require any cognitive endorsement, the assertion that there is a computational discipline of ontology requires the endorsement of a theory of signification. Unlike programming language semantics, information system semantics (and ontology with it) is not theoretically innocent, so to speak.

If we take the rather general view that an ontonomy is a set of symbol and of relations between them then, with respect to the problem of meaning, one might ask whether these relations are constitutive or not. A negative answer leads to an atomism á la Fodor, while a positive answer leads to a point of view resembling very much what Fodor himself calls *inference rôle semantics*. I will begin by assuming that the answer is negative, that is that conceptual atomism is the theory of choice.

* * *

The possibility that symbols signify "by themselves" that is, independently of the relations between them requires the endorsement of a very strong form of conceptual atomism found, as far as I can tell, only in Fodor's *informational semantics*:

> Informational semantics denies that "dog" means *dog* because of the way it is related to other linguistic expressions [...]. Correspondingly, informational semantics denies that the concept DOG has its content in virtue of its position in a network of conceptual relations[4].

Note that the "correspondingly" here requires a fairly important metaphisical investment since it maps conceptual structures to linguistic ones. This, *passim,* is the same investment that ontology requires when it takes a linguistic structure (constituted of words and relations) and calls it a conceptual model.

Informational semantics has to struggle hard to eradicate itself from radical nativism: by the account of representational theories of mind, only composed concepts can be acquired (through inference from their components), thus conceptual atomism seems to imply that *all* concepts are innate. For Fodor, acquiring a concept means "getting *nomologically locked* to the property that the concept represents"[5] but the way to acquire a concept is having the right kinds of experiences. So, if one doesn't want to throw away the conceptual atomism baby together with the radical nativism bath water, the problem that one faces is "why is it so often experience with doorknobs, and so rarely experience with whipped cream or giraffes, that leads one to lock to doorknobhood?"[6]

Explanations that rely on hypothesis testing turn out to deny atomism, so they can't be applied. Fodor's solution to this problem is to stipulate that doorknobhood is *constituted by how its strikes us,* viz. "*being a doorknob* is having the property that minds like ours come to resonate to in consequence to relevant experience with stereotypical doorknobs"[7]

The serious flaw of this notion is that, since it needs to avoid any oppositional or structural definition of meaning in order to save atomism, it can't take into account the dependence of a single concept on the way in which different cultures divide the

---

[4] [3], p. 73.

[5] ibid. p. 125, emphasis in the original.

[6] ibid. p. 127.

[7] ibid. p. 137, emphasis in the original.

semantic field. To stay on Fodor's example, the English words "doorknob" and "door handle" correspond (roughly) to the Italian words "pomello" and "maniglia." But the areas covered by these concepts are not the same: while pomelli are, in general, doorknobs, some of the things that English speakers call doorknobs would qualify, for the Italian, as maniglie. The schema is more or less the following:

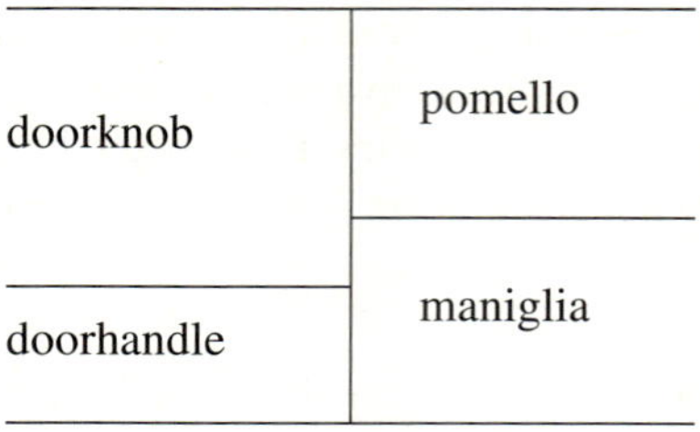

Why is it then that Italian minds "resonate" with doorknobs differently than English minds? By Fodor's account, there must be something different between English and Italian minds. A consequence of the consumption of wine and olive oil?

It appears, in other words, that we can't give a sensible explanation of the difference between doorknobs and pomelli unless we consider them differentially and oppositionally in the context of their respective languages. Doorknob is not a positive term, but serves to establish a distinction, an opposition in the semantic field of a language. Different languages break the semantic field in different ways, and concepts arise at the fissures of these divisions. Consider, as an example, the way in which adjectives of old age are constituted in Italian, Spanish and French[8]. The basic adjective, *vecchio/viejo/vieux* is applied both to things and to persons. There are specific forms, however: in Spanish, *añejo* is an appreciative form used mainly for alcoholic beverages *(un ron añejo)*. The Italian adjective *anziano* applied mainly to people, and the correspondence is roughly *anziano/anciano/âgé*, but *anziano* has a broader meaning that the other two adjectives, being used in expressions such as "il sergente anziano" to denote seniority in a function, a situation in which the Spanish would use *antiguo* and the French *ancien*. Note that the Spanish also has the possibility of using the word *mayor* as a softer and more respectful form of denoting a person of old age, while the corresponding Italian and French words are never used in this sense. The correspondence is, in other words, according to this schema

Italian	Spanish	French
	añejo	
vecchio	viejo	vieux
anziano	anciano	âgé
	mayor	
	antiguo	ancien
antico		antique

[8] I am taking this example, with some adaptation, from [5].

Here too, in order to save atomism and the nomological relation between concepts and world that goes with it, one should explain why it is that Italian, Spanish, and French minds resonate differently with age and, this, of course, by making reference only to the relation between individual concepts and the state of affairs in the world: differential or oppositional explanations related to the semantic field are not allowed by atomism.

At the origin of these problems there is, among other things, a certain confusion that computational ontologists have been known to make between signification and *designation*: the general idea in ontology seems to be that A means B if and only if A designates B. It is important however to keep the distinction between the two and, for this, I will just consider a famous example from Husserl ([9], p. 47): *the winner at Jena/the loser at Waterloo*. We notice that the *meaning* of tehse two phrases is different, although their *designatum* is the same: Napoleon.

Designation is a relation between a linguistic plane and an extra-linguistic one, but signification is a purely linguistic relation. That is, *pace* Fodor, meaning is not a nomological relation between mind and world, but a collection of relations and oppositions within the language.

* * *

These facts point quite strongly away from atomism that is, away from the (admittedly naïve) hypothesis that a symbol in an ontonomy possesses meaning *qua* symbol, by virtue of its name alone, without reference to the other elements of the ontonomy[9].

We are thus led to considering the second hypothesis given in the opening of this section, namely that the relations that one finds in an ontonomy are *constitutive* of meaning. Consider, for instance, the following ontonomy:

$$\begin{aligned}\text{car} &\sqsubseteq \text{motorvehicle} \sqcap \text{roadvehicle} \sqcap \exists\text{size.small}\\ \text{pickup} &\sqsubseteq \text{motorvehicle} \sqcap \text{roadvehicle} \sqcap \exists\text{size.big}\\ \text{motorvehicle} &\sqsubseteq \exists\text{uses.gasoline}\\ \text{roadvehicle} &\sqsubseteq \exists^4\text{has.wheels}\end{aligned} \tag{4}$$

The meaning of the word "car" is not given here by the juxtaposition of the three letters /c/, /a/, and /r/, but by its (structural) relation with the terms "motorvehicle," "roadvehicle," "size," and "small," together with the relation of these terms with other terms and so on. In other words, one can say that the meaning of the word "car" is given by the following structure

$$\begin{aligned}D &\sqsubseteq B \sqcap C \sqcap \exists\rho_3.F\\ E &\sqsubseteq B \sqcap C \sqcap \exists\rho_3.G\\ B &\sqsubseteq \exists\rho_1.A\\ C &\sqsubseteq \exists^4\rho_2.H\end{aligned} \tag{5}$$

[9] This is not conceptual atomism á la Fodor, which is all but naïve, but the naïve interpretation that of it has been given in computing science.

which we can represent by the following diagram

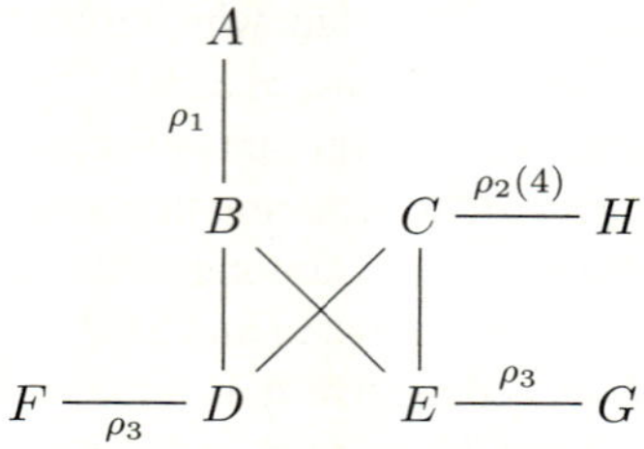

(6)

The meaning of the word "car" is to be found in the *structure* of this definition that is, essentially, in the following diagram:

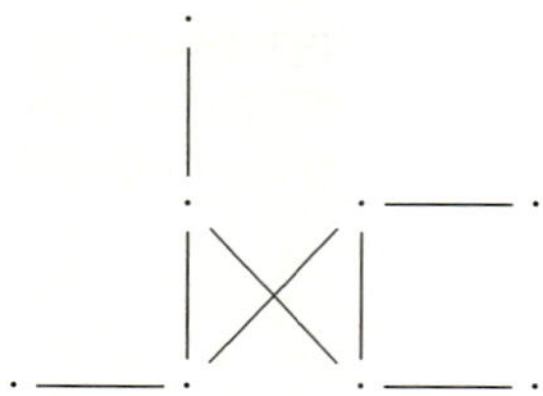

(7)

Replacing D with "car" in (6), we obtain the structural meaning of the concept CAR. (Here I am using capitalization to denote concepts and words in quotes to denote linguistic entities; a Saussurean semiotician would say that "car" is a signifier and CAR the corresponding signified.)

The problem with the position that the structure (6) is the meaning of the word "car" (that is, to be completely clear, that (6) *is* CAR) comes from the following structure:

$$\begin{aligned} \text{dog} &\sqsubseteq \text{animal} \sqcap \text{quadruped} \sqcap \exists\text{size.small} \\ \text{horse} &\sqsubseteq \text{animal} \sqcap \text{quadruped} \sqcap \exists\text{size.big} \\ \text{animal} &\sqsubseteq \exists\text{ingests.food} \\ \text{quadruped} &\sqsubseteq \exists^4\text{has.leg} \end{aligned} \tag{8}$$

which is isomorphic to (6), that is, to CAR. Unless one is ready to concede that CAR = DOG (and I expect quite a few people to object to this identification on ground of affection either toward their poodle or toward their BMW), one must admit that there is something wrong in our definition.

The structural definition of meaning can be saved, in this circumstance, by noticing that quadrupeds are animals, while road vehicles are not necessarily motor vehicles (a horse-drawn cart, a small omnibus, or one of those four wheels bicycles that are often rented out at seaside resorts are examples of road vehicles with four wheels but no engine) so, in (8) we can affirm

$$\text{quadruped} \sqsubseteq \text{animal} \tag{9}$$

and change the first two relations to

$$\text{dog} \sqsubseteq \text{quadruped} \sqcap \exists\text{size.small} \tag{10}$$

$$\text{horse} \sqsubseteq \text{quadruped} \sqcap \exists\text{size.big} \tag{11}$$

If this new structure is still not enough to differentiate between different concepts, we can add more predicates. The question is: when can we stop? The answer is that we can't: if meaning is in the structure (and we have already ruled out the hypothesis that meaning is in the symbols themselves), then the meaning of a sign is given by the *trace* on it of all the other signs of the language, and no part of the system can self-sustain once detached from the whole.

* * *

But even an hypothetical (and impossible) macrostructure containing the whole language and its lexical relations would not be sufficient to save the semantic programme of ontology: the ontological meaning would still be normative, the codification of an author's intention at the time the text was written, and would omit the essential active rôle of the reader in the construction of meaning. In order to maintain the possibility of recording meaning once and for all, ontology must anchor it to a pre-linguistic intentional act of the author: reconstructing meaning means reconstructing this intentional status. The only way in which ontology can keep a stable meaning is by constant policing and an authoritarian normativism that sets, once and for all, the 'true' intentions of the author. There is no social participation in this construction of meaning: the reader can be replaced by an algorithm. To the Barthesian death of the author, ontology opposes a drastic "death of the reader." The underlying philosophy here is that of signification as a market, an old pre-structuralist view associated with the bourgeois individualism: meaning belongs to the author like a commodity, and language is just the currency that allows one to exchange this meaning-commodity with someone who is also an owner of meaning. But it is unlikely that such a privately owned, pre-linguistic intentional act may exist: meaning arises in language, and it is a product of a shared system of signification. What can be articulated and understood depends on this shared code. One can no longer see an intentional act that pre-dates language and that language simply reflects (the essentialist view of the ontologists notwithstanding). Reality, and the writing subject, are the product of language. And just as language interacts with other social and cultural systems, so does the act of reading. It is reading—historically and conceptually situated—that constructs meaning connecting the cues that the text gives with the complex network of conventions, discourses, and situatedness in which it occurs.

Consider a sign on a door that says "trespassers will be prosecuted." The context necessary to understand this sign is considerable. I must understand, for instance, that this sign is not informative in the sense that a newspaper headline is: I am not being informed that there have been trespassers somewhere and that they will be prosecuted sometime in the future: in western societies at least, information of this kind is not written on signs hanging from doors, especially if we see that the sign is made of plastic or wood (and therefore is durable) and the writing is not dated. Such a sign typically is a threat, the word "trespasser" refers to me (the reader) in case I decide to walk through the door, and it threatens me of prosecution if I do so. The threat also implies that prosecution is likely to result in punishment. I must understand that trespassing in this context means to cross *this* door, not some door in the palace of the king of Siam. I have to have a general knowledge of private property to understand that preventing people from entering into a building is one of the rights that society grants to proprietors (while, for instance, preventing people from looking at the building is in general not such a right), that there are authorities that will guarantee the respect of these rights, and that they will punish people who infringe these rights, that the sign has been placed there with their tacit approval, and so on...

None of these elements, necessary for understanding, is *in* the text: they must be supplied by a specific situation. The text here takes meaning by being situated (viz. placed in a situation: a door on a building rather than, say, a shelf on a store that sells signs) and in a certain relation with other texts that are not present, namely the political discourse that regulate private property, the speech through which certain customs have been implanted in the reader, and so on. Finally, all this linguistic discourse rests on a substratum of human practices and action: the political relation of power between authority and citizens, and the fact that in order to understand punishment one must understand pain (psychological pain, at least).

There is more to meaning, in other words, than just relations between terms: the creation of signification is a back-and-forth process between the text and the reader; the reader, influenced by the text, creates a frame of reference in which the text itself can be given meaning. This is what Gadamer [4] called the *hermeneutic circle:* the parts of the text can be understood in terms of the whole context, and the context becomes intelligible by means of the parts.

Ontology is trying to break this circle by removing the reader from it: it removes the creative act of the reader and tries to encode the *essence* of the meaning in such a way that it can be read without interpretation.

In this, it falls into the trap of believing that a text is just an author's intended meaning, and that therefore it is possible to re-code the text leaving the meaning unaltered. But if the meaning arises through an historically situated interaction of the reader with the text, then the text is the only possible closure of the hermeneutic circle, the only possible representation of itself, and changing the code will change the meaning. There is, in other words, no objective, essential or immutable meaning that can be encoded, either through ontological or other means in such a way that its interpretation will not require the active, culturally and historically situated, participation of the reader.

4 The Pragmatics of Ontology

The previous section suggested quite decisively and conclusively that the abmitious semantic programme of ontology is unattainable. Yet, as we all know, ontonomies are eagerly sought after, to the point of being hailed as a cornerstone of the constituenda semantic web. It is interesting to question why this is the case. A full answer to this question would require investigating in some depth the sociology of the computing enterprise and its relation with other economic forces, and analysis that is in the absolutest terms beyond the scope of this paper. I will venture only the briefest of comments.

The view of meaning as a commodity and of signification as a market transaction fit quite well, of course, with certain commercial aspects of the web, and it is no surprise that, in an age in which intellectual property rights are expanded to levels never dreamt before, a view of signification that allows the commodification of meaning (and thus, potentially, its patentability) should be regarded with more than a passing interest in the semantic web area. It is, in other words, not a surprise that the semantic web is these days probably the more fertile ground for the application of ontology.

It is also not surprising that the idea that meaning is to be sought in a series of taxonomies (naïve as it might be) should have arisen in an environment close to the programming profession, where taxonomies have been popularized as a programming discipline by object oriented methods: a lot of the ontological vocabulary, especially in the vicinity of the semantic web, shows a definite debt to that of the programming profession. Of course, the wide adoption of a taxonomy in a certain discipline tends to confine the discourse around certain terms an to establish an orthodoxy which might stifle alternative discourses: whether this is useful depends on the status of the discipline. The taxonomy of Linneus was a great help to the relatively mature discipline of zoology, but the taxonomization of all the elements into air, water, fire, and earth contributed to the failure of the Greek to develop a science of nature. Given the pervasiveness of computers, and the social pressure to use them, the terms and taxonomies that they impose tend to become strong norms. By forcing computerized data bases, normative semantics, and taxonomies on a vital but not yet settled discipline we might take away its vitality more than help it.

5 Conclusions

Semantics (in the sense of information systems semantics) seems to have become a most powerful "buzz-word" in the computing profession (a profession that is becoming, alas, very responsive to hype and word clout), and ontology seems occasionally to ascend to the status of a panacea. But, from within the point of view of computing science, there are at least two serious problems with this panacea.

The first is that, while we appear eager to use ontonomies in the most diverse applications, we are quite unable to define them with precision. More than a specific ontological problem, this issue is a symptom of a preoccupying relaxation of the standards of rigor of computing and, as such, should not be taken lightly, even from researchers not directly connected with ontology.

The second problem is in the idea of semantics to which ontology makes reference, an idea that is clearly insufficient in the light of all that is known about the process of signification. In a sense, the choice of such a model of signification reveals a certain cultural autism, so to speak, of computing science, and a certain historical arrogance. The problem of signification has been studied at least since the debate between the Stoics and the Epicureans on the nature of the sign, has been an important concern in medieval philosophy, and has been absolutely central in the philosophy of the XX century. But, faced with the problem of signification, computing scientists chose to disregard all this and to start from zero.

This problem is not specific to computing science, but it appears to be fairly common among technologists: "High tech, in fact, appears not only as optimistic about the future but also more indifferent toward and, in other contexts, more manipulative of the past than earlier technologies have been"[10]. Computing science is falling here in the very typical technological fallacy of considering history—cultural history, in this case, as "irrelevant save as the supposed contrast with the golden age ahead. It is as if high tech arrived and flourished in an historical vacuum of no more than a few decades and

[10] [11], p. 177.

as if everything before it can simply be forgotten"[11]. But, of course, to think this way is illusory. The problem of signification and the viable relations between a syntactic manipulation device such as a computer and semantics are much more complex than the simple schematism of ontology would imply.

Given the importance that the presence of computing devices has in the disciplines in which they are used; given the influence that these devices have in promoting or constraining certain discourses in these disciplines, the computing profession has the responsibility of rejecting facile solutions. It has the responsibility of understanding the different perspectives on semantics, of being aware of the history of such problem and, ultimately, to re-analyze the relations between computers and the process of signification. Computers are syntactic machines, and it not immediately obvious that they can be of any help in dealing with semantics. The problem is worth exploring, but in a more complex way, without prejudices: the first question should not be *how* to we use a computer to represent semantics, but *whether* we should do so. We computing professional must have the acumen to discover the answer, and the cultural humility to accept it, whatever it might be.

References

1. T. Bench-Capon and G. Malcom. Formalizing ontologies and their relations. In T. Bench-Capon, G. Soda, and M. Toja, editors, *Proceedings of DEXA 99*, pages 250–259, 1999.
2. D. Fensel, F. van Harmelen, I. Horrocks, D. McGuinness, and P. Patel-Schneider. Oil: an ontology infrastructure for the semantic web. *IEEE intelligent systems*, March-April 2001.
3. Jerry Fodor. *Concepts*. Oxford:Oxford University Press, 1997.
4. H. G. Gadamer. *Truth and Method*. London, 1975.
5. Horst Geckeler. *Semántica estructural y teoría del campo léxico*. Madrid:Gredos, 1976. Spanish translation of *Strukturelle semantik und wortfeldtheorie* by Marcos Martínez Hernández.
6. J. Goguen and J. Meseguer. Order;sorted algebras I: equational deduction for multiple inheritance, overloading, exceptions, and p[artial operations. *Theoretical computer science*, 105(2):217–273, 1992.
7. Thomas Gruber. Towards principles for the design of ontologies used for knowledge sharing. In N. Guarino and R. Poli, editors, *Formal ontology in conceptual analysis and knowledge representation*. Kluwer Academic Publishers, 1993.
8. N. Guarino. Formal ontology and information systems. In *Proceedings of FOIS 98, Trento, Italy, 6–8 June*, pages 3–15. Amsterdam:IOS Press, 1998.
9. E. Husserl. *Logische Untersuchungen, Part II: Untersuschungen zur Phänomenologie und Theorie der Erkenntnis*. Halle, 1901.
10. S. Russell and P. Norvig. *Artificial inteligence, a modern approach*. Upper Saddle River:Prentice Hall, 1995.
11. H. Segal. The cultural contradictions of high tech: or the many ironies of contemporary technological optimism. In Y. Ezrani, E. Mendelsohn, and H. Segal, editors, *Technology. pessimism, and postmodernism*. Amhrest:University of Massachusetts Press, 1994.
12. H. Wache, T. Vöegle, U. Visser, H. Stuckenschmidt, G. Schuster, H. Neumann, and S. Hübner. Ontology-based integration of information–a survey of existing approaches. In *Proceedings of IJCAI/01 Workshop: ontologies and information sharing*, pages 108–117, 2001.

[11] ibid. p. 187.

Dynamic Plan Migration for Snapshot-Equivalent Continuous Queries in Data Stream Systems*

Jürgen Krämer[1], Yin Yang[2], Michael Cammert[1], Bernhard Seeger[1], and Dimitris Papadias[2]

[1] University of Marburg, Germany
[2] Hong Kong University of Science and Technology, China

Abstract. A data stream management system executes a large number of continuous queries in parallel. As stream characteristics and query workload change over time, the plan initially installed for a continuous query may become inefficient. As a consequence, the query optimizer will re-optimize this plan based on the current statistics. The replacement of the running plan with a more efficient but semantically equivalent plan at runtime is called *dynamic plan migration*. In order to have a sound semantic foundation for query optimization, we investigate dynamic plan migration for snapshot-equivalent plans. We develop a general method for dynamic plan migration that treats the old and new plan as snapshot-equivalent black boxes. This enables the query optimizer to apply the conventional transformation rules during re-optimization. As a consequence, our approach supports the dynamic optimization of arbitrary continuous queries expressible in CQL, whereas existing solutions are limited in their scope.

1 Introduction

Dynamic query optimization at runtime is important for a data stream management system (DSMS) because the subscribed queries are long-running and the underlying stream characteristics such as arrival rates and data distributions may vary over time. In addition, the query workload may gradually change. In this case, dynamic query optimization may be useful to enable a DSMS to save system resources by subquery sharing.

There are two major steps in dynamic query optimization. First, the query optimizer needs to identify a plan with optimization potential. For this purpose, a DSMS keeps a plethora of runtime statistics, e. g., on stream rates, and selectivities. In the second step, the query optimizer replaces the currently running, inefficient plan by a semantically equivalent but more efficient new plan. This transition at runtime is called *dynamic plan migration* [1]. Dynamic plan migration is easy as long as query plans only consist of *stateless* operators, such

* This work has been supported by the German Research Foundation (DFG) under grant no. SE 553/4-3.

T. Grust et al. (Eds.): EDBT 2006 Workshops, LNCS 4254, pp. 497–516, 2006.

as selection and projection, and inter-operator queues. In order to perform the migration, it is sufficient to pause the execution of the old plan first, drain out all existing elements in the old plan afterwards, replace the old plan by the new plan, and resume the execution finally. In contrast to *stateless* operators, *stateful* operators like join and aggregation must maintain information derived from previously received elements as state information to produce correct results. Migration strategies for query plans with stateful operators are complex because it is non-trivial to appropriately transfer the state information from an old plan to a new plan.

Besides the essential requirement of correctness, a migration strategy should take the following performance objectives into account. It should (i) not stall query execution for a significant timespan as catching up with processing could cause system overload afterwards, (ii) continuously produce results during migration – the smoother the output rate the better, and (iii) minimize the migration duration and migration overhead in terms of system resources like memory and CPU costs.

To the best of our knowledge, dynamic plan migration has only been addressed in [1] so far. The authors proposed two different migration strategies, *moving states* (MS) and *parallel track* (PT). MS computes the state of the new plan instantly from the state of the old plan at migration start. Afterwards the old plan is discarded and the execution of the new plan is started. In order to apply MS, the query optimizer requires a detailed knowledge about the operator implementations because it needs to access and modify state information. Despite the fact that it may be possible to define those transitions correctly for arbitrary transformation rules involving joins, aggregation, duplicate elimination etc., the implementation will be very complex and inflexible. For that reason, we prefer the second strategy proposed in [1], namely PT, as starting point for our black box migration approach. In contrast to MS, PT runs both plans in parallel for a certain timespan to initialize the new plan gradually with the required state information. Although [1] claims that PT is generally applicable to continuous queries over data streams, we identified problems if stateful operators other than joins occur in a plan, e. g., duplicate elimination and aggregation. In this paper we develop a general migration strategy which overcomes these deficiencies.

The basis of our approach is the temporal semantics for continuous queries over data streams defined in [2]. The algebraic transformation rules known from conventional database systems can be transferred to the stream algebra in [2] because the stream-to-stream operators are *snapshot-reducible* [3,4] to their counterparts in the extended relational algebra. Snapshot-reducibility is also the reason why the semantics and stream algebra in [2] are in accordance with CQL [5], an extension of SQL for continuous queries. Based on this semantic foundation, our migration strategy requires for correctness that both plans – the old and new – produce snapshot-equivalent results. Note that applying conventional transformation rules guarantees this property for the algebra in [2].

As we generalize PT, we treat the old and new plan as snapshot-equivalent black boxes which can consist of arbitrary operators. The basic idea of our approach is to define a split time. For all time instants before the split time, results are computed by the old plan, whereas the new plan computes the results for all other time instants. The migration is finished as soon as the timestamps of the elements in all input streams reached the split time.

The contributions of this paper can be summarized as follows:

- We show that PT fails to cope with plans involving stateful operators other than joins.
- We propose our general solution for dynamic plan migration of arbitrary CQL queries, called *GenMig*, prove its correctness, and discuss implementation issues. Besides a straightforward implementation, we suggest two optimizations.
- We analyze the performance of GenMig with regard to the objectives mentioned above, and compare it to PT.

The rest of this paper is organized as follows. Section 2 introduces semantic foundations and briefly summarizes implementation techniques for continuous queries over data streams. In Section 3, we demonstrate that PT fails for plans with other stateful operators than joins. Our general plan migration strategy is presented in Section 4. Section 5 shows the results of our experimental studies. Related work is discussed in Section 6. Finally, Section 7 concludes the paper.

2 Preliminaries

In order to understand the rationale of our approach, it is important to know the underlying semantics and compatible implementations. In analogy to traditional database management systems, we distinguish between a *logical* and a *physical* operator algebra. The logical stream algebra defines the semantics of the operations, whereas the physical algebra provides implementations.

2.1 Semantic Foundations

Time. The notion of time is of utmost importance in stream processing. As common in most approaches, we assume each stream element to be equipped with a timestamp, and streams to be ordered by this timestamp attribute. Furthermore, we assume that only a finite number of elements has the same timestamp. Let $\mathbb{T} = (T, \leq)$ be a discrete time domain with a total order $\leq$. We use $\mathbb{T}$ to model the notion of application time, not system time. For the sake of simplicity, let T be the non-negative integers $\{0, 1, 2, 3, \ldots\}$.

Sliding Window Queries. Sliding window queries are the most common and important type of continuous queries in DSMS. Without loss of generality, we assume time-based sliding window queries in this paper. A sound semantics for this query type has been established in recent years [2,5] based on the operations of the well-known extended relational algebra [6,7].

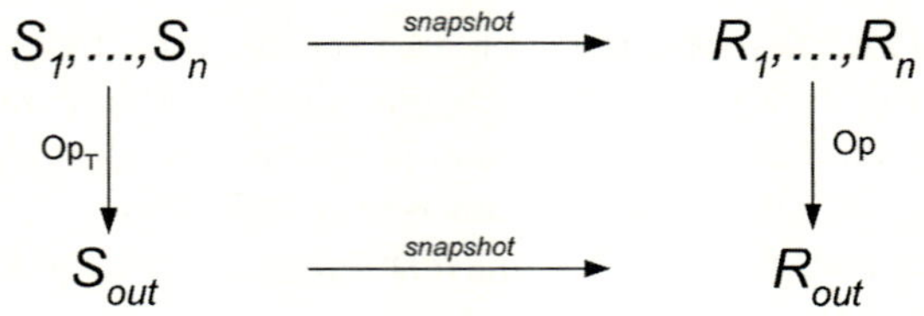

Fig. 1. Snapshot reducibility

The operators in [2] can be classified into two categories: *window* operators and *standard* operators. The window operators model the sliding window semantics. In a logical query plan, a window operator is placed downstream of each source for which a window has been specified in the corresponding query representation, e. g., CQL [5]. The rest of the plan consists of standard operators borrowed from the temporal relational algebra [3]. The standard operators are *snapshot-reducible* to their relational counterparts and are used in the same way.

Definition 1 (Snapshot-Reducibility). *We denote a stream-to-stream operation op_T with inputs $S_1, \ldots, S_n$ as snapshot reducible if for each time instant $t \in T$, the snapshot at t of the results of op_T is equal to the results of applying its relational counterpart op to the snapshots of $S_1, \ldots, S_n$ at time instant t.*

Figure 1 illustrates the temporal concept of snapshot reducibility [3,4]. A snapshot of a stream at a time instant t can be considered as a relation since it represents all tuples valid at that time instant.

Definition 2 (Snapshot-Equivalence). *Two streams are snapshot-equivalent if for all time instants t, the snapshots at t of both streams are equal.*

We denote two query plans as equivalent if they produce *snapshot-equivalent* results. Note that conventional transformation rules applied to snapshot-reducible operators preserve snapshot-equivalence [3]. Snapshot equivalence is the reason why the common relational transformation rules are still applicable to the stream algebra [2] and make query optimization feasible.

Remark 1. Figure 1 can also be used to motivate that [2] and [5] basically have the same expressiveness. The abstract semantics proposed for STREAM transforms the input streams into relations, uses operations of the relational algebra for processing, and transforms the output relations back into streams. The window specifications are included in the mappings from streams to relations. Hence, the stream-to-stream approach in [2] works completely on the left side of Figure 1, whereas STREAM goes the way round on the right side.

2.2 Interval-Based Implementation

There currently exist two major implementation techniques compatible with the semantics introduced above: the interval-based implementation [2,8], and the positive-negative tuple approach [5,9]. We describe the implementation of GenMig for the interval-based approach, but additionally outline how it can be adapted to the positive-negative approach.

The stream-to-stream operator algebra in [2] relies on so-called physical streams.

Definition 3 (Physical Stream). *A physical stream S is a potentially infinite, ordered sequence of elements $(e, [t_S, t_E))$ composed of a tuple e belonging to the schema of S and a half-open time interval $[t_S, t_E)$ where $t_S, t_E \in T$. A physical stream is non-decreasingly ordered by start timestamps.*

The interpretation of a physical stream element $(e, [t_S, t_E))$ is that a tuple e is valid during the time interval $[t_S, t_E)$.

Input Stream Conversion. Input streams of many stream applications provide elements with a timestamp attribute, but no time interval. As those streams are usually ordered by timestamps, a physical stream can be generated easily by mapping each incoming element e with its internal timestamp t to $(e, [t, t+1))$, where $+1$ indicates a time period at finest time granularity.

Window Operator. The window operator assigns a validity according to its window size to each element of its input stream. For a *time-based* sliding window, the window size $w \in T$ represents a period in application time. For each element $(e, [t_S, t_S + 1))$, the window operator extends its validity by adding the window size to its end timestamp, i. e., $(e, [t_S, t_S + 1 + w))$. This is intuitive for a time-based sliding window query since a stateful operation downstream of a window operator has to consider an element for additional w time instants. In the general case, where nesting of continuous sliding window queries is permitted, the window operator produces for each incoming element $(e, [t_S, t_E))$ a set of elements by extending the validity of each single time instant by the window size w. Note that a window operator does not affect stateless operations, such as selection and projection.

Query Plans. Query plan construction is basically the same as in conventional database systems, except that the query optimizer has to place the window operators in addition. The window operators are placed downstream of the source for which a window has been specified. This placement is performed by the query optimizer when transforming the posed query into the corresponding logical query plan. Thereafter, the query optimizer computes the physical plan by choosing a physical operator for each logical one.

Temporal Expiration. Besides the desired semantics, windowing constructs (i) restrict the resource usage and (ii) ensure non-blocking behaviour of stateful operators over infinite streams [10]. For stateful operators like joins, elements in the state expire due to the validity assigned by the window operator. A stateful operator considers an element $(e, [t_S, t_E))$ in its state as expired if it is guaranteed that it will not be involved in the result production any more. That means, no element in one of its input streams will arrive in the future whose time interval will overlap with $[t_S, t_E)$. According to the total order maintained for each physical stream, this condition holds if the minimum of all start timestamps of the latest incoming element from each input stream is greater than t_E. A stateful operator can delete all expired elements from its state. In those cases where application-time skew between streams and latency in streams becomes an issue, *heartbeats* [11] can be used to explicitly trigger additional expiration steps.

Examples. Our examples throughout the paper are based on two stateful operators: join and duplicate elimination. The snapshot-reducible join satisfies the following conditions [2,8]: (a) for two participating stream elements, the join predicate has to be fulfilled and (b) their time intervals have to intersect. The time interval associated with the join result is set to the intersection of the two participating time intervals. The snapshot-reducible duplicate elimination removes duplicate tuples at each single snapshot. That means, the output must not contain two elements with identical tuples and intersecting time intervals.

2.3 Positive-Negative Implementation

Another common implementation technique for continuous queries is the Positive-Negative (PN) tuple approach, used in STREAM [12] and Nile [9] for instance. The PN implementation is based on streams with elements of the following format: a tuple e, a timestamp $t \in T$, and a sign, $+$ or $-$. A stream is ordered by timestamps. The signs are used to define the validity of elements. The standard operators are modified to handle positive and negative tuples, in particular with regard to temporal expiration. For each incoming stream element with application timestamp t, the window operator sends a positive element with that timestamp, and after $w + 1$ (window size $+ 1$) time units, a negative element is sent with timestamp $t + w + 1$ to signal the expiration. For further details, we refer the reader to [9,12].

A pair consisting of a positive and its corresponding negative element can be used to express a stream element in the interval-based approach. Namely, $(e, [t_S, t_E))$ can be implemented by sending a positive element $(e, t_S, +)$ and negative element $(e, t_E, -)$. Hence, positive elements refer to start timestamps, whereas negative elements refer to end timestamps. Even at this physical level, the semantic equivalence of both approaches becomes obvious. However, the interval approach does not have the drawback of doubling stream rates due to sending positive and negative tuples.

3 Problems of the Parallel Track Strategy

After outlining PT, we demonstrate that PT produces incorrect results if applied to plans involving stateful operators other than joins. Note that the authors in [1] claim that their migration strategies are generally applicable. We assume a global time-based window of size w as in [1]. We use the term *box* to refer to the implementation of a plan, i. e., the physical query plan actually executed.

3.1 Parallel Track Strategy

At migration start PT pauses the processing only shortly to plug in the new box. Then, it resumes the old box and runs both boxes in parallel. The results of both plans are merged. Finally, when the states in the old box solely consist of elements that arrived after migration start, the migration is over and the old box can be safely removed. This implies that all elements stored in the state before migration start have been purged due to temporal expiration.

The following aspects guarantee the correctness of the PT strategy according to [1]: (i) Although all elements arriving during migration are processed by both plans, the combined output must not contain duplicates, that means results produced by both plans for the same snapshot. This is achieved by marking the elements with flags, *old* and *new*, which indicate if an element arrived before and after the migration start time, respectively. For combined results, e. g., join results, a *new* flag is assigned if all involved elements had a *new* flag. To guarantee correctness, PT removes all results of the old box that are assigned with a *new* flag as those are additionally produced by the new box. (ii) In order to preserve temporal ordering, the output of the two boxes has to be synchronized. PT simply buffers the output of the new box during migration.

3.2 Problems

The PT strategy as proposed in [1] works well for join reordering but fails if other stateful operators are involved. We illustrate this by a concrete example. Let us consider the migration scenario given in Figure 2 consisting of an equi-join ($\bowtie$) and a duplicate elimination (δ) which is pushed down for optimization purposes. Recall that this is a standard transformation rule which holds in the stream algebra due to our semantic foundations. Figure 2 shows the query plans as well as the inputs and outputs of the operators.

Example 1. We have two input streams A and B delivering the elements listed in the upper right table. The table labelled with $\bowtie$ depicts the correct results of the join inside the old box. The table labelled with δ contains the correct results of the duplicate elimination of the old box. The tables δ'_1, δ'_2, and $\bowtie'$ correspond to the operator results of the new box. Correctness here refers to the snapshot-reducible semantics assumed. Although we use our notation with half-open time intervals to denote the validity of elements, the example solely relies on snapshot-reducible operator semantics and thus is implementation independent. Recall that a time interval just describes a contiguous set of time instants.

All input elements are considered to be valid for 100 time units, which is the global window size. The migration start is at time instant 40. The element $(a, [20, 121))$ from input B, which is marked as *old*, joins with the element $(a, [50, 151))$ from input A. Hence, the join result $(a, [50, 121))$ is marked as *old*. As $[50, 121)$ overlaps with the time interval of the duplicate elimination's result $(a, [111, 121))$, this is also marked as *old*. Therefore, it definitely belongs to the output of the old box. Unfortunately, $(a, [111, 121))$ has a temporal overlap with $(a, [70, 151))$ which is a result of the new box. Consequently, the complete output

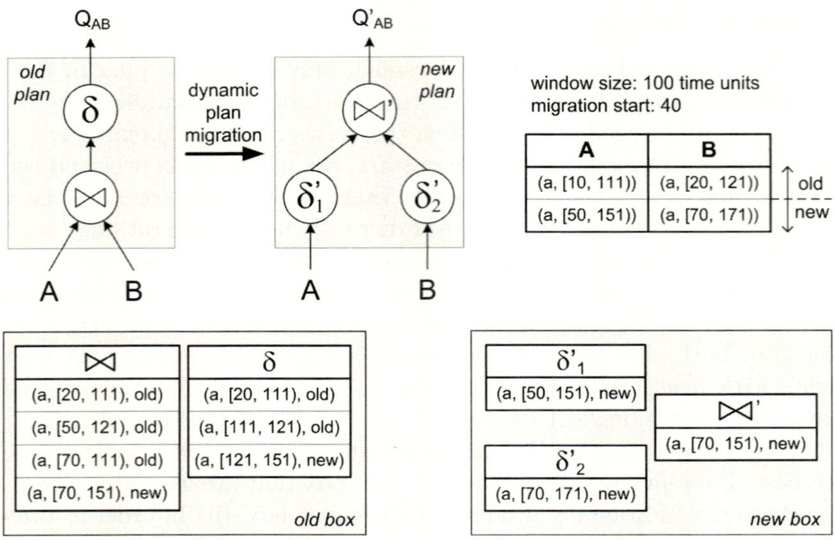

Fig. 2. Plan migration with duplicate elimination

contains tuple a for the snapshots 111 to 120 twice. Thus, PT does not produce correct results.

The reason for this problem is that the validity of results of the old box can refer to points in time which are beyond the plan migration start time. These time instants may additionally be addressed by the new box. Since the new box has no information about the old box, duplicates at those time instants may occur in the output, which is the union of both boxes. GenMig overcomes this problem by introducing a split time which is greater than all time instants occurring in the old box.

Note 1. The problem of PT is not restricted to duplicate elimination but arises for other operators as well, e. g., aggregation and difference. Although join reordering is a very important transformation rule which is covered by PT, there exist rules for other stateful operators [3,13] for which PT will fail in a similar way as shown above.

4 A General Strategy for Plan Migration

In this section we propose *GenMig* which overcomes the problems of PT while maintaining its merits, namely (i) a gradual migration from the old to the new plan, and (ii) generating results during migration.

4.1 Logical View

We first present the basic idea of GenMig from a purely logical and semantic perspective.

GenMig Strategy. Given two snapshot-equivalent plans, the query optimizer determines a point in application time denoted as T_{split}. At this time instant the time domain is split into two partitions.

- For all time instants $t < T_{split}$ the results are produced by the old plan.
- For all time instants $t \geq T_{split}$ the results are produced by the new plan.

The union of both plans represents the total results. T_{split} refers to the plan migration end because up from this point in time the new plan produces the output by itself, and thus the old plan can be discarded. The migration duration is the period from migration start to T_{split}.

Correctness. Under the assumption that the old and new plan produce a snapshot-equivalent output, the total output of GenMig is complete. The output is computed for every single time instant. Due to snapshot-equivalence it does not matter if the results for a snapshot are produced by either the old or the new plan. The duplicate elimination problem does not arise because the results of the two plans are disjoint in terms of timestamps.

4.2 Physical View

GenMig is very clear and easy at the logical level. However, at the physical level it is impractical to compute the query results for every single snapshot separately.

Algorithm 1. GenMig

Input : streams $I_1, \ldots, I_n$, old plan with state information, new plan without state information, global window constraint w
Output : streams $O_1, \ldots, O_m$, new plan with state information

foreach *input stream* $I_i, i \in \{1, \ldots, n\}$ **do**
  Start monitoring the start timestamps;
  Keep the most recent start timestamps of I_i as t_{S_i};
Pause the execution of the old plan as soon as t_{S_i} has been set for each input;
$T_{split} \leftarrow max\{t_{S_i} | i \in \{1, \ldots, n\}\} + w + 1 + \varepsilon$;
Insert a *Split* operator downstream of each source of the old plan;
Insert a *Coalesce* operator at the top of both plans for each output stream;
Resume the execution of the old plan and start the execution of the new plan;
while $min\{t_{S_i} | i \in \{1, \ldots, n\}\} < T_{split}$ **do**
  Continue the execution of both plans;
Signal the end of all input streams to the old plan;
Stop the execution of the old plan;
Pause the execution of the new plan;
Remove the old plan, coalesce and split operators;
Connect inputs and outputs directly with the new plan;
Resume the execution of the new plan;

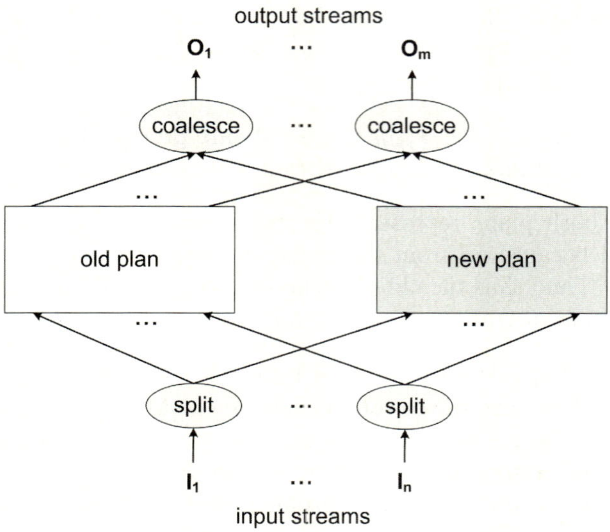

Fig. 3. GenMig strategy

Interval-Based Implementation of GenMig. Algorithm 1 shows the implementation of GenMig for the interval-based approach [2,8]. The input consists of the old currently running box, the corresponding input streams, and the new box without any state information. In contrast to the PT strategy, GenMig does not start with plan migration instantly. It starts monitoring the start timestamps instead.

Remark 2. In contrast to [1] where a single migration start time is used, our approach maintains a migration start time for each input. This has the advantage that GenMig does not require the scheduling to obey the global temporal ordering by start timestamps, which would be in conflict with sophisticated scheduling strategies [14,15,16] otherwise.

Algorithm 2. Split

Input : stream I, split time T_{split}
Output : streams O_{old}, O_{new}

foreach *new incoming stream element* $(e, [t_S, t_E)) \in I$ **do**
  if $t_S < T_{split}$ **then**
    if $t_E \leq T_{split}$ **then** Append $(e, [t_S, t_E))$ to O_{old};
    else
      Append $(e, [t_S, T_{split}))$ to O_{old};
      Append $(e, [T_{split}, t_E))$ to O_{new};
  else
    Append $(e, [t_S, t_E))$ to O_{new};

Algorithm 3. Coalesce

Input : streams I_0 (from old plan), I_1 (from new plan), hash maps M_0, M_1, heap H, split time T_{split}
Output : stream O

foreach *new incoming stream element* $(e, [t_S, t_E)) \in I_i, i \in \{0, 1\}$ **do**
  $t_{out} \leftarrow 0$;
  if $t_E < T_{split} \vee t_S > T_{split}$ **then**
    Append $(e, [t_S, t_E))$ to H;
  else
    if $i = 0$ **then**
      if $\exists (e', [t'_S, t'_E)) \in M_1$ *where* $e = e'$ **then**
        Append $(e, [t_S, t'_E))$ to H and remove it from M_1;
      else Insert $(e, [t_S, t_E))$ into M_0;
    if $i = 1$ **then**
      if $\exists (e', [t'_S, t'_E)) \in M_0$ *where* $e = e'$ **then**
        Append $(e, [t'_S, t_E))$ to H and remove it from M_0;
        $t_{out} \leftarrow t'_S$;
      else Insert $(e, [t_S, t_E))$ into M_1;
  while $t_{out} \geq H.top.t_S$ **do**
    Append $H.top$ to O and remove it from H;
if *migration finished* **then**
  Flush H and append its elements to O;

After initialization, i. e., when for each input stream a timestamp t_{S_i} has been determined, the old box is paused. The split time T_{split} is set to the maximum of all t_{S_i} plus the window size w plus 1 plus ε. This setting ensures that T_{split} is greater than any time instant in the old box.

Remark 3. Without loss of generality, we assume ε to be chosen so that T_{split} neither occurs as start nor end timestamp in any input stream. This can for instance be achieved if T_{split} is expressed at a finer time granularity [17] and ε refers to a chronon according to that granularity. From the implementation side, this assumption can be assured easily but is omitted in the algorithms due to clarity reasons.

In addition to setting the split time, two novel operators – split and coalesce – are inserted at the inputs and outputs, respectively. Figure 3 illustrates this placement. For their implementations, see Algorithms 2 and 3. The stateless split operator splits the time interval of an incoming element at T_{split} into two disjoint intervals. The tuple e associated with the first interval is sent to the old box, e associated with the second interval is sent to the new box.

The coalesce operator inverts the effects of splitting. Coalesce merges two equivalent tuples, each of one input, with adjacent time intervals. Contrary to split, coalesce is a stateful operator because it has to maintain data structures,

e. g., hash maps, for the detection of equivalent tuples. Furthermore, a heap ordered by start timestamps is required to ensure the ordering property of the output stream.

The migration end is defined as the point in application time when the monitored start timestamps of all input streams are equal or greater than T_{split}. Then, the optimizer signals the end of all input streams to the old box in order to drain out intermediate elements. After that, the heap inside the coalesce operator containing the new results can be flushed. Finally, the optimizer shortly interrupts the processing to discard the old box as well as the split and coalesce operators before it continues to execute the new plan stand-alone.

4.3 Correctness

Lemma 1. *GenMig produces correct results and preserves the temporal ordering.*

Proof. (sketch)

1. No elements are lost during the insertion and removal of the split and coalesce operators because the processing of the boxes is suspended during these steps.
2. The split operator guarantees that all elements valid at snapshots smaller than T_{split} are transferred to the old box, while the elements with snapshots equal or greater than T_{split} are processed by the new box. This matches with the logical view of GenMig (see Section 4.1). Since no snapshot is lost under this partitioning and each box produces snapshot-equivalent results, the union of both plans contains the entire result.
3. PT uses a marking mechanism to detect duplicates, i. e., results at the same snapshot produced by both plans. We showed in Section 3 that this marking fails for stateful operators other than joins. GenMig overcomes these problems because the split operator ensures that the results of both boxes are disjoint in terms of snapshots due to the choice of T_{split}. As T_{split} is greater than any snapshot referenced in the old box, the corresponding snapshot-reducible operators in that box will never produce a result with a snapshot equal or larger than T_{split}. Moreover, the new box will never generate results for snapshots smaller than T_{split}. Consequently, GenMig inherently avoids the generation of duplicates as addressed for PT.
4. The temporal ordering is preserved as (i) all operators inside a box produce a correctly ordered output, (ii) the split operators are stateless and do not affect the ordering, and (iii) the coalesce operator explicitly synchronizes the results of the old and the new box according to the start timestamp ordering.
5. The coalesce operator combines the results of both plans. It does not have any semantic effects as coalesce preserves snapshot-equivalence [3]. Because it merges stream elements with identical tuples and adjacent time intervals, it rather serves as an optimization which inverts the negative effects of the split operator on stream rates.

6. Due to the global window constraint of w time units, the maximum interval length in a plan is limited to w time units (see window operator in Section 2). Snapshot-reducibility implies that the time intervals in the output stream of a standard operator can only have shorter time intervals. Hence, setting T_{split} to $max\{t_{S_i} | i \in \{1, \ldots, n\}\} + w + 1 + \varepsilon$ ensures that T_{split} is greater than any time instant occurring in the old box. □

4.4 Performance Analysis

Given the sufficient-system-resources assumption as in [1], the difference between system and application becomes negligible. We can thus identify durations in application time with those in system time. The migration duration of GenMig is determined by $T_{split} - min\{t_{S_i}\}$ where t_{S_i} denotes the migration start time of input i. For negligible application time skew between streams and negligible latency in streams, the migration duration is approximately w time units due to the choice of T_{split}.

Compared to PT, GenMig has the following advantages:

- For join trees with more than one join, the required time for migration is only w time units instead of $2w$. GenMig requires at most w time units because all elements in the old plan have become outdated at T_{split}. GenMig does not need to wait until all *old* elements were purged from states in the old box as done for PT. Consequently, the allocated memory for the old box can be released earlier.
- GenMig does not require any mechanisms to detect duplicates at the output of the old box. Hence, those costs for duplicate detection can be saved.
- GenMig does not need to buffer the entire results of the new box during migration for ordering purposes. All results produced by the new box during migration can be coalesced and emitted. The size of the heap and hash maps inside the coalesce operator is predominantly determined by the application time skew between the input streams. Heartbeats [11] and sophisticated scheduling strategies can be used to minimize application time skew and thus the memory allocation of the coalesce operator.
- According to [1], the migration for PT is finished if all *old* elements have been removed from the old box. For join trees with more than one join, this happens after $2w$ time units. Interestingly, the old box only produces output during the first w time units. The other w time units are used to purge all *old* elements from the states. For snapshot-reducible query plans, there will be no output during this timespan. Therefore, PT has the following output rate characteristics. For the first w time units, the output rate corresponds to the output rate of the old box. The next w time units there is no output. At the migration end there is a burst when the buffer on top of the new box is flushed. In contrast, GenMig directly switches from the output rate of the old box to the one of the new box at migration end (T_{split}).

4.5 Optimizations

Optimization 1 - Reference Point Method The reference point method [18,19] is a common technique for index structures to prevent duplicates in the output. We can use this method as an optimization of GenMig if the following modifications are performed. The split operator has to be modified to send the elements to the old plan without splitting, i. e., with the full intervals. The coalesce operator is removed and replaced by a simple selection and a union. The selection is placed on top of the new box and drops all elements with a start timestamp equal to T_{split}. The union of the old box and the selection generates the final output. We treat the start timestamp of results of the new box as reference point. This reference point is compared with T_{split}. If it is larger than T_{split}, the element is not a duplicate and sent to the output.

Using the reference point method makes coalescing superfluous. Hence, it saves the memory and processing costs spent on the coalesce operator. Both boxes produce their output correctly ordered. As we use the start timestamp as reference point, all results from the old box have a smaller start timestamp than those from the new box. Therefore, it is sufficient to first output the results of the old box and afterwards those of the new box. Under the assumptions of a global temporal scheduling as in [1], no buffer is needed to synchronize the output of both boxes. Note that all additional operators required for GenMig with reference point optimization (split, union, and selection) have constant costs per element.

Optimization 2 - Shortening Migration Duration The migration duration could be shortened if T_{split} is set to the maximum end timestamp inside the old box plus 1 plus ε. This setting still satisfies the correctness condition that T_{split} has to be greater than any time instant occurring in the old box. However, such an optimization requires to monitor the end timestamps in addition. If a DSMS provides this information as some kind of metadata, it could be effectively used to reduce the migration duration and thus gain savings of system resources. This optimization is particularly effective if the plan to be optimized is not close to window operators. In this case, it is likely that the time intervals are significantly shorter than the window size.

4.6 Positive-Negative Implementation for GenMig

The GenMig algorithm can easily be transferred to the positive-negative tuple approach [9,5]. Instead of monitoring the start timestamps, the timestamps of the positive elements are monitored. T_{split} is set as proposed in Algorithm 1. The split operator sends all incoming positive and associated negative elements to the new box and additionally to the old box if their timestamps are smaller than T_{split}. Using the timestamp of an element, independent of its sign, as reference point, we accept results from the old box if their timestamps are less than T_{split}, and from the new box if it is greater than T_{split}. Since the results generated by both plans are correctly ordered, it is sufficient to first output the results of the old box and afterwards those from the new box. The migration end is reached if all input streams passed T_{split}.

5 Experimental Evaluation

Although the primary focus of this work is on the semantics, generality, and correctness of GenMig, we conducted a set of experiments that compares GenMig with PT for join reordering. We observed that even in this case, where PT is only applicable, GenMig is at least as efficient as PT. In addition, we validated GenMig for a variety of transformation rules beyond join reordering. However, those experiments only show the correctness of GenMig and point out the potential of dynamic query optimization. As these do not contribute further insights into our approach, we omitted them due to space limitations.

We implemented PT and GenMig in our PIPES framework [20,21] with Java 5. Our hardware was a PC with an Intel Pentium 4 processor (2.8 GHz) and 1 GB of RAM running Windows XP Professional. To have a fair comparison with the original PT implementation in [1], we executed the plans in a single thread according to the global temporal ordering. Since a comparison with PT is only possible for joins, we executed 4-way nested-loops joins as done in [1].

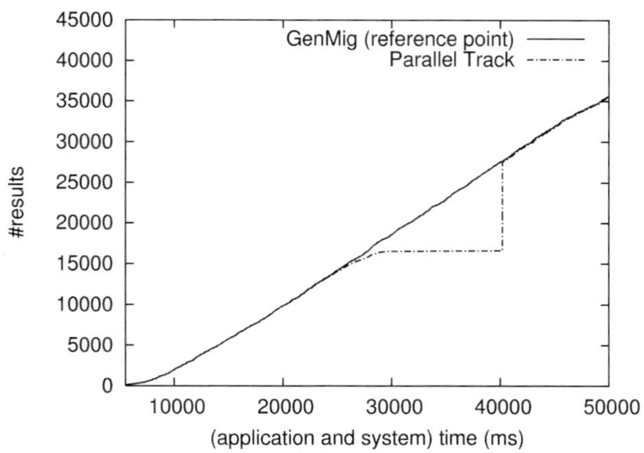

Fig. 4. Characteristics of Parallel Track and GenMig

In our first experiment, we ensured the sufficient-system-resources assumption which means that query execution can keep up with stream rates. Each input stream delivered 5000 random numbers with a rate of 100 elements per second. The random numbers were distributed uniformly between 0 and 500 for streams A and B, and between 0 and 1000 for streams C and D. We performed time-based sliding window equi-joins with a global window size of 10 seconds. The old plan was set to the left-deep join tree $((A \bowtie B) \bowtie C) \bowtie D$ which was rather inefficient due to the huge intermediate result produced by $A \bowtie B$. The goal of the dynamic plan migration was to switch to the more efficient right-deep join tree $A \bowtie (B \bowtie (C \bowtie D))$. The migration started after 20 seconds.

GenMig finished the migration w time units (10 seconds) after migration start as expected. In contrast, PT requires $2w$ time units due to purging all *old* elements from the old box. This complies with the analysis in [1]. During migration the output rate of PT decreases because the results of the new box are buffered as shown in Figure 4. For PT, after 30 seconds the output rate is 0 for 10 seconds. During this period the purging of *old* elements took place. At the migration end for PT after 40 seconds (migration start + 2 · window size $= 20 + 2 \cdot 10 = 40$), the results of the new box which had been buffered during migration were immediately released. This caused the significant burst in the output rate. Such a burst may lead to a temporary system overload and should be avoided whenever possible. In contrast to PT, GenMig produces results with a smooth output rate during migration.

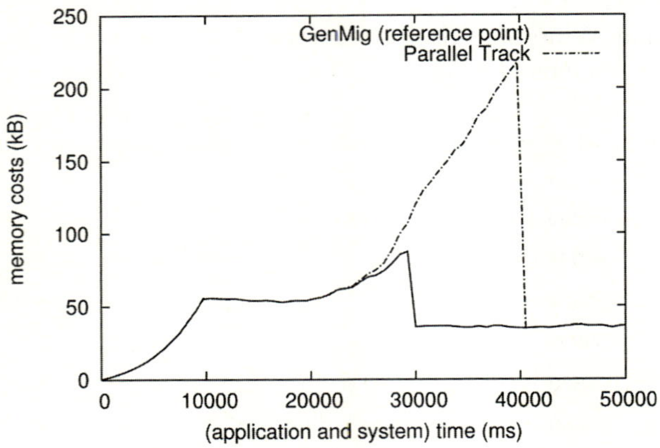

Fig. 5. Memory usage of Parallel Track and GenMig

Figure 5 shows the memory usage of GenMig and PT during the experiment. For sake of comparability, we only measured the memory allocated for the values. We omitted the overhead of timestamps – GenMig requires two timestamps per element (time interval), whereas PT needs up to four. Note that the memory usage can only differ during migration. Figure 5 demonstrates that PT continuously requires more memory than GenMig during this period. Overall, the system has an increased memory usage during plan migration but profits from the reduced memory usage of the new plan afterwards. This temporary increase of memory usage is smaller for GenMig.

Our second experiment was aimed at comparing the total system load of PT, GenMig with coalesce, and GenMig with reference point optimization. We processed the same random numbers associated with the same application timestamps as before. But this time, we processed the input streams as fast as possible. This means, we no longer synchronized application and system time, and

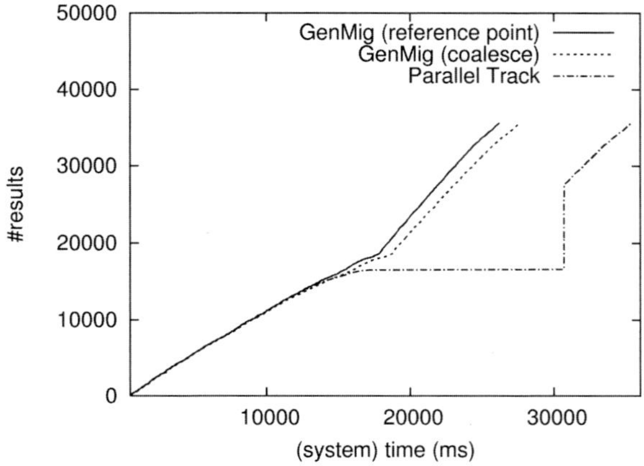

Fig. 6. Performance comparison of Parallel Track, GenMig with coalesce, and GenMig with reference point optimization

the system was saturated. This is a widely accepted approach to determine the efficiency of stream join algorithms [22]. Furthermore, we simulated a more expensive join predicate to emphasize the effects of complex join computations. Figure 6 depicts our performance measurements. At the beginning the slope of the curves, which corresponds to the output rate, is less steep than at the end because the left-deep join plan is not as efficient as the right-deep plan. During migration the slope reaches its minimum as both plans run in parallel. The total runtimes demonstrate that GenMig is superior to PT. Moreover, the reference point optimization improves the coalesce variant of GenMig slightly as it avoids the CPU costs caused by the coalesce operator.

To sum up the experiments, GenMig is not only more general than PT but also more efficient for the case of join reordering where both strategies are applicable.

6 Related Work

In recent years adaptivity issues for query processing and optimization have attracted research attention. The following discussion is limited to work related to stream processing. The interested reader is referred to [23] for a survey beyond streams.

Our work directly refers to the dynamic plan migration strategies proposed in [1] as it generalizes PT towards arbitrary continuous query plans. To the best of our knowledge, the strategies published in [1] are the only methods for dynamic plan migration in DSMS.

There are several papers on different topics of runtime optimizations for DSMS but these do not tackle plan migration issues explicitly. In [24] the problem of executing continuous multiway join queries is addressed for streaming environments with changing data characteristics. GenMig does not aim at optimizing multiway join performance by materializing intermediate join views. In contrast, it is designed more general and treats join reordering as one possible transformation rule. Proactive re-optimization [25] is a novel optimization technique in stream processing in which the optimizer selects the initial query plan with the background information that this plan is likely to be re-optimized in future due to uncertainty in estimates of the underlying statistics. However, the choice of a suitable plan is not the focus of GenMig. It rather describes how to migrate from one plan to another snapshot-equivalent plan.

Eddies [26] perform a very flexible kind of adaptive runtime optimization for continuous queries. Unlike traditional approaches where elements are processed according to a given query plan until the plan is re-optimized, all operators of a query plan are connected with the eddy. For each incoming element, the eddy determines an individual query plan. PT and GenMig are by far not as flexible as eddies, but the per-element routing is expensive and only profitable in highly dynamic environments. Moreover, eddies are limited to queries with selection, projection, and join, whereas GenMig considers more general plans.

Cross-network optimization issues for continuous queries are discussed in [27] for the Borealis stream processing engine, but not at a semantic level with concrete techniques for plan migration as presented in this paper. How GenMig can be adapted to a distributed environment remains as an open issue for future work.

7 Conclusions

In this paper we first identified shortcomings of the parallel track strategy, an existing solution for the dynamic plan migration problem in DSMS. We showed that this strategy fails to cope with plans involving stateful operators other than joins. We consequently proposed a general approach to dynamic plan migration, called *GenMig*, which enables a DSMS to optimize arbitrary CQL queries at runtime. Our analysis and performance comparison shows that GenMig with its optimizations is at least as efficient as parallel track, while being more general. Due to the underlying semantics, the whole set of conventional transformation rules can be applied for optimization purposes. Moreover, GenMig does not require any specific knowledge about the operator states and implementations because it treats the old and new plans as black boxes which only have to produce snapshot-equivalent results to ensure correctness. Due to its generality and ease of use, GenMig is likely to be integrated into existing and future DSMS as a basic mechanism for the dynamic query optimization of continuous queries.

References

1. Zhu, Y., Rundensteiner, E.A., Heineman, G.T.: Dynamic Plan Migration for Continuous Queries Over Data Streams. In: Proc. of the ACM SIGMOD. (2004) 431–442
2. Krämer, J., Seeger, B.: A Temporal Foundation for Continuous Queries over Data Streams. In: Proc. of the Int. Conf. on Management of Data (COMAD). (2005) 70–82

3. Slivinskas, G., Jensen, C.S., Snodgrass, R.T.: Query Plans for Conventional and Temporal Queries Involving Duplicates and Ordering. In: Proc. of the IEEE Conference on Data Engineering (ICDE). (2000) 547–558
4. Böhlen, M.H., Busatto, R., Jensen, C.S.: Point-Versus Interval-Based Temporal Data Models. In: Proc. of the IEEE Conference on Data Engineering (ICDE). (1998) 192–200
5. Arasu, A., Babu, S., Widom, J.: An Abstract Semantics and Concrete Language for Continuous Queries over Streams and Relations. In: Proc. of the Int. Conf. on Data Base Programming Languages (DBPL). (2003) 1–19
6. Dayal, U., Goodman, N., Katz, R.H.: An Extended Relational Algebra with Control Over Duplicate Elimination. In: Proc. of the ACM SIGMOD. (1982) 117–123
7. Albert, J.: Algebraic Properties of Bag Data Types. In: Proc. of the Int. Conf. on Very Large Databases (VLDB). (1991) 211–219
8. Krämer, J., Seeger, B.: A Temporal Foundation for Continuous Queries over Data Streams. Technical report, University of Marburg (2004) No. 45.
9. Hammad, M., Aref, W., Franklin, M., Mokbel, M., Elmagarmid, A.: Efficient Execution of Sliding Window Queries over Data Streams. Technical report, Purdue University (2003) No. 35.
10. Golab, L., Özsu, M.T.: Issues in Data Stream Management. SIGMOD Record **32**(2) (2003) 5–14
11. Srivastava, U., Widom, J.: Flexible Time Management in Data Stream Systems. In: Symp. on Principles of Database Systems (PODS). (2004) 263–274
12. Arasu, A., Babu, S., Widom, J.: The CQL Continuous Query Language: Semantic Foundations and Query Execution. Technical report, Stanford University (2003) No. 57.
13. Galindo-Legaria, C., Joshi, M.: Orthogonal Optimization of Subqueries and Aggregation. In: Proc. of the ACM SIGMOD. (2001) 571–581
14. Babcock, B., Babu, S., Datar, M., Motwani, R.: Chain: Operator Scheduling for Memory Minimization in Data Stream Systems. In: Proc. of the ACM SIGMOD. (2003) 253–264
15. Carney, D., Cetintemel, U., Zdonik, S., Rasin, A., Cerniak, M., Stonebraker, M.: Operator Scheduling in a Data Stream Manager. In: Proc. of the Int. Conf. on Very Large Databases (VLDB). (2003) 838–849
16. Jiang, Q., Chakravarthy, S.: Scheduling Strategies for Processing Continuous Queries over Streams. Lecture Notes in Computer Science **3112** (2004) 16–30
17. Cammert, M., Krämer, J., Seeger, B., Vaupel, S.: An Approach to Adaptive Memory Management in Data Stream Systems. In: Proc. of the IEEE Conference on Data Engineering (ICDE). (2006) 137–139
18. Seeger, B.: Performance Comparison of Segment Access Methods Implemented on Top of the Buddy-Tree. In: Advances in Spatial Databases. Volume 525 of Lecture Notes in Computer Science., Springer (1991) 277–296
19. van den Bercken, J., Seeger, B.: Query Processing Techniques for Multiversion Access Methods. In: Proc. of the Int. Conf. on Very Large Databases (VLDB). (1996) 168–179
20. Krämer, J., Seeger, B.: PIPES - A Public Infrastructure for Processing and Exploring Streams. In: Proc. of the ACM SIGMOD. (2004) 925–926
21. Cammert, M., Heinz, C., Krämer, J., Riemenschneider, T., Schwarzkopf, M., Seeger, B., Zeiss, A.: Stream Processing in Production-to-Business Software. In: Proc. of the IEEE Conference on Data Engineering (ICDE). (2006) 168–169

22. Golab, L., Öszu, M.T.: Processing Sliding Window Multi-Joins in Continuous Queries over Data Streams. In: Proc. of the Int. Conf. on Very Large Databases (VLDB). (2003) 500–511
23. Babu, S., Bizarro, P.: Adaptive Query Processing in the Looking Glass. In: Proc. of the Conf. on Innovative Data Systems Research (CIDR). (2005) 238–249
24. Babu, S., Munagala, K., Widom, J., Motwani, R.: Adaptive Caching for Continuous Queries. In: Proc. of the IEEE Conference on Data Engineering (ICDE). (2005) 118–129
25. Babu, S., Bizarro, P., DeWitt, D.: Proactive Re-Optimization. In: Proc. of the ACM SIGMOD. (2005) 107–118
26. Deshpande, A., Hellerstein, J.M.: Lifting the Burden of History from Adaptive Query Processing. In: Proc. of the Int. Conf. on Very Large Databases (VLDB). (2004) 948–959
27. Abadi, D.J., Ahmad, Y., et al. M.B.: The Design of the Borealis Stream Processing Engine. In: Proc. of the Conf. on Innovative Data Systems Research (CIDR). (2005) 277–289

Unsatisfiability Reasoning in ORM Conceptual Schemes

Mustafa Jarrar[1] and Stijn Heymans[2]

[1] STAR Lab, Vrije Universiteit Brussel, Belgium
mjarrar@vub.ac.be
[2]TINF, Vrije Universiteit Brussel, Belgium
sheymans@vub.ac.be

Abstract. ORM (Object-Role Modeling) is a rich and well-known conceptual modeling method. As ORM has a formal semantics, reasoning tasks such as satisfiability checking of an ORM schema naturally arise. Satisfiability checking allows a developer to automatically detect contradicting constraints. However, no *complete* satisfiability checker is known for ORM. In this paper, we revisit existing patterns from literature that indicate unsatisfiability of ORM schemes i.e., schemes that cannot be populated, and we propose refinements as well as additions for them. Although this does not yield a complete procedure – there may be ORM schemes passing the pattern checks while containing unsatisfiable roles – it yields an efficient and easy to implement detection mechanism (specially in interactive modeling tools) for the most common conceptual modeling mistakes.

1 Introduction

ORM (Object-Role Modeling) is a conceptual modeling approach and the historic successor of the NIAM (Natural-language Information Analysis Method) [VB82]. ORM schemes can be translated into pseudo natural language statements. The graphical representation and the translation into pseudo natural language make it a lot easier, also for non-computer scientists, to create, check and adapt the knowledge about the Universe of Discourse (UoD) needed in an information system.

Although ORM was originally developed as a database modeling approach, it has been also successfully reused in other conceptual modeling scenarios, such as *ontology modeling* [J05], business rule modeling [H97,N99,DJM02a], XML-Schema conceptual design [BGH99], etc. Hence, we shall regard an ORM schema, in this paper, as a general conceptual model independently of a certain modeling scenario or domain[1].

ORM has a well-defined formal semantics (see e.g. [H89,BHW91,T96,TM95]). This formal semantics naturally leads to the question of satisfiability checking, i.e. given a concept/role in a schema, is there a model (an interpretation/population of the schema that satisfies all constraints) such that the concept/role has a non-empty population. From a practical perspective, such reasoning procedures can help the

[1] We sometimes interchange the term "ORM schema" with the term "axiomatization" to refer to the same thing.

T. Grust et al. (Eds.): EDBT 2006 Workshops, LNCS 4254, pp. 517 – 534, 2006.

developer in analyzing the *validity* of the constructed schema for the domain. In particular, it allows to detect concepts and roles in a schema that always have an empty population, symptoms of a faulty model: there are too many constraints or constraints are too harsh[2].

For example, consider Fig. 1, stating that Students and Employees are types of Persons where no Student can be an Employee (and vice versa), and a PhD Student is both a Student and an Employee. Thus, the PhDStudent type cannot be populated. Otherwise, a PhD Student would be both a student and an employee which contradicts with the fact that Student and Employee need to be disjoint types (by the exclusion constraint). Although there are types in the schema in Fig. 1 that cannot be satisfied, there is a formal model satisfying the global schema: e.g. let PhDStudent have an empty population, Student and Employee disjoint populations, and Person some superset of the union of the populations of Student and Employee.

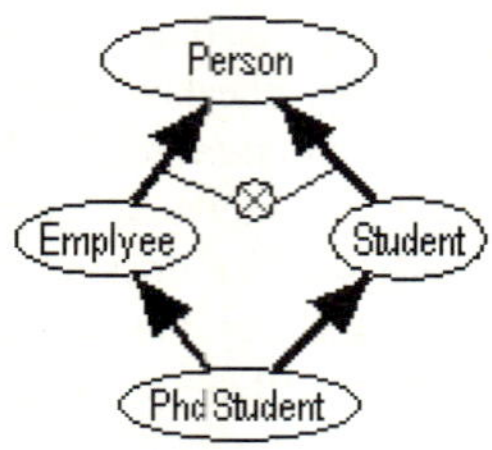

Fig. 1. Unsatisfiability of ORM schema

Types of Satisfiability. Formally, we distinguish between three types of satisfiability of an ORM schema [BHW91]. First, *schema satisfiability checking* of an ORM schema is checking whether there exists a model of the schema (or less abstract, some population for the schema) as a whole. A satisfiable ORM schema does not need to satisfy any concepts or roles per se, as exemplified in Fig. 1. The only condition is that all constraints are satisfied by the (possibly empty) populations. Second, *concept satisfiability checking* amounts to checking whether *all* concepts (i.e. object-types) are satisfied (can be populated) by a model (by a population) of the schema. Concept satisfiability is thus stronger than schema satisfiability as a model of the schema that satisfies all concepts is, by definition, also a model of the schema. Finally, *role satisfiability checking* amounts to checking whether there exists a model of the schema that satisfies (populates) *all* roles in the schema. This is the strongest form of satisfiability checking as it implies concept satisfiability: if a role is satisfied, the corresponding concept that plays the role is also satisfied. Given these implications (*role then concept then schema satisfiable)*, we refer to role satisfiability as *strong satisfiability* and to *schema satisfiability* as *weak satisfiability.*

In this context, we are particularly interested in strong satisfiability: checking whether *all* roles in the schema are satisfiable: since a weakly satisfiable model may contain empty roles, problems with contradictory constraints are not necessarily detected. Note that if the schema does not contain roles we will also look at concept satisfiability.

[2] We assume the UoD itself is consistent, such that faults in the model have their origin in the modeling and not in the UoD.

In this paper, we refine, optimize, and re-represent existing ORM "formation rules" found formed in [H89,DMV,BHW91], as well as introduce new ones for detecting unsatisfiable roles (we call it *unsatisfiability constraint patterns*). Furthermore, we indicate how a significant part of these existing rules are not aimed at detecting unsatisfiability but are guidelines for good modeling, e.g., to avoid redundant/implied constraints.

Our patterns approach for detecting unsatisfiable models is motivated by the needs that *unsatisfiability procedures should be easy to implement and applicable in interactive modeling.* The latter requirement enforces that the procedures should be fast as well. We shall come back to this motivation in Sec. 4, and illustrate how our approach can be applied in *interactive* ontology modeling tools, which indeed help ontology builders to quickly detect unsatisfiability in the early phases of ontology modeling. Our experience in applying this approach for the development of a customer complaint ontology (developed by 10s of lawyers) will be reported in Sec. 4 as well.

Although our approach covers the most common unsatisfiability cases in practice, it cannot be complete, i.e., there are ORM schemas that are not strongly satisfiable but will fail to be detected by our patters. This is because of the general problem of determining consistency for all possible constraint patterns in ORM is undecidable [H97], e.g., the use of transitivity combined with frequency constraints is problematic with regards to decidability. In Sec. 4, we shall discuss and compare our patterns approach with the work that we have done on mapping (large part of) ORM into description logics (DLs) [JF05]. We shall discuss that the patterns approach (which we present in this paper) offers fast and easy to implement and understand reasoning mechanism specially for interactive modeling. We believe that both approaches complement each other.

The remainder of the paper is organized as follows. In Sec. 2, we introduce 9 patterns for detecting unsatisfiability of ORM models. Section 3 discusses related work, Sec. 4 illustrates the implementation of the patterns, and Sec. 5 contains discussion, conclusions and directions for future work.

2 Unsatisfiability Patterns in ORM Conceptual Schemes

In this section, we present and discuss 9 patterns that can be used to detect unsatisfiability in an ORM conceptual schema[3]. We adopt the ORM formalization and syntax as found in [H89,H01], except three things. First, although ORM supports n-ary predicates, only binary predicates are considered. Second, our approach does not support objectification, or the so-called nested fact-types in ORM. Finally, our approach does not support the derivation constraints that are not part of the ORM graphical notation.

Pattern 1 (Top common supertype)

In this pattern, subtypes that do not have a top common supertype are detected. In ORM, all object-types are assumed by definition to be mutually exclusive, except

[3] An extended version of this work can be found in [J05].

those that are subtypes of the same supertype. Thus, if a subtype has more than one supertype, these supertypes must share a top supertype; otherwise, the subtype cannot be satisfied. In Fig. 2 the object-type C cannot be satisfied because its supertypes A and B do not share a common supertype, i.e. A and B are mutually exclusive.

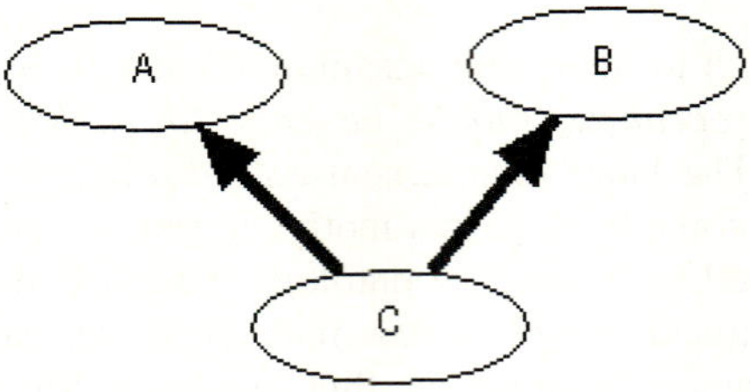

Fig. 2. Subtype without a top common supertype

Formally, for each subtype T in the schema, let $T.\mathrm{DirectSupers}$ be the set of all n direct supertypes of T. Let $T.\mathrm{DirectSupers}_i.\mathrm{Supers}$ be all supertypes of the i-th direct supertype of T. If $(T.\mathrm{DirectSupers}_1.\mathrm{supers} \cap \ldots \cap T.\mathrm{DirectSupers}_n.\mathrm{supers}) = \varnothing$, then the object-type T cannot be satisfied. See the appendix for the implementation detail.

Pattern 2 (Exclusive constraint between types)

In this pattern, subtypes of mutually exclusive supertypes (caused by an exclusive constraint) are detected. Fig. 3 shows a case where D cannot be satisfied because its supertypes are mutually exclusive. The set of instances of D is the intersection of the instances of B and C, which is an empty set according to the exclusive constraint between B and C.

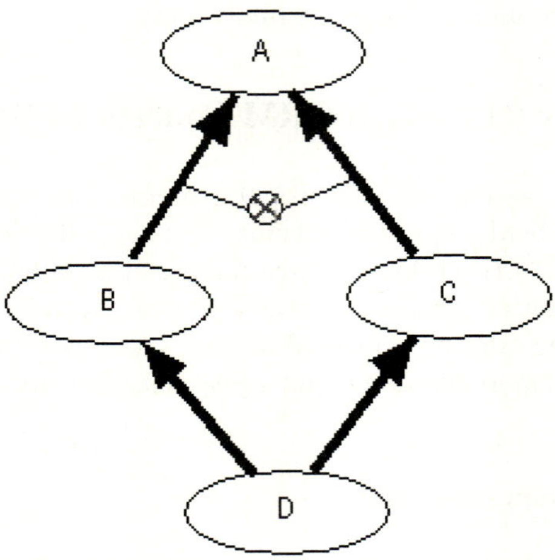

Fig. 3. Subtype with exclusive supertypes

Formally, for each exclusive constraint between a set of object-types $T = \{T_1, \ldots T_n\}$, let $T_i.\mathrm{Subs}$ be the set of all possible subtypes of the object-type T_i, and $T_j.\mathrm{Subs}$ be the set of all possible subtypes of the object-type T_j, where $i \neq j$, the set $(T_i.\mathrm{Subs} \cap T_j.\mathrm{Subs})$ must be empty. See the appendix for the implementation detail.

Pattern 3 (Exclusion-Mandatory)

In this pattern, contradictions between exclusion and mandatory constraints are detected. In Fig. 4, we show three examples of unsatisfiable schemes.

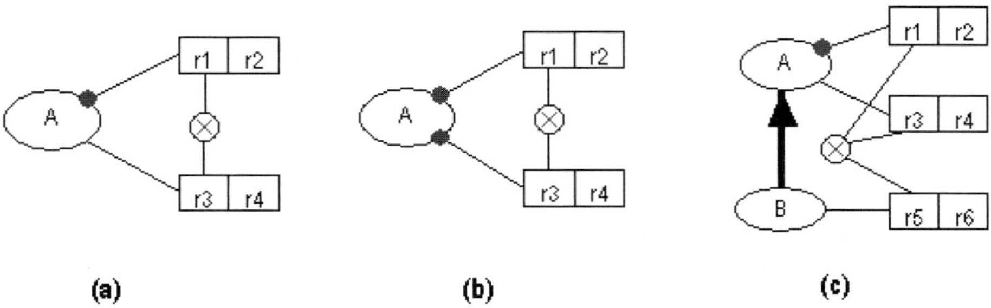

Fig. 4. Unsatisfiable schemes because of mandatory and exclusion conflicts

In the first case (a), the role r3 will never be played. The mandatory and exclusion constraints restrict that each instance of A must play r1 and the instance that plays r1 cannot play r3. In the second case (b), both r1 and r3 will never be played. According to the two mandatory constraints, each instance of A must play both r1 and r3. At the same time, according to the exclusion constraints, an instance of A cannot play r1 and r3 together. Likewise, in the third case (c), r3 and r5 will never be played. As B is a subtype of A, instances of B inherit all roles and constraints from A. For example, if an instance of B plays r5, then this instance – which is also instance of A – cannot play r1 or r3. However, according to the mandatory constraint, each instance of A must play r1 and, according to the exclusion constrain, it cannot play r1, r3 and r5 all at the same time. In general, a contradiction occurs if an object-type plays a mandatory role that is exclusive with other roles played by this object-type or one of its subtypes. Formally, for each exclusion constraint between a set of single roles R, let $R_i.T$ be the object-type that plays the role R_i, $R_i \in R$. For each (R_i, R_j), where $i \neq j$ and R_i *is mandatory*, If $R_i.T = R_j.T$ or $R_j.T \in R_i.T.Subs$ -where $R_i.O.Subs$ is the set of all subtypes of the object-type $R_i.O$, then some roles in R cannot be populated.

Pattern 4 (Frequency-Value)

In this pattern, contradictions between value and frequency constraints are detected.

In Fig. 5, the role r1 cannot be populated. If the frequency constraint FC(3 - 5) on r1 is satisfied, each instance of A must play r1 at least three times, and thus three

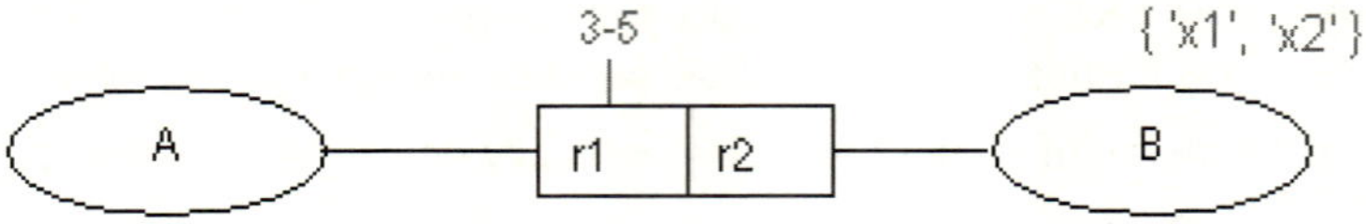

Fig. 5. Contradiction between value and frequency constraints

different instances of B are required. However, there are only two possible instances of B, which are declared by the value constraint {'x1', 'x2'}. For each fact-type ($A\ r\ B$), let c be the number of the possible values of B that can be calculated from its value constraint, and let FC($n-m$) be a frequency constraint on the role r, then c must be equal or more than n. Otherwise, the role r cannot be satisfied, as the value and the frequency constraints contradict each other.

Pattern 5 (Value-Exclusion-Frequency)

In this pattern, contradictions between value, exclusion, and frequency constraints are detected. Fig. 6 shows a particular contradiction between those three constraints. Due to the frequency constraint, there should be at least two different values to populate r1. In order to populate r3, we need, by the exclusion constraint, a value different from the two for role r1. In total, we thus need three different values in order to be able to populate both r1 and r2, but this contradicts with the value constraint on object-type A: we only have 2 values at our disposal. Note that any combination with only two of the three constraints does not amount to unsatisfiability; we explicitly need the combination of the three of them.

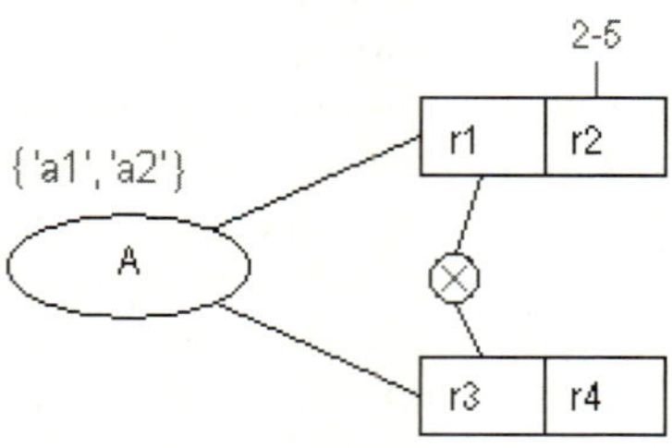

Fig. 6. Contradiction between value, exclusion, and frequency constraints

A special case occurs in the absence of frequency constraints, e.g., Fig. 7: according to the exclusion constraint, there should be at least three different values of A to play r1, r2 and r3. However, according to the value constraint, there are only two possible values of A.

We assume that exclusion constraints are in their most compact form. For example, the exclusion constraint in Fig. 7 is the compact representation of three different exclusion constraints: between r1 and r3, r3 and r5, and r1 and r5.

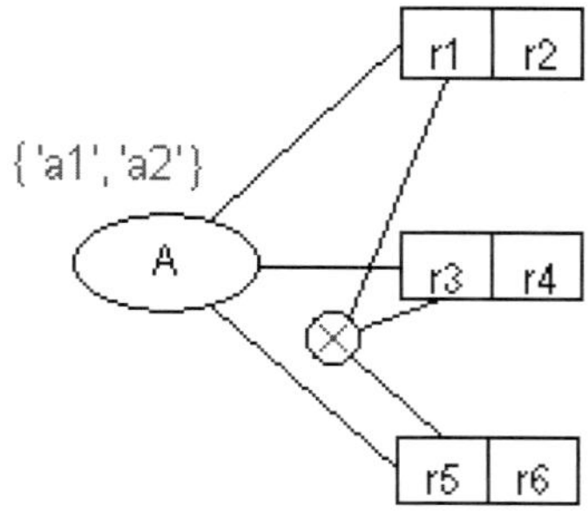

Fig. 7. Contradiction between value and exclusion constraints

Formally, for each exclusion constraint, let $R=\{R_1,\ldots,R_n\}$ be the set of roles participating in this constraint. With each of those roles R_i, we associate the inverse role S_i, and we let f_i be the minimum of the frequency constraint on S_i (if there is no frequency constraint on S_i, we take f_i equal to 1). Let T be the object-type that plays all roles in R. Let C be the number of the possible values of T, according to the value constraint. C *must always be more than or equal to* $f_1+\ldots+f_n$. Otherwise, some roles in R cannot be satisfied. See the appendix for the implementation detail. Note that this pattern is actually a generalization of the previous pattern where there are no exclusion constraints. However, the current pattern explicitly focuses on the exclusion constraints attached to a role, taking into account the frequency constraints, to decide whether some roles are unsatisfiable. As pattern 4 does not contain exclusion constraints, a similar strategy would not work.

Pattern 6 (Set-comparison constraints)

In this pattern, contradictions between exclusion, subset, and equality constraints are detected. Fig. 8 shows a contradiction between the exclusion and the subset constraints. This contradiction implies that both predicates cannot be populated.

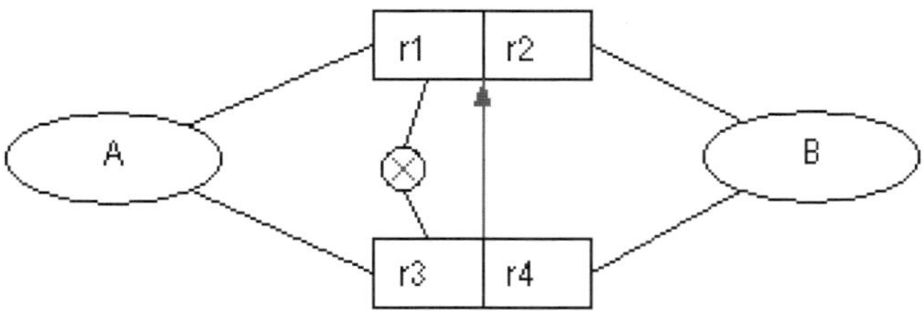

Fig. 8. A non fact-type populatable schema

The exclusion constraint between the two roles r1 and r3 means that their populations should be distinct. However, in order to satisfy the subset constraint between (r1, r2) and (r3, r4), the populations of r1 and r3 should not be distinct. In other words, the exclusion constraint between r1 and r3 implies an exclusion constraint between (r1, r2) and (r3, r4) [H89], which contradicts any subset or equality constraint between both predicates. Fig. 9 shows the implications for each set-comparison constraint that might be declared between parts of role sequences. These implications are taken into account when reasoning for contradictions between the three set-comparison constraints.

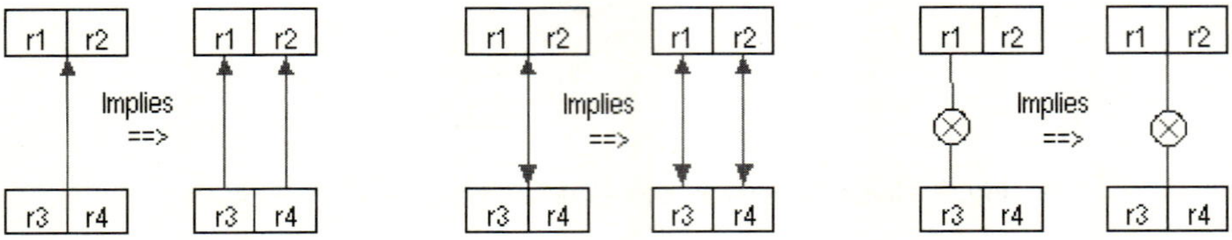

Fig. 9. Main set-comparison implications

In addition, an equality constraint is equivalent to two subset constraints. Hence, we refer to a subset or an equality constraint as a SetPath. Formally, for each exclusion constraint between A and B: If A and B are two predicates, there should not be any (direct or implied) SetPath between these predicates; If A and B are single roles, there should not be any (direct or implied) SetPath between both roles or between the predicates that include these roles. Otherwise, the two predicates cannot be populated, as the two constraints contradict each other. See the appendix for the implementation detail.

Pattern 7 (Uniqueness-Frequency)

In this pattern, all occurrences of a uniqueness constraint that contradicts with a frequency constraint on the role are detected. E.g., in Fig. 10 the uniqueness constraint indicates that the role r1 should be played by at most one element, while the frequency constraint demands that there are at least 2 and at most 5 participants in the role (denoted as FC(2-5)). It is thus impossible to populate r1. Formally, unsatisfiability of a role occurs if there is a frequency constraint FC(min-max) and a uniqueness constraint on some role (or predicate) r where min is strictly greater than 1. See the appendix for the implementation detail.

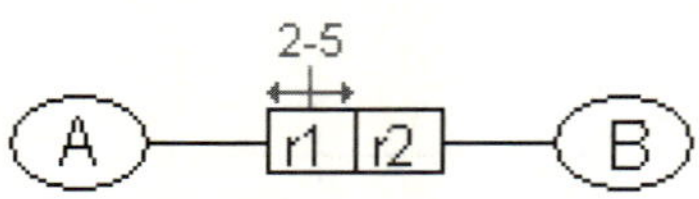

Fig. 10. Unsatisfiability of frequency and uniqueness constraint

Pattern 8 (Ring constraints)

ORM allows ring constraints to be applied to a pair of roles that are connected directly to the same object-type in a fact-type, or indirectly via supertypes. Six kinds of ring constraints are supported by ORM: antisymmetric (ans), asymmetric (as), acyclic (ac), irreflexive (ir), intransitive (it), and symmetric (sym) [H01,H99]. For

Fig. 11. Irreflexivity on the ring constraint

example, Fig. 11 shows an irreflexivity on the *Sister Of* role, indicating that no woman is her own sister.

The relationships between the six ring constraints are formalized by [H01] using the Euler diagram as in Fig. 12. This formalization indeed helps to visualize the implication and incompatibility between the constraints. For example, one can see

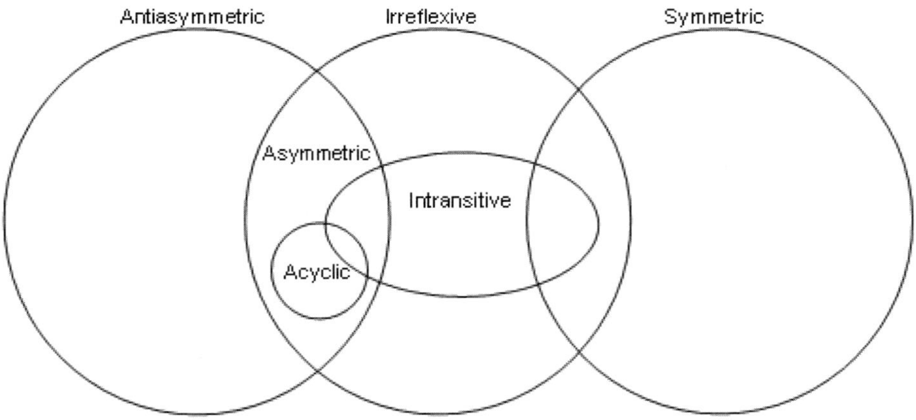

Fig. 12. Relationships between ring constraints [H01]

Table 1. All possible compatible combinations or ring constraints

No.	Constraint$_1$	Constraint$_2$	Combination
1	Ans	Ir	As
2	Ans	As	as
3	Ans	It	Ans, it
4	Ans	Ac	ac
5	Ir	Sym	Ir, sym
6	Ir	As	as
7	Ir	It	It
8	Ir	Ac	Ac
9	Sym	It	Sym, it
10	As	It	As, it
11	As	Ac	ac
12	it	ac	It, ac
13	Ans, it	Ans	Ans, it
14	Ans, it	Ir	Ans, it
15	Ans, it	As	Ans, it
16	Ans, it	It	Ans, it
17	Ans, it	Ac	it, ac
18	Ir, sym	Ir	Ir, sym
19	Ir, sym	Sym	Ir, sym

No.	Constraint$_1$	Constraint$_1$	Combination
20	Ir, sym	It	It, sym
21	Sym, it	Ir	Sym, it
22	Sym, it	Sym	Sym, it
23	Sym, it	It	Sym, it
24	As, it	Ans	As, it
25	As, it	Ir	As, it
26	As, it	As	As, it
27	As, it	It	As, it
28	As, it	Ac	Ac, it
29	It, ac	Ans	It, ac
30	It, ac	Ir	It, ac
31	It, ac	As	It, ac
32	It, ac	It	It, ac
33	It, ac	Ac	It, ac
34	Ans, it	As, it	it, as
35	Ans, it	It, ac	it, ac
36	Ir, sym	Sym, it	sym, it
37	As, it	It, ac	it, ac

that acyclic implies reflexivity, intransitivity implies reflexivity, the combination between antisymmetric and irreflexivity is exactly asymmetric, and acyclic and symmetric are incompatible, i.e. their combination leads to unsatisfiability).

In general, unsatisfiability occurs if two ring constraints that are disjoint in the Euler diagram are used. Based on the Euler diagram, we derive in Table 1. all possible compatible combinations of the six ring constraints. Combinations that do not appear in the table are incompatible and lead to unsatisfiable roles, e.g., (Sym, it) and (Ans), (Sym, it) and (It, ac), or (Ans, it) and (Ir, sym).

Pattern 9 (Loops in Subtypes)

In this pattern, loops in the subtype relation are detected. Since in ORM, the population of a subtype is a strict subset, i.e. a subset and not equal, of the population of its supertype [H01], one cannot have loops. Otherwise, one would have that a population is a strict subset of itself, which is not possible. In Fig. 13, none of the object-types A, B, or C can be satisfied since they form a loop.

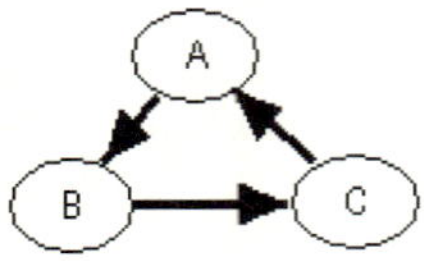

Fig. 13. Loop in subtypes

Formally, for each subtype T in the schema, let T.Supers be the set of all supertypes of T. If T in T.Supers, then the object-type T cannot be satisfied. See the appendix for the implementation detail. Note that there is no analogous pattern for subset constraints; no strict subset relation is required for subset constraints, such that loops in subset constraints imply equality of the involved roles but do not lead to unsatisfiability in general.

3 Related Work

In [H89], 7 formation rules for constraints on ORM conceptual schemes are described. We discuss to which extent these rules can also be used for detecting unsatisfiability of roles and how they relate to the patterns described in the previous section.

Formation rule 1 *(A frequency constraint of 1 is never used (the uniqueness constraint must be used instead))* and rule 2 *(A frequency constraint cannot span a whole predicate)* prefer one syntactical form over another (rule 1) or prohibit a, from a logical perspective, nonsensical[4] frequency constraint (rule 2). Rule 1 is, however, not relevant, where we call a rule *relevant* if it is relevant from an unsatisfiability detection perspective, i.e. a rule is relevant, if in case it is violated, there is an

[4] Nonsensical, since predicates are interpreted as sets, where each element in a set is, by definition of sets, unique in that set.

unsatisfiable role. Regarding rule 2, as the population of an ORM predicate is basically a set, any frequency constraint FC(min-max) where min is strictly greater then 1 leads to unsatisfiability. Rule 2 is, however, too strict in the sense that a frequency constraint FC(1-max), although redundant, does not lead to unsatisfiability. Pattern 7 takes care of the latter case (where it is assumed, as is implicit in ORM, that a predicate is spanned by a uniqueness constraint). Note that we are only interested in unsatisfiability; from a modeling perspective the formation rules are most certainly useful, in the sense that they, e.g., avoid adding redundant constraints to the schema.

Rule 3 *(No role sequence exactly spanned by a uniqueness constraint can have a frequency constraint)* is again too strict by itself to be relevant for unsatisfiability. For example, a constraint FC(1 – 5) and a uniqueness constraint on the same role do not yield an unsatisfiable role. They are, however, equivalent with FC(1 – 1) or with a mandatory plus a uniqueness constraint, thus, from a modeling perspective, formation rule 3 makes sense, but it does not necessarily lead to an unsatisfiable role. We loosened up rule 3 to take this into account in pattern 7.

Rule 4 *(No uniqueness constraint can be spanned by a longer uniqueness constraint)* is again not relevant for unsatisfiability. Rule 5 *(An exclusion constraint cannot be specified between roles if at least one of these roles is marked as mandatory)* is exactly pattern 3; we made it explicit that the rule applies to subtypes as well.

Rule 6 *(An exclusion constraint cannot be specified between two roles attached to object-types one of which is specified as a subtype of the other)* is not relevant for unsatisfiability. There are ORM conceptual schemes violating rule 6, although all roles are satisfiable, e.g., Fig. 14.

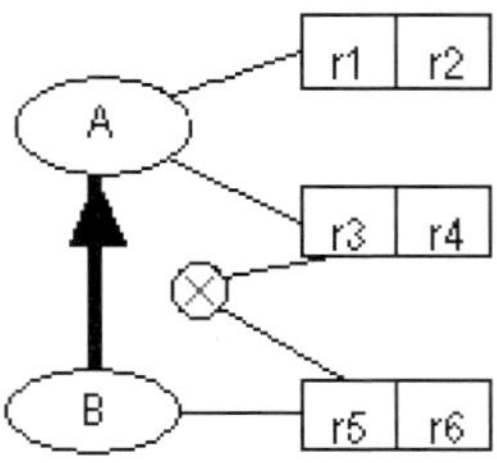

Fig. 14. ORM schema violating formation rule 6 but with satisfiable roles

For example, populate r5 with some 'a', then 'a', by the subtyping, must play one of the roles r1 or r3. It cannot play r3 due to the exclusion constraint but nothing keeps it from playing r1.

The last formation rule, rule 7 *(A frequency constraint with upper bound n cannot be specified on a role sequence if n is less than the product of the maximum cardinalities of the other role populations for the predicate)*, is covered by pattern 4 since we restrict ourselves to binary predicates[5]. The 7 ORM formation rules thus provide useful criteria for constructing ORM schemes: in a lot of cases they avoid unsatisfiability as well as implied (redundant) constraints. However, the rules mix

[5] Maximal cardinalities in [H89] correspond to value constraints.

both syntactical and semantical criteria, occasionally yielding too strict criteria for detecting unsatisfiability. The constraint patterns, described in Sec. 3, focus on the semantical aspect of unsatisfiability only.

In [DMV], the RIDL-A module of the RIDL* workbench, a database engineering tool based on the NIAM methodology [VB82], checks whether a conceptual schema is correctly constructed. Since NIAM is the predecessor of ORM, it is interesting to compare the criteria RIDL-A employs to our patterns. Of particular interest in the RIDL-A module are the Validity Analysis (rules V1-V6) and Set Constraint Analysis (rules S1 – S4) parts.

It appears that none of the Validity Analysis rules are relevant for unsatisfiability. The Set Constraint Analysis part contains 4 rules dealing with three types of constraints: subset, equality, and exclusion. S1 and S3 say that a subset (resp. equality) constraint may not be superfluous[6]. Although interesting from a modeling perspective, neither S1 nor S3 lead to unsatisfiability of roles in itself. S2 *(A subset constraint may not contain any loops)* is not relevant for unsatisfiability; the population of the roles would be equal but can be non-empty. Note that we use the definition of subset constraints on predicates as in [H89], i.e. a role r1 is a subset of r2 if every element playing role r1 also plays r2. In particular, r1 does not need to be a *strict* subset of r2: they may be equal. S2 is relevant for subset constraints between subtypes since those are strict; we covered this with pattern 9.

Finally, S4 *(The OTSETS[7] involved on an exclusion constraint may not have a common subset)* is a valid condition for detecting inconsistency. It is, however, too general, in the sense that it is actually the definition of an exclusion constraint, and does not indicate how the exclusion might yield unsatisfiable roles.

4 Implementation and Discussion

The DogmaModeler, an ontology and business rules engineering tool, implements the patterns described in this paper. Fig. 15 displays these patterns as a menu in the DogmaModeler Validator Settings window[8]. Users can choose to enable or disable the enforcement of these validation patterns when reasoning about the satisfiability of an ORM model. The DogmaModeler typically implements the satisfiability patterns that we have developed in Sec. 2. In the appendices, we present 9 algorithms, which are written in a JAVA-like code, to implement the 9 patterns in DogmaModeler. One can see, from these algorithms, that DogmaModeler does not only detect unsatisfiable ORM models, but also, it gives (through the generated message) details about the detected problems, such as, which constraints cause the unsatisfiability, the problems with the other constraints, etc.

Experience in developing ontologies in DogmaModeler shows that detecting unsatisfiability in an interactive manner helps ontology builders in quick detection of mistakes. In other words, we found that interactive detection of unsatisfiability improves the modeling skills of ontology builders, especially those who are not well trained in ontology modeling and logics.

---

[6] A constraint is superfluous – or implied – if it can be derived from other constraints.

[7] The OTSET of a role corresponds, roughly, to the population of a role.

[8] The specification of the last three implication patterns is adopted from [H89].

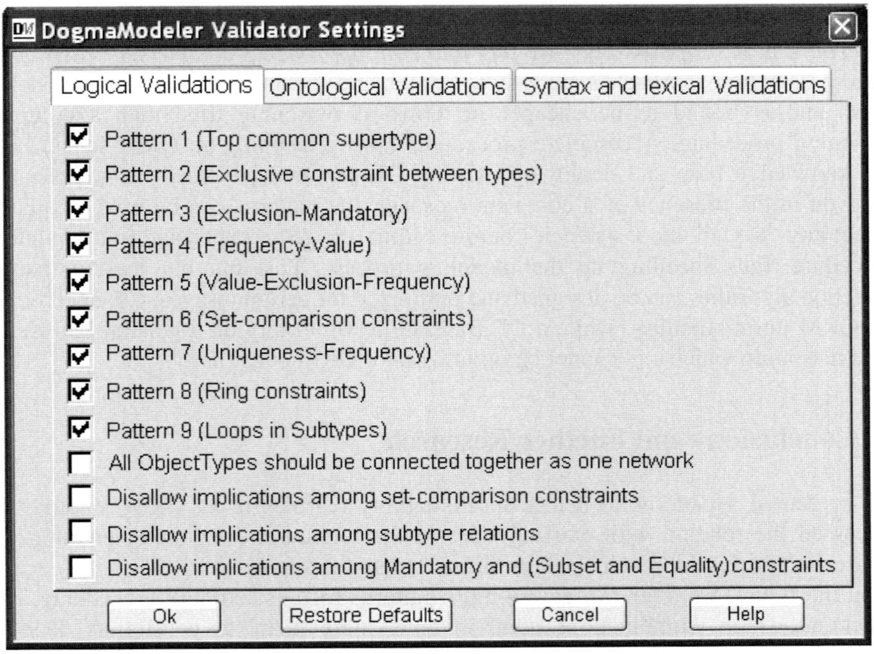

Fig. 15. DogmaModeler's support of logical validations

It is probably worth to note that our motivation for developing this patterns-approach was derived from our experience in using ORM to develop a Customer Complaint Ontology [J05,JVM03], which was done within the CCFORM project, IST-2001-38248. This ontology was built by 10s of lawyers, and the presented reasoning patters were applied to guide those lawyers to detect inconsistency problems in early phases. One of the interesting lessons we have learned in this project is that the implementation of the patterns (*in an interactive manner* during the ontology modeling process) enabled the lawyers to learn how to avoid such mistakes the next time. Some of them even admitted that they understood some logics from their experience in using DogmaModeler[9].

As we have mentioned earlier, we have also tackled the ORM satisfiability problem in another way. We have mapped ORM into the ***DLR*** Description Logic [JF05], DLR is a powerful and decidable fragment of first order logic [CDLNR98]. This mapping[10] provides us a complete reasoning support for ORM schemes, i.e. users are able to check (strong and weak) satisfiability of an ORM schema by satisfiability checking of the corresponding ***DLR*** knowledge base, which can be done using RACER[11].

[9] More details about DogmaModeler and our experience in CCFORM are not presented in this paper because of the space limitations, but can be found e.g. in [J05], [J06], [JVM03] and [JDM03].

[10] Some ORM constrains (but are rarely used in practice) cannot be mapped into DLR such as ring constraints, frequency constraints on several roles, etc.

[11] http://www.racer-systems.com/products/download/index.phtml (July 2005).

On comparison between pattern detection approaches and a complete reasoning procedure in description logic, we find that both approaches complement each other. Pattern detection approaches are easy to implement, specially in interactive modeling tools, and is bound to be cheaper in terms of reasoning time than a complete reasoning procedure. A complete procedure, e.g. by mapping an ORM schema to a DL knowledge base and deploying existing DL reasoners, typically is exponential. So even in the presence of a complete reasoner, the patterns can be used to quickly detect any "trivial" inconsistencies before calling the more expensive (but complete) procedure, thus speeding up the modeling process. Last but not least, a pattern detection algorithm can be designed and optimized for certain usages, e.g. specifically for ORM unsatisfiability, while a DL translation would rely on a general knowledge base reasoning which e.g. cannot be optimized for ORM constructs.

5 Conclusions and Further Research

We presented 9 patterns to detect unsatisfiability of roles in an ORM schema, and discussed the relation with existing rules in the literature. The implementation and application of this approach has been illustrated and discussed.

In the future, we intend to devise more patterns for unsatisfiability checking, e.g., checking which combinations that involve more than 2 constraints lead to unsatisfiability while leaving out one constraint would not lead to unsatisfiability (as in pattern 5). Moreover, we intend to extend our approach to detect unsatisfiability for ORM derivation rules, assertional knowledge, etc.

Although the 9 patterns are patters that arise frequently in faulty modeling, they are by no means complete. E.g., one could demand that for irreflexive roles at least 2 different values need to be present.

One may notice that our patterns can be easily translated to other knowledge representation languages, especially for ontology and business-rules modeling tools[12].

References

[BCMNP03] F. Baader, D. Calvanese, D. McGuinness, D. Nardi, and P. Patel-Schneider. *The Description Logic Handbook. Cambridge University Press*, 2003.

[BGH99] Bird, L., Goodchild, A., Halpin, T.A.: Object Role Modelling and XML-Schema. In: Laender, A., Liddle, S., Storey, V. (eds.): *Proc. of the 19th International Conference on Conceptual Modeling (ER'00)*. LNCS, Springer, 1999.

[BHW91] P. van Bommel, A.H.M. ter Hofstede, and Th.P. van der Weide. Semantics and verification of object role models. *Information Systems*, 16(5), pp. 471-495, 1991.

[BvHHHMP04] S. Bechhofer, F. van Harmelen, J. Hendler, I. Horrocks, D. L. McGuinness, P. F. Patel-Schneider, and L. A. Stein. OWL Web Ontology Language Reference. `http://www.w3.org/TR/owl-ref/`, 2004.

[CDLNR98] D. Calvanese, G. De Giacomo, M. Lenzerini, D. Nardi, R. Rosati. Information integration : Conceptual Modeling and reasoning support. In *Proceedings of the 6th International Conference on Cooperative Information Systems (CoopIS'98)*, pp. 280-291, 1998.

[12] One of our master students aims to implement these patterns in Protégée, as part of his thesis on interactive ontology modeling.

[DJM02a]: Demey, J., Jarrar, M., Meersman, R.: A Conceptual Markup Language that supports interoperability between Business Rule modeling systems. *Proc. of the Tenth International Conference on Cooperative Information Systems (CoopIS 02)*. Springer LNCS 2519, pp. 19-35, 2002.

[DMV] O. De Troyer, R. Meersman, and P. Verlinden. RIDL* on the CRIS case: A Workbench for NIAM. *Technical report*. INFOLAB, Tilburg University, The Netherlands.

[H] T. Halpin. Object-Role Modeling: an overview. White paper, *http://www.orm.net*.

[H01] T. Halpin. Information Modeling and Relational Databases. 3rd edn. Morgan-Kaufmann, 2001.

[H89] T. Halpin. A logical analysis of information systems: static aspects of the data-oriented perspective. *PhD thesis*, University of Queensland, Brisbane, Australia, 1989.

[H97] Halpin, T.: An Interview- Modeling for Data and Business Rules. *In: Ross, R. (eds.): Database Newsletter*. vol. 25, no. 5. (Sep/Oct 1997). -This newsletter has since been renamed Business Rules Journal and is published by Business Rules Solutions, Inc.

[J06]: Jarrar, M.: Towards the notion of gloss, and the adoption of linguistic resources in formal ontology engineering. Proceeding of the 15th International World Wide Web Conference, WWW2006. Edinburgh, Scotland. May 2006. ACM, 2006.

[J05] M. Jarrar. Towards Methodological Principles for Ontology Engineering. *PhD thesis*, Vrije Universiteit Brussel, 2005.

[JF05] Jarrar, M., Franconi, E.: Mapping ORM into the DLR description logic. Technical Report, August 2005.

[JVM03] Jarrar, M., Verlinden, R., Meersman, R.: Ontology-based Customer Complaint Management. In: Jarrar M., Salaun A., (eds.): Proceedings of the workshop on regulatory ontologies and the modeling of complaint regulations, Catania, Sicily, Italy. Springer Verlag LNCS. Vol. 2889. November (2003) pp. 594–606

[N99] North, K.: Modeling, Data Semantics, and Natural Language. *In: New Architect magazine*, 1999.

[T96] O. De Troyer. A formalization of the binary Object-role Model based on Logic. *Data & Knowledge Engineering* 19, North-Holland, Elsevier, pp. 1-37, 1996.

[TM95] O. De Troyer and R. Meersman. A Logic Framework for a Semantics of Object-Oriented Data Modelling. In *Proc. Of 14th International Conference Object-Orientation and Entity-Relationship Modelling (OO-ER'95)*, LNCS 1021, pp. 238-249, Springer, 1995.

[VB82] G. Verheijen and P. van Bekkum. NIAM, aN Information Analysis Method. In Proc. Of the *IFIP Conference on Comparative Review of Information Systems Methodologies*, North-Holland, 537-590, 1982

Appendix: Algorithms

Pattern 1

```
For each subtype T[x] {
 Let T[x].DirectSupers = the set of all direct supertypes of T[x].
 n = T[x].DirectSupers.size
 If ( n > 1)  {
   For (i = 1 to i=n)    {
     Let T[x].DirectSupers[i].Supers = the set of all possible supertypes
                                        of T[x].DirectSupers[i]   }
  // if the intersection of all T[x].DirectSupers[i].supers is not empty,
     then the composition is not satisfiable.
```

```
if (Intersection(T[x].DirectSupers[1].supers, ... T[x].DirectSupers[n].supers))
   is empty {
    Satisfiability = false
    Message= ("The subtype T[x].DirectSupers[i] cannot
        be satisfied as its supertypes do not have a top common supertype.")      }} }
```

Pattern 2

```
For each exclusive constraint Exv[x] {
  Let Exv[x].T = the set of the object-types participating in Exv[x].
  //For each pair of object-types participating in the exclusion constraint:
  For (i = 1 to i = Exv[x].T.size) {
    For (j = 1 to j = Exv[x].T.size) {
      If (i not equal j) {
         Let Exv[x].T[i].Subs = the set of subtypes of the object-type Exv[x].T[i].
         Let Exv[x].T[j].Subs = the set of subtypes of the object-type Exv[x].T[j].
         S = IntersectionOf(Exv[x].T[i].Subs, Exv[x].T[j].Subs)
         If (S is not empty) {
           Satisfiability = false
           Message = ("all subtypes in <S> cannot be instantiated because of <Exv[x]>") }}}}   }
```

Pattern 3

```
For each exclusion constraint Exs[x] between a set of single roles {
  Let Exs[x].roles = the set of all roles participating in Exs[x].
  For (i=1 to Exs[x].roles.size)
    If (Exs[x].roles[i].Mandatory = true) {
      For (j=1 to Exs[x].roles.size) {
        If (I not equal j){
         Let Exs[x].roles[i].T = the object-type that plays the role Exs[x].roles[i]
         Let Exs[x].roles[j].T = the object-type that plays the role Exs[x].roles[j]
         Let Exs[x].roles[i].T.Subs = the set of all subtypes of Exs[x].roles[i].T
         If (Exs[x].roles[i].T = Exs[x].roles[j].T) OR
                                  In(Exs[x].roles[j].T, Exs[x].roles[i].T.Subs ) {
             Satisfiability = false
             Message = ("There are some roles in <Exs[x].roles> that cannot
               be instantiated because of the <Exv[x]>")}}}}}
```

An alternative but more compact algorithm can be:

```
For each exclusion constraint Exs[x] between a set of single roles {
  Let Exs[x].roles = the set of all roles participating in Exs[x].
  Let MandRoles = the set of all mandatory roles from Exs[x].roles.
  If (MandRoles  is not empty)
    For (i=1 to ManRoles.size)
      For (j=1 to Exs[x].roles.size)
        Let MandRoles[i].T = the object-type that plays the role MandRoles[i]
        Let Exs[x].roles[j].T = the object-type that plays the role Exs[x].roles[j]
        Let Exs[x].roles[j].T.Subs = the set of all subtypes of Exs[x].roles[j].T
        If Not In(MandRoles[i].T, Exs[x].roles[j].T.Subs)
            Satisfiability = false
            Message= ("There are some roles in
              <Exs[x].roles> that cannot be populated because of the <Exv[x]>")}}}}  }
```

Pattern 4

```
For each frequency constraint F[x] {
   Let F[x].min = the lower bound of the frequency constraint F[x].
   Let T = the object-type that is played by the role holding F[x].
   Let T.Values = the value constraint on T.
   // if there is no value constraint on T, then T.Values = null
   If (T.Values is not null) and (T.Values.size < F[x].min) {
```

```
      Satisfiability = false.
      Message =("the role <T.r> cannot be instantiated because the
         <F[x]> and the <T.Values> contradict each other"). } }
```

Pattern 5

```
For each exclusion constraint Exs[x] between a set of single roles {
  Let Exs[x].Roles = the set of roles participating in the exclusion Exs[x].
  Let Exs[x].InvRoles = the set of inverse roles of Exs[x].Roles.
  For ( Si in  Exs[x].InvRoles) {
           If ( there is frequency constraint on Si )
                    fi = minimum freq. const. on Si;
           else fi = 1;  }
  Let F = sum(fi).
  Let O = the object-type that plays all roles in Exs[x].Roles.
  Let O.Values = the value constraint on O.
  // if there is no value constraint on O, then O.Values = null
  If (O.Values is not null) and (O.Values.size < F) {
      Satisfiability = false.
     Message =("Some roles in <Exs[x].Roles> cannot be instantiated because
         the <Exs[x]> and the <O.Values> contradict each other").} }
```

Pattern 6

```
For each exclusion constraint Exs[x] {
 If (Exs[x] between predicates) {
   Let Exs[x].predicates = the set of all predicates participating in Exs[x].
   \\ For each pair of predicates participating in the exclusion
   For (i = 1 to i = Exs[x].predicates.size) {
     For (j = 1 to j = Exs[x].predicates.size) {
       If (i not equal j) {
         Sp = GetSetPathsBetween(Exs[x].Predicates[i], Exs[x].Predicates[j])
         // Sp is the set of all subset or equality constraints that specify or imply a
         // SetPath between the current tuple of predicates.
         If (Sp is not empty) {
           Satisfiability = false.
           Message = ("the exclusion constraint <Exs[x]> contradicts some subset
                   and/or equality constraints on the predicates in <Sp>").}}}}}
 Else { // then the Exs[x] is between roles
   Let Exs[x].roles = the set of all roles that participate in Exs[x].
   \\ For each pair of roles participating in the exclusion constraint
   For (i = 1 to i = Exs[x].roles.size) {
     For (j = 1 to j = Exs[x].roles.size) {
       If (i not equal j) {
         Sr = GetSetPathsBetween(Exs[x].roles[i], Exs[x].roles[j])
         // Sr is the set of all subset or equality constraints that specify or imply a
         // SetPath between the current tuple of roles.
         Sp = GetSetPathsBetween(Exs[x].Predicates[i], Exs[x].Predicates[j])
         // Sp is the set of all subset or equality constraints that specify or imply a
         // SetPath between the predicates of the current tuple of roles.
         If (Sr is not empty) OR (Sp is not empty) {
           Satisfiability = false.
           Message = ("the exclusion constraint <Exs[x]> contradicts some Subset
               and/or equality constraints on the predicates in Sp"). }}}}}}}
```

Pattern 7

```
For each frequency constraint F[x] {
   Let F[x].min = the lower bound of the frequency constraint F[x].
  Let R = the role (predicate) on which F[x] is placed.
```

```
  If ( there is uniqueness constraint on R ) and ( F[x].min > 1 )
    Satisfiability = false
     Message= ("The frequency constraint F[x] cannot  be satisfied as it conflicts with a
uniqueness constraint.") }
```

Pattern 8

```
For each role R {
  Let RC = the set of ring constraints on R
   If ( RC not allowed according to Table 1.)
        Satisfiability = false
        Message= ("The ring constraints RC cannot  be satisfied.") }
```

Pattern 9

```
For each subtype T[x] {
 Let T[x].Supers = the set of all supertypes of T[x].
If ( T[x] in T[x].Supers )   {
        Satisfiability = false
        Message= ("The subtype T[x] is part of a loop, thus it cannot be satisfied.")      }}}
```

Inferring with Inconsistent OWL DL Ontology: A Multi-valued Logic Approach*

Yue Ma, Zuoquan Lin, and Zhangang Lin

Department of Information Science, Peking University, Beijing, China
{mayue, lz, zglin}@is.pku.edu.cn

Abstract. Web ontology language OWL DL has two-valued model theory semantics so that ontologies expressed by it become trivial when contradictions occur. Based on classical description logic $\mathcal{SHOIN}(\mathcal{D})$, we propose the four-valued description logic $\mathcal{SHOIN}(\mathcal{D})4$ which has the ability to reason with inconsistencies. By transformation technic, we convert the reasoning problems of $\mathcal{SHOIN}(\mathcal{D})4$ to the counterparts of $\mathcal{SHOIN}(\mathcal{D})$. So $\mathcal{SHOIN}(\mathcal{D})4$ provides us with an approach to deal with contradictions by classical reasoning mechanism.

1 Introduction

The semantic web which is full of semantic information makes computers process information automatically. Kinds of standard semantic web languages provided by W3C[1], such as OWL DL and OWL Lite [1], are based on a rigorous logic basis — description logic which proves to be very useful for defining, integrating and maintaining ontologies [2]. Among the family of description logics is $\mathcal{SHOIN}(\mathcal{D})$ which is very close to OWL DL [3].

Description logics inherit the triviality from first order logic, that is, a single contradiction in the knowledge base leads to the only trivial logic consequence which includes everything. Therefore, a description logic knowledge base is ill when inconsistent. Considering a fragment of an ontology in medical treatment [4]: the one in surgical team does not belong to the team permitted to read patient's private record, while the one in urgency team does. We can express the knowledge by $\mathcal{SHOIN}(\mathcal{D})$ as follows:

$$SurgicalTeam \sqsubseteq \neg ReadPatientRecordTeam$$
$$UrgencyTeam \sqsubseteq ReadPatientRecordTeam$$

When we know the fact that $john$ belongs both to $SurgicalTeam$ and to $UrgencyTeam$, we find that there is a contradiction about whether $john$ is allowed to read patient's record. Under two-valued semantics, this knowledge base has no model so that anything can be deduced from it, even irrelative information like $Patient(john)$.

Decomposing the connections between information of being true and information of being false, thus yielding an extended semantics for ontology language, is the approach

* This work is supported by NSFC (grant number 60496322).

[1] http://www.w3c.org

T. Grust et al. (Eds.): EDBT 2006 Workshops, LNCS 4254, pp. 535–553, 2006.

adopted in this paper to deal with inconsistencies. Actually, our work is based on multi-valued logic, whose truth value set is extended so that we can assign the contradiction to an additional truth value denoting contradiction. In the literature, the theory which describes contradiction but is nontrivial is called paraconsistent logic [5,6,7]. The underlying idea of this paper is Belnap's four-valued logic [8,9] , which proves basic and important both in multi-valued logic and in para-consistent logic.

Terminological logic is an early version of description logic. Patel-Schneider [10] has proposed four-valued semantics for a terminological logic system which provides a tractable inclusion by the weaker inference ability of four-valued logic. In [10], *structural subsumption algorithm* is used to compute inclusion relation between classes (concepts), which is the first generation reasoning system of DLs and cannot treat complex constructors, such as disjunction ($\sqcup$), full negation ($\neg$), and full existence restriction ($\exists R.C$). Therefore, the language studied in [10] does not include these constructors which are important for OWL DL. Moreover, the semantics of inclusion has direct effect on complexity, thus defining more kinds of inclusion relations is difficult in [10]. In this paper, we propose a kind of four-valued semantics for all of these constructors as well as a complete algorithm for reasoning with $\mathcal{SHOIN}(\mathcal{D})4$ in a framework of two-valued $\mathcal{SHOIN}(\mathcal{D})$.

There are three main approaches to deal with inconsistent ontologies. The first is to reason with one(several) consistent subset(s) selected according to some principles, such as syntax/semantics relevance principle [11] and priority principle [4]. The second is to diagnose and repair contradictions when encountered. The third is through non-classical reasoning theory under new semantics. In this paper, we extend propositional four-valued semantics to ontology languages, thus forming $\mathcal{SHOIN}(\mathcal{D})4$ which is a four-valued version of $\mathcal{SHOIN}(\mathcal{D})$. The underlying idea is that we value the whole original theory instead of only choosing some sub-theory to take part in reasoning. However, ours is different from the third method in that we propose the decomposition of four-valued semantics to the two-valued, whereby existing reasoning systems for OWL DL remain useful for $\mathcal{SHOIN}(\mathcal{D})4$. $\mathcal{SHOIN}(\mathcal{D})4$ includes all the constructors of $\mathcal{SHOIN}(\mathcal{D})$ so that it can be used as an ontology language which is compatible with OWL DL but has the ability to deal with inconsistencies.

In the rest, we first briefly review description logic $\mathcal{SHOIN}(\mathcal{D})$ and Belnap's four-valued $\mathcal{FOUR}$. Then we describe $\mathcal{SHOIN}(\mathcal{D})4$ in details in section 3, and prove its inference can be reduced to that of $\mathcal{SHOIN}(\mathcal{D})$ in section 4. At last, we conclude this paper, compare it with related work, and point out our future work.

2 Description Logic and Four-Valued Logic

2.1 OWL DL and Description Logic $\mathcal{SHOIN}(\mathcal{D})$

OWL DL is a subset of ontology web language OWL that has close relation with $\mathcal{SHOIN}(\mathcal{D})$. The main semantic relationship for OWL DL is entailment between pairs of OWL ontologies. An ontology O_1 entails an ontology O_2, written $O_1 \models O_2$, if and only if all interpretations that satisfy O_1 also satisfy O_2 [1]. Moreover, the OWL DL entailment can be transformed into $\mathcal{SHOIN}(\mathcal{D})$ knowledge base (un)satisfiability [3].

Generally, a description logic system includes: the set of concept and role constructors, inclusion assertions in TBox, fact assertions in ABox, and reasoning mechanism on TBox and ABox. The semantics of $\mathcal{SHOIN}(\mathcal{D})$ is given by means of an interpretation $I = (\Delta^I, \cdot^I)$ consisting of a non-empty domain Δ^I, disjoint from the datatype (or concrete) domain Δ^I_D, and a mapping $\cdot^I$, which interprets atomic and complex concepts, roles, and nominals according to Table 1 [3]. All the axiom forms contained in TBox and ABox of $\mathcal{SHOIN}(\mathcal{D})$ are also shown in Table 1. An interpretation satisfies a knowledge base K iff it satisfies each axiom in K; K is satisfiable (unsatisfiable) iff there exists (does not exist) such an interpretation.

Table 1. Syntax and Semantics of $\mathcal{SHOIN}(\mathcal{D})$

Constructor Name	Syntax	Semantics
atomic concept A	A	$A^I \subseteq \Delta^I$
datatypes D	D	$D^{\mathrm{D}} \subseteq \Delta^I_{\mathrm{D}}$
abstract role R_A	R	$R^I \subseteq \Delta^I \times \Delta^I$
datatype role R_D	U	$U^I \subseteq \Delta^I \times \Delta^I_{\mathrm{D}}$
individuals I	o	$o^I \in \Delta^I$
data values	v	$v^I = v^{\mathrm{D}}$
inverse role	R^-	$(R^-)^I \subseteq \Delta^I \times \Delta^I$
top concept	$\top$	Δ^I
bottom concept	$\bot$	$\emptyset$
conjunction	$C_1 \sqcap C_2$	$C^I \cap D^I$
disjunction	$C_1 \sqcup C_2$	$C^I \cup D^I$
negation	$\neg C$	$\Delta^I \setminus C^I$
oneOf	$\{o_1, ...\}$	$\{o_1^1, ...\}$
exists restriction	$\exists R.C$	$\{x \mid \exists y, (x, y) \in R^I \wedge y \in C^I\}$
value restriction	$\forall R.C$	$\{x \mid \forall y, (x, y) \in R^I \rightarrow y \in C^I\}$
atleast restriction	$\geq n.R$	$\{x \mid card(\{y.(x, y) \in R^I\}) \geq n\}$
atmost restriction	$\leq n.R$	$\{x \mid card(\{y.(x, y) \in R^I\}) \leq n\}$
datatype exists	$\exists U.D$	$\{x \mid \exists y, (x, y) \in U^I \wedge y \in D^I\}$
datatype value	$\forall U.D$	$\{x \mid \forall y, (x, y) \in U^I \rightarrow y \in D^I\}$
datatype atleast	$\geq n.U$	$\{x \mid card(\{y.(x, y) \in U^I\}) \geq n\}$
datatype atmost	$\leq n.U$	$\{x \mid card(\{y.(x, y) \in U^I\}) \leq n\}$
datatype oneOf	$\{v_1, ...\}$	$\{v_1^I, ...\}$
Axiom Name	**Syntax**	**Semantics**
concept inclusion	$C_1 \sqsubseteq C_2$	$C_1^I \subseteq C_2^I$
object role inclusion	$R_1 \sqsubseteq R_2$	$R_1^I \subseteq R_2^I$
object role transitivity	$\mathrm{Trans}(R)$	$R^I = (R^I)^+$
datatype role inclusion	$U_1 \sqsubseteq U_2$	$U_1^I \subseteq U_2^I$
individual inclusion	$a : C$	$a^I \in C^I$
individual equality	$a = b$	$a^I = b^I$
individual inequality	$a \neq b$	$a^I \neq b^I$

2.2 Bilattice and Four-Valued Logic

For a given $Domain$, $(\{< P, N >\}, \leq_k, \leq_t)$ constructs a bilattice space [12], where P and N are subsets of $Domain$ which stand for the information set of being true and of being false, respectively; and where the two partial orders $\leq_k$ and $\leq_t$ reflect differences in the amount of *truth* and the amount of *information*, respectively. The logical operators on the bilattice are defined as follows:

- Negation($\neg$) on direction $\leq_t$: $\neg < P, N > = < N, P >$
- Lower bound($\wedge$) and upper bound($\vee$) on direction $\leq_t$:

$$< P_1, N_1 > \wedge < P_2, N_2 >=< P_1 \cap P_2, N_1 \cup N_2 >$$

$$< P_1, N_1 > \vee < P_2, N_2 >=< P_1 \cup P_2, N_1 \cap N_2 >$$

The negation as well as lower and upper bounds on direction $\leq_k$ are also defined by Fitting in [12], but the above is enough for this paper since we only consider logic constructors in truth direction $\leq_t$.

Belnap's four-valued logic $\mathcal{FOUR}$ [8,9,13], whose truth value set is $FOUR = \{t, f, \top, \bot\}$ (also written as $\{t\}$, $\{f\}$,$\{t, f\}$, and $\emptyset$, respectively), is a special bilattice logic. The designated set of $\mathcal{FOUR}$ is $\{t, \top\}$ and three kinds of implications of it are material implication($\mapsto$), internal implication($\supset$) and strong implication($\rightarrow$) defined as follows [13,14]:

$$\varphi \mapsto \psi \stackrel{\text{def}}{=} \neg\varphi \vee \psi.$$

$$\varphi \supset \psi \stackrel{\text{def}}{=} \begin{cases} \psi & \text{if } \varphi \in \{t, \top\}, \\ t & \text{if } \varphi \in \{f, \bot\}. \end{cases}$$

$$\varphi \rightarrow \psi \stackrel{\text{def}}{=} (\varphi \supset \psi) \wedge (\neg\psi \supset \neg\varphi).$$

$$\varphi \leftrightarrow \psi \stackrel{\text{def}}{=} (\varphi \rightarrow \psi) \wedge (\psi \rightarrow \varphi).$$

Note that, exception could occur for material implication, while it is not the case for internal and strong implications, since $\varphi \mapsto \psi = \top$ still holds when $\varphi = \top$ and $\phi \in \{f, \bot\}$. Intuitively, it is the contradictions in the precondition that bring exceptions for material implication, that is, material implication tolerates the situation that the conclusion is not true (valuing f or $\bot$) when we have information asserting the truth of the precondition (valuing $\top$ which includes truth information). For the other two implications, conclusions must be true when the preconditions are true. Therefore, internal and strong implications cannot characterize exceptions. Furthermore, when we lack the information about precondition, i.e. its truth value is $\bot$, the conclusion of material implication must value t or $\top$ which means it has information of being true; the conclusion of strong implication should value f or $\bot$, which means we lack information of it being true; the conclusion of internal implication accepts any truth value of $FOUR$. However, internal implication corresponds to the basic consequence of the four-valued logic as the following proposition says:

Proposition 1. *[14]*

- $\Gamma, \psi \models^4 \phi, \Delta$ *iff* $\Gamma \models^4 \psi \supset \phi, \Delta$.
- *If* $\Gamma \models^4 \psi, \Gamma \models^4 \psi \supset \phi$, *then* $\Gamma \models^4 \phi$.

The following counterexamples show that material and strong implications don't have the above property:

- $\{\psi, \neg\psi, \neg\phi\} \models^4 \psi \mapsto \phi$, but $\{\psi, \neg\psi, \neg\phi\} \not\models^4 \phi$.
- $\{\psi, \phi, \neg\phi\} \models^4 \phi$, but $\{\phi, \neg\phi\} \not\models^4 \psi \rightarrow \phi$.

Strong implication characterizes a class of stricter implication relationship: on one hand, when there is information of being true about the precondition, its conclusion must have information of being true; on the other hand, when there is information of being false about the conclusion, its precondition must have information of being false. The following proposition shows that the four-valued equality between two formulas can be defined through strong implication instead of material and internal implications.

Proposition 2. *[14] For every schemata* $\Theta, \psi \leftrightarrow \phi \models^4 \Theta(\psi) \leftrightarrow \Theta(\phi)$.

3 Four-Valued Description Logic $\mathcal{SHOIN}(\mathcal{D})4$

3.1 Syntax

The inclusion axiom in $TBox$ characterizes human's exact knowledge of concept classifications. For example, $surgeon \sqsubseteq doctor$ means "whenever an instance is a surgeon, he/she must be a doctor". Salem et al. [4] declare that there are three types of information in a knowledge base (KB for short): facts, assertions without exception, and assertions with exception. Without distinguishing different information, contradictions easily occur in KB. Consider the following KB: (1) Generally, the person who is not a stuff of the hospital is not allowed to check patient's record; (2) However, the person who is doing temporary study practices in the hospital is generally allowed to do so. For this KB, some graduate of a medicine college may become an exception of the first axiom of KB — that is, although he/she is not a stuff of the hospital, he/she has the permission to read patient's record. The inclusion described in $\mathcal{SHOIN}(\mathcal{D})$ is exact knowledge without exceptions.

The concept constructors and fact axioms in $\mathcal{SHOIN}(\mathcal{D})4$ are the same as those in $\mathcal{SHOIN}(\mathcal{D})$. In addition, three kinds of inclusion axioms, denoted by $C \mapsto D$, $C \sqsubset D$, and $C \rightarrow D$ called material inclusion, internal inclusion and strong inclusion respectively, are defined in $\mathcal{SHOIN}(\mathcal{D})4$. These three inclusions are corresponding to the three implications in four-valued logic $\mathcal{FOUR}$. The first allows exceptions, and the other two do not. These three subsumptions help us to describe various class hierarchies. The exactnesses expressed by them increase one by one. For example, "$Bird \mapsto Fly$" means that birds can fly with exceptions, that is, there may be some bird which cannot fly; "$Bird \sqsubset Fly$" means that every bird must can fly. Note that, if we have some information indicates that some bird cannot fly, this implication still cannot tell us whether it is not a bird; "$Bird \rightarrow Fly$" means that an instance can fly whenever it is known to be a bird. Moreover, it can not be a bird if we know it cannot fly. Similarly, three kinds of inclusion axioms both of object and of datatype roles are defined in $\mathcal{SHOIN}(\mathcal{D})4$.

Knowledge with different exactness surely exists in human mind. So does it in the Semantic Web. However, all standard ontology languages for semantic web don't consider it. The main goal of this paper is to propose $\mathcal{SHOIN}(\mathcal{D})4$ which provides us with a way to characterize them.

3.2 Semantics

Generally speaking, there are four situations describing whether an individual is an instance of a concept: we surely know it is an instance of the concept; we surely know it is not an instance of the concept; we neither know it is an instance of the concept nor not (the situation of lacking information); or we have data indicating both it is an instance of the concept and not (the contradictory situation). So we define the semantic of $\mathcal{SHOIN}(\mathcal{D})4$ concepts by bilattice in this subsection.

For any given domain Δ and a concept C, we assign C an extended truth value $< P, N >$, where P is the subset of Δ that supports C to be true and N is the subset of Δ that supports C to be false. Cancelling the requirements $P \cap N = \emptyset$ and $P \cup N = \Delta$ in classical semantic conditions of $\mathcal{SHOIN}(\mathcal{D})$, an extended semantics forms and we will show that inconsistencies and uncertainty can be properly handled under this semantics.

For brevity, we first define positive projecting operator and negative projecting operator as follows:

Definition 1. *$proj^+(\cdot)$ and $proj^-(\cdot)$ are respectively positive projecting operator and negative projecting operator on bilattice space $(\{< P, N >\}, \leq_k, \leq_t)$, such that for any $< P, N >$,*

$$proj^+(< P, N >) = P;$$

$$proj^-(< P, N >) = N.$$

Definition 2. *A four-valued interpretation $I = (\Delta^I, \cdot^I)$ of $\mathcal{SHOIN}(\mathcal{D})4$ includes an object domain Δ^I, a datatype domain Δ^I_D, and a function $\cdot^I$ which satisfies all the interpretation requirements as shown in Table 2. (In Table 2, $\wedge$ and $\vee$ are the lower and upper bound of bilattice on direction $\leq_t$, respectively. $\sharp$ stands for set cardinality.)*

The following definition indicates why we use the name "four-valued interpretation" in definition 2.

Definition 3. *For any given instance $a, b \in \Delta^I$, concept name C and object/datatype role name R:*

- $C^I(a) = t$, *iff* $a^I \in proj^+(C^I)$ *and* $a^I \notin proj^-(C^I)$;
- $C^I(a) = f$, *iff* $a^I \notin proj^+(C^I)$ *and* $a^I \in proj^-(C^I)$;
- $C^I(a) = \top$, *iff* $a^I \in proj^+(C^I)$ *and* $a^I \in proj^-(C^I)$;
- $C^I(a) = \bot$, *iff* $a^I \notin proj^+(C^I)$ *and* $a^I \notin proj^-(C^I)$.
- $R^I(a, b) = \top$, *iff* $(a^I, b^I) \in proj^+(R^I)$ *and* $(a^I, b^I) \in proj^-(R^I)$;
- $R^I(a, b) = f$, *iff* $(a^I, b^I) \notin proj^+(R^I)$ *and* $(a^I, b^I) \in proj^-(R^I)$;
- $R^I(a, b) = t$, *iff* $(a^I, b^I) \in proj^+(R^I)$ *and* $(a^I, b^I) \notin proj^-(R^I)$;
- $R^I(a, b) = \bot$, *iff* $(a^I, b^I) \notin proj^+(R^I)$ *and* $(a^I, b^I) \notin proj^-(R^I)$;

where, $t, f, \top, \bot$ are truth values of four-valued logic.

The semantics of material inclusion axioms, internal inclusion axioms, and strong inclusion axioms, as shown in Table 3, are corresponding to the sematics of material implication, internal implication, and strong implication in four-valued logic, respectively.

Table 2. Syntax and Semantics of $\mathcal{SHOIN(D)}4$

Constructor Syntax	Semantics
A	$A^I =< P, N >$, where $P, N \subseteq \Delta^I$
D	$D^{\mathrm{D}} \subseteq \Delta^I_{\mathrm{D}}$
R	$R^I =< P_1 \times P_2, N_1 \times N_2 >$, where $P_i, N_i \subseteq \Delta^I$ for $i = 1, 2$
U	$U^I =< P_1 \times P_2, N_1 \times N_2 >, P_i \in \Delta^I, N_i \subseteq \Delta^I_D$ for $i = 1, 2$
o	$o^I \in \Delta^I$
v	$v^I = v^{\mathrm{D}}$
R^-	$(R^-)^I = (R^I)^-$
$\top$	$< \Delta^I, \emptyset >$
$\bot$	$< \emptyset, \Delta^I >$
$C_1 \sqcap C_2$	$C^I \wedge D^I$
$C_1 \sqcup C_2$	$C^I \vee D^I$
$\neg C$	$(\neg C)^I =< N, P >$,$C^I =< P, N >$
$\{o_1, ...\}$	$< \{o_1^I, ...\}, N >$
$\exists R.C$	$< \{x \mid \exists y, (x, y) \in proj^+(R^I) \wedge y \in proj^+(C^I)\}$, $\{x \mid \forall y, (x, y) \in proj^+(R^I) \Rightarrow y \in proj^-(C^I)\} >$
$\forall R.C$	$< \{x \mid \forall y, (x, y) \in proj^+(R^I) \Rightarrow y \in proj^+(C^I)\}$, $\{x \mid \exists y, (x, y) \in proj^+(R^I) \wedge y \in proj^-(C^I)\} >$
$\geq n.R$	$< \{x \mid \#(y.(x, y) \in proj^+(R^I)) \geq n\}$, $\{x \mid \#(y.(x, y) \notin proj^-(R^I)) < n\} >$
$\leq n.R$	$< \{x \mid \#(y.(x, y) \notin proj^-(R^I)) \leq n\}$, $\{x \mid \#(y.(x, y) \in proj^+(R^I)) > n\} >$
$\exists U.D$	$< \{x \mid \exists y, (x, y) \in proj^+(U^I) \wedge y \in D^I\}$, $\{x \mid \forall y, (x, y) \in proj^-(U^I) \Rightarrow y \in D^I\} >$
$\forall U.D$	$< \{x \mid \forall y, (x, y) \in proj^+(U^I) \Rightarrow y \in D^I\}$, $\{x \mid \exists y, (x, y) \in proj^-(U^I) \wedge y \in D^I\} >$
$\geq n.U$	$< \{x \mid \#(y.(x, y) \in proj^+(U^I)) \geq n\}$, $\{x \mid \#(y.(x, y) \notin proj^-(U^I)) < n\} >$
$\leq n.U$	$< \{x \mid \#(y.(x, y) \notin proj^-(U^I)) \leq n\}$, $\{x \mid \#(y.(x, y) \in proj^+(U^I)) > n\} >$
oneOf $\{v_1, ...\}$	$\{v_1^I, ...\}$

A four-valued interpretation I satisfies a $\mathcal{SHOIN(D)}4$ knowledge base $\mathcal{K}$ iff it satisfies each axiom in $\mathcal{K}$. $\mathcal{K}$ is satisfiable (unsatisfiable) iff there exists (does not exist) such an interpretation.

For an interpretation $I = (\Delta^I, \Delta^I_D, \cdot^I)$ of a $\mathcal{SHOIN(D)}4$ ontology, the semantics of an object concept C in it is some element, say $< P_0, N_0 >$, of the bilattice space $(< P, N >, \leq_t, \leq_k)$ which is formed based on Δ^I (i.e., $P, N \in \Delta^I$). If we restrict that $P_0 \cap N_0 = \emptyset$ and $P_0 \cup N_0 = \Delta^I$, then it is the classical two-valued semantics of C. The situation is the same for object role name and datatype role name. Therefore, the semantics of $\mathcal{SHOIN(D)}4$ is an extension of that of $\mathcal{SHOIN(D)}$.

In the following two propositions, we show that the semantics defined above has the similar intuition as the classical two-valued semantics.

Table 3. Syntax and Semantics of axioms in $\mathcal{SHOIN}(\mathcal{D})4$

Axiom Name	Syntax	Semantics
concept material inclusion	$C_1 \mapsto C_2$	$\Delta^I \setminus proj^-(C_1^I) \subseteq proj^+(C_2^I)$
concept internal inclusion	$C_1 \sqsubset C_2$	$proj^+(C_1^I) \subseteq proj^+(C_2^I)$
concept strong inclusion	$C_1 \rightarrow C_2$	$proj^+(C_1^I) \subseteq proj^+(C_2^I)$ and $proj^-(C_2^I) \subseteq proj^-(C_1^I)$
object role material inclusion	$R_1 \mapsto R_2$	$\Delta^I \times \Delta^I \setminus proj^+(R_1^I) \subseteq proj^+(R_2^I)$
object role internal inclusion	$R_1 \sqsubset R_2$	$proj^+(R_1^I) \subseteq proj^+(R_2^I)$
object role strong inclusion	$R_1 \rightarrow R_2$	$proj^+(R_1^I) \subseteq proj^+(R_2^I)$ and $proj^-(R_2^I) \subseteq proj^-(R_1^I)$
datatype role material inclusion	$U_1 \mapsto U_2$	$\Delta^I \times \Delta_{\mathrm{D}}^I \setminus proj^+(U_1^I) \subseteq proj^+(U_2^I)$
datatype role internal inclusion	$U_1 \sqsubset U_2$	$proj^+(U_1^I) \subseteq proj^+(U_2^I)$
datatype role strong inclusion	$U_1 \rightarrow U_2$	$proj^+(U_1^I) \subseteq proj^+(U_2^I)$ and $proj^-(U_2^I) \subseteq proj^-(U_1^I)$
object role transitivity	$\mathrm{Trans}(R)$	$R^I = (R^I)^+$
individual inclusion	$a : C$	$a^I \in proj^+(C^I)$
individual equality	$a = b$	$a^I = b^I$
individual inequality	$a \neq b$	$a^I \neq b^I$

Proposition 3. *Let C, D be concepts. For any $\mathcal{SHOIN}(\mathcal{D})4$ interpretation I,*

$$(C \sqcap \top)^I = C^I, (C \sqcup \top)^I = \top^I,$$
$$(C \sqcap \bot)^I = \bot^I, (C \sqcup \bot)^I = C^I.$$

Proof. For any given interpretation $I = (\Delta^I, \cdot^I)\top^I =< \Delta^I, \emptyset >, \bot^I =< \emptyset, \Delta^I >$. Without loss of generalitysuppose $C^I =< P, N >$. By definition 2

$$\begin{aligned}
(C \sqcap \top)^I &= < P \cap \Delta^I, N \cup \emptyset >=< P, N >= C^I \\
(C \sqcup \top)^I &= < P \cup \Delta^I, N \cap \emptyset >=< \Delta^I, \emptyset >= \top^I \\
(C \sqcap \bot)^I &= < P \cap \emptyset, N \cup \Delta^I >=< \emptyset, \Delta^I >= \bot^I \\
(C \sqcup \bot)^I &= < P \cup \emptyset, N \cap \Delta^I >=< P, N >= C^I.
\end{aligned}$$

□

Proposition 4. *Let C, D be concepts, R be an object role name or a datatype role name. For any $\mathcal{SHOIN}(\mathcal{D})4$ interpretation I,*

$$\begin{aligned}
&(\neg\neg C)^I = C^I, (\neg\top)^I = \bot^I, (\neg\bot)^I = \top^I, \\
&(\neg(C \sqcup D))^I = (\neg C \sqcap \neg D)^I, (\neg(C \sqcap D))^I = (\neg C \sqcup \neg D)^I, \\
&(\neg(\forall R.C))^I = (\exists R.\neg C)^I, (\neg(\exists R.C))^I = (\forall R.\neg C)^I, \\
&(\neg(\geq n.R))^I = (< n.R)^I, (\neg(\leq n.R))^I = (> n.R)^I.
\end{aligned}$$

Proof. For any interpretation $I = (\Delta^I, \cdot^I), \top^I =< \Delta^I, \emptyset >, \bot^I =< \emptyset, \Delta^I >$ Without loss of generalitysuppose $C^I =< P, N >, D^I =< P', N' >$. By definition 2, the first three formulae hold obviously. Since

$$\begin{aligned}
(\neg(C \sqcup D))^I &= \neg < P \cup P', N \cap N' >=< N \cap N', P \cup P' >, \\
(\neg C \sqcap \neg D)^I &=< N, P > \wedge < N', P' >=< N \cap N', P \cup P' > .
\end{aligned}$$

$(\neg(C \sqcup D))^I = (\neg C \sqcap \neg D)^I$.

$(\neg(C \sqcap D))^I = (\neg C \sqcup \neg D)^I$ follows in the same way.

Note that $proj^+(C^I) = proj^-((\neg C)^I) = P, proj^-(C^I) = proj^+((\neg C)^I) = N$. By definition 2

$$\begin{aligned}(\neg(\forall R.C))^I &= \neg < \{x \mid \forall y, (x,y) \in proj^+(R^I) \Rightarrow y \in proj^+(C^I)\},\\ &\quad \{x \mid \exists y, (x,y) \in proj^+(R^I) \wedge y \in proj^-(C^I)\} >\\ &= < \{x \mid \exists y, (x,y) \in proj^+(R^I) \wedge y \in proj^-(C^I)\},\\ &\quad \{x \mid \forall y, (x,y) \in proj^+(R^I) \Rightarrow y \in proj^+(C^I)\} >\\ &= < \{x \mid \exists y, (x,y) \in proj^+(R^I) \wedge y \in proj^+((\neg C)^I)\},\\ &\quad \{x \mid \forall y, (x,y) \in proj^+(R^I) \Rightarrow y \in proj^-((\neg C)^I)\} >\\ &= (\exists R.\neg C)^I\end{aligned}$$

Therefore, $(\neg(\forall R.C))^I = (\exists R.\neg C)^I$.

By the same approach, we can prove that $(\neg(\exists R.C))^I = (\forall R.\neg C)^I$, $(\neg(\geq n.R))^I = (< n.R)^I$, and $(\neg(\leq n.R))^I = (> n.R)^I$. □

3.3 Expressivity of $\mathcal{SHOIN}(\mathcal{D})4$

We explain the expressivity of $\mathcal{SHOIN}(\mathcal{D})4$ by following examples.

Example 1. *Let knowledge base K be as follows*

$$TBox = \exists hasPatient.Patient \sqsubseteq Doctor. \text{ (The one who has a patient must be a doctor)}$$
$$\begin{aligned}ABox = \{&Doctor(john), \neg Doctor(john), Patient(mary),\\ &hasPatient(bill, mary)\}.\end{aligned}$$

Obviously, there is a contradiction in $ABox$. If it is a $\mathcal{SHOIN}(\mathcal{D})$ knowledge base, we can conclude anything from $\mathcal{K}$. But as a $\mathcal{SHOIN}(\mathcal{D})4$ knowledge base, we get positive answer to the query "is there any information indicating bill is a doctor?", since for each four-valued model of K, the following holds: $(bill, mary) \in proj^+(hasPatient^I)$, $mary \in proj^+(Patient^I), john \in proj^+(Doctor^I)$, and $john \in proj^-(Doctor^I)$. By definition 2, $bill \in proj^+((\exists hasPatient.Patient)^I)$, so $bill \in proj^+(Doctor^I)$. But we cannot get positive answer to the query " is there any information indicating bill is not a doctor?", since for the following model I of K,

$$\begin{aligned}&Doctor^I =< \{john, bill\}, \{john\} >, Patient^I =< \{mary\}, \emptyset >,\\ &hasPatient^I =< \{(bill, mary)\}, \emptyset >\end{aligned}$$

we see that $bill \notin proj^-(Doctor^I)$.

Therefore, the $\mathcal{SHOIN}(\mathcal{D})4$ knowledge base can tolerate inconsistency without destroying useful inferences, that is it reasons para-consistently.

Example 2. *Let $\mathcal{K}$ be the following knowledge base*

$$TBox4 = \begin{cases} SurgicalTeam \sqsubset \neg ReadPatientRecordTeam \\ UrgencyTeam \sqsubset ReadPatientRecordTeam \end{cases}$$

$$ABox = \{SurgeicalTeam(john), UrgentTeam(john)\}.$$

The $\mathcal{SHOIN}(\mathcal{D})4$ knowledge base is satisfiable since it has a model as followings:

$$SurgicalTeam^I \in \{<\{john\}, \emptyset>, <\{john\}, \{john\}>\},$$
$$UrgencyTeam^I \in \{<\{john\}, \emptyset>, <\{john\}, \{john\}>\},$$
$$ReadPatientRecordTeam^I =<\{john\}, \{john\}> .$$

When queried "is there any information declining that john is allowed to read patient's record", it answers "yes" since $john \in proj^+(ReadPatientRecordTeam^I)$ for every models of $\mathcal{K}$; when queried "is there any information declining that john is not allowed to read patient's record", it answers "yes" because for every model of $\mathcal{K}$, $john \in proj^-(ReadPatientRecordTeam^I)$. However, when queried "is there any information declining that john is (not) a patient", it answers "no" since for some model of $\mathcal{K}$, $john \notin proj^{+(-)}(Patient^I)$.

In short, $\mathcal{SHOIN}(\mathcal{D})4$ gives the positive answers to both aspects of a contradiction, while remains other information not contrary. In this sense, $\mathcal{SHOIN}(\mathcal{D})4$ reflects system's information actually.

Let us consider an example including material and internal inclusion axioms:

Example 3. *We have the following knowledge: "generally speaking, the bird with a pair of swings can fly. Penguin is a kind of bird and has a pair of swings, but it cannot fly. $Tweety$ is a penguin with a pair of swings w." We can describe it by $\mathcal{SHOIN}(\mathcal{D})$ ontology ($TBox$, $ABox$) and $\mathcal{SHOIN}(\mathcal{D})4$ ontology ($TBox4$, $ABox$) as follows:*

$$TBox = \begin{cases} Bird \sqcap \exists hasWing.Wing \sqsubseteq Fly \\ Penguin \sqsubseteq Bird \\ Penguin \sqsubseteq \exists hasWing.Wing \\ Penguin \sqsubseteq \neg Fly \end{cases}$$

$$TBox4 = \begin{cases} Bird \sqcap \exists hasWing.Wing \mapsto Fly \\ Penguin \sqsubset Bird \\ Penguin \sqsubset \exists hasWing.Wing \\ Penguin \sqsubset \neg Fly \end{cases}$$

$$ABox = \{Bird(tweety), Penguin(tweety), Wing(w), hasWing(tweety, w)\}.$$

$\mathcal{K} = (TBox, ABox)$ is an unsatisfiable $\mathcal{SHOIN}(\mathcal{D})$ knowledge base from which everything follows. But $\mathcal{K}4 = (TBox4, ABox)$ is a satisfiable $\mathcal{SHOIN}(\mathcal{D})4$ knowledge base. Among its models is the following $I = (\{tweety, w\}, \cdot^I)$:

$Bird^I =<\{tweety\}, \{tweety\}>$, $Fly^I =<\emptyset, \{tweety\}>$, $Penguin^I =<\{tweety\}, \emptyset>$, $Wing^I =<\{w\}, \emptyset>$, $hasWing^I =<\{tweety\}, \{w\}>$.

Under this interpretation, $tweety \in proj^+(Bird^I) \cap proj^-(Bird^I)$, that is the value of $Bird^I(tweety)$ is $\top$. Similarly, $Fly^I(tweety) = f, Penguin^I(tweety) = t, Wing^I(w) = t, hasWing^I(tweety, w) = t$. We see that exceptions can be expressed by $\mathcal{SHOIN}(\mathcal{D})4$ system. We will continue to discuss the reasoning of this example in section 4.2.

Let us consider another example with number restriction constructor:

Example 4. *"The one who has at least one child is a parent. Generally speaking, parent is married. We have the fact that single Smith adopts a child Kate." This is a possible ontology. But it can not be expressed by any classical OWL DL ontology language without contradiction. We can express it by $\mathcal{SHOIN}(\mathcal{D})4$ in a novel way:*

$$TBox = \begin{cases} \geq 1.hasChild \sqsubset Parent \\ Parent \mapsto Married \end{cases}$$

$$ABox = \{hasChild(smith, kate), \neg\, Married(smith)\}$$

This is a satisfiable $\mathcal{SHOIN}(\mathcal{D})4$ knowledge base. For example, the following is its models with domain $\{smith, kate\}$:

- M1-M4: $(\geq 1.hasChild)^I =< \{smith\}, \emptyset >, Married^I =< \{smith\}, \{smith\} >,$ $hasChild^I =< \{(smith, kate)\}, \emptyset > \mathit{or} < \{(smith, kate)\}, \{(smith, kate)\} >,$ $Parent^I =< \{smith\}, \emptyset > \mathit{or} < \{smith\}, \{smith\} >;$
- M5-M6: $(\geq 1.hasChild)^I =< \{smith\}, \emptyset >, Parent^I =< \{smith\}, \{smith\} >,$ $hasChild^I =< \{(smith, kate)\}, \emptyset\} > \mathit{or} < \{(smith, kate)\}, \{(smith, kate)\} >,$ $Married^I =< \emptyset, \{smith\} >;$
- M7-M8: $hasChild^I =< \{(smith, kate)\}, \{(smith, kate), (smith, smith)\} >,$ $(\geq 1.hasChild)^I =< \{smith\}, \{smith\} >, Married^I =< \{smith\}, \{smith\} >,$ $Parent^I =< \{smith\}, \emptyset > \mathit{or} < \{smith\}, \{smith\} >;$
- M9: $hasChild^I =< \{(smith, kate)\}, \{(smith, kate), (smith, smith)\} >,$ $(\geq 1.hasChild)^I =< \{smith\}, \{smith\} >, Parent^I =< \{smith\}, \{smith\} >,$ $Married^I =< \{smith\}, \emptyset >;$

The corresponding four-valued semantics of the above models are as shown in Table 4 (s is Smith for short and k is Kate for short).

Table 4. Four-valued Models of Example 4

	$hasChild(s,k)$	$\geq 1.hasChild(s)$	$Parent(s)$	$Married(s)$
M1-M4	$t/\top$	t	$t/\top$	$\top$
M5-M6	$t/\top$	t	$\top$	f
M7-M8	$\top$	$\top$	$t/\top$	$\top$
M9	$\top$	$\top$	$\top$	f

Since the role $hasChild$ is not reflexive (namely, no one will relate itself by this role), we declare that the semantics of $\mathcal{SHOIN}(\mathcal{D})4$ had better not refer to unreasonable interpretation like $hasChild(smith, smith)$ for nonreflexive roles. The effect of distinguishing reflex roles to DL systems is to be study.

4 Reducing $\mathcal{SHOIN}(\mathcal{D})4$ to $\mathcal{SHOIN}(\mathcal{D})$

Because we don't consider the four-valued semantics of datatype concepts, in the rest, we only denote an interpretation of $\mathcal{SHOIN}(\mathcal{D})4$ as $I = (\Delta^I, \cdot^I)$ instead of $I = (\Delta^I, \Delta^I_D, \cdot^I)$ for simpleness.

For any interpretation $I = (\Delta^I, \cdot^I)$ of $\mathcal{SHOIN}(\mathcal{D})4$ and any concept C, we can decide the semantics of C by the positive projection of C^I and $(\neg C)^I$ according to the equation $proj^+((\neg C)^I) = proj^-(C^I)$, although there's no relation between $proj^+(C^I)$ and $proj^-(C^I)$.

We introduce the following notations to characterize the relationship between four-valued and two-valued semantics.

Definition 4. *(Decomposability) The four-valued semantics of $\mathcal{SHOIN}(\mathcal{D})4$ can be decomposed into two-valued semantics of $\mathcal{SHOIN}(\mathcal{D})$, iff for any $\mathcal{SHOIN}(\mathcal{D})4$ knowledge base $\mathcal{K}$ and its concept C and object (datatype) role R, there is an two-valued $\mathcal{SHOIN}(\mathcal{D})$ knowledge base $\overline{\mathcal{K}}$ and its two concepts $\overline{C_1}$,$\overline{C_2}$ and two object (datatype) roles $\overline{R_1}$,$\overline{R_2}$ such that for any four-valued interpretation I of $\mathcal{K}$, there's a two-valued interpretation $\overline{I}$ of $\overline{\mathcal{K}}$, such that*

$$C^I =< P, N > \text{ iff } \overline{C_1}^{\overline{I}} = P, \overline{C_2}^{\overline{I}} = N.$$

$$R^I =< P_1 \times P_2, N_1 \times N_2 > \text{ iff } \overline{R_1}^{\overline{I}} = P_1 \times P_2, \overline{R_2}^{\overline{I}} = \Delta^I \times \Delta^I \setminus N_1 \times N_2.$$

where P, N, P_1, P_2, N_1 and N_2 are subsets of Δ^I.

The decomposability of $\mathcal{SHOIN}(\mathcal{D})4$ means that the four-valued semantics of concept C and role R can be divided into the two-valued semantics of two $\mathcal{SHOIN}(\mathcal{D})$ concepts $\overline{C_1}, \overline{C_2}$ and roles $\overline{R_1}, \overline{R_2}$. Arieli [15,16] provides some techniques to reduce some models of four-valued logic to classical two-valued semantics. Yue [17] proposes a formula transformation technique to distinguish material implication and internal implication of four-valued logic. We will further study transformation technique to decompose the four-valued semantics of $\mathcal{SHOIN}(\mathcal{D})4$ in the next section. Furthermore, we will see that the decomposability of $\mathcal{SHOIN}(\mathcal{D})4$ enables the inference of $\mathcal{SHOIN}(\mathcal{D})4$ to be reduced to that of $\mathcal{SHOIN}(\mathcal{D})$.

4.1 Concept, Role and Axiom Transformations

Let $\mathcal{L}$ be a $\mathcal{SHOIN}(\mathcal{D})4$ language, $\mathcal{L} = \{C, R, a \mid C$ is a concept name, R is a role name, a is an individual$\}$. $\mathcal{A}(\mathcal{L})$ is set of atomic concepts of $\mathcal{L}$. $\overline{\mathcal{L}} = \{\overline{C}, \overline{\neg C}, R^+, R^=, \overline{a} \mid C, R, a \in \mathcal{L}, \overline{C}, \overline{\neg C}$ are the concept transformations of C and $\neg C$ respectively, $R^+, R^=$ are two role transformations of role R. $\overline{a}$ is the renamed name of individual a in $I\}$.

Concept transformation and role transformation of a $\mathcal{SHOIN}(\mathcal{D})4$ concept C and a role R are defined as follows:

Definition 5. *For any given concept $C \in \mathcal{L}$, $\overline{C} \in \overline{\mathcal{L}}$ is the concept transformation of C, such that*

(1) If $C = A$, $A \in \mathcal{A}(\mathcal{L})$, then $\overline{C} = A^+$;
(2) If $C = \neg A$, $A \in \mathcal{A}(\mathcal{L})$, then $\overline{C} = A^-$;
(3) If $C = \top$, then $\overline{C} = \top$;
(4) If $C = \bot$, then $\overline{C} = \bot$;
(5) If $C = E \sqcap D$, then $\overline{C} = \overline{E} \sqcap \overline{D}$;
(6) If $C = E \sqcup D$, then $\overline{C} = \overline{E} \sqcup \overline{D}$;

(7) *If* $C = \exists R.D$ *where* R *is an object role or a datatype role, then* $\overline{C} = \exists R^+.\overline{D}$;
(8) *If* $C = \forall R.D$ *where* R *is an object role or a datatype role, then* $\overline{C} = \forall R^+.\overline{D}$;
(9) *If* $C = \geq n.R$ *where* R *is an object role or a datatype role, then* $\overline{C} = \geq n.R^+$;
(10) *If* $C = \leq n.R$ *where* R *is an object role or a datatype role, then* $\overline{C} = \leq n.R^=$;
(11) *If* $C = \neg\neg D$, *then* $\overline{C} = \overline{D}$;
(12) *If* $C = \neg(E \sqcap D)$, *then* $\overline{C} = \overline{\neg E} \sqcup \overline{\neg D}$;
(13) *If* $C = \neg(E \sqcup D)$, *then* $\overline{C} = \overline{\neg E} \sqcap \overline{\neg D}$;
(14) *If* $C = \neg(\exists R.D)$ *where* R *is an object role, then* $\overline{C} = \forall R^+.\overline{\neg D}$;
(15) *If* $C = \neg(\forall R.D)$ *where* R *is an object role, then* $\overline{C} = \exists R^+.\overline{\neg D}$;
(16) *If* $C = \neg(\geq n.R)$ *where* R *is an object role or a datatype role, then* $\overline{C} = \leq (n-1).R^=$;
(17) *If* $C = \neg(\leq n.R)$ *where* R *is an object role or a datatype role, then* $\overline{C} = \geq (n+1).R^+$;
(18) *If* $C = \{o_1, ...\}$ *where* o_i *is an individual, then* $\overline{C} = \{\overline{o}_1, ...\}$;
(19) $(R^-)^+ = (R^+)^-, (R^-)^= = (R^=)^-$

Based on the concept and role transformations, we give the axiom transformations as follows:

Definition 6. *The transformation of axioms of* $\mathcal{SHOIN}(\mathcal{D})4$ *are defined as follows:*

(1) $\overline{C_1 \mapsto C_2} = \neg\overline{\neg C_1} \sqsubseteq \overline{C}_2$;
$\overline{C_1 \sqsubset C_2} = \overline{C_1} \sqsubseteq \overline{C}_2$;
$\overline{C_1 \rightarrow C_2} = \{\overline{C_1} \sqsubseteq \overline{C}_2, \overline{\neg C_2} \sqsubseteq \overline{\neg C_1}\}$.
where, $C_i (i = 1, 2)$ *is a concept.*
(2) $\overline{R_1 \mapsto R_2} = R_1^= \sqsubseteq R_2^+$;
$\overline{R_1 \sqsubset R_2} = R_1^+ \sqsubseteq R_2^+$;
$\overline{R_1 \rightarrow R_2} = \{R_1^+ \sqsubseteq R_2^+, R_1^= \sqsubseteq R_2^=\}$.
where, $R_i (i = 1, 2)$ *is an object role or a datatype role.*
(3) $\overline{Trans(R)} = \{Trans(R^+)\}$
where, R *is an object role.*
(4) $\overline{a : C} = \overline{a} : \overline{C}$, $\overline{a = b} = \overline{a} = \overline{b}$, $\overline{a \neq b} = \overline{a} \neq \overline{b}$
where, a, b *are individuals,* C *is a concept.*

Definition 7. *(Classical Induced KB) We say the* classical induced KB *of any given* $\mathcal{SHOIN}(\mathcal{D})4$ *knowledge base* $\mathcal{K}$, *written* $\overline{\mathcal{K}}$, *if all axioms in* $\overline{\mathcal{K}}$ *are exactly the transformations of axioms in* $\mathcal{K}$.

Obviously, concept, role and axiom transformations can be finished in polynomial time.

4.2 $\mathcal{SHOIN}(\mathcal{D})4$ Reasoning

In this section we first show the decomposability of $\mathcal{SHOIN}(\mathcal{D})4$, and then prove that the standard reasoning problems of $\mathcal{SHOIN}(\mathcal{D})4$ can be reduced to those of classical $\mathcal{SHOIN}(\mathcal{D})$.

Definition 8. *(Classical Induced Interpretation) Let* $I = (\Delta^I, \cdot^I)$ *be an interpretation of* $\mathcal{SHOIN}(\mathcal{D})4$, *and* $\overline{\mathcal{K}}$ *be the classical induced KB of* $\mathcal{K}$. I*'s classical induced interpretation* $\overline{I} = (\Delta^{\overline{I}}, \cdot^{\overline{I}})$ *is defined as follows:*

- *I and $\overline{I}$ have the same domain, i.e. $\Delta^{\overline{I}} = \Delta^I$;*
- *I and $\overline{I}$ interpret instance names in the same way, i.e. $\overline{a}^{\overline{I}} = a^I$;*
- *For any atomic concept A, if $A^I =< P, Q >$, then $(A^+)^{\overline{I}} = P, (A^-)^{\overline{I}} = Q$;*
- *For any object or datatype role R, if $R^I =< P_1 \times P_2, N_1 \times N_2 >$, then $(R^+)^{\overline{I}} = P_1 \times P_2$, and $(R^=)^{\overline{I}} = \Delta^{\overline{I}} \times \Delta^{\overline{I}} \setminus N_1 \times N_2$.*

The semantics of complex concepts are obtained in the standard way.

Definition 9. *(Four-valued Induced Interpretation) Let $\overline{I}$ be the interpretation of an $\mathcal{SHOIN}(\mathcal{D})$ knowledge base $\mathcal{K}$, $\overline{I}$'s four-valued induced interpretation $I = (\Delta^I, \cdot^I)$ is defined as follows*

- *I and $\overline{I}$ have the same domain, i.e. $\Delta^{\overline{I}} = \Delta^I$;*
- *I and $\overline{I}$ interpret instance names in the same way, i.e. $\overline{a}^{\overline{I}} = a^I$;*
- *For any primitive concept A, if $(A^+)^{\overline{I}} = P, (A^-)^{\overline{I}} = Q$, then $A^I =< P, Q >$;*
- *For any object and datatype role R, if $(R^+)^{\overline{I}} = P_1 \times P_2$, and $(R^=)^{\overline{I}} = Q_1 \times Q_2$, then $R^I =< P_1 \times P_2, \Delta^I \times \Delta^I \setminus Q_1 \times Q_2 >$.*

The semantics of complex concepts are obtained according to definition 2.

From definitions 8 and 9, the classical induced KB of a $\mathcal{SHOIN}(\mathcal{D})4$ knowledge base $\mathcal{K}$ is two-valued theory, whose constructors are those of $\mathcal{SHOIN}(\mathcal{D})$. Therefore, we can change a $\mathcal{SHOIN}(\mathcal{D})4$ knowledge base into a $\mathcal{SHOIN}(\mathcal{D})$ one by transformation technique.

Lemma 5. *The semantics of $\mathcal{SHOIN}(\mathcal{D})4$ can be decomposed to two-valued semantics of $\mathcal{SHOIN}(\mathcal{D})$.*

Proof. Let $\mathcal{K}$ be a $\mathcal{SHOIN}(\mathcal{D})4$ knowledge base and C be a concept. For any interpretation I, we prove by structure induction that $C^I =< P, N >$ iff $\overline{C}^{\overline{I}} = P, \overline{\neg C}^{\overline{I}} = N$, where $\overline{I}$ is the Classical Induced Interpretation of I.

Case: C is an atomic concept A is easy by definition 9, 8.

Case: $C = \neg D$. $\overline{C} = \overline{\neg D}, \overline{\neg C} = \overline{D}$,

- Suppose $C^I =< P, N >$. Then $D^I =< N, P >$. By induction assumption, we know $\overline{D}^{\overline{I}} = N, \overline{\neg D}^{\overline{I}} = P$. That is $\overline{\neg C}^{\overline{I}} = N, \overline{C}^{\overline{I}} = P$.
- Whereas, suppose $\overline{C}^{\overline{I}} = P, \overline{\neg C}^{\overline{I}} = N$. Then $\overline{D}^{\overline{I}} = N, \overline{\neg D}^{\overline{I}} = P$. By induction assumption, we know $D^I =< N, P >$. Through the semantics of negation, we know $C^I =< P, N >$.

Case: $C = D \sqcup E$. $\overline{C} = \overline{D} \sqcup \overline{E}$, and $\overline{\neg C} = \overline{\neg D} \sqcap \overline{\neg E}$,

- Suppose $C^I =< P, N >$,$D^I =< P_1, N_1 >, E^I =< P_2, N_2 >$. Then $P_1 \cup P_2 = P, N_1 \cap N_2 = N$. By induction hypothesis, we know $\overline{D}^{\overline{I}} = P_1, \overline{\neg D}^{\overline{I}} = N_1, \overline{E}^{\overline{I}} = P_2$, and $\overline{\neg E}^{\overline{I}} = N_2$. Therefore $\overline{C}^{\overline{I}} = \overline{D}^{\overline{I}} \cup \overline{E}^{\overline{I}} = P_1 \cup P_2 = P$, and $\overline{\neg C}^{\overline{I}} = \overline{\neg D}^{\overline{I}} \cap \overline{\neg E}^{\overline{I}} = N_1 \cap N_2 = N$.

- Whereas, suppose $\overline{C}^{\mathcal{I}} = P, \overline{\neg C}^{\mathcal{I}} = N, \overline{D}^{\mathcal{I}} = P', \overline{\neg D}^{\mathcal{I}} = N'$, and $\overline{E}^{\mathcal{I}} = P'', \overline{\neg E}^{\mathcal{I}} = N''$. By the definition of semantics, $P = P' \cup P'', N = N' \cap N''$. By induction hypothesis, $D^I =< P', N' >, E^I =< P'', N'' >$. Therefore, $C^I =< P' \cup P'', N' \cap N'' >=< P, N >$ by definition of semantics of $\mathcal{SHOIN}(\mathcal{D})4$.

Case: $C = D \sqcap E$. the proposition holds likewise.
Case: $C = \forall R.D$. $\overline{C} = \forall R.\overline{D}$ and $\overline{\neg C} = \exists R.\overline{\neg D}$,

- Suppose $C^I =< P, N >$, $D^I =< P_1, N_1 >$. By semantics definition, we know $P = \{x \mid \forall y, R(x,y) \Rightarrow y \in proj^+(D^I)\}$, $N = \{x \mid \exists y, R(x,y) \wedge y \in proj^-(D^I)\}$. By induction hypothesis, $\overline{D}^{\mathcal{I}} = P_1$ and $\overline{\neg D}^{\mathcal{I}} = N_1$. Therefore, $N_1 = proj^-(D^I)$. (Note that $P_1 = proj^+(D^I)$)

$$\begin{aligned}\overline{C}^{\mathcal{I}} &= (\forall R.\overline{D})^{\mathcal{I}} = \{x \mid \forall y, R(x,y) \Rightarrow y \in (\overline{D})^{\mathcal{I}}\}\\ &= \{x \mid \forall y, R(x,y) \Rightarrow y \in P_1\} = P,\\ \overline{\neg C}^{\mathcal{I}} &= (\exists R.\overline{\neg D})^{\mathcal{I}} = \{x \mid \exists y, R(x,y) \wedge y \in (\overline{\neg D})^{\mathcal{I}}\}\\ &= \{x \mid \exists y, R(x,y) \wedge y \in N_1\} = N.\end{aligned}$$

- Whereas, suppose $\overline{C}^{\mathcal{I}} = P, \overline{\neg C}^{\mathcal{I}} = N, \overline{D}^{\mathcal{I}} = P', \overline{\neg D}^{\mathcal{I}} = N'$. By the definition of semantics,

$$\begin{aligned}P &= \overline{C}^{\mathcal{I}} = (\forall R.\overline{D})^{\mathcal{I}} = \{x \mid \forall y, R(x,y) \Rightarrow y \in P'\},\\ N &= \overline{\neg C}^{\mathcal{I}} = (\exists R.\overline{\neg D})^{\mathcal{I}} = \{x \mid \exists y, R(x,y) \wedge y \in N'\}.\end{aligned}$$

By induction hypothesis, $D^I =< P', N' >$. Furthermore, by the semantics of $\mathcal{SHOIN}(\mathcal{D})4$, we know

$$C^I =< \{x \mid \forall y, R(x,y) \Rightarrow y \in P'\}, \{x \mid \exists y, R(x,y) \wedge y \in N'\} >=< P, N >$$

Case: $C = \exists R.D$. the lemma holds likewise.
Case: $C =\geq n.R$. $\overline{C} =\geq n.R^+, \overline{\neg C} =\leq (n-1).R^=$:

- Suppose $C^I =< P, N >, R^I =< P_1 \times P_2, N_1 \times N_2 >$. By definition 2,

$$\begin{aligned}P &= \{x \mid \sharp(y.(x,y) \in proj^+(R^I)) \geq n\} = \{x \mid \sharp(y.(x,y) \in P_1 \times P_2) \geq n\}\\ &= \{x \mid \sharp(y.(x,y) \in (R^+)^{\mathcal{I}}) \geq n\} = (\geq n.R^+)^{\mathcal{I}} = \overline{C}^{\mathcal{I}},\\ N &= \{x \mid \sharp(y.(x,y) \notin proj^-(R^I)) < n\}\\ &= \{x \mid \sharp(y.(x,y) \in \Delta^I \times \Delta^I \setminus N_1 \times N_2) < n\}\\ &= \{x \mid \sharp(y.(x,y) \in (R^=)^{\mathcal{I}}) < n\} = (\leq (n-1).R^=)^{\mathcal{I}} = \overline{\neg C}^{\mathcal{I}},\end{aligned}$$

Note that $(R^+)^{\mathcal{I}} = P_1 \times P_2, (R^=)^{\mathcal{I}} = \Delta^I \times \Delta^I \setminus N_1 \times N_2$ by definition 8.
- Whereas, Suppose $(\geq n.R^+)^{\mathcal{I}} = P, (\leq (n-1).R^=)^{\mathcal{I}} = N, (R^+)^{\mathcal{I}} = P_1 \times P_2, (R^=)^{\mathcal{I}} = \Delta_1 \times \Delta_2 \setminus N_1 \times N_2$. Then $P = \{x \mid \sharp(y.(x,y) \in P_1 \times P_2) \geq n\}, N =$

$\{x \mid \sharp(y.(x,y) \notin N_1 \times N_2) < n\}$. By definition 9, $R^I =< P_1 \times P_2, N_1 \times N_2 >$. By definition 2,

$$C^I = < \{x \mid \sharp(y.(x,y) \in P_1 \times P_2) \geq n\}, \{x \mid \sharp(y.(x,y) \notin N_1 \times N_2) < n\} > \\ = < P, N > .$$

Case: $C = \leq n.R$. the lemma can be proven in the same way.

In all, let $C_1 = \overline{C}, C_2 = \overline{\neg C}$, we see that for any concept C, $C^I =< P, N >$ iff $C_1^{\overline{I}} = P$ and $C_2^{\overline{I}} = N$.

For any role R, from definition 9 and 8, we can see that $R^I =< P_1 \times P_2, N_1 \times N_2 >$ iff $\overline{R_1}^{\overline{I}} = P_1 \times P_2, \overline{R_2}^{\overline{I}} = \Delta^I \times \Delta^I \setminus N_1 \times N_2$. □

Theorem 6. *The interpretation $I = (\Delta^I, \cdot^I)$ is a model of knowledge base $\mathcal{K}$ iff there is a model of $\overline{\mathcal{K}}$, say $\overline{I} = (\Delta^{\overline{I}}, \cdot^{\overline{I}})$, which is the classical induced knowledge base of $\mathcal{K}$.*

Proof. (Necessity) For any interpretation I of $\mathcal{K}$, let the interpretation $\overline{I}$ be I's classical induced interpretation. According to the relationship between $\overline{\mathcal{K}}$ and $\mathcal{K}$, for any $\overline{\mathcal{K}}$'s inclusion of the form $\neg\overline{\neg C} \sqsubseteq \overline{D} \in \overline{\mathcal{K}}, C \mapsto D \in \mathcal{K}$. Suppose $C^I =< P_1, N_1 >$, $D^I =< P_2, N_2 >$. By lemma 5, $\overline{\neg C}^{\overline{I}} = N_1, \overline{D}^{\overline{I}} = P_2$. Therefore, $(\neg\overline{\neg C})^{\overline{I}} = \Delta^{\overline{I}} \setminus N_1 = \Delta^I \setminus N_1$. I satisfies $C \mapsto D$. So $\Delta^I \setminus N_1 \subseteq P_2$. Therefore, $(\neg\overline{\neg C})^{\overline{I}} \subseteq \overline{D}^{\overline{I}}$. That is, $\overline{I}$ satisfies $\neg\overline{\neg C} \sqsubseteq \overline{D}$.

For any $\overline{\mathcal{K}}$'s inclusion of the form $\overline{C} \sqsubseteq \overline{D} \in \overline{\mathcal{K}}, \overline{\neg C} \sqsubseteq \overline{\neg D} \notin \overline{\mathcal{K}}, C \sqsubset D \in \mathcal{K}$. Suppose $C^I =< P_1, N_1 >$, $D^I =< P_2, N_2 >$. By lemma 5, $\overline{C}^{\overline{I}} = P_1, \overline{D}^{\overline{I}} = P_2$. I satisfies $C \sqsubset D$. Therefore, $P_1 = proj^+(C^I) \subseteq proj^+(D^I) = P_2$, that is $\overline{I}$ satisfies $\overline{C} \sqsubseteq \overline{D}$.

For any $\overline{\mathcal{K}}$'s inclusion pair of the form $\{\overline{C} \sqsubseteq \overline{D}, \overline{\neg D} \sqsubseteq \overline{\neg C}\} \subseteq \overline{\mathcal{K}}$, $C \rightarrow D \in \mathcal{K}$. Suppose $C^I =< P_1, N_1 >, D^I =< P_2, N_2 >$. By lemma 5, $\overline{C}^{\overline{I}} = P_1, \overline{D}^{\overline{I}} = P_2, \overline{\neg C}^{\overline{I}} = N_1, \overline{\neg D}^{\overline{I}} = N_2$. I satisfies $C \rightarrow D$. Therefore, $P_1 = proj^+(C^I) \subseteq proj^+(D^I) = P_2, N_2 = proj^-(D^I) \subseteq proj^-(C^I) = N_1$, that is $\overline{I}$ satisfies $\{\overline{C} \sqsubseteq \overline{D}, \overline{\neg D} \sqsubseteq \overline{\neg C}\}$.

For any assertion of the form $\overline{a}:\overline{C}$. $a:C$ belongs to the $\mathcal{K}$. Suppose $C^I =< P, N >$, $a^I = \delta_0 \in \Delta^I$, then $(\overline{C})^{\overline{I}} = P, \overline{a}^{\overline{I}} = \delta_0$. Because I satisfies $a:C$, $\delta_0 \in P$, that is $\overline{I}$ satisfies $\overline{a}:\overline{C}$. Finally, since $a^I = (\overline{a})^{\overline{I}}, b^I = (\overline{b})^{\overline{I}}$, $(\overline{a})^{\overline{I}} = (\overline{b})^{\overline{I}}$ iff $a^I = b^I$, $(\overline{a})^{\overline{I}} \neq (\overline{b})^{\overline{I}}$ iff $a^I \neq b^I$.

For any $\overline{\mathcal{K}}$'s role inclusion $R_1^{=} \sqsubseteq R_2^{+}, R_1 \mapsto R_2 \in \mathcal{K}$. Assume $R_1^I =< P_1^1 \times P_2^1, N_1^1 \times N_2^1 >$, $R_2^I =< P_1^2 \times P_2^2, N_1^2 \times N_2^2 >$. By definition 8, $(R_2^+)^{\overline{I}} = P_1^2 \times P_2^2$, $R_1^{=} = \Delta^I \times \Delta^I \setminus N_1^1 \times N_2^1$. I satisfies $R_1 \mapsto R_2$, so $(R_1^)\overline{I} == \Delta^I \times \Delta^I \setminus N_1^1 \times N_2^1 \subseteq P_1^2 \times P_2^2 = (R_2^+)^{\overline{I}}$. That is. $\overline{I}$ satisfies $R_1^{=} \sqsubseteq R_2^{+}$.

For any $\overline{\mathcal{K}}$'s role inclusion $R_1^{+} \sqsubseteq R_2^{+}, R_1 \sqsubset R_2 \in \mathcal{K}$. Suppose $R_1^I =< P_1^1 \times P_2^1, N_1^1 \times N_2^1 >$, $R_2^I =< P_1^2 \times P_2^2, N_1^2 \times N_2^2 >$. By definition 8, $(R_2^+)^{\overline{I}} = P_1^2 \times P_2^2$, $R_1^+ = P_1^1 \times P_2^1$. I satisfies $R_1 \sqsubset R_2$, so $(R_1^+)\overline{I} = P_1^1 \times P_2^1 \subseteq P_1^2 \times P_2^2 = (R_2^+)^{\overline{I}}$. That is. $\overline{I}$ satisfies $R_1^+ \sqsubseteq R_2^+$.

For any $Tran(R^+) \in \overline{I}, Trans(R) \in \mathcal{K}$. Suppose $R^I =< P_1^1 \times P_2^1, N_1^1 \times N_2^1 >$. I satisfies $Trans(R)$, then $R^I = (R^I)^+$, that is $P_1 \times P_2 = (P_1 \times P_2)^+$. By definition 8, $(R^+)^{\overline{I}} = ((R^+)^{\overline{I}})^+$. That is, $Trans(R^+)$.

(sufficiency) For any interpretation $\overline{I} = (\Delta^{\overline{I}}, \cdot^{\overline{I}})$ of $\overline{K}$, let I be the four-valued semantics of $\overline{I}$. By the similar approach, we can prove that the proposition holds. □

For $\mathcal{SHOIN}(\mathcal{D})$, the inclusion axioms can be reduced to unsatisfiability of concepts. The following corollary shows similar results of inclusion axioms and concept satisfiability of $\mathcal{SHOIN}(\mathcal{D})4$.

Corollary 7. *For a $\mathcal{SHOIN}(\mathcal{D})4$ ontology $\overline{\mathcal{K}}$, the material inclusion axiom $C \mapsto D$ holds in $\mathcal{K}$ iff $\overline{\neg\neg C} \sqcap \overline{\neg D}$ is unsatisfiable in $\overline{\mathcal{K}}$; The internal inclusion axiom $C \sqsubset D$ holds in K iff $\overline{C} \sqcap \overline{\neg D}$ is unsatisfiable in $\overline{\mathcal{K}}$; The strong inclusion axiom $C \rightarrow D$ holds in $\mathcal{K}$ iff $\overline{C} \sqcap \overline{\neg D}, \overline{\neg D} \sqcap \overline{\neg\neg C}$ is unsatisfiable in $\overline{\mathcal{K}}$.*

We explain by the following example that $\mathcal{SHOIN}(\mathcal{D})4$ can express inconsistency in a knowledge base, meanwhile inference is done by calling existing reasoning techniques which is based on two-valued semantics.

Example 5. *(Example 3 contd.) By transformations, we obtain the following classical induced KB, $\overline{\mathcal{K}}$, of the example 3:*

$$\overline{TBox} = \begin{cases} \neg Bird^- \sqcap \neg\forall.\overline{hasWing}.Wing^- \sqsubseteq Fly^+ \\ Penguin^+ \sqsubseteq Bird^+ \\ Penguin^+ \sqsubseteq \exists\overline{hasWing}.Wing^+ \\ Penguin^+ \sqsubseteq Fly^- \end{cases}$$

$\overline{ABox} = \{Peguin^+(\overline{tweety}), Bird^+(\overline{tweety}), Wing^+(\overline{w}), hasWing^+(\overline{tweety}, \overline{w})\}$.

By classical tableaux algorithm, $Fly^-(\overline{tweety})$ holds, that is, tweety cannot fly. But $Fly^+(\overline{tweety})$ does not holds, which means that $\overline{\mathcal{K}}$ is not trivial. So is the original $\mathcal{SHOIN}(\mathcal{D})4$ knowledge base by theorem 6.

5 Related Work

Patel-Schneider [10] has proposed four-valued semantics for a terminological logic to equip it with a tractable inclusion relation, while we use the similar method but with some extensions to equip ontology language OWL DL with the ability to represent and reason with contradictions. The direct effect of inclusion form on the validity of algorithm makes the inclusion get only very easy cases in [10]. The algorithm used in [10] for computing inclusion is tractable, while it cannot treat concept union, full negation and exist quantification. Therefore, Patel-Schneider restricts the language without these constructors in [10]. However, the description logic $\mathcal{SHOIN}(\mathcal{D})4$ studied in this paper includes all of these constructors. Moreover, we proves that the standard inferences of $\mathcal{SHOIN}(\mathcal{D})4$ can be converted to those of $\mathcal{SHOIN}(\mathcal{D})$. Thus, both the complexity and decidability of $\mathcal{SHOIN}(\mathcal{D})4$ are the same as those of $\mathcal{SHOIN}(\mathcal{D})$.

The material inclusion proposed in this paper is a method to deal with knowledge with exceptions, which is based on four-valued logic. Salem et al. [4] adopt possibilistic logic and lexicographical inference combining MSP algorithm [18] which can make a stratification among the knowledge with exceptions according to the principle that the ones with higher stratification will be preferential to others which conflict with the former and are of lower stratifications. Huang [11] introduces syntax relevance to selection function whereby some consistent sub-theory(sub-theories) can be selected to be reasoned with. Both approaches mentioned above infer on a consistent sub-theory, while the approach in this paper acknowledges contradictions and allow them to join in reasoning instead of ignoring them. Note that conclusions deduced in this way may contain contradiction also. However, as we have seen, the inconsistencies are localized without destroying useful conclusions.

In this paper, four-valued ontology can be changed into a two-valued one so that we can make full use of existing inference systems instead of studying new mechanism. Formula transformations have been used to compute complex model [15,16,17]. However, those works are all based on propositional language. The extension of transformation techniques to ontology language is a core work of this paper as well.

6 Conclusion

We defined four-valued semantics for concepts, object (datatype) roles, and axioms, thus forming an inconsistent tolerance description logic $\mathcal{SHOIN}(\mathcal{D})4$. Mature reasoning mechanisms of classical description logic remain useful for $\mathcal{SHOIN}(\mathcal{D})4$ because of concept and axiom transformations. Since $\mathcal{SHOIN}(\mathcal{D})$ is the underlying logic system of OWL DL, $\mathcal{SHOIN}(\mathcal{D})4$ provides us with an approach to infer with inconsistent OWL DL ontology by classical inference mechanism.

The underlying idea through this paper is considering contradiction as static or hidden — that is, it is based on paraconsistent logic. Another method to treat contradiction is nonmonotonic logic which views inconsistency as dynamic and modifiable. We will further compare and combine these two methods to find out excellent methods for semantic web to reason with inconsistencies in the future work.

References

1. F. Patel-Schneider Peter and Horrocks Ian. Owl web ontology language semantics and abstract syntax. *W3C Recommendation*, 10 February, 2004.
2. Baader Franz, Horrocks Ian, and Ulrike Sattler. Description logic as ontology languages for the semantic web. *In Proceedings of the Workshop on Methods for Modalities 2001*, 2001.
3. Horrocks Ian and F. Patel-Schneider Peter. Reducing owl entailment to description logic satisfiability. *J. Web Sem.*, 1(4):345–357, 2004.
4. Salem BENFERHAT, Rania EL BAIDA, and Frédéric CUPPENS. A stratification-based approach for handling conflicts in access control. *Symposium on Access Control Models and Technologies (SACMAT'03)*, June 2-3, 2003.
5. Zuoquan Lin and Wei Li. Para-consistent logic(I)— the study of traditional para-consistent logic. *Computer Science*, 21(5), 1994.

6. Zuoquan Lin and Wei Li. Para-consistent logic(II)— the study of new para-consistent logic. *Computer Science*, 21(6), 1994.
7. Zuoquan Lin and Wei Li. Para-consistent logic(III)— the logic base of para-consistent logic. *Computer Science*, 22(1), 1995.
8. N.D.Belnap. A useful four-valued logic. *Modern uses of multiple-valued logic*, pages 7–73, 1977.
9. N.D.Belnap. How a computer should think. *Comtemporary Aspects of Philosophy: Proceedings of the Oxford International Symposium*, pages 30–56, 1977.
10. Peter F.Patel-Schneider. A four-valued semantics for terminological logics. *Artificial Intelligence*, 38:319–351, 1989.
11. Zhisheng Huang, Frank van Harmelen, and Annette ten Teije. Reasoning with inconsistent ontologies. In Leslie Pack Kaelbling and Alessandro Saffiotti, editors, *IJCAI*, pages 454–459. Professional Book Center, 2005.
12. Melvin Fitting. Bilattices are nice things. *proceedings of Conference on Self-Reference*, 2002.
13. Ofer Arieli and Arnon Avron. The value of the four values. *Artificial Intelligence*, 102:97–141, 1998.
14. Ofer Arieli and Avron A. Reasoning with logical bilattices. *J.Logic,Language and Information*, 5(1):25–63, 1996.
15. Ofer Arieli and Marc Denecker. Modeling paraconsistent reasoning by classical logic. In Thomas Eiter and Klaus-Dieter Schewe, editors, *FoIKS*, volume 2284 of *Lecture Notes in Computer Science*, pages 1–14. Springer, 2002.
16. Ofer Arieli. Paraconsistent preferential reasoning by signed quantified boolean formulae. In Ramon López de Mántaras and Lorenza Saitta, editors, *ECAI*, pages 773–777. IOS Press, 2004.
17. Anbu Yue, Yue Ma, and Zuoquan Lin. Four-valued semantics for default logic. In Luc Lamontagne and Mario Marchand, editors, *Canadian Conference on AI*, volume 4013 of *Lecture Notes in Computer Science*, pages 195–205. Springer, 2006.
18. Salem Benferhat, Didier Dubois, and Henri Prade. Nonmonotonic reasoning, conditional objects and possibility theory. *Artif. Intell.*, 92(1-2):259–276, 1997.

Configuring Intelligent Mediators Using Ontologies

Gennaro Bruno, Christine Collet, and Genoveva Vargas-Solar

LSR-IMAG Laboratory
681, rue de la passerelle
38402, St. Martin d'Hères
France
{Gennaro.Bruno, Christine.Collet, Genoveva.Vargas-Solar}@imag.fr
http://www-lsr.imag.fr/

Abstract. This paper presents a new intelligent mediators configuration approach which exploits high expressive description logics to represent metadata, and reasoning tasks in order to build more flexible mediation systems. A user specifies a *needs expression* in terms of (i) an interesting view over a given application domain, (ii) sources preferences and (iii) architectural requirements. A well-adapted mediator, is automatically configured according to these needs through a reasoning-based configuration process. A configured mediator can therefore be adapted in order to build knowledge-based mediation systems with an arbitrary architecture.

1 Context and Motivations

Mediation systems [1] were introduced to provide an integrated view over distributed and heterogeneous data sources for accessing them in a transparent way. During these last years, their role has constantly evolved. Several mediation approaches, providing different modeling and implementing solutions, have been proposed.

In order to provide query expression and metadata management with more semantics, a particular kind of data integration approach, commonly called *knowledge-based* mediation system, has been proposed. Differently from classical mediation systems, they use high expressive knowledge representation formalisms, i.e., description logics, as basis for data integration. This allows to have a more precise semantic representation of application domains, and to improve classical mediation tasks with inference capabilities.

This work focuses on knowledge-based mediation systems. For this reason, we analyzed many existing approaches according to several aspects such as the integration approach, data model and associated query language, and more particularly the mediation system architecture. According to this latter aspect, knowledge-based mediation systems can be mainly divided into two main categories (cf. Figure 1):

T. Grust et al. (Eds.): EDBT 2006 Workshops, LNCS 4254, pp. 554–572, 2006.

- *centralized mediation systems* [2,3,5,7,8,6] are based on a *domain ontology* acting as an integrated view over a set of distributed and heterogeneous data sources. A user formulates a query over the domain ontology. Then the query is rewritten into a set of local expressions over local sources, which are consequently accessed in a transparent way. The mediator represents the single access point to the system, and local sources are directly accessible from it.
- *distributed mediation systems* [4,9] aim to integrate a very large number of distributed data sources. This makes the construction of an integrated view over them a very difficult task to achieve. Therefore, query processing becomes a distributed task and the centralized mediator is replaced by a net of cooperative components commonly called *peers*. Each peer provides a *local ontology* modeling one or more underlying local sources. A user formulates a query over a peer. If locally retrieved data does not fulfill user expectatives, the query is forwarded to some neighbors peers[1] for execution in order to retrieve mode data.

To our knowledge, no mediation system, being able to adapt to both applicative contexts, exists today.

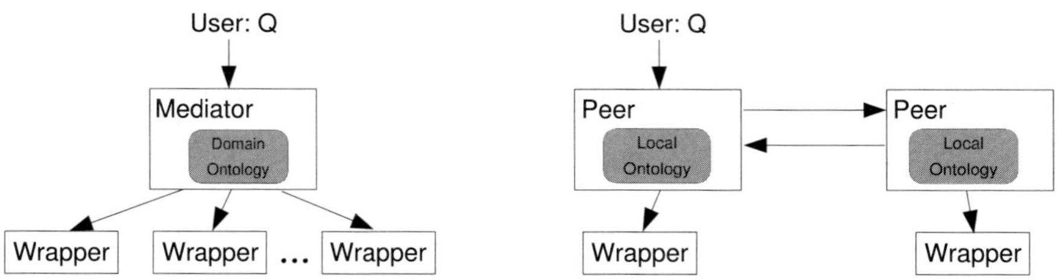

Fig. 1. Existing approaches

This paper focuses on the intelligent mediator configuration process of ADEMS[2] and on the role of mediators within a knowledge-based mediation system. The architecture of ADEMS has been previously presented in [10], therefore, the paper gives no details on the mediator internal architecture and on query expression and processing.

ADEMS exploits the high expressive description logic $\mathcal{SHIQ}(\mathcal{D})$ [12] to represent metadata, and exploits reasoning tasks in order to automatically configure well-adapted mediators. A user specifies a *needs expression* in terms of (i) the interesting view over a given application domain, (ii) sources preferences and, (iii) architectural requirements. ADEMS configures a well-adapted mediator according to these needs, being able to adapt centralized as well as distributed architectures. A configured mediator manages metadata as knowledge within a

[1] Neighbor peers are those ones that a peer can directly access. Differently from centralized approach, not all resources are directly accessible from a peer (mediator).
[2] ADEMS, an *ADaptable and Extensible Mediation Service*.

set of ontologies, and exploits inference in order to semantically improve the query processing task. Nevertheless, for a lack of space, this paper mainly focuses on the mediator configuration process, and on the role of mediators within a knowledge-based mediation system. No details on the mediator internal architecture and functions are given.

The remainder of this document is organized as follows. Section 2 presents the ADEMS approach. It describes the general architecture of a mediation system, its components, i.e. a set of mediators and sources, and the way they interact. Then it introduces the mediator configuration process. Section 3 illustrates the needs expression structure and shows how its ontological representation allows to better represent the semantics of metadata. Section 4 shows how a needs expression is analyzed and a mediator is configured accordingly, by exploiting reasoning tasks. Metadata involved in such a process is also illustrated. Section 5 discusses on implementation issues and experimental validations. Finally, Section 6 concludes the paper.

2 Approach

In our approach, a mediation system consists of a net of interconnected mediators giving access to a set of heterogeneous and distributed local sources (cf. Figure 2). Each mediator corresponds to a user access point to the mediation system. No assumptions about the system topology are done. The system architecture is not fixed a priori and it is adaptable to different applicative contexts/user requirements.

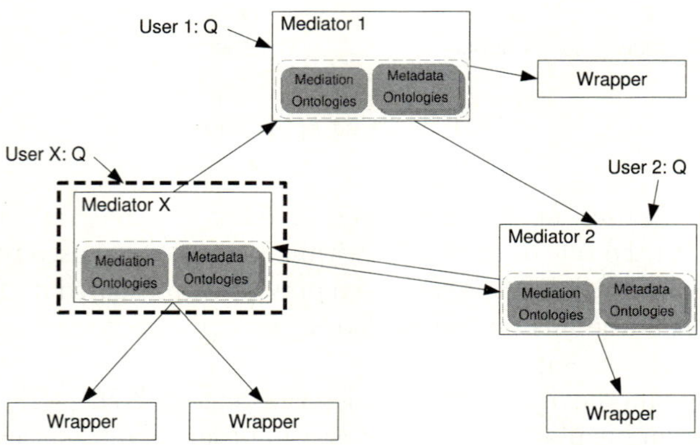

Fig. 2. ADEMS mediation system

For doing so, a mediator is modeled a general-purpose reusable mediation component. It becomes a specific ad-hoc component through a *configuration process*, whose goal is to adapt a mediator to a particular user needs definition. The mediator configuration process consists of building a set of ontologies describing the behavior of a mediator: a (i) *mediation ontology* represents a user-defined view over a domain description and acts as a global schema (integrated or not) over a set of underlying local *resources* (sources as well as other mediators), and (ii) a set of *metadata ontologies* representing all necessary metadata about available resources, the data they manage and the way to access them. Therefore, from a *user X* point of view (cf. dashed box in the Figure 2), a mediation system consists of a *mediator X* accessing a set of resources. A user formulates a query over its mediation ontology and the query is evaluated over the mediator resources in a transparent way. The user perception of the whole mediation system is limited to his/her own configured mediator, representing his/her access point to data. We will show later in this paper how, according to the way a mediator is configured, our approach allows to emulate both centralized and distributed knowledge-based mediation systems, and to enable more complex architectures.

Configuring a mediator in such a way is a difficult and tedious task for a human operator. For this reason, in order to help users with this task, we propose the ADEMS *mediator configuration service* (cf. Figure 3). The service manages all

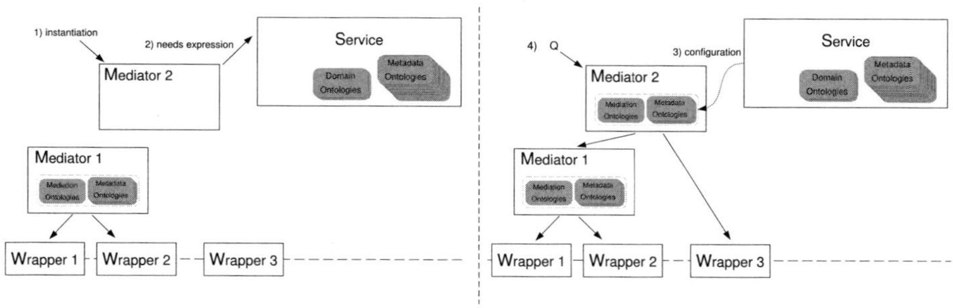

a) b)

Fig. 3. The ADEMS approach

necessary metadata as knowledge within a set of ontologies. For each application domain, the service manages (i) a *domain ontology*, modeling its entities and acting as a shared vocabulary, e.g., bioinformatics, and (ii) a set of *metadata ontologies* representing all necessary metainformation to access available local sources for a domain, e.g., mappings and sources capabilities. A user specifies a *needs expression* (cf. Fig 3-a) in terms of an interesting domain, and a view over it, architectural and source requirements. The service analyzes the user-defined needs expression and exploits reasoning tasks to extract pertinent metadata to configure the mediator (cf. Fig 3-b): the mediation ontology is built as a view over the selected domain ontology, and metadata ontologies as a subset of metadata ontologies within the service.

3 Needs Expression

A needs expression is modeled as a complex concept definition within the *needs expression ontology*. This is the most important metadata ontology of the service as it plays a key role during the whole mediator configuration process. This ontology is built around a main central concept Need, representing a whole needs expression. The goal of this ontology is to exploit reasoning tasks to classify needs expressions in order to deduce containment relations, and to exploit this knowledge to discover when a mediator can exploit another mediator as a possible resource. For this reason, metadata in this ontology is manipulated at the intensional level, i.e., classes. Each new needs expression is represented in this ontology as a new subclass of Need. The satisfiability and subsumption verifications can then be exploited, to verify all needs expressions consistency and to classify them.

A needs expression is composed of three main parts, that we call *metadata categories*. Each category represents a set of *metadata aspects*. The concept Need is defined as follows:

$$\begin{aligned}\mathsf{Need} \equiv\ & \exists \mathit{hasConceptSet}.\mathsf{ConceptSet} \wedge \\ & \exists \mathit{hasArchitecture}.\mathsf{Architecture} \wedge \\ & \exists \mathit{hasSourcePreference}.\mathsf{SourcePreference}\end{aligned}$$

where the three main categories are: ConceptSet, representing the interesting view the domain; SourcePreference and Architecture, specifying source preferences and architectural requirements respectively.

Given a new needs expression, a new class, representing it, is defined as follows:

$$\begin{aligned}\mathsf{Need\_i} \equiv\ & \exists \mathit{hasConceptSet}.\mathsf{ConceptSet\_i} \wedge \\ & \exists \mathit{hasArchitecture}.\mathsf{Architecture\_i} \wedge \\ & \exists \mathit{hasSourcePreference}.\mathsf{SourcePreference\_i}\end{aligned} \tag{1}$$

where, Need_i is deduced to be subclass of Need, and classes ConceptSet_i, Architecture_i and SourcePreference_i represent values for each category. In the remainder of this section, we present details on the three needs expression categories: ConceptSet, Architecture and SourcePreference.

3.1 ConceptSet

A user defines an interesting view over a domain by selecting a set of concepts from the corresponding domain ontology. An algorithm (not shown here) analyzes selected concepts and generates a mediation ontology accordingly. In order to classify needs, in our approach, a whole view over an application domain is represented by a single concept definition called *concept set*. A concept set is defined as follows:

$$\begin{aligned}\mathsf{ConceptSet\_i} &\equiv \mathsf{C}_1 \vee ... \vee \mathsf{C}_n \\ \mathsf{ConceptSet\_i} &\sqsubseteq \mathsf{ConceptSet}\end{aligned}$$

Clearly, this concept must be explicitely defined as a subclass of ConceptSet in order to exploit reasoning capabilities. Given two concept sets ConceptSet_i and ConceptSet_j defined as follows:

$$\mathsf{ConceptSet\_i} \equiv \mathsf{C}_1 \vee ... \vee \mathsf{C}_{n-1} \vee \mathsf{C}_n$$
$$\mathsf{ConceptSet\_j} \equiv \mathsf{C}_1 \vee ... \vee \mathsf{C}_{n-1}$$

the subsumption relation $\mathsf{ConceptSet\_j} \sqsubseteq \mathsf{ConceptSet\_i}$ is interpreted as a containment relation between their corresponding views. This motivates the use of a union of concepts to represent this aspect.

By default, when a domain concept, e.g., Person, is added to a concept set, it is considered with all its associated attributes. However, it is possible to explicitely specify a view over a class in order to consider interesting attributes only. For this purpose, our model provides a special property definition *_without* to specify a restriction over an atomic concept. In order to conserve a meaningful subsumption relation between concept sets, this property restriction models attributes that are not taken into account in the view. Here is an example:

$$\mathsf{ConceptSet\_i} \equiv \mathsf{C}_1$$
$$\mathsf{ConceptSet\_j} \equiv \mathsf{C}_1 \wedge \exists\_\mathit{without}.\mathsf{ATT}_1 \wedge ... \wedge \exists\_\mathit{without}.\mathsf{ATT}_n$$

Subsumption verification allows to infer that ConceptSet_j is subclass of ConceptSet_i. Clearly, the subsumption relation between concept sets reflects the containment relation between their respective mediation ontologies.

More complex views may so be defined. Here is an example:

$$\mathsf{ConceptSet\_1} \equiv \mathsf{Person} \vee \mathsf{Car} \vee \mathsf{Job}$$
$$\mathsf{ConceptSet\_2} \equiv \mathsf{Person} \vee \mathsf{Car}$$
$$\mathsf{ConceptSet\_3} \equiv (\mathsf{Person} \wedge \exists\_\mathit{without}.\mathsf{Age}) \vee \mathsf{Car}$$
$$\mathsf{ConceptSet\_4} \equiv (\mathsf{Person} \wedge \exists\_\mathit{without}.\mathsf{Age} \wedge \exists\_\mathit{without}.\mathsf{Gender}) \vee \mathsf{Car}$$

Reasoning tasks allow to deduce the following subsumption relation between views:

$$\mathsf{ConceptSet\_4} \sqsubseteq \mathsf{ConceptSet\_3} \sqsubseteq \mathsf{ConceptSet\_2} \sqsubseteq \mathsf{ConceptSet\_1}$$

3.2 Architecture

Architectural aspects are modeled as follows:

$$\mathsf{Architecture} \equiv \exists \mathit{hasImportDegree}.\mathsf{ImportDegree} \wedge \exists \mathit{hasExportDegree}.\mathsf{ExportDegree} \wedge \exists \mathit{hasMatDegree}.\mathsf{MatDegree} \wedge \exists \mathit{hasIntDegree}.\mathsf{IntDegree}$$

where Architecture represents a category containing the four aspects ImportDegree, ExportDegree, MatDegree and IntDegree.

ImportDegree: this dimension defines the possible strategies to adopt when exploiting other running mediators as resources. We refer to this feature as resource *import*. Each strategy is enabled by one of the following values:

- ImportAll: the mediator may import any pertinent resource, independently of its ownership. This value is modeled as an atomic class.
- ImportGroup: specifies the group of trusted users/owners from which mediators can be imported. Any specified group is modeled as a subclass of ImportGroup.
- ImportNone: specifies that no mediator is imported. This value corresponds to an atomic class definition.

According to the semantic of this aspect, in order to guarantee the containment relation between two needs, the following subsumption relations must be stated:

$$\mathsf{ImportNone} \sqsubseteq \mathsf{ImportGroup} \sqsubseteq \mathsf{ImportAll} \tag{2}$$

In order for a mediator M_1 to be potentially imported by M_2, the group of users specified by the M_1's import degree must be contained by the one of M_2. In other words, M_2 cannot import M_1 if M_1's import degree contains at least a user which is not considered in M_2's import degree, as this will violate the M_2 strategy.

These considerations motivate the use of union of classes to model a group of trusted users in the import degree. Here is an example:

$$\mathsf{User\_1} \vee \mathsf{User\_2} \sqsubseteq \mathsf{ImportGroup} \tag{3}$$

$$\mathsf{ImportNone} \sqsubseteq \mathsf{User\_1} \vee \mathsf{User\_2} \tag{4}$$

Statement (3) specifies a new group composed by User_1 and User_2. This is done by stating the union of classes as a subclass of ImportGroup class. Statement (4) guarantees the containment relation between any group and the empty one.

Figure 4-a shows an example of import groups classification. In this example, eight groups have been specified, and each of them corresponds to a different independently defined needs expression. Let us suppose that a user wants to retrieve all resources which may be imported by a mediator configured according the need Need_1. As Need_1 imports resources from users Jim, Jack and John, only needs Need_3, Need_5, Need_6 and Need_7 can be normally be imported. Modeling import groups as union of classes allows to retrieve importable resources for a mediator by asking for synonyms and descendants of the class representing its import degree value.

ExportDegree: this dimension specifies the reusability degree of a new defined mediator in the context of future user needs expressions. We refer to this feature as resource *export*. Three strategies are allowed and represented by the following values:

- ExportNone: specifies that no further defined mediator can reuse this mediator in the future. Its values correspond to an atomic class.

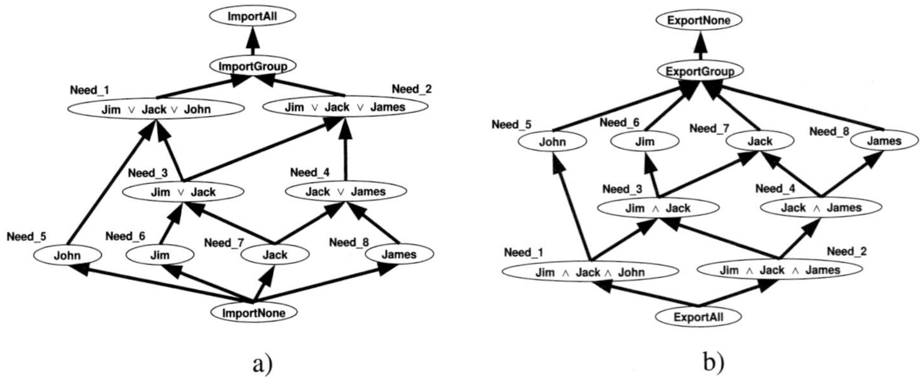

Fig. 4. Import and export degrees classification

- ExportGroup: specifies the group of users that can reuse the mediator in future configurations. Any specified group is modeled as subclass of ExportGroup.
- ExportAll: specifies that any further defined mediator can reuse this mediator in the future. No user restriction are given.

In order to respect the needs containment according to this aspect, the following subsumption relations must be respected:

$$\text{ExportAll} \sqsubseteq \text{ExportGroup} \sqsubseteq \text{ExportNone} \quad (5)$$

In order for a mediator M_1 to be importable by M_2, the set of users specified by the M_1's export degree must contain the one of M_2. In other words, M_2 cannot import M_1 and, at the same time, export itself to other user than the ones allowed for M_1, because this will violate the M_1 strategy. Consequently, M_1's export degree must be subclass of the M_2's one, what justifies the use of a conjuction of classes to represent the export degree value. A group is defined as the conjuction of classes representing user names. Here is an example:

$$\text{User\_1} \wedge \text{User\_2} \sqsubseteq \text{ExportGroup} \quad (6)$$

$$\text{ExportAll} \sqsubseteq \text{User\_1} \wedge \text{User\_2} \quad (7)$$

Statement (6) specifies a new group composed by User_1 and User_2. This is done by stating the conjunction of classes as a subclass of ExportGroup class. Statement (7) guarantees the containment relation between any group and the whole set of users.

Figure 4-b shows an example of export groups classification. In this example, eight groups have been specified, and each of them corresponds to a different independently defined needs expression. Let us suppose that a user wants to retrieve all resources which may be imported by a mediator configured according the need Need_3. As Need_3 exports to users Jim and Jack, only needs Need_1 and Need_2 can be normally be imported. Similarly to the import degree aspect, modeling an export group as a conjunction of classes allows to retrieve importable resources for a mediator by asking for synonyms and descendants of the class representing its export degree value.

Notice that, differently from the ImportDegree, the ExportDegree must necessarily contain the name of the user defining the need. This is motivated by the fact that a user always exports to himself his own resources. However, a user does not necessary import resources from himself.

MatDegree : this dimension specifies the materialization strategy to adopt within a mediation system. This dimension may take the following two values, modeled as atomic classes:

- Materialized: specifies that the materialization is allowed in all mediators composing the mediation system. Retrieved data can be materialized at the mediator level as well as into its imported resources. When data freshness is not a priority, this allows for a faster data retrieval.
- NoMaterialized: specifies that no materialization is allowed. This corresponds to a fully virtual approach and only non-materializing resources will be imported.

In order to respect the needs containment, the following subsumption relation is stated:

$$\mathsf{NoMaterialized} \sqsubseteq \mathsf{Materialized}$$

stating that a materialized mediator can import materialized as well as non-materialized resources, but not viceversa.

IntDegree: this dimension specifies the integration degree for the mediator, which may essentially take two possible values:

- Integrated: specifies that the mediator provides the user with an integrated global representation over underlying resources. This latter corresponds to the mediation ontology which is built as a subgraph of the domain ontology. A mediator configured in such a way can import integrated as well as non-integrated resources. This strategy is typical adopted in approaches providing a transparent access to underlying local sources, e.g. centralized mediation systems.
- Non-integrated: specifies that the mediator provides the user with a non-integrated global representation. The mediation ontology consists of a set of local ontologies. This feature can be interesting for expert users, which prefer to deal with local sources, or in highly distributed mediation systems, where no integrated global representation is required. In this approach, only non-integrated resources can be imported. This feature enables peer-to-peer mediation systems.

In order to respect the need containment, the following subsumption relation is stated:

$$\mathsf{Non\text{-}integrated} \sqsubseteq \mathsf{Integrated}$$

stating that an integrated mediator can import non-integrated as well as integrated resources, but not viceversa.

Given a new needs expression definition Need_i, a new class Architecture_i is defined. Here is an example:

$$\begin{aligned}\mathsf{Architecture\_i} \equiv\ & \exists \mathit{hasImportDegree}.(\mathsf{Jim} \ \vee \ \mathsf{Jack}) \wedge \\ & \exists \mathit{hasExportDegree}.\mathsf{Jim} \wedge \\ & \exists \mathit{hasMatDegree}.\mathsf{Materialized} \wedge \\ & \exists \mathit{hasIntDegree}.\mathsf{Integrated}\end{aligned}$$

stating that the corresponding mediator imports previously defined mediators from users *Jim* and *Jack*, but can be reused only by *Jim*. Materialization is allowed and the mediator provides an integrated view over underlying resources.

3.3 Source Preference

Source preferences are modeled in the needs expression ontology as follows:

$$\begin{aligned}\mathsf{SourcePreference} \equiv\ & \exists \mathit{hasQuality}.\mathsf{Quality} \wedge \\ & \exists \mathit{hasAvailability}.\mathsf{Availability} \wedge \\ & \exists \mathit{hasCost}.\mathsf{Cost}\end{aligned}$$

where Quality, Availability and Cost represent three metadata sub-categories. Notice that these aspects are given for explanation purpose. We do not propose in this paper a source annotation model. Our goal is to show how to apply ontologies and reasoning tasks to model such kind of metadata and deduce knowledge about it. Consequently, other pertinent aspects and categories could be used instead, e.g. local source capabilities. In our approach this can be easily done by simply modifying the needs ontology.

Quality: this metadata category specifies the required quality level for local sources. The class Quality is defined as follows:

$$\begin{aligned}\mathsf{Quality} \equiv\ & \exists \mathit{sourceQuality}.z \wedge \exists \mathit{dataQuality}.z \wedge \\ & \exists \mathit{dataFreshness}.z\end{aligned}$$

where *sourceQuality*, *dataQuality* and *dataFreshness* are integer attributes modeling some possible quality criteria.

Availability: it describes the required availability level for pertinent local sources. The class Availability is defined as follows:

$$\begin{aligned}\mathsf{AlwaysAvailable} &\sqsubseteq \mathsf{Availability} \\ \mathsf{TemporarilyAvailable} &\equiv \mathsf{Availability} \wedge \\ & \quad \exists \mathit{begin\_d}.z \wedge \exists \mathit{end\_d}.z \wedge \\ & \quad \exists \mathit{begin\_h}.z \wedge \exists \mathit{end\_h}.z\end{aligned}$$

A selected source may be always available or in a period only. In our example, the period is specified by four integer attributes. *begin_d* and *end_d* represent respectively the first day and the last day of the period. *begin_h* and *end_h* represent the initial and final hour of service in the day. This simple source availability model could be easily improved by specifying more complex class definitions and/or constraints.

Cost: this class is used to represent the cost of accessing a data source. It is defined as follows:

$$\mathsf{Cost} \equiv \exists \mathit{fixedCost}.z \wedge \exists \mathit{variableCost}.z \wedge \exists \mathit{connectionSpeed}.z$$

where the three attributes represent respectively fixed access cost, variable access cost, e.g., euros per hour, and the connection speed for accessing the data source.

When a new needs expression Need_i is defined, a new class SourcePreference_i representing source preferences is specified. Here is an example:

$$\begin{aligned}\mathsf{SourcePreference\_i} \equiv\ & \exists \mathit{hasQuality}.(\exists \mathit{sourceQuality}.\mathbf{min_3} \wedge \\ & \quad \exists \mathit{dataQuality}.\mathbf{min_1} \wedge \\ & \quad \exists \mathit{dataFreshness}.\mathbf{max_5}) \wedge \\ & \exists \mathit{hasAvailability}.(\exists \mathit{begin\_d}.\mathbf{max_1} \wedge \\ & \quad \exists \mathit{end\_d}.\mathbf{min_{31}} \wedge \\ & \quad \exists \mathit{begin\_h}.\mathbf{max_0} \wedge \\ & \quad \exists \mathit{end\_h}.\mathbf{min_{23}}) \wedge \\ & \exists \mathit{hasCost}.(\exists \mathit{fixedCost}.\mathbf{equal_0} \wedge \\ & \quad \exists \mathit{variableCost}.\mathbf{equal_0} \wedge \\ & \quad \exists \mathit{connectionSpeed}.\mathbf{min_{10}})\end{aligned}$$

where the user requires the source quality to be at least 3, data quality to be at least 1 and data freshness no more than 5 days. Sources must be available 24 hours a day, during the month of January. They must be accessible for free and provide a connection speed which corresponds at least to 10Mbps.

4 Mediator Configuration

Given a valid needs expression, represented within the needs ontology, a mediator can be configured accordingly. Therefore, a needs expression is first analyzed in order to identify pertinent metadata by exploiting reasoning tasks. Then the corresponding set of ontologies, i.e., mediator configuration, is generated and made available in a web repository for download. This allows a mediator to access the repository in order to download its configuration at runtime. Thanks to this approach, no mediator recompilation is needed, and the configuration can be updated at any time.

The remainder of this section focuses on the three main configuration steps which are: *architecture identification*, *mediators importation*, *candidate source selection*. For a lack of space, no details on the *mediator ontologies generation* are given.

4.1 Architecture Identification

The first step of the mediator configuration consists of identifying the architecture of a mediation system. For doing so, firstly, the *integration degree* is analyzed. According to its value, two main mediation system categories may be identified:

- *integrated mediation systems*: the mediation ontology is built as a view over the domain ontology. The domain ontology acts as a shared domain vocabulary. Centralized knowledge-based mediation systems are included in this category.
- *non-integrated mediation systems*: are characterized by a mediation ontology consisting of a non-integrated view over a set of local sources ontologies. It gives access to underlying sources by applying their local vocabulary. Distributed knowledge-based mediation systems are in this category.

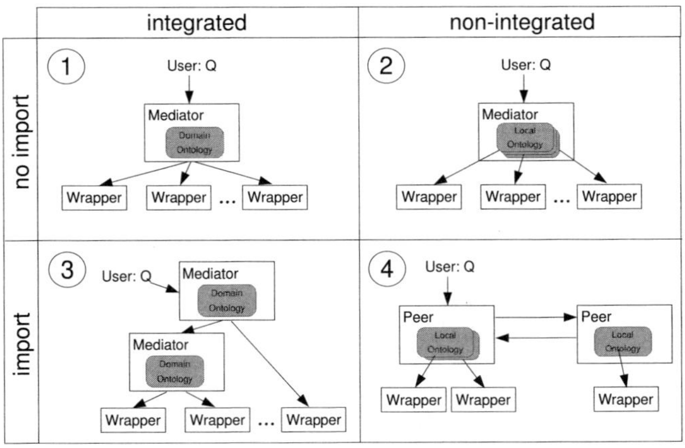

Fig. 5. Integration and import degrees

Secondly, the *import degree* aspect is analyzed. According to its value, combined with the integration degree aspect, four main mediation systems architectures can be identified (cf. Figure 5). If mediators importation is not enabled (`ImportNone`), mediation systems are composed of only one mediator accessing underlying local sources. When an integrated mediation ontology is defined (cf. configuration `1` in the Figure), the resulting mediation system allows to emulate a centralized architecture.If the mediation ontology consists of a non-integrated view over local sources (cf. configuration 2), the mediation system represents a kind of *multidatabase system* [13].

If mediators importation is enabled, the mediation system may be composed of more than one mediator. When a configured mediator provides an integrated mediation ontology (cf. configuration 3), it may import both integrated and non-integrated mediators as resources. This allows to build more complex architecture such as hierachical mediation in [11]. However, when a non-integrated mediation ontology is adopted, imported mediators act as neighbour peers into a distributed mediation system (cf. configuration 4). This allows to emulate existing knowledge-based distributed mediation systems.

Thirdly, after having identified all resources of the new configured mediator, the way the mediator accesses them is analyzed. Two possible methods may be applied to access imported resources [3]:

- *rewriting* is needed when a mediation ontology X and a resource ontology Y (mediator or wrapper) adopt two different vocabularies. In this case a query expressed over the mediation ontology X (or a part of it) is rewritten according to the target vocabulary Y by exploiting *inter-ontology* semantic correspondences.
- *dispatching* is applied when a mediation ontology X and a resource ontology Y adopt the same vocabulary. In this case no rewriting is needed and a query (or a part of it) can be dispatched to the underlying resource for execution.

Independently of the mediation system architecture, a configured mediator is always characterized by:

- a mediation ontology (integrated or not), acting as a global schema, and
- a set of resources accessible by rewriting and/or dispatching.

Therefore, a mediator can easily be adapted to several mediation system architectures. Figure 6 gives some architecture examples (rewriting is represented by a continous arrow, while dispatching by a dashed one). For instance, in a centralized mediation system, a mediator X is configured so that all of its resources (i) correspond to wrapped sources and (ii) are accessed by rewriting. This is due to the fact that local sources are described by their own ontologies, independently of the mediator vocabulary. On the other hand, building a distributed mediation system means to cope with both mediators and wrappers as resources. The mediator (or peer) X accesses its underlying local sources by dispatching queries. This is due to the fact that each mediator in the distributed mediation system applies the local vocabulary to describe underlying data. Therefore, accessing other mediators requires a rewriting task through inter-ontology correspondences. More complex architecture can be configured, e.g. hierachical architecture allows to exploit previously defined mediators as resources by dispatching (partial) queries to them.

4.2 Mediators Importation

This task consists of identifying which running mediators can be imported as resources by a new configured mediator. This task is performed by exploiting

[3] Remember that resources are local sources and imported mediators.

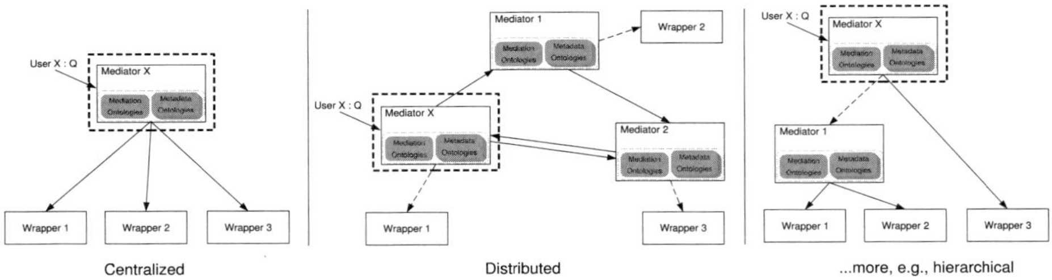

Fig. 6. Mediation system architectures

the concepts classification in the needs ontology. Let the need N_i be composed of n aspects, whose values are represented by classes $\{\mathsf{D}_{i1}, ..., \mathsf{D}_{in}\}$. Let a mediator M_i be configured according to the needs expression N_i. Given two needs N_1 and N_2, if:

- $\forall_{j=\{1..n\}}\ \mathsf{D}_{1j} \equiv \mathsf{D}_{2j}$, then it is deduced that $\mathsf{N}_1 \equiv \mathsf{N}_2$. This means that M_1 and M_2 have equivalent characteristics and consequently M_1 can be reused by M_2 as a resource and viceversa.
- $\forall_{j=\{1..n\}}\ \mathsf{D}_{1j} \sqsubseteq \mathsf{D}_{2j}$, then it is deduced that $\mathsf{N}_1 \sqsubseteq \mathsf{N}_2$. ADEMS interprets such a relation as a *needs containment*, which means that a mediator M_1 can be reused by a mediator M_2 as a pertinent resource.

In all other cases, N_1 and N_2 cannot be classified, and therefore, nothing can be stated.

Given a set of independently defined needs expressions, they are automatically classified by exploiting reasoning tasks. Let us suppose that two needs expression are defined as follows:

$$\begin{aligned}\mathsf{Need\_1} \equiv\ & \exists \mathit{hasConceptSet}.\mathsf{ConceptSet\_1}\\ \wedge\ & \exists \mathit{hasArchitecture}.\mathsf{Architecture\_1}\\ \wedge\ & \exists \mathit{hasSourcePreference}.\mathsf{SourcePref\_1}\end{aligned}$$

$$\mathsf{ConceptSet\_1} \equiv \mathsf{Person} \vee \mathsf{Car} \vee \mathsf{Job}$$

$$\begin{aligned}\mathsf{Architecture\_1} \equiv\ & \\ & \exists \mathit{hasImportDegree}.(\mathsf{Jim} \vee \mathsf{Jack})\\ \wedge\ & \exists \mathit{hasExportDegree}.\mathsf{Jim}\\ \wedge\ & \exists \mathit{hasMatDegree}.\mathsf{FullMaterialized}\\ \wedge\ & \exists \mathit{hasIntDegree}.\mathsf{Centralized}\end{aligned}$$

$$\begin{aligned}\mathsf{SourcePref\_1} \equiv\ & \\ & \exists \mathit{hasQuality}.(\exists sourceQuality.\mathbf{min_3}\\ & \quad \wedge \exists dataQuality.\mathbf{min_1}\\ & \quad \wedge \exists dataFreshness.\mathbf{max_5})\\ \wedge\ & \exists \mathit{hasAvailability}.\mathbf{AlwaysAvailable}\\ \wedge\ & \exists \mathit{hasCost}.(\exists fixedCost.\mathbf{max_{10}}\\ & \quad \wedge \exists variableCost.\mathbf{equal_0}\\ & \quad \wedge \exists connectionSpeed.\mathbf{min_{10}})\end{aligned}$$

$$\begin{aligned}\mathsf{Need\_2} \equiv\ & \exists \mathit{hasConceptSet}.\mathsf{ConceptSet\_2}\\ \wedge\ & \exists \mathit{hasArchitecture}.\mathsf{Architecture\_2}\\ \wedge\ & \exists \mathit{hasSourcePreference}.\mathsf{SourcePref\_2}\end{aligned}$$

$$\mathsf{ConceptSet\_2} \equiv \mathsf{Person} \vee \mathsf{Car}$$

$$\begin{aligned}\mathsf{Architecture\_2} \equiv\ & \\ & \exists \mathit{hasImportDegree}.(\mathsf{Jim} \vee \mathsf{Jack})\\ \wedge\ & \exists \mathit{hasExportDegree}.\mathsf{Jim}\\ \wedge\ & \exists \mathit{hasMatDegree}.\mathsf{FullMaterialized}\\ \wedge\ & \exists \mathit{hasIntDegree}.\mathsf{Centralized}\end{aligned}$$

$$\begin{aligned}\mathsf{SourcePref\_2} \equiv\ & \\ & \exists \mathit{hasQuality}.(\exists sourceQuality.\mathbf{min_3}\\ & \quad \wedge \exists dataQuality.\mathbf{min_3}\\ & \quad \wedge \exists dataFreshness.\mathbf{max_2})\\ \wedge\ & \exists \mathit{hasAvailability}.\mathbf{AlwaysAvailable}\\ \wedge\ & \exists \mathit{hasCost}.(\exists fixedCost.\mathbf{equal_0}\\ & \quad \wedge \exists variableCost.\mathbf{equal_0}\\ & \quad \wedge \exists connectionSpeed.\mathbf{min_{10}})\end{aligned}$$

Subsumption allows to deduce the following relations:

$$\mathsf{ConceptSet\_2} \sqsubseteq \mathsf{ConceptSet\_1} \tag{8}$$

$$\mathsf{Architecture\_2} \equiv \mathsf{Architecture\_1} \tag{9}$$

$$\mathsf{SourcePref\_2} \sqsubseteq \mathsf{SourcePref\_1} \tag{10}$$

The subsumption relation (8) is evident and does not require more explanation. Identical architectural choices (9) give as result an equivalence relation between classes Architecture_2 and Architecture_1. This equivalence has no impact on the needs classification. In (10) SourcePref_2 is deduced to be subclass of SourcePref_1. This is due to the fact that all of its role restrictions are more restrictive or as much as the ones of SourcePref_2. For instance, the data freshness for Need_2, i.e., data must not be older than 2 days, is more restrictive than the Need_1 one, i.e. days must not be older than 5 years. Therefore the following subsumption relation is deduced:

$$\mathsf{Need\_2} \sqsubseteq \mathsf{Need\_1}$$

Now, let us suppose that architectural requirements for both needs were defined differently:

$$\begin{aligned}\mathsf{Architecture\_1} \equiv\ & \exists \mathit{hasImportDegree}.(\mathsf{Jim}) \\ \wedge\ & \exists \mathit{hasExportDegree}.\mathsf{Jim} \\ \wedge\ & \exists \mathit{hasMatDegree}.\mathsf{FullMaterialized} \\ \wedge\ & \exists \mathit{hasIntDegree}.\mathsf{Centralized}\end{aligned}$$

$$\begin{aligned}\mathsf{Architecture\_2} \equiv\ & \exists \mathit{hasImportDegree}.(\mathsf{Jim} \vee \mathsf{Jack}) \\ \wedge\ & \exists \mathit{hasExportDegree}.\mathsf{Jim} \\ \wedge\ & \exists \mathit{hasMatDegree}.\mathsf{FullMaterialized} \\ \wedge\ & \exists \mathit{hasIntDegree}.\mathsf{Centralized}\end{aligned}$$

Given the fact that the mediator M_1 can import resources from Jim, but not from Jack, the following subsumption relations are deduced:

$$\mathsf{ConceptSet\_2} \sqsubseteq \mathsf{ConceptSet\_1}$$

$$\mathsf{Architecture\_2} \sqsupseteq \mathsf{Architecture\_1}$$

$$\mathsf{SourcePref\_2} \sqsubseteq \mathsf{SourcePref\_1}$$

therefore, Need_2 and Need_1 cannot be classified and the mediator M_2 will not be deduced to be a potential resource for M_1.

A similar effect can be obtained if a disjointness relation between the two needs can be inferred for at least one aspect. Let us suppose that source preferences for both needs were defined as follows:

$$\begin{aligned}\mathsf{SourcePref\_1} \equiv\ & \\ & \exists \mathit{hasQuality}.(\exists \mathit{sourceQuality}.\mathbf{min_3} \\ & \quad \wedge \exists \mathit{dataQuality}.\mathbf{min_1} \\ & \quad \wedge \exists \mathit{dataFreshness}.\mathbf{max_5}) \\ & \wedge \exists \mathit{hasAvailability}.\mathbf{AlwaysAvailable} \\ & \wedge \exists \mathit{hasCost}.(\exists \mathit{fixedCost}.\mathbf{equal_5} \\ & \quad \wedge \exists \mathit{variableCost}.\mathbf{equal_0} \\ & \quad \wedge \exists \mathit{connectionSpeed}.\mathbf{min_{10}})\end{aligned}$$

$$\begin{aligned}\mathsf{SourcePref\_2} \equiv\ & \\ & \exists \mathit{hasQuality}.(\exists \mathit{sourceQuality}.\mathbf{min_3} \\ & \quad \wedge \exists \mathit{dataQuality}.\mathbf{min_3} \\ & \quad \wedge \exists \mathit{dataFreshness}.\mathbf{max_2}) \\ & \wedge \exists \mathit{hasAvailability}.\mathbf{AlwaysAvailable} \\ & \wedge \exists \mathit{hasCost}.(\exists \mathit{fixedCost}.\mathbf{equal_0} \\ & \quad \wedge \exists \mathit{variableCost}.\mathbf{equal_0} \\ & \quad \wedge \exists \mathit{connectionSpeed}.\mathbf{min_{10}})\end{aligned}$$

Due to their incompatible values for the aspect *fixedcost*, SourcePref_2 and SourcePref_1 are deduced to be disjoint classes. Consequently Need_2 and Need_1 cannot be classified.

4.3 Candidate Sources Selection

A *candidate source* is a source that respects user-defined source preferences in the needs expression, i.e., availability, quality and cost requirements, but it does not necessarily fulfil the view definition, i.e. concept set. We refer as a *pertinent source*, a candidate source which also respects the user-defined view definition.

Metadata about sources is modeled within the *source metadata ontology*, whose structure is quite similar to the source preference category in the needs expression ontology. Let us imagine that the source metadata ontology contains the following two definitions:

$$\begin{aligned}\mathsf{Source\_1} \equiv\ & \exists \mathit{hasQuality}.(\exists \mathit{sourceQuality}.\mathbf{equal_3} \\ & \quad \wedge \exists \mathit{dataQuality}.\mathbf{equal_{10}} \\ & \quad \wedge \exists \mathit{dataFreshness}.\mathbf{equal_1}) \\ & \wedge \exists \mathit{hasAvailability}.\mathbf{AlwaysAvailable} \\ & \wedge \exists \mathit{hasCost}.(\exists \mathit{fixedCost}.\mathbf{equal_5} \\ & \quad \wedge \exists \mathit{variableCost}.\mathbf{equal_0} \\ & \quad \wedge \exists \mathit{connectionSpeed}.\mathbf{equal_{15}}) \\ & \wedge \exists \mathit{hasKeyword}.\mathbf{Person} \\ & \wedge \exists \mathit{hasKeyword}.\mathbf{Car}\end{aligned}$$

$$\begin{aligned}\mathsf{Source\_2} \equiv\ & \exists \mathit{hasQuality}.(\exists \mathit{sourceQuality}.\mathbf{equal_1} \\ & \quad \wedge \exists \mathit{dataQuality}.\mathbf{equal_1} \\ & \quad \wedge \exists \mathit{dataFreshness}.\mathbf{equal_5}) \\ & \wedge \exists \mathit{hasAvailability}.\mathbf{AlwaysAvailable} \\ & \wedge \exists \mathit{hasCost}.(\exists \mathit{fixedCost}.\mathbf{equal_0} \\ & \quad \wedge \exists \mathit{variableCost}.\mathbf{equal_0} \\ & \quad \wedge \exists \mathit{connectionSpeed}.\mathbf{equal_{10}}) \\ & \wedge \exists \mathit{hasKeyword}.\mathbf{Car} \\ & \wedge \exists \mathit{hasKeyword}.\mathbf{Motorbike}\end{aligned}$$

The set of candidate sources, is retrieved by executing a reasoning-based query over the source metadata ontology. This query is built by using knowledge about user-defined source preferences in the needs expression.

In *integrated* mediation systems, candidate sources are firstly retrieved by comparing the source preferences with metadata contained within the source metadata ontology. This is done by defining a new class based on the user-defined source preferences. Here is an example:

$$\begin{aligned}\mathsf{SourcePref\_1} \equiv\ & \exists \mathit{hasQuality}.(\exists \mathit{sourceQuality}.\mathit{min}_3\ \wedge \\ & \quad \exists \mathit{dataQuality}.\mathit{min}_1\ \wedge \\ & \quad \exists \mathit{dataFreshness}.\mathit{max}_5)\ \wedge \\ & \exists \mathit{hasAvailability}.\mathsf{AlwaysAvailable}\ \wedge \\ & \exists \mathit{hasCost}.(\exists \mathit{fixedCost}.\mathbf{max_5}\ \wedge \\ & \quad \exists \mathit{variableCost}.\mathit{equal}_0\ \wedge \\ & \quad \exists \mathit{connectionSpeed}.\mathit{min}_{10})\end{aligned}$$

The candidate sources are retrieved by asking for synonyms and descendants of this class definition over the source metadata ontology. In our example, a query based on the class SourcePref_1, retrieves the source Source_1 only. Once candidate sources are discovered, pertinent ones are identified by exploiting the concept set information and semantic correspondences. This task is performed during the generation of the mediator configuration ontologies.

In *non-integrated* mediation systems, the pertinence of sources can be verified during the candidate sources retrieval. This is made possible by the presence of source annotations as a set of *keywords*. Let us illustrate this aspect with an example:

$$\begin{aligned}\mathsf{SourcePref\_1} \equiv\ & \exists \mathit{hasQuality}.(\exists sourceQuality.min_3\ \wedge \\ & \quad \exists dataQuality.min_1\ \wedge \\ & \quad \exists dataFreshness.max_5)\ \wedge \\ & \exists \mathit{hasAvailability}.\mathsf{AlwaysAvailable}\ \wedge \\ & \exists \mathit{hasCost}.(\exists fixedCost.\mathbf{max_{15}}\ \wedge \\ & \quad \exists variableCost.equal_0\ \wedge \\ & \quad \exists connectionSpeed.min_{10}) \\ & \exists \mathit{hasKeyword}.(\mathbf{Person}\ \vee\ \mathbf{House})\end{aligned}$$

In this example, source preferences establish that the fixed cost must not exceed 15. This would make both sources Source_1 and Source_2 two valid candidate sources. In order to identify pertinent sources, the concept set information is exploited to filter pertinent sources thanks to their keywords annotation. For example, let us suppose that the specified concept set in the needs expression corresponds to (Person $\vee$ House). The query SourcePref_1 is modified in order to take into account the concept set information as shown above. This allows to deduce that the only pertinent source is Source_1 (Person $\sqsubseteq$ Person $\vee$ House). Clearly this requires a source annotation effort in terms of the domain ontology vocabulary. Anyway, if the keywords information is not available for each source description, or deduced sources do not satisfy the user expectatives, a non-integrated mediation system requires the user to manually select pertinent sources among candidate ones.

5 Implementation and Validation

We have implemented prototypes of the service and of the general purpose mediator. They have been implemented by using the Java platform and by exploiting the RACER [14] inference engine. RACER allows for an efficient $\mathcal{SHIQ}(\mathcal{D})$ ontologies management, and permits importing their description in several emerging standard languages such as OWL[4] and DAML+OIL[5]. RACER allows us to guarantee sound and complete reasoning tasks and provides highly optimized algorithms for terminology classification and reasoning on concrete datatypes [15].

Our approach has been validated in the context of computer assisted instruction (CAI) through the configuration of an integrated mediation system named

[4] W3C-OWL - http://www.w3.org/2004/OWL/

[5] DAML+OIL - http://www.daml.org/

SKIMA [16]. A graphical application, built on top of a configured mediator gives a transparent access to distributed material, e.g. documents. The domain ontology represents concepts and relations regarding the PI (programmed instruction) context, e.g. course, learner, section, document, exercise. Sources are modeled via a $\mathcal{SHIQ}(\mathcal{D})$ representation and integrate, via semantic correspondences, data about students and teachers, available courses with associated material and exercises. Students work through the programmed material by themselves at their own speed and after each step test their comprehension by answering questions.

We are currently conducting a validation experience in bioinformatics in the context of the Mediagrid project[17]. Mediagrid provides an infrastructure for giving a transparent access to biological sources. Using such an infrastructure, biologists can correlate expression levels of a gene and observe their evolution using data stored in a set of distributed data sources. Our goal is to exploit the ADEMS service in order to configure knowledge-based mediators being:

- able to exploit the current Mediagrid query evaluation capabilities, and
- adaptable to biologists needs in terms of view of interests over a biological domain ontology, architectural requirements and sources preferences.

6 Conclusions

This paper shows how to use ontologies for describing metadata and configuring mediators in an intelligent way. Given a user needs expression, ADEMS configures a mediator by generating a set of ontologies describing its necessary metadata. Reasoning tasks are also fully exploited for processing queries expressed in terms of the mediation ontology entities. Satisfiability and subsumption checking allow for query consistency verification and containment. Moreover, the knowlege-based query processing allows to enable approximative as well as partial query plans generation.

Being our approach strongly based on reasoning tasks, performances of the mediator configuration process are tightly related to the efficiency of the exploited reasoner. Currently, our approach allows fast metadata classification and mediator configuration, thanks to our metadata model and the use of RACER that provides efficient reasoning algorithms. More tests still have to be done in the presence of a very large amount of metadata. Recent research works, aiming to provide efficient reasoning algorithms on large ontologies, let us believe that future advances of inference engines will enable large-scale knowledge management. Future improvements in this research domain will validate our approach on huge number of data sources providing important volumes of distributed data.

Acknowledgements

We thank Eng. Hector Manuel Perez Urbina for his careful reading. Eng. Perez is the implementor of the SKIMA prototype, and he strongly participated in the implementation of the first ADEMS service prototype.

References

1. Wiederhold, G.: Mediators in the architecture of future information systems. Computer (1992) 25(3):38–49
2. Collet, C., Huhns, M., Shen, W.-M.: Resource integration using a large knowledge base in carnot. Computer (1991) 24(12):55–62
3. Arens, Y., Knoblock, C.-A., Shen, W.-M.: Query reformulation for dynamic information integration. Journal of Intelligent Information Systems - Special Issue on Intelligent Information Integration, (1996) 6(2/3): 99–130
4. Mena, E., Kashyap, V., Sheth, A.-P., Illarramendi, A.: OBSERVER: An approach for query processing in global information systems based on interoperation across pre-existing ontologies. Conference on Cooperative Information Systems, (1996), 14–25
5. Calvanese, D., De Giacomo, G., Lenzerini, M., Nardi, D., Rosati, R.: Schema and data integration methodology for DWQ. Technical Report DWQ-UNIROMA-004, Dipartimento di Informatica Sistemistica, Universita' di Roma La Sapienza, (1998)
6. Goasdoué, F., Lattes, V., Rousset, M.-C.: The use of CARIN language and algorithms for information integration: The PICSEL system. International Journal of Cooperative Information Systems, (2000), 9(4):383 – 401
7. Baker, P.-G., Brass, A., Bechhofer, S., Goble, C., Paton, N., Stevens, R.: TAMBIS: Transparent access to multiple bioinformatics information sources. Int. Conf. on Intelligent Systems for Molecular Biology, (1998), 25–34
8. Peim, M., Franconi, E., Paton, N., Goble, C.: Query processing with description logic ontologies over object-wrapped databases. In SSDBM '02: Proceedings of the 14th International Conference on Scientific and Statistical Database Management, (2002), 27–36
9. Adjiman, P., Chatalic, P., Goasdoue, F., Rousset, M.-C., Simon, L.: Somewhere in the semantic web. Technical report, LRI, (2004)
10. Bruno, G., Vargas-Solar, G., Collet, C.: ADEMS, an adaptable and extensible mediation framework: application to biological sources. Electronic Journal e-Gnosis (2004)
11. Li, C., Yerneni, R., Vassalos, V., Garcia-Molina, H., Papakonstantinou, Y., Ullman, J., Valiveti, M.: Capability based mediation in TSIMMIS, (1998), 564–566
12. Horrocks, I., Sattler, U., Tobies, S.: Reasoning with individuals for the description logic shiq. In CADE-17: Proceedings of the 17th International Conference on Automated Deduction, (2000), 482–496
13. Litwin, W., Mark, L., Roussopoulos, N.: Interoperability of multiple autonomous databases, (1990), 22(3):267–293
14. Haarslev, V., Möller, R.: Practical reasoning in racer with a concrete domain for linear inequations. In Proceedings of the International Workshop on Description Logics, (2002), 91–98
15. Haarslev, V., Möller, R.: Description logic systems with concrete domains: Applications for the semantic web. In KRDB, (2003)
16. Perez-Urbina, H., Bruno, G., Vargas-Solar, G.: SKIMA: Semantic Knowledge and Information Management. In Proceedings of the Encuentro Internacional de Computacion, (2005)
17. Collet, C., et al.: Towards a mediation system framework for transparent access to largely distributed sources. In Proceedings of the International Conference on Semantics of a Networked World (sematics for Grid databases), (2004)

OntoBuilder: Fully Automatic Extraction and Consolidation of Ontologies from Web Sources Using Sequence Semantics

Haggai Roitman and Avigdor Gal

Technion – Israel Institute of Technology
Technion City, Haifa 32000, Israel

1 Introduction

Ontologies, formal specifications of domains, have evolved in recent years as a leading tool in representing and interpreting Web data. The inherent heterogeneity of Web resources, the vast amount of information on the Web, and its non-specific nature requires a semantically rich tool for extracting the essence of Web source content. The OntoBuilder project [5] supports the extraction of ontologies from Web interfaces, ranging from simple Search Engine forms to multiple-pages, complex reservation systems. Ontologies from similar domains are then matched to identify ontology mappings.

Given a sample form, filled by the user, and given a new form, from another Web site, OntoBuilder finds the best mapping between the two forms. This, in turn, can serve a system in automatically filling the fields, a sort of a query rewriting.

Unlike systems such as Protégé [2] OntoBuilder enables fully-automatic ontology matching, and therefore falls within the same category as GLUE [1]. The use of ontologies, as opposed to relational schema or XML, as an underlying data model allows a flexible representation of metadata, that can be tailored to many different types of applications. OntoBuilder contains several unique matching algorithms, that can match concepts (terms) by their data types, constraints on value assignment, and above all, the sequencing of concepts within forms (termed *precedence*), capturing sequence semantics that reflect business rules.

2 Overview of OntoBuilder

OntoBuilder was developed using Java, which makes it portable to various platforms and operating system environments. OntoBuilder generates dictionary of terms by extracting labels and field names from Web forms, and then it recognizes unique relationships among terms, and utilize them in its matching algorithms. There are two types of relationships OntoBuilder is specifically equipped to deal with, namely composition and precedence. The latter is discussed later in this section.

OntoBuilder is a generic tool and serves as a module for several projects at the Technion. For example, we have designed a framework for evaluating automatic schema matching algorithms [4], and we use OntoBuilder both for evaluation and for improving our methodology. This framework provides a sufficient condition (we term *monotonicity*) for a matching algorithm to generate “good” ontologies. Our empirical results

T. Grust et al. (Eds.): EDBT 2006 Workshops, LNCS 4254, pp. 573–576, 2006.

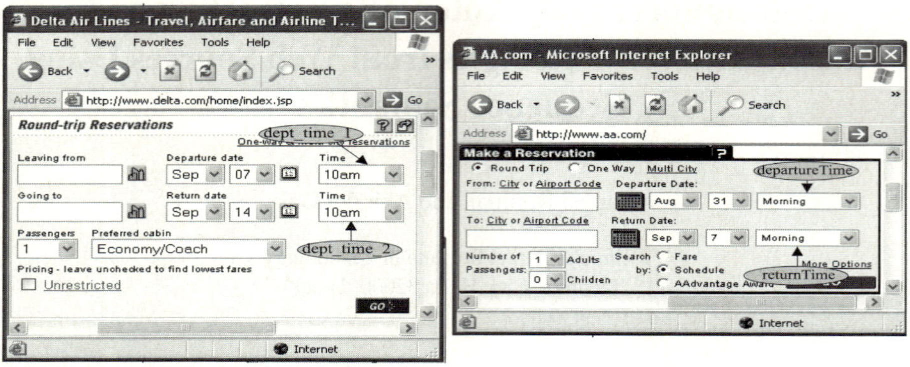

(a) (b)

Fig. 1. AA versus Delta

with OntoBuilder show that its algorithms satisfy one of the forms of monotonicity we present in [4]. Also, algorithms from OntoBuilder are being employed in an agent negotiation protocol for trading information goods [6]. Finally, OntoBuilder is used as a testbed for experimenting with simulataneous top-*K* mapping evaluation [3].

The rest of this section presents the main features and highlights of OntoBuilder, focusing on the sequence semantics. The detailed description can be found in [5,7]. The process of ontology extraction and matching is divided into four phases. The input to the system is an HTML page representing a Web site main page. First, the HTML page is parsed and all form elements and their labels are identified. Next, the system produces an initial version of global (target) ontology and local (candidate) ontologies. Finally, the ontologies are matched to produce amapping.

Ontology matching aims at refining domain information by mapping various ontologies **within the same domain**. OntoBuilder supports an array of matching and filtering algorithms. Additional algorithms can be implemented and added to the tool as plug-ins. Algorithm parameters (such as weights) are specified using an XML configuration file which can be edited using a user-friendly interface.

Ontology matching is based on term and value matching, the former compares labels and field names using string matching, while the latter provides a measure of similarity among domains, as reflected by constrained data fields, such as drop-down lists and radio buttons. OntoBuilder provides several preprocessing techniques, based on Information Retrieval well-known algorithms such as *stoplists* and *dehyphenation*. It also supports automatic domain recognition and normalization to enhance the matching.

Once terms are extracted, OntoBuilder analyzes the relationships among them to identify ontological structures of composition and precedence. We focus here on the latter. **Precedence** determines the order of terms in the application according to their relative order within a page and among pages. In any interactive process, the order in which data are provided may be important. In particular, data given at an earlier stage may restrict the availability of options for a later entry. For example, car rental forms will present pickup information before return information. Also, airline reservation systems will introduce departure information before return information. Such precedence relationships can usually be identified by the activation of a script, such as

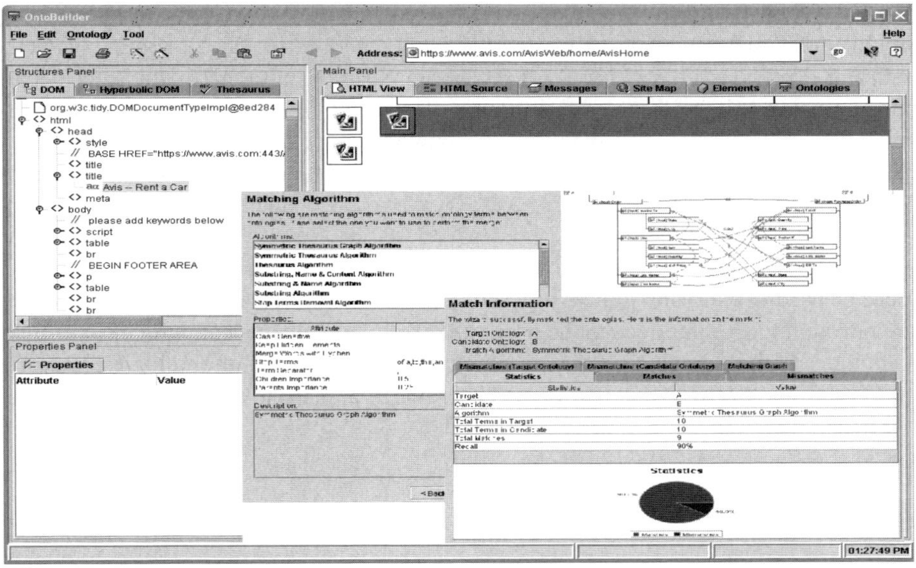

Fig. 2. The OntoBuilder user interface

(but not limited to) the one associated with a SUBMIT button. It is worth noting that the precedence construct rarely appears as part of basic ontology constructs. This can be attributed to the view of ontologies as static entities whose existence is independent of temporal constraints. It is our conjecture (supported by experiments) that precedence reflects time constraints of the application business rules and thus can be used to match better heterogeneous ontologies.

OntoBuilder employs unique algorithms for identifying structure similarity using **composition** and **precedence** constructs. Structure similarity is determined based on structure partitioning into subontologies, using terms as pivots, and comparison of subontologies. For example, using the precedence construct and two terms in two ontologies as pivots within their own ontology, OntoBuilder computes the similarity of subontologies that contain all terms that precede the pivots and also the subontologies that contain all terms that succeed the pivots (recall that Web forms enforce complete ordering of fields). A higher similarity among subontologies increases the similarity of the pivot terms themselves. This simple, yet powerful algorithm, has proven to be successful in a series of experiments performed with OntoBuilder on variety of Web sites. For example, consider Figure 1. The form of Delta airline reservation system contains two time fields, one for departure and the other for return. Due to bad design (or designer's error), the departure time entry is named `dept_time_1` while return time is named `dept_time_2`. Both terms carry an identical label, `Time`, since the context can be easily determined (by a human observer of course) from the positioning of the time entry with respect to the date entry. For American Airlines reservation system (see Figure 1 on the right), the two time fields of the latter were not labeled at all (relying on the proximity matching capabilities of an intelligent human observer), and therefore were assigned, using composition by association, with the label `Departure Date` and `Return Date`.

The fields were assigned the names departureTime and returnTime. Term matching would prefer matching both Time(dept_time_1) and Time(dept_time_2) of Delta with Return Date(returnTime) of American Airlines (note that 'dept' and 'departure' do not match, neither as words nor as substrings). Value matching cannot differentiate the four possible combinations. Using precedence matching, OntoBuilder was able to correctly map the two time entries, since the subontologies of the predecessors of Time(dept_time_2) and Return Date(returnTime) match better than subontologies of other combinations.

OntoBuilder provides an easy to use environment for ontology authoring. Therefore, it can be used to build ontologies from scratch or refine extracted ontologies. In order to provide an intuitive interface to the user, the system implements common visualization techniques such as graph representations and hyperbolic views for ontologies, Web site maps, and document structures. Figure 2 provides a snapshot of OntoBuilder's user interface.

3 System Demonstration

We will demonstrate OntoBuilder using an easy-to-follow example of matching Car rental ontologies. The system will create ontologies of car rental Web sites on-the-fly, and combine them into a global ontology. The benefits of OntoBuilder in resolving, in an automatic manner, semantic heterogeneity, including synonyms and designer errors, will be highlighted. In particular, we will focus on the use of the precedence construct in correctly identifying mappings.

OntoBuilder is available at http://ie.technion.ac.il/OntoBuilder.

References

1. A. Doan, J. Madhavan, P. Domingos, and A. Halevy. Learning to map between ontologies on the semantic web. In *Proceedings of the eleventh international conference on World Wide Web*, pages 662–673. ACM Press, 2002.
2. N. Fridman Noy and M.A. Musen. PROMPT: Algorithm and tool for automated ontology merging and alignment. In *Proceedings of the Seventeenth National Conference on Artificial Intelligence (AAAI-2000)*, pages 450–455, Austin, TX, 2000.
3. A. Gal. Managing uncertainty in schema matching with top-k schema mappings. *Journal of Data Semantics*, (6):90–114, 2006.
4. A. Gal, A. Anaby-Tavor, A. Trombetta, and D. Montesi. A framework for modeling and evaluating automatic semantic reconciliation. *VLDB Journal*, 14(1):50–67, 2005.
5. A. Gal, G. Modica, H.M. Jamil, and A. Eyal. Automatic ontology matching using application semantics. *AI Magazine*, 26(1), 2005.
6. G. Koifman, O. Shehory, and A. Gal. Negotiation-based price discrimination for information goods. In *Proc. of the Third International Conference on Autonomous Agents & Multi Agent Systems*, NY, NY, 2004.
7. G. Modica. A framework for automatic ontology generation from autonomous web applications. Master's thesis, Mississippi State University, July 2002.

Query Transformation of SQL into XQuery Within Federated Environments

Heiko Jahnkuhn, Ilvio Bruder, Ammar Balouch,
Manja Nelius, and Andreas Heuer

Department of Computer Science, University of Rostock,
18051 Rostock, Germany
{hj016, ilr, ab006, manel, ah}@informatik.uni-rostock.de

Abstract. Federated information systems integrate various heterogeneous autonomic databases and information systems. Queries respect to the federation have to be translated into the local query language and must be transformed with respect to the local data model. This paper deals with the problem of a global query according to an object-relational federation service. This SQL query is to be translated into an equivalent XQuery expression, so that it can be processed by the corresponding XML component database system according to the local schema.

1 Introduction

Federated database and information systems (FDBIS) represent system architectures for multidatabase systems [1]. In general, one characteristic of FDBIS is that component database systems are not restricted concerning the underlying data model or query language. As a result, the participants of the federation may be very heterogeneous. A general architecture of a federation is shown in Fig. 1.

The approach introduced in this paper deals with the heterogeneity between the object-relational and the XML-based data model, for which the query languages SQL and XQuery are applied respectively. However, this paper does not focus on transformation from XQuery into SQL, because there are several approaches and implementation techniques, for example considered in [4,10]. It mainly focuses on the transformation of SQL into XQuery, for which two essential scenarios are possible.

In the first case, there is an XML-based federation service, which uses XQuery as query language and an object-relational component database system, which is accessed by a local application via SQL. If the local application queries the federation with respect to the local schema, this statement has to be transformed into XQuery and must correspond to the global schema. This scenario is handled e.g. in [6].

In the second case, to which the introduced algorithm refers, the federation service is based upon the object-relational data model, which is queried by SQL. These SQL queries according to the global schema have to be transformed for

T. Grust et al. (Eds.): EDBT 2006 Workshops, LNCS 4254, pp. 577–588, 2006.

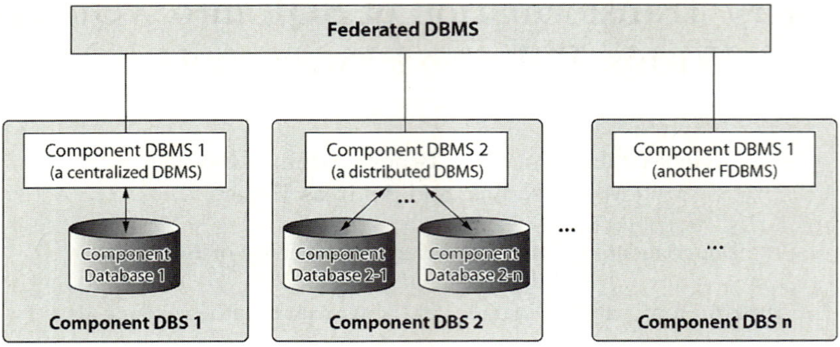

Fig. 1. General architecture of a federation (according to [3])

every participant of the federation. In case of an XML database, every query must be translated into an XQuery request respect to a single document or a collection of XML documents.

Using a rule-based system for such a transformation, as described in [5] for other languages, can cause an unreasonably high administration costs. An XML database system (XMLDBS) usually does not manage only one document collection which is valid relating to a schema, but uses a multitude of variably structured documents and diverse schemata. On the contrary, rule systems are static and cause problems within dynamic applications. However, as data, and hence the underlying schema descriptions, of XMLDBS in most cases are changed frequently, every modification would cause an adaptation of the rule system.

To counter these effects, this paper introduces an algorithm, which is able to automatically perform such a transformation relating to diverse schema descriptions. Former approaches need a valid XML and/or relational representation of the data. E.g., [6] needs a predefined schema for the transformation. This approach uses only a set of paths as mapping description of a federation system. A schema for the query transformation can be automatically and arbitrarily generated (it depends possibly on the federated system). Changing the schema causes only the adaptation of the mapping between the local and the global schema; an adaptation of the algorithm is not required. However, this paper only presents the fundamental algorithm, which is restricted to the basic SQL statements. This means, only elementary logical operators (e.g. `<`, `>`, `=`), which can be linked with `AND`, `OR`, and `NOT`, are allowed for the clauses `WHERE` and `HAVING`. Furthermore, aggregate functions are possible within the `HAVING` clause. [7] goes into details concerning the realisation of other SQL constructs (e.g., `between`, `exists`, and `contains`) and describes further phases and problems occurring at query processing in federated information systems.

The purpose of this algorithm is to generate a tuple (schema description, XQuery statement) based on the mapping of the local schema onto the global schema and of the SQL query with respect to the global schema. The XQuery expression within the tuple represents the local equivalent of the global SQL request and is queried respect to the document collection whose documents are valid according to the given schema. Then, the federation system sends this tuple to the appropriate XML CDBS, which processes the request.

2 Query Processing

Starting point of the query processing is a SQL request in turns of the federation service's global schema. Assuming a semantics conserving mapping between the local schema description and the global federation schema, a translation table is created prior to the actual transformation. This table contains a list of all global attribute names as well as the local schema's corresponding path expressions, which are assigned to the respective global attributes. The global SQL request in conjunction with this translation table is the basis of the query processing, which can be subdivided into four separate phases described below and demonstrated with an example within the next section.

Phase 1

The first step of the algorithm analyses and classifies the query which must be transformed. For this purpose all occurrences of global attribute names within the query are determined and substituted with their corresponding path expression by applying the translation table. As a result of this substitution a list of paths is generated, which can be interpreted as a tree structure. This tree, in the following called query tree, represents a sub tree of that one that is described by the underlying federated schema, and is restricted to that information, which is relevant to the query.

The nodes of the created query tree are now tagged with three different flags, which classify the query tree. These flags are called *return elements*, *where elements* and *splitting nodes*.

The *return elements* result from those path expressions, which occur within the `SELECT`, `GROUP BY`, `HAVING`, and `ORDER BY` clauses after the substitution of all global attribute names.

The `WHERE` clause of the query has to be processed to determine the *where elements*. Because of a missing schema every element of the query tree has to be considered as a potential list of path expressions. Therefore, by using the where elements it is specified which part of the `WHERE` clause references which element of the query tree. By regarding the selection condition as a conjunction of selection conditions, every conjunction term refers to the bottom element in the query tree, which contains all occurring path expressions in the descendant-or-self axis. Therefore, the `WHERE` clause is decomposed into a list of conjunctions via the distributive law. Consequently, this list consists of either disjunctions or atomic comparisons and would fit the primal `WHERE` clause if joined with `AND`. All elements of the list include at least one path expression after the substitution of the global attributes. Then, the most common path (mcp) is determined for every element within the list. This one is the last element of the query tree, which includes all elements of the current list element within the descendant-or-self axis. As a result every mcp now represents a where element in the query tree.

Finally, the *splitting nodes* have to be determined. Splitting nodes describe nodes, which lead to a new FLWR expression within the result query for each subtree of this node. Therefore, for each element of the query tree is checked, whether it matches one of the patterns shown in Fig. 2. In case it does, the element is marked as a splitting node. Pattern a) represents the context of the query, that is that tree element, which contains all XML elements concerning the request. Patterns b) to e) analyse, whether the current element includes where elements as well as return elements within the descendant-or-self axis.

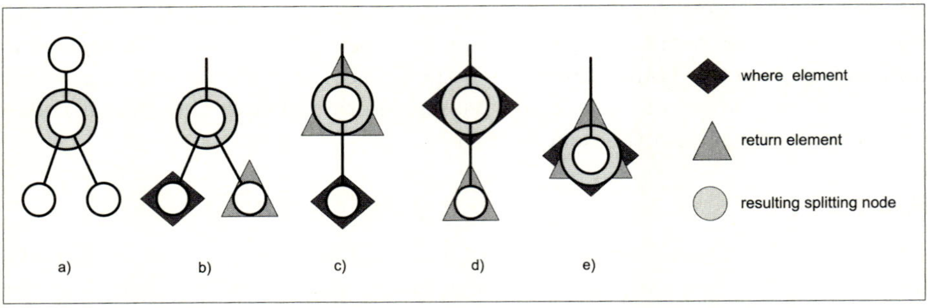

Fig. 2. Patterns of splitting nodes

Consequently, the result of the first transformation step is a tagged query tree, which is shown exemplarily in Fig. 3. This tree represents the input for the next phase of the transformation.

Phase 2

The second transformation step is a mapping algorithm which generates a For-Let-Where-Return (FLWR) expression for every splitting node within the query tree. The result is a nested XQuery statement representing the tagged query tree. The mapping uses a top-down method by determining the first splitting node beginning from the root element. This is the context node the SQL-query refers to. The outermost FLWR expression is now composed of a `for` clause, which declares the splitting node as context node, a `where` clause, which corresponds to a conjunction of the selection conditions of the where elements, and a `return` clause. For generating the `return` clause the descendant axis of each node is checked, whether it contains return elements only; in this case, the return elements are output out directly as path expressions. If the descendant axis includes a splitting node, it will be used as context node for a new FLWR statement. Then, the mapping algorithm is repeated, whereby the context node is considered relatively to the superior splitting node, and the `where` clause represents a conjunction of all where elements within the descendant-or-self axis of the current splitting node. Fig. 3 shows an example of this mapping algorithm. The XQuery statement generated during this second transformation step already represents a relational SET-OF-TUPLE-OF structure. Consequently, the result

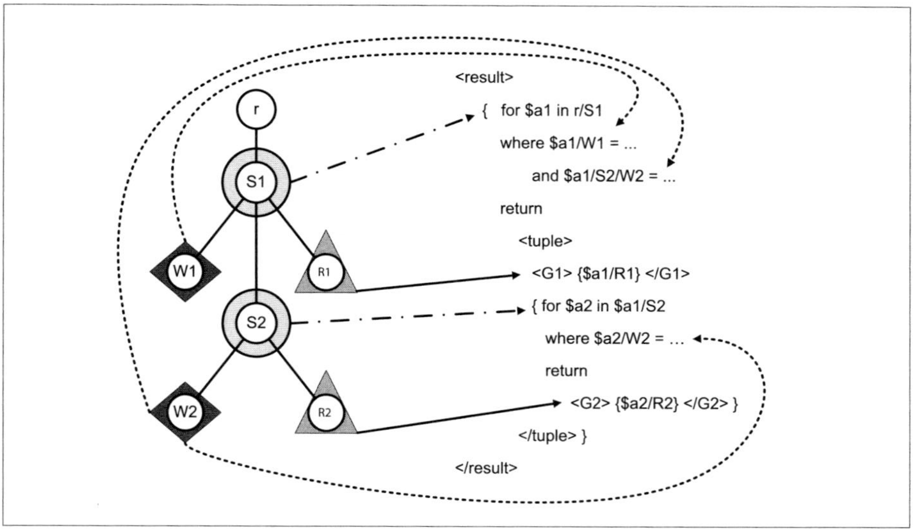

Fig. 3. Example of a mapping

of the XQuery expression is a set of tuple elements, which are valid with respect to the `SELECT` clause and contain the specified return elements to emulate the relational SET-OF-TUPLE-OF representation. This structure is the basis of the third transformation phase.

Phase 3

The third transformation step realises the optionally specified `GROUP BY` and `HAVING` clauses. As the second phase already generated a relational structure, the handling of these clauses is not a serious problem anymore. Thereby, this phase is subdivided into two stages, because a `HAVING` clause is optional. The first partial stage realises the grouping by generating a new FLWR statement, which uses the output of the second transformation step as input. Here, every grouping attribute is referenced within the `for` clause, so that an n-dimensional vector space is spanned. Afterwards, every tuple element is assigned to a point inside this vector space via the `let` clause. Every non-empty point, that means a combination of values at least one tuple element is assigned to, represents a grouping. Thereupon, by the `return` clause a result set is created which consists of a set of group elements. A group element includes the grouping attributes as well as the tuple elements, which have identic values regarding the grouping attributes.

Based on this generated structure the selection concerning the`HAVING` clause can be realised. Again a FLWR expression is created, which uses the previous one as input. Thereby, every group element is passed through sequentially by using the group element inside the `for` clause as context node. The `where` clause results directly from the `HAVING` clause; only the global attribute names must be substituted with the corresponding paths and be considered relatively to the context node. The result set generated within the `return` clause matches that one of the first stage. The procedure of this third transformation step is explained graphically in Fig. 4.

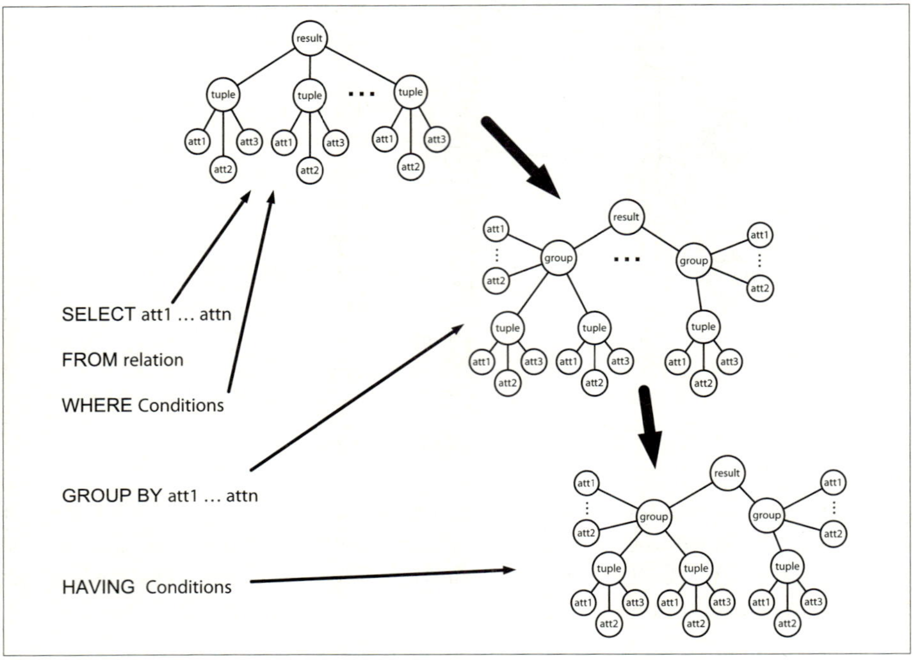

Fig. 4. Realisation of `GROUP BY` and `HAVING` clauses

Phase 4

The fourth transformation phase realises the possibly specified `ORDER BY` clause as well as the `SELECT` clause, which may include aggregate functions and renamings. For this a new FLWR expression is generated again. Three different circumstances have to be considered to determine the context node:

1. The global `SELECT` clause contains aggregate functions only and no attributes. If a grouping exists, the aggregate functions refer to the result's group element, otherwise they refer to the result element, thus the whole result set. In both cases, the aggregate functions refer to the parent node of the tuple element.
2. The global `SELECT` clause contains attributes only, no aggregate functions. If a grouping exists, the attributes have to be declared inside the `GROUP BY` clause and consequently refer to the group element. In case of no `GROUP BY` clause the attributes refer to every single tuple element. In both cases, the attributes refer to all direct children of the result element.

3. The global `SELECT` clause contains attributes as well as aggregate functions. Hence a `GROUP BY` clause was specified with respect to those attributes that occur within the `SELECT` clause as direct attributes. This also means that these attributes are identical within all tuple elements of the grouping. Consequently, this case is to be handled analogically to the second one.

The `ORDER BY` clause of the FLWR statement can be determined analogically to the `HAVING` clause, which was described in the third transformation step. Now the `return` clause contains aggregate functions, which are referenced directly via `Agg(/tuple/attribute)`, and attributes, which can be output immediately via `/attribute`. Thereby, every output is enclosed in tags which are named either after the attribute name, after the specified alias, or after the concatenation of the aggregate function name and the attribute name. The so defined output is enclosed in `<tuple>` tags again. In this way, a SET-OF-TUPLE-OF representation of the requested output is created.

The output generated during this phase represents the final result of the query transformation. Now, the tuple (schema name, XQuery statement) can be transmitted to the respective XML CDBS for evaluation. It is also possible to optimise or minimise the XQuery expression first. There are several proposals, [9] describes one of them.

3 Transformation Example

The described algorithm is demonstrated by an example in the following section. Therefore, the following query example is used:

```
SELECT   Name, Address->City AS City
FROM     Hotels
WHERE    Name LIKE "Beach%" AND
         (Address->ZIP < 20000 OR
          Address->City = "Freiburg")
GROUP BY Name, Address->City
```

During the first step of the transformation a list of all occurring path expressions is determined. Based on the underlying schema description the list may look like this:

```
hotels/hotel/name
hotels/hotel/address
hotels/hotel/address/zip
hotels/hotel/address/city
```

With this list of path expressions a sub tree of the underlying schema is described, which is marked with `where` elements, `return` elements and splitting nodes. In the example the `return` elements only result from the substituted path expressions within the `SELECT` and `GROUP BY` clause. On the one hand, the list of `where` elements contains the atomic comparison

```
W1 = Name LIKE "Beach%",
```

on the other hand, it includes the disjunction

```
W2 = Address->ZIP < 20000 or
     Address->City = "Freiburg".
```

After substituting all global attributes the most common paths of the where elements are:

```
mcp(W1) = hotels/hotel/name,
mcp(W2) = hotels/hotel/address.
```

By applying the patterns in Fig. 2 three splitting nodes can be derived from this result. This transformation step as well as the marked query tree and the resulting splitting nodes are shown in Fig. 5.

The second step of the transformation uses the marked query tree in Fig. 5 as input for the mapping algorithm. Starting from the root element the first splitting node (`hotels/hotel`) is determined as context node, whereupon the first FLWR expression is generated accordingly. As both child elements also contain splitting nodes, two FLWR expressions are generated for them. These new expressions are positioned relatively to the first splitting node. Within these splitting nodes, the return elements can be directly referenced as a result. This transformation phase is illustrated in Fig. 6

As a result of the generated XQuery expression a structure is created, which is valid respect to the following generic DTD:

```
<!ELEMENT result (tuple*)>
<!ELEMENT tuple  (Name, City)>
<!ELEMENT Name   ANY>
<!ELEMENT City   ANY>
```

From this DTD it is recognisable, that the step already created a relational SET-OF-TUPLE-OF representation of the primary hierarchic structure. This structure is used again as an input for the third transformation step, which implements the grouping. Therefore, a new FLWR expression, consisting of a `let` and `return` clause, is generated. Within the `let` clause a variable is bound to the output of the second transformation step, which is rearranged within the `return` clause. This is done by generating a new FLWR statement, which references the grouping attributes inside the `for` clause as well as `name` and `city`. As a result, every possible combination of both attributes is considered. After that, those tuple elements, which contain the same combination of values, are assigned to every combination inside the `let` clause. Finally, within the `return` clause is ensured that no empty combinations are accepted for the result and a group element is created. The latter consists of the combination of all values as well as of those tuple elements which contain the respective combination. This grouped structure is used as an input for the fourth step of the transformation.

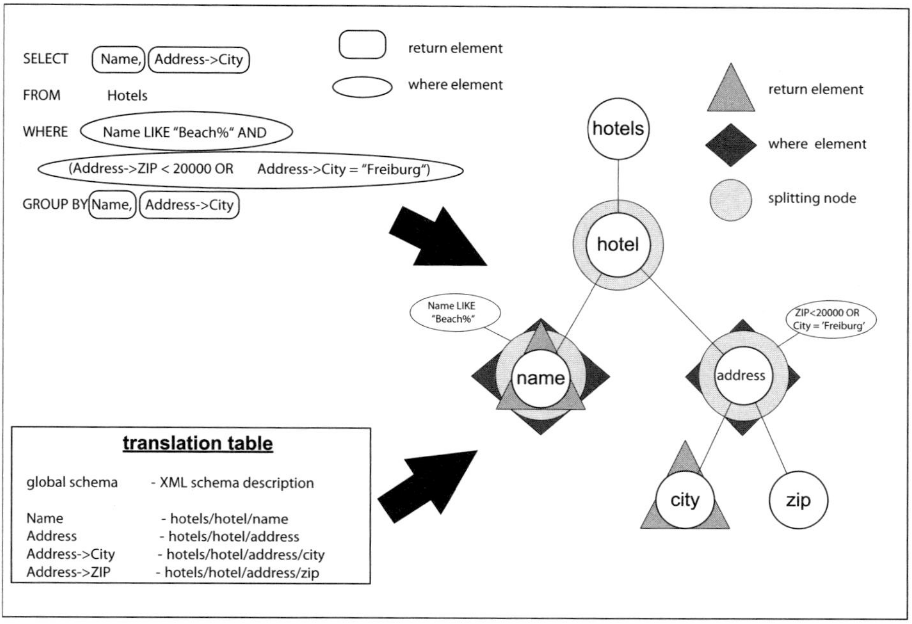

Fig. 5. Process of the first transformation step

Based on the case differentiation concerning the SELECT clause, the second condition is fulfilled (the SELECT clause contains only attributes, but no aggregate functions). Hence, the selection is applied to the child elements of the result element, which is the tuple element in the example. The just generated FLWR expression references the tuple element as context node, and the selection attributes can be output inside the return clause directly. The XQuery statement created during this transformation step represents the overall result of the transformation algorithm[1]:

```
for $final in (
  let $result :=(
    <result>
      { for $a1 in hotels/hotel
        where $a1/name LIKE "Beach%" and
              ($a1/address/zip < 20000
               or $a1/address/city = "Freiburg")
        return
          <tuple>
            { for $a2 in $a1/name
              where $a2 LIKE "Beach%"
              return
```

[1] The LIKE operator acts only as an interim solution and has to be transformed in accordance with the rules described in [7]. The corresponding XQuery expression depends on the function fn:substring().

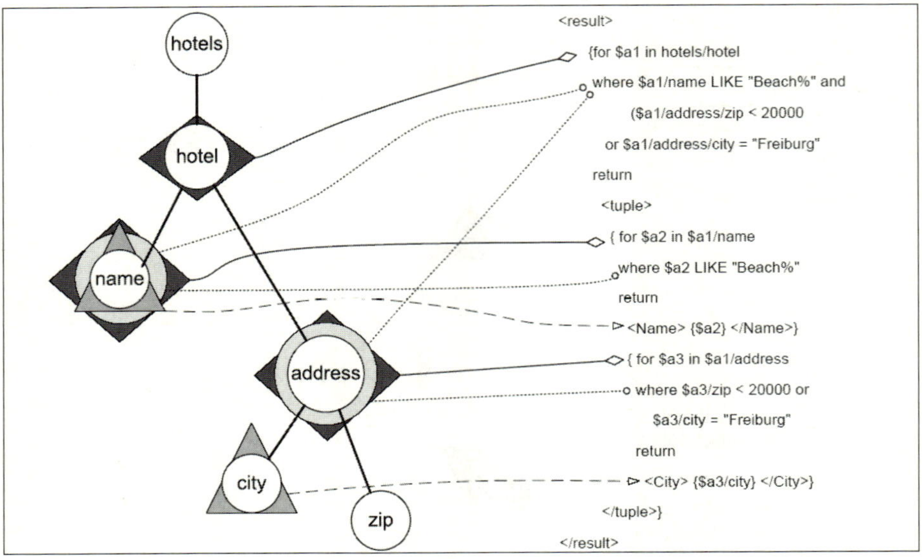

Fig. 6. Process of the second transformation step

```
                <Name> {$a2 } </Name>,
                for $a3 in $a1/address
                  where $a3/zip < 20000 or
                        $a3/city = "Freiburg"
                  return
                    <City> {$a3/city } </City>}
          </tuple>}
    </result>)
  return
   <result>
     { for $groupBy1 in distinct-values($result/tuple/Name ),
           $groupBy2 in distinct-values($result/tuple/City )
       let $new := $result/tuple[Name = $groupBy1 and
                                 City = $groupBy2]
       return
         if ($new != " ") then (
           <group>
             <Name> {$groupBy1 } </Name>
             <City> {$groupBy2 } </City>
             {$new }
           </group> ) }
  </result> )/child::node()
return
  <tuple>
    <Name> {$final/Name } </Name>
    <City> {$final/City } </City>
  </tuple>
```

This XQuery statement along with the name of the corresponding schema can be forwarded to the XML CDBS. Based on these information, the latter is able to determine a document collection whose documents are valid respect to the given schema and can apply the generated query to this collection.

4 Related Work

With the exception of the approach of Escobar et al. mentioned in Sect. 1, we are not aware of other architectures which realise an algorithm for transforming SQL queries into XQuery statements. Though, there are many commercial systems which integrate disparate data sources (in most cases (object-)relational and XML-based data) into a global schema, these systems either allow only one query language according to the global data model or they forward the XQuery and SQL statements only to the corresponding data sources.

The commercial BizQuery Suite by ATS [2], for instance, is a software system for virtual integration of disparate data, which are provided by a unified XML-based view. In this way, XQuery requests across multiple data sources are possible, but no transformation of SQL into XQuery statements is performed. The same approach is realised by the first type 4 JDBC driver for XML files by Sunopsis [8]. The driver loads (upon connection or user request) the XML, EDI or IDoc structure and data into a relational schema, using an XML to SQL mapping. After that, the user works on the relational schema, manipulating data through regular SQL statements or specific driver commands. Upon disconnection or user request, the XML driver is able to synchronise the data and the structure stored in the schema back to the XML file. Similar to the BizQuery system the JDBC driver implements the querying according to heterogeneous data sources by mapping the data into a global schema, which is either object-relational or XML-based, but not by translating the requests.

5 Summary and Future Prospects

The aim of the introduced algorithm is the fully automatic transformation of a global SQL request into an equivalent XQuery expression which can be delivered to an XML component database system with relating to an XML document collection. The only precondition for that is a semantics conserving mapping of the local schema description onto the federation service's global schema. Based on this mapping and the current SQL request, the corresponding XQuery statement is generated. The presented example of such a transformation demonstrates the application of the algorithm.

However, the algorithm as introduced here is restricted to simple structured queries and was implemented prototypically to demonstrate the feasibility in principle. The realisation of further constructs, as for instance the `LIKE` operator or nested queries, is discussed in [7]. The application to SQL extensions is also imaginable. An interesting SQL extension in this context is MM/Full-Text. By the provided information retrieval techniques, which allow comparisons with stemming or distance based queries, the full-text supplement of XQuery could also be realised by this algorithm.

References

1. Bell, D., Grimson, J.: Distributed Database Systems. Addison-Wesley (1992)
2. BizQuery: A Software System for Virtual Integration of Disparate Data. ATS. `http://www.atssoft.com/products/bizquery.htm` (22 August 2005)
3. Sheth, A. P., Larson, J. A.: Federated Database Systems for Managing Distributed, Heterogeneous, and Autonomous Databases. ACM Computing Surveys, Vol. 22, No. 3 (September 1990)
4. DeHaan, D., Toman, D., Consens, M.P., Özsu, M.T.: A comprehensive XQuery to SQL translation using dynamic interval encoding. In Proceedings of the 2003 ACM SIGMOD Int. Conf. San Diego (2003)
5. Elmagarmid, A., Rusinkiewicz, M., Sheth, A.: Management of Heterogeneous and Autonomous Database Systems. Morgen Kaufmann Publishers Inc. (1999)
6. Escobar, F., Espinosa, E., Lozano, R.: XML Information Retrieval Using SQL2Xquery. Tecnolgico de Monterrey-Campus cd. De México. Departmento do Computacin (2002)
7. Jahnkuhn, H.: Transformation von SQL- in XQuery-Anfragen innerhalb föderierter Informationssysteme. University of Rostock. Department of Computer Science. Student research project (2005)
8. JDBCforXML: Sunopsis XML Driver (JDBC Edition) `http://www.sunopsis.com/corporate/us/products/jdbcforxml/` (22 August 2005)
9. Michiels, P.: XQuery Optimization. In Proceedings of VLDB 2003 PhD-Workshop. Berlin (2003)
10. Rost, G.: Implementierung von XQuery auf objektrelationalen Datenbanken. University of Rostock. Department of Computer Science. Diploma thesis (2002)

A Foundation for the Replacement of Pipelined Physical Join Operators in Adaptive Query Processing

Kwanchai Eurviriyanukul, Alvaro A.A. Fernandes, and Norman W. Paton

University of Manchester, Manchester M13 9PL, United Kingdom
{eurvirik, alvaro, norm}@cs.man.ac.uk

Abstract. Adaptive query processors make decisions as to the most effective evaluation strategy for a query based on feedback received while the query is being evaluated. In essence, any of the decisions made by the optimizer (e.g., on operator order or on which operators to use) may be revisited in an adaptive query processor. This paper focuses on changes to physical operators (e.g., the specific join operators used, such as hash-join or merge-join) in pipelined query evaluators. In so doing, the paper characterizes the runtime properties of pipelined operators in a way that makes explicit when specific operators may be replaced, and that allows the validity of operator replacements to be proved. This is illustrated with reference to the substitution of join operators during their evaluation.

1 Introduction

The execution plan of a query describes how the query is to be evaluated. The plan makes explicit the decisions made by the query optimizer, e.g., with respect to the order of evaluation of operators, the algorithms and auxiliary data structures to be used, the allocation of plan fragments to resources, and the level of partitioned parallelism. An adaptive query processor (e.g., [5]) may revise any of these different kinds of decision at query runtime.

Many proposals have been made for adaptive query processing techniques (see [2] for a recent survey). However, few of the proposals provide a formal characterization of the adaptations undertaken, and thus the validity of the runtime changes proposed is rarely addressed in a rigorous manner. We cannot point to any cases in which published adaptive strategies have subsequently been shown to produce incorrect results, but contend that certain forms of adaptation may benefit from a more formal approach. We observe that adaptive strategies may be associated with complex protocols for halting, revising and resuming execution plans (e.g., [14]), and that certain categories of runtime change may only be fully explored when the safety net of a formal foundation is in place. One such category, which is the focus of this paper, is the replacement of operators in pipelined query plans.

In pipelined plans, which have been shown to be effective for increasing resource usage and reducing response times in parallel and distributed settings,

T. Grust et al. (Eds.): EDBT 2006 Workshops, LNCS 4254, pp. 589–600, 2006.

many operators may be being evaluated simultaneously. As such, if a particular operator is ineffective in a specific context, the replacement of that operator without disrupting its suppliers or consumers may provide effective and focused adaptation. However, during evaluation an operator may maintain internal data structures, and at any point in time may have partially processed some of its inputs. This paper presents an approach to the description of partially-evaluated operators that makes explicit the issues associated with in-flight operator replacement, and enables the validity of specific transformations to be proved. This is illustrated with reference to the substitution of physical join operators.

We observe that operator replacement for pipelined evaluation has not been extensively investigated to date. Several strategies that may lead to changes in the physical operators used by a plan do not adapt during operator evaluation (e.g., [15,9,8]). POP [10] explores several approaches to adaptation that materialize the results of complete sub-plans, but when an operator is replaced during its evaluation, the replacement operator starts evaluating from scratch, thus repeating work that was done by its predecessor. Rio [3] tests the suitability of an operator at a place in a plan by sampling and caching its inputs, and, like POP, when an algorithm is replaced it is rerun from scratch over its input buffers. This paper complements existing work by investigating finer-grained operator replacement and by providing a formal characterization of the changes made.

The remainder of the paper is structured as follows. Section 2 describes the technical context for the material that follows. Section 3 provides a notation for describing partially evaluated operators, characterizes the states in which an operator can safely be replaced, and illustrates the overall approach by considering the replacement of physical join operators, including a proof of validity for an example transformation. Section 4 presents some conclusions.

2 Technical Context

This section defines some terms and notions that are used later in the paper.

A query plan P can be represented by a tree consisting of a set of query operator nodes and a set of edges representing data that flows from child nodes to parent nodes. Given a node N, P^N denotes the sub-plan of P rooted at N. Given a query plan P, $[\![P]\!]$ denotes the result obtained by evaluating P.

In this paper, the nodes of a plan are considered to be drawn from a physical algebra, i.e., one in which the node identifies the algorithm to be used. Examples are presented later in the paper of adaptations where one physical join operator replaces another. Five representative join algorithms, viz., hash join, nested-loop join, merge join, index nested-loop join and symmetric hash join are considered. An equality join condition and bag semantics are assumed throughout. Assume that R is the left, and S the right, input of a join. Let $\overset{H}{\bowtie}$, $\overset{NL}{\bowtie}$, $\overset{M}{\bowtie}$, $\overset{IN}{\bowtie}$ and $\overset{SH}{\bowtie}$, respectively, denote the above physical join operators, the algorithms for which are described briefly below:

- **Hash Join** [7]**:** All R-tuples are read and stored in a hash table, indexed on the join attribute(s). Then, each S-tuple is read in turn and used to probe the hash table. Any matching R-tuples are retrieved.
- **Nested-Loop Join** [11]**:** Each R-tuple is read in turn and compared with all S-tuples to find which ones match.
- **Merge Join** [11]**:** Given inputs sorted on the join attribute(s), the tuples are read from either R or S in turn and to find which ones is S or R (respectively) match.
- **Index Nested-Loop Join** [4]**:** Each R-tuple is read in turn and its join attribute(s) are then used to search an index on S and retrieve the tuples that match.
- **Symmetric Hash Join (Pipelined Hash Join)** [16]**:** Each tuple from either R or S is read in turn and is both stored in the hash table for R (or S, respectively) and used to to probe the hash table for S (or R, respectively). Any matching R- (or S-) tuples (respectively) are retrieved.

In this paper, pipelined evaluation is assumed to be implemented using the iterator model [7], which has three principal functions: OPEN, NEXT and CLOSE. The OPEN function prepares the operator for result production. The NEXT function produces the results one at a time, and the CLOSE function performs cleaning up. When combined with communication operators such as *exchange* [6], the iterator model supports pipelined parallelism.

A state-transition diagram can be used to capture the evaluation trace of operators implemented using the iterator model. These states are labelled as $\mathbb{I}, \mathbb{O}, \mathbb{O}', \mathbb{N}, \mathbb{N}', \mathbb{C}$ and $\mathbb{C}'$ in Figure 1.

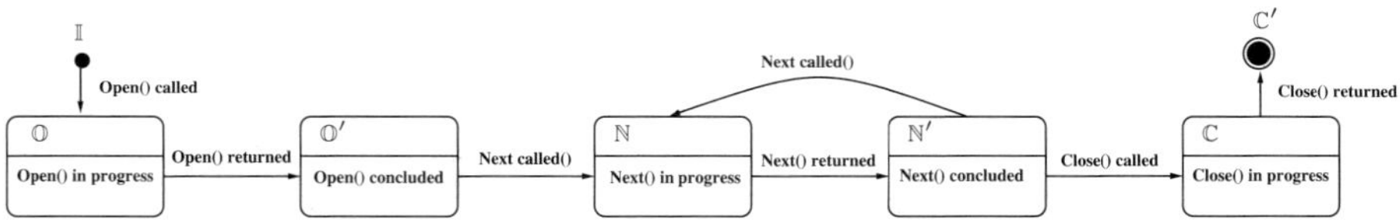

Fig. 1. The state-transition diagram of an iterator

In this paper, the emphasis is on adapting query plans in the state $\mathbb{N}'$, as other states are either in-progress states or else are only reached before or after the operator as a whole has been evaluated. In state $\mathbb{N}'$, a call to the NEXT function has been evaluated and its result returned. If the operator has not returned all its results, the NEXT function will be called again, and the operator returns to state $\mathbb{N}$. On the other hand, if the operator has returned all its results, the CLOSE function is called and the operator moves to state $\mathbb{C}$ and then $\mathbb{C}'$.

3 Replacing Physical Operators

This section presents an approach to the description and validation of operator replacement for pipelined query plans. The following issues are addressed:

1. The provision of a notation for describing partially evaluated query plans.
2. The identification of points during operator evaluation, referred to as *quiescent* states, in which the results produced by an operator in state $\mathbb{N}'$ can be defined precisely in terms of the inputs read by the operator up to then.
3. The description, for different physical operators, of the data produced and the results that remain to be produced, in quiescent states.
4. The provision of an approach to proving that specific operator replacements are result-neutral, i.e., that they have no effect on the result that is output.

3.1 A Notation for Partially Evaluated Query Plans

Expressions in logical or physical algebras, such as $(R \bowtie S)$, describe query plans, but provide no way of describing the runtime properties of the plan, such as the data produced by an operator at a point in time. To describe not only the plan, but also its evaluation status, some additional notation is introduced.

Given a sub-plan P^N, let I be a child node of N.

- $I^+_{[N:\mathbb{S}]}$ is the portion of $[\![I]\!]$ that has been returned by a previously made call to the NEXT() function of I when node N is in state $\mathbb{S}$, where $\mathbb{S} \in \{\mathbb{I}, \mathbb{O}, \mathbb{O}', \mathbb{N}, \mathbb{N}', \mathbb{C}, \mathbb{C}'\}$. Therefore, $I^+_{[N:\mathbb{S}]} \subseteq [\![I]\!]$.
- $I^-_{[N:\mathbb{S}]}$ is the portion of $[\![I]\!]$ that has yet to be returned to N by subsequent calls to the NEXT() function of I. As a result, $I = (I^+_{[N:\mathbb{S}]} \cup I^-_{[N:\mathbb{S}]})$.
- $last(I^+_{[N:\mathbb{S}]})$ is the set containing the last tuple added into $[\![I^+_{[N:\mathbb{S}]}]\!]$.

3.2 Quiescent States

Section 3.1 provided a notation for describing the state of the inputs to an operator during operator evaluation. However, the relationship between the input read by an operator and the output produced by an operator at a point in time may be different at different points in the trace, i.e., at different occurrences of $\mathbb{N}'$. Thus, during the evaluation of a hash join $R\overset{H}{\bowtie}S$, the operator is in state $\mathbb{N}'$, and the inputs read by the algorithm are $R^+_{[N:\mathbb{N}']}$ and $S^+_{[N:\mathbb{N}']}$, where N is the relevant instance of $\overset{H}{\bowtie}$ in the plan. Assuming that the left operand is used to populate the hash table, $R^+_{[N:\mathbb{N}']} = [\![R]\!]$. The tuples produced so far by the algorithm may not be denoted by $R^+_{[N:\mathbb{N}']} \bowtie S^+_{[N:\mathbb{N}']}$, because the last tuple read from S may join with many tuples in R. As such, the tuples produced by the operator will only be $R^+_{[N:\mathbb{N}']} \bowtie S^+_{[N:\mathbb{N}']}$ if $last(S^+_{[N:\mathbb{N}']})$ has been joined with every matching tuple in R.

A *quiescent* state for an operator is one in which the result produced by the operator in state $\mathbb{N}'$ can be precisely defined in terms the input to the operator at that point in time. The test as to whether or not an operator is in a quiescent state is operator-specific. To make possible a quiescence test, we extend the interface to an operator with an ISQUIESCENT function, which determines from the internal state of the operator whether or not it is in a quiescent state.

Algorithm 3.1: NESTED-LOOP JOIN(*Operator R*, *Operator S*)

```
comment: R and S are the outer and the inner inputs, respectively
Tuple r, s, eof      comment: the state of the operator

boolean procedure OPEN()
 if (R.OPEN() and S.OPEN())
   then { r ← R.NEXT()   comment: set up the outer loop
        { return ( true )
   else return ( false )

Tuple procedure NEXT()
 while ( true ) {
   s ← S.NEXT()
   if (s ≠ nil and r ≠ nil)
     then { if (r.JOINATT() = s.JOINATT())
          {   then return (CONCAT(r,s))
          {   else continue
     else { comment: no s ∈ S to match with r ∈ R
          { r ← R.NEXT()
          { if (r ≠ nil)
          {   then { comment: restart S
          {        { S.CLOSE()
          {        { S.OPEN()
          {   else { comment: R was consumed
          {        { break ;
 return (eof ← nil)

boolean procedure CLOSE()
 if (R.CLOSE() and S.CLOSE())
   then return ( true )
   else return ( false )

boolean procedure HASNEXT()
 return (eof ≠ nil)

boolean procedure ISQUIESCENT()
 comment: returns true if the inner input been consumed
 return (¬(S.HASNEXT()))
```

The following are characterizations of the quiescent states for the example join operators, assuming that R is the left, and S the right, input of a join.

- **Hash Join:** The last S-tuple read has been joined with all matching R-tuples in the hash table.
- **Nested-Loop Join:** The last R-tuple read has been joined with all matching S-tuples.
- **Merge Join:** The last R-tuple read has been joined with all matching S-tuples and the join attribute value(s) of the next R-tuple is different from that of the last R-tuple read.
- **Index Nested-Loop Join:** The last R-tuple read has been joined with all matching S-tuples that were retrieved by a lookup on an index on S.
- **Symmetric Hash Join:** The last tuple read from either R or S has been joined with all matching tuples in the hash table for S or R, respectively.

Algorithm 3.1 defines NESTED-LOOP JOIN(R,S) and formalizes the quiescent-state test for this algorithm, viz., that a state is quiescent if there are no more S-tuples to read (in that pass).

Related notions include *moments of symmetry*, from the work on eddies, which determine when the order of the inputs to a join can be changed [1]; this is a narrower notion than that of a quiescent state, as it defines conditions for a specific adaptation. In [12], operators are classified, with respect to their ability to participate in adaptations, on the basis of properties shared by groups of algorithms (e.g., that they have fixed memory consumption); here, quiescent states are used not so much to identify different forms of algorithm as to support the algebraic-level description of operator states, as described in Section 3.3.

3.3 Describing Partial Results

When an operator is in a *quiescent* state, it is possible to define its result precisely in terms of the data it has consumed. As a consequence, it is also possible to define precisely the portion of the result that remains to be produced.

Table 1 describes both the intermediate results produced by the different operators at quiescent states and the corresponding portion of the result that has yet to be returned. As an example, for hash join with operands R and S, at a quiescent state, every tuple that has been read into the hash table (i.e., $R^{+}_{[N:\mathbb{N}']} = [\![R]\!]$) has been joined with every tuple that has been read from the other operand (i.e., $S^{+}_{[N:\mathbb{N}']}$). To complete the evaluation, every tuple in $R^{+}_{[N:\mathbb{N}']} = [\![R]\!]$ needs to be joined with the tuples that have yet to be read from S (i.e., $S^{-}_{[N:\mathbb{N}']}$). A similar justification lies behind the other entries in Table 1.

When one join operator is to be replaced with another operator at a quiescent state, the rightmost column in Table 1 describes the work that remains to be done by the new operator. Section 3.4 describes how the validity of the entries in Table 1 can be proved.

Table 1. The intermediate result and the remainder of $R \bowtie S$ in a quiescent $\mathbb{N}'$

Physical Join Operator ($\overset{X}{\bowtie}$)	Intermediate Result	Remainder
Hash Join ($\overset{H}{\bowtie}$)	$\llbracket R^{+}_{[\overset{H}{\bowtie}:\mathbb{N}']} \bowtie S^{+}_{[\overset{H}{\bowtie}:\mathbb{N}']} \rrbracket$	$\llbracket R^{+}_{[\overset{H}{\bowtie}:\mathbb{N}']} \bowtie S^{-}_{[\overset{H}{\bowtie}:\mathbb{N}']} \rrbracket$
Nested-Loop Join ($\overset{NL}{\bowtie}$)	$\llbracket R^{+}_{[\overset{NL}{\bowtie}:\mathbb{N}']} \bowtie S \rrbracket$	$\llbracket R^{-}_{[\overset{NL}{\bowtie}:\mathbb{N}']} \bowtie S \rrbracket$
Merge Join ($\overset{M}{\bowtie}$)	$\llbracket (R^{+}_{[\overset{M}{\bowtie}:\mathbb{N}']} - last(R^{+}_{[\overset{M}{\bowtie}:\mathbb{N}']}))$ $\bowtie (S^{+}_{[\overset{M}{\bowtie}:\mathbb{N}']} - last(S^{+}_{[\overset{M}{\bowtie}:\mathbb{N}']})) \rrbracket$	$\llbracket (last(R^{+}_{[\overset{M}{\bowtie}:\mathbb{N}']}) \cup R^{-}_{[\overset{M}{\bowtie}:\mathbb{N}']})$ $\bowtie (last(S^{+}_{[\overset{M}{\bowtie}:\mathbb{N}']}) \cup S^{-}_{[\overset{M}{\bowtie}:\mathbb{N}']}) \rrbracket$
Index Nested-Loop Join ($\overset{IN}{\bowtie}$)	$\llbracket R^{+}_{[\overset{IN}{\bowtie}:\mathbb{N}']} \bowtie S \rrbracket$	$\llbracket R^{-}_{[\overset{IN}{\bowtie}:\mathbb{N}']} \bowtie S \rrbracket$
Symmetric Hash Join ($\overset{SH}{\bowtie}$)	$\llbracket R^{+}_{[\overset{SH}{\bowtie}:\mathbb{N}']} \bowtie S^{+}_{[\overset{SH}{\bowtie}:\mathbb{N}']} \rrbracket$	$\llbracket (R^{+}_{[\overset{SH}{\bowtie}:\mathbb{N}']} \bowtie S^{-}_{[\overset{SH}{\bowtie}:\mathbb{N}']})$ $\cup (R^{-}_{[\overset{SH}{\bowtie}:\mathbb{N}']} \bowtie S^{+}_{[\overset{SH}{\bowtie}:\mathbb{N}']})$ $\cup (R^{-}_{[\overset{SH}{\bowtie}:\mathbb{N}']} \bowtie S^{-}_{[\overset{SH}{\bowtie}:\mathbb{N}']}) \rrbracket$

3.4 Replacing Operators

To compute the remainder of the result, an adaptive system may choose to replace an operator in a plan with one that it is predicted will perform better in a specific setting. For example, a nested-loop join may have been selected by the optimizer based on inaccurate predictions for the cardinalities of the inputs to a join; if in practice the cardinalities used by the optimizer are revealed to be underestimates, it may be appropriate to migrate to a hash join instead. Alternatively, a hash join may have been assigned on the assumption that the selectivity of the right hand operand was quite high; if it turns out to be low, it may be more effective to complete the evaluation using an index nested-loop join. There could also be resource restrictions that, e.g., lead to a hash table within a join exceeding the available memory, which in turn leads to options being explored such as changing to a join algorithm that uses less memory, e.g., nested-loop join.

In essence, with reference to Table 1, an operator in a quiescent state can be replaced by any other operators if the remainder of the result can be computed. The complete result is then the union of that produced by the original operator with that produced by the replacement operators; this union may not be carried out explicitly, as replacement operators may simply be planted within a suspended plan, which then resumes evaluation. The suspension and resumption of plans has been discussed in the literature (e.g., [14]).

Using the notation from Section 3.3, the following rule could be used to indicate that a nested-loop join can be replaced during its evaluation at a quiescent state by a hash join, where the value to be computed by the hash join is that described in the *Remainder* column in Table 1. For any quiescent $[\overset{NL}{\bowtie} : \mathbb{N}']$:

$$[\![R \bowtie S]\!] = [\![R^{+}_{[\overset{NL}{\bowtie}:\mathbb{N}']} \bowtie S]\!] \cup [\![R^{-}_{[\overset{NL}{\bowtie}:\mathbb{N}']} \overset{H}{\bowtie} S]\!] \tag{1}$$

The decision as to whether or not a specific operator replacement is appropriate in a context could be made with reference to a cost model that compares the cost of completing the existing plan with the cost of changing from one plan to another plus the cost for the evaluation of the replacement plan.

The next step is to prove that an operator replacement is result-neutral. To do so, there are two proof obligations:

1. To show that the value of intermediate the join result from Table 1 in the quiescent state $\mathbb{N}'$ is correct.
2. To show that the union of the value produced by the original plan and the value computed by the transformed plan provides a correct result for the query.

Such proofs must be provided on a case-by-case basis, reflecting the fact that different algorithms have different quiescent states, which leave different amounts of work to be carried out by other algorithms. Due to limited space, proofs are only provided for the replacement of a nested-loop join with a hash join operator. Similar proofs for other physical join operators have been conducted in an analogous manner but space constraints preclude their presentation here.

Proof by induction shows that, for a nested-loop join operator in a quiescent state $\mathbb{N}'$, the value of the intermediate join result is as stated in Table 1. Given a sub-plan $P^{\overset{NL}{\bowtie}}$, for all integers $i \geq 1$, let $\mathbb{N}'(i)$ represent the i-th occurrence of the quiescent state in the execution trace of this operator's evaluation.

Theorem 1 (Value of the Intermediate Result for Nested-Loop Join)

$$[\![P^{\overset{NL}{\bowtie}}{}_{[\mathbb{N}'(i)]}]\!] = [\![R^{+}_{[\overset{NL}{\bowtie}:\mathbb{N}'(i)]} \bowtie S]\!] \tag{2}$$

Proof

Basis step: *If $i = 1$, then (2) becomes:*

$$[\![P^{\overset{NL}{\bowtie}}{}_{[\mathbb{N}'(1)]}]\!] = [\![R^{+}_{[\overset{NL}{\bowtie}:\mathbb{N}'(1)]} \bowtie S]\!] \tag{3}$$

Let the first matching tuple read from R be t_{r_1}. Then, $R^{+}_{[\overset{NL}{\bowtie}:\mathbb{N}'(1)]} = \{t_{r_1}\}$. Substituting $R^{+}_{[\overset{NL}{\bowtie}:\mathbb{N}'(1)]}$ in (3) yields:

$$[\![P^{\overset{NL}{\bowtie}}{}_{[\mathbb{N}'(1)]}]\!] = [\![\{t_{r_1}\} \bowtie S]\!] \tag{4}$$

which holds, because given that the quiescent-state test for NESTED-LOOP JOIN *in Section 3.2 is satisfied in the first quiescent* $\mathbb{N}'$*, it follows that the first matching tuple from R has been joined with all matching tuples in S.*

Induction step: *In a quiescent state* $\mathbb{N}'$*, for any integer* $k \geq 1$*, the induction hypothesis states that:*

$$[\![P^{\overset{NL}{\bowtie}}{}_{[\mathbb{N}'(k)]}]\!] = [\![R^{+}_{[\overset{NL}{\bowtie}:\mathbb{N}'(k)]} \bowtie S]\!] \tag{5}$$

Assuming (5), we prove that

$$[\![P^{\overset{NL}{\bowtie}}{}_{[\mathbb{N}'(k+1)]}]\!] = [\![R^{+}_{[\overset{NL}{\bowtie}:\mathbb{N}'(k+1)]} \bowtie S]\!] \tag{6}$$

Firstly, following from the quiescent-state test for NESTED-LOOP JOIN *in Section 3.2, the value of a sub-plan in the subsequent quiescent state to a quiescent state k (i.e.,* $[\![P^{\overset{NL}{\bowtie}}{}_{[\mathbb{N}'(k+1)]}]\!]$*) equals the intermediate result at k (i.e.,* $[\![P^{\overset{NL}{\bowtie}}{}_{[\mathbb{N}'(k)]}]\!]$*) unioned with the result of joining the tuples in S with the most recently read tuple of R (i.e.,* $last(R^{+}_{[\overset{NL}{\bowtie}:\mathbb{N}'(k+1)]})$*):*

$$[\![P^{\overset{NL}{\bowtie}}{}_{[\mathbb{N}'(k+1)]}]\!] = [\![P^{\overset{NL}{\bowtie}}{}_{[\mathbb{N}'(k)]}]\!] \cup [\![last(R^{+}_{[\overset{NL}{\bowtie}:\mathbb{N}'(k+1)]}) \bowtie S]\!] \tag{7}$$

Using the right-hand side of (5) to substitute $[\![P^{\overset{H}{\bowtie}}{}_{[\mathbb{N}'(k)]}]\!]$ *in (7) gives:*

$$[\![P^{\overset{NL}{\bowtie}}{}_{[\mathbb{N}'(k+1)]}]\!] = [\![R^{+}_{[\overset{NL}{\bowtie}:\mathbb{N}'(k)]} \bowtie S]\!] \cup [\![last(R^{+}_{[\overset{NL}{\bowtie}:\mathbb{N}'(k+1)]}) \bowtie S]\!] \tag{8}$$

Since the value of *symbol* ($[\![\;]\!]$) *denotes the result set of evaluating a plan fragment, two or more results can be unioned, so (8) becomes:*

$$[\![P^{\overset{NL}{\bowtie}}{}_{[\mathbb{N}'(k+1)]}]\!] = [\![(R^{+}_{[\overset{NL}{\bowtie}:\mathbb{N}'(k)]} \bowtie S) \cup (last(R^{+}_{[\overset{NL}{\bowtie}:\mathbb{N}'(k+1)]}) \bowtie S)]\!] \tag{9}$$

From (9), by the distributivity of join with respect to union, it follows that:

$$[\![P^{\overset{NL}{\bowtie}}{}_{[\mathbb{N}'(k+1)]}]\!] = [\![(R^{+}_{[\overset{NL}{\bowtie}:\mathbb{N}'(k)]} \cup last(R^{+}_{[\overset{NL}{\bowtie}:\mathbb{N}'(k+1)]})) \bowtie S]\!] \tag{10}$$

By the definition of the quiescence condition in Section 3.2, it follows that:

$$last(R^{+}_{[\overset{NL}{\bowtie}:\mathbb{N}'(k+1)]}) \not\subseteq R^{+}_{[\overset{NL}{\bowtie}:\mathbb{N}'(k)]} \tag{11}$$

Therefore, the left operand of the join in the right-hand side of (10) becomes:

$$(R^+_{[\overset{NL}{\bowtie}:\mathbb{N}'(k)]} \cup last(R^+_{[\overset{NL}{\bowtie}:\mathbb{N}'(k+1)]})) = R^+_{[\overset{NL}{\bowtie}:\mathbb{N}'(k+1)]} \tag{12}$$

Substituting the right-hand side of (12) in (10) gives (6), as desired. □

We note that this proof is independent of the join operator that is to replace the nested-loop, and thus that the proof need not be repeated for different target operators. Next, we have to prove that changing from $\overset{NL}{\bowtie}$ to $\overset{H}{\bowtie}$ is result-neutral.

Given a sub-plan P^J, where J is quiescent in state $\mathbb{N}'$, we show that replacing J with J' is result-neutral when J is a nested-loop join and J' is a hash join.

Theorem 2 (Validity of Replacing Nested-Loop Join with Hash Join)

$$[\![P^J]\!] = [\![P^{J_{[\mathbb{N}']}}]\!] \cup [\![P^{J'}]\!] \tag{13}$$

Proof

According to Table 1, we get $[\![P^J]\!] = [\![R\overset{NL}{\bowtie}S]\!], [\![P^{J_{[\mathbb{N}']}}]\!] = [\![R^+_{[\overset{NL}{\bowtie}:\mathbb{N}']}\bowtie S]\!]$ *and* $[\![P^{J'}]\!] = [\![R^-_{[\overset{NL}{\bowtie}:\mathbb{N}']}\overset{H}{\bowtie}S]\!]$. *Substituting into (13) gives:*

$$[\![R\overset{NL}{\bowtie}S]\!] = [\![R^+_{[\overset{NL}{\bowtie}:\mathbb{N}']}\bowtie S]\!] \cup [\![R^-_{[\overset{NL}{\bowtie}:\mathbb{N}']}\overset{H}{\bowtie}S]\!] \tag{14}$$

Since the value of *symbol* ($[\![\ ]\!]$) *denotes the result set of evaluating a plan fragment, two or more results can be unioned, so (14) becomes:*

$$[\![R\overset{NL}{\bowtie}S]\!] = [\![(R^+_{[\overset{NL}{\bowtie}:\mathbb{N}']}\bowtie S) \cup (R^-_{[\overset{NL}{\bowtie}:\mathbb{N}']}\overset{H}{\bowtie}S)]\!] \tag{15}$$

Assuming the correctness of Nested-Loop Join *(i.e.,* $\overset{NL}{\bowtie}$*) and* Hash Join *(i.e.,* $\overset{H}{\bowtie}$*) in implementing the semantics of logical join operation (i.e.,* $\bowtie$*), (15) becomes:*

$$[\![R\bowtie S]\!] = [\![(R^+_{[\overset{NL}{\bowtie}:\mathbb{N}']}\bowtie S) \cup (R^-_{[\overset{NL}{\bowtie}:\mathbb{N}']}\bowtie S)]\!] \tag{16}$$

From (16), by the distributivity of join with respect to union, it follows that:

$$[\![R\bowtie S]\!] = [\![(R^+_{[\overset{NL}{\bowtie}:\mathbb{N}']} \cup R^-_{[\overset{NL}{\bowtie}:\mathbb{N}']})\bowtie S)]\!] \tag{17}$$

By the definitions of I^+ *and* I^- *in Section 3.1, it follows that* $(R^+ \cup R^-) = R$. *Substituting into (17) gives:*

$$[\![R\bowtie S]\!] = [\![R\bowtie S]\!] \tag{18}$$

Thereby establishing (13), i.e., that replacing J with J' is result-neutral when J is a nested-loop join and J' is a hash join. □

We observe that no re-computation for the initial segment of the join result is needed.

4 Conclusion

Adaptive query processing shows promise for improving the performance of query evaluation, especially in settings in which available statistical information may be unreliable or out-of-date.

This paper adds the following to existing results on adaptive query processing:

1. A notation for describing the properties of partially evaluated query plans; this notation enables systematic and precise description of transformations to query execution plans at runtime.
2. A demonstration of the use of the notation for describing changes to physical join operators within pipelined plans, including an example of how the validity of such transformations can be proved.

The notation and proof strategies contributed in this paper can be generalized to other pipelined physical operators. The paper is thus best thought of as contributing a framework for such formal analysis task.

The above results seek to contribute to ongoing work on adaptive databases by:

1. Encouraging the formal description of adaptations, thereby providing assurances as to the correctness of changes made to execution plans at runtime. Although a few adaptive strategies have received a formal treatment (e.g., [13] includes several proofs of properties of eddies and their extensions), such a practice does not seem to be widespread.
2. Providing a formal underpinning for the replacement of physical operators during their evaluation, thereby allowing finer-grained adaptations than have been supported by most previous work that changes plans at runtime (e.g., [15,9,8,10]).

Acknowledgement. K. Eurviriyanukul thanks Rajamangala University of Technology Lanna, Chiang Mai, Thailand, for their financial support.

References

1. R. Avnur and J.M. Hellerstein. Eddies: Continuously Adaptive Query Processing. In *ACM SIGMOD*, pages 261–272, 2000.
2. S. Babu and P. Bizarro. Adaptive Query Processing in the Looking Glass. In *CIDR*, pages 238–249, 2005.

3. S. Babu, P. Bizarro, and D. DeWitt. Proactive Re-Optimization. In *Proc. ACM SIGMOD*, pages 107–118, 2005.
4. H. Garcia-Molina, J. Widom, and J.D. Ullman. *Database System Implementation.* Prentice-Hall, Inc., 1999.
5. A. Gounaris, J. Smith, N. W. Paton, R. Sakellariou, and A. A. A. Fernandes. Adapting to Changing Resources in Grid Query Processing. In *Proc. 1st International Workshop on Data Management in Grids.* Springer-Verlag, 2005.
6. G. Graefe. Encapsulation of Parallelism in the Volcano Query Processing System. In *Proc. SIGMOD*, pages 102–111, 1990.
7. G. Graefe. Query Evaluation Techniques for Large Databases. *ACM Comput. Surv.*, 25(2):73–170, 1993.
8. Z.G. Ives, D. Florescu, M. Friedman, A. Y. Levy, and D. S. Weld. An Adaptive Query Execution System for Data Integration. In *SIGMOD Conference*, pages 299–310, 1999.
9. N. Kabra and D. J. DeWitt. Efficient Mid-Query Re-Optimization of Sub-Optimal Query Execution Plans. In *SIGMOD Conference*, pages 106–117, 1998.
10. V. Markl, V. Raman, D. E. Simmen, G. M. Lohman, and H. Pirahesh. Robust Query Processing through Progressive Optimization. In *SIGMOD Conference*, pages 659–670, 2004.
11. P. Mishra and M. H. Eich. Join Processing in Relational Databases. *ACM Comput. Surv.*, 24(1):63–113, 1992.
12. Kenneth W. Ng, Zhenghao Wang, and Richard R. Muntz. Dynamic Reconfiguration of Sub-Optimal Parallel Query Execution Plans. Technical Report CSD-980033, UCLA, 1998.
13. V. Raman, A. Deshpande, and J. M. Hellerstein. Using State Modules for Adaptive Query Processing. Technical Report UCB/CSD-03-1231, University of California Berkeley, 2003.
14. M. A. Shah, J. M. Hellerstein, S. Chandrasekaran, and M. J. Franklin. Flux: An Adaptive Partitioning Operator for Continuous Query Systems. In *ICDE*, pages 25–36, 2003.
15. Tolga Urhan, Michael J. Franklin, and Laurent Amsaleg. Cost Based Query Scrambling for Initial Delays. In *SIGMOD Conference*, pages 130–141, 1998.
16. A. N. Wilschut and P. M. G. Apers. Dataflow Query Execution in a Parallel Main-memory Environment. *Distributed and Parallel Databases*, 1(1):103–128, 1993.

Implementing a Linguistic Query Language for Historic Texts

Lukas C. Faulstich, Ulf Leser, and Thorsten Vitt

Institut für Informatik
Humboldt-Universität zu Berlin
Unter den Linden 6, D-10099 Berlin
{faulstic, leser, vitt}@informatik.hu-berlin.de

Abstract. We describe the design and implementation of the linguistic query language DDDquery. This language aims at querying a large linguistic database storing a corpus of richly annotated historic German texts. We use a graph-based data model that supports multiple independent annotation layers on a shared text layer as well as alignments of text layers representing the same text or related texts (e.g., translations). The corpus is stored in an object-relational database system with a text retrieval extension.

DDDquery is based on XPath to leverage the familiarity of many users with this language. It is translated to SQL in a two phase compilation with first order logic as an intermediate language. This approach effectively decouples the query language from the schema of the underlying corpus.

We provide an overview of DDDquery, the underlying ODAG data model, its implementation as relational schema, the predicates of the intermediate language, and describe both phases of the translation process.

1 Introduction

The project DDD[1] is a large interdisciplinary project of linguists of historical German, corpus linguists, computational linguists, and computer scientists for creating a *diachronic corpus* of German, i.e., a collection of German texts ranging from the 8th century to modern German carefully selected to cater linguistic research interests. Most texts in the DDD corpus will be richly annotated, i.e., words will be annotated with morphological, lexical, and grammatical information; sentences will be annotated with their syntactic structure; and whole texts will be annotated with respect to the structure of their content as well as with bibliographic and other meta-data [1].

In the DDD project, we are developing methods to store and manage large collections of richly annotated historic texts such as the Sachsenspiegel[2] in an RDBMS [2]. The project is faced with non-tree-shaped annotation graphs and multiple annotation hierarchies with conflicting structure that cannot be represented naturally in XML. For instance, the logical organization of a text in sections, paragraphs, sentences, and words

[1] www.deutschdiachrondigital.de

[2] The "Sachsenspiegel" is the earliest code of common law written in German. The Heidelberg manuscript, a Middle High German version of the "Sachsenspiegel", is available at http://digi.ub.uni-heidelberg.de/cpg164; a detail is shown in Fig. 1

T. Grust et al. (Eds.): EDBT 2006 Workshops, LNCS 4254, pp. 601–612, 2006.

Fig. 1. Detail from page 1r of the "Heidelberger Sachsenspiegel"

often conflicts with the structure of its physical source (e.g., a manuscript) in pages, lines, and whitespace-separated groups of characters: sentences may cross several lines, logical words may be hyphenated etc. Historical linguists use several parallel text layers (e.g., a so-called *diplomatic* version close to the original text witness, a more readable *normalized* version, a word-by-word translation, alternative versions from different text witnesses etc.) which need to be carefully aligned with each other (cf. Fig. 2). Searching within text layers, in different annotation layers and across alignments in combination with hierarchical and spatial relationships (e.g., precedence, inclusion, intersection of text spans) poses further challenging requirements to the query language.

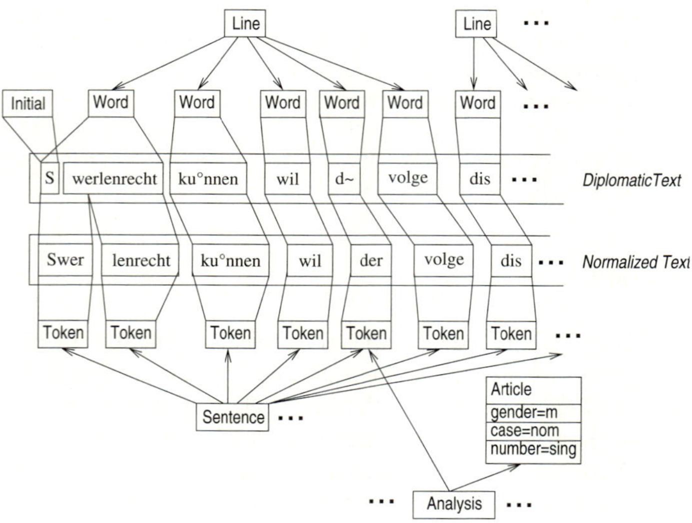

Fig. 2. Exemplary annotation of the Sachsenspiegel (detail; cf. Fig. 1)

While in principle XML together with a reference mechanism such as XPointer can be used to encode richly annotated corpora by means of so-called stand-off annotation, we believe (with others [3,4]) that specialized data models are a more natural and promising way to cope with the requirements of such corpora. Hence we have introduced [5] the graph-based ODAG data model presented in Sec. 2 that extends the XML data model. The particular requirements of linguists for querying corpora have led to the development of various linguistic query tools and specialized query languages such as CQP [6] and TigerSearch [7]. Recently, there have been proposals for XML-based linguistic query languages such as LPath [8]. While LPath is designed for querying tree banks encoded in XML, we propose the query language DDDquery for querying richly annotated corpora represented in our ODAG model. It goes beyond LPath by supporting queries on text spans, on multiple annotation layers, and across aligned texts.

1.1 Requirements and Design Decisions

Our query language should build on an established and popular standard to leverage the familiarity of users with this base language. We have decided to base the *syntax* of our language on XPath due to its popularity, its simplicity (compared to XQuery) and the similarity of our data model to XML. We need to extend XPath with linguistic query operations such as projection through alignments and selection of text spans by content (full-text retrieval) or according to spatial relationships (textual order).

As search results neither lists of whole documents (like in Information Retrieval) nor linear sequences of nodes (like in XPath) are sufficient. A query needs to specify several targets (e.g., a sentence together with a verb and noun phrase within this sentence) the matches of which must be shown in their textual context together with selected annotations. The result of a DDDquery query is a subgraph of the corpus where matches of particular targets are specially tagged to facilitate highlighting by the presentation layer that is in charge of formatting the results. Hence construction of arbitrary XML documents (as supported by XQuery) is deliberately not offered by DDDquery.

While the DDD corpus will be stored in a object-relational database system, the language should be independent from the implementation of this storage layer. Hence we choose first-order logic over a fixed set of primitive predicates as an intermediary language that abstracts from the underlying database schema.

With the corpus still in its planning stage, user requirements cannot be fully predicted. Hence we need an easily extensible language. Using the JavaCC and JJTree tools facilitates syntactical extensions. New primitive predicates can easily be defined in the logic-based intermediate layer in terms of SQL templates without changing our logic-to-SQL compiler LoToS. Moreover, changes of the underlying relational schema can be compensated to some extent by adapting the SQL templates.

1.2 Structure of the Paper

In the next section we discuss the underlying ODAG data model and how it is implemented as relational schema. Then, in Sec. 3 we give an overview of DDDquery. The intermediate language is presented in Sec. 4. Then we discuss the two translation phases in Sec. 5 and Sec. 6 before we conclude the paper with Sec. 7.

2 The ODAG Linguistic Data Model

The principle elements of the ODAG linguistic data model are depicted in Fig. 3: Text layers are represented by a text ID and the actual text content. Spans are continuous intervals of texts, represented by their left and right border and by an optional score (which may result from an approximate full text search). Elements, characterized by a

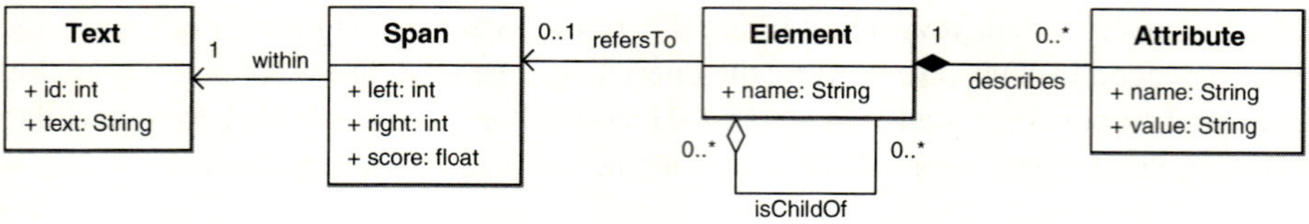

Fig. 3. The ODAG data model in form of an UML class diagram

name and further described by a set of Attributes, may refer to a span. An element may have an ordered sequence of children and one or more parents, thus forming a DAG. Cycles however are forbidden.

The relational schema presented here is a straight-forward implementation of this data model. It is based on [9]. Text layers are stored in a table

`text(id, content)`

where `content` is a string (CLOB) storing the text of the text layer identified by attribute `id`. ODAG elements are stored in table

`element(id, name, tid, left, right, score)`

where `tid` refers to the identifier of a text layer. If `tid` is not null, then the tuple `(tid,left,right,score)` refers to a text span associated with the element.

The children of each element are stored in table

`child(parent, pos, child)`

where `parent` and `child` reference `element.id` and `pos` indicates the position of a child within its siblings.

Since the ODAG data model generalizes XML to acyclic directed graphs, our storage concept is based on a shredded interval-based storage scheme similar to [10]. In this model, each document node is stored together with its so-called pre- and post-order ranks. These ranks result from traversing the document tree depth-first and numbering each node before (pre-order rank) and after (post-order rank) visiting its children. This representation allows queries for the XPath axes to be translated into simple conditions on rank-intervals. This approach has been generalized in [11] to support graph-based data models such as ODAG. An ODAG element that can be reached on different paths will be visited multiple times during a complete traversal of the ODAG. Hence for each visit a different rank is attached to the element:

`rank(element, pre, post)`

Attribute `pre` stores a pre-order rank of the element referenced by attribute `element` and attribute `post` stores the corresponding post-order rank.

The attributes of ODAG elements are stored in table

`attribute(element, name, value)`

An attribute is uniquely identified by the `id` of the element it describes (referred to by attribute `element`) and its `name`.

3 Overview of the Query Language DDDquery

This section gives a brief overview of DDDquery. For a detailed presentation see [12]. DDDquery extends XPath to fulfill the linguists' requirements and to handle the data model outlined in Sec. 2.

As in XPath, DDDquery's fundamental language element is a *path expression* composed of *location steps*. Each step consists at least of an *axis* and a *node test* and may optionally contain *predicates* (which further constrain the set of matched nodes) and *variables* (explained below). A path expression in a query matches a set of paths in the corpus graph such that the steps match graph nodes and the axes describe the relations between the respective nodes.

3.1 Complex Query Features

Linguists' requirements [13] for corpus query languages include regular expressions on path components and correlation of subqueries. For instance, sample query Q_1 from [8] "Noun phrases *NP* that immediately follow a verb *V*" (within the same Sentence *S*) can be expressed in DDDquery using a shared variable `$NP` by

```
//S$S//V$V//immediately-following::NP$NP & $s//NP$NP
```

While this query can be expressed as well in LPath (but not in XPath), queries involving more complex correlations can not. Further features that go beyond LPath such as alignments and multiple layers are supported using dedicated axes and elements.

3.2 Complex Search Results

Unlike XPath, where the path's result is simply a sequence of nodes "pointed at" by the path expression, DDDquery needs to offer more complex query results, e. g. context information. Hence for each step the matching nodes can be selected for output by binding the step to a variable. The variable name will be used to annotate the respective nodes in the result, such that users and front-ends can recognize the mapping between result nodes and query steps. The subgraph induced by the nodes selected for output will be the result of the query. For example, `//S$s//VP//NP$np` selects all NP elements which are descendants of VP elements which are descendents of S elements, but only outputs the NP and S elements, marking them with "s" and "np", respectively.

The purpose of DDDquery is to provide structured results containing all necessary information needed for their presentation in a Web interface, but not to prepare documents in a presentation format such as HTML. Hence it does not provide constructs for assembling arbitrary XML documents but returns the results in a fixed XML format, which can then be post-processed using, for instance, XSLT.

3.3 Spans and Full Text Search

Spans (i. e. continuous intervals of text) are first class objects of the corpus data model. They may be initially obtained either by following an association with an element node or by a full text search in the document. We cope with spans by introducing special node tests. For instance, DDDquery provides a node test `exact-match('Siegfried')` which matches all text spans consisting of the exact string "Siegfried". A similar test is defined for regular expression matching, and the language is open for extension with additional tests like a fuzzy text search.

To describe relations between spans there are respective axes like, e. g.,`contained`. In particular, the semantics of the horizontal XPath axes like `following` and `preceding` have been adapted to refer to relations between spans. To allow navigation from an element to the associated span and vice versa, we provide special axes. E. g., the path fragment

```
exact-match("XPath") / containing-element::sentence /
  contained::exact-match("grammar")
```

navigates from a text span with the content *XPath* to a text span *grammar* which must be contained in the same sentence.

3.4 Syntactic Sugar

Like XPath, DDDquery provides a simple, but rather verbose normative syntax able to express all language features plus a set of abbreviations for common constructs. In particular there are, like in LPath [8], shortcut symbols for axis steps using many common axes (so `a/following::b` may be abbreviated as `a --> b`).

4 Intermediate Language

Queries in DDDquery are translated to an intermediate language called DDDlog that is based on first-order logic with a fixed set of predicates. In DDDlog a query q is defined as a horn clause $H \leftarrow F$. The head $H = h(X_1,\ldots,X_m)$ defines the variables $X_1,\ldots,X_m$ as parameters of q. F is a Boolean formula defined recursively as $F ::= F_1 \vee F_2 | F_1 \wedge F_2 | \neg(F_1) | p(t_1,\ldots,t_n) | p(t_1,\ldots,t_n)^+$. h and p are predicate symbols. The call parameters t_j are either constants or variables. The transitive closure operator $()^+$ provides a limited form of recursion that can be handled by current DBMS. A call $p(t_1,\ldots,t_n)^+$ is equivalent to a call $r(t_1,\ldots,t_n)$ to a recursive predicate r/n defined as

$$r(X_1,\ldots,X_n) \equiv p(X_1,X_2,\ldots,X_{n-1},Y) \wedge (Y = X_n \vee r(Y,X_2,\ldots,X_{n-1},X_n))$$

A query result is a substitution σ for all free variables in q such that the result $F\sigma$, i.e., applying σ to F, is true.

A predicate is either a *macro* or a *primitive*. Macros are defined by a set of non-recursive horn clauses, i.e., a macro defines an intensional database predicate. Macros are expanded before query translation. Primitives are defined in terms of templates that can be instantiated to SQL code. Templates are discussed in Sec. 6.

4.1 Representation of Corpus Nodes

The semantics of DDDquery is defined in terms of *(corpus) nodes*. Similar to document nodes in XML there are different types of corpus nodes.

A corpus node is either a span, an instance of an element, or an instance of an attribute. An element instance is an element together with a pre- and post-order rank for this element and the optional span associated with this element. For each instance of an element in combination with one of the element's attributes there exists an attribute instance. Since our FO-to-SQL compiler does not support polymorphic types, we represent all nodes by the same tuple type

$$(\mathit{EltId}, \mathit{Name}, \mathit{Value}, \mathit{Pre}, \mathit{Post}, \mathit{TextId}, \mathit{Left}, \mathit{Right}, \mathit{Score})$$

For spans only the last four components are not null. For element instances, component *Name* stores the element name while *value* is null. For attribute instances, name and value of the attribute are stored in the respective components. Attribute instances are not associated with spans, hence the last four components are always null.

4.2 Predicates of the Intermediate Language

DDDlog defines a set of predicates for node tests (discussed in Sec. 5.1) and axis steps (presented in Sec. 5.2). They are defined as macros building on other predicates: (i) primitives providing the relational tables presented in Sec. 2 as extensional database predicates, (ii) auxiliary predicates (s. Table 1) for accessing components of nodes, (iii) basic predicates (s. Table 2) defining relationships between nodes, and (iv) primitives providing access to various SQL functions.

Due to space limitations we cannot describe all predicates of the intermediate language but must limit the presentation to some examples.

Table 1. Auxiliary Predicates

Predicate	Definition
$nodeRank(E,P,Q)$	$E = (I,N,V,P,Q,T,L,R,C)$
$span(E,T,L,R,S)$	$T \neq null \wedge E = (I,N,V,P,Q,T,L,R,S)$
$elementId(E,I)$	$E = (I,N,V,P,Q,T,L,R,C)$

Table 2. Basic Predicates defined as macros

Predicate	Definition
$ancestor(A,D)$	$nodeRank(A,P_A,Q_A) \wedge nodeRank(D,P_D,Q_D) \wedge P_A < P_D \wedge Q_D < Q_A$
$immPrec(X,Y)$	$span(X,T_X,L_X,R_X,S_X) \wedge span(Y,T_Y,L_Y,R_Y,S_Y) \wedge T_X = T_Y \wedge R_X = L_Y$
$alias(X_1,X_2)$	$X_1 = (I,N,V,P_1,Q_1,T,L,R,C) \wedge X_2 = (I,N,V,P_2,Q_2,T,L,R,C)$

With the help of the auxiliary predicate $nodeRank/3$ we can define predicate $ancestor/2$ as a relation on nodes. Similarly we can define spatial predicates such as $immPrec/2$ on nodes that have spans on the same text layer. $immPrec(X,Y)$ is satisfied if the right boundary of the span of X coincides with the left boundary of the span of Y.

The predicate $alias/2$ tests whether two nodes are instances of the same element.

The textual content of a node associated with a span is computed by the primitive predicate $content(X,S)$ that is defined by a SQL template since it needs to use the SQL function `SUBSTR()` for computing a substring of a text layer (s. Example 2 in Sec. 6.1).

For full-text retrieval we assume several primitives like $matches(P,S,M)$ that take a string P conforming to a certain syntax (e.g., for regular expressions) and a node S with a span and return all sub-spans M that match P. Variants include predicates for matching a pattern only against the whole span S or against prefixes or suffixes of S. Since SQL and typical full-text retrieval extensions in existing database systems do not support this type of operation well, we may need to support these primitives by appropriate table functions.

5 Translation to DDDlog

The DDDquery-to-DDDlog translation is implemented in JavaCC and JJTree.

5.1 Translation of Node Tests

Node tests are used to generate bindings for node variables. In Table 3 node tests for element and attribute instances are presented that take an (optional) argument N specifying the element/attribute name. Node tests for spans are treated in Sec. 5.3.

Table 3. Node tests

Predicate	**Definition**
$elementNode(N,E)$	$element(I,N,T,L,R,C) \wedge rank(I,P,Q) \wedge E = (I,N,null,P,Q,T,L,R,C)$
$attributeNode(N,A)$	$attribute(I,N,V) \wedge rank(I,P,Q) \wedge A = (I,N,V,P,Q,null,null,null,null)$

5.2 Translation of Axes

Each axis is implemented by a predicate that defines a node relation (s. Table 4) without necessarily computing node bindings for the target nodes. Note that $ancestorAxis/2$

Table 4. Axis steps

Predicate	**Definition**
$childAxis(P,C)$	$elementId(P,E_P) \wedge elementId(C,E_C) \wedge child(E_P,\_,E_C)$
$parentAxis(C,P)$	$elementId(C,E_C) \wedge elementId(P,E_P) \wedge child(E_P,\_,E_C)$
$descendentAxis(A,D)$	$ancestor(A,D)$
$ancestorAxis(D,A)$	$elementNode(\_,D') \wedge alias(D,D') \wedge ancestor(A,D')$

needs to find also ancestors A not on the path on which the descendent D has been reached. Hence we need first to find all alias nodes D' of D (i.e., all element instances sharing the element with D, but representing different paths to reach this element).

5.3 Combination of Axis Steps and Node Tests

The primitives for text pattern matching mentioned in Sec. 4 conceptually combine an axis step (e.g., computing all sub-spans of a span) with a node test (e.g., testing whether the text content of a sub-span equals a given string). It would be extremely inefficient to actually generate a large number of spans and then filter those spans satisfying the node test. Hence we translate combinations of axis steps on spans and node tests involving text pattern matching together. For instance, the query fragment

```
contains::exact-match('word')
```

is translated to a call $exactMatchSubstring($`"word"`$,S,M)$. The query fragment

```
following::re-match('be.{1,5}en')
```

is translated to $\mathit{suffixAfter}(S,T) \wedge \mathit{regexpMatchSubstring}(\texttt{"be.\{1,5\}en"},T,M)$ where $\mathit{suffixAfter}(S,T)$ returns for a span S the suffix T of the whole text layer starting at the right border of S.

In some cases, it is more efficient to bind spans in some other part of the query and just test whether they match the pattern. This results in a different translation that avoids to call a table function for text pattern matching. For instance,

```
contains::exact-match('where')/element::word
```

translates to $\mathit{elementNode}(\_, \texttt{"word"}, W) \wedge \mathit{content}(W, \texttt{"where"})$.

5.4 Example

The sample query `//S$S//V$V//immediately-following::NP$NP & $s//NP$NP` introduced in Sec. 3.1 is translated to the following predicate definition:

$$\begin{aligned} Q_1(S,V,NP) \equiv\ & \mathit{elementNode}(\texttt{'S'},S) \wedge \\ & \mathit{ancestor}(S,V) \wedge \mathit{elementNode}(\texttt{'V'},V) \wedge \mathit{immPrec}(S,NP) \\ & \mathit{ancestor}(S,NP) \wedge \mathit{elementNode}(\texttt{'NP'},NP) \end{aligned}$$

6 Translation from DDDlog to SQL

6.1 Templates

A primitive predicate p is defined by one or more templates T, each of which provides an SQL implementation for a certain binding pattern that can be instantiated to an SQL SELECT statement. The FO-to-SQL compiler combines these templates in such a way that for every variable in a query there is a template that binds this variable. Primitives are not necessarily extensional database predicates since their templates may combine data from multiple tables of the underlying database and may contain calls to SQL functions (e.g., for full-text search).

Definition 1 (Template)

A template T for a predicate $p(a_1,\ldots,a_m)$ has the form (A,I,R,σ,τ,w) where

- $A = \langle a_1,\ldots,a_m\rangle$ *is the parameter vector of p.*
- $I \subseteq \{a_1,\ldots,a_m\}$ *is a set of* input parameters *that must be bound externally.*
- $O = \{a_1,\ldots,a_m\} - I$ *is the set of* output parameters *that can be computed by p.*
- $R = \{r_1,\ldots,r_n\}$ *is a finite set of* table aliases
- $\mathscr{E}_{R,I}$ *is the set of SQL expressions over aliases R and free variables I.*
- $\sigma : O \rightarrow \mathscr{E}_{R,I}$, *the* output substitution, *assigns expressions to output parameters.*
- $\tau : R \rightarrow \mathscr{T} \cup \mathscr{Q}_{R,I}$, *the* table assignment, *assigns each table alias an element from the set $\mathscr{T}$ of table names or from the set $\mathscr{Q}_{R,I}$ of sub-queries over R and I.*
- $w \in \mathscr{E}_{R,I}$ *is an SQL condition that must be satisfied for each solution of p.*

Example 1. The template for predicate $\mathit{element}(E,N,T,L,R,C)$ may be defined as

$$\begin{aligned} T_{element} &= (\langle E,N,T,L,R,C\rangle, \{\texttt{e}\}, \sigma_{element}, \{\texttt{e} \mapsto \texttt{element}\}, \mathit{true}) \\ \sigma_{element} &= \{E \mapsto \texttt{e.id}, N \mapsto \texttt{e.name}, \\ &\quad T \mapsto \texttt{e.tid}, L \mapsto \texttt{e.left}, R \mapsto \texttt{e.right}, C \mapsto \texttt{e.score}\} \end{aligned}$$

A call to EDB predicate *element*, for instance *element*("e21",N,T,L,R,C), induces a binding β for all (here: zero) input parameters and some output parameters, i.e., $\beta(E) =$ "e21". The template can be expanded then to the following SQL query which retrieves the name and span for element "e21":

```
SELECT e.name, e.tid, e.left, e.right, e.score
FROM element e
WHERE e.id= "e21"
```

Example 2. The content of a span is the substring of the underlying text layer starting from the left span boundary up to the right span boundary. The predicate *content*(T_0,S,X) is fulfilled if node X is associated with a span in text layer T_0 whose content is string S. The following template supports the binding pattern where $X = (I,N,V,P,Q,T,L,R,C)$ is given while T_0 and S are requested:

$$\begin{aligned} T_{content} = (&\langle T_0,S,I,N,V,P,Q,T,L,R,C\rangle,\\ &\{T,L,R\},\\ &\{\mathtt{t}\},\\ &\{T_0 \mapsto \mathtt{t.id}, S \mapsto \mathtt{SUBSTR}(\mathtt{t.content},L,R-L)\},\\ &\{\mathtt{t} \mapsto \mathtt{text}\},\\ &(\mathtt{t.id} = T\ \mathtt{AND}\ \mathtt{T.id} <> \mathtt{null})) \end{aligned}$$

6.2 Translation Algorithm

Although FO-to-SQL translation is standard textbook knowledge, we are not aware of any ready-to-use implementation. Moreover, we wanted to support the transitive closure operator by using the recursive SQL constructs provided now by several DBMS. Hence we developed the **Lo**gic **To** **S**QL compiler LoToS[3] described in [14]. Depending on the underlying database system the transitive closure operator is translated into a `WITH RECURSIVE ... SELECT` statement (e.g., DB2) or using the `SELECT ... CONNECT BY` construct (Oracle).

6.3 Result Construction

Executing a DDDquery compiled to SQL produces a result table in which each tuple represents the bindings of the query variables to corpus nodes. Our goal is to generate a result document in which all relevant variable bindings are highlighted. Hence we need a post-processing step in which the union of all variable bindings is computed and sorted by pre-order rank to allow for the construction of a result document tree.

6.4 Example

The DDDlog representation of sample query Q_1 (cf. Sec. 5.4) is translated by LoToS to the SQL query listed in Table 5 that can be executed against a corpus stored using the schema presented in Sec. 2.

[3] Available at `http://www.informatik.hu-berlin.de/ faulstic/projects/DDD/software/LoToS/`

Table 5. SQL code for sample query Q_1

```
SELECT
  element1.id,
  element3.id,
  element2.id
FROM
  element element1,
  rank ancestor1,
  rank descendant1,
  rank ancestor2,
  rank descendant2,
  element element2,
  element element3
WHERE element1.name="S"
AND element2.name="V"
AND element3.name="NP"
AND element1.id=ancestor1.element
AND ancestor1.element=ancestor2.element
AND descendant1.element=element2.id
AND descendant2.element=element3.id
AND ancestor1.pre=<descendant1.pre
AND descendant1.pre<ancestor1.post
AND ancestor2.pre=<descendant2.pre
AND descendant2.pre<ancestor2.post
AND (element2.tid IS NOT NULL)
AND (element3.tid IS NOT NULL)
AND element2.tid=element3.tid
AND element2.right=element3.left;
```

7 Conclusion and Future Work

We have given an overview of the linguistic query language DDDquery and its implementation. We are currently integrating the DDDquery parser developed in [12] with the generic FO-to-SQL compiler LoToS [14] into a linguistic query processor. This processor will be tested on a small sample corpus. Thorough performance tests on large corpora need to be undertaken. Until a significant part of the DDD corpus becomes available, we need to use synthetic data or data from existing corpora. Another open point is how to support full-text retrieval on historic texts. The requirements of historic linguists go beyond what is supported in typical full-text indexing solutions: proper Unicode support, regular expression and substring matching, finding all matches within texts rather than all matching texts etc. The two-phase compilation approach taken by DDDquery allows to tune its relational implementation easily without touching the first translation stage and the generic FO-to-SQL compiler.

References

1. Lüdeling, A., Poschenrieder, T., Faulstich, L.C.: DeutschDiachronDigital - Ein diachrones Korpus des Deutschen. In: Jahrbuch für Computerphilologie 6 (2004). Mentis Verlag (2005) 119–136
2. Faulstich, L.C., Leser, U., Lüdeling, A.: Storing and Querying Historical Texts in a Relational Database. Informatik-Bericht 176, Inst. für Informatik, Humboldt-Universität zu Berlin (2005)
3. Carletta, J., Kilgour, J., O'Donnell, T., Evert, S., Voormann, H.: The NITE object model library for handling structured linguistic annotation on multimodal data sets. In: 3rd Workshop on NLP and XML, NLPXML-2003. (2003)
4. Dekhtyar, A., Iacob, I.E.: A framework for management of concurrent XML markup. Data and Knowledge Engineering **52** (2005) 185–208
5. Dipper, S., Faulstich, L.C., Leser, U., Lüdeling, A.: Challenges in Modelling a Richly Annotated Diachronic Corpus of German. In: Workshop on XML-based richly annotated corpora, Lisbon, Portugal (2004)

6. Christ, O.: A modular and flexible architecture for an integrated corpus query system. In: COMPLEX'94, Budapest (1994)
7. Lezius, W.: Ein Suchwerkzeug für syntaktisch annotierte Textkorpora. PhD thesis, Institut für maschinelle Textverarbeitung (IMS), Universität Stuttgart (2002)
8. Bird, S., Chen, Y., Davidson, S., Leea, H., Zheng, Y.: Extending XPath to Support Linguistic Queries. In: Workshop on Programming Language Technologies for XML (PLAN-X). (2005)
9. Vitt, T.: Speicherung linguistischer Korpora in Datenbanken. Studienarbeit, Institut für Informatik, Humboldt Universität zu Berlin (2004)
10. Grust, T., Keulen, M.V., Teubner, J.: Accelerating XPath evaluation in any RDBMS. ACM Transactions on Database Systems **29**(1) (2004) 91–131
11. Trissl, S., Leser, U.: Querying ontologies in relational database systems. In: 2nd Conference on Data Integration in the Life Sciences (DILS05). (2005)
12. Vitt, T.: DDD*query*: Anfragen an komplexe Korpora. Diplomarbeit, Institut für Informatik, Humboldt-Universität zu Berlin (2005)
13. Lai, C., Bird, S.: Querying and updating treebanks: A critical survey and requirements analysis. In: Proceedings of the Australasian Language Technology Workshop. (2004)
14. Faulstich, L.C., Leser, U.: Implementing Linguistic Query Languages Using LoToS. Informatik-Bericht 195, Institut für Informatik, Humboldt-Universität zu Berlin (2005)

NeuroQL: A Domain-Specific Query Language for Neuroscience Data

Hao Tian[1,*], Rajshekhar Sunderraman[1], Robert Calin-Jageman[2], Hong Yang[1], Ying Zhu[1], and Paul S. Katz[2,*]

[1] Department of Computer Science, Georgia State University, Atlanta, GA 30303, USA
{haotian, raj, hyang9, yzhu}@gsu.edu
[2] Department of Biology, Georgia State University, Atlanta, GA 30302, USA
{rcalinjageman, pkatz}@gsu.edu

Abstract. In this paper, we propose a domain-specific query language called NeuroQL for the neuroscience domain. NeuroQL is designed primarily for neuroinformatics database users and aims to enable users to directly interact with neuroscience databases in their professional concepts and terms with the help of a conceptual data model. NeuroQL is DBMS independent and can be translated into traditional query language such as SQL, OQL and XQuery. It integrates some object-oriented features, and supports neuron domain-specific data types and query operators, which can dynamically evolve when the underlying database schema evolves.

1 Introduction

In recent years, neuroscientists have been accumulating data at an exponential rate. To accommodate this expansion of data, a variety of neuroscience databases have been developed to let neuroscientists store, retrieve, manipulate, and analyze their data. A list of neuroscience databases can be found at the society for Neuroscience website [2]. Usually users are provided a graphical query interface, through which users can create their queries. However the major problem of the query GUI solution is that it is application-dependent and supports limited types of queries. To provide a more flexible and powerful tool for neuroscientists to interface with neuroscience databases, we are proposing a neuron domain-specific query language (NeuroQL).

The concept of domain-specific language (DSL) is not new. There are many domain-specific languages for different application domains. Best known are classic examples like PIC, SCATTER, CHEM, LEX, YACC, and Make, which are described in [6]. For a variety of domain-specific problems, domain-specific languages are more attractive than general-purpose languages (GPL) because of the features of easier programming, systematic re-use, and easier verification in DSLs [4, 5]. However, designing and developing a domain-specific language is not an easy task, sometimes it is even harder than developing the application itself. SQL can be considered as a domain-specific language focusing on the database domain. But it is still too general

* This work is funded in part by a Georgia State University Brains & Behavior Program, and by grants to Paul S. Katz from NIH and NSF.

T. Grust et al. (Eds.): EDBT 2006 Workshops, LNCS 4254, pp. 613 – 624, 2006.

and not application-user-friendly for life science database applications as mentioned above. So far, only a few domain-specific query languages (DS-QL) have been proposed [7, 8, 9] for life-science data. Hammer and Schneider proposed a high-level data model and object-oriented query algebra for genomic information [10]. However, none of them can be adapted or extended to neuroscience due to the significant difference on the underlying data structure and semantics. To our knowledge, no domain-specific query language exists for neuroscience.

NeuroQL is motivated by the development of the NeuronBank system [1], which is an effort to develop an online reference source and informatics tool for exploring the vast knowledge of identified neurons and the circuits that they form. During the design of the NeuronBank system, neuroscientists expressed a desire of having a simple query language in their familiar concepts and terms so that they can query the database directly in a way close to their research language. This new query language will provide an advanced query function for experienced users as a supplement to the naïve query GUI, and should work on most types of DBMSs. Obviously, the current common query languages such as SQL, OQL [12], and XQuery [13] do not meet the requirements because they are all DBMS-dependent, and do not have built-in support to the neuroscience domain-specific data types and functions. Therefore, NeuroQL is designed for use by neuroinformatics database users, rather than the database administrators or developers. And it is mostly based on the neuron domain knowledge, unlike SQL and OQL that are based on the underlying relational database schema (see Fig. 1.).

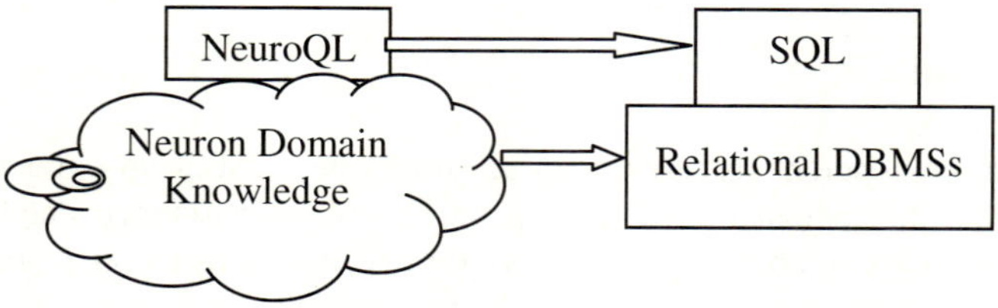

Fig. 1. The bases of NeuroQL and SQL

NeuroQL is a high-level canonical query language, whose basic idea was firstly introduced in [3]. The initial format and syntax of NeuroQL was proposed by the neuroscientists in our NeuronBank team. It integrates object-oriented concepts and supports most of neuron domain-specific data types, for example, neuron, soma, axon, and so on. These data types are systematically derived from the conceptual neuron data model - NeuroDM [3]. NeuroDM defines a small core data structure that holds on the neuron data in all species. It should not be changed in any neuron data model extension for an application. The underlying database schema is generated from NeuroDM as well. Thus, it is easy to set up the mapping between the database schema and the NeuroQL data types, which can dynamically update the data types in NeuroQL whenever the database schema evolves. NeuroQL also defines many advanced neuron domain-specific query operators corresponding to the functions among some common objects in neuroscience. For example, the operator "bilateral" represents the bilateral function between two neurons, and the operator "project" represents the projection function from a neuron's axon to a nerve. The conceptual and implementation architecture of NeuroQL is shown in Fig. 2. The domain-specific data types and query operators are the major constructs of NeuroQL so that the NeuroQL query statements are very close to the questions or queries that the neuroscientists ask in their research.

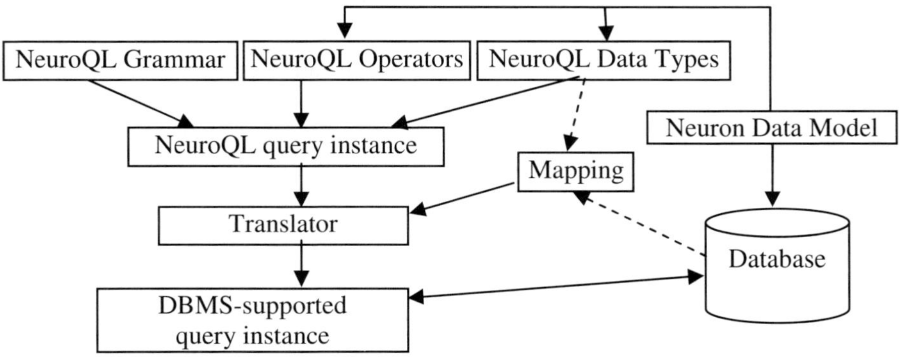

Fig. 2. The conceptual and implementation architecture of NeuroQL

In NeuronBank system, NeuroQL is used in the Meta Search Engine (Fig. 3) to provide the advanced query functionality on integrated heterogeneous species databases. Although each species database represents the neuron data in different ways, they have the same core structure defined in NeuroDM. They can be built on different types of DBMS such as relational DBMS, object-oriented DBMS, and XML native database. The NeuroQL queries will be translated into corresponding SQL, OQL or XQuery queries according to the type of the underlying DBMS.

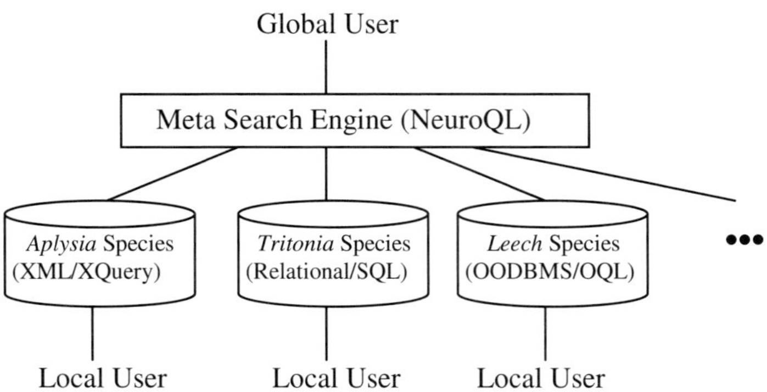

Fig. 3. NeuroQL in NeuronBank

Overall, NeuroQL supports neuroscientists to query the databases using their professional concepts and operators after they understand the abstract conceptual data structures in the data models. We believe that understanding a conceptual data diagram (close to the users' domain knowledge) is much easier than figuring out and remembering the details of the relational database schema, especially the referential constraints.

2 Data Types and Query Operators in NeuroQL

2.1 Data Types

In addition to the common primitive data types, such as Integer, Float, Character, and Boolean, NeuroQL supports most of neuron domain-specific data types as well, such as neuron, soma, axon, nerve, ganglion, firing_pattern, connection, molecule, electrical synapse, chemical synapse, neuromodulation, and component. These domain-specific data types are systematically derived from the entities in the conceptual neuron data model. Fig. 4 shows an extension of NeuroDM used in the *Tritonia* species database of NeuronBank system.

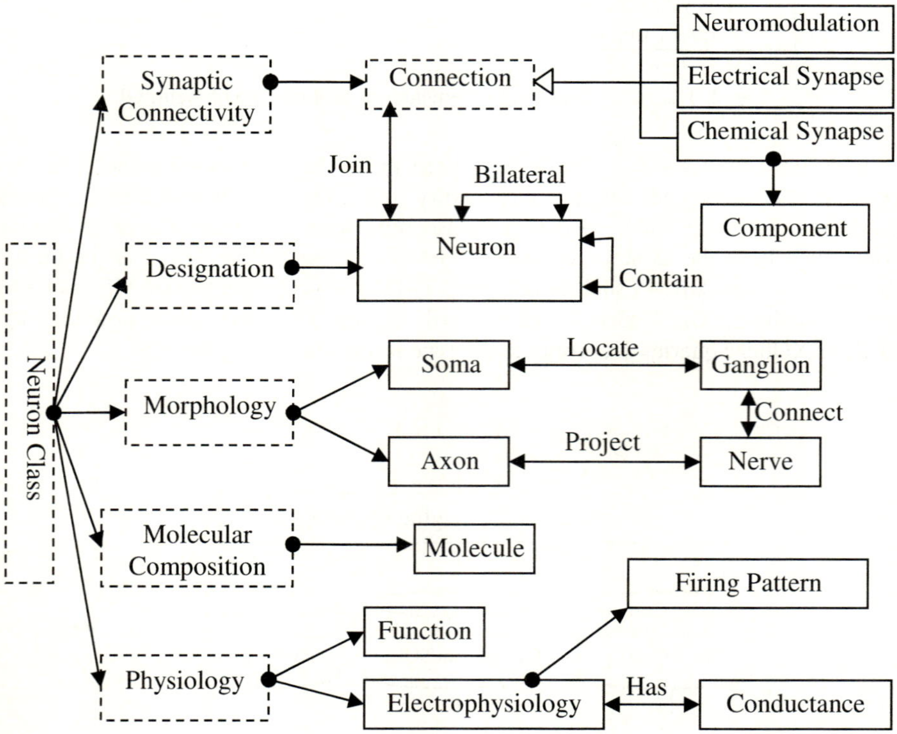

Fig. 4. An extension of NeuroDM [3] used in NeuronBank *Tritonia* species database

The algorithm translating a neuron data model into the data types of NeuroQL should be straightforward because it is similar to the process of converting an ER data model to the object-oriented classes. Following is an algorithm that generates the NeuroQL data types in the NeuronBank system from the NeuroDM, an extended ER data model with some OO features.

NeuroQL_Data_Type_Generation_Algorithm:

```
Input: NeuroDM
Output: NeuroQL data types

Begin:
For each entity in NeuroDM
   Create a new NeuroQL data type
   For each attribute of the entity
      If it is an atomic attribute
         Create an atomic property
      Else
         Create a container property for that attribute
   End of For
   For each inheritance relationship
      Inherit all properties and functions from the
                super data type to the new data type
   End of For
   For each aggregation relationship
      If the maximum number of members == 1
         Create a new property for the aggregated data
      Else
         Create a container for the aggregated data
   End of For
   For each association relationship
      Create a function returning the associated data
   End of For
End of For
For each special table in NeuroDM
   Create a new NeuroQL data type
   For each column in the table
      If it has an atomic data
         Create an atomic property
      Else
         Create a container property for that attribute
   End of For
End of For
End of Algorithm;
```

Next is a data type example ‘neuron’ that is derived from the entity ‘neuron’ in NeuroDM. We adopt object-oriented concept in our data type definition as well.

```
Data Type: neuron

    Properties:
    //Properties derived from the entity 'Neuron'
       neuronID                 String
       name                     String
       synonym                  Set[String]
       type                     String
       genus                    String
       species                  String
       minSize                  Integer
       maxSize                  Integer
       functionCategory         String
       remark                   String

    //Properties derived from the aggregation
    //relationships
       itsSoma                  Soma
       itsAxon                  Axon
       itsFunctions             Set[Function]
       itsElectrophysiology     Electrophysiology
       itsMolecules             Set[Molecule]
       itsFlaggedFeatures       Set[String]

    Functions:
    //Functions derived from the association
    //relationships
       Neuron  bilateral();
       Set[Neuron]  homologue();
       Set[Neuron]  contains();
       Set[Connection]  connect_neuron(Neuron);
```

Since the mapping between NeuroQL data types and database schema is set up systematically, NeuroQL can be updated dynamically when the database schema evolves. This mapping will be used by NeuroQL Translator to translate a NeuroQL query instance to a corresponding DBMS-supported query instance like SQL query. By adding, deleting and changing the entities in the neuron data model, NeuroQL can be easily extended and customized. This feature is especially useful when NeuroQL is integrated into the database applications focusing on the neuron data in different species.

2.2 Query Operators in NeuroQL

The query operators (see Table 1) in NeuroQL are divided into 2 categories: primitive query operators and advanced query operators. Primitive query operators includes the common operators used in traditional query languages, and advanced query operators are corresponding to the functions among the objects in neuroscience The introduction of advanced query operators makes the NeuroQL query statements much

Table 1. Some query operators in NeuroQL

Category	Operators
Primitive query operators	+ - * / % > >= = <= < != . LIKE IN
Advanced query operators	connect, parent, children, neighbors, project, electricalSynapse, chemicalSynapse, location neuromodulation, hasComponent, pass, circuit, itsFiringPatterns, presynapticCell, postsynapticCell.

closer to the questions and queries asked by the neuroscientists in their research. The semantics of the query operators are discussed in the next section.

3 Syntax and Semantics

3.1 Syntax

Following is the BNF grammar of NeuroQL and the interpretation of terminals is given in Table 2:

```
<NeuroQL_query> ::= ( <result_list> ) [ <condition_list> ]
<result_list> ::= <result_term> | <result_term> , <result_list>
<result_term> ::= <single_class_term> | <single_class_term>.SET_PROPERTY
<condition_list> ::= <condition_term> | <condition_term> , <condition_list>
<condition_term> ::= /*EMPTY*/ |<declaration_term> | <comparison_term>
<declaration_term> ::= <single_class_term> IDENTIFIER
              | <single_class_term>.SET_PROPERTY IDENTIFIER
              | <non_bool_op_term> IDENTIFIER
<comparison_term> ::= <bool_op_term>
              | <operand> COMPARISON_OP <operand>
<single_class_term> ::= DATATYPE | IDENTIFIER
              | <single_class_term>.SINGLE_PROPERTY
<bool_op_term> ::= ADV_BOOL_OP(<parameter_list>)
              | <single_class_term>.ADV_BOOL_OP(<parameter_list>)
<non_bool_op_term> ::= ADV_NON_BOOL_OP (<parameter_list>)
              | <single_class_term>.ADV_NON_BOOL_OP (<parameter_list>)
<parameter_list> ::= <parameter> | <parameter>,<parameter_list>
<parameter> ::= /*empty*/ | <operand>
<operand> ::= CONSTANTS | <single_class_term> | <non_bool_op_term>
              | <arithmetic_operand> ARITHMETIC_OP <arithmetic_operand>
<arithmetic_operand> ::= CONSTANTS
              | <single_class_term>.SINGLE_PROPERTY
```

Table 2. The interpretation of terminals in NeuroQL grammar

Terminals	Interpretation
DATATYPE	{dt | dt is the name of a neuron-domain data type in NeuroQL}
SINGLE_PROPERTY	{p | p is a property of a neuron-domain data type in NeuroQL, which references to a single object}
SET_PROPERTY	{sp | sp is a property of a neuron-domain data type in NeuroQL, which references to a set of objects}
IDENTIFIER	{id | id ::= [_a-zA-Z][_a-zA-Z0-9]*}
ADV_BOOL_OP	{bop | bop is an advanced query operators in NeuroQL, which returns a Boolean value}
ADV_NON_BOOL_OP	{nbop | nbop is an advanced query operators in NeuroQL, which returns a non_boolean value}
CONSTANTS	{c | c is a constant value of a primitive data type}
COMPARISON_OP	{'>', '>=', '=', '<=', '<', '!=', 'LIKE', 'IN'}
ARITHMETIC_OP	{'+', '-', '*', '/', '%'}

We adopt the dot notation in NeuroQL, which simplifies the reference to a class or its properties. For example, the path expression of neuronA.itsSoma.colorPattern references the property "colorPattern" of a soma of a neuron instance, neuronA. And in SQL, this is usually done by joining multiple tables based on some referential constraints.

3.2 Semantics

A NeuroQL query has a very simple structure like *(<result_list>)[<condition_list>].* The <result_list> is similar to the SELECT clause in SQL, which consists of a list of objects (i.e. <result_term> in grammar). Each object in the <result_list> can be an instance of a NeuroQL data type or a property of it. The <condition_list> lists all query criteria (<comparison_term>), that is, the conditions that the query result must satisfy.

Let's use RT_1, RT_2, …, RT_n to represent the domain of each <result_term> respectively, then the domain of <result_list>, RL, is the set of n-tuples, whose first element is from RT_1, the second element is from RT_2, and so on. The query result includes the tuples in RL, which satisfy all conditions in the <condition_list>.

The advanced query operators (Table 3) can be used in <condition_list> in order to simplify the expression of a query, and make it closer to a professional expression in the neuron research domain.

Table 3. The signatures and semantics of some advanced query operators in NeuroQL

Operators	Signatures	Semantics
Parent	parent()	parent: {t ǀ t is a neuron instance } → {n ǀ n is the neuron instance in cluster type, and t is a member cell of n.}
Children	children()	children: {t ǀ t is a neuron instance in cluster type } → { n ǀ n is a neuron instance that is a member cell of t.}
Neighbors	Neighbors (double r)	neighbors: {(t, r) ǀ t is a neuron instance, r ∈ R} → {n ǀ n is a neuron instance, and the distance between t and n is less than or equal to r}
Project	Project (nerve v)	project: {(t, v) ǀ t is a neuron instance, v is a nerve instance} → {bool ǀ bool = true if the axon of t projects to v, otherwise bool = false}
Connect	connect(String name, String type)	connect:{(t, name, type) ǀ t is a neuron instances, $name is a name of another neuron instance s, and $type ∈ {'electrical', 'chemical', 'neuromodulation', 'any'}} → {bool ǀ bool = true if there is a connection from t to s or from s to t , whose type matches the value of input $type, otherwise, bool=false.}
electricalSynapse	electricalSynapse (neuron s)	electricalSynapse: {(t, s) ǀ t and s are two neuron instances} → {bool ǀ bool=true if there is an electrical_synapse instance between t and s; otherwise, bool=false}
chemicalSynapse	chemicalSynapse (neuron s, String pos)	chemicalSynapse: {(t, s, pos) ǀ t and s are two neuron instances, and pos ∈ {'pre', 'post', 'any'}} → {bool ǀ bool=true if there is a chemical_synapse instance from t to s if pos= 'pre', or from s to t if pos= 'post', or between t and s if pos= 'any'; otherwise, bool=false}
itsFiringPatterns	itsFiringPatterns()	itsFiringPattern: {t ǀ t is a neuron instance } → {fp ǀ fp is a firingpattern instance that t has}
Location	location()	location: {t ǀ t is a neuron instance } → {g ǀ g is a ganglion instance, at which t is located}
presynaptic_cell	presynaptic_cell()	presynaptic_cell: {t ǀ t is a neuron instance } → {n ǀ n is a neuron instance, and there is a chemical synapse from n to t}
postsynaptic_cell	postsynaptic_cell()	postsynaptic_cell: {t ǀ t is a neuron instance } → {n ǀ n is a neuron instance, and there is a chemical synapse from t to n}
circuit	circuit(Vector[neuron] v)	circuit: {n ǀ n ∈ v, and v is a set of neuron instances} → {c ǀ c is a circuit instance whose nodes include all neuron instances in v}
hasComponent	hasComponent (component p)	hasComponent: {(t, p) ǀ t is a neuron instance and p is a component instance} → {bool ǀ bool = true if p is a component of a chemical_synapse instance, whose presynaptic cell is t, otherwise bool = false}

*: In order to simplify the syntax of NeuroQL, there is an implicit input of a neuron instance for all advanced query operators.

4 Some NeuroQL Query Examples

In this section, we illustrate some NeuroQL query statements and their corresponding SQL query statements. Comparing the two kinds of query statements, it is obvious that it is easier for neuroscientists to write a NeuroQL query than an SQL query.

Example 1:
Query statement: all neurons that project to Nerve 'Pd N 1'.
(Note: 'Pd N 1' is the name of a nerve)
NeuroQL query:
```
(neuron)[project(v), v.name = 'Pd N 1']
```
SQL query generated by SQL-Generator:
```
SELECT   n.neuronid, n.name, n.synonym
FROM     nb_neuron n, nb_nerve v, nb_project p
WHERE    n.neuronid = p.neuronid AND
        v.nerveid = p.nerveid AND v.name = 'Pd N 1'
```

Example 2:
Query statement: all neurons that have an electrical synapse connection with the neuron "R3-13".
NeuroQL query:
```
(neuron)[connect('R3-13','electrical')]
```
SQL query generated by SQL-Generator:
```
SELECT    n.neuronid, n.name, n.synonym
FROM      nb_neuron n, nb_neuron s, nb_esynapse e_syn
WHERE    n.neuronid =e_syn.presyncell AND
          s = e_syn.postsyncell AND s.name = 'R3-13'
UNION
SELECT    n.neuronid, n.name, n.synonym
FROM      nb_neuron n, nb_neuron s, nb_esynapse e_syn
WHERE    n.neuronid =e_syn.postsyncell AND
          s = e_syn.presyncell AND s.name = 'R3-13'
```

Example 3: This is a complicated query example.
Query statement: all neurons satisfying following conditions: 1) they have molecule '5HT'; 2) they are the post-synaptic cell of some chemical synapse; 3) the pre-synaptic cell of the chemical synapse in condition 2) has a firing pattern 'Irregular with Burst'.
NeuroQL query:
```
(neuron)[hasMolecules('5HT'),chemicalSynapse(s,'post'),
    s.itsFiringPatterns sfp, sfp.name= 'Irregular with
    Burst']
```

SQL query generated by SQL-Generator:
```
SELECT   n.neuronid, n.name, n.synonym
FROM    nb_neuron n, nb_molecule m, nb_hasmolecule hm
```

```
WHERE    n.neuronid=hm.neuronid AND
     m.moleculeid=hm.moleculeid AND m.name='5HT' AND
     n.neuronid IN
        (SELECT  c_syn.postsyncell
         FROM    nb_neuron s, nb_csynapse c_syn
         WHERE s.neuronid = c_syn.presyncell AND
           s.neuronid IN
              (SELECT fp.neuroid
                FROM  nb_firingpattern fp
                WHERE fp.name='Irregular with Burst'))
```

The SQL-Generator is being implemented using Java compiling tools JFlex and JCup. The application is a terminal based interpreter in which the user can enter NeuroQL queries and see responses. The system checks for syntax, generates and executes SQL code and displays the answers to the query.

5 Conclusions and Future Work

In this paper, we propose a domain-specific query language (NeuroQL) specifically for the neuroscience domain. The motivation is from the neuroscientists' desire of having a neuron query language supporting neuroscience concepts and functions so that they can directly interact with their data. Therefore, NeuroQL is designed primarily for neuroinformatics databases users, rather than the database administrators or developers. Based on the initial format and syntax proposed by the neuroscientists, we design NeuroQL as a high-level canonical query language, and implement it as an advanced query tool that can be used on any NeuroDM compatible neuroinformatics database applications. NeuroQL can be translated into most common types of query language such as SQL, OQL, and XQuery. Therefore, it is DBMS independent. NeuroQL integrates some object-oriented features, such as the dot notation, from OQL, and supports most of neuron domain-specific data types, for example, neuron, soma, axon, nerve, ganglion, synapse, molecule, firing-pattern, and so on. These data types are systematically derived from the conceptual neuron data model and mapped to the underlying database schema. This mapping will dynamically update NeuroQL data types whenever the database schema evolves. NeuroQL also defines many advanced neuron domain-specific query operators corresponding to the functions among the objects in neuroscience. The domain-specific data types and query operators are the major constructs of NeuroQL so that NeuroQL query statements are very close to the way, in which the neuroscientists ask questions or make a query in their research.

Writing an common query statement like SQL requires the users to know exactly what the database schema and constraints are, for example, table names, column names, foreign keys, etc. The common solution to this problem is that most of database applications provide users some graphical query interface with some predefined query functions. But these graphical query interfaces are usually application-dependent, and provide only limited and predefined query functions to users. NeuroQL solves this problem by providing users an abstract and succinct conceptual data model diagram. This diagram models the neuron data structure in the database from the neuroscience point of view. Therefore, it is very close to neuron domain knowledge and easy to understand. With the conceptual data model diagram, neuroscientists can write a NeuroQL query in their familiar concepts and operators. Besides, the object-oriented concept, built-in domain-specific data types, and advanced query operators all help neuroscientists master NeuroQL quickly.

Because NeuroQL is designed for the database application users, it does not have the data definition and data update operations as in SQL, such as CREATE, ALTER, UPDATE, and INSERT operations. In the future, we will add some data update functions with restricted access to support neuroscientists to manipulate their data. Another future project is to develop more advanced query operators to facilitate interaction between neuroscientists and the database.

References

1. NeuronBank: Knowledgebase of Identified Neurons & Synaptic Connections. Website: http://www.neuronbank.org
2. The SfN Neuroscience Database Gateway. Website: http://big.sfn.org/NDG/site/
3. Tian, H., Wang, Y., Yang, H., Sunderraman, R., Katz, P.S., Zhu, Y.: A Novel Neuron Data Model with Domain-Specific Query Language. 27th Annual International Conference of the IEEE Engineering In Medicine and Biology Society (2005).
4. Deurse, A.V., Klint, P., Visser, J.: Domain-Specific Languages: an Annotated Bibliography. SIGPLAN Notices, ACM, Vol. 35 (2000) 26-36.
5. Domain-Specific Languages – An Overview. Website: http://compose.labri.fr/documentation/dsl/dsl_overview.php3
6. Bentley, J. L.: Programming Pearls: Little Languages. Communications of the ACM, Vol. 29, (1986) 711-721.
7. Amarall, V., Helmer, S., Meorkottel, G.: A Visual Query Language for HEP Analysis. Conference Proceedings of Nuclear Science Symposium, IEEE (2003).
8. Collberg, C.S.: A Fuzzy Visual Query Language for a Domain-Specific Web Search Engine. Proceedings of the Second International Conference on Diagrammatic Representation and Inference (2002) 176-190.
9. Goodman, N., Rozen, S., Stein, L.: Requeirements for a Deductive Query Language in the Mapbase Genome-Mapping Database. Workshop on Programming with Logic Databases, ILPS (1993) 18-32.
10. Hammer, J., Schneider, M.: The GenAlg Project: Developing a New Integrating Data Model, Language, and Tool for Managing and Querying Genomic Information. SIGMOD Record, ACM, Vol. 33 (2004).
11. Chen, P.P.: The Entity-Relationship Model: Toward a Unified View of Data", ACM Transactions on Database System. Vol. 1 (1976) 9-36.
12. Object Data Management Group. Website: http://www.odmg.org
13. XQuery 1.0. Website: http://www.w3.org/TR/xquery

Querying Semistructured Temporal Data

Carlo Combi[1], Nico Lavarini[2], and Barbara Oliboni[1]

[1] Dipartimento di Informatica, Università degli Studi di Verona
[2] Expert System S.p.A.

Abstract. In this paper we propose the *GEM* Language (*GEL*), a SQL-like query language, which is able to extract information from semistructured temporal databases represented according to the Graphical sEmistructured teMporal (*GEM*) data model.

1 Introduction

In the last years the database research community has devoted some efforts to the development of methods for representing and querying *semistructured data* [1] (i.e., data that have no absolute schema fixed in advance, and whose structure may be irregular or incomplete). In this context, several approaches have been proposed, in which labeled graphs are used to represent semistructured data [9,11]. Recently, it has been recognized and emphasized that time is an important aspect to consider also in the semistructured data context; thus, the problem of representing and querying changes in semistructured data has been considered in the database research field and some temporal data models, based on labeled graphs [5,6,7], have been studied.

In this work, we consider the Graphical sEmistructured teMporal (*GEM*) data model [6], which is general enough to include the main features of semistructured data representation. GEM allows one to model either valid or transaction times: the *valid time* (VT) of a fact is the time when the fact is true in the modeled reality, whereas the *transaction time* (TT) of a fact is the time when the fact is current in the database and may be retrieved [10].

In this paper we propose the *GEM* Language (*GEL*), a SQL-like query language, which is able to extract information from semistructured temporal databases represented by means of the *GEM* data model. *GEL* is a language designed for semistructured data and, similarly to Lorel [2], can be seen as an extension of OQL [4]. In particular, the most important features which add some novelty to *GEL*, with respect to the other main proposal, namely Chorel [5], are the following: we allow for querying databases which manage either valid time — and we will focus on it in the rest of the paper — or transaction time, while most of the others only allow for managing transaction time; we can exploit the generality of the *GEM* model, and thus build and query about general relationships between objects: it provides expressive power both to the model and to the language, without constraining the database to be tree-shaped and to use just the containment relationship; we introduce suitable temporal predicates and specific clauses and keywords for allowing the user to manage temporal aspects of data.

T. Grust et al. (Eds.): EDBT 2006 Workshops, LNCS 4254, pp. 625–636, 2006.

2 Related Work

In [2], the authors propose the *Lorel* query language, a semistructured query language based on the Object Exchange Model (OEM) [11]. OEM is a simple graph-based data model, with objects as nodes and object-subobject relationships represented as labeled arcs. Nodes are not labeled, labels are represented only on the edges and represent the node the edge point to. In the OEM data model each entity is represented by means of an object with an *oid* (*object identifier*). Lorel queries are intuitive, based on a syntax similar to that of the statement `SELECT FROM WHERE` of OQL [4], and use *Path Expressions.* A path expression represents a path on the graph, and thus it identifies the objects composing the path itself.

Chorel (*Change Lorel*) [5] is a query language for semistructured temporal data and is an extension of the Lorel query language. The Chorel query language is based on the *DOEM* (*Delta-OEM*) [5] data model, which is a temporal extension of OEM. Change operations (i.e., node insertion, update of node values, addition and removal of labeled arcs) are represented in DOEM by using *annotations* on nodes and arcs of an OEM graph for representing the history. Intuitively, annotations are the representation of the history of nodes and edges as it is recorded in the database: indeed, this proposal takes (implicitly) into account the *transaction time* dimension. DOEM and Chorel are implemented by means of a method that encodes DOEM databases as OEM databases and translates Chorel queries into equivalent Lorel [2] queries over the OEM encoding. Chorel queries are similar to Lorel queries, and can contain *annotation expressions.* For example, the query

```
SELECT Guide.<add>restaurant;
```

requires the restaurants having an `add` annotation, i.e., those restaurants which have been added to the database after its creation.

Chorel is a very flexible and powerful language, but is limited by the data model it is based on. As an example, neither OEM nor DOEM allow for the representation of general relationships: they represent only the containment relationship.

In [14], the authors extend the XPath [13] data model and query language to include valid time. In particular, they extend XPath's data model by adding to each node a list of disjoint intervals or instants representing valid time, and impose that the valid time of a node is constrained to be a subset of the valid time of a node's parent. Moreover, a valid-time axis is added to the query language to retrieve nodes according a valid time view. The valid-time axis of a node contains the valid-time information of the node itself. The main focus of [14] is the extension of the XPath data model to represent valid time, and thus the authors do not introduce any extension of XPath with temporal predicates and aggregates.

In [8], the author presents an extension of XPath to support transaction time. The proposed extension allows the representation of the history of an XML document as a sequence of XML documents representing the versions of the considered XML document. According to the data model extension, the author extends the query language to query the transaction time. At this aim several new axes, node tests, and temporal constructs are added.

3 Representing Temporal Semistructured Data

In this work, we suppose to represent temporal semistructured data by means of the Graphical sEmistructured teMporal data model (*GEM*), which represents semistructured temporal data by means of rooted, connected, directed, labeled graphs, where the temporal dimension is explicitly reported on node and edge labels and is described as an interval. *GEM* allows the database designer to model either transaction or valid times, by properly defining suitable constraints [6].

In designing *GEL*, we focus on the valid time dimension, as we want to focus on query aspects related to changes in the represented real world. In this section, we briefly describe the data model, by considering an example taken from a medical scenario. Figure 1 shows a *GEM* graph, representing information about the patient David Johnson.

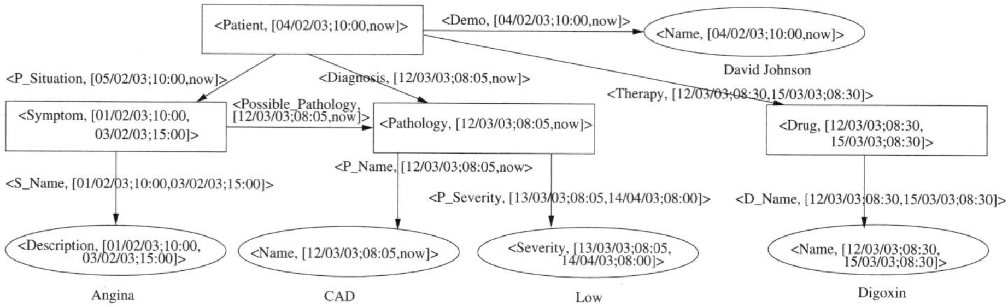

Fig. 1. An example of a *GEM* graph

A *GEM* graph is composed by two kinds of nodes: *complex* and *simple* nodes. The former represent abstract entities, whereas the latter represent primitive values and are leaves. Complex nodes are depicted as rectangles, while simple nodes are depicted as ovals. In the *GEM* data model [6], the symbol `now` is used to define respectively the objects that are valid at the present time in the considered reality, when considering the valid time dimension. Considering the example depicted in Figure 1, the node *Patient* is a complex node, while the node *Name* (child of *Patient*) is a simple node having value *David Johnson*.

In Figure 1, the nodes *Patient* and *Name*, and the edge *Demo* have valid time interval[1] *[04/02/03;10:00,*`now`*]*. The time interval represents that *David Johnson* becomes a *Patient* from 10:00 of 04/02/03, and he is still a *Patient*.

Several constraints and relationships could exist between valid times of nodes and edges: as an example, the valid time of a simple node could be contained in the valid time of the related complex node: indeed, the simple node represents a

[1] In this paper we adopt the format `DD/MM/YY;HH:mm` for timestamps.

property of the related complex node. Figure 1 depicts the simple node *Severity* having a valid time interval contained into the valid time of its related complex node *Pathology*. As a further example, the valid time of the node *Symptom* starts before the valid time of the related node *Patient* (i.e., the symptom appeared before the patient was enrolled), and the valid time of the edge between *Patient* and *Symptom* represents the fact the symptom has been reported after the patient was enrolled.

4 A Query Language for Semistructured Temporal Data

Semistructured (temporal) data may be irregular and incomplete and do not necessarily conform to a fixed schema, thus flexibility in querying is needed. *GEL* is able to manage irregularity by means of flexible statements and allows one to extract and evaluate temporal information. Moreover, *GEL* supports the filtering of query results based on temporal information.

GEL is similar to Lorel [2] and to OQL [4], and has a SQL-like syntax. *GEL* queries are composed through the classical clauses `SELECT`, `FROM`, `WHERE`. The expressions specified in each clause are *path expressions*, i.e., expressions representing paths, which allows one to reach a given object on the *GEM* graph.

In an OEM graph [11], edges between nodes represent only the containment relationship, thus Lorel path expressions are based on this kind of relationship, and use the "dot notation"; in a *GEM* graph, edges represent different relationships and thus in the *GEL* syntax we decided to adopt the object-oriented notation related to methods. For example, the *GEL* path expression `Patient.has(Symptom)` can be read as "the `Patient has` the `Symptom`", and more formally, "the object `Patient` is related, by means of the relationship `has`, to the object `Symptom`".

An example of a *GEL* query is the following:

```
SELECT Patient.Demo(Name)
FROM Patient
WHERE Patient.P_situation(Symptom).S_name(Description) = "Angina"
```

Intuitively, this query requires to extract the `Name` object, identified by the path expression in `SELECT` clause, starting from the object reported in the `FROM` clause, but only if the required object satisfies the constraint imposed in the `WHERE` clause. Temporal clauses `TIME-SLICE` and `MOVING WINDOW` can be used to specify temporal features of required data, as detailed in Section 4.5.

As for the type system, in the semistructured data context flexibility is needed. In order to convert data having different types, *GEL* adopts the Lorel [2] approach, based on *type coercion*.

The `FROM` clause could be left implied in the *GEL* queries. This characteristic, rising from Lorel [2], derives from the fact that usually the value of this clause is the object from which the path expressions, in the `SELECT` clause, start. If the `FROM` clause is not specified, then it is automatically produced from the `SELECT` clause, introducing in the `FROM` clause a path expression for each path expression in the SELECT clause. If the FROM clause is implied, then all the path expressions in the SELECT clause must start with the root of the graph. For example, the query

```
SELECT Patient.Diagnosis(Pathology)
WHERE Patient.Demo(Name) = "Smith"
```

becomes

```
SELECT Patient.Diagnosis(Pathology)
FROM Patient
WHERE Patient.Demo(Name) = "Smith"
```

In this way, the queries can be simplified leaving implied the FROM clause.

4.1 *GEL* Statements

A *GEL* query is based on the SELECT statement, as for OQL and SQL [4,12]. In the same way as OQL and SQL, in *GEL* the expression in the SELECT clause states for the objects of the database which have to be retrieved, the expression in the FROM clause specifies the objects to consider in the search, and the expression in the WHERE clause represents the constraints the retrieved objects have to satisfy. Obviously, like in other syntactically similar languages, when there is no constraint to be used in the WHERE clause, the whole clause itself can be missing. In the following, we will adopt a *current* semantics for the query evaluation [12], i.e., the query will return only the current objects which satisfy the query, for all the cases where time dimensions are not referred to in the query. When variables are used in the query to refer to the temporal dimensions of nodes/edges, the adopted semantics will be the *non-sequenced* one [12]: all the objects of the database, even the non current ones, will be considered for the query evaluation.

The result of a *GEL* query is a *multiset* or *bag* of tuples of attribute values. Each value can be either an atomic value or a node identifier; each attribute is named according to the content of the SELECT clause. It is possible to use set operators (intersect, union, except) to combine different queries (SQL-style).

4.2 Attribute Naming

In *GEL*, attributes can be renamed, as in SQL statements:

```
SELECT P.Diagnosis(Pathology).P_name(Name) as Path_name
FROM Patient P
```

in this case, Path_name is the label of the retrieved object, i.e., in the original graph the pathology name is labeled Name, while in the result it is labeled Path_name.

4.3 Variables

Variables can be used also inside an expression and can have different roles. *GEL* allows one to use variables (i) as *aliases* to avoid to repeat long expressions, and (ii) to identify each element to be instantiated in the query evaluation.

```
SELECT P.P_name(Name) as Path_name
FROM Patient.Diagnosis(Pathology) P
```

In this case, the variable P is used to identify the Pathology object, in order to avoid to refer to it repeating all the expression, as for example:

```
SELECT Patient.Diagnosis(Pathology).P_name(Name) as Path_name
FROM Patient.Diagnosis(Pathology)
```

The variables inside the path allow for retrieving (and for naming) the needed objects, without the need of repeating the common portions of the path for each expression we want to name, as in the following example.

```
SELECT P.Diagnosis(Pathology)<T>.P_name(Name)<N>
FROM Patient P
WHERE T.P_Severity(Severity)="high" AND N="CAD"
```

This query allows one to retrieve the objects T and N, without specifying two similar expressions in the FROM clause; at the same time T and N are used as names for the corresponding objects.

The query without using Intra-path variables should be

```
SELECT P.Diagnosis(Pathology) as T,
       P.Diagnosis(Pathology).P_name(Name) as N
FROM Patient P, P.Diagnosis(Pathology) T,
       P.Diagnosis(Pathology).P_name(Name) N
WHERE T.P_Severity(Severity)="high" AND N="CAD"
```

Variables in the path expressions can be used to force two expressions to be distinct. For example, the query

```
SELECT P.Demo(Name)
FROM Patient P
WHERE P.Diagnosis(Pathology).P_name(Name) = "CAD" AND
      P.Diagnosis(Pathology).P_name(Name) = "Pneumonia"
```

cannot be used to extract the patients who suffer of CAD and Pneumonia, because the two paths in the WHERE clause have a common prefix (in this case the complete path expression) and thus they are instantiated on the same objects. For this reason the previous query does not retrieve the desired result.

It is possible to assign two distinct variables to the two desired results, thus they are instantiated separately on the two paths of the graph, related to two (possibly) different nodes with label Name (if they exist), in the following way:

```
SELECT P.Demo(Name)
FROM Patient P
WHERE P.Diagnosis(Pathology)<X1>.P_name(Name) = "CAD" AND
      P.Diagnosis(Pathology)<X2>.P_name(Name) = "Pneumonia"
```

In this way, the two paths P.Diagnosis(Pathology).P_name(Name), which are considered as distinct by the user, are not forced to be the *same* path.

The variables can be used also to identify a constraint expressing the fact that an object must be reachable on several paths. Indeed a GEM database, as the one in Figure 1, is not expressed as a tree, but as a DAG (Directed Acyclic Graph): in our case, for example, edges `Possible_Pathology` and `Diagnosis` are directed to the same node `Pathology`. In this case, we can use variables to define queries on objects with several ingoing edges:

```
SELECT Patient.Demo(Name)
FROM Patient.Diagnosis(Pathology)<X>,
  Patient.P_Situation(Symptom).Possible_Pathology(Pathology)<X>
```

The previous query asks for the name of patients having a diagnosed pathology and presenting also a connected symptom.

4.4 Wildcards

The path expression power, with respect to objects and paths representation, can be increased by using *wildcards*.

The simplest type of wildcard comes directly from SQL, and is represented by the special characters '`#`'[2] and '`%`'.

As in SQL, these characters can be considered "special" in the *pattern matching* between the query strings and the labels of *GEM* graph elements, as they can be used for comparisons with string literals and also, differently from SQL, as wildcards for the edge labels.

The '`#`' character represents *any character*. The '`%`' character represents a sequence of characters with an arbitrary length. These wildcards can be used in the node and edge names contained in the path expressions, or instead of their names. Moreover, in a path expression, specifying an edge/node, having label "`%`", means "an edge/node with any label". For example, the path expression `Patient.%(Pathology)` means that we are looking for a node with label `Patient`, linked by means of any edge, to a node with label `Pathology`. In the same way, the path expression `Patient.%(%).P_name(Name)` means that we are looking for a node with label `Patient` linked by means of any edge to any node, which has an outgoing edge with label `P_name` ending in a node with label `Name`. Since in the path expressions, nodes and edges are represented in different ways, when a node or an edge is only represented by the wildcard '`%`' we can abbreviate it with an empty string.

Another kind of wildcard allows one to specify some properties of each element in the path expression by using some simple *regular expression*.

It is possible to specify how many times a given edge has to appear in a sequence, and to give a choice between different possible labels. For example the path expression `A.[(B)]?.(C)` means that between the nodes `A` and `C`, either 0 or 1 nodes `B` can exist.

---

[2] The choice of the character '`#`' instead of the traditional SQL '`_`' to mean any character, is based on the fact that '`_`' is often used as word separator in labels for nodes and edges, and thus it is too used to be protected by escape sequences.

The | character, used between two or more elements, allows one the choice of any element in the set. This operator is particularly effective when it is used together with the previous one, in the characters [and]. For example A.[(B)|(C)]*.(D) means that between the nodes A and D, a sequence exists, and is either empty or each element of it is B or C

These regular expressions can be combined with the string wildcards to obtain a powerful and flexible query system. As an example, the following query

```
SELECT S.%(Name)
FROM Symptom S
WHERE S.[Possible_Pathology(Pathology)]+.P_name(Name) = "Hepatitis"
```

extracts the Name of the Symptom (connected by any edge to the node) which is related (to a degree) to Hepatitis. The WHERE clause actually requires the node S to be connected by a path made of Possible_Pathology edges and Pathology nodes to the simple node labeled Hepatitis. The length of the path must be greater than 0, so a path Symptom.p_name(Name) would not make the clause true, while a path Symptom.Possible_Pathology (Pathology).P_name(Name) would do.

The following query

```
SELECT P.Demo(Name)
FROM Patient P
WHERE P.[P_situation(Symptom)|Diagnosis(Pathology)].%(%)="Hemicrania"
```

extracts the name of a Patient for which the symptom or the pathology is connected to any node labeled Hemicrania. In this case what is required is the existence, starting from a Patient node, of the edge P_situation and the node Symptom, or of the edge Diagnosis and the node Pathology. When this condition is met, any edge connected to any simple node labeled Hemicrania would make the clause true.

4.5 Temporal Aspects

Nodes and edges of a *GEM* graph have in the label a time interval representing their validity with respect to a considered time dimension (see Section 3). In particular, in this work, we focus on the valid time dimension, i.e., the time when the fact represented by the object is true in the considered reality.

Temporal Clauses

In the WHERE clause, conditions expressing constraints that must be satisfied by the requested objects are specified. To consider temporal aspects, we introduce the new clauses TIME-SLICE and MOVING WINDOW. Moreover, temporal constraints can be specified in the WHERE clause.

The TIME-SLICE clause allows the user to query along the temporal dimension of nodes and edges, by considering only those nodes and edges having a valid time interval intersecting the specified interval. In general, the result of the query will be composed by nodes (edges), requested in the SELECT clause, satisfying general constraints expressed in the WHERE clause, and having a time interval intersecting the time interval specified in the TIME-SLICE clause.

In the TIME-SLICE clause, the considered time interval can be specified in different ways:

– by the FROM ... TO ... keywords it is possible to require objects intersecting an interval starting at a given instant, and ending at a second given instant. For example, the query requiring the name of the patients considering only the period from 08:00 of 01/02/03 to 08:00 of 01/03/03 is:

```
SELECT Patient.Demo(Name)
FROM Patient
TIME-SLICE FROM 01/02/03;08:00 TO 01/03/03;08:00
```

– by the FROM keyword it is possible to require objects having an interval ending after a given instant. In this case, the ending time is not specified. For example, the query requiring the name of the patients after 08:00 of 01/02/03 is:

```
SELECT Patient.Demo(Name)
FROM Patient
TIME-SLICE FROM 01/02/03;08:00
```

– by the TO keyword it is possible to require objects having an interval starting before a given instant. For example, the query requiring the name of the patients before 08:00 of 01/03/03 is:

```
SELECT Patient.Demo(Name)
FROM Patient
TIME-SLICE TO 01/03/03;08:00
```

The interval constraint expressed by the TIME-SLICE clause can be forced to be either a strict containment, or a left strict containment, or a right strict containment. For example, in the first case, the objects satisfy the requested constraints only if they have a time interval strictly contained in the specified time interval. This kind of containment is expressed by means of the keyword STRICT.

```
SELECT Patient.Demo(Name)
FROM Patient
STRICT TIME-SLICE FROM 01/02/03;08:00 TO 01/03/03;08:00
```

In Figure 2 we suppose that $[t_i, t_j]$ is the time interval of a node (edge) and $[t_h, t_k]$ is the time interval specified in the TIME-SLICE clause, and report examples of time intervals satisfying the temporal constraints expressed in the TIME-SLICE clause with respect to the specified keywords.

The MOVING WINDOW clause allows the user to consider nodes and edges through a (moving) temporal window. The window is specified in the clause and moves along the temporal axis. The general constraints expressed in the other clauses are checked only on the nodes and edges visible through the window, i.e., only on the nodes and edges having a time interval satisfying the temporal constraints expressed in the MOVING WINDOW clause. For example, the following query requires the name of the patients having had both CAD and pneumonia within a period of 40 days:

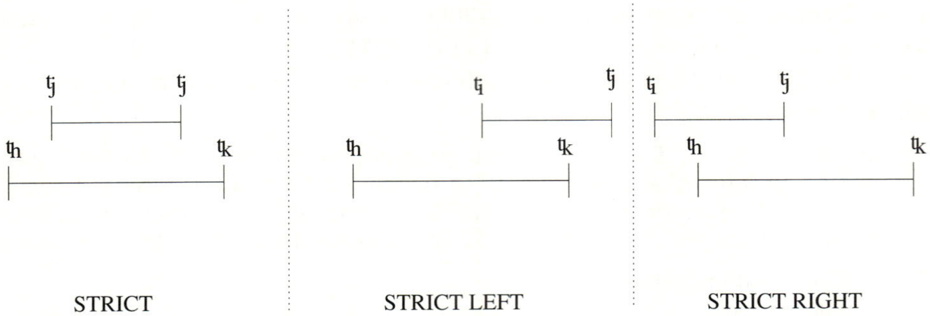

Fig. 2. Examples of time intervals satisfying constraints in the `TIME-SLICE` clauses

```
SELECT P.Demo(Name)
FROM Patient P
WHERE P.Diagnosis(Pathology)<X1>.P_name(Name) = "CAD" AND
      P.Diagnosis(Pathology)<X2>.P_name(Name) = "Pneumonia"
MOVING WINDOW 40 days
```

Temporal Predicates

To compare valid times of different nodes and edges, *GEL* provides the support of standard comparison predicates both for intervals, instants, and for comparing intervals and instants.

Variables can be suitably assigned both to the overall valid time and to the starting and ending instants of the valid time. The syntax is based on the symbol `@`, and is used as in the following example:

```
Patient.Diagnosis@[X1,X2](Pathology).P_name(Name)@[Y1,Y2]
```

This path expression identifies a graph element and extracts the values of the start and end times of the element itself. In particular, it identifies the edge `Diagnosis` and extracts its start and end times, and the node `Name` and extracts its start and end times.

To assign a single variable to the overall valid time, the previous symbol `@` must be used as in the following example:

```
Patient.Diagnosis@[X](Pathology).P_name(Name)@[Y]
```

This path expression identifies a graph element and extracts the interval values of the valid time of the element itself. In particular, it identifies the edge `Diagnosis` and extracts its time interval, and the node `Name` and extracts its time interval.

The variables used to extract the times could be used as selection for the query, as in the following case:

```
SELECT N as PatientName, X1 as DiagStart, X2 as DiagEnd
FROM Patient.Diagnosis@[X1,X2](Pathology).P_name(Name)<N>
```

The result of this query is a set of tuples; each tuple is composed by the string representing the name of the patient, the start time and the end time of the diagnosis related to the patient itself.

This is a case, where the query evaluation considers all the nodes/edges and not only the current ones, with the application of a non-sequenced temporal semantics [12]: the condition in the query may involve the explicit comparison of nodes/edges at different times.

GEL also offers the way to compose temporal predicates on time instants and intervals in the WHERE clause. The temporal predicates can be *point-point predicates*, which compare two time instants, *point-interval predicates*, which compare a time instant with a time interval, and *interval-interval predicates*, which compare two time intervals.

A *point-point predicate* is composed by a variable, a temporal comparison operator, and a time instant, which can be either a variable or a constant. The temporal comparison operators are: =, <>, <, <=, >, >=.

Point-interval predicates verify whether a time instant belongs to a time interval. This time interval is represented with the *GEL* syntax by means of a couple of time instants separated from a comma, and contained in "[" and "]". One or both of these instants can be replaced by a variable, which can be extracted from another element. Thus, a point-interval predicate is composed by a variable, an interval operator, and an interval (variable or constant). The interval operators are in (the instant belongs to the interval) and out of (the instant does not belong to the interval).

Interval-interval predicates verify whether two time intervals satisfy the well known Allen's relations (before, meets, overlaps, ...) [3].

As a final example, let us consider the following query requiring the name of the patients having had CAD either starting or ending during pneumonia and pneumonia holding on an interval overlapping the period from May 23, 2003 8:00 a.m. to July 21, 2003 8:00 a.m.

```
SELECT P.Demo(Name)
FROM Patient P
WHERE P.Diagnosis(Pathology)<X1>@[I1,I2].P_name(Name) = "CAD" AND
      P.Diagnosis(Pathology)<X2>@[T].P_name(Name) = "Pneumonia" AND
      (I1 in T OR I2 in T) AND
      T overlaps [23/05/03;08:00,21/07/03;08:00]
```

5 Conclusions

In this work, we proposed the temporal query language *GEL* for semistructured data, which explicitly considers the temporal dimensions of data and their comparison as well as specific temporal clauses and keywords. As for future work, we plan to focus on some main topics, such as allowing the specification of a (temporal) graph structure for the query result, i.e., providing the language with the closure property, supporting several time semantics for graph-based data models, and extending the query language to deal with both valid and transaction times, to obtain a fully fledged bitemporal query language.

References

1. S. Abiteboul. Querying Semi-Structured Data. In *Proceedings of the International Conference on Database Theory*, volume 1186 of *LNCS*, pages 262–275, 1997.
2. S. Abiteboul, D. Quass, J. McHugh, J. Widom, and J. L. Wiener. The Lorel query language for semistructured data. *International Journal on Digital Libraries*, 1(1):68–88, 1997.
3. J. F. Allen. Towards a general theory of action and time. *Artificial Intelligence*, 23(2):123–154, 1984.
4. R. G. G. Cattell, Douglas K. Barry, Mark Berler, Jeff Eastman, David Jordan, Craig Russell, Olaf Schadow, Torsten Stanienda, , and Fernando Velez. *The Object Data Standard: ODMG 3.0.* Series in Data Management Systems. Morgan Kaufmann Series in Data Management Systems, 2000.
5. S. S. Chawathe, S. Abiteboul, and J. Widom. Managing historical semistructured data. *Theory and Practice of Object Systems*, 5(3):143–162, 1999.
6. C. Combi, B. Oliboni, and E. Quintarelli. A graph-based data model to represent transaction time in semistructured data. In *Proceedings of DEXA 2004*, volume 3180 of *LNCS*, pages 559–568. Springer-Verlag, Berlin, 2004.
7. C. E. Dyreson, M. H. Böhlen, and C. S. Jensen. Capturing and Querying Multiple Aspects of Semistructured Data. In *VLDB'99, Proceedings of 25th International Conference on Very Large Data Bases*, pages 290–301. Morgan Kaufmann, 1999.
8. Curtis E. Dyreson. Observing transaction-time semantics with ttxpath. In *WISE (1)*, pages 193–202, 2001.
9. M. Fernandez, D. Florescu, J. Kang, A. Levy, and D. Suciu. STRUDEL: A web site management system. In *Proceedings of the ACM SIGMOD International Conference on Management of Data*, volume 26,2 of *SIGMOD Record*, pages 549–552. ACM Press, 1997.
10. C. S. Jensen, C. E. Dyreson, and M. H. Bohlen et al. The consensus glossary of temporal database concepts - february 1998 version. In *Temporal Databases: Research and Practice*, volume 1399 of *Lecture Notes in Computer Science*, pages 367–405. Springer, 1998.
11. Y. Papakonstantinou, H. Garcia-Molina, and J. Widom. Object Exchange Across Heterogeneous Information Sources. In *Proceedings of the Eleventh International Conference on Data Engineering*, pages 251–260. IEEE Computer Society, 1995.
12. R. T. Snodgrass. *Developing Time-Oriented Database Applications in SQL.* Series in Data Management Systems. Morgan Kaufmann, 2000.
13. World Wide Web Consortium. XML Path Language (XPath) version 1.0. http://www.w3.org/TR/xpath.html. W3C Reccomendation 16 November 1999.
14. Shuohao Zhang and Curtis E. Dyreson. Adding valid time to xpath. In *Databases in Networked Information*, volume 2544 of *LNCS*, pages 29–42, 2002.

A Query Algebra for XML P2P Databases*

Carlo Sartiani

Dipartimento di Informatica - Università di Pisa
Largo B. Pontecorvo 3 - 56127 - Pisa - Italy
sartiani@di.unipi.it

Abstract. One missing point in the current research about p2p XML databases is the definition of a proper query algebra that addresses p2p-specific issues, such as the dissemination and replication of data, the dynamic nature of the system, and the transient nature of data and replicas.

This paper describes a query algebra for queries over XML p2p databases that provides explicit mechanisms for modeling data dissemination and replication constraints.

1 Introduction

Peer-to-peer (p2p) database systems are usually composed by a *dynamic*, *open-ended* network of *autonomous* or semi-autonomous peers, which contribute data to the system and query data exported by other peers. These systems affirmed as an interesting evolution of distributed and integration systems as well as an attempt to overcome their limitations, namely the heavy administration load, the need for centralization points, and their quite limited scalability, as they blur the distinction between clients and servers, each peer being able to submit service requests and (simultaneously) support other peer requests.

Several *ongoing* projects focus on the the design and the implementation of p2p database systems, mostly for XML data and for supporting Semantic Web applications [1,2,3]. One missing point in the current research about p2p XML databases is the definition of a proper query logical algebra. In this context, a query algebra can be profitably used in the following tasks.

Query distribution. Algebraic expressions are a convenient form into which queries and sub-queries can be translated and packaged, so to be distributed across the network; since algebraic expressions are independent from the actual implementation of the query engine in local nodes and from the local data organization (e.g., indexes, etc), they can be locally translated into highly optimized physical query plans, hence allowing for the best exploitation of local data structures and computational capabilities.

* Carlo Sartiani was funded by the FIRB GRID.IT project and by Microsoft Corporation under the BigTop project.

T. Grust et al. (Eds.): EDBT 2006 Workshops, LNCS 4254, pp. 637–648, 2006.

Distributed query rewriting. As in distributed database systems, algebraic expressions can be manipulated to perform *global-scale* optimizations, such as query unnesting and replica selections, while pushing most of the optimization load to the local peers.

Existing query algebras for XML data, most notably the *official* algebra by W3C [4], have been defined in the context of static and centralized database systems, and cover issues ranging from query result analysis and query type-checking to the rigorous definition of the statical and dynamic semantics of XML query languages. As a consequence, they lack support for three key issues in p2p database systems:

- data are disseminated in multiple peers, which may appear and disappear unpredictably;
- data are usually *replicated* into multiple peers, and, due to the dynamic nature of the system, the replicas have a limited time validity;
- data distribution and replication may change during query execution.

Our contribution. This paper describes a logical query algebra for queries over XML p2p databases. The relevance of the contribution is twofold. First, the algebra provides an abstraction from physical or system-specific issues, hence it can be used for reasoning about p2p query processing (p2p distributed optimization, in particular) without worrying about the peculiar issues of a given system. Second, it provides explicit mechanisms for modeling data dissemination and replication constraints: in particular, the algebra data model incorporates the notion of *locations*, which model peer content, as well as the notion of data freshness; moreover, the algebra provides operators for manipulating locations, and for expressing replication constraints, together with the related rewriting rules.

The proposed query algebra supports a relevant fragment of the XQuery query language [5] (FLWR queries with free nesting), and provides corresponding rewriting rules.

Paper outline. The paper is organized as follows. Section 2 identifies some requirements for a p2p logical query algebra. Section 3, then, describes the algebra data model and operators. Next, Section 4 discusses rewriting rules that can be applied to algebraic expressions. Section 5, then, illustrates some related works. Section 6 concludes.

2 Requirements for a p2p Query Algebra

The design of the proposed query algebra has been guided by three main requirements that emerge in XML p2p databases (in addition to the obvious requirement of supporting queries on XML data). These requirements are discussed below.

Data dissemination. Since data are dispersed on multiple peers, the algebra should model the notion of peer as well as the distribution of data into peers. Hence, the data model should not be limited to represent XML trees, but also peers with their content. A clear benefit of having explicit peer information inside algebraic expressions is the ability to support routing decisions taken at both the global and the local level.

Data replication. To increase the robustness of p2p systems as well as their performance, data are usually replicated in high-speed/high-capacity peers. As a consequence, information about replicas (who is replicating what) should be part of the algebraic vision of the database, i.e., the data model should record both the data provenance and the data replication. Moreover, since replicas in a p2p context are usually not up-to-date (2PL/2PC synchronization protocols are too restrictive for this setting), replica information should be enhanced with details about the validity of these replicas, e.g., the period of time during which a replica can be *safely* used in place of the original data.

Data freshness. Peer-to-peer database systems are chaotic systems, where some data are very frequently updated and others remain untouched for a long period of time. This chaotic nature, together with the presence of loosely synchronized replicas, makes important the explicit representation of data freshness information into algebraic expressions. This allows for the support of queries where the user can choose between *fresh* data, at the price of a potentially higher evaluation cost, and *older* data, potentially not up-to-date, retrieved much more quickly.

3 Query Algebra

The proposed algebra is based on that of [6]. The most important extensions concern the representation of peer contents and replicas, the introduction of a *data freshness* notion, as well as algebraic operators for manipulating them.

For reasons of space, we focus here on the description of new operators and refer the reader to [6] for more detail about the others.

3.1 Data Model and Term Language

The query algebra represents XML data as unordered forests of node-labeled trees. According to the term grammar shown in Fig. 1, each tree node (n) has a unique *object identifier* (oid) that can be accessed by the special-purpose function *oid*; an algebraic support operator ν is used to generate new oids and to refresh existing ones. Furthermore, each node is augmented with the indication of the hosting peer (*location* in the following) as well as with a freshness parameter fr, which indicates when the last update on the node was performed ($\perp$ indicates that the freshness is undefined, and it is necessary to ensure the closeness of the model).

The label, the location, and the freshness of a node can be accessed by means of the auxiliary functions *label*, *loc*, and $freshness$, which are used thorough

$$
\begin{array}{ll}
t ::= t_1, \ldots, t_n \mid n[t] \mid n & \text{trees} \\
n ::= (oid, loc, fr)label & \text{nodes} \\
loc : (dbname \rightarrow t, (dbname, loc) \rightarrow t) & \text{locations} \\
\text{where } label \in \Sigma^*,\ fr \in \mathbb{N} \cup \{\perp\}, \text{ and} & \\
loc^1 \text{ and } loc^2 \text{ are partial functions.} &
\end{array}
$$

Fig. 1. Term grammar

the whole algebra. For the sake of simplicity, we assume that peers perform leaf updates only (deletions, insertions, and value changes), hence the model satisfies the following parent/child freshness constraint.

Property 1 (Structural freshness constraint). Given a data tree t, it holds that:

$$t = n[t_1] \Rightarrow freshness(n) \leqslant freshness(t_1)$$
$$t = n[t_1, \ldots, t_k] \Rightarrow freshness(n) \leqslant min_i freshness(t_i)$$

Locations model the content of peers, hence they are represented as a pair of partial functions: the first function (loc^1) returns, for each database identifier, the trees contributed to the database by the given peer, if any; the second function (loc^2), instead, describes the replication services offered by a given peer, i.e., it returns, for each database identifier and location, the replicated trees for such database and location, if any. Replicas are further described by a (distributed) set *replicas*, which contains dynamic replication constraints. A replication constraint has the form $(loc_1, loc_2, db, \delta_1, \delta_2)$, and it states that loc_2 replicates the content of loc_1 for the database db from time δ_1 to time δ_2 (δ_2 may assume the special value ∞, which indicates that the replica is always kept up to date); given the dynamic nature of the system, we expect replication constraints to evolve over time.

Location content can be accessed through the function *content*, as shown below:

$$content(loc) = \bigcup_{id} loc^1(id)$$
$$AllLocs(id) = \{loc \mid loc^1(id) \neq \emptyset\}$$

The set of locations containing data relevant for a given database db is returned by the function *AllLocs*. The way *AllLocs* is computed and updated goes far beyond the scope of this paper, as it depends on the physical organization of the system; we only assume that the system will provide a set supposed to comprise an exhaustive list of locations containing relevant data. As usual in p2p systems, we also expect this set to be incomplete or even incorrect. The same considerations apply to *replicas*.

3.2 Global Time

For the sake of supporting freshness parameters, the data model has a universal constant τ, which denotes the current global time in the system. The hypothesis of the existence of a global time, shared by all peers in the network, even though unrealistic, is not restrictive and does not affect the well-foundness of the algebra. Indeed, as shown in [2], query results are usually incomplete in p2p systems, and their incompleteness implies, in many cases, their incorrectness, so the assumption of the existence of a universal shared time does not significantly affect the quality of query results.

To support dynamic replication constraints, we assume that each query has two time parameters: the query issuing time τ', and the maximum replica time $\delta_{\tau'}$, which indicates that replication constraints of the form $(loc_1, loc_2, db, \delta_1, \delta_2)$ with $\delta_2 \geqslant \tau' - \delta_{\tau'}$ can be considered during query compilation.

3.3 *Env* Structures

Most algebraic operators manipulate unordered sequences of tuples, each tuple containing the variable bindings collected during query evaluation. These sequences (called *Env* structures as they mimic an environment) allow one to define algebraic operators that manipulate sequences of tuples, instead of trees; hence, common optimization and execution strategies (which are based on tuples rather than trees) can be easily adapted to XML.

Tuples in a given *Env* structure are *flat*, hence they cannot be nested one another. Each variable binding associates a variable to a collection, possibly a singleton, of node identifiers.

To ensure the closure of the algebra, intermediate structures are themselves represented as node-labeled trees conforming to the algebra data model; this kind of representation also allows one to apply useful optimization properties to border operators.

3.4 *path* and *return*

path and *return* represent the interface between XML data and intermediate *Env* structures. They allow for creating *Env* structures from XML trees (*path*) and for creating new documents from existing *Env* structures.

path. The main task of the *path* operator is to extract information from the database, and to build variable bindings. The way information is extracted is described by an *input filter*; a filter is a tree, describing the paths to follow into the database (and the way to traverse these paths), the variables to bind and the binding style, as well as the way to combine results coming from different paths. Input filters, hence, are just a way to describe query twigs, according to the grammar shown in Table 3.1.

A simple filter $(op, var, binder)label[F]$ tells the *path* operator a) to traverse the current context by using the navigational operator *op*, b) to select those elements or attributes having label *label*, c) to perform the binding expressed by *var* and *binder*, and d) to continue the evaluation by using the nested filter F.

An input filter fully describes the behavior of its enclosing *path* operator. In addition to an input filter, the *path* takes as input a data model instance, that is browsed according to the specification given by the input filter; hence, a *path* operator has the syntax $path_F(t)$, where F is the input filter and t the data

Table 3.1. Input filters grammar

$F ::= F_1, \ldots, F_n$	conjunctive filters	$op \in \{/, //, \_\}$	navigational axes
$\mid F_1 \vee \ldots \vee F_n$	disjunctive filters	$var \in String \cup \{\_\}$	variable names
$\mid (op, var, binder) label[F]$	simple input filter	$binder \in \{\_, in, =\}$	binders
$\mid \emptyset$	empty filter		

model instance. The result of the evaluation of a *path* operator is a sequence of tuples containing the variable bindings described in the filter. The following examples show the behavior of *path*.

Example 1. Consider a real-estate p2p market database, and consider the following query fragment.

```
for $b in input()//building,
    $d in $b/desc,
```

This clause retrieves descriptions for buildings at any level in the database. Assuming that the query plan generation layer found only one relevant location loc_1, the clause can be translated into the following *path* operation:

$path_{(//,\$b,in)building[(/,\$d,in)desc[\emptyset]]}(loc_1^1(db1))$

which returns the following *Env* structure:

$\$b : o_1$	$\$d : o_{11}$
$\$b : o_1$	$\$d : o_{12}$
$\$b : o_3$	$\$d : o_{24}$
...	...

Example 2. Consider the following XQuery fragment:

```
for $b in input()//building
let $d_list := $b/desc,
```

This query retrieves buildings and building descriptions in the database; unlike the previous example, descriptions of the same building are grouped together in *$d_list*. This query fragment can be expressed by the following *path* operation:

$path_{(//,\$b,in)building[(/,\$d\_list,=)desc[\emptyset]]}(loc_1^1(db1))$

which returns the following *Env* structure:

$\$b : o_1$	$\$d\_list : \{o_{11}, o_{12}, \ldots\}$
$\$b : o_3$	$\$d\_list : \{o_{24}, \ldots\}$

As shown by the filter grammar, multiple input filters can be combined to form more complex filters. The algebra allows filters to be combined in a *conjunctive* way, or in a *disjunctive* way. In the first case, the *Env* structures built by simple filters are joined together, hence imposing a product semantics; in the second case, partial results are combined by using an *outer union* operation. Therefore, disjunctive filters can be used to map occurrences of $op : union$ inside paths into input filters, as well as more sophisticated queries; the use of outer union ensures that the resulting *Env* has a uniform structure, i.e., all binding tuples have the same fields.

return. While the *path* operator extracts information from existing XML documents, the *return* operator uses the variable bindings of an *Env* to produce new XML documents. *return* takes as input an *Env* structure and an *output filter*, i.e., a skeleton of the XML document being produced, and returns a data model instance (i.e., a well-formed XML document) conforming to the filter. This instance is built up by filling the XML skeleton with variable values taken from the *Env* structure: this substitution is performed once per each tuple contained in the *Env*, hence producing one skeleton instance per tuple.

Output filters satisfy the following grammar:

$$\begin{array}{l}(1)\ OF ::= OF_1, \ldots, OF_n \quad | \quad n[OF] \quad | \quad val \\ (2)\ val ::= n \quad | \quad var \quad | \quad \nu var\end{array}$$

An output filter may be an *element constructor* ($n[OF]$), which produces an element tagged n and whose content is given by OF, a value constructor (n), or a combination of output filters ($OF_1, \ldots, OF_n$). The production describing values (val) needs further comments. The algebra offers two ways to publish information contained in an *Env* structure: by copy (νvar) and by reference (var). Referenced elements are published as they are in query results; in particular, their object ids are not changed, as well as their location and freshness information. Copied elements, instead, are published with *fresh* oids, while their location and freshness information remains untouched. Finally, newly created elements ($OF ::= n[OF]$) and values ($val ::= n$) are managed as copied nodes with undefined freshness, so they have fresh oids, empty location, and are marked with the undefined time information ($\perp$).[1]

The following example shows the use of the *return* operator.

Example 3. Consider the following XQuery query:

```
for $b in input()//building,
    $d in $b/desc,
    $p in $b/price
return <entry> {$d, $p} </entry>
```

This query returns the description and the price of each building in the market, and it can be represented by the following algebraic expression:

$$\begin{array}{l} return_{entry[\nu\$d,\nu\$p]}(\\ \quad path_{(//,\$b,in)building[(/,\$d,in)desc[\emptyset],(/,\$p,in)price[\emptyset]]}(\\ \quad\quad loc_1^1(db1))) \end{array}$$

[1] Any freshness comparison w.r.t $\perp$ is true, so the freshness structural constraint still holds.

3.5 Operators on Locations

Operators on locations are crucial for retrieving data coming from multiple peers, and for exploiting, if necessary, replicas of the content of some location. The query algebra offers two location operators: *LocUnion* and *Choice*.

LocUnion ($\bullet$) takes as input two locations loc_1 and loc_2, and it returns a new location obtained by uniting the content and the replica functions of the arguments, as shown in Table 3.2.

Table 3.2. Formal definition of *LocUnion*

$$\begin{aligned}
loc_1 \bullet loc_2 &= ((loc_1^1 \oplus loc_2^1), (loc_1^2 \cup loc_2^2)) \\
loc_1^1 \oplus loc_2^1 &= \{(dbname, t) \mid (dbname, t) \in loc_1^1 \wedge \nexists t' : (dbname, t') \in loc_2^1\} \cup \\
&\quad \{(dbname, t) \mid (dbname, t) \in loc_2^1 \wedge \nexists t' : (dbname, t') \in loc_1^1\} \cup \\
&\quad \{(dbname, (t_1, t_2)) \mid (dbname, t_1) \in loc_1^1 \wedge (dbname, t_2) \in loc_2^1\}
\end{aligned}$$

LocUnion is primarily used for expressing queries retrieving data from multiple peers. The following example shows the use of *LocUnion*.

Example 4. Consider our real-estate market database, and assume that new locations (loc_{11}, loc_{13}, and loc_{17}) contribute data about buildings. Then, the query of Example 3 can be expressed by the following algebraic expression:

$$\begin{aligned}
&return_{entry[\nu\$d,\nu\$p]}(\\
&\quad path_{(//,\$b,in)building[(/,\$d,in)desc[\emptyset],(/,\$p,in)price[\emptyset]]}(\\
&\qquad (\bullet_{i=1,11,13,17} loc_i)^1(db1)))
\end{aligned}$$

As shown in Section 4.1, *LocUnion* operations can be extruded from *path* operators, hence the previous expression can be rewritten as follows:

$$\begin{aligned}
&return_{entry[\nu\$d,\nu\$p]}(\cup_{i=1,11,13,17} \\
&\quad path_{(//,\$b,in)building[(/,\$d,in)desc[\emptyset],(/,\$p,in)price[\emptyset]]}(\\
&\qquad loc_i^1(db1)))
\end{aligned}$$

The *Choice* ($|_{db}^{\delta}$) operator is a convenient way to encapsulate replication constraints into query plans. $loc_1 \,|_{db}^{\delta}\, loc_2$ indicates that loc_2 replicates $loc_1^1(db)$ until time δ, so, if permitted, it can serve requests for data in $loc_1^1(db)$. As a consequence, $loc_1 \,|_{db}^{\delta}\, loc_2$ can be rewritten (in *path* operations concerning *db*) as loc_1 or as $loc_2^2(loc_1)$.

The following example shows the use of *Choice*.

Example 5. Consider the query of the previous example, and assume that $loc_{11}(db1)$ is replicated at loc_{17} till time δ; furthermore, assume that the query was submitted at time τ' so that $\tau' < \delta$. Then, the query can be expressed by the following algebraic expression:

$$\begin{aligned}
&return_{entry[\nu\$d,\nu\$p]}(\\
&\quad path_{(//,\$b,in)building[(/,\$d,in)desc[\emptyset],(/,\$p,in)price[\emptyset]]}(\\
&\qquad (loc_1 \bullet (loc_{11} \,|_{db1}^{\delta}\, loc_{17}) \bullet loc_{13} \bullet loc_{17})^1(db1)))
\end{aligned}$$

4 Optimization Properties

Four main classes of algebraic rewriting rules can be applied to the query algebra. The first class contains *classical* equivalences inherited from relational and OO algebras (e.g., *push-down* of *Selection* operations and commutativity of joins); the second class consists of path decomposition rules, which allows the query optimizer to break complex input filters into simpler ones; the third class contains equivalences used for unnesting nested queries; the last class, finally, contains rewriting rules for location operators. For the sake of brevity, we focus here on location rewritings (the reader can see [6] for a detailed list of equivalence rules for the core of this algebra).

4.1 Location Rewriting Rules

Operators on locations represent a crucial fragment of a query algebra for p2p databases; as a consequence, rules for simplifying location operators as well as for splitting complex location unions are a *must*. The algebra offers three main rewriting rules for location operators: extrusion of *LocUnion* operations from *path* operations; simplification of *Choice* operators; and introduction of *Choice* operations.

Proposition 1 (Extrusion of *LocUnion* operations)
Given a database db disseminated on loc_1 and loc_2, it holds that:

$$path_f((loc_1 \bullet loc_2)^1(db)) = path_f((loc_1)^1(db)) \cup path_f((loc_2)^1(db))$$

This property states that *LocUnion* operations inside path operations can be split and distributed across the query; this, in turn, allows the system to more easily decompose a query in single-location subqueries.

Proposition 2 (Rewriting of location choices)
Given a database db hosted at loc_1 and replicated at loc_2, it holds that:

$$path_f((loc_1 \,|^{\delta}_{db}\, loc_2)^1(db)) = path_f(loc_1^1(db))$$
$$path_f((loc_1 \,|^{\delta}_{db}\, loc_2)^1(db)) = path_f(loc_2^2(loc_1)(db))$$

This property shows how a *Choice* operation inside a *path* operation can be rewritten; we expect that this rewriting will be guided by additional information about network conditions, peer computing power, etc.

Proposition 3 (Choice introduction)
Given a database db, if $(loc_1, loc_2, db, \delta_1, \delta_2) \in replicas$, and $\delta_2 \geqslant \tau' - \delta_{\tau'}$, then $loc_1^1(db) \rightarrow (loc_1 \,|^{\delta_2}_{db}\, loc_2)^1(db)$

Corollary 1 (Guarded choice introduction). *Given a database db disseminated on loc_1, ..., loc_m, if $(loc_i, loc_j, db, \delta_1, \delta_2) \in replicas$, and $\delta_2 \geqslant \tau' - \delta_{\tau'}$, then*

$$path_f((loc_1 \bullet loc_i)^1(db)) \rightarrow path_f((loc_1 \bullet (loc_i \,|^{\delta_2}_{db}\, loc_j))^1(db))$$

These properties back the introduction of *Choice* operations in query plans.

The following example illustrates how these properties can be used during query compilation.

Example 6. Consider the real-estate database of Section 3, and assume that peer p_i submits the query of Example 4 to the system (we report it below for the sake of clarity).

```
for $b in input()//building,
    $d in $b/desc,
    $p in $b/price
return <entry> {$d, $p} </entry>
```

Assuming, as in Example 4, that relevant data for the query are hosted at locations loc_1, loc_{11}, loc_{13}, and loc_{17}, then the system compiles this query into the following algebraic expression.

$$\begin{array}{l} return_{entry[\nu\$d,\nu\$p]}(\\ \quad path_{(//,\$b,in)building[(/,\$d,in)desc[\emptyset],(/,\$p,in)price[\emptyset]]}(\\ \quad\quad (\bullet_{i=1,11,13,17} loc_i)^1(db1))) \end{array}$$

In the case that no suitable replicas are available, the system can just apply Proposition 1, so to push down *path* operations and to maximize the query fragments to be delivered to remote peers, as shown below.

$$\begin{array}{l} return_{entry[\nu\$d,\nu\$p]}(\cup_{i=1,11,13,17} \\ \quad path_{(//,\$b,in)building[(/,\$d,in)desc[\emptyset],(/,\$p,in)price[\emptyset]]}(\\ \quad\quad loc_i^1(db1))) \end{array}$$

Assume now that *replicas* contains two relevant replication constraints for the query: $(loc_{11}, loc_1, db1, \tau_1, \tau_2)$ and $(loc_{11}, loc_{24}, db1, \tau_3, \tau_4)$. If loc_{24} models a very reliable and fast peer, the system may decide to apply Corollary 1 and Proposition 2, so to speed up query execution, as shown below.

$$\begin{array}{l} return_{entry[\nu\$d,\nu\$p]}(\\ \quad path_{(//,\$b,in)building[(/,\$d,in)desc[\emptyset],(/,\$p,in)price[\emptyset]]}(loc_1^1(db1))\cup \\ \quad path_{(//,\$b,in)building[(/,\$d,in)desc[\emptyset],(/,\$p,in)price[\emptyset]]}(loc_{24}^2(loc_{11})(db1))\cup \\ \quad path_{(//,\$b,in)building[(/,\$d,in)desc[\emptyset],(/,\$p,in)price[\emptyset]]}(loc_{13}^1(db1))\cup \\ \quad path_{(//,\$b,in)building[(/,\$d,in)desc[\emptyset],(/,\$p,in)price[\emptyset]]}(loc_{17}^1(db1))) \end{array}$$

Alternatively, the system may decide, on the basis of network traffic conditions and other parameters, to exploit the first replication constraint, so to concentrate the query load to the peer corresponding to loc_1. In this case, the application of Corollary 1 and Proposition 2 leads to the following algebraic expression.

$$\begin{array}{l} return_{entry[\nu\$d,\nu\$p]}(\\ \quad path_{(//,\$b,in)building[(/,\$d,in)desc[\emptyset],(/,\$p,in)price[\emptyset]]}(loc_1^1(db1))\cup \\ \quad path_{(//,\$b,in)building[(/,\$d,in)desc[\emptyset],(/,\$p,in)price[\emptyset]]}(loc_1^2(loc_{11})(db1))\cup \\ \quad path_{(//,\$b,in)building[(/,\$d,in)desc[\emptyset],(/,\$p,in)price[\emptyset]]}(loc_{13}^1(db1))\cup \\ \quad path_{(//,\$b,in)building[(/,\$d,in)desc[\emptyset],(/,\$p,in)price[\emptyset]]}(loc_{17}^1(db1))) \end{array}$$

It should be noted that, unlike Proposition 1, which is always applicable, the application of Corollary 1 and Proposition 2 is subject to conditions that may change over time, hence, after a certain period of time, the algebraic expressions reported above may become invalid.

5 Related Works

Current research about the algebraic treatment of queries in p2p database systems mostly focuses on *physical* query algebras for relational databases. [7] presents a physical query algebra for a DHT-based relational p2p database system. This algebra provides low-level operators for supporting relational queries on a DHT, which cannot be generalized to other contexts. In particular, no abstract notions of locations and replicas are provided, and all operators strictly depend on the presence of a DHT.

In [8] a more sophisticated approach is described. Queries are posed against *virtual* tables by means of a standard relational algebra, and are then translated into relational *concrete* queries over *local* and *distributed* tables; concrete queries are expressed through a concrete query algebra, which contains operators inspired by traditional distributed systems. Distributed tables are attached to peers, so they can be used to implicitly denote locations. While this approach is more general than that of [7], the lack of explicit modeling of locations and replicas is a significant difference with our algebra.

The explicit modeling of locations is not new. For instance, [9] contains a formalization of *static* p2p systems in terms π-calculus expressions. The main limitation of the work is the lack of support for dynamic topologies.

6 Conclusions

This paper describes a query algebra for XML p2p database systems. The algebra features mechanisms for dealing with p2p-specific issues, namely the dissemination and replication of data across an unstable network, as well as for incorporating replication constraints into query plans.

Even though designed for a specific class of systems (XML databases), the key ideas of the proposed algebra can be generalized to p2p systems with different data models.

The proposed algebra is now being used in the XPeer [10] p2p system: XPeer is a scalable and self-organizing p2p system for XML data designed for resource discovery applications.

The proposed algebra represents the first step in the development of a p2p query optimization systems. Its definition will be the starting point for the further investigation of suitable rewriting rules and for the design of a proper query optimizer.

References

1. Halevy, A.Y., Ives, Z.G., Mork, P., Tatarinov, I.: Piazza: data management infrastructure for semantic web applications. In: Proceedings of the Twelfth International World Wide Web Conference, WWW2003, Budapest, Hungary, 20-24 May 2003, ACM (2003) 556–567

2. Papadimos, V., Maier, D., Tufte, K.: Distributed Query Processing and Catalogs for Peer-to-Peer Systems. In: CIDR 2003, First Biennial Conference on Innovative Data Systems Research, Asilomar, CA, USA, January 5-8, 2003. (2003)
3. Abiteboul, S., Benjelloun, O., Manolescu, I., Milo, T., Weber, R.: Active XML: Peer-to-Peer Data and Web Services Integration. In: 28th International Conference on Very Large Data Bases (VLDB 2002), Hong Kong, China, August 20-23, 2002, Proceedings, Morgan Kaufmann (2002) 1087–1090
4. Draper, D., Fankhauser, P., Fernandez, M., Malhotra, A., Rose, K., Rys, M., Siméon, J., Wadler, P.: XQuery 1.0 and XPath 2.0 Formal Semantics. Technical report, World Wide Web Consortium (2005) W3C Working Draft.
5. Boag, S., Chamberlin, D., Fernandez, M.F., Florescu, D., Robie, J., Siméon, J.: XQuery 1.0: An XML Query Language. Technical report, World Wide Web Consortium (2005) W3C Candidate Recommendation.
6. Sartiani, C., Albano, A.: Yet Another Query Algebra For XML Data. In Nascimento, M.A., Özsu, M.T., Zaïane, O., eds.: Proceedings of the 6th International Database Engineering and Applications Symposium (IDEAS 2002), Edmonton, Canada, July 17-19, 2002. (2002)
7. Sattler, K.U., Rösch, P., Buchmann, E., Böhm, K.: A physical query algebra for dht-based p2p systems. In: Proceedings of 6th Workshop on Distributed Data and Structures (WDAS'2004), Lausanne, Switzerland, July 8-9, 2004. (2004)
8. Boncz, P., Treijtel, C.: Ambientdb: relational query processing in a p2p network. Technical report, CWI - INS (2003)
9. Gardner, P., Maffeis, S.: Modelling dynamic web data. In Lausen, G., Suciu, D., eds.: DBPL. Volume 2921 of Lecture Notes in Computer Science., Springer (2003) 130–146
10. Sartiani, C., Ghelli, G., Manghi, P., Conforti, G.: XPeer: A self-organizing XML P2P database system. In: Proceedings of the First EDBT Workshop on P2P and Databases (P2P&DB 2004), 2004. (2004)

Apuama: Combining Intra-query and Inter-query Parallelism in a Database Cluster*

Bernardo Miranda[1], Alexandre A. B. Lima[1,3], Patrick Valduriez[2], and Marta Mattoso[1]

[1] Computer Science Department, COPPE, Federal University of Rio de Janeiro
[2] Atlas Group, INRIA and LINA, University of Nantes – France
[3] School of Engineering and Computer Science, University of Grande Rio – Brazil
{bmiranda, assis, marta}@cos.ufrj.br, Patrick.Valduriez@inria.fr

Abstract. Database clusters provide a cost-effective solutionn for high performance query processing. By using either inter- or intra-query parallelism on replicated data, they can accelerate individual queries and increase throughput. However, there is no database cluster that combines inter- and intra-query parallelism while supporting intensive update transactions. C-JDBC is a successful database cluster that offers inter-query parallelism and controls database replica consistency but cannot accelerate individual heavy-weight queries, typical of OLAP. In this paper, we propose the Apuama Engine, which adds intra-query parallelism to C-JDBC. The result is an open-source package that supports both OLTP and OLAP applications. We validated Apuama on a 32-node cluster running OLAP queries of the TPC-H benchmark on top of PostgreSQL. Our tests show that the Apuama Engine yields super-linear speedup and scale-up in read-only environments. Furthermore, it yields excellent performance under data update operations.

1 Introduction

Competitive organizations typically optimize their business processes using decision support systems (DSS) [9]. A DSS includes On-Line Analytical Processing (OLAP) tools and a data warehouse (DW) capable of efficiently handling large amounts of data [3]. Due to the important role played by DSS, much research has been devoted to provide high performance for OLAP queries.

High performance query processing on data warehouses can be achieved using a relational database management system (DBMS) running on top of a PC cluster. PC clusters can scale to very large configurations [8]. Examples of cluster-aware DBMSs are Oracle RAC 10g [5] and DB2 ICE [6]. However, software licensing, hardware specific requirements or database migration costs may prevent their use by many applications. An alternative approach for high-performance data warehousing using PC clusters is a database cluster [1, 2, 14, 18]. A database cluster (DBC) consists of a set of independent DBMSs (not cluster-aware) distributed over a set of cluster nodes,

* Work partially funded by CNPq, Finep, Capes, Cofecub and ACI "Massive Data" in France.

T. Grust et al. (Eds.): EDBT 2006 Workshops, LNCS 4254, pp. 649 – 661, 2006.

and orchestrated by a middleware, responsible for offering a single external view of the whole system, like a virtual DBMS. Applications need not be modified when database servers are replaced by their cluster counterparts. Their queries are sent to the middleware which provides data distribution transparency. Previous work as PowerDB [1], Leg@net [4], C-JDBC [2] and SmaQ [13] have shown the effectiveness of the DBC approach.

Two kinds of parallelism can be exploited in a DBC for query processing: inter-query parallelism and intra-query parallelism. Inter-query parallelism consists of executing many queries at the same time, each at a different node. Inter-query works fine for On-Line Transactional Processing (OLTP) application support, where queries are usually light-weight. However, OLAP applications typically have heavy-weight queries, i.e., queries that access large amounts of data and perform complex operations, thus taking a long time to be processed. Using only inter-query parallelism is not appropriate for heavy-weight query processing as it does not reduce the processing time of individual queries. In such case, intra-query parallelism is the most adequate solution as shown in [14].

Intra-query parallelism consists of using many nodes to process each single query. In this case, each node addresses only a subset of query data and/or query operations. The main goal is to reduce the execution time of individual heavy-weight queries while improving the overall throughput.

Inter- and intra-query parallelisms can be combined in a DBC implementation. Moreover, a DBC with both kinds of parallelism and support for concurrent data updates can be used in both OLAP and OLTP applications. However, current DBC solutions [1], [4], [2] and [14], exclusively support inter-query for OLTP or intra-query for OLAP applications. First, because current DBC solutions for OLAP applications usually consider that database refresh operations are not controlled by them and takes place on a specific predefined time which the DSS is offline. The second reason is that combining inter- with intra-query parallelism can be conflicting. Intra-query parallelism requires the presence of data subsets which are typically produced by physical database design. When the data is physically partitioned among cluster nodes, inter-query parallel processing becomes very limited, since most queries need to scan all partitions in parallel. Depending on the data partitioning design, a simple OLTP query must be processed by intra-query parallelism and becomes very inefficient. On the other hand, OLAP queries without data partitioning cannot be performed efficiently.

Our goal is to provide a high-performance and low-cost DBC solution that supports OLTP and OLAP workloads. To avoid the problems with physical database partitioning, we adopt dynamic virtual partitioning to a replicated database. We use C-JDBC, an industrial quality open-source DBC solution that offers support for inter-query parallelism and database replica consistency. C-JDBC provides excellent performance for OLTP applications [2] but does not support intra-query parallelism. Thus, we extend C-JDBC with a non-intrusive intra-query solution.

In this paper, we present the Apuama[1] Engine as an extension of C-JDBC. The main goal is to provide an environment to process OLAP queries using intra-query parallelism while keeping the effectiveness of C-JDBC to support OLTP transactions.

[1] *Apuama* means *fast* in Tupi-Guarani, a primitive language of South America.

No source code was changed in C-JDBC. Apuama acts as a connection proxy between C-JDBC and the DBMSs. It does not interfere with the C-JDBC query processing and is only used for OLAP query processing. Unlike all other DBC intra-query solutions, Apuama also provides for database replica consistency during intra-query processing.

To evaluate Apuama, we ran experiments based on the TPC-H benchmark [19] (specific for OLAP applications) on a 32-node cluster using PostgreSQL [16]. Query processing speedup and throughput scalability were measured on experiments with read-only queries and a mix of read-only queries and concurrent data updates. In most cases, Apuama achieves super-linear speedup and scale-up. Since there has been no change to C-JDBC inter-query processing, successful OLTP results are sustained.

The paper is organized as follows. Section 2 introduces the basic concepts for intra-query parallelism in DBC. Section 3 explains intra-query support in Apuama. Section 4 presents the architecture of Apuama as an extension to C-JDBC. Section 5 describes experimental results. Section 6 discusses related work. Section 7 concludes.

2 Intra-query Parallel Processing in DBC

Intra-query parallelism consists of having each query being processed by many nodes in parallel. This can be achieved in different ways. The most frequent solutions are through data parallelism, where the same query is executed against different parts of a partitioned database in parallel. A DBMS that has parallel capabilities usually offers several data partitioning techniques that are used during physical database design. Such DBMS provides transparent access to the partitioned database and has full control over the parallel query execution plan. This is not the case for DBC.

In DBC, independent DBMSs are used by a middleware as "black-box" components. It is up to the middleware to implement and coordinate parallel execution. This means that query execution plans generated by such DBMSs are not parallel. Furthermore, as "black-boxes", they cannot be modified to become aware of the other DBMS and generate parallel plans.

When the database is replicated at all nodes of the DBC, inter-query parallelism is almost straightforward. Any read query can be sent to any node and execute in parallel. On the other hand, to implement intra-query in a DBC, the application database must be partitioned and distributed among the DBC nodes. The use of a replicated database or a partitioned database can also impact on the way the update transactions are processed. For replicated databases, the DBC must send a notification to all replicas in order to complete an update transaction. Using a partitioned database, the update transaction processing is faster because the DBC has to notify a smaller number of nodes. The notification is sent just to the owners of updated tuples. However, physical data partitioning can be complex to design, hard to maintain, and can cause severe data skew. In addition, automatically generating a parallel query execution plan can be quite complex.

An interesting solution to combine inter- and intra-query parallelism is to keep the database replicated and design partitions using *virtual partitioning* (VP) [1]. VP is based on replication and dynamically designs partitions. The basic principle of VP is to take one query, rewrite it as a set of sub-queries "forcing" the execution of each one over a different subset of the table. In the PowerDB DBC [1], this is implemented in a simple way called Simple Virtual Partitioning (SVP) that works as follows. First, the database is fully replicated over all cluster nodes. Then, when a query Q is submitted to a DBC with n nodes, a set of sub-queries $Q_{i=1..n}$ is produced. Each Q_i is formed by the addition of a different range predicate to Q at the where clause. The goal is to make each sub-query to run over a different subset of the data that must be accessed by Q. Then, each sub-query is sent to a different node, where it is executed by the local DBMS. After sub-query execution, the DBC produces the final result based on the partial results of each node. Let us take the following query Q to be executed in a DBC with four nodes:

```
Q: select sum(l_extendedprice) from lineitem        (1)
```

According to SVP, Q would be rewritten as follows:

```
Qi: select sum(l_extendedprice) from lineitem       (2)
    where l_orderkey >= :v1 and l_orderkey < :v2
```

The difference between Q and Q_i is the range predicate "l_orderkey > :*v1* and l_orderkey <= :*v2*". We call *virtual partitioning attribute* (VPA) the attribute chosen to virtually partition the table. The values used for parameters *v1* and *v2* vary from node to node and are computed according to the total range of the VPA values and the number of nodes. Assuming that the interval of values of l_orderkey is [1; 6,000,000] and we have 4 nodes, then, 4 sub-queries must be generated. The intervals covered by each sub-query are the following: Q_1: *v1*=1 and *v2*=1,500,001; Q_2: *v1*=1,500,001 and *v2*=3,000,001; and so on. Although all nodes have a replica of lineitem, VP forces each Q_i to process a different and disjoint subset of lineitem's tuples.

However, this approach does not guarantee that different physical parts of lineitem will be scanned. If the tuples of the added range are scattered along the table storage, all disk pages occupied by the table might be accessed. For SVP to be effective, the tuples of the virtual partition must be physically clustered according to the VPA and there must be an index associated to this attribute, i.e., there must exist a clustered ordered index on lineitem based on l_orderkey. Furthermore, the DBMS optimizer must choose the clustered index to be used in the execution plan.

Query re-writing is not trivial. We base our transformations on some typical query templates from OLAP queries, adopting some hints from [1]. To leverage this complexity we only apply VP on fact tables, which makes it easier to re-write queries with complex joins. Some SQL functions require a more complex query modification. For example, the avg() function of a query must be rewritten in the sub-queries as a sum() function followed by a count() function to address a global average. Still some queries, such as complex nested queries, cannot be transformed. In those cases, intra-query is not explored.

3 Query Processing with Apuama

Apuama is an extension of C-JDBC responsible for providing intra-query parallelism. It is implemented as an external component, without changing C-JDBC. OLTP transactions are processed by C-JDBC without any change. In this section we explain how OLAP queries are handled by Apuama through intra-query processing, result composition and update transactions.

Apuama implements intra-query parallelism based on SVP. Query speedup with SVP is DBMS-dependent since the partitioned table must be accessed through a clustered index associated to the partitioning attribute. If, for any reason, the DBMS optimizer chooses a full table scan to execute a sub-query, the virtual partition is ignored and the performance of SVP can be severely hurt. Even though a full table scan can be more efficient for an isolated query execution, in Apuama it is also important trying to keep most of the virtual partition data at the cache. Thus, in order to guarantee effective exclusive access to the virtual partition tuples, Apuama directly interferes in DBMS optimizer choices in order to force index usage. This is done by asking the DBMS to disable full table scans during heavy-weight intra-query processing. This can be done in many popular open-source DBMSs, e.g. MySQL [7] and PostgreSQL.

Apuama disables full scans only before starting to process a query using intra-query parallelism. When the query processing is finished, the original DBMS settings are reestablished. This strategy is not DBMS-independent because the command used to do that is not standard, although it is common knowledge for the most of DBAs. Thus, Apuama must detect which DBMS driver is being used to make DBMS-specific changes on the query execution plan. This information is part of Apuama's metadata and it is set during software installation.

Sub-queries produced by SVP in Apuama are independently processed by each node and their partial results must be combined in order to form the final query result. Apuama uses HSQLDB [10], a fast in-memory DBMS, to perform result composition. This method proved to be very efficient during our experiments. In many experiments, aggregations performed by HSQLDB took no more than one second to be processed even with large partial results involving several columns.

Updates in Apuama are propagated to all nodes in the same order to guarantee consistency among different replicas. The time needed to broadcast updates over all nodes increases according to the number of nodes in the cluster. With full replication, this can impact performance in update-intensive situations. Fortunately, this is not the case for most decision-making environments. Although C-JDBC does not require full replication, we adopted it to maximize speedup through intra-query parallelism. Solutions using the replica freshness techniques [15] are out of the scope of this work.

In order to produce consistent results for heavy-weight queries, Apuama must guarantee that, before beginning to process a query using intra-query parallelism, all node replicas are consistent with each other. Distributed updates are performed by C-JDBC, which is not aware of the existence of sub-queries generated by SVP. With C-JDBC only, we can assure that updates are executed in the same order in all nodes but we cannot assure that updates and SVP sub-queries are executed in the same order. Different execution threads, executing update and read-only operations, may be scheduled in different orders by the operating systems of different nodes. Therefore, Apuama provides a blocking mechanism to avoid performing updates along SVP sub-queries of the same query. Apuama has a transaction counter for each node. When a query must be processed with SVP, Apuama waits until a consistent state is reached by all nodes. This happens when all transaction counters are equal. If new update transactions arrive, they are blocked. Then, Apuama starts executing SVP, dispatching all sub-queries to their respective nodes. When all sub-queries are sent and started by the DBMSs, update transactions are unblocked and can be executed. The transaction isolation provided by the DBMS makes it possible to have the updates executed before each sub-query finishes, thereby improving throughput.

4 Apuama Architecture

This section describes the Apuama architecture and its integration within C-JDBC. Fig. 1(a) shows our architecture that contains only C-JDBC components relevant to our explanation and the Apuama Engine extension. The main purpose of C-JDBC is to offer transparent access to a cluster of databases without any modification on the client application. The unique requirement is to use a JDBC driver [11]. Instead of having the application directly connected to the DBMS, it is connected to C-JDBC controller using a C-JDBC JDBC driver.

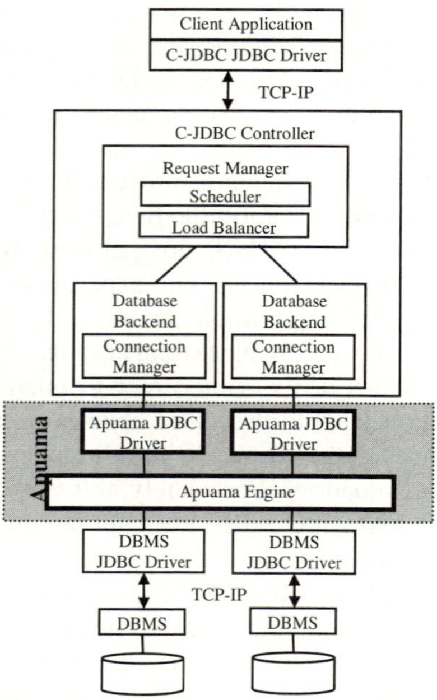

(a) C-JDBC with Apuama extension

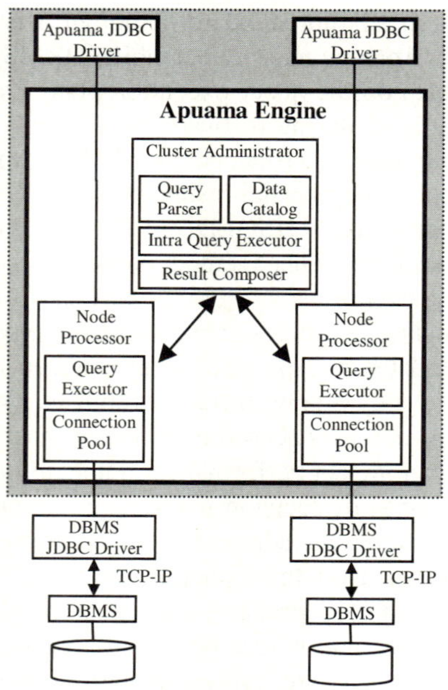

(b) Apuama Engine internals

Fig. 1. Apuama architecture

The *C-JDBC controller* is a Java process that manages all database resources. It has a *Database Backend* component that manages a pool of connections to running DBMSs. Each request received by C-JDBC is submitted to the *Scheduler* component that controls concurrent request executions and makes sure that update requests are executed in the same order by all DBMSs. The Scheduler can be configured to enforce different parallel levels of concurrency. In our experiments, it was set to concurrently execute read and write requests. After a request is scheduled to run, the *Load Balancer* component chooses which Database Backend will execute it. If it is a write request, the same query is executed in every Database Backend to maintain consistency. But if it is a read request, the Load Balancer chooses the best node to execute it. This choice is based on a previously established policy. We configured the Load Balancer to select the node with the least number of pending requests.

Apuama does not require any changes in C-JDBC source code. Fig. 1(a) shows that Apuama is a layer between C-JDBC and the DBMSs. C-JDBC no longer makes any direct connection to DBMSs. Each Database Backend connects to Apuama through a JDBC driver. It is Apuama that connects to the DBMSs.

Fig. 1(b) shows a detailed architecture of Apuama. It has two kinds of components: one that manages intra-query parallel executions, called *Cluster Administrator*, and a set of *Node Processor* components. For each connection established by C-JDBC using Apuama, a Node Processor is created and is responsible for mediating and monitoring requests sent to its corresponding DBMS. To be able to process multiple requests, the Node Processor creates a pool of connections.

The Cluster Administrator has a *Query Parser* component capable of determining which tables are referenced by a query and a *Data Catalog* that contains information about tables that can be virtually partitioned. They are used to determine if a current OLAP query can be processed using intra-query parallelism or not. If not, the Node Processor simply redirects the request to the corresponding DBMS. Otherwise, the Cluster Administrator takes the query and processes it through the *Intra-Query Executor* (IQE) component. When all sub-queries are ready to be processed, they are sent in parallel to the *Query Executor* of each Node Processor. The Query Executor is responsible for sending the sub-query to its corresponding DBMS and waiting for results, which are sent to the IQE that forwards it to the *Result Composer*. It uses HSQLDB to store the partial results and perform final result composition. When all partial results are collected, the Result Composer produces the final result that is sent back to the client application.

5 Experiments

In this section, we evaluate the intra-query parallel processing capabilities added to C-JDBC by Apuama in different scenarios. We ran experiments based on the TPC-H benchmark. We stress Apuama in situations of high concurrency levels, even while executing database refresh operations.

All tables are replicated, but only the fact tables are virtually partitioned (orders and lineitem). Typically, fact tables have the highest cardinality in the database and they are frequently involved in OLAP queries, particularly in heavy joins. Thus, their reduced number of tuples can improve IO and CPU processing. Dimension tables are not virtually partitioned because they are small tables and represent 14% of total database size. We employ virtual partitioning on orders, based on its primary key (o_orderkey). The first attribute of the primary key of lineitem (l_orderkey) is a foreign key to orders. So, by choosing l_orderkey we generate a derived partitioning on lineitem. Tuples of the fact tables are physically ordered according to their partitioning attributes and indexes were built over them. Also, indexes are built for all foreign keys of all tables. As TPC-H assumes *ad-hoc* queries, we perform no other optimization, as determined by the benchmark.

The TPC-H queries that involve a fact table can benefit from the virtual partitioning. Exceptionally, some queries that contain subqueries involving fact tables cannot be rewritten using virtual derived partitioning. We use a subset of 8 queries from TPC-H. As in the specification, we identify queries by their numbers: Q1, Q3, Q4, Q5, Q6, Q12, Q14 and Q21. We chose such queries because they represent OLAP queries of different complexities. Q1 accesses only the lineitem table and performs many aggregate operations. The "where" predicate of Q1 is not very selective since around 99% of tuples are retrieved. This is a very costly query. Q3 joins lineitem, orders and a dimension table. Differently from other queries, its result contains a large number of rows. Q4 contains a reference to lineitem table and a sub-query with another reference to lineitem. Q5 joins lineitem, orders and four dimension tables. It performs only one aggregate operation. As Q1, Q6 accesses just the lineitem table. The main differences between them are that Q6 has only one aggregate operation and its "where" predicate is much more selective, retrieving only 1.5% of tuples. Q12 joins lineitem and orders tables and has two aggregation operations. Q14 joins lineitem table and a dimension table. Q21 contains three references to lineitem table. Two of those references are part of two sub-queries, respectively.

There are three kinds of experiments: first, we analyze speedup obtained with Apuama when processing isolated individual queries. Then, we evaluate the system overall throughput with sequences of read-only queries. Finally, we evaluate throughput obtained while simultaneously processing read-only and update queries.

We ran experiments on top of a 32-node shared-nothing cluster system from the Paris Team at INRIA [17]. Each node has two 2.2 GHz Opteron processors with 2 GB RAM and 30 GB HD. The network is a Gigabit ethernet. An instance of PostgreSQL 8 was running at each node. The total database size on disk, including all tables and indexes, is about 11 GB, for a TPC-H database with a scale factor of 5. We use HSQLDB to compute the final results.

In the following, we present results that show query execution times and throughput rates for an increasing number of nodes (from 1 to 32). Every execution was repeated five times and the final metric is the mean value obtained in such runs, not considering the first one. In some cases, metrics were also normalized by dividing their value by the value obtained during the same kind of experiment with one node. In order to ease reading and analysis, values are presented in logarithmic scale to give a clear notion of linearity [14].

The first experiment (Fig. 2) evaluates the speedup obtained with Apuama when executing isolated queries in different cluster configurations. With 2 nodes, query execution time for all queries is reduced by almost 50%, when compared to the sequential execution. With 4 nodes, query execution time is decreased from 45% to 20% for all queries, except for Q4 and Q6 that were decreased to 1.2% and 6.8% of the original time, respectively. As Q4 and Q6 are highly selective queries, fragments obtained by virtual partitioning are small enough to fit in main memory with just four nodes, resulting in super-linear speedup. For such configurations, we could observe that, after the first query execution, no page faults occur, thus avoiding disk accesses. However, we continue to see a linear speedup with 8, 16 and 32 nodes showing the effectiveness of virtual partitioning even for in-memory databases. Because Q1 and

Q21 are CPU-bound queries, they do not benefit from IO improvement. Still their speed-up is always near linear.

In the next experiment, read-only query sequences are executed in parallel against the DBC. All sequences are composed by the same 8 queries, sorted in different ways, according to TPC-H specification. Each sequence submits the next query after the completion of the current query. This is how TPC-H simulates a decision-making user formulating new queries based on previous query results. Queries from different sequences are submitted in parallel.

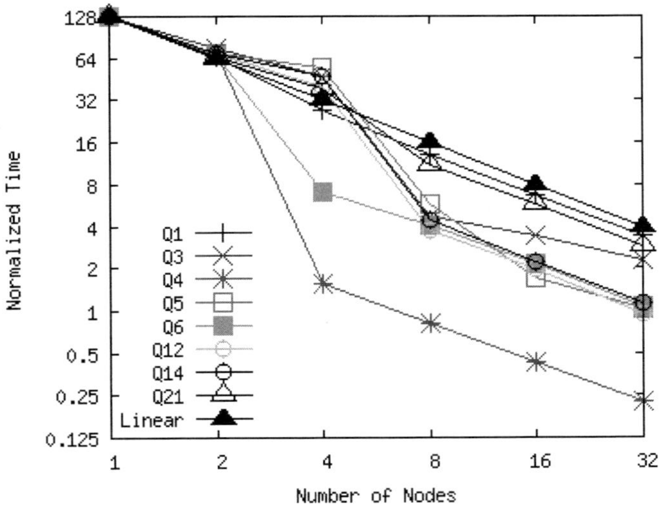

Fig. 2. Speedup experiments - normalized query execution times

Fig. 3(a) shows the throughput rate (in queries per minute) obtained during the execution of three concurrent query sequences in different cluster configurations. It also shows the throughput that would be achieved if linear scale-up throughput was obtained. The number of query sequences was defined according to TPC-H, which recommends this level of concurrency for OLAP databases with a scale factor of 5. For all configurations, the throughput rises super-linearly. With 2 nodes, it is near linear. With 4 nodes, the throughput is almost 2 times higher than if a linear gain was obtained. From 8 to 32 nodes, the throughput is constantly about 6 times higher than linear gain showing excellent performance.

Fig. 3(b) shows the scale-up throughput rate when Apuama is processing sequences of read-only queries. In this experiment, the number of concurrent query sequences is equal to the number of nodes being used. Therefore, the ideal situation is that the execution time would be the same for all cluster configurations, as the "Linear" curve shows. As in the previous experiment, the performance obtained with 2 nodes is better than expected. With 4 nodes, the performance is more than two times better than expected. From 8 to 32 nodes, the performance is always about 3 times better than expected, showing very good scalability with respect to query load.

Therefore, Apuama can be used to successfully reduce OLAP individual query execution time and increase system throughput in a typical OLAP scenario and even in the presence of high-concurrency.

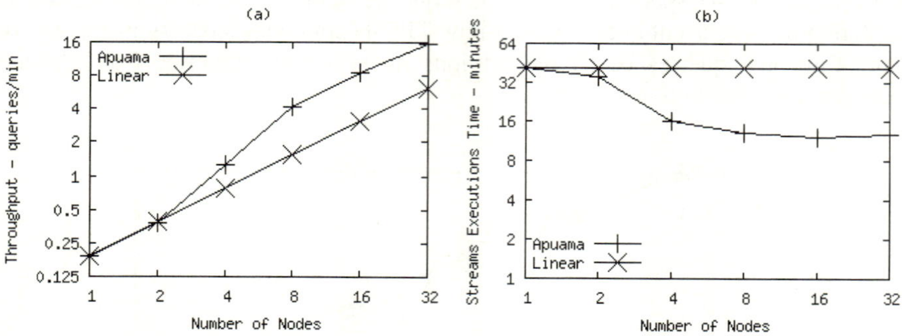

Fig. 3. Read-only query sequences experiment - (a) throughput with 3 concurrent sequences, (b) execution time with *n* concurrent sequences, where *n* is equal to the number of nodes

In the following experiment, we mix read-only query sequences with an update query sequence. The update operations consist of 52,500 transactions for all cluster configurations. First, the update queries insert an amount of data on the lineitem and orders tables. In a second step, the updates remove all inserted tuples from lineitem and orders tables.

Fig. 4(a) shows throughput (in queries per minute) obtained while concurrently processing 3 read-only query sequences and an update query sequence. Again, it shows the throughput that would be achieved if linear gain was obtained. From 2 to 8 nodes, performance of Apuama is near linear. For 16 and 32 nodes, the consistency protocol makes the update propagation delay hurt performance. There is almost no performance gain from 16 to 32 nodes. Fig. 4(b) shows scalability in Apuama with a concurrent updates. Here, the number of read-only sequences equals the number of nodes while there is always one update sequence. There is a performance gain up to

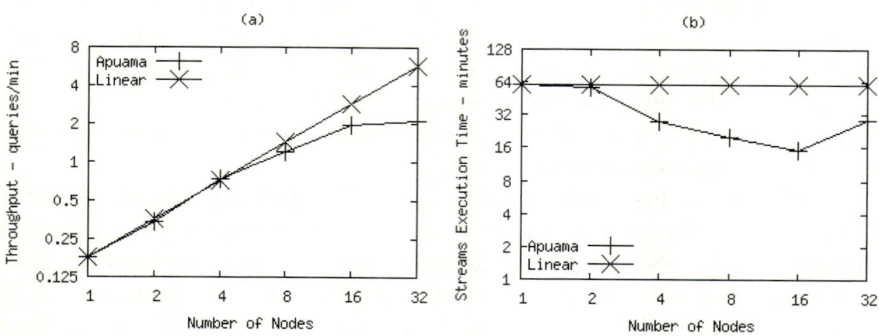

Fig. 4. Mixed workload experiment - (a) throughput with 3 read-only and 1 update sequence (b) execution time with 1 update and n read-only queries, where n is equal to the number of nodes

16 nodes. However, for 32 nodes, the performance is almost the same as with 4 nodes. This is due to the replica synchronization when using a large number of nodes.

In summary, these experiments show that Apuama provides excellent performance in processing read-only query workloads. This is true for typical OLAP scenarios and for those with a high degree of concurrency. With mixed workloads (consisting of read-only and update queries), reasonable performance can still be obtained and the system does not need to be unavailable for end-users while data refresh operations are carried out. Thus, in typical OLAP scenarios, where such operations occur only from time to time, we can conclude that Apuama is a good solution for DSS.

6 Related Work

The main DBC projects that can be found in the literature are C-JDBC [2], PowerDB [1], PowerDB-FAS [18], SmaQ [13] and Leg@net [4]. C-JDBC, PowerDB-FAS and Leg@net only support inter-query parallelism. Apuama was developed as an extension to C-JDBC to support OLAP applications through intra-query parallelism.

PowerDB provides intra-query parallelism, but does not guarantee query speedup because it depends on a DBMS-specific query execution optimization. Thus their results are unstable. Furthermore, in contrast with our motivation to offer a low-cost solution, PowerDB software is not freely available.

SmaQ is also focused on OLAP. It uses a technique called "adaptive virtual partitioning" (AVP) [14] that reduces query execution time and allows for dynamic load balancing during query execution. Although SmaQ can support both inter- and intra-query parallelism, it does not support update transactions. The main difference between SmaQ and Apuama is the existence of a replica consistency management. Besides, experiments showed that execution of OLAP queries in environments with high levels of concurrency can lead to poor performance. Apuama uses a simpler virtual partition technique than AVP that allows for better concurrent queries support. Since AVP locally subdivides the local sub-query it increases the level of concurrency while inducing a bad memory cache use.

7 Conclusion

We proposed the Apuama Engine as an extension to C-JDBC, a successful open-source DBC. Apuama adds intra-query parallel processing capabilities. The result is a low-cost powerful and unique DBC that can simultaneously support OLTP and OLAP applications. We implemented intra-query parallelism using SVP, an efficient technique that can be used with different DBMSs requiring standard, non-intrusive techniques and almost "black-box" DBMS components.

To validate our solution, we implemented Apuama on a 32-node cluster system and ran experiments with typical queries of the TPC-H benchmark. By varying the number of nodes in our experiments, it was possible to examine the query processing performance in cases that the virtual partition size is larger or smaller than the amount of available memory in a node. Although the performance improvement is better when the virtual partition fits in memory, the query super-linear speedup occurs in both cases. When processing isolated queries, super-linear speedup was obtained in most situations. When processing parallel sequences of read-only queries, the performance gain of Apuama is super-linear for all cluster configurations, even in scenarios with high levels of concurrency. With mixed workloads that combine parallel sequences of read-only queries and large amounts of data updates, the performance gain is also very good. The performance gain is near-linear for most experiments of speed-up test and super-linear for throughput scale-up test. Thus, Apuama is a good solution for high-performance DSS. In the presence of updates, Apuama presented performance deterioration when a large number of nodes were employed due to the replica consistency protocol. As a future work we plan to focus on this limitation using an alternative replication policy that relaxes consistency. The tradeoff between OLAP query result correctness and update transaction performance would be analyzed.

Apuama is released as an open source software protected under the terms of LGPL [12] license. It can be downloaded from http://www.cos.ufrj.br/~bmiranda/apuama.

References

1. Akal, F., Böhm, K., Schek, H.-J.: OLAP Query Evaluation in a Database Cluster: A Performance Study on Intra-Query Parallelism. Proceedings of the 6th East-European Conference on Advances in Databases and Information Systems (ADBIS), Bratislava, Slovakia (2002) 218-231
2. Cecchet, E.: C-JDBC: a Middleware Framework for Database Clustering. Proceedings of IEEE Data Engineering Bulletin Vol. 27 (2004) 19-26
3. Chaudhuri, S., Dayal, U.: An Overview of Data Warehousing and OLAP Technology. ACM SIGMOD Record Vol. 26 (1997) 65-74
4. Coulon, C., Pacitti, E., Valduriez, P.: Scaling Up the Preventive Replication of Autonomous Databases in Cluster Systems. Proceedings of 6th International Conference on High Performance Computing for Computational Science (VECPAR), Valencia, Spain (2004) 170-183
5. Cruanes, T., Dageville, B., Ghosh, B.: Parallel SQL Execution in Oracle 10g. Proceedings of the ACM SIGMOD International Conference on Management of Data, Paris, France (2004) 850-854
6. DB2 ICE. Retrieved 11/09/2005, from http://ibm.com/software/data/db2/linux/ice.
7. MySQL 5.0 Documentation. Retrieved 11/09/2005, from http://mysql.com.
8. Gançarski, S., Naacke, H., Pacitti, E., Valduriez, P.: Parallel Processing with Autonomous Databases in a Cluster System. Proceedings of International Conference on Cooperative Information Systems (CoopIS), Los Angeles, USA (2002) 410-428
9. Gorla, N.: Features to Consider in a Data Warehousing System. Communications of the ACM Vol. 46 (2003) 111-115
10. HSQL Database Engine. Retrieved 11/09/2005, from http://hsqldb.org/.
11. JDBC. Retrieved 11/09/2005, from java.sun.com/products/jdbc.
12. LGPL. Retrieved 11/09/2005, from http://www.gnu.org/copyleft/lesser.html.
13. Lima, A.A.B.: Intra-Query Parallelism in Database Clusters. COPPE/UFRJ, D.Sc. Thesis, Rio de Janeiro (2004)
14. Lima, A.A.B., Mattoso, M., Valduriez, P.: Adaptive Virtual Partitioning for OLAP Query Processing in a Database Cluster. Proceedings of 19h Brazilian Symposium on Databases (SBBD), Brasilia, Brazil (2004) 92-105

15. Pape, C.L., Gançarski, S., Valduriez, P.: Refresco: Improving Query Performance Through Freshness Control in a Database Cluster. Proceedings of International Conference on Cooperative Information Systems (CoopIS), Agia Napa, Cyprus (2004) 174-193
16. PostgreSQL 8.0.1 Documentation. Retrieved 11/09/2005, from http://postgresql.org.
17. Paris Project. Retrieved 11/09/2005, from http://www.irisa.fr/paris/General/cluster.htm.
18. Röhm, U., Böhm, K., Schek, H.-J., Schuldt, H.: FAS - A Freshness-Sensitive Coordination Middleware for a Cluster of OLAP Components. Proceedings of the 28th International Conference on Very Large Data Bases (VLDB), Hong Kong, China (2002) 754-765
19. TPC-H Benchmark. Retrieved 11/09/2005, from http://tpc.org/tpch.

Querying Along XLinks in XPath/XQuery: Situation, Applications, Perspectives

Erik Behrends, Oliver Fritzen, and Wolfgang May

Institut für Informatik, Universität Göttingen, Germany
{behrends, fritzen, may}@informatik.uni-goettingen.de

Abstract. This paper summarizes the situation about using XLink for connecting XML instances. We discuss applications where XLink functionality can be useful, and derive requirements how the basic XLink technology should be supported in these scenarios. We compare several proposals dealing with interlinked XML data with our dbxlink approach which is a minimal extension to XLink and XPath, and we show how its semantics can be added to arbitrary XPath-based query engines.

1 Introduction

We start the presentation with a short introduction to XLink and the current, unsatisfying state of the art of dealing with XLinks in XQuery. Section 2 then points out tasks where XLinks can be applied successfully and show what features would be nice to be supported. We describe our dbxlink proposal and correlate it with existing proposals in Section 3. We give a high-level description here since the formal details of dbxlink can be found in [BFM06], and then report our experiences with extending a "common" XML database system with this functionality in Section 4 before closing with some concluding remarks.

XML and XLink. XML has been designed and accepted as *the* framework for semi-structured data. XML data is not required to be self-contained on an individual server, but may include *links* to XML data on other servers. Such references inside XML data can be expressed by the *XML Linking Language (XLink)* [XLi01, XLi06]. XLink provides special tags in the xlink namespace that tell an application that an element is equipped with link semantics. The well-known HTML <a href="..."> construct is a simple XLink element whose href attribute references a document. XLink defines general functionality of such references: (i) *arbitrary* elements can be distinguished as *XLink* elements, (ii) the allowed values of the href attribute are enhanced for addressing XML data, and (iii) the behavior of the link can further be specified.

The essential step in (ii) is to allow to specify the remote resource not only as usual in HTML by a URL optionally extended with an *anchor* (e.g., `http://www.example.org#foo`), but, suitable for the XML data model, for addressing *nodes*. The extended addressing functionality is provided by the XPointer Framework [XPt03] and the XPointer addressing scheme [XPt02]. XPointer in turn is based

T. Grust et al. (Eds.): EDBT 2006 Workshops, LNCS 4254, pp. 662–674, 2006.

on XPath expressions: An XPointer expression of the form *url*#xpointer(*xpointer-expr*) (where the syntax of *xpointer-expr* is a slight extension of XPath) identifies a fragment inside the XML document located at *url*. E.g., the following XPointer (see also Figure 1 and Example 1 below)

```
http://www.foo.de/countries.xml#xpointer(//country[@car_code="D"])
```

addresses the node that represents Germany in http://www.foo.de/countries.xml.

XLink defines several types of links, i.e., *simple links* that provide *referencing* functionality similar to the HTML <a> element, and *extended links* that allow for *connecting* sources by *arcs*. In this paper, the focus of our interest is on *simple links*, where one XLink element with an XPath expression in place of the *xpointer-expr* references one or more nodes from a remote document. A simple link has the following form:

```
<qname xlink:type="simple" xlink:href="xpointer" further-xlink-attributes>
  content
</qname>
```

Example 1 (Simple XLinks). *The document* countries.xml *in Figure 1 contains basic data about countries, and for each country,* cities-XX.xml *(where* XX *is the country's car code) contains information about the cities in this country.*

Query Support for XLink References. How can the instance be queried – e.g., for finding out how many inhabitants the capital of Belgium has? Although the W3C's *XML Query (XQuery) Requirements* [XMQ05, Sec. 3.3.4/3.4.12 (References)] explicitly state that

> *"the XML Query Data Model MUST include support for references, including both references within an XML document and references from one XML document to another",*

and XLink is a well-established W3C Recommendation, neither XPath nor XQuery support navigation along XLink references. While for intra-document references, the id(...) function does this task, and the doc(...) function allows for accessing remote documents, there is not yet complete support for XPointer in XPath/XQuery: users can select the pointer with

```
for $pointer in
doc("http://.../countries.xml")//country[@car_code="B"]/capital/@xlink:href
```

but XQuery cannot be told to resolve it.

The crucial point of handling XLink references is the evaluation of a *data item* (i.e., the value of the href attribute) as a query. This is currently not possible in XPath/XQuery, neither in the base language, nor by the functions and operators given in *XQuery 1.0 and XPath 2.0 Functions and Operators* [XPQ05].

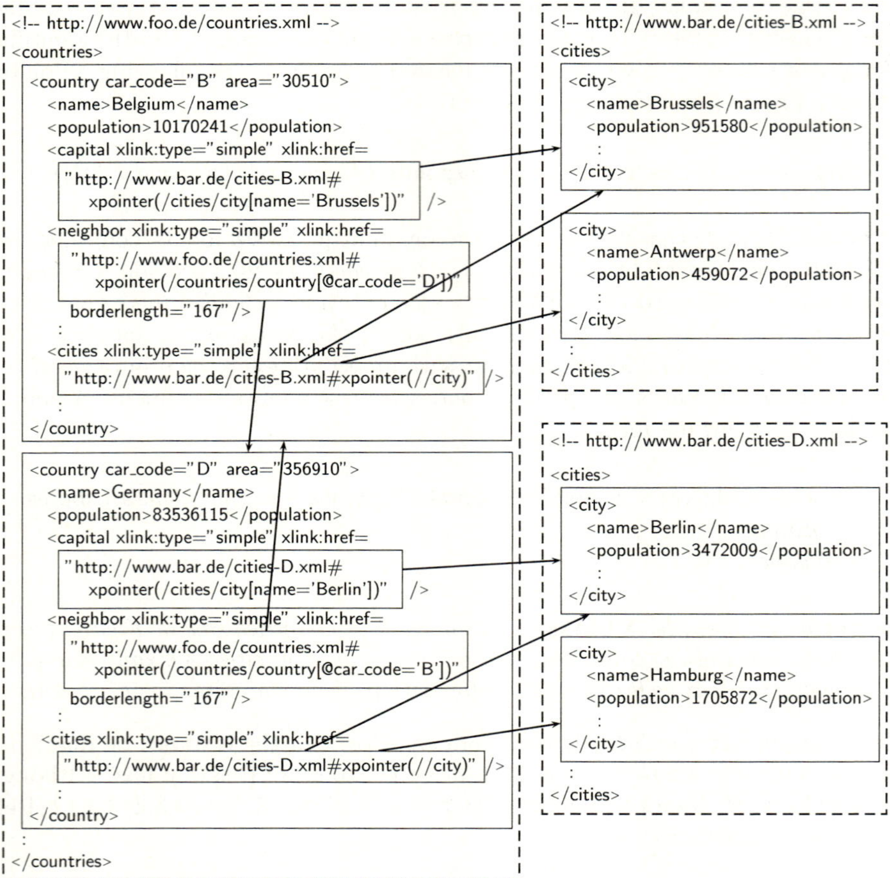

Fig. 1. Excerpt of the Distributed MONDIAL XML Database [May01b]

Simple XPointers. Simple XPointers actually consisting of an fn:id() function application of the form *url*#xpointer(id(*string*)) (equivalent to the "shorthand pointers" like http://.../country.xml#D in [XPt03]) can be resolved by combining the doc() and id() functions. In [LS04, Section 7.4.2], a solution by an XQuery user-defined function is given which is restricted to such simple XPointers:

```
declare namespace fu = "http://www.example.org/functions";
declare function fu:follow-xlink($href as xs:string) as item()*
{ let $docValue := fn:substring-before($href,"#")
  let $x := fn:substring-after($href,"#xpointer(id('")
  let $idValue := fn:substring-before($x,"')")
  return fn:doc($docValue)/fn:id($idValue) };
```

XPath Expressions in XPointers. In the general case, instead of fn:id($idValue), any XPointer expression must be allowed:

```
declare function fu:follow-xlink($href as xs:string) as item()*
{ let $docValue := fn:substring-before($href,"#")
  let $path := fn:substring-before(fn:substring-after($href,"#xpointer("),")")
  return fn:doc($docValue)/ $path };
```

Such functionality must evaluate a dynamically constructed XPath expression. This is not yet available in XQuery (and can also not be programmed by the current *XQuery 1.0 and XPath 2.0 Functions and Operators* [XPQ05]; note that the function given in [LS04, Section 7.4.2] explicitly returns a message "XPointer Syntax nicht unterstützt/XPointer syntax not supported" in this case).

The required functionality is available in Saxon [saxon] as an *extension function* saxon:evaluate(*string*) where the above function can be expressed as

```
declare function fu:follow-xlink($href as xs:string) as item()*
{ let $docValue := fn:substring-before($href,"#")
  let $path := fn:replace($href, "^.*#xpointer.(.*).$", "$1")
  return fn:doc($docValue)/saxon:evaluate($path) };
```

[RBHS04] proposes another XQuery extension as "execute at *url* xquery {*xquery*}". Then, queries use –similar to the id function– an *explicit* dereferencing, e.g.

```
doc("http://.../countries.xml")//country[@car_code="B"]/
                  capital/ fu:follow-xlink(@xlink:href) /population .
```

With respect to the applications where XLink references are used, we argue that *implicit* dereferencing is preferable, seeing XLink elements as embedded views, like doc("http://.../countries.xml")//country[@car_code="B"]/capital/population.

2 Applications

Data Integration. An integrated view over distributed, autonomous data can be defined according to a given target DTD or XML Schema. In this case, the integration approach is realized by the *Global as View (GAV)* [Len02] approach, i.e., queries are answered by *view unfolding* which in this case amounts to evaluating the XPointer and integrating its result into the surrounding structure. By this, also calls to Web Services can be integrated via XLink.

Example 2. *Consider a similar structure as in Example 1, but instead of the parts of the distributed* MONDIAL *database, not the "own" city data is referenced, but remote, autonomous city data residing at* http://www.geohive.com/. *Here, referencing remote data (e.g.,* http://www.geohive.com/cy/c_de.xml *for German cities) guarantees that in case that this data is updated, subsequent queries always return the most up-to-date results.*

Data Integration Process. Not only the final result of an integrated view can be expressed by XLink references: we have shown in [May05] how to carry out the integration process by partial materialization of an integrated XML instance. Nodes that are only *referenced* from the so far integrated fragment are integrated by suitable XLinks. When the integration process proceeds, the materialized fragment is minimally extended just by the structure that is generated by the integration, still referencing as much as possible the remote data-carrying nodes. Queries are actually evaluated against (i) the partially materialized integrated database, and (ii) remaining parts that reside in the original sources. This has the advantage that in case that remote data is modified, any query against the integrated model uses the up-to-date modified data.

Data Reorganization and Splitting. When XML documents grow, it is sometimes preferable or necessary to split them over several documents or even servers. In this case, the original schema should be kept, seeing the integrated document as a GAV view over the –now distributed– data. Then, the same queries that were stated against the original instance can also be used against the split-up instance.

Requirements. The above list shows that XLinks can be applied as a basic mechanism for *syntactical representation* of references in several scenarios. This basic mechanism has to be equipped with a *semantics* that supports the application and defines how actually to deal with the references:

1. modeling: how to integrate the referenced nodes with the referencing document in a logical model,
2. querying: how to express and evaluate queries against this model.

It is preferable that the result of (1) is a standard XML document according to a given target DTD or XML Schema. Then, the semantics of (2) is obvious since common XML query concepts (i.e., XPath, XQuery, XSLT) can be immediately used *without* the need for explicit dereferencing.

In contrast, the proposals described in Section 1 are directly based on the original XML structure (the *XML Infoset* [XML99]) and do not use any logical model of the XLink elements. All of them require that the query expressions include *explicit* dereferencing operations. The use of an explicit navigation operator requires non-semantic navigation steps along the xlink:href attribute. The above applications for **data integration** and **splitting** with obtaining/retaining an original DTD or XML schema are not possible with them.

Thus, a transparent modeling as an XML-to-XML transformation where the XLink elements are present only on the syntactical level, but queries navigate in a *logical* model along semantic notions is desirable.

3 Proposed Solutions

Several solutions have been proposed up to now that deal with distributed and/or linked XML documents. We start with our dbxlink approach as described in detail in [BFM06], which keeps close to XML and XPath, and then discuss other approaches that cover similar topics and can be used for such issues.

3.1 The DBXLink Approach

In [BFM06], we presented the dbxlink approach for handling distributed XML data where XLink elements are extended with attributes in the dbxlink namespace that specify the *modeling*, *evaluation strategies*, and *caching of remote query results* of the links. Here, links are *transparent*, i.e., we define a logical, transparent model for mapping distributed, XLinked XML documents virtually to an integrated XML instance: The XLink elements are seen as view definitions that integrate the referenced data within the referencing XML instance where the XLink element contains the following attributes (see [BFM06] for details):

- specification of the referenced nodes by xlink:href,
- how they are mapped into the surrounding instance by dbxlink:transparent,
- when (at parsing time or at query answering time) the XPointer is actually evaluated by dbxlink:actuate,
- where (query shipping, data shipping or hybrid shipping) the evaluation takes place by dbxlink:eval, and
- whether intermediate results are cached by dbxlink:cache.

This virtual instance can then be processed by standard languages like XPath, XQuery, or XSLT. The variety of modeling variants (e.g., replacing the link element by the referenced nodes, or keeping the link element and inserting the contents of the referenced nodes into it, or attaching the referenced nodes as reference attributes to the element that surrounds the XLink element) is formally discussed in [BFM06]. There, also implementation aspects and pitfalls (ancestor axis, cycles) are discussed.
Concerning the above scenarios, this modeling flexibility allows

- to define an integrated view over remote data sources according to a given target DTD or XML Schema, and
- splitting an existing XML instance at arbitrary edges (i.e., subelement edges and also reference attributes) while keeping the original DTD or XML Schema.

Since the logical model is an XML instance, XPath, XQuery and XSLT can be applied to it as usual. dbxlink allows for controlling when, and whether, the virtual instance is actually materialized; usually, it is not materialized, but queries are just evaluated against the logical model via appropriate algorithms.

XPath vs. XQuery and XSLT. Note that the actual work is only concerned with extending XPath for smoothly dereferencing of XLinks according to the logical model: The *addressing* of nodes is done completely within XPath. Thus, extending the XPath module of an XQuery and/or XSLT system makes this functionality also available for XQuery and XSLT. The approach has been implemented as an extension to the eXist [exi] XML database system, an open-source implementation of the common languages of the XML area, supporting XPath/XQuery as query languages.

We will discuss the general applicability of this approach in Section 4.

3.2 Comparison with Related Approaches

XLink for Browsing. Up to now, the XLink approach is primarily interpreted for browsing, as it is mirrored by the W3C XLink Recommendation [XLi01] where several attributes for link elements are defined that specify the *behavior* of the link element during browsing. The show='embed' behavior of XLink can be seen as one special case of the above approach, specified by transparent="drop-element insert-nodes" replacing the XLink by the referenced contents. In this case, also a logical model is defined that is directly materialized and presented as XHTML.

XInclude. A restricted approach for distributed documents is proposed with XInclude [XIn04]: the <xi:include href="*uri*" xpointer="*xpointer*"> element provides also a *uri* and an *xpointer*. XInclude defines a fixed XML-to-XML transformation where the xi:include elements are replaced by the corresponding included items. In fact, this model generalizes XLink's browsing behavior for show='embed', replacing the XLink by the referenced contents. The specification of XInclude also corresponds to the dbxlink specification transparent="drop-element insert-nodes" and actuate="parse", i.e., the target is included when the document is loaded/parsed, materializing the model completely.

General Investigations on Distributed Semistructured Data. In [Suc02], distributed query evaluation for general semistructured data graphs is investigated. Queries are split into *decomposed queries*, then, their parts are evaluated independently at each site, and the result fragments are reassembled. The logical modeling of [Suc02] is similar to XInclude. In [BG03], distribution of XML repositories is investigated, focussing on index structures for answering queries.

Other approaches to distributed XML data apply a schema-based distribution. There are no explicit references in the data, but schema components are associated with databases and identified by their types and key attributes. During query answering the different databases are queried (here, a database dictionary is needed which tells where the data to certain schema components can be found) and the fragments are put together in the answer.

Example 3 (Schema-based Distribution). *Consider a similar structure as in Example 1. For a schema-based distribution, all country data is still in one database, but also all city data is together in one database.*

In contrast, by using XLinks, the city data for each country can reside in an individual database, or even on different hosts. Explicit references in the data here allow for full flexibility without need for a central database dictionary.

Active XML. A general approach for integrating intensional data generated by Web Services into XML documents is proposed by *Active XML* [ABM$^+$02]. With this technology, calls to Web Services are embedded into XML documents by <axml:call> elements.

Active XML on the one hand and XInclude or dbxlink on the other hand differ significantly wrt. generality (Active XML) and specialization (XInclude and dbxlink) and in the degree of integration with the database functionality. While XInclude and dbxlink are incremental extensions to the existing concepts of XLink and XPointer, targeting to provide a transparent data model and support XPath/XQuery for them from the database point of view, Active XML is a generic extension of functionality towards Web Services. Nevertheless, dbxlink and Active XML can be used to implement each other: on one hand, an Active XML service that implements the dbxlink modeling and takes a dbxlink-extended XLink element as input could return the appropriate XML fragment. On the other hand, XLink elements with dbxlink evaluation that refer to Web Services can be used for implementing functionality like Active XML, providing higher modeling flexibility (which is the main focus of the approach), but less operational alternatives (i.e., no active functionality).

4 Enabling XPath/XQuery Engines for Handling XLinks

Between XInclude on the one side and Active XML on the other side, the dbxlink approach is *specialized* to XLink, and provides functionality that we think is necessary and sufficient for using XLink for references between XML instances, and for querying these. In this section, we discuss how query engines have to be modified in order to handle queries on distributed, interlinked XML instances according to the dbxlink model. Recall that the queries are stated wrt. the DTD of the integrated GAV view and must be evaluated based on the original documents.

Naive Approach. An intuitive, naive approach to achieve this would consist of two steps. First, materialize the whole virtual instance induced by all interlinked XML instances wrt. the contained XLinks and their dbxlink directives. Then, tell the query engine to evaluate the given XPath expression on this new instance. This approach is not suitable for two reasons. In case of many distributed documents, it might be time-consuming to fetch all partaking XML documents and to compute the virtual instance, and usually, not the whole instance is needed to answer the given query. Even worse, the materialized view might contain cycles and thus the straightforward materialization process might not terminate.

4.1 Dynamic Query Evaluation

Given an XPath expression, we assume that it has the following form

$$\mathsf{doc}(url)/\mathsf{step}_1/\mathsf{step}_2/\ldots/\mathsf{step}_n.$$

In our distributed setting, we require XPath queries to start with the doc() function for specifying an XML document which shall serve as a starting point for evaluating the query. The query itself consists of n *location steps.*

There are several possibilities how XPath query engines evaluate XPath queries. We discuss different approaches and show how the navigation across XLinks can be integrated accordingly.

Stepwise Result Set Evaluation. The most common and intuitive method (which is also induced by the semantics definition by the W3C in [XPa99] or other sources, e.g., [Wad99]) for evaluating XPath queries is to subsequently apply all location steps. In every step, the set of nodes selected by the previous step is called the current *context*; in the first step, the document node is the initial context. Then, for each node of the current context, the current step is evaluated, selecting a sequence of matching items, i.e. attribute or element nodes, or atomic values that form the context for recursively applying the next step. Note that not complete intermediate results are materialized, but only local contexts on the way to the next step. Most XPath engines like Saxon, Xalan, and eXist, the native XML database system we chose for an implementation, use this strategy.

Extension of the Stepwise Evaluation. In order to implicitly replace all relevant link elements during navigation in an XML tree, thus making the navigation transparent, all subelements of every node belonging to the *context* have to be analyzed: any XLink subelement of the current context node can potentially be replaced by one or more nodes that are relevant for the next step. Thus, a kind of lookahead evaluation in order to make the required nodes available for the next step has been implemented, temporarily materializing fragments of the virtual instance on-demand.

4.2 Example Evaluation

In the general case, the navigation across XLinks takes place as follows. Consider an expression *xpath-expr*$_1$/*xpath-expr*$_2$, where a result node of *xpath-expr*$_1$ contains a simple XLink element with an XPointer *url*#xpointer(*xpath-expr*$_x$). For the most "intuitive" case, assume that the remote server is capable of answering XPath queries. The query *xpath-expr*$_x$ is thus submitted to the server at *url* that transfers the result which is then mapped into the current context. Then, the local query evaluation continues with (the first step of) *xpath-expr*$_2$.

Consider again the example "capital" query whose evaluation is illustrated in Figure 2: /countries/country[@car_code="B"]/id(@capital)/population (note that we chose the modeling dbxlink:transparent="make-attribute insert-nodes" which turns the capital into a reference attribute to adhere to a "given" target DTD). In the distributed MONDIAL database (cf. Figure 1), after evaluating *xpath-expr*$_1$:= /countries/country[@car_code="B"], the capital XLink subelement is a child node of the context element that represents *Belgium* and it has to be expanded. The rest of the query is then *xpath-expr*$_2$:= id(@capital)/population, and *xpath-expr*$_x$:= "http://dbis05/cities-B.xml#xpointer(//city[name='Brussels'])" is the XPointer expression.

As illustrated in Figure 2, *xpath-expr*$_x$ is sent to the remote server which returns the city node for Brussels. The screenshot in Figure 3 illustrates the communication between two servers when resolving the XPointer in the capital XLink subelement of Belgium traced by the *Apache Axis TCPMonitor*. On the left hand side, the corresponding GET request for http://dbis05/cities-B.xml//city[name="Brussels"] from the country server (ap34) to the city server (dbis05) can be seen, whose result, i.e., the XML fragment representing Brussels, is shown on the right hand side.

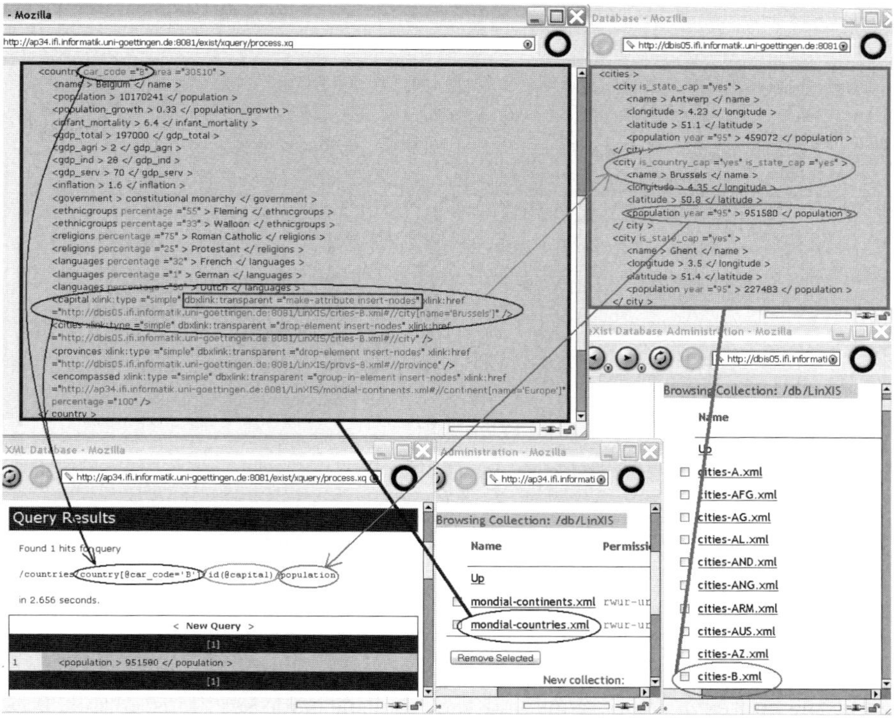

Fig. 2. Querying the Distributed MONDIAL Database

Once the local server has received the XML data for Brussels, it maps it into a reference attribute of its parent element *Belgium* (as required by the modeling dbxlink:transparent="make-attribute insert-nodes"): The new, local *Brussels* node is extended with a (local) ID attribute with value *brus-id*. Additionally, an IDREF attribute node capital="*brus-id*" is added to the *Belgium* element in the currently materialized context. Then, the remaining part of the original query, $xpath\text{-}expr_2$ = id(@capital)/population is evaluated locally (using the new IDREF/ID attributes to navigate from the *Belgium* element to *Brussels*).

4.3 Extending Alternative Evaluation Strategies

Iterator-based Evaluation. Relational database systems usually do not materialize intermediate results except when needed for aggregations; instead combinations of iterators are used that implement the algebra tree. Here, the lookahead evaluation can be covered inside the iterators that smoothly return the actual sequence of children or attributes in the logical model. Such an evaluation has been used in first experiments when extending the LoPiX system [May01a].

[GKP05] present an algorithm that reduces the worst-case complexity of XPath from exponential (in the size of the query) to polynomial time. For

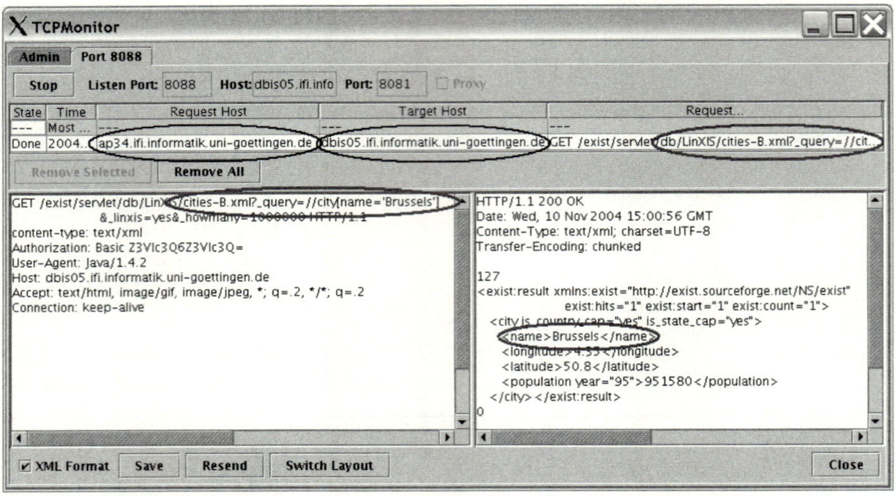

Fig. 3. Communication: Answer Shipping

this, the proposed algorithm uses a kind of *tabling* via dynamic programming where earlier results are stored for later lookup. These *context-value-tables* contain combinations of contexts (given as node, position in the context and size of the context), expressions and the resulting node set. This approach can easily be combined with the caching of the results of XPointers in the dbxlink approach.

Non-XPath-based Query Languages. Since the core of the dbxlink approach is only concerned with defining an XML-to-XML mapping, its usage is not restricted to XPath-based, or navigation-based at all, environments. For example, the Xcerpt language [BS02] uses positional *query terms* that are *matched* against an underlying XML instance via *unification simulation*. Since in fact individual bisimulation paths are again navigational, integrating the expansion of XLinks into these navigation steps (using the same basic functionality and mappings as in our eXist reference implementation) would provide the required functionality.

Distributed Query Evaluation. In the above example, the actual evaluation of the XPointer took place at the referenced host and evaluating the remaining query locally (hybrid shipping). Other evaluation strategies allow to fetch the whole referenced document (data shipping) and evaluate the remaining query locally, or to rewrite the remaining query with the XPointer and evaluate both remote (query shipping). Intermediate results can be cached. The above functionality has been implemented in the eXist-based system.

Approaches that focus on distributed XML query evaluation in general like [Suc02, BG03] are orthogonal to ours (where the focus is on the modeling and handling of the interplay of links seen as views) and could probably be applied for a more efficient implementation.

5 Conclusion and Perspectives

We discussed the situation of employing the XLink mechanism for expressing references between XML instances. We have shown how the support for querying along XLinks given by the dbxlink approach can be integrated into XPath/XQuery evaluation algorithms and engines, providing a proof-of-concept implementation. The more elaborate and efficient handling of distributed queries poses a lot of questions that call for combinations with results of other work.

Projecting XML Fragments. For reducing the amount of data transmitted from one server to another, the techniques of projecting XML documents proposed in [MS03] can be applied. Given the remaining part $xpath\text{-}expr_2$, the referenced XML fragment can be reduced significantly to the projection relevant wrt. the query before transmitting it.

XPointer Containment. When an XML document containing XLinks is parsed and stored, the static set of links can be detected. XPath query containment algorithms as suggested e.g. in [MS04] can be used for the corresponding XPointer expressions. Then, assuming hybrid shipping and caching, queries that are subsumed by other links that are already cached, can be answered using the cached knowledge.

Further relevant work that might be worthwhile to be incorporated into our framework comprise parallel evaluation of remote queries, refined caching strategies, optimization strategies for local evaluation of XPath queries and stream processing of the results of XPointers, as well as strategies based on metadata, schema reasoning, and path indexes for finding out which XLinks will contribute to the result of a given query. In a global scale, such strategies require a sophisticated P2P-based infrastructure with appropriate communication. Hence more specialized research results, some of which are mentioned above, can be applied.

Acknowledgements. This work is supported by the German Research Foundation (DFG) under grant no. MA 2539 within the LinXIS project.

References

[ABM+02] S. Abiteboul, O. Benjelloun, I. Manolescu, T. Milo, and R. Weber. Active XML: Peer-to-Peer Data and Web Services Integration. In VLDB, 2002.

[BFM06] E. Behrends, O. Fritzen, and W. May. Handling Interlinked XML Instances on the Web. In EDBT, Springer LNCS 3986, pp. 792–810, 2006.

[BG03] J.-M. Bremer and M. Gertz. On Distributing XML Repositories. In *WebDB*, pp. 73–78, 2003.

[BS02] F. Bry and S. Schaffert. Towards a declarative query and transformation language for XML and semistructured data: Simulation Unification. In ICLP, Springer LNCS 2401, pp. 255–270, 2002.

[exi] eXist: an Open Source Native XML Database. `http://exist-db.org/`.

[GKP05] G. Gottlob, C. Koch, and R. Pichler. Efficient Algorithms for Processing XPath Queries. *ACM Transactions on Database Systems (TODS)*, 30(2), 2005.

[Len02] M. Lenzerini. Data integration: a theoretical perspective. In *ACM Intl. Conference on Management of Data (SIGMOD)*, pp. 233–246, 2002.

[LS04] W. Lehner and H. Schöning. *XQuery.* dpunkt, 2004.

[May01a] W. May. LoPiX: A System for XML Data Integration and Manipulation. In *Intl. Conf. on Very Large Data Bases (VLDB)*, 2001.

[May01b] W. May. The MONDIAL Database, 2001. http://dbis.informatik.uni-goettingen.de/Mondial/.

[May05] W. May. Logic-based XML data integration: A semi-materializing approach. *Journal of Applied Logic*, (3):271–307, 2005.

[MS03] A. Marian and J. Siméon. Projecting XML Documents. In VLDB, 2003.

[MS04] G. Miklau and D. Suciu. Containment and Equivalence for a Fragment of XPath. *Journal of the ACM*, 51(1):2–45, 2004.

[RBHS04] C. Re, J. Brinkley, K. Hinshaw, and D. Suciu. Distributed XQuery. In *Workshop on Information Integration on the Web (IIWEB)*, 2004.

[saxon] M. Kay. SAXON: The XSLT and XQuery processor. http://saxon.sf.net/.

[Suc02] D. Suciu. Distributed Query Evaluation on Semistructured Data. *ACM Transactions on Database Systems (TODS)*, 27(1):1–62, 2002.

[Wad99] P. Wadler. Two semantics for XPath. 1999. http://www.cs.bell-labs.com/who/wadler/topics/xml.html

[XIn04] XML Inclusions (XInclude). http://www.w3.org/TR/xinclude/, 2004.

[XLi01] XML Linking Language (XLink). http://www.w3.org/TR/xlink, 2001.

[XLi06] XML Linking Language (XLink) Version 1.1. http://www.w3.org/R/Txlink11, 2006.

[XML99] XML Information Set. http://www.w3.org/TR/XML-infoset, 1999.

[XMQ05] XML Query Requirements. http://www.w3.org/TR/xmlquery-req, 2005.

[XPa99] XML Path Language (XPath) Version 1.0: 1999. http://www.w3.org/TR/xpath, 1999.

[XPQ05] XQuery 1.0 and XPath 2.0 Functions and Operators. http://www.w3.org/TR/xquery-operators, 2005.

[XPt02] XPointer xpointer() Scheme. http://www.w3.org/TR/xptr-xpointer, 2002.

[XPt03] XPointer Framework. http://www.w3.org/TR/xptr-framework, 2003.

Towards Similarity-Based Topological Query Languages

Alberto Belussi[1], Omar Boucelma[2], Barbara Catania[3], Yassine Lassoued[2], and Paola Podestà[3]

[1] DI, University of Verona, Italy
[2] LSIS-CNRS, Université Paul Cézanne Aix-Marseille III, France
[3] DISI, University of Genova, Italy

Abstract. In recent times, the proliferation of spatial data on the Internet is beginning to allow a much larger audience to access and share data currently available in various Geographic Information Systems (GISs). Unfortunately, even if the user can potentially access a huge amount of data, often, she has not enough knowledge about the spatial domain she wants to query, resulting in a reduction of the quality of the query results. This aspect is even more relevant in integration architectures, where the user often specifies a global query over a global schema, without having knowledge about the specific local schemas over which the query has to be executed. In order to overcome such problem, a possible solution is to introduce some mechanism of query relaxation, by which approximated answers are returned to the user. In this paper, we consider the relaxation problem for spatial topological queries. In particular, we present some relaxed topological predicates and we show in which application contexts they can be significantly used. In order to make such predicates effectively usable, we discuss how GQuery, an XML-based spatial query language, can be extended to support similarity-based queries through the proposed operators.

1 Introduction

The proliferation of spatial data on the Internet is beginning to allow a much larger audience to access and share data currently available in various Geographic Information Systems (GISs). As spatial data increase in importance, many public and private organizations need to disseminate and have access to the latest data at a minimum (right) cost and as fast as possible. One of the main problems in making this objective feasible is due to the gap existing between the data made available on the Web and the user's knowledge of such data during query specification. Indeed, the user may not exactly know the spatial domain she wants to query, in terms of properties, available features, and geometric types used to represent such features. This aspect is even more relevant in integration architectures, where a global query is expressed over a global schema, without having knowledge about the specific local schemas over which the query has to be executed. Differences in data sources may depend on how each single data

T. Grust et al. (Eds.): EDBT 2006 Workshops, LNCS 4254, pp. 675–686, 2006.

source models spatial objects in terms of their descriptive attributes (length of a river, population in a town), their type (region, line, point), their geometric type, and their topology. For example, one dataset $M1$ may represent roads and bridges as regions, another dataset $M2$ may represent roads as regions and bridges as lines, a third dataset $M3$ may represent both as lines.

The gap between stored data and user knowledge may impact the quality of the results obtained by a query execution, reducing user satisfaction in using a given application. The main cause of this unsatisfaction relies on the usage of equality-based queries, by which the user specifies in an exact way the constraints that data to be retrieved must satisfy. In order to overcome such problems, similarly to what has been done in the multimedia context, a possible solution is to introduce some mechanism of query relaxation, by which approximated answers are returned to the user, possibly introducing some false hits, but at the same time making query answers more satisfactory from the user point of view.

In this paper, we consider a specific sub-problem of the one cited above, concerning the relaxation problem for spatial topological queries, representing one of the most important classes of queries in spatial applications. In particular: (i) we present some relaxed topological predicates, that we call *weak*; (ii) we show in which application contexts they can be significantly used; (iii) we extend an existing spatial query language to cope with weak topological operations, discussing implementation issues.

Weak topological predicates are obtained from the usual one, that we call *strong*, by specifying an error threshold. Such threshold is used by the query processor to relax the topological predicate into a set of predicates, whose semantic distance from the given one is lower than or equal to the specified threshold. The definition of weak topological predicates thus relies on the usage of a similarity function between topological predicates. To this purpose, in this paper we consider the function presented in [1]. Such function extends other previously defined functions by considering pairs of topological predicates applied over pairs of objects with possibly different dimension. We then show how weak topological predicates can be used in the Web and other integration contexts and, since XML is becoming the de-facto standard for data representation and processing in such environments, we discuss how weak topological predicates can be represented using XML-like standards. In the GIS context, the OpenGIS consortium (OGC) has adopted GML (Geography Markup Language) for the XML representation and transport of geographic data [14]. GML data can be manipulated through Web Feature Services (WFSs), by which it is possible to describe or get features from a spatial data source on the Web. However, WFS is not a real query language and cannot be used to join data from different sources or to perform spatial analysis. Based on these limitations and the large diffusion of XQuery as query language for XML data, GQuery has been recently defined to overcome some of these limitations, by extending XQuery with the ability of using GML geometric types and specifying functions manipulating such types [7]. Due to its characteristics, in this paper we show how GQuery can be extended to deal with weak topological predicates, from a syntax and implementation point of view.

We remark that, even if several similarity functions for topological predicates have been defined (see for example [4,8,10]), the only work we are aware of dealing with similarity-based processing for spatial data is presented in [11], addressing spatial similarity for queries with multiple constraints. A methodology is proposed for spatial similarity retrieval in response to complex queries formed by combinations of logical or relational operators, in presence of null values. Spatial similarity is however considered from a conceptual rather than implementation point of view. On the other hand, here we consider a specific sub-problem of what considered in [11] and we provide concrete and easily implementable solutions. The approximation concept we consider in this paper is also different from that presented in [5], where uncertainty on object representation, due to broad boundaries, leads to the definition of approximated topological relationships.

The remainder of the paper is organized as follows. The reference model and topological distance are introduced in Section 2. Section 3 presents some scenarios of possible usage of weak topological predicates and formally introduce them. The proposed similarity-based language is then presented in Section 4, together with the discussion of some implementation issues. Finally, Section 5 presents some conclusions and outlines future work.

2 The Reference Spatial Data Model

The spatial model. We define a *map schema* as a set of feature types, object classes representing real word entities (such as lakes, rivers, etc.). Each feature type has some descriptive attributes, including a feature identifier and a *spatial attribute*, having a given dimension. We assume that values for the spatial attribute are modeled according to the OGC (Open GeoSpatial Consortium) *simple feature* geometric model [13]. In such a model, the geometry of an object can be of type: point, describing a single location in the coordinate space (dimension 0, also denoted with P); line, representing a linear interpolation of an ordered sequence of points (dimension 1, also denoted with L); polygon - more generally called region -, defined as an ordered sequence of closed lines defining the exterior and interior boundaries (holes) of an area(dimension 2, also denoted by R); recursively, a collection of disjoint geometries. We assume that the same feature type may belong to one or more map schemas, possibly with different dimensions. The instance of a map schema is called *map* and is a set of features, instances of the feature types belonging to the map schema. The same feature may belong to one or more maps, associated with possibly different geometries and dimensions according to the map schemas.

Topological relationships. Features inside a map are related by topological relationships. Topological relationships can be formally defined by using the 9-intersection model [9]. In the 9-intersection model, each spatial object A is represented by 3 point-sets: its interior A°, its exterior A^-, and its boundary ∂A. A topological relation can be represented as a 3x3-matrix, called *9-intersection matrix*, defined as follows:

Table 1. Definition of the reference set of topological relationships

Name	Definition	Object type
Disjoint (d)	$f_1 \cap f_2 = \emptyset$	All
Touch (t)	$(f_1^\circ \cap f_2^\circ = \emptyset) \wedge (f_1 \cap f_2) \neq \emptyset)$	R/R, R/L, R/P, L/L, L/P
In (i)	$(f_1 \cap f_2 = f_1) \wedge (f_1^\circ \cap f_2^\circ) \neq \emptyset)$	R/R, L/L, L/R, P/R, P/L
Contains (c)	$(f_1 \cap f_2 = f_2) \wedge (f_1^\circ \cap f_2^\circ) \neq \emptyset)$	R/R, R/L, R/P, L/L, L/P
Equal (e)	$f_1 = f_2$	R/R, L/L, P/P
Cross (r)	$dim(f_1^\circ \cap f_2^\circ) = (max(dim(f_1^\circ), dim(f_2^\circ)) - 1) \wedge$ $(f_1 \cap f_2) \neq f_1 \wedge (f_1 \cap f_2) \neq f_2$	L/R L/L
Overlap (o)	$dim(f_1^\circ) = dim(f_2^\circ) = dim(f_1^\circ \cap f_2^\circ) \wedge$ $(f_1 \cap f_2) \neq f_1 \wedge (f_1 \cap f_2) \neq f_2$	R/R L/L
Covers (v)	$(f_2 \cap f_1 = f_2) \wedge (f_2^\circ \cap f_1^\circ) \neq \emptyset) \wedge (f_1 - f_1^\circ) \cap (f_2 - f_2^\circ) \neq \emptyset$	R/R, R/L, R/P, L/L, L/P
CoveredBy (vb)	$(f_1 \cap f_2 = f_1) \wedge (f_1^\circ \cap f_2^\circ) \neq \emptyset) \wedge (f_1 - f_1^\circ) \cap (f_2 - f_2^\circ) \neq \emptyset$	R/R, L/L, L/R, P/R, P/L

$$R(A,B) = \begin{pmatrix} A^\circ \cap B^\circ & A^\circ \cap \partial B & A^\circ \cap B^- \\ \partial A \cap B^\circ & \partial A \cap \partial B & \partial A \cap B^- \\ A^- \cap B^\circ & A^- \cap \partial B & A^- \cap B^- \end{pmatrix}$$

The obtained relations are mutually exclusive and represent a complete coverage. In [6], this model has been extended by considering for each 9 intersection its dimension, obtaining the *extended 9-intersection model.* Since the number of such relationships is quite high, a partition of extended 9-intersection matrices has been proposed, grouping together similar matrices and assigning a name to each group. The result is the definition of the following set of binary, mutually exclusive topological relationships, refining those presented in [6]: $TREL = \{Disjoint, Touch, In, Contains, Equal, Cross, Overlap, Covers, CoveredBy\}$.[1] The semantics of such topological relationships is presented in Table 1. It is easy to show that not all relationships can be defined for any pair of dimensions. In the following, we use the notation θ_{d_1,d_2} to denote the topological relation θ applied to pairs of objects having dimension d_1 and d_2 and $REL(d_1, d_2)$ to denote the set of topological relationships defined over pairs of objects having dimension d_1 and d_2.

Topological distance. In this paper, we consider the topological distance presented in [1], defined over topological relationships represented according to the 9-intersection model. Since each topological relationship in $TREL$ corresponds to a set of 9-intersection matrices, topological distance is a total function defined in two steps: first a distance function between two 9-intersection matrices is defined, then such function is used in computing the final result.

[1] *Covers* and *CoveredBy* have been defined as refinements of relations *Contains* and *In* and are not considered in [6].

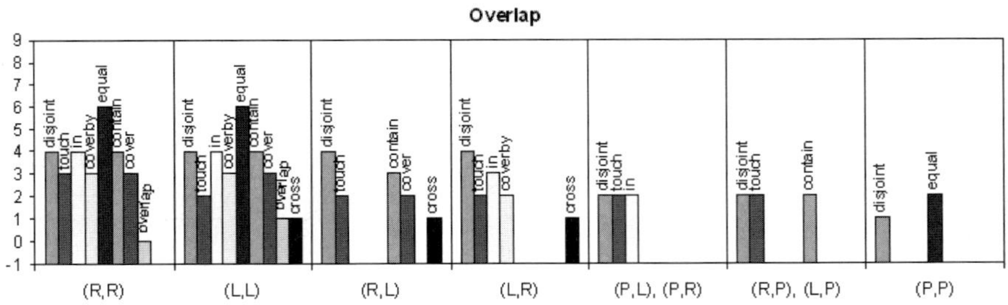

Fig. 1. Distance values (times 9) for the $Overlap_{R,R}$ topological relationship

The distance between two 9-intersection matrices ψ_1 and ψ_2 has been first defined in [8] as the number of different cells in the two matrices. Two cells are considered different if one corresponds to a non-empty intersection (whatever is its dimension) and the other to an empty intersection. Here, we normalize such distance by dividing it by the total number of cells (9).

Since each relationship in $TREL$ corresponds to a set of 9-intersection matrices, we can then compute the distance between two topological relationships $\theta^1_{d_1,d_2}$ and $\theta^2_{d_3,d_4}$ as the minimum distance between any 9-intersection matrix defining $\theta^1_{d_1,d_2}$ and any 9-intersection matrix defining $\theta^2_{d_3,d_4}$. We denote this distance by $d(\theta^1_{d_1,d_2}, \theta^2_{d_3,d_4})$.

Based on the topological distance, given a topological relationship $\theta^1_{d_1,d_2}$, all topological relationships $\theta^2_{d_3,d_4}$ can be ordered with respect to $\theta^1_{d_1,d_2}$ depending on the distance value. All values for $d(\theta^1_{d_1,d_2}, \theta^2_{d_3,d_4})$ can be found in [1]. Figure 1 just presents distances $d(Overlap_{R,R}, \theta^2_{d_3,d_4})$.

3 Weak Topological Predicates

In the following, we present two contexts in which similarity-based topological predicates can be useful. The first scenario concerns query specification in a Web context, the second scenario concerns query execution under a mediator architecture. Then, we formally introduce weak topological predicates.[2]

In the following scenarios, we use three distinct maps M_1, M_2, and M_3, sketched in Figure 2. They represent roads (identified by r_i) and bridges (identified by b_i) with different dimensions: $(2,2)$ in M_1, $(2,1)$ in M_2, and $(1,1)$ in M_3. We also assume that the following topological relationships holds:[3] (i) $Overlap(r1, b1)$, $Overlap(r2, b2)$, $Cover(r6, b6)$ in M_1; (ii) $Cross(r1, b1)$, $Cross(r2, b2)$, $Cross(r3, b3)$, $Cover(r6, b6)$ in M_2; (iii) $Overlap(r1, b1)$, $Cross(r2, b2)$, $Cross(r7, b7)$, $Overlap(r5, b5)$ in M_3.

[2] In the following, the term 'topological predicate' is used to denote the predicate induced by a topological relation and both notations $a\theta b$ and $\theta(a, b)$ $\theta \in TREL$ are used.

[3] For the sake of simplicity, we do not list relationships based on $Disjoint$.

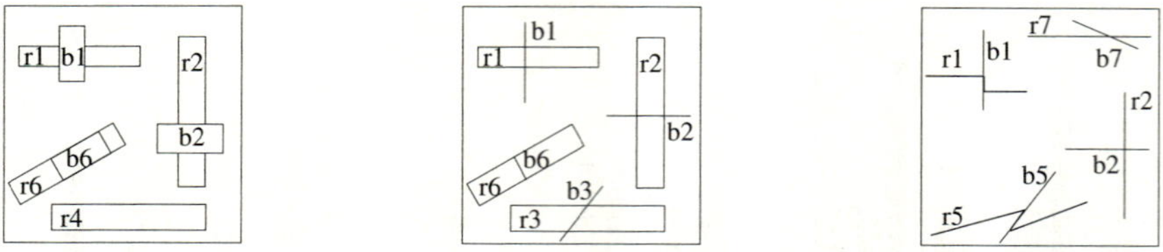

Fig. 2. Sketch of the content of the map examples

3.1 Scenario 1

Consider a user that wants to query some spatial data available on the Web, without having a detailed knowledge about such data. When the user specifies the query, she may not know the resolution of the underlying database, therefore she may not be able to specify the query in an exact way since topological predicates are not always defined when changing object dimensions. As a consequence, the quality of the obtained result may be reduced since interesting pairs may not be returned.

For example, suppose she wants to determine which pairs of roads and bridges *Overlap*, i.e., intersect and the intersection has the same type of the input objects. This query can be specified as follows: $GQ = \{(r, b)|\ r$ is a road, b is a bridge, $r\ Overlap\ b\}$. If roads and bridges are represented as regions, as in map M_1, the correct predicate would be *Overlap*. However, if roads and bridges are represented as lines, as in map M_3, besides *Overlap*, also predicate *Cross*, checking for intersections having dimension lower than those of input spatial objects, could be relevant for the user. If roads are represented as regions and bridges as lines, as in map M_2, *Overlap* is not defined and, based on the topological distance, *Cross*, which is the most similar predicate to *Overlap*, could be used.

In this context, a similarity-based approach could be very useful. The user could specify the query by: (i) assuming data have the maximal dimension, i.e., all polygons (in order to made available to the user the larger set of available topological predicates); (ii) providing a threshold value. Such value can be used to increase the quality of the generated result, e.g., to return more information even if not necessarily significant for the user.

For example, suppose the user wants to execute query GQ up to an error ϵ. Actually, this error depends on the user's application and needs. Let us suppose, for instance, that $\epsilon = 22\%$. If the dimension of roads and bridges in the map where the query has to be executed are d_3 and d_4, the query processor can use the topological distance introduced in Section 2 to rewrite the topological predicate *Overlap* into a set of topological predicates $\theta^1_{d_3,d_4}, ..., \theta^n_{d_3,d_4}$ such that $d(Overlap_{R,R}, \theta^i_{d_3,d_4}) \leq 0.22, i = 1, ..., n$. The union of the result sets is then returned to the user. According to Figure 1, we have that:

$d(Overlap_{R,R}, \theta_{R,R}) \leq 0.22$ for $\theta \in \{Overlap\}$
$d(Overlap_{R,R}, \theta_{R,L}) \leq 0.22$ for $\theta \in \{Cross, Cover, Touch\}$
$d(Overlap_{R,R}, \theta_{L,L}) \leq 0.22$ for $\theta \in \{Overlap, Cross, Touch\}$

Thus, the query processor rewrites GQ as follows:

- M_1: $GQ_1 = \{(r, b) |\ r$ is a road, b is a bridge, $r\ Overlap\ b\ \}$
- M_2: $GQ_2 = \{(r, b) |\ r$ is a road, b is a bridge, $r\theta b, \theta \in \{Cross, Cover, Touch\}\}$
- M_3: $GQ_3 = \{(r, b) |\ r$ is a road, b is a bridge, $r\theta b, \theta \in \{Overlap, Cross, Touch\}\}$

We notice that the user may initially not know what is the right threshold to be used in the query. However, as usual in similarity-based approaches, she may refine the threshold value, depending on the results obtained in previously executed queries, in the context of the same querying session.

3.2 Scenario 2

The second scenario deals with mediation systems. Mediation systems provide users with a uniform access to a multitude of data sources, without duplicating such data, via a common model. The user poses her query against a virtual global schema and the query is in turn rewritten into queries against the real local sources, taking into account differences in the models and query languages. The basic architecture of a mediation system is based on two main components: the mediator and the wrappers. The mediator allows "semantic translations" by rewriting the user's query into queries over data sources expressed in a common query language, which is specific to the mediator. Each data source is accessed through a wrapper. When a query is posed against a data source, the corresponding wrapper translates it according to the data source query language.

In the context of GIS data, VirGIS is a mediation system based on OpenGIS standards that addresses the issue of integrating GIS data and tools [2,3]. In the VirGIS system, adding a new data source is easy thanks to two main things: (i) wrappers are replaced by WFS servers and there is no need to define new ones when adding a new source; (ii) VirGIS uses a mediation approach in which adding a new data source consists only in declaring its capabilities to the mediator and describing its schema (mappings) according to the global one. VirGIS supports topological operators, which are executed at the mediator level.

In general, mediator systems, including VirGIS, take into account differences concerning feature representation in local sources. However, mediators usually do not usually consider the impact of topological information on query rewriting. The problem here is that different topological predicates should be considered for execution at the local level, in order to return results that are consistent with the global request.

As an example, assume that the maps in Figure 2 represent three local sources to be integrated. Suppose that at the global level features are represented with the maximum dimension by which they appear in the local sources, in order to made available to the user the larger set of available topological predicates. In our example, this means that at the global level, *road* and *bridges* will be both represented as regions. Actually, in more general cases, the features representation, in terms of dimensions, depend on users and their applications. Specific interfaces to the users' applications can be used and may impose their own features representations. That is, for each application, we can assume that such an interface generates queries according to predefined features dimensions that are suitable for the application. Assume now that the user, at the global level, wants to execute the query $GQ = \{(r, b)|$ r is a road, b is a bridge, r *Overlap* $b\}$.

Under this scenario, a reasonable approach for query execution at the local level would be that of rewriting the global predicate into the most similar ones (i.e., into those having the minimum distance from the global predicate) in each local source. According to Figure 1, GQ will be rewritten in the following three queries and the obtained results integrated using ad hoc merge operators:

- M_1: $GQ_1 = \{(r, b)|$ r is a road, b is a bridge, r *Overlap* $b\}$.
- M_2: $GQ_2 = \{(r, b)|$ r is a road, b is a bridge, r *Cross* $b\}$.
- M_3: $GQ_3 = \{(r, b)|$ r is a road, b is a bridge, $r\ \theta\ b$, $\theta \in \{Overlap, Cross\}\}$

We notice that in M_3 two predicates are considered since, according to the distance function, they have the same (minimum) distance with respect to the global predicate.

3.3 Weak Topological Predicates

In order to formally support the queries introduced above, spatial query languages should be extended with the ability of specifying similarity-based topological predicates. Such predicates relax the usual ones by allowing a certain distance between the specified predicate and those really executed. For this reason, we call them *weak topological predicates*, to distinguish them from the usual predicates, that we call *strong*. Strong predicates correspond to partial functions, on the other hand weak predicates are always defined. Given a topological relation θ_{d_3,d_4}, we also define its Nearest Neighbor relations in $REL(d_1, d_2)$ as the topological relations in $REL(d_1, d_2)$ at the minimum distance from θ_{d_3,d_4}.

Definition 1 (Strong and Weak topological predicates). *Let SO be the set of spatial objects. Let dim be a function that, given an object $o \in SO$, returns its dimension (i.e., R, L, or P). Let $d_1, d_2, d_3, d_4 \in \{R, L, P\}$. Let $\theta \in TREL$.*

- *The strong topological predicate for θ is defined as $\theta : SO \times SO \rightarrow Bool$ and $\theta(o_1, o_2) = true$ if and only if $\theta \in REL(dim(o_1), dim(o_2))$ and the conditions pointed out in Table 1 are true for o_1 and o_2. If $\theta \notin REL(dim(o_1), dim(o_2))$, $\theta(o_1, o_2)$ is undefined.*
- *The weak topological predicate for θ with respect to d_3 and d_4 is defined as $\theta^{w:d_3,d_4} : SO \times SO \times [0...1] \rightarrow Bool$ and $\theta^{w:d_3,d_4}(o_1, o_2, \rho) = true$ if there exists $\overline{\theta} \in \{\psi | \psi \in REL(dim(o_1), dim(o_2)), d(\psi, \theta_{d_3,d_4}) \leq \rho\}$ such that $\overline{\theta}(o_1, o_2)$ is true.*
- *A Nearest Neighbor topological relation in $REL(d_1, d_2)$ for θ_{d_3,d_4} is a topological relation $\overline{\theta} \in REL(d_1, d_2)$ such that $d(\overline{\theta}, \theta_{d_3,d_4}) = min\{d(\psi, \theta_{d_3,d_4}) | \psi \in REL(d_1, d_2)\}$. This set of relations is denoted by $NN^{d_3,d_4}_{d_1,d_2}(\theta)$.* □

Example 1. Consider Scenario 1. If the user queries are specified over objects with the maximum resolution, GQ can be specified as follows: $GQ = \{(r, b)|$ r is a road, b is a bridge, $Overlap^{w:R,R}(r, b, 0.22)\}$. In Scenario 2, the global query $GQ = \{(r, b)|$ r is a road, b is a bridge, $Overlap(r, b)\}$ can be locally re-written as follows:

- M_1: $GQ_1 = \{(r,b)|\ r$ is a road, b is a bridge, $\theta \in NN^{R,R}_{R,R}(Overlap),\ r\ \theta\ b\}$. In this case, $NN^{R,R}_{R,R}(Overlap) = \{Overlap\}$.
- M_2: $GQ_2 = \{(r,b)|\ r$ is a road, b is a bridge, $\theta \in NN^{R,R}_{R,L}(Overlap),\ r\ \theta\ b\}$. In this case, $NN^{R,R}_{R,L}(Overlap) = \{Cross\}$.
- M_3: $GQ_3 = \{(r,b)|\ r$ is a road, b is a bridge, $\theta \in NN^{R,R}_{L,L}(Overlap),\ r\ \theta\ b\}$. In this case, $NN^{R,R}_{L,L}(Overlap) = \{Overlap, Cross\}$. □

4 GQuery^s: A Similarity-Based Spatial Query Language

Weak topological predicates can be used to extend existing spatial query languages, in order to directly support similarity-based computations. Since motivations for the usage of weak topological predicates come from distributed architectures where XML is becoming the de-facto standard for data representation and processing, we discuss how weak topological predicates can be represented using XML-like standards. To this purpose, we consider GQuery [7,2], an XML-like spatial data query language based on XQuery, for query specification, and GML, for data representation.

GML is an XML-like language for representing spatial data, proposed by the OpenGIS consortium. The basic concept is the Feature, i.e., an (object) abstraction of the real world phenomena, with spatial and non-spatial attributes. Spatial attributes may be points, lines, or polygons, as defined in Section 2. Figure 3 reports an example of GML representation for a road feature, represented as a polygon, and a bridge feature, represented as a line. Note that a polygon is defined as a (set of) LineRing, i.e., lines where the first and the last point coincide. In the following, we first present the proposed extension of GQuery, called GQuery^s, and then we discuss a possible approach for its implementation.

4.1 GQuery^s: The Syntax

A GQuery query is composed of expressions. Each expression is made up of built-in or user-defined functions. An expression is either a function call, a value, or generates an error. The result of an expression can be the input of a new one. A value is an ordered sequence of items. An item is a node or an atomic value. There is no distinction between an item and a sequence containing one value. Nodes are those defined for XQuery: document, element, attribute, text, comment, processing-instruction and namespace nodes. Writing a query consists in combining simple expression (like atomic values), path expressions (from XPath [18]), FLOWER expression (For-Let-Where-Return), test expressions (if-then-return-else-return), or (pre- or user defined) functions. Non spatial operators are arithmetic operators (+,-,×,/,mod), operators over sequences (concatenation, union, difference), comparison operators (between atomic values, nodes, and sequences), and boolean operators.

Spatial operators are applied to sequences. We have three types of spatial operators. The first two categories perform spatial analysis, the third implements

```
<Road name = 'A12'>
  <geometry>
    <gml:Polygon gid='98217'
                 srsName='http://www.opengis.net/gml/srs/epsg.xml#4326'>
      <gml:LinearRing>
        <gml:coordinates> ... </gml:coordinates>
      </gml:LinearRing>
    </gml:Polygon>
  </geometry>
</Road>

<Bridge name = 'main_bridge'>
  <geometry>
    <gml:LineString gid='45234'
                    srsName='http://www.opengis.net/gml/srs/epsg.xml#4326'>
      <gml:coordinates>....</gml:coordinates>
    </gml:LineString>
  </geometry>
</Bridge>
```

Fig. 3. An example of GML data representation

strong topological predicates (in the following *node* is a GML data node having a geometric type):

- operators which perform spatial analysis and return numeric values:
  $area, length : (node) \rightarrow numeric\,value$
  $distance : (node, node) \rightarrow numeric\,value$
- operators which perform spatial analysis and return GML values:
  $convexhull, centroid : (node) \rightarrow node$
- strong topological operators:
  $\theta : (node, node) \rightarrow boolean$ where $\theta \in TREL$.

GQuery^s is obtained from GQuery by introducing weak topological operators and a Nearest Neighbor operator is_NN, checking the Nearest Neighbor relation between two topological predicates, according to Definition 1:

- Weak topological operators are defined as follows:
  $\theta^w : (node, node, dim, dim, numeric\,value) \rightarrow boolean$
  where $\theta \in TREL$, $dim \in \{R, L, P\}$, $numeric\,value = [0, 1]$.
  $\theta^w(n_1, n_2, d_3, d_4, \epsilon)$ returns true if and only if $\theta^{w:d_3,d_4}(o_1, o_2, \epsilon) = true$ and o_i is the spatial object corresponding to n_i.
- The is_NN operator is defined as follows:
  $is\_NN : (TREL, dim, dim, TREL, dim, dim) \rightarrow boolean$
  where $dim \in \{R, L, P\}$.
  $is\_NN(r_1, d_1, d_2, r_2, d_3, d_4)$ returns true if and only if $r_1 \in NN^{d_3,d_4}_{d_1,d_2}(r_2)$.

The result of a GQuery expression is another GML document, thus GQuery is closed. Errors are raised when input parameters have not the right geometric

Determine all roads overlapping some bridge.

```
for $x in document(bridge.xml), $y in document(road.xml)
where overlap($x/geometry, $y/geometry) = true
return $x
```

Determine all roads overlapping some bridge, up to a 22% error.

```
for $x in document(bridge.xml), $y in document(road.xml)
where overlap^w($x/geometry, $y/geometry,R,L,0.22) = true
return $x
```

Fig. 4. GQuery^s examples

type. For example, the function call $overlap(node_1, node_2)$ returns a boolean value if and only if $node_1$ and $node_2$ are both polygons or lines, otherwise it raises an error. Figure 4 presents some examples of GQuery^s queries.

4.2 GQuery^s Query Processing

The GQuery^s model extends the XQuery model to deal with spatial and topological operators. This means that the GQuery^s implementation must rely on the usage of external functions. The main steps to process a query that requires a spatial processing are the following:

1. translate GML documents representing the input of the GQuery query into the right format of the input of external functions involved in the spatial computation;
2. use external spatial functions to perform the spatial computation;
3. translate the result into GML format.

GQuery^s uses as external functions the Java Topology Suite (JTS) [12], an Open Source API providing spatial object model and fundamental geometry function and strong topological relations. However, such API does not support weak topological and Nearest Neighbor operators and do not provide methods for converting JTS results into GML format. As a first step, JTS has therefore been extended in two ways, obtaining the JTS^s API:

- a new method *ConvertToGML* is added to JTS, converting JTS Geometry Objects into GML;
- one new method is added for any weak topological predicates and one for computing the *is_NN* predicate. Such methods rely on Definition 1 and on the JTS implementation of strong topological predicates.

5 Conclusions and Future Work

In this paper we have presented an approach for similarity-based specification and execution of topological queries. The proposed solution relies on the definition of weak topological predicates, relaxing the traditional ones with the specification of the maximal error allowed in executing such predicates. Topological distance between topological predicates is computed according to the function defined in [1]. In order to show the usability of the proposed concepts, we have also presented some reference application scenarios. We have finally discussed how such operators can be implemented in the context of GQuery, an XQuery-based spatial query language that can be effectively used in the identified applications. We are currently extending the VirGIS architecture [3] to deal with weak topological predicates. Future works include the extension of the proposed approach to other spatial relations, such as directional ones, the definition of a weak algebra and the analysis of its properties, the definition of query processing strategies for weak topological predicates, and an exhaustive experimentation, based on real and synthetic data.

References

1. A. Belussi, B. Catania, and P. Podestà. Towards Topological Consistency and Similarity of Multiresolution Geographical Maps. In *Proc. of ACM GIS*, pages 220–229, 2005.
2. O. Boucelma, M. Essid, and Z. Lacroix. A WFS-based Mediation System for GIS interoperability. In *Proc. of ACM GIS*, pages 23–28, 2002.
3. O. Boucelma, M. Essid, Z. Lacroix, J. Vinel, J-Y. Garinet, and A. Betari. VirGIS: Mediation for Geographical Information Systems. In *Proc. of ICDE*, pages 855–856, 2004.
4. H.T. Burns and M. J. Egenhofer. Similarity of Spatial Scenes. In *Proc. of SDH*, pages 31–42, 1996.
5. E. Clementini and P. Di Felice. A Spatial Model for Complex Objects with a Broad Boundary Supporting Queries on Uncertain Data. *Data & Knowledge Engineering*, 37(3): 285-305, 2001.
6. E. Clementini, P. Di Felice, and P. van Oosterom. A Small Set of Formal Topological Relationships Suitable for End-User Interaction. In *LNCS 692: Proc. of SSD*, pages 277–295, 1993.
7. F-M. Colonna and O. Boucelma. Querying GML Data. In *Proc. of CopSTIC*, pages 11–13, 2003.
8. M. J. Egenhofer and K. Al-Taha. Reasoning about Gradual Changes of Topological Relationships. In *LNCS 639: Theory and Methods of Spatio-Temporal Reasoning in Geographic Space*, pages 196–219, 1992.
9. M. J. Egenhofer and J. Herring. Categorizing Binary Topological Relations Between Regions, Lines, and Points in Geographic Databases. *Tech. Rep., Dep. of Surveying Engineering, University of Maine*, 1990.
10. M. J. Egenhofer and D. Mark. Modeling Conceptual Neighborhoods of Topological Line-Region Relations. *Int. Journal of Geographical Information Systems*, 9(5):555–565, 1995.
11. K. Nedas and M. Egenhofer. Spatial Similarity Queries with Logical Operators. In *LNCS 2750: Proc. of SSTD*, pages 430-448, 2003.
12. JTS Topology Suite. http://www.vividsolutions.com/jts/jtshome.htm
13. OpenGeoSpatial Consortium. OpenGIS Simple Features Specification for SQL. *Tec. Rep., OGC 99-049*, 1999.
14. OpenGIS. Geography Markup Language (GML) 3.0. http://www.opengeospatial.org.

A Data and Query Model for Streaming Geospatial Image Data*

Michael Gertz, Quinn Hart, Carlos Rueda, Shefali Singhal, and Jie Zhang

Department of Computer Science, University of California, Davis, CA 95616, U.S.A.
{gertz, qjhart, carueda, sssinghal, jiezhang}@ucdavis.edu

Abstract. Most of the recent work on adaptive processing and continuous querying of data streams assume that data objects come in the form of tuples, thus relying on the relational data model and traditional relational operators as basis for query processing techniques. Complex types of objects, such as multidimensional data sets or the vast amounts of raster image data continuously streaming down to Earth from satellites have not been considered.

In this paper, we introduce a data and query model as a comprehensive and practically relevant basis for managing and querying streams of remotely-sensed geospatial image data. Borrowing basic concepts from Image Algebra, we detail a data model that reflects basic properties of such streams of imagery. We present a query model that includes stream restrictions, transforms, and compositions, and provides a sound basis for formulating expressive and practically relevant queries over streams of image data. Finally, we outline how the data and query model is currently realized in a data stream management system for geospatial image data that supports geographic applications.

1 Introduction

Data products generated from remotely-sensed (satellite) imagery and used in emerging applications areas such as global climatology, environmental monitoring, land use, and disaster management currently require costly and time consuming efforts in processing data [12,13,25]. For geographic applications, data is typically replicated using file-based approaches and has to undergo several batch-oriented processing steps before it eventually can be processed to obtain a data product. These processes are often duplicated at many sites for different and even the same type of applications.

Many satellite instruments transmit data in continuous streams to receiving stations. Multi- and hyper-spectral imagery for different wavebands that describe radiometric reflectance from the Earth's surface is typically transmitted in the form of *raster images*. Existing systems for processing the data, however, neither utilize the stream nature of the imagery nor do they expose database like concepts and architectures that provide users and applications with expressive and efficient operators to retrieve and manipulate streams of geospatial image data.

* This work is in part supported by the NSF under award IIS-0326517.

T. Grust et al. (Eds.): EDBT 2006 Workshops, LNCS 4254, pp. 687–699, 2006.

On the other hand, there have recently been considerable advancements in data stream management systems (DSMS), where data arrives in continuous and time-varying data streams and does not take the form of persistent relations [1,5,7]. Most of the proposed techniques, such as adaptive query processing, operator scheduling, and load shedding, exclusively concentrate on simple structured, usually relational data. Query operators and query processing techniques are based on those known and studied in the context of relational databases.

The above observations suggest that there is a strong potential benefit in adopting techniques developed for relational DSMS to the management of streaming remotely-sensed image data. However, the complexity and heterogeneity as well as various non-traditional (compared to relational) operations on geospatial image data pose several challenges. First, remotely-sensed imagery exhibits characteristics of spatio-temporal data. That is, image data taken at a particular point in time describes some properties of a spatial extent on the Earth's surface. In addition, remotely-sensed data is *geo-referenced*, i.e., image data (pixels) can be mapped to locations on the Earth based on some coordinate system. Second, image data is transmitted at a very high rate; well-known satellites such as GOES [8], Landsat [15] or Aqua/Terra [20] each continuously stream about 20-60GB of remotely-sensed image data to receiving stations every day. Third, operators on geospatial image data are more complex than traditional (relational) operators and have to take characteristics of the remotely-sensed data into account, in particular their geographic and stream organization properties.

In this paper, we present a data and query model as basis to formulate (continuous) queries over streaming geospatial image data. Our focus is on the characteristics of remotely-sensed data originating from satellites and used in geographic applications. We formulate a data model that takes both the spatio-temporal and geo-referenced nature of image data into account. We describe three classes of operators: stream restrictions, transforms, and compositions. These allow the formulation of queries to (1) select image data of interest based on its spatio-temporal properties, such as spatial regions of interest and time intervals, (2) perform different types of neighborhood operations and spatial transforms on image data, and (3) combine image data from different streams (corresponding to different spectral channels). We also study some properties of the operators in terms of space and time complexity, as these heavily depend on the organization of the image data in a stream. Overall, our goal is to establish a framework to build a stream management system particularly designed to operate on streaming remotely-sensed data and to stream data products to clients and geographic applications in real-time.

The rest of the paper is organized as follows. In Section 2, we present the data model underlying streaming geospatial image data. Section 3 introduces the query model and presents different types of operators, including stream restrictions, transforms, and compositions. In Section 4, we give an overview of our prototypical query processing infrastructure. After a review of related work in Section 5, we conclude the paper with a summary and outlook in Section 6.

2 Data Model

The primary types of objects in our stream processing framework are *images* and *streams*. Although an image has a fairly intuitive description, such as a (rectangular) set of pixels together with their pixel values, some more formal definitions are necessary to establish a sound framework for describing operations on individual images and in particular streams of images. In the following, we first give some basic definitions adopted from Image Algebra [23] and then extend these definitions to account for fundamental properties of (streaming) geospatial image data.

Roughly speaking, in Image Algebra, an image consists of two things, a *set of points* in some n-dimensional space and a *set of values* associated with points.

Definition 1 (Point Set). *A* point set *is some topological space, consisting of* points *and a* topology *that provides for notions such as distance between two points and neighborhood of a point.*

Typical point sets are discrete subsets of the n-dimensional Euclidean space $\mathbb{R}^n$, together with a discrete topology that provides for a metric space. With points, values from a value set can be associated.

Definition 2 (Value Set). *A* value set $\mathbb{V}$ *is an instance of a homogeneous algebra, that is, a set of values together with a set of operands.*

In Image Algebra there is no application specific semantics associated with points sets, components of points, or point values. For the processing of streaming geospatial image data, however, such a semantics is crucial to build an expressive query model and processing framework. For this, we consider point sets of the form $\mathbf{X} = \mathbf{S} \times \mathbf{T}$, where $\mathbf{S}$ is the *spatial* domain, e.g., $\mathbf{S} = \mathbb{R}^2$ or $\mathbf{S} = \mathbb{R}^3$, and $\mathbf{T}$ is the temporal domain of the point set, typically $\mathbf{T} = \mathbb{R}$.

Each point $\mathbf{x}$ in a point set $\mathbf{X}$ is of the form $\mathbf{x} = \langle s, t \rangle$, where $s \in \mathbf{S}$ describes the *spatial location* of the point, and $t \in \mathbf{T}$ is a *timestamp*. The timestamp t specifies a logical point in time when the value of that point has been obtained. This can be the point in time when the value actually has been measured or the identifier of a satellite scan sector to which the point $\mathbf{x}$ belongs.

Moreover, we only consider point sets $\mathbf{X}$ whose spatial domain is a *regularly-spaced lattice* in $\mathbb{R}^n$, thus providing a *spatial resolution* pertinent to $\mathbf{X}$. For brevity, throughout the paper we will use the term *point lattice* to indicate a point set with the above restrictions. Point lattices exhibit fundamental characteristics of spatio-temporal data and allow for standard vector space and point operations. In particular, they provide a basis for a formal definition of a stream.

Definition 3 (Stream). *Given a point lattice* $\mathbf{X}$ *and a value set* $\mathbb{V}$*, a* $\mathbb{V}$*-valued stream* $\mathbf{G}$ *is a function* $\mathbf{G}\colon \mathbf{X} \rightarrow \mathbb{V}$ *that maps points from the point lattice* $\mathbf{X}$ *to values from the value set* $\mathbb{V}$*.*

Let $\mathbb{V}^{\mathbf{X}}$ denote the set of all functions from a point lattice $\mathbf{X}$ to a value set $\mathbb{V}$. Besides the functional notation of a stream $\mathbf{G} \in \mathbb{V}^{\mathbf{X}}$, in the following we also use the set notation $\mathbf{G} = \{(\mathbf{x}, \mathbf{G}(\mathbf{x})) \colon \mathbf{x} \in \mathbf{X}\}$, where $\mathbf{x}$ denotes the *spatio-temporal point location* and $\mathbf{G}(\mathbf{x})$ denotes the *value* at location $\mathbf{x}$.

Definition 4 (Image). *An* image *of a stream* $\mathbf{G}$ *is a subset* $\mathbf{i} \subset \mathbf{G}$ *whose points all have the same timestamp.*

A *raster image* consisting of a rectangular grid of pixels is a typical instance of an image. In a raster image all points (pixels) in the point lattice have the same timestamp value, and point values are taken from, e.g., $\mathbb{Z}$ (for grey-scale images), $\mathbb{Z}^3$ (for color images), or $\mathbb{Z}^n, n > 3$, for multi-spectral images.

To support geographic applications, there is one important property of streams and images that needs to be recognized. With every point lattice $\mathbf{X}$, or more precisely its spatial component $\mathbf{S}$, a *coordinate system* must be associated. A coordinate system, such as latitude/longitude or Universal Transverse Mercator (UTM), provides the basis for mapping points to pairs of numbers and vice versa. As we will see in Section 3, one precondition for applying operations on pairs of image data is that their point lattices are based on the same coordinate system. Note that the spatial resolution of two point lattices still can be different, although they are based on the same coordinate system.

Based on the above notions, we define the concept of streaming geospatial image data, called a GeoStream, as follows.

Definition 5 (GeoStream). *A stream* $\mathbf{G} \in \mathbb{V}^{\mathbf{X}}, \mathbf{X} = \mathbf{S} \times \mathbf{T}$, *is a* GeoStream *if a* coordinate system *is associated with the spatial component* $\mathbf{S}$.

In general, a GeoStream $\mathbf{G}$ is homogeneous in the sense that all points are based on the same coordinate system and that all points have the same spatial resolution. Yet there is no restriction on the shape or orderliness that points in a GeoStream can take. For the definition of operations on one or more GeoStreams, however, it is important to recognize typical point organizations that result from different remote-sensing instruments. Figure 1 illustrates this aspect.

Airborne cameras typically obtain data in an image-by-image fashion, as shown in Fig. 1(a). That is, there are several consecutive frames that cover possibly different spatial regions. Most satellite instruments obtain data in a row-by-row fashion where strips of image data arrive at a time, shown in Fig. 1(b). In this case, a single line of neighboring points constitutes a frame. Some instruments, such as LIDAR [16], have non-uniform point lattice structures, and points are only ordered by time, as shown in the Fig. 1(c).

An important feature of the GeoStreams data model that does not have a counterpart in traditional (relational) stream processing frameworks is that *consecutive points in a GeoStream have a close spatial proximity.* This is true except for the case where the last point of one frame is followed by the first point of a new frame (as shown in in Fig. 1(a)) that covers a different spatial region. In this case there is only a close temporal proximity between points. This feature has a significant impact on how operators are realized on one or more GeoStreams, as we will show in the following section.

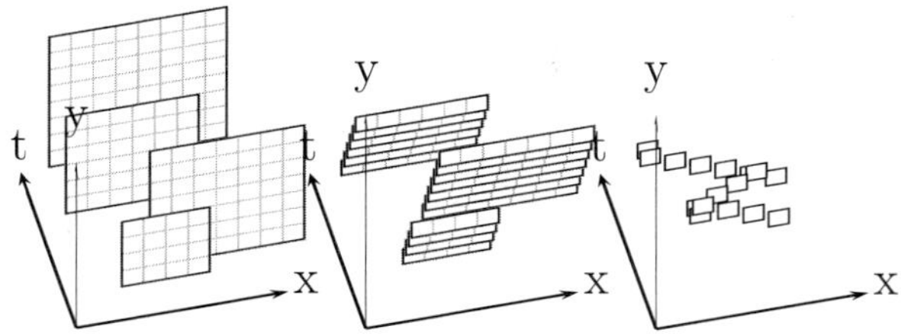

Fig. 1. Point set organization in a GeoStream for different remote-sensing instruments: (a) image-by-image (left); (b) row-by-row (middle); (c) point-by-point (right)

3 Query Model

In the following, we present a set of operators that, together with the concept of GeoStreams, build a basic algebraic model for querying streaming geospatial image data. Our primary focus is on operators that are used in typical geographic applications to derive different data products from geospatial image data. We put less emphasis on image processing operators, such as linear image transforms (e.g., Fourier and Wavelet transforms) or shape and pattern detection (see, e.g., [23]), which are often applied as post-processing steps to individual frames and images rather than streams of geospatial image data.

An important feature of our query algebra is that it is *closed*. That is, the result of applying an operator to one or two GeoStreams is again a GeoStream. This allows the formulation of complex queries over streaming geospatial image data, and it also provides a basis for query optimization techniques, such as query rewriting. In the following section, we present three classes of stream restriction operators, followed by stream transform operators in Section 3.2. Both types of operators operate on a single GeoStream. In Section 3.3, we then discuss stream composition operators. For the operators introduced, we also discuss their cost and practical realization. In Section 3.4, we briefly illustrate formulation techniques for complex queries and query rewriting.

3.1 Stream Restrictions

Assume a GeoStream $\mathbf{G} \in \mathbb{V}^{\mathbf{X}}$, $\mathbf{X} = \mathbf{S} \times \mathbf{T}$. A restriction operator can be thought of as a filter that only selects points from a stream that satisfy a certain condition on the spatial, temporal, or point value component. For a point $\mathbf{x} \in \mathbf{X}$, we denote these components $\mathbf{x}.s$, $\mathbf{x}.t$, and $\mathbf{G}(\mathbf{x})$, respectively.

The most important type of restriction and frequently used operator in typical queries is a *spatial restriction.*

Definition 6 (Spatial Restriction). *Given a point lattice* $\mathbf{R} \subset \mathbf{S}$, *the* spatial restriction *of* $\mathbf{G}$ *to* $\mathbf{R}$, *denoted* $\mathbf{G}_{|\mathbf{R}}$, *is defined as* $\mathbf{G}_{|\mathbf{R}} := \{(\mathbf{x}, \mathbf{G}(\mathbf{x})) \colon \mathbf{x} \in \mathbf{G} \wedge \mathbf{x}.s \in \mathbf{R}\}$.

Although many remote-sensing instruments may cover large regions, users and applications are often only concerned with particular *regions of interest.* A spatial restriction allows to filter only those incoming point data that are spatially located in the region $\mathbf{R}$ of interest. Conceptually, there are several ways in which $\mathbf{R}$ can be specified: (1) as an enumeration of all x, y value pairs in $\mathbf{R} \subset \mathbf{S}$ (assuming a 2-dimensional space), (2) expressions of a constraint data model, i.e., polynomials on variables x, y [22, Chap. 4], or (3) by specifying two corner points of a rectangle that describes the bounding box of the points of interest. In practice, approach (3) is commonly used in graphical user interfaces.

A temporal restriction operator is defined as follows.

Definition 7 (Temporal Restriction). *Let* $\mathbf{T} \subset \mathbb{R}$ *be a set of timestamps. The* temporal restriction *of* $\mathbf{G}$ *to* $\mathbf{T}$*, denoted* $\mathbf{G}_{|\mathbf{T}}$*, is defined as*

$$\mathbf{G}_{|\mathbf{T}} := \{(\mathbf{x}, \mathbf{G}(\mathbf{x}))\colon \mathbf{x} \in \mathbf{G} \,\wedge\, \mathbf{x}.t \in \mathbf{T}\}$$

For this operator, too, there are several ways in which $\mathbf{T}$ can be described: as a collection of points in time, as an open interval or as a set of (re-occurring) intervals, e.g., if an application requires only data during a specific time period every day. Finally, a value restriction operator, denoted $\mathbf{G}_{|\mathbf{V}}$, over a set $\mathbf{V} \subseteq \mathbb{V}$ of point values is defined as $\mathbf{G}_{|\mathbf{V}} \equiv \{(\mathbf{x}, \mathbf{G}(\mathbf{x}))\colon \mathbf{G}(\mathbf{x}) \in \mathbf{V}\}$.

It is obvious that all three restriction operators can process incoming image data on a point-by-point basis and thus can be evaluated without storage for any intermediate point data. That is, all restriction operators are non-blocking and have constant cost per point, independent of the size of the input stream.

3.2 Stream Transforms

Assume again a GeoStream $\mathbf{G}$ over point lattice $\mathbf{X}$ and value set $\mathbb{V}$. Conceptually, a transform operator maps the point or value set associated with $\mathbf{G}$ to a new point and value set. There are two types of transforms: *value transforms* and *spatial transform.* We start with the simpler one, the value transform.

Definition 8 (Value Transform). *Given a function* $f_{val}\colon \mathbb{V} \rightarrow \mathbb{W}$*, with* $\mathbb{V}, \mathbb{W}$ *being value sets, a* value transform*, denoted* $f_{val} \circ \mathbf{G}$*, changes a stream over* $\mathbb{V}^{\mathbf{X}}$ *to a stream over* $\mathbb{W}^{\mathbf{X}}$*, and is defined as* $f_{val} \circ \mathbf{G} := \{(\mathbf{x}, f_{val}(\mathbf{G}(\mathbf{x})))\colon \mathbf{x} \in \mathbf{X}\}$.

A simple form of a value transform operator is one that transforms color point values with $\mathbb{V} \subset \mathbb{Z}^3$ to gray-scale point values with $\mathbb{W} \subset \mathbb{Z}$. Clearly, such an operator allows for processing on a point-by-point basis. However, not all value transform operators show such a behavior. For example, in order to fully utilize the complete range of values in $\mathbb{V}$, point values can be *scaled.* Typical approaches include linear contrast stretch, histogram equalization, and Gaussian stretch [19]. In order to perform a respective value transform on a point, information about previous point values needs to be maintained, in particular the minimum and maximum point values seen so far. In the context of streaming image data, this is typically done on individual frames of the stream $\mathbf{G}$, and not the complete stream. If a frame has a large number of points, all points of that frame need to be stored before they can be output with new point values. Thus, the cost of a "stretch" transform operator is determined by the size of the largest frame that can occur in **G**. For most satellites and satellite imagery, such frame sizes are known (e.g., for GOES, the maximum frame size is about 20,840 by 10,820 points for the visible band at $1km$ resolution, requiring approx. 280MB storage).

An important type of operator for processing streaming geospatial image data is a spatial transforms. They allow for magnification (zooming), rotation, and general affine transformations. For geographic point lattices with associated coordinate system, re-projection of points into a new coordinate system is also a transformation.

Definition 9 (Spatial Transform). *Given a function* $f_{spat}\colon \mathbf{Y} \rightarrow 2^{\mathbf{X}}$*, with* $\mathbf{X}, \mathbf{Y}$ *being point lattices. A* spatial transform*, denoted* $\mathbf{G} \circ f_{spat}$*, changes a stream over* $\mathbb{V}^{\mathbf{X}}$ *to a stream over* $\mathbb{V}^{\mathbf{Y}}$*, and is defined as*

$$\mathbf{G} \circ f_{spat} := \{(\mathbf{y}, \mathbf{G}(f_{spat}(\mathbf{y})))\colon \mathbf{y} \in \mathbf{Y}\}.$$

How does a spatial transform operator actually work on a GeoStream? Assume a scenario where image data from **G** is coming in and one wants to change the spatial resolution associated with the point lattice **X**. An operator that increases the spatial resolution would take an incoming point **x** and produce a rectangular lattice of $k \times k$ (k being the magnification factor) of points in **Y**, all with the point value $\mathbf{G}(\mathbf{x})$. No neighboring points for **x** are required to accomplish this transform, and thus the spatial transform actually would be of the form $f_{spat}\colon \mathbf{Y} \rightarrow \mathbf{X}$. However, neighboring points are needed in case one wants to decrease the resolution. For a point $\mathbf{x} \in \mathbf{X}$, a rectangular lattice of $k \times k$ neighboring points "surrounding" **x** is needed to compute the value $\mathbf{G}(f_{spat}(\mathbf{y}))$ of a point $\mathbf{y} \in \mathbf{Y}$ (see Fig. 2(a)). Thus, the operator has to buffer a sufficient number of points in **X** in order to compute the value of a point $\mathbf{y} \in \mathbf{Y}$.

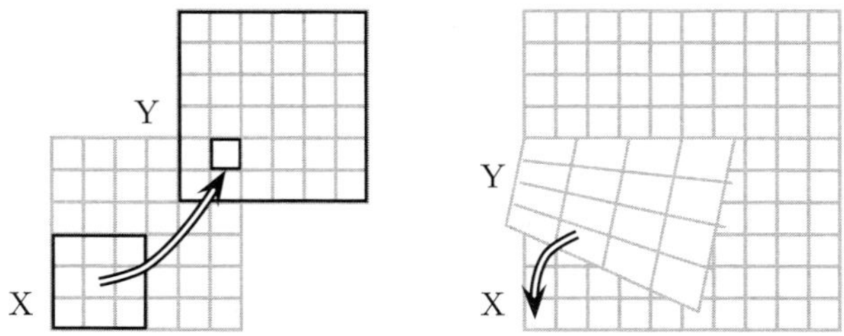

Fig. 2. Spatial transform operators: (a) decreasing the spatial resolution by $\frac{1}{3}$ (left); (b) re-projection to a new coordinate system (right)

Without any knowledge about the point lattice organization in **G**, such an operator could *potentially block forever*, e.g., when the rightmost lower point in a frame has been received and no suitable neighboring points follow. In an implementation, such a scenario (which in general can occur for any point in a frame) can be avoided by utilizing auxiliary information about the spatial region currently scanned by an instrument and added as metadata to the stream of image data. The operator then can use such metadata and execute appropriate boundary point interpolations.

From a geographic application point of view, an important functionality is to re-project geospatial data from one coordinate system to another one [11,26]. One can think of a re-projection as a mathematical framework that specifies for every point $\mathbf{y} \in \mathbf{Y}$ what points in $\mathbf{X}$ are necessary to compute $\mathbf{y}$ and its point value. Often, the transformation strives for an approximate one-to-one correspondence between points in point lattices $\mathbf{X}$ and $\mathbf{Y}$, and a regular lattice corresponding in size and aspect to the lattice of the original point set $\mathbf{X}$ is overlayed over the spatial extent of the new point lattice. In traditional GIS applications, for a point $\mathbf{y} \in \mathbf{Y}$, either the nearest point in the original point lattice is chosen to supply the point value, or a function is applied to a neighborhood of pixels of $\mathbf{x}$ to provide the point value. Respective functions f_{spat} include linear interpolations or higher-order fitting routines. In general, there is no single best solution, considering the multitude of coordinate systems and types of re-projections.

From a query processing point of view, it is important to note that such types of spatial transform operators may block for a considerable amount of time, as the computation of the value of a point $\mathbf{y} \in \mathbf{Y}$ may require any number of points from $\mathbf{X}$. An implementation of individual operators corresponding to specific spatial transform and re-projections, however, can be again tailored by utilizing metadata about the spatial extent of the current scan sector and the spatial resolution associated with $\mathbf{X}$ and $\mathbf{Y}$.

3.3 Stream Compositions

Geographic applications often derive data products by combining information from different spectral bands. For example, the normalized difference vegetation index (NDVI) describing the health of vegetation combines pixel data from the near-infrared and visible band to compute a single NDVI value for a spatial location. In our model, combining image data from different spectral bands is realized through a generic stream composition operator where each stream represents a single spectral band.

Definition 10 (Stream composition). *Let* $\mathbf{G}_1, \mathbf{G}_2$ *be two streams over a point lattice* $\mathbf{X}$ *and value set* $\mathbb{V}$. *A* stream composition operator γ *over* $\mathbf{G}_1, \mathbf{G}_2$, *denoted* $\mathbf{G}_1\ \gamma\ \mathbf{G}_2$ *is a binary operator defined as*

$$\mathbf{G}_1\ \gamma\ \mathbf{G}_2 \equiv \{(\mathbf{x}, \mathbf{G}_1(\mathbf{x})\ \gamma\ \mathbf{G}_2(\mathbf{x}))\colon \mathbf{x} \in \mathbf{X}\}.$$

Typical stream composition operators include addition, difference, division, supremum and infimum, i.e., $\gamma \in \{+, -, \div, \vee, \wedge\}$. There are several important observations regarding the behavior of these operators. First, although both streams are based on the same point lattice $\mathbf{X}$, it can happen that there is no single point that occurs in both streams. This obviously is the case when the two streams cover different spatial regions.

Second, and more important for practical applications, note that in order to apply γ to two point values $\mathbf{G}_1(\mathbf{x})$ and $\mathbf{G}_2(\mathbf{x})$, the points must match in the spatial dimension and in the timestamp. This has considerable consequences on how timestamping for points is realized and, consequently, how much intermediate image data an operator needs to store in order to output new image data.

For example, assume a satellite that scans a spatial region first for the visible band and then for the near-infrared band. If incoming points are timestamped based on when the points were measured, a stream composition operator would never produce new image data as respective timestamps would never match. That is why in practice, point data is timestamped using *scan-sector identifiers*: a satellite scans a spatial region for different spectral bands, each band resulting in a single GeoStream. A point in each of the imagery obtained for the spectral bands for the scan sector is assigned the scan-sector identifier as timestamp, facilitating the comparison of point data from different bands and streams, respectively.

Finally, although for a single scan, all point data from the different streams have the same timestamp, the space complexity of a stream composition operator depends on the point organization in which the image data is transmitted (see also Fig.1). If the data is transmitted on an image-by-image basis, the operator has to buffer a complete image whereas for a row-by-row organization, it only has to buffer a single row of one stream before it can combine it with a matching row from another stream.

In summary, the realization of a stream composition operator, which conceptually might seem straightforward, very much depends on the scan characteristics of the remote-sensing instrument that generates the image data streams.

3.4 Complex Queries and Query Rewriting

In geographic applications, data products are typically obtained by applying a sequence of operators to imagery. Our query model and the closure property of operators in particular naturally facilitate the formulation of complex queries. However, unlike queries in a relational database context where queries can have complex nested subqueries, continuous queries over streams of remotely-sensed image data typically tend to be less complex; in fact, they are often "sequential".

Due to space constraints we cannot describe all query composition and rewriting techniques for the previously presented operators, but we illustrate a few key aspects of our query model by means of an example. Assume two GeoStreams $\mathbf{G}_1$ and $\mathbf{G}_2$ corresponding to the near-infrared and visible band of a satellite instrument. Consider the following query

$$((f_{val} \circ ((\mathbf{G}_1 - \mathbf{G}_2) \div (\mathbf{G}_2 + \mathbf{G}_1))) \circ f_{UTM})_{|\mathbf{R}}$$

which can be read as follows: (1) compute the NDVI over streams $\mathbf{G}_1, \mathbf{G}$ as stream composition $((\mathbf{G}_1 - \mathbf{G}_2) \div (\mathbf{G}_2 + \mathbf{G}_1))$, (2) perform a value transform f_{val} on the result point lattice, (3) re-project to the UTM coordinate system (f_{UTM}), and finally (4) select only point data for the region $\mathbf{R}$ of interest. Assume $\mathbf{G}_1$ and $\mathbf{G}_2$ are based on a coordinate system C. Rather than performing the composition of *all point data* from the two streams, followed by a value and spatial transform on all the resulting points, the final spatial restriction $_{|\mathbf{R}}$ can be pushed "inwards" and applied first to $\mathbf{G}_1$ and $\mathbf{G}_2$ before any composition.

However, because in the query **R** is based on the UTM coordinate system, **R** needs to be mapped to the coordinate system C. The query optimizer has to identify such rewrites in particular for spatial selections, as these result in the most significantly space and time gains for query evaluation.

4 Query Processing Framework

Some of the operators introduced in Section 3 have been realized in the context of the *GeoStreams* project [6]. In the following, we give a brief overview of the prototypical system being developed in this project to illustrate the data flow and stream processing components.

Remotely-sensed imagery from the GOES satellites [8] is received by the Data Stream Management System (DSMS) server, and the raw data is converted by the stream generator into GeoStream point lattices that have a row-by-row organization. The streams correspond to the different spectral channels that are generated by the imager instrument on-board the GOES satellite. In the DSMS server, a spatial transform operator converts the GeoStream point sets, which come in a satellite specific coordinate system (called GOES Variable Format), into point lattices based on latitude/longitude. Multiple users can connect to the DSMS server and formulate queries over the GOES data streams generated within the DSMS. Users use a Web-based graphical interface to specify spectral channels (streams) of interest, regions of interest, and certain spatial transforms (e.g., zooming). The coordinate system used in this interface is latitude/longitude.

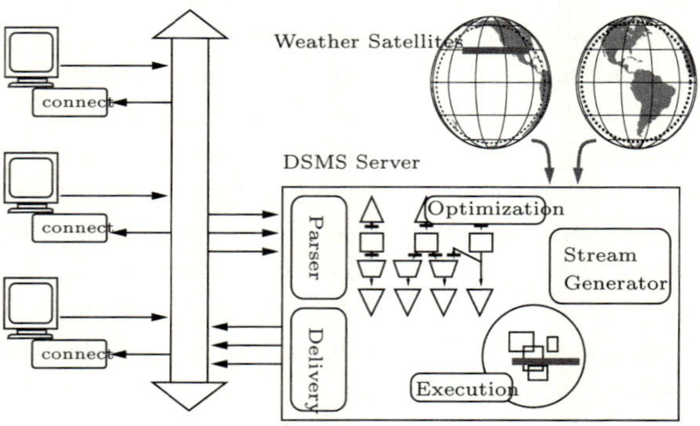

Fig. 3. Architecture of the Stream Management System for Geospatial Image Data

User queries, which are converted by the interface to specialized HTTP requests, are transmitted to the server, parsed, and registered. Multiple queries against a single GeoStream are optimized using a dynamic cascade tree structure [10], which acts as a single spatial restriction operator and efficiently streams only the point data of interest to current continuous queries to subsequent operators. As indicated in Section 3.4, optimizing queries with respect to regions of interest has the greatest benefit. This spatial restriction operator then streams the point data to a specialized stream delivery operator that ships stream results back to clients using the PNG image format. Other operators that are currently being implemented and integrated with the query execution engine include different types of re-projections (using extensions to PROJ.4 [21]) and specialized macro operators that compute specific data products, such as NDVI. Such data products can be directly selected in the user interface, without the need to compose otherwise complex queries.

5 Related Work

Our work borrows several fundamental concepts from Ritter and Wilson's Image Algebra [23], in particular the functional representation of images and some operations on images. Our data and query model provides an extension of these concepts in that we (1) consider streams of image data instead of (static) images and (2) explicitly introduce the notion of spatio-temporal data, which is geo-referenced, and specialized operations on geo-referenced data.

Query processing techniques for multi-dimensional arrays have been studied by Marathe and Salem [18] and Libkin et al. [14]. General types of operations on raster image data, which can be considered as a specialized form of arrays, have been proposed by Baumann [2,3,4]. While these works study frameworks for operations and query processing on array data and raster images, they do not consider the aspect of streaming geospatial image data. The operators are not specific to streaming spatio-temporal data and in particular do not consider the specifics of typical computations performed on remotely-sensed imagery. As we have illustrated in Section 3, knowing about point lattice organizations in a stream of image data and properties of satellite scan sectors can have a significant impact on how image data is processed.

A work closely related to ours is the one by Mokbel et al. [17] on continuous query processing of spatio-temporal data streams in the context of pervasive location-aware computing environments. In their work, they primarily focus on object-based spatio-tempporal data (moving objects), whereas our approach exclusively focuses on field-based spatio-temporal data, in particular satellite imagery and its specific operators.

The large body of work on spatial and spatio-temporal data (for an overview, see, e.g., [22,24]) in general neither considers streaming geospatial image data nor remotely-sensed data.

6 Conclusions and Outlook

Remotely-sensed imagery from the numerous satellites orbiting the Earth provides a great opportunity to develop novel data stream management and processing systems, leveraging techniques and models developed for relational data streams to improve processing streaming geospatial image data. In this paper, we have presented the foundation of a data and query model that allows the formulation and processing of continuous queries over streams of such image data. In particular, we have discussed the specifics of stream restriction, transform, and composition operators with a focus on the properties of remotely-sensed data and processing techniques relevant for typical geographic applications.

We are currently extending the set of operators, with a particular focus on spatial transforms, because they represent the most demanding types of operators in terms of space and time complexity. We are also investigating the full integration of a spatio-temporal aggregate operator for streaming image data. This operator has been proposed in [27], and will provide an important addition to the functionality of our stream management system.

References

1. A. Arasu, S. Babu, J. Widom: The CQL Continuous Query Language: Semantic Foundations and Query Execution. The VLDB Journal 15(2):121–142, 2006.
2. P. Baumann: Management of Multidimensional Discrete Data. The VLDB Journal 3(4):401–444, 1994.
3. P. Baumann: Database Array Algebra for Spatio-Temporal Data and Beyond. In *Next Generation Information Technologies and Systems, 4th International Workshop (NGITS'99)*, LNCS 1649, Springer, 76–93, 1999.
4. P. Baumann, A. Dehmel, P. Furtado, R. Ritsch, N. Widmann: Spatio-Temporal Retrieval with RasDaMan. In *Proceedings of 25th International Conference on Very Large Data Bases*, 746–749, 1999.
5. B. Babcock, S. Babu, M. Datar, R. Motwani, J. Widom: Models and Issues in Data Stream Systems. In *Proceedings of the Twenty-first ACM SIGACT-SIGMOD-SIGART Symposium on Principles of Database Systems (PODS 2002)*, 1–16, 2002.
6. GeoStreams: Adaptive Query Processing Architectures for Streaming Geospatial Image Data. University of California at Davis, `http://geostreams.ucdavis.edu`.
7. L. Golab, M. T. Özsu: Issues in Data Stream Management. SIGMOD Record 32(2):5–14, 2003.
8. NOAA Satellite and Information Service. Geostationary Satellite Server. http://www.goes.noaa.gov.
9. Q. Hart, M. Gertz: Querying Streaming Geospatial Image Data: The GeoStreams Project. In *17th International Conference on Scientific and Statistical Database Management (SSDBM 2005)*, 2005.
10. Q. Hart, M. Gertz, J. Zhang: Evaluation of a Dynamic Tree Structure for Indexing Query Regions on Streaming Geospatial Data. In *9th International Symposium on Spatial and Temporal Databases (SSTD05)*, LNCS 3633, Springer, 145–162, 2005.
11. J. C. Iliffe: Datums and Map Projections. CRC Press, 2000.
12. J. R. Jensen: Remote Sensing of the Environment: An Earth Resource Perspective. Prentice-Hall, 2000.
13. J. R. Jensen: Introductory Digital Image Processing: A Remote Sensing Perspective (3rd Edition). Prentice-Hall, 2005.
14. L. Libkin, R. Machlin, L. Wong. A Query Language for Multidimensional Arrays: Design, Implementation, and Optimization Techniques. In *Proc. of the 1996 SIGMOD International Conference on Management of Data*, 228–239, 1996.
15. Landsat 7, `http://landsat.gsfc.nasa.gov`.
16. LIDAR Tutorial. `www.ghcc.msfc.nasa.gov/sparcle/sparcle_tutorial.html`.

17. M.F. Mokbel, X. Xiong, M.A. Hammad, W.G. Aref: Continuous Query Processing of Spatio-temporal Data Streams in PLACE. GeoInformatica 9(4):343–365, 2005.
18. A. P. Marathe, K. Salem: Query Processing Techniques for Arrays. The VLDB Journal 11(1):68–91, 2002.
19. P. M. Mather: *Computer Processing of Remotely-Sensed Images.* Wiley, 2004.
20. Moderate Resolution Imaging Spectroradiometer (MODIS). `http://modis.gsfc.nasa.gov`.
21. PROJ.4 - Cartographic Projections Library. `http://proj.maptools.org`.
22. P. Rigaux, M. Scholl, A. Voisard: *Spatial Databases with Application to GIS.* Morgan Kaufmann, 2002.
23. G. X. Ritter, J. N. Wilson: *Handbook of Computer Vision Algorithms in Image Algebra (2nd Edition).* CRC Press, 2001.
24. S. Shekar, S. Chawla: Spatial Databases: A Tour. Prentice Hall, 2003.
25. A. Skidmore (Editor): *Environmental Modeling with GIS and Remote Sensing.* Taylor & Francis, 2002.
26. J. P. Snyder, W. R. Tobler, O.H. Yang, J.P. Snyder, Q.H. Yang: Map Projection Transformation: Principles and Applications. CRC Press, 2000.
27. J. Zhang, M. Gertz, D. Aksoy: Spatio-Temporal Aggregates over Raster Image Data. In *12th ACM International Workshop on Geographic Information Systems (ACM-GIS 2004)*, 39–46, 2004.

Enhanced Regular Path Queries on Semistructured Databases

Dan Stefanescu[1] and Alex Thomo[2]

[1] Suffolk University, Boston, USA
dan@mcs.suffolk.edu
[2] University of Victoria, Victoria, Canada
thomo@cs.uvic.ca

Abstract. Regular path queries are the basic navigational component of virtually all the mechanisms for querying semistructured data commonly found in information integration applications, Web and communication networks, biological data management etc. We start by proposing weight-enhanced regular path queries with semantics that allow user-assigned preference (query) weights to be naturally combined with quantitative database link-information for driving the navigation.

Motivated by the fact that the main applications of semistructured data involve distributed data sources, we focus next on the distributed evaluation of the weight-enhanced path queries. We present a distributed algorithm for evaluating our proposed queries in a *multi-source* setting. Our algorithm is general in the sense that it does not assume a known topology of the network and it can work using asynchronous communication. This algorithm can also be used to solve multi-source shortest path problems for which the full graph is not known in advance. To the best of our knowledge our algorithm is the first to address this problem in such a setting.

1 Introduction

Nowadays, modeling and/or representing the data as labeled graphs has become very common in many areas such as communication and traffic networks, Web information systems, data integration, biological data management, cartography, etc (see e.g. [8,7,13]). As it has been recognized by seminal works (see [1,12]), the basic querying mechanism for such data are (regular) path queries, which are formulated using regular expressions, that provide to the user a recursive way of navigating (partially unknown) graph data.

As an example from airline networks, imagine a user who wants to find all the pairs of cities that can be reached from each other by taking Air Canada. Notably, this can easily be captured by using a path query such as $aircanada^*$, which has to be evaluated starting from each city Air Canada flies from.

In order to evaluate our example path query, a query processor would try to find all the paths consisting of *aircanada*-labeled edges. However, there are two problems associated with path queries like the above. First, a selective query

T. Grust et al. (Eds.): EDBT 2006 Workshops, LNCS 4254, pp. 700–711, 2006.

(such as *aircanada**) may return too few answers. For example, two cities such as Vancouver (*YVR*) and San Diego (*SAN*) might not have an all-*aircanada* labeled route[1] and thus, the pair (*YVR*, *SAN*) will not be in the returned answer for the query. On the other hand, partnerships between airlines are a well known fact, and clearly the system should be able to return the pair (*YVR*, *SAN*) even in the absence of an Air Canada route from Vancouver to San Diego. In the particular example there is a jointly operated route with Air Canada flying from Vancouver to Los Angeles and continuing with United Airlines from Los Angeles to San Diego. It might seem that this is a simple matter of specifying the disjunctive path query *aircanada* + *united* instead. However, this second query does not differentiate between purely Air Canada routes (that the user might prefer) and the joint partnership routes. Hence, the system should allow the user to specify alternative choices, which can be weighted by her preferences. Furthermore, the system should also be able to present a ranking of the returned answers with respect to the expressed user preferences.

In this paper, we address this problem by proposing weight-enhanced path queries (WEPQ's). Intuitively, we allow the user to specify weighted edge alternatives in path queries. For example, instead of *aircanada**, the user could specify the weighted path query

$$(aircanada{:}0+united{:}1+usairways{:}3)^*+(aircanada{:}0)^*\cdot(alaska{:}0)\cdot(aircanada{:}0)^*$$

to express her preferences, which in plain language are: "I would like to take Air Canada routes (paths with weight 0), or United Airlines routes but with lower preference (weight 1), or US Airways but with even lower preference (weight 3). Furthermore, I can accept at no cost a single Alaska segment connecting two Air Canada routes."

The second problem with simple path queries is that their semantics do not take into consideration other properties of the traversed links other than the mere link label. To illustrate with the above example, a query such as *aircanada**, would return all the pairs of cities connected through an aircanada route without any indication of the length of the path used to compute the answers. This is just an example of what other information might be present at the database links, and clearly, there are other examples of useful information such as frequency of flights for a particular link, time of the day, special service offered, etc. Notably, it is easy to map such information into (virtual) link weights as we navigate the database.

After introducing an "edge importance aware" generalization of graph databases, we formally define the notion of weighted answers to WEPQ's on such databases. The computed weights of the answers enable their ranking according to the user preference for following certain database paths. Moreover, we propose query semantics in which the weight of an automaton transition is further scaled up or down by the importance of the traversed database edge. Thus, in our spatial example, the edge importance could simply be the edge-length, and so, traversing a 1000 *miles united*-edge would be less preferable than traversing a

[1] A route may contain intermediate cities.

300 *miles usairlines*-edge, even though initially in the query, flying with United Airlines was more preferable than flying with US Airways.[2]

Analogous to the airline example, we can also describe our semantics in a Web scenario. Here, the database edges are hyperlinks, and the values assigned to each edge could be based on the inverse of the page-rank of the linked page, using an algorithm similar to the one used to rank pages in a search engine.

In almost every scenario where the data is represented in a graph based fashion, prime examples of which are information integration, Web based information systems, airline reservation systems etc, the data is distributed among many different sources. Clearly, it is imperative to not only show how a query can be evaluated in a centralized way, but also to devise truly distributed algorithms for this purpose. With "truly" in this context we want to say that the data shipping paradigm, commonly used by the today's XQuery processors, is not to be considered as a viable distributed solution. Instead, a query shipping paradigm should be used, where the queries are appropriately decomposed, and where each source works towards accomplishing specific tasks related to the local data only. Hence, we turn our attention to devising a distributed algorithm for the evaluation of our proposed WEPQ's. Our assumption is that the database graph is partitioned into several autonomous processors which do not share memory. Communication between these processors is achieved exclusively through message passing.

In our setting, we tackle the more challenging problem of evaluating a query starting from multiple database nodes. Clearly, multi-source path queries impose a much higher load on the system, since we need to find all the possible paths spelling words in the query language, as opposed to finding paths starting from some root only. Moreover, the database paths that one has to follow starting from different nodes might have a great amount of overlap and a naive processing would do extensive redundant work. To see this, imagine we want to evaluate *aircanada*:0 + *united*:1, starting from Vancouver and Toronto. Such routes will have many intersections such as for example in Los Angeles. An intelligent query processing would not follow more than once sub-paths starting from Los Angeles.

We present a distributed algorithm that completely avoids traversing database paths multiple times. Through an iterative weight-correcting process, our algorithm computes and ranks the query answers. A nice feature of our algorithm is that any snapshot of the query answer at any point in time will be a partial answer to the user query. The practical consequence of this is that the user would very soon see some partial answers to her query, and along the time that she is willing to wait, new answers will show up, while the existing answers will possibly be improved.

Related Work. Similar queries have been also introduced in [2] in the context of Web data. However, our query semantics are more general, and furthemore we explore in detail different aspects of handling, generating, and evaluating such queries.

[2] We assume that the user is not interested in optimizing the distance traveled. Thus, our problem is not about multi-feature ranking. Rather we assume that the user is interested in optimizing her preferences, which she can tolerate to be weighted by the cost of satisfying them.

Interestingly, our expression syntax is similar with the one used in [4,5]. Syntactically, the difference is that in [4,5], the expressions were on symbol-weight-symbol triples as opposed to symbol-weight pairs that we use. Semantically, the expressions of [4,5] were used for capturing knowledge or constraints about databases.

We also want to mention here the work of [3] and [9] on how to produce ranked XPath answers in XML information retrieval (IR) systems. In [3] and [9], the focus is on ranking the node answers according to the text contents of the selected (by XPath) XML nodes. Namely, the node texts are ranked using IR relevance criteria. We want to stress here that our approach is very different from [3] and [9]. We rank the node answers according to the "quality" (based on user preferences) of the paths used for reaching the nodes. Thus, we present a graph *structural* approach to ranking the query answers, which is inherently different from IR text approaches of [3] and [9].

Surprisingly, to the best of our knowledge only very few works have dealt with a distributed evaluation of path queries. The most important works in this direction are [1], [11], and [10]. In [1], the architecture is similar with ours but the queries are simple path queries without weights, and furthermore the evaluation is considered starting from some root node only. The single root assumption is also made in [10], focusing in a generalization of path queries that is different from the one in the present paper. Similarly with [1] and [10] , [11] also studies the single root scenario for simple (unweighed) path queries. However, in [11], the main objective is to minimize the number of communication messages and for achieving this [11] suggests an approach, which distributes the load unevenly among processors.

Our distributed query evaluation algorithm is inherently different from the algorithms in [1,11,10] because here we solve the more difficult problem of evaluating the query starting from multiple database objects (or all objects).[3] Moreover, our queries are semantically different from those considered in [1,11,10].

The rest of the paper is organized as follows. In Section 2, we introduce weight-enhanced path queries (WEPQ's) and their semantics. Section 3 provides a short review of the evaluation of classical path queries and the intuition behind the algorithm for evaluating WEPQ's. In Section 4, we present our distributed algorithm and discuss its message complexity.

2 Databases and Weight-Enhanced Path Queries

We consider a database to be an edge-labeled graph with real values assigned to the edges. Intuitively, the nodes of the database graph represent objects and the edges represent relationships (and their importance) between the objects.

Formally, let Δ be an alphabet. Elements of Δ will be denoted $R, S, \ldots$. As usual, Δ^* denotes the set of all finite words over Δ. Words will be denoted by

[3] Even for simple shortest path problems, the algorithms for multi-source variants are inherently different from the algorithms for single-source variants. Usually, the former are dynamic programming approaches, while the latter are greedy approaches.

$u, w, \ldots$. We also assume that we have a universe of objects, and objects will be denoted $a, b, c, \ldots,$. A *database* DB is then a weighted graph (V, E), where V is a finite set of objects and $E \subseteq V \times \Delta \times \mathbb{R} \times V$ is a set of directed edges labeled with symbols from Δ and weighted with numbers from $\mathbb{R}$.

Before introducing weighted preference path queries, it will help to first review the classical path queries.

A *path query* (PQ) is a regular language over Δ. For the ease of notation, we will blur the distinction between regular languages and regular expressions that represent them. Let Q be a PQ and $DB = (V, E)$ a database. Then, the *answer* to Q on DB is defined as

$$Ans(Q, DB) = \{(a, b) \in V : a \xrightarrow{w} b \text{ in } DB \text{ for some } w \in Q\},$$

where $\longrightarrow$ denotes a path in the database.

Now, let $\mathbb{N} = \{0, 1, 2, \ldots\}$. A *weight enhanced path query* (WEPQ) is a regular language over $\Delta \times \mathbb{N}$. The "words" of such a language are in fact pairs in $\Delta^* \times \mathbb{N}$. Observe that, given a WEPQ Q, and a word w on Δ, w can be weighted in Q by different real numbers. As an example, it could be that there exist $r_1, r_2 \in \mathbb{R}$ (there can many more such numbers) such that both (w, r_1), and (w, r_2) are in Q. In order to capture the best preference that query Q gives to the word w, we define the *Q-preference* of w, denoted with $pref_Q(w)$, to be the smallest of the values associated with with w in Q.

Next, we define the *weighted answer (WAns)* to a WEPQ Q on DB starting from some object o as

$$WAns(Q, DB) = \{(a, b, k) \in V \times V \times \mathbb{N} : k = inf\,\{pref_Q(w) : a \xrightarrow{w} b \text{ in } DB\}\}$$

Naturally, WEPQ's can be represented by "weighted automata." Formally, a *weighted automaton* $\mathcal{A} = (P, \Delta, \tau, p_0, F)$ consists of a finite set of states P, an input alphabet Δ, an initial state p_0, a set of final states F, and a transition relation $\tau \subseteq P \times \Delta \cup \{\epsilon\} \times \mathbb{N} \times P$.

Given a weighted automaton $\mathcal{A} = (P, \Delta, \tau, p_0, F)$, we say that a word $w \in \Delta^*$ is *accepted through a k-weighted transition path* if there exists a sequence $(p_0, w_1, k_1, p_1), \ldots, (p_{n-1}, w_n, k_n, p_n)$ of state transitions of τ (where $\{w_1, \ldots, w_n\} \subseteq \Delta \cup \{\epsilon\}$), such that $p_n \in F$, $w = w_1 \ldots w_n$, and $k = k_1 + \cdots + k_n$. When referring to a transition path as the above, we could also say that it is a "$(k_1, \ldots, k_n)$-weighted transition path" in order to concisely specify that such a path consists of n transitions with respective weights $k_1, \ldots, k_n$. We denote the set of all accepted words of $\mathcal{A}$ (regardless of transition path followed) by $\mathcal{A}(L)$.

Now, we can equivalently define $pref_Q(w)$ using weighted automata. Thus, let $\mathcal{A}_Q$ be an arbitrary weighted automaton for Q. For w on Δ, the *Q-preference* of w is

$$pref_Q(w) = \begin{cases} inf\,\{k : w \text{ is accepted though a } k\text{-weighted transition path in } \mathcal{A}_Q\} \\ \infty, \text{ if } w \notin \mathcal{A}_Q(L). \end{cases}$$

In our definition of $WAns(Q, DB)$, we do not use the real values that could possibly be assigned to the edges of the database graph. As mentioned in the

Introduction, such values can be used to scale up or down the transitions during the query evaluation.

In order to take into consideration the edge values, we define the *scaled Q-preference* of a word w (of length n) through a scaling vector $\mathbf{scale} = (r_1, \ldots, r_n) \in \mathbb{R}^n$, as

$$pref_Q(w, \mathbf{scale}) = \begin{cases} inf\,\{r : w \text{ is accepted though a } (k_1, \ldots, k_n)\text{-weighted} \\ \quad \text{transition path in } \mathcal{A}_Q, \text{ and } r = k_1 r_1 + \cdots + k_n r_n\} \\ \infty, \text{ if } w \notin \mathcal{A}_Q(L). \end{cases}$$

For a path π in DB, we define $\mathbf{scale}_\pi$ to be the scaling vector obtained in the natural way from the values of each edge along π. We are ready now to define the path *scaled weighted answer (SWAns)* of a WEPQ Q on DB as

$$\begin{aligned} SWAns(Q, DB) = \{(a, b, r) \in V \times V \times \mathbb{R} :& \\ k = inf\,\{pref_Q(w, \mathbf{scale}_\pi) :& \\ \pi \text{ is a path } a \xrightarrow{w} b \text{ in } DB\}\}.& \end{aligned}$$

Next, we show how to efficiently transform a weighted automaton $\mathcal{A}$, into one with ϵ-free transitions, in such a way that the essential features of $\mathcal{A}$ are preserved. The ϵ-freeness is essential in properly computing the answer of a WEPQ.

From the automaton $\mathcal{A}$ we will construct another "weight equivalent" automaton $\mathcal{B}$. We will use ϵ-*closure*(p), similarly to [6], to denote the set of all states q, such that there is path π, from p to q in $\mathcal{A}$, spelling ϵ.

Obviously, we will keep all the non-ϵ transitions of $\mathcal{A}$ in the automaton $\mathcal{B}$, that we are constructing.

Now, we will insert an R-transition ($R \neq \epsilon$) in $\mathcal{B}$ from a state p to a state q whenever there is in $\mathcal{A}$ a path π, spelling ϵ, from p to an intermediate state r and there is an R-transition, from that state r to the state q. We take special care here for computing the weight of these transitions. Formally, if $\mathcal{A} = (P, \Delta, \tau_\mathcal{A}, p_0, F)$, then $\mathcal{B} = (P, \Delta, \tau_\mathcal{B}, p_0, G)$, where $G = F \cup \{p_0 : \text{ if } \epsilon\text{-}closure_\mathcal{A}(p_0) \cap F \neq \emptyset\}$ and

$$\begin{aligned} \tau_\mathcal{B} = \{(p, R, n, q) : (p, R, n, q) \in \tau_\mathcal{A}\} \cup& \\ \{(p, S, m+n, q) : \exists r \in \epsilon\text{-}closure_\mathcal{A}(p),& \\ \text{such that } (r, S, n, q) \in \tau\},& \end{aligned}$$

where the weight m is the weight of the cheapest path from p to r in $\mathcal{A}$ spelling ϵ, and (r, S, n, q) is the cheapest S-transition from r to q.

It is easy to verify about the above constructed automaton $\mathcal{B}$ that

Theorem 1. *For a given word w, there is k-weighted transition path spelling w in $\mathcal{B}$ if and only if there is such a path in $\mathcal{A}$.*

Also observe that in the above construction, although there can be exponentially many ϵ-paths from state p to state r, we insert only one transition from p to

q for each symbol labeling a transition from r to q. Hence, we have that the size of $\mathcal{B}$ is polynomial on the size of $\mathcal{A}$. Moreover, note that there can be many transitions from r to s labeled with the same symbol but having different weight. However, we only consider the cheapest of them.

3 Path Queries, Reachability, and Shortest Paths

Before presenting the distributed (weighted) query evaluation, we will review the classical method of query evaluation. In essence, the evaluation proceeds by creating state-object pairs from the query automaton and the database. For this, let $\mathcal{A}$ be an NFA that accepts a query Q. Starting from some object a of a database DB, we first create the pair (p_0, a), where p_0 is the initial state in $\mathcal{A}$. Then, we create all the pairs (p, b) such that there exist a transition from p_0 to p in $\mathcal{A}$, and an edge from a to b in DB, and furthermore the labels of the transition and the edge match. In the same way, we continue to create new pairs from the existing ones, until we are not anymore able to do so. At that point, we produce as the answer to the query the set of object pairs (a, b), such that b has been associated with some final state of the query automaton $\mathcal{A}$.

It is worth mentioning here that the state-object pairs induce an (implicit) edge labeled graph with these pairs as its nodes. Regarding the edges, let (q, b) be obtained by another pair, say (p, a), through a database edge and automaton transition both labeled by R. Then, we consider an R-labeled edge from (p, a) to (q, b) in the induced graph.

Now, when having a weighted query automaton, we can modify the classical matching algorithm to build instead a weighted state-object graph. This can be achieved by assigning to the edges of this graph the corresponding automaton transition weights scaled by the corresponding database edge-values.

It is not difficult to see that, in order to find the weighted answers to the query, we have to find, in the state-object graph, the shortest paths from the "sources" (p_0, a) to all the nodes (p, b), where p is a final state in the query automaton $\mathcal{A}$.

However, the challenge is that when the database is very large and distributed, we cannot afford to construct the above graph, and then use some centralized shortest path algorithm on it.

In the next section, we present a distributed algorithm which computes the multi-source shortest paths in the state-object graph, while constructing it on the fly and achieving all the possible overlap in the computations starting from each source.

4 Distributed Evaluation of Path Queries

Our algorithm has two interwoven components: the computation of query answers and its termination detection. In this paper, we focus on the computation of query answers. The termination detection will be discussed in a companion paper.

The central idea of our algorithm is to overlap computations starting from different objects. We assume that each database object, say a, is being serviced by a dedicated process for that object P_a.

Each process starts by creating an initial task for itself. The tasks are "keyed" by the automaton states, with the initial tasks being keyed by the initial state, say p_0. Each task $\langle p, \ldots \rangle$ corresponding to some object a (serviced by P_a), is eventually selected for "expansion," which is the creation and sending of new tasks to other processes whenever there is an automaton transition originating at state p that matches a database edge originating at the object a. Let (p, R, q, k) be such a transition matching a database edge (a, R, b, t). Then the process P_a will send the task $\langle q, \ldots \rangle$ to the process P_b servicing the object b. The process P_b, upon receival of the task $\langle q, \ldots \rangle$, will establish a virtual communication channel with the process P_a for the originating task $\langle p, \ldots \rangle$. This channel is weighted by kt. In a sense, the completion of the task $\langle p, \ldots \rangle$ in P_a depends on the completion of the task $\langle q, \ldots \rangle$ in P_b.

Notably, overlapping of computations happens when a process receives the same task multiple times from different neighboring processes. In such a case the receiving process does not accept the "new" task, but instead it creates only a virtual communication channel with the sending process as explained above. The overlapping of computations is reminiscent of view-based optimization of queries.

Whenever a process receives (the first time) a task keyed by a final state, it sends as an answer, through the backward communication channels, the *id* of the object that it services. The receiving processes will back-propagate such answers, through their *appropriate* backward communication channels, satisfying along the way the p_0 keyed tasks. The meaning of "appropriate" will become clear in the detailed algorithm that follows. The back-propagated answers will be weighted by the cost of traversing the communication channel paths. Recall that the cost of a communication channel is the product of the corresponding automaton transition and database edge weights. At the joint points, i.e. at the tasks receiving the same answer from different paths, we "relax" the weight of the answer by setting it equal to the smallest received weight.

Now, we formally present our algorithm, which, as we mentioned earlier, emphasizes the distributed computation of query answers ignoring (for the moment) the termination detection of the computation.

Algorithm 1

Input:

1. A database DB. For simplicity we assume that each database object, say a, is being serviced by a dedicated process for that object P_a.
2. A weighted automaton $\mathcal{A} = (P, \Delta, \tau, p_0, F)$ for a WEPQ Q. This automaton is sent first to all the processes.[4]

[4] This does no harm to the true distribution of computation. Instead of transferring whole parts of the data (as in the XQuery paradigm), we simply send (once only) the query automaton, which is polynomial in the size of the regular expression given by the (human) user.

Output: The weighted answers to the query Q evaluated on the database DB.
Method: Each process P_a creates a task $\langle p_0, \{\}, \texttt{unexpanded}\rangle$ for itself. If p_0 is also a final state, insert $(a, 0)$ in the pair-set of the above p_0-task, which would become $\langle p_0, \{(a, 0)\}, \texttt{unexpanded}\rangle$.

1. Repeat 2, 3, and 4 at each process P_a in *parallel*, until termination is detected.
2. For each unprocessed yet task $\langle p, \{\ldots\}, \texttt{unexpanded}\rangle$
   (a) **if** there is a t-weighted R-edge, from object a to some object b in DB, and there is a k-weighted R-transition from state p to some state q in automaton $\mathcal{A}$
   then (P_a will expand the task to P_b)
   P_a creates a message $\langle a, p, q, u\rangle$, where $u = kt$, and sends it to process P_b.
   else P_a is "stuck" with respect to this task, and sends an empty message $\langle\rangle$ through each communication channel (see step 3) $\langle(a, p), (\_, \_), x\rangle$, to the processes at the other end of the channels.
   (b) Task $\langle p, \{\}, \texttt{unexpanded}\rangle$ will change to $\texttt{expanded}$.
3. Upon receival of a message $\langle c, r, p, v\rangle$ (due to expansion of an r-keyed task of P_c)
   (a) **if** P_a does not have yet a task $\langle p, \{\ldots\}, \_\rangle$
   then P_a creates a corresponding task $\langle p, \{\}, \texttt{unexpanded}\rangle$ for itself, and establishes a virtual communication channel $\langle(a, p), (c, r), v\rangle$ between this task and the r-keyed task of P_c.
   if p is a final state
   then P_a inserts $(a, 0)$ in the pair set of $\langle p, \{\}, \texttt{unexpanded}\rangle$, which becomes $\langle p, \{(a, 0)\}, \texttt{unexpanded}\rangle$.
   else (P_a has already a task $\langle p, \{\ldots\}, \_\rangle$)
   If there is not already a communication channel $\langle(a, p), (c, r), v\rangle$, create one as above.
   (b) Next, for each object-weight pair (d, y) in the p-task pair-set, P_a sends a message $\langle d, y + v\rangle$ through the communication channel $\langle(a, p), (c, r), v\rangle$.
4. Upon receival of a message $\langle e, z\rangle$ through some channel, say $\langle(\_, \_), (a, p), y\rangle$:
   (a) P_a checks whether there exists a pair $(e, \_)$ in the p-task pair-set. If there exists such a pair, say (e, w), update (relax) it with $(e, \texttt{min}\{z, w\})$; otherwise insert (e, z).
   (b) **if** in step (a) a change, which is an update or insertion, did happen (say we got (e, z) in the above pair-set)
   then P_a propagates the change upwards by sending through each channel $\langle(a, p), (\_, \_), v\rangle$ the message $\langle e, z + v\rangle$.
   else (when in step (a) there was no change) P_a does nothing. It has already good object weights for the p-keyed task, which have been (or will be soon) propagated upwards.

Finally upon termination, which happens when there are no more messages sent but not yet received, set

$$eval(\mathcal{A}, DB) = \{(a, b, r) : (b, r) \text{ is in the pair-set of the } p_0\text{-task of process } P_a\}.$$

It is easy to verify that the following theorem is true.

Theorem 2. *Upon termination of the above algorithm, we have that*

$$eval(\mathcal{A}, DB) = SWAns(Q, DB).$$

Now, we illustrate the Algorithm 1 by the following example. Consider the database and the query automaton in Figure 1, *left* and *right* respectively. Due to space constraints, we have abbreviated *unexpanded* by u, and *expanded* by e. A possible sequence of actions for Algorithm 1 is given in Table 1. In the first column labeled "T" we number the hypothetical time (break)points in which we observe the system. An explanation for the (possible) actions at each time point follows.

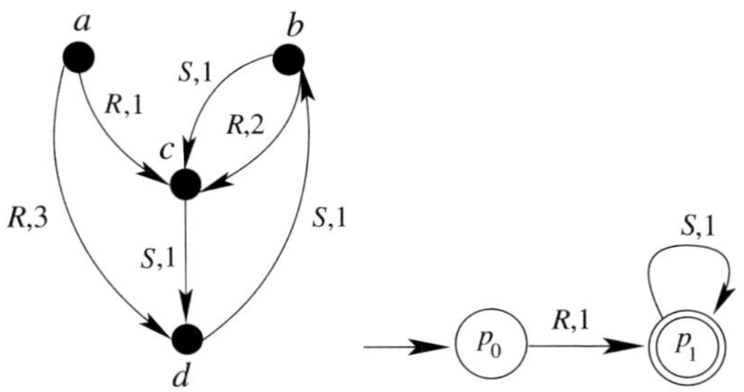

Fig. 1. A database and a query automaton

1. All the processes create a task $\langle p_0, \{\}, u\rangle$ for themselves.
2. P_a expands the tasks $\langle p_0, \{\}, u\rangle$ and sends the task $\langle p_1, \{\}, u\rangle$ to both P_c and P_d. P_c and P_d observe that p_1 is a final state and insert $(c, 0)$ and $(d, 0)$ respectively in their p_1-task pair-set. Next, P_c and P_d send $\langle c, 1\rangle$ and $\langle d, 3\rangle$ respectively to P_a through the appropriate virtual channels.
3. P_b expands the tasks $\langle p_0, \{\}, u\rangle$ and sends a p_1-task to P_c. Since P_c has already received such a task before (from P_a), it does not create a new task, but only establishes a virtual channel with P_b for the originating p_0-task. Also, P_c sends $\langle c, 2\rangle$ to P_b.
4. P_c expands the tasks $\langle p_0, \{\}, u\rangle$. It gets stuck.
5. P_c expands the tasks $\langle p_1, \{\}, u\rangle$ and sends a p_1-task to P_d. Since P_d has already received such a task before, it does not create a new task, but only establishes a virtual channel with P_c for the originating p_1-task. Also, P_d sends $\langle d, 1\rangle$ to P_c. P_c in turn sends $\langle d, 2\rangle$ to P_a, and $\langle d, 3\rangle$ to P_b. P_a will update(relax) the weight for d from 3 to 2.
6. P_d expands the task $\langle p_0, \{\}, u\rangle$. It gets stuck.
7. P_d expands the tasks $\langle p_1, \{(d, 0)\}, u\rangle$ and sends a p_1-task to P_b. P_b observes that p_1 is a final state inserts $(b, 0)$ in its p_1-task pair-set. Also, P_b sends $\langle b, 1\rangle$ to P_d through the appropriate virtual channel. P_d propagates this new answer by sending $\langle b, 4\rangle$ to P_a, and $\langle b, 2\rangle$ to P_c.
8. Further computation occurs leading, upon termination, to this final snapshot.

Table 1. A possible sequence of snapshots for Algorithm 1

T	P_a	P_b	P_c	P_d
1	$\langle p_0, \{\}, u\rangle$	$\langle p_0, \{\}, u\rangle$	$\langle p_0, \{\}, u\rangle$	$\langle p_0, \{\}, u\rangle$
2	$\langle p_0, \{(c,1),(d,3)\}, e\rangle$	$\langle p_0, \{\}, u\rangle$	$\langle p_0, \{\}, u\rangle$ $\langle p_1, \{(c,0)\}, u\rangle$	$\langle p_0, \{\}, u\rangle$ $\langle p_1, \{(d,0)\}, u\rangle$
3	$\langle p_0, \{(c,1),(d,3)\}, e\rangle$	$\langle p_0, \{(c,2)\}, e\rangle$	$\langle p_0, \{\}, u\rangle$ $\langle p_1, \{(c,0)\}, u\rangle$	$\langle p_0, \{\}, u\rangle$ $\langle p_1, \{(d,0)\}, u\rangle$
4	$\langle p_0, \{(c,1),(d,3)\}, e\rangle$	$\langle p_0, \{(c,2)\}, e\rangle$	$\langle p_0, \{\}, e\rangle$ $\langle p_1, \{(c,0)\}, u\rangle$	$\langle p_0, \{\}, u\rangle$ $\langle p_1, \{(d,0)\}, u\rangle$
5	$\langle p_0, \{(c,1),(d,2)\}, e\rangle$	$\langle p_0, \{(c,2),(d,3)\}, e\rangle$	$\langle p_0, \{\}, e\rangle$ $\langle p_1, \{(c,0),(d,1)\}, e\rangle$	$\langle p_0, \{\}, u\rangle$ $\langle p_1, \{(d,0)\}, u\rangle$
6	$\langle p_0, \{(c,1),(d,2)\}, e\rangle$	$\langle p_0, \{(c,2),(d,3)\}, e\rangle$	$\langle p_0, \{\}, e\rangle$ $\langle p_1, \{(c,0),(d,1)\}, e\rangle$	$\langle p_0, \{\}, e\rangle$ $\langle p_1, \{(d,0)\}, u\rangle$
7	$\langle p_0, \{(b,4),(c,1),(d,2)\}, e\rangle$	$\langle p_0, \{(c,2),(d,3)\}, e\rangle$ $\langle p_1, \{(b,0)\}, u\rangle$	$\langle p_0, \{\}, e\rangle$ $\langle p_1, \{(b,2),(c,0),(d,1)\}, e\rangle$	$\langle p_0, \{\}, e\rangle$ $\langle p_1, \{(d,0),(b,1)\}, e\rangle$
8	$\langle p_0, \{(b,3),(c,1),(d,2)\}, e\rangle$	$\langle p_0, \{(b,4),(c,2),(d,3)\}, e\rangle$ $\langle p_1, \{(b,0),(c,1),(d,2)\}, e\rangle$	$\langle p_0, \{\}, e\rangle$ $\langle p_1, \{(b,2),(c,0),(d,1)\}, e\rangle$	$\langle p_0, \{\}, e\rangle$ $\langle p_1, \{(b,1),(c,2),(d,0)\}, e\rangle$

It is worth mentioning that any snapshot of $eval(\mathcal{A}, DB)$ at any time during the execution of the above algorithm is a partial answer to the query. The answer would be partial because: (a) there could still be objects to be discovered during the navigation, and (b) the weights of the already discovered objects could be further improved, i.e. lowered, should we wait further for the algorithm to continue. However, depending on the application a "quicker" partial answer could be more desirable than the complete answer.

Complexity. Here we are interested in the number of messages since to send a message is an order of magnitude more expensive than to perform a main memory operation. We show the following.

Theorem 3. *The number of messages in Algorithm 1 is bounded by* $(E \cdot |\tau|)^2$, *where* E *is the number of edges in DB, and* $|\tau|$ *is the cardinality of the transition relation of* $\mathcal{A}$.

Proof Sketch. Each physical database edge can "accommodate" in the worst case $|\tau|$ virtual communication channels. To set up a communication channel one "forward" message is needed. Now the question is how many times a communication channel is traversed "backward," by the update $\langle d, y\rangle$ messages. It is not difficult to see that a new wave of possible update messages can be propagated backwards for each forward message $\langle c, r, p, v\rangle$ in step 3 of the algorithm. As a wave of updates could have in the worst case up to $E \cdot |\tau|$ backward messages, we get the claimed upper bound. □

We can make a tradeoff between the time the nodes wait before initiating an update-wave, and the query response time. If each process waits a certain time before back-propagating query answers (as opposed to immediately sending all the answers that the process knows), then it is possible that better weighted answers will arrive to the processes, and many back-propagation messages will be cancelled. Not sending right away might be good for "throughtput" when we have a big number of executing queries. Such a strategy might significantly reduce the stress to the system making it possible to execute faster a set of queries.

As mentioned before, (due to space constraints) we do not present here the termination detection algorithm. It will be found in a future companion paper.

References

1. S. Abiteboul, V. Vianu. Regular Path Queries with Constraints. *Journal of Computing and System Sciences* 58(3) 1999, pp. 428-452.
2. Flesca, S., Furfaro, F., and Greco, S. Weighted path queries on web data. *In Proceedings of the 4th International Workshop on the Web and Databases (WebDB '01).* Informal Proceedings, pp. 7–12.
3. Grabs T., and H.-J. Schek ETH Zürich at INEX: Flexible Information Retrieval from XML with PowerDB-XML *Proc. INEX Workshop 2002: pp. 141–148*
4. Grahne, G., and Thomo, A. Approximate reasoning in semistructured data. *In Proceedings of the 8th International Workshop on Knowledge Representation meets Databases (KRDB '01).* Online Proceedings, http://ceur-ws.org/Vol-45/03-thomo.ps
5. Grahne, G., and Thomo, A. Query answering and containment for regular path queries under distortions. *In Proceedings of the 3rd International Symposium on Foundations of Information and Knowledge Systems (FoIKS '04).* Lecture Notes in Computer Science 2942, Springer, 2004, pp. 98–115.
6. Hopcroft, J., E., and Ullman, J., D. *Introduction to Automata Theory, Languages, and Computation.* Addison-Wesley, Reading, MA, 1979.
7. Mendelzon, A., O., Mihaila, G., A., and Milo, T. Querying the World Wide Web. *International Journal on Digital Libraries,* 1 (1), 1997, pp. 57–67.
8. Mendelzon A. O., and P. T. Wood, Finding Regular Simple Paths in Graph Databases. *SIAM J. Comp.* 24 (6) : 1235–1258, 1995.
9. Meyer, H., I. Bruder, A. Heuer, and G. Weber The Xircus Search Engine. *INEX Workshop 2002, pp. 119–124*
10. Stefanescu D. C., Thomo, A, and Thomo, L. Distributed evaluation of generalized path queries *Proc. Proceedings of the 2005 ACM Symposium on Applied Computing* 2005 pp. 610–616.
11. Suciu D., Distributed query evaluation on semistructured data. *ACM Transactions on Database Systems,* 27 (1), 2002, pp. 1–62.
12. Vardi. M. Y. A Call to Regularity. *Proc. PCK50 - Principles of Computing & Knowledge, Paris C. Kanellakis Memorial Workshop '03*, pp. 11.
13. Lacroix, Zoe and Raschid, Louiqa and Naumann, Felix and Vidal, Maria Esther. Exploring Life Sciences Data Sources Technical report 2003.

A Calculus for Propagating Semantic Annotations Through Scientific Workflow Queries*

Shawn Bowers[1] and Bertram Ludäscher[1,2]

[1] UC Davis Genome Center
[2] Department of Computer Science
University of California, Davis

Abstract. Scientific workflows facilitate automation, reuse, and reproducibility of scientific data management and analysis tasks. Scientific workflows are often modeled as dataflow networks, chaining together processing components (called *actors*) that query, transform, analyse, and visualize scientific datasets. Semantic annotations relate data and actor schemas with conceptual information from a shared ontology, to support scientific workflow design, discovery, reuse, and validation in the presence of thousands of potentially useful actors and datasets. However, the creation of semantic annotations is complex and time-consuming. We present a calculus and two inference algorithms to *automatically propagate* semantic annotations through workflow actors described by relational queries. Given an input annotation α and a query q, *forward propagation* computes an output annotation α'; conversely, *backward propagation* infers α from q and α'.

1 Introduction

Scientific workflows aim at automating repetitive scientific data management, analysis, and visualization tasks and provide scientists with a mechanism to seamlessly "glue" together different local and/or remote applications and (web) services into complex data analysis pipelines. Fig. 1 shows a simple ecology analysis workflow for computing two biodiversity quantities called Richness and Productivity using the KEPLER scientific workflow system [17]. As can be seen from the figure, scientific workflows are often modeled as networks of computational steps (called *actors*) that query, transform, and analyse input datasets (here, two datasets containing measurement data) via intermediate steps and derived datasets, resulting in a number of data products (here, containing the desired Richness and Productivity information). Scientific workflow systems (*e.g.*, KEPLER, TAVERNA [21], TRIANA [19] and many others [24]) are emerging as flexible and extensible problem-solving environments for designing, documenting, sharing, and executing scientific workflows [18]. In contrast to the use of shell scripts or spreadsheets, scientific workflows offer a versatile and controlled mechanism for automating data analysis pipelines, tracing data provenance [7,23], reproducing results, etc. As more and more workflow components and datasets become available, however,

* Work supported by NSF/ITR SEEK (DBI-0533368), NSF/ITR GEON (EAR-0225673), and DOE SDM (DE-FC02-01ER25486). We also thank Alin Deutsch and Alan Nash for insightful discussions on the Chase and mapping composition, respectively.

T. Grust et al. (Eds.): EDBT 2006 Workshops, LNCS 4254, pp. 712–723, 2006.

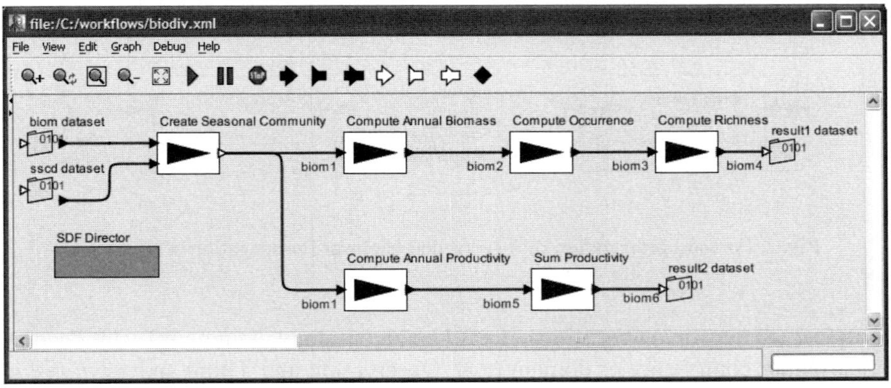

Fig. 1. Simple scientific workflow for computing species richness and productivity [9]

users face the problem of selecting from thousands of possibly relevant workflow components (*e.g.*, given as web service operations, command-line tools, functions from statistics packages such as R, or native application components), and an even larger set of possible datasets. Similarly, once candidate actor components and datasets have been identified, there is the problem of whether it is possible to "chain" them together in the desired form. Generic programming language data types (such as `string` or arrays of integers) do *not* provide any guidance as to whether it is meaningful to chain together the output(s) of one actor with the input(s) of another actor. While the use of WSDL or XML Schema types can guide workflow composition, this requires that a single common schema is adopted, which is often impractical. To at least partially capture information about a dataset or analysis component, informal metadata annotations are often used in practice.

Example 1 (Informal Annotation). Consider a dataset D with the relational schema $S = \{\mathtt{R(Obs, La, Lo, T, V)}\}$. D might be given as a csv (comma-separated values) file, with an accompanying documentation saying that `R.Obs` identifies an *observation* at *time* `R.T`, conducted at a point having *latitude* and *longitude* `R.La` and `R.Lo`, respectively, and having as *value* `V`, which is a *temperature* measurement in degrees *celsius*. □

While such informal annotations are useful for the scientist when manually inspecting and interpreting data, a scientific workflow system cannot make use of this information, *e.g.*, to check whether the annotation of a dataset D is compatible with the annotation of a workflow actor A that consumes or produces D, or whether the output annotation of A_1 is compatible with the input annotation of A_2 in a chain of actors $(\cdots A_1 \xrightarrow{D} A_2 \cdots)$.

To address these problems, formal semantic annotations have been proposed [4,5]. A *semantic annotation* α: $S \to \mathcal{O}$ associates elements of a data schema S with concepts and relationships of an ontology $\mathcal{O}$. [1] Thus, α can be seen as a "hybrid type" [5], linking structural information given by S with conceptual level ("semantic") information from a shared community ontology (or controlled vocabulary) $\mathcal{O}$.

[1] We consider ontologies expressed in description logic, *e.g.*, OWL-DL.

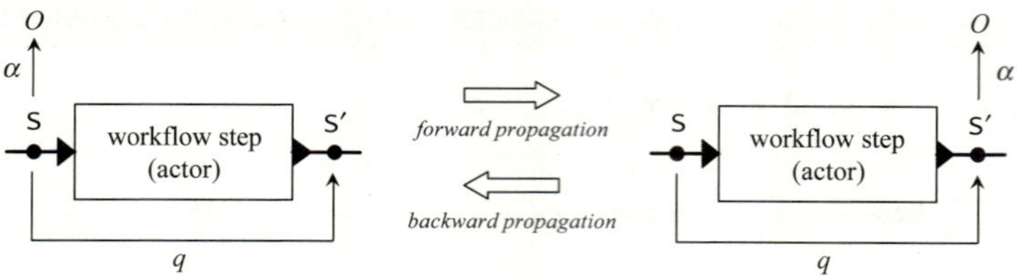

Fig. 2. Forward propagation $\alpha, q \rightsquigarrow \alpha'$ and backward propagation $\alpha', q \rightsquigarrow \alpha$

Example 2 (Semantic Annotation). Let $\mathcal{O}$ be an ontology defining relevant *concepts* of a particular community or domain (*e.g.*, Observation and Time) and *relationships* (*e.g.*, hasUnit and hasLatitude) between concepts. The informal annotation above can be formalized by logic rules (constraints) of the form α: $S \rightarrow \mathcal{O}$:

$$\underbrace{\mathtt{R}(o,x,y,t,v)}_{\text{query over schema } S} \longrightarrow \underbrace{\mathsf{Observation}(o) \wedge \mathsf{hasUnit}(o,\mathsf{celsius}) \wedge \mathsf{hasVal}(o,v) \wedge \mathsf{Time}(t)}_{\text{assertion over ontology } \mathcal{O}}$$

This rule states that $\mathtt{R}.o$ identifies an Observation, having a unit celsius, and a value $\mathtt{R}.v$, and that $\mathtt{R}.t$ is a Time. Similar rules α are used to map other columns or subsets of R to concepts and relationships in $\mathcal{O}$. □

By capturing semantic annotations as sets of logic rules α, a scientific workflow or data integration system can exploit these constraints, *e.g.*, for checking semantic type correctness of data-to-actor and actor-to-actor connections, and for suggesting semantically type-correct connections during workflow design [5].

In this paper we study the problem of automatically propagating a set of semantic annotations α "through" workflow actors which are described by relational queries q.[2] We consider the *forward propagation problem* $\alpha, q \rightsquigarrow \alpha'$ of deriving from an input annotation α: $S \rightarrow \mathcal{O}$ and a query q: $S \rightarrow S'$ an output annotation α': $S' \rightarrow \mathcal{O}$. Similarly, the *backward propagation problem* $\alpha', q \rightsquigarrow \alpha$ is to derive from knowledge of an output annotation α' and query q an input annotation α. The forward and backward propagation problems are summarized in Fig. 2.

Example 3 (Forward Propagation). Consider a simple actor A that selects from the above dataset R (input schema) only those observations with temperature measurements below 0°C and locations that fall into a particular region of interest $\mathtt{R}_{roi}(x,y)$ resulting in a dataset R′ (output schema). We can describe A with a query q as follows:

$$\mathtt{R}'(o,v) \ :\!-\ \mathtt{R}(o,x,y,t,v), \mathtt{R}_{roi}(x,y), v < 0. \qquad (q)$$

Given the semantic annotation α of the actor input R in Example 2, the forward problem is to *automatically* derive an output annotation α' for R′. Here, we obtain

$$\mathtt{R}'(o,v) \longrightarrow \mathsf{Observation}(o) \wedge \mathsf{hasUnit}(o,\mathsf{celsius}) \wedge \mathsf{hasVal}(o,v) \qquad (\alpha')$$

[2] The actor may not be implemented as a relational query q. Instead, q is another form of metadata, a *query annotation*, which describes or approximates an actor's workflow function.

since we "know" from α and q that v is the value of an observation o with unit celsius. Note that to infer this α', we use the "only if" direction $q_{head} \rightarrow q_{body}$ of the (Datalog) rule q_{head} :- q_{body} defining the query q above.[3] Since annotations α and α' have a particular form (source-to-ontology constraints in a language $\mathcal{L}^{\alpha}_{S \rightarrow \mathcal{O}}$), α' may not include all deducible information: *e.g.*, here we omit in the consequent of α' the fact that $v < 0$ and possibly other information about $\mathtt{R}$ and $\mathtt{R}_{roi}$ (as these are not $\mathcal{O}$ expressions). □

The manual creation of semantic annotations can be a complex and time-consuming task. Thus providing automated solutions for deriving annotations is desirable for supporting scalable frameworks of "semantics-aware" scientific workflows. In addition, solving the propagation problem also provides new opportunities for *semantic type checking*: if both an input annotation α and an output annotation α' for an actor are given, then employing forward and backward propagation allows us to check the consistency of the given annotations relative to the inferred ones.

Contributions and Previous Work. We first present a formal framework for semantic annotations α and define the associated forward and backward propagation problems. We then present inference rules of our annotation propagation calculus (APC) and two general propagation algorithms f-APC and b-APC for forward and backward propagation, respectively. These algorithms proceed by structural induction on the operator tree corresponding to a relational query q. We use such queries q to represent individual actors of a workflow. An advantage of the APC approach is that it can be "scaled" to different query languages $\mathcal{L}^q$, *i.e.*, for certain query classes we obtain the exact (*i.e.*, most specific) annotation as the propagation result, but we also obtain results (not necessarily most specific) for more expressive classes $\mathcal{L}^q$ for which no exact solution exists.

We introduced semantic annotations in [4,5] to facilitate scientific data integration and workflow design and composition, and proposed to automatically propagate such annotations through workflows [6]. This paper extends our previous work [6] in several ways: (i) by considering both forward and backward propagation, (ii) by introducing the f-APC and b-APC algorithms for annotation propagation, and (iii) by considering propagation challenges in terms of the annotation and query languages used.

The f-APC and b-APC algorithms employ a specific goal-directed resolution strategy for annotation propagation. Similary, goal directed resultion strategies are also used for solving schema mapping composition problems [13,20] as well as query rewriting problems in data integration/exchange settings, where the corresponding rewriting techniques can be understood as specialized versions of resolution [3], but for which certain termination and efficiency guarantees can be given (unlike for general resolution).

Other Related Work. Annotation mechanisms in other related work are generally more restricted than our approach in that they consider only single attribute or value annotations. In [2], annotations are stored in a special attribute, and the user must specify how to propagate such value-based annotations through SQL queries, while we are able to capture more expressive schema-based annotations, and also propagate them automatically. Our approach also does not require a special semantics for interpreting relational algebra queries. [14] present an approach to scientific annotations which

[3] This is correct, since the symbol ':-' stands for an equivalence $q_{head} \leftrightarrow q_{body}$, corresponding to a sound and *complete* definition of the query answer (*a.k.a.* "Clark's completion" [10]).

allows *value associations* (as opposed to annotations to individual values only [2]). Such associations between different schema columns can be easily expressed in our approach as conjunctive conditions in the body of α.

Propagating annotations is also related to the issue of (*why* and *where*) data provenance [7]. For example, [8] present an approach to propagate annotations through views, but consider again simple text-based instance (*i.e.*, value) annotations. In contrast, our annotations are applied at the schema level, but can also specify subsets of the input data (through the "query part", *i.e.*, the body of α), including individual values just like previous approaches. In [11] methods are presented for lineage tracing of data (within the context of data warehouses), which take advantage of known structure or properties of transformations, similar to our queries q. The lineage problem and propagation methods considered in [11] are related but different from our approach. For example, in their case, for first-order (relational) queries, an exact data lineage can be computed. Conversely, in general, the problem of propagating a semantic annotation through a first-order query may not have a solution in the desired annotation language. This indicates that propagating semantic annotations is in general harder than computing data lineage. The problem of propagation is also related to type inference in programming languages, where types are generally given in less expressive langauges (*e.g.*, compared to dependency constraints) but programs are written in more expressive languages (*e.g.*, compared to relational algebra queries).

2 Formalization of the Annotation Propagation Problem

Here we present our framework for semantic annotations and show how the propagation problem can be formalized and reduced to a constraint implication problem.

Scientific Workflows. These are often modeled as *dataflow process networks* [15,16],[4] consisting of a set of computational components called *actors*, which can run as independent processes or threads, and which exchange data tokens (*e.g.*, scalars, vectors, files, XML fragments, etc.) through unidirectional, buffered FIFO *channels*. Channels connect *output ports* of source actors with *input ports* of target actors (*cf.* Fig. 1).

Mappings. A schema *mapping* is a binary relation[5] on instances D_S, $D_{S'}$ of disjoint schemas S (input) and S' (output). Given S, S', and a set of (logic) constraints Σ, we associate with (S, S', Σ) the mapping $m = \{ \langle D_S, D_{S'} \rangle \mid (D_S \cup D_{S'}) \models \Sigma \}$, *i.e.*, the set of pairs $\langle D_S, D_{S'} \rangle$ of instances of S and S' for which the combined instance $D_S \cup D_{S'}$ satisfies Σ. For example, a *query* q corresponds to a (functional) mapping m_q: (S, S', Σ_q). We write q: $S \rightarrow S'$ to emphasize the input/output signature of q.

Actor Schemas and Semantic Annotations. With the input and output ports of an actor A, we associate two disjoint relational schemas, S and S', describing the input and

[4] Many scientific workflow systems (*e.g.*, INFORSENSE, KEPLER, PIPELINEPILOT, TAVERNA, TRIANA), scientific problem-solving environments (*e.g.*, SCIRUN), and commercial LIMS systems (*e.g.*, LABVIEW) are based on this dataflow process network model.

[5] We follow the convention to call such relations "mappings" [1,13,20], although they are *not* (functional) mappings in the traditional sense: *e.g.*, unlike conventional mappings, a (non-functional) "mapping" $\langle D_S, D_{S'} \rangle$ always has an inverse "mapping" $\langle D_{S'}, D_S \rangle$.

output data structures of A, respectively. The input/output behavior of A is described (or approximated) via a query $q\colon S \to S'$, mapping instances of the input schema S to instances of the output schema S' (see Fig. 2). An instance D_S of a schema S is called a *dataset*. A *semantic annotation* $\alpha\colon S \to \mathcal{O}$ is a mapping from instances of a (concrete) data schema S to instances of an (abstract, virtual) ontology $\mathcal{O}$. Here, an ontology is a (finite) first-order structure. Given a query $q\colon S \to S'$ for an actor A, we call $\alpha\colon S \to \mathcal{O}$ an *input annotation*, and $\alpha'\colon S' \to \mathcal{O}$ an *output annotation* of A (Fig. 2). Using the above notation, a semantic annotation α corresponds to a mapping $m_\alpha\colon (S, \mathcal{O}, \Sigma_\alpha)$, where Σ_α is a set of logic constraints capturing α.

Annotation Propagation as Composition of Mappings. The forward propagation problem $\alpha, q \rightsquigarrow \alpha'$ can be seen as a mapping composition problem [13,20]. The given signatures $\alpha\colon S \to \mathcal{O}$, $q\colon S \to S'$, and $\alpha'\colon S' \to \mathcal{O}$ suggest the definition

$$\alpha' := \alpha(q^-) \qquad \text{(f-prop)}$$

i.e., obtain the propagated annotations as the composition $\alpha'\colon (S', \mathcal{O}, \Sigma_{\alpha'})$ of α and q^-. Here $q^-\colon (S', S, \Sigma_q)$ is the *inverse mapping* of q, which is exactly like q but with the roles of inputs and outputs reversed. Similarly, for the backward propagation:

$$\alpha := \alpha'(q) \qquad \text{(b-prop)}$$

one could apply $\alpha'\colon (S', \mathcal{O}, \Sigma_{\alpha'})$ on top of $q\colon (S, S', \Sigma_q)$, resulting in $\alpha\colon (S, \mathcal{O}, \Sigma_\alpha)$.

To view annotation propagation in this way as mapping composition helps to understand some aspects of the subsequent annotation propagation calculus (APC) rules and inference algorithm: *e.g.*, in the foward case we are looking for a constraint $\alpha'\colon S' \to \mathcal{O}$. Given $\alpha\colon S \to \mathcal{O}$ and $q\colon S \to S'$, we can "go" from S' to $\mathcal{O}$ by first applying q in the inverse direction $q'\colon S' \to S$, then applying $\alpha\colon S \to \mathcal{O}$ to the result (cf. Fig. 2), hence we can think of the propagated result as $\alpha' = \alpha(q^-)$. By similar reasoning, we obtain $\alpha = \alpha'(q)$ for the backward propagation.

The Annotation Propagation Problem. We now formally define the annotation propagation problem by relating it to constraint implication as follows:

Definition 1. Consider a semantic annotation $\alpha\colon (S, \mathcal{O}, \Sigma_\alpha)$ expressed in an annotation language $\mathcal{L}^\alpha$, and a query $q\colon (S, S', \Sigma_q)$. Let $q^-\colon (S', S, \Sigma_{q^-})$ be the inverse of q.

We say that $\alpha'\colon (S', S, \Sigma_{\alpha'})$ is a *forward $\mathcal{L}^\alpha$-propagation* of α *through* q, if $\Sigma_{\alpha'}$ is the *most specific* annotation in $\mathcal{L}^\alpha$ that is implied by Σ_α and Σ_{q^-}, denoted $\Sigma_\alpha \cup \Sigma_{q^-} \models \Sigma_{\alpha'}$. We say α_1 is *more specific* than α_2, if $\Sigma_{\alpha_1} \models \Sigma_{\alpha_2}$. The *backward $\mathcal{L}^\alpha$-propagation* is defined analogously: Find the most specific $\Sigma_\alpha \subseteq \mathcal{L}^\alpha$ with $\Sigma_{\alpha'} \cup \Sigma_q \models \Sigma_\alpha$. □

This formalization has several advantages: First, under this propagation semantics, a result annotation may exist even in cases where the mapping composition semantics cannot be expressed in the constraint language of choice. Second, this formalization naturally applies to inference-based (logic) approaches like the APC below.

3 Annotation Propagation Calculus (APC)

We first present the basic annotation propagation calculus (APC), then present two goal-directed inference algorithms f-APC and b-APC for forward and backward propagation.

(σ) $\forall \mathbf{x}\, R(\mathbf{x}) \wedge \psi(\mathbf{x}) \rightarrow S'(\mathbf{x})$	(σ^-) $\forall \mathbf{x}\, S'(\mathbf{x}) \rightarrow R(\mathbf{x}) \wedge \psi(\mathbf{x})$
(π) $\forall \mathbf{x} \forall \mathbf{y}\, R(\mathbf{x},\mathbf{y}) \rightarrow S'(\mathbf{x})$	(π^-) $\forall \mathbf{x}\, S'(\mathbf{x}) \rightarrow \exists \mathbf{y}\, R(\mathbf{x},\mathbf{y})$
$(\times)$ $\forall \mathbf{x} \forall \mathbf{y}\, R_1(\mathbf{x}) \wedge R_2(\mathbf{y}) \rightarrow S'(\mathbf{x},\mathbf{y})$	$(\times^-)$ $\forall \mathbf{x} \forall \mathbf{y}\, S'(\mathbf{x},\mathbf{y}) \rightarrow R_1(\mathbf{x}) \wedge R_2(\mathbf{y})$
$(\setminus)$ $\forall \mathbf{x}\, R_1(\mathbf{x}) \wedge \neg R_2(\mathbf{x}) \rightarrow S'(\mathbf{x})$	$(\setminus^-)$ $\forall \mathbf{x}\, S'(\mathbf{x}) \rightarrow R_1(\mathbf{x}) \wedge \neg R_2(\mathbf{x})$
$(\cup)$ $\forall \mathbf{x}\, R_1(\mathbf{x}) \vee R_2(\mathbf{x}) \rightarrow S'(\mathbf{x})$	$(\cup^-)$ $\forall \mathbf{x}\, S'(\mathbf{x}) \rightarrow R_1(\mathbf{x}) \vee R_2(\mathbf{x})$
a) q: $S \rightarrow S'$ direction for b-APC	b) q^-: $S' \rightarrow S$ direction for f-APC

Fig. 3. Relational algebra operators (atomic queries) expressed as logic constraints

Query Operators as Logic Constraints. The core idea of APC is the observation that annotation propagation is easy for primitive (atomic) query operators. Therefore, we start by representing a complex (first-order) query q_c in the form of a relational algebra expression, or equivalently, as an operator tree, consisting of atomic query operators $q \in \{\sigma, \pi, \times, \setminus, \cup\}$. Each relational operator q defines a mapping q: (S, S', Σ_q) for the "standard" (*i.e.*, forward) direction $S \rightarrow S'$ of q, and an inverse mapping q^-: (S', S, Σ_{q^-}) for the opposite (*i.e.*, backward) direction $S' \rightarrow S$. Here, Σ_q and Σ_{q^-} are as defined in Fig. 3(a) and Fig. 3(b), respectively.

3.1 Inference Rules of APC

The formalization of annotation propagation using logic constraints (see Definition 1), suggests a natural inference procedure for the forward problem $\alpha, q \rightsquigarrow \alpha'$, *i.e.*, by "applying" the constraints Σ_α to Σ_{q^-}, thus obtaining $\Sigma_{\alpha'}$. Similarly, one can combine Σ_q and $\Sigma_{\alpha'}$ to obtain Σ_α to solve the backward problem. This is the core idea behind the APC inference rules.

Fig. 4 shows the rules for backward propagation, which take an output annotation α' and an atomic query operator q and infer the input annotation α. Similary, Fig. 5 shows how forward propagation is solved by applying the input annotation α on the inverse query q^- to obtain the output annotation α'. The inference rules in both figures are depicted with their *premises* above the horizontal line, and their *consequent*(s) below the line. Each inference rule corresponds to an algebra operator q: $S \rightarrow S'$ or its inverse q^-: $S' \rightarrow S$. Moreover, with every rule for q (in b-APC) and q^- (in f-APC), we associate at least one *goal atom*, marked as $[\![A]\!]$ in the head of q (Figure 4) or the head of q^- (Figure 5). The basic idea of annotation propagation is to "resolve" the goal atom in q (or in q^-) with some literal of the given semantic annotation α' (or α), to obtain the desired propagated annotation.

Applying Substitutions. To simplify the exposition of the rules in Fig. 4 and Fig. 5, the application of unifiers is not shown but implicit. More precisely, let θ be an *mgu* (most-general-unifier) of a goal atom $[\![R(\mathbf{u})]\!]$ in q (or q^-) with a corresponding atom $R(\mathbf{x})$ on the left-hand side of an annotation α' (or α). The unifier θ is a (most general) substitution under which both atoms become identical, *i.e.*, $\theta(R(\mathbf{u})) = \theta(R(\mathbf{x}))$. In the figures, with the b-APC and f-APC rules, we assume that this θ is applied to the consequent rule (below the line) to obtain the propagated annotation.

Additional Remarks for f-APC. For f-APC we assume that annotations α and the constraint q_π^-, capturing the inverse of relational projection π, have been "skolemized"

$$B_\sigma\ \frac{\begin{array}{l}\alpha'\colon\ S'(\mathbf{x}),\ \varphi(\mathbf{x}) \rightarrow \exists \mathbf{z}\,\omega(\mathbf{x},\mathbf{z})\\ q\colon\ R(\mathbf{u}),\ \psi(\mathbf{u}) \rightarrow [\![S'(\mathbf{u})]\!]\end{array}}{\alpha\colon\ R(\mathbf{u}),\ \psi(\mathbf{u}),\ \varphi(\mathbf{x}) \rightarrow \exists \mathbf{z}\,\omega(\mathbf{x},\mathbf{z})}$$

$$B_\pi\ \frac{\begin{array}{l}\alpha'\colon\ S'(\mathbf{x}),\ \varphi(\mathbf{x}) \rightarrow \exists \mathbf{z}\,\omega(\mathbf{x},\mathbf{z})\\ q\colon\ R(\mathbf{u},\mathbf{v}) \rightarrow [\![S'(\mathbf{u})]\!]\end{array}}{\alpha\colon\ R(\mathbf{u},\mathbf{v}),\varphi(\mathbf{x}) \rightarrow \exists \mathbf{z}\,\omega(\mathbf{x},\mathbf{z})}$$

$$B_\times\ \frac{\begin{array}{l}\alpha'\colon\ S'(\mathbf{x},\mathbf{y}),\ \varphi(\mathbf{x},\mathbf{y}) \rightarrow \exists \mathbf{z}\,\omega(\mathbf{x},\mathbf{y},\mathbf{z})\\ q\colon\ R_1(\mathbf{u}),\ R_2(\mathbf{v}) \rightarrow [\![S'(\mathbf{u},\mathbf{v})]\!]\end{array}}{\alpha\colon\ R_1(\mathbf{u}),\ R_2(\mathbf{v}),\ \varphi(\mathbf{x},\mathbf{y}) \rightarrow \exists \mathbf{z}\,\omega(\mathbf{x},\mathbf{y},\mathbf{z})}$$

$$B_\cup\ \frac{\begin{array}{l}\alpha'\colon\ S'(\mathbf{x}),\ \varphi(\mathbf{x}) \rightarrow \exists \mathbf{z}\,\omega(\mathbf{x},\mathbf{z})\\ q\colon\ R_1(\mathbf{u}) \rightarrow [\![S'(\mathbf{u})]\!]\\ \quad\ \ R_2(\mathbf{u}) \rightarrow [\![S'(\mathbf{u})]\!]\end{array}}{\alpha\colon\ R_1(\mathbf{u}),\ \varphi(\mathbf{x}) \rightarrow \exists \mathbf{z}\,\omega(\mathbf{x},\mathbf{z})}$$

$$B_\setminus\ \frac{\begin{array}{l}\alpha'\colon\ S'(\mathbf{x}),\ \varphi(\mathbf{x}) \rightarrow \exists \mathbf{z}\,\omega(\mathbf{x},\mathbf{z})\\ q\colon\ R_1(\mathbf{u}),\ \neg R_2(\mathbf{u}) \rightarrow [\![S'(\mathbf{u})]\!]\end{array}}{\alpha\colon\ R_1(\mathbf{u}),\ \neg R_2(\mathbf{u}),\ \varphi(\mathbf{x}) \rightarrow \exists \mathbf{z}\,\omega(\mathbf{x},\mathbf{z})}$$

Fig. 4. Backward propagation (b-APC) rules for $\alpha', q \rightsquigarrow \alpha$

(replacing $\exists$-quantified variables by symbolic identifiers while keeping track of the $\forall$-variables they depend on). In the rule F_σ, we denote by $(\varphi(\mathbf{x}) \wedge \neg\psi(\mathbf{u}))^*$ that φ has ψ "factored out", *i.e.*, we simplify $\varphi \wedge \neg\psi$.

3.2 Operator-Driven Annotation Propagation in APC

The above APC rules for forward and backward propagation based on atomic query operators induce two natural inference algorithms for complex queries, *i.e.*, consisting of nested expressions of operators. The approach is to drive the application of inference rules by the structure of the operator tree of a given complex query q. To illustrate this structural induction over the operator tree, consider first the backward problem $\alpha', q \rightsquigarrow \alpha$. Let $q\colon S \rightarrow S'$ be a complex query, expressed as a nested relational algebra expression of unary or binary operators q_i: $q = q_n(q_{n-1}(\cdots q_1 \cdots)$ where q_n corresponds to the top-most (root) node of the operator tree, and leaf nodes (such as q_1) are applied to the input relations of q (cf. Fig. 6). Recall the "composition solution" $\alpha := \alpha'(q)$ to the backward problem (see (b-prop) on page 717). Applying α' to the nested expression for q yields $\alpha = \alpha'(q) = \alpha'(q_n(q_{n-1}(\cdots)))$. As mapping composition is associative, we can first apply α' to q_n (the root node), obtaining an intermediate annotation α_1, which is applied to q_{n-1}, yielding α_2, which is further propagated downward in the tree, etc. This process is repeated until the leaf nodes are reached. Fig. 6 (a) illustrates this top-down process for b-APC.

Similarly, for the forward problem $\alpha, q \rightsquigarrow \alpha'$, we have the "composition solution" (f-prop) of the form $\alpha' := \alpha(q^-)$. First note that the "inverse reading" of the operator tree can be seen as an expression $q^- = q_1^-(q_2^-(\cdots))$ in which the root node q_n becomes an innermost node. Applying α to this expression, and again exploiting associativity, we obtain a bottom-up annotation propagation for f-APC: Fig. 6 (b) depicts this process.

Strictly speaking, the notation (nested expressions) used for q and q^- above were based on unary operators. However, it should be clear how the top-down approach for b-APC and the bottom-up approach for f-APC work in the case of binary operators. For the case of b-APC we perform a *preorder* traversal of the operator tree. At each operator node we propagate (1) each source annotation given as input to the operator

$$F_\sigma\ \frac{\begin{array}{l}\alpha\colon\ R(\mathbf{x}),\ \varphi(\mathbf{x}) \to \omega(\mathbf{x},\mathbf{f}(\mathbf{x}))\\ q^-\colon\ S'(\mathbf{u}) \to [\![R(\mathbf{u})]\!],\ \psi(\mathbf{u})\end{array}}{\alpha'\colon\ S'(\mathbf{u}),\ (\varphi(\mathbf{x}) \wedge \neg\psi(\mathbf{u}))^* \to \omega(\mathbf{x},\mathbf{f}(\mathbf{x}))} \qquad F_\pi\ \frac{\begin{array}{l}\alpha\colon\ R(\mathbf{x}),\ \varphi(\mathbf{x}) \to \omega(\mathbf{x},\mathbf{f}(\mathbf{x}))\\ q^-\colon\ S'(\mathbf{u}) \to [\![R(\mathbf{u},\mathbf{g}(\mathbf{u}))]\!]\end{array}}{\alpha'\colon\ S'(\mathbf{u}),\ \varphi(\mathbf{x}) \to \omega(\mathbf{x},\mathbf{f}(\mathbf{x}))}$$

$$F_\times\ \frac{\begin{array}{l}\alpha\colon\ R_1(\mathbf{x}),\ \varphi(\mathbf{x}) \to \omega(\mathbf{x},\mathbf{f}(\mathbf{x}))\\ q^-\colon\ S'(\mathbf{u},\mathbf{v}) \to [\![R_1(\mathbf{u})]\!],\ R_2(\mathbf{v})\end{array}}{\alpha'\colon\ S'(\mathbf{u},\mathbf{v}),\ \varphi(\mathbf{x}) \to \omega(\mathbf{x},\mathbf{f}(\mathbf{x}))} \qquad F_\setminus\ \frac{\begin{array}{l}\alpha\colon\ R_1(\mathbf{x}),\ \varphi(\mathbf{x}) \to \omega(\mathbf{x},\mathbf{f}(\mathbf{x}))\\ q^-\colon\ S'(\mathbf{u}) \to [\![R_1(\mathbf{u})]\!],\ \neg R_2(\mathbf{u})\end{array}}{\alpha'\colon\ S'(\mathbf{u}),\ \varphi(\mathbf{x}) \to \omega(\mathbf{x},\mathbf{f}(\mathbf{x}))}$$

$$F_\cup\ \frac{\begin{array}{l}\alpha_1\colon\ R_1(\mathbf{x}),\ \varphi_1(\mathbf{x}) \to \omega_1(\mathbf{x},\mathbf{f}(\mathbf{x}))\\ \alpha_2\colon\ R_2(\mathbf{y}),\ \varphi_2(\mathbf{y}) \to \omega_2(\mathbf{y},\mathbf{g}(\mathbf{y}))\\ q^-\colon\ S'(\mathbf{u}) \to [\![R_1(\mathbf{u})]\!] \vee [\![R_2(\mathbf{u})]\!]\end{array}}{\alpha'\colon\ S'(\mathbf{u}),\ \varphi_1(\mathbf{x}),\ \varphi_2(\mathbf{y}) \to \omega_1(\mathbf{x},\mathbf{f}(\mathbf{x})) \vee \omega_2(\mathbf{y},\mathbf{g}(\mathbf{y}))}$$

Fig. 5. Forward propagation (f-APC) rules for $\alpha, q^- \rightsquigarrow \alpha'$

propagation step, and (2) all unique annotations that can be derived (including those that contain intermediate relation symbols) by repeatedly applying the corresponding inference rule of the operator. Once all nodes of the operator tree have been visited, the subset of source-to-target annotations (not mentioning intermediate relations) are propagated through the query. We apply a similar procedure for f-APC, but instead use a postorder traversal (*i.e.*, bottom up), as shown in Fig. 6 (b). The following example illustrates the inference steps of b-APC:

Example 4. Let $\mathtt{R}_1(o,x,y,t,v)$, $\mathtt{R}_2(u,p)$ be input schemas, $\mathtt{S}'(o,x,y,v,u,p)$ the output schema (Fig. 6), where $\mathtt{S}'$ is the given output annotation

$\alpha'\colon\ \mathtt{S}'(o,x,y,v,u,p) \to \mathsf{Observation}(o),\ \mathsf{hasVal}(o,v),\ \mathsf{Species}(p)$

Also consider the query shown in the figure, which combines all $\mathtt{R}_1$ observations, made at a particular time $\mathtt{c}$, with species observed at a location $\mathtt{d}$ (*e.g.*, assuming the spatial extent of $\mathtt{R}_1$ is $\mathtt{d}$, the query extends $\mathtt{R}_1$ with its corresponding species). We follow the navigation path given in Fig. 6 (a) to compute the backward propagation. The first step derives $\alpha_1 := \alpha'(q_4)$ by applying $B_\times$ to α' and q_4 (the goal atom is in double brackets):

$q_4\colon\ \mathtt{R}_1''(o,x,y,v),\ \mathtt{R}_2'(u,p) \to [\![\mathtt{S}'(o,x,y,v,u,p)]\!]$

The resulting annotation $\alpha_1 = \alpha'(q_4)$ is propagated downwards the operator tree:

$\alpha_1\colon\ \mathtt{R}_1''(o,x,y,v),\ \mathtt{R}_2'(u,p) \to \mathsf{Observation}(o),\ \mathsf{hasVal}(o,v),\ \mathsf{Species}(p)$

The next step is $\alpha_2 = \alpha_1(q_3)$ via rule B_π, *i.e.*, applying α_1 to q_3 (= $\pi_{oxyv}(\mathtt{R}_1')$):

$q_3\colon\ \mathtt{R}_1'(o,x,y,t,v) \to [\![\mathtt{R}_1''(o,x,y,v)]\!]$

which results in

$\alpha_2\colon\ \mathtt{R}_1'(o,x,y,t,v),\ \mathtt{R}_2'(u,p) \to \mathsf{Observation}(o),\ \mathsf{hasVal}(o,v),\ \mathsf{Species}(p)$

Next we apply α_2 to q_2 (= $\sigma_{t=\mathtt{c}}(\mathtt{R}_1)$)

$q_2\colon\ \mathtt{R}_1(o,x,y,t,v), t{=}\mathtt{c} \to [\![\mathtt{R}_1'(o,x,y,t,v)]\!]$

and using rule B_σ we obtain $\alpha_3 = \alpha_2(q_2)$:

$\alpha_3\colon\ \mathtt{R}_1(o,x,y,t,v), t{=}\mathtt{c},\ \mathtt{R}_2'(u,p) \to \mathsf{Observation}(o),\ \mathsf{hasVal}(o,v),\ \mathsf{Species}(p)$

Finally, on the second, parallel branch we have a selection q_1 (= $\sigma_{u=\mathtt{d}}(\mathtt{R}_2)$):

$q_1\colon\ \mathtt{R}_2(u,p), u{=}\mathtt{d} \to [\![\mathtt{R}_2'(u,p)]\!]$

We obtain the final result $\alpha_4 := \alpha_1(q_1)$ via B_σ:

α_4: $\mathtt{R}_1(o,x,y,t,v), t{=}\mathsf{c}$, $\mathtt{R}_2(u,p), u{=}\mathsf{d}$ $\rightarrow$ $\mathsf{Observation}(o)$, $\mathsf{hasVal}(o,v)$, $\mathsf{Species}(p)$ □

The forward algorithm f-APC proceeds similarly but bottom-up instead of top-down:

Example 5. Consider two relations $\mathtt{R}_1$ and $\mathtt{R}_2$ with semantic annotations α_a and α_b:

α_a: $\mathtt{R}_1(o,x,y,t,v) \rightarrow \mathsf{Observation}(o),\ \mathsf{hasVal}(o,v)$

α_b: $\mathtt{R}_2(u,p) \rightarrow \mathsf{Site}(u),\ \mathsf{Species}(p),\ \mathsf{observedIn}(p,u)$

and the same query q as in the previous example. We follow the navigation path given in Fig. 6 (b) to compute the forward propagation. The first step derives $\alpha_1 := \alpha(q_2^-)$ by applying F_σ to α_a and the inverse q_2^- of the operator $\sigma_{t=\mathsf{c}}(\mathtt{R}_1)$

q_2^-: $\mathtt{R}_1'(o,x,y,t,v) \rightarrow [\![\mathtt{R}_1(o,x,y,t,v)]\!],\ t=\mathsf{c}$

α_1: $\mathtt{R}_1'(o,x,y,t,v) \rightarrow \mathsf{Observation}(o),\ \mathsf{hasVal}(o,v)$

The next step derives $\alpha_2 \leftarrow \alpha_1, q_3^-$ by applying F_π to α_1 and operator $\pi_{o,x,y,v}$ (q_3^-)

q_3^-: $\mathtt{R}_1''(o,x,y,v) \rightarrow [\![\mathtt{R}_1'(o,x,y,g(o,x,y,v),v)]\!]$

α_2: $\mathtt{R}_1''(o,x,y,v) \rightarrow \mathsf{Observation}(o),\ \mathsf{hasVal}(o,v)$

The next step derives $\alpha_3 \leftarrow \alpha_b, q_1^-$ by applying F_σ to α_b and the operator $\sigma_{u=\mathsf{d}}$ (q_1^-)

q_1^-: $\mathtt{R}_2'(u,p) \rightarrow [\![\mathtt{R}_2(u,p)]\!],\ u=\mathsf{d}$

α_3: $\mathtt{R}_2'(u,p) \rightarrow \mathsf{Site}(u),\ \mathsf{Species}(p),\ \mathsf{observedIn}(p,u)$

The last step derives α' (denoted α_a' and α_b' below) by applying $F_\times$ twice, once to α_2 and the operator $\times$ (q_4^-) and then to α_3 and q_4^-.

q_4^-: $\mathtt{S}'(o,x,y,v,u,p) \rightarrow [\![\mathtt{R}_1''(o,x,y,v)]\!],\ \mathtt{R}_2'(u,p)$

α_a': $\mathtt{S}'(o,x,y,v,u,p) \rightarrow \mathsf{Observation}(o),\ \mathsf{hasVal}(o,v)$

q_4^-: $\mathtt{S}'(o,x,y,v,u,p) \rightarrow \mathtt{R}_1''(o,x,y,v),\ [\![\mathtt{R}_2'(u,p)]\!]$

α_b': $\mathtt{S}'(o,x,y,v,u,p) \rightarrow \mathsf{Site}(u),\ \mathsf{Species}(p),\ \mathsf{observedIn}(p,u)$

Soundness and Termination of APC Rules and Algorithms. Applications of APC inference rules correspond to one or more first-order resolution steps [22,3]. Thus, from the soundness of resolution, the soundness of f-APC and b-APC is immediate.

Proposition 1 (Soundness of b-APC and f-APC). *For Σ_α' and Σ_q as in Fig. 4:*

If $\Sigma_{\alpha'} \cup \Sigma_q \vdash_{\text{b-APC}} \Sigma_\alpha$ then $\Sigma_{\alpha'} \cup \Sigma_q \models \Sigma_\alpha$

Similarly, for Σ_α and Σ_{q^-} as in Fig. 5:

If $\Sigma_\alpha \cup \Sigma_{q^-} \vdash_{\text{f-APC}} \Sigma_{\alpha'}$ then $\Sigma_\alpha \cup \Sigma_{q^-} \models \Sigma_{\alpha'}$

Annotation propagation in both the forward and backward versions of APC proceeds by structural induction on the operator tree of q. Since there are only finitely many rule applications per node in the tree, and since each node in the tree is visited once, termination follows. Note however, that we assume here that annotations and query operators are strictly source-to-target (*e.g.*, for recursive (Datalog) queries, termination is not guaranteed).

Proposition 2 (Termination of b-APC and f-APC). *For any relational query q and any finite set of annotations, the algorithms b-APC and f-APC terminate.*

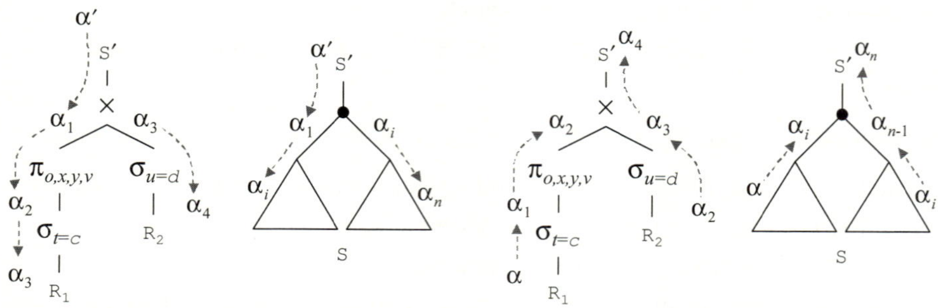

Fig. 6. Structural inductions on operator trees for queries q, where (a) shows a preorder navigation for b-APC and (b) a postorder navigation for f-APC

4 Discussion

Semantic annotations are a promising approach for ensuring compatibility and reuse of actors in scientific workflows. However, the current manual process of generating semantic annotations limits their utility. We have proposed a method for automatically propagating semantic annotations forward and/or backward through a dataflow process networks of actors, described by relational queries. We have shown how the problem of propagation can be recast as one of constraint implication, and presented a calculus of annotation propagation (APC) and developed two algorithms (b-APC and f-APC), corresponding to a top-down and bottom-up propagation of annotations through a query's operator tree. Both algorithms have been implemented in Prolog. Despite the initial results presented here, several interesting problems remain. The presented approach can be seen as a specialized first-order resolution procedure which is guided by the operator structure of a query. In general, resolution methods, including specialized versions such as the Chase (see *e.g.* [12]), may not terminate, *e.g.*, due to recursive rules and Skolem symbols. In contrast, our approach terminates, because we guide and limit the inference steps using the structure of the operator tree. However, we cannot always guarantee to obtain the most specific annotation via our propagation algorithm. In future work we plan to identify classes of queries and annotations where most specific annotations can be effectively computed. Similarly, we are interested in deriving approximate solutions even in cases where a most specific annotation does not exist. relationship between the formalization of annotation propagation as mapping composition (only sketched in this paper) and the one as constraint implication (used in this paper as the basis for APC).

References

1. P. A. Bernstein. Applying Model Management to Classical Meta-Data Problems. *Conference on Innovative Data Systems Research (CIDR)*, pages 209–220, 2003.
2. D. Bhagwat, L. Chiticariu, W. C. Tan, and G. Vijayvargiya. An Annotation Management System for Relational Databases. *Intl. Conf. on Very Large Data Bases (VLDB)*, 2004.

3. J. Biskup and A. Kluck. A New Approach to Inferences of Semantic Constraints. *Proc. of Advances in Databases and Information Systems*, 1997.
4. S. Bowers, K. Lin, and B. Ludäscher. On Integrating Scientific Resources through Semantic Registration. *Intl. Conf. on Scientific and Statistical Database Management (SSDBM)*, 2004.
5. S. Bowers and B. Ludäscher. Actor-Oriented Design of Scientific Workflows. *Intl. Conference on Conceptual Modeling (ER)*, Klagenfurt, Austria, 2005.
6. S. Bowers and B. Ludäscher. Towards Automatic Generation of Semantic Types in Scientific Workflows. *Intl. Workshop on Scalable Semantic Web Knowledge Base Systems*, 2005.
7. P. Buneman, S. Khanna, and W. C. Tan. Why and Where: A Characterization of Data Provenance. *Intl. Conference on Database Theory (ICDT)*, volume 1973 of *LNCS*, 2001.
8. P. Buneman, S. Khanna, and W. C. Tan. On Propagation of Deletions and Annotations Through Views. *ACM Symposium on Principles of Database Systems (PODS)*, 2002.
9. D. Chalcraft, J. Williams, M. Smith, and M. Willig. Scale Dependence In The Species-Richness-Productivity Relationship: The Role Of Species Turnover. *Ecology*, 85(10), 2004.
10. K. L. Clark. Negation as Failure. *Logic and Databases*. Plemum Press, 1977.
11. Y. Cui and J. Widom. Lineage Tracing for General Data Warehouse Transformations. *Intl. Conference on Very Large Data Bases (VLDB)*, Rome, Italy, 2001.
12. A. Deutsch, L. Popa, V. Tannen. Query Reformulation with Constraints. *SIGMOD Record*, 2006, to appear.
13. R. Fagin, P. G. Kolaitis, L. Popa, and W. C. Tan. Composing Schema Mappings: Second-Order Dependencies to the Rescue. *ACM Symposium on Principles of Database Systems (PODS)*, Paris, France, 2004.
14. F. Geerts, A. Kementsietsidis, and D. Milano. MONDRIAN: Annotating and Querying Databases through Colors and Blocks. *Intl. Conference on Data Engineering (ICDE)*, 2006.
15. G. Kahn and D. B. MacQueen. Coroutines and Networks of Parallel Processes. In B. Gilchrist, editor, *Proc. of the IFIP Congress 77*, pages 993–998, 1977.
16. E. A. Lee and T. Parks. Dataflow Process Networks. *Proceedings of the IEEE*, 83(5):773–799, May 1995.
17. B. Ludäscher, I. Altintas, C. Berkley, D. Higgins, E. Jaeger, M. Jones, E. A. Lee, J. Tao, and Y. Zhao. Scientific Workflow Management and the Kepler System. *Concurrency and Computation: Practice & Experience*, 2006. to appear.
18. B. Ludäscher and C. A. Goble, editors. *Guest Editors' Introduction to the Special Section on Scientific Workflows*, volume 34(3). ACM SIGMOD Record, September 2005.
19. S. Majithia, M. S. Shields, I. J. Taylor, and I. Wang. Triana: A Graphical Web Service Composition and Execution Toolkit. *Proceedings of the IEEE International Conference on Web Services (ICWS'04)*, pages 514–524. IEEE Computer Society, 2004.
20. A. Nash, P. A. Bernstein, and S. Melnik. Composition of Mappings Given by Embedded Dependencies. *ACM Symposium on Principles of Database Systems (PODS)*, 2005.
21. T. M. Oinn, M. Addis, J. Ferris, D. Marvin, M. Senger, R. M. Greenwood, T. Carver, K. Glover, M. R. Pocock, A. Wipat, and P. Li. Taverna: A Tool for the Composition and Enactment of Bioinformatics Workflows. *Bioinformatics*, 20(17), 2004.
22. J. A. Robinson. A Machine-Oriented Logic Based on the Resolution Principle. *Journal of the ACM*, 12(1):23–41, 1965.
23. Y. Simmhan, B. Plale, D. Gannon. A Survey of Data Provenance in e-Science. In [18].
24. J. Yu, R. Buyya. A Taxonomy of Scientific Workflow Systems for Grid Computing. In [18].

ShareEnabler: Policy-Driven Access Management for Ad-Hoc Collaborative Sharing

Jing Jin[1], Gail-Joon Ahn[1], and Mukesh Singhal[2]

[1] Department of Software and Information Systems
University of North Carolina at Charlotte
Charlotte, NC 28223, USA
{jjin, gahn}@uncc.edu
[2] Department of Computer Science
University of Kentucky
Lexington, KY 40506, USA
singhal@cs.uky.edu

Abstract. The rise of the Internet has introduced dramatic changes in managing and sharing digital resources among widely dispersed groups. This paper presents a policy-driven access management approach for ad-hoc collaboration to enable secure information sharing in heterogeneous network environments. In particular, we attempt to incorporate the features of distributed role-based access control, delegation and dissemination control to meet the fundamental access control requirements associated with resource originators. These features are realized in a set of XACML-based Role-based Originator Authorization policies (ROA). We propose a security architecture, called ShareEnabler, to achieve effective authorization and enforcement mechanisms in the context of Peer-to-Peer (P2P) networking oriented file sharing. We briefly discuss our proof-of-concept prototype implementation based on an existing P2P file sharing toolkit developed by Lawrence Berkeley National Laboratory.

1 Introduction

The rise of Internet has led collaborators to face dramatic changes in managing and sharing their resources. Subsequently, it has extremely influenced to the traditional information sharing fashion. Firstly, collaborative information sharing has increasingly turned outward to connect distributed participants across enterprises and research institutes. By removing the barriers of the time and geographical distance from research collaborations, people are able to work together regardless of their locations. And new terms such as *virtual organization*, *virtual laboratory*, and *collaboratorium* have been introduced consequently. Also, the heterogeneous network environments demand more open and flexible infrastructures as well as system architectures to enable collaborative sharing. In addition, there is a need for ad-hoc collaborative sharing systems to support autonomous and spontaneous collaboration among diverse participants, minimizing administrative complexity.

Traditionally, collaborative information sharing heavily relies on client-server based approach or email systems. By recognizing the inherent deficiencies such

T. Grust et al. (Eds.): EDBT 2006 Workshops, LNCS 4254, pp. 724–740, 2006.

as a central point of failure and scalability issue, several alternatives have been proposed to support collaborative sharing of resources, including Grid computing [1] and Peer-to-Peer (P2P) networking [2]. While Grid suits for highly structured collaborations with centralized infrastructures, P2P works well on heterogeneous network environments and promises to be more flexible and reliable for smaller ad-hoc collaborative interactions [3]. Especially, with the decentralized structure and load balancing feature, P2P based file sharing system offers better scalability and robustness. As demonstrated in the newly proposed SciShare system [3,4] from Lawrence Berkeley National Laboratory (LBNL), P2P file sharing has great potentials to support collaborative sharing. However, most P2P technologies mainly focus on sharing services such as availability and scalability. Ad-hoc collaborative sharing requires the resource sharing be highly controlled and the confidentiality and integrity be properly protected during sharing sessions. On one hand, systematic techniques such as secure group communication protocols are needed to protect the communication traffic for each sharing session. On the other hand, access control mechanisms should be in place to allow resource owners, also called originators, to define and enforce access control policies for participating peers. Although some researchers have investigated secure group communication protocols and technologies [5,6,7], there are few attempts in exploring practical access control models and mechanisms for such environments. Our immediate motivation of this paper is to provide effective and practical policy-driven access management mechanisms for fulfilling access control requirements associated with ad-hoc collaborative sharing environments. Our approach emphasizes the originator as the principal source of policy to determine the collaboration control space and delegate fine-grained access capabilities to collaborators. The policy framework incorporates the features of distributed role-based access control, delegation and dissemination control. The policy enforcement system is then proposed to guarantee the policies being propagated and enforced appropriately.

The rest of the paper is organized as follows. In Section 2, we give an overview of motivation and background technologies. Section 3 introduces our access management framework, including the originator-initiated approach and role-based management framework followed by the underlying policy specification framework. We then realize the proposed policy framework in a concrete collaborative sharing example and show the detailed policy evaluation procedures. Our proposed ShareEnabler system and implementation issues are also discussed in this section. Section 4 concludes the paper.

2 Problem Statements and Background Technologies

To better understand the ad-hoc collaborative sharing environments, we proceed with a typical example of collaborative sharing [8], from which we identify the key concepts involved in the environment and derive generic access control requirements for our approach:

NIH sponsored large-scale biomedical science collaborations involve a consortium of universities and research groups participating in several testbed projects related to the brain imaging of human neurological disease and associated animal models. Researchers from any of the groups may contribute their research results and data to be shared by other members in the collaboration group. Suppose Regional Medical Center (RMC), jointly initiated with Bioinformatics Department at University of XYZ, administers a local magnetic resonance imaging (MRI) data repository and would like to share the data with other collaborators for testing new hypotheses on human neurological diseases.

RMC needs to protect and control the data access and dissemination during the collaborative sharing. Due to the large group of collaborators, RMC would like to have a flexible and easy way to define the sharing collaborators as well as the access privileges for them. For faster and more convenient sharing, instead of contacting all the researchers in collaborating labs, RMC may need to notify the director or the coordinator of each collaborator's lab. The data are then shared with all other lab members through them. Furthermore, to protect the patentable data, any dissemination of the data should be under RMC's agreement. Meanwhile, Bioinformatics Department at University of XYZ as a co-owner of the data also would like to have the control on the data.

From the example above, we first identify several key concepts in an ad-hoc collaborative sharing environment that are used through the rest of this paper:

- **Originator:** In collaborative sharing environments, we refer the *resource owner* or the *initial information provider* as an originator. An originator plays a critical role in providing the resource to be shared and in controlling how the resource is shared among collaboration participants. The originator could be an individual principal or an organizational entity. For a particular resource, there may be one or multiple joint originators. In our scenario, RMC and XYZ University, both as organizational entities, act as joint originators for the MRI data repository.
- **Collaborative sharing space:** In general, collaborative sharing space refers to the *control domain* of the collaborative sharing. An originator needs to define her collaborative sharing space by including a collection of, mostly distributed, people or organizations and granting fine-grained access privileges to them. In our example, the whole NIH sponsored biomedical science consortium or a subgroup of consortium could be considered as the collaboration space. This should be determined at the originator's discretion.
- **Collaborator:** Each entity that is included inside the collaborative sharing space is referred as a collaborator. These collaborators are the actual *recipients* or *consumers* of the shared resource(s). Similar to the originator, a collaborator could be an individual principal such as independent researcher or an organizational research lab.
- **Disseminator:** We define two types of disseminators, namely, the *root disseminator* and the *designated disseminator*. The root disseminator refers to the originator since the originator triggers the initial sharing process with other ad-hoc collaborators. Designated disseminator, on the other hand, refers to a group of collaborators, with the consent of originator, to further distribute the resource. This can be achieved through the notion of delegation.

Indeed, designated disseminator is a subgroup of ad-hoc collaborator. In our case, the directors/coordinators of collaboration laboratories are the designated disseminators.

2.1 Access Control Requirements

From the above-mentioned example, we derive several generic access management requirements for ad-hoc collaborative sharing:

- **Flexible and manageable access control:** Collaborative sharing may involve a large amount of distributed collaborators across domains. The diversity and unpredictability of the involved participants determine that the authorization cannot be established on per-individual basis like the way ACL does. The access control system needs to provide appropriate abstraction of collaborators and privileges to achieve the flexibility and reduce the complexity of security administration.
- **Flexible delegation/revocation:** The nature of distributed resource sharing requires delegation in place to allow the access privileges as well as administrative responsibilities of an originator to be distributed among different collaboration parties. Especially, it should also allow an originator to delegate not only all of the privileges, but also partial privileges. In addition, revocation as the counterpart of delegation should be supported as well.
- **Effective originator-controlled dissemination:** As the shared information leaves the originator's domain, it is hard for the originator to have control on such information. With the originator-initiated control, originators should be able to control and track down the re-dissemination of their resources to make sure the dissemination happens within the collaborative sharing space, and only the legitimate collaborators could share the resources.

2.2 Background Technologies

Role-based Access Control (RBAC): RBAC is a proven technology for managing and enforcing security in large-scale and enterprise-wide systems [9,10]. The essential idea of RBAC is that permissions are associated with roles, and users acquire permissions by being members of appropriate roles. With the abstraction between users and permissions, RBAC could tremendously reduce the complexities of security management for system administrators. Meanwhile, many role-based delegation models [11,12,13] have been proposed as a complementary to RBAC in leveraging an effective way of propagating authorities as well as responsibilities among various distributed entities. Our framework is built on existing role-based delegation models by applying decentralized user assignments.

ORCON, UCON and DCON: Originator control (ORCON) is a special access control policy defined by a resource originator to control the dissemination of restricted resources [14,15]. ORCON policy requires that resource recipients obtain an originator's permission to re-disseminate protected resources to users who are not originally designated as authorized recipients by the originator. Traditional ORCON solutions used a non-discretionary access control list, which limits the ability to enforce ORCON policies in a closed centralized control environment [16]. The concept of Usage Control (UCON) is introduced in [16,17] for controlling access and usage of digital information objects. The re-dissemination control in ORCON is also one of the key concerns in UCON. By introducing license and ticket [16], UCON has the potential to support and enforce ORCON policies in more versatile and flexible ways for distributed environments. Most recently, the notion of dissemination control (DCON) has been proposed in [18]. DCON involves a much richer and broader concept than ORCON and UCON concerning with controlling information during the dissemination activities.

SciShare File Sharing Infrastructure: Traditional P2P sharing applications, such as Gnutella [19], allow end users to search and download information from other peers, and make their own information available to other peers. The search component often broadcasts a query to all known peers, while sending response and downloading information are unicast communications. LBNL's framework, called Scishare [4], is a security enhanced version of P2P file sharing system. SciShare leverages X.509 public key certificate as the central security component. The certificate can be either self-signed or signed by a trusted organizational certification authority (CA). To facilitate new peers joining the community quickly, the system allows the new peers (called pseudo user) to create self-signed X.509 certificates. However, the pseudo user cannot gain higher level of trust or privileges in the system. The instantiation of secure and reliable multicast communication is provided by Secure Group Layer (SGL) [5], while TLS [20] is used to achieve confidentiality and integrity in unicast communication when peers play traditional role of client in some cases and the traditional role of a server in others. SciShare also supports access control that is primitive and limited to group-based discretionary access control approach.

3 Policy-Driven Access Management Framework

In this section, we describe a policy-driven access management framework to provide a means of comprehensive access management model beyond SciShare. The framework emphasizes originator-initiated role-based access control and delegation. Originators dynamically create and include roles in their collaborative sharing space while delegating fine-grained access and dissemination capabilities to the roles. Distributed role-assignment is achieved through *Delegation of Delegation Authority*. These features are expressed in a set of Role-based Originator Authorization policies (ROA). ROA policies serve as the foundation of our framework and are further evaluated and enforced in our proposed security architecture for P2P based file sharing.

3.1 Supporting Originator Control and Role-Based Approach

An originator, as the resource owner, is responsible for initiating the controls to secure her respective resources over sharing and dissemination activities among other peer collaborators. To accommodate the originator-initiated control approach, it is essential for an originator to define her collaborative sharing space in a set of access management policies and delegate fine-grained privileges through these policies. The specified policies should be propagated and enforced properly by the underlying security system during the resource re-dissemination.

RBAC provides an effective way to abstract privileges using roles. Instead of including every individual ad-hoc collaborator, the originator could simply define the collaborative sharing space in a collection of specific roles, such as "engineer" and "investigator". And each peer collaborator is dynamically included in the sharing space to gain access privileges by claiming their role. Therefore, bringing "role" in our framework becomes a natural choice to achieve the manageability in the ad-hoc collaboration environments. In addition, we introduce role-based delegation as another layer of privilege and authority decentralization to accommodate the needs of distributed role assignment and fine-grained privilege propagation in collaborative sharing environments. In particular, our framework incorporates the following types of delegation relationships for ad-hoc collaboration:

- **Delegation of access capabilities:** The permission-role assignment in traditional RBAC usually deals with the abstraction of privileges in a closed organizational domain. In a distributed collaborative sharing environment, an originator delegates fine-grained access capabilities to certain roles in the collaboration space so that the privileges are propagated and distributed across various participating entities through these roles.
- **Constrained dissemination delegation:** To achieve better resource availability and continuous resource dissemination, besides the normal access privileges, the resource dissemination privilege can be delegated by an originator to a certain set of roles, so that the collaborators who are assigned to these roles are allowed to further disseminate the pre-obtained resources on the originator's behalf. These collaborators, in another words, are the designated disseminators. As "constrained" delegation, the scope of delegation should be within the originators and the designated disseminators.
- **Delegation of delegation authority:** This is a special form of administrative delegation that enables an originator to partially delegate the role assignment privilege to trusted third parties. In our example, the originator defines a set of roles in her collaborative sharing space and delegates the role assignment authority to the directors/coordinators of each collaboration group so that these directors/coordinators may assign roles to their members on the originator's behalf.

3.2 Designing Policies

In our policy framework, an originator defines her access management policies in a set of authorization policies using XACML (eXtensible Access Control Markup Language) [21]. We introduce two major types of policies, Root Meta PolicySet (RMPS) and Role-based Originator Authorization PolicySet (ROA).

Root Meta Policy Set (RMPS) is the starting point of the originator's authorization policies for the shared resources. Since the shared resources may have single or multiple distributed originators, their authorization policies may be maintained in multiple administrative domains. We need a policy to identify these originators and locate their policies so that the underlying enforcement system could retrieve and enforce these distributed policies. RMPS is designed for this purpose. In RMPS policy schema, the *Target* element specifies the resource to which ROA authorization policies are applied. The resource is represented as a URI that conforms to RFC2396 standard format [22]. The *PolicySet* contains one ownership *Policy* and one or more *PolicySetIdReference* elements to specify ROA policy locations in the format of LDAP URLs. In the ownership *Policy*, originators are identified as *Subject* attributes in their X.500 DNs. The ownership is specified as "*own*" in *Action* element. Figure 1(a) illustrates the schema of RMPS.

ROA policy sets are the real role-based authorization policies where an originator defines her collaborative sharing space and delegates fine-grained capabilities. We extend OASIS RBAC profile [23] to support the delegation and distributed role assignment in our framework. ROA contains four major sub-components: role specification policy (RPS), capability specification/role-capability assignment policy (CPS), user-role assignment policy (RAPS), and delegation of delegation authority policy (DoDPS).

- Role *PolicySet* (RPS) is a role specification *PolicySet*. The originator defines the collaborative sharing space in a set of RPSs, and associates each role RPS with a Capability *PolicySet* (CPS) that actually contains capabilities of the given role. The role is specified as a *Subject* attribute, the corresponding CPS is referenced through *PolicySetReference*. Figure 1(b) shows the schema of RPS.
- Capability *PolicySet* (CPS) specifies the actual capabilities assigned to the given role. CPS contains *Policy* and *Rule* elements that describe the delegated capabilities as the resources and actions. By granting the "*disseminate*" action to a specific role, the originator delegates her dissemination privilege to the role. The collaborator who is assigned to that role then becomes a designated disseminator to re-disseminate the resources. The CPS may also contain references to the CPSs associated with other roles that are junior to the given role, thereby achieving the role hierarchies through the capability aggregation. Figure 1(c) shows the schema of CPS.
- Role Assignment *PolicySet* (RAPS) is specified by an originator or a delegated third party authority to define which roles are assigned to which collaborators. In RAPS, the principals are specified in their X.500 DNs as *Subject* attributes. The assigned role is specified as *Resource* attribute. And the term"*enable*" is used as *Action* attribute to indicate the assignment relationship. Figure 1(d) shows the schema of RAPS.
- Delegations of Delegation Authority *PolicySet* (DoDPS) reflects the type of "*delegation of delegation authority*" with originators specifying which role assignments are delegated to which specific trusted authorities. The construction of DoDPS is similar to RAPS, except that the *Subjects* are the trusted

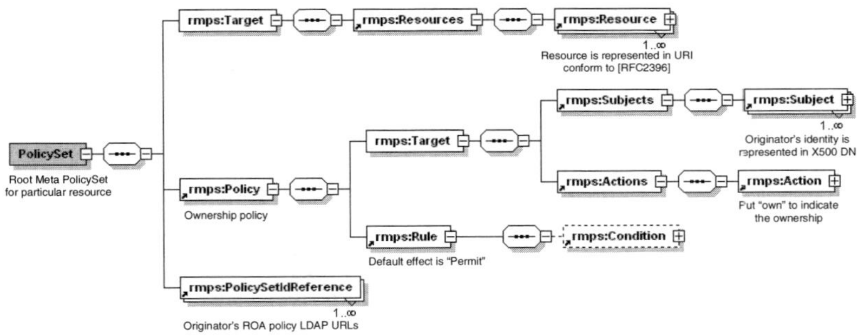

(a) RMPS Policy Schema

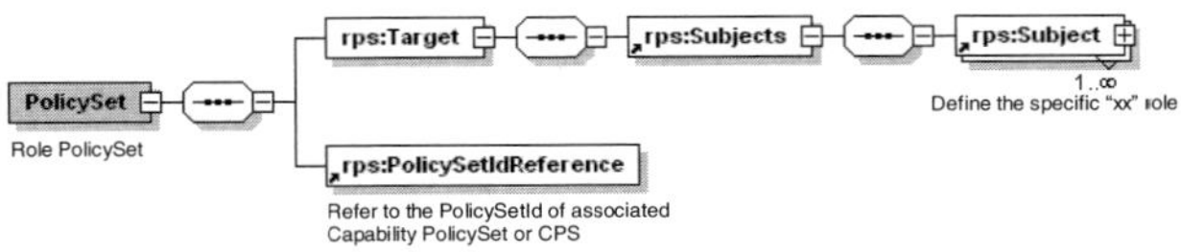

(b) RPS Policy Schema

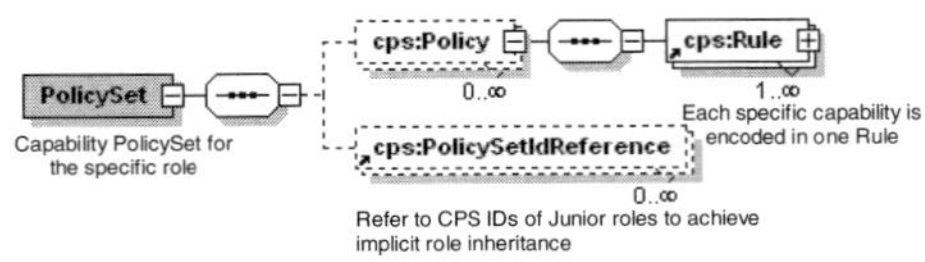

(c) CPS Policy Schema

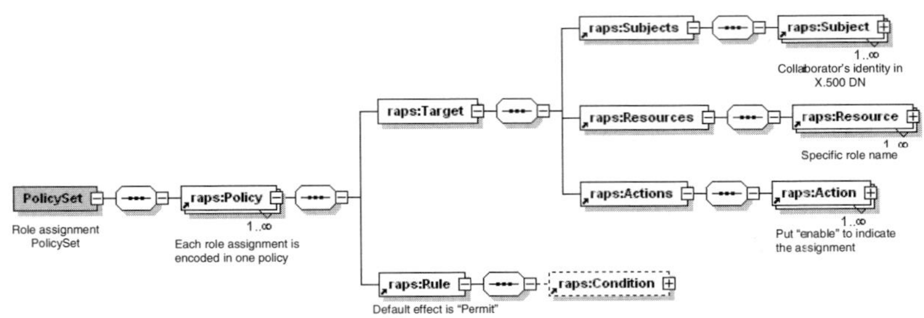

(d) RAPS Policy Schema

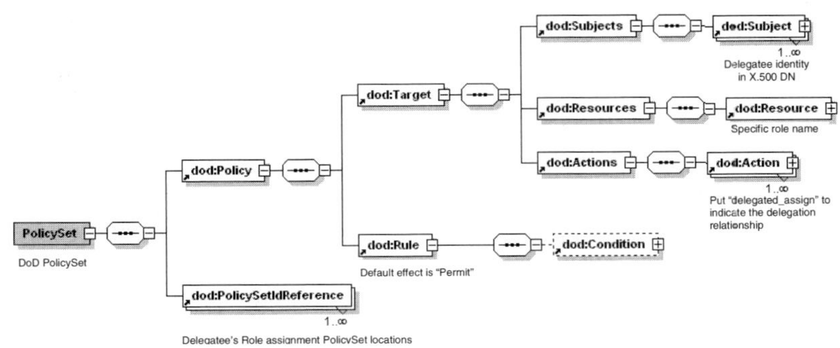

(e) DoDPS Policy Schema

Fig. 1. Policy Set Schemas

delegatees and the delegation relationship is indicated as "*delegated_assign*" in *Action*. Figure 1(e) shows the schema of DoDPS.

3.3 Policy Framework Realization and Policy Evaluation

In this section, we extend the earlier discussed collaborative sharing scenario into a concrete example and proceed implementing a set of access management policies to realize our proposed policy framework. We then show how the authorization system evaluate these policies and make decisions.

Inside the NIH biomedical science research community, a team of biologists from LIISP research lab, with John as the team leader and Dave as one of the team members, is conducting research tasks related to animal modeling comparisons and analysis. John's team needs to collaborate with RMC and use RMC's data to verify a new hypothesis drawn from their research.

As discussed earlier, both *RMC* and *XYZ University* are joint originators for the *MRI data* resource. For simplicity, we focus on how RMC develops the ROA policies and omit the control from the XYZ University. End each individual member in *LIISP* lab, *John* and *Dave*, is considered as an ad-hoc collaborator that needs to be authorized individually in *RMC*'s collaborative sharing space. To authorize accesses to the members in *LIISP* lab, *RMC* defines two roles such as *Coordinator* role and *Investigator* role, where the *Coordinator* role is senior to the *Investigator* role. *RMC* delegates the capabilities of "*query*" and "*acquire*" to the *Investigator* role, and further delegates the capability of "*re-disseminate*" to the *Coordinator* role. *RMC* then assigns the team leader *John* to the *Coordinator* role and delegates *John* to perform the user-*Investigator* role assignment through the delegation of delegation authority, so that *John* is able to assign his other team members (i.e. *Dave*) to the *Investigator* role and re-disseminate the resource to them as a designated disseminator.

Figure 2(a) shows the overall structure of our policy framework and the relationships among the individual policy components. In particular, RMPS specifies the resource with the originator(s) who "*own*" the resource, and locates the originators' ROA policy sets. In the example scenario, *RMC* and *XYZ University*, both represented as *Subject* attributes in their X.509 DNs, are joint originators of the "*MRI data*" resource. Since we focus on the control of *RMC*, only the URL location of *RMC*'s ROA policy sets is referenced through the *PolicySetIdReference* element. In RMC's ROA policies, there is a set of RPSs and CPSs, a RAPS and a DoDPS. As shown in Figure 2(b), RPSs define two roles in RMC's collaborative sharing space, namely the *Coordinator* role and the *Investigator* role. CPSs specify the corresponding capabilities associated with these two roles. The reference link between each pair of RPS and CPS reflects the permission-role assignment relation where the originator delegates the fine-grained access and dissemination capabilities to the role. By referencing to the CPS of the *Investigator* role, the *Coordinator* role inherits all the capabilities that are assigned to the *Investigator* role. In this context, the role hierarchy is achieved indirectly through capabilities aggregation. As shown in Figure 2(c), the RAPS specifies

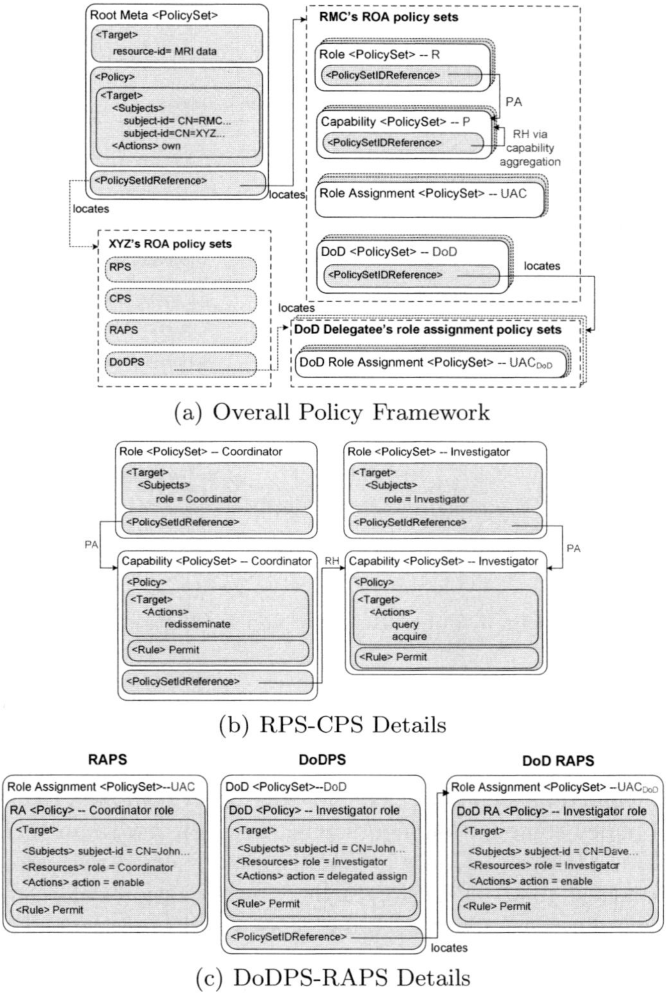

(a) Overall Policy Framework

(b) RPS-CPS Details

(c) DoDPS-RAPS Details

Fig. 2. Policy Framework Realization

the user-role assignment relation that RMC assigns *John* to the *Coordinator* role. By being assigned to the role, *John* is included in RMC's collaborative sharing space, and thus obtains the delegated capabilities. DoDPS realizes the *delegation of delegation authority* where RMC delegates the user-*Investigator* role assignment to *John*. And *John*'s RAPS policy is finally referenced in the DoDPS where *John* assigns his team member *Dave* to the *Investigator* role.

As our policy framework conforms to the XACML standard, the policy evaluation and authorization decision making can be done as specified in [21]. The typical setup is that the Policy Enforcement Point (PEP) forms an access request based on the requester's attributes (X.509 identities, roles, etc.), the resource in question, and the action towards the resource. The request is sent to a Policy

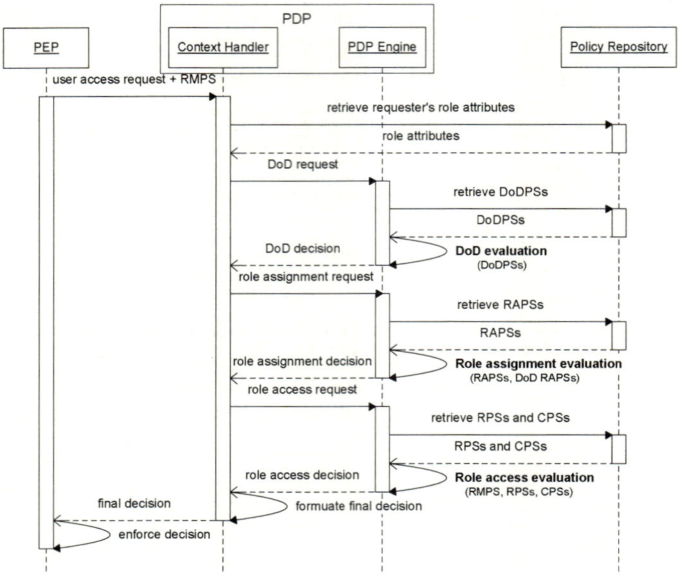

Fig. 3. Policy Retrieval and Evaluation

Decision Point (PDP) for policy retrieval and policy evaluation. Basically, the PDP first finds the top-level policy elements that the *Target* elements match the attributes specified in the access requests, and then evaluates the boolean expressions included in each *Rule* elements and finally combines the results using the specified policy combination algorithms. A response with an access *Decision* element of value "*Permit*", "*Deny*", "*Indeterminate*" or "*NotApplicable*" will be made and returned to the PEP for further authorization enforcement. In our system, we introduce the Context Handler as a subcomponent of the PDP to conduct a series of query-generation and decision-making process for a single access query sent by the PEP. In this section, we focus on how the PEP, Context Handler and PDP interact with each other and how the PDP evaluates an access request against the originator's ROA policies. The detailed system design and implementation will be discussed shortly in next section.

Figure 3 shows the detailed sequence diagram of the policy retrieval and policy evaluation. The PEP formulates an access request with the requester's X.509 identity and the action towards the requested resource. For instance, the PEP may generate an access request for the PDP to evaluate whether a requester Dave (*CN=Dave...*) is allowed to "*acquire*" the "*MRI data*" resource. Along with the associated RMPS for the "*MRI data*", the request is sent to the PDP. The Context Handler parses the RMPS and locates *RMC*'s policy directory. The role attributes that are assigned to the user's identity are retrieved from the originator's policy repository. In our case, the *Investigator* role is assigned to *Dave* by *John*. Since the attribute is assigned by an entity other than the originator, the Context Handler will prompt to formulate a DoD request for the

PDP to evaluate whether the role attribute issuer (*CN=John...*) is a legitimate delegated authority to conduct the user-*Investigator* role assignment. The PDP Engine conducts the ***DoD Evaluation*** based on DoDPS and confirms the delegation of delegation authority relationship. The Context Handler then formulates the role assignment request for the PDP Engine to check whether the requester (*CN=Dave...*) is "*enabled*" with the *Investigator* role attribute that is retrieved earlier. The PDP Engine conducts the ***Role Assignment Evaluation*** against the retrieved RAPSs defined by the originator and/or the DoD RAPSs defined by the DoD delegatee (in our case, only the DoD RAPS is evaluated). Finally, the Context Handler formulates the role access request for the PDP Engine to check whether the assigned *Investigator* role is able to perform the "*acquire*" action towards the "*MRI data*" resource as specified in the PEP's access request. The PDP Engine conducts the ***Role Access Evaluation*** against the RMPS, RPSs and CPSs. Based on the authorization decisions of these three evaluations, the Context Handler generates the final user access decision and sends back to the PEP for further decision enforcement process.

3.4 ShareEnabler System Architecture and Discussions

In this section, we give an overview of our system architecture, called ShareEnabler. ShareEnabler casts our proposed framework as detailed authorization services and mechanisms which are bound to specific communication infrastructure from LBNL's SciShare toolkit [4].

In our collaborative sharing system, each participant is represented by a ShareEnabler (SE) agent that executes sharing services on the collaborator's behalf. Similar to most of existing P2P file sharing systems, the resource discovery involves broadcasting a query to all known peers. As shown in Figure 4, ShareEnabler Agent 1 sends a broadcasting query message to all known peers in the collaborative sharing group. Upon receiving the query message, SE Agents 2 - 5 look up their own posted contents. SE Agent 2 finds the matched content(s), evaluates the originator's ROA policies and sends a unicast query response with the metadata of the authorized content(s) to SE Agent 1, while SE Agents 3 - 5 are not necessary to respond to the requester. We call this process as metadata sharing. SE Agent 1 then can send out the download request, while the SE Agent 2 will further check with the originator's ROA policies and initiate the data transferring process if the requester is authorized to download to resource.

Figure 4 also shows the detailed components inside the ShareEnabler Agent and their interactions in the process of metadata sharing between the SE Agent 1 (as the requester) and the SE Agent 2 (as the responder). Each ShareEnabler agent is composed of five components: Graphical User Interface (GUI), Executive Services, Access Management/Enforcement, SGL/IG and TLS/TCP. GUI is the interface through which the user operates and executes the sharing services. Executive Services are the real services required by collaborative sharing behaviors, which include Search, Download and Share Services. All these services are based on the underlying Data Management Service, which provides data storage and cache functionalities. The Data Management Service also serves as the

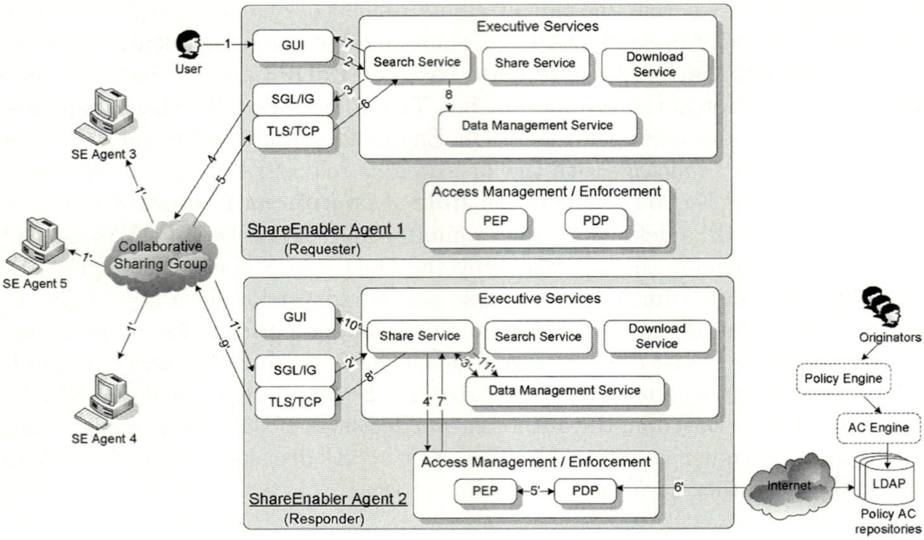

Fig. 4. ShareEnabler System Architecture

background database in the system. The Access management/enforcement is the central component for the core access and dissemination control. The PEP is responsible for the request processing and access decision enforcement. The PDP, which consists of the Context Handler and the PDP Engine, is designed for the policy retrieval and authorization decision making. Secure Group Layer (SGL) and the underlying InterGroup protocol provide the secure group communication services. Similarly, Transport Layer Security (TLS) and the underlying TCP protocol provide the secure communication between two ShareEnabler agents, which in the category of unicast communication. The functionalities for both SGL/IG and TLS/TCP are adopted from SciShare [4].

In the context of metadata sharing, on the requester agent side (ShareEnabler Agent 1), a user interacts with the GUI to specify the keywords and search criteria (step 1). GUI invokes the Search Service to formulate the query message and broadcast to all known peers in the collaborative sharing group through the SGL/IG protocol (step 2 - 4). Upon receiving responses from other peers, the TLS/TCP module notices the Search Service with the response messages (step 5 - 6), and these responses are parsed and then shown in the GUI (step 7), through which the user may further interact to download the data resource. The search results are finally cached through the Data Management Service (step 8).

On the responder agent side (ShareEnabler Agent 2), the SGL/IG module notices the Sharing Service (step 1' - 2') upon receiving the request. The Sharing Service then invokes the Data Management Service to find matched resources against the query (step 3'). When a list of matched resources is returned back to the Sharing Service, the Access Management/Enforcement component is invoked for access checking (step 4' - 6'). The PEP enforces the decision by removing unauthorized resources from the list and returns the updated list back to the Sharing Service (step 7'). Finally, the Sharing Service formulates the response message with the metadata of a list of matched and authorized resources, and sends back to the requester through the TLS/TCP module (step 8' - 9'). The metadata sharing result is shown in the GUI and cached in the Data Management Service (step 10' - 11').

As also shown in Figure 4, ROA policies are deployed separately from the major ShareEnabler application and its enforcement components. These ROA policies will be retrieved and enforced at run time whenever the ShareEnabler agent needs to respond to other peer's requests. In doing so, an originator can easily maintain and change the policies without requiring changes to sharing service systems. We decide to apply X.509 attribute certificates to encapsulate access management policies. X.509 attribute certificate (AC) is a basic data structure in Privilege Management Infrastructure (PMI) [24] to bind a set of attributes to its holder. With its portability and flexibility, AC is considered as an ideal container of subject attributes as well as authorization policies in ShareEnabler. We also developed a Policy Administration Facility application to provide the utility modules for originator to create and maintain ROA policies. Especially, originators use the *Policy Engine* to create their ROA policy sets. *Attribute Certificate Engine* is then invoked to generate the ROA policy ACs and store them in distributed LDAP policy repositories.

The goal of access and dissemination control of ShareEnabler is to guarantee the resource is shared within the collaborative sharing space defined by ROA policies. Our system applies a distributed policy propagation and enforcement scheme with decentralized, self-enforcing, and self-monitoring features at each ShareEnabler agent level. Especially, each disseminator ShareEnabler agent should ensure that ROA policies are enforced locally by the Access Management/Enforcement component, and these ROA policies are propagated to other ShareEnabler agents while those agents may further act as disseminators to respond to other peers' requests. Since the Root Meta Policy Set (RMPS) plays an important role for the ShareEnabler Agent to locate and enforce originator's policies. It is essential to make sure the RMPS is propagated along with the data dissemination and the confidentiality and integrity are properly protected . In achieving these goals, we design a new data structure that strongly encapsulates the data resource together with the associated RMPS policy. As the originator initiates the sharing process, instead of sending out the original data resource, originator's ShareEnabler agent disseminates the encapsulated data structure to other agents, which can only be decrypted at runtime by the ShareEnabler Agent. By doing this, we leave the ShareEnabler Agent with full enforcement power and make it extensible for more advanced dissemination tracking mechanisms.

In our prototype, we use JDK1.4 core packages as well as other necessary libraries to develop the components specified in the system architecture. Especially, we adopt SciShare's Reliable and Secure Group Communication (RSGC) package for the implementation of SGL/TLS communication protocol as well

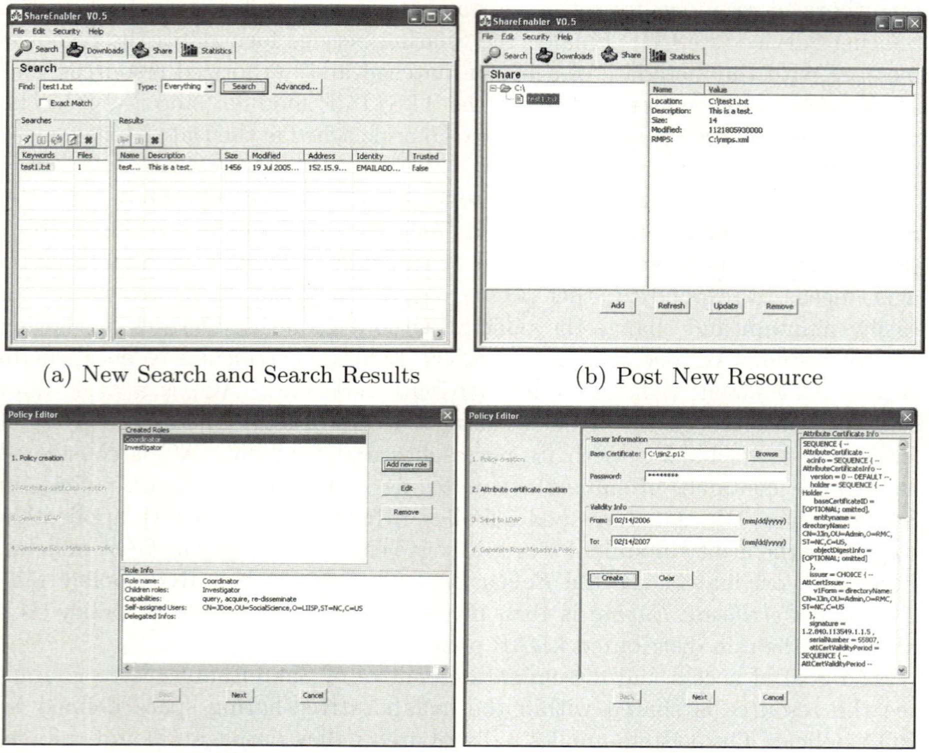

(a) New Search and Search Results

(b) Post New Resource

(c) Policy Creation

(d) Attribute Certificate Generation

Fig. 5. ShareEnabler User Interfaces

as the basic authentication mechanisms. We extend Sun's XACML implementation to accommodate the functionalities in PDP and PEP. IAIK's java crypto library is used to implement the major components of cryptography and attribute certificate. And IPlanet Directory Server serves as the back-end LDAP policy repository. The beta version of ShareEnabler system implementation has been completed for further testing and evaluation. Figure 5(a) shows a user interface of an SE Agent for searching for specific file resource and displaying search results based on the responses from other peers. Figure 5(b) shows an originator posts new resource to be shared with other collaborator peers. The Figure 5(c) shows the user interface of the policy creation that allows an originator to create new roles in her collaborative sharing space and delegate fine-grained capabilities to the roles. The ROA policies will then be generated automatically based on the originator's input. Finally, Figure 5(d) shows the interface of policy attribute certificate generation with the originator specifying the validity period of the attribute certificate and using her private key (encapsulated in an X.509 Personal Information Exchange Certificate [25]) to sign the attribute certificate.

4 Conclusion

In this paper, we have presented a policy-driven access control framework for ad-hoc collaborative sharing. Especially, we articulated distinctive access control requirements in ad-hoc collaborative sharing and proposed a family of XACML-based policy schemas that are comprehensive and flexible enough to meet the identified requirements. In addition, we briefly described the enforcement mechanisms as well as a proof-of-concept prototype of P2P based file sharing system, called ShareEnabler. An important contribution of this work includes special features of originator control, delegation and dissemination control. Our approach allows originators to authorize distributed collaborators and control over the resources being shared. The delegation of delegation authority was introduced to systematically achieve user-role assignments in distributed environments.

Our future works are geared towards several directions. We would investigate and apply more advanced system-level dissemination control enforcement mechanisms. In collaborative sharing environment, the resources are stored and updated in distributed places. This causes another control issue of how to maintain the originator-initiated control of data usage and modification after the dissemination, which in turn, relates to the enforcement mechanisms. Furthermore, the inconsistency of data representation and instances needs to be dealt with while the resources are shared and updated. Developing an integrated infrastructure would be another research direction as well.

Acknowledgments

The work was partially supported by the grants from National Science Foundation (NSF-IIS-0242393). The work of Gail-J Ahn and Jing Jin was also supported by the grants from Department of Energy Early Career Principal Investigator Award (DE-FG02-03ER25565).

References

1. Baker, M., Buyya, R., Laforenza, D.: The Grid: International efforts in global computing. International Journal of Software Practice and Experience. (2002)
2. Oram, A. (ed.): Peer-to-peer: Harnessing the power of disruptive technologies. O'Reilly. (2001)
3. Berket, K., Agarwal, D.: Enabling secure ad-hoc collaboration. In: Proceedings of the Workshop on Advanced Collaborative Environments. (2003)
4. Berket, K., Essiari, A., Muratas, A.: PKI-based security for peer-to-peer information sharing. In: Proceedings of the Fourth IEEE International Conference on Peer-to-Peer Computing. (2004)
5. Agarwal, D., Chevassut, O., Thompson, M.R., Tsudik, G.: An integrated solution for secure group communication in wide-area networks. In: Proceedings of the 6th IEEE Symposium on Computers and Communications. (2001) 22–28
6. Kihlstrom, K.P., Moser, L.E., Melliar-Smith, P.M.: The securering protocols for securing group communication. In: Proceedings of 31st IEEE HICSS. (1998) 317–326

7. Reiter, M.K.: Secure group membership protocol. In: Proceedings of IEEE Symposium on Research in Security and Privacy. (1994)
8. NIH: NIH data sharing workbook. http://grants.nih.gov/grants/policy/data_sharing/data_sharing_workbook.pdf (2004)
9. Sandhu, R., Coyne, E.J., Feinstein, H.L., Youman, C.E.: Role based access control models. IEEE Computer **29** (1996)
10. Ferraiolo, D., Sandhu, R., Gavrila, S., R. Kuhn, R.: Proposed NIST standard for role-based access control. ACM Transactions on Information and System Security (TISSEC) **4** (2001) 224–274
11. Zhang, L., Ahn, G.J., Chu, B.T.: A rule-based framework for role-based delegation and revocation. ACM Transactions on Information and System Security (TISSEC) **6** (2003) 404–441
12. Ahn, G.J., Mohan, B.: Secure information sharing using role-based delegation. Journal of Network and Computer Applications **2** (2005)
13. Barka, E., Sandhu, R.: Framework for role-based delegation models. In: Proceedings of the 16th Annual Computer Security Applications Conference (ACSAC), IEEE Computer Society (2000) 168
14. Abrams, M.D., Heaney, J., King, O., LaPadula, L.J., Lazear, M., Ol, I.M.: Generalized framework for access control: Towards prototyping the orgcon policy. In: Proceedings of the 14th National Computing Security Conference. (1991) 257–266
15. McCollum, C.J., Messing, J.R., Notargiacomo, L.: Beyond the pale of MAC and DAC — defining new forms of access control. In: Proceedings of IEEE Symposium on Security and Privacy. (1990) 190–200
16. Park, J., Sandhu, R.: Originator control in usage control. In: Proceedings of the 3rd International Workshop on Policies for Distributed Systems and Networks (POLICY'02). (2002)
17. Park, J., Sandhu, R.: Towards usage control models: beyond traditional access control. In: Proceedings of the 7th ACM Symposium on Access Control Models and Technologies (SACMAT 2002). (2002) 57–64
18. Thomas, R., Sandhu, R.: Towards a multi-dimensional characterization of dissemination control. In: Proceedings of the 5th IEEE International Workshop on Policies for Distributed Systems and Networks (POLICY04). (2004)
19. Gnutella. http://www.gnutella.com/
20. RFC2246: The TLS protocol version 1.0. http://www.ietf.org/frc/rfc2246.txt (1999)
21. OASIS: XACML 2.0 core: extensible access control markup language (xacml) version 2.0. http://docs.oasis-open.org/xacml/2.0/access_control-xacml-2.0-core-spec-os.pdf (2005)
22. RFC2396: Uniform resource identifiers (URI): Generic syntax. http://rfc.net/rfc2396.html (1998)
23. OASIS: Core and hierarchical role based access control (rbac) profile of xacml v2.0. http://docs.oasis-open.org/xacml/2.0/access_control-xacml-2.0-rbac-profile1-spec-os.pdf (2005)
24. ITU-T: The directory: Public-key and attribute certificate frameworks. ISO/IEC 9594-8:2001 (2001)
25. RSA: PKCS #12: Personal information exchange syntax standard. ftp://ftp.rsasecurity.com/pub/pkcs/pkcs-12/pkcs-12v1.pdf (1999)

Context Consistency Management Using Ontology Based Model*

Yingyi Bu, Shaxun Chen, Jun Li, Xianping Tao, and Jian Lu

National Laboratory for Novel Software Technology, Nanjing University
Nanjing City, P.R. China, 210093
byy@ics.nju.edu.cn, buyingyi@nju.org.cn

Abstract. Inconsistent contexts are death-wounds which usually result in context-aware applications' incongruous behaviors and users' perplexed feelings, therefore the benefits of context-aware computing will become less believed. This problem occurs in most sensor based applications due to the intrinsic drawbacks of fallible physical sensors which can only detect some evidence of real world's situations rather than global views of them. In this paper, we extend ontology based context modeling approach with some descriptive information added to contexts, modify reasoners to support time information, bring in a context life-cycle management strategy, establish a context exploitation mechanism, and propose an inconsistency resolution algorithm, fostering timely, exact and conflict-free contexts. Besides, evaluations and a case study are carried out to attest our design principles.

1 Introduction

Context-awareness which aims at decreasing people's attentions to various computational devices is an attractive feature of pervasive computing paradigms. Context informs both recognition and mapping by providing a structured, unified view of the world in which the system operates [1]. However, context is different from knowledge in traditional views because of its dynamic, transient, and fallible characteristics.

It is widely acknowledged that a good context model can lead to well designed and easily understood context-aware applications. Recently emerging ontology based context modeling approach [2][3][4] is an elegant solution towards context sharing, reasoning and reusing. However, in practice, context-aware applications are so fragile that their behaviors often make users bewildered, due to mismatching between contexts in computer systems and contexts in real world. Concretely speaking, inconsistent contexts often appear in context-aware systems on account of failures from either physical sensors or software infrastructures. For example, contexts like "Tom is giving a lecture" and "Tom is talking to Jim on the Aisle" may appear at the same time. How do we know which context is correct? Our previous work [5][6] focuses on context model and fusion infrastructure design, but context management and conflict resolution are simply considered so that applications based on the infrastructure are not so robust.

* This work is funded by NSFC (60233010, 60273034, 60403014), 973 Program of China (2002CB312002), 863 Program of China (2005AA113160) and NSF of Jiangsu Province (BK2002203, BK2002409).

T. Grust et al. (Eds.): EDBT 2006 Workshops, LNCS 4254, pp. 741–755, 2006.

Nevertheless, we find ontology based context model can largely facilitate inconsistency detection and resolution. In this work, we first extend ontology based context model by adding some descriptive information such as time, frequency and state to contexts. Based on the context model, a context management device is established, which not only aims at timely and accurate contexts but also facilitates inconsistency resolution. Then, we design an inconsistency resolution algorithm to provide correct and consistent contexts. Through experiments and an application case study, we find that our modified approach is rather acceptable for fetching up those disadvantages in previous work and the quality of contexts is largely improved.

The rest of this paper is organized as follows. In Section 2, we discuss some related work. The extended context model is presented in Section 3. Our context management mechanism is proposed in Section 4. Section 5 introduces our context inconsistency resolution algorithm CIR. The evaluations are given in Section 6. Section 7 presents a case study to verify our design principles. Finally, we conclude in Section 8.

2 Related Work

In the past decade, many context-aware systems are developed both in research communities and industrial companies which all contribute a lot to context-aware computing.

Active Badge [7] is the earliest context-aware applications that redirects phone calls based on people's locations. Salber developed Context-Toolkit [8] which is a well designed object-oriented framework supporting context-aware computing. Context Fabric [9] is an infrastructure for building context-aware applications, which provides a context specification language. Solar [10] is a middleware system that consists of various information sources such as sensors, gathering physical or virtual context information, together with filters, transformers and aggregators modifying context to offer the application usable context information. CoBrA [11] is an agent-based architecture employing ontology based context model for smart room environments. SOCAM [4][3] proposed an ontology based context model addressing context sharing, reasoning and knowledge reusing, and built a service oriented middleware infrastructure for applications in a smart home. Cooltown [12] is a web based context-aware system. The CORTEX [13] project has built a context-aware middleware based on the Sentient Object Model, in which there is an event-based communication mechanism supporting loose coupling between sensors, actuators and application components. CASS [14] enables developers to overcome the memory and processor constraints of small mobile computer platforms with supporting a large number of low-level sensor and other context inputs, and opens the way for context-aware applications configurable by users. Context Cube [15] gives a good context management mechanism based on the techniques of data warehousing and data mining. Siren [16] is a good real-time context-aware system used in fire fighting domain. Sparkle [17] is a flexible platform to support context-aware services with migrations on difference type of devices.

In previous systems and researches, many context modeling approaches are proposed, either formal or informal, including key-value, object, XML, ER-UML, ontology and so on [18]. Ontology based context model and reasoning mechanism proposed in [2][4][3] displays its potential value for most non-time-critical applications. Kalyan

[19] presented a hybrid context model based on multilevel situation theory and ontology to handle complex user's queries by creating simple entity specific situations and enable efficient context reasoning. Strimpakou [20] built a well designed context management architecture in distributed environments.

But none of the works above concern context conflict resolution in one computational node nor introduce their conflict resolution algorithm. Dey [21] gave a novel solution for ambiguity resolution by user mediation, while Xu established a context consistency management mechanism by providing a sophisticated architecture for inconsistency detection and resolution [22], and using a well-designed incremental consistency checking approach [23]. But differently, our intention is to resolve context ambiguity automatically in software infrastructure layer. Although Myllymaki [24] proposed a good solution for resolving conflicts in location information, the strategy is difficult to be extended for inconsistency detection and resolution of various contexts.

In addition, our modifications of ontology based context model is totally different from temporal databases [25] because we deal with time constraints during context fusions upon ontology based model, and those time constraints are used in inconsistency resolution .

3 pvCM—The Extended Context Model

3.1 Conceptual Model

Our modeling approach is still ontology based, but for convenient context management and inconsistency resolution, some extensions are brought in. The extended context model called pvCM consists of 2 parts: ontology and its instances(including both persistent contexts and dynamic contexts). The ontology is a set of shared vocabularies of concepts and the interrelationships among these concepts. Persistent contexts are instances of the ontology and they can be combined with dynamic contexts during inferences. Triples described as (subject, predicate, object) are used to model persistent contexts which can last a long period. For example, the context "Tim is a student" is modeled as (Tim, type, Student). Dynamic contexts with transient characteristics only have a short life in the system, such as "Jimmy in NJU". Octuples (subject, predicate, object, ttl, starttime, updatetime, frequency, state) are used to represent them. Ttl means the life period of the context. "Starttime" is the UNIX time when the context begins existing in the system while "updatetime" denotes the UNIX time when the context is lately updated. A more important element of dynamic contexts is the "frequency" value which indicates how many times the context is updated from its first appearance. The "state" value describes contexts' life status: "Beginning", "Updated", "Inert", or "Disappearing", the details of which will be explained in Section 4.

3.2 Implementations

The ontology of pvCM is constructed by OWL-Lite[1]. Fig. 1 shows part of our ontology for laboratory office domain. Persistent contexts are serialized in RDF[2] files. For

[1] OWL reference: http://www.w3.org/TR/owl-ref

[2] RDF reference: http://www.w3.org/TR/rdf-ref

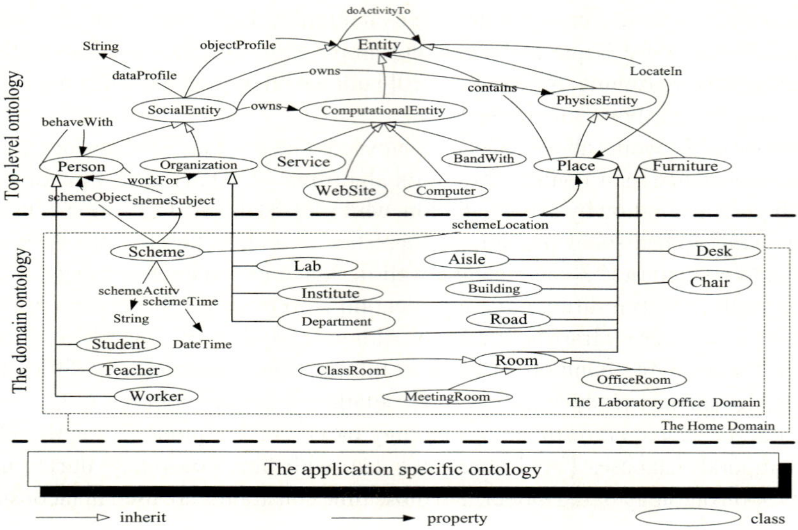

Fig. 1. Part of Our Ontology

example, persistent context triple (Tom, type, Teacher) is a piece of RDF file like Fig. 2. Dynamic contexts are messages containing both RDF messages and other descriptive information. Dynamic context octuple (Tom, giveLecture, Room305, 15s, 116943354000, 116943388123, 2, Updated) is implemented like Fig. 3. This means context "Tom gives a lecture in Room305" is updated for the 2nd time at the UNIX time 116943588123, and if it doesn't be updated in the next 15 seconds, its state will become "Inert".

```
<rdf:resource rdf:ID= "Tom">
        < rdf:type rdf:about="Teacher"/>
</rdf:resource>
```

Fig. 2. The Serialized Format of A Persistent Context

```
Ttl=15s                 Updatestime = 1116943388123
  <person rdf:resource= "Tom">
        <giveLecture rdf:resource="Room305"/>
  </person>
Frequency = 2                    State = "Updated"
        Starttime = 1116943354000
```

Fig. 3. The Serialized Format of A Dynamic Context

4 Context Management Mechanism

4.1 Context Reasoning

For reasoning high-level semantic contexts, we apply rule based reasoning and ontology based reasoning orderly on low-level contexts. The rules for reasoning are just horn clauses for the consideration of system performance. Whereas the process is similar to [3], some significant improvements are brought in.

Firstly, time information is added to high-level contexts during inferences because this information is obviously important toward timely and accurate contexts. But how do we know exactly the starttime, updatetime and ttl value of each high-level inferred context? There are only intersection operations among a horn clause formed rule's antecedents without negation and union operations so that if a premise context become demoded, the inferred context should also correspondingly disappear from the system. Therefore, an approximate approach is implemented. When a high-level context $context_i$ is inferred by raw contexts and a rule, we select the earliest dying one which has the smallest value of ttl plus updatetime from $context_i$'s premises corresponding with the rule, and finally set the $context_i$'s ttl and updatetime the same as the selected one. The default starttime, state and frequency of $context_i$ are respectively set as its updatetime, "Beginning" and 1.

Secondly, the two reasoners are configured as traceable. Because derivation information is often needed for both judging which contexts will be discarded during inconsistency resolution and preventing future conflicts, the reasoning process is stored in the memory until a inconsistency resolution algorithm is performed.

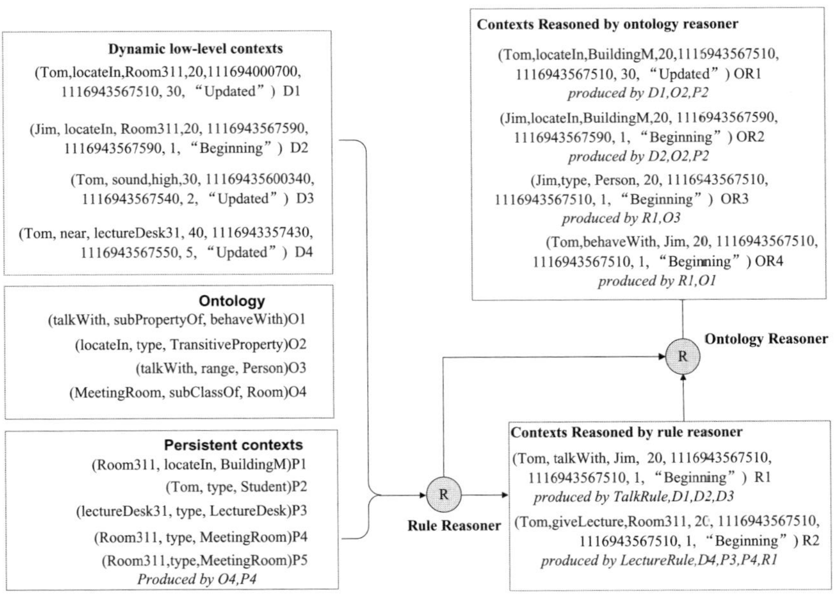

Fig. 4. Context Reasoning Example

An example of our modified reasoning flow is shown in Fig. 4. According to the first modification, inferred context R_1,R_2,OR_1, OR_3, OR_4's ttl and updatetime are set the same as D_1, the similar processes are applied on high-level contexts OR_2.

4.2 Context Lifecycle Management

In our prototype, an enhanced context lifecycle management strategy is carried out for every dynamic context. As described in Section 3, dynamic contexts have 4 life states:

"Beginning", "Updated", "Inert", and "Disappearing". "Beginning" denotes the context is newly generated and no other replicas already exist in the system. "Updated" means the context has been refreshed recently. The design consideration for state "Inert" is to have those contexts which are existing in the real world but delayed in computer systems accidently due to either weakening of sensors' physical signals or bottlenecks of software infrastructures live for a little while. "Disappearing" means the context disappears in computer's view and will be discarded after a short period. It is obvious that using lifecycle states can make computers' contexts more timely and accurate so as to largely approximate real world contexts. Another intention for employing context lifecycle is that applications needs contexts depending on not only their contents but also their life status, for example, an application may open slides at the beginning of a seminar(exploiting beginning contexts) while close the slide at the end of the seminar(requiring disappearing contexts).

The 9 context life state transitions in the system are shown in Fig. 5. Transition 0, 1, 3, 5 and 8 are invoked for the reason that there are new contexts generated, either low-level ones from sensors or high-level ones from reasoning. The pseudocode for those transitions is shown as follow.

---

a new context $context_{new}$ is generated.
if $\exists$ $context_e$ in memory, $context_e$ has the same S-P-O triple with $context_{new}$
  if $context_e.state ==$ "Disappearing"
    $context_{new}$ substitute $context_e$
    (Transition 8 is performed)
  else
    $context_e.state =$"Updated",
    $context_e.updatetime = context_{new}.updatetime$
    $context_e.frequency = context_e.frequecny + 1$
    discard $context_{new}$
    (Transition 1 or 3 or 5 is performed)
else
  add $context_{new}$ into memory,
  (Transition 0 is performed)

A background thread runs periodically to tick the life period for every live context. When a "Beginning" or "Updated" context $context_i$'s ttl is no more than zero, its state turns to "Inert" (transition 2 or 4). After a fixed time, if $context_i$ is still not refreshed, it will become "Disappearing" and removed to historical context storage (transition 6 and 7). We store demoded contexts in persistent storage rather than discard them because historical contexts may be useful for various applications.

In practice, we found that using this lifecycle management can greatly abridge the gap between computers' contexts and real world's . Besides, context exploitation will become easier and more unambiguous.

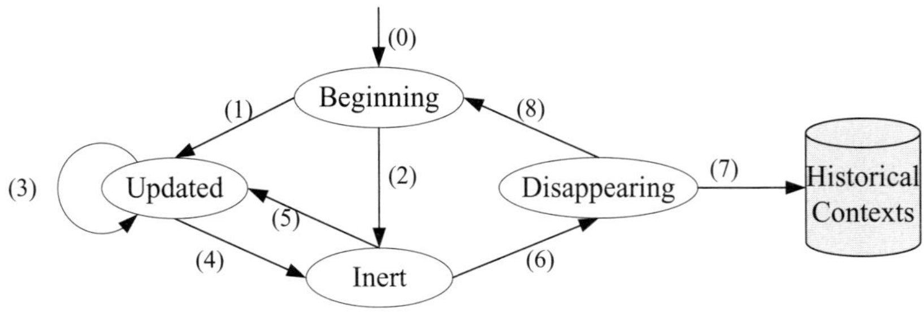

Fig. 5. State Transitions of Dynamic Contexts

4.3 Context Exploitation

Context Query. In our prototype system, we use RDQL[3] as context query language. But we extend RDQL for the particular features of contexts. Applications can query contexts by specifying a RDQL sentence with a state of contexts. For instance, we can use sentence "select ?x where (?x giveLecture Room311)(?x Type Teacher), Beginning" to search if there is a teacher who begins giving a lecture in Room311. Also, we can look up historical contexts conveniently by attaching time ranges to RDQL sentence.

Context Callback. Applications can exploit contexts not only by querying but also by registering callbacks. However, context callback mechanism should be much different from conventional event-callback mechanisms due to particularity of contexts. Contexts are varied with time and callbacks must exactly match to real world's requirements. For example, if a context-aware application's function is to open slides for lecturers automatically, with a badly designed callback mechanism, the application may open the slides more than once so that users are confused. Focusing on this, we invokes callbacks after every inferences and time tick, and use a replica pool to store consumed context for every applications respectively. When the callback is being invoked, the system check each replica pool and do not call those stored consumed contexts' callback function. Unless those consumed contexts have some changes, they will not be cleared out of every replica pool. This device embraces the particularity of contexts and leads to jarless applications in practice. The view of callback architecture is shown in Fig. 6.

5 Context Inconsistency Resolution

5.1 Conflict Detection

For inconsistency resolution, the first step is to detect conflicts. Ontology based context model can largely facilitate conflict detection. For example, if there are 2 dynamic contexts: d_1(Tom, giveLecture, Room311, 15s,1116943120489, 1116943567511, 10, Updated) and d_2(Tom, giveLecture, Aisle3, 25s, 1116943111897, 1116943567599, 1, Beginning), 2 persistent contexts: p_1(Room311, type, Room) and p_2(Aisle3, type, Aisle),

[3] RDQL tutorial: http://jena.sourceforge.net/tutorial/RDQL/index.html

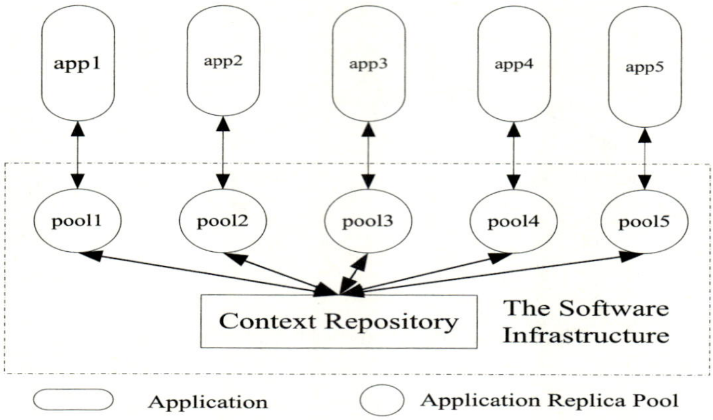

Fig. 6. The Callback Architecture

and 2 assertions in ontology: o_1(Room, disjointWith, Aisle) and o_2(giveLecture, type, FunctionalProperty), a conflict will be detected in ontology model because there is an instance of both Room and Aisle. However, d_1's derivations and d_2's usually implicitly conflict, therefore we need to find their derivations and resolve them completely in order to prevent future conflicts. Most semantic web APIs support conflict detection like that, and a validity report which indicate all first-hand conflicting pairs such as (d_1, d_2) will be easily obtained.

5.2 Several Definitions

Conflict pair set. A set consisting of pairs such as ($context_a$,$context_b$) that $context_a$ conflicts with $context_b$ is a conflict pair set.

Conflict set. Imaging a context set $ContextSet$, if its members are conflicting with each other, we call $ContextSet$ a Conflict set.

Derivation. If $context_a$ is a premise of high-level $context_b$, then we call $context_a$ is one of $context_b$'s Derivation. Furthermore, the relationship of Derivation is transitive and reflexive.

Derivation set. All of $context_c$'s Derivations compose a set called $context_c$'s Derivation Set.

Relative frequency$-rf$. A formula that calculates the rf value of a context $context_i$ is shown as follow.

$$context_i.rf = \begin{cases} \dfrac{context_i.ttl \cdot context_i.frequency}{currenttime - context_i.starttime} \\ \text{(for dynamic contexts)} \\ \\ infinite \\ \text{(for persistent contexts)} \end{cases}$$

5.3 CIR—Context Inconsistency Resolution Algorithm

The CIR(Context Inconsistency Resolution) algorithm is shown below.

---

1. Initialize
1). obtain a firsthand conflict pair set CFS from conflict detection results.
2). for every pair (a,b) $\in CFS$
    add both a and b into set $allContext$
3). for every $context_i \in allContext$
    a. Construct its derivation set $derivations_i$
    b. Construct $dynamicderivations_i$ which only contains dynamic contexts in $derivations_i$
2. Discard Contexts
while there are conflicts in $allContext$
  1). partition $allContext$ into several maximum conflict sets.
  2). for every conflict set $conflicts$
      select a context $context_{max}$ with largest rf.
      for every $context_i \in conflicts$ $(i \neq max)$
        for every $context_j \in dynamicderivation_i$
          if $\exists k, i \neq k$, $context_j \in dynamicderivation_k$
            reserve $context_j$
          else
            discard $context_j$
        delete $dynamicderivation_i$

Our design principle is that more frequent dynamic contexts are prior. However, different sorts of contexts are hard to compare their frequencies. For example, voice contexts may be inherently varied more frequently than temperature contexts, but we can't say that voice contexts have more priorities. Due to this reason, we use the rf value to measure each context's relative frequency because ttl value may often imply the context is inherently frequent or infrequent. We believe that those contexts with larger rf value emerge more relatively frequently recently, therefore they are more possible to be correct contexts. Also, persistent contexts are ensured to be consistent when they are been deployed to the platform so that they are always reserved.

It is ensured that after the algorithm, there is no conflict existing in the context repository. The step of partitioning $allContext$ uses a greedy algorithm, in which we begin to search from a random element, and form a maximum conflict set circularly until the partition is completely formed. Although the worst case time complexity of CIR is polynomial with the number of total contexts, we found in experiments that it is still such an expensive task that we can only run it periodically.

5.4 Example

Fig. 7 shows an example of the inconsistency resolution algorithm. In the example, we have two conflict sets: conflict set A and conflict set B. We first resolve conflicts for

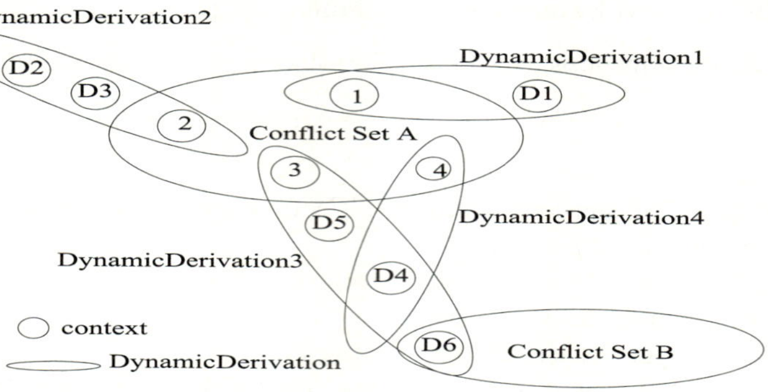

Fig. 7. An Example of the Inconsistency Resolution

A, and then for B. Assume that in A, $context_1$, $context_2$, $context_3$ and $context_4$ are ordered by their rf value increasingly. After A is resolved by the algorithm, there are 3 contexts$-context_4$, $context_{D4}$, $context_{D6}$ left.

6 Evaluations

During implementations, the semantic web API we choose is Jena2.2[4], the rules are in the form of Jena Generic Rules, and the ontology reasoner we used is entailed by OWL-Lite. We have modified Jena source code by adding time information to triples during reasoning, as described in section 4. The performance and effect of CIR algorithm are evaluated by 2 experiments.

First, we test the performance of CIR on a Linux Workstation with 4G RAM and 2 Xeon CPUs, and find that the efficiency is decreasing proportionally to the increasing of total contexts in memory. At the level of $1000-2000$ contexts, the time used is 1.5 seconds-2.0 seconds, but at the level of 3000-4000, about 6 seconds are needed.

Second, for evaluating the effect of CIR, another experiment is designed. There are 3 computers involved, one Linux workstation with 4G RAM and 2 Xeon CPUs and two PC clients, connecting through LAN. The meeting room and aisle for the experiment are equipped with mica sensors[5] to detect noise and cricket sensors[6] to find persons' locations. One of the clients plays the role of raw context provider while the other acts as context consumer. In the experiment, a person adorning a cricket beacon stands in a meeting room to act as giving a lecture, and during this, he/she goes out to the aisle with immediately coming back to the meeting room at different frequencies which vary from 10s once to 40s once at the step of 5s (horizontal axis in Fig. 8), and maintains each frequency for 10 minutes. This activity can lead to many context conflicts among high-level contexts in the system because two raw context triples: ($person_x$, locateIn, $MeetingRoom_x$) and ($person_x$, locateIn, $Aisle_x$) are obtained. Meanwhile, the context consumer client continues querying contexts 10 times a minute to see the

[4] Jena2 Semantic Web Toolkit: http://www.hpl.hp.com/semweb/jena2.htm
[5] The Mica Sensor: http://www.xbow.com
[6] The Cricket indoor location system: http://cricket.csail.mit.edu/

probability of context correctness(vertical axis in Fig. 8). In this way, for every going out frequency, 100 samples about context quality can be gained. It is apparent that with the decreasing of the person's going out frequency, the incorrectness and inconsistency of contexts will decline. For comparing the effect with other solutions, 3 configurations of the context fusion infrastructure are carried out respectively: without any inconsistency resolution(without IR), with a simplistic resolution strategy that later updated and persistent contexts are prior(with SIR), with our proposed algorithm CIR(with CIR). The results are shown in Fig. 8.

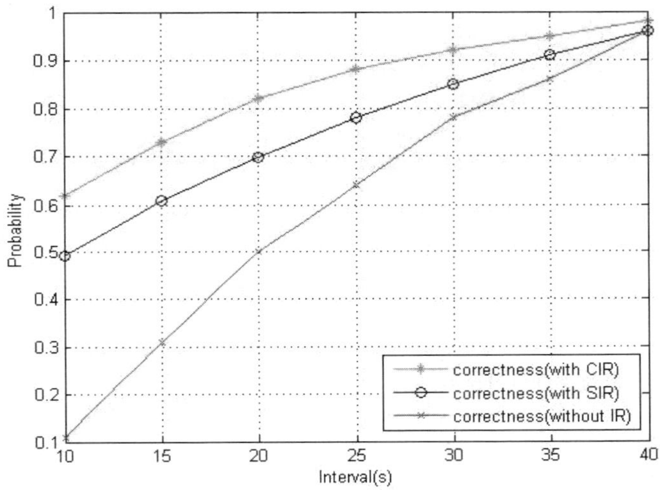

Fig. 8. Effect Analysis of the Inconsistency Resolution

Hence, although CIR is a computational intensive task, it is still necessary to run periodically. Although there are only 2 types of sensors used in the experiments, our architecture and algorithm can suit to more sensor types without modifications because they are designed for semantic contexts rather than physical sensors. And the only thing we need to do is to add specific raw context providers when new sensor types are brought in.

7 Application Case Study

7.1 Scenario

In research groups, seminars are often held. When someone gives a lecture, he/she should copy the slides to his/her flash disk, carry it to the meeting room, copy the slides to the computer in the meeting room, and then open them. The work is dull and trivial, and many of people's attentions are consumed. In our context-aware computing environment, the lecturer needs to do nothing other than edit his/her lecture notes. When he/she enters the meeting room, and stands near the lectern, his/her slides will be opened automatically. During the seminar, if some strangers come in, a warning balloon will pop up on the screen. At the end of the seminar, the slides will be closed automatically.

Fig. 9. The Runtime Effect of Seminar Assistant

7.2 Implementation

We implement two versions of the scenario, one of which is based on our context management mechanism(with CIR), the other of which is based on an earlier version which employs a simplistic inconsistency resolution strategy that later updated and persistent contexts are prior(with SIR).

The application called Seminar Assistant has two parts. One called User Assistant runs at all users' computers while the other called Meeting Assistant runs at the computer in the meeting room. When the User Assistant detects the context that the user it serves will give a lecture in the next few days, it will upload the slides he has edited recently, the name of which matches the lecture to an http server. When the lecturer starts to give the lecture in the meeting room, the Meeting Assistant will obtain the right context, and then download and open the previous uploaded slides. Then the Meeting Assistant starts detecting if strangers come in. When the Meeting Assistant detects the context that the lecturer leaves the room, it will close the slides. In this application, we've used the in-door location sensor Cricket to detect a person's location in a room, and also the Mica sensor to detect the noise in a room. Fig. 9 shows the runtime action of Seminar Assistant when a stranger comes into the meeting room during a seminar(a warning balloon is popped up). Part of the context reasoning process for this example is already shown in Fig. 4.

7.3 Application Error Rate Comparison

We compare the two versions of "Seminar Assistant" by investigating their average error rates. Since both of the applications are very small, they are debugged exhaustively before our error rate comparison so that most errors occurring in the comparison should attribute to context mismatching. For the comparison, we run the two applications respectively for 20 days, use them according to the scenario for 400 times(20 times each

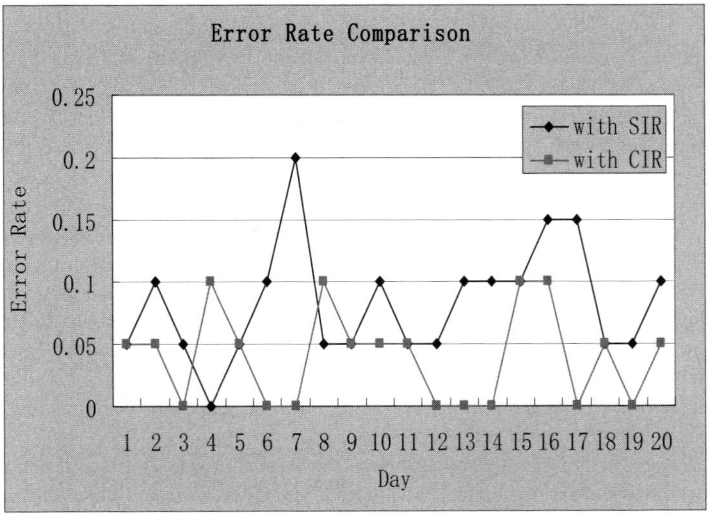

Fig. 10. Error Rate Comparison of The Two Versions

day), and record the error rates of each day. In the experiments, all the errors recorded are application's incongruous behaviors such as opening the slides before the reporter entering the meeting room, and system failures such as out of memory error are not included. Fig. 10 shows the results, in which the horizontal axis denotes the day while the vertical axis denotes the error rate. It can be concluded from the experiment results that our context consistency management mechanism(with CIR) has largely improved context-aware applications' robustness since over 50 percent incongruous behaviors are reduced(from 33 errors of 400 to 16 errors of 400).

8 Conclusions and Future Work

With experiences of developing context-aware applications, we find that the inconsistency of contexts is a serious problem which can threaten the prevalence of context-aware computing. Aiming at this problem, we propose an extended ontology based context model called pvCM, establish a context management mechanism and design an inconsistency resolution algorithm. Through the evaluations and case study, the necessity and feasibility of our design principles are verified. The work of this paper is part of our ongoing research project–FollowMe [6] which is designed towards a workflow-driven, service-oriented, pluggable and programmable software infrastructure for context-awareness.

In the near future, we plan to explore novel approaches to improve runtime performances of context reasoning, using technologies such as distributed context fusion and so on. Also, we are working towards a better inconsistency resolution approach in which context conflicts are resolved during the reasoning process, with sophisticated reasoning technologies.

References

1. Joelle Coutaz, James L. Crowley, Simon Dobson, and David Garlan. Context is key. *Communications of ACM*, 48(3):49–53, 2005.
2. Harry Chen, Timothy W. Finin, Anupam Joshi, Lalana Kagal, Filip Perich, and Dipanjan Chakraborty. Intelligent agents meet the semantic web in smart spaces. *IEEE Internet Computing*, 8(6):69–79, 2004.
3. Xiaohang Wang, Jin Song Dong, ChungYau Chin, SankaRavipriya Hettiarachchi, and Daqing Zhang. Semantic space: An infrastructure for smart spaces. *IEEE Pervasive Computing*, 3:32–39, July-September 2004.
4. Tao Gu, H. K. Pung, and Da Qing Zhang. Towards an osgi-based infrastructure for context-aware applications in smart homes. *IEEE Pervasive Computing*, December 2004.
5. Yingyi Bu, Jun Li, Shaxun Chen, Xianping Tao, and Jian Lu. An enhanced ontology based context model and fusion mechanism. In *Proceedings of IFIP 2005 International Conference on Embedded and Ubiquitous Computing (EUC2005). Nagasaki, Japan.*, volume 3824 of *LNCS*, pages 920–929. Springer, 2005.
6. Jun Li, Yingyi Bu, Shaxun Chen, Xianping Tao, and Jian Lu. Followme: On research of pluggable infrastructure for context-awareness. In *Proceedings of the 20th International Conference on Advanced Information Networking and Applications (AINA2006)*, volume 1, pages 199–204. IEEE Computer Society, 2006.
7. Roy Want, Andy Hopper, Veronica Falcao, and Jonathan Gibbons. The active badge location system. *ACM Transactions on Information Systems*, 10(1):91–102, 1992.
8. Daniel Salber, Anind K. Dey, and Gregory D. Abowd. The context toolkit: Aiding the development of context-enabled applications. In *Proceeding of the CHI 99 Conference on Human Factors in Computing Systems: The CHI is the Limit (CHI99), Pittsburgh, PA, USA. ACM, 1999*, pages 434–441, 1999.
9. Jason I. Hong and J.A. Landa. An infrastructure approach to context-aware computing. *Human-Computer Interaction (HCI) Journal*, 16, 2001.
10. Guanlin Chen. Solar: Building a context fusion network for pervasive computing. *Ph.D. Thesis. Dartmouth College*, August 2004.
11. Harry Chen, Timothy W. Finin, and Anupam Joshi. Semantic web in the context broker architecture. In *Proceedings of the Second IEEE International Conference on Pervasive Computing and Communications (PerCom 2004), 14-17 March 2004, Orlando, FL, USA*, pages 277–286, 2004.
12. Tim Kindberg and John J. Barton. A web-based nomadic computing system. *Computer Networks*, 35(4):443–456, 2001.
13. Gregory Biegel and Vinny Cahill. A framework for developing mobile, context-aware applications. In *Proceedings of the Second IEEE International Conference on Pervasive Computing and Communications (PerCom 2004), 14-17 March 2004, Orlando, FL, USA*, pages 361–365. IEEE Computer Society, 2004.
14. Fahy P. and Clarke S. Cass: Middleware for mobile context-aware applications. In *ACM MobiSys Workshop on Context Awareness, Boston, USA*, 2004.
15. Lonnie D. Harvel, Ling Liu, Gregory D. Abowd, Yu-Xi Lim, Chris Scheibe, and Chris Chatham. Context cube: Flexible and effective manipulation of sensed context data. In *Proceedings of the Second International Conference on Pervasive Computing(Pervasive 2004), Vienna, Austria*, volume 3001 of *LNCS*, pages 51–68. Springer, 2004.
16. Xiaodong Jiang, Nicholas Y. Chen, Jason I. Hong, Kevin Wang, Leila Takayama, and James A. Landay. Siren: Context-aware computing for firefighting. In *Proceedings of The Second International Conference on Pervasive Computing(PERVASIVE2004), Vienna, Austria*, pages 87–105, 2004.

17. Pauline P. L. Siu, Nalini Moti Belaramani, Cho-Li Wang, and Francis C. M. Lau. Context-aware state management for ubiquitous applications. In *Proceedings of International Conference on Embedded and Ubiquitous Computing*, pages 776–785, 2004.
18. T. Strang and C. Linnhoff-Popien. A context modeling survey. In *Workshop on Advanced Context Modelling, Reasoning and Management as part of UbiComp 2004 - The Sixth International Conference on Ubiquitous Computing*, September 2004.
19. Anupama Kalyan, Srividya Gopalan, and V. Sridhar. Hybrid context model based on multilevel situation theory and ontology for contact centers. In *Proceedings of the 3rd IEEE Conference on Pervasive Computing and Communications Workshops (PerCom 2005 Workshops), 8-12 March 2005, Kauai Island, HI, USA*, pages 3–7. IEEE Computer Society, 2005.
20. Maria Strimpakou, Ioanna Roussaki, Carsten Pils, Michael Angermann, Patrick Robertson, and Miltiades E. Anagnostou. Context modelling and management in ambient-aware pervasive environments. In *Proceedings of First International Workshop on Location- and Context-Awareness (LoCA), Oberpfaffenhofen, Germany, May 12-13, 2005*, volume 3479 of *LNCS*, pages 2–15. Springer, 2005.
21. Anind K. Dey and Jennifer Mankoff. Designing mediation for context-aware applications. *ACM Transactions on Computer-Human Interaction(TOCHI)*, 12(1):53–80, 2005.
22. Chang Xu and S.C. Cheung. Inconsistency detection and resolution for context-aware middleware support. In *Proceedings of the Joint 10th European Software Engineering Conference and 13th ACM SIGSOFT Symposium on the Foundations of Software Engineering (ESEC/FSE 2005), Lisbon, Portugal*, pages 336–345, September 5-9 2005.
23. Chang Xu, Shing-Chi Cheung, and W. K. Chan. Incremental consistency checking for pervasive context. In *Proceedings of the 28th International Conference on Software Engineering(ICSE 2006), Shanghai, China, May 20-28, 2006*, pages 292–301, 2006.
24. Jussi Myllymaki and Stefan Edlund. Location aggregation from multiple sources. In *Proceedings of the Third International Conference on Mobile Data Management (MDM 2002), Singapore, January 8-11, 2002*, pages 131–138. IEEE Computer Society, 2002.
25. Gadia and Sunil S. Nair. Temporal databases: A prelude to parametric data. In *Temporal Databases*, pages 28–66. 1993.

Activity Policy-Based Service Discovery for Pervasive Computing

Woohyun Kim, Saehoon Kang, Younghee Lee, Dongman Lee, and Inyoung Ko

Information and Communications University
119, Munjiro, Yuseong-gu, Daejeon 305-732, Korea
{woorung, kang, yhlee, dlee, iko}@icu.ac.kr

Abstract. Service discovery is an essential technique to provide applications with appropriate resources. However, user mobility and heterogeneous environments make the discovery of appropriate resources difficult. The execution environments will be rapidly changed, so developers cannot predict available resources exactly in design time. Thus, service discovery frameworks for pervasive computing must guarantee transparent development environments to application developers. In this paper, we introduce how to semantically describe and discover a variety of services in different environments. This approach helps applications to find appropriate services even though the required ones are not available or not found. For this, we propose a fine-grained effect ontology which is used to reasonably evaluate functional similarity among different services, and a policy-based query coordination which is used to dynamically apply different resource constraints according to human activities. Finally, we show with a feasible scenario how to find appropriate services in different environments. Our approach helps applications to seamlessly perform their tasks across a dynamic range of environments.

1 Introduction

Pervasive computing environments are surrounded by a variety of computing devices, software services, and information sources. Applications must adapt to dynamically changing environments to seamlessly perform their tasks [1, 2]. However, different environments have different resources, and their capabilities are also different. Even though developers specify in design time all the resources required by applications, appropriate resources may not always be available across a dynamic range of environments [1, 8]. Suppose that there are some real instances such as "AlarmClock," "TV," "Audio," and "Light" in a home environment. A developer would like to use an instance "AlarmClock" to wake a user out of a deep sleep. Unfortunately, if the instance was not available or not found in real time, which instances could be found and used instead of the "AlarmClock"?

Traditional service discovery systems (i.e., Jini, UPnP, SLP, and Salutation) are not proper for pervasive computing since syntactic matching is mainly used [3, 4]. They do not support alternative representations of semantically similar services. In contrast, context-aware service discovery systems [3-7] take advantage of contextual information (i.e. location) syntactically or semantically to provide appropriate

T. Grust et al. (Eds.): EDBT 2006 Workshops, LNCS 4254, pp. 756–768, 2006.

services in pervasive computing environments. Similarly, semantic service discovery systems [1, 2, 7, 8, 9] make use of abstract representations in various aspects of services to transparently provide appropriate services despite different environments. Nevertheless, these approaches do not seem to deal with yet systematically the semantics in various aspects of services: data semantics (requirement), functional semantics (capability), QoS semantics (effect), and execution semantics (execution pattern) [15]. In this point, Semantic Web [16] which semantically describes and discovers Web services in the IOPE (Input, Output, Precondition, Effect) level gives us a noble idea to reasonably provide substitutable services which are functionally similar to the required ones when they are not available or not found.

In the earlier "AlarmClock" example, some sophisticated inference processes are required to semantically evaluate functional similarity among other available candidates such as "TV," "Audio," and "Light." Note that "AlarmClock" has a sound effect, and "TV" and "Audio" also have another type of sound effects. In this paper, we define an *effect* as a process to change the state of the world to other state. Each sound effect has its own properties as follows: impact factor (*alarm volume*, *TV volume*, and *audio volume*), behavior pattern (*sound delivery*, *multimedia delivery*, and *music delivery*), and human perceptibility (*auditory sense*). The enumerated properties are constructed in some semantic hierarchies. That is, *TV volume* and *audio volume* have equivalent semantics to *alarm volume* with intensity beyond a certain level. Similarly, *multimedia delivery* and *music delivery* have equivalent semantics in the aspect of *sound delivery*. These semantic associations play an important role in evaluating which service can substitute the originally required service.

In this paper, we propose a fine-grained effect ontology which is used to reasonably evaluate functional similarity among different services, and a policy-based query coordination which is used to dynamically apply different resource constraints according to human activities. The goal of our approach aims at enabling applications to take full advantage of local resources across a dynamic range of environments.

The remainder of this paper is as follows. In Section 2, we describe existing efforts on service discovery for pervasive computing. Section 3 covers design considerations, and we introduce our approach in detail in Section 4. The implementation details of the proposed scheme are addressed in Section 5. Finally, we describe our conclusions and suggest future work in Section 6.

2 Related Works

Several research efforts have been done on a high level of abstract representations to solve the problems of mobility and heterogeneity. Gaia [1] introduces an application as a set of structural components , MPACC(model, presentation, adaptor, controller, and coordinator). To make applications polymorphic, such a component is represented as abstract functionalities in ontologies. The actual components are dynamically bound in a given environment. And yet, Gaia does not mention how systematically the ontologies are constructed. The ontologies are predefined by rule of thumb and made by hand. Aura [2] introduces a service as one of abstract semantics of coarse-grained functionalities required to perform a user task. It proposes an idea to be automatically able to bring up all the resources associated with a given task. It works on a higher level of abstractions such as tasks as coalitions of abstract services. In other words, Aura does not tell what properties of a service are equivalent to those of its similar service(s).

On the other hand, several approaches use some policies to find appropriate resources. Olympus [10] proposes the separation of class and instance discovery to allow alternative services to be found, which is based on the functionality required by an original service. When resolving virtual entities into actual ones, it considers developer-specific constraints, space-level policies, class-/instance-level context-awareness, and utility function. Olympus insists that even entities of classes that are highly different from the class specified by the developer can be discovered and used. In this aspect, Olympus is very similar to the proposed scheme. CARISMA [22] uses application-specific policies to enable mobile applications to behave according to contexts such as bandwidth, CPU performance, and even other applications' behaviors. CARMEN [23] uses declarative management policies for migration, binding, access control, user preferences, device capabilities, and service component characteristics. However, these approaches do not consider that the semantics of exact or abstract representations might be dynamically changed in different situations.

3 Design Considerations

Service discovery for pervasive computing has to deal with a user's mobility and environment heterogeneity. This leads to the issue of how to formally describe a diversity of services and transparently discover appropriate services despite different environments. Thus, we consider two key issues in this paper: *transparent accessibility* and *high availability*.

3.1 Transparent Accessibility

Figure 1 illustrates some processes to discover the *Alarm* service in pervasive computing environments. In the developer's point of view, the *Alarm* service keeps an abstract representation level. However, in the system's point of view, the real semantics of the required *Alarm* service can be dynamically changed as *SoundAlarm*, *VibrationAlarm*, or *DisplayAlarm* according to users' current location. It means that the *Alarm* service can be bound with some real instances in the current execution environments which have sound effects, vibration effect, or display effect. The binding to real instances is determined in real time, so the *Alarm* service is transparently kept in abstract level. In conclusion, service discovery should work on abstract representations to describe and discover all of the services in pervasive computing environments.

3.2 High Availability

Figure 1 shows a need to find substitutable services when the best matching instance "AlarmClock" is not available or not found in a given environment. Suppose that a user sleeps late in the morning. An application should find the *Alarm* service to wake him up. But there is no available instance "AlarmClock." Which instance can be used instead of the "AlarmClock"?

In the user's point of view, a certain function such as *StartAlarming* of "AlarmClock" is supposed to be somewhat equivalent to other functions such as *TVTurnOn* function of "TV," *AudioPlayCD* function of "Audio," or even *LightTurnOn* function of "Light." To take full advantage of local resources, consequently, service discovery frameworks for pervasive computing must provide applications with other substitutable instances which are functionally similar to the best matching instance "AlarmClock."

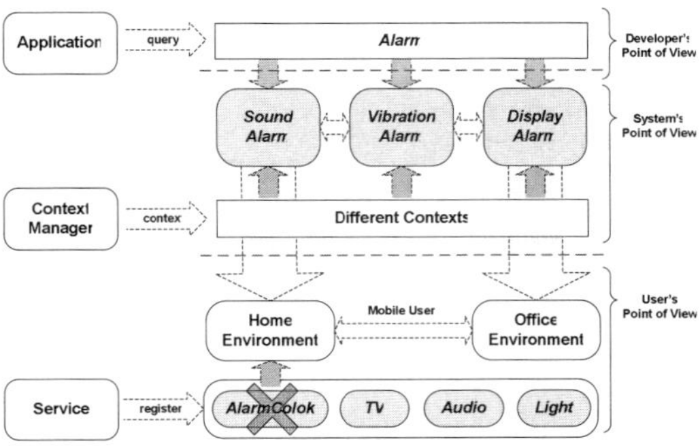

Fig. 1. The Discovery of the *Alarm* Service in Pervasive Computing Environments

4 Proposed Approach

Task-based computing [11, 12] and activity-based computing [8] focus on a higher level of abstraction level such as *tasks* or *activities* to enable computing environments to be aware of users' intents or requirements. In this paper, we especially pay our attentions to a high level of context model, *human activity* which means anything that users intend to do in a specific region by using some resources. The model is for representing what a user intends to do, what resources can be utilized for an activity, and where services can be performed. Thus, we use the *activity policy* which describes different resource constraints according to locations, humans, and activities. Furthermore, we use the IOPE model of Semantic Web [16] to describe the capabilities of services in a fine-grained level, and provide upper ontologies to reasonably evaluate functional similarity among different services.

4.1 Activity Policy-Based Query Coordination

To describe different resource constraints according to human activities, Figure 2 shows how to define activity policies and how the user query is coordinated with the appropriate resource constraints in service discovery processes.

At first, some policies, the notation "P := A*n*(A*c*, H, L, O)" is described. An application sends queries (Q) for services and the name of the next activity(A*n*). Our service discovery framework receives the contextual information such as the name of the current activity (A*c*), target user (H) for the activity to influence, target place (L) for the activity to be performed in, and other contexts (O). In this point, an appropriate policy is selected, and then some resource constraints (C) are extracted according to the current contexts. The given queries and the selected resource constraints are adjusted in the query coordination part. Thus, the proposed scheme can reflect the dynamic changes of real semantics between abstraction (queries) and context-awareness (policies).

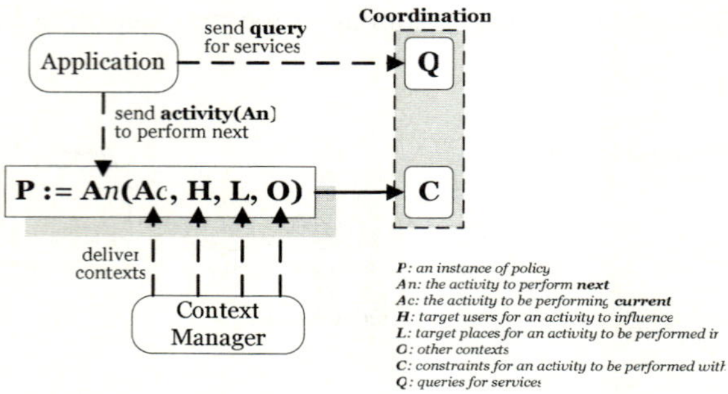

Fig. 2. Activity Policy and Query Coordination

Suppose that Alice should receive business-related messages. Location sensors recognize her current position, and deliver the sensed values of (x, y, z) coordinates or logical/physical space names to ContextManager. Here, ContextManager [21] is a part of context-aware middleware to aggregate contexts and interpret their semantics. Authentication sensors could also deliver the ID number of Alice to ContextManager. If ContextManager could recognize even human activities, our service discovery framework would infer appropriate resource constraints according to Alice's activities as Figure 3. In this point, the context model of Gaia [14] based on first order logic would be useful for such a context fusion.

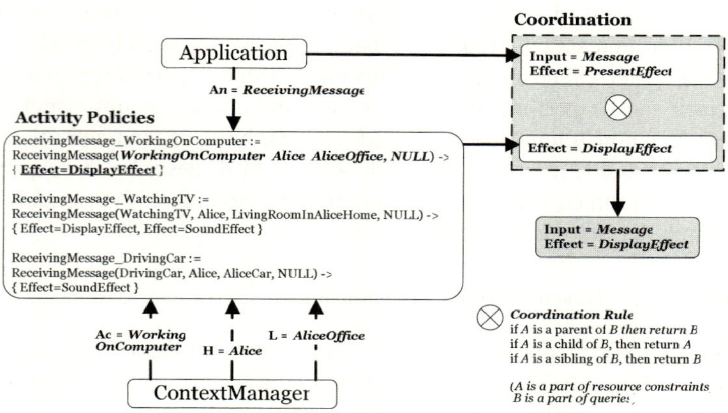

Fig. 3. An Example of Activity Policy-based Query Coordination

The application intends to find some local resources to present the messages to Alice as the query, Input=*Message* and Effect=*PresentEffect*. Our service discovery framework knows that Alice works with a computer at the office and the application wants to deliver some messages to her. Thus, the framework selects an appropriate resource constraint, Effect=*DisplayEffect*, and start coordinating it with the given query, Input=*Message* and Effect=*PresentEffect*. In this point, the effect parts between the query and the constraint trigger a conflict in the coordination part. To resolve this conflict, simple coordination rules are used with some subsumption relations such as the *parent*, the *child*, and the *sibling* relation in our ontologies as following.

- If *A* is a parent of *B*, then we select *B*;
- If *A* is a child of *B*, then we select *A*;
- If *A* is a sibling of *B*, then we select *B*;
  (*A is a part of resource constraints, B is a part of queries*)

Finally, the new coordinated query, Input=*Message* and Effect=*DisplayEffect*, enables Alice to receive the messages through "WindowsPopupMessage," when Alice works at the office not to distract other co-workers.

4.2 IOPE-Based Semantic Matching

To maximize high availability of services in heterogeneous environments, it is very important to define how to semantically describe and discover services by using ontologies [15]. In this paper, we use the IOPE model to formally describe the capabilities of services in a fine-grained level. This enables services to be richly represented in data semantics, functional semantics, and QoS semantics.

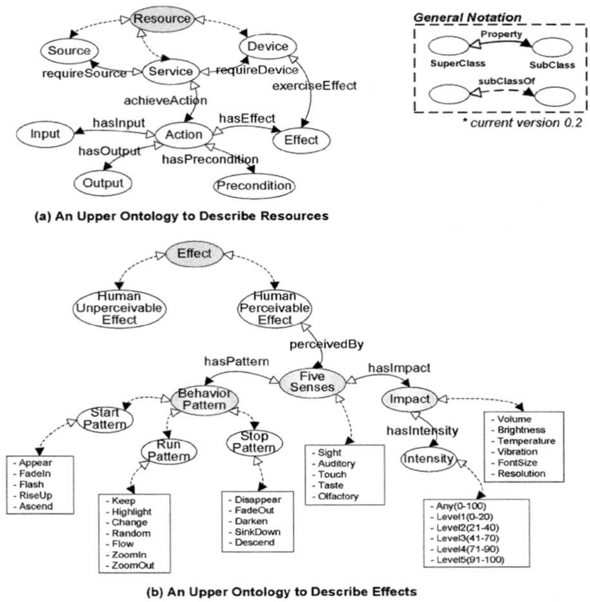

Fig. 4. Upper Ontologies to Formally Describe Various Resources

Figure 4 shows two upper ontologies designed by OWL [18] to describe the diversity of services and effects in pervasive computing environments. Ovals represent classes (or concepts), black arrows represent characterized properties (or roles), white arrows represent inverse properties, and dotted lines represent subsumption (parent and child) relations among some classes. In Figure 4 (b), the rectangle means some value instances of the parent class. That is, the parent class *Intensity* can be instantiated to one of the instance values such as *Any*, *Level1*, *Level2*, *Level3*, *Level4*, and *Level5*. Specific intensities can be defined in this way. In case of the volume of "TV" or "Audio," as an instance of the class *Impact*, a specific instance *SmallVolume* can be defined with the instance *Level1* as the value of the property *hasIntensity*. Similarly, another specific instance *LargeVolume* can be defined with the instance *Level5* as the value of the *hasIntensity*. In case of the brightness of "Light," some specific instances such as *WeakBrightness*, *ModerateBrightness*, and *StrongBrightness* can be respectively defined with some value instances of the *Intensity*. Therefore, we can make use of such a specific instance to evaluate functional similarity among some services.

At first, we define *effect* as a process to change the states of the world to other states. According to this definition, we consider three main properties: *perceivedBy*, *hasImpact*, and *hasPattern*. We understand some effects of services in human-centric aspects, so the effects which we deal with in this paper are those which can be perceived by the five senses of human beings. Moreover, the effects give some impacts on the states of the world, and those kinds of changes are achieved in the specific behavior patterns. Figure 4 (b) illustrate how to define the effects with the classes such as *FiveSenses*, *Impact*, and *BehaviorPattern*. To more easily explain, the following BNF format is used.

<*HumanPerceivableEffect*> := <*perceivedBy*> | <*perceivedBy*> <*op*> <*HumanPerceivableEffect*>
<*perceivedBy*> := <*FiveSenses*> (<*hasImpact*>, <*hasPattern*>)
<*op*> := and | or
<*FiveSenses*> := Sight | Auditory | Touch | Olfactory | Taste | …
<*hasImpact*> := Volume | Brightness | Temperature | Vibration | FontSize | Color
| Message | Music | Document | Multimedia | Image | …
<*hasPattern*> := Appear | Disappear | Increase | Decrease | Maximize | Minimize | FadeIn
| FadeOut | ZoomIn | ZoomOut | Deliver | Reserve | KeepInLimitTime | …

For example, the effect of "TVVolumeUP" action is to increase the volume of TV to a certain level. The effect is perceived by the auditory sense of human beings. Its impact factor is the volume of TV, and its behavior pattern is to increase. That is, the effect can be described as *TVVolumeIncreaseEffect* := *Auditory*(*TVVolume*, *Increase*). Similarly, the effect of "AudioVolumeUP" action is to increase the volume of Audio, so it can be described as *AudioVolumeIncreaseEffect* := *Auditory*(*AudioVolume*, *Increase*). In this way, we define a diversity of effects, and the effects are associated with some semantic hierarchies. Consequently, the effect of "TVVolumeUP" is similar to the effect of "AudioVolumeUP." Thus, both of them have the effect to make the volume of sound increased in a specific region. It is quite an interesting feature in pervasive computing environments since it shows that the different functions, "TVVolumeUP" and "AudioVolumeUP," can trigger some equivalent effects in a specific region. Such a feasible example is shown in Figure 5.

When Alice sleeps late in the morning, an intelligent application checks her schedule and recognizes that she has an important business meeting today. Suppose that the application tries to find "AlarmClock" in the bedroom, but fails to find it. In this case, it knows that some substitutable services such as "LotteAudio" or "SamsungTV" can

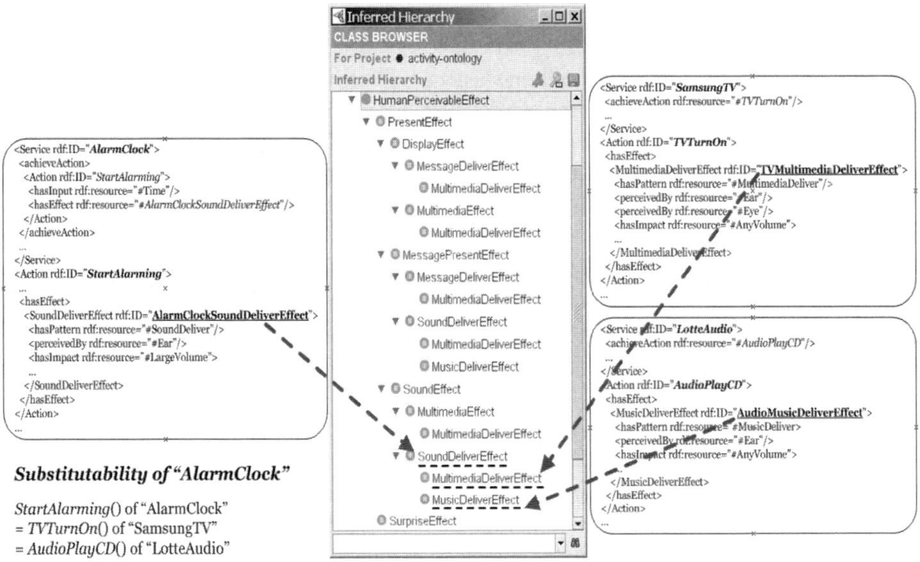

Fig. 5. Substitutability of "AlarmClock," "SamsungTV," "LotteAudio" in the Effect Ontology

be used instead of "AlarmClock." To make it possible, "AlarmClock," "LotteAudio," and "SamsungTV" are described as Figure 5. "AlarmClock" service has a function "StartAlarming." The function gives the effect *AlarmClockSoundDeliverEffect* on a target user. Similarly, "AudioPlayCD" function of "LotteAudio" has *AudioMusicDeliverEffect*, and "TVTurnOn" function of "SamsungTV" has *TVMultimediaDeliverEffect*. All the effects can be perceived by the auditory sense of human beings. Moreover, they have the behavior patterns to deliver some impact factors with different levels of intensities. Through the common properties, we have an inferred hierarchy in the effect ontology as shown in Figure 5. *AlarmClockSoundDeliverEffect* is an instance of *SoundDeliverEffect*, and *MultimediaDeliverEffect* and *MusicDeliverEffect* are inferred as subclasses of the *SoundDeliverEffect*. Each subclass has the instance *TVMultimediaDeliverEffect* and *AudioMusicDeliverEffect*, respectively. In conclusion, we can see that the different effects have a semantic hierarchy in the effect ontology by dynamically inferring the relative relations of the properties such as *FiveSenses*, *Impact*, and *BehaviorPattern*.

In the earlier part, we have already shown how to define some specific semantics related to *Intensity* and *Impact*. In Figure 5, each service was described with these specific instances. Initially, *AlarmClockSoundDeliverEffect* would be different from *AudioMusicDeliverEffect* and *TVMultimediaDeliverEffect* in the aspect of *Intensity*. Later, *AudioMusicDeliverEffect* and *TVMultimediaDeliverEffect* would have volume intensities beyond a certain level, which might be corresponded to that of *AlarmClockSoundDeliverEffect*. Through these processes, we can finally make sense that the effects of "TVTurnOn" function and "AudioPlayCD" function can be provided instead of that of "StartAlarming" function.

5 Implementation

We implemented the proposed scheme as the service discovery part in Active Surroundings [21], which is a middleware for pervasive computing environments. Figure 6 shows home appliances, location sensors, and IR (Infrared Rays) transceiver deployed in our prototype smart home environment. Especially, the IR transceiver is used to convey an IR signal corresponding to a user command to a target device.

Fig. 6. Home Appliances, Location Sensors, and IR Transceiver in the Prototyped Home

Each agent program corresponding to the devices is extended from the basic class ServiceProxy which has the fundamental interfaces such as discovery, registry, and invocation. The agent automatically registers its description file to the proposed service discovery server, which uses soft-state mechanism to maintain the state information of each service. Our communications are implemented on HTTP protocols. Therefore, end-users can use local services in familiar ways. In addition, each service works as a server to allow other applications to invoke its service in peer-to-peer ways. Our framework manages all of the services in our ontologies, which are developed by using OWL [18] and Protégé [19]. Activity policies will be also managed in the ontologies, and inferred by Racer [20].

5.1 Activity Policy-Based Service Discovery Framework

Figure 7 shows a hierarchical architecture of the proposed service discovery framework. ServiceProxy includes some operations to register, discover, and invoke services. Communications between ServiceProxy and ServiceDiscoveryServer are achieved on HTTP protocols. That is, the operations such as WWWRegister, WWWDiscover, WWWShow, and WWWCall are implemented as GET or POST methods of HTTP servers. ServiceProxy hides complex protocols required for the operations. Applications just use the given functions such as register(), discover(), and invoke(). In addition, general users can use the proposed scheme by using Web browsers such as Internet Explorer because we provide the operations as GET or POST methods of HTTP protocols.

On the other hand, all of the services must be extended from ServiceProxy to periodically register the service description files to ServiceDiscoveryServer. When the register() function is executed in each service, ServiceProxy creates a thread to automatically register the specific description file. The thread sleeps and wakes with the given lifetime which is described in the description file. The descriptions are stored in description repository and ontologies. Furthermore, ServiceProxy provides functionalities of micro-HTTP server to the services to support remote invocations. When applications invoke some functions in remote services, ServiceDiscoveryServer provides the reference to the desired services such as IP address, port number, class name, and method name, and then the ServiceProxy in the side of applications invokes the remote calls to the micro-HTTP server of the target services. ServiceManager governs most of the operations which are occurred in ServiceDiscoveryServer. It closely interacts with the reasoning engine, RacerPro [20]. Activity policies and ontologies are operated with the reasoning engine. ServiceManager uses JRacer and nRQL [17] to perform policy-based query coordination and IOPE-based semantic matching.

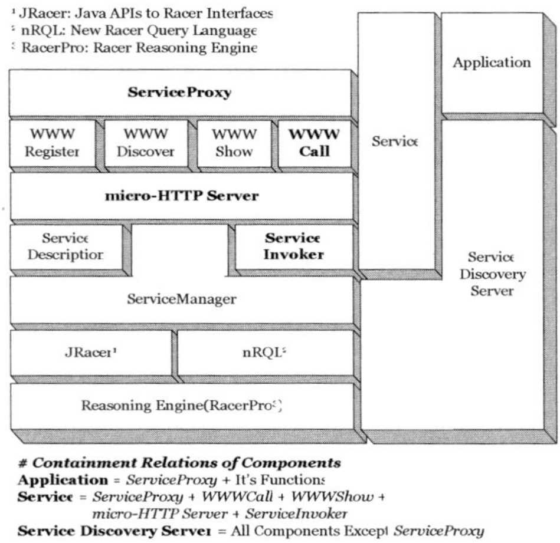

Fig. 7. Activity Policy-based Service Discovery Framework

5.2 Message Delivery Example

To illustrate the effectiveness of the proposed scheme, we use the activity ReceivingMessage introduced in Figure 3. We compare two types of service discovery approaches. Type 1 does not use policies, but use IOPE-based queries, while Type 2 uses policies with IOPE-based queries.

Table 1 present the experiment results of the ReceivingMessage activity. Note that the queries are not changed according to different environments in the developer's aspect. However, in the system's aspect, the queries are dynamically coordinated in the QueryPolicyCoordinator component. When working on a computer in the office, Alice would like to receive message through "WindowsPopupMessage" not to distract other people. When driving a car, she wants to use "NateTTS" function for the sake of safety. In result, Type 1 might provide inappropriate services, while Type 2 provides appropriate services according to context aware resource constraints. Furthermore, our approach can take full advantage of local resources although mobile users move from one to another place. In this case, Alice can use a variety of local resources such as VoiceSpeech, WindowsPopupMessage, NateCarNavigation, FreeTTS, and CaptionMaker to receive messages.

Table 1. Experiment Results of the Activity Policy, ReceivingMessage

<table>
<tr><th></th><th>Application (Query)</th><th>ContextManager (Context)</th><th>PolicyManager (Constraints)</th><th>QueryPolicyCoordinator (Coordinated Query)</th><th>Service Discovery (Found Services)</th></tr>
<tr><td>Type 1 (Office)</td><td>discover("Message", null, null, "PresentEffect");</td><td>(WorkingOnComputer , Alice, AliceOffice)</td><td>N/A</td><td>(retrieve (?service ?action) (and (?input |Message|) (?effect PresentEffect|) (?action ?input |hasInput|) (?action ?effect |hasEffect|) (?service ?action |achieveAction|) (?service |AliceOffice| |locatedIn|)))</td><td>(((?SERVICE VoiceSpeech|) (?ACTION |SpeakMessage|)) ((?SERVICE WindowsPopupMessage|) (?ACTION |PopupMessageDialog|)))</td></tr>
<tr><td>Type 2 (Office)</td><td>discover("Message", null, null, "PresentEffect", 'ReceivingMessage");</td><td>(WorkingOnComputer , Alice, AliceOffice)</td><td>(?effect DisplayEffect|)</td><td>(retrieve (?service ?action) (and (?input |Message|) (?effect DisplayEffect|) (?action ?input |hasInput|) (?action ?effect |hasEffect|) (?service ?action |achieveAction|) (?service |AliceOffice| |locatedIn|)))</td><td>(((?SERVICE WindowsPopupMessage|) (?ACTION |PopupMessageDialog|)))</td></tr>
<tr><td>Type 1 (Car)</td><td>discover("Message", null, null, "PresentEffect");</td><td>(DrivingCar, Alice, AliceCar)</td><td>N/A</td><td>(retrieve (?service ?action) (and (?input |Message|) (?effect PresentEffect|) (?action ?input |hasInput|) (?action ?effect |hasEffect|) (?service ?action |achieveAction|) (?service |AliceCar| |locatedIn|)))</td><td>(((?SERVICE NateCarNavigation|) (?ACTION |NateTTS|)) ((?SERVICE NateCarNavigation|) (?ACTION |NatePopupMessageBox|)))</td></tr>
<tr><td>Type 2 (Car)</td><td>discover("Message", null, null, "PresentEffect", 'ReceivingMessage");</td><td>(DrivingCar, Alice, AliceCar)</td><td>(?effect SoundEffect|)</td><td>(retrieve (?service ?action) (and (?input |Message|) (?effect SoundEffect|) (?action ?input |hasInput|) (?action ?effect |hasEffect|) (?service ?action |achieveAction|) (?service |AliceCar| |locatedIn|)))</td><td>(((?SERVICE NateCarNavigation|) (?ACTION |NateTTS|)))</td></tr>
<tr><td>Type 1 (Home)</td><td>discover("Message", null, null, "PresentEffect");</td><td>(WatchingTV, Alice, LivingRoomInAliceHome)</td><td>N/A</td><td>(retrieve (?service ?action) (and (?input |Message|) (?effect PresentEffect|) (?action ?input |hasInput|) (?action ?effect |hasEffect|) (?service ?action |achieveAction|) (?location |Home|) (?service ?location |locatedIn|)))</td><td>(((?SERVICE FreeTTS|) (?ACTION |FreeTTSVoiceSpeak|)) ((?SERVICE CaptionMaker|) (?ACTION |ShowSubtitle|)))</td></tr>
<tr><td>Type 2 (Home)</td><td>discover("Message", null, null, "PresentEffect", 'ReceivingMessage");</td><td>(WatchingTV, Alice, LivingRoomInAliceHome)</td><td>(or (?effect DisplayEffect|) (?effect SoundEffect|))</td><td>(retrieve (?service ?action) (and (?input |Message|) (or (?effect |DisplayEffect|) (?effect SoundEffect|)) (?action ?input |hasInput|) (?action ?effect |hasEffect|) (?service ?action |achieveAction|) (?location |Home|) (?service ?location |locatedIn|)))</td><td>(((?SERVICE CaptionMaker|) (?ACTION |ShowSubtitle|)) ((?SERVICE FreeTTS|) (?ACTION |FreeTTSVoiceSpeak|)))</td></tr>
</table>

6 Conclusions and Future Work

We introduce a service discovery framework using activity policies. Existing research efforts on service discovery have focused on context-awareness and semantics support. However, due to the dynamic changes of semantics according to different contexts, the instances acquired in real environments might not be permitted or not exercise great influence on target users in certain situations. In order to resolve these problems, activity policies provide flexible and reusable resource constraints according to dynamically changing contexts. Thus, our approach enables developers to transparently make use of appropriate services despite heterogeneous environments.

In the future, we must refine activity policies into a dynamic range of environments as well as a home environment. Human activities will be divided to domain-independent and domain-specific activities. The predefined policies can be reused or customized by users, developers, or policy designers. Therefore, we need to provide them with some manners to simply manage the policies.

Acknowledgements

This research was supported in part by the Ubiquitous Autonomic Computing and Network Project, 21st Century Frontier R&D Program of the Ministry of Information and Communication (MIC) and by the Digital Media Lab. Support Program of the MIC and the Institute of Information Technology Assessment (IITA), in Korea.

References

1. A. Ranganathan, S. Chetan, R. Campbell, "Mobile Polymorphic Applications in Ubiquitous Computing Environments," In Mobiquitous 2004 : The First Annual International Conference on Mobile and Ubiquitous Systems:Networking and Services, August 22-25, 2004 - Boston, Massachusetts, USA.
2. J. Sousa and D. Garlan, "Aura: an architectural framework for user mobility in ubiquitous computing environments," In 3rd Working IEEE/IFIP Conference on Software Architecture, pages 29--43, 2002.
3. T. Broens, S. Pokraev, M. van Sinderen, J. Koolwaaij, P. D. Costa, "Context-Aware, Ontology-Based Service Discovery," EUSAI 2004: 72-83.
4. C. Lee and A. Helal, "Context Attributes: An Approach to Enable Context-awareness for Service Discovery," In proceedings of third IEEE/IPSJ Symposium on Applications and the Intrnet, Orlando, Florida, January 2003.
5. Guanling Chen and David Kotz, "Context-sensitive resource discovery," In Proceedings of the First IEEE International Conference on Pervasive Computing and Communications (PerCom 2003), pages 243-252, Fort Worth, TX, March 2003.
6. A. Harter, A. Hopper, P. Steggles, A. Ward, and P. Webster, "The anatomy of a context-aware application," In Mobicom 99, ACM Press, pages 59–68, 1999.
7. A. Toninelli, A. Corradi, R. Montanari, "Semantic Discovery for Context-Aware Service Provisioning in Mobile Environments," 9th MCMP 2005, Ayia Napa, Cyprus
8. J. E. Bardram, "Activity-Based Service Discovery – An Approach for Service Composition, Orchestration and Context-Aware Service Discovery," CfPC 2004-PB-67, 2004, http://www.daimi.au.dk/~bardram/pvc/papers/absd.pdf
9. Z. Song, Y. Labrou, and R. Masuoka, "Dynamic Service Discovery and Management in Task Computting," presented at First Annual International Conference on Mobile and Ubiquitous Systems: Networking and Services(MobiQuitous'04), 2004.
10. A. Ranganathan, S. Chetan, J. Al-Muhtadi, R. H. Campbell, M. D. Mickunas, "Olympus: A High-Level Programming Model for Pervasive Computing Environments," In IEEE International Conference on Pervasive Computing and Communications (PerCom 2005), Kauai Island, Hawaii, March 8-12, 2005.
11. Z. Wang and D. Garlan, "Task-Driven Computing," Technical Report CMU-CS-00-154, School of Computer Science, Carnegie Mellon University, May 2000
12. R. Masuoka, B. Parsia, and Y. Labrou, "Task Computing—The Semantic Web Meets Pervasive Computing," Proc. 2nd Int'l Semantic Web Conf. 2003 (ISWC 03), Springer-Verlag, 2003
13. Roman M. and Campbell R. H., "A User-Centric, Resource-Aware, Context-Sensitive, Multi-Device, Application Framework for Ubiquitous Computing Environments," University of Illinois at Urbana-Champaign UiUCDCS-R-2002-2284 UILU-ENG-2002-1728, 2002
14. A. Ranganathan, and R. H. Campbell, "An Infrastructure for Context-Awareness based on First Order Logic," Journal of Personal and Ubiquitous Computing, Vol. 7, Issue 6, Dec. 2003, pp. 353-364.
15. Sivashanmugam, K., Sheth A., Miller J., Verma K., Aggarwal R., Rajasekaran P., "Metadata and Semantics for Web Services and Processes," Book Chapter, Datenbanken und Informationssysteme, Festschrift zum 60. Geburtstag von Gunter Schlageter, Publication Hagen, October 2003-09-26.
16. "Semantic Web projects," http://www.semanticweb.org/

17. "New Racer Query Lanauge," http://www.cs.concordia.ca/~haarslev/racer/racer-queries.pdf
18. "OWL," http://www.w3.org/2004/OWL/
19. "Protégé," http://protege.stanford.edu/
20. "Racer," http://www.racer-systems.com/
21. D. Lee, S. Han, I. Park, S. Kang, K. Lee, S. J. Hyun, Y. H. Lee, and G. Lee, "A Group-Aware Middleware for Ubiquitous Computing Environments," ICAT 2004, http://as.icu.ac.kr/www/pdf_paper/icat04-final.pdf.
22. L. Capra, W. Emmerich, and C. Mascolo, "CARISMA: Context-Aware Reflective Middleware System for Mo-bile Applications," IEEE Transactions on Software Engineering, 29(10), 2003
23. P. Bellavista, A. Corradi, R. Montanari, and C. Stefanelli, "Context-Aware Middleware for Resource Management in the Wireless Internet," IEEE Transactions on Software Engineering, Vol. 29, No. 12, December 2003

Data Stream Sharing*

Richard Kuntschke and Alfons Kemper

Institut für Informatik, Technische Universität München, Munich, Germany
{richard.kuntschke, alfons.kemper}@in.tum.de

Abstract. Recent research efforts in the fields of data stream processing and data stream management systems (DSMSs) show the increasing importance of processing data streams, e. g., in the e-science domain. Together with the advent of peer-to-peer (P2P) networks and grid computing, this leads to the necessity of developing new techniques for distributing and processing continuous queries over data streams in such networks. In this paper, we present a novel approach for optimizing the integration, distribution, and execution of newly registered continuous queries over data streams in grid-based P2P networks. We introduce *Windowed XQuery (WXQuery)*, our XQuery-based subscription language for continuous queries over XML data streams supporting window-based operators. Concentrating on filtering and window-based aggregation, we present our stream sharing algorithms as well as experimental evaluation results from the astrophysics application domain to assess our approach.

1 Introduction

Over the past few years, data stream processing and data stream management systems (DSMSs) have been very active research areas. This trend is promoted by the increasing need to process streaming data on-the-fly whenever possible, instead of storing intermediate results or buffering whole input data sets before processing. Newly upcoming and evolving fields, such as e-science applications in physics and astronomy, deal with huge volumes of data and render storing all of the delivered data increasingly impractical. Also, transmitting all the data over physically limited and therefore eventually congested network connections is a problem. This is especially true if only small subsets of the data or some processing results—which usually constitute a much smaller data volume than the input data—are actually needed.

We propose *data stream sharing* as a new optimization technique addressing these issues. Data stream sharing is based on two main optimization approaches. These are (1) *in-network query processing* for distributing and executing newly registered continuous queries in the network and (2) *multi-subscription optimization* for enabling the reuse of existing (parts of) data streams that were generated to satisfy previously registered subscriptions.[1]

* This research is supported by the German Federal Ministry of Education and Research within the D-Grid initiative under contract 01AK804F and by Microsoft Research Cambridge under contract 2005-041.

[1] The terms *query*, *continuous query*, and *subscription* are treated as synonyms throughout this paper.

T. Grust et al. (Eds.): EDBT 2006 Workshops, LNCS 4254, pp. 769–788, 2006.

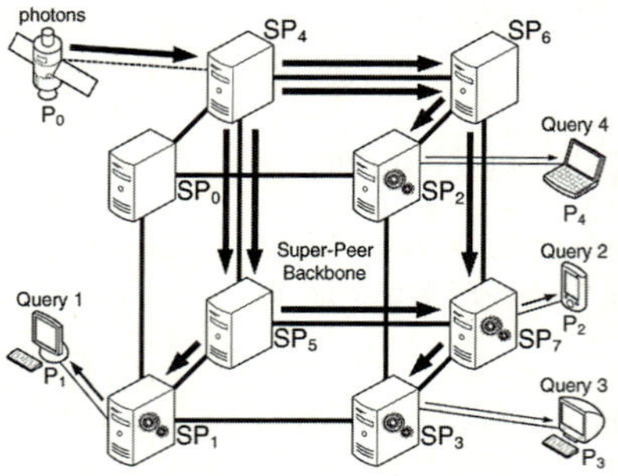

Fig. 1. No stream sharing

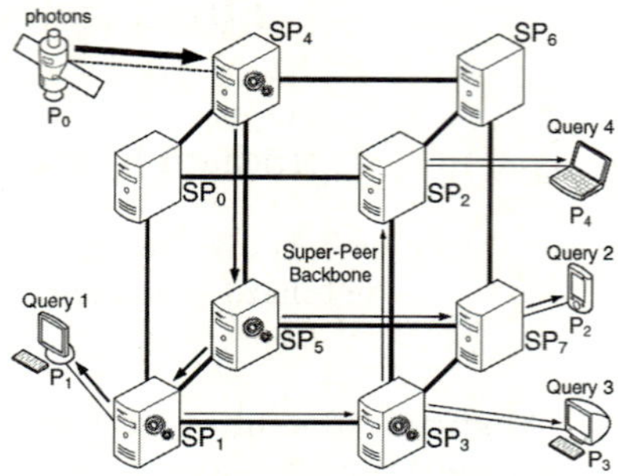

Fig. 2. Stream sharing

These optimizations are an integral part of our *StreamGlobe* system [1,2]. To enable them, we use *peer-to-peer (P2P) networking* techniques. In contrast to the conventional use of P2P networks for *file sharing*, StreamGlobe uses P2P-based networks for *data stream sharing*. The system architecture is based on a P2P overlay backbone network that is organized as a *super-peer network* [3], i. e., peers are classified into *super-peers* and *thin-peers*. Super-peers are powerful servers which form a stationary super-peer backbone network. Thin-peers—often simply called peers in the following—are less powerful devices that can be registered at a super-peer and deliver data streams or register queries in the network. The StreamGlobe implementation adheres to established *grid computing* standards (OGSA) and therefore fits seamlessly into existing e-science platforms.

As a motivating example, we introduce an astrophysical e-science application. Consider Figures 1 and 2 which both illustrate the same exemplary network. Here, SP_0 to SP_7 are the super-peers that constitute the super-peer backbone network and P_0 to P_4 are thin-peers. Peer P_0 is a satellite-bound telescope that detects photons and registers a data stream called `photons` at super-peer SP_4. This data stream contains real astrophysical data collected during the ROSAT All-Sky Survey (RASS) which we obtained through our cooperation partners from the Max Planck Institute for Extraterrestrial Physics (MPE).

In our scenario, we deal with streams of XML data. The data items in stream `photons` comply to a DTD with the tree structure shown below. As its name implies, the data stream delivers a stream of photons detected by the telescope's photon detector. Each photon contains its celestial and detector pixel coordinates, its detector pulse, its energy, and its detection time.

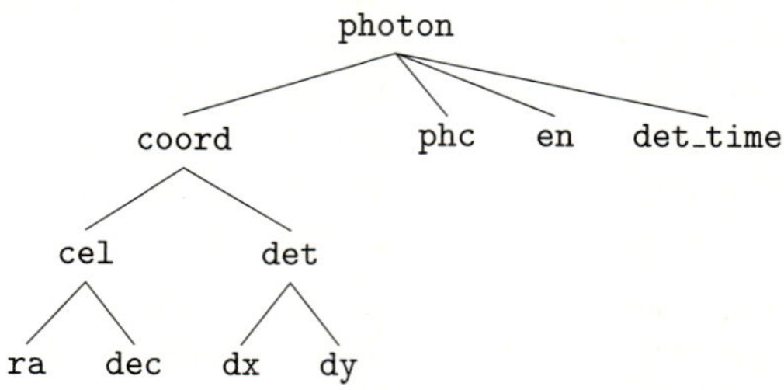

We assume that peers P_1 to P_4 in the example network are devices of astrophysicists used to register subscriptions in the network referencing the available data stream as input. Subscriptions are registered using *WXQuery*, our XQuery-based subscription language that will be introduced in detail in Section 2. We will only consider Queries 1 and 2 of Figures 1 and 2 here. Queries 3 and 4 will be presented in Section 2. All queries reference data stream `photons` as their single input. Query 1 (Q1) is shown below.

```
Q1:  <photons>
       { for $p in stream("photons")/photons/photon
         where $p/coord/cel/ra >= 120.0 and $p/coord/cel/ra <= 138.0
           and $p/coord/cel/dec >= -49.0 and $p/coord/cel/dec <= -40.0
         return <vela> { $p/coord/cel/ra } { $p/coord/cel/dec }
                       { $p/phc } { $p/en } { $p/det_time } </vela> }
     </photons>
```

This query selects the area of the *vela supernova remnant*. The `stream` function was newly introduced by us and indicates a possibly infinite data stream used as input to the query. Query 2 (Q2) below filters a smaller section of the sky.

```
Q2:  <photons>
       { for $p in stream("photons")/photons/photon
         where $p/en >= 1.3
           and $p/coord/cel/ra >= 130.5 and $p/coord/cel/ra <= 135.5
           and $p/coord/cel/dec >= -48.0 and $p/coord/cel/dec <= -45.0
         return <rxj> { $p/coord/cel/ra } { $p/coord/cel/dec }
                      { $p/en } { $p/det_time } </rxj> }
     </photons>
```

This query selects the area of the *RX J0852.0-4622 supernova remnant* which is situated within the area of *vela*. Note that the section of the sky selected by Query 2 is completely contained in the section selected by Query 1. Also, Query 2 is only interested in photons having an energy value of at least 1.3 keV.

We first consider Figure 1 which shows the traditional scenario of data shipping. The thickness of the arrows associated with the various network connections indicates the size of the data streams transmitted over these connections. Each of the four queries in the system only needs a certain part of the original data stream. However, in each case, the whole stream gets transmitted from the data source to the data sink leading to the transmission of unnecessary data. Since query execution for each subscription takes place at the super-peer that the subscribing peer is connected to, queries that perform the same operations on the same input data streams cause redundant execution of operators.

Figure 2 shows the benefits of using our stream sharing approach which answers newly registered subscriptions using (parts of) data streams already present in the network. This includes data streams which have been generated earlier for satisfying previously registered continuous queries. We assume that Queries 1 to 4 have been registered one after another in ascending order in our example. Obviously, network traffic and processing overhead can be significantly reduced by avoiding redundant transmissions and computations through sharing previously generated data streams. For example, when Query 1 is registered, its execution can be pushed into the network and computed at SP_4 instead of SP_1. The result is then routed to P_1 via SP_5 and SP_1. When Query 2 is registered afterwards, it can reuse the stream constituting the answer for Query 1 at SP_5 because the result of Query 2 is completely contained in the answer for Query 1. The result data stream of Query 1 is duplicated at SP_5, yielding two identical streams. One is used to answer Query 1, the other is filtered using the selection and projection specified by Query 2. This results in a new stream that constitutes the result of Query 2 which is subsequently routed to P_2 via SP_7.

The contributions presented in this paper are as follows. First, we introduce *Windowed XQuery (WXQuery)*, our XQuery-based subscription language for continuous queries over XML data streams enabling the formulation of queries including window-based aggregation operators. Second, we present a properties representation of data streams and subscriptions, a cost model, and algorithms for optimizing the evaluation of newly registered continuous queries in a data stream management system by sharing possibly preprocessed data streams. Eventually, we show experimental evaluation results to assess our approach.

The paper is organized as follows. In Section 2, we introduce WXQuery. Our new data stream sharing approach is presented in Section 3. Section 4 shows some evaluation results. Related work is presented in Section 5. Finally, Section 6 concludes and states ongoing and future work.

2 Subscription Language

In StreamGlobe, subscriptions over XML data streams are registered using *Windowed XQuery (WXQuery)*. WXQuery is a fragment of XQuery [4] that has been augmented with support for window-based operators.

In Definition 2.1 below, α and β are WXQuery expressions and χ denotes a condition. A tag name is denoted by t. Further, $\$x$ and $\$y$ are variables representing XML trees, where $\$y$ can also start with a function call to reference a document node or the stream node of a data stream like `stream("photons")` in the example subscriptions. A variable representing the result of a window-based aggregation operation is denoted by $\$a$. The variable $\$z$ can represent any of the three kinds of variables $\$x$, $\$y$, or $\$a$ as described above. We use $\overline{\pi}$ to denote a relative path that only employs the child axis ("`/`"). It does not include wildcards ("`*`"), conditions ("`[`p`]`"), or other axes (e.g., "`//`"). A relative path π differs from $\overline{\pi}$ in that it can also contain conditions. An aggregation operator is denoted by Φ, i.e., $\Phi \in \{$`min,max,sum,count,avg`$\}$.

Expressions enclosed in $[\![\,]\!]^?$, $[\![\,]\!]^*$, or $[\![\,]\!]^+$ in the definition are optional, can occur zero or more times, or can occur one or more times, respectively. A vertical bar ($|$) indicates an alternation. An expression of the form $\alpha_{i_1,\ldots,i_n}$ represents a WXQuery expression from a restricted set of expressions. For example, $\alpha_{1,2}$ stands for any one of the two element constructor expressions numbered 1 and 2 in the definition below and $\alpha_{3,4,5,6,7}$ stands for any one of the remaining expressions numbered 3 to 7.

Definition 2.1 (WXQuery). *The WXQuery subscription language comprises all subscriptions that consist only of the following expressions:*

1. <t/> (empty direct element constructor)
2. <t> $[\![\alpha_{1,2} \mid$ `{`$\alpha_{3,4,5,6,7}$`}`$]\!]^*$ </t> (direct element constructor)

3. $[\![\texttt{for } \$x \texttt{ in } \$y[\![/\pi]\!]^? [\![\texttt{|count } \Delta\ [\![\texttt{step } \mu]\!]^? \texttt{|} \mid \texttt{|}\bar{\pi} \texttt{ diff } \Delta\ [\![\texttt{step } \mu]\!]^? \texttt{|}]\!]^? \mid \texttt{let } \$a \texttt{ := } \Phi\texttt{(}\$y[\![/\pi]\!]^?\texttt{)}]\!]^+\ [\![\texttt{where } \chi]\!]^? \texttt{ return } \alpha$ (FLWR expression)
4. $\texttt{if } \chi \texttt{ then } \alpha \texttt{ else } \beta$ (conditional expression)
5. $\$y/\pi$ (output of subtrees reachable from node $\$y$ through path π)
6. $\$z$ (output of subtree rooted at node $\$z$)
7. $\texttt{(}[\![\alpha[\![\texttt{,}\beta]\!]^*]\!]^?\texttt{)}$ (sequence)

The FLWR expression in the WXQuery definition introduces our new syntax for expressing data windows, e. g., for use with window-based aggregation operators. Query 3 (Q3) in the network of Figures 1 and 2 is an example for the use of such an operator.

```
Q3:  <photons>
       { for $w in stream("photons")/photons/photon
           [coord/cel/ra >= 120.0 and coord/cel/ra <= 138.0
            and coord/cel/dec >= -49.0 and coord/cel/dec <= -40.0]
           |det_time diff 20 step 10|
         let $a := avg($w/en)
         return <avg_en> { $a } </avg_en> }
     </photons>
```

Query 4 (Q4) employs a different window.

```
Q4:  <photons>
       { for $w in stream("photons")/photons/photon
           [coord/cel/ra >= 120.0 and coord/cel/ra <= 138.0
            and coord/cel/dec >= -49.0 and coord/cel/dec <= -40.0]
           |det_time diff 60 step 40|
         let $a := avg($w/en)
         where $a >= 1.3
         return <avg_en> { $a } </avg_en> }
     </photons>
```

The definition of a data window is enclosed in "|" characters. Item-based windows—indicated by the keyword `count`—contain a fixed number of items given by the numeric value of Δ. Optionally, a step size μ determining the update interval of the data window can be specified. For example, the window `|count 20 step 10|` defines a data window that always contains 20 data items and, during each update, removes the 10 oldest entries from the window while adding the next 10 new data items arriving in the stream. If omitted, the step size defaults to the value of Δ, meaning the contents of the window are completely replaced by new ones during each update. The situation is analogous for time-based windows, except that Δ indicates the size of the window in time units and the step size indicates the time interval between two successive data windows. Again, the step size defaults to Δ if omitted. Time-based windows can only be applied on data streams that are sorted according to the values of a particular *reference element* that is used to control the window. This premise could be somewhat relaxed to a fuzzy order by requiring that a fixed sized buffer is sufficient to derive the total order. The value of the reference element of a time-based data window can either be a real or an abstract timestamp. An example for a time-based window is `|det_time diff 60 step 40|` in Query 4. Note that the path inside the window is not meant to be evaluated yielding a sequence as defined by the conventional XPath semantics. Rather, it specifies the reference element controlling the window.

Conditions in our context, whether they appear in a `where` clause ("χ") or within a path ("[p]"), are conjunctions of *atomic predicates*. Atomic predicates are of the form $\$v\ \theta\ c$ or $\$v\ \theta\ \$w{+}c$, where $\$v$ and $\$w$ represent paths of the form $\overline{\pi}$, c represents a constant value, and $\theta \in \{=, <, \leq, >, \geq\}$. Constant values can be negative and are either integer values or decimal values with a finite number of decimal places.

Restructuring (introducing new elements, reordering or renaming output elements, etc.) is done in a post-processing step at the super-peer that is connected to the peer that registered the subscription. The result of the post-processing is delivered to the final destination and is not considered for reuse in the network. Since attributes in XML data can always be converted into corresponding elements, we restrict ourselves to dealing with elements.

3 Data Stream Sharing

This section introduces our properties-based approach for representing subscriptions and data streams, our cost model, and the algorithms for searching, identifying, and choosing appropriate streams for satisfying new subscriptions.

3.1 Properties

Subscriptions and data streams are treated symmetrically in our context. This is due to the fact that a subscription can always be seen as producing a result data stream and a data stream can always be seen as the result of a subscription. Therefore, subscriptions and data streams are also represented by the same properties data structure.

The properties of subscriptions and data streams consist of three parts and describe how the associated (result) data stream was generated. An abstract schematic illustration of the properties of Query 1 from Section 1 is shown in Figure 3. A subscription or data stream is described by a set of original input data streams, a set of operators for each input data stream used to transform the respective input data stream into the represented (result) data stream and, for each operator, a set of conditions specifying the operator, i. e., selection predicates, projection elements, data window specifications, or aggregation operators together with the identifier of the corresponding aggregated element. Predicates, e. g., selection predicates, are stored using a graph representation as shown in Figure 3. Data window specifications are also stored in a specific format that contains the ordered reference element (only for time-based windows), the window type (`count` or `diff`), the window size (Δ) and the step size (μ). This approach supports flat WXQueries without nesting. An advanced approach supporting nested queries is part of future work.

Note that the properties as described above serve two purposes. First, they represent the parts of the originally queried input data streams that are needed by the corresponding subscription. Second, they describe the contents—relative

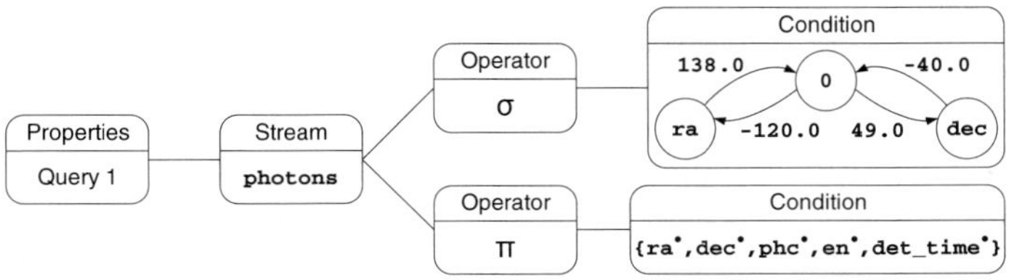

Fig. 3. Abstract properties of Query 1

to the contents of the input data streams—of the data stream produced as a result of that subscription. Also note that properties do not need to represent transformation details like the exact structure of query results as stated in a query's return clause.

3.2 Cost Model

We now introduce the cost model used in our optimizations. The cost function C focuses on the amount of additional network traffic and peer load caused by answering a new subscription. Other parameters, e. g., latency of network connections, could easily be added. To define C, we need to introduce some notation. Let p be the properties of a new continuous query q that is to be registered in the network. Then $\overline{size}(p)$ denotes the average size of one data stream item (e. g., one `photon`) of the stream represented by p. Let P_q be the set of properties of all input data streams of q, $\overline{occ}(n_s)$ the average occurrence and $\overline{size}(n_s)$ the average size of element n_s in the input stream represented by properties s, and Π_{p_s} the set of projection elements of p concerning the input stream represented by s. Then, for a subscription that only contains selection and projection operators, $\overline{size}(p)$ is calculated using the following formula:

$$\overline{size}(p) := \sum_{s \in P_q} \left(\overline{size}(s) - \sum_{n_s \notin \Pi_{p_s}} \left(\overline{occ}(n_s) \cdot \overline{size}(n_s) \right) \right)$$

Note that, in the above formula, $\overline{size}(p)$ denotes the average size of one data stream item in the stream represented by p, e. g., one `photon` element in stream `photons`, whereas $\overline{size}(n_s)$ denotes the average size of one subelement n_s, e. g., the `phc` subelement of a `photon`. For aggregate queries, the result data stream is a stream of aggregate result values. The average result data stream size is therefore independent of the input stream size in this case and is computed as the sum of the sizes of the aggregate values and their surrounding element tags. For queries returning the contents of data windows, the average size of a data window needs to be determined. For item-based data windows this can be done by multiplying the window size with the average size of the items contained in the window and adding the sizes of the enclosing window tags. For time-based data windows this works analogously except that the average number of data items contained in the window must be estimated as the product of the input stream frequency and the window size.

The average frequency of data items in the stream represented by p is denoted by $\overline{freq}(p)$. With $sel(\sigma_p)$ denoting the selectivity of the subscription represented by p, $\overline{freq}(p)$ can be computed as follows:

$$\overline{freq}(p) := sel(\sigma_p) \cdot \sum_{s \in P_q} \overline{freq}(s)$$

Note that the expression $\sum_{s \in P_q} \overline{freq}(s)$ in this formula depends on the semantics of the employed operators in q. The above formula is valid for selection operators. Projection operators do not influence $\overline{freq}(p)$. For window-based queries, $\overline{freq}(p)$ depends on the step size defined for the data window and the average frequency of the input data stream. For item-based data windows, $\overline{freq}(p)$ corresponds to the frequency of the respective input data stream divided by the step size μ of the data window. For time-based data windows, $\overline{freq}(p)$ depends on the distribution of the values of the reference element. To be able to estimate the frequency of the result data stream in such a case, we keep track of the average increment of the reference element value between two successive data items arriving in the stream. Dividing the step size μ of the time-based data window by this average increment yields the average number of data items that need to be read from the stream before the window update is complete. Then, as with item-based data windows, the frequency of the input data stream is divided by this estimated number of data items to obtain the estimated average frequency of the result data stream.

Introducing $b(e)$ as the maximum bandwith of a network connection e, we can characterize the relative amount $u_b(e)$ of bandwith of e used by the additional data streams routed over e for answering q using the following formula:

$$u_b(e) := \frac{\sum_{p \in P_e} \left(\overline{size}(p) \cdot \overline{freq}(p)\right)}{b(e)}$$

Here, P_e denotes the set of properties of all additional data streams added over e to answer q.

The average computational load caused by an operator o on a peer v with a set of input stream properties P_o is denoted $\overline{load}(o, v, P_o)$. The maximum load of a peer v is represented by $l(v)$. The relative amount $u_l(v)$ of computational load on a peer v caused by the additional operators in O_v installed at v for answering a new subscription can be computed as follows:

$$u_l(v) := \frac{\sum_{o \in O_v} \overline{load}(o, v, P_o)}{l(v)}$$

Cost function inputs like average frequencies of data stream items, average sizes and occurences of elements, and selectivities of operators are obtained from statistics and selectivity estimations. The average load $\overline{load}(o, v, P_o)$ of an operator o on a peer v with a set of input stream properties P_o depends on the performance of the executing peer, expressed by a performance index ($pindex(v)$), and the characteristics of the operator itself. For example, assuming a linear dependency of the load caused by a selection operator σ from the frequency $\overline{freq}(s)$ of its only input stream represented by properties s, the average load caused by σ on a peer v can be defined as $\overline{load}(\sigma, v, s) := bload(\sigma) \cdot pindex(v) \cdot \overline{freq}(s)$. Here, $bload(\sigma)$ represents a base load factor for the selection operator. Factors like base loads of operators and performance indices of peers as well as formulas for combining these factors yielding realistic load estimations have to be determined, e. g., on the basis of reference values.

The cost function C is then defined as follows:

$$C(\mathcal{P}) := \gamma \cdot \left(\sum_{e \in E_{\mathcal{P}}} \left(u_b(e) + \max(0, (u_b(e) - a_b(e))) \cdot e^{(u_b(e) - a_b(e))} \right) \right) + \\ (1-\gamma) \cdot \left(\sum_{v \in V_{\mathcal{P}}} \left(u_l(v) + \max(0, (u_l(v) - a_l(v))) \cdot e^{(u_l(v) - a_l(v))} \right) \right)$$

In this function, $\mathcal{P}$ denotes the evaluation plan of the new subscription, i. e., the operators that have to be installed, the peers on which they have to be installed, and the additional data streams that are generated and routed through the network. Furthermore, $E_{\mathcal{P}}$ is the set of network connections and $V_{\mathcal{P}}$ is the set of peers affected by plan $\mathcal{P}$. A weighting factor $\gamma \in [0, 1]$ determines, which part of the cost function should be more dominant—network traffic or peer load. An exponential penalty is given for overload situations on peers and network connections. The relative amount of available bandwith on network connection e and of available computational load on peer v is represented by $a_b(e)$ and $a_l(v)$, respectively. A plan $\mathcal{P}$ is better than another plan $\mathcal{P}'$ according to cost function C, expressed by $\mathcal{P} \prec_C \mathcal{P}'$, if and only if $C(\mathcal{P}) < C(\mathcal{P}')$.

3.3 Stream Sharing Algorithms

We now describe our stream sharing algorithms for registering and efficiently satisfying new continuous queries in P2P data stream management systems. The algorithms search for shareable data streams in the network, compare the properties of new subscriptions with those of existing data streams, and decide which streams to reuse at which peers.

Query Registration. The algorithm for continuous query registration searches for shareable data streams in the network and decides if a certain available data stream can actually be shared for answering a new query by comparing the corresponding properties. Further, it decides whether a newly found evaluation plan for the new query is better than the previously best plan.

The algorithm is divided into four parts. The SUBSCRIBE algorithm shown in Algorithm 1 describes the discovery of shareable data streams and the generation of corresponding query evaluation plans. The MATCHPROPERTIES and MATCHPREDICATES algorithms which are detailed in Algorithms 2 and 3 handle the matching of properties and predicates, respectively. Finally, the matching of aggregation operators is dealt with in the MATCHAGGREGATIONS algorithm. Beginning with Algorithm 1, the inputs p_q and v_q are the properties of the new subscription q and the network node where q is registered, respectively. The output of the algorithm is the evaluation plan $\mathcal{P}$, describing how the network has to be changed in terms of installed operators and routed data streams in order to satisfy q. Note that there will always be at least one plan that is suitable for answering q—provided that q refers to existing inputs—namely the plan using the originally registered versions of q's input streams. The goal of our approach is to find possibly transformed versions of these streams—generated by projection, selection, or aggregation operators in the network for answering previously registered continuous queries—that can also be used to answer q, possibly by applying some further transformations.

The SUBSCRIBE algorithm starts with an empty evaluation plan $\mathcal{P}$ (line 1 in Algorithm 1) and iterates over the properties of all input data streams of q (line 2). For each such input data stream, the algorithm performs some initialization tasks (lines 3–6). First, a FIFO queue L_V for network nodes (peers) and another queue L_P for properties are initialized. Then, the properties p_s of the currently considered input data stream s and the network node where this input data stream is registered are stored in p_b and v_b, respectively. The variables p_b and v_b represent the properties of the currently best solution for the data stream chosen as input for satisfying q and the network node where to find and reuse that stream. Installing the whole new subscription at the super-peer at which it is registered and using the original input streams, routed to the subscription via shortest paths in the network, is set as the initial evaluation plan. Therefore, the part of the query evaluation plan that deals with input stream s, called $\mathcal{P}_s$, is initially set to routing s from the peer where it is registered to the peer where q is registered via the shortest path in the network and performing any query evaluation tasks on data stream s at the target peer. This plan is generated by means of the *generatePlan* function that takes as inputs the properties p_b of the data stream chosen for reuse, the node v_b where to reuse that stream, and the node v_q where the query to be answered is registered and where the query result is needed. At each time during the remaining execution of the algorithm, the current best plan for input data stream s is represented by $\mathcal{P}_s$. Finally, the start node v_b of the search is added as first node to L_V.

If a subscription references more than one input stream, each stream is handled individually by the subscription algorithm. The algorithm assures that at least the relevant parts of each input stream are delivered to the super-peer connected to the peer that registered q. Any combination of input data streams as demanded by the subscription is performed at this peer during the final post-processing step and the result of this combination is not considered for reuse in the network. This is the same as with any restructuring of the query result as described in Section 2.

After the initialization, the algorithm performs a breadth-first search in the network graph for each input stream, starting at the node that corresponds to the super-peer at which the corresponding original input stream of q is registered. Using LIFO queues for L_V and L_P instead of FIFO queues would cause the algorithm to perform depth-first search which would be equally possible. The peers in L_V are dequeued one after another (line 8). Each peer in L_V is marked in order to handle circles in the network graph, i. e., consider each node at most once. For each dequeued peer, all properties of data streams that are available at the currently handled peer and that are variants of p_s are subsequently inserted

Algorithm 1. SUBSCRIBE

Input: The properties p_q of the subscription q to be registered and the node v_q where q is to be registered.
Output: A query evaluation plan $\mathcal{P}$.

1: $\mathcal{P} \leftarrow \emptyset$;
2: **for all** $p_s \in getInputDS(p_q)$ **do**
3: $L_V \leftarrow \emptyset$; $L_P \leftarrow \emptyset$;
4: $p_b \leftarrow p_s$; $v_b \leftarrow getTNode(p_b)$;
5: $\mathcal{P}_s \leftarrow generatePlan(p_b, v_b, v_q)$;
6: $add(L_V, v_b)$;
7: **while** $L_V \neq \emptyset$ **do**
8: $v \leftarrow dequeue(L_V)$; $mark(v)$;
9: **for all** data streams available at v that are variants of p_s **do**
10: enqueue all associated properties in L_P;
11: **end for**
12: **while** $L_P \neq \emptyset$ **do**
13: $p \leftarrow dequeue(L_P)$;
14: **if** MATCHPROPERTIES(p, p_s) **then**
15: $n \leftarrow getTNode(p)$;
16: **if** $(\neg(isMarked(n)) \wedge (n \notin L_V))$ **then**
17: $add(L_V, n)$;
18: **end if**
19: $\mathcal{P}'_s \leftarrow generatePlan(p, v, v_q)$;
20: **if** $\mathcal{P}'_s \prec_C \mathcal{P}_s$ **then**
21: $p_b \leftarrow p$; $v_b \leftarrow v$; $\mathcal{P}_s \leftarrow \mathcal{P}'_s$;
22: **end if**
23: **end if**
24: **end while**
25: **end while**
26: unmark all nodes;
27: $add(\mathcal{P}, \mathcal{P}_s)$;
28: **end for**
29: **return** $\mathcal{P}$;

into L_P (lines 9–11). These properties are then consecutively taken out of the queue and matched against the properties p_q of q using Algorithm 2 (lines 12–14). This will be described in detail below. Network connections that do not have any associated properties because they do not carry any data streams are ignored during the breadth-first search. Also, non-matching properties do not add any peers to L_V since following these paths cannot yield a reusable data stream. Pruning the search in this way leads to the breadth-first search traversing only the relevant part of the network instead of the whole network.

If a property p has been successfully matched, its corresponding stream can be reused for answering q. If the target peer of p, i. e., the peer to which the stream corresponding to p is delivered, is still unmarked, it is added to L_V to be processed later on during the breadth-first search (lines 15–18). For any found solution, a new plan $\mathcal{P}'_s$ is generated, again using the *generatePlan* function (line 19). Then, the value of the cost function C for the plan reusing the found data stream is computed and compared against the current best solution (line 20). Only if the new solution is better according to C, it replaces the current best solution and is stored along with its cost function value for future comparisons (lines 20–22). When there are no properties left in queue L_P, the next node of L_V is considered. If there are no more nodes left in L_V, the best plan $\mathcal{P}_s$ found for input stream s is added to the overall plan $\mathcal{P}$ for evaluating q (line 27). When all input streams of q have been considered, the algorithm terminates and returns the current best solution for plan $\mathcal{P}$ as the final result.

Matching Properties. Next, we explain how Algorithm 2 matches properties. For each input data stream of a subscription, the properties of the subscription reflect which operators and operator conditions are employed to transform the respective input stream into the subscription result. These properties have to be matched with the properties of data streams already present in the network to find shareable streams for each input stream of the new subscription. The inputs for the properties matching algorithm are the properties p of the data stream that is considered for reuse and the properties p' of the newly registered subscription. The algorithm returns true if these properties match and false otherwise.

If the input streams of both properties match—checked in lines 1–4 of Algorithm 2—the sets of operators used to transform the inputs are fetched from the properties data structures (line 5) and assigned to O and O', respectively. For each operator in O there must be a corresponding operator in O'. For example, if O contains a selection operator, the data stream represented by p is only considered for sharing if p' also contains a corresponding selection. Otherwise, the stream represented by p would not contain all the necessary data for the query represented by p'. If a corresponding operator is found in O', it has to be assured that the conditions of the two operators, which are fetched from the properties data structures in line 10 of the algorithm, are compatible. We distinguish four cases (lines 11–30), i. e., selection, projection, window-based aggregation, and unknown operators. If the corresponding operators are selection operators (lines 11–15), the algorithm retrieves the graphs representing the selection predicates (line 12) and tries to match them using Algorithm 3. In case of a projection (lines 16–20), the set $\overline{R}$ of projection elements of p that are actually returned in the result data stream of the query represented by p—these are the projection elements marked with bullets in the properties of Query 1 in Figure 3—has to be a superset of the set R' of all the elements referenced by the query, marked as well as unmarked, in order for the stream represented by p to be reusable. If o and o' are one of the window-based aggregation operators `min`, `max`, `sum`, `count`, or `avg`, it has to be assured that the conditions and data windows are compatible (lines 21–24). This is done by the MATCHAGGREGATIONS algorithm described further below. All other operators are handled in the fourth and final case (lines 25–30). These are unknown operators, in particular user defined functions. Nothing is known about the semantics of these operators. We only require them to be deterministic, meaning that the same operator applied to the same inputs must always yield the same result. The algorithm then demands that not only the operators but also their input vectors, i. e., their parameter lists retrieved in line 26 of the algorithm, are the same for shareability. More sophisticated techniques for identifying shareable user defined operators involve the development

Algorithm 2. MATCHPROPERTIES

Input: The properties p of a data stream considered for sharing and p' of a subscription to be registered.
Output: true if p and p' match, false otherwise.

```
s ← getDS(p); s' ← getDS(p');
if s ≠ s' then
  return false;
end if
O ← getOps(s); O' ← getOps(s');
for all o ∈ O do
  match ← false;
  for all o' ∈ O' do
    if o = o' then
      C ← getConds(o); C' ← getConds(o');
      if o = σ then
        G ← getPGraph(C); G' ← getPGraph(C');
        if MatchPredicates(G, G') then
          match ← true; break;
        end if
      else if o = Π then
        R̄ ← getOutElems(C); R' ← getRefElems(C');
        if R̄ ⊇ R' then
          match ← true; break;
        end if
      else if o ∈ {min,max,sum,count,avg} then
        if MatchAggregations(C, C'); then
          match ← true; break;
        end if
      else
        i⃗ ← getParams(C); i⃗' ← getParams(C');
        if i⃗ = i⃗' then
          match ← true; break;
        end if
      end if
    end if
  end for
  if match = false then
    return false;
  end if
end for
return true;
```

of suitable operator descriptions providing the necessary meta data. Developing such techniques and operator descriptions is part of future work.

Matching Predicates. A predicate is represented by a weighted directed graph $G = (V, E)$ within the corresponding properties. The construction and representation of predicate graphs are an extension of related work on the processing of conjunctive predicates [5]. In addition to integer valued variables and constants, we also allow decimal values with a finite number of decimal places. First,

Algorithm 3. MATCHPREDICATES

Input: The predicate graphs $G = (V, E)$ of a data stream considered for sharing and $G' = (V', E')$ of a subscription to be registered.

Output: true if the predicates represented by G match the predicates represented by G', false otherwise.

```
for all v ∈ V do
   vmatch ← false;
   for all v' ∈ V' do
      if v ≙ v' then
         vmatch ← true;
         for all x ∈ {e ∈ E | e connected to v} do
            ematch ← false;
            for all y ∈ {e' ∈ E' | e' connected to v'} do
               if ζ(x) ⇐ ζ(y) then
                  ematch ← true; break;
               end if
            end for
            if ematch = false then
               return false;
            end if
         end for
         break;
      end if
   end for
   if vmatch = false then
      return false;
   end if
end for
return true;
```

predicates are normalized to contain only comparisons of the form $\$v \geq c$, $\$v \leq c$ and $\$v \leq \$w + c$ where $\$v$ and $\$w$ represent variables and c represents a constant integer or decimal value. Each variable in the predicate becomes a node in V and an atomic predicate of the form $\$v \leq \$w + c$ is represented by a weighted directed edge in E from node $\$v$ to node $\$w$ with weight c. Further, V contains a node for the constant zero. An atomic predicate of the form $\$v \leq c$ is represented by an edge from node $\$v$ to node zero with weight c and an atomic predicate of the form $\$v \geq c$, which can be expressed as $0 \leq \$v - c$, by an edge from node zero to node $\$v$ with weight $-c$. As an illustrating example, consider Figure 3 which contains the predicate graph of the selection in Query 1. After the construction of G, the predicate can be checked for satisfiability and is minimized using techniques introduced in earlier related work [5]. If an operator's predicate is unsatisfiable, the corresponding subscription can be rejected. A minimized predicate does not contain any redundant atomic predicates. Note that the construction of the properties together with all the steps described in this paragraph is performed only once for each new subscription during the registration process.

Algorithm 3 can match any predicates in the described graph representation, e. g., selection and join predicates. In this paper, it is used to match the predicates

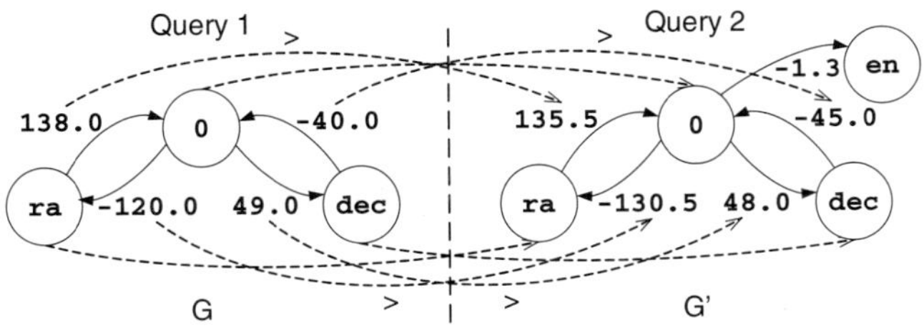

Fig. 4. Matching predicates

of selection operators. The algorithm takes the data structures G and G' of the weighted directed graphs representing the selection predicates of the existing data stream and the new subscription which are to be compared and returns true if the predicates of G' imply those of G, i. e., reusability of the data stream is not prevented by the predicates. One prerequisite for the possibility of data stream sharing is that, for each node v in the node set V of G, there exists an equivalent node v' in the node set V' of G', denoted by $v \hat{=} v'$ in line 4 of Algorithm 3. Nodes are equivalent if the variables represented by them refer to the same element. Furthermore, if two equivalent nodes v and v' have been found, for each edge x connected to v there must be an edge y connected to v' such that the atomic predicate represented by x, denoted by $\zeta(x)$, is compatible with the atomic predicate represented by y, denoted by $\zeta(y)$. In our algorithm, this is the case if $\zeta(x) \Leftarrow \zeta(y)$ in line 9. An example matching for the predicate graphs of Queries 1 and 2 is shown in Figure 4. For brevity, only the variable names instead of the full paths are shown as node labels in the figure. The definition of $\zeta(e)$ for any edge e in a predicate graph G can be formally expressed as

$$\zeta(e) := (sourcelabel(e) \leq targetlabel(e) + weight(e))$$

where $sourcelabel(e)$ and $targetlabel(e)$ denote the absolute path to the variable represented by the source and the target node of edge e, respectively, and $weight(e)$ denotes the weight of edge e.

Window-Based Aggregation. Sharing results of window-based aggregation operators has been studied before [6]. Our approach differs from this previous solution in two ways. First, we introduce a step size in our windows which allows us to explicitly specify when a new aggregate value shall be computed. Second, we consider existing results of other subscriptions for sharing instead of precomputing aggregation results that might never be used. As usual, we categorize aggregation operators using three classes. These classes are distributive (e. g., `min`, `max`, `sum`, `count`), algebraic (e. g., `avg`), and holistic aggregates (e. g., `quantile`). We concentrate on the above mentioned distributive and algebraic aggregation operators here.

The MatchAggregations operation is used in Algorithm 2 to compare the conditions of window-based aggregation operators. Such operators are compared by examining their input data, their results, and their data windows as follows. First, MatchAggregations checks whether the aggregate considered for reuse

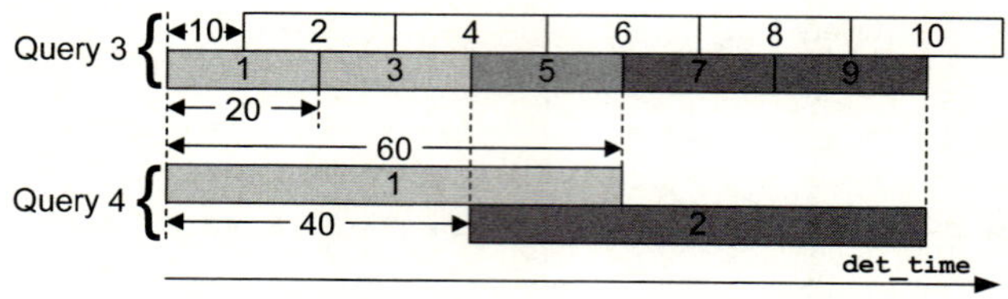

Fig. 5. Reusing window-based aggregates

and the new aggregate employ the same aggregation operator, are based on the same input data, and aggregate the same element. Furthermore, selections in aggregate subscriptions have to be handled more strictly than in other subscriptions. It has to be assured that any selection performed on the aggregated data stream prior to the aggregation is the same in both the reused and the new aggregate subscription. Second, it is checked whether the aggregation result which is considered for sharing has been filtered in any way. As an example consider Query 4 which filters its aggregation result `$a` using the predicate `$a > 1.3`. Reusing such aggregate values for computing more coarse-grained window aggregates is not possible in general since a part of the necessary data might have been filtered out. However, they can still be reused for aggregates that apply the same or a more restrictive filter on the aggregation result as long as all other prerequisites for reusability are fulfilled.

Eventually, the data windows of both operators are examined. For time-based windows, reuse is only possible if both windows have the same ordered reference element, e. g., `det_time` in Queries 3 and 4. For both, time-based and item-based windows, we require the window size and the step size of the windows to be compatible for being able to reuse existing aggregate values without any further complex optimizations or transformations. One requirement for this is that the window size of the new subscription is a multiple of the window size of the data stream considered for reuse. This guarantees that a fixed number of reused windows fits into one new window. Furthermore, the size of a reused aggregate's data window must be a multiple of its step size. This assures that a sequence of non-overlapping windows, i. e., aggregate values, covering the whole input data can be obtained—possibly by ignoring some windows. Note that ignored aggregate values might have to be temporarily buffered to be reused for computing subsequent values of the new aggregate. The situation for the step sizes of both windows is analogous to their window sizes as described above, guaranteeing that the reused aggregate delivers an aggregate value at least each time the new aggregate has to produce one. These three conditions for data window shareability can be expressed as $\Delta' \bmod \Delta = 0$, $\Delta \bmod \mu = 0$, and $\mu' \bmod \mu = 0$. The sharing of result data streams of window-based aggregation operators is illustrated in Figure 5, using Queries 3 and 4 of Section 2 as examples.

Note that for the values of `avg` aggregates to be shareable, we internally represent such aggregates by their appropriate `sum` and `count` values. These values are actually transmitted in the super-peer network. The final aggregate value is computed at the super-peer at which the corresponding subscription is registered by evaluating `(sum/count)`. The described internal representation of `avg` aggregates also enables their reuse for computing `sum` and `count` aggregates, i. e., the requirement of equal aggregate operators for shareability as introduced above can be relaxed.

4 Evaluation

This section presents the results of some performance evaluations that we conducted using our prototype implementation in the StreamGlobe system. For the evaluation, the system was installed on a blade server. Each super-peer ran on one blade. The blades had a 2.8 GHz Xeon Processor and 1 GB of main memory each. They were interconnected by a 100 MBit/s LAN. We report on two scenarios here. The first one is based on the network topology of the example scenario of Section 1 and involves 8 super-peers, 1 data stream, and 25 queries. The second scenario uses a 4 × 4 grid topology with 16 super-peers, 2 data streams, and 100 queries. All data streams and queries are based on real astrophysical data. The queries were generated using query templates for selection, projection, and aggregation queries. Constant values, e. g., in selection predicates or data window definitions, were chosen uniformely from a predefined set of values to enable a certain degree of shareability.

For each scenario, we compare three strategies. *Data shipping* simply transmits the whole input data stream for each query from the data source to the target super-peer using a shortest path in the network. The whole query evaluation takes place at the target super-peer. *Query shipping* evaluates each query completely at the super-peer that the data source is registered at. The query result is transmitted to the target peer again using a shortest path in the network. This of course only works for queries that reference a single input data stream, which is the case in our example queries used here. Finally, *stream sharing* uses our previously described optimization algorithms.

Benchmark results in terms of average CPU load in percent and average network traffic on network connections in kbps are shown in Figure 6 for the first scenario. As can be clearly seen from the diagrams, query shipping leads to massive peaks of CPU load at data stream source peers since all computation on the respective stream is executed there. On the other hand, network traffic caused by this strategy is comparatively low. Data shipping, as expected, causes much more network traffic but also relatively high CPU load over the whole range of super-peers in the network since all the data needs to be forwarded over many peers and network connections, often even multiple times. Stream sharing distributes computational load much better over the peers in the network than query shipping and causes less overall CPU load than data shipping. Furthermore, network traffic is also greatly reduced compared to the other two strategies due to the effects of reusing streams for multiple queries.

The results for the second scenario in terms of average CPU load in percent and accumulated network traffic in MBit including both, incoming and outgoing traffic for each super-peer are shown in Figure 7. The results clearly indicate, that our approach significantly reduces network traffic at single peers as well as overall in the network. Note that, while data shipping transmits the whole original data stream through the network multiple times, once for each subscription referencing the stream as input, query shipping already significantly reduces

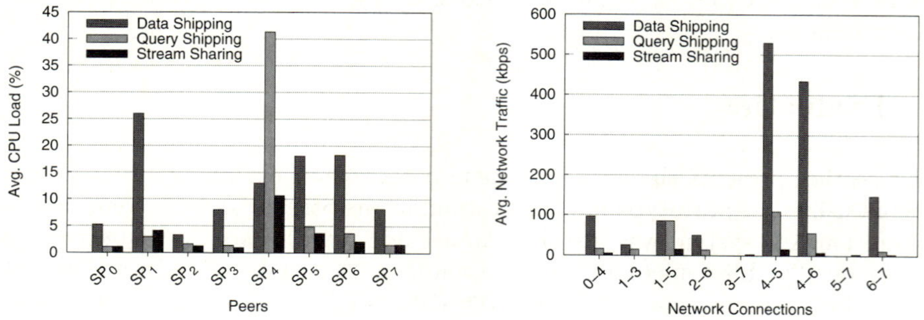

Fig. 6. Extended example scenario: 8 super-peers, 1 data stream, 25 queries

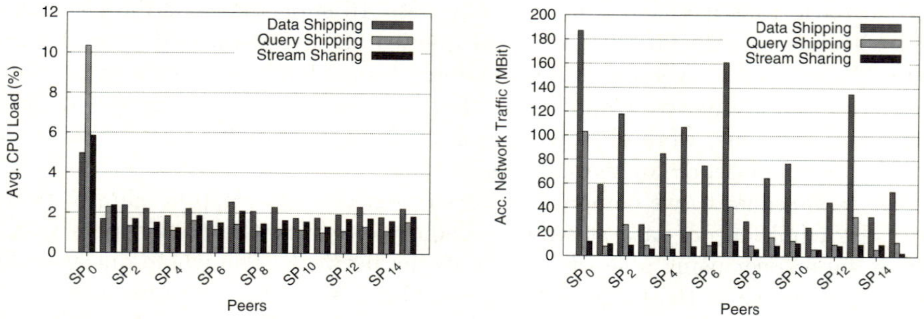

Fig. 7. 4 × 4 grid scenario: 16 super-peers, 2 data streams, 100 queries

network traffic by means of early filtering at the data stream source. However, like data shipping, query shipping still transmits one data stream per query in the network. Stream sharing is able to further reduce network traffic greatly by using multi-subscription optimization, i. e., transmitting data streams in the network only once and sharing them for satisfying multiple similar or equal queries. CPU load is comparable to the other approaches on most peers in this scenario, except for the peak at the data stream source node for query shipping.

We expect our approach to distribute load better over peers in larger scenarios than the other two approaches. This expectation is confirmed by the results of an additional test where we limited the maximum CPU load of peers to 10 % of their actual capacity and the maximum bandwith of network connections between peers to 1 MBit/s. We then used the second scenario and determined how many queries had to be rejected by the system because no query evaluation plan without causing overload on peers or network connections could be found. While data shipping had to reject 47 and query shipping had to reject 35 out of the 100 queries that we tried to register, our stream sharing approach only rejected 2 queries in this scenario.

Of course, stream sharing does not come for free. Table 1 shows the times in milliseconds a query took from the beginning of its registration until it was successfully installed and executed in the network in the two benchmark scenarios. The stream sharing approach stays within a factor of 3 of the other two much simpler approaches. This is acceptable, since we are dealing with continuous queries that usually remain registered over long periods of time.

Table 1. Query registration times

Time (ms)	Average		Minimum		Maximum	
Scenario	1	2	1	2	1	2
Data Shipping	931	1363	390	265	2078	4953
Query Shipping	890	1287	284	250	2032	4802
Stream Sharing	2153	3558	509	672	5025	11855

5 Related Work

Numerous DSMSs have been proposed in recent years [7,8,9,10,11,12]. The contributions presented in this paper can be used to augment existing DSMSs to support the efficient integration of incrementally subscribed continuous queries.

The approach of optimizing query execution by computing identical or similar parts of queries only once and reusing them multiple times for various queries is similar to multi-query optimization [13]. However, instead of optimizing a set of queries all at once, we incrementally optimize queries one after another when they are registered in the network, based on the current network state. Sharing of work between queries over streams has also been addressed in previous work [14,15]. Our solution differs from these approaches in that we can adaptively distribute subscription evaluation among peers in a network.

Of further interest is the problem of query containment, which has also been discussed in the context of XML queries with nesting [16]. Query containment, especially for XML queries, is a difficult problem. We were able to make it manageable by exploiting the properties of our distributed system architecture.

Finally, for more details on data stream sharing, we refer to an extended version of this paper [17].

6 Conclusion

In this paper, we have presented a subscription language, a properties approach, a cost model, and algorithms for registering continuous queries over data streams in P2P networks using data stream sharing. Our approach takes three steps. First, the properties of a newly registered subscription are constructed. Second, shareable data streams generated for answering previously registered subscriptions in the network are identified by matching properties. An appropriate stream for answering the new subscription is chosen according to a cost model that focuses on the reduction of network traffic and peer load. Finally, operators are placed in the network to execute the new subscription. An experimental evaluation confirms the effectiveness of our approach.

We are currently working on an enhanced version of the approach presented in this paper that is able to handle nested queries and to widen data streams. This enables the system to consider data streams for sharing that initially do not contain all the necessary data for a new query but can be altered to do so by changing some operators in the network. Apart from that, there are numerous opportunities for future work. One is to address the issue of scalability by introducing a hierarchical network organization with several interconnected subnets where each subnet is optimized separately.

References

1. Stegmaier, B., Kuntschke, R., Kemper, A.: StreamGlobe: Adaptive Query Processing and Optimization in Streaming P2P Environments. In: Proc. of the Intl. Workshop on Data Management for Sensor Networks, Toronto, Canada (2004) 88–97
2. Kuntschke, R., Stegmaier, B., Kemper, A., Reiser, A.: StreamGlobe: Processing and Sharing Data Streams in Grid-Based P2P Infrastructures. In: Proc. of the Intl. Conf. on Very Large Data Bases, Trondheim, Norway (2005) 1259–1262
3. Yang, B., Garcia-Molina, H.: Designing a Super-Peer Network. In: Proc. of the IEEE Intl. Conf. on Data Engineering, Bangalore, India (2003) 49–60
4. W3C: XQuery 1.0: An XML Query Language (W3C Candidate Recommendation, November 3rd, 2005) (2005) `http://www.w3.org/TR/xquery/`.
5. Rosenkrantz, D.J., Hunt, H.B.: Processing Conjunctive Predicates and Queries. In: Proc. of the Intl. Conf. on Very Large Data Bases, Montreal, Canada (1980) 64–72
6. Arasu, A., Widom, J.: Resource Sharing in Continuous Sliding-Window Aggregates. [18] 336–347
7. Abadi, D.J., Ahmad, Y., Balazinska, M., Çetintemel, U., Cherniack, M., Hwang, J.H., Lindner, W., Maskey, A.S., Rasin, A., Ryvkina, E., Tatbul, N., Xing, Y., Zdonik, S.: The Design of the Borealis Stream Processing Engine. In: Proc. of the Conf. on Innovative Data Systems Research, Asilomar, CA, USA (2005) 277–289
8. Arasu, A., Babcock, B., Babu, S., Datar, M., Ito, K., Motwani, R., Nishizawa, I., Srivastava, U., Thomas, D., Varma, R., Widom, J.: STREAM: The Stanford Stream Data Manager. IEEE Data Engineering Bulletin **26**(1) (2003) 19–26
9. Chandrasekaran, S., Cooper, O., Deshpande, A., Franklin, M.J., Hellerstein, J.M., Hong, W., Krishnamurthy, S., Madden, S., Raman, V., Reiss, F., Shah, M.A.: TelegraphCQ: Continuous Dataflow Processing for an Uncertain World. [19]
10. Chen, J., DeWitt, D.J., Tian, F., Wang, Y.: NiagaraCQ: A Scalable Continuous Query System for Internet Databases. In: Proc. of the ACM SIGMOD Intl. Conf. on Management of Data, Dallas, TX, USA (2000) 379–390
11. Cherniack, M., Balakrishnan, H., Balazinska, M., Carney, D., Çetintemel, U., Xing, Y., Zdonik, S.B.: Scalable Distributed Stream Processing. [19]
12. Yao, Y., Gehrke, J.: The Cougar Approach to In-Network Query Processing in Sensor Networks. ACM SIGMOD Record **31**(3) (2002) 9–18
13. Sellis, T.K.: Multiple-Query Optimization. ACM Trans. on Database Systems **13**(1) (1988) 23–52
14. Madden, S., Shah, M.A., Hellerstein, J.M., Raman, V.: Continuously Adaptive Continuous Queries over Streams. In: Proc. of the ACM SIGMOD Intl. Conf. on Management of Data, Madison, WI, USA (2002) 49–60
15. Krishnamurthy, S., Franklin, M.J., Hellerstein, J.M., Jacobson, G.: The Case for Precision Sharing. [18] 972–986
16. Dong, X., Halevy, A.Y., Tatarinov, I.: Containment of Nested XML Queries. [18] 132–143
17. Kuntschke, R., Stegmaier, B., Kemper, A.: Data Stream Sharing. Technical Report TUM-I0504, Technische Universität München (2005)
18. Proc. of the Intl. Conf. on Very Large Data Bases. In: Proc. of the Intl. Conf. on Very Large Data Bases, Toronto, Canada (2004)
19. Proc. of the Conf. on Innovative Data Systems Research. In: Proc. of the Conf. on Innovative Data Systems Research, Asilomar, CA, USA (2003)

Flexible Pattern Management Within PSYCHO

Barbara Catania and Anna Maddalena

Dipartimento di Informatica e Scienze dell'Informazione
Università degli Studi di Genova, Italy
{catania, maddalena}@disi.unige.it

Abstract. Patterns are concise, but rich in semantic, representation of data. The approaches proposed in the literature and by commercial systems for pattern management usually deal with few types of knowledge artifacts and mainly concern pattern extraction issues. Little effort has been posed in designing an overall framework dedicated to the management of different types of patterns, possibly user-defined, in an homogeneous way. PSYCHO (Pattern based SYstem arCHitecture prOtotype) is a recently developed tool, built on top of Oracle technologies, for generating, representing, and manipulating heterogeneous patterns, possibly user-defined. The aim of this paper is to present the PSYCHO system, by discussing the underlying theory, the reference architecture, and providing concrete examples of its usage.

1 Introduction

A pattern can be defined as a *compact* and *rich in semantics* representation of raw data. Clusters, association rules, frequent itemsets, symptom-diagnosis correlation, and moving object trajectories are common examples of patterns. Pattern management is an important issue in many different contexts, such as data mining, information retrieval, image processing, and clickstream analysis.

The specific characteristics of patterns make traditional DBMSs unsuitable for pattern representation and management. In particular, patterns can be generated from different application contexts resulting in very heterogeneous structures. Moreover, patterns can be mined (*a-posteriori patterns*) but also known by the users and used for example to check how well some data source is represented by them (*a-priori patterns*). To maintain the semantic alignment between patterns and raw data it is also important to determine whether existing patterns, after a certain time, still represent the data source from which they have been generated, possibly being able to update pattern information. Finally, all kinds of patterns should be manipulated (e.g. extracted, synchronized, deleted) and queried through dedicated languages. All the previous reasons motivate the need for ad hoc *Pattern Management Systems (PBMSs)*, i.e., *systems for handling (storing/processing/retrieving) patterns defined over raw data* [10].

Recently, several approaches have been provided for pattern management. Scientific community efforts mainly deal with the definition of a pattern management framework providing a full support for heterogeneous patterns. In the

T. Grust et al. (Eds.): EDBT 2006 Workshops, LNCS 4254, pp. 789–800, 2006.

3W Model [5] and in the PANDA framework [10], raw data are stored and managed in a traditional way by using a DBMS whereas patterns are stored and managed by a dedicated PBMS. In the inductive databases approach, mainly investigated in the context of the CINQ project [6], raw data and patterns are stored together, by using the same data model, and managed in the same way. On the other hand, industrial proposals mainly deal with standard representation purposes for patterns resulting from data mining, in order to support their exchange between different architectures. Examples of such approaches are the Predictive Model Markup Language (PMML) [11] and the Java Data Mining API (JDM) [8]. PMML simply deals with pattern representation issues, providing an XML-based format to represent data mining results and the used mining algorithm. JDM represents patterns within the Java environment and provides manipulation support through JAVA primitives. In all these cases, no user-defined patterns can be specified. Concerning commercial systems, the most important DBMSs (e.g., Oracle and MS-SQL Server) provide an applicational layer offering features for representing and managing typical data mining patterns.

Even if several approaches have been proposed, an integrated environment satisfying the requirements introduced above is still missing. Starting from these limitations and relying on the results achieved in the context of the PANDA Project [10], we have designed and implemented PSYCHO (*Pattern based System arCHitecture prOtotype*) [4,12], a system built on top of Oracle technologies, for generating, representing, and manipulating heterogeneous patterns, possibly user-defined. According to our knowledge, PSYCHO is the first proposal of a PBMS system coping with most of the features cited above. Differently from existing proposals, that are mainly focused on common data mining patterns (e.g. association rules, frequent itemsets, and clusters), PSYCHO allows the design of user-defined pattern types and the management of both a-posteriori and a-priori patterns. Moreover, by exploiting the logical model proposed in [3], it allows the representation of pattern validity information and pattern hierarchies. Besides basic manipulation operations, PSYCHO supports synchronization between patterns and raw data. Concerning query capabilities, PSYCHO, by exploiting the power of the logical model, supports interesting queries combining both data and patterns in order to get a deeper knowledge of their correlations.

This paper is organized as follows. In Section 2, the model underlying the PSYCHO development is briefly discussed. Details about the PSYCHO architecture are presented in Section 3, while Section 4 is focused on PSYCHO usage. Finally, Section 5 presents some concluding remarks and outlines future work.

2 PSYCHO: The Model

PSYCHO is a prototype of a Pattern Based Management System (PBMS) exploiting the logical framework for pattern management proposed in the context of the PANDA Project [10]. In particular, it relies on the logical model and the languages for pattern generation, manipulation, and querying introduced in [2,3,4]. The PSYCHO logical model used to represent patterns is based on three basic concepts: *pattern type*, *pattern*, and *class* (see [3,10] for further details).

A *pattern type* gives a formal description of the pattern structure of each of its instances. It is characterized by six components: (i) the *pattern name* n; (ii) the *structure schema* ss, which defines the structure of the patterns instances of the pattern type; (iii) the *source schema* ds, which describes the dataset from which patterns, instances of the pattern type being defined, are constructed; (iv) the *measure schema* ms, which is a tuple describing the measures which quantify the quality of the source data representation achieved by the pattern; (v) the *formula* f, carrying the semantics of the pattern. f is a constraint-based formula describing, possibly in an approximate way, the relation between data represented by the pattern and the pattern structure; (vi) the *validity period schema* vs, defining the schema of the temporal validity interval associated with each instance of the pattern type.

Patterns are instances of a specific pattern type, containing the proper instantiation of the corresponding schema components in the pattern type. In particular, the formula component of a pattern is obtained from the one in the corresponding pattern type pt by instantiating each attribute appearing in ss with the corresponding value, and letting the attributes appearing in ds range over the source space.

We remark that the data source represents the overall dataset over which the pattern has been extracted (in case of a-posteriori patterns). On the other hand, the formula represents, in an intensional and possibly approximated way, the specific subset of data represented by the pattern.

A *class* is a set of semantically related patterns and constitutes the key concept in defining a pattern query language. A class is defined for a given pattern type and contains only patterns of that type. A pattern may belong to any number of classes. If it does not belong to any class, it cannot be queried.

In the context of the PANDA Project [10], some interesting relationships supporting hierarchical pattern definition have also been proposed. Among them, we recall: the *composition* relationship - between a pattern and those used to define its structure - and the *refinement* relationship - between a pattern and those belonging to its data source. PSYCHO supports the definition of complex patterns based on refinement and composition hierarchy notions.

Based on the considered pattern model, PSYCHO provides three languages for the management of both a-priori and a-posteriori patterns: (i) the *Pattern Definition Language (PSY-PDL)*, used for defining new pattern types, classes, and *mining functions*, used for pattern generation; (ii) the *Pattern Manipulation Language (PSY-PML)*, used to perform operations such as insertion, extraction, deletion, update, synchronization of patterns, as well as insertion or removal of patterns into or from a class defined for the proper pattern type; (iii) the *Pattern Query Language (PSY-PQL)*, used to retrieve patterns and correlate them with data they represent (*cross-over queries*). For all these languages, an SQL-like syntax has been provided.

3 PSYCHO: The Architecture

The PSYCHO [4] architecture relies on Oracle and Java technologies and it is composed of three distinct layers as depicted in Fig.1: (i) the physical layer, containing both patterns and data (possibly residing at different sites); (ii) the middle layer, coinciding with the kernel of the system and supporting all functionalities for pattern manipulation and retrieval; (iii) the external layer, corresponding to a set of user interfaces from which the user can send requests to the engine and import/export data in other formats. Due to design and implementation choices, the current version of PSYCHO is tightly coupled with Oracle technology and, when possible, it allows the user to exploit the Oracle Data Mining (ODM) server functionalities [9].

In the following, we describe each one of the PSYCHO layer (Sections 3.1, 3.2, and 3.3); then, in Section 3.4, we discuss the technology adopted for the communication between layers.

3.1 Physical Layer

The Physical Layer contains both the *Pattern Base* and the *Data Source.*

The *Pattern Base* component contains pattern types, a-priori and a-posteriori patterns, and classes. PSYCHO relies on the object-relational model of Oracle 10g [9] for pattern storage. Concerning the pattern formula, we consider two distinct representations: an operational one, by which the formula is indeed a predicate over data source elements implemented as an Oracle PL/SQL stored function; a declarative one, by which the formula is just a representation of a linear constraint formula (see the Formula Handler). Since the provided implementation of the Pattern Base exploits the Oracle logical model, the PSY-PML and PSY-PQL interfaces are realized using PL/SQL functions and procedures which are invoked by the Java application implementing the PBMS Engine.

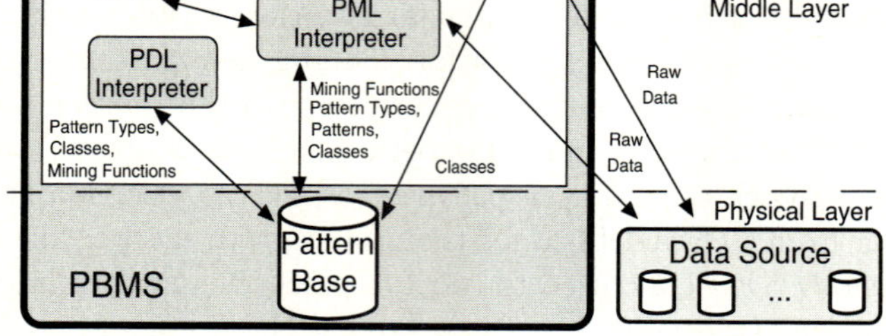

Fig. 1. The 3 layers architecture of PSYCHO

The *Data Source* is a distributed repository containing raw data from which patterns have been extracted (in case of a-posteriori patterns). Various technology can be used to store the source datasets: relational or object-relational DBMSs, XML dataset, streams, etc. In the current PSYCHO version, raw data are stored in Oracle 10g DBMS.

3.2 Middle Layer

The Middle Layer consists of the *PBMS Engine* component, which supports all functionalities for pattern manipulation and retrieval, by adequately using the Pattern Base and Data Sources when required. The PBMS Engine and the Pattern Base represent the core of the PSYCHO prototype. The PBMS Engine has been implemented in Java and is logically divided into three main submodules, each of which is dedicated to parse, interpret, and execute PSY-PQL, PSY-PML, and PSY-PDL requests, respectively, that are sent to the physical layer components. There is also a dedicated component to handle intensional pattern-data mapping, i.e. the pattern formula component.

The *PDL Interpreter* takes as input, from the higher layer, a PSY-PDL request for a pattern type or class definition and translates it into calls to the right functions and procedures defined in the Pattern Base.

The *PML Interpreter* takes as input a PSY-PML request and translates it into calls to the right functions/procedures of the Pattern Base. Some manipulation operations, such as, for instance, pattern extraction and synchronization, require an interaction with the Data Source to get the data from which patterns have to be generated. In the current release, pattern extraction is performed by using either mining functions provided by ODM server (i.e., a variant of the A-priori algorithm for association rules or the K-means or the proprietary O-cluster algorithm for clusters) or other mining functions (possibly defined by the user) stored in the PBMS. We outline that the Query Processor has to be invoked by the PML Interpreter in case patterns have to be filtered (e.g. only patterns with specific measures have to be generated, synchronized, deleted, or inserted in a given class).

The *Query Processor* translates an input PSY-PQL query into calls to the right functions and procedures defined in the Pattern Base. For non cross-over queries, only the Pattern Base and, eventually, the Formula Handler are involved in the query process. On the other side, to execute cross-over queries, the Data Source may also be required. We point out that queries can also use formulas for pattern comparison and selection. When formulas are used under the operational semantics, the queries are executed directly by the Query Processor. On the other hand, when they are used under the declarative semantics, the Formula Handler module is required to execute the query. As already said, some query requests can be generated by the PML Interpreter; in this case the Query Processor computes the answer and sends it directly to the PML Interpreter.

The *Formula Handler* deals with the declarative management of formulas, i.e., with constraints. It is used by the PSY-PML and PSY-PQL interpreters when computations over formula constraints are required. Within PSYCHO, the Formula

Handler is implemented as a Java module, using the Jasper package [7] for interacting with SICStus Prolog environment [13]. Computations over formulas concern comparisons (equivalence, containment) between the specific sets of data from which patterns have been extracted and are implemented by the Formula Handler through typical logical operations such as equivalence or subsumption.

3.3 External Layer

The External Layer corresponds to a set of user interfaces from which the user can send requests to the engine and import/export data in other formats. User requests can be specified through a *GUI*, providing a visual environment (in the current release, it is a simple shell), where the user can specify his/her request using an SQL-like syntax. The *Import/Export module* supports the import and the export in the PBMS of patterns already represented in standard formats (e.g. PMML models [11]).

3.4 Communication Between Layers

As already stated, the Pattern Base is integrated within the Oracle DBMS managing the Data Source. The PBMS Engine is placed immediately above the Pattern Base. It creates and manages the connection with the Oracle DBMS and the calls to the stored functions and procedures defined in the Pattern Base. The communication between the Pattern Base and the PBMS Engine is, therefore, the classical communication between a Java application and a DBMS, through a JDBC driver. On the other hand, the communication between the PSYCHO Engine and the external layer is established using the mechanism of sockets. In this way the whole system is more flexible and a completely distributed architecture can be realized, where the different PSYCHO components - i.e., the pattern base, the data sources, the PBMS engine, and the external modules - can be placed on different hosts. In details, the PBMS Engine opens a socket on a fixed port and waits for connections from the outside. Whenever an external module needs to communicate with the engine, it makes a connection, creates a serializable object that encapsulate the request, and sends it to the PBMS Engine.

4 PSYCHO: Usage

In the following, PSYCHO usage and its peculiarities in pattern management are highlighted by considering a typical data mining scenario dealing with market-basket association rules. Additional examples can be found at [12]. Association rules are a well-known data mining pattern type, therefore they are managed by any commercial system dealing with data mining [9,8]. However, PSYCHO allows one to perform several operations that are not directly supported by other existing tools.

We assume source data is stored in a table with schema $(DSid, Item_1, ..., Item_n)$, where each tuple represents a sale transaction identified by $DSid$; $Item_i$

```
n:  AssociationRule
ss: TUPLE(head: SET(String),
          body: SET(String))
ds: BAG(transaction: SET(String))
ms: TUPLE(confidence: REAL,
          support: REAL)
f:  ∀x(x ∈ head ∨ x ∈ body ⇒
       x ∈ transaction)
vs: [start : DAY, end : DAY)
```

(a)

```
pid: 512
s:   < head={'Boots'},
       body={'Socks','Hat'} >
d:   'SELECT SETOF(article) AS transaction
     FROM sales
     GROUP BY transactionId'
m:   < confidence=0.75, support=0.55 >
f:   {transaction : ∀x(
     x ∈ {'Boots','Socks','Hat'}
     ⇒ x ∈ transaction)}
v:   [1-DEC-2005,31-MAR-2006)
```

(b)

Fig. 2. Association Rules modeling: (a) the pattern type *AssociationRule* and (b) one of its pattern instance

is either 1 or 0, and $Item_i = 1$ means that the corresponding transaction contains $Item_i$. According to the PANDA model, the pattern type for modeling association rules and one of its pattern instances are shown in Fig.2(a) and 2(b).

Besides the structure - i.e., head and body in the case of association rules - and the measures - i.e., support and confidence in the case of association rules - in PSYCHO each pattern type is associated with three additional components: the extensional formula, the intensional formula, and the validity period. The extensional formula is just a PL/SQL function that takes a source dataset and returns the subset of such dataset (possibly approximatively) represented by the pattern. The intensional formula has the same meaning, but it is intensionally represented through a Prolog predicate, defined by a set of linear constraints. Note that the two formulas used by PSYCHO (i.e., the extensional one and the intensional one) implement the formula component of the underlying logical model under an operational and a declarative perspective, respectively. The validity period is just a temporal interval inside which we assume the information represented by the pattern is reliable. The PSY-PDL command to create the pattern type *AssociationRule* is sketched in Fig.3(a).

In the following, we show a concrete example of PSYCHO usage by describing typical steps of a data mining process concerning pattern generation and system population, pattern analysis and querying, and pattern maintenance.

PBMS Population and Class Management. In this step, we show how PSYCHO can be used to: (i) use various mining functions to extract a-posteriori patterns; (ii) directly insert a-priori patterns; (iii) create new patterns by recomputing existing ones; (iv) handle pattern classes.

Pattern extraction. Given a pattern type, several mining functions can be used to extract patterns of that type from a given dataset. For example, to mine association rules, we can use a PSYCHO proprietary Java mining function *apriori* implementing the well-known Apriori algorithm. [1]. We

```
CREATE PATTERN TYPE AssociationRule
STRUCTURE head CharArray, body CharArray /* CharArray is an already
defined type*/
...
MEASURE support REAL, confidence REAL
...
FORMULA EXTENSIONAL ON varDS ...
/* retrieve items in the source dataset effectively represented by a
pattern of type AssociationRule*/
FORMULA INTENSIONAL ARFormula_INT; /* ARFormula_INT is an existing
Prolog predicate */
```

(a)

```
CREATE PATTERN TYPE ClusterOfAR
STRUCTURE ruleset ARSET
/*ARSET is an already defined type modeling arrays of AssociationRule
references*/
...
MEASURE Svalidity REAL
...
FORMULA EXTENSIONAL ON varDS ...
/* retrieve items in the source dataset effectively represented by a
pattern of this type*/
```

(b)

Fig. 3. (a) PSY-PDL definition of the pattern type *AssociationRules* and (b) PSY-PDL definition of the pattern type *ClusterOfAR*

may specify that the support of the extracted rules must be higher than 0.4 and the confidence higher than 0.7; the validity period of the extracted rules is set from 01-jul-2005 to 10-aug-2005. Before extracting patterns, it may be useful to create a class, called *AR_PSY*, where extracted patterns are stored (if no class is used, patterns are stored in the system but they cannot be used in queries) (see Fig. 4(a)). Moreover, it is also possible to mine association rules by using different mining functions. For instance, other association rules can be extracted by using the mining function *Apriori_ODM* calling the one available in ODM [9] within a PSY-PML command similar to the previous one.

Direct insertion. Single association rules can also be directly inserted in PSYCHO by using the 'DIRECT INSERT' PSY-PML command (see Fig.4(b)).

Recomputation. New patterns can also be generated by recomputing measures of existing ones over a new data source. Various functions recomputing measure values for instances of a given pattern type, upon a given dataset can be defined. For association rules, PSYCHO provides a measure function for computing confidence and support over a given data source, named *AR_mf*. Fig. 4(c) reports an example of pattern recomputation using this measure function.

```
CREATE CLASS AR_PSY OF
AssociationRule;

EXTRACT PATTERNS OF
AssociationRule ar
FROM itemsDS_30
USING Apriori(0.4,0.7)
VALID FROM '01-jul-2005'
      TO '10-aug-2005'
INTO CLASS AR_PSY;
```

(a)

```
DIRECT INSERT PATTERN
OF AssociationRule ar
FROM itemsDS_30
STRUCTURE (
chararray('BREAD','MILK'),
chararray('JAM','BUTTER','WINE')
)
MEASURE (0.5,0.7)
VALID FROM '01-aug-2005'
      TO '15-aug-2005'
INTO CLASS AR_PSY;
```

(b)

```
RECOMPUTE PATTERNS
OF AssociationRule ar
ON itemsDS_5
USING AR_mf;
```

(c)

```
CREATE CLASS AR_high_support
OF AssociationRule;

INSERT INTO CLASS
AR_high_support ar
WHERE ar.m.support >= 0.5;
```

(d)

Fig. 4. Manipulation operations over *AssociationRules*: (a) Extraction of association rules using the *apriori* mining function; (b) Direct insertion of association rules into class *AR_PSY*; (c) Recomputation of association rules over dataset *itemsDS_5* by using function *AR_mf*; (d) Definition and population of class *AR_high_support*

Class Management. Suppose the user wants to define a class containing all association rules having support greater than 0.5%. Such class, named *AR_high_support*, can be created and association rules satisfying the previous condition can be inserted in it (see Fig.4(d)). The class can then be used for query purposes.

Querying. PSY-PQL supports the following querying features: (i) simple queries involving predicates dealing with pattern components; (ii) pattern composition; (iii) nested queries; (iv) pattern-data reasoning (cross-over queries). In the following, we discuss each class of queries.

Simple queries. Simple queries allow one to select patterns from a given class, according to a variety of predicates. In particular, PSYCHO supports selection based on two validity notions: temporal validity and semantic validity. A pattern is temporally valid with respect to a certain date if its validity period contains the specified date. A pattern is semantically valid with respect to a certain dataset and a set of thresholds if the pattern measures computed over the input datasets are better than those provided as input. Several examples of queries checking temporal and semantic validity are shown in Table 1 (e.g. Q2,Q4,Q7).

Pattern composition. Within PSYCHO, different types of joins are available. In the actual release, two types of join are provided: a general one (*CJOIN*)

Table 1. Several PSY-PQL queries over class *AR_PSY*

QID	Query	PSY-PQL statement
Q1	Retrieve all association rules from *AR_PSY* with confidence greater than or equal to 0.75	SELECT * FROM AR_PSY ar WHERE ar.m.confidence >= 0.75;
Q2	Retrieve all association rules that are valid on July 20, 2005	SELECT * FROM AR_PSY ar WHERE isTvalid(ar,'20-jul-2005')=1;
Q3	Retrieve all association rules valid during the period August,1 - August,10 2005	SELECT * FROM AR_PSY ar WHERE during(ar.v, valPeriod('01-aug-2005','10-aug-2005'))=1;
Q4	Retrieve all semantically valid rules (with respect to their data source), with support and confidence greater than or equal to 0.4	SELECT * FROM AR_PSY ar WHERE isSvalid(ar,ar.d,'AR_mf', AssociationRuleMeasure(null,0.4,0.4))=1;
Q5	Determine all association rules with confidence greater or equal to 0.75 or which are temporally valid in August,15 2005	SELECT * FROM AR_PSY ar WHERE ar.m.confidence >= 0.75 OR isTvalid(ar,'15-aug-2005')=1;
Q6	Determine all association rules, obtained as the transitive closure of two existing association rules, having at least two items in the body	SELECT * FROM AR_PSY ar1 CJOIN AR_PSY ar2 WITH Trans_closure_ar WHERE ar2.s.body.count >= 2;
Q7	Select among rules with at least confidence value equal to 0.7 the ones which are temporally valid in 15-aug-2005	SELECT * FROM (SELECT * FROM AR_PSY ar WHERE ar.m.confidence >= 0.7) rule WHERE isTvalid(rule,'15-aug-2005') = 1;
Q8	Which data are represented by association rules with confidence greater than 0.75?	DRILL THROUGH (SELECT * FROM AR_PSY ar WHERE ar.m.confidence > 0.75) rule;
Q9	Determine whether the association rule with PID=1001348 is suitable for representing a certain dataset *itemsDS_30*	DATA COVERING (SELECT * FROM AR_PSY pr WHERE pr.PID = 1001348) ar FOR itemsDS_30;
Q10	Determine which patterns, belonging to class *AR_PSY* and having a confidence higher than 0.8, represent dataset *itemsDS_30*	PATTERN COVERING itemsDS_30 FOR AR_PSY ar WHERE ar.m.confidence >= 0.8;

and a specific one ($INTERSECTIONJOIN$). The $CJOIN$ takes two classes and, for each pair of patterns, the first belonging to the first class, the second belonging to the second one, it applies a specified composition function, specifying the structure of the resulting patterns. On the other hand, the $INTERSECTIONJOIN$ takes two classes and returns new patterns, whose structure is a combination of the input structures and whose intensional formula is the conjunction of input intensional formulas. For instance, the user may be interested in calculating an association rule obtained as the transitive closure of two existing association rules $A \leftarrow B$ and $B \leftarrow C$ extracted from data sources D_1 and D_2, respectively. The new association rule $A \leftarrow C$ can be obtained by applying function $Trans\_closure\_ar$, which generates such a new rule by computing also a new data source, which is the union of D_1 and D_2, and a new validity period, which is the intersection of the validity periods of the two input rules. PSY-PDL supports the specification of such composition function (see [12] for more details). Query Q6 in Table 1 is an example of PSY-PQL CJOIN query.

Nested queries. PSY-PQL queries can also be nested. In the current version, nesting is provided in the *FROM* clause (see Q7 in Table 1).

Cross-over queries. PSY-PQL supports pattern-data reasoning, i.e., it allows the user to specify queries involving both data and patterns. Such kind of queries are quite important in pattern management, since they allow the user to discover interesting (possibly new) correlations between patterns and data. Some examples of such queries are reported in Table 1 (Q8,Q9,Q10).

Advanced manipulation operations. Differently from most existing systems and standards, PSYCHO supports various types of update operations (see Table 2): (i) synchronization, (ii) set validity, and (iii) validate.

Synchronization. It allows the user to synchronize pattern measures with the current data source, that may be changed with respect to its status at extraction time, using a specific measure function. In order to perform this operation a measure function defined for the pattern type of the patterns you want to synchronize has to be used.

Validate. Validating a pattern means synchronizing it, using a certain measure function, if the new measures are better then the original ones, or recomputing it, if this condition is not satisfied.

Set Validity. Since PSYCHO supports a time validity associated with patterns, a manipulation operation to update the validity period of a pattern is provided.

Pattern Hierarchies. PSYCHO supports hierarchies of patterns, by implementing refinement and composition relationships (see Section 2). Suppose we are interested in clusters of association rules describing correlations among sold products based on some grouping criteria (for instance, a simple clustering criteria could just divide a set of association rules into two clusters based on their

Table 2. PSY-PML update operations over class *AR_PSY*

Update Operation	PSY-PML statement
Synchronize all association rules using measure function *AR_mf*	UPDATE PATTERNS OF AssociationRule ar SYNCHRONIZE USING AR_mf WHERE INCLASS(ar,'AR_PSY')=1;
Validate rules in class *AR_PSY*	UPDATE PATTERNS OF AssociationRule ar VALIDATE USING AR_mf WHERE inclass(ar, 'AR_PSY')=1 INTO CLASS AR_PSY;
Set the validity period of all association rules starting at 10-*jun*-2005 and ending at 31-*aug*-2005	UPDATE PATTERNS OF AssociationRule ar SET VALIDITY FROM '10-jun-2005' TO '31-aug-2005' WHERE INCLASS(ar,'AR_PSY')=1;

semantic validity with respect to a certain dataset). By using PSY-PDL, a new pattern type *ClusterOfAR* can be defined exploiting the refinement relationship, i.e., classes of association rules previously created can be considered the data source (see Fig.3(b)). As in the case of non-hierarchical patterns, PSYCHO supports the manipulation and querying of hierarchical patterns.

5 Concluding Remarks

In this paper, we have presented PSYCHO, a prototype system for pattern management developed on top of Oracle. After briefly presenting the underlying data model and architecture, we have presented an example of PSYCHO usage, based on a common market-basket scenario. The current PSYCHO version can be extended in several ways. For example, in the current PSYCHO release, the user interacts with the system through a simple textual shell. As a future work, we plan to extend PSYCHO with a user-friendly GUI. Another important issue under investigation consists in defining an open-source version of PSYCHO, relying on open-source technologies. To this purpose, we are currently investigating the opportunity of using the WEKA library [14], a collection of machine learning algorithms for data mining tasks written in Java, as part of the PSYCHO backend. Finally, we plan to investigate the relationships between our manipulation operations and adaptive/incremental mining solutions, with the aim of designing an incremental mining environment based on database solutions.

References

1. R. Agrawal, R. Srikant. Fast Algorithms for Mining Association Rules in Large Databases. In *Proc. of VLDB'94*, 487-499, 1994.
2. E. Bertino, B. Catania, and A. Maddalena. Towards a Language for Pattern Manipulation and Querying. In *Proc. of PaRMa'04*, 2004.
3. B. Catania, A. Maddalena, M. Mazza, E. Bertino, and S. Rizzi. A Framework for Data Mining Pattern Management. In *Proc. of PKDD'04*, pp 87-98, 2004.
4. B. Catania, A. Maddalena, and M. Mazza. PSYCHO: A Prototype System for Pattern Management. In *Proc. of VLDB'05*, pp 1346–1349, 2005.
5. L.V.S. Lakshmanan S. Johnson and R.T. Ng. The 3W Model and Algebra for Unified Data Mining. In *Proc. of VLDB'01*, pp 21–32, 2001.
6. The CINQ project. `http://www.cinq-project.org`.
7. Jasper Java Interface. `http://www.sics.se/sicstus/docs/latest/html/sicstus/Jasper.html`.
8. Java Data Mining API. `http://www.jcp.org/jsr/detail/73.prt`.
9. Oracle10g Database. `http://www.oracle.com/technology/ products/database/oracle10g/index.html`.
10. The PANDA Project. `http://dke.cti.gr/panda/`, 2002.
11. Predictive Model Markup Language (PMML). `http://www.dmg.org/pmmlspecs_v2/pmml_v2_0.html`.
12. PSYCHO Site. `http://www.disi.unge.it/person/CataniaB/psycho/`.
13. SICStus Prolog (v.3). `http://www.sics.se/isl/sicstuswww/site/index.html`.
14. WEKA site. `http://www.cs.waikato.ac.nz/~ml/weka/index.html`

NaviMoz: Mining Navigational Patterns in Portal Catalogs

Eleni Christodoulou, Theodore Dalamagas, and Timos Sellis

School of Electr. and Comp. Engineering
National Techn. University of Athens,
Athens, GR 15773
{hchristo, dalamag, timos}@dblab.ece.ntua.gr

Abstract. Portal Catalogs is a popular means of searching for information on the Web. They provide querying and browsing capabilities on data organized in a hierarchy, on a category/subcategory basis. This paper presents mining techniques on user navigational patterns in the hierarchies of portal catalogs. Specifically, we study and implement navigation retrieval methods and clustering tasks based on navigational patterns. The above mining tasks are quite useful for portal administrators, since they can be used to observe users' behavior, extract personal preferences and re-organize the structure of the portal to satisfy better user needs and navigational habits. These mining tasks have been implemented in the NaviMoz, a prototype system for mining navigational patterns in portal catalogs.

1 Introduction

Portal catalogs provide querying and browsing capabilities on data organized in a hierarchy on a category/subcategory basis. Users can navigate these hierarchies to identify data of their preference. Examples of such catalogs can be found in all popular search engines, e.g. in Google, Yahoo, OpenDirectory Project. Also, portal catalogs of a specific subject or domain (e.g. e-marketplaces for hardware, portals for cultural information) are provided by user communities on the Web. Such catalogs, known as vertical portals, is a valuable collection of resources for anyone who needs to search for information relevant to the interests of those communities. Portal catalogs maintain large volumes of information resources which is not possible for a single user to classify and exploit. For this reason, they are quite popular as a means for searching information on the Web.

A key point for maintaining portal catalogs is to observe users' behavior and extract personal preferences in order to re-organize the structure of the portal to satisfy better user needs. To support such tasks, current approaches [8,10,1] examine the pages that users visit by investigating the web logs of proxy servers. However, observing visited pages, without also paying attention to the categories in which these pages have been classified, cannot give an indication of the user *navigational habits*.

T. Grust et al. (Eds.): EDBT 2006 Workshops, LNCS 4254, pp. 801–813, 2006.

Navigational habits are related with how users search and browse in the paths of a hierarchy in a portal catalog. Paths in hierarchies provide a conceptual clustering of Web pages in groups sharing common properties. During a Web page search and browsing in a portal catalog, users may visit categories, go forward in subcategories if they look for pages with specific content or go backwards in more general categories if they look for Web pages with general content. We call *navigational patterns* the paths that users follow in the hierarchy of a portal catalog during a Web page search and browsing. Observing *navigational patterns* can give an indication of the concepts that users are interested in, and their navigational habits, and better support the maintenance of the portal catalog. For example, knowing that the navigational pattern `/gadgets/sound/mp3-players` is quite popular among users, the portal administrator may decide to put a link for the category `mp3-players` in the first level of the portal hierarchy to provide users with instant access to the list of mp3 players available. Also, discovering that many users go back and forth several times within a navigational pattern, might be an indication that the specific part of portal hierarchy is not well-designed and users cannot easily determine which category to follow. In this case, the administrator may decide to change that part, providing new categories or eliminating some of the old ones.

This paper develops mining techniques on user navigational patterns in the hierarchies of portal catalogs. Specifically, the work studies and implements navigation retrieval capabilities and clustering tasks based on common navigational patterns. The above mining tasks are quite useful for portal administrators for customizing the structure of portal catalog according to user and navigational habits. We next summarize the contributions of our work:

1. We introduce navigational patterns for hierarchies of portal catalogs.
2. We suggest a metric to capture the structure and content similarity between two navigational patterns.
3. We study and implement mining tasks for user navigational patterns in the hierarchies of portal catalogs. We develop navigation retrieval methods, and clustering tasks based on navigational patterns. In navigation retrieval methods, given navigational patterns as input, we determine users that follow navigational patterns which have common characteristics compared to those input patterns. In clustering tasks, we determine user groups that share common navigational habits.
4. The above tasks are implemented in the NaviMoz, a prototype system for mining navigational patterns in portal catalogs.

1.1 Related Work

Bioinformatics is one of the research fields where mining patterns (similar to navigational patterns that we study here) is a popular research issue. Biological entities, such as proteins and molecules, consist of sequences of elements, in the same way that the navigational patterns consist of sequences of categories of the portal hierarchy [7,9,5]. However, in this field, user requirements are different and, thus, mining tasks needed are different, too (e.g. one can ask for the co-factors of a reaction) [7].

Also, there are many approaches that exploit Web logs of proxy servers to observe users behavior in Internet sites [4,8,10,11,17]. They are based on the words related to the hyper-links that users click and on the keywords related to the target Web pages. Some of those approaches [2,10] assist the creation of user communities, that is groups of users with similar interests. In [17], a new algorithm is presented, which supports sequence discovery from multidimensional data, allowing the detection of sequences across monitored attributes, such as URLs and http referees. As noted in the introduction, observing visited pages, without also paying attention to the categories in which these pages have been classified, cannot give an indication of the user navigational habits, as studied in this paper. Thus, we believe that our work is complementary to the approaches that exploit Web logs. For a detailed discussion on web mining techniques for web personalization see [1].

The shape definition language (SLD) presented in [18] is also related to our work. The SDL language is used to retrieve objects based on shapes contained in the histories associated with these objects. The notion of shapes is close to the notion of navigational patterns.

The rest of the paper is organized as follows. Section 2 introduces navigational patterns in the hierarchies of portal catalog, and defines a similarity metric for navigational patterns. Section 3 presents the mining tasks developed. Section 4 describes our prototype system, and finally, Section 5 concludes the paper.

2 Hierarchies and Navigational Patterns in Portal Catalogs

Portal catalogs classify information resources in a semantically meaningful way. Their purpose is to develop and maintain specific communities of interests on the Web. Portal catalogs maintain large volumes of information resources, organized in thematic categories. The overall structure of a portal catalog is actually a hierarchy on a category/subcategory basis.

We can represent a hierarchy of a portal catalog as a graph structure $G = (V, E)$. V is the set of nodes representing categories included in the hierarchy, and E is the set of edges representing category/subcategory relationship. Since we represent a hierarchy of a portal catalog as a graph structure, a user can reach a category following different paths. For example, one reaches the category `History` through either `Science/Social Science/History` or through `Society/History`.

A user, during a Web page search and browsing in a portal catalog, may visit several categories. We call the sequence of categories in those visits `navigational patterns`. We note that such patterns may include multiple occurrences of categories. This might be the result of users going back and forth several times within a path in the graph of hierarchy.

A key issue for developing mining tasks for navigational patterns is to be able to estimate how similar two navigational patterns are. In the next subsection we present a similarity metric to estimate the similarity degree between two navigational patterns in terms of structure and content.

2.1 A Similarity Metric for Navigational Patterns

We design a similarity metric for navigational patterns in hierarchies of portal catalogs that takes into consideration both the structure of the pattern and the keywords used as labels for the categories.

1. To estimate the structure similarity between two navigational patterns, we consider the elements of navigational patterns as character sequences and we exploit the metric suggested in [12]. Such a metric is based on the minimum cost sequence of *edit operations* needed to change one string to become identical to another string. The set of edit operations include deletion of a character, insertion of a character and replacement of a character with another one. The calculation of the metric is based on a dynamic programming algorithm. The final result is the sum of the costs of the considered operations divided by the sum of the lengths of the navigational patterns. The result expresses a distance d. Thus, in order to have the similarity we should calculate $1 - d$.
2. To estimate the content similarity between two navigational patterns, we calculate the ratio of the number of occurrence of the common categories in both patterns to the total number of categories in both patterns.

The similarity metric is calculated as the average of structure and content similarity.

Let for example A =`/Health/Medicine/Fitness` and B=`/Health/Fitness/Running/Training/Coaching/Training` be two navigational patterns. Their structural distance is 0.55 (delete `Medicine` from A and insert `/Running/Training/Coaching/Training` : 5 operations, total length=9). Thus, their structural similarity is 0.45. The ratio of the number of occurrence of the common categories in both patterns to the total number of categories in both patterns is $4/9 = 0.44$. Thus, the similarity between these two navigational patterns is 0.445.

3 Mining Tasks

We study and implement mining tasks for user navigational patterns in the hierarchies of portal catalogs. Specifically, we develop navigation retrieval tasks and clustering tasks based on navigational patterns.

3.1 Navigation Retrieval Tasks

In all navigational retrieval tasks, a navigational pattern is given as input. Based on this input pattern, we can determine users that follow navigational patterns with common characteristics compared to the input pattern. All tasks can be performed for a certain time period provided by the user. Specifically, we have developed the following navigation retrieval tasks:

– *Retrieval of navigations which are supersets of the input pattern.* This task identifies users whose navigational patterns contain all the categories from the input pattern (but these are not the only ones in the user pattern), keeping their ordering. For example, given that `/Arts/Radio` is an input pattern, the following navigational patterns will be part of the answer:
  • `/Arts/Radio/Personalities/Henrie_Phil/Personalities/Radio/Personalities/Programs/Voice_Actors`
  • `/Arts/Radio/Guides/Directories/Directories`
– *Retrieval of navigations which are subsets of the input pattern.* This task identifies users whose navigational patterns contain only categories from the input pattern (but these are not the only ones in the user pattern), keeping their ordering. For example, given that `/Arts/Radio/Guides` is an input pattern, the following navigational patterns will be part of the answer:
  • `/Arts/Radio`
  • `/Arts/Guides`
– *Retrieval of navigations which are identical to the input pattern.* This task identifies users whose navigational patterns contain all the categories from the input pattern (and these are the only ones in the user pattern), keeping their ordering.
– *Retrieval of the navigations which are similar to the input pattern.* This task identifies users whose navigational patterns are similar to the input pattern, given a similarity threshold. The threshold is provided by the user. A navigational pattern is retrieved as part of the answer if the similarity metric (introduced in the previous section) between itself and the input pattern gives a value that exceeds the threshold provided. We note that the suggested similarity metric takes into consideration both the structure of the pattern and the keywords used as labels for the categories. For example, given that `/Arts/Music` is an input pattern, and the threshold is 0.70, the pattern `/Arts/Radio/Music` will be retrieved (similarity=0.81), but the pattern `/Arts/Radio` will not (similarity=0.62).

3.2 Clustering Tasks

In clustering tasks, we can determine user groups that share common navigational habits. All tasks can be performed for a certain time period provided by the user. Specifically, we have developed the following tasks:

– *Grouping users that follow similar navigational patterns.* To support this task we have implemented two clustering algorithms: the K-means and the single link hierarchical clustering algorithm [13,14]. For both clustering algorithms we exploit the similarity metric suggested in the previous section.
– *Retrieval of the most popular navigations.* This task identifies the navigational patterns which have been followed by the majority of users. We consider such patterns as popular patterns.

– *Retrieval of the most undecided users.* This task identifies users whose navigational habits indicate that they are undecided during their search and browse in the portal hierarchy. Also, it ranks the users according to how much undecided they are. We suppose that when a user goes back and forth during searching and browsing, he/she is an undecided user. An example of a navigational pattern which shows that the respective user is undecided is the following: `/Arts/Music/Pop/Music/Pop/Concerts/Pop/Music/Rock/Concerts`. A user whose navigational pattern is `/Arts/Music/Rock/Music/Rock/Concerts` is less undecided than the former, due to lower number of *back and forth* (*B&F*) movements.

Next, we give an overview of clustering techniques and we discuss in detail the single link implementation. The key point of our implementation is that the estimation of the clustering level for single link is performed exploiting the C-index method [16].

Clustering Algorithms. Clustering methods are usually divided into two broad categories. *Non-hierarchical methods* group a data set into a number of clusters. *Hierarchical methods* produce nested sets of data (hierarchies), in which pairs of elements or clusters are successively linked until every element in the data set becomes connected. Non-hierarchical methods have low computational requirements, ($O(kn)$, if for example n documents need to be grouped into k clusters), but certain parameters like the number of formed clusters must be known a priori. Hierarchical methods are computationally expensive, with time requirements of $O(n^2)$, if n documents need to be clustered. However, hierarchical methods have been used extensively as a means of increasing the effectiveness and efficiency of retrieval [20,21,22]. For a wide ranging overview of clustering methods one can refer to [13,14]. *Single link*, *complete link* and *group average link* are known as hierarchical clustering methods. All these methods are based on a similar idea:

1. Each element of the data set to be clustered is considered to be a single cluster.
2. The clusters with the minimum distance (i.e. maximum similarity) are merged and the distance between the remaining clusters and the new, merged one is recalculated.
3. While there are more than one clusters, go again to step 2.

In single link (complete link), the distance between two non-single clusters is defined as the minimum (maximum) of the distances between all pairs of elements so that one element is in the first cluster and the other element is in the second cluster. In group average link, the distance between two non-single clusters is defined as the mean of the distances between all pairs of elements so that one element is in the one cluster and the other element is in the other cluster.

We implemented a single link clustering algorithm using Prim's algorithm [23] for computing the *minimum spanning tree (MST)* of a graph. Given a graph G

with a set of weighted edges E and a set of vertices V, a MST is an acyclic subset $T \subseteq E$ that links all the vertices and whose total weight $W(T)$ (the sum of the weights for the edges in T) is minimized. It has been shown [24] that a MST contains all the information needed in order to perform single link clustering.

Given n navigational patterns, we form a fully connected graph G with n vertices $\in V$ and $n(n-1)/2$ weighted edges $\in E$. The weight of an edge corresponds to the similarity distance between the vertices (trees) that this edge connects. The single link clusters for a *clustering level* l_1 can be identified by deleting all the edges with weight $w \geq l_1$ from the MST of G. The connected components of the remaining graph are the single link clusters. Figure 1(a) shows a graph with 7 nodes that correspond to 7 navigational patterns, and 10 edges. The weight of an edge is the similarity distance between the involved navigational patterns. For example the similarity distance between patterns 1 and 2 is 0.2. The missing edges, that is the extra edges that make the graph fully connected, are those that have weight 1. Figure 1(b) shows the minimum spanning tree of (a). Figure 1(c) presents the graph remaining after deleting all edges with weight ≥ 0.4. There are 2 connected components that include nodes $(1, 2, 3, 6)$ and nodes $(7, 5)$, respectively. This indicates the presence of 2 clusters: cluster 1 with $(1, 2, 3, 6)$ as members and cluster 2 with $(7, 5)$ as members. Nodes which are not connected to other nodes will be considered as single-node clusters.

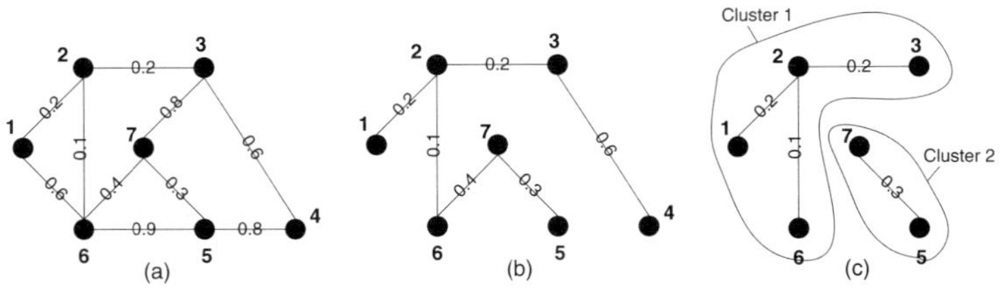

Fig. 1. Minimum Spanning Tree (MST) detection and single link clustering at level 0.6

A stopping rule is necessary to determine the most appropriate clustering level for the single link hierarchies. Milligan et al. present 30 such rules [25]. Among these rules, $C-$index [16] exhibits excellent performance (found in the top 3 stopping rules). We next present the way we adopt the $C-$index in a hierarchical clustering procedure for navigational patterns.

$C-$index for Hierarchical Clustering. $C-$index is a vector of pairs $((i_1, n_1), (i_2, n_2), \ldots, (i_p, n_p))$, where $i_1, i_2, \ldots, i_p$ are the values of the index and $n_1, n_2, \ldots, n_p$ the number of clusters in each clustering arrangement produced by varying the clustering level of a hierarchical clustering procedure in p different steps. Let l_1 be the first selected clustering level, which produces an arrangement of N_1 clusters (that is $n_1 = N_1$): C_1 with c_1 elements, C_2 with c_2 elements, ..., C_{N_1} with c_{N_1} elements. We can calculate i_1 in order to have the first pair (i_1, n_1) of C-index vector:

$$i_1 = (d_w - min(d_w))/(max(d_w) - min(d_w))$$

where:

1. $d_w = Sum(d_{w_1}) + Sum(d_{w_2}) + \ldots + Sum(d_{w_{N_1}})$, with $Sum(d_{w_i})$ to be the sum of pairwise similaritites of all members of cluster $C_i, 1 \leq i \leq n_1$,
2. $max(d_w)$: the sum of the n_d highest pairwise similaritites in the whole set of data (that is, sort distances, highest first, and take the Top-n_d sum),
3. $min(d_w)$: the sum of the n_d lowest pairwise similaritites in the whole set of data (that is, sort distances, highest first, and take the Bottom-n_d sum),

with $n_d = c_1 * (c_1 - 1)/2 + c_2 * (c_2 - 1)/2 + \ldots + c_{N_1} * (c_{N_1} - 1)/2$ (that is the number of all within cluster pairwise similaritites). Similarly we calculate all values of C–index for all different p clustering levels, getting the vector $((i_1, n_1), (i_2, n_2), \ldots, (i_p, n_p))$. We point out that:

- Although all pairwise similaritites are needed to compute the C-Index, this doesn't require any additional computation because these similaritites need to be computed anyway for the hierarchical clustering procedure itself.
- Since multiple successive clustering levels can generate the same number of clusters, we compute the C–Index not for each level but for each number of clusters generated by different levels.
- The number of clusters with the lowest C–Index is chosen as the correct clustering, as [25] suggests.

We next present the algorithm exploited to retrieve the most undecided users.

Undecided Users. To support this task, we have implemented an algorithm which counts how many $B\&F$ movements a user has made. The term $B\&F$ refers to a pair of categories in the hierarchy of a portal catalog. A pair of categories (A, B) is $B\&F$ if:

- Both A and B belong to the same navigational pattern P.
- $label(A) = label(B)$: the categories are the same.
- There is an odd number of categories (different than A and B) between A and B in pattern P.
- $label(after(A)) = label(before(B))$ (after(A) gives the category which is after A in the examined navigational pattern, while before(A) gives the category which is before A in the examined navigational pattern).

According to the above, a $B\&F$ pair appears in the primitive navigational pattern `A/B/A`. We call such $B\&F$ pairs as *basic* $B\&F$s, since the patterns in which can appear are of minimum length. The algorithm first detects the basic $B\&F$s, and then the others.

Input: navigational pattern
Output: number of the $B\&F$ pairs in the pattern.
Algorithm:
array BF: For every category of the input pattern, it contains its $B\&F$ partner (i.e., the category with which it constitutes a $B\&F$).

Vector P: Contains all category pairs (A, B) which are candidates for $B\&F$s, and the number of categories that exist between A and B.
Vectors valueVector: One vector for each category, having the place where the category occurs in the navigational pattern.
int counter: Contains the number of $B\&F$.

/*Find basic B&F */

```
for all categories
   if the size of the current category valueVector >1
      Check whether there are two successive occurrences in
      places i and j of the category in the pattern, such that
      no other category exists between places i and j.
      If there are not such successive occurrences then
         if one category exists between places i and j.
            B&F exists for category in i and category in j
            Add B&F to array BF
         else
            if N categories exist between places i and j,
            with N odd
               candidate B&F exists for category in i and
                    category in j
               add this category pair to Vector P

Sort Vector P according to the number of categories that exist
between categories which constitute a candidate B&F.
```

/*Find the rest B&F */

```
for every pair (A,B) of the sorted Vector P
   Check if the categories after(A) and before(B) form a pair in
   array BF, and if so, the pair (A,B) is B&F.
      Update array BF
   else
      Find the category in array BF that constitutes a B&F pair
            together with after(A)
      If that category is before(B)
         Add the B&F pair to array BF
      else
         Find the category in array BF that constitutes a B&F pair
            together with BF[after(A)]
```

/*Computation of the total number of B&F */

```
For every non-zero element of array BF, increase counter by 1.
Return counter.
```

An example is given in case the input to the algorithm is the navigational pattern: `r/s/m/d/m/o/m/s/f/s/f/w/f/w`. The algorithm first detects the basic $B\&F$s,

which are the category pairs $(2,4)$[1] (i.e., m and m), $(4,6)$, $(11,13)$, $(7,9)$, $(8,10)$ and $(10,12)$ (i.e., f and f), and updates the array BF . Vector P keeps the category pair $(1,7)$ as a candidate $B\&F$. The algorithm examines the category pair $(2,6)$ and finds that there exist $B\&F$ pairs $(1,4)$ and $(4,6)$. Thus, the pair $(1,7)$ is $B\&F$.

3.3 User Identification Tasks

These tasks provide useful information regarding user identification. Specifically, the system provides (a) user navigation retrieval for a given time period, and (b) user session retrieval for a given time period.

4 System Description

The above tasks are implemented in the NaviMoz, a prototype system for mining navigational patterns in portal catalogs. NaviMoz system consists of three basic modules:

1. User Manager Module. This module provides user login operations and maintains the user access to the portal catalog. The users' navigations are stored in the database and they are further explored by the system's manager.
2. Mining Module. This module provides all the mining tasks for navigational patterns described in this paper.
3. Storage Module. This module is responsible for maintaining an RDBMS used for storing users information and their navigational patterns.

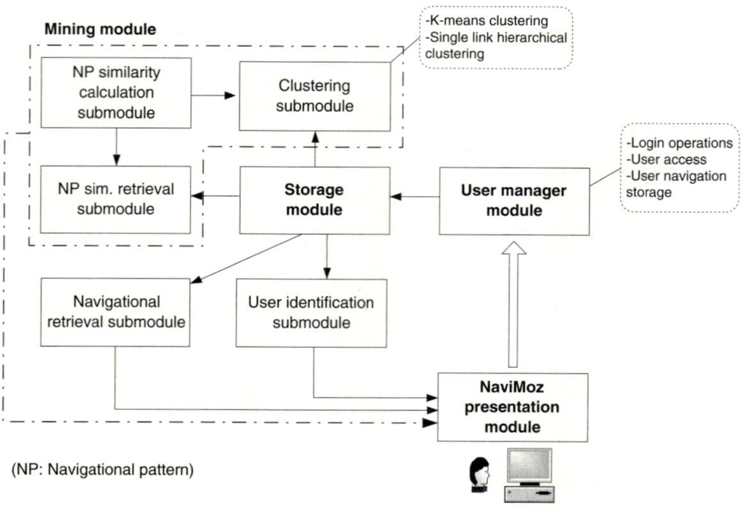

Fig. 2. Architecture of NaviMoz

[1] Numbers denote places in the navigational pattern.

4. Presentation Module. This module supports the graphical interface of NaviMoz.

The architecture of NaviMoz is presented in Figure 2, while a screen dump showing a clustering task running is illustrated in Figure 3. Clustering has identified a cluster involving three users (Christodoulou Eleni, Kalimerh Maria and Kanellakopoulos Haralampos) whose navigational habits are similar.

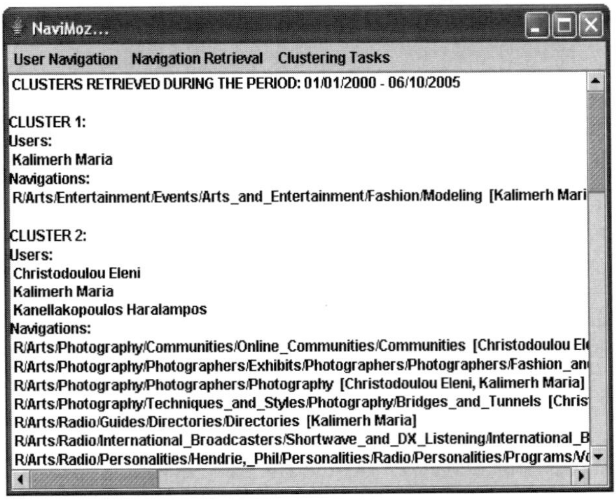

Fig. 3. Clustering task in NaviMoz

5 Conclusions

Observing user behavior and extracting personal preferences is crucial for maintaining portal catalogs. Certain navigational habits can indicate the need to re-organize the structure of the portal to satisfy better user needs. Observing visited pages in a portal catalog, without also paying attention to the categories in which these pages have been classified, cannot give an indication of the user navigational habits.

This paper suggests a set of mining tasks on user navigational patterns in the hierarchies of portal catalogs. Those mining tasks can help portal administrators for customizing the structure of portal catalog according to user and navigational habits. In our work, we introduced navigational patterns for hierarchies of portal catalogs, and we designed a metric to capture their structure and content similarity. Based on this metric, we implemented several mining tasks, like navigation retrieval methods and clustering methods, for user navigational patterns in the hierarchies of portal catalogs.

The navigational patterns can be considered as simplified Xpath queries [19]. We will extend our work to employ complex navigational patterns (e.g., branching path expressions), expressed as Xpath pattern queries. Our future plan for

NaviMoz is to become a full-fledged generic portal management system that will provide editing operations fully supported by the mining tasks described in this paper.

References

1. M. Eirinaki, M. Vazirgiannis, Web mining for web personalization. ACM Transactions on Internet Technology (TOIT), 3(1), 2003.
2. C. R. Anderson, E. Horvitz. A Dynamic Personalized Start Page. In Proceedings of the 11th WWW Conference 2002.
3. A. Ajijth, V. Ramos. Web Usage Mining Using Artificial Ant Colony Clustering and Genetic Programming. Congress on Evolutionary Computation, IEEE Press ISBN 078-0378-04-0 pp 1384-1391, Canberra, Australia, Dec 2003.
4. X. Fang, O. R. Liu Sheng. Designing a Better Web Portal for Digital Government: A Web-Mining Based Approach, http://diggov.org/library/library/dgo2005/demosb/fang_designing.pdf
5. Y. Kaneta, M. Md. Munna Ahaduzzaman, T. Ohkawa. A Method of Extracting Sentences Related to Protein Interaction from Literature using a Structure Database. In Proceedings of the 2nd European Workshop on Data Mining and Text Mining for Bioinformatics (ECML/PKDD'04), Italy, September 2004.
6. T. Kamdar. A. Joshi. On Creating Adaptive Web Sites using Web Log Mining, TR-CS-00-05. Department of Computer Science and Electrical Engineering University of Maryland, Baltimore Country, (2000).
7. L. Krishnamurthy, J. Nadeau, G. Ozsoyoglu, M. Ozsoyoglu, G. Schaeffer, M. Tasan, W. Xu . Pathways Database System: An integrated set of tools for biological pathways. Bioinformatics 19(8) 2003.
8. B. Mobasher, H. Dai, T. Luo, Y. Sung, J. Zhu.: Integrating Web Usage and Content Mining for More Effective Personalization. In Proceedings of the International Conference on E-Commerce and Web Technologies, Greenwich, UK, 165-176, 2000.
9. R. G. Pensa, C. Leschi, J. Besson and J. Boulicaut. Assessment of discretization techniques for relevant pattern discovery from gene expression data. In Proceedings of the 2nd Workshop on Data Mining in Bioinformatics, Seattle, USA, August 2004.
10. D. Pierrakos, G. Paliouras, C. Papatheodorou, V. Karakaletsis and M. Dikaiakos. Web community directories: A new approach to web personalization. In Lecture Notes in Artificial Intelligence (LNAI), 3209, Springer-Verlag, 2004.
11. F. Toolan, N. Kusmerick. Mining web logs for personalized site maps. In Proceedings of the 3rd International Conference on Web Information Systems Engineering (WISE'02), 2002.
12. R. A. Wagner, M. J. Fischer, The String to String Correction Problem, Journal of the Association for the Computer Machinery, Vol 21, No.1, pp.168-173, January 1974.
13. E. Rasmussen, Clustering algorithms, in: W. Frakes, R. Baeza-Yates (Eds.), Information Retrieval: Data Structures and Algorithms, Prentice Hall, 1992.
14. M. Halkidi, Y. Batistakis, M. Vazirgiannis, Clustering algorithms and validity measures. In Proceedings of the SSDBM Conference, Virginia, USA, 2001.
15. T. Dalamagas, T. Cheng, K.J. Winkel, T. Sellis, A Methodology for Clustering XML Documents by Structure, Information Systems, Elsevier, 2004.
16. L. J. Hubert, J. R. Levin, A general statistical framework for accessing categorical clustering in free recall, Psychological Bulletin 83 (1976) 1072–1082.

17. Matthias Baumgarten, Alex G. Buchner, Sarabjot S. Anand, Maurice D. Mulvenna, John G. Hughes: User-Driven Navigation Pattern Discovery from Internet Data. 74-91
18. Agrawal, R., Psaila, G., Wimmers, E.L., Zat, M.: Querying shapes of histories. In: Proceedings of 21st International Conference on Very Large Data Bases, Morgan Kaufmann (1995) 502–514
19. XML path language (XPath: www.w3.org/TR/xpath)
20. N. Jardine, C. J. van Rijsbergen, The use of hierarchical clustering in information retrieval, Information storage and retrieval 7 (1971) 217–240.
21. E. Voorhees, The effectiveness and efficiency of agglomerative hierarchic clustering in document retrieval, Ph.D. thesis, Cornell University, Ithaca, New York (Oct. 1985).
22. M. Hearst, J. O. Pedersen, Reexamining the cluster hypothesis: Scatter/gather on retrieval results, in: Proceedings of the ACM SIGIR Conference, Zurich, Switzerland, 1996, pp. 76–84.
23. T. Cormen, C. Leiserson, R. Rivest, Introduction to algorithms, MIT Press, 1990.
24. J. C. Gower, G. J. S. Ross, Minimum spanning trees and single linkage cluster analysis, Applied Statistics 18 (1969) 54–64.
25. G. W. Milligan, M. C. Cooper, An examination of procedures for determining the number of clusters in a data set, Psychometrika 50 (1985) 159–179.

An XML-Based Database for Knowledge Discovery

Rosa Meo[1] and Giuseppe Psaila[2]

[1] Università di Torino, Dipartimento di Informatica, corso Svizzera 185, I-10149, Torino, Italy
meo@di.unito.it

[2] Università di Bergamo, Facoltà di Ingegneria, Viale Marconi 5, I-24044 Dalmine (BG), Italy
psaila@unibg.it

Abstract. Pattern Management Systems and Inductive Databases, are proposed as a new generation of general purpose databases with the aim to manage data mining patterns and work as knowledge bases in support to the deployment of the KDD process. One of the main problems to be solved is the integration between data and patterns and pattern maintenance when data update. Unfortunately, the heterogeneity of the patterns that represent the extracted knowledge and of the different conceptual tools used to find the patterns make difficult this integration in a unique framework.

In this paper, we explore the feasibility of using XML as the unifying framework for inductive databases, and present a model, named XDM (XML for Data Mining). We will show the basic features of the model, such as the storage in the same database of both data and patterns. To store patterns, we consider determinant for their interpretation the storage of the pattern derivation process which is described by the concept of statement, based on data mining operators. Some of the statements are automatically generated by the system while maintaining consistence between source and derived data. Furthermore, we show how the use of XML namespaces allows the effective coexistence of different data mining operators and provides extensibility to new operators. Finally, we show that with the use of XML-Schema we are able to define the schema, the state and the integrity constraints of an inductive database.

1 Introduction

Data mining applications are called to extract descriptive and predictive patterns, typically used for decision making, from the data contained in traditional databases and from other unconventional information systems such as the web.

Inductive Databases (IDB) have been launched in [8] as general-purpose databases in which both the data and the patterns can be represented, retrieved and manipulated with the goal to assist the deployment of the *Knowledge Discovery Process* (KDD). Thus, KDD becomes a querying sequence in a query

T. Grust et al. (Eds.): EDBT 2006 Workshops, LNCS 4254, pp. 814–828, 2006.

language designed for a specific data mining problem. Pattern Management Systems (PMS) [12] have been proposed instead with the main concern of representing and managing in a unique system a collection of heterogeneous patterns. Consequently, both of them should integrate several heterogeneous data mining patterns that deal with very different, and complex data models. For example, classification tools usually adopt a data model that is a classification tree or rules, while basket analysis usually represent patterns by means of set enumeration models. In [12] a logic-based model of a pattern management system is studied which satisfies the basic requirements of generality, extensibility and reusability. In [5] object oriented modeling techniques have been applied to obtain a uniform model of a pattern management database. In [11] UML has been applied, instead.

In this paper, we present a semi-structured data model specifically designed for inductive databases and, more generally, for *Knowledge Discovery Systems*. This model is called XDM (XML for Data Mining). It is based on XML and is devised to cope with several distinctive features at the same time. At first, it is semi-structured, in order to be able to represent an apriori infinite set of data models. Second, it is based on two simple and clear concepts, named *Data Item* (Section 2) and *Statement* (Section 3): a data item is a container of data and/or patterns; a statement is a description of an operator application. Third, with XDM the inductive database state is defined (Section 5) as the collection of data items and statements, and the knowledge discovery process is represented as a set of relationships between data items and statements. Fourth, with the aid of XML-Schema[1] (see the official documents [13,2] for detailed descriptions) we define (Section 5) the concept of database schema which provides the set of integrity constraints over the operators' inputs and outputs and constitutes part of the meta-data of the KDD process. The above detailed features of the model set the foundations for the interoperability of the operators inside a unique framework. Finally, the adoption of XML as syntactic format provides several benefits; in particular, the concept of *namespace* opens the way to the integration of several data formats and operators inside the same framework. Throughout the paper we demonstrate the feasibility of the model to support KDD processes presenting a sample process (Section 4).

A similar set of functionalities, i.e. the application of XML to the deployment of the KDD process, is available also in [1] while [3] provides a framework for extracting knowledge from XML documents. XDM, however, provides a set of features that is peculiar to the integration of different patterns and models in inductive databases. At first, source data and patterns are represented at the same time in the model. Patterns may be stored either extensionally or intensionally, i.e. by storing only the statements that generate the patterns. Second, the pattern derivation process is stored in the database: this is determinant in many situations, such as for the maintenance of the patterns (that are a kind of

[1] XML-Schema specifications constrain the structure of XML documents and overcome the limitations of classical DTDs by adding the concept of data type for attributes.

derived data) when the original data is updated, in the phase of pattern interpretation and allows pattern reuse. Furthermore, the framework can be easily extended with new data mining operators (thanks to the embedding provided by namespaces). Thus IDB based on XDM really become open systems and a unifying framework in which various KDD data transformation phases take place. Finally, the use of XML allows the inclusion in IDB of semi-structured data.

To conclude, we want to highlight an important difference of XDM w.r.t. other XML formats for data mining and knowledge discovery, such as PMML [6]. PMML is a format to exchange patterns among different systems, thus it is focused on the description of patterns. XDM is not focused on the description of specific patterns; it is a framework for knowledge discovery activities, and the XML structure is the suitable format to host in a flexible way different representations for data and patterns, included PMML documents.

2 XDM Data Items

Tree Model. An XML document or fragment is represented as a tree of nodes, called *ElementNodes*. An *ElementNode* n has a possibly empty set of *attributes*, denoted as *n.Attributes*, i.e. pairs $(Name : String, Value : String)$ (they are the attributes defined by the XML syntax within tags). Furthermore, an *ElementNode* has the following properties: the element name $n.Name$ and the prefix associated to the name space $n.Prefix$ (that, with the notation $Prefix$:*Name*, we will use to refer to *ElementNodes*); the name space *r.NameSpace* specifying the name space URI. Finally, an element node has a content *n.Content*, which is a possibly empty sequence of *ElementNode*.

Definition 1: An *XDM Data Item* is a tree fragment defined as follows.

• The root r is an *ElementNode* `XDM:DATA-ITEM`, belonging to the standard XDM name space whose prefix is `XDM`. In the content *r.Content*, only `XDM:DERIVATION` and `XDM:CONTENT` nodes are allowed (defined hereafter).
• The root node r has a set of attributes, *r.Attributes*, denoting the data item features: `Name`, `Date` and `Version`. `Virtual` denotes if the data item is materalized. □

Definition 2: The `XDM:CONTENT` node is an *ElementNode* (defined in the XDM name space), denoted as c. The `XDM:CONTENT` node has no attributes, and only one child *ElementNode* n in *c.Content*. □

Example 1: Consider the following XDM data item.

```
<XDM:DATA-ITEM Name="Purchases" Version="1"
     Date="..." Virtual="NO" xmlns:XDM="http://.../NS/XDM">
  <XDM:CONTENT>
    <TRANSACTIONS>
      <PRODUCT TID="1" CUST="c1" ITEM="A"  PRICE="25"/>
      <PRODUCT TID="1" CUST="c1" ITEM="B"  PRICE="12"/>
      <PRODUCT TID="2" CUST="c3" ITEM="C"  PRICE="30"/>
```

```
   . . .
  </TRANSACTIONS>
 </XDM:CONTENT>
</XDM:DATA-ITEM>
```

The start tag XDM:DATA-ITEM defines the attributes for the XDM data item named Purchases. Notice the name space definition xmlns:XDM="http://.../NS/XDM", which says that all element nodes prefixed as XDM belong to the name space identified by the specified URI.

This data item is materialized (Virtual="NO"); therefore the content of the Purchases data item consists of the actual set of purchase transactions, with the details of each purchase. □

Definition 3: A XDM:DERIVATION node is an *ElementNode* (defined on the standard XDM name space), here denoted as *d*. In this case, *d.Attributes* contains only one mandatory attribute, statement, which contains the identifier of the XDM *statement* that generated the data item (see next sections for a detailed discussion on derivation). This is the statement that defines how the derived data item is generated and can be used later to recover the definition of that data item (for instance for documentation purposes or when original data is updated and the system needs to maintain consistency between the derived data item and the original data).

In addition, in derived data items *d.Content* could be empty. This is a case of a virtual data item (with Virtual="YES") that is very useful in the management and derivation of large data volumes. In fact, a virtual data item is not materialized, but only the statement that will be used to generate the data item is stored. This statement could be executed later, at the most convenient time for load-balancing of the system. □

Note that the XDM:DERIVATION node is required for derived data items (it stores the derivation process of the data item). On the contrary, a non-derived data item contains the XDM:CONTENT node only.

Example 2: The following XDM code shows the first version of a derived XDM data item, named Rules, containing the association rules extracted from the source data given in input, and materialized in the database. These data items are shown in the left hand side of Figure 1 that shows a sample KDD process.

```
<XDM:DATA-ITEM Name="Rules" Version="1" Date="..." Virtual="NO"
 xmlns:XDM="http://.../NS/XDM">
 <XDM:DERIVATION Statement="00128"/>
 <XDM:CONTENT>
 <AR:ASSOCIATION-RULE-SET xmlns:AR="http://...NS/DATA/AssRules">
     <AR:RULE>
         <AR:BODY>
             <AR:ELEMENT Name="ITEM">A</AR:ELEMENT>
             <AR:ELEMENT Name="ITEM">B</AR:ELEMENT>
         </AR:BODY>
         <AR:HEAD>
```

```
            <AR:ELEMENT Name="ITEM">C</AR:ELEMENT>
        </AR:HEAD>
        <AR:MEASURES>
            <AR:SUPPORT VALUE="0.5">
            <AR:CONFIDENCE VALUE="0.8">
            <AR:AVG-PRICE VALUE="22.33">
        </AR:MEASURES>
    </AR:ASSOCIATION-RULE>
    Other association rules
 </AR:ASSOCIATION-RULE-SET>
 </XDM:CONTENT>
</XDM:DATA-ITEM>
```

The XDM:DERIVATION node specifies (attribute Statement) the statement whose execution generated the item (statements will be described in Section 3). In particular, this item is generated by a statement based on the MR:MINE-RULE operator (see Section 3) which extracts association rules from a data item. The generated set of association rules is included in the XDM:CONTENT element. The description of association rules included here can be in PMML or XML-compliant. The version presented is an extension of PMML for the presence of the ELEMENT and MEASURES nodes. ELEMENT describes (by means of Name) the schema of the antecedent and consequent itemsets (named BODY and HEAD) in terms of their constituting elements, as defined in the data mining statement that generated them (generally speaking, BODY and HEAD schemas could be different). MEASURES helps the introduction by the users of new evaluation measures that define the validity of association rules and that can satisfy the different requirements of the various applications.

This XML fragment is based on a specific name space (with prefix AR: and its own URI) defined for association rule sets descriptions. Note that this difference w.r.t. the standard XDM name space is due to the fact that XDM is independent of the operators, that can be added to the XDM-based system when necessary. In the example, the association rule {A,B} ⇒{C} with the values of three evaluation measures (support, confidence and an aggregate value, average of the items price involved in the rule). □

Schema for XDM Data Items. The XML syntactic structure of XDM data items is very rich. However, Behind this structure, we can identify the concept of *Schema*. Given an XDM data item *di*, the schema of *di*, denoted as *Schema*(*di*), is a four-tuple $Schema(di) = \langle NameSpace, Prefix, Root, xsd \rangle$ where *NameSpace* is the namespace URI on which the content of the XDM data item is defined, *Prefix* is the namespace prefix associated to the namespace URI, *root* is the root node element of the XML fragment within the XDM:CONTENT element in the data item; finally, *xsd* is the name of the file containing the XML-Schema definition that defines the XML structure for documents belonging to the specified namespace URI. For example, the schema of item in Example 2 is ⟨"http://...NS/DATA/AssRules","AR","ASSOCIATION-RULE-SET","ar.xsd"⟩

3 XDM Statements

The XDM model is devised to capture the KDD process and therefore it provides also the concept of *statement*. This one specifies the application of an operator (for data manipulation and analysis tasks) whose execution causes the generation of a new, derived data item.

Definition 4: An XDM statement s is specified by an XML fragment, whose structure is the following.

- The root of the fragment is an element node `XDM:STATEMENT` denoted as s. s has the attribute `ID`, which is the statement identifier.
- The *Content* of `XDM:STATEMENT` is a non empty list of `XDM:SOURCE-ITEM` nodes (where each of them specifies an operator input), followed by an `XDM:OPERATOR` node (describing the application of the operator), followed by a non empty list of `XDM:OUTPUT-ITEM` nodes (that specify the operator output). □

Example 3: The following example shows the main features of a statement of `MR:MINE-RULE` (see [9] for a complete description).

```
<XDM:STATEMENT ID="00128" xmlns:MR="http://.../NS/XDM">
 <XDM:SOURCE-ITEM Role="RawData" Name="Purchases" Version="1"/>
 <XDM:OPERATOR>
  <MR:MINE-RULE xmlns:MR="http://.../NS/MINE-RULE">
   <MR:GROUPING select="TRANSACTIONS/PRODUCT" common-value="@TID"/>
    <MR:RULE-ELEMENT name="ITEM" select="@ITEM"/>
     <MR:MEASURES>
      <MR:SUPPORT threshold="0.4"/>
      <MR:CONFIDENCE threshold="0.75"/>
     </MR:MEASURES>
  </MR:MINE-RULE>
 </XDM:OPERATOR>
<XDM:OUTPUT-ITEM Name="Rules" Role="AssociationRules"
  Root="MR:RULE-SET" NS="http://.../NS/DATA/Rules"/>
</XDM:STATEMENT>
```

The operator and its specific element nodes are defined in the name space prefix `MR`. `SOURCE-ITEM` specifies the input of the operator providing `Name` and `Version` number of the XDM data item while `OUTPUT-ITEM` identifies the output node by means of the `Name` and the `Root` node of its tree fragment, as well as the name space in which the output format is defined (attribute `NS`). The `Role` attribute is exploited by the operator to distinguish the role of each data item w.r.t. the operator application.

The `MINE-RULE` operator analyzes the source item named `Purchases` (shown in Example 2) looking for association rules which associate values of attribute `ITEM` (see `MR:RULE-ELEMENT`); items are selected from elements `TRANSACTIONS/PRODUCT` logically grouped by the value of attribute `TID`, (see `MR:GROUPING`) since association rules must denote regularities w.r.t. single transactions. Finally, rules are extracted if their evaluation measures (support and confidence) are greater than the respective thresholds (see `MR:MEASURES`). □

Schema for XDM Statements. Statements are based on the XML Syntactic structure and, as well as XDM data items, it is possible to identify the concept of *schema*. Given an XDM statement s, the schema of s, denoted as $Schema(s)$, is a four-tuple $Schema(s) = \langle NameSpace, Prefix, Root, xsd \rangle$ where $NameSpace$ is the namespace URI associated to the operator application described in `XDM:STATEMENT`, $Prefix$ is the namespace prefix associated to the namespace URI, *root* is the root element of the XML fragment describing the operator application, xsd is the XML-Schema definition that defines the XML structure for the operator application belonging to the specified namespace URI. For example, the schema of the `MINE-RULE` statement of Example 3 is

⟨`"http://.../NS/MINE-RULE","MR","MINE-RULE","mr.xsd"` ⟩

It is important to note that data items and statements have the same concept of schema. This is important, because it shows that they are dual: data items and statements are really two faces of the same coin, i.e. the KDD process.

4 A Sample KDD Process

In the following we present a sample instance of a knowledge discovery process that involves the presented XDM data items and is instantiated by the excution of data management and data mining operators. This example will show how XML, and XDM in particular, is suitable for the inductive database framework and to provide effective support to the deployment of the KDD process. Figure 1 shows the sample KDD process: data items are rectangles; statements are circles labeled with operator name and `ID`; edges are labeled with input/output roles (written in italic).

In the figure, we find the application of the `MINE-RULE` operator on market basket data that produces the data item `Rules`. Then, another operator, namely `EVALUATE-RULE`, computes cross-references between rules and original data. It is discussed in detail in the Example 4, where it retrieves the list of customers that satisfy each association rule. Customers are then selected by a data manipulation operator, `SELECT-DATA-ITEM`, that performs selection on customers, according to the association rules they satisfy. Later selected customers are joined by operator `JOIN-DATA-ITEM` with the data item containing customers' details (named `Customers`). Finally, a clustering operator analyzes better the selected customers by clustering them on their detailed data. In the following examples we will discuss the operators and the data items generated.

Example 4: The operator `EVALUATE-RULE` retrieves the original data (stored in XDM data items) for which already extracted association rules (in other XDM data items) are satisfied. A complete description of this operator, in an SQL version for relational databases, can be found in [10].

The application of an `EVALUATE-RULE` statement is shown in Figure 1. This instance of the operator (identified by `ID="00133"` and reported in the following)

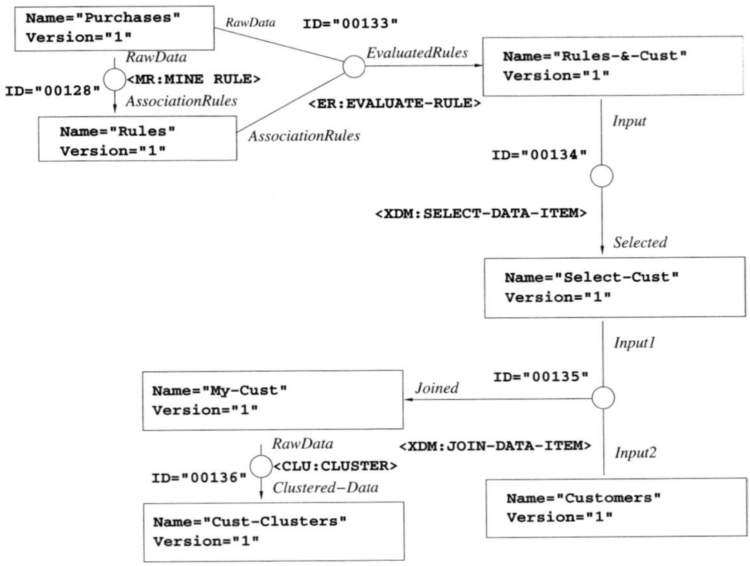

Fig. 1. A sample knowledge discovery process based on XDM

takes in input two `XDM` data items: with the role of `RawData` it takes the first version of the data item named `Purchases`, and with the role of `AssociationRules` the first version of the data item named `Rules`. It gives in output the first version of a new data item, named `Rules-&-Cust` containing for each association rule the list of customers for which it holds; this data item has the role `Evaluated Rules`. For lack of space we omit the details of the clauses in the operators.

```
<XDM:STATEMENT ID="00133" xmlns:ER="http://.../NS/XDM">
  <XDM:SOURCE-ITEM Role="RawData" Name="Purchases" Version="1"/>
  <XDM:SOURCE-ITEM Role="AssociationRules" Name="Rules" Version="1"/>
  <XDM:OPERATOR>
    <ER:EVALUATE-RULE xmlns:ER="http:.../NS/EVALUATE-RULE">
      . . . tags with operator clauses . . .
    </ER:EVALUATE-RULE>
  </XDM:OPERATOR>
  <XDM:OUTPUT-ITEM Name="Rules-&-Cust" Version='1'
   Virtual="NO" Role="EvaluatedRules" Root="DATA-AND-RULE-SET"
   NS="http://xdm.unito.it/NS/DATA/Data-With-Rules"/>
</XDM:STATEMENT>
```

Notice that the specific element nodes of the operator are defined in the namespace `ER:`, corresponding to the URI `"http:.../NS/EVALUATE-RULE"`, outside the standard XDM namespace.

The first `SOURCE-ITEM` node specifies the data item with the role of `RawData`; it is the data set over which rules are evaluated. The second `SOURCE-ITEM` node specifies the data item with the role of AssociationRules, i.e. the set of association rules to evaluate.

The operator produces a new data item, which contains the same rules extended with the list of customers for which each rule holds. The output data item is specified by the XDM:OUTPUT-ITEM. Evaluated association rules have a specific role (EvaluatedRules) and in the case of this statement will be materialized (attribute Virtual=NO). The name of the output node is defined by the Root attribute and its namespace (ERD) is defined by a NS specification. □

The data item produced by the previous statement is the following.

```
<XDM:DATA-ITEM Name="Rules-&-Cust" Version="1" Virtual="NO"
     Date="..." xmlns:XDM="http://.../NS/XDM">
 <XDM:DERIVATION Statement="00133"/>
 <XDM:CONTENT>
   <EAR:EVALUATED-ASSOCIATION-RULE-SET
     xmlns:AR="http://.../NS/DATA/EvAssRules">
      <EAR:RULE>
        <EAR:BODY>
          <EAR:ELEMENT Name="ITEM"> A </EAR:ELEMENT>
          <EAR:ELEMENT Name="ITEM"> B </EAR:ELEMENT>
        </EAR:BODY>
        <EAR:HEAD>
          <EAR:ELEMENT Name="ITEM"> C </EAR:ELEMENT>
        </EAR:HEAD>
        <EAR:SUPPORT value="0.5"/>
        <EAR:CONFIDENCE value="0.8"/>
        <EAR:EVALUATED-FOR>
          <EAR:ELEMENT Name="CUST"> c1 </EAR:ELEMENT>
          <EAR:ELEMENT Name="CUST"> c3 </EAR:ELEMENT>
        </EAR:EVALUATED-FOR>
      </EAR:RULE>
   </EAR:EVALUATED-ASSOCIATION-RULE-SET>
 </XDM:CONTENT>
</XDM:DATA-ITEM>
```

Notice that this data item is structurally similar to the one shown in Example 2, named Rules. In particular, it is defined on a different namespace associated with the prefix EAR; furthermore, for each rule an element named EAR:EVALUATED-FOR is added, which contains the set of customers for which the rule holds (notice that each customer is described by an occurrence of element EAR:ELEMENT, whose attribute Name specifies the feature whose value is reported in the content).

Example 5: We want to select now the customer identifiers that satisfy a particular association rule of interest, such as {A, B}⇒ {C}, shown in Example 2. We perform a selection operation on Rules-&-Cust data item. The operator SELECT-DATA-ITEM, in the XDM namespace, makes use of the SOURCE-ITEM and OUTPUT-ITEM nodes for the specification of the input and output, while the OPERATOR node introduces the kind of operator. Notice the roles for the input and output data items. The SELECT-DATA-ITEM statement follows, for which we omitted the details for lack of space.

```
<XDM:STATEMENT ID="00134" xmlns:XDM="http://.../NS/XDM">
  <XDM:SOURCE-ITEM Role="Input" Name="Rules-&-Cust" Version="1"/>
  <XDM:OPERATOR>
     <XDM:SELECT-DATA-ITEM>
      . . . tags with operator clauses . . .
     </XDM:SELECT-DATA-ITEM>
  </XDM:OPERATOR>
  <XDM:OUTPUT-ITEM Name="Select-Cust" Role="Selected" Version='1'
   Virtual="NO" Root="CONTENT"
   NS="http://xdm.unito.it/NS/XDM"/>
</XDM:STATEMENT>
```

The output of this SELECT-DATA-ITEM statement is the first version of the data item named Select-Cust. It will be materialized and will contain the list of customer identifiers in EAR:ELEMENT nodes under the root node CONTENT. The role of the data item puts in evidence that this object is a selected version of the input. □

Example 6: Consider the XDM data item storing the details of customers.

```
<XDM:DATA-ITEM Name="Customers" Version="1"
     Date="..." Virtual="NO" xmlns:XDM="http://.../NS/XDM">
 <XDM:CONTENT>
 <CUST ID="c1" SALARY="53.000" AGE="56" SEX="M" COUNTRY="FL"/>
 <CUST ID="c2" SALARY="46.500" AGE="32" SEX="M" COUNTRY="VA"/>
 <CUST ID="c3" SALARY="60.000" AGE="44" SEX="F" COUNTRY="CA"/>
      .  .  . Other customers  . . .
 </XDM:CONTENT>
</XDM:DATA-ITEM>
```

Now we would like to better analyze the customers that satisfy the association rule of interest and whose identifiers are listed in Select-Cust. In particular we would like to perform a clusterization step that groups similar customers according to their details. Therefore, we retrieve the details of selected customers by joining Select-Cust with the data-item Customers. We use a data manipulation operator named JOIN-DATA-ITEM, shown in the following, which combines the element nodes in the first source data item with the element nodes in the second data item specified by the SOURCE-ITEM nodes. The element nodes from the first and second source items are retrieved according to a select condition that consists in an XPath expression. Its application results in a set of valid node pairs included under the first version of the output data item named My-Cust under the root node CONTENT. In the following the details of the condition are omitted for lack of space.

```
<XDM:STATEMENT ID="00135" xmlns:XDM="http://.../NS/XDM">
  <XDM:SOURCE-ITEM Role="Input1" Name="Select-Cust" Version="1"/>
  <XDM:SOURCE-ITEM Role="Input2" Name="Customers" Version="1"/>
  <XDM:OPERATOR>
     <XDM:JOIN-DATA-ITEM>
      . . . tags with operator clauses . . .
     </XDM:JOIN-DATA-ITEM>
  </XDM:OPERATOR>
  <XDM:OUTPUT-ITEM Name="My-Cust" Role="Joined"
   Version='1' Virtual="NO" Root="CONTENT"
   NS="http://xdm.unito.it/NS/XDM"/>
</XDM:STATEMENT>
```

The ouput of this JOIN-DATA-ITEM statement, under the XDM namespace, has role Joined that puts in evidence the nature of the output whose content is determined by the operator inputs. Follows the new data item, named My-Cust:

```
<XDM:DATA-ITEM Name="My-Cust" Version="1"
     Date="..." Virtual="NO" xmlns:XDM="http://.../NS/XDM">
  <XDM:DERIVATION Statement="00135"/>
  <XDM:CONTENT>
    <EAR:ELEMENT Name="CUST"
     xmlns:AR="http://.../NS/DATA/EvAssRules> c1 </ELEMENT>
    <CUST ID="c1" SALARY="53.000" AGE="56" SEX="M" COUNTRY="FL"/>
    <EAR:ELEMENT Name="CUST"
     xmlns:AR="http://.../NS/DATA/EvAssRules> c3 </ELEMENT>
    <CUST ID="c3" SALARY="60.000" AGE="44" SEX="F" COUNTRY="CA"/>
       . . . Other customers . . .
  </XDM:CONTENT>
</XDM:DATA-ITEM>
```

Notice the DERIVATION node referring to the statement that generated this derived data item. Notice also the customer identifier in EAR:ELEMENT that comes from evaluated rules generated by EVALUATE-RULE. It is still in the namespace EAR of that operator, since it could still be checked and modified by that operator. □

Example 7: Finally, to conclude our sample knowledge discovery process by XDM, we would like to perform a clusterization step that groups similar customers according to their details. A clustering operator is called:

```
<XDM:STATEMENT ID="00136" xmlns:CLU="http://.../NS/CLU">
  <XDM:SOURCE-ITEM Role="RawData" Name="My-Cust" Version="1"]"/>
  <XDM:OPERATOR>
     <CLU:CLUSTER>
      . . . tags with operator clauses . . .
     </CLU:CLUSTER>
  </XDM:OPERATOR>
  <XDM:OUTPUT-ITEM Name="Cust-Clusters" Role="Clustered-Data"
```

```
  Version='1' Virtual="NO" Root="CONTENT" NS="http://.../XDM"/>
</XDM:STATEMENT>
```

This operator has the namespace CLU for clustering. It specifies the source data item with the role RawData and the ouput one with a specific role. □

5 XDM Database Schema and State

Defined the two basic XDM concepts, we can formally define the concepts of XDM *database schema* and XDM *database state*. They help us to define some integrity constraints over the possible inputs and outputs of a given statement, or, dually, over the possible statements that can be applied to a given data item. These are meta data on the KDD process that can be exploited by querying the schema of the XDM database to check (automatically by the system or explicitly by the user) the consistence among the operations performed over the data.

Definition 5: The *schema of an XDM database* is a 4-tuple $\langle \overline{S}, \overline{I}, \overline{In}, \overline{Out} \rangle$, where $\overline{S}$ is a set of statement schemas, and $\overline{I}$ is a set of data item schemas.

$\overline{In}$ is a set of tuples $\langle Operator, InputRole, InputFormat \rangle$, where $Operator$ is an operator whose schema is described by a tuple in S (in the form $prefix : root$); $InputRole$ is the role expected by the operator for the input data; $InputFormat$ is a data item content root (whose schema is described by a tuple in I) allowed for the role (if the operator does not require any particular data format for the specified role, $InputFormat$ is $*$).

$\overline{Out}$ is a set of tuples $\langle Operator, OutputRole, OutputFormat \rangle$ where $Operator$, $OutputRole$ and $OutputFormat$ are analogously defined. □

Example 8: With reference to the KDD scenario described in previous examples, this is the schema of our database.

$\overline{In}$={⟨MR:MINE-RULE, RawData,*⟩, ⟨ER:EVALUATE-RULE, RawData,*⟩,
⟨ER:EVALUATE-RULE, AssociationRules, AR:ASSOCIATION-RULE-SET⟩,
⟨XDM:SELECT-DATA-ITEM, Input,*⟩,⟨XDM:JOIN-DATA-ITEM, Input1,*⟩,
⟨XDM:JOIN-DATA-ITEM, Input2,*⟩,⟨CLU:CLUSTER, RawData,*⟩}
$\overline{Out}$={⟨MR:MINE-RULE, AssociationRules,AR:ASSOCIATION-RULE-SET⟩,
⟨ER:EVALUATE-RULE, EvaluatedRules,ERD:DATA-AND-RULE-SET⟩,
⟨XDM:SELECT-DATA-ITEM,Selected,*⟩,⟨XDM:JOIN-DATA-ITEM,Joined,*⟩,
⟨CLU:CLUSTER, Clustered-Data, CLU:CLUSTERS⟩} □

Definition 6: The state of an XDM database is represented as a pair

$$\langle DI : Set\ Of(DataItem), ST : Set\ Of(Statement) \rangle$$

where DI is a set of XDM data items (see Definition 1), and ST is a set of XDM statements (see Definition 4). The following constraints hold.

- *Data Item Identity.* Given a data item d and its mandatory attributes Name, and Version, the pair ⟨Name, Version⟩ uniquely identifies the data item d in the database state.
- *Statement Identity.* Given a statement s and its mandatory attribute ID, its value uniquely identifies the statement s in the database state.

Table 1. Database states for the example of Figure 1

State	*DI*	*ST*
S_0	{⟨Purchases,1⟩},⟨Customers,1⟩}	∅
S_1	{⟨Purchases,1⟩,⟨Customers,1⟩,⟨Rules,1⟩}	{00128}
S_2	{⟨Purchases,1⟩,⟨Customers,1⟩,⟨Rules,1⟩,⟨Rules-&-Cust,1⟩}	{00128,00133}
S_3	{⟨Purchases,1⟩,⟨Customers,1⟩,⟨Rules,1⟩,⟨Rules-&-Cust,1⟩, ⟨Select-Cust,1⟩}	{00128,00133, 00134}
S_4	{⟨Purchases,1⟩,⟨Customers,1⟩,⟨Rules,1⟩,⟨Rules-&-Cust,1⟩, ⟨Select-Cust,1⟩,⟨My-Cust,1⟩}	{00128,00133, 00134,00135}
S_5	{⟨Purchases,1⟩,⟨Customers,1⟩,⟨Rules,1⟩,⟨Rules-&-Cust,1⟩, ⟨Select-Cust,1⟩,⟨My-Cust,1⟩, ⟨Cust-Clusters,1⟩}	{00128,00133, 00134,00135, 00136}

• *Relationship between statements and source data items.* Consider an XDM statement *s*. The attributes `Name` and `Version` of each `XDM:SOURCE-ITEM` appearing in *s* must denote one and only one XDM data item.

• *Relationship between derived data items and statements.* Consider a derived XDM data item *d*. The value specified by the `Statement` attribute of the `XDM:DERIVATION` element must identify one and only one XDM data item. □

Example 9: With reference to the KDD process described in Figure 1 the database has moved between five states that are reached after the application of each statement, to some of the data items in `DI`. After each statement execution, the statement identifier is added to `ST` and the output data items are added to `DI`. □

Observe that an XDM database is both a data item base and a statement base. When a new statement is executed, the new database state is obtained by adding both the executed statement and the new data item. This structure represents the two-fold nature of the knowledge discovery process: data and patterns are not meaningful if considered in isolation; in contrast, patterns are significant if the overall process is described, because their meaning is clarified by the data mining operators that generated them. Considering this, the patterns representation provided by PMS [12] does not seem to be so specifically defined.

6 Implementation of a Prototype of the XDM System

We implemented a prototype based on the XDM framework. This prototype demonstrated the feasibility of the approach and gave us useful indications to study practical problems related with extensibility issues and performance issues.

The XDM System is fully realized in Java, and is based on open source components only. The architecture of the XDM System (Figure 2) is organized in four overlapped layers, each of them hiding the lower layers to the upper ones.

The top-most components are The *User Interface* and the *XDM API* allow to interact with the XDM System: the *XDM API* is used by applications; the *User Interface* is used in interactive sessions with the system.

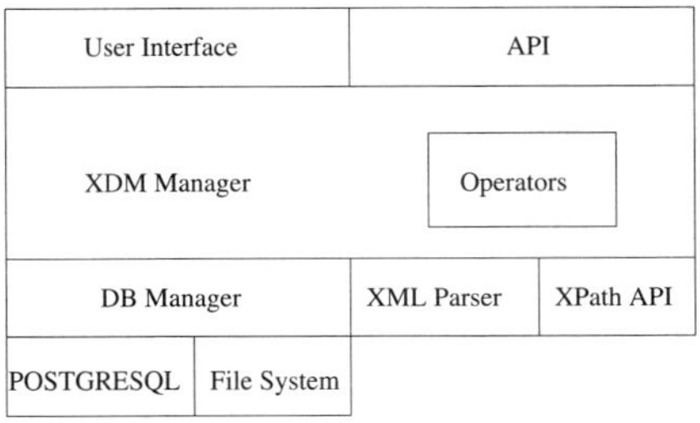

Fig. 2. XDM System Architecture

The second layer is constituted by the *XDM Manager*, and by *Operators*, i.e. components which implement data management or data mining operators. *XDM Manager* interprets statements coming from interfaces, activates execution of tools, exploits *DB Manager* to access and store both meta data and data items. *Operators*, are responsible to implement the actual semantics given to the operators; they can interact with the system through an API provided by *XDM Manager*. This embedding is beneficial because it provides an inner and immediate compatibility and security check on which operations are allowed by operators. This is a fundamental feature of an open system where new operators are allowed to be added freely by users at any time.

XDM Manager exploits components in the third layer: these are *DB Manager*, *XML Parser* and *XPath API* components; in particular, since both *XML Parser* and *XPath API* might be used by *Operators* for reading data items, *XDM Manager* provides a controlled access to these components (in the sense that these latter components can be exploited by various tools in *Operators*). For both *XML Parser* and *XPath API* we adopted `xerces` XML Parser and the XPath API library available in the `xalan` XSLT processor (open source implementations developed by the *Apache Software Foundation*).

DB Manager encapsulates all data management operations. In particular, it currently exploits `POSTGRESQL` DBMS to manage the meta-schema of the XDM framework, and the file system to store unstructured and semi-structured data items. This latter choice is motivated by efficiency reasons. However, we plan to study the integration of an XML DBMS in *DB Manager*.

In the current version, operators read XDM items by a SAX parser, which has the advantage of avoiding the construction and storage of the DOM tree corresponding to their XML structure. For the future, we also plan the development of a fast XPath interpreter on top of the parser so that only the relevant XML fragments are identified and sent through the channel (avoiding to send the entire XML document). Another possible solution is the usage of XML compressors. Furthermore, we also plan to investigate the problem of getting data items from different data sources, such as relational databases or native XML database. Finally, we plan to evolve XDM system into a distributed, grid like, system, where both distributed data sources and distributed computational sources are connected through the Internet.

7 Conclusions

In this paper we presented an XML-based data model, named XDM. It is designed to be adopted inside the framework of inductive databases. XDM allows the management of semi-structured and complex patterns thanks to the semi-structured nature of the data that can be represented by XML.

In XDM the pattern definition is represented together with data. This allows the reuse of patterns by the inductive database management system. In particular, XDM explicitly represents the statements that were executed in the derivation process of the pattern. The flexibility of the XDM representation allows extensibility to new pattern models and new mining operators: this makes the framework suitable to build an open system, easily customized by the analyst. We experimented the XDM idea by means of a system prototype that resulted to be easily and quickly extendible to new operators.

References

1. P. Alcamo, F. Domenichini, and F. Turini. An xml based environment in support of the overall kdd process. In *FQAS*, 2000.
2. P. V. Biron and A. Malhotra. Xml schema part 2: Data types. Technical Report REC-xmlschema-2-20010502, World Wide Web Consortium, http://www.w3.org/TR/2001/REC-xmlschema-2-20010502/, May 2001.
3. D. Braga, A. Campi, S. Ceri, M. Klemettinen, and P. L. Lanzi. Discovering interesting information in xml data with association rules. In *ACM SAC*, 2003.
4. A.G. Buchner and M.Baumgarten. Data mining and xml: Current and future issues. *Int. Conf. on Web Information Systems Engineering*, 2000.
5. B. Catania, M. Maddalena, Mazza, E. Bertino, and S. Rizzi. A framework for data mining pattern management. In *Proc. of ECML-PKDD 2004*, Italy, Sept. 2004.
6. DMG. The pmml language. *http://www.dmg.org/pmml-v2-0.htm.*
7. A. N. Edmonds. Xmlminer, xmlrule and metarule white paper. Technical report, Scientio, Inc., http://www.kdnuggets.com/news/2001/n14/7i.html, 2002.
8. T. Imielinski and H. Mannila. A database perspective on knowledge discovery. *Coomunications of the ACM*, 39(11):58–64, November 1996.
9. R. Meo, G. Psaila, and S. Ceri. An extension to SQL for mining association rules. *Journal of Data Mining and Knowledge Discovery*, 2(2), 1998.
10. G. Psaila. Enhancing the kdd process in the relational database mining framework by quantitative evaluation of association rules. In *Knowledge Discovery for Business Information Systems*. Kluwer Academic Publisher, January 2001.
11. S. Rizzi. Uml-based conceptual modeling of pattern-bases. In *Proc. of PaRMA'04*.
12. S. Rizzi, E. Bertino, B. Catania, M. Golfarelli, M. Halkidi, M. Terrovitis, P. Vassiliadis, M. Vazirgiannis, and E. Vrachnos. Towards a logical model for patterns. In *ER*, pages 77–90, 2003.
13. H: S. Thompson, D. Beech, M. Maloney, and N. Mendelsohn. Xml schema part 1: Structures. Technical Report REC-xmlschema-1-20010502, World Wide Web Consortium, http://www.w3.org/TR/2001/REC-xmlschema-1-20010502/, May 2001.

Pattern-Based Query Answering

Alkis Simitsis[1] and Georgia Koutrika[2]

[1] National Technical University of Athens,
Department of Electrical and Computer Engineering,
Athens, Greece
asimi@dbnet.ece.ntua.gr
[2] University of Athens,
Department of Computer Science,
Athens, Greece
koutrika@di.uoa.gr

Abstract. Users without knowledge of schemas or structured query languages have difficulties in accessing information stored in databases. Commercial and research efforts have focused on keyword-based searches. Among them, précis queries generate entire multi-relation databases, which are logical subsets of existing ones, instead of individual relations. A logical database subset contains not only items directly related to the query selections but also items implicitly related to them in various ways. Existing approaches to précis query answering assume that a database is pre-annotated with a set of weights, and when a query is issued, an ad-hoc logical subset is constructed on the fly. This approach has several limitations, such as dependence on users for providing appropriate weights and constraints for answering précis queries, and difficulty to capture different query semantics and user preferences. In this paper, we propose a pattern-based approach to logical database subset generation. Patterns of logical subsets corresponding to different queries or user preferences may be recognized and stored in the system. Each time a user poses a question, the system searches in a repository of précis patterns to extract an appropriate one. Then, this is enriched with tuples extracted from the database, in order to produce the logical database subset.

1 Introduction

The need for facilitating access in information stored in a database for users with no specific knowledge of schemas or structured query languages has been acknowledged, especially in the context of web accessible databases, as libraries, museums, and other organizations publish their electronic contents on the Web. Towards this direction, current commercial and research efforts have focused on keyword-based searches. Among them, *précis queries* are free-form queries that generate entire multi-relation databases, which are logical subsets of existing ones, instead of individual relations [10]. The logical subset of a database generated by a précis query contains not only items directly related to the query selections but also items implicitly related to them in various ways. This subset is useful in many cases and provides to the user much greater insight into the original data.

T. Grust et al. (Eds.): EDBT 2006 Workshops, LNCS 4254, pp. 829 – 841, 2006.

For instance, a user asking about "Woody Allen" would probably like to know a little bit more than that "*Woody Allen is a director*". A more meaningful response would be in the form of the following précis:

> "*Woody Allen was born on December 1, 1935 in Brooklyn, New York, USA. As a director, Woody Allen's work includes Match Point (2005), Melinda and Melinda (2004), Anything Else (2003). As an actor, Woody Allen's work includes Hollywood Ending (2002), The Curse of the Jade Scorpion (2001).*"

This response provides sufficient information to help someone learn about Allen and identify new keywords for further searching. For example, the user may decide to explicitly issue a new query about "*Anything Else*" or implicitly by following underlined topics (hyperlinks) to pages containing more relevant information. On the other hand, given large databases, enterprises often need smaller subsets that conform to the original schema and satisfy all of its constraints in order to perform realistic tests of new applications before deploying them to production. Likewise, software vendors need such smaller but correct databases to demonstrate new software product functionality. Based on the above, support of précis queries over databases and generation of logical database subsets comprises an advanced searching paradigm helping users to gain insight into the contents of a database.

Given a précis query, a system would first determine the schema of the logical database subset, i.e. the database part that contains information related to the query, and then extract tuples from the database with the use of appropriate SQL queries in order to populate this subset. The schema of the subset that should be extracted from a database given a précis query may vary depending on the type of the query issued and the user issuing the query. For instance, the logical subset corresponding to a query about movies would probably contain the title, year and duration of movies along with the names of directors and actors; whereas the logical subset corresponding to a query about actors would most likely contain detailed information about actors such as name, date and location of birth, and nationality and only titles of movies an actor has starred in. Furthermore, different users or groups of users, e.g., movie reviewers vs. filmgoers, would be interested in different logical subsets for the same query.

Existing approaches to précis query answering assume that each entity and relationship of a database is pre-annotated with a weight determining its significance for a certain user [10]. When a query is issued, the appropriate logical subset is constructed on the fly based on syntactic criteria issued by the user at query time or pre-stored in the system. This approach has several drawbacks: dependence on users for providing appropriate weights and criteria for answering précis queries, difficulty to capture different query semantics and user preferences in the same time, and inefficient execution since a logical subset is generated from scratch each time a query is issued.

However, as the examples above illustrate, patterns of logical subsets corresponding to different queries or groups of users may be recognized and stored in the system. For instance, different patterns would be used to capture preferences of movie reviewers and filmgoers. In this context, each time a user poses a question, the system searches in a repository of *précis patterns* to extract an appropriate one. Then, this précis pattern is enriched with tuples extracted from the database according to the query keywords, in order to produce the logical database subset.

Furthermore, apart from the benefit of getting a pre-stored schema for a logical subset of a database instead of creating from scratch a new one, we exploit the presence of précis patterns in our framework in a two-fold manner: (a) incremental population of a logical database subset, and (b) pre-storing answers for the most frequent précis queries.

Contributions. In brief, the contributions of our paper are the following.

- We propose a pattern-based approach to logical database subset generation. Précis patterns may capture semantics of different précis queries or preferences of different user groups and improve the efficiency of generation of logical database subsets from précis queries.
- We present the architecture of a system that produces logical database subsets according to précis queries posed by individuals using précis patterns extracted from the repository and describe methods that implement the required functionality.
- We discuss two optimization techniques that are used to further improve the efficiency and effectiveness of the system: incremental population of a logical database subset and using pre-stored answers.

Outline. The rest of the paper is structured as follows. In Section 2, we present related work. In Section 3, we describe the general framework of précis queries and introduce précis patterns. In Section 4, we describe our approach of answering queries using précis patterns and we sketch the techniques used for incremental population of a logical database subset and pre-storing answers in the system. Finally, in Section 5, we conclude our results with a prospect to the future.

2 Related Work

The need for free-form queries has been early recognized in the context of databases. Motro [14] described the idea of using tokens, i.e. value of either data or metadata, when accessing information instead of structured queries, and proposed an interface that understands such utterances by interpreting them in a unique way, i.e. complete them to proper queries. With the advent of the World Wide Web, the idea has been revisited. In particular, recent approaches on keyword searches in databases [1, 2, 3, 6, 7, 11] extended the idea of tokens to values that may be part of attribute values. An answer to a keyword search is a set of ranked tuples. Oracle 9i Text [15], Microsoft SQL Server [12] and IBM DB2 Text Information Extender [9] create full text indexes on text attributes of relations and then perform keyword queries. Keyword search over XML databases has also attracted interest recently [4, 5, 8].

Existing keyword searching approaches focus on finding and possibly interconnecting tuples in relations that contain the query terms. For example, the answer for "Woody Allen" would be in the form of relation-attribute pair, such as (Director, Name). In many cases, this answer may suffice, but in many practical scenarios it conveys little information about "Woody Allen". A more complete answer containing, for instance, information about this director's movies and awards would be more meaningful and useful instead. In the spirit of the above, recently, précis queries have been proposed [10] that instead of simply locating and connecting values in tables, they also consider information around these values that may be related to them. Therefore, the answer to a précis query might also contain information found in other parts of the database, e.g., movies directed by Woody Allen. This information needs to be "assembled" -in perhaps unforeseen ways- by joining tuples from multiple relations. Consequently, the answer to a précis query is a whole new database, a logical database subset, derived from the original database compared to flatten out results returned by other approaches. Additionally, a complementary research effort provides a method towards the translation of a précis query answer into a narrative form, in order to return results such the one in the introduction about "Woody Allen" [19].

In this paper, we built upon the approach suggested in [10] and we revisit the idea of a logical database subset generated by a précis query by recognizing the existence of précis patterns, i.e. patterns of logical database subsets that capture semantics of different précis queries or preferences of different user groups and improve the efficiency of a précis query answering system.

3 The Précis Query Framework

3.1 Preliminaries

We consider the *database schema graph* **G(V, E)** as a directed graph corresponding to a database schema D. There are two types of nodes in **V**:

- *relation nodes,* **R**, one for each relation in the schema;
- *attribute nodes*, **A**, one for each attribute of each relation in the schema.

Likewise, edges in **E** are the following:

- *projection edges*, **Π**, each one connects an attribute node with its container relation node, representing the possible projection of the attribute in the system's answer;
- *join edges*, **J**, from a relation node to another relation node, representing a potential join between these relations. These could be joins that arise naturally due to foreign key constraints, but could also be other joins that are meaningful to a domain expert. Joins are directed for reasons explained later. For simplicity in presentation, we assume (a) that primary keys are not composite; thus, an attribute from a relation joins to an attribute from another relation, and (b) that these attributes have the same name. For convenience, we do not depict the joining attributes in both relations; instead, the common name of the joining attributes is tagged on the respective join edge between the two relations.

Therefore, a database graph is formally defined as a directed graph **G(V, E)**, where: $\mathbf{V} = \mathbf{R} \cup \mathbf{A}$, and $\mathbf{E} = \mathbf{\Pi} \cup \mathbf{J}$. The notation for the graphical representation of a database schema graph is depicted in Fig. 1.

A *weight*, w, is assigned to each edge of the graph **G**. This is a real number in the range [0, 1], and represents the significance of the bond between the corresponding nodes. Weight equal to 1 expresses strong relationship; in other words, if one node of the edge appears in an answer, then the edge should be taken into account making the other node appear as well. If a weight equals to 0, occurrence of one node of the edge in an answer does not imply occurrence of the other node.

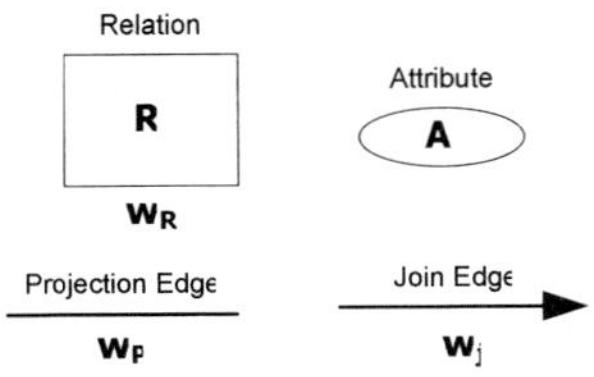

Fig. 1. Representation of graph elements

Based on the above, two relation nodes could be connected through two different join edges, in the two possible directions, between the same pair of attributes, but carrying different weights. A directed join edge expresses the dependence of the source relation of the join on the target one. The source relation indicates the relation already considered for the answer and the target corresponds to the relation that may be included, if the join is taken into account. For simplicity, we assume that there is at most one edge from one node to the same destination node.

A directed path between two relation nodes, comprising adjacent join edges, represents the "implicit" join between these relations. Similarly, a directed path between a relation node and an attribute node, comprising a set of adjacent join edges and a projection edge represents the "implicit" projection of the attribute on this relation. The weight of a path is a function of the weight of constituent edges. In principle, one may imagine several functions. All of them, however, should satisfy the condition that the weight decreases as the length of the path increases, based on human intuition and cognitive evidence [17].

Consider a database D properly annotated with a set of weights and a *précis query* Q, which is a set of tokens, i.e. $Q=\{k_1,k_2,\ldots,k_m\}$. We define as *initial relation* any database relation that contains at least one tuple in which one or more query tokens have been found. A tuple containing at least one query token is called *initial tuple*.

A *logical database subset* D′ of D satisfies the following:

- The set of relation names in D′ is a subset of that in the original database D.
- For each relation R_i' in the result D′, its set of attributes in D′ is a subset of its set of attributes in D.
- For each relation R_i' in the result D′, the set of its tuples is a subset of the set of tuples in the original relation R_i in D (when projected on the set of attributes that are present in the result).

The result of applying query Q on a database D given a set of constraints C is a logical database subset D′ of D, such that D′ contains initial tuples for Q and any other tuple in D that can be transitively reached by (foreign-key) joins on D starting from *some* initial tuple, subject to the constraints in C [10]. Possible constraints in C could include the maximum number of attributes in D′, the minimum weight of paths in the database schema graph, the maximum number of joins, the maximum number of tuples in D′ and so forth. Using different constraints and weights on the edges of the database schema allows generating different answers for the same query.

Weights and constraints may be provided in different ways. They may be set by the user at query time using an appropriate user interface. This option is attractive in many cases since it enables interactive exploration of the contents of a database. This bears a resemblance to query refinement in keyword searches. In case of précis queries, the user may explore different regions of the database starting, for example, from those containing objects closely related to the topic of a query and progressively expanding to parts of the database containing objects more loosely related to it. Although this approach is quite elegant, there is a major disadvantage: apart of the difficulty of browsing efficiently a database schema, per se, the user should spend some time with a procedure that does not seem relevant to his/her need for a certain answer. Weights and criteria may be pre-specified by a designer, or may be stored as part of a profile corresponding to a user or a group of users.

However, finding an appropriate set of weights to annotate a database is difficult as we explain below. Depending on users for providing appropriate weights for producing meaningful answers to précis queries is not acceptable, at least for the majority of them. Furthermore, weights may depend on the query and the user issuing the query, thus finding a unique set of weights for a database capturing different query semantics and user preferences altogether may not be possible. Finally, in the case of a system serving a large number of users, generating a logical subset from scratch each time a query is issued turns to be time consuming.

Therefore, in this paper, we propose a different approach. Patterns of logical subsets corresponding to different queries or groups of users may be recognized and stored in the system. For instance, different patterns would be used to capture preferences of movie reviewers and filmgoers.

3.2 Précis Patterns

Formally, given the database schema graph G of a database D, a *précis pattern* is a directed rooted tree $\mathcal{P}$**(V,E)** on top of G annotated with a set of weights. Given a query Q over database D, a précis pattern $\mathcal{P}$**(V,E)** is *applicable* to Q, if its root relation coincides with an initial relation for Q.

The result of applying query Q on a database D given an applicable pattern $\mathcal{P}$ is a logical database subset D′ of D, such that:

- The set of relation names in D′ is a subset of that in $\mathcal{P}$.
- For each relation R_i′ in the result D′, its set of attributes in D′ is a subset of its set of attributes in $\mathcal{P}$.
- For each relation R_i′ in the result D′, the set of its tuples is a subset of the set of tuples in the original relation R_i in D (when projected on the set of attributes that are present in the result).

In order to produce the logical database subset D′, a pattern $\mathcal{P}$ is enriched with tuples derived from the database based on constraints in C. Possible constraints can be the maximum number of attributes, the maximum number of tuples, and so forth.

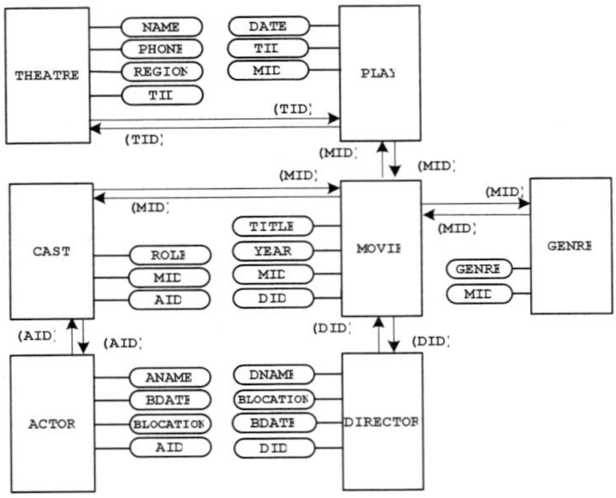

DIRECTOR(did,dname,blocation,
bdate)
THEATRE(tid,name,phone,region)
PLAY (tid,mid,date),
GENRE(mid,genre)
MOVIE(mid,title,year,did)
CAST (mid,aid,role)
ACTOR(aid,aname,blocation,bdate)

Fig. 2. An example database graph

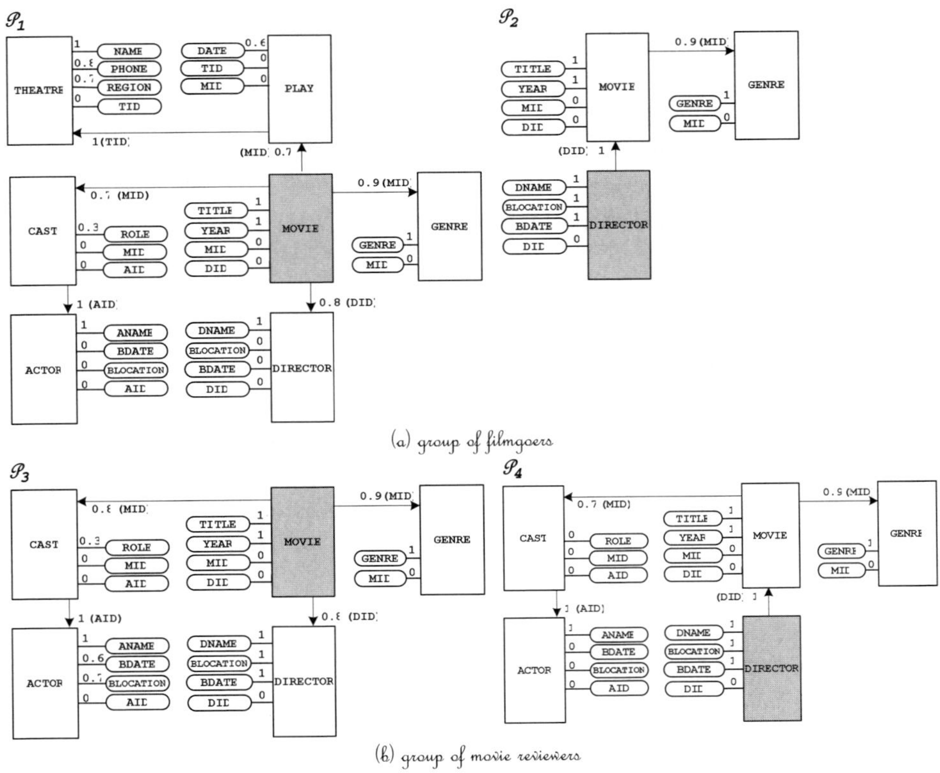

Fig. 3. Example précis patterns

3.3 An Example Database

Consider a movies database [16] described by the schema presented in Fig. 2; primary keys are underlined. The corresponding database graph is depicted in Fig. 2 too. On top of this graph, précis patterns may be recognized and stored in the system. Patterns may correspond to different queries. In Fig. 3, $\mathcal{P}_1$ and $\mathcal{P}_2$ are patterns corresponding to different types of queries, i.e. regarding movies and directors, respectively (as indicated by the initial relations colored grey in each pattern). Different précis patterns may be also used to capture preferences of different groups of users. For instance, $\mathcal{P}_3$ and $\mathcal{P}_4$ are different patterns regarding movies and directors, respectively. $\mathcal{P}_1$ and $\mathcal{P}_2$ might capture preferences of filmgoers whereas $\mathcal{P}_3$ and $\mathcal{P}_4$ might correspond to movie reviewers. Assume that, $\mathcal{P}_1$ captures the fact that a filmgoer would be interested in information about theatres playing specific movies, while a movie-reviewer would not, as expressed in $\mathcal{P}_3$.

From the discussion above, it becomes apparent that there is an *n*-to-*m* correspondence between (group/user) profiles and patterns. As Fig. 4 shows, a pattern $\mathcal{P}_i$ may be used by more than one profile and a profile G_j may involve more than one pattern.

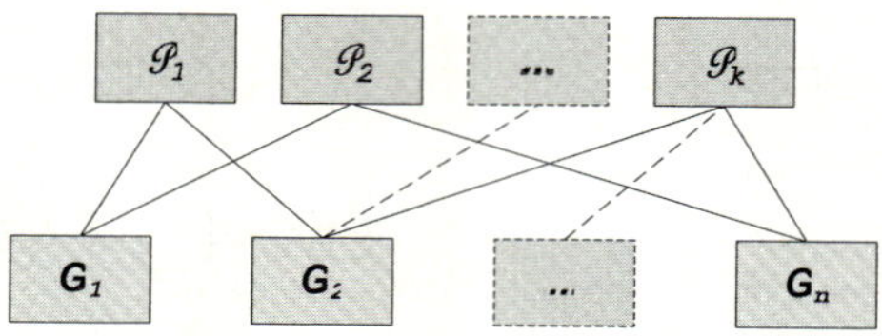

Fig. 4. Correspondence between patterns and profiles

Although an extensive analysis of précis patterns creation procedures is out of the scope of this paper, as an example, we refer two typical ways:

Manual creation. Pre-specified patterns may be created by a designer targeting different groups of users and different types of queries for a specific domain.

Semi-automatic creation. The system is trained using logs of queries that domain users have issued in the past. No matter how précis patterns are initially created, the system may adapt those associated with a specific user by learning from the queries this user submits to the system. In this way, the system may provide personalized answers to précis queries.

4 Answering Queries Using Précis Patterns

In this section, we describe a framework that generalizes the usage of précis queries based on patterns.

System Architecture. The system architecture of our approach is depicted in Fig. 5. Each time a user poses a question, the system finds the initial relations that match this query, i.e. database relations containing at least one tuple in which one or more query tokens have been found (Keyword Locator). Then, it searches in a repository of précis patterns to extract an appropriate one (Précis Manager). If an appropriate pattern is not found, then a new one is created and registered in the repository. Next, this précis pattern is enriched with tuples extracted from the database according to the query keywords, in order to produce the logical database subset (Database Generator).

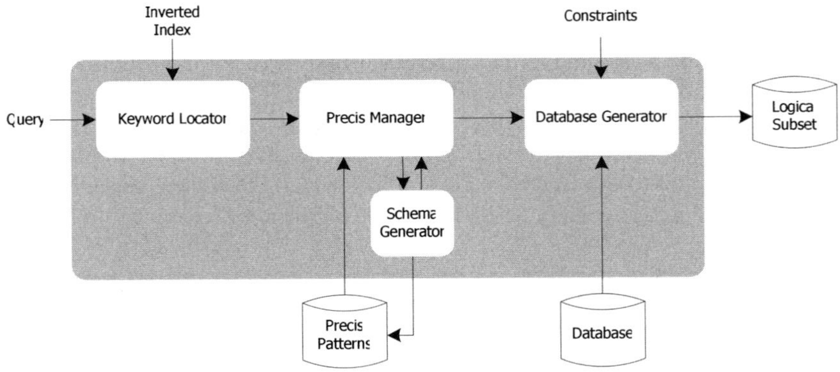

Fig. 5. System architecture

In more details, first, the user submits a précis query $Q=\{k_1, k_2, \ldots, k_m\}$. A set of constraints C may be additionally provided to determine tuples extracted from the database, in order to produce the logical database subset. The following steps are performed.

Keyword Locator. An inverted index associates each keyword that appears in the database with a list of occurrences of the keyword. Modern RDBMS' provide facilities for constructing full text indices on single attributes of relations (e.g., Oracle9i Text). However, in our approach, we chose to create our own inverted index (technical details are out of the scope of this paper, but can be found in [18]), basically due to the following reasons: (a) a keyword may be found in more than one tuple and attribute of a single relation and in more than one relation; and (b) we consider tokens of other data types as well, such as date and number. Based on this inverted index, *Keyword Locator* returns for each term k_i in Q, a list of all initial relations, i.e. $k_i \rightarrow \{R_j\}$, $\forall k_i$ in Q. (If no tuples contain the query tokens, the following steps are not executed.)

Précis Manager. Next, instead of creating an ad-hoc logical subset for the particular query and user, *Précis Manager* searches into the repository of précis patterns to extract those that are appropriate for the situation. If users are categorized into groups, then this module examines only patterns assigned to the group the active user belongs to. Based on the initial relations identified for query Q, one or more applicable patterns may be identified.

Précis patterns are directed rooted trees $\mathcal{P}(\mathbf{V},\mathbf{E})$ that are stored in a graph database depicted as Précis Patterns in Fig. 5. An indexing mechanism `Index` is needed for the search in the graph database. For this purpose, we adopt GraphGrep presented by Shasha et al. [20]. Recall that a précis pattern $\mathcal{P}(\mathbf{V},\mathbf{E})$ is applicable to Q, if its root relation coincides with an initial relation for Q. Thus, given the initial relations and a group of users, the index outputs the appropriate patterns. If none is returned for a certain initial relation, then the request is propagated to the *Schema Generator*. This module is responsible for finding which part of the database schema may contain information related to Q. The output of this step is the schema D' of a logical database subset comprised of: (a) relations that contain the tokens of Q; (b) relations transitively joining to the former, and (c) a subset of their attributes that should be present in the result, according to the preferences registered for the user that poses the query. (For more details, we refer the interested reader to [18].) After its creation, the schema of the logical database subset is stored in the graph database as a pattern associated with the group that the user submitting the query belongs to. Moreover, it is further propagated to the Database Generator through the Précis Manager module. The whole procedure is formally described by the algorithm EP depicted in Fig. 6.

Algorithm Extraction of a Précis Pattern (EP)
Input: a set of initial relations **R**, a group of users U, a set of stored patterns **P**
Output: a set of logical database subsets **D'**

```
Begin
  D'={};
  For each initial relation R∈R
    If (Index(R,U)!=null) {
      P = Index(R,U);
    else
      P = Schema_Generator(R,U);
      P = P ∪ P;
    }
    D' = D' ∪ P;
  End for
  Return D';
End.
```

Fig. 6. The algorithm EP

For instance, a user belonging to the group of filmgoers of Fig. 3 issues the query "1960". Keyword Locator returns two initial relations, DIRECTOR and MOVIE, because this token is found in the field BDATE of the former and in the field YEAR of the latter. Then, Précis Manager identifies two applicable patterns, $\mathcal{P}_1$ and $\mathcal{P}_2$.

Database Generator. Subsequently, *Database Generator* enriches patterns with tuples extracted from the database. On each pattern, it starts from the initial relation where tokens in Q appear. Then, more tuples from other relations are retrieved by (foreign-key) join queries starting from the initial relation and transitively expanding on the database schema graph following edges of the pattern. Joins on a précis pattern are executed in order of decreasing weight. In this way, relations that are most related to a query are populated first. Any relations that may not be eventually populated due to constraints in C would be the ones most weakly connected to the query. In other words, a précis pattern comprises a kind of a "plan" for collecting tuples matching the query and others related to them. At the end of this phase, the logical database subset has been produced.

Formally, given are a database D, a pattern $\mathcal{P}$, and optionally a set of constraints C (e.g., maximum total number of tuples, maximum number of tuples per relation and so forth). For the initial relation of $\mathcal{P}$, the list of tuples containing query tokens is considered. This is an initial logical database subset D_o corresponding to pattern $\mathcal{P}$. The set of possible logical database subsets corresponding to $\mathcal{P}$ in order of increasing cardinality is defined as follows:

$$D_1 \leftarrow D_o \bowtie R_1 \quad , \quad D_2 \leftarrow D_1 \bowtie R_2 \quad , \quad \ldots \quad , \quad D_{nj} \leftarrow D_{n_{j-1}} \bowtie R_{n_j}$$

At any point, a relation R_i is joined to D_{i-1} if there is a join edge in $\mathcal{P}$ between this relation and a relation already populated in D_{i-1}. If more than one join may be executed, these are considered in order of decreasing weight. In this way, relations in D that are most related to the query are populated first. Any relations that may not be eventually populated due to the constraints would be the ones most weakly connected to the query. A logical database subset D_i contains all tuples also contained in D_{i-1} plus any tuples from D that join to those through the corresponding join. According to the constraints, the result database D' is a database D_c, such that:

$$c = \max(\ \{ t \mid t \in [0, n_J] : \text{constraints in } D_t \text{ hold} \}\ )$$

For each relation R_i, a subset of its tuples, R_i', is found in the result D', projected on the set of attributes that are present in the result.

Optimization Issues. Apart from the benefit of getting a pre-stored schema for a logical subset of a database instead of creating from scratch a new one, we further exploit the presence of précis patterns in our framework in a two-fold manner: (a) incremental population of a logical database subset, and (b) pre-stored answers to the most frequent précis queries.

Consider the following scenario: a user submits a query, and the system returns an answer, similar to the one presented in the introduction, in which certain keywords are hyperlinks. Clicking one of them fires a new query involving the corresponding keywords. The latter query is executed by the system and returns a new subset of information. The interesting problem is that this new query may specify results that have already been part of the initial system answer. We discriminate two possible cases: these results may be either presented to the user or not. However, in both cases, it would be desired to avoid re-computing them again.

For instance, assume that the initial query contained a keyword that identifies a director. Then, a possible system answer would contain, among others, a set of several movies, along with the names of their star actors, which could be transformed to hyperlinks. If the search continues with one of the actors, then the movies that he/she has participated in are a superset of the movies presented in the precedent answer. In such case our system incrementally populates the respective pattern for the new query.

Moreover, as practice shows, several keywords are more often posed than some others. According to this, we can keep track of the search history and maintain in the inverted index an extra attribute that stores for each keyword the frequency of its occurrences in queries submitted in the past. In our approach, we take into account the most frequently used keywords along with other parameters, such as the complexity of a pattern, in order to decide which patterns should be populated in advance. The threshold that determines which logical subsets should be populated is subject of further experimentation and tuning, inasmuch as the extent to which each database differs from another.

At this point, it is noteworthy to underline the difference between the notion of a précis pattern and the classical definition of a view. A view returns a single relation, whereas a précis pattern represents the schema of a full-fledged database, which is the logical subset of another database, thus, containing multiple relations along with their relationships and constraints.

5 Conclusions

In this paper, we revisit the idea of a logical database subset generated by a précis query by recognizing the existence of précis patterns, i.e. patterns of logical database subsets that capture semantics of different précis queries or preferences of different user groups and improve the efficiency of a précis query answering system. In this context, each time a user poses a question, the system searches in a repository of précis patterns to extract an appropriate one. Then, this précis pattern is enriched with tuples extracted from the database according to the query keywords, in order to produce the logical database subset. Further optimization techniques are discussed.

Future work includes extension of the aforementioned methods toward the efficient capture and maintenance of précis patterns, the treatment of précis queries with complex semantics, e.g., involving multiple keywords as input combined with several operators, and the tuning of Database Generator. Another challenging issue is the extension of précis queries to provide ranked or top-k results.

Acknowledgments

This work is co-funded by the European Social Fund (75%) and National Resources (25%) - Operational Program for Educational and Vocational Training II (EPEAEK II) and particularly the Program PYTHAGORAS.

References

[1] S. Agrawal, S. Chaudhuri, and G. Das. DBxplorer: A system for keyword-based search over relational databases. In *ICDE*, pp. 5-16, 2002.

[2] A. Balmin, V. Hristidis, and Y. Papakonstantinou. Objectrank: Authority-based keyword search in databases. In *VLDB*, pp. 564-575, 2004.

[3] G. Bhalotia, A. Hulgeri, C. Nakhe, S. Chakrabarti, and S. Sudarshan. Keyword searching and browsing in databases using banks. In *ICDE*, pp. 431-440, 2002.

[4] D. Florescu, D. Kossmann, and I. Manolescu. Integrating keyword search into xml query processing. *Computer Networks*, 33(1-6), 2000.

[5] L. Guo, F. Shao, C. Botev, and J. Shanmugasundaram. Xrank: Ranked keyword search over xml documents. In *SIGMOD*, pp. 16-27, 2003.

[6] V. Hristidis, L. Gravano, and Y. Papakonstantinou. Effcient IR-style keyword search over relational databases. In *VLDB*, pp. 850-861, 2003.

[7] V. Hristidis and Y. Papakonstantinou. Discover: Keyword search in relational databases. In *VLDB*, pp. 670-681, 2002.

[8] V. Hristidis, Y. Papakonstantinou, and A. Balmin. Keyword proximity search on XML graphs. In *ICDE*, pp. 367-378, 2003.

[9] IBM. *DB2 Text Information Extender.* *url: www.ibm.com/software/data/db2/extenders/textinformation/.*

[10] G. Koutrika, A. Simitsis, and Y. Ioannidis. Précis: The essence of a query answer. In *ICDE*, 2006.

[11] U. Masermann and G. Vossen. Design and implementation of a novel approach to keyword searching in relational databases. In *ADBIS-DASFAA*, pp. 171-184, 2000.

[12] Microsoft. *SQL Server 2000. url:msdn.microsoft.com/library/.*

[13] A. Motro. Baroque: A browser for relational databases. *ACM Trans. Inf. Syst.*, 4(2):164-181, 1986.

[14] A. Motro. Constructing queries from tokens. In *SIGMOD*, pp. 120-131, 1986.

[15] Oracle. *Oracle 9i Text.* *url: www.oracle.com/technology/products/text/index.html.*

[16] IMDB. Internet Movies DataBase. *url: www.imdb.com.*

[17] A. Collins and M. Quillian. Retrieval time from semantic memory. J. of Verbal Learning and Verbal Behaviour, 8:240-247, 1969.

[18] G. Koutrika, A. Simitsis, and Y. Ioannidis. Précis: The essence of a query answer. TR-2006-1. *url: www.dblab.ntua.gr.*

[19] A. Simitsis and G. Koutrika. Comprehensible Answers to Précis Queries. In *CAiSE*, 2006.

[20] D. Shasha, J. Tsong-Li Wang, R. Giugno. Algorithmics and Applications of Tree and Graph Searching. In PODS, pp. 39-52, 2002.

Twelve Theses on Reactive Rules for the Web

François Bry and Michael Eckert

University of Munich, Institute for Informatics
Oettingenstr. 67, D-80538 München
{bry, eckert}@pms.ifi.lmu.de
http://www.pms.ifi.lmu.de

Abstract. Reactivity, the ability to detect and react to events, is an essential functionality in many information systems. In particular, Web systems such as online marketplaces, adaptive (e.g., recommender) systems, and Web services, react to events such as Web page updates or data posted to a server.

This article investigates issues of relevance in designing high-level programming languages dedicated to reactivity on the Web. It presents twelve theses on features desirable for a language of reactive rules tuned to programming Web and Semantic Web applications.

1 Introduction

A common perception of the Web is that of a distributed repository of hypermedia documents with clients (in general browsers) that download documents, and servers that store and update documents. Although reflecting a widespread use of the Web, this perception is not completely accurate.

In fact, many Web applications build upon servers or clients updating data in reaction to events or to messages exchanged on the Web. Examples are online marketplaces, adaptive (e.g., recommender) systems, and Web services. The Web's communication protocol, HTTP, provides an infrastructure for exchanging events or messages. In addition, SOAP provides conventions for exchanging structured and typed information on the Web as XML messages. For transport of messages between Web nodes, SOAP can use HTTP (or other protocols).

This article first argues that complementing HTTP and SOAP with high-level languages for updates and reactivity is needed for both standard Web and Semantic Web applications. It then presents twelve theses on features desirable for a language of reactive rules tuned to programming Web applications.

After providing motivation and background (Section 2), this article successively addresses the need for ECA rules on the Web (Section 3), paradigms for communicating events between Web sites (Section 4), specifying composite events (Section 5), specifying conditions as Web queries (Section 6), specifying state-changing actions (Section 7), structuring constructs for rules and programs (Section 8), and additional issues (Section 9). The views reported about in this article have emerged during the design of the Web and Semantic Web query language Xcerpt [1,2] and of the reactive Web language XChange [3,4], as well as from experiences with programming in Xcerpt and XChange [5,6].

T. Grust et al. (Eds.): EDBT 2006 Workshops, LNCS 4254, pp. 842–854, 2006.

2 Motivation and Background

Updates on the Web Many Web applications build upon servers that update data according to client requests or actions. This is the case in online marketplaces that receive and process orders, e-learning systems that select and deliver teaching materials depending on a student's test performances, recommender systems that select goods or services depending on a customer's previous orders or expressed preferences, and communication platforms such as Wikis, where several users modify the same documents. Conversely, some Web applications also build upon clients that update data according to server requests: a server can request a client to store information in a cookie. Typically a cookie is used to store information such as user identification or the contents of a user's shopping basket on the client-side. The server can then later retrieve this information, thus freeing the client-side user from reentering this information.

Reactivity on the Web. Many Web applications not only build upon the updating of data, but also upon complex reactions to messages or events exchanged not only between clients and servers but also (via servers) between clients. This is the case when contributors to a Web-based communication platform are informed of other contributors joining or leaving a session. It is the case for Web-based business management systems, e.g., for business travel applications, planning, and reimbursement in large companies, that rely upon complex workflows of actions and messages, possibly realized using Web services. It is also the case for Web-based systems offering context-dependent services, e.g., a time- and location-dependent car park directory that adapts the information it delivers and reacts to changes.

Updates and Reactivity on the Semantic Web. Updates and reactivity are as much a Semantic Web issue as they are a standard Web issues. The application scenarios stressed above might involve both standard Web and Semantic Web data and techniques, such as HTML, XML, RDF, Topic Maps, and OWL data, as well as inference from RDF triples. For example, e-commerce offers might be described by RDF meta-data and an e-learning system might refer to inference rules expressed in terms of RDF triples, RDF Schema, and OWL.

Infrastructure. The basis for updates and reactivity is that Web sites inform each other about update requests and events by exchanging messages. The Hypertext Transfer Protocol (HTTP) [7], the Web's communication protocol, allows Web sites to send data to each other. The important commands are GET, which is primarily used to retrieve data identified by a URI, and POST, which is primarily used to send data to some Web resource (again identified by a URI).[1] A framework for message exchange on the Web is given by SOAP [8].[2] SOAP's

[1] Data can also be sent from the client to the server using GET. Though against the original philosophy of HTTP (GET should not have side-effects), this use is quite common.

[2] "SOAP" was originally an acronym for "Simple Object Access Protocol," but this name has been dropped with SOAP 1.2 as the concern is rather object interoperability than object access.

main components are (1) message envelope and (2) transport binding. The envelope defines an XML format for representing message content and processing information. It consist of the header, which provides information about the message (e.g., date when sent), and the body, which carries application-dependent data (the "payload"). The transport binding specifies the method used to communicate a message from one node to the other via some lower-level protocol such as HTTP or SMTP (Simple Mail Transfer Protocol [9]).

High-level Languages. Cost-efficient development of Web applications such as those mentioned above requires high-level languages tailored to updates and reactivity. Although HTTP and SOAP help implement updates and reactivity on the Web, more abstract and higher-level languages are needed that

- abstract away network communication and system issues,
- ease the specification of complex updates of Web resources (e.g., XML, RDF, and OWL data),
- are convenient for specifying complex flows of actions and reactions on the Web.

The need for high-level Web update and reactive languages is similar to the need for high-level (Semantic) Web query languages (see [10] for a survey). High-level reactive languages will complement, not replace, HTTP and SOAP.

3 The Need for ECA Rules on the Web

Thesis 1: **High-level reactive languages are needed on the Web. Event-Condition-Action rules are well-suited to specify reactivity on the Web. In particular, they are better suited than production rules for a large class of Web applications.**

High-level reactive languages are needed on the Web. Programming reactive behavior using the primitives of the Hypertext Transfer Protocol, HTTP, (such as POST and GET) is rather cumbersome and distracts from the principal task. Efforts like the Common Gateway Interface (CGI) or Application Programming Interfaces to access Web Services and exchange SOAP messages such as the Java API for XML Web Services (JAX-WS) seek to overcome this burden of low-level programming. These efforts are based on general purpose programming languages not specifically tailored for the Web and for reactivity.

Rules are very convenient for a high-level expression of reactive behavior. This is amply demonstrated by the intensive use of reactive, also called "dynamic," rules among other kinds of "business rules."

A rule-based approach to reactivity on the Web provides the following benefits over the conventional approach using (imperative or object-oriented) general purpose programming languages:

- Rules are easy to understand for humans. Requirements specification often already comes in the form of rules expressed either in a natural or formal language.

- Rule-based specifications are flexible, therefore easy to adapt, alter, and maintain as requirements change, which is quite frequently the case with business rules.
- Rules are well-suited for processing and analyzing by machines. Methods for automatic optimization, verification, and transformation into other types of rules (e.g., derive ECA rules from integrity constraints) have been well-studied and applied successfully in the past.
- Rules can be managed in a single rule base as well as in several rule bases possibly distributed over the Web.

Common reactive rules are production rules, also called Condition-Action (CA) rules, and Event-Condition-Action (ECA) rules.[3] Production rules have the form "if *condition* do *action*" and specify to execute the *action* automatically when the *condition* (typically expressed as a query to data in some fact base) becomes true (in general due to previous actions). In contrast, ECA rules have the form "on *event* if *condition* do *action*" and specify to execute the *action* automatically when the *event* happens, provided the *condition* holds.

On the Web, reactive rules explicitly referring to events, i.e., Event-Condition-Action (ECA) rules, are more appropriate than production rules without explicit reference to events for the following reasons:

- "Real-world reactive rules" often come with an explicit specification of an event, for example: "a credit card application (event) will be granted (action) if the applicant has a monthly income of more than EUR 1 500 and no outstanding debts (condition)."
- Events exchanged as messages between Web nodes are a natural, high-level communication paradigm, also exploited in Service-Oriented and Event-Driven Architecture.
- Events can carry data between Web nodes that is relevant for the condition and action part of a rule.
- ECA rules allow an easy handling of errors and exceptional situations that can conveniently be expressed as (special) events.

Finally, in situations where production rules are more appropriate, it is often possible to derive ECA rules automatically or semi-automatically from production rules[4] and provide an efficient implementation mechanism this way.

[3] In some works, the term production rules is used to mean both ECA and CA rules. We use it here in the more customary sense meaning only CA rules.

[4] It is tempting to claim that the production rule "`if` C `do` A" can be trivially expressed as the ECA rule "`on` *true* `if` C `do` A", where *true* matches any event. In general, this is however not the case: the production rule fires *only once*, when the condition becomes true. The ECA rules fires *every time* an event happens, as long as the condition holds. Only with further assumptions, such as that the action is idempotent (executing it a second time has no further effects, e.g., insertion into a set) and not undone by some other action while the condition holds (e.g., once the insertion of an item is made, it will not be deleted), the above production rule and ECA rule are equivalent.

Thesis 2: **Reactive Web rules should be processed locally and act globally through event-based communication and access to persistent Web data.**

Reactive Web rules should be processed locally at each Web site. In particular, each Web site manages its own rule base and determines locally which of the rules fire. Approaches assuming a central rule processing entity are not suitable for the Web's highly distributed and loosely coupled architecture. Even distributed approaches that assume collaboration and cooperation between different Web sites for rule processing are too tightly coupled for the Web.

Observe that requiring rules to run locally does not make any restrictions on their source: rule interchange formats such as the one developed at W3C [11] allow a Web site to incorporate rules from documents anywhere on the Web or receive rules as messages from other Web sites. An example where rule exchange by messages is necessary will be given in Thesis 11.

Global behavior can be achieved by using event-based communication. Local reactive rules can generate new events which are sent to remote Web sites, where they in turn trigger other (remote) reactive rules. This also enables Web sites to coordinate and synchronize activities in a choreography-based manner without a central coordinator. Further, reactive rules should be able to access data from anywhere on the Web, for example, query a (remote) RDF document identified by its URI. (See Thesis 4 for the distinction of event data and persistent Web data.)

4 Event Communication Paradigms

Thesis 3: **Events are best exchanged directly between Web sites in a push manner.**

Because of the Web's decentralized architecture, events must be exchanged directly, point-to-point, between Web sites without the involvement of central servers, super-peers, and the like.

Events are best sent in a push manner from the Web sites where the event happens or originates to other interested Web sites. Periodical polling, where interested Web sites retrieve remote Web resources periodically to check if an event has happened, is less favorable since it causes more network traffic, increases reaction time, and requires more local resources.

5 Specifying Composite Events: Towards High-Level Event Query Languages

Thesis 4: **Events are volatile data and should be kept distinct from persistent data.**

On a reactive Web, there are two kinds of data: "normal" data from Web resources such as XML or RDF documents ("persistent data") and data from events ("volatile data"). "Normal" Web data is retrieved upon request in a pull manner, *persistent*, and can be *modified*. It typically signifies a *state* of (an abstraction of) the world. Event data is communicated between Web nodes (typically in a push manner), *volatile*, and *not modifiable*. It is typically used to signal *changes in state*.

The distinction of persistent data and volatile data can be illustrated with a metaphor. Persistent data is like (computer-)*written text*. Once produced, it is available permanently for anyone to read (or rather anyone who is allowed to do so). Later, the text can be modified directly by editing it. Volatile data is like *spoken words*. Once a sentence is spoken, its information is available only to the listeners and only as long as they remember. A spoken sentence cannot be changed; the only way to correct, complete, or invalidate its information then is through speaking new sentences.

Due to their different nature, there should be a clean separation of persistent Web data and volatile event data in a reactive language. It should be ensured that volatile data stays volatile, i.e., is disposed of after finite time. This avoids growing storage requirements for event data. If some data from an event must be stored indefinitely, it should explicitly be made persistent in a Web resource. Most importantly, not having a clean separation of Web data and event data could lead to a "shadow Web," a hidden collection of (then non-volatile) event data that lives in parallel to the normal Web with its persistent Web resources.

Thesis 5: **Recognizing composite events is essential for a reactive Web language. Composite events are conveniently specified by (event) queries. There are (at least) four complementary dimensions to event queries: data extraction, event composition, temporal conditions, and event accumulation.**

Often, a situation that requires a reaction cannot be detected from a single incoming event (called *atomic event* henceforth). For example, the cancellation of a flight (atomic event) might not by itself require a reaction by a passenger. However, if a flight has been canceled, and there is no notification within the next two hours that the passenger is put onto another flight, this might well require a reaction.

Such situations are called *composite events* (as opposed to single atomic events), and they are especially important on the Web: In a carefully developed application, atomic events might suffice as designers have the freedom to choose events according to their goal. On the Web, however, many different applications are integrated and have to cooperate. Situations which have not been considered in an application's design must then be inferred from several atomic events.

Composite events as patterns of events do not exists explicitly "by themselves" in the stream of incoming atomic events. Rather they are implicit and the patterns are conveniently specified by event queries.

There are at least the following four complementary dimensions that need to be considered for an event query language:

- Data extraction: Event messages contain data that is relevant to whether and how to react. The data must be provided (typically as bindings for variables) to the condition and action part of an ECA rule.

- Event composition: To support composite events, event queries must support composition constructs such as the conjunction, disjunction, and negation of events (or more precisely of event queries).
- Temporal conditions: Time plays an important role in many reactive Web applications. Event queries must be able to express temporal conditions such as "events A and B happen within 1 hour and A happens before B."
- Event accumulation: Event queries must be able to accumulate events of the same type to aggregate data or detect repetitions. For example, a stock market application might require notification if "the average over the last 5 reported stock prices raises by 5%," or a service level agreement might require a reaction when "3 server outages have been reported within 1 hour."

Some applications might also require features not mentioned above such as event instance selection (choose only one out of several available answers to an event query) or event instance consumption ("use-up" atomic events so they are not available for generating future answers) [12].

Thesis 6: **A data-driven, incremental evaluation of event queries is the approach of choice.**
A data-driven evaluation of (composite) event queries is the best-suited approach. It can work incrementally and is thus preferable for efficiency reasons: work done in one evaluation step of an event query should not be redone in future evaluation. For example, the composite event query "events A and B happen" requires to check every incoming event if it is A or B and thus multiple evaluation steps. When event A is detected, we want to remember this for later when B is detected to signal the composite event. In contrast, a non-incremental, query-driven (backward-chaining) evaluation would have to check the entire history of events for an A when a B is detected.

6 Specifying Conditions: Embedding a Web Query Language

Thesis 7: **Data from persistent Web resources plays an essential role for Web reactivity. A reactive language thus should embed or build upon a Web query language.**
A reactive Web language has to integrate in the current Web of retrievable, persistent data sources. Programmers must be able to easily access and query persistent Web data. Querying XML, RDF, and other Web data is well-studied and a multitude of query languages have been devised [10]. Instead of reinventing the wheel, a reactive language should thus embed or build upon an existing Web query language.

Data from Web resources is usually persistent and reflects a state (see Thesis 4). The natural place to deploy a Web query language in ECA rules is thus the condition part. However, the Web query language should also be used to query data in atomic events in the event part of ECA rules — after all, the same data models (XML, RDF, etc.) are used. This gives language coherency [13] and makes learning the new reactive language much faster. The language coherency can be even further increased if an update language based on the query language is available for the action part.

Criteria to be considered for a Web query language include:

- What is the query language's notion of answers (variable bindings, newly constructed data)?
- How are answers delivered, can they be used to "parameterize" further queries or the action? Can, for example, a variable bound in an event query be a parameter in a condition query, i.e., the value delivered by the event query be accessed and used in the condition query?
- What evaluation methods for queries are possible (backward chaining, forward chaining)?
- Which data models are supported (XML, RDF, OWL)? Is it possible to access data in different data models within one query?
- How does the query language deal with identity (see Thesis 10)?
- Which reasoning or deductive capabilites does the query language provide (views, deductive rules; see also Thesis 9)?

The choice of a Web query language has significant influence on the design of a reactive language and should thus be made carefully.

7 Specifying State-Changing Actions

Thesis 8: **The Web is a dynamic, state-changing system. Reactions to state changes (events) through reactive rules are state-changing actions such as updates to persistent data. Reactive rules are needed where compound actions can be constructed from primitive actions.**

The Web is a dynamic, state-changing system. To act in this world, reactive rules need the ability to perform state-changing actions such as updates to persistent data. The drawback that this makes reactive languages less declarative than pure (side-effect free) logic or functional programming languages is inherent to the task and should not withhold efforts to make reactive languages as declarative as possible.

The most important actions are updating persistent data on the Web and communicating with other Web sites (through raising new events). Complex reactions can conveniently be built as compounds of primitive actions such as insertions, deletions, or modifications of XML elements, RDF triples, or OWL facts. The most common compound is a sequence of actions, but other compounds such as a the specification of alternative actions are needed, too.

8 Structuring Rules and Rule Programs

Thesis 9: **Development and maintenance of reactive rule programs can be considerably supported by structuring mechanisms such as:**

branching in rules, deductive rules for event queries and Web queries, procedural abstractions for actions, and grouping of rules.

Like in any other programming language, development and maintenance of reactive rule programs can be considerably supported by a language's structuring mechanisms. In particular, we propose that reactive rule languages have the following structuring mechanisms:

- Branching in rules: it is more convenient to write one rule "`on` E `if` C `do` A_1 `else` A_2" than writing two rules "`on` E `if` C `do` A_1" and "`on` E `if` $\neg C$ `do` A_2". Rules of this kind are sometimes called ECAA rules (since they specify an action and an alternative action), and there are also more general forms such as $\mathrm{EC}^n\mathrm{A}^n$ rules [14], which specify several condition-action pairs. Rules of this kind are not only more convenient to write, but also are easier to maintain because replication (of C in this example) is avoided. Avoiding replication is also good for execution efficiency: the condition C is only tested once in an ECAA rule.[5]
- Deductive rules for event queries and Web queries: deductive rules can be compared to views in relational databases and their advantages for Web data (XML documents, RDF sources, etc.) are well understood. They avoid replication of complicated queries, allow to derive intensional data from extensional data, and can be used to mediate data in different schemas. The same advantages apply for querying and reasoning with event data, and we propose to also have deductive rules for events. However, since event queries have to be evaluated very frequently, a reactive language can be made more restrictive about rules for events for efficiency reasons (e.g., reject recursive rules and rule sets).
- Procedural abstractions for actions: often several rules will share the same action. For example, an electronic shop will have rules for different forms of payment, all having the same reaction (e.g., ship item). The reaction can be rather complicated and composed of many smaller actions (e.g., update the customer database and the warehouse database, e-mail the customer the expected date of delivery and the tracking number). A procedure mechanism, where the action is specified once and given a name, is clearly a better approach than writing the same code in several rules.
- Grouping of rules: a flat, unstructured set or list of rules offers no guidance where a certain functionality is to be found and which rules interact. Virtually all wide-spread programming languages offer modules, packages, or similar constructs to structure programs. Grouping rules into separate, named rule sets and possibly also building hierarchies of rule sets exposes the structure of a rule program and eases considerably human understanding. Also, rule sets could introduce scopes for identifiers, alleviating the danger of unwanted interaction of rules due to name-clashes of identifiers.

These structuring mechanisms aim primarily at avoiding redundancy, i.e., write code needed in several places only once, and at exposing the organization

[5] Testing C only once for the two ECA rules with C and $\neg C$ is of course possible, but requires optimization techniques detecting and exploiting similarities in rules.

of a program, i.e., keep related pieces code together and unrelated code separate in the program layout. This not only eases authoring and maintenance for human programmers; it is also good for the execution of the rules on a machine: recognizing redundancy becomes less important for query optimization and division of programs allows to execute smaller units.

9 Miscellanea

Thesis 10: **Identity of data items is an issue for reactive languages due to their ability to react to changes of data objects on the Web.**

Reactive languages with the ability to monitor data items (or objects) and react to their changes need to deal with identity of the data items. Consider monitoring a news Web site for updates to a particular article: for this task, it is necessary to (uniquely) identify the article of interest.

There are basically two approaches to identity: extensional identity and surrogate identity.

Extensional identity defines identity based on an object's structure or value (its extension). Objects which are equal in structure and value are thus treated as identical. Examples of this are relational databases (forgetting multi-set semantics for the moment), logic programming, and functional programming. When an object's value changes, it looses its identity. To alleviate this, objects are often given an auxiliary attribute such as a primary key having a unique value for each object. Of course, with a change of the value of the key, identity is lost.

Surrogate identity (also called object identity) defines identity independent from an object's extension as an external surrogate (e.g., the object's address in memory). It is thus possible for objects to be non-identical, even though they have the same structure and value, leading to a distinction of identity and equality. Examples of this are object-oriented databases and object-oriented programming languages. An important advantage of surrogate identity is that it allows an object to keep its identity when its value changes.

For monitoring changes of objects, surrogate identity is advantageous. However, to communicate with remote Web sites, surrogate identity has to become part of the data, i.e., made extensional. Even worse, Web resources such as XML or RDF documents usually do not provide a surrogate identity for their data at all and only rarely provide auxiliary identity-defining attributes (keys such as `xml:id` attributes) as part of the extension.

Thesis 11: **Meta-programming and meta-circularity, that is, the ability to use rules to exchange and evaluate (other) rules, are needed in some important cases.**

Certain important reactive Web applications require a mutual exchange and evaluation of rules. An example are (automatic) policy-based trust negotiations [15]. Consider the following scenario of online-shopping. Customer and (electronic) shop do not know (or trust) each other in advance and are thus sensitive about giving out certain information (e.g., credit card number) or committing to certain actions (e.g., shipping without prior payment). Using policy-based negotiation they establish a basis of trust sufficient to make a deal.

1. Customer Franz requests to buy ten soccer balls from `fussbaelle.biz`, an online shop which he has found with a Web search and not heard of before.
2. In reply, the shop sends its policy governing sales and payment, that is, a set of rules describing, e.g., what identification the customer has to provide and which methods of payment (credit card, check, money transfer, etc.) are acceptable under what conditions.
3. Franz determines that paying by credit card satisfies the shop's policy as well as his own preferences. However, he is not willing to provide sensitive information such as his credit card number to some untrusted shop. Instead he sends back to the shop a policy stating conditions under which he is willing to disclose it.
4. `fussbaelle.biz` evaluates the customer's policy, determines that its membership in the Better Business Bureau of Internet satisfies the customer's conditions, and sends its membership certificate.
5. Franz checks the certificate, reveals his credit card information, and closes the deal.

Observe that in this example, customer and shop do not give out all their policies at once. Instead they exchange policies reactively during the course of the trust negotiation. Which policies are actually exchanged depends on the previous course of action. Such a reactive approach has several advantages: (1) it is more efficient since only small sets of relevant rules are exchanged, (2) policies themselves can be sensitive information and thus only given out when a certain stage in the negotiation (e.g., trust level) has been reached, (3) it allows policies to be determined dynamically (e.g., using game-theoretic approaches in the fashion of [16]).

Realizing the above exchange of rules and rule sets (policies) with reactive rules leads to a requirement for meta-programming or meta-circularity in reactive, rule-based languages. In meta-programming, programs can "have other programs as data and exploit their semantics"[17]. A particular form of meta-programming is meta-circularity, where the same language is used on both levels (i.e., the rules realizing the exchange and the rules being exchanged are written in the same language).

Thesis 12: **Reactivity in the Web's open and uncontrolled world requires language support for authentication, authorization, and accounting.**

The Web is an open, uncontrolled system allowing for anyone to retrieve data from anywhere on the Web in an anonymous way. For reactive Web applications this is usually not acceptable; services such as electronic shops or on-demand computing require controlled access, in particular:

– authentication to establish that users of the service really are who they claim to be,

- authorization to control access to sensitive information or services, and
- accounting to monitor and log service accesses and resource consumption for management, planning, and billing (the latter in particular when pay-per-use pricing is employed).

These "three As" are non-functional requirements;[6] a reactive language should thus come to the programmers aid and provide easy-to-use support for them, so programmer can concentrate on the functional requirements.

We discuss only accounting in more detail since it is maybe the most interesting issue, as far as reactivity is concerned. Authentication and authorization are relatively static issues which can be treated, e.g., as simple conditions in ECA rules (though they can be negotiated dynamically, see the previous thesis) and also exist for pure information access on the non-reactive Web.

Accounting in contrast is a dynamic issue: it reacts to incoming service request to monitor and log them. This leads to a "double reactivity": on the one hand there is the reactive service itself, on the other hand the accounting service, which in turn reacts to uses of the reactive service. Note, however, that these are orthogonal axes of reactivity and no meta-programming (see previous thesis) has to be employed: the accounting service does not contain the reactive service or have to reason about its interiors.

10 Conclusion

In this article we have presented twelve theses on reactive rules for the Web. We have argued that reactivity in the Web needs reactive rules, in particular ECA rules, and established a list of desiderata for reactive, ECA-rule-based languages.

The theses reflect our experiences from designing the reactive language XChange [4,18,3,19] and programming in it. An initial design and a prototype implementation of XChange are complete, and we hope for the positions presented in this paper to provide directions in the future development of XChange.

Many of the desiderata postulated in this article are very general. They apply not only to reactive languages based on ECA rules, but also to other rule-based reactive languages (e.g., based on production rules) and even languages, frameworks, and program libraries not based on rules at all.

Acknowledgments

The ideas expressed in this article have been significantly influenced by the research project REWERSE (Reasoning on the Web with Rules and Semantics, `http://rewerse.net`) and the W3C RIF Working Group

[6] In software engineering, non-functional requirements are constraints on the functionality offered by the system (e.g., performance, security). Functional requirements, in contrast, are statements about the actual functionality of a system (e.g., accepted input, produced output).

(`http://w3.org/2005/rules`). The authors thank their colleagues of REWERSE and of the W3C RIF Working Group for many fruitful exchanges on the subject of this article.

The authors thank Tim Furche, Paula-Lavinia Pătrânjan, and Inna Romanenko for their insights and numerous discussions.

References

1. Schaffert, S., Bry, F.: Querying the Web reconsidered: A practical introduction to Xcerpt. In: Proc. Extreme Markup Languages. (2004)
2. Xcerpt. http://xcerpt.org (2006)
3. Bailey, J., Bry, F., Eckert, M., Pătrânjan, P.L.: Flavours of XChange, a rule-based reactive language for the (Semantic) Web. In: Proc. Intl. Conf. on Rules and Rule Markup Languages for the Semantic Web. Volume 3791 of LNCS, Springer (2005)
4. Bry, F., Eckert, M., Pătrânjan, P.L.: Reactivity on the Web: Paradigms and applications of the language XChange. J. of Web Engineering **5**(1) (2006) 3–24
5. Kraus, S.: Use Cases fr Xcerpt: Eine positionelle Anfrage- und Transformationssprache für das Web. Master's thesis (in German), Inst. for Informatics, Univ. of Munich (2004)
6. Romanenko, I.: Use cases for reactivity on the Web: Using ECA rules for business process modeling. Master's thesis, Inst. for Informatics, Univ. of Munich (2006)
7. Fielding, R., et al.: Hypertext transfer protocol – HTTP/1.1. RFC 2616, The Internet Society (1999)
8. Gudgin, M., et al.: SOAP version 1.2. W3C recommendation, World Wide Web Consortium (2003)
9. Klensin, J.: Simple mail transfer protocol. RFC 2821, The Internet Society (2001)
10. Bailey, J., Bry, F., Furche, T., Schaffert, S.: Web and Semantic Web query languages: A survey. In: Reasoning Web, Int. Summer School. Volume 3564 of LNCS, Springer (2005) 35–133
11. World Wide Web Consortium: Rule interchange format working group charter. `http://www.w3.org/2005/rules/wg/charter` (2005)
12. Zimmer, D., Unland, R.: On the semantics of complex events in active database management systems. In: Proc. Int. Conf. on Data Engineering. (1999)
13. Bry, F., Marchiori, M.: Ten theses on logic languages for the Semantic Web. In: Proc. Int. Workshop on Principles and Practice of Semantic Web Reasoning. Volume 3703 of LNCS, Springer (2005) 42–49
14. Knolmayer, G., Endl, R., Pfahrer, M.: Modeling processes and workflows by business rules. In: Business Process Management, Models, Techniques, and Empirical Studies. Volume 1806 of LNCS, Springer (2000) 16–29
15. Winslett, M.: An introduction to trust negotiation. In: Proc. Int. Conf. on Trust Management (iTrust). Volume 2692 of LNCS, Springer (2003) 275–283
16. Preibusch, S.: Implementing privacy negotiations in e-commerce. In: Proc. Asia-Pacific Web Conference. Volume 3841 of LNCS, Springer (2006) 604–615
17. Apt, K.R., Turini, F., eds.: Meta-Logics and Logic Programming. MIT Press (1995)
18. Bry, F., Eckert, M., Pătrânjan, P.L.: Querying composite events for reactivity on the Web. In: Proc. Int. Workshop on XML Research and Applications (XRA) at APWeb 2006. Volume 3842 of LNCS, Springer (2006) 38–47
19. XChange. http://www.reactiveweb.org/xchange (2006)

Event-Condition-Action Rule Languages for the Semantic Web

Alexandra Poulovassilis, George Papamarkos, and Peter T. Wood

London Knowledge Lab, Birkbeck, University of London, London WC1E 7HX
{ap, gpapa05, ptw}@dcs.bbk.ac.uk

Abstract. The Semantic Web is based on XML and RDF as standards for exchanging and storing information on the World Wide Web. Event-Condition-Action rules are a possible candidate technology for distributed web-based applications that require timely notification and propagation of events and information between different sites. This paper discusses the provision of ECA rules for XML and RDF data, and highlights some of the challenges that arise.

1 Introduction

XML and RDF are becoming dominant standards for storing and exchanging information on the World Wide Web, and are being increasingly used in distributed web-based applications in areas such as e-business, e-science, e-learning and e-government. Such applications may need to be *reactive*, i.e. to be able to detect the occurrence of specific events or changes within information repositories, and to respond by automatically executing the appropriate application logic. Event-condition-action (ECA) rules are one way of providing this kind of functionality. An ECA rule is of the form `on` *event* `if` *condition* `do` *actions*. The event part specifies when the rule is *triggered*. The condition part is a query which determines if the information system is in a particular state, in which case the rule *fires*. The action part states the actions to be performed if the rule fires. These actions may in turn cause further events to occur, which may in turn cause more ECA rules to fire[1].

References [24,20] discuss ECA rules (triggers) in databases. More broadly, ECA rules are used in workflow management, network management, personalisation, publish/subscribe technology, and specifying and implementing business processes. In the distributed web-based applications that we envisage, rules are likely not to be hand-crafted but automatically generated by higher-level presentation and application services.

For some applications, content-based publish/subscribe [9] may be an alternative or complementary technology to ECA rules. Publish/subscribe systems

[1] Non-termination of rule execution is generally a possibility and thus much research has focussed on the development of static and dynamic analysis techniques for detecting possibly non-terminating ECA rule sets. There has also been considerable research into techniques for verifying the confluence of ECA rules.

T. Grust et al. (Eds.): EDBT 2006 Workshops, LNCS 4254, pp. 855–864, 2006.

such as [7,23] support more sophisticated distributed event definition and detection than ECA rules. On the other hand, ECA rules allow the definition and execution of more complex actions than just simple notifications.

This paper discusses the provision of ECA rules for XML and RDF data, and highlights some of the issues that arise in the context of such data. This work has been motivated by our participation in the EU FP5 "SeLeNe: Self e-Learning Networks" project (see `http://www.dcs.bbk.ac.uk/selene/`). The aim of this project was to investigate techniques for managing evolving distributed repositories of educational metadata and for providing a variety of services over such repositories, including syndication, notification and personalisation services. Peers in a SeLeNe (self e-learning network) store metadata relating to learning objects (LOs) registered with the SeLeNe, and also metadata relating to users of the SeLeNe. SeLeNe's reactive functionality includes features such as propagating changes in the description of a LO to those of composite LOs dependent on it; propagating changes in a learner's history of accesses to LOs to the learner's personal profile; notifying users of the registration of new LOs of interest to them; and notifying users of changes in the description of LOs of interest to them. We investigated the provision of this kind of reactive functionality by means of ECA rules over SeLeNe's metadata, considering first XML and then RDF encodings of the metadata.

2 ECA Rules for XML

In [4,5] we introduced a language for defining ECA rules on XML data, based on XPath and XQuery. This language uses a fragment of XPath for selecting and matching sub-documents of XML documents within the event and condition parts of ECA rules, while a fragment of XQuery is used within insertion actions where there is a need to be able to construct new XML sub-documents. We also developed techniques for analysing the triggering and activation relationships between such rules[2] which can be 'plugged into' existing generic frameworks for ECA rule analysis and optimisation.

The semistructured nature of XML data gives rise to a number of issues in the context of ECA rules:

- *Event semantics*: For relational data, the semantics of data manipulation events is straightforward, since insert, delete or update events occur when a relation is inserted into, deleted from, or updated. With XML, specifying where data has been inserted or deleted within an XML document is more complex, and path expressions that identify locations within the document are necessary.

[2] A rule r_i *may trigger* a rule r_j if execution of the action of r_i may generate an event which triggers r_j. A rule r_i *may activate* another rule r_j if r_j's condition may be changed from False to True after the execution of r_i's action. A rule r_i *may activate* itself if its condition may be True after the execution of its action.

- *Action semantics*: Again for relational data, the effect of data manipulation actions is straightforward, since an insert, delete or update action can only affect tuples in a single relation. With XML, actions now manipulate entire subdocuments, and the insertion or deletion of subdocuments can trigger a set of different events.
- *Rule analysis*: The determination of triggering and activation relationships between ECA rules is more complex for XML data than for relational data. The associations between actions and events/conditions are more implicit, and more sophisticated semantic comparisons between sets of path expressions are required.

Details of the syntax and rule execution semantics of our XML ECA rule language can be found in [5]. Reference [3] describes a prototype implementation the language: A *Parser* component parses and checks the syntactic validity of new ECA rules. Valid rules are stored in a *Rule Base*. An *Execution Engine* encapsulates the rule processing functionality, comprising an *Event Dispatcher*, a *Condition Evaluator* and an *Action Scheduler*. All of these components interface with a *Wrapper* which sends/receives data to/from the underlying XML files. The Action Scheduler places the updates resulting from rules that have fired at the head of an *Execution Schedule*. If multiple rules have fired, then the updates that result from their actions are prefixed to the schedule in order of the rules' specified priorities[3].

A number of other ECA rule languages for XML have also been proposed, although none of this other work has focussed on analysing rule behaviour. Most notably, Active XQuery [6] is an ECA rule language for XML based on the SQL3 triggers standard [13]. This language is more complex than ours as it allows full XPath in the event parts of rules, and full XQuery in the condition and action parts. However, analysing the behaviour of ECA rules expressed in this more complex language has not been considered. The rule execution model is also different to ours: we treat insertions or deletions of XML fragments as atomic updates and ECA rule execution is invoked only after the completion of such an update, whereas in Active XQuery such updates are broken up into a sequence of finer granularity requests each of which may invoke the ECA rule execution. In general, these semantics may produce different results for the same initial update.

ARML [8] provides an XML-based rule description for rule sharing among different heterogeneous ECA rule processing systems. In contrast to our language and Active XQuery, conditions and actions are defined abstractly as XML-RPC methods which are later matched with system-specific methods. Active XML [1] provides similar functionality to that provided by XML ECA rules by embedding calls to web services within XML documents via special tags, aiming to integrate distributed data and distributed computation in P2P architectures.

---

[3] This prefixing to the schedule is `Immediate` rule scheduling, and other rule scheduling alternatives would also be possible e.g. `Deferred` and `Detached`, where updates are appended to the transaction or are executed as a separate transaction, respectively.

In the commercial arena, triggers on XML data are now supported by all the major relational DBMS vendors and also by some native XML repository vendors. However, this is confined to document-level triggering and only events concerning the insertion, deletion or update of an XML document can be caught. In relational DBMS it is however possible to decompose XML documents into a set of relational tables, potentially allowing developers to exploit existing relational triggering functionality in order to define finer-grain triggers over XML data.

3 ECA Rules for RDF

XML ECA rule languages can be used for RDF data which has been serialised as XML. However, we have also developed an RDF ECA rule language, RDFTL, that will operate directly on a graph/triple representation [17,18]. To our knowledge, this is the first ECA rule language developed specifically for RDF.

Languages for updating RDF descriptions have been considered in [15,14]. The Modification Exhange Language (MEL) of [15] is based on an RDF representation of Datalog and is used for updating RDF in the distributed environment of Edutella [16] while RUL (RDF Update Language) [14] is based on the RQL [12] query language.

RDFTL operates over RDF graphs and it is assumed that these RDF graphs conform to one or more RDFS schemas, in the sense that (a) every resource in the RDF graph belongs to an RDFS class (in addition to belonging to the default `rdfs:Resource` class); (b) every property in the RDF graph is declared in the RDFS schema, along with domain and range constraints; (c) the subject and object of every property in the RDF graph are of the declared subject and object type of the property in the RDFS schema.

RDFTL uses a path-based query sublanguage, syntactically similar to XPath, for defining queries over an RDF graph. Each RDFTL rule has an optional preamble consisting of one or more namespace definition clauses and a set of *let-expressions* of the form `let` *variable* := *e* associating a variable with a query.

The event part of an RDFTL rule describes updates whose occurrence will cause the rule to trigger, and is an expression of one of the following three forms:

1. `(INSERT | DELETE)` *e* `[AS INSTANCE OF` *class*`]`
2. `(INSERT | DELETE)` *triple*
3. `UPDATE` *upd_triple*

Form 1 detects insertions or deletions of resources specified by the expression *e*. *e* is a query, which evaluates to a set of nodes. Optionally, *class* is the name of the RDFS schema class to which at least one of the nodes identified by *e* must belong in order for the rule to trigger. The rule is triggered if the set of nodes returned by *e* includes any new node (in the case of an insertion) or any deleted node (in the case of a deletion) that is an instance of *class*, if specified. The system-defined variable `$delta` is available for use within the condition and actions parts of the rule, and its set of instantiations is the set of new or deleted nodes that have triggered the rule.

Form 2 detects insertions or deletions of arcs specified by *triple*, which has the form *(source_node, arc_name, target_node)* where *source_node* and *target_node* may be expressions of the form *e* or variables defined in the rule's preamble. The wildcard '_' is allowed in the place of any of a triple's components. The rule is triggered if an arc labelled *arc_name* from *source_node* to *target_node* is inserted/deleted. The variable `$delta` has as its set of instantiations the triples which have triggered the rule; the individual components of these triples are identified by `$delta.source`, `$delta.arc_name` or `$delta.target`.

Form 3 similarly detects updates to the target nodes of arcs, specified by *upd_triple* which has the form *(source, arc_name, old_target* → *new_target)*. The wildcard '_' is allowed in the place of any of these components. The rule is triggered if an arc labelled *arc* from *source* changes its target from *old_target* to *new_target*. The variable `$delta` has as its set of instantiations the triples which have triggered the rule and the components of these triples can be obtained by `$delta.source`, `$delta.arc_name`, `$delta.old_target` or `$delta.new_target`.

The condition part of rule is a boolean-valued expression which may consist of conjunctions, disjunctions and negations of queries.

The actions part of a rule is a sequence of one or more actions. Actions can `INSERT` or `DELETE` a resource — specified by its URI — and `INSERT`, `DELETE` or `UPDATE` an arc. The actions language has the following form for each one of these cases, where triples in the actions part have a similar form as in the event part:

1. `INSERT` *e* `AS INSTANCE OF` *class*
   `DELETE` *e* `[AS INSTANCE OF` *class*`]`
   for expressing insertion or deletion of a resource, where the `AS INSTANCE OF` keyword classifies the resource to be deleted or inserted.
2. `(INSERT | DELETE)` *triple* `(',' ` *triple*`)*`
   for expressing insertion or deletion of the arcs(s) specified.
3. `UPDATE` *upd_triple* `(',' ` *upd_triple*`)*`
   for updating arc(s) by changing their target node.

The condition and action parts of a rule may contain occurrences of the `$delta` variable in place of a named resource in a query, or a component of a triple. If neither the condition nor the action part contain occurrences of `$delta`, then the rule is a *set-oriented rule*, otherwise it is an *instance-oriented rule*. A set-oriented rule *fires* if it is triggered and its condition evaluates to true. A copy of the rule's action part is executed as a new transaction (i.e. Detached rule coupling). An instance-oriented rule fires if it is triggered and its condition evaluates to true for some instantiation of `$delta`. A copy of the rule's action part is executed as a new transaction for each value of `$delta` for which the rule's condition evaluates to true, in each case substituting all occurrences of `$delta` within the action part by one specific instantiation for `$delta`.

We refer the reader to [18] for full details of the syntax and execution semantics of RDFTL, and that paper also discusses conservative tests for determining the termination and confluence of sets of RDFTL rules.

3.1 RDFTL Rules in P2P Environments

We have developed a system for processing RDFTL rules in P2P environments. The rule processing functionality is provided by a set of services that constitute the *RDFTL ECA Engine*. This acts as a wrapper over a distributed set of RDF/S repositories, exploiting their query, storage and update functionality. In the current version of our system we are using ICS-FORTH RSSDB [2] as the RDF repository. For the future we plan also to support Jena2 [11].

Our system architecture is similar to the superpeer-based architecture of Edutella [16]. Each peer in the network is supervised by a superpeer (each superpeer supervises itself). The set of peers supervised by a superpeer is termed its *peergroup*. At each superpeer there is an ECA Engine installed. Each peer or superpeer hosts a fragment of an overall global RDFS schema. As in Edutella, the metadata distribution in RDFTL allows hybrid fragmentation, with possible replication between peers. The fragment of the global RDFS schema stored at a peer may change as a result of changes in the peer's RDF/S descriptions. Peers notify their supervising superpeer of any updates to their local RDF/S repository. Peers may dynamically join or leave the network at any time.

Each superpeer's RDFS schema is a superset of its peergroup's individual RDFS schemas. Each superpeer defines access privileges over the classes and properties in its RDFS schema describing the corresponding access level to the instances of each class and property. More fine-grained access privileges are also allowed on specific RDF resources and triples. These facilities allow a superpeer to specify which information can be shared with other superpeers outside its peergroup.

An ECA rule generated at one site of the network might be replicated, triggered, evaluated, and executed at different sites. Within the event, condition and action parts of ECA rules there might be references to specific RDF resources.

Whenever a new ECA rule r is generated at a peer P, it is sent to P's superpeer for syntax validation, translation into the local repository's query and update language, and storage. From there, r will also be forwarded to all other superpeers, and a replica of it will be stored at those superpeers where an event may occur that may trigger r's event part, i.e. those superpeers that are *e-relevant* to r (see below). A rule r has a globally unique identifier of the form $SP_i.j$, where SP_i is the originating superpeer identifier and j a locally unique identifier for the rule in SP_i's rule base.

At run-time rules are triggered by events occurring within a single peer's local RDF repository, i.e. there is no distributed event detection. Also, each particular copy of a rule's action part executes within a single peer's RDF repository, i.e. there is no distributed update execution. If there is a need to distribute a sequence of updates across a number of peers in reaction to some event, then rather than specifying one rule of the form `on` e `if` c `do` $a_1; \ldots; a_n$ instead, n rules $r_1, \ldots, r_n$ can be specified, where each r_i is `on` e `if` c `do` a_i and r_1 has a higher precedence than r_2, which has a higher precedence than r_3 etc.

There are three types of *relevance* of a rule r to an RDF schema S:

- r is *e-relevant* to S if each of the queries that either appear in the event part of r or are used by the event part through variable references, can be evaluated on S, i.e., each step in each path expression exists in S.
- r is *c-relevant* to S if some step in one of the queries referenced by the condition part of r can be evaluated on S (unlike events and actions, conditions may be evaluated at multiple sites).
- r is *a-relevant* to S if all actions in the action part of r are *a-relevant* to S. An individual action is a-relevant to S if it satisfies one of the following:
  - If it is a deletion or insertion of resources that uses `AS INSTANCE OF` *`class`*, then *`class`* must be in S.
  - If it is a deletion of resources that does not use `AS INSTANCE OF` *`class`*, then the most specific class of resources that the path expression in the deletion would return must be in S.
  - If it is an action over triples that uses a property p, then p must be in S. If it is a deletion of triples that uses the wildcard '_' instead of a property (the only action allowed to do this), then the classes of resources returned by the path expressions involved in the deletion must exist in S.

A peer or superpeer is e-relevant, c-relevant or a-relevant to a rule r if r is e-, c- or a-relevant, respectively, to the peer or superpeer's RDFS schema.

At each superpeer, each rule is annotated with the IDs of local peers that are e-relevant, c-relevant and a-relevant to it. These annotations are kept synchronised with changes in peers' and superpeers' schemas.

3.2 P2P Rule Execution

The RDF graph is fragmented, and possibly replicated, amongst the peers, and each superpeer manages its own local rule execution schedule. Each execution schedule at a superpeer is a sequence of updates which are to be executed on the fragment of the global RDF graph which is stored at the superpeer or its local peergroup. Each superpeer coordinates the execution of transactions that are initiated by that superpeer, or by any peer in its local peergroup.

Whenever an update u is executed at a peer P, P notifies its supervising superpeer SP. SP determines whether u may trigger any ECA rule whose event part is annotated with P's ID. If a rule r may have been triggered, then SP will send r's event query to P to evaluate.

If r has indeed been triggered, its condition will need to be evaluated, after generating an instantiation of it for each value of the `$delta` variable if this is present in the condition. If a condition evaluates to true, SP will send each instance of r's action part (one instance if r is a set-oriented rule, and one or more instances if r is an instance-oriented rule) to the local peers that are a-relevant to it. All instances of r's actions part will also be sent to all other superpeers of the network. All superpeers that are a-relevant to r will consult their schemas and access privileges in order to determine whether the updates they have received can be scheduled and executed on their local peergroup.

In summary therefore, local execution of the update at the head of a local schedule may cause events to occur. These events may cause rules to fire, modifying the local schedule or remote schedules with new updates to be executed. We refer the reader to [18] for full details of the P2P implementation of RDFTL.

Our current RDFTL implementation does not yet support any concurrency control or recovery mechanisms. In principle, any distributed concurrency control protocol could be adapted to a P2P environment. For example, the AMOR system adopts optimistic concurrency control [10]. The serialisation graph is distributed amongst those peers responsible for transaction coordination (analogous to our superpeers). The AMOR system assumes that conflicts are only possible between those transactions that are accessing a particular 'region' of resources (analogous to our peers) and thus subgraphs of the global serialisation graph are stored and replicated amongst those coordinators which service a particular region. The regions are not static and these subgraphs are dynamically merged and replicated as transactions execute and regions evolve.

In the classical approach to distributed transactions, global transactions hold on to the resources necessary to achieve their ACID properties until such time as the whole transaction commits or aborts. In a P2P environment this may not be feasible: the resources available at peers may be limited, peers may not wish to cooperate in the execution of global transactions, and peers may disconnect at any time from the network, including during the execution of a global transaction in which they are participating. The cascaded triggering and execution of ECA rules will cause longer-running transactions which may further exacerbate these problems. It is therefore necessary to relax the Atomicity and Isolation properties of transactions.

In particular, subtransactions executing at different peers may be allowed to commit or abort independently of their parent transaction committing or aborting, and parent transactions may be able to commit even if some of their subtransactions have failed. Subtransactions that have committed ahead of their parent transaction committing can be reversed, if necessary, by executing compensating subtransactions. These can be generated as transactions execute and they reverse the effects of a transaction by compensating each of the transaction's updates in reverse order of their execution. Generating compensating updates is straight-forward for RDFTL updates: the insertion of a triple is reversed by deletion of the triple, the deletion of a triple by an insertion, and an update by the restoration of the original value. If transactions have read from committed (sub)transactions which are subsequently reversed, then a cascade of compensations will result.

3.3 Performance

We have developed an analytical performance model for our P2P RDFTL rule processing system, which is described in [19]. We use as the main performance criterion the update response time i.e. the mean time required to complete all rule processing resulting from a top-level update submitted to one of the peers in the network. In [19] we examine how the update response time varies with the network topology, number of peers, number of rules, and degree of data replication between peers. We also describe a simulation of the system, and present the results of similar performance and scalability experiments with the simulator.

The two sets of experimental results show good agreement. Both sets of experiments show that the system performance is significantly reliant on the network topology between superpeers. In particular, if a Hypercup topology [22] is used for interconnecting the superpeers, then rule processing shows good scalability, pointing to its practical usefulness as a technology for real applications. For the future we would like to conduct large-scale experiments with the actual RDFTL system itself, possibly using the PlanetLab [21] infrastructure. As well as giving insight into the actual system behaviour in a real P2P environment, this will allow measurements on actual system workloads and rule sets, which can then be fed into the analytical performance model and the simulator to allow more accurate predictions from these.

4 Concluding Remarks

In this paper we have discussed the provision of ECA rules for XML and RDF data, and have highlighted some of the new issues that arise in the context of such data. We have described a language for ECA rules over XML data, a language for ECA rules over RDF data, implementations of these languages, and the results of a study into the performance and scalability of our RDF ECA rule processing system in P2P environments.

Although conducted in the context of ECA rules operating on RDF, we expect that similar behaviour would occur for P2P ECA rules operating on other types of data e.g. XML and relational, and this is an area of planned future work. Also planned for the future is a distributed version of our XML ECA rule system, and a deeper study into expressiveness of our languages, in terms of their update and constraint enforcement capabilities.

References

1. S. Abiteboul, O. Benjelloun, I. Manolescu, T. Milo, and R. Weber. Active XML: peer-to-peer data and web services integration. In *Proc. 28th Int. Conf. on Very Large Data Bases*, pages 1087–1090, 2002.
2. S. Alexaki, V. Christophides, G. Karvounarakis, D. Plexousakis, and K. Tolle. The ICS-FORTH RDFSuite: Managing Voluminous RDF Description Bases. In *Proc. 2nd. Int. Workshop on the Semantic Web*, 2001.
3. J. Bailey, G. Papamarkos, A. Poulovassilis, and P. T. Wood. An Event-Condition-Action Rule Language for XML. In M. Levene and A. Poulovassilis, editors, *Web Dynamics*. Springer, 2004.
4. J. Bailey, A. Poulovassilis, and P.T. Wood. An Event-Condition-Action Language for XML. In *Proc. 11th Int. Conf. on the World Wide Web*, pages 486–495, 2002.
5. J. Bailey, A. Poulovassilis, and P.T. Wood. Analysis and optimisation for event-condition-action rules on XML. *Computer Networks*, 39:239–259, 2002.

6. A. Bonifati, D. Braga, A. Campi, and S. Ceri. Active XQuery. In *Proc. 18th Int. Conf. on Data Engineering*, pages 403–418, 2002.
7. P. Chirita, S. Idreos, M. Koubarakis, and W. Nejdl. Publish/subscribe for RDF-based P2P networks. In *Proc. ESWS 2004, Heraklion, Crete*, pages 182–197, 2004.
8. E. Cho, I. Park, S. J. Hyun, and M. Kim. ARML: an active rule mark-up language for heterogeneous active information systems. In *Proc. RuleML 2002*, Sardinia, June 2002.
9. P. T. Eugster, P. A. Felber, R. Guerraoui, and A. Kermarrec. The many faces of publish/subscribe. *ACM Comput. Surv.*, 35(2):114–131, 2003.
10. K. Haller, H. Schuldt, and H.J. Schek. Transctional peer-to-peer information processing: The AMOR approach. In *4th Int. Conf. on Mobile Data Management*, pages 356–362. Springer, 2003.
11. Jena: A Semantic Web Framework for Java. http://jena.sourceforge.net/.
12. G. Karvounarakis, A. Magkanaraki, S. Alexaki, V. Christophides, D. Plexousakis, M. Scholl, and K. Tolle. RQL: A Functional Query Language for RDF. In *Functional Approaches to Computing Data*, pages 592–603. Springer, 2003.
13. K. Kulkarni, N. Mattos, and R. Cochrane. Active database features in SQL3. In N. Paton, editor, *Active Rules in Database Systems*, pages 197–219. Springer, 1999.
14. M. Magiridou, S. Sahtouris, V. Christophides, and M. Koubarakis. RUL: A declarative update language for RDF. In *Proc. Fourth Int. Semantic Web Conference*, pages 506–521, 2005.
15. W. Nejdl, W. Siberski, B. Simon, and J. Tane. Towards a modification exchange language for distributed RDF repositories. In *Proc. First Int. Semantic Web Conference*, pages 236–249, 2002.
16. W. Nejdl, B. Wolf, C. Qu, S. Decker, M. Sintek, A. Naeve, M. Nilsson, M. Palmer, and T. Risch. EDUTELLA: a P2P networking infrastructure based on RDF. In *Proc. 11th Int. Conf. on the World Wide Web*, pages 604–615, 2002.
17. G. Papamarkos, A. Poulovassilis, and P. T. Wood. RDFTL: An Event-Condition-Action Language for RDF. In *Proc. 3rd Int. Workshop on Web Dynamics (in conjunction with WWW2004)*, 2004.
18. G. Papamarkos, A. Poulovassilis, and P. T. Wood. Event-Condition-Action Rules on RDF metadata in P2P environments, Technical Report BBKCS-05-05, to appear in Computer Networks, 2006.
19. G. Papamarkos, A. Poulovassilis, and P. T. Wood. Performance Modelling and Evaluation of Event-Condition-Action Rules RDF in P2P networks, Technical Report BBKCS-06-02, 2006.
20. N. Paton. *Active Rules in Database Systems*. Springer, 1999.
21. PlanetLab. `http://www/.planet-lab.org`.
22. M. Schlosser, M. Sintek, S. Decker, and W. Nejdl. HyperCuP – hypercubes, ontologies and efficient search on p2p networks. In *First Int. Workshop on Agents and P2P Computing*, pages 112–124, 2002.
23. W. W. Terpstra, S. Behnel, L. Fiege, A. Zeidler, and A. P. Buchmann. A peer-to-peer approach to content-based publish/subscribe. In *DEBS '03: Proceedings of the 2nd international workshop on Distributed event-based systems*, pages 1–8, New York, NY, USA, 2003. ACM Press.
24. J. Widom and S. Ceri. *Active Database Systems*. Morgan-Kaufmann, San Mateo, California, 1995.

ActiveXQBE: A Visual Paradigm for Triggers over XML Data

Daniele Braga[1], Alessandro Campi[1],
Davide Martinenghi[2], and Alessandro Raffio[1]

[1] Politecnico di Milano
Dip. di Elettronica e Informazione
p.zza L. da Vinci 32, 20133 Milano, Italy
{braga, campi, raffio}@elet.polimi.it
[2] Free University of Bozen/Bolzano
Faculty of Computer Science
p.zza Domenicani, 3, 39100 Bolzano, Italy
martinenghi@inf.unibz.it

Abstract. While XQuery is becoming a standard, the W3C is currently discussing the features of an update language for XML, and its requirements. Therefore, time is ripe for designing and defining the language features and extensions that are usually needed when updates are supported: reaction policies to constraint violations, business rules, and more. In the past years, several languages have been proposed for updates as well as for triggers in XML, such as *XUpdate* and *Active XQuery*.

In this paper, we propose a visual approach to the formulation of active rules building on XQBE, a graphical query language for XML data. Our approach is motivated by the need to provide unskilled users with the ability to express business rules in an intuitive fashion. Visual triggers are then translated into statements that can be interpreted by query engines.

1 Introduction

According to a well-known classification [6], data semantics can be represented declaratively under the form of *normative rules*, *constructive* (or passive) *rules*, and *reactive* (or active) *rules*.

Normative rules, also known as *integrity constraints* in the terminology of databases, are properties that the data must always satisfy. In the context of XML data, some forms of integrity constraints can be expressed through schema definition languages, such as DTDs and XML Schema. Although some attempts exist (e.g., [3]), a universally accepted paradigm for specifying general constraints (in the sense of SQL assertions) still seems to be missing for XML.

Constructive rules (*views* in databases) allow one to specify how to derive new data from data already available. Integrity constraints can also be expressed in this form and, thus, evaluated as constructive rules. Again, there is no standard for the specification of constructive rules in XML, although some support to

T. Grust et al. (Eds.): EDBT 2006 Workshops, LNCS 4254, pp. 865–875, 2006.

views is intrinsically available in XQuery. The issues concerning the materialization and maintenance of views in XML are discussed, for instance, in [1].

Finally, reactive rules specify how data should change depending on the current state of the store and, possibly, on events.

The above rules eventually serve the purpose of formally specifying process flows or business level requirements of the system to be described. According to good design principles, these so-called *business rules* should be expressed as part of the schema, so that the knowledge they carry is decoupled from the rest of the application. Business rules are used to describe the operations and constraints that apply to organizations. As such, they should be business owned and oriented and should be specified in the easiest and most intuitive way, so as to appeal to the broadest audience. Ideally, it should be possible to allow users to maintain the rules without the intervention of an IT professional. In this regard, an intuitive visual paradigm can simplify the specification, via user-friendly interfaces, of essential data management features and policies, such as queries and updates, of requirements of compliance with data constraints, and of consistency repairing actions that ought to take place upon violations of constraints. Complex rules are best specified by domain experts, who, however, may lack knowledge in data definition and manipulation languages. A number of applications can be envisaged, where XML is already established as the *de facto* data representation model, e.g., in the medical domain, where health care professionals sharing information stored in clinical records may need to impose constraints, say, on treatments and compatibility between medicines and patients' profiles.

The ActiveXQBE paradigm presented in this paper stands out from previous attempts for incorporating a visual approach with an emphasis on usability and intuitiveness, yet without heavily sacrificing generality and expressiveness. In particular, to achieve these goals, we designed and propose the visual tool ActiveXQBE for the specification of active rules, building on XQBE [5], a graphical query language for XML. XQBE as well as ActiveXQBE are based on annotated trees, so as to adhere to the hierarchical nature of the XML data model. Both XQBE and ActiveXQBE have a quite steep learning curve; although no formal tests were performed, our experience with under-graduated students has shown that a couple of lessons are enough to get acquainted with the visual paradigm.

Visual ActiveXQBE triggers can be translated into textual representations to be executed by external rule engines. To this end, we provide an algorithm for translating visual triggers into *Active XQuery* rules [4].

2 XQBE: A Visual XML Query Language

XQBE (XQuery By Example) [5] is a graphical query language for XML designed to be intuitive and capable of running on top of XQuery engines. XQBE includes most of the expressive power of XPath, allows for arbitrarily deep nesting of XQuery FLWOR expressions, supports the construction of new XML elements, and permits to restructure existing documents. Figure 1 shows a query reading "*List books published by Addison-Wesley after 1991, including their year*

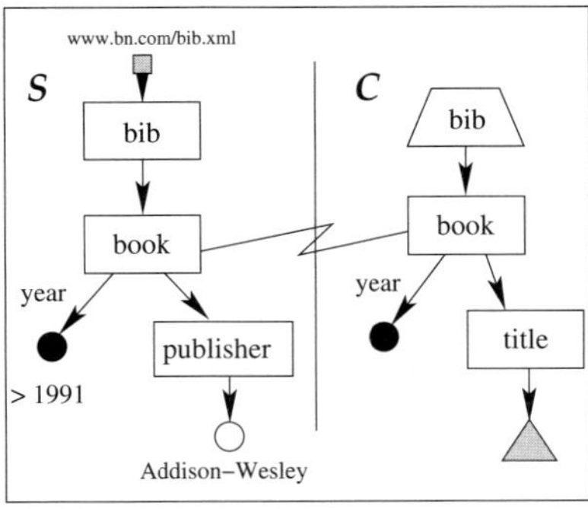


```
<bib>
 { for  $b in
    doc("www.bn.com/bib.xml")/
                      bib/book
   where $b/publisher=
             "Addison-Wesley"
    and $b/@year>1991
   return
    <book year="{ $b/@year }">
     { $b/title }
    </book> }
</bib>
```

Fig. 1. XQBE and XQuery versions of the same query

and title". All XQBE queries have a vertical line in the middle, separating the *source* part (on the left) from the *construct* part (on the right); both parts contain labeled graphs that represent XML fragments and express properties of such fragments: the source part specifies the properties of the XML data to be included in the result, while the Construct Part describes the structure of the result in terms of newly generated XML items, together with the projection of the elements extracted from the source documents. The correspondence between the components of the two parts is expressed by means of explicit *binding edges* across the vertical line; these edges connect the nodes of the Source Part to the nodes that will take their place in the output document. The paths that branch out of a bound node in the Construct Part indicate which of its sub-items are to be retained, thus "projecting" the node. All the XML *elements* in the Source Part of the target documents are represented as labeled rectangles; *attributes* are represented as black circles, with the *attribute name* on the arc between the rectangle and the circle; *PCDATA content* is represented as an empty circle. Attribute and PCDATA nodes in the Source Part may be labeled, so as to express conditions on the values they represent.

In Figure 1 the Source Part matches all the `book` elements with a `year` attribute whose value is greater than 1991 *and* a `publisher` sub-element whose PCDATA content equals "Addison-Wesley". By means of a binding edge, the selected `books` are sent to the Construct Part, where only the `title` and publication `year` are retained. Note the use of the triangular node to project the entire fragment rooted in the `title` element. The binding edge between the `book` nodes states that the query result shall contain *as many* `book` elements *as* those matched in the Source Part. Rectangular nodes in the Construct Part represent XML elements in direct correspondence with some XML data extracted from the source documents (either by a direct binding or by projection and renaming). Elements with no counterpart in the source documents are rendered by means of trapezoidal nodes, such as the `bib` node in the Construct Part of the example.

Other nodes allow one to express more complex queries with joins, aggregates, sorting, negation and more. Figure 2 shows all the defined constructs. For a full and formal description of the language, refer to [5].

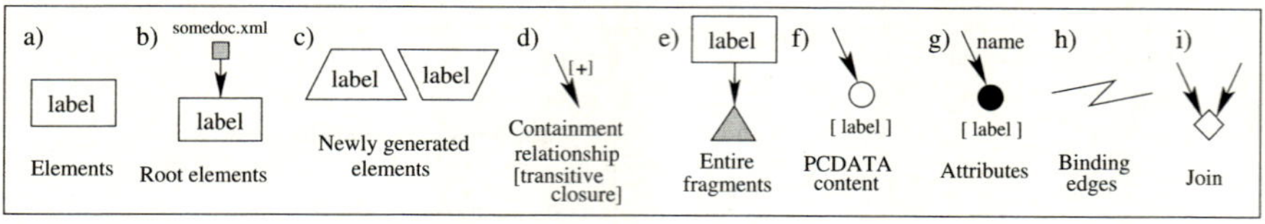

Fig. 2. Summary of the core XQBE constructs

3 ActiveXQBE

ActiveXQBE extends XQBE: while XQBE uses two regions to extract data and construct results, ActiveXQBE uses three regions (Figure 3a):

$\mathcal{S}$: the region on the left is the *Source Part* ($\mathcal{S}$); the graphs in this region locate the XML nodes on which the triggering events are defined, as well as the conditions that apply to such nodes for the rules to be triggered. Any valid XQBE source graph is allowed in $\mathcal{S}$; besides, one (and only one) node in this region *must* be tagged as the node on which the event occurs (the *event node*). One *action arrow* can go out of a node and point to an element in the action part $\mathcal{A}$, described below.

$\mathcal{C}$: the region on the right is the *Construct Part* ($\mathcal{C}$); the trees contained in this region, when present, define the constructed data structures to be inserted into suitable documents (as defined by the third region $\mathcal{A}$); such insertions may implement the actions of the active rules. If $\mathcal{C}$ is not empty, an *action arrow* *must* connect the root of the tree in $\mathcal{C}$ and a node in $\mathcal{A}$. Any regular XQBE construction tree is allowed in $\mathcal{C}$.

$\mathcal{A}$: a new region, the *Action Part* ($\mathcal{A}$) is placed below $\mathcal{S}$ and $\mathcal{C}$, where the action of the trigger is represented. ActiveXQBE supports different kinds of actions: insertions, updates, deletions and denials. If the action is a denial of the operation, a *stop sign* is placed in this region (Figure 3e). For the other three kinds of action, a tree in $\mathcal{A}$ expresses the selection of the XML fragments which must be affected. Such tree can be either rooted in a *Root Element*, or in a *Rectangular Element* bound to a node in $\mathcal{S}$. If the action of the rule is an update or an insertion, then the target of the action is the node reached by the

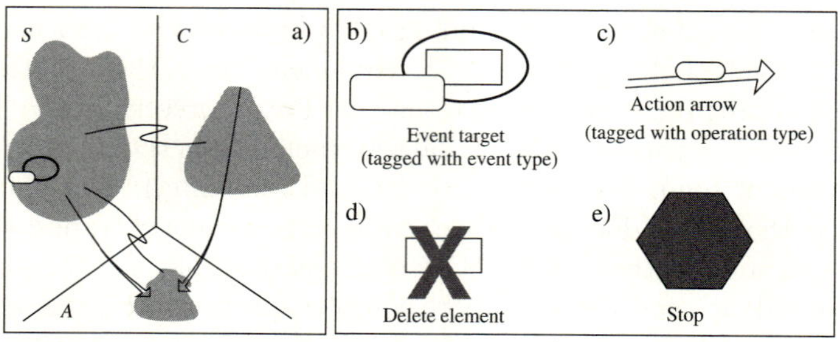

Fig. 3. Summary of the ActiveXQBE constructs

```
<dept>                                  <!ELEMENT dept
 <budget>1000000</budget>                       (budget, manager, emp*)>
 <manager>                              <!ELEMENT manager
  <name>Smith</name>                            (name, salary, numOfEmps)>
  <salary>10000</salary>                <!ELEMENT emp (name, salary)>
  <numOfEmps>9</numOfEmps>              <!ELEMENT name (#PCDATA)>
 </manager>                             <!ELEMENT numOfEmps (#PCDATA)>
 <emp> <name>Jones</name>               <!ELEMENT salary (#PCDATA)>
       <salary>8000</salary> </emp>
</dept>
```

Fig. 4. An XML document and its DTD schema

action arrow (described below), which is tagged with the type of operation. If the action is a deletion, then a red cross identifies the element to be deleted. ActiveXQBE triggers can only perform one action, so at most one action arrow can reach $\mathcal{A}$, either originating from $\mathcal{S}$ or $\mathcal{C}$.

Figure 3b shows the syntax for specifying the target of the event: a blue oval surrounds the target node (which can be either an Element, an attribute or a PCDATA node), and a tag specifies the type of event.

The syntax for actions is shown in Figure 3c, d, and e: an *action arrow* is used to *insert* or *update* an element with data extracted from the original document, or built on purpose. The arrow starts from the element to be inserted and reaches the element that will be updated (or below which the new item will be inserted). The tag on the arrow specifies the kind of action to be performed (insert-before, insert-after[1], update). A *red cross* is used to mark a node that must be deleted. A *stop sign* is used to indicate that the event should be prevented. In other words, if the trigger is evaluated *before* the event, then the action is stopped so that the update that activates the trigger is not even executed; if the trigger is evaluated *after* the event, then a rollback is performed that cancels the effect of the event itself.

In order to describe our approach, we show some triggers that apply to an XML data set exemplified in Figure 4.

Example 1 (Rollback).
As a first example, consider the trigger of Figure 5(a), which blocks insertion of salaries greater than 40000\$ to an employee. In this example the Construct Part is empty, since there is no need to build any new elements; the symbol in the action part states that the insertion is to be undone.

The `salary` node is the subject of the event: as stated by the label attached to the oval surrounding it, the trigger is evaluated *after* a `salary` node is inserted as a child of `emp`. Then, the action (in this case, a rollback of the insertion) is performed only when all the conditions of the source graph apply, i.e., only when the value of the `salary` is greater than 40000\$. Note that the trigger would also be evaluated after the insertion, for instance, of an `emp` element, because a `salary` sub-element would be inserted too.

[1] As in the XML update language proposal XUpdate [16], the "-before" and "-after" suffixes are to be interpreted with respect to the position of the pointed node.

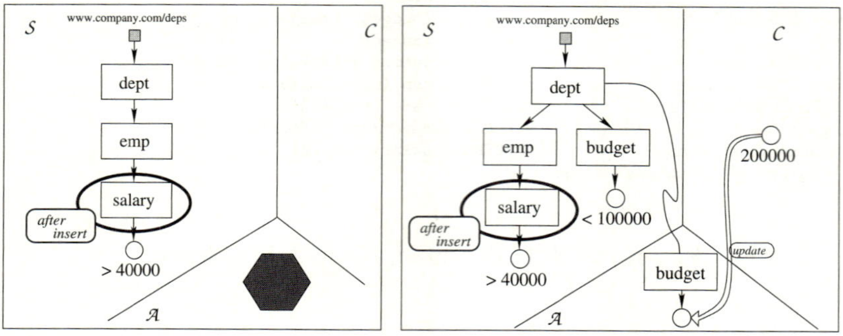

(a) (b)

Fig. 5. (a) Trigger 1: denying too high salaries (b) Trigger 2: updating budget

Example 2 (Update).
The example of Figure 5(b) extends the previous one with the addition of a condition and an action; in particular, when a salary greater than 40000$ is inserted for an employee belonging to a department with low budget (say, less than 100000$), this budget is updated to 200000$.

Note that the `dept` element in the action part is bound to the `dept` element in $\mathcal{S}$: the binding edge toward the action part transfers the context from $\mathcal{S}$, so, when a high salary is set to an employee, only the budget of his department is updated. The Construct Part of this trigger is used to build a new constant value of 200000$, that is used to update the budget of the department by means of an action arrow.

Example 3 (Adding complexity).
In Figure 6 we compare the newly inserted salary of an employee with the manager's salary. If the manager's salary is lower, then the employee's salary is updated to be the same as the manager's. The peculiarities of this trigger are

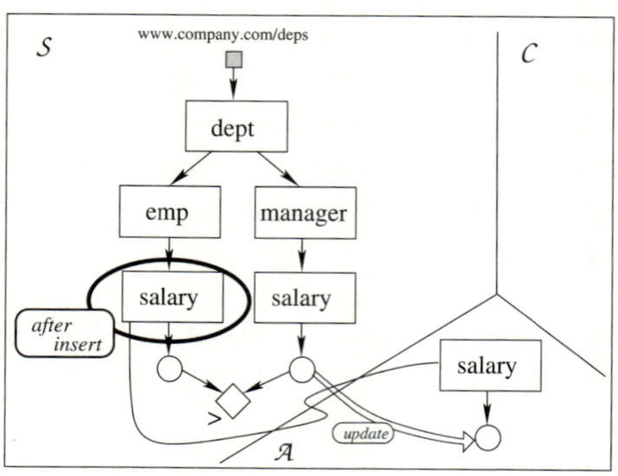

Fig. 6. Trigger 3: updating salary

the *join node* used to compare salaries (the small rhombus in Figure 6) and the action arrow, which comes from the Source Part. The Construct Part is unused.

Note that the action updates the newly inserted salary (i.e., the salary is removed and inserted again). This causes the trigger to be evaluated again, but the second time the comparison between salaries definitely fails, since the contents of the elements selected by the paths `emp/salary` and `manager/salary` are equal.

4 Graph Translation Algorithm

ActiveXQBE triggers are not interpreted by a specific engine; rather, they are translated into *Active XQuery* triggers and evaluated by existing rule engines.

As with many declarative languages, there are many ways to express the same operation in Active XQuery. Here we first define a *canonical Active XQuery form* and then show how to translate an ActiveXQBE graph into such form. Note that every well-formed ActiveXQBE graph can be translated into canonical Active XQuery, while nothing can be stated about the contrary.

Active XQuery triggers comply with the following syntax:

```
1. CREATE TRIGGER Trigger-Name [WITH PRIORITY Signed-Integer-Number]
2. (BEFORE|AFTER) (INSERT|DELETE|REPLACE|RENAME) OF
       XPathExpression (,XPathExpression)*
3. [FOR EACH (NODE|STATEMENT)]
4. [XQuery-Let-Clauses]
5. [WHEN XQuery-Where-Clause]
6. DO XUpdate-UpdateOp
```

The trigger can be divided into five main blocks: lines 1 and 3 are a sort of *header*, where the name and priority[2] of the trigger are defined, as well as its granularity[3]; line 2 describes the triggering *event*; in line 4 the *variables* useful to express conditions and actions can be defined; line 5 contains the trigger *conditions*; line 6 describes the *action* to be performed when the rule is triggered, which can either be an update statement written in XUpdate.

We say that a trigger is in *canonical form* when (a) the triggering event is monitored for target nodes which are identified by a *single path expression* and (b) the triggering conditions are expressed by stating the *non-emptiness* of *node sequences*, defined by means of *XQuery let-clauses*. Any trigger can be expressed in canonical form. We define the semantics (and perform the translation) of ActiveXQBE graphs in terms of canonical Active XQuery triggers. The translation algorithm operates with the steps described below.

[2] When the same event fires multiple rules, their actions are executed in priority order; within the same priority level, an implicit creation order is followed. This behavior is independent of ActiveXQBE, since it is enforced by the Active XQuery rule engine.

[3] I.e., whether the trigger must react on a per-statement basis, or once for each node affected by the event. In the latter case, the corresponding `$new` and `$old` variables will be available.

Source Graph Reduction. The first step is to locate and mark some nodes in the *source* graph which are said to be *relevant.* These nodes are the **event target** (the node on which the event occurs); the nodes with **binding edges**, both towards the construct and the action part; the nodes involved in an **action**. A variable will be generated for each such relevant node in the textual counterpart of the trigger.

Variable Generation. The event target represents the node on which the event occurs and is implicitly associated to a variable named *$new* or *$old*, according to the type of the event; this straightforwardly corresponds to the notion of "transition data" in SQL triggers. This variable, available for use in any part of the trigger, implicitly and automatically fixes the context of evaluation for other expressions.

All the other *relevant* nodes will be associated to a variable by means of suitable *let clauses*, which in turn can be used within other let-clauses, when-conditions, and during action specification (see below). The construction of such let clauses relies on topological analysis of the nodes surrounding the relevant ones.

As the Source Part of an XQBE query is always a directed acyclic graph, a partial order is implicitly defined over the set of relevant nodes. The nodes are considered in an order which is compliant with such partial order (namely, as encountered in a left-pre-ordered traversal that starts from the *initial* nodes, considered in left-to-right order). Each relevant node is associated to a path expression which corresponds to a path in the graph. For the first nodes considered, such path expression is rooted in one of the initial nodes (those corresponding to root nodes in the XML documents). For the other nodes such paths are rooted in the nearest ancestor chosen between the already considered relevant nodes (which are all already bound to a variable). The selection conditions of the XQuery statement that constitutes the body of the let clause associated to each variable (namely: the conjuncts of a where clause) are generated considering all the nodes reachable from the node currently under consideration, up to the not yet visited relevant nodes. In other words, starting from each relevant node, a set of conditions is generated, considering a subgraph that contains the current relevant node and is limited by the other relevant nodes. Some of the considered branches may have bifurcations at some point; in this case, an internal variable is generated for the node with the bifurcation, which is local to one specific let clause. Nodes with bifurcations, though, are not considered as relevant, and they are not involved in any separated let-clauses.

WHEN Clauses. All the conditions on the triggering of the rule, as represented by the query structures, have already been considered in the variable generation process; therefore, the WHEN clause can be reduced to a conjunction of non-emptiness statements over the node sequences returned by the previously defined let-clauses. Note that only the conjunction of *all* these statements ensures that all the conditions expressed in the Source Part will be correctly evaluated.

Action Specification. The last part of the trigger is the action to be performed. The Active XQuery language allows for any update language inside the `DO` block. Here, we choose XUpdate.

If the action part of ActiveXQBE contains special directives, such as a ROLLBACK, the corresponding textual command is simply generated within the action block. In general, when the action part contains a graph, an XUpdate variable is generated to select the target elements; moreover, if the action is not a deletion, another variable is generated to describe the elements to be inserted or updated. These elements are obtained either from the source or the Construct Part, based on the origin of the action arrow.

Figure 7 shows the trigger of figure 5(b) and its translation into Active XQuery.

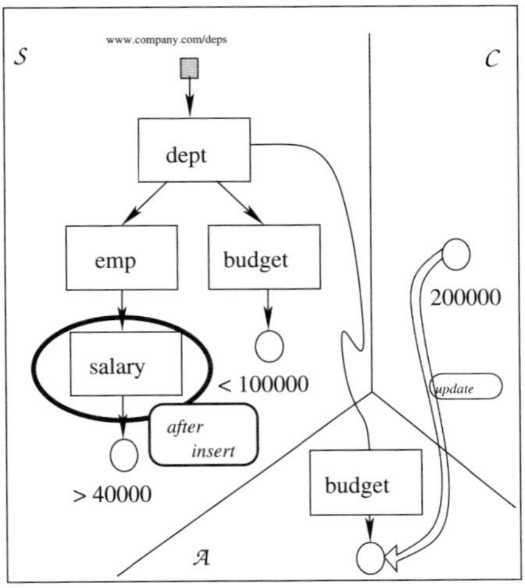


```
CREATE TRIGGER t
AFTER INSERT OF
  doc("...")/dept/emp/salary
FOR EACH NODE
let $dept_s := (
  for $dept in doc("...")/dept
  where $dept/emp/salary = $new
  return $dept )
let $new_s := (
  for $new in $new
  where $new/text() > 40000
  return $new )
let $budget_s := (
  for $budget in $dept_s/budget
  where $budget/text() < 100000
  return $budget )
WHEN
  not(empty($dept_s)) AND
  not(empty($new_s)) AND
  not(empty($budget_s))
DO (
  <XUpdate:update select="$budget_s">
    200000
  </XUpdate:update> )
```

Fig. 7. An ActiveXQBE trigger and its Active XQuery translation

5 Related Work

Querying XML documents content has been extensively studied within the database and semi-structured data communities and, ultimately, within the W3C. Once established, query languages have a natural extension in supporting content-based updates or in extracting views of XML documents. XQuery has been extended to support updates as a result of a research work [20], and the first working draft on the XQuery Update Facility has been recently published[4]. XQuery update operations include deletion, insertion, replacement and renaming of XML data. The XUpdate language is described in [16]. An XQuery-based XML update language is described in [19].

[4] http://www.w3.org/TR/2006/WD-xqupdate-20060127/

Active rules to enforce correctness of update operations and to automatically maintain views over data have been extensively studied in database systems [9]. Several research projects have provided substantial contributions to the field of active databases (e.g., Starburst [21], Hipac [15], Reach [8], Sentinel [10]).

Active XQuery [4], our target language, aims at emulating the trigger definition and execution model of SQL3 with respect to the XML data model. It builds on the XML update language and model defined in [20]. Other XML trigger languages are XChange [7] and ECA rules for XML [2]. None of these languages offers a graphical approach.

XQBE[5] comes after a long stream of research on visual and graph-based languages, started many years ago with QBE [22]. The first graphical query languages were G and G+ [13,14]. Graphlog [12] is a direct descendant of G+. A uniform notation for object databases where nodes represent objects and edges represent relationships was used in Good [17]. A Good-like notation was used by G-Log [18], a logic-based graphical language that allows one to represent and query complex objects by means of directed labeled graphs. An evolution of this language is XML-GL [11]. XQBE can be considered a successor of XML-GL, albeit with several new features.

6 Conclusion

In this paper we presented a framework for the visual specification of active rules for XML data. We showed that ActiveXQBE is a suitable tool for visually designing triggers in an intuitive fashion, as was demonstrated through a number of examples. These triggers can then be translated to Active XQuery and, thus, executed by implemented engines.

Among the possible future directions of research, we are studying the creation of an XQBE-based tool, to be integrated with ActiveXQBE, for the automatic or semi-automatic generation of optimized versions of the visual triggers that respond to given events and integrity constraints. Such tool would be designed along the lines of optimization frameworks for integrity constraints in deductive databases, but based on graph grammars to define rewrite rules for graphs.

References

1. Serge Abiteboul, Jason McHugh, Michael Rys, Vasilis Vassalos, and Janet L. Wiener. Incremental maintenance for materialized views over semistructured data. In *VLDB*, pages 38–49, 1998.
2. James Bailey, Alexandra Poulovassilis, and Peter T. Wood. Analysis and optimisation of event-condition-action rules on xml. *Computer Networks*, 39(3):239–259, 2002.
3. Michael Benedikt, Glenn Bruns, Julie Gibson, Robin Kuss, and Amy Ng. Automated Update Management for XML Integrity Constraints. In *PLAN-X*, 2002.
4. A. Bonifati, D. Braga, A. Campi, and S. Ceri. Active xquery. In *Proc. of the 18th ICDE, IEEE Computer Society Press, San José, California*, Feb. 2002.

5. D. Braga, A. Campi, and S. Ceri. XQBE (XQuery By Example): a visual interface to the standard XML query language. *ACM TODS*, 30(2):398–443, 2005.
6. François Bry and Massimo Marchiori. Ten theses on logic languages for the semantic web. In *W3C WS on Rule Languages for Interoperability*. W3C, 2005.
7. François Bry and Paula-Lavinia Patranjan. Reactivity on the web: paradigms and applications of the language xchange. In *SAC*, pages 1645–1649, 2005.
8. A. P. Buchmann, H. Branding, T. Kudrass, and J. Zimmermann. Reach: A real-time, active and heterogeneous mediator system. *IEEE Data Eng. Bull.*, 15(1-4):44–47, 1992.
9. S. Ceri, R.J. Cochrane, and J. Widom. Practical applications of triggers and constraints: Successes and lingering issues. In *VLDB*, pages 254–262, 2000.
10. S. Chakravarthy, E. Anwar, and L. Maugis. Design and implementation of active capability for an object-oriented database. Technical report, Univ. Florida, 1993.
11. S. Comai, E. Damiani, and P. Fraternali. Computing graphical queries over xml data. *ACM TOIS*, 19(4):371–430, 2001.
12. M. P. Consens and A. O. Mendelzon. The g+/graphlog visual query system. In *Proc. of the 1990 ACM SIGMOD, Atlantic City, NJ, May 23-25*, page 388, 1990.
13. I. F. Cruz, A. O. Mendelzon, and P. T. Wood. A graphical query language supporting recursion. In *Proc. of the ACM SIGMOD*, pages 323–330, 1987.
14. I. F. Cruz, A. O. Mendelzon, and P. T. Wood. G+: Recursive queries without recursion. In *2nd Int. Conf. on Expert Database Systems*, pages 355–368, 1988.
15. U. Dayal, A. P. Buchmann, and S. Chakravarthy. *Active Database Systems*, chapter The HiPAC Project, pages 177–205. Morgan Kauffmann, 1996.
16. Andreas Laux and Lars Matin. XUpdate working draft. Technical report, `http://www.xmldb.org/xupdate`, October 2000.
17. J. Paredaens, J. Van den Bussche, M. Andries, M. Gemis, M. Gyssens, I. Thyssens, D. Van Gucht, V. Sarathy, and L. V. Saxton. An Overview of GOOD. *SIGMOD Record*, 21(1):25–31, 1992.
18. J. Paredaens, P. Peelman, and L. Tanca. G-log a declarative graph-based language. *IEEE Trans. on Knowledge and Data Eng.*, 7(3):436–453, 1995.
19. Gargi Sur, Joachim Hammer, and Jerome Siméon. UpdateX - An XQuery-Based Language for Processing Updates in XML. In *PLAN-X 04*, pages 40–53, 2004.
20. I. Tatarinov, Z. G. Ives, A. Y. Halevy, and D. S. Weld. Updating XML. In *ACM SIGMOD*, pages 413–424, 2001.
21. J. Widom. The starburst active database rule system. *IEEE TKDE*, (4):583–595,1996.
22. Moshé M. Zloof. Query-by-example: A data base language. *IBM Systems Journal*, 16(4):324–343, 1977.

Visual Modeling of ReActive Web Applications

Federico Michele Facca and Florian Daniel

Dipartimento di Elettronica e Informazione, Politecnico di Milano
P.zza Leonardo da Vinci 32, I-20133 Milano, Italy
{facca, daniel}@elet.polimi.it

Abstract. In our previous research we have proposed a new high-level model for the specification of Web applications that takes into account the way in which users interact with the application in order to actively react and supply appropriate contents or gather profile data. In this context, we have realized a proper execution framework to develop ReActive Web applications specified by means of the novel modeling paradigm. In this paper we discuss an e-learning case study implemented using our framework and introduce the visual design tools we have extended and developed in order to support the development of ReActive Web applications.

1 Introduction

Reactivity on the Web is becoming a hot topic, and aims at addressing new issues within emerging e-business and e-learning Web applications, where retrieval and update of data plays an essential role. In this context, monitoring the behaviors of users may enable Web applications to react to such behaviors and to improve the users navigation comfort and interactivity with the application. This paper is based on our previous research on ReActive Web applications [1,2]; the result of this research is a visual Event-Condition-Action (ECA) paradigm to describe reactivity triggered by a user's interactions with the Web application.

The ECA rule paradigm was first implemented in active database systems in the early nineties [3] to improve the robustness and maintainability of database applications. Recently, it has also been exploited in other contexts, such as XML [4] to incorporate reactive functionality in XML documents, Semantic Web [5] to allow reactive behaviors in ontology evolution, Web applications [6] to realize reactive behaviors involving distributed applications on the Web.

In our framework it is possible to specify arbitrary composite and timed behaviors depending on a user's navigations and to react by adapting the Web application and the application's data. A composite behavior is a behavior including different user interactions with the Web application, i.e., user's inspections of different portions of the Web application and data instances; a timed behavior is a behavior where the time gaps between the the users' actions are specified by time constrain. In this paper we highlight the potentialities of our framework by presenting an e-learning case study and by introducing the visual design tools we used to automatically generate the application presented in the case study.

T. Grust et al. (Eds.): EDBT 2006 Workshops, LNCS 4254, pp. 876–886, 2006.

This paper is organized as follows: Section 2 introduces the two background models that we adopt for modeling ReActive Web applications: WebML and WBM. Section 3 combines WebML and WBM for defining proper ECA rules. Section 4 illustrates an applicative example, and Section 5 introduces some details on the framework used to develop ReActive Web applications. Finally, in Section 6 we address future research efforts and draw some conclusions.

2 Background Models

Our ReActive framework is based on two models, WebML [7] and WBM [2], which are properly combined to obtain a visual paradigm for ECA rules, enabling the specification of reactivity of user behaviors.

2.1 Web Modeling Language

The *Web Modeling Language*, WebML, is a conceptual model for the design of Web applications [7], supported by a proper CASE tool [8]. The WebML method fosters a strong separation of concerns, by separating the information content from its composition into hypertext, navigation, and presentation, which can be defined and evolved independently. The modeling language offers a set of visual primitives for defining structural schemas that represent the organization and navigation of hypertext interfaces on top of the application data, while for specifying the organization of data the well known Entity-Relationship model is adopted. Also, primitives for specifying data manipulation operations for updating the site content or interacting with arbitrary external services are provided.

For further details on WebML, the reader is referred to [7].

2.2 Web Behavior Model

The *Web Behavior Model*, WBM, is a timed state-transition automaton for representing classes of user behaviors on the Web. Graphically, WBM models are expressed as labeled graphs, allowing for an easy to understand syntax (cf. Figure 1). A *state* represents the user's inspection of a specific portion of hypertext (i.e., a page or a collection of pages). State labels are mandatory and correspond to names of pages or page collections. A *transition* represents a navigation from one such portion to another and, thus, the evolving from one state to another. Each WBM specification, called *script*, has at least an initial state, indicated by an incoming unlabeled arc, and at least one accepting state, highlighted by double border lines. Initial states cannot also be accepting states. Each transition from a source to a target state may be labeled with a pair $[t_{min}, t_{max}]$, expressing a time interval within which the transition must occur in order to cause a state transition.

Finally, the expressive power of WBM has been augmented to better describe WebML-based applications: *state constraints* – referring to data contained within a page – and *link constraints* – referring to a particular incoming or outgoing link – have been introduced. For further details on the WBM model and its tailoring to WebML, the reader is referred to [2].

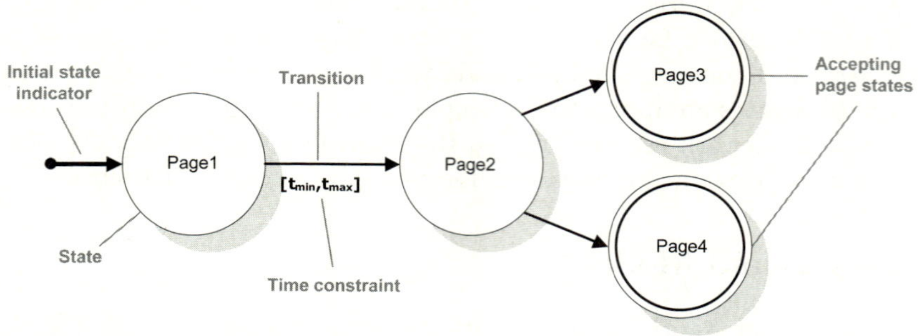

Fig. 1. Example of WBM script with state, link, and time constraints and multiple exiting transitions from one state

3 Reacting to User Behaviors

In order to be able to react to observed behaviors and to adapt the running application to novel requirements, we combined WebML and WBM. In our framework possible reactions comprise: (i) adaptivity of contents published by specific pages; (ii) automatic execution of navigation actions toward other pages; (iii) automatic execution of operations or services; (iv) adaptivity of the overall hypertext structure.

Although independent from one another, expressing adaptation as a combination of WBM scripts and WebML adaptivity constructs intrinsically leads to a high-level ECA paradigm for specifying adaptivity. Commonly, ECA rules respect the general syntax: `on` *event* `if` *condition* `do` *action*, where the event part specifies *when* the rule should be triggered, the condition part assesses whether given *constraints* are satisfied, and the action part states the *actions* to be automatically performed if the condition holds. When specifying behavior-aware Web applications, the event consists of a *page* or *operation request*, the condition checks the state of the WBM scripts associated with the current page, and the action part specifies some actions to be forced on the Web application which are expressed as a WebML *operations chain*, i.e., a sequence of WebML operation units. The condition is satisfied and, thus, actions are performed, only when the page's scripts reaches an accepting state. Actions are executed only when pages associated with the respective rules are accessed. ReActive pages are labeled in the WebML hypertext model with `A`, standing for "Active". To avoid multiple rule activation conflicts a priority can be associated with each rule, thus if the condition holds for two ore more rules, only the one with the highest priority is fired.

Figure 2 graphically summarizes the outlined rule construct: The rule reacts to a user's visit to *Page1* followed by a visit to *Page2* at some stage after his/her visit to *Page1*. The expressed rule condition only holds when the script reaches the accepting state *Page2*. In this case the operations associated to that page (abstracted as the cloud in Figure 2) are executed and possible reactions may be performed.

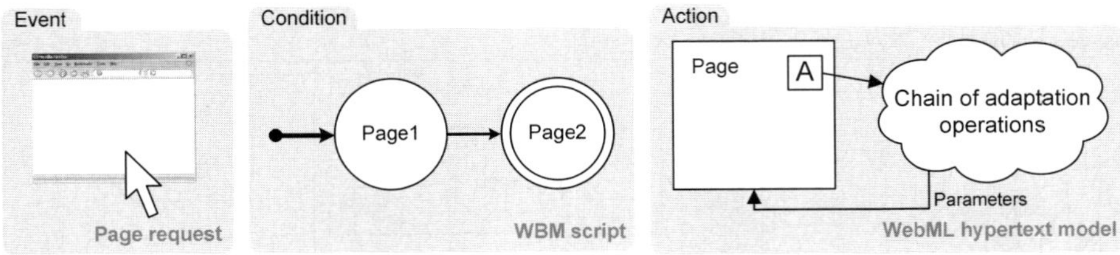

Fig. 2. High-level ECA rule components

For further details on WebML operations chain and adaptivity in WebML, the reader is referred to [9].

4 An E-Learning Case Study

This section provides an e-learning reference scenario modelled in WebML. Later we will enrich the scenario with proper reactivity constructs by means of visual ECA rules as shown in Section 3. This way of presenting the Web application fully reflects our development method.

The non-adaptive application allows users to browse courses according to their personal expertise level on the topic of the course and to test the acquired knowledge by answering related questions, thus possibly enhancing their knowledge level on a topic. Figure 3 depicts the E/R schema underlying the e-learning application: each user has a set of favorite topics and an associated level of expertise for each topic. Each course is related to one or more levels of expertise and to one topic. For each level of expertise and each topic there is a set of questions; each question is associated to a set of possible answers and to one correct answer. Results achieved by users and their answers to each question are stored. To simplify the diagram, derived relationship are not shown.

A simplified WebML model for the *Student* siteview of the e-learning application is depicted in Figure 4. The *Home* page contains *User Data*, a list of

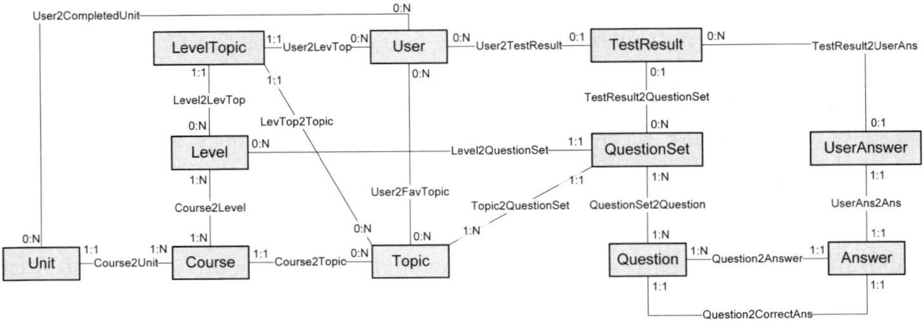

Fig. 3. Entity-Relationship schema for the ReActive e-learning application

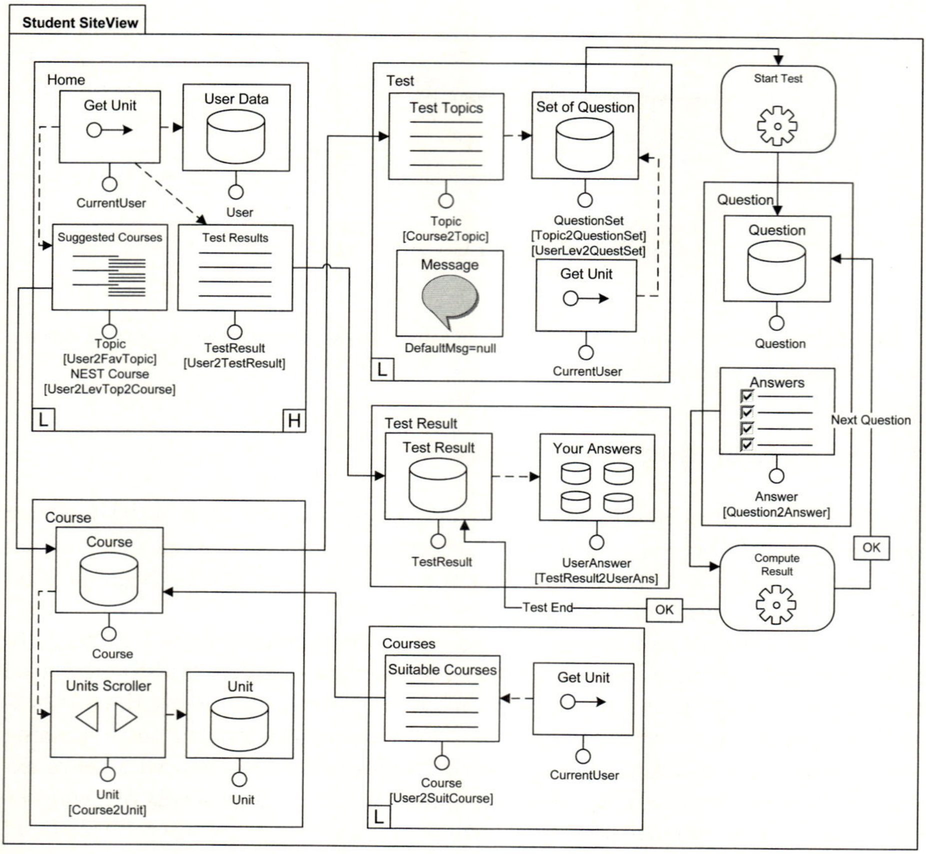

Fig. 4. The WebML model of the proposed educational Web site

Suggested Courses, grouped by topic and selected according to the user's knowledge level on the topic[1] and a list of the *Test Results* scored. The *Get Unit* allows accessing the user's identifier, while the selector conditions below the units allow binding a unit to a data entity and personalizing the displayed items by applying filter conditions. From the *Home* page the user can ask for the *Courses* page or the *Test Result* page. L-labeled pages – *Home*, *Test* and *Courses* – are landmark pages and can be accessed from any page within the hypertext. The *Test* page presents a list of *Topic* and for each of them a *Set of Question* is selected according to the individual knowledge on the selected topic. Once the user has selected a topic on which he/she wants to test his/her knowledge, he/she can start a test. Hence a *Question* is presented with the relative set of possible *Answers*. Submitting an answer, its correctness is evaluated and a score is associated to the the user by the *Compute Result* operation unit. Then, this unit sends the

[1] When a new student registers for the first time to the Web application, his/her level of knowledge is assumed to be 0 for each topic.

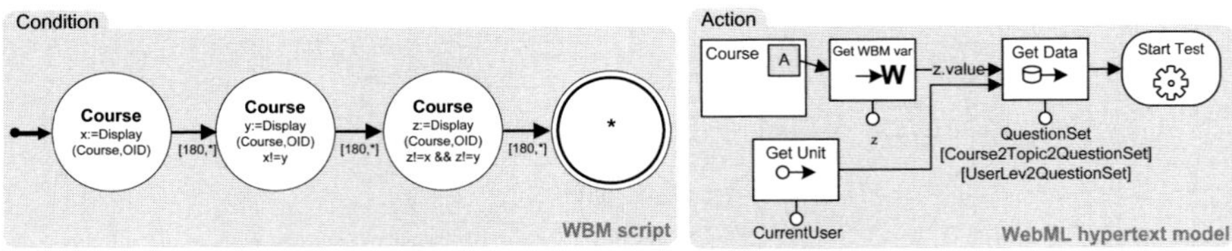

Fig. 5. An ECA rule to trigger the evaluation of a student's knowledge level. The event part (user click) is omitted for simplicity.

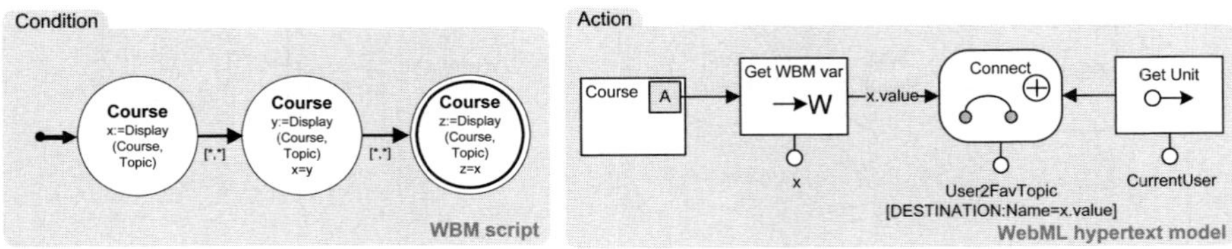

Fig. 6. An ECA rule to profile user preferences

user to the next question, or, finally, computes the new expertise level of the user on the topic he/she wanted to test and redirects the user to the *Test Result* page. In this page, the *Test Result* scored is reported to the user together with the set of answers he/she selected during the test. In the *Courses* page, *Suitable Courses* according to the user's knowledge level are presented. From here, the user can browse a (*Course* page) where each *Course* is organized into a set of smaller contents that can be scrolled.

In the sequel we describe some examples that add a ReActive layer to the Web application.

Example 1. Evolving the Level of User Expertise. Figure 5 models an ECA rule to redirect the user to the *Test* page for the next experience level after having visited 3 courses (i.e., 3 different instances of *Course* pages), spending at least 3 minutes over each different Course page. The $*$ in the final state of the WBM script specifies the acceptance of any arbitrary page. The WebML operation chain for adaptation is thus performed when the user asks again for a *Course* page. When the chain is activated, the appropriate question set is retrieved by the `Get Data` unit using parameters passed by the `Get` unit and the `Get WBM Variable` unit, hence the test starts.

Example 2. Student Profiling. Suppose we want to personalize the application according to the user's preferences traceable from his/her navigational choices (cf. Figure 6). The script detects that a user is interested in a certain topic, whenever he/she navigates at least three different *Course* pages presenting three courses belonging to the same topic. The identified topic is stored within the variable x. In response to this behavior, the WebML operation chain stores the derived preference: the value of the variable x is retrieved by the `Get WBM`

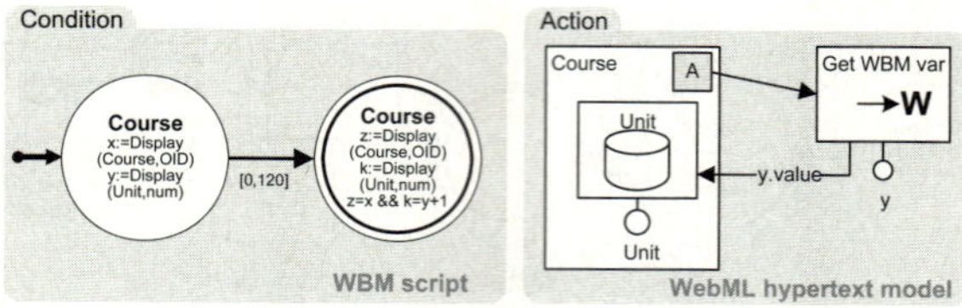

Fig. 7. An ECA rule to oblige student to spend enough time on a course unit

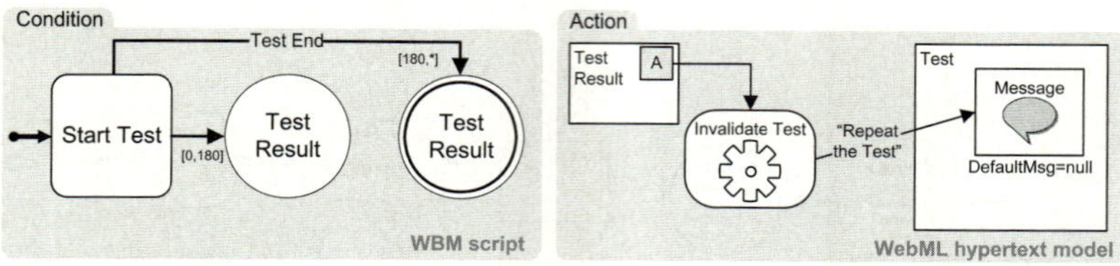

Fig. 8. An ECA rule to invalidate too long tests

`Variable` unit and the identified topic is associated to the current user. Now, when the user enters the *Home* page, courses belonging to the same topic are automatically presented by means of the *Suggested Courses* unit (cf. Figure 4).

Example 3. Imposing time of page browsing. Figure 7 depicts an ECA rule to oblige students to spend enough time on a course unit before accessing the next one: the WBM script tracks users that access a course *Unit* within the *Course* page and then ask for the next course *Unit* of the same course in less than 2 minutes. In such case, we suppose the user has not carefully read the unit, and hence the action part of the rule forces him to stay on the same course *Unit*.

Example 4. Invalidating a Test. Suppose it is not enough for us that a student successfully passes a test to improve his/her level, but we also want him/her to pass it within a certain amount of time (cf. Figure 8). The WBM script reaches a success state only if the user starts a test and reaches the *Test Result* page in more than 180 seconds, in such case he/she is redirected to the *Test* page where the *Message* unit asks him/her to repeat the test.

Further ECA rules that can be applied to the e-learning Web application may include: dynamical increase/decrease of the difficulty level of the question according to the answer time of a user to each single question; forcing students to browse the same contents as the teacher (a sort of "collaborative" reaction); monitoring of effectively active students on the Web application (not only logged into the application but also actively interacting with it); determination of effectively completed course units (units where the student spent at least the minimum required time).

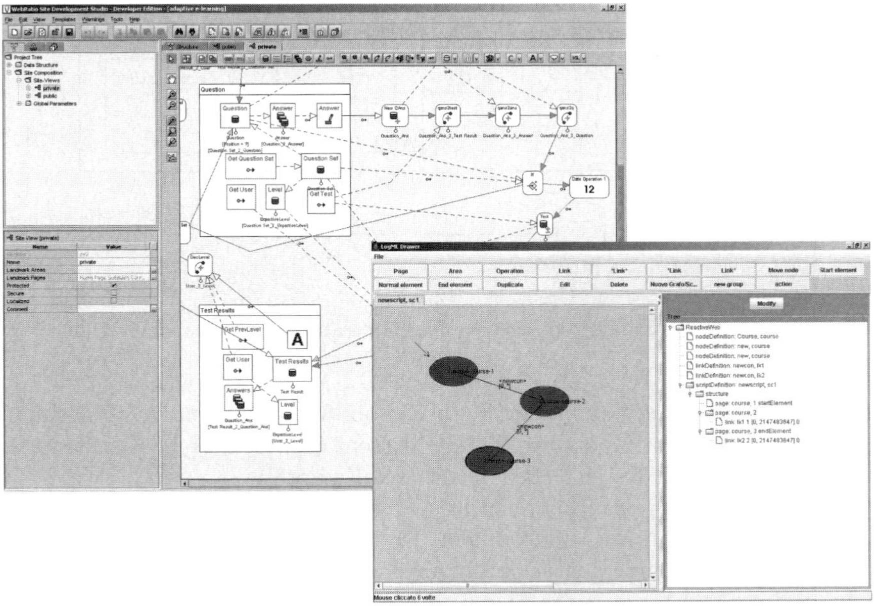

Fig. 9. The WebRatio modeling tool, extended with the new reactivity-supporting units and the WBM CASE tool

5 A Framework for Building ReActive Web Applications

In our framework, Web application code generation is based on WebRatio [8], a CASE tool for WebML that supports the visual design of the application schema and the automatic code generation, starting from WebML schemas and using a proprietary, extensible runtime engine. Automatic code generation is based on parametric code components corresponding to WebML units. Parametric components are configured at runtime using XML descriptors that contain SQL queries and parameters for retrieving contents from the application data source. The implementation of the extension introduced in this paper exploits WebRatios native extension mechanisms that allow adding new features by means of so-called custom units, a mechanism that has already demonstrated its power when extending the CASE tool to support other functions. The so achieved extension fully reflects the proposed (visual) design method, and supports the automatic generation and deployment of ReActive Web applications. We implemented the ReActive pages as described in Section 3 and introduced a new unit to retrieve WBM variables (`Get WBM Variable`). The implementation of ReActive pages required an extension of the page logic, yielding a further new unit (called `Active` unit), to be used in place of the `A`-label associated to reactive pages. This unit triggers the operation chains, indicated by the outgoing links from the `A`-label, when a WBM script associated to a page and to the current user terminates successfully (cf. Figure 9).

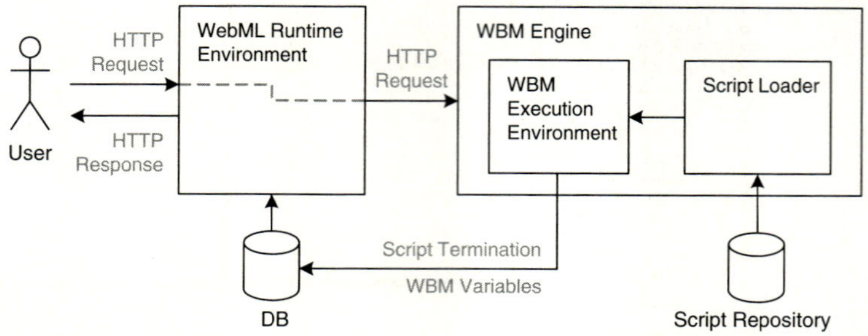

Fig. 10. Functional architecture of the overall behavior-aware system

To support WBM script's modeling based on WebML schemas, we developed a visual tool that can import the XML representation of a WebML schema and use retrieved data to design WBM script (see Figure 9).

Executing Web applications reacting to users' behaviors – in addition to the standard WebML runtime environment – requires proper runtime support for WBM scripts. The implementation of rule engines for active databases is a well known and studied topic in the literature on database systems. Our problem of handling user sessions and WBM scripts resembles to the problem of handling transactions and rules in active databases. For more details on the implementation of the WBM engine refer to [2].

5.1 ReActive Architecture

Figure 10 reports the architecture of our framework: HTTP requests toward the Web application are automatically forwarded to the WBM engine by the WebML runtime environment, which hosts the actual application. Users interact only with the Web application itself and are not aware of the WBM engine behind it.

The WBM engine collects and evaluates tracked, user-generated HTTP requests for (i) instantiating new scripts at runtime, and (ii) enhancing the states of possible running WBM scripts, as well as (iii) communicating possible script terminations. Script instantiation is managed by a proper *Script loader* module and the set of scripts that can be instantiated for a particular application is retrieved from a *Script Repository*. Finally a dedicated *WBM Execution Environment*, is in charge of progressing instantiated, running scripts. Once a script reaches its accepting state, the execution environment communicates the successful termination to the Web application by modifying suitable data structures within the shared database.

After the successful termination of a WBM script, the Web application possesses all the necessary data for executing the possibly associated actions. As soon as a user requests one of the pages within the scope of the high-level rule whose condition is satisfied by the terminated WBM script, the Web application executes the operations associated to the requested page. For this purpose, page computation starts by checking whether scripts connected to the page have terminated or not, before proceeding with the actual rendering of the page. If there are terminated scripts for that page, one or more rules could be executed. Thus, computation proceeds with the determined adaptation operations, producing effects as described in Section 3. Only afterward, if no automatic navigation actions are triggered, computation continues with the actual page, and a suitable HTTP response is produced.

6 Conclusion and Future Work

In this paper we introduced a practical case study showing a potential application of the general purpose approach for building ReActive Web applications. Furthermore, we presented our current implementation of the WBM engine and the CASE tools we used to design advanced ReActive Web sites. The adopted CASE tools prove that combining WebML and WBM yields a very powerful visual ECA model, with adequate expressive power for capturing highly sophisticated Web dynamics and providing suitable reactivity mechanisms.

In our future work, we are planning to enrich the proposed ECA paradigm, including not only events related to user behaviors but also data events and other Web events. We also intend to better integrate the two CASE tools presented for providing a unique and complete tool to easily design and deploy Web applications reacting to user behaviors.

Acknowledgement

We acknowledge the commitment of Luca Sonzogni and Cristian Rossi to the implementation of the WBM engine and the prototype application, and Luca Cavagnoli who developed the WBM CASE tool.

References

1. F. M. Facca, S. Ceri, J. Armani, V. Demaldé, Building reactive web applications, in: Proceedings of the 14th international conference on World Wide Web, WWW 2005, Chiba, Japan, May 10-14, 2005 - Special interest tracks and posters, ACM, 2005, pp. 1058–1059.
2. S. Ceri, F. Daniel, , F. M. Facca, Modeling web applications reacting to user behaviors, to appear on a Special Issue of the Computer Networks journal on *Web Dynamics*.
3. J. Widom, The Starburst Active Database Rule System, IEEE Trans. Knowl. Data Eng. 8 (4) (1996) 583–595.
4. A. Bonifati, S. Ceri, S. Paraboschi, Active rules for XML: A new paradigm for E-services, The VLDB Journal 10 (1) (2001) 39–47.
5. G. Papamarkos, A. Poulovassilis, P. T. Wood, Event-Condition-Action Rule Languages for the Semantic Web, in: Proceedings of SWDB'03, Berlin, Germany, September 7-8, 2003, 2003, pp. 309–327.

6. F. Bry, P.-L. Pătrânjan, Reactivity on the web: Paradigms and applications of the language XChange, in: Proceedings of ACM Symposium on Applied Computing, Santa Fe, New Mexico, USA (13th–17th March 2005), 2005.
7. S. Ceri, P. Fraternali, A. Bongio, M. Brambilla, S. Comai, M. Matera, Designing Data-Intensive Web Applications, Morgan Kauffmann, 2002.
8. WebModels srl: WebRatio. `http://www.webratio.com`.
9. S. Ceri, F. Daniel, M. Matera, Extending WebML for Modeling Multi-Channel Context-Aware Web Applications, in: Proceedings of Fourth International Conference on Web Information Systems Engineering Workshops (WISEW'03), Rome, Italy, December 12 -13, 2003, IEEE Press, 2003, pp. 225–233.

An ECA Engine for Deploying Heterogeneous Component Languages in the Semantic Web

Erik Behrends, Oliver Fritzen, Wolfgang May, and Daniel Schubert

Institut für Informatik, Universität Göttingen
{behrends, fritzen, may, dschuber}@informatik.uni-goettingen.de

Abstract. We describe a generic ECA service for implementing behavior using heterogeneous languages in the Semantic Web. The module details and implements our recent work on an ontology and language concept for a modular approach to ECA rules in the Semantic Web. The ECA level provides generic functionality independent from the actual languages and semantics of event detection, queries, and actions.

1 Introduction

In [MAA05b], we presented an ontology-based approach for specifying (reactive) behavior of the Web and evolution of the Web that follows the *Event-Condition-Action (ECA)* paradigm. The approach provides a modular framework for *composing* languages for event detection, queries, conditions, and actions by separating the ECA semantics from the underlying semantics of events, queries, and actions. We deal with the heterogeneity of the components (i.e., event, query and action languages) by associating every rule component with a language. The language descriptions (as resource descriptions) provide pointers to appropriate Web Services that implement the respective languages in a service-oriented architecture. An accompanying proposal for a rule markup language has been given in [MAA05a]. In the present paper, we describe a prototypical implementation (in Java) of an ECA engine for this framework: Section 2 shortly reviews the underlying ontology and language model of the general framework for ECA rules. Section 3 describes the global semantics of the rules, focusing on the handling of variables. Section 4 then describes the actual evaluation and communication with the component language services and illustrates it by a running example. Section 5 concludes the paper.

2 Language Heterogeneity: Rule Components and Languages

For dealing with the different languages for events, queries and tests, and actions, we prefer a *declarative* approach with a *clean, modular* design as a "Normal Form": First detect just the dynamic part of a situation (event), then optionally obtain additional information by queries (that can be stated using different languages), evaluate a *boolean* test, and, if "yes", then actually *do* something – as

T. Grust et al. (Eds.): EDBT 2006 Workshops, LNCS 4254, pp. 887–898, 2006.

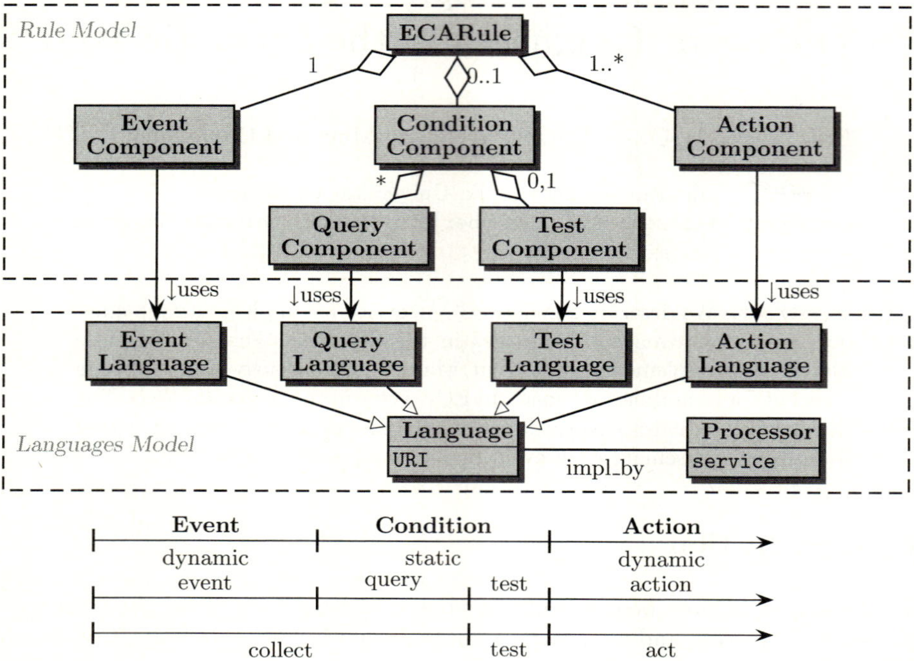

Fig. 1. ECA Rule Components and Languages (simplified from [MAA05a])

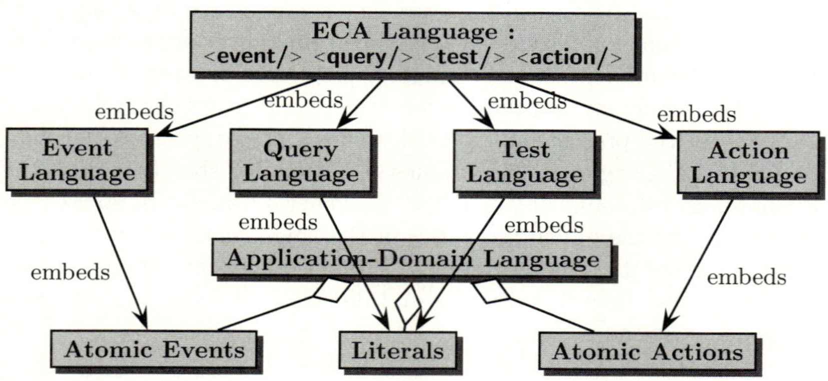

Fig. 2. Hierarchy of Languages (simplified from [MAA05a])

shown in Figure 1. Thus, every rule uses an event language, one or more query languages, a test language, and one or more action languages for the respective components. Rules and their components are objects of the Semantic Web, i.e., subject to a generic *rule ontology* as shown in the UML model. Every component is associated with its language (seen as a resource), identified by a URI. With this URI, further information is associated that allows to address a suitable Web Service that implements the language; details about the service-oriented architecture can be found in [MAA05b].

The framework defines a hierarchical structure of language families (wrt. embedding of language expressions) as shown in Figure 2: the ECA language embeds event, query, test, and action languages. Rules combine one or more languages of each of the families. In general, each such language consists of an application-independent syntax and semantics (e.g., event algebras, query languages, boolean tests, process algebras) which is then applied to a domain (e.g. travelling). The domain ontologies define the static and dynamic notions of the application domain, i.e., predicates or literals (for queries and conditions), and events and actions (e.g. events of delayed flights, actions of reserving tickets).

3 Semantics of ECA Rules and Variables

For classical deductive rules, there is a *bottom-up* evaluation where the body is evaluated and produces a set of tuples of variable bindings. Then, the rule head is "executed" by *iterating* over all bindings, for *each* binding instantiating the structure described in the head (in some languages also executing actions in the head). We define the semantics of ECA rules as close as possible to this semantics, adapted to the temporal aspect of an event:

ON *event* AND *additional knowledge*, IF *condition* THEN DO *something*.

Logical variables are used in the same way as in Logic Programming for communication between the different components of a rule: the semantics of rules is based on sets of tuples of (answer) variable bindings. In case that a variable occurs more than once in a rule, it is handled as a join variable. While in Logic Programming rules, variables must be bound by a positive literal in the body to serve as join variables in the body and to be used in the head, in ECA rules we have four components: A variable must be bound in the rule, in an "earlier" (Event < Query < Test < Action) or at least the same component as where it is used. Usage can be as a join variable in case of the Event, Query, or Test component, or to execute ("derive") an action in the Action component (that corresponds to the rule head). Variables can be bound to values/literals, references (URIs), XML or RDF fragments, or events (marked up as XML or RDF fragments).

While the semantics of the ECA *rules* provides the infrastructure and global semantics, the *component languages* provide the local semantics. For dealing with heterogeneous languages, the ECA level does only minimally constrain the component languages. Communication between the ECA engine and the Event, Query, Test, and Action components is done by exchanging variable bindings. Component languages use variables in two different ways: Logic Programming-style languages match free variables, e.g. query languages like Datalog, F-Logic [KL89], XPathLog [May04], or Xcerpt [BS02]; similar techniques can also be applied to design languages for the event component. Functional-style languages act as functions over a database or an event stream, and some input/environment variables. In the XML world, such languages return an XML fragment (e.g. XQuery). In most classical approaches for event languages (e.g., as in SNOOP [CKAK94]), the "result" of an expression is often considered to be the sequence of detected events that "matched" the event expression in an event stream. Variables can be bound on the rule level for binding results of functional expressions by borrowing from XSLT as <eca:variable name="*name*">*content*</eca:variable> where *content* can be any expression whose value is then bound to the variable (i.e., an event specification or a query). Similar constructs are recommended to use in the component languages. We will focus here on the ECA level, keeping the component expressions as simple as possible.

4 The ECA Engine

4.1 Architecture

The architecture is shown in Figure 3. The ECA engine controls the evaluation of a rule, i.e., *when* to evaluate *which* rule component, and keeps the state information during the evaluation. The communication with the autonomous remote component language processors is done via the *Generic Request Handler (GRH)*, using an XML markup for requests and answers. Using the namespace declaration of the components, the GRH determines an appropriate language processor and sends the request and the relevant variable bindings to it in an appropriate form. After receiving the answer, the obtained variable bindings are communicated back to the ECA engine.

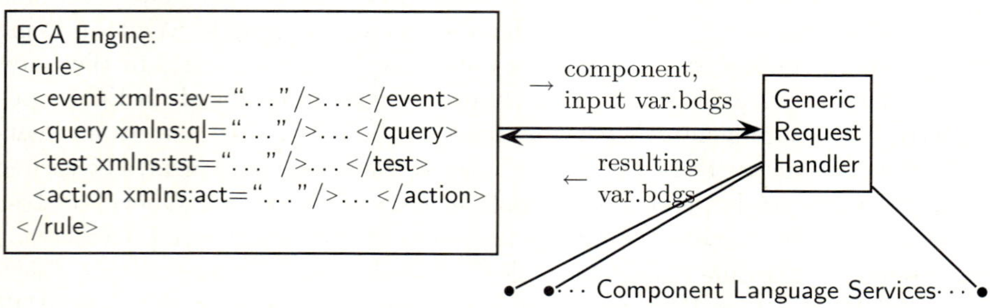

Fig. 3. Global Service-Oriented Architecture

This process is described below and illustrated by an exemplary ECA rule of a car-rental company: when a customer books a flight, cars similar in size to his own cars are offered at the given destination (see Figure 4).

4.2 Firing ECA Rules: The Event Component

Upon registration of a rule in the ECA engine, its event component is submitted to the GRH. The GRH inspects the namespace of the event language and submits

```
<eca:rule xmlns:eca="http://www.semwebtech.org/06/eca-ml">
  <eca:event><!-- detect a booking by a person --></eca:event>
  <eca:variable name="OwnCar">
    <eca:query><!-- query the person's cars --></eca:query>
  </eca:variable>
  <eca:variable name="Class">
    <eca:query><!-- map the cars to the appropriate classes --></eca:query>
  </eca:variable>
  <eca:query>
    <!-- query cars that are available at the destination. -->
  </eca:query>
  <eca:action><!-- inform the customer about suitable cars --></eca:action>
</eca:rule>
```

Fig. 4. Outline of the Sample Rule

the event component to an appropriate event detection service (see Figure 5). In our simple example, the event component consists only of an atomic event pattern. The event pattern is thus sent directly to an *Atomic Event Matcher* that is aware of relevant events.

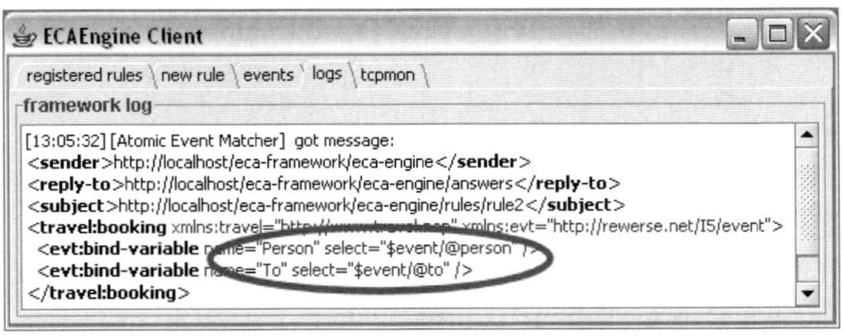

Fig. 5. Registration of the Event Component

The event detection service evaluates the event specification against the stream of events. When an (atomic) event that matches the specification, e.g.,

<travel:booking person="John Doe" from="Munich" to="Paris"/>

occurs, the detection of the event component pattern is signalled from the event detection service to the GRH (containing the identification of the rule, the event sequence that matched the pattern and the collected variable bindings). The GRH forwards it to the ECA engine as shown in Fig. 6(1), using an XML markup for answers and tuples of variable bindings. The arrival of the event detection message marks the starting point of the rule evaluation at the ECA engine. The ECA engine creates one or more instances of the rule with appropriate variable bindings according to the number of answer elements in the message (Fig. 6(2)).

Languages for Composite Events. The event component can also use *arbitrary* language for specifying composite events – as far as a service that actually does the event detection is provided. In this case, the event component is of the form

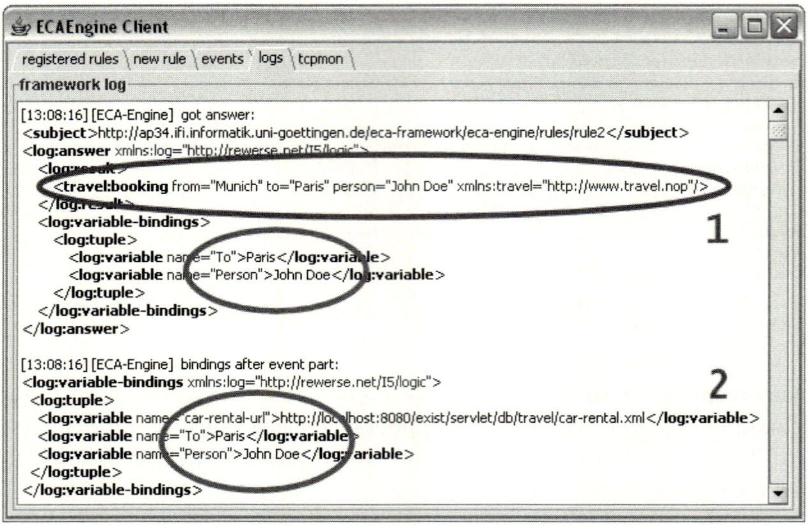

Fig. 6. Detection of the Event Component

<eca:event xmlns:evt="*uri of the event language*">
<evt:*operator*> *nested expression in the event language* </evt:*operator*>
</eca:event>

and the component is then registered and processed at an appropriate service associated with the language's URI [MAA05b].

Possible languages here are e.g. an extension of SNOOP [CKAK94] with logical variables where a framework-aware service has been implemented in [Spa06] (with input in XML markup), or XChange [BP05]. Both languages return the event sequence as functional result and bind/use logical (join) variables.

4.3 The Query Components

The query components serve for obtaining *static* information from Web resources based on the information contained in the event. The query component is very similar to the evaluation of rule bodies in Logic Programming, extending the set of tuples of variable bindings (and also probably restricting it via join conditions). Since we also allow answers of functional query languages, the semantics is adapted accordingly: when bound to a variable at the rule level, each answer yields a separate variable binding.

In our example, at this time, the following facts are known: the name of the person who booked the flight and the destination city (Fig. 6(2)). The name is used to ask for the cars that this person owns at home. Note that here, the query is stated as an "opaque" XQuery code fragment (against an XML document on the Web) without markup. The query code together with the values of the input variables is communicated to the GRH as shown in Figure 7.

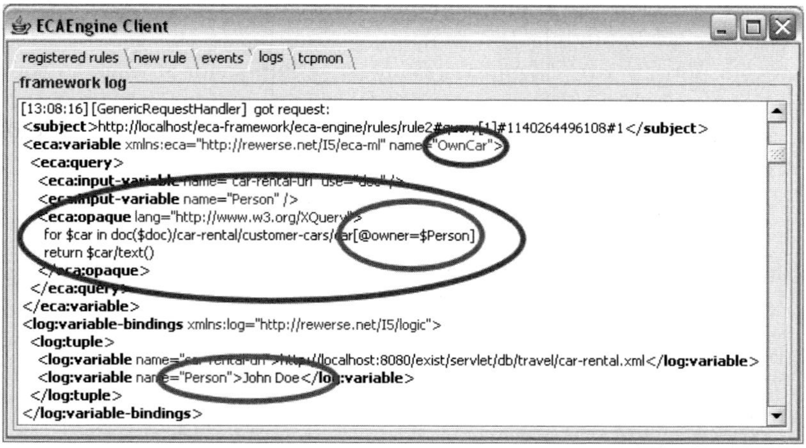

Fig. 7. Sending the First Query Component to the GRH: Own Cars

Languages for the Query Component. In contrast to the event component, many query languages for SQL, XML and RDF data are around, and many Web nodes already support interfaces for them. Thus, for current applications, *opaque* query components where the query is just given as a string and submitted to such a service (using e.g. HTTP, or calling a saxon-based [saxon] wrapper for XQuery) are expected to be frequently used:

```
<eca:query>
  <eca:opaque (language= "name of the language"|url= "URL of WebService)">
    query
  </eca:opaque>
</eca:query>
```

4.4 The Generic Request Handler

The Generic Request Handler acts as a mediator for dealing with remote services. It inspects the namespace declaration of the components (or the language attribute in case of opaque fragments) for determining an appropriate language processor and forwards the request to it in an appropriate form. For framework-aware services, the incoming requests can just be forwarded. To integrate non-framework-aware services, the GRH uses information about the communication protocol and method in addition to the processor's capabilities wrt. the handling of variable bindings (cf. the second query discussed later).

The first query is forwarded together with the input variable bindings from the GRH to a framework-aware wrapped Saxon [saxon] XQuery processor node. The node evaluates the query and returns one <log:answer> for each result to the GRH as shown in Figure 8(1). For such processors that return a functional result (in an <log:result> element), the query component is surrounded by a

<eca:variable> element (as in our example, see Figure 4). The GRH extends the input bindings with binding the functional result(s) to the given variable. It generates an appropriate <log:answers> message and sends it back to the ECA engine as shown in Figure 8(2) where it is then joined with the existing variable bindings. Note that since John Doe owns two cars at home, a *Golf* and a *Passat*, there are now two tuples of variable bindings (Figure 8(3)).

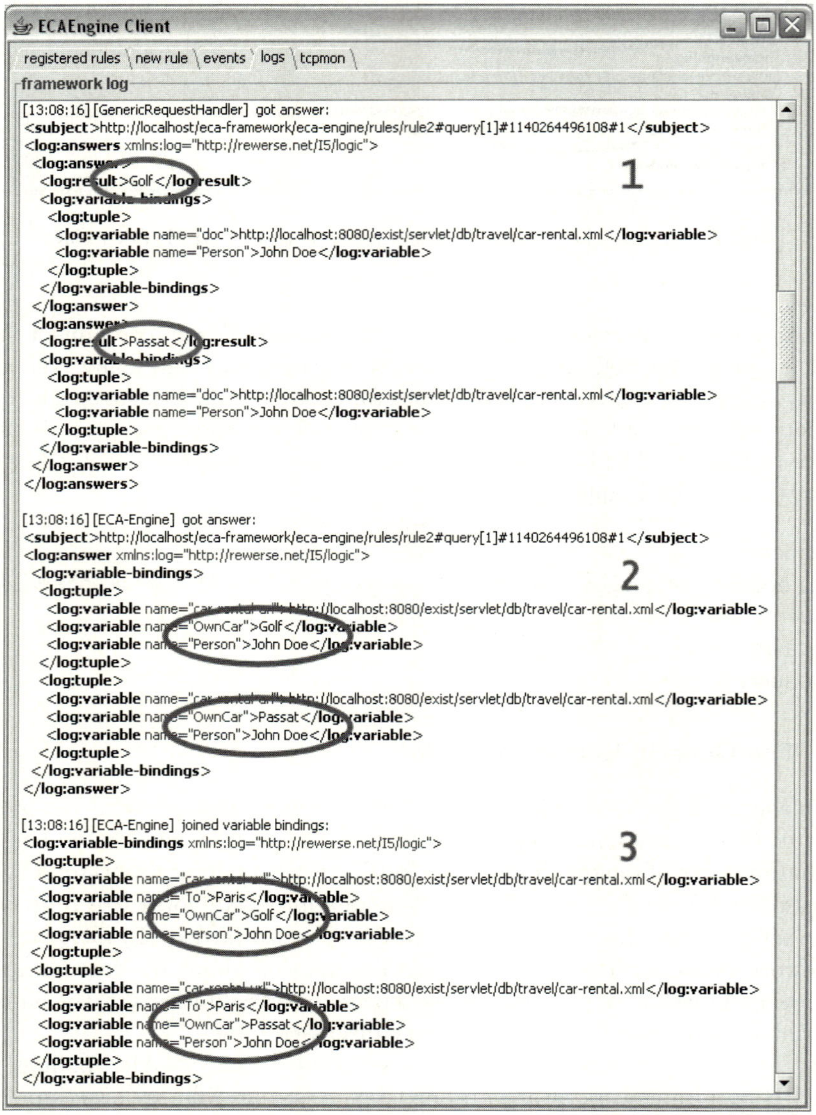

Fig. 8. Answer to the First Query Component: Own Cars

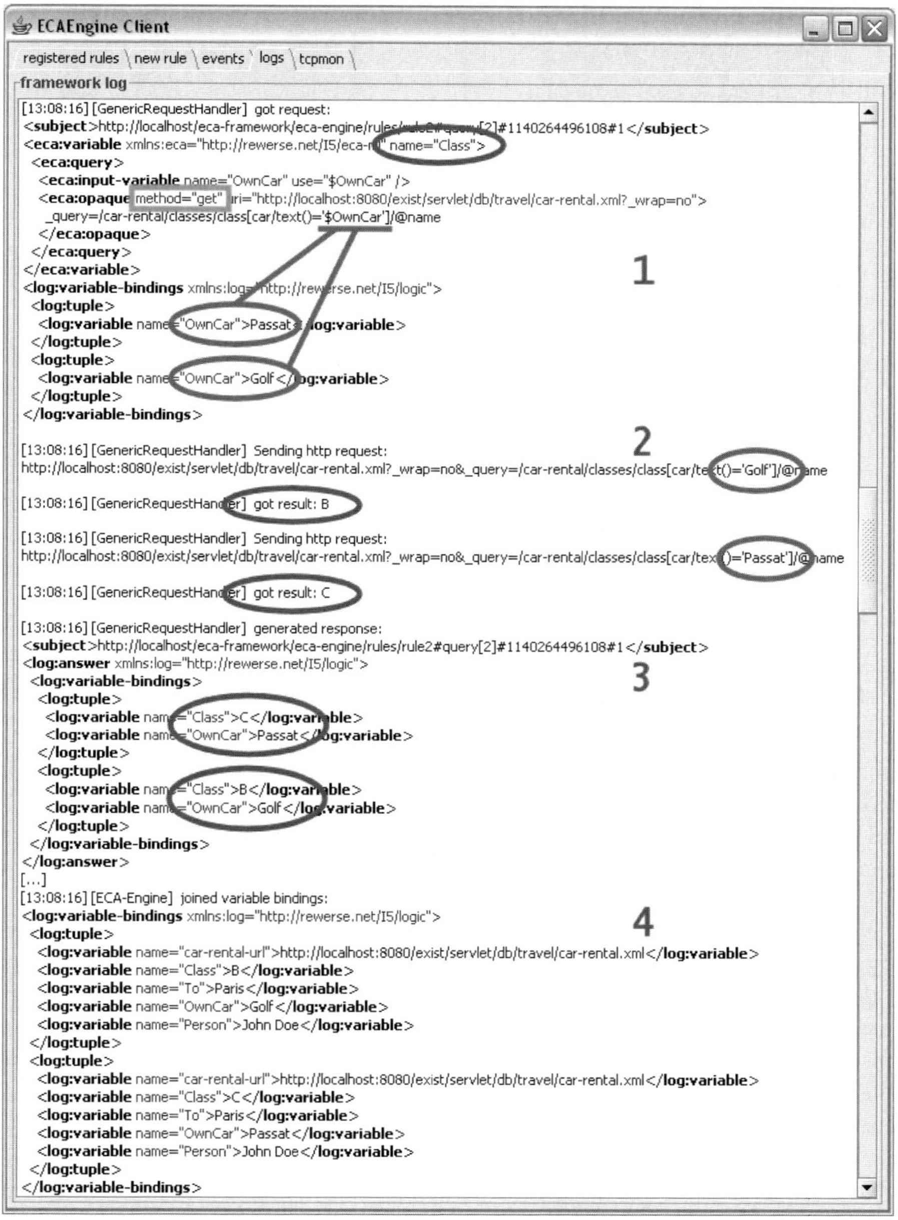

Fig. 9. Evaluation of the 2nd Query against a Framework-Unaware Service

In the next query, another database is queried for the classes (sizes) of the respective cars as shown in Figure 9(1). The <eca:opaque> element specifies to contact an unwrapped, framework-unaware XQuery node (an eXist database) via HTTP GET. Variables in the query string are replaced by their values and the

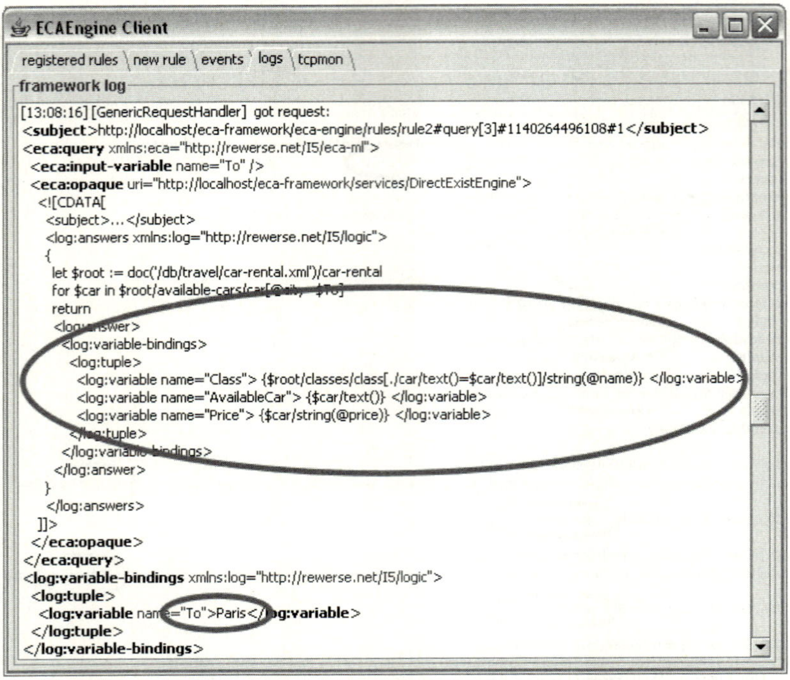

Fig. 10. Query Against Available Cars, Generating a <log:answers> Structure

query is submitted. In the example, the GRH executes the request for every tuple of the input variable bindings, once for "Golf" and once for "Passat" (Fig. 9(2)), and binds the results to the variable Class. The resulting variable bindings are then sent as the content of an <log:answers> message back to the ECA engine (Fig. 9(3)) where they are joined with the existing tuples (Fig. 9(4)).

Next, another query retrieves all cars that are available at the destination city (see Figure 10). Here an XQuery engine is addressed directly with a query that generates the required <log:answers> structure to "fake" a framework-aware service. The available cars (of classes B and D) are compared to the classes of the cars owned by the customer (B and C) as shown in Figure 11. The join semantics (natural join over class) eliminates tuples containing a car either of class "C" or of class "D", and only those with class "B" remain.

4.5 The Test and Action Components

These two components follow the same principle. The test component (which corresponds to the WHERE clause in SQL and is empty in our example) contains a condition over the bound variables which discards those tuples that do not satisfy the condition. In general, it is evaluated locally, using only simple comparison predicates. The action component then is the one where *actually* something is done: for each tuple of variable bindings, the action component is executed, again via the GRH. This can include commands on the database level, explicit message sending, or actions on the domain ontology level.

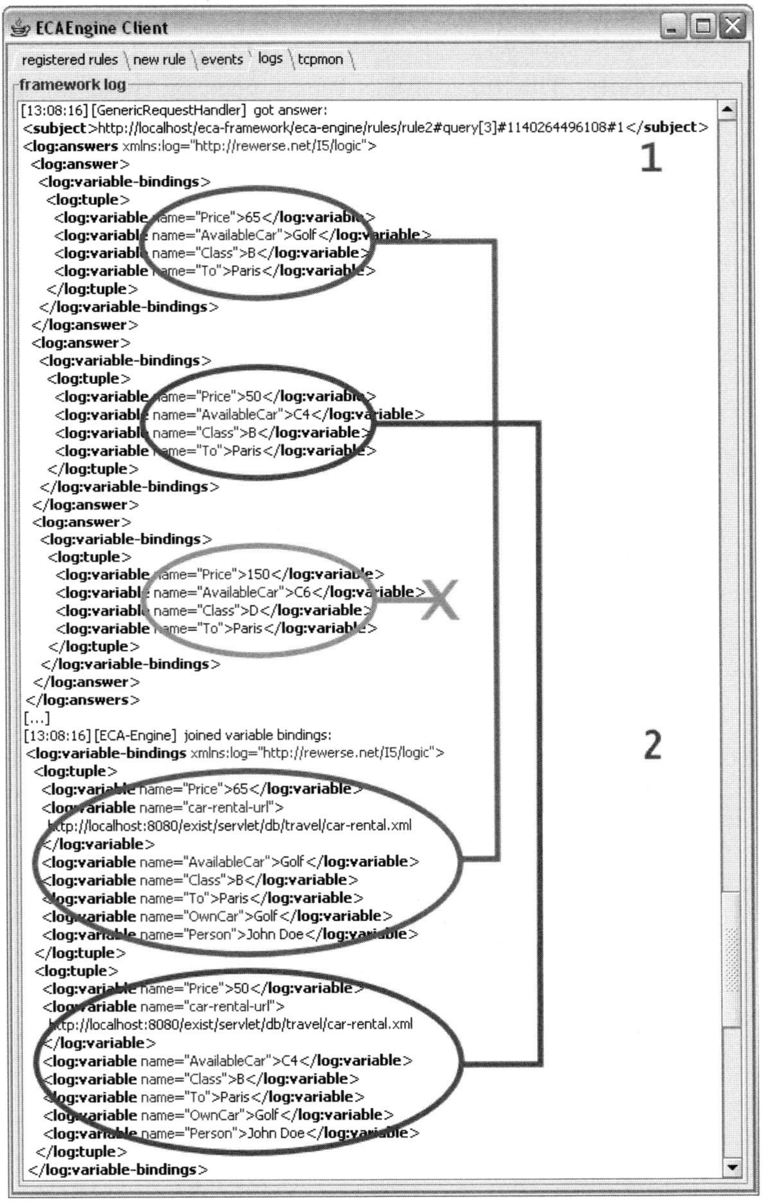

Fig. 11. Evaluation of the Available Cars

5 Conclusion

The above *ECA engine* and *Generic Request Handler* implement the upper level of the generic ECA framework proposed in [MAA05a, MAA05b]. They can be used for combining arbitrary event detection, query and action languages and respective engines. A variety of such engines, including sample domain services are currently being developed.

Acknowledgements. This research has been funded by the European Commission within the 6th Framework Programme project REWERSE, no. 506779.

References

[BP05] F. Bry and P.-L. Pătrânjan. Reactivity on the Web: Paradigms and Applications of the Language XChange. In *ACM Symp. Applied Computing*. ACM, 2005.

[BS02] F. Bry and S. Schaffert. Towards a declarative query and transformation language for XML and semistructured data: Simulation Unification. In *Intl. Conf. on Logic Programming (ICLP)*, Springer LNCS 2401, pp. 255–270, 2002.

[CKAK94] S. Chakravarthy, V. Krishnaprasad, E. Anwar, and S.-K. Kim. Composite Events for Active Databases: Semantics, Contexts and Detection. *VLDB*, 1994.

[KL89] M. Kifer and G. Lausen. F-Logic: A higher-order language for reasoning about objects, inheritance and scheme. In J. Clifford, B. Lindsay, and D. Maier, editors, *ACM Intl. Conference on Management of Data (SIGMOD)*, pp. 134–146, 1989.

[MAA05a] W. May, J. J. Alferes, and R. Amador. Active Rules in the Semantic Web: Dealing with Language Heterogeneity. In *Rule Markup Languages (RuleML)*, Springer LNCS 3791, pp. 30–44, 2005.

[MAA05b] W. May, J. J. Alferes, and R. Amador. An Ontology- and Resources-Based Approach to Evolution and Reactivity in the Semantic Web. In *Ontologies, Databases and Semantics (ODBASE)*, Springer LNCS 3761, pp. 1553–1570, 2005.

[May04] W. May. XPath-Logic and XPathLog: A Logic-Programming Style XML Data Manipulation Language. *Theory and Practice of Logic Progr.*, 4(3):239–287, 2004.

[saxon] Michael Kay. SAXON: an XSLT processor. `http://saxon.sourceforge.net/`.

[Spa06] Sebastian Spautz. Automatenbasierte Detektion von Composite Events gemäss SNOOP in XML-Umgebungen. *Diplomarbeit, TU Clausthal (in german)*, 2006.

Prova: Rule-Based Java Scripting for Distributed Web Applications: A Case Study in Bioinformatics

Alex Kozlenkov[2], Rafael Penaloza[1], Vivek Nigam[1], Loïc Royer[1], Gihan Dawelbait[1], and Michael Schroeder[1]

[1] Biotec, Dresden University of Technology, Germany
ms@biotec.tu-dresden.de
[2] Dept. of Computing, City University, London, UK

Abstract. Prova is a language for rule-based Java scripting to support information integration and agent programming on the web. Prova integrates Java with derivation and reaction rules supporting message exchange with various comminication frameworks. Prova supports transparent access to databases, retrieval of URLs, access to web services, and querying of XML documents. We briefly illustrate Prova and show how to implement a distributed bioinformatics application, which includes access to an ontology stored in a database and to XML data for protein structures. Finally, we compare Prova to other event-condition-action rule systems.

1 Introduction

Prova is a language for rule based Java scripting for information integration, and agent programming [6,3]. Prova is suitable for use as a rule-based backbone for distributed web applications in biomedical data integration. It has been designed to meet the following goals:

- Combine the benefits of declarative and object-oriented programming;
- Combine the syntaxes of Prolog and Java to appeal to programmers in both worlds;
- Expose logic and agent behaviour as rules;
- Access data sources via wrappers written in Java or command-line shells like Perl;
- Make all Java APIs from available packages directly accessible from rules;
- Run within the Java runtime environment;
- Enable rapid prototyping of applications;
- Offer a rule-based platform for distributed agent programming with common messaging protocols.

These design goals are especially important for integration tasks where location and format transparency are important. The latter means that the language should support the work with databases, RDF, HTML, XML, and flat file formats. Prova's rule-based approach is particularly important for two applications: derivation rules to reason over ontologies and reaction rules to specify reactive behaviour of possibly distributed agents.

T. Grust et al. (Eds.): EDBT 2006 Workshops, LNCS 4254, pp. 899–908, 2006.

Let us consider examples to illustrate these two types of rules. As a declarative language with derivation rules Prova follows a Prolog-style syntax as the next example shows:

Example 1. (Declarative programming)
Graph traversal is a typical example for declarative programming. A standard example is the same generation problem, in which all nodes in a tree are returned, which belong to the same generation. Two nodes are in the same generation if they are siblings or if their parents are in the same generation. The corresponding Prova programme is identical to standard Prolog, the execution semantics of Prova follow the usual top-down, left to right resolution.

Listing 1.1. Prova example

```
parent(anna, gerda).
parent(anna, fritz).
parent(asif, anna).
parent(asif, yanju).
parent(yanju, anja).

sg(X,Y) :- parent(Z,X), parent(Z,Y).
sg(X,Y) :- parent(Z1,X), parent(Z2,Y), sg(Z1,Z2).
```

The query `:- solve(sg(gerda,X)).` will return `X=gerda`, `X=fritz`, and `X=anja`.

Thus, Prova follows classical Prolog closely by declaratively specifying relationships with facts and rules. Now let us consider two examples, where access to Java methods is directly integrated into rules.

Example 2. (Object-oriented programming)
The code below represents a rule whose body consists of three Java method calls: the first to construct a String object, the second to append something to the string, and the third to print the string to the screen.

Listing 1.2. Prova example

```
hello(Name):-
  S = java.lang.String("Hello "),
  S.append(Name),
  java.lang.System.out.println(S).
```

2 Prova and Reactivity

Prova's reaction rules can comprise events, conditions, and actions in any order, as both events and actions are raised by built-in predicates for receiving and sending messages. Both allow for various communication frameworks such as the agent messaging language Jade, the Java messaging system JMS [1] or even Java events generated by Swing components. Due to the natural integration of Prova with Java, Prova's reaction rules

[1] `java.sun.com/products/jms/`

offer a syntactically economic and compact way of specifying agents behaviour while allowing for efficient Java-based extensions to improve performance of critical operations. JMS in general has the advantage of being a guaranteed delivery messaging platform. Intuitively it means that when computer A sends a message to computer B the latter is not required to be operational. Once B goes online the messages will be delivered.

2.1 Main Features of Prova's Reaction Rules

Prova provides three main constructs for enabling agent communication:

- sendMsg predicates, which can be used as actions anywhere in the body of a derivation or reaction rule,
- reaction rules, which have a blocking rcvMsg in the head and which fire upon receipt of a corresponding event, and
- inline reactions, which are encoded by blocking receipt of messages using rcvMsg or rcvMult anywhere in the body of derivation or reaction rules.

Communication actions with sendMsg. The sendMsg predicate can be embedded into the body of an arbitrary derivation or reaction rule. It can fail only if the parameters are incorrect and the message could not be sent due to various other reasons including the dropped connection (note that in the JMS case, the message may be sent anyway even if the network is down).

The format of the predicate is:

```
sendMsg(Protocol,Agent,Performative,[Predicate|Args]|Context)
```

or

```
sendMsg(Protocol,Agent,Performative,Predicate(Args)|Context)
```

where Protocol can currently be either jade, jms, self, or queue. Jade and JMS use the corresponding communication layers, while self and queue send the message to the agent itself or to another agent running locally in the same process but in another thread. Agent denotes the target of the message. For the self, jade, and jms methods, Agent is the name of the target agent. For the queue option, Agent is the object representing the message queue of the target agent. For Jade messages, the agent name takes the form agent@machine while for jms messages the agent locations are read from configuration files and are not specified in the Agent parameter. Performative corresponds to the semantic instruction the broad characterisation of the message. A standard nomenclature of performatives is FIPA Agents Communication Language ACL (www.fipa.org).

[Predicate|Args] corresponds to the bracketed form and Predicate(Args) corresponds to functional form of the message content sent in the message envelope. The first form can be useful to match any literal including arity-0 predicates (in which case, query() is the represented as [query]) or arity-1 predicates (in which case, query(arg1) is represented as [query,arg1]). The problem with the functional form is that it is impossible to specify a general pattern accommodating predicates of arbitrary arity while the bracketed version is compatible with any arity. Context includes an arbitrary length list of comma-separated parameters that can be used to identify the message or to distinguish the replies to this particular message from other messages. In particular, it can be useful to include the protocol as part of context for the recipient of the message to be able to reply by using the same protocol.

The following code shows a complete rule that sends a code base (a fragment of Prova code) from an external File to the agent Remote that will then assimilate the rules being sent. The rules are encapsulated in a serializable Java StringBuffer object and sent with the literal for the built-in predicate consult. The particular version of consult will then read on the Remote machine the Prova statements from a StringBuffer (in contrast to the standard version of consult that reads statements from the specified file provided as an input string).

Listing 1.3. sendMsg Example

```

% Upload a rule base read from File to the host at address Remote

upload_mobile_code(Remote,File) :-
        % Opening a file returns an instance of java.io.BufferedReader in Reader
        fopen(File,Reader),
        Writer = java.io.StringWriter(),
        copy(Reader,Writer),
        Text = Writer.toString(),
        % SB will encapsulate the whole content of File
        SB = StringBuffer(Text),
        sendMsg(jade,Remote,eval,consult(SB)).
```

Reaction rules with rcvMsg. In Prova, reaction rules are implemented as rules whose head consists of a rcvMsg predicate, which has the same syntax as the sendMsg predicate:

```
rcvMsg(Protocol,To,Performative,[Predicate|Args]|Context)
```

The agent reacts to the message based on its pattern including the protocol, sender, performative, message content, and context. The following code shows a general purpose but simplified reaction rule for the FIPA queryref performative. The first rule triggers a non-deterministic derivation of the literal [Pred|Args] sent as the message content. Based on the agent's knowledge-base derive will instantiate Pred|Args and send corresponding replies. The second rule sends a special end_of_transmission message to inform the querying agent of the completion of the query. The Protocol parameter available as the first parameter allows the recipient of queryref to know the protocol (jade, jms etc.) that should be used for replies.

Listing 1.4. rcvMsg Example

```
% Reaction rule to general queryref
rcvMsg(Protocol,From,queryref,[Pred|Args]|Context) :-
        derive([Pred|Args]),
        sendMsg(Protocol,From,reply,[Pred|Args]|Context).
rcvMsg(Protocol,From,queryref,[Pred|Args],Protocol) :-
        sendMsg(Protocol,From,end_of_transmission,[Pred|Args]|Context).
```

Now we will show how to deploy Prova's derivation and reaction rules to implement a distributed web-based bioinformatics application.

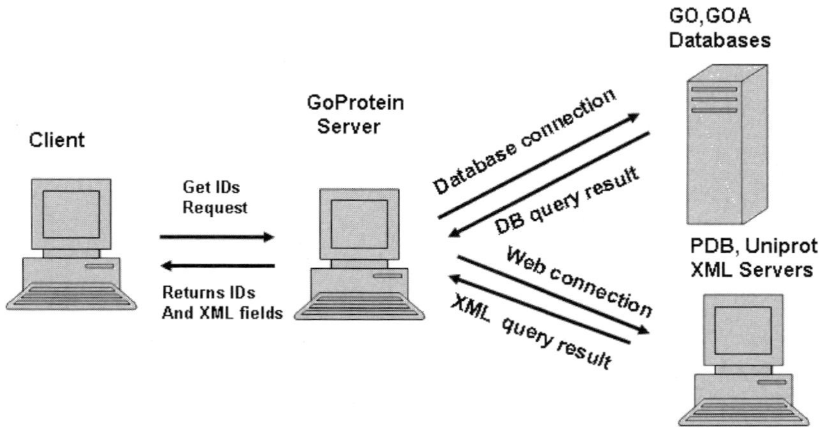

Fig. 1. Sketch of the GoProtein tool workflow: The user interacts locally with a GUI on a client machine. Queries for all proteins annotated with a given term from the ontology are sent to the server. The server can access a database server to obtain protein IDs, which are annotated with the given term. The remote protein database returns an entry for protein as XML file given the protein ID. The protein database is used to display relevant information to the user.

3 The GoProtein Tool

Biological databases are growing rapidly. Currently there is much effort spent on annotating these databases with terms from controlled, hierarchical vocabularies such as the GeneOntology [5]. It is often useful to be able to retrieve all entries from a database, which are annotated with a given term from the ontology. We want to build such a query engine according to the scheme shown in Fig. 1. The application consists of four agents, whose interaction is driven by reaction rules. The agents are a thin client, which contains nothing but a GUI to interact with the user, a server, which handles queries of the client, a database server, which contains the ontology and the protein IDs annotated with the ontology terms, and a protein database which contains detailed information on the protein in XML format. The client's GUI displays the ontology. If the user selects a term from the ontology, an event is fired, which triggers a request being sent to the GoProtein server. The server in turn queries the GeneOntology database server for protein IDs, which have been annotated with the ontology term. If the user selects a specific protein on the GUI, a query is sent to the server, which reacts by retrieving an XML file from the remote protein database and by extracting relevant information from the file and returning it to the client.

For this specific implementation of the GoProtein workflow we want to use the GeneOntology [5] as annotation vocabulary and the Protein Databank PDB [1] as protein database. The Gene ontology (GO) contains over 19.000 terms organised in three sub-ontologies relating to biological processes, molecular functions, and cellular components. GeneOntology is available in XML, OWL, or database dump. Here we use the database dump of the GeneOntology. The protein databank PDB is a database with over 25.000 3D protein structures. Entries contain protein names, species, literature

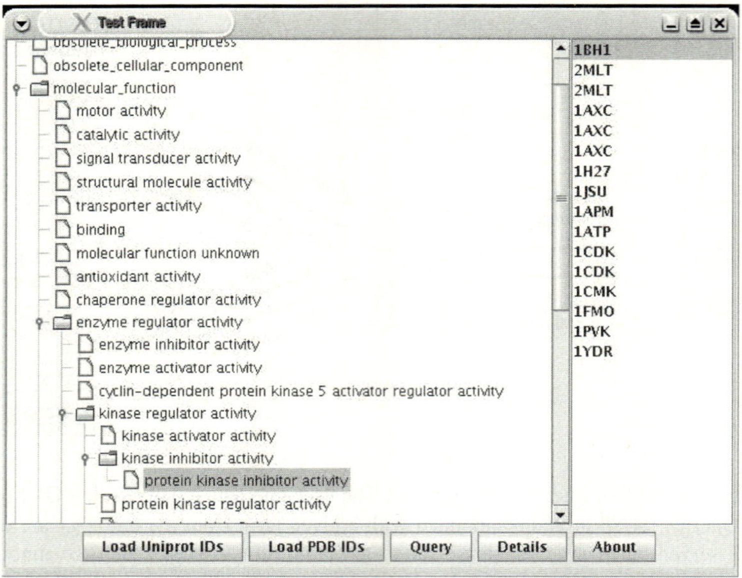

Fig. 2. Screenshot of GoProtein: The left panel shows the ontology including the term "protein kinase inhibitor" and on the right the PDB entries annotated with the term

references, and most important the 3D coordinates of all the atoms of the protein. PDB is available as flat file format and XML.

4 Prova Code for GoProtein

The client agent comprises the GUI and therefore makes heavy use of Java's Swing methods. For example, the MutableTreeNode class is used to display the GeneOntology tree as shown on Fig. 2.

Listing 1.5. Client agent

```
gui() :-
        println(["==========Window Loading=========="]),
        % create the tree and a placeholder for the IDs
        Node1 = javax.swing.tree.DefaultMutableTreeNode("all"),
        TreeModel = javax.swing.tree.DefaultTreeModel(Node1),
        Tree = javax.swing.JTree(Node1),
        Panel1 = javax.swing.JScrollPane(Tree),
        IdList = javax.swing.JList(),
        Panel2 = javax.swing.JScrollPane(IdList),
    ...
```

For large knowledge bases such as the 19.000 GeneOntology terms it is important to keep data on disc and load it into main memory only as needed. For this purpose, the code snippet below defines the location of the database and uses built-in predicates such as dbopen to open a database connection and sql_select to issue database queries. The concat statements are used to assemble the query string.

Listing 1.6. The Server Agent

```

:- eval(consult("utils.prova")).

% Define database location
location(database,"GO","jdbc:mysql://myserver","guest","guest").

% get description of term
desc(Term, Desc) :-
        dbopen("GO",DB),
        unescape("\'", Quote),
        concat(["term_definition.term_id = term.id AND term.name =", Quote, ...
             ...Term, Quote],A),
        concat(["term, term_definition"],From),
        sql_select(DB,From,['term_definition.term_definition',Desc],[where,A]).
```

The user can also issue a request to extract specified fields from URLs of XML entries for a selected term. The code below shows the ability of Prova to connect to different URLs, process their XML contents and retrieve the requested fields using the built-in predicate descendantValue.

Listing 1.7. XML Handler

```

searchPDB("http://pdbbeta.rcsb.org/pdb/displayFile.do?structureId=").

% get the xml file
searchPDB(Query,XML):-
        print(["Query for ",Query," at PDB"]),
        searchPDB(BaseURL),
        concat([BaseURL,Query, "&fileFormat=xml"],URLString),
        retrieveXML(URLString,XML),
        println(["done"]).

% search for "sequence length" values in the xml file of a PDB ID
doSearchPDB(Term, Lst):-
        searchPDB(Term,XML),
        PDB = "PDBx:",
        concat([PDB,"length_a"],La),
        descendantValue(XML,La,A),!,
        concat([PDB,"length_b"],Lb),
        descendantValue(XML,Lb,B),!,
        concat([PDB,"length_c"],Lc),
        descendantValue(XML,Lc,C),!,
        Lst = [A,B,C].

%%%%%%%%%%%%%%%% UTILITIY predicates %%%%%%%%%%%%%%%%%%%%%%%%

retrieveXML(URLString,Root):-
        URL = java.net.URL(URLString),
        print(["."]),
        Stream = URL.openStream(),
        print(["."]),
        ISR = java.io.InputStreamReader(Stream),
        XMLResult = XML(ISR),
        Root = XMLResult.getDocumentElement(),
        print(["."]).
```

The communication between the client and server agents is performed by using the Prova massaging and reaction rules to specify behaviour of the two agents. The predicate remote in line 1 takes as an argument the specification of the target machine we are communicating with. The reaction rule in line 5, 8, 10 are triggered by an event from the GUI's Swing component, while the one on line 15 is triggered by a message sent by the server. One of the actions triggered by the reaction rule in line 5 is a message sent to the server (last line).

Listing 1.8. The Client Agent

```
1  remote("ils_assign_server@servername").
2
3  % message transfer for the listeners:
4  % Reaction to button actions
5  rcvMsg(XID,Protocol,From,swing,[action,Cmd,Source|Extra]) :-
6          process_button(Source,Cmd).
7  % Reaction to incoming swing mouse clicked messages.
8  rcvMsg(XID,Protocol,From,swing,[mouse,clicked,Src|Extra]) :-
9          process_mouse(clicked,Src|Extra).
10 rcvMsg(XID,Protocol,From,swing,[mouse,entered,Src|Extra]) :-
11         process_mouse(entered,Src|Extra).
12
13 % message transfer with the server
14 % actions after receiving the results of a query
15 rcvMsg(XID,Protocol,From,reply_qry,[IDs]|Context) :-
16         mainlist(List),
17         buildList(List, IDs).
18
19 % process executed when the "Load Uniprot IDs" button is clicked
20 % it finds the selected node, finds all its associated Uniprot IDs, and loads ...
       ...them in the List
21 process_button(Button, "Load Uniprot IDs") :-
22         Tree = Button.getTree(),
23         Path = Tree.getSelectionPath(),
24         Node = Path.getLastPathComponent(),
25         Term = Node.toString(),
26         List = Button.getList(),
27         buildList(List, ["contacting server...","please wait"]),
28         % ask for the list of associated uniprod IDs
29         remote(Remote),
30         sendMsg(XID,jade,Remote,uniprot,[Term],"context").
```

5 Comparison and Conclusion

The World Wide Web is a rich heterogenous media following a pattern of growth that is uncentralized, directed by trends, and resistant to initiatives to enforce strong conformance to standards. A language for reactivity on the Web should be simple, offer 'out of the box' ability to handle most current de facto standards and offer specification robustness through clear declarative semantics. The many recent efforts that have been initiated to bring proper semantics to the Web - the Semantic Web - must also be kept in mind, as they delineate what the Web could eventually become. One can thus enumerate some 'must have' features for a Reactive Web Language:

- Ability to read and write XML, RDF, OWL, RSS and their variants;
- Possibility to interface to systems written in Java and/or embed java code;
- Connectivity to public/private databases, through different media (direct, web or web-services);

- Simple access to URL-based resources: Web page, XML file, RSS feed;
- Reactivity through the listening, processing and sending of events and actions;
- Declarative semantics and Event-Condition-Action paradigm.

In the following, we briefly compare Prova with other languages to address the problem of reactivity on the web: JESS, a java based rule engine, XChange based on the Xcerpt web query language, and ruleCore, an XML-based active rule engine.

5.1 JESS

Jess is a forward-chaining rule engine based on the Rete algorithm for the Java platform [4]. Jess supports the development of rule-based systems which can be tightly coupled to code written in the Java language. The syntax of the Jess language is Lisp-based. Java functions can be called from Jess, and Jess can be extended by writing Java code. Jess rules can be embedded in Java applications. Jess inherits from Java all the XML libraries to read, process and write XML data. However, it does not provide rule-based wrappers that provide these facilities in a transparent manner. The same holds for connectivity to databases: it is possible through Java libraries but not truly integrated in the system. This is one of the main differences between Prova and Jess, Prova has specialized predicates that allow easy and transparent access to databases, XML data, message exchange frameworks, and even events from Swing components. The fact that Jess is essentially a rule engine, provides a very natural setup to write Event-Condition-Action rules in the context of event propagation in the Web. Thus Business rules can be stated in a declarative and transparent manner.

5.2 XChange

XChange is a declarative language built upon the declarative web query language Xcerpt [2]. It provides Web-specific capabilities such as propagation of changes on the Web and event-based communications between Web sites. XChange is a research project and has a prototype implementation as proof-of-concept implementation. Among the interesting characteristics of XChange is its use of explicit temporal constructs to describe sequences of events, their overlapping and composition. Reactivity is achieved by having Event-Condition-Action rules at the core of the language. The main difference between Prova and XChange is that Prova is a full featured programming language built-upon the robustness and richness of Java, whereas XChange is geared towards XML and HTML contents.

5.3 ruleCore

Of proved industrial strength, the ruleCore Engine (`www.rulecore.com/`) is a robust implementation of an active rule engine server. The ruleCore Engine implements Event-Condition-Action rules that are organised in situation trees. The goal of ruleCore is to detect situations that arise as the temporal and logical composition of events. The rule engine itself does not rely on a generic programming language as in the case of Prova and Jess, but instead on the definition of situations as event detector trees. Connectivity to other media and systems is achieved through the use of event and action wrappers, most of which are provided 'out of the box' for databases and standard industrial messaging frameworks like XML-RPC, Web Services, TIBCO Rendezvous, plain sockets or IBM WebSphere MQ. The main difference between Prova and the ruleCore engine is, as in the case of XChange, that Prova is a generic rule language extending Java, whereas ruleCore is a language-independent rule engine.

Prova is the choice of a Java programmer with Prolog experience who aims to develop a system which needs a possibly thin layer of rules for reasoning with backward chaining and for defining business rules and workflows with agent communication. Prova is available at www.prova.ws.

References

1. H. M. Berman, J. Westbrook, Z. Feng, G. Gilliland, T. N. Bhat, H. Weissig, I. N. Shindyalov, and P. E. Bourne. The protein data bank. *Nucleic Acids Res*, 28(1):235–242, 2000.
2. F. Bry and P. Patranjan. Reactivity on the web: Paradigms and applications of the language xchange. In *Proceedings of 20th Annual ACM Symposium on Applied Computing (SAC'2005)*. ACM, March 2005.
3. J. Dietrich, A. Kozlenkov, M. Schroeder, and G. Wagner. Rule-based agents for the semantic web. *Journal on Electronic Commerce Research Applications*, 2(4):323–38, 2003.
4. Ernest Friedman-Hill. *Jess in Action Java Rule-based Systems*. Manning, 2003.
5. GeneOntologyConsortium. The Gene Ontology (GO) database and informatics resource. *Nucleic Acids Res.*, 1(32):D258–61, 2004.
6. A. Kozlenkov and M. Schroeder. PROVA: Rule-based Java-scripting for a bioinformatics semantic web. In E. Rahm, editor, *International Workshop on Data Integration in the Life Sciences DILS*, Leipzig, Germany, 2004. Springer.

Reactivity in Online Auctions

Adriano Pereira[1], Fernando Mourão[1], Paulo Góes[2], and Wagner Meira Jr.[1]

[1] Federal University of Minas Gerais
Av. Antônio Carlos 6627 - ICEx - room 4010 - CEP 31270-010
Belo Horizonte – Minas Gerais – Brazil
{adrianoc, fhmourao, meira}@dcc.ufmg.br
[2] University of Connecticut
School of Business Administration
2100 Hillside Road – Storrs, CT 06269 – USA
Paulo.Goes@business.uconn.edu

Abstract. Interactive computer systems, that is, systems in which users cyclically interact by getting and providing information, have already a widespread and increasing use in all areas of our society. One characteristic of such systems is that the user behavior affects the system behavior and vice-versa. There is strong evidence that much of the user behavior is reactive, that is, the user reacts to the instantaneous conditions at the action time. This paper presents the reactivity concept and describes a framework to model it in interactive systems, in particular Internet-based systems. We analyze an online auction within the framework. Based on *eBay* data, we identify attributes that affect the winner bidders' behavior, such as the auction time to finish. This paper presents the first findings towards the formal description and understanding of reactivity patterns in an e-commerce application, which will be useful in improving the application and building novel mechanisms.

1 Introduction

Interactive computer systems, that is, systems in which users cyclically interact by getting and providing information, have become very useful in our society. From bank transactions to cell phones, we are continuously interacting with systems and even with other users through these systems. A significant part of the interactions is synchronous, that is, users submit information to the system and wait for a response, then submit more information and so on. The Web is an example of such a rich environment for interaction pattern.

User-system interactions are usually complex and intriguing. It is quite hard to determine exactly the factors that lead a user to behave as we may observe. The information we have about users is sparse and variable, in terms of both the instantaneous conditions surrounding the observed behavior and the users' background. It is important to note that the interactions are not isolated, but successive interactions become a loop feedback mechanism, where the user behavior affects the system behavior and vice-versa.

There is strong evidence that a significant part of the user behavior is reactive, that is, the user reacts to the instantaneous conditions. As a consequence, user behavior varies according to some factors related to the server and the application.

T. Grust et al. (Eds.): EDBT 2006 Workshops, LNCS 4254, pp. 909–918, 2006.

This work presents the reactivity concept, describing how to model it in interactive systems, in particular Internet-based systems. We propose a framework to model reactivity in interactive systems and present a case study of applying it to online auctions, based on *eBay* data.

The paper is organized as follows. Section 2 provides an overview of related work in the realm of online auctions. Section 3 explains the concept of reactivity, discussing how it may be modeled. Section 4 presents our case study showing the reactivity modeling online auctions. Finally, Section 5 presents the conclusions and outlines ongoing work.

2 Related Work

An auction is the process of buying and selling goods by offering them up for bid, taking bids, and selling the item to the highest bidder. In economic theory, an auction is a method for determining the value of a commodity that has an undetermined or variable price. Online auctions present several aspects that violate the common assumptions made by the traditional economic auction theory. The auction duration is typically much longer than in traditional auctions; bidders can come and exit at any time; bidders are geographically dispersed all over the world; they have very distinct backgrounds and it is hard to predict how many bidders will end up participating in the auction. Instantaneous reactivity in such environments plays an important role, which we plan to address in our research.

Online auctions have been studied extensively lately. Many studies focus on testing results from the classic economic theory of auctions in the online environment. For example, Lucking-Reiley [1] tests the well-known results of revenue equivalence. Bajari and Hortacsu [2] address how the starting bid set by the seller affects the winner's course. Gilkeson and Reynolds [3] show the importance of a proper starting bid price to attract more bidders and make an auction successful.

The widespread use of reputation and feedback systems and their impact on the outcome of online auctions has also received considerable attention. Resnick and Zeckhauser [4] and Ba and Pavlou [5] examine the effects of bidder and seller reputations on auction outcomes, concluding that seller reputations are correlated with auction success on eBay.

In addressing the issue of reactivity in online auctions, it is important to consider the work that has been done on analyzing bidders' and sellers' behavior in online environments. Roth and Ockenfels [6] study the timing of bids, and the impact of different methods of specifying auction deadlines. Comparing eBay and Amazon auctions, they find evidence that auctions held with a "soft" ending time discourage late bidding or "sniping", common on eBay. Using data from ubid.com, Bapna et al. [7] develops a cluster analysis approach to classify online bidders into four categories: participators, evaluators, opportunists and sip-and-dippers. In another paper, Bapna et al. [8] develop a simulation model emulating bidders' behavior to analyze their impact in the outcome of the auctions.

Looking at sellers' strategies, Anderson et al. [9] find that various types of sellers have diversified strategies for PDAs listed in eBay. They also show that sellers with higher feedback scores are more likely to release more information about the items for sale. Kauffman and Wood [10] model opportunistic sellers' behavior in coin auctions in eBay because of information asymmetry.

Although there are several detailed studies of online auctions, none of them deals with reactivity. We believe that this concept will allow a better characterization of online auctions and other distributed applications, qualifying and quantifying, for instance, temporal aspects. We have already studied reactivity in system's performance. In [11] we model reactivity in this context and [12] quantifies its impact on the performance of Internet services.

Reactivity has been widely studied in the database context [13,14], and more recently has been applied also in Web semantic research [15]. Also, event-condiction action (ECA) paradigm [16,17] is an interesting topic in this context.

Our reactivity concept can be considered in any Web-based systems characterized by user-system interactions. The reactivity concept we are presenting in this paper has a novel semantic, once its objective is to model the dynamics of e-business applications, like online auctions. In this context, there are not specific related works.

3 Reactivity Modeling

This section introduces our concept of reactivity. Reactivity emerges naturally whenever there is the possibility of a feedback on the user-system interaction. Our approach is based on the concepts of action and perception. Actions are all activities performed by users while interacting with the systems. On the other hand, perceptions are the set of criteria through which the user evaluates the service being provided.The goal of our analysis is to correlate actions and perceptions, as a means of identifying the user behaviors.

We define reactivity as the set of pairs perception-action associated with each user, that is, we model how the user acts as a function of his/her perception of some criterion. We classify reactivity according to two dimensions: (1) Performance: in this case, the user action considers performance measures, such as response time; (2) Business Rules: in this case, the user action considers business rules, such as the negotiation parameters of an e-business application.

Our approach may be divided into three steps: (1) the framework is instantiated for an application and reactivity dimension; (2) application-related data is translated into framework elements; and (3) behaviors are characterized in terms of action-perception pairs.

In this paper we focus on Internet-based services where the business-rules dimension is important. One example of such service is an auction, where the negotiation characteristics may affect directly the bidder's behavior.

We model the reactivity as a tuple $< App, Ses_{App}, S, E, Ac, P, PC >$, where App is the application, Ses_{App} is an application session (an instance of the application by a user), S is the set of states that the application may assume, E represents the set of entities that participate, Ac is the set of actions that may be executed by the entities, P is the application protocol, and PC is the set of perception criteria that characterize the reactivity.

App describes the service or object being provided. The Ses_{App} is adopted once it describes the set of actions performed by the entities that will define the interaction process. P represents the protocol, that is, the application functioning - rules that define which actions can be executed by the entities according to the application states. Each rule has the form: Source State $\xrightarrow[Action]{Entity}$ Target State. The protocol rules define the state transition graph.

Once we have a reactivity model, we can try to identify some correlation between the perception criteria (PC) and the set of actions that an entity may execute. This function will be used to add the reactivity concept to the traditional interactivity model. Once we instantiate the framework, we translate observations in terms of the framework components, so that we may analyze them.

4 Case Study: On Line Auction

In an auction there are two entities, the buyer and the seller. The English auction [18,19] is an ascending-price auction. Each auction instance is a session of the auction engine, that is, the sequence of bids related to the sell of a given item. Thus, the seller putting an item for sale is the start of a session. The last bid delimits the end. There are many states in which an auction session may be: *Active*, *Active with Bids*, *Active with Buy-it-now Option*, *Active with Bids and Buy-it-now Option*, *Cancelled*, *Ended with Buy-it-now Option*, *Ended with Sale*, and *Ended without Sale*. The seller may create an auction session, cancel it, and set the "Buy it now" option. The buyer may bid, the most common action, or perform a "Buy it now" offer. During the auction, the "Buy it now" option permits an immediate purchase. There are many attributes that may affect the buyer's action, such as: the number of bids, the current price, the seller's feedback, and the payment method. It is important to stand out that we are interested in this work in business rules as reactivity dimension, that is, we analyse how the business rules tailor user actions. Instantiating the reactivity framework to this scenario we get the result presented in Table 1.

eBay [20] was founded in 1995. eBay boosters claim that, in terms of revenue growth, eBay [9,2,4] is among the fastest-growing companies of all time. It has revolutionized the collectible market by bringing together buyers and sellers world-wide in a huge, never-ending yard sale and auction. As of June 2005, there were over 15,000 members in the eBay Developers Program, comprising a broad range companies creating software applications to support eBay buyers and sellers as well as eBay affiliates.

This case study is based on eBay data. The data consists of auction data of three different products: Nintendo GameCube, Sony PlayStation 2, and Microsoft Xbox System. The data was collected from $05/25/2005$ to $08/15/2005$, almost three months. Table 2 presents basic information about the auction data, where we can see that there is a significative number of auctions and bids to analyze.

Table 3 presents general statistics, concerning the number of buyers and sellers that participate in the auctions, the auction pricing, the average number of bids per auction, and the average number of unique bidders per auction. STD represents the standard deviation. As can be observed, the STDs are big, showing there are significant variations

Table 1. Reactivity Model - Auction

App	Auction Engine
Ses_{App}	Each Auction Instance
S	Created , Active, Active with Bids, Active with Buy-it-now (BIN) Option, Active with Bids and Buy-it-now (BIN) Option, Cancelled, Ended with Buy-it-now (BIN) Option, Ended with Sale, Ended without Sale
E	Buyer, Seller
Ac	Buyer: MakeBid, MakeBuyItNowOffer Seller: Cancel, SetBuyItNow
P	Created $\xrightarrow[Cancel]{Seller}$ Cancelled Active $\xrightarrow[MakeBid]{Buyer}$ Active with Bids Active $\xrightarrow[SetBuyItNow]{Seller}$ Active with BIN Option Active with Bids $\xrightarrow[MakeBid]{Buyer}$ Active with Bids Active with Bids $\xrightarrow[SetBuyItNow]{Seller}$ Active with Bids and BIN Option Active with BIN Option $\xrightarrow[MakeBid]{Buyer}$ Active with Bids and BIN Option Active with BIN Option $\xrightarrow[MakeBuyItNowOffer]{Buyer}$ Ended with BIN Option Active with BIN Option $\xrightarrow[Cancel]{Seller}$ Cancelled Active with Bids and BIN Option $\xrightarrow[MakeBid]{Buyer}$ Active with Bids and BIN Option Active with Bids and BIN Option $\xrightarrow[MakeBuyItNowOffer]{Buyer}$ Ended with BIN Option Active with Bids and BIN Option $\xrightarrow[Cancel]{Seller}$ Cancelled
PC	Number of Bids, Current Price, Seller's Feedback, Starting Bid, Seller Location, Item's Condition, Shipment Fee, Item's Pictures, Shipment Insurance, Payment Method

over the data. This aspect motivates even more the reactivity analysis, once it can be used to explain them. A first analysis on these statistics shows that:

- The number of successful auctions varies from 63% to 69%.
- The number of distinct sellers is high, showing that auctions are not concentrated among a small number of sellers. The top seller has created 186 Nintendo, 223 Sony, and 116 Xbox auctions for each product.
- The number of distinct buyers is also high, guaranteeing high level of competition in this e-market. On the other hand, from this set of buyers, just very few of them become winners.
- The mean variation of price between new and used products is small, however the standard deviation of the prices is very high.
- There is a significant number of bids per auctions, which indicates the level of competition during the negotiation. This information is confirmed by the average number of unique bidders per auction being greater than 5.

The following two aspects are important to reactivity in online auctions, once they are related to dynamic aspects of the auction bids: (1) The inter-bidding time (IBT), i.e.,

Table 2. Basic information about the eBay dataset

Information	Product			Total
	Nintendo	Sony	Xbox	
# Auctions	8855	17234	9928	36017
# Bids	85803	179057	120021	384881

Table 3. General statistics about the eBay dataset

Statistics	Product		
	Nintendo	Sony	Xbox
Number of auctions with winner	6103	10884	6466
Number of unique sellers	5453	9340	6466
Number of unique buyers that win	735	795	548
Number of unique buyers	18073	39026	26358
Average winner price (overall)	US$ 32.04	US$ 44.21	US$ 49.63
STD winner price (overall)	37.04	51.36	58.87
Average winner price (new)	US$ 35.32	US$ 48.71	US$ 52.97
STD winner price (new)	37.53	60.26	66.10
Average winner price (used)	US$ 31.90	US$ 41.71	US$ 50.34
STD winner price (used)	38.14	49.09	58.12
Average number of bids per auction	11.59	12.38	14.13
STD number of bids per auction	9.43	10.82	11.27
Average number of unique bidders per auction	5.39	5.71	6.48
STD number of unique bidders per auction	3.58	4.23	4.57

the time between two consecutive bids; and (2) The price difference, i.e., the difference of price between two consecutive bids.

Due to space constraints, only the characterization of Nintendo auctions is presented here. Figure 1 shows the difference of price and time between each consecutive bid for Nintendo. As can be seen, there exists a huge concentration of points where the IBT and the difference of price have small values. However the variation of these two metrics shows that there exists a significant variation over them. In the case of IBT, this variation is very high. Moreover it is not possible to identify a clear correlation between these two metrics. This observation holds for the three different auction products.

We analyze the histogram of auction duration for Nintendo, Sony and Xbox. The three sets of auctions present similar duration behavior. Nintendo has more than 40% of auctions during a week and around 15% of them during one day. For Sony and Xbox, the number of auctions with 7-day duration is 40% and 1-day is 20%. The other durations are similar: 20% of three days long and 15% of five days long. Around 5% of the auctions has durations of 2, 4, 6 and 10 days. As can be noted, duration of odd number of days predominate.

In order to analyze the bidders' behavior, we classify them isolating the winner attribute to evaluate how some attributes affect the result of the auction. Initially, we identify the most relevant attributes using an attribute selection algorithm. From 31

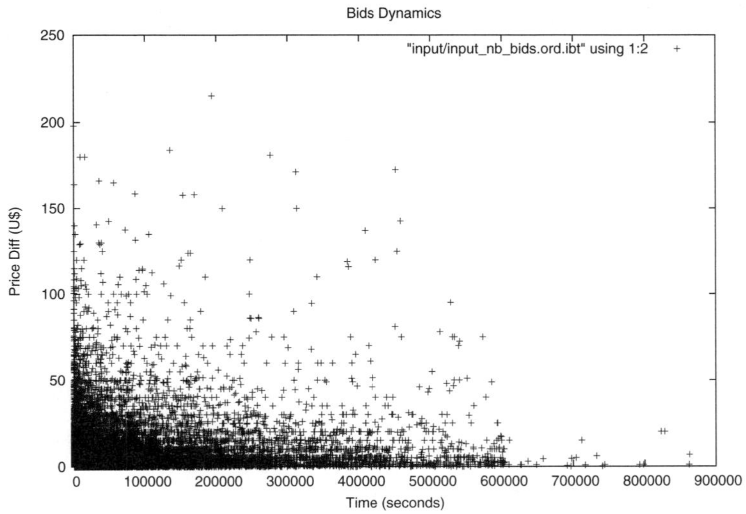

Fig. 1. Bid Dynamics - Nintendo

attributes, all of them related to business-rules dimension, we select the following attributes to apply the classification technique: BIDDER BIDS REL (Relative Quantity of Bidder Bids), ACTIVE TIME REL (Relative Time between the First and Last Bidder's Bid), BID ENTRANCE REL (Relative First Bid Date), BID LEFT REL (Relative Last Bid Date), AVG DELTA TIME REL (Relative average time difference between two bids of the same bidder in an auction), and AVG DELTA PRICE REL (Relative average price difference between two bids of the same bidder in an auction).

Figure 2 presents the classification tree for the Nintendo auctions dataset. This decision tree is a simple structure where non-terminal nodes represent tests on one or more attributes and terminal nodes reflect decision outcomes. From its analysis it is possible to identify some interesting results:

- 43% of winning bidders make the last bid almost at the end of the auction, their bids represent less than 90% of auction bids, and their average relative delta price consists of small values.
- 34% of winning bidders have made more than 90% of the bids of the auction.
- 9.3% of winning bidders present a small average relative price difference between bids (less or equal than 0.02), a small average relative delta time between bids (less or equal than 0.0145), make less bids than 38.5% of the total number of the auction bids, and make the last bid almost at the end of the auction (BID_LEFT_REL > 0.9993).
- 8.5% of winners present an average relative delta time between bids greater or equal than 0.0145, make less bids than 38.5% of the total number of the auction bids, and make the last bid almost at the end of the auction (BID_LEFT_REL > 0.9996).
- 4.5% of winners present a small average relative price difference between bids (less or equal than 0.0227), make 38.5% to 89.5% of the total number of the auction bids, and make the last bid almost at the end of the auction (BID_LEFT_REL > 0.9993).

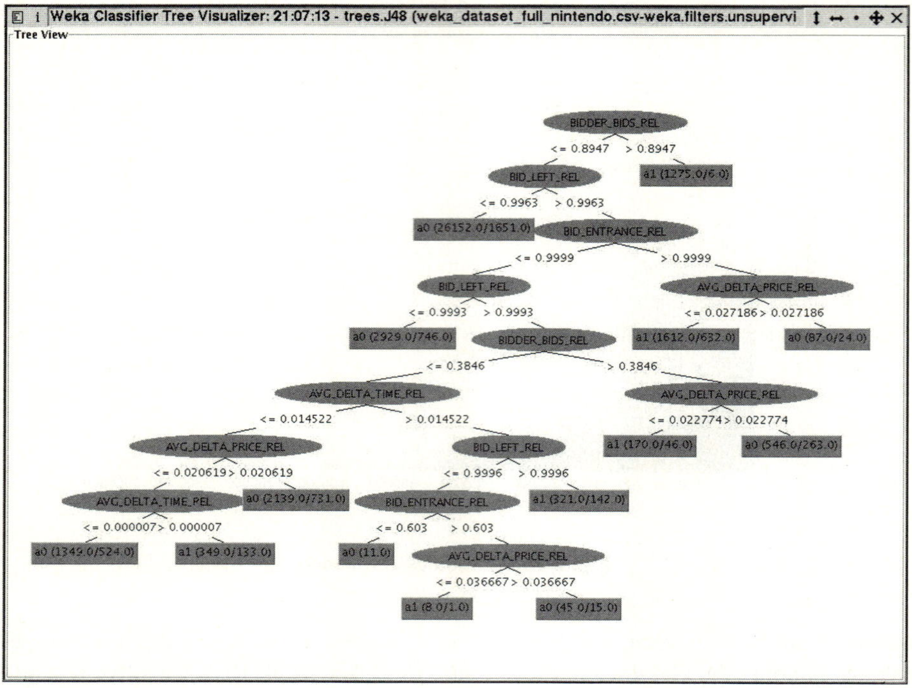

Fig. 2. Classification Tree - Nintendo

From the results of this case study it is possible to identify that there are some aspects that affect the winning bidders' behavior, such as the auction time to finish. Another interesting aspect is that most of the winning bidders make a large amount of bids and/or present a small inter-bidding time. As an expected result, the winning bid has been made near the end of the auction.

The results of the classification for Sony and Xbox auctions are similar to Nintendo. From this analysis, we conclude that is of interest to divide the auction duration in periods to analyze separately. These will help us to understand which factors directly affect the result of the auction, such as the correlation between inter-bidding time and bidding price difference. It will also help in identifying reactivity determinants that explain bidders' behaviors at different stages of the auction.

5 Conclusions and Ongoing Work

This work presents the reactivity concept, describing how to model it in interactive systems, in particular Internet-based systems. We present a case study of an online auction, based on *eBay* data. Although there are some related works of online auctions, none of them models reactivity.

The case study shows some aspects that affect the winner bidders' behavior, such as the auction time to finish and the number of bids of each bidder according to the total amount of auction bids. We identify that winners make a large amount of bids and/or presents a small inter-bidding time.

As ongoing work we divide the auction duration in periods and analyze them separately. These will help us understand which factors directly affect the result of the auction, such as the correlation between inter-bidding time and bidding price difference. This case study motivates us to continue working on improving the reactivity characterization of e-commerce environment.

Modeling reactivity in online auction can contribute to understand the business dynamics and to design more complete automatic agents. We are also confident that by understanding the reactivity patterns in relation to the negotiation features and specific business rules that govern the auction environment we will be able to conceptualize and design a comprehensive framework to model reactivity. Also, studying reactivity can benefit the economic analysis of Web-based environments, such as marketplaces.

References

1. Lucking-Reiley, D.: Using field experiments to test equivalence between auction formats: Magic on the internet. American Economic Review **89**(5) (1999) 1063–1080 available at http://ideas.repec.org/a/aea/aecrev/v89y1999i5p1063-1080.html.
2. Bajari, P., Hortacsu, A.: The winner's curse, reserve prices, and endogenous entry: Empirical insights from ebay auctions. RAND Journal of Economics **34**(2) (2003) 329–55 available at http://ideas.repec.org/a/rje/randje/v34y2003i2p329-55.html.
3. Gilkeson, J.H., Reynolds, K.: Determinants of internet auction success and closing price: An exploratory study. Psychology & Marketing **20**(6) (2003) 537–566
4. Resnick, P., Zeckhauser, R.: Trust among strangers in internet transactions: Empirical analysis of ebay's reputation system. The Economics of the Internet and E-Commerce. Amsterdam: Elsevier Science B.V. (2002) 127–157
5. Ba, S., Pavlou, P.A.: Evidence of the effect of trust building technology in electronic markets: Price premiums and buyer behavior. MIS Quarterly **26**(3) (2002)
6. Roth, A., Ockenfels, A.: Last-minute bidding and the rules for ending second-price auctions: Evidence from ebay and amazon auctions on the internet. American Economic Review **92**(4) (2002) 1093–1103
7. Bapna, R., Goes, P.B., Gupta, A., Jin, Y.: User heterogeneity and its impact on electronic auction market design: An empirical exploration1research essays. MIS Quarterly **28**(1) (2004)
8. Bapna, R., Goes, P.B., Gupta, A.: Replicating online yankee auctions to analyze auctioneers' and bidders' strategies. Information Systems Research **14**(3) (2003) 244–268
9. Anderson, S., Friedman, D., Milam, G., Singh, N.: Seller strategies on ebay. Industrial Organization 0412004, Economics Working Paper Archive EconWPA (2004) available at http://ideas.repec.org/p/wpa/wuwpio/0412004.html.
10. Kauffman, R., Wood, C.: Why does reserve price shilling occur in online auctions? In: International Conference on Electronic Commerce (ICEC 2003), Pittsburg, PA (2003)
11. Pereira, A., Franco, G., Silva, L., Meira, Jr., W., Santos, W.: The *usar* characterization model. In: Proceedings of the IEEE 7th Annual Workshop on Workload Characterization (WWC-7), Austin, Texas, USA, IEEE Computer Society (2004)
12. Pereira, A., Silva, L., Meira Jr., W., Santos, W.: Assessing the impact of reactive workloads on the performance of web applications. In: ISPASS-2006: IEEE International Symposium on Performance Analysis of Systems and Software, Austin, TX, USA, IEEE Computer Society (2006)

13. Widom, J., Ceri, S.: Active Database Systems: Triggers and Rules For Advanced Database Processing. Morgan Kaufmann (1996)
14. Paton, N.W., ed.: Active Rules in Database Systems. Springer, New York (1999)
15. Bry, F., Patranjan, P.L.: Reactivity on the web: paradigms and applications of the language xchange. In: SAC '05: Proceedings of the 2005 ACM symposium on Applied computing, New York, NY, USA, ACM Press (2005) 1645–1649
16. Facca, F.M., Ceri, S., Armani, J., Demaldé, V.: Building reactive web applications. In: WWW '05: Special interest tracks and posters of the 14th international conference on World Wide Web, New York, NY, USA, ACM Press (2005) 1058–1059
17. Ceri, S., Daniel, F., Demaldé, V., Facca, F.M.: An Approach to User-Behavior-Aware Web Applications. In Lowe, D., Gaedke, M., eds.: Web Engineering, 5th International Conference, ICWE 2005, Sydney, Australia, July 27-29, 2005, Proceedings. Volume 3579 of Lecture Notes in Computer Science., Springer (2005) 417–428
18. Lopomo, G.: Optimality and robustness of the english auction. Working Papers 95-03, New York University, Leonard N. Stern School of Business, Department of Economics (1995) available at http://ideas.repec.org/p/ste/nystbu/95-03.html.
19. David, E., Azoulay-Schwartz, R., Kraus, S.: Bidders' strategy for multi-attribute sequential english auction with a deadline. In: AAMAS '03: Proceedings of the second international joint conference on Autonomous agents and multiagent systems, New York, NY, USA, ACM Press (2003) 457–464
20. EBay: eBay, Inc. (2005) http://www.ebay.com/.

Event Correlation and Pattern Detection in CEDR

Roger S. Barga[1] and Hillary Caituiro-Monge[2]

[1] Microsoft Research, One Microsoft Way, Redmond WA
barga@microsoft.com
[2] UC Santa Barbara, Computer Science Department, Santa Barbara, CA
caituiro@cs.ucsb.edu

Abstract. Event processing will play an increasingly important role in constructing distributed applications that can immediately react to critical events. In this paper we describe the **CEDR** language for expressing complex event queries that *filter* and *correlate* events to match specific patterns, and transform the relevant events into new composite events for the use of monitoring applications. Stream-based execution of these standing queries offers instant insight for users to see what is occurring in their systems and to take time-critical actions.

1 Introduction

"By 2008 event processing will be mainstream, with most new business systems in large companies set up to emit vast amounts of event information. Applications are going to start to get very chatty..." *David McCoy, Gartner Group 2005*

A vendor receives a purchase order from a customer, a physician orders a medication change for a patient, an investor executes a trade, a new employee joins a company, a retail outlet makes a sale. Every kind of business is driven by a myriad of such events that occur in its environment. It is not an exaggeration to say that business events are the real drivers of business processes because events represent changes in the state of the business. This is not to say that enterprise web services are not key participants in business processes—they are, but as providers of data and function not as drivers of the process state. Events are also central to creating views of business processes, whether automated or not.

Over the last few years a great deal of attention has been focused on making service level interactions uniform across the industry, such as those based on the WS-* standards, and much progress has been made. Far less attention has been paid to the variety of ways in which events are defined, handled and propagated. Major platform vendors offer event brokers as a feature of their message oriented middleware, and also offer business activity monitoring (BAM) as a feature of their business process stack. But, as in the case of data management in pre-database days, every usage area of events today tends to build its own special purpose infrastructure for defining, handling and propagating events. We see the need for a common event fabric running across web services. Such fabric should allow event sources to fire events "into the

T. Grust et al. (Eds.): EDBT 2006 Workshops, LNCS 4254, pp. 919–930, 2006.

event cloud", without caring who consumes them, the subscribers to events can register "standing queries" describing what they are interested in. The queries can be as simple as simply filtering events or require that events be *filtered* and *correlated* for pattern detection, and that these events are then *transformed* to composite events that reach a semantic level appropriate for end applications. These requirements constitute a unique class of queries that perform real-time transformation of events describing a physical world into information more useful to end applications and users.

2 Events, Messages and Data

An event is a record of some occurrence in the physical or digital world. Each event explicitly (as part of its data) or implicitly (interpretation rule) has a type that indicates what happened, and schematized data that describes the details. A message is a means of transmitting data from a source to one or more targets. A message also typically has a type and schematized data. It is thus natural to ask if the two are different. The difference between them is not in form but in semantics. Unlike a message, an event has neither a targeted receiver nor an interaction pattern—there is no such thing as a reply to an event. Instead, the important part of the semantics of an event is causality – what events caused this to occur and what will be the consequences of the current event. This *causality* is not in the event itself – it can only be inferred interpretation of the payload of multiple events, possibly from different sources.

Of course, events can be caused by messages and messages are used to transmit events to interested observers and processors. We illustrate the message/event relationship and idea of causality with an example. A purchasing subsystem receives a shipment status message. The status code and details inform the recipient that a shipment is delayed by 3 weeks. The purchasing subsystem is configured to generate a specific type of event when processing shipment delay messages. There are event transformation services installed in the "event fabric" to process events of this type based on the reference numbers in the content by fetching relevant application data to transform the event into a more meaningful event such as "delivery for Intel processor parts order 72134 delayed by 3 weeks". This same type of "parts delivery delayed" event can also occur as a result of manual action by a purchasing agent receiving a phone call or FAX, illustrating that different occurrences of the same type of event may have different causality chains. Through a further chain of rule-based event transformations, an event "PC production-line 4 in Memphis at risk of closure in 3 weeks" is generated. The "Memphis PC Production-line Managers" group has an alert subscription for this type of, and the final event generates an alert message sent to the group.

3 Complex Event Queries over Event Streams

In this section we outline the event correlation and pattern detection language for CEDR, short for **C**omplex **E**vent **D**etection and **R**esponse, an event processing system currently under development at MSR.

3.1 From Web Service Message Streams to Event Streams for Query Processing

This discussion outlines how we go from a *physical message stream* flowing over an event bus or WS-Event channel, to a *logical event stream* for processing against a set of standing queries. Our raw input stream consists of messages with an arbitrary but known schema for each message type that provides the necessary metadata information about the *message payload.* Input to our processing system is an infinite sequence of events, referred to as an *event stream.* An event represents an instantaneous and atomic occurrence of interest at a point in time. Similar to the distinction between types and instances in programming languages, our model includes event types that describe a set of attributes that a class of events must contain. Each event instance, denoted by a lower-case letter (e.g., '*e*'), consists of the name of its type, denoted by an upper-case letter (e.g., '*E*'), and a set of values corresponding to the attributes defined in the event type which we refer to as the *payload.* In order to *transform* a message into an event for processing we augment the record with the following fields:

- Start_Valid_Time: the time at which the event instance can be considered for query processing. If an operator in our system is processing an event instance at a time before (less than) this timestamp, this event instance can not yet be considered (seen) by the operator.
- End_Valid_Time: the time at which an event instance can no longer be considered for query processing. This value can be set by a time-to-live (ttl) attribute or sliding window specification, expressed in the query, or by a corresponding delete (retraction) of the event coming into the system.

So, the schema of an event instance for processing is a union of message schemas or possibly some mapping of incoming message type to its associated event type, and temporal schema: <start valid time, end valid time>. Most messages will already have a timestamp from a discrete ordered time domain. We assume timestamps are assigned by a separate mechanism before events enter our system and reflect the true occurrence time of these events in the "real world", so we use this timestamp as start valid time – if an incoming event does not have a timestamp, we assign the value of the system clock. The corresponding end valid time value is set to infinity by default – we assume the fact this event represents will stand true forever, but will adjust depending on the semantics of the query. It is important to note the transformation from a raw message to logical input event preserves the arrival order of event instances.

3.2 CEDR Language

In this section, we present the CEDR language for expressing queries over event streams. The language is declarative and based on three independent aspects: 1) an event pattern expression that identifies event types and order, using operators and constructs that specify how event instances are *filtered*, and how multiple events are *correlated* via time-based and value-based constraints to detect *patterns*; 2) an optional *lifetime* during which the pattern may be detected; 3) an optional *selection* expression that specifies how complex events are constructed from correlated events.

The overall structure of the CEDR language is:

EVENT_NAME <string>
EVENT_PATTERN <event type and order expression>
WHERE < temporal and data qualification predicates>
[LIFETIME <window>]
NOTIFY <selection conditions for the construction of a complex event>

To introduce the constructs in our language, we use examples drawn from systems monitoring in which operations management monitors events stemming from network servers, database servers and network devices across the company. The first query (Q1) looks for events that indicate a software upgrade is being installed on a machine.

Q1: UPDATE_MACHINE
EVENT_PATTERN **INSTALL**
WHERE (*software_type* = 'SP' AND *version_id* = '2')

In Q1, the EVENT PATTERN clause contains a filter for ***event type*** "*INSTALL*" that retrieves only event instances of the *INSTALL* type from the input stream. The WHERE clause further filters these event instances by evaluating two ***predicates*** applied to their attributes: the first predicate requires the value of attribute *software_type* to be 'SP' and the second predicate requires the value of attribute *version_id* to be '2'. In general, the WHERE clause is responsible for *filtering* event instances and can be a boolean combination, using logical connectives AND and OR, of predicates that use one of the six comparison operators $(=, \neq, >, <, \geq, \leq)$.

Our second example, Q2 detects a failed software upgrade by filtering the event stream to retrieve only those events that report an upgrade was installed on a machine, followed by a *shutdown* without the occurence of a subsequent *restart*. The EVENT clause of this query contains a SEQUENCE construct that specifies events must occur in a particular order; the components of the sequence are the occurrences and non-occurrences of events of interest. In this query, the SEQUENCE construct specifies the occurrence of an *INSTALL* event followed by a *SHUTDOWN* event, and the non-occurrence of a *RESTART* within a fixed window of time. Non-occurrences of events are expressed using the **NOT** operator and bounded by a time interval, expressed by the WITHIN operator. For the use of subsequent clauses, the SEQUENCE construct also includes a variable in each component to refer to the corresponding event.

Q2: FAILED_UPGRADE
EVENT_PATTERN **SEQUENCE**(*INSTALL x*, *SHUTDOWN y*,
NOT (*RESTART z*, **WITHIN** 5 minutes))
WHERE *((x.machine_id = y.machine_id)* AND *(y.machine_id = z.machine_id))*
/* shorthand for this test is **CorrelationKey**(machine_id, Equal) */

The WHERE clause in Q2 uses variables defined previously to form predicates that compare attributes across different events. One of the more powerful aspects of any language for event pattern detection is *correlation*, the ability of an event instance to be linked to specific instances of other events through payload values. To distinguish this from simple predicates that compare to a constant, such as those in the first example, we refer to such predicates as ***parameterized predicates.*** The parameterized predicates in Q2 compare the *machine_id* attributes of all three events in the

SEQUENCE construct for equality. Since this is such a common comparison, we introduce shorthand to simplify writing such parameterized predicates.

Equality comparisons on a common payload attribute across entire event sequences are typical in distributed monitoring applications. For ease of use, we refer to the common attribute used for this purpose as a *correlation key*, and the set of comparisons on this attribute as the ***similarity test*** that checks for equality or inequality. Our language offers simple shorthand for an equivalence test on common attributes, specifically **CorrelationKey**(*attribute*, *Equal* | *Unique*). In addition, we offer predefined operators for temporal correlation, such "**BEFORE**", "**AFTER**", "**EQUAL**", "**WITHIN**" which automatically extract the timestamp field from all event instances.

In CEDR an optional LIFESPAN clause is used to define a temporal interval during which a query is active or "*of interest*" and may be detected. In our model, a lifespan is either *Active* or *Inactive* and is controlled by two events, referred to as *initiator* and *terminator*. An occurrence of an initiator event activates the lifespan, while the occurrence of a terminator event deactivates the lifespan. A lifespan can also expire, as defined by its maximal duration. While *active*, any query associated with the lifespan is also *active* and CEDR will attempt to detect the pattern in the event stream.

Lifespan Pattern
Name – *name of the lifespan pattern*
Initiator – *conditions for lifespan initiation*
Event: identifies the initiating event;
Condition: optional conditions the event must satisfy;
Terminator – *describes conditions for lifespan termination*
Event: identifies the initiating event;
Condition: optional conditions the event must satisfy;
Duration: max duration the lifespan will remain active;

A lifespan can be used to implement *state based* pattern detection – when the system is in a particular state, as indicated by the activation of a lifespan, a select set of queries is activated. Each state can define a unique set of queries (events to watch for) and filters to eliminate (drop) redundant events. In short, LIFESPAN enables a system to compartmentalize functionality and provide context for event processing. CEDR is not the only system to include lifetimes – the concept is identified in [2] and implemented in AMIT [22] and Rapide [1].

Given a sequence of event instances as input, the output of a standing query in CEDR is also a sequence of event instances, where each output event instance represents a unique match or *detection*. The NOTIFY clause allows a programmer to specify exactly how the complex event that signifies detection is composed. Using query Q2 for example, a resulting event can be created to indicate an upgrade has failed to install on the machine. Unlike previous work that focuses only on the detection of standing queries, but not reporting how the query was actually satisfied, we provide the means to explicitly report the events used to match the query. This significantly increases the complexity of the underlying runtime, since it must accurately track event instances.

In CEDR, the NOTIFY clause can specify for each *event type* in the pattern expressing which individual *instances* of this event type are to be chosen. CEDR supports four options, which can be specified for each operand in the pattern expression: *First*, *Last*, *Each* and *Cond*; the default is *First*. *First* and *Last* are minimum-oriented selection strategies [2]. *First* (*Last*) selects from the event collection instances with the oldest (youngest) timestamps. *Each* selects all permissible event instances associated with the operand, possibly resulting in the creation of multiple complex events after pattern detection. The final option, *Cond*, is a user supplied predicate that is applied to each event instance associated with the operand – only if the condition is satisfied will the instance be selected.

In example Q2, the pattern expression includes a sequence operator and two operands (event types) to detect an **INSTALL** event followed by a **SHUTDOWN** event. There may be several instances of the install event, each indicating installation of a different patch, before a shutdown is detected. If the pattern indicating a flawed upgrade is detected, the user may wish to raise a complex event identifying *all software patches* installed, which can be easily accomplished using the selection condition *Each*. We hasten to note, typically NOTIFY creates an instance of an event type and selection conditions are used to *bind* variables for composing this new event instance (marshaling the payload for the new event instance) but we omit this discussion for brevity.

Q2: FAILED_UPGRADE
EVENT_PATTERN **SEQUENCE**(*INSTALL x*, *SHUTDOWN y*,
NOT (*RESTART z*, **WITHIN** 5 minutes))
WHERE **CorrelationKey**(machine_id, Equal)
NOTIFY *Each* x, *First* y

The simple examples presented in this section were intended to highlight constructs of CEDR. Our language builds on event languages [20, 16, 2] originally developed for active databases, triggers [17] and continual queries [19]. In addition to event constructs such as *sequence*, CEDR offers additional features, such as i) the use of negation in event sequences, ii) *parameterized predicates* in the WHERE clause for correlating events via value-based constraints and iii) *time to live (TTL) and various sliding windows for event instances* in the LIFETIME clause for expressing additional temporal constraints for pattern detection. Finally, CEDR enables event composition, which allows the output of one query to be used as input to another. The fact that a CEDR query can take a sequence of input events and produce a sequence of composite (complex) events as output enables full compositionality. Together these features provide rich functionality and control over event pattern specification and detection.

3.3 Semantics of the Language

In this section, we present the semantics of CEDR by translating selected language constructs to algebraic query expressions. Each event type E_i is a query expression. An event operator connects query expressions to form a new expression. Semantics is added to a query expression by treating it as a function mapping the underlying discrete time domain onto the boolean values *True* or *False*. For example, the semantics of a base expression E_i, represented as $E_i(t)$, is that at a given point t in time, $E_i(t)$ is *True* if an E_i type event occurred at t, and is *False* otherwise. Below, we describe the set of operators that CEDR supports and the semantics of expressions that they form.

Event Sequencing (Order) – The ability to synthesize events based upon the ordering of previous events is a basic and powerful event language construct.

Operator	Description
ALL [E1 . . . ,Ek]	A conjunction of events *E*1. . .*Ek* with no order importance. It takes a set of event types as input and evaluates to *True* if instances of each event type occur. Formally, defined as: **ALL**($E1, E2, \ldots, En)(t) \equiv \forall\ 1 \leq i \leq n\ E_i(t)$. It outputs all instances that occurred at time *t* as a result.
ANY [E1...,Ek]	It takes a set of event types as input and evaluates to *True* if an event of any of these types occurs. Formally, it is defined as follows: **ANY**($E1, E2, \ldots, Ek)(t) \equiv \exists\ 1 \leq i \leq k\ E_i(t)$. It outputs the event that occurred at time *t* as a result.
SEQUENCE [E1… Ek]	SEQUENCE takes a list of *n* (*n*>1) event types as its parameters – these parameters specify a particular order in which events must occur. Arbitrary events may appear between any two events in the sequence. The formal definition is: SEQUENCE($E1, E2, \ldots, En)(t) \equiv \exists\ t_1<t_2<\ldots<t_n \bullet E_1(t_1) \wedge E_2(t_2) \wedge \ldots \wedge E_n(t_n)$. The operators ANY and ALL can be used inside a SEQUENCE, e.g., SEQUENCE(E_1, ANY($E_{21}, \ldots, E_{2m}$), …). The semantics of the resulting expressions are defined by combining semantics of SEQUENCE along with ANY (or ALL).

Counting – Counting operators reduce the number of events flowing to the application, thus reducing the amount of state required in the process. State is maintained by CEDR and there is value in this separation. For example, a "valuable customer" pattern may be triggered after three consecutive purchases. To change it to four purchases requires simply changing the event pattern definition – not the business application.

Operator	Description
ATLEAST [n, E1...Ek]	A minimal conjunction of *n* events out of *E*1. . .*Ek* with no order importance. ATLEAST takes a list of k (k>1) event types as its parameter, along with an integer n, and evaluates to *True* if n or more of these k events occur. **ATLEAST** (n, $E1, E2, \ldots, Ek)(t) \equiv \Sigma\ 1 \leq i \leq k\ E_i(t) \geq$ n. It outputs all event instances true at time *t* as a result.
ATMOST [n, E1...Ek]	A maximal conjunction of *n* events out of *E*1. . .*Ek* with no order importance. While the definition of **ATMOST** follows directly from the definition of **ATLEAST**, an important difference is that some temporal expression must be supplied to cancel the accumulation of state for patterns that use this operator.

Absence – The event service can track the *non-occurrence* of an expected event, such as a customer not answering an email within a specified time. So-called *non-events* have great utility in business processes. Further, set operations apply to non-events: for example, events indicating that *none* of a group of customers has responded, or *all* or some *threshold number* of customers has answered are valid and useful events.

Operator	Description
NOT [E1,…,Ek, scope]	None of the events *E*1…*Ek* has occurred within the detection lifespan. The **NOT** operator requires an explicit bound on the detection window, which can be specified using an optional **SCOPE** clause, which specifies the amount of time in the detection lifespan.
UNLESS [E1, E2]	Designates the occurrence of the first operand and non-occurrence of the second within the detection lifespan.

Constraints and Event Cancellation – Event patterns normally do not "pend" indefinitely; conditions or constraints may be used to cancel the accumulation of state for a pattern (which would otherwise remain to aggregate with future events to generate a composite event). Such temporal constraints limit event generation to within a particular time window. The CANCEL-WHEN operator is used to describe such constraints. CANCEL-WHEN may be followed either by a temporal expression *time-expr*, and is commonly used with a timer event but may use any other base or pattern event, including patterns that mix timer events with other events (e.g., Approval & T [Approval.t + 20hours]).

Operator	Description
E **CANCEL-WHEN** *EXPR*	Used to cancel or invalidate specific event instances or a complete sub-expression in a pattern query. This effectively removes the event instances being held in the event collection for this pattern.

Use of **CANCEL-WHEN** has a number of interesting applications, which we touch on only briefly. Since multi-term patterns rely upon the asynchronous delivery of multiple events, it is possible that one required event will arrive but the others will not. To avoid the unbounded accumulation of event instances (state) temporal constraints are used to remove them; normally this is thought of as a form of garbage collection. In this case the **CANCEL-WHEN** predicate is used to bound the valid time of an event pattern. As an example: ((E & F) **CANCEL-WHEN** *time-expr*). In this case event E and event F *must* occur before the value in *time-expr* is reached.

The use of **CANCEL-WHEN** can be generalized to include other sorts of pattern cancellation; for example: (E & F **CANCEL-WHEN** G). In this case if event G arrives before both E and F then event pattern detection is aborted.

4 Pattern Detection and Event Processing

In this section, we illustrate the functionality of components in CEDR by walking thru the processing of events and pattern detection. The initial stage is *event filtering*. For each incoming event, the CEDR *filter manager* will determine if it has the potential to impact an active pattern. While at any given time the total number of active pattern instances can be quite large, typically the number affected by an incoming event instance is orders of magnitude lower. We leverage this to construct a restrictive filter on event instances and fine tune filtering by pushing *event instance conditions* into the filter. In the system monitoring application, for example, we filter event instances using event type = **install** with context (instance condition) = **SP2**. Once detected, the filter is updated to include event type = **shutdown** with context = **MachineID**, where the value of **MachineID** is extracted from the **install** event instance. We also use indexes to efficiently identify pattern instances affected by the incoming event.

The decision process in CEDR to determine whether or not an event pattern has actually been detected is divided into three separate stages, where each stage is based on a separate aspect of the pattern language definition.

Stage 1: Event Collection – An *event collection* designates the event instances that are considered for pattern detection, if they occur while the pattern is active. In this stage all event instances that may contribute to an active pattern are collected. An instance *contributes* to a pattern if the event type matches an operand type in the pattern expression, and satisfies all conditions defined for the operand. Each candidate in the event collection is associated with the operand to which it matches and forms a *candidate list* for the operand. An event instance may contribute to more than one active patterns, so to avoid storing multiple copies CEDR maintains a shared collection of event instances and stores only a reference to the instance in the candidate list; reference counting is used to manage (clean up) this shared collection. To decide if the pattern is satisfied it is sufficient to base detection on these event instances only.

Stage 2: Detection – The decision about whether a pattern occurred is based on a combination of operators and event instance conditions. It is possible that multiple event instances of the same event type satisfy the detection conditions.

Stage 3 Selection – When a pattern is detected, instances that contributed to detection are *selected* from the event collection following the pattern's *selection policy* and used to create the composite event. This new event is then published (broadcast). Finally, the event instances that triggered the detection are removed from the candidate list of that operand. CEDR actually supports a range of consumption policies [2] to update the event instance collection, but this is outside the scope of this paper.
To summarize, filtering permits only select event types to pass into the detection engine. While a standing query is active, all event instances that may contribute to a pattern are collected (step 1). If all conditions that define the standing query have been met (step 2), the event instances in the collection that triggered detection are selected to generate a new complex event and removed from the collection (step 3).

5 Related Work

Throughout the paper we have attempted to point out closely related work, so in this section we briefly discuss other related work in a broader set of areas.

A number of event processing systems have been recently developed. HiFi [7] aggregates events in a tree-structured network on various temporal and geographic scales and offers limited support for complete event processing [9]. Siemens RFID middleware [10] offers a temporal data model and declarative rules for managing RFID data but no solid implementation is described. Overall, these systems lack the expressiveness to support our target applications, which is distributed monitoring.

Conventional publish/subscribe systems [4][6] support predicate-based filtering of individual events. CEDR extends this approach with the ability to handle both temporal and data value correlations among events and transform primitive events into a new composite event. More recent work on enhanced publish/subscribe [5] provides expressive language support to specify subscriptions spanning multiple events, similar to the language in CEDR. However, it supports the absence of events, or negation, in a rather limited way. Moreover, Cayuga does not address issues related to creating composite events as a result of detection and managing event instance state, whereas CEDR exposes commands and techniques to compose complex events after detection.

In a broader context, our system is related to sequence databases [17] since raw input streams are a temporally ordered sequence of records. However, the semantics of SQL-style sequence languages includes one-time, but not continuous queries. The chronicle data model [16] provides operators over relations and chronicles, which can be considered as a raw input stream, but focuses on the space complexity of an incremental maintenance of materialized views over chronicles; it does not include continuous queries or aspects of data-driven processing. None of these offer the flexible use of negation. In the context of continuous queries over streams, there has also been considerable research. Tribeca [18] introduces fixed and moving window queries over single network streams. TelegraphCQ [14] defines a declarative language to express a sequence of windows over a stream. Aurora [11, 13] builds a query graph of stream operators parameterized by functions and predicates while abstracting from a certain query language. The Tapestry system [19] transforms a continuous query into an incremental query that is run periodically, which ensures snapshot-reducibility but can not detect patterns (sequences) in the event stream. We refer the interested reader to [12, 15] for a broader overview on data stream processing.

6 Conclusion

Event processing will play an increasingly important role in constructing distributed enterprise applications over web services that can immediately react to critical events. In this paper we have illustrated the need for a common event fabric across web services. This fabric will allow any event source to contribute its events into the "event cloud". Subscribers can register their interest in receiving both the raw events from sources and the result of complex standing queries against events streaming through the cloud. In this paper we introduced CEDR, a runtime service for event correlation and pattern detection. Our presentation outlined CEDR's language for defining event patterns, along with its event processing and detection model. CEDR builds on and extends previous work on event processing in several directions. It introduces a declarative language for specifying patterns that includes high level event operators, support for detection lifetime and flexible instance selection and consumption conditions. Our detection model, currently built using nondeterministic finite automata

(NFA) supports a time model to manage temporal correlations across event instances and timeouts, and can efficiently handle predicates in patterns. This paper represents a current snapshot of our design and language development.

References

1. Luckham, David "The Power of Events: An Introduction to Complex Event Processing in Distributed Enterprise Systems", Addison Wesley Publishers, 2002.
2. Zimmer D, Unland R On the semantics of complex events in active database management systems. In the Proceedings of ICDE, March 1999, pp 392–399.
3. RS Barga and H. Caituiro-Monge, CEDR – a runtime service for event correlation and pattern detection, ACM Middleware'05 Conference, *demo presentation and short paper.*
4. Aguilera, M.K., Strom, R.E., Sturman, D.C., Astley, M., and Chandra, T.D. Matching events in a content-based subscription sys-tem. In *Proc. of Principles of Distributed Computing*, 1999.
5. Demers, A., Gehrke, J., Hong, M., Riedewald, M., et al. Towards expressive publish/subscribe systems. In *EDBT*, 627-644, 2006.
6. Fabret, F., Jacobsen, H.A., Llirbat, Pereira, J., Ross, K.A., and Shasha, D. Filtering algorithms and implementation for very fast publish/subscribe systems. In *SIGMOD*, 115-126, 2001.
7. Franklin, M.J., Jeffery, S., Krishnamurthy, S., Reiss, F., Rizvi, S., Wu, E., Cooper, O., Edakkunni, A., and Hong, W. Design considerations for high fan-in systems: The HiFi approach. In *CIDR*, 2005.
8. Hinze, A. Efficient filtering of composite events. In *Proc. of the British National Database Conference*, 207-225, 2003.
9. Rizvi, S., Jeffery, S.R., Krishnamurthy, S., Franklin, M.J., Burkhart, N., et al. Events on the edge. In *SIGMOD*, 885-887, 2005.
10. Wang, F. and Liu, Peiya. Temporal management of RFID data. In *VLDB*, 1128-1139, 2005.
11. D. J. Abadi, D. Carney, U. Cetintemel, M. Cherniack, C. Convey, S. Lee, M. Stonebraker, N. Tatbul, and S. B. Zdonik. Aurora: A New Model and Architecture for Data Stream Management. VLDB Journal, 12(2):120–139, 2003.
12. A. Arasu, S. Babu, and J. Widom. The CQL Continuous Query Language: Semantic Foundations and Query Execution. Technical report, Stanford University, 2003.
13. D. Carney, U. Cetintemel, M. Cherniack, C. Convey, S. Lee, G. Seidman, M. Stonebraker, N. Tatbul, and S. B. Zdonik. Monitoring Streams: A New Class of Data Management Applications. In Proc. of the Conf. on Very Large Databases (VLDB), pages 215–226, 2002.
14. S. Chandrasekaran, O. Cooper, and A. D. et al. TelegraphCQ: Continuous Dataflow Processing for an Uncertain World. In Proc. of the Conference on Innovative Data Systems Research (CIDR), 2003.
15. L. Golab and M. T. Ozsu. Issues in Data Stream Management. SIGMOD Record, 32(2):5–14, 2003.
16. H. V. Jagadish, I. S. Mumick, and A. Silberschatz. View Maintenance Issues for the Chronicle Data Model. In Proc. of the ACM SIGMOD, pages 113–124, 1995.
17. P. Seshadri, M. Livny, and R. Ramakrishnan. The Design and Implementation of a Sequence Database System. In the Proceedings of the Conference on Very Large Databases (VLDB), pages 99–110, 1996.

18. M. Sullivan and A. Heybey. Tribeca: A System for Managing Large Databases of Network Traffic. In In Proc. of the USENIX Annual Technical Conference, pages 13–24, 1998.
19. D. B. Terry, D. Goldberg, D. Nichols and B. M. Oki. Continuous Queries over Append-Only Databases. In Proc. of the ACM SIGMOD, pages 321–330, 1992.
20. Chakravarthy, S., Krishnaprasad, V., Anwar, E. and Kim, S. Composite events for active databases: Semantics, contexts and detection. In *VLDB*, 606-617, 1994.
21. Gehani, N.H., Jagadish, H.V., and Shmueli, O. Composite event specification in active databases: Model and implementation. In *VLDB*, 327-338, 1992.
22. Opher Etzion, Complex Event Processing. In the Proc. of the Intl Conf on Web Services (*ICWS*) 185-197, 2004.

Author Index

Lecture Notes in Computer Science

For information about Vols. 1–4168

please contact your bookseller or Springer

Vol. 4270: H. Zha, Z. Pan, H. Thwaites, A.C. Addison, M. Forte (Eds.), Interactive Technologies and Sociotechnical Systems. XVI, 547 pages. 2006.

Vol. 4265: N. Lavrač, L. Todorovski, K.P. Jantke (Eds.), Discovery Science. XIV, 384 pages. 2006. (Sublibrary LNAI).

Vol. 4264: J.L. Balcázar, P.M. Long, F. Stephan (Eds.), Algorithmic Learning Theory. XIII, 393 pages. 2006. (Sublibrary LNAI).

Vol. 4254: T. Grust, H. Höpfner, A. Illarramendi, S. Jablonski, M. Mesiti, S. Müller, P.-L. Patranjan, K.-U. Sattler, M. Spiliopoulou, J. Wijsen (Eds.), Current Trends in Database Technology – EDBT 2006. XXXI, 932 pages. 2006.

Vol. 4253: B. Gabrys, R.J. Howlett, L.C. Jain (Eds.), Knowledge-Based Intelligent Information and Engineering Systems, Part III. XXXII, 1301 pages. 2006. (Sublibrary LNAI).

Vol. 4252: B. Gabrys, R.J. Howlett, L.C. Jain (Eds.), Knowledge-Based Intelligent Information and Engineering Systems, Part II. XXXIII, 1335 pages. 2006. (Sublibrary LNAI).

Vol. 4251: B. Gabrys, R.J. Howlett, L.C. Jain (Eds.), Knowledge-Based Intelligent Information and Engineering Systems, Part I. LXVI, 1297 pages. 2006. (Sublibrary LNAI).

Vol. 4249: L. Goubin, M. Matsui (Eds.), Cryptographic Hardware and Embedded Systems - CHES 2006. XII, 462 pages. 2006.

Vol. 4248: S. Staab, V. Svátek (Eds.), Engineering Knowledge in the Age of the Semantic Web. XIV, 400 pages. 2006. (Sublibrary LNAI).

Vol. 4247: T.-D. Wang, X. Li, S.-H. Chen, X. Wang, H. Abbass, H. Iba, G. Chen, X. Yao (Eds.), Simulated Evolution and Learning. XXI, 940 pages. 2006.

Vol. 4243: T. Yakhno, E.J. Neuhold (Eds.), Advances in Information Systems. XIII, 420 pages. 2006.

Vol. 4241: R.R. Beichel, M. Sonka (Eds.), Computer Vision Approaches to Medical Image Analysis. XI, 262 pages. 2006.

Vol. 4239: H.Y. Youn, M. Kim, H. Morikawa (Eds.), Ubiquitous Computing Systems. XVI, 548 pages. 2006.

Vol. 4238: Y.-T. Kim, M. Takano (Eds.), Management of Convergence Networks and Services. XVIII, 605 pages. 2006.

Vol. 4236: L. Breveglieri, I. Koren, D. Naccache, J.-P. Seifert (Eds.), Fault Diagnosis and Tolerance in Cryptography. XIII, 253 pages. 2006.

Vol. 4234: I. King, J. Wang, L. Chan, D. Wang (Eds.), Neural Information Processing, Part III. XXII, 1227 pages. 2006.

Vol. 4233: I. King, J. Wang, L. Chan, D. Wang (Eds.), Neural Information Processing, Part II. XXII, 1203 pages. 2006.

Vol. 4232: I. King, J. Wang, L. Chan, D. Wang (Eds.), Neural Information Processing, Part I. XLVI, 1153 pages. 2006.

Vol. 4229: E. Najm, J.F. Pradat-Peyre, V.V. Donzeau-Gouge (Eds.), Formal Techniques for Networked and Distributed Systems - FORTE 2006. X, 486 pages. 2006.

Vol. 4228: D.E. Lightfoot, C.A. Szyperski (Eds.), Modular Programming Languages. X, 415 pages. 2006.

Vol. 4227: W. Nejdl, K. Tochtermann (Eds.), Innovative Approaches for Learning and Knowledge Sharing. XVII, 721 pages. 2006.

Vol. 4225: J.F. Martínez-Trinidad, J.A. Carrasco Ochoa, J. Kittler (Eds.), Progress in Pattern Recognition, Image Analysis and Applications. XIX, 995 pages. 2006.

Vol. 4224: E. Corchado, H. Yin, V. Botti, C. Fyfe (Eds.), Intelligent Data Engineering and Automated Learning – IDEAL 2006. XXVII, 1447 pages. 2006.

Vol. 4223: L. Wang, L. Jiao, G. Shi, X. Li, J. Liu (Eds.), Fuzzy Systems and Knowledge Discovery. XXVIII, 1335 pages. 2006. (Sublibrary LNAI).

Vol. 4222: L. Jiao, L. Wang, X. Gao, J. Liu, F. Wu (Eds.), Advances in Natural Computation, Part II. XLII, 998 pages. 2006.

Vol. 4221: L. Jiao, L. Wang, X. Gao, J. Liu, F. Wu (Eds.), Advances in Natural Computation, Part I. XLI, 992 pages. 2006.

Vol. 4219: D. Zamboni, C. Kruegel (Eds.), Recent Advances in Intrusion Detection. XII, 331 pages. 2006.

Vol. 4218: S. Graf, W. Zhang (Eds.), Automated Technology for Verification and Analysis. XIV, 540 pages. 2006.

Vol. 4217: P. Cuenca, L. Orozco-Barbosa (Eds.), Personal Wireless Communications. XV, 532 pages. 2006.

Vol. 4216: M.R. Berthold, R. Glen, I. Fischer (Eds.), Computational Life Sciences II. XIII, 269 pages. 2006. (Sublibrary LNBI).

Vol. 4213: J. Fürnkranz, T. Scheffer, M. Spiliopoulou (Eds.), Knowledge Discovery in Databases: PKDD 2006. XXII, 660 pages. 2006. (Sublibrary LNAI).

Vol. 4212: J. Fürnkranz, T. Scheffer, M. Spiliopoulou (Eds.), Machine Learning: ECML 2006. XXIII, 851 pages. 2006. (Sublibrary LNAI).

Vol. 4211: P. Vogt, Y. Sugita, E. Tuci, C. Nehaniv (Eds.), Symbol Grounding and Beyond. VIII, 237 pages. 2006. (Sublibrary LNAI).

Vol. 4210: C. Priami (Ed.), Computational Methods in Systems Biology. X, 323 pages. 2006. (Sublibrary LNBI).

Vol. 4209: F. Crestani, P. Ferragina, M. Sanderson (Eds.), String Processing and Information Retrieval. XIV, 367 pages. 2006.

Vol. 4208: M. Gerndt, D. Kranzlmüller (Eds.), High Performance Computing and Communications. XXII, 938 pages. 2006.

Vol. 4207: Z. Ésik (Ed.), Computer Science Logic. XII, 627 pages. 2006.

Vol. 4206: P. Dourish, A. Friday (Eds.), UbiComp 2006: Ubiquitous Computing. XIX, 526 pages. 2006.

Vol. 4205: G. Bourque, N. El-Mabrouk (Eds.), Comparative Genomics. X, 231 pages. 2006. (Sublibrary LNBI).

Vol. 4204: F. Benhamou (Ed.), Principles and Practice of Constraint Programming - CP 2006. XVIII, 774 pages. 2006.

Vol. 4203: F. Esposito, Z.W. Raś, D. Malerba, G. Semeraro (Eds.), Foundations of Intelligent Systems. XVIII, 767 pages. 2006. (Sublibrary LNAI).

Vol. 4202: E. Asarin, P. Bouyer (Eds.), Formal Modeling and Analysis of Timed Systems. XI, 369 pages. 2006.

Vol. 4201: Y. Sakakibara, S. Kobayashi, K. Sato, T. Nishino, E. Tomita (Eds.), Grammatical Inference: Algorithms and Applications. XII, 359 pages. 2006. (Sublibrary LNAI).

Vol. 4200: I.F. C. Smith (Ed.), Intelligent Computing in Engineering and Architecture. XIII, 692 pages. 2006. (Sublibrary LNAI).

Vol. 4199: O. Nierstrasz, J. Whittle, D. Harel, G. Reggio (Eds.), Model Driven Engineering Languages and Systems. XVI, 798 pages. 2006.

Vol. 4198: O. Nasraoui, O. Zaiane, M. Spiliopoulou, B. Mobasher, B. Masand, P. Yu (Eds.), Advances in Web Minding and Web Usage Analysis. IX, 177 pages. 2006. (Sublibrary LNAI).

Vol. 4197: M. Raubal, H.J. Miller, A.U. Frank, M.F. Goodchild (Eds.), Geographic, Information Science. XIII, 419 pages. 2006.

Vol. 4196: K. Fischer, I.J. Timm, E. André, N. Zhong (Eds.), Multiagent System Technologies. X, 185 pages. 2006. (Sublibrary LNAI).

Vol. 4195: D. Gaiti, G. Pujolle, E. Al-Shaer, K. Calvert, S. Dobson, G. Leduc, O. Martikainen (Eds.), Autonomic Networking. IX, 316 pages. 2006.

Vol. 4194: V.G. Ganzha, E.W. Mayr, E.V. Vorozhtsov (Eds.), Computer Algebra in Scientific Computing. XI, 313 pages. 2006.

Vol. 4193: T.P. Runarsson, H.-G. Beyer, E. Burke, J.J. Merelo-Guervós, L. D. Whitley, X. Yao (Eds.), Parallel Problem Solving from Nature - PPSN IX. XIX, 1061 pages. 2006.

Vol. 4192: B. Mohr, J.L. Träff, J. Worringen, J. Dongarra (Eds.), Recent Advances in Parallel Virtual Machine and Message Passing Interface. XVI, 414 pages. 2006.

Vol. 4191: R. Larsen, M. Nielsen, J. Sporring (Eds.), Medical Image Computing and Computer-Assisted Intervention – MICCAI 2006, Part II. XXXVIII, 981 pages. 2006.

Vol. 4190: R. Larsen, M. Nielsen, J. Sporring (Eds.), Medical Image Computing and Computer-Assisted Intervention – MICCAI 2006, Part I. XXXVVIII, 949 pages. 2006.

Vol. 4189: D. Gollmann, J. Meier, A. Sabelfeld (Eds.), Computer Security – ESORICS 2006. XI, 548 pages. 2006.

Vol. 4188: P. Sojka, I. Kopeček, K. Pala (Eds.), Text, Speech and Dialogue. XV, 721 pages. 2006. (Sublibrary LNAI).

Vol. 4187: J.J. Alferes, J. Bailey, W. May, U. Schwertel (Eds.), Principles and Practice of Semantic Web Reasoning. XI, 277 pages. 2006.

Vol. 4186: C. Jesshope, C. Egan (Eds.), Advances in Computer Systems Architecture. XIV, 605 pages. 2006.

Vol. 4185: R. Mizoguchi, Z. Shi, F. Giunchiglia (Eds.), The Semantic Web – ASWC 2006. XX, 778 pages. 2006.

Vol. 4184: M. Bravetti, M. Núñez, G. Zavattaro (Eds.), Web Services and Formal Methods. X, 289 pages. 2006.

Vol. 4183: J. Euzenat, J. Domingue (Eds.), Artificial Intelligence: Methodology, Systems, and Applications. XIII, 291 pages. 2006. (Sublibrary LNAI).

Vol. 4182: H.T. Ng, M.-K. Leong, M.-Y. Kan, D. Ji (Eds.), Information Retrieval Technology. XVI, 684 pages. 2006.

Vol. 4180: M. Kohlhase, OMDoc – An Open Markup Format for Mathematical Documents [version 1.2]. XIX, 428 pages. 2006. (Sublibrary LNAI).

Vol. 4179: J. Blanc-Talon, W. Philips, D. Popescu, P. Scheunders (Eds.), Advanced Concepts for Intelligent Vision Systems. XXIV, 1224 pages. 2006.

Vol. 4178: A. Corradini, H. Ehrig, U. Montanari, L. Ribeiro, G. Rozenberg (Eds.), Graph Transformations. XII, 473 pages. 2006.

Vol. 4177: R. Marín, E. Onaindía, A. Bugarín, J. Santos (Eds.), Current Topics in Artificial Intelligence. XV, 482 pages. 2006. (Sublibrary LNAI).

Vol. 4176: S.K. Katsikas, J. Lopez, M. Backes, S. Gritzalis, B. Preneel (Eds.), Information Security. XIV, 548 pages. 2006.

Vol. 4175: P. Bücher, B.M.E. Moret (Eds.), Algorithms in Bioinformatics. XII, 402 pages. 2006. (Sublibrary LNBI).

Vol. 4174: K. Franke, K.-R. Müller, B. Nickolay, R. Schäfer (Eds.), Pattern Recognition. XX, 773 pages. 2006.

Vol. 4173: S. El Yacoubi, B. Chopard, S. Bandini (Eds.), Cellular Automata. XV, 734 pages. 2006.

Vol. 4172: J. Gonzalo, C. Thanos, M. F. Verdejo, R.C. Carrasco (Eds.), Research and Advanced Technology for Digital Libraries. XVII, 569 pages. 2006.

Vol. 4169: H.L. Bodlaender, M.A. Langston (Eds.), Parameterized and Exact Computation. XI, 279 pages. 2006.